MODERN TWANG

An Alternative Country Music
Guide & Directory

by David Goodman

DOWLING PRESS NASHVILLE, TENNESSEE

Cover Design by Jesse Marinoff Reyes

Modern Twang logo by Jeff Geib

First edition

CONTENTS

In 1969 when I was a junior in high school, I joined the Columbia Record Club. Among my eight choices for $1 were three albums which would have a major impact not only on my musical consciousness but also that of many others in my generation and several generations to come. The Byrds' **Sweetheart of the Rodeo** and Bob Dylan's **John Wesley Harding** and **Nashville Skyline** were radical departures for these artists who had already established themselves as major rock stars. Their engaging folk-rock sounds had won me and many others over but to hear country music from them was something else altogether! Growing up in a Dallas suburb, my exposure to country music was limited but steady. A collection of 78s given to me by my grandmother included some old-time country performers; traditional and/or hard-core country came over the border radio stations and Saturday afternoon TV shows like *Buck Owen's Ranch* and Ft. Worth's *Cowtown Jamboree* or sometimes on national programs such as *The Beverly Hillbillies, Andy Griffith Show, Hee Haw,* or *The Johnny Cash Show.* But, I also remember hearing another type of country, namely, "country politan" or the "Nashville Sound," the lush, string laden pop country that became dominant in Music City in the 1960s-early 1970s. And while Nashville remained an important recording and songwriter mecca and the symbolic center of traditional country, that style was pushed more and more to the fringes in favor of the pop country industry. Countrypolitan was way too cheesy for a teenage rocker like me, but there was something in traditional/hard-core country I found strangely appealing. However, I didn't spread this news around to my middle class relatives and peer group because if anything, the long time stigma attached to "hillbilly" or "redneck" culture and music had intensified in the 1960s. But, suddenly, when Dylan went to Nashville to do his country recordings and the Byrds turned out **Sweetheart**, I gained a whole new perspective on and respect for country music. What I subsequently realized was that the Byrds' and Dylan's experimentation was part of a more widespread rediscovery of American roots music in general and traditional country in particular by a generation of young people raised on rock (in many ways this was an extension of the earlier "folk scare" of the early 1960s). And though the country-rock fusion that started in the late 1960s and intensified in the early 1970s with a succession of California performers including Neil

Young, the Grateful Dead, the Dillards, Gram Parsons and his protégé Emmylou Harris, the Flying Burrito Brothers, Creedence Clearwater Revival, and the New Riders of the Purple Sage got most of the attention, this phenomenon was happening throughout the nation. In upstate New York, The Band, who had secretly cut the monumental **Basement Tapes** with Dylan in 1967, were working on their special brand of rock Americana; in West Texas, Joe Ely, Jimmie Dale Gilmore, and Butch Hancock were developing a unique country-rock sound with the Flatlanders; the "Outlaws" and "Cosmic Cowboys" in Austin, Texas led by Willie Nelson and Waylon Jennings' rebellion against Nashville were blending honky tonk and rock while Doug Sahm was putting down "Texas rock for country rollers" (and incidentally introducing Tex-Mex/*conjunto* to a wider audience by collaborating with Flaco Jimenez). Moreover, all of the major styles of traditional country were affected: old-time was refreshed by groups such as the New Lost City Ramblers and the Highwoods String Band; bluegrass took a "progressive" turn under the guidance of the Seldom Scene, the Country Gentlemen, Old and In the Way, and the New Grass Revival; Western swing experienced a major renaissance with Commander Cody, Asleep at the Wheel, and Dan Hicks; the Balfa Brothers from south Louisiana appeared at the 1967 Newport Folk Festival and helped lay the foundations for a Cajun music renaissance in the 1970s; and a bewildering array of singer/songwriters emerged with a new take on all types of country music and themes. These developments constituted the first wave of what has recently become known as "Alternative Country," that is, the reinterpretation and enhancement of traditional country music styles, themes, and images by incorporating a variety of modern musical and non-musical influences. Throughout the history of country music a number of precedents for this had been set: Bill Monroe remade string band music into bluegrass beginning in the late 1930s; Bob Wills combined Eastern swing with country and western in the 1930s-1940s; honky tonkers in Texas and southern California electrified country in the 1940s-1950s; early rockabilly acts like Bill Haley and Elvis' melded hillbilly and rock into "Western Beat." The waves of alternative country that began in the late 1960s and recurred in three subsequent cycles (late 1970s-mid 1980s; late 1980s-early 1990s; mid 1990s-present) built on and redefined these and other country music styles gradually expanding into other musical genres, joining several genera-tions, and crossing geographical boundaries until, in the late 1990s, it was possible to speak of alternative country not just as a tradition but a full blown musical movement.

Of course, most traditional country purists were horrified by the first wave of alternative country although there were a few cease fires such as Dylan's sessions with Johnny Cash in 1969, Earl Scruggs' recordings with the Byrds and Dylan, and the grand summit between "a bunch of Hippies" (the Nitty Gritty Dirt Band) and old-time/bluegrass giants to record the land-mark, **Will the Circle Be Unbroken**, in 1972. Not surprisingly, the increasingly monolithic Nashville establishment initially chose to ignore it and continued churning out tepid (though very lucrative) pop country. However, due in part to the popularity of light weight country rock acts (the Eagles, the Amazing Rhythm Aces et al.) and Southern Rock (Lynyrd Skynyrd, Marshall Tucker et al.) but, most especially, the phenomenal rise of Outlaw or Redneck Rock," Music Row finally responded in 1980 with the "Urban Cowboy" campaign. This major coup for country pop marked the beginning of Nashville's rise to almost total dominance of the country music field in the 1980s-1990s. A group of Music City acts known as the "new traditionalists" (Ricky Skaggs, Randy Travis, George Strait) reacted with a sound based more on country roots but only slightly less polished than urban cowboy. The really hard-core country music rebellion came from a combination of fans and musicians from alternative country's first wave and a new generation of rockers who were seeking alternatives to the stagnancy of popular, mainstream rock and roll. One answer was a return to and reconstruction of traditional country styles that wasn't so much a reaction to Nashville as part of a much larger resurgence of interest in Americana much like the one that occurred in the late 1960s. This second alternative country wave built on the first but contributed new forms as well. Roots-rockers like the Blasters, Joe Ely, the LeRoi Brothers, the Del Lords, Green on Red, Giant Sand, and the Long Ryders expanded on earlier country-rock by adding a variety of Ameri-cana plus the sound, energy, and/or attitude of punk which hit in the late 1970s and early 1980s. Several groups including Rank and File, Jason & the Scorchers, the Beat Farmers, the Mekons, and Lone Justice took the country punk connection one step further by developing the romping, stomping style known as cowpunk. (It was also popular in Great Britain for a brief time and produced a 1985 compilation album, **Leather Chaps and Lace Petticoats**, whose subtitle "Welcome to Alternative Country" is the earliest use of that phrase I have seen). Sur-prisingly, one of the most influential alternative country

recordings from this period was Elvis Costello's **Almost Blue** (recorded in Nashville) which covered a variety of artists from Hank Williams to Gram Parsons and in the process exposed punkers to country and not a few country fans (like me) to punk.

At the same time, other branches of traditional country under-went a similar rediscovery and reinterpretation. Rounder, Flying Fish, and Philo Records were home to a host of innovators in new old-time (the Horseflies, the Chicken Chokers, the Red Clay Ramblers), progressive bluegrass (J. D. Crowe, Hot Rize), and "newgrass" (David Grisman, Tony Rice); these labels also reissued classic material by a host of forgotten but important old-time and bluegrass musicians. Rounder and a number of other independent labels (e.g. Arhoolie) were instrumental in Cajun music's second major renaissance (in the U.S. and the U.K.) and in the rise of Tex-Mex/*conjunto* which gained in popularity due mainly to Flaco Jimenez and his work with Peter Rowan and Ry Cooder. And, many of the singer/songwriters of the 1960s-1970s were joined by a new generation based mainly in Texas.

In the "post-punk" era of the late 1980s as urban cowboy mutated into "Hot New Country," there came a third cycle of alternative country even more diverse and widespread than its predecessors. Once again, it did not arise mainly as a response to Nashville's all-out pop country blitz, but as part of the continuing and ever increasing rebirth of Americana and all types of roots music. Combining and elaborating on previous trends, this round of alternative country sprang up all across North America and beyond. In California, the "Bakersfield Sound" was revived in L.A. by the "Town South of Bakers-field" generation from which came, most notably, Dwight Yoakum but also many key alternative country performers including Dale Watson, Rosie Flores, Ronnie Mack, the Lonesome Strangers, and James Intveld; farther up the Pacific Coast, in Seattle, the Picketts, the Walkabouts, and Ranch Romance helped set the stage for that city's rise to alternative country prominence in the 1990s; on the East Coast, in New York City, a spate of bands led by the World Famous Bluejays, Five Chinese Brothers, and the Blue Chieftains played and recorded what they called "Rig Rock" for the new Diesel Only label (the "Rig Rock" net eventually spread wider across the U.S. to encompass such acts as Go To Blazes from Philadelphia, Jean Caffeine out of Austin, and the punkgrass band Killbilly based in Dallas); Boston became quite a little alternative country hotbed with the Swinging Steaks and the Blood Oranges and so did Washington, D.C. with the Slim Jims, the Wanktones, Ruthie & the Wranglers, and Bill Kirchen among others. The exposure of the alternative country scenes in L.A., New York City, and D.C. to a national audience was greatly enhanced by a series of pioneering compilations: **A Town South of Bakersfield, Vols. 1-3**; **Rig Rock Juke Box** & **Rig Rock Truck Stop**; **The Big D.C. Jamboree, Vols. 1-3**. Austin continued as a major music focal point with the arrival of a wide range of performers including the Wagoneers, Chaparral, High Noon, Lucinda Williams, and Jimmie Dale Gilmore; several other key players in alternative country's future who emerged at this time were the Mavericks, Steve Earle, the Cowboy Junkies, and two left-field acts, k.d. lang and Lyle Lovett, who invaded and for a time succeeded in Nashville. All over North America, Europe, and "down under" in Australia and New Zealand, new old-time, progressive bluegrass, Cajun, and Tex-Mex remained strong, and the roster of alternative country singer/songwriters continued to grow as well. However, the most important developments in alternative country came in America's heartland. Minneapolis became a major scene through the Gear Daddies and the Jayhawks as did Columbus, Ohio with Ricky Barnes, Hank McCoy, the Schramms, and the Gibson Brothers. But, without doubt, the most influential group of the period came from Belleville, Illinois, a tiny Midwestern town near St. Louis. In their seven years together (1987-1994), Uncle Tupelo developed a distinctive country/roots/rock style that set the tone for much of the fourth wave of alternative country in the mid-1990s and beyond.

By 1994, the number and variety of alternative country acts and fans drawn to them world wide had increased dramatically. For the first time, the term alternative country was being used regularly to describe the music (Gregory Himes may have been the first to use it as a separate category in the 1994 edition of *Blackwell's Guide to Recorded Country Music*). Several other names were suggested including "No Depression," "Insurgent Country," "Twangcore," "Western Beat," "Rural Contemporary," "Hillbilly Noir," and "Y'alternative." And while "Americana" (see Terms) ran a close second, "Alternative Country" became the most widely accepted term and over the next few years, predominantly under that label, the music really began to take off. This fourth wave of alternative country benefited from an even larger upsurge in Americana and a growing disillusionment with Nashville's pop country imperialism (an associated phenomenon was the rise of interest in "Redneck"/"White Trash" culture that generated a number of musical acts and events celebrating and/or exploiting this stereotype). Pioneer fans and musicians from alternative country's first three waves joined with a whole new generation of converts (influenced mainly by Uncle Tupelo and its offshoots, Wilco and Son Volt) and built nearly three decades of tradition into a full scale movement. They accomplished this through an ever expanding grassroots network that used a variety of strategies. Compilation CDs which had been important during the third alternative country cycle in spreading word of local and regional scenes became an even more vital marketing technique for independent labels that handled alternative country. Bloodshot Records, out of Chicago, with lots of inspiration and guidance from Jon Langford (the Mekons), led the way in 1994 with the first (**For a Life of Sin**) of its series of landmark "Insurgent Country" compilations, but other labels quickly followed suit with anthologies for Atlanta's Redneck Underground (**Bubbapalooza**), Austin (**Austin Country Nights**; **True Sounds of the New West**), St. Louis (**Out of the Gate Again**), and North Carolina (**Revival**). Closely related were widely publicized tribute albums to country's greats (Jimmie Rodgers, Woody Guthrie, Merle Haggard, Willie Nelson) showcasing a variety of old and new alternative country performers. Overseas, the U.K.'s Vinyl Junkie and Sweden's Sound Asleep labels produced several alternative country collections with both veteran and new artists while Germany's Glitterhouse issued a number of CDs filled with the music of many of alternative country's best singer/songwriters past and present (Glitterhouse also increasingly became Europe's leading label for a host of established and up and coming American and European acts). Several rockabilly labels in North America and Europe put together compilations with new hillbilly boppers like High Noon, Big Sandy, Ray Condo, and the Barnshakers while Rounder made available many first rate collections of the best in contemporary old-time, bluegrass, cowboy/Western, Cajun, and Tex-Mex. Finally, acknowledgement by the new crop of alternative country performers of the influence of alternative country pioneers and a general upswing of interest in alternative country's history led to the reissue and/or first time release (on CD) of material from the key figures in its evolution.

Alternative country also grew through the proliferation of radio shows on stations around the globe. Many alternative country related programs including general Americana and bluegrass, old-time, and classic country shows had been on continuously for twenty years or more, but their ranks swelled greatly in the 1990s. Individual alternative country programs came on the air while some stations offered a variety of Americana and alternative country programming throughout the day; in 1996, Gavin, the long time radio information clearinghouse, allowed Rob Bleetstein to create an Americana section and sponsored a growing list of Gavin Americana stations. And though most of the stations offering alternative country and Americana were at the lower, less powerful end of the broadcast spectrum, their range was greatly increased through the introduction of services like Bitcaster and RealAudio which allowed online broadcasting on the World Wide Web. Meanwhile, nightclubs remained crucial as always, but, now, an alternative country circuit emerged throughout North America and beyond and many venues began to present weekly and/or monthly alternative country events. Festivals of all shapes and sizes throughout the world provided wider forums for alternative country performers; since its inception in 1987 South By Southwest in Austin has been a major showcase boosting its proportion of alternative country acts each year, but other international, national and a variety of regional alternative country events such as Bubbapalooza, Twangfest, Sleazefest, Torch & Twang Fest, and Extravaganza were very influential as well. The new breed of old-time, bluegrass, Cajun, Tex-Mex, et al. set up many separate festivals at which they could be seen and heard by a variety of audiences. An expanding list of independent labels (Bloodshot, Hightone, Checkered Past, Freedom, Dead Reckoning, E-Squared, Little Dog, Watermelon) devoted themselves to alternative country acts while many performers took advantage of advances in CD recording technology to do-it-themselves and get their music to the public in a completely unique way. Articles, interviews, reviews, and other information appeared in an ever growing number of publications beginning with pioneering American roots music magazines like *Blue Suede News* and *Music City Texas/3rd Coast Music* in the late 1980s through early alt. country periodicals such as *Twangin'*, *Maybelle*, *Cornfed*, and *The Feedlot* in the early 1990s down to the first landmark issue of *No Depression: The Alternative Country (Whatever That Is) Bi-Monthly* in 1995. The latter grew out of a discussion group on AOL devoted to Gram Parsons, the Jayhawks, Uncle Tupelo, et al. and was a reflection of the power of the single most important factor in the growth and development of alternative country in the last five years. Through web pages (band, company, fan), mailing lists and discussion groups, Real Audio, e-mail, and more, alternative country fans, musicians, promoters, writers, and others interested in the music linked up in an unprecedented way and as the *All Music Guide to Country* has observed the shorthand "alt. country" vividly demonstrates "the role the Internet has played in the growth and publicity of this movement." Still, there was debate over just what to call this music and some, including a few of its most prominent names, rejected the label altogether or dismissed it as nothing more than another musical fad. However, for an ever growing

number of fans and performers the name stuck, and there were many signs in the late 1990s that alternative country was here to stay: more acts and labels emerging all the time; alt. country artists signing long term contracts with independents and an increasing number of majors; big labels setting up alternative country subsidiaries; independents and larger companies making distribution deals; more feature articles on alt. country and individual artists in music magazines in the U.S. and overseas; wider radio coverage and TV programs; movie soundtracks involving alt. country artists; constant new events and festivals; planned tributes, compilations, and other projects involving big names in both alternative rock and alternative country; ongoing collaborations between several generations of alt. country artists; a steady stream of reissues and anthologies of the pioneers in alt. country; and exponential growth on the Internet. Heck, even Nashville has re-emerged as a twang center with acts like Paul Burch, BR5-49, Farmer Not So John, Tom House, et al. Given the vagaries of musical trends and the music business, it is hard to predict just how far and how long alternative country will go. But, as a fan of alternative country for more than thirty years, I am more excited and optimistic about its future than ever before. (*After the publication of the 1st edition of *Modern Twang* in March 1998, the trends mentioned above accelerated, renewed my faith in the music, and increased my desire to do a 2nd, expanded edition.)

I have been very fortunate as an avid fan, concert goer, dancer, record collector, promoter, teacher, and writer to have experienced the four major waves of alternative country first hand. As a teenager, through the miracle of recorded sound, I got to hear the first stirrings of country-rock in the late 1960s and in the process gained a greater appreciation for country music's rich heritage. During the early 1970s, when I was attending college in Waco, Texas my exposure to early alternative country was increased by frequent visits to Austin (100 miles away) where I was treated to great local and national alt. country acts at places like Soap Creek Saloon and the Armadillo World Headquarters. When the second wave of alternative country took shape in the late 1970s-mid 1980s I was living in Albuquerque, New Mexico where I was lucky to fall in with a music/dance crowd that not only showed me just how widespread and varied alternative country had become but also furthered my education in country music's roots. Into the late 1980s and early 1990s, I kept touch with alt. country's third wave through reading, chronic visits to record stores, and regular pilgrimages to Austin. While working toward a Ph.D. in American Studies, I taught a class on "Country Music and American Culture" in which I managed to convince a few of my students that Garth Brooks was the anti-Hank and opened them up to traditional and alternative country. Finally, in 1993, I fulfilled a long time dream when I moved to Austin where I planned to finish my dissertation by day and roam the "live music capital of the world" by night. Then, as my interest in and money for completing my doctorate ran out, I dropped out of school, took a series of jobs (construction, substitute teacher) and threw myself more intensely into music and dancing. For an alternative country music fan, the mid-1990s were an exciting time to live in Austin. A new generation of top notch acts (Junior Brown, the Derailers, the Bad Livers, Don Walser, et al.) were emerging and as a major musical mecca, the city's clubs (and SXSW) played host to the increasing number and variety of alt. country performers that were arising at the time. As alternative country really began to heat up after 1994, I continued to collect recordings by acts past and present and then began keeping a list which eventually grew into note cards full of biographical, discographical, and other information. Slowly, the idea for a book on alternative country began to take shape, but the big question was, what kind of book? Initially, I thought about putting my History and American Studies training to use and writing a history of alternative country from the late 1960s-present, but that sounded too formal and too reminiscent of what I had recently left behind. Instead, I decided I could do something more useful and fun by putting together a guide to alternative country modeled roughly on other music guides (e.g. *Trouser Press* and *Rolling Stone Guides to Rock*; *Blackwell's Guide to Recorded Country Music*; *All Music Guides*). For a couple of years I accumulated information on alternative country acts, labels, publications, venues, radio stations, and more from a variety of sources, and in the process filled several filing cabinets. My archive was dramatically expanded by an avalanche of data that came via the Internet; the growth of the Web and alternative country ran parallel during this time and in just a few years, I watched a trickle of alternative country related pages and sites accelerate into a veritable flood. This development made my task both harder and easier, and in truth, on a number of levels, this project would have been impossible without the Internet. As I began to write profiles and compile discographies and a variety of other data, *Modern Twang* took shape and evolved. In the course of writing the book, several general country music guides (*Definitive Country*; *All Music Guide to Country*; *Music Hound Country*) were published that profile vintage and new country performers along side the more prominent names in alternative country in the last 30 years. They also guide the reader in the sense of

rating recordings or telling you what to buy and/or what to avoid, and one (*Music Hound*) has some simple listings of labels, radio stations, festivals, and web pages. However, what I wanted to do with *Modern Twang* was provide a separate book for alternative country featuring not only the major names in the field but also obscure but important figures from the past and the many regionally popular and/or up-and-coming acts that have emerged in the last four to five years. I also wanted to emphasize alternative country as a world wide phenomenon by including performers from Canada, the U.K., Europe, and Australia/New Zealand (incidentally, some of alt. country's most dedicated and knowledgeable fans come from outside the U.S.). And while I do express my opinions about individual performers and recordings, I have down played detailed critiques in favor of profiles which give biographical data, personnel, interesting anecdotes, cross-references, the very latest news (through January 1999), and complete (as possible) discographies including singles, EPs, promos, imports and bootlegs. To supplement the performer profiles, there are annotated appendices for alternative country compilations and sound-tracks, labels, publications, promotion, web pages, Internet mailing lists and newsgroups, venues, festivals, and radio stations/programs from around the world. In addition, I've taken *Modern Twang* a step further than other guides by making it a directory as well with snail mail, e-mail, and/or web page addresses for individual artists plus labels, publications, venues, festivals, and radio stations/shows. My hope is that *Modern Twang*, as both guide and directory, will be a useful source of information and at the same time strengthen the bonds connecting the alternative country network around the globe. (*Response to the 1st edition was very positive with the most consistent comments being that it was helpful—some called it "their bible" and that it put them in touch with artists and fans from all over the world.)

While putting together *Modern Twang*, I have had to deal with a number of sticky questions and problems. First of all, as mentioned before, the term "Alternative Country" is quite controversial, but I feel comfortable with it because I believe that at a time when 90%+ of the public associates "Country" music with Garth Brooks, Shania Twain, and the rest of the Nashville establishment, there needs to be a way to delineate performers who have provided an important option by drawing on and enhancing traditional country through the addition of contemporary styles and ideas. Secondly, not everyone will agree with my definition of alternative country, but I believe all the styles included here fit comfortably under my "big tent." Related to this problem is my choices of who to include and exclude. In making these selections, I relied on liner notes, reviews, articles, and friends' opinions (many suggestions came in after the 1st edition), but ultimately my own eyes and ears. Of course, there is always the concern for accuracy of information, and I have tried to verify and cross check all facts using a variety of sources. Any errors in grammar or content, choices of what to put in and leave out, and of course, opinions expressed are fully my responsibility.

In the long run, the incentives for doing *Modern Twang* have far outweighed the deterrents. Not only has it given me a chance to combine work and play but more importantly has allowed me to give something back to a musical tradition that has given me so much over the years. In the process of compiling, writing, and publishing *Modern Twang*, I have had help and inspiration from many sources. First and foremost, I want to thank Jane, my dance partner for life, who through the ups and downs, goods and bads was always there with love and understanding and much more. My parents, Richard and Jerry Goodman, probably thought, "Oh boy, another one of David's hair-brained schemes" but kept it to themselves and gave me constant encouragement. My brother Terry, the real brain in the family, put up with my weird country music tapes and has always been supportive. Jane's parents, Bill and Dean Vaughan, really think I'm crazy but don't mind because I love their daughter, and they have provided a variety of assistance. I especially want to thank my brother-in-law, Jeff Geib who drew the excellent *Modern Twang* logo and contributed his immense musical knowledge and friendship as well; his wife, Dana, and kids Becky and Billy have also been an inspiration. Scott Bookman of Lancaster, Pennsylvania gave much needed proofreading support and was also a great source of information. I must also acknowledge the Austin alternative country music/dance crowd especially Judy Frels who has been a valued friend, gave much needed marketing tips, and helped with advertising at a crucial time; John Conquest (*3rd Coast Music*) and Jason Shields (*Texas Jamboree*) were both fountains of information and gave consistently good advice and support. I also want to thank the alternative country community including musicians, fans, club owners, DJs, et al. but especially the members of the Postcard, Postcard 2, and No Depression online alt. country discussion groups for consistently entertaining dialogue and valuable information. And, of course, I am very grateful to Maryglenn McCombs and Andy Scheinman at Dowling Press for having faith in *Modern Twang* and being such great people to work with.

After the publication of the first edition, I received kind words and support from many individuals but especially want to thank Dan Aloi, Sophie Best, Peter Blackstock, Rob Bleetstein, Skule Boie, David Bowling, Marc Bristol, George Bullfrog, Chris Butler, Martin Caraher, Bryan Chapman, Cheryl Cline, Paul Comeau, Rick Cornell, Autumn Deuel, Jerker Emanuelson, Violet and Randy Geib, Mike Hays, Dave Henderson, Joe Horn, Ben Ieven, Kathy James, Roy Kasten, Kelly Kessler, David Klug, Chip Lamey, Mike Lynam, Curtis Lynch, Tom Mahnke, Vinny and Judy Macey, John Matterface, Kathryn Meador, Karl Mullen, Marc Nolis, Peter Olmstead, Howard Owens, Pete Peterson, Jeffrey Remz, Brian Straub, Bruce Sylvester, Agusti Baillo Tubau, Stacey Taylor, Stephen Terrell, Bob Timmers, Archa Vaughan, Lynn Vaughan, Maurice Vaughan, Jeff Wagner, Jeff Weiss and Corrie Gregory, James Willett, Don Yates, Zellem Printing, and Carl Zimring. Finally, all my catitude to Wild Boy, Nicky, and Rambo, the three coolest kitties I know.

Questions? Comments? Suggestions? Please write to me:

David Goodman
c/o Modern Twang
P.O. Box 443
East Petersburg, PA 17520-0443
twirlyd@lancnews.infi.net

TERMS

Alternative Country

Umbrella term for a wide array of performers from the late 1960s to the present who, generally working outside of the Nashville country mainstream, have reinterpreted and enhanced traditional country music styles and themes by incorporating a variety of modern musical and non-musical influences.

Americana

Often used interchangeably with Alternative Country but here defined more broadly as any musical genre native to America including blues, country, jazz, rock, etc.

Austin Sound

Central Texas alternative country tradition from the Outlaws, Cosmic Cowboys, and singer/songwriters of the 1970s through the cowpunks and roots-rockers of the 1980s to the current generation of honky tonkers and singer/songwriters.

Bakersfield Sound

Honky tonk style that emerged in Southern California in the 1950s-1960s with artists like Merle Haggard and Buck Owens; it has been kept alive through several generations of performers and has had a major influence on alt. country from the late 1960s to the present.

Cajun

Accordion and fiddle fueled dance music native to southern Louisiana that since the early 20th century has absorbed many musical influences (country, rock, etc.) and instruments (electric guitar, steel guitar, etc.) and experienced several major revivals making it one of the most popular styles throughout North America and Europe.

Close Harmony

Beautiful, twangy vocalizing first made famous by brother/sister groups of the 1930s-1940s then revived by the Everlys in the 1950s-1960s and very influential on a number of contemporary alt. country acts.

Country Rock

Highly elastic term but here used to refer to artists who combine various styles of traditional/hard-core country and rock.

Cowboy/Western

Country music created by "real" cowboys in the American and Canadian West, made popular by Hollywood and Nashville cowboys in the 1930s-1950s, and revived several times in the 1970s-1990s.

Cowpunk

A short-lived 1980s hybrid combining the energy and attitude of punk with country/western themes, images, and music.

Desert Rock

Alt. country sound that evolved in the Phoenix/Tucson area in the 1980s by joining country, roots rock, and Southwestern musical styles.

Gay Country

Small but very dedicated contingent of homosexual performers usually with strong leanings toward parody and/or sociopolitical commentary.

Gothic Country

Extremely laid back style with an intense focus on the supernatural, death, sorrow, and other themes and images found in Southern/Gothic literature.

Grain Belt Rock

Alternative country acts (mostly country rock and roots rock) found in the Mid West from Missouri to Minnesota.

Grange Rock

Play on "grunge rock" used to designate Seattle's alternative country performers.

Hillbilly Bop

Rockabilly with a heavy dose of Western swing and honky tonk.

Honky Tonk

Hard core, electrified country music born in Texas beer joints and dives in the 1940s-1950s and spread to Bakersfield, California and beyond.

Hot New Country

Mega-commercial enterprise from the 1990s Nashville establishment obsessed with hits and glitz from a seemingly endless stream of interchangeable pretty girls and boys epitomized by Shania Twain and the anti-Hank himself, Garth Brooks.

Insurgent Country

Originated by Bloodshot Records to refer to alternative country performers combining traditional and/or hard core country with a punk attitude and energy. Initially applied for the most part to Chicago's alt. country contingent, it has come to include a growing number of like-minded performers throughout the U.S.

Lo-Fi Country

Played and sung at a snail-on-quaaludes pace, setting a mood ranging from dreary to downright menacing.

Lubbock Mafia

West Texas' stellar collection of singer/songwriters (and supporting musicians) that first emerged in the early 1970s and have continually exerted a powerful influence on the face of alternative country (not sure of the derivation of this phrase).

New Old-Time

Contemporary take on early 20th century Appalachian/hillbilly music that modernizes its conventional instrumentation and themes with the addition of different techniques, Western and non-Western musical styles, and an array of other influences.

Newgrass

Also known as the "new acoustic music," it starts with a bluegrass base but is even more experimental than progressive bluegrass in its incorporation of various types of music.

No Depression

Drawn from the name of Uncle Tupelo's landmark 1990 album (which they took from an A. P. Carter song) and generally referring to that branch of alternative country that like UT/Son Volt/Wilco combines country, roots rock, and punk elements. Also the name of an AOL discussion group and alt. country's leading publication.

Okra

Designates the excellent stable of alternative country groups on Columbus, Ohio based Okra Records in the late 1980s-early 1990s.

Outlaw

Often used synonymously with "progressive country" and alluding to those country performers led by Willie Nelson, Waylon Jennings, Billy Joe Shaver, Kinky Friedman, and David Allan Coe who, in the 1970s, split with Nashville and created an appealing and very popular country rock hybrid. The music and the attitude has had a big impact on alt. country in the 1980s-1990s and was also a factor in Nashville's launching of the "urban cowboy" campaign in the late 1970s.

Progressive Bluegrass

Bluegrass incorporating blues, rock, country, and other modern musical styles.

Psychocountry

Off the deep end style characterized by frenzied playing, deranged vocals (including yelling, wooping, and various animal sounds), and demented lyrics (the hard core rockabilly version of this is called psychobilly).

Punkgrass

Fusion of bluegrass with a punk music edge and attitude (sometimes called "thrashgrass").

Redneck Underground

Coined by local celebrity Deacon Lunchbox to refer to the Atlanta/Athens, Georgia alternative country movement that developed in the early 1990s.

Rig Rock

Diesel Only Records expression for the hard core country/rock sound found on DO singles and Rig Rock compilations. Initially, it referred mostly to New York City's alt. country movement of the late 1980s-early1990s but eventually included an ever-widening body of U.S. performers.

Rockabilly

Progenitor to rock and roll combining hillbilly music with a hard driving, electric beat; early on associated mainly with Sun Records (Elvis, Jerry Lee, Johnny Cash), Gene Vincent, Buddy Holly, and Bill Haley but has since split off into many forms from hillbilly bop to neo-rockabilly to psychobilly.

Roots Rock

A return of rock music to its blues and country roots that began in the 1980s and continues unabated into the 1990s.

Singer/Songwriter

Basically, poets and storytellers who, solo or with minimal accompaniment, set their writings to music.

Tex-Mex/Conjunto

Type of music developed by the Mexican-Americans of central and south Texas; *conjunto* refers to a group style that in its simplest form features accordion, *bajo sexto* (12 string bass guitar), and *toloche* (upright bass) but can also include electric guitar, steel guitar, and drums. Its earliest practitioners played *nortenos*, *corridos*, *rancheras*, and other forms native to Mexico but, over the years, new generations of players have incorporated other Latin styles (e.g. *huapango, cumbia*) and Americana including country and rock. In turn, country and rock have absorbed Tex-Mex influences.

Tobacco Row

Alternative country from North Carolina's Triangle area (Raleigh/Durham/Chapel Hill) that arose with a vengeance in the 1990s (this phrase is my feeble attempt to humorously combine Tobacco Road and Music Row).

Town South of Bakersfield (TSOB)

L.A.'s late 1980s and early 1990s alternative country movement that produced three influential compilations (**A Town South of Bakersfield, Vols. 1-3**) introducing some of the leading names in today's alt. country.

Twangtrust

Partnership between Steve Earle and Ray Kennedy that created E-Squared Records (1996) which has produced recordings by the V-Roys, 6 String Drag, Bap Kennedy, and Cheri Knight.

White Trash Parody

Take off (in music and image) on one of America's most enduring stereotypes that, depending on your perspective, can be seen as celebratory or condescending, fun loving or exploitative.

REFERENCES

BOOKS

All Music Guide, ed. Michael Erlewine, San Francisco: Miller Freeman Books, 1994.

All Music Guide to Country, ed. Michael Erlewine et al., San Francisco: Miller Freeman Books, 1997.

Blackwell Guide to Recorded Country Music, ed. Bob Allen, Oxford: Blackwell, 1994.

Country Music USA, Bill Malone, Rev. Ed. Austin: University of Texas Press, 1985.

Creating Country Music: Fabricating Authenticity, Richard A. Peterson, Chicago: University of Chicago Press, 1997.

Definitive Country: The Ultimate Encyclopedia of Country Music & Its Performers, ed. Barry McCloud, New York: Perigee, 1995.

Desperados: The Origins of Country Rock and the Roots of New Country, John Einarson, Quarry Press, 1998.

Encyclopedia of Folk, Country & Western Music, Irwin Stambler and Grelun Landon, 2nd ed., New York: St. Martin's Press, 1984.

Go Cat Go: Rockabilly Music and Its Makers, Craig Morrison, Carbondale: University of Illinois Press, 1995.

Gram Parsons—A Music Biography, Sid Griffin, 4th ed., Pasadena, CA: Sierra, 1997.

Guinness Encyclopedia of Popular Music, 4 vols. Chester, CT: New England Publishing Assn., 1992.

In The Country of Country: People and Places in American Music, Nicholas Dawidoff, New York: Pantheon Books, 1997.

Invisible Republic: Bob Dylan's Basement Tapes, Greil Marcus, New York: Holt, 1997.

Let the Good Times Roll!: A Guide to Cajun & Zydeco Music, David Babb, Pat Nyhan, and Brian Rollins, Upbeat Books, 1997.

Music Hound Country: The Essential Album Guide, ed. Brian Mansfield and Gary Graff, Detroit: Visible Ink, 1997.

Music Hound Folk: The Essential Album Guide, ed. Neal Walters, Brian Mansfield, and Gary Graff, Detroit: Visible Ink, 1998.

No Depression, ed. Grant Alden and Peter Blackstock, Nashville: Dowling Press, 1998.

Prairie Nights to Neon Lights: The Story of Country Music in West Texas, Joe Carr and Alan Munde, Lubbock: Texas Tech, 1995.

Rolling Stone Album Guide, ed. Anthony DeCurtis and James Henke, New York: Random House, 1992.

South to Louisiana: The Music of the Cajun Bayous, John Broven, 3rd prntg., Gretna, Louisiana: Pelican, 1992.

Steve Earle in Quotes, Joanna Serrais, 1997.

Texas Rhythm, Texas Rhyme: A Pictorial History of Texas Music, Larry Willoughby, Austin: Tonkawa Free Press, 1990.

Trouser Press Guide to '90s Rock, ed. Ira A. Robbins, New York: Fireside, 1997.

Trouser Press Record Guide, ed. Ira A. Robbins, 4th ed., New York: Collier Books, 1991.

World Music: The Rough Guide, ed. Simon Broughton, et al., London: The Rough Guides, 1994.

PUBLICATIONS

(Print and/or Online)

3rd Coast Music/Music City Texas

The Austin American-Statesman

The Austin Chronicle

Blue Suede News

Cornfed

Country Standard Time

Creative Loafing

Dirty Linen

The Feedlot

FolkRoots

Gavin

Grindstone

Happenstance

Jelly

The Journal of Country Music

Maybelle

Mojo

MoMZine

Nash!

Nashville Scene

No Depression

Roadhouse Fever

Roots World

Rural Route Twangzine

Southern & Rocking

Texas Jamboree

Twangin'

Uncut

Third Coast Music Network

Twanger's Home Page

Western Swing.Com

WHOAAH!!: The Home of Hot Rockabilly and Cool Twang

WEB PAGES

Akers Mic: Country & Western

AlternativeCountry.Com

Americana A-Z

Americana Archives

Americana Music

Bluegrass Roots

Cybergrass

Down Home and Free Roots Home Page

Electric L.A.

Freight Train Boogie

Gumbo Pages

Hellcountry

Insurgent Country Home Page

Juke Joint

Tommy Nordeng's No Depression Page

Bob Paterson's Home Page

Postcard2

Progressive Torch & Twang

RealCountry.Net

Renegade Texas

Rockabilly Hall of Fame

Rockin' Roots, Country Casanovas and Southern Sliders

Rodney's Essential Music Page

Roots 66

The Rural Route to Insurgent Country

Sleazefest

Southern & Rocking Music

Stephen Terrell's Web Page

Texas Music

A Select List of Alternative Country Articles

Many of the following articles are archived online in the web pages of individual newspapers and magazines (see Publications section of *Modern Twang* for urls). Articles from independent weeklies such as *The Austin Chronicle*, *Nashville Scene*, *Tucson Weekly*, et al. are archived in an online digest called the Weekly Wire (//:weeklywire.com). Metro-Active preserves articles from the CA indies (//:www.metroactive.com).

"Whatever Happened to the New Country Rock?," Jimmy Guterman, *The Journal of Country Music*, Late 1980s (article on Jason, Steve Earle, and other 1980s country rockers).

"Diesel Only Records: Where Singles Keep on Truckin'," Jonathan Marx, *The Journal of Country Music*, c.1992.

"Austin Country Roundup," Lee Nichols et al., *The Austin Chronicle*, July 23, 1993, pp. 31-32, 37, 43 (articles on Junior Brown, Wayne Hancock, Cornell Hurd, Don McCalister).

"Are You Ready for the Country?," Daniel Durchholz, *Request*, November 1993 (Uncle Tupelo).

"Heart of the Country," Jason Fine, *Option*, November-December 1993 (Uncle Tupelo).

"Cosmic Cowboys," Chet Flippo and "Progressive Country," Craig Hillis, *The Austin Chronicle*, January 14, 1994, pp. 33-36.

"The Last Uncle Tupelo Interview. Ever!," Jim Saah and Sohrab Habibion, *Uno Mas*, February 19, 1994.

"Country Influence and Rock 'n' Roll Attitude: Post-Punk Roots Movement in Danger of Becoming Hip," Don McLeese, *The Austin American-Statesman*, April 13, 1995, pp. 5-6.

"Buck and Hag Revisited: The Faces of 'New' Country," Lee Nichols, *The Austin Chronicle*, May 26, 1995, 41-43 (The Derailers, Dale Watson).

"Hubba Bubbas: Exploring the Rise of the Redneck Underground," Bob Ruggiero, *Creative Loafing*, July 15, 1995.

"God Bless Americana," Bill Wyman, *The Chicago Reader*, October 13, 1995.

"What Hath Uncle Tupelo Wrought?: Alternative Country's Second Wave," Lee Nichols, *The Austin Chronicle*, November 16, 1995.

"Alternative Country, Indy Scene Grows," Jeffrey B. Remz, *Country Standard Time*, 1996.

"Is Country Music Cool?, Or Why Should I Listen to Uncle Tupelo?," *Heckler*, 1996.

"The Children of Detroit City," David Cantwell, *Rock & Rap Confidential*, 1996 & *Twangin'* 1997.

"Searchin' For a Truer Sound," Bill Wyman, *Addicted to Noise*, January 1996.

"Hicksville: The Other Side of Country," Greg Cahil, *The Sonoma Independent*, January 11, 1996.

"Twang and Shout: Hard Country Sound Has Found a Nurturing Home on the Edge of Chicago's Music Scene," Greg Kot, *The Chicago Tribune*, January 25, 1996 (about Bloodshot Records).

"Revival of the Fittest: Hightone's Roadhouse Revival Tour," Michael Point, *The Austin American-Statesman*, February 8, 1996, pp. 5-7.

"Wanted: Adventurous Radio Programmers for Twangy Insurrection," Seana Baruth, *Gavin* #2095, March 8, 1996.

"Testy Outlaws Regroup For New Raid On The Charts," David Zimmerman, *USA Today*, March 12, 1996.

"Whose Alternative Is This, Anyway? Or My Dinner With Rob Bleetstein," Max Tolkoff, *Gavin* #2096, March 15, 1996.

"Call It Cowpunk or Call It Hip Country, It's a Fine Place To Be," Don McLeese, *The Austin American-Statesman*, March 17, 1996, pp. 8-10.

"Twangapalooza," Jon Maples, *The San Francisco Bay Guardian*, March 20, 1996.

"Tupelo Honey 1996: Alternative Country Breaks Through," Jim Caligiuri, *Pulse!*, May 1996, p. 55.

"Same Train, A Different Time: Austin's Country Music Scene Regenerates," Lee Nichols, *The Austin Chronicle*, May 10, 1996, pp. 46-53.

"Lard Almighty," Kelly Luker, *Metro Santa Cruz*, June 27, 1996. (feature on legendary Americana radio station KFAT/KPIG)

"No Depression?: Looking For the Next Merle in Alt. Country," Michael McCall, *Pulse!*, August 1996, pp. 42-43.

"Hank Williams. Garth Brooks. BR5-49?," Peter Applebome, *The New York Times Magazine*, October 27, 1996, pp. 38-43.

"Threadgill's Supper Sessions, Watermelon & Buddy Records, and Walter Hyatt," Arthur Wood, *Country Music People*, November 1996.

"The 'No Depression' Family Tree," David Fenigsohn, *MSNBC*, November 15, 1996.

"Underground Country," William Athey, *The Event*, November 21, 1996 (on the rise of alt. country).

"The Great Roots-Rock Scare of '96: The Americana Chart, Alternative Country, and Austin," Jim Caligiuri, *The Austin Chronicle*, December 1996.

"It's a Free Range, Baby: The Alt-Country Non-Movement," Rick Cornell, *Music Monitor Online*, 1997.

"The Hightone Story," Patrick Carr, *Country Music*, January/February 1997, pp. 39-42.

"Hillbilly Noir? Postmodern Traditional? Southern Goth?: It All Adds Up to...Insurgent Country," Wayne Wise, *In Pittsburgh Newsweekly*, January 2, 1997.

"Eclectic Bands Play Rough Hewn Hybrid," William Porter, *The Arizona Republic*, January 19, 1997.

"Offering a Slice of 'Americana': Local Station Blazing a Trail With Country Radio Format," Mario Tarradell, *The Dallas Morning News*, January 19, 1997.

"Alternative Acts Creep Into Country," David Zimmerman, *USA Today*, January 24, 1997.

"A Little Bit Country, A Little Bit Rock 'N' Roll: Nashville Grows Self-Conscious," Ben Ratliff, *Slate Magazine*, January 28, 1997.

"Hank Williams Interpreted Two Ways," Greg Kot, *The Chicago Tribune*, February 4, 1997 (BR5-49 vs. The Waco Brothers)

"Grange Grunge?: Alt Is Country's New Guerilla Movement, And It Seems To Be Burgeoning In Ballard," Tom Phalen, *The Seattle Times*, February 20, 1997.

"Tangled Roots: The Would-Be Revolution of Alternative Country," Jim Ridley, *Nashville Scene*, February 27, 1997 (lengthy article with lots on the Nashville scene and alt. country in general).

"The Biblical Hillbillies," Greil Marcus, *Addicted to Noise*, March 1997.

"Dead Recknoners Are Alive and Well, On Their Own," Joel Bernstein, *Country Standard Time*, March/April 1997.

"Americana Rides the Waves: A Name Helped Alternative Country Creep Onto Radio and Catch the Ear of the Music Industry," Andrew C. Revkin, *The Montreal Gazette*, March 9, 1997 or "Sounds Like a Piece of Americana: Rough-Edged, Homespun Music Rising," *The Los Angeles Daily News*, March 10, 1997 or "Rootsy Americana Music Is Moving Up," *The San Diego Union-Tribune*, March 12, 1997.

"Music City: Country's Establishment Begins to Note Americana's Promise," Jay Orr, *The Nashville Banner*, March 11, 1997.

"A Whole Lot Country and a Bit Rock and Roll Add Up to No Depression Music," Brad Tyer, *The Houston Press*, March 13, 1997.

"Slow Depression: SXSW Finds Alt Country Moving Ahead Slow But Steady," Jon Maples, *The San Francisco Bay Guardian*, March 19, 1997.

"No Depression's Bull Market," Peter Margasak, *The Chicago Reader*, March 21, 1997.

"Country's Cool (Really): Y'Alternative Music Finding an Audience Ignored By Nashville," Jim Beal, Jr., *The San Antonio Express-News*, March 26, 1997.

"Pop on the Rocks: Alternative Country," Chris Dickinson, *The St. Louis Post-Dispatch*, April 3, 1997.

"Alternative' Country Proving That 'Good Songs Still Matter'", Walter Tunis, *Lexington Herald-Leader*, April 6, 1997.

"Alternative Sound: Wilco Takes Country Music Downtown," Chris Wodskou, *The Toronto Globe and Mail*, April 11, 1997 (several pages on general alt. country).

"Hooked on Twang: A New Generation Goes Honky-Tonkin'", Holly George-Warren, *Rolling Stone*, April 17, 1997, pp. 36, 48 (The Derailers, Junior Brown, Wayne Hancock).

"Rock-and-Roll's Haute Lonesome," Eric Brace, *The Washington Post*, April 20, 1997, p. G04.

"Wellsprings of Change: An Alternative-Country Movement Is Bubbling Up From the Underground," Dan De-Luca, *The Philadelphia Inquirer*, April 20, 1997.

"Lost Highways: Between Seattle and Nashville Lies Alt-Country," David Browne, *Entertainment Weekly*, April 25, 1997.

"Tupelo Money: Whither Goest the Future of Country Music?," Bill Friskics-Warren, *Pulse!*, May 1997, pp. 46, 57.

"The Rise of No Depression Country Rock," Bud Scoppa, *Addicted to Noise*, May 1997 (lengthy with "No Depression Essentials," a list of key alt. country albums)

"Alternative Country Call It What You Will, It Rocks the Boat," Dan DeLuca, *The Charleston Gazette*, May 22, 1997.

"Chicago's Bloodshot Label Attracts Insurgent Acts," Catherine Cuellar, *The Dallas Morning News*, June 22, 1997, 6C.

"A Whole Other Country," Thor Christensen, *The Dallas Morning News*, June 22, 1997, pp. 1C, 6C (with "Where It All Comes From," a time line of alt. country 1967-1997).

"C&W's Hitkickers," Christopher Weir, *Metro Santa Cruz*, July 3, 1997 (brief profiles of Dale Watson, Chris Wall, The Derailers, Don Walser).

"Up From the Roots. The Next Big Thing: The Thing That Started It All," Michael Podolsky, *Tucson Weekly*, July 24, 1997.

"Take Back the Country," Robert Christgau, *The Village Voice*, August 5, 1997.

"God Bless Americana," Stephen L. Bets, *Country Spotlight*, August 14, 1997.

"Alternative Country: Or How I Learned to Like Country and Western," Jessica Holliday, *MusicMatch On-Line*, August 29, 1997.

"Catching On: No Depression Magazine," Michael Bertin, *The Austin Chronicle*, September 5, 1997.

"This Ain't Your Daddy's Old Country Rock: No Depression Blending Twang, Crunch," Fred Shuster, *The Los Angeles Daily News*, September 10, 1997.

"Western Where? 'Insurgent Country,' A Little Bit Rock-and-Roll," Richard Harrington, *The Washington* Post, September 17, 1997, p. D07.

"Garage Notes: Country Music Monstrosities," Bob Pomeroy, *Focus*, September 18, 1997.

"The Life and Times of Americana—In The Pines," Rob Bleetstein, *Gavin*, September 19, 1997.

"Tony Brown on Americana: The Next Wave Is Now," Rob Bleetstein, *Gavin*, September 19, 1997.

"Alternative Country Music Getting Big Labels' Attention," Dan DeLuca, *The Greensboro News & Record*, November 13, 1997.

"Twangcore Acts Take Back the Country," Daniel Aloi, *Elmira Star-Gazette*, November 20, 1997.

"Return of the Grievous Angels," *Uncut* (UK), December 1997 or January 1998 (general alt. country article).

"Yuletide Resuscitation: Big Iron Comes Back for Another Round," Matt Weitz, *Dallas Observer*, December 18, 1997 (on the **Honkey-Tonk Holidays** compilation from Dallas record label that was the original home of the Old 97s, Cartwrights, and other Big-D alt. country bands of the early 1990s).

"Bashing Nashville: Panning for Country Gold Outside the Mainstream," Michael McCall, *Nashville Scene*, December 29, 1997.

"Radio's Newest Format Gets to Its Roots," Craig P. Havighurst, *The Wall Street Journal*, January 7, 1998 (on Americana; reprinted *Gavin*, January, 21, 1998).

"Country Punks," Jon Wiederhorn, *Swing Generation*, February 1998.

"Past Guides Roots Musicians," David Hoekstra, *The Chicago Sun-Times*, February 15, 1998 (about Checkered Past Records).

"Americana May Be Music's Big Comer," Phil Gallo, *Reuters*, February 20, 1998.

"Alejandro Escovedo: Artist of the Decade," Peter Blackstock, *No Depression*, March/April 1998, pp. 66-80 (See *3rd Coast Music*, July 1998 and *XLent, Austin-American Statesman*, January 21, 1999 for different candidates).

"Austin: A Musical History Tour," Chris Marino, *Gavin*, March 25, 1998 (focus on the best of Austin's Americana venues).

"The Horse Whisperer: Can a Star-Studded Soundtrack Bring Americana to the Masses?," Alexandra Russell, *Gavin*, March 25, 1998.

"A Little Bit Country, A Little Bit Rock 'n' Roll: Can Alt-Country Find a Voice of Its Own?," Amy Carlson, *AE:ONLINE*, April 1, 1998.

"Country Music: Down Home on Avenue C, An 'Opry' Neither Grand Nor Ole," Peter Applebome, *The New York Times*, April 23, 1998 (on Greg Garing's Alphabet City Opry).

"It's a Cheatin' Situation: Musicians Gather to Celebrate the Sinful in Country Songs," John T. Davis, *XLent, Austin-American Statesman*, April 30, 1998 (The Wandering Eyes).

"Exhuming Hank," Brandon Barber, *Jacked*, May 4, 1998.

"Under (ground) Achievers: Can Nashville's Creative Underbelly Save Country From Music Row?," Rob Patterson, *The Houston Press*, May 28, 1998 (on Earle, Burch, Morris, Moorer, et al.).

"Alt. Country Gazette," Daniel Durchholz, *Pulse!*, June 1998, pp. 55, 65 (on *No Depression* magazine).

"Bringing It Home: Americana Radio's Community Ties," Laura Sweezy with Chris Marino, *Gavin*, June 4, 1998 (on charitable projects by various stations).

"Alternative Country: All Twanged Out?," Mark Guarino, *Chicago Daily Herald*, June 5, 1998.

"Country Rock Reels With Comings and Goings," David Menconi, *The Raleigh News & Observer*, June 5, 1998 (about the woes of the Backsliders and Whiskeytown).

"Country Music Roots," Scott Simon, *NPR*, June 20, 1998 (radio interview with historian Bill Malone on the radical roots of country with a bit on Steve Earle and insurgent/no depression country).

"Southern to the Roots: The New Country Synthesis Mixing in Blues, Rock, Pop, and Soul," Bill Friskics-Warren, *The Washington Post*, June 24, 1998.

"Alternative Country: A Primer on How the Nashville Sound Fused With the Power of Punk Rock," Monica Eng, *Chicago Tribune*, June 25, 1998.

"Got a Woody. With Mermaid Avenue, Billy Bragg and Wilco Turn a Myth Into a Man," Robert Wilonsky, *Dallas Observer*, June 25, 1998.

"The House Is Rockin'...A Hankerin' for Hank, Buck, Gram and Their Musical Ilk is Rising Like a Prairie Twister," Lisa Weeks, *Tucson Weekly*, June 29, 1998.

"Dave Alvin: Artist of the Decade," John Conquest, *3rd Coast Music*, July 1998.

"Everything Old is Young Again. New Music From the Veterans of Old Country is Roping in Rock Audiences," Bill C. Malone, *Salon*, July 2, 1998 (on the current influence of Guthrie, Stanley, Cash, and Nelson).

"Gram Parsons: Genius & Grief," *Mojo, The Music Magazine*, July 1998.

"Supersonic Nursery Rhymes: Billy Bragg and Woody Guthrie," Michael Bertin, *The Austin Chronicle*, July 5, 1998.

"This Machine Kills Preconceptions," Dave Marsh, *Addicted to Noise*, July 5, 1998 (on Mermaid Avenue).

"Why Aren't Mainstreamers Buying Alternative Country?" and "Who's Hot and Who's Not in Alt. Country," Dave Ferman, *Ft. Worth Star-Telegram*, July 29, 1998 (also as "Alternative Country Isn't Yet Everyone's Cup of Tea," *The Milwaukee Journal Sentinel*, August 2, 1998.

"The Other Country Music: Alternative-Country Fans Are Tuning Out the Slick Sounds of Mainstream Nashville Stars for Country's Raw Roots," Dave Ferman, *The Ottawa Citizen*, August 10, 1998.

"Another Country Heard From" & "Movers and Shakers in Alt-Country," Dave Ferman, *The Bergen Record Online*, August 11, 1998.

"The Incomplete Guide to Roots Music," Buddy Seigal, *OC Weekly*, August 14, 1998 (on alt. country/Americana/roots in Orange County, California).

"Sleazy Not Easy," Mary Jessica Hammes & Melissa Jane Link, *Flagpole*, August 19, 1998 (on Sleazefest).

"From Little Acorns: Oakhill Music is An Online Growth Industry," Jack W. Hill, *Arkansas Democrat Gazette*, August 21, 1998 (on the excellent alt. country record store based in Little Rock).

"Americana All-Stars: The Format's Top Performers," Chris Marino, *Gavin*, August 27, 1998 (profiles of the best according to Americana radio and music industry professionals).

"Country's Grave Condition: Jon Langford Came to Nashville to Bury Country, Not to Praise It," Bill Friskics-Warren, *The Washington Post*, August 30, 1998 (on controversial Nashville/Chicago art exhibition on the "Death of Country Music").

"Sounds of the New West," *Uncut*, September 1998 (special section devoted to Alternative Country with accompanying CD of the same name featuring cuts by the Flying Burrito Brothers, Emmylou, Hazel-

dine, Neal Casal, Freakwater, Lambchop, et al.).

"How the West Was Won: Everything You Need to Know About Alternative Country," Stewart Lee and Allan Jones, *Uncut*, September 1998 (lengthy A-Z guide with profiles of selected artists, labels, 'zines, and venues).

"Take Me Back to Those Black Hills That I Ain't Never Seen: The Kinks Invent Alternative-Kountry," Gary Pig Gold, *Rural Route Twangzine*, September 1998 (on the 1971 **Muswell Hillbillies** as a pioneering country-rock album).

"Special Section: Local Label Round-Up," *The Austin Chronicle*, September 4-10, 1998 (profiles of Austin record companies including alt. country labels Freedom, Lazy SOB, Doolittle, and Cold Spring).

"Parsons Still on the Edge. Late Country-Rock Pioneer Gains a Growing Cult Status," James Sullivan, *The San Francisco Chronicle*, September 9, 1998.

"Gram Parsons Retrospective," Sean O'Hagan, *The Guardian*, September 12, 1998.

"Time to Develop: Record Company Does Things the Old-Fashioned Way," Bill Friskics-Warren, *Nashville Scene*, September 14, 1998 (on Dejadisc/KOCH).

"MC Hank. According to a Couple of Modern-Day Country Punks, Hank Williams Would Probably Be a Rapper Today," *Amazon.Com*, September 17, 1998 (interview with Jon Langford and Robbie Fulks).

"Y'All-Ternative Country: Who Will Win Isn't Who Should at Tonight's CMA Awards," Buzz McCalin, *The Ft. Worth Star-Telegram*, September 23, 1998 (HNC vs. Alt. Country).

"The Legacy of Gram Parsons," Michael Goldberg, *Addicted To Noise*, September 24, 1998.

"Alternative Country Is What Punks Play When They Grow Up," Tom Cox, *The Guardian*, October 16, 1998.

"Bloodshot Records: On the Fringe and Loving It," Derek Caney, *Reuters/Variety*, October 20, 1998.

"Texas Troubadours: 10 Quintessential Lone Star Songwriters Shine on Lyle Lovett's New CD," Punch Shaw, *The Fort Worth Star-Telegram*, October 21, 1998.

"Country and Midwestern: The Best of Alt-Country Lot Salute the Majesty of the Past While Defining the Future," Mark Athitakis, *The Dallas Observer*, October 22, 1998.

"Outside Regular Channels: The Texas Music Round-Up," Andy Langer, *The Austin Chronicle*, October 22, 1998. (about the independent label mail order company formed by Cold Spring, Freedom, and Lazy SOB Records).

"Bluegrass Fiddlin' Around: Long a Musical Mainstay Here, 'True Country' Suddenly Is Spreading Like a Weed and Cropping Up All Over," Judy Raphael, *The Los Angeles Times*, October 29, 1998 (on the resurgence of bluegrass in the L.A. Area).

"Hands Up! Outlaw Country: Willie, Waylon and the Nashville Rebels," Stanley Booth, *Gadfly*, November, 1998.

"Post-Depression: The Legacy of Uncle Tupelo," Greg Bottoms, *Gadfly*, November 1998, p. 34.

"The Originators of Alt-Country—It Ain't What You Think," Jeff Wall, *Rural Route Twangzine*, November 1998.

"The Third Coast Music Network", *Action: The Texas Entertainment Magazine*, November 1998 (on Joe Horn's great alt. country/Americana program on station KSYM in San Antonio).

"Sa-Lute! Say Howdy to the Area's New Wave of Country Insurgents", Michael Powell, *Ft. Worth Weekly*, November 26, 1998 (on up-and-coming Dallas/Ft. Worth acts like Jasper Stone, Woodeye, and Eleven-Hundred Springs).

"Opry Fever Afflicts Big Apple," Brian Steinberg, *Country Standard Time*, December 1998 (Greg Garing's Alphabet City Opry in New York City).

"Postcards From the (Alt-Country) Edge," Don Yates, *Gavin*, December 1998.

"The Originators of Alt-Country, Part I—Country Rock," Jeff Wall, *Rural Route Twangzine*, December 1998.

"The New Roots Explosion: The Lonesome Trail From Hank Williams to Beck," *Mojo*, December 1998 (Includes "The Shock of the Old" and "The Woodchuck Nation," an article and timeline which trace the moments from 1968-1998 when rock returned to its roots).

"Breaking the Rules of Country Radio: www.TwangCast.com," Rural Route *Twangzine*, January 1999 (Mike Hays/RealCountry netcast).

"The History of Alt. Country, Part II," Jeff Wall, *Rural Route Twangzine*, January 1999.

"Hillbilly Boogie," *Journal of Country Music*, January 1999 (cover story featuring Big Sandy, Ray Condo, Ronnie Dawson, Dave & Deke, Rose Maddox, and more).

"Alt-Country Spreads From the Heartland to the Fringes," Daniel Aloi, *Elmira Star-Gazette*, January 7, 1999.

"Artist of the Decade: Jeff Tweedy," Michael Corcoran, *XLent, Austin-American Statesma*n, January 21, 1999.

---

*Many thanks to Phil Connor of the Postcard 2 online mailing list for regularly posting alt. country & Americana articles!

Modern Twang

ABBREVIATIONS

acc	accordion		l.s.	lap steel
a.g.	acoustic guitar		l.v	lead vocals
b	bass		md	mandolin
bj	banjo		mda	mandola
bj sx	bajo sexto		m.o.	mail order
boot	bootleg recording		No	Norway
b.v.	background vocals		org	organ
b/w	backed with		p	piano
Can.	Canada		perc	percussion
cl	clarinet		pp	previous performers
clo	cello		p.s.	pedal steel
cs	cassette		rb	rubboard
d	drums		r.g.	rhythm guitar
db	dobro		sax	saxophone
dulc	dulcimer		s.g.	steel guitar
e.g.	electric guitar		sl. g.	slide guitar
EP	recording with 3-6 tracks		s/s	singer/songwriter
f	fiddle		Swe.	Sweden
Fin.	Finland		Switz.	Switzerland
Fr.	France		tba	tuba
g	guitar		trb	trombone
Ger.	Germany		tri	triangle
hm	harmonica		tp	trumpet
h.v.	harmony vocals		u.b.	upright bass
Ita.	Italy		U.K.	United Kingdom
Jp.	Japan		v	vocals
ky	keyboards		vio	violin
l.g.	lead guitar		wb	washboard

Accident Clearinghouse

Honky Tonk; Country Rock; Rockabilly; New Old-Time
Champlin, Minnesota; 1993-

Formed in the early 1990s, Accident Clearinghouse was originally an acoustic trio made up of Quillan Roe on guitar and lead vocals with Mike Brady and Jeff Tranberry trading off on banjo, bass, guitar, and mandolin. With the addition of Dan Gerber on spoons, washboard, and Tide bottle, the group began writing songs and playing basement parties, art gallery openings, and local clubs. By the middle of 1996, they had stockpiled a large body of original material and seriously considered putting out a 38 song, double CD but decided instead to make two separate recordings. The first, **The Simple-Hearted Sounds of Accident Clearinghouse, Volume 1: Saginaw Sweetheart**, is fairly easy-going old-time and honky tonk as interpreted by country rock groups from the Byrds/Flying Burrito Brothers through the Jayhawks and Uncle Tupelo/Son Volt. Relying mainly on acoustic instruments, Accident Clearinghouse probes standard country themes (heartbreak, violence, death, substance abuse) giving them whimsical twists on "Big City Trouble," "I Got Friends," "The Night That Daddy Got His Gun," "What Was Your Name in the States," "I Wanna Forget Your Mine," and "Flamin' Hair." Early in 1997, the Minnesota Academy of Music nominated their debut for Best Country Recording, and in 1998, the same organization nominated them as Best Country Group. Meanwhile, with drummer Scott Berndt replacing percussionist Gerber, AC set to work on a sequel, **Volume 2: Absolute Collision**, which retains much of the feel of **Volume 1** ("Claire & Leo," "Loraine," "Pink, Not Blue," "Your Angel Above") but also adds straight ahead rockabilly with "Bye-Bye, Pain," "Speedin'," "Queen of Double Vision," "Trash Talkin' Mama," and "I Sold My Soul." Late in 1998, with new drummer Kevin Riach and washboard man Tim Armstrong, AC released an EP, **Live at Bryant Lake Bowl**, with five new songs and "candid" interviews. They also worked on a third full-length recording tentatively titled **Walking Heart Attack**.

Tim Armstrong (wb, v); Scott Berndt (d,b.v.,1996); Mike Brady (bj,md,l.g.,b.v.); Dan Gerber (bottle,wb,1993-1996); Kevin Riach (d); Quillan Roe (r.g., l.v.); Jeff Tranberry (ub,bj,l.g.,md)

The Simple-Hearted Sounds of Accident Clearinghouse, Volume 1: Saginaw Sweetheart/ OBT/1996
Accident Clearinghouse: Live at The Fine Line/ AC/1997
The Simple-Hearted Sounds of Accident Clearinghouse, Volume 2: Absolute Collision/ OBT/1998
"Bedtime for Boogie Town" on **Welcome to Swingland: Lee's Liquor Bar Swing Compilation**/KLBB/1998
Live at Bryant Lake Bowl/OBT/1998 (EP)
The Simple-Hearted Sounds of Accident Clearinghouse, Volume 3: Walking Heart Attack/OBT/1999

Accident Clearinghouse, P.O. Box 41271, Plymouth, MN 55441-0271; 612-425-5174

Accident Clearinghouse Home Page //www.accidentclearinghouse.com

jtranberry@accidentclearinghouse.com

Acetone

Lo-Fi Country Rock
Los Angeles, California; 1987-

Named for a powerful industrial solvent, Acetone has made its reputation primarily as a very low-energy garage rock band combining Crazy Horse noise and Velvet Underground psychedelia into a sound most often described as languid, dreamy, or mellow. However, they've occasionally detoured down a country road, most notably on **I Guess I Would** which uses whispery vocals and spare accompaniment to set a slower-than-molasses-in-December tone suggestive of the Cowboy Junkies, the Handsome Family, Palace, and Souled American. Side A is extremely laid back covers of "Juanita" (Parsons/Hillman instrumental), "The Late John Garfield Blues" (John Prine), "All For the Love of a Girl" (Johnny Horton), "Sometimes You Just Can't Win" (Smokey Stover), "How Sweet I Roamed" (Ed Sanders-Fugs/William Blake), and the title track (Jerry Cole). Side B is an extended (11 minutes), grungy version of Kris Kristofferson's "Border Lord" beginning with distorted fuzzy guitar and vocals and then easing down into a drowsy jam reminiscent of the psychedelic 60s.

Dropped by their original label in 1996, Acetone's self-titled CD/double LP became the first release on Neil Young's Vapor Records at the end of 1997. Described by its label as "Gram Parsons hijacking the sessions for the third Velvet Underground album," **Acetone** continues the band's patented lo-fi drone with just a hint of twang thanks, in part, to the contribution of pedal steel ace Greg Leisz.

Steve Hadley (d); Richie Lee (a.g.,b,fuzz g.,v); Mark Lightcap (g,v.)

Cindy/Vernon Yard/1993
I Guess I Would/Vernon Yard/1994

If You Only Knew/Vernon Yard/1996
Acetone/Vapor/1997

Acetone Home Page
//yin.interaccess.com/~bmaki/acetone/home.htm

Acetone/Vapor Records Web Page
//www.vaporrecords.com/acetone.htm

Hasil Adkins

Psychocountry
Boone County, West Virginia; April 29, 1937-

The undeniable godfather of psychocountry or psychobilly is Hasil Adkins. Beginning in the 1950s, this demonic one-man band, began recording the rawest, most demented hillbilly music in a homemade studio set back in the hills of Boone County, West Virginia. Through the release of 45s (on very obscure labels) and live performances, Adkins gained a reputation as "The Wild Man" whose style both lyrically (severed heads, neanderthals, weird dances) and musically (distorted guitar, crazy rhythms, screaming) bordered on total insanity. In 1957, he introduced a dirty new dance called "The Hunch," and while Hasil gained a local following and was popular in Europe (mostly through bootlegs), his recording career flagged in the 1960s and 1970s. Then, in the late 1980s, Norton Records began reissuing Adkins early recordings as well as new releases like **The Wild Man** that were as over-the-edge as ever. And although the bulk of his output is of the whacked out variety, The Haze has shown an ability to do more straight ahead country on **Moon Over Madison** and **Achy Breaky Ha Ha**. The resurgence of psychobilly in recent years and appearances at events such as Sleazefest helped make Adkins popular with a new generation of fans and musicians such as Southern Culture on the Skids. For an up close and personal look, check out the 1993 documentary: *The Wild World of Hasil Adkins.*

In 1998, Adkins signed with Fat Possum and shortly thereafter came **What The Hell Was I Thinking?** which presents a slightly more "subdued" wild man on country and country blues. During the summer and fall of that year, Hasil joined the Fat Possum Eye-Scratchers & Ball Kickers Tour with label mates T-Model Ford and Spum, Elmo Williams, and Hezekiah Early. Late in December 1998, he invaded the Empty Glass in Charleston, West Virginia for a live recording set for release in 1999. Meanwhile, his legions of fans launched a drive to give The Haze his rightful place in the Rock & Roll Hall of Fame.

>   **Out to Hunch**/Norton/1986 (LP)
>   **Chicken Walk**/Dee-Jay Jamboree/1986
>   **The Wild Man**/Norton/1987 (LP)
>   **Peanut Butter Rock & Roll**/Norton/1990 (from
>   1958-1963)
>   **Moon Over Madison**/Norton/1990 (LP)
>   **Look at That Caveman Go!**/Norton/1993 (LP,CD)
>   **Rock & Roll Tonight (Live)**/Dee-Jay Jamboree/
>   **Haze's House Party**/Norton/ (EP)
>   "Big Red Satellite" b/w "Ellen Marie"/Norton/ (7")

"Sally Wally Woody Waddy Weedy" b/w "Miami Kiss"/Norton/ (7")
"Boo Boo the Cat" b/w "Mathilda"/Norton/ (7")
"Chicken Shake" b/w "She's Mine #2"/Norton/ (7")
Achy Breaky Ha Ha/Norton/1995 (LP,CD)
"Seaside Cruise" b/w "Chocolate Milk Honeymoon"/
   Norton/1997 (7")
Live From Chicago/Bughouse/1997
What The Hell Was I Thinking?/Fat Possum/1998
The Wild World of Hasil Adkins/1993 (28 min. video)

Hasil Adkins, P.O. Box 668, Madison, WV 25130;
304-369-3466

The Hasil Adkins Hunch Club (Official)
//members.tripod.com/~hasil_adkins/

Hasil Adkins: The Haze
//www.iserv.net/~jakeb/hazemain.html

The Hasil Motel Page //www.sleazefest.com

See Southern Culture on the Skids

Christine Albert (Boxcars)

Singer/Songwriter; Austin
New York; September 12, 1955-

A native of upstate New York, Christine Albert got her first exposure to country music when she moved to New Mexico in the 1970s. She played in country/swing bands in Santa Fe and Albuquerque and met Junior Brown (at that time J. B. Brown) who was a member of the locals' favorite honky-tonk band the Last Mile Ramblers. He introduced her to the rich traditions of country music, and she got to open as a solo for Texas performers (Asleep at the Wheel, Guy Clark, Joe Ely, Townes Van Zandt, et al.) when they toured northern New Mexico. Eventually, Albert made the move to Austin (1982) where with the help of these earlier contacts, she began performing and recording. She was also active as an organizer, co-founding the Austin Songwriters Group in 1987. In the late 1980s and early 1990s, Christine Albert was tabbed as the next Austin singer/songwriter to "make it big" but due to a number of factors, it just didn't happen. An album cut for CBS in 1988 was never released, and she was dropped from their label in the wake of a corporate take over; at the same time, Albert became a mother and devoted more time to her new family. In the early 1990s, Christine recorded several solid Texas country rock albums, **The High Road** and **Underneath the Lone Star Sky**, using some of Austin's best talent (Paul Glasse, Gene Elders, Mitch Watkins, Danny Levin, Jimmy LaFave). She also did a "French Show" and a very popular bilingual recording (**Texafrance**) reflecting her French-Swiss heritage and long standing love affair with the music of Edith Piaf, Jacques Brel, and other notable French vocalists. In spite of mixed success in attracting major label attention, Albert continued doing the kind of music she wanted to do and maintained a strong following in Central Texas (Kerrville Outstanding Female Vocalist 1996) as well as in Europe. While working on a new album in the spring of 1997, she teamed with guitarist/vocalist Chris Gage (ex-Jimmie Dale

Gilmore) as the country/roots/rock duo Boxcars (named for a Butch Hancock song). Their debut, **Jumpin' Tracks**, expands Albert's country rock into a more folksy, rhythm and bluesy sound.

Across the Miles/Gambini Global/1986
You Are Gold/Gambini Global/1990 (CS)
Texafrance/Gambini Global/1992
"Pastures of Plenty" on **Pastures of Plenty: An Austin Celebration of Woody Guthrie**/ Dejadisc/1993
The High Road/Gambini Global/1993
Underneath the Lone Star Sky/dos/1995
Jumpin' Tracks (Boxcars)/Flatrock/1997
"Haunt Your Heart" on **The Women of Kerrville**/ Silverwolf/1998

Christine Albert/Boxcars, P. O. Box 33294, Austin, TX 78764; 512-707-1720 (fax) 512-707-1763

boxcars@juno.com

The Alien Rebels
Hillbilly Bop; Novelty
Calgary, Alberta, Canada; 1991-

Although they call what they do "post ancient earth music," Canada's Alien Rebels actually play a combination of rock-abilly, surf, and old-time tilted heavily toward the bizarre and just outright silly. The members were veterans of various Canadian alt. country bands (Willie P. Bennett, Jr. Gone Wild) before getting together in 1991 as a result of some jam sessions at the Black Diamond Hotel south of Calgary. Modeled loosely on the classic rockabilly acts of the 1950s, their name was chosen by leader Mark Sadlier-Brown because it was the dumbest he could think of and because he thought it might get them more attention. Establishing themselves as mainstays on the Alberta club scene, the Alien Rebels made their debut with **UFO** which contained the Sadlier-Brown composition, "Your Heart is As Cold as the TV Dinner You Threw at Me Last Night" (later covered by Amos Garrett). In 1996, they self-released **Strange Feelings** with covers of Screamin Jay Hawkins (title cut), Webb Pierce ("Teenage Boogie"), Roosevelt Sykes ("Drivin' Wheel"), Jack Earles ("Slow Down"), Crazy Cavan ("Bop"), Pinkard & Bowden ("I Lobster But Never Flounder"), and playfully twisted originals "Laundromat Love," "Dance of the Strange," "Don Armando's Campground," "Surfin' the Net," and "Aliens." The Rebels received greater coverage through appearances on Canadian television, air play on the CBC for their "All I Want for Christmas Is a Red Guitar," and inclusion of "Strange Feelings" on Air Canada's in flight enter-tainment menu.

Terry Anderson (d,v); Lance Loree (hm,l.g.,v); Mark Sadlier-Brown (jug,r.g.,v); Suitcase James Stanley (b,v)

UFO/AR/1993
Strange Feelings/AR/1996
"All I Want For Christmas Is a Red Guitar"/AR/1996 (7")

The Alien Rebels, 621 9th Ave. NW, Ste. 200, Calgary, Alberta, Canada T2N 1E3; 403-283-9452
The Alien Rebels Home Page
//www.candisc.com/alien_rebels/
Alienreb@cadvision or alien_rebels@hotmail.com

Terry Allen
Lubbock Mafia; Singer/Songwriter
Wichita, Kansas; May 7, 1943-

West Texas has contributed more than its fair share of great singer/songwriters: Joe Ely, Jimmie Dale Gilmore, and Butch Hancock. A more obscure but in many ways the most talented artist to come from this region is Terry Allen. Like the aforementioned musicians, Allen grew up in Lubbock and was heavily influenced by the unique landscape and culture of the Texas Panhandle. Early on, he rebelled against the starkness of both the land and the people through painting, writing, and music. Allen was especially encouraged in the latter by his family; his mother taught him piano while his father, Sled, owned and operated a large arena that booked wrestling and a variety of local and national musicians. While working there, Allen was exposed on a regular basis to country, blues, and rock 'n' roll and inspired to make his musical debut at a high school assembly where he performed an original song, "Roman Orgy." Allen was rewarded with a suspension which was the capper to a generally forgettable high school career. Not surprisingly, after graduation, he got out of Lubbock, pronto, and headed to California where he entered the Chouinard Art Institute in Los Angeles. Earning a B.F.A. in 1966, Allen remained in California into the 1970s where he developed his artistic style and musical skills as well. In 1974, trading art for studio time, he recorded his first album, **Juarez**, a soundtrack for an imaginary film exploring the special relationship between Texas and Mexico. Shortly afterward, Allen and a partner set up Fate Records, and he began working on a new concept album focusing on his hometown. Initially, he planned to record it in L.A. and Lubbock, but the success of Ely and Hancock in the late 1970s convinced him to do the whole thing at Lubbock's Caldwell Studios which was at the heart of the resurgent West Texas music scene. There, Allen teamed with producer and steel guitar wiz Lloyd Maines, Richard Bowden, Jesse Taylor, and members of the Maines Brothers to form the Panhandle Mystery Band. In 1977, they recorded the double LP, **Lubbock (On Everything)**, which many consider Allen's definitive musical work. Here, he paints a brilliant and refreshingly honest portrait of life in West Texas by using familiar country music idioms but in a way that is wholly original. The unique characters and experiences of the region shine through on "Amarillo Highway," "The Great Joe Bob," "Highplains Jamboree," "Wolfman of Del Rio," and a host of other great songs. After the release of the album in 1979, Allen and band toured and followed up **Lubbock** with two albums covering similar territory, **Smokin' the Dummy** and **Bloodlines**. Then, in the mid-1980s, Allen expanded his musical and artistic horizons: from 1983-1986, he worked on a project called "Youth in Asia" about the emotional shocks of the Vietnam experience (including the music for a documentary, **Amerasia**, about American servicemen in Thailand); in 1984, Allen composed an award winning score for a dance piece, **Pedal Steel**, for the San Francisco Dance Company and followed it up with a similar project, **Rollback**; in 1986, he contributed several songs for the David Byrne/Talking Heads film, *True Stories*; beginning in 1987, Allen did four commissioned works for radio, *Torso Hell*, *Bleeder*, *Reunion: Return to Juarez*, and *Dugout* which presented music and vocal performances by Allen and his wife Jo Harvey (an Allen "self-interview" and excerpts from his radio plays can be found at the New American Radio web site); with Jo Harvey, he co-wrote the play *Chippy, The Diary of a West Texas Hooker* which ran off Broadway and in selected U.S. cities in the early 1990s. The music from it was released as the soundtrack **Songs From Chippy** and includes selections by the Allens, Jimmie Dale Gilmore, Joe Ely, Butch Hancock, Wayne Hancock, and Jo Carol Pierce. On top of all this, Allen has developed into a top notch visual artist winning several NEA grants, a Guggenheim Fellowship, and international acclaim.

After a hiatus from recording studio albums, in 1996 Allen returned with **Human Remains** which offers more of his signature West Texas commentary with help from David Byrne, Joe Ely, and the Sexton Brothers. Sugar Hill Records has steadily reissued Allen's classics including **Lubbock on Everything**, **Smokin' the Dummy**, and **Bloodlines**. Late in 1998, he made a long overdue appearance on *Austin City Limits* and worked on two recordings for release in 1999: a collaboration with Guy Clark and a solo tentatively titled **Crosshairs** (supposedly the cover would be a picture of a hairy crucifix) but later renamed **Salivation** (with a funky drawing of Jesus on the front). Allen called it "gospel...with a limp and a lurch."

Juarez/Landfall/1975; Fate/1981
Lubbock on Everything/Fate/1979; Sugar Hill/1996
Smokin' the Dummy/Fate/1982
Bloodlines/Fate/1983
Amerasia/Fate/1984
Pedal Steel/Fate/1985
Rollback/Fate/1988
The Silent Majority: Terry Allen's Greatest Hits Missed/Fate/1993
Songs From Chippy/Hollywood/1994
Human Remains/Sugar Hill/1996
Smokin' the Dummy/Bloodlines/Sugar Hill/1997
"Ourland" (live) on **Viva Americana**/Boka UK/1998
Salivation/Sugar Hill/1999

Terry Allen/Davis McLarty Agency Page
//www.davismclarty.com/terry.htm

Terry Allen/New American Radio Page
//somewhere.org/nar/workexcerpts/allen/media/interview.htm

See Joe Ely; Butch Hancock; Lloyd Maines; Jo Carol Pierce

Amy Allison (The Maudlins; Parlor James)
Rig Rock; Gothic Country
Brooklyn, New York; June 24, 1958-

One of the great things about a really sad country song is that it can often cheer you up when you're down. Just listen to the pitiful moanings of some "tears in my beer" singer and chances are you'll end up laughing out loud and feeling better about your own miserable life. Such an understanding of the effect of country music informs the songwriting and singing of Amy Allison. Her unrivaled nasally twang and wry sense of humor transform what at first appear to be excruciatingly sad situations into stories that make you chuckle in spite of yourself. Allison's knack for turning pathos to mirth comes at least in part from her father Mose, the jazz pianist who was noted for his humorous take on the blues ("Your Mind is On Vacation, But Your Mouth is Working Overtime"; "I Don't Worry 'Bout a Thing, 'Cause I Know Nothin's Gonna Turn Out Right"). Beginning, in 1987, Allison and her aptly named band, the Maudlins, began presenting their "citybilly" sound in New York nightclubs. Their first recording was "Cheater's World" for the **Rig Rock Truckstop** compilation in 1993. However, the band's first full length effort didn't appear until 1996 with the release of **The Maudlin Years**, which is full of Allison's catchy little gems including "Hate at First Sight," "The Whiskey Makes You Sweeter Than You Are," "Garden State Mall," and "Holding the Baby."

In the last few years, Allison has explored the decidedly darker traditions of country life and music with a band called Parlor James. Here, she teams with Ryan Hedgecock (co-founder of the 1980s country rock band, Lone Justice) who knew of Amy through her album work with the Silos. When they finally met in 1994 at a songwriters' showcase at New York City's Mercury Lounge, Allison's live performance sealed the deal for Hedgecock; they began singing together and did several demos including the traditional song "Snow Dove" which got the attention of Discovery Records. Joined by former Lone Justice mate Don Heffington on drums and Malcolm Burn on keyboards, Allison and Hedgecock formed Parlor James and recorded the **Dreadful Sorry** EP in 1996. From the CD artwork (flower draped open casket cover; distraught angel statue on the inner sleeve) to the songs about fear ("Lost My Way"), poverty ("Hell to Pay"), suicide ("Snow Dove"), darkness ("Devil's Door"), the record oozes Gothic Americana rivaling the eeriest of Palace and 16 Horsepower. However, contrary to expectations, Parlor James full length debut, **Old Dreams**, veered off their previous course toward a more electronica/pop rock sound with Allison's undisguiseable twang now backed by programmed effects and Daniel Lanoisesque guitars. Still, a few remnants of the traditional country feel remain, most notably on

"Captain, Captain," "Don't Go Downtown," "The Pain I'm In," and a startling remake of the old classic, "Clementine." Comparable experiments have come from Greg Garing, the Handsome Family, and Emmylou Harris on **Wrecking Ball**. As with these recordings, critics were about evenly divided over whether **Old Dreams** is sacrilege or respectful innovation. Fans of Allison's "citybilly" can still find her playing with the Maudlins (now with Hedgecock on bass) in New York City.

The Maudlins: Amy Allison (l.v.); Mark Amft (b); Simon Heathcote (l.g.); Ryan Hedgecock (b); Steven Lewis (l.s.); Rob Meador (r.g.); Charlie Shaw (d).
Parlor James: Amy Allison (v); Malcolm Burn (b); Ryan Hedgecock (g,v); Don Heffington (perc)

"Cheater's World" on **Rig Rock Truck Stop**/Diesel
    Only/1993
The Maudlin Years/KOCH/1996
Dreadful Sorry (Parlor James)/Discovery/1996 (CD EP)
Old Dreams (Parlor James)/Sire/1998

Amy Allison/KOCH Home Page //kochint.com/
Parlor James iMusic Showcase
//www.imusic.com/showcase/contemporary/parlorjames.html

Dave Alvin; Phil Alvin

See The Blasters

Eric Ambel (The Del Lords; Roscoe's Gang)

Roots Rock; Producer
Brooklyn, New York

While most of the bands that led the country/roots/rock resurgence of the mid-1980s were from the Left Coast, on the East Coast the band at the forefront was New York City's Del Lords. Their effective blending of basic country and city rock resulted in a string of rocking and sometimes twangy albums. Prime mover (along with Scott Kempner) behind the group was Eric "Roscoe" Ambel who previously played guitar for Joan Jett and the Blackhearts. After six years with the Del Lords, Ambel decided to go it alone recording **Roscoe's Gang** in 1988. In the 1990s, Ambel became renowned as producer for alt. country artists—the Blood Oranges, Blue Mountain, the Bottle Rockets, Go To Blazes, Cheri Knight, Mojo Nixon, the Cowslingers, and the Blacks. Beside his vast experience, Ambel brought a distinctive guidance that accentuated the rock edge of these bands but never allowed it to overpower their country influences. Roscoe also lent his considerable guitar skills to albums by many artists including Angry Johnny & the Killbillies. He has continued to record and produce his own roots rock albums (**Loud and Lonesome**) as well, performing occasionally with Roscoe's Gang (has included the Skeletons, Will Rigby, Peter Holsapple) and collaborating with Dan Baird (ex-Georgia Satellites), Thomas Anderson, and Keith Christopher as the Yayhoos. In late 1998, Ambel contributed a cover

of "Revolution Blues" to a Dutch produced Neil Young tribute called **This Note's For You, Too!**

The Del Lords: Eric Ambel (g,v); Manny Caiti (b); Frank Funaro (d); Scott Kempner (g)
Roscoe's Gang: The Skeletons; Peter Holsapple; Will Rigby; Skid Roper

Frontier Days (Del Lords)/Enigma EMI/1984
Johnny Comes Marching Home (Del Lords)/
    Enigma/1986
Based on a True Story (Del Lords)/Enigma/1988
Howlin' at the Halloween Moon (Del
    Lords)/Restless/1989
Roscoe's Gang (Eric Ambel solo)/Enigma/1989
Lovers Who Wander (Del Lords)/Enigma/1990
Loud and Lonesome (Eric Ambel solo)/ESD/1995
"Highway Junkie" (The Yayhoos) on **Rig Rock Deluxe**/
    Upstart Diesel Only/1996
"Revolution Blues" on **This Note's for You Too!: A
    Tribute to Neil Young**/Inbetweens Dut./1999

American Music Club (Clodhopper)

Roots Rock; New Old-Time
San Francisco, California; 1983-1995

American Music Club was a forerunner of the many San Francisco alt. country groups (Dieselhed, Granfaloon Bus, Tarnation, U.S. Saucer) that emerged in the 1990s. They joined country, blues, and rock with modern elements drawn from punk and pop; their recordings (particularly **Engine**, **California**, **United Kingdom**, **Everclear**, and **San Francisco**) generally had a stripped-down, lo-fi roots rock sound made memorable by the effective use of moody pedal steel (Bruce Kaphan), mandolin, and guitar and the stellar songwriting of leader Mark Eitzel who dampened his angst-ridden songs of desperation with wit and even a little hope. *Spin* magazine called **Everclear** "a pedal steelists megalomaniac fantasy" while *Rolling Stone* labeled AMC's overall style as "post-punk honky tonk." A music critic's darling (especially with *Rolling Stone*) and very popular in England, AMC remained mostly an underground favorite in the U.S. despite several major label recordings in the early 1990s. When the "big breakthrough" failed to materialize, the band called it quits in 1995 with Eitzel going on to a solo career and maintaining a very loyal following. Meanwhile, AMC alumni, Dan Pearson and Tim Mooney, put together Clodhopper with Tim Bierman and several different bass players including Pearl Jam's Jeff Ament. Originally based in Missoula, Montana, and then San Francisco, Clodhopper is rooted in old-time mountain music (clawhammer banjo) but with a modern twist thanks to Pearson's electric mandolin and Bierman's fuzz guitar. Their debut, **Red's Recovery Room**, features covers of traditional tunes ("900 Miles"; "Dinah"; "Moonshiner") and Pearson originals (from his AMC days) with some fine steel work by old bandmate Bruce Kaphan.

AMC: Mark Eitzel (g,v); Bruce Kaphan (g,ky,p.s.,v); Tom Mallon (g); Tim Mooney (d,g,v); Dan Pearson (b,g,md,v); Vudi (g,v)
Clodhopper (1997-): Jeff Ament (b); Tim Bierman (g); Joe Goldring (b); J.C. Hawkins (org); Tim Mooney (d); Danny Pearson (bj, md,g,v)

> **The Restless Stranger**/Grifter/1986
> **Engine**/Grifter Frontier/1987
> **California**/Grifter Frontier/1988
> **United Kingdom**/Demon UK/1990
> **Everclear**/Alias/1991
> **Rise**/Alias/1991 (EP)
> **Songs of Love** (Mark Eitzel)/Demon UK/1991
> **Mercury**/Reprise/1993
> **60 Watt Silver Lining** (Mark Eitzel)/Warner Bros./1993
> **San Francisco**/Reprise/1994
> **Hello Amsterdam**/Reprise/1995 (EP)
> **West** (Mark Eitzel)/Warner Bros./1997
> **Red's Recovery Room** (Clodhopper)/My Own
>   Planet/1998

AMC/Warner Bros. Reprise Web Page
//www.iuma.com/warner/html/american_music_club.html

Clodhopper Web Page
//www.imusic.com/labels/myownplanet/clodhopper/

See Dieselhed; Granfaloon Bus; Tarnation; U.S. Saucer

Pete Anderson

See Dwight Yoakam

Angry Johnny and The Killbillies

Cowpunk
Easthampton, Massachusetts; 1991-

Many commentators have pointed out the connections between hard core country and punk: anger, iconoclasm, substance abuse, destruction, etc. Since the 1980s, many cowpunk or country punk bands have joined these traditions together; one of the most recent and most intense is Angry Johnny and the Killbillies. Hailing from the wilds of Western Massachusetts, Angry Johnny (a nickname given by his father, now his legal name) started out in a punk band in the early 1980s but when that played out was drawn to country music and particularly songs about failed relationships in which the jilted lover exacts retribution on himself or others. Angry had been a multiple loser in love but rather than acting on his destructive impulses channeled his anger into songwriting and performing. To support him, he assembled a band, first called the Snots, then the Millrats, and then the Killbillies with Al Camino, Jim Joe Greedy, and Sleepy Animall Kaisla. On record and on stage, the band alternates between acoustic numbers and rip-roaring, brain pounding country punk rock. Up until 1996, the Killbillies output consisted of one 45 and several independent LPs and cassettes, but a contract with Tar Hut Records resulted in **Hankenstein** whose cartoon cover depicts a green-skinned, heavily-stitched Hank standing before a microphone with guitar in hand (talk about your monster stars!). Equally

disturbing are Angry Johnny's songs which take many of country's tried and true themes way beyond the pale. AJ lives up to his name scratching and clawing through tunes about vengeance ("Life, Love, Death and the Meter Man" and "Chainsaw Charlie" which give new meaning to "you're in luck when you got a McCulloch chainsaw"; "Jawbone"; "Brand New Girl"; "Big Bang"), death ("Mr. Undertaker"; "202"; "Meet My Maker"), and losers ("Prison Walls"; "The Creep"). The most lighthearted moment on the album is about roadkill ("Poor Little Raccoon"). Serious, tongue-in-cheek, pretentious? Certainly not everyone's cup of meat but undoubtedly a breath of fresh air compared to the current crop of Nashville anti-Hanks.

A new recording in 1998, produced by Eric Ambel and titled **What's So Funny?** further sealed Angry Johnny's self-styled reputation as "the world's most whacked-out band." Its cartoon cover depicting a fat clown wielding a bloody axe is a dead give away you're in for more raw boned backwoods country centered on wretched refuse ("All American Girl"; "Disposable Boy"; "Shitty Day") and lots and lots of violence ("High Noon in Killville"; "The Joneses"; "Henry"; "Kill Again").

Angry Johnny (hm, l.v.); Al Camino (g,md); Jim Joe Greedy (b); Sleepy Animall Kaisla (d)

> "Henry" + 2/Chunk/1993 (7")
> "Nuclear Man" on **Hotel Massachusetts**/Chunk/1994
> **Hankenstein**/Tar Hut/1996
> **What's So Funny?**/Tar Hut/1998

Angry Johnny Home Page //members.aol.com/killbillie/
Angryjohn@aol.com

Angry Johnny/Tar Hut Page //www.tarhut.com
info@tarhut.com

Asleep at the Wheel

Western Swing
Paw Paw, West Virginia; 1971-

In 1995, a gala celebration was held at Bass Concert Hall in Austin, Texas to commemorate the 25th anniversary of Asleep at the Wheel. On hand were fans, friends, and a good number of the 70+ musicians who played in the band over the years. At center stage was the imposing figure of Ray Benson, founder and only member to have been with the group all the way through. Born and raised in Philadelphia, Ray Benson Siefert absorbed a variety of music in the 1950s and 1960s, but his introduction to country was mainly through the West Virginia Jamboree over radio station WWVA. After a brief stay at Antioch College (Ohio), in 1970 Benson moved to a farm in West Virginia where with steel player Reuben Gosfield aka Lucky Oceans and drummer LeRoy Preston, he began playing Western swing in local dives. With the addition of Jim Haber aka Floyd Domino on piano and vocalist Chris O'Connell,

Asleep at the Wheel was born (name thought up by Oceans while sitting in an outhouse). Encouraged by Commander Cody's manager, they moved to California in 1971 and quickly built a large following in the Berkeley area. By 1973, AATW was ready to record their first album **Comin' Right at You** for United Artists. Produced by Tommy Allsup and aided by the great fiddler and Texas Playboy alumnus Johnny Gimble, it presented winning covers of Bob Wills ("Take Me Back to Tulsa"), Ernest Tubb ("Drivin' Nails in My Coffin"), Hank ("I'll Never Get Out of This World Alive"), and Moon Mullican ("Cherokee Boogie") as well as some fine originals penned by Preston. Then, on the advice of Gimble, the band moved to Austin in 1974 where they became regulars at the Armadillo World Headquarters. That year, the band made a self-titled record catching them at their best on swing standards ("Choo Choo Ch'boogie"; "Jumpin' at the Woodside"; "Miss Molly"), country classics ("Last Letter"), and excellent originals. In 1975, it was re-released as a double LP paired with a collection of great Bob Wills and the Texas Playboys songs. Entitled **Fathers and Sons**, it represented a symbolic passing of the Western swing torch to a new generation (Bob Wills died the same year), and AATW followed it up with another gem, **Texas Gold**, which produced two hits including the Top 10 song "The Letter That Johnny Walker Read." Two more charted songs ("Miles and Miles of Texas"; "Route 66") came out of the 1976 **Wheelin' and Dealin'** with Playboys Gimble, Tiny Moore, and Eldon Shamblin and more terrific swing, country, and even Cajun. AATW won their first Grammy (Best Instrumental Performance) for "One O'Clock Jump" off **The Wheel** (1977) and then came **Collision Course** (1978) and **Served Live** (1979), recorded at the Austin Opera House. However, as sensational as they were in the studio and as a live dance band, the truth was they simply didn't sell many records and in 1980 the wheels began to come off as Oceans left and the band was dropped by Capitol. Former Dan Hicks & His Hot Licks vocalist, Maryann Price, was brought on board for **Framed** which had a few bright spots but overall was pale in comparison with their previous material. Although AATW continued to tour, Benson moved more into producing but returned to recording in 1985 with **Pasture Prime** which, with the exception of O'Connell, had a completely new line up including Texas fiddle champion Larry Franklin, steel player John Ely, pianist Tim Alexander, and drummer David Sanger. It went nowhere but two years later, the group (sans O'Connell) got a contract with Epic and in the wake of a country music resurgence put out **10** which charted several songs ("House of Blue Lights"; "Way Down Texas Way"; "Boogie Back to Texas") and earned a second Grammy for the instrumental "String of Pars." In 1988 came a third Grammy instrumental award for "Sugarfoot Rag" off **Western Standard Time**. But, once again, in spite of these successes, low record sales pushed them on to another label (Arista) where they did **Keepin' Me**

Up Nights and **Greatest Hits Live and Kickin'**. The former produced the hit "Boot Scootin' Boogie" (actually a bigger hit for Brooks & Dung) while the latter captured the band as they are at their best...in person. Benson revamped the band yet again in 1993 and undertook a very ambitious recording project, **Tribute to the Music of Bob Wills and the Texas Playboys**. Here, Benson brought together Playboy alumni, "New Country" stars (Garth, Vince, B&D) plus Lyle Lovett, Dolly Parton, Marty Stuart, and Merle Haggard to cover Wills' classics. Not surprisingly, the results were mixed as were the reviews. This album was later packaged in a 3 CD box set, **Still Swingin'**, with the best of AATW's Capitol recordings plus a long lost live set from 1977. Now, into their third decade, AATW continues to tour over 200 days per year and record although, **The Wheel Keeps on Rollin'** (1996), left critics cold. In early 1997, a big surprise came when it was announced that California alt. country veteran, Rosie Flores, would be joining the band as lead female vocalist. This was followed by a new live album, **Back to the Future Now**, done live in Las Vegas and marking the return (for this album only) of original alumni Oceans, O'Connell, and Preston plus guest appearances by new country singer Tracy Byrd. If you want a taste of AATW-in-their-prime check out the Western swing duo Ethyl & Methyl (Chris O'Connell and Maryann Price) and Lucky Oceans who did a fine solo recording (**Lucky Steels the Wheel**) and another great one with his Australian band (where he now lives) Dude Ranch. Also carrying on the country swing tradition was LeRoy Preston (**Country Pedigree**, 1997) and original piano pounder Floyd Domino who worked with Cornell Hurd and as a solo.

Signing on with Dreamworks Nashville in 1998, Benson and The Wheel decided to do a sequel to their multiple Grammy winning tribute to Bob Wills. Released in 1999, **Ride With Bob** once again presents a variety of classic, alt., and new country performers doing their versions of classic Texas Playboys songs.

Original Members: Ray Benson (l.g.,l.v.); Floyd Domino (p); Lucky Oceans (p.s.); Chris O'Connell (g,l.v.,h.v.); Leroy Preston (d,g,v)
Current Members: Tim Alexander (acc,p,h.v.); Tommy Beavers (d); Ray Benson; Cindy Cash Dollar (l.s.,p.s.); Rosie Flores (v,1997); Michael Francis (sax); David Earl Miller (b,h.v.)

Comin' Right at Ya/United Artists/1973; Edsel UK/1987
Asleep at the Wheel/Epic/1974; Edsel UK/1988 (as **Jumpin' at the Woodside**)
Fathers and Sons/Epic/1974 (2 LPs: **Asleep at the Wheel/Bob Wills**)
Texas Gold/Capitol/1975
Wheelin' and Dealin'/Capitol/1976
The Wheel/Capitol/1977
Collision Course/Capitol/1978
Served Live/Capitol/1979
Framed/MCA/1980

Pasture Prime/1985
Ten/Epic/1987
Western Standard Time/Epic/1988
Keepin' Me Up Nights/Arista/1990
Swingin' Best of Asleep at the Wheel/Epic/1992
Greatest Hits (Live and Kickin')/Arista/1992
**Tribute to the Music of Bob Wills and the Texas
   Playboys**/Liberty/1993
Still Swinging/Liberty/1995 (3 CD box set)
The Wheel Keeps On Rollin'/Liberty/1996
Back to the Future Now (Live at Arizona Charlie's)/
   Sony/1997
Boogie Woogie (Floyd Domino)/Hightower/1997
Country Pedigree (LeRoy Preston)/Alcazar/1997
Merry Texas Christmas, Y'All!/High Street/1997
*Learn to Play Western Swing Steel Guitar for Lap and
   Non-Pedal Models, Vols. 1 & 2* (Cindy Cashdollar)/
   Homespun Video/1997
Ride With Bob/Dreamworks Nashville/1999

Asleep at the Wheel Fan Club 1745 Houston Ct.,
New Albany, IN 47150

Official Asleep at the Wheel Home Page
//www.asleepatthewheel.com

Asleep at the Wheel iMusic Showcase
//imusic.com/showcase/country/

Asleep at the Wheel AOL Folder:
Entertainment>Music>Chat & Messages>Music
Community>Country/Folk>Country & Western, A-K

See Ethyl & Methyl, Lucky Oceans

The Ass Ponys
Okra; Roots Rock
Cincinnati, Ohio; 1989-

Based in Cincinnati, the Ass Ponys were created in 1989 by
Chuck Cleaver and Dan Kleinger who had previously played
together in several local rock bands (including the Lunch-
buddies). Randy Cheek on bass and John Erhardt on guitar and
pedal steel rounded out the initial line up. Their first recording,
Mr. Superlove, was completed under the guiding hand of John
Curley (Afghan Whigs) and released in 1990 by Okra. Unfortu-
nately, the label's parent company went under shortly thereafter
so distribution of their debut was very limited. However, the
Ass Ponys went on an Eastern U.S. tour and then returned to
Ohio to record **Grim** which surfaced in 1992 on the German
Normal label (took over Okra) and a year later on Safehouse.
And, in spite of more label and distribution hassles, they did
manage to get the attention of critics and a contract with A&M.
This resulted in **Electric Rock Music** (1994) and **The Known
Universe** (1996) with a new guitar player, Bill Alletzhauser
replacing Erhardt who was tired of touring and wanted to return
to running The Sock Store in Cincinnati. As with many other alt.
country bands, the critics and even the band itself have a hard
time pinning down exactly where the Ass Ponys fit. Thematically, their lyrics reflect the grimmer side of rural/small town
life ("God Tells Me Too"; "Cancer Show"; "Laughing At the
Ghost"; "Shoe Money"; "Redway") while their sound shows

influences ranging from bluegrass to country to modern rock. In
late 1996, the Ass Ponys got word that three of their songs
would be on the soundtrack of *Tromeo and Juliet* from the
infamous schlock movie studio Troma (*Class of Nuke 'Em
High*; *Toxic Avenger*). However, in early 1997, they learned
A&M had dropped them from their roster leaving the Ass Ponys
looking for a label to sponsor their next record which as of 1998
was still in the "pre-production" stage.

Bill Alletzhauser (g,1996-); Randy Cheek (b, b.v.); Chuck
Cleaver (g,v); John Erhardt (g,p.s.,sl.g,1989-1996); Dan
Kleinger (d,1989-1991); Dave Morrison (d,org,perc)

> **Mr. Superlove**/Okra/1990
> "Laughing at the Ghost" and "Peanut" on **Sample Some
>   Okra**/Okra/1991
> **Grim**/Normal Ger./1992; Safehouse/1993
> **Earth to Grandma**/A&M/1994 (EP)
> **Little Bastard**/A&M/1994 (EP)
> **Electric Rock Music**/A&M/1994
> **The Known Universe**/A&M/1996

The Ass Ponys Home Page //www2.eos.net/knownuniverse/
davem@eos.net

The Asylum Street Spankers
New Old-Time
Austin, Texas; 1994-

On stage, the Asylum Street Spankers look more like a
convention than a band; a boisterous meeting of traditional
Americana at which the various members represent old-time
blues, country, jazz, ragtime, and gospel straight out of the
heyday of vaudeville. Since 1994, when blues guitarist Guy
Forsyth and torch singer Christina Marrs began performing
together, the Spankers have continually added members
committed to playing music "the way God intended, without the
use of demon electricity." Their ranks have been filled by
alumni from a variety of Austin groups; Kevin Smith (High
Noon), Olivier Giraud (8½ Souvenirs), Stan Smith (the Jazz
Pharoahs), Pops Bayless and Mysterious John (both from
Duckie Duncan) plus Josh Arnson and local celebrity poet,
Wammo. With a reputation for live shows filled with hilarious
hijinks (do they really spank people from the audience?) and hot
playing, the ASS built a loyal following especially for their
"Original Gospel Sunday Brunch" at La Zona Rosa. In 1995,
they did a live cassette of classics ("Deep Ellum Blues"; "Mama
Don't Allow"; "Sittin' on Top of the World"; "Chinatown";
"Walkin' Blues"; etc.) and the quirky, "Children of the
Cornuts." It was reissued as a CD in 1997 with four extra cuts
produced by the Bad Livers' Mark Rubin who also guided their
first "studio" (a living room with one mic) recording, **Spanks
For the Memories**, in 1996. Once again, the Spankers cover
some standards but also offer memorable novelties, "Lee
Harvey Was a Friend of Mine" (Homer Henderson) and
originals, "Startin' to Hate Country." Every member con-

tributes to the overall effect, but the real standout is Marrs' belting blues numbers. Late in 1997, Billy Horton of the hillbilly bop band, the Horton Brothers replaced Kevin Smith, Olivier Giraud dropped out, and violinist Eamon McLaughlin was added to the ensemble. Around the same time, a collection of Spanker covers of naughty ditties from the 1920s-1930s (**Nasty Novelties**) was issued by Freedom Records, and into 1998-1999, the Spankers continued their popular Sunday brunch shows plus a regular Wednesday night session at the Electric Lounge. Guitar ace Dave Biller (ex-Dale Watson; ex-Wayne Hancock; Panhandlers) joined up with the Spankers in time to play (as Leroy Biller) on their 1999 release **Hot Lunch**.

Josh Arnson (g,v); Pops Bayless (bj,md,uke,v); Dave Biller (g,1999-); Adam Booker (u.b.,1998-); Jimmie Dean (snare, 1994-1998); Olivier Giraud (g,v,1994- 1997); Guy Forsyth (g,hm,v); Billy Horton (u.b.,1997-1998); Christina Marrs (uke,v); Eamon McLaughlin (vio,v,1997-); John Salmon (d,1998-); Kevin Smith (u.b.,1994-1997); Stan Smith (cl,v); Wammo (wb,v)

> **Asylum Street Spankers Live**/ASS/1995 (CS);
> Watermelon/1997 (CD with extra. trks.)
> **Spanks For the Memories**/Watermelon/1996
> **Nasty Novelties**/Freedom/1997
> **Hot Lunch**/Cold Spring/1999

The Official Asylum Street Spankers Home Page
//www.eden.com/~spankers/

spankers@eden.com

Unofficial Asylum Street Spankers Home Page
//www.seething-prod.com/spankers/

See The Blue Rags; High Noon; The Horton Brothers

Atomic Deluxe

Honky Tonk; Rockabilly; Swing
Salt Lake City, Utah; 1995-

Blasting out from the heart of Mormon Country, Atomic Deluxe delivers a potent fusion of honky tonk, rockabilly, and swing. At the core of the band are the rough and tough vocals of Lara Jones and the "blues-a-billy" guitar of Paul "Shorty" Kreutz who had known each other since the early 1990s when she was in the Broken Hearts/Rattlekings and he in Voodoo Swing, one of the best rockabilly bands to ever emerge from the Mountain West. On several occasions, the two bands played gigs together and even combined forces along with Greg Swanholm of Flathead to record an unreleased tape as Stardust and the High Lonesome Hillbillies. Eventually, as the Broken Hearts and Voodoo Swing wound down, Jones, Kreutz, Leeroy Aidukatis (Voodoo Swing), and "Kid" Kelly Larson formed Atomic Deluxe and released **Swing Time Shoot 'Em Up** in 1996. Their rockabilly/honky tonk/swing sound was subsequently given a big boost by the addition of Dan Salini on fiddle and steel, and they soon began to establish themselves as the top alt. country band in the area. That position was cemented

in 1998 when Atomic Deluxe won the Salt Lake City Showdown to Austin (to determine who would represent the city at SXSW) and released their second CD, **Stories From the New West**. Jones and Kreutz wrote and/or co-wrote 13 of the recording's 16 cuts and have a definite knack for tender ballads, peppy two-steps, rollicking hillbilly, and jumping swing centered on everybody's favorite twins, heartbreak ("Wish You Well," "Another Day," "10 Shades of Blue," "Sometimes," "Beggin' for Love," "You Used to Call Me Baby," "The Desert is Crying) and drinking ("Pass That Bottle," "Too Much Drinkin'," "Seein' Double Boogie"). They also do credible covers of Jimmie Skinner ("Doin' My Time"), George Jones ("You're Still on My Mind"), and the Western standard "Along the Navajo Trail." The fall-out from Atomic Deluxe's recordings and energetic live performances got them closer to the alt. country core in 1999.

Leeroy Aidukatis (d,1995-1996); Lara Jones (g, l.v.); Paul "Shorty" Kreutz (l.g.,l.v.); Kelly "Kid" Larson (b,1995-1997); Nick Lloyd (b,1997-); Dan Salini (f,p.s.); Jay Wetmore (d)

> **Swing Time Shoot 'Em Up**/Cool Cat/1996
> **Stories From the New West**/Cool Cat/1998

Atomic Deluxe/Cool Cat Productions, 1213 W. Crystal River Dr., Murray, UT 84123; 801-685-2993

Atomic Deluxe Web Page
//music.slweekly.com/atomic/atomic.html

Austin Lounge Lizards
Progressive Bluegrass; Satire
Austin, Texas; 1980-

In 1980, two Princeton history majors (Hank Card and Conrad Deisler) began singing and writing songs in a band called Canyon City Limits. Four years later, while in law school at the University of Texas, they teamed with a banjo/pedal steel playing philosophy grad student (Tom Pittman) and began playing bluegrass in local nightclubs as the Austin Lounge Lizards. Just three years later, after the addition of a bass player (first Tom Ellis then Mike Stevens) and mandolinist (first Tim Wilson then Paul Sweeney in 1984), they took Best Band honors at the 1983 Kerrville Folk Festival. After a number of years of recording and performing part time, the Lizards went full time in 1991. And although they probably could have succeeded on their bluegrass/country vocal and playing skills alone, what sets the ALL apart is clever satire and social commentary which Deisler once described as "guerrilla warfare on the conventions of country music." Throughout the 1980s and into the 1990s, on a series of acclaimed recordings (**Creatures From the Black Saloon, Highway Cafe of the Damned, Lizard Vision, Paint Me on Velvet, Small Minds**), they took aim at every type of insanity and excess in American culture: right-wing Christians ("Jesus Loves Me, But He Can't Stand You"), Nashville country ("Put the Oak Ridge Boys in the

Slammer"), pompous politicians ("Gingrich the Newt"; "The Ballad of Ronald Reagan"), illegal alien hysteria ("Teenage Immigrant Welfare Mothers on Drugs"), and the gradual lowering of the American IQ ("Life is Hard, But Life is Hardest When You're Dumb"; "Shallow End of the Gene Pool" by Emily Kaitz). Their humor and daring approach to bluegrass (they cover Pink Floyd's "Brain Damage") garnered the Lizards numerous awards including *The Austin Chronicle*'s Best None of the Above Band and Kerrville's 1994 Band of the Year. They bill themselves as "the most laughable band in show business," but around the world, fans know them affectionately as "the band less reverent than Spike Jones but more punctual than George...the fearless, flamboyant Austin Lounge Lizards!!" Those growing legions breathlessly awaited the ALL's 1998 recording, **Employee of the Month**, which delivers more knee slappers including "Stupid Texas Song," "The Dogs, They Really Miss You," and "Leonard Cohen's Day Job." A supporting tour to the UK (their first ever) was followed by a return to Austin to participate in the gala KUT radio 40th anniversary in November 1998.

Richard Bowden (f); Hank Card (g,v); Conrad Deisler (g,md); Tom Pittman (bj,ps,v); Boo Resnick (b,1995-); Michael Stevens (b,v,1980-1984); Paul "Tex" Sweeney (md,v,1984-1993); Kirk Williams (b,v,1984-1995); Tim Wilson (md,f,v,1980-1984)

> **Creatures From the Black Saloon**/ Watermelon/1984
> **Highway Cafe of the Damned**/Watermelon/1988
> **Lizard Vision**/Flying Fish/1991
> **Paint Me on Velvet**/Flying Fish/1994
> **Small Minds**/Watermelon/1995
> **Live Bait**/Watermelon/1996 (EP)
> **Employee of the Month**/Sugar Hill/1998

Austin Lounge Lizards, P.O. Box 49152, Austin, TX 78765

Official Austin Lounge Lizards Home Page
//www.austinlizards.com

Allizards@io.com

Annie's Completely Unofficial Austin Lounge Lizards Hangout //www.midplains.net/~drshrink/lizards.htm

Unofficial Austin Lounge Lizards Home Page
//www.webcom.com/~yeolde/all/allhome.html

Unofficial Austin Lounge Lizards Tribute Page
//www.geocities.com/Nashville/7340/

The Backsliders

Tobacco Row; Country Rock; Honky Tonk
Raleigh, North Carolina; 1991-

In recent years, North Carolina has become quite a little alternative country hotbed with such bands as Whiskeytown, Jolene, $2 Pistols, 6 String Drag, and the Backsliders who have been playing around the Raleigh area in one form or another since 1991. The nucleus for the band was initially Steve Howell (previously in the Shady Grove bluegrass band) and Chip Robinson whose background was in rock. They later added

fiddle and lap steel (Larry Hutcherson) for a straight ahead honky tonk sound, but in 1995 went to a line up consisting of bass, drums, and a trio of guitars highlighted by the searing punk fueled leads of Brad Rice. Self described as a "hard core honky-tonk" band, the Backsliders began to specialize in country rock *a la* Gram and the Flying Burrito Brothers but could also crank it up a notch *a la* Jason & the Scorchers. Setting up shop at The Brewery, a popular local club, the group's fiery live shows attracted Mammoth Records which released an EP, **From Raleigh, North Carolina** (live at The Brewery) in 1996. This impressive debut led to great anticipation among alt. country circles for the Backsliders full length CD **Throwing Rocks at the Moon**. Produced by Pete Anderson, this recording presents a potent collection of original honky tonk/country rock that pleases from beginning to end (the cover art is great too!). Robinson's twangy Southern vocals and the rest of the Backsliders solidly hit the mark on country rockers ("My Baby's Gone"; "Cowboy Boots"), honky tonk shuffles ("If You Talk to My Baby"; "Lonesome Teardrops"), ballads ("Crazy Wind"; "Last Train"), and even a bit of menacing swamp ("Hey Sheriff"). Released in early 1997, **Throwing Rocks at the Moon** catapulted the Backsliders into the forefront of contemporary country rock bands. A follow-up produced by Eric Ambel at his Roscoe's Place studio was recorded in early 1998 but shortly thereafter, the Backsliders bandwagon bogged down. In the wake of a rumored split over the band's musical direction, Howell accepted an offer from the Two Dollar Pistols, Rice moved to California, and Kurtz and Dennis went on to other groups. Undaunted, Robinson quickly put together a new lineup with Eric Ambel, Terry Anderson, Roger Gupton, and Erik Kristiansen to tour in anticipation of **Southern Lines** (originally titled **Hicktopia**) which was delayed several times before finally being released in mid-1999.

Jeff "J.D." Dennis (d, 1991-1998); Steve Howell (e.g.,v,1991-1998); Danny Kurtz (b,1991-1998); Brad Rice (e.g.,1994-1998); Chip Robinson (a.g.,l.v.);

> **From Raleigh, North Carolina**/Mammoth/1996 (EP)
> **Throwing Rocks at the Moon**/Mammoth/1997
> "Doin' What I Did" on **Will Sing for Food: The Songs of Dwight Yoakam**/Lucky Dog/1998
> **Southern Lines**/Mammoth/1999

The Backsliders/Mammoth Records Home Page
//www.mammoth.com/mammoth/bands/bsliders/

Bcksldr@aol.com

Billy Bacon and The Forbidden Pigs

"Rock and Roll Tex-Mex Bluesabilly"
San Diego, California; Tucson, Arizona; 1984-

They call their sound "rock and roll Tex-Mex bluesabilly" and in the late 1980s, Billy Bacon and Forbidden Pigs became one of the Southwest's premier good time roots bands in spite of the fact that none of their albums have used the same lead guitarist or drummer. The mainstay of the group has been bassist and lead vocalist Billy Bacon (W. Seth Russell) who looks like Rush Limbaugh's long lost hip kid brother, slaps a mean standup, writes top notch songs, and possesses a silky smooth set of pipes. Formed in San Diego in 1984 and originally known as just the Forbidden Pigs, the band's early line-up was Bacon, Mario Moreno, and Esten Cooke. They became popular on the Southwest club circuit and were brought to the attention of Triple X Records by Mojo Nixon. They debuted on that label in 1991 with **Una Mas Cerveza**, produced by Buddy Blue (the Beat Farmers) and introduced by a typically manic Mojo. It nicely captures their trademark mix of rockabilly, Tex-Mex, honky-tonk, blues, and swing. Two years later, with a new lead guitarist (Tom Upthegrove) and drummer (Joey Myers) plus assistance from Michael Doucet (Beausoleil), Country Dick Montana, Chris Gaffney, Dave Alvin, and Mojo Nixon, the Pigs unleashed **Dressed to Swill**, another fine collection of original country/roots/rock. After yet another band shakeup, Bacon returned with **The Other White Meat** (produced by Dave Alvin) which has a variety of Americana with a strong supporting cast (Alvin, Gaffney, Candye Kane, Joe Walsh) but generally lacks the spark and consistency of earlier efforts. In 1997, Bacon tried, tried again with new lead guitarist Jerry "Hot Rod" DeMink and drummer Randy "The Hammer" Willert. After a warm up tour, they made a "live" in the studio recording, **Thirteen Years of Bad Road**, showcasing eight of the best from the Pigs previous recordings plus seven new honky tonk/ rockabilly songs. Then, with yet another drummer change, Billy and the Pigs launched into the next 13 years of life on the road.

Billy Bacon (b,l.v.); David Bernson (d,1995-); Esten Cook (d,1984-1992); Adrian Demain (l.g.,1995-); Jerry DeMink (l.g.,1997-); Mario Moreno (acc,l.g.,v,1984-1992); Joey Myers (d,1993-1995); George Sluppick (d,1998-); Tom Upthegrove (l.g.,v,1993-1995); Randy Willert (d,1997-1998)

Una Mas Cerveza/Triple X/1991
Dressed to Swill/Triple X/1993
The Other White Meat/Triple X/1995
Thirteen Years of Bad Road/Swine Song/1997
"You Don't Know" on **L.A. County Line: A Country Compilation From the City of Angels**/ Strawdog/1998

Billy Bacon and The Forbidden Pigs,
P.O. Box 2063, Tucson, AZ 85702

Billy Bacon and The Forbidden Pigs Home Page
//www.bleybrothersgarage.com/bacon/bacon.htm

billybacon@bleybrothersgarage.com

Bad Livers
Punkgrass?; Thrashgrass?
Austin, Texas; 1990-

The Bad Livers are undoubtedly one of the most unique "bluegrass" groups to emerge in the 1990s. Bass player Mark

Rubin cut his musical teeth mainly on classical and then punk while growing up in Oklahoma but a move to Dallas in the mid-1980s exposed him to the music of the controversial Killbilly which combined bluegrass with a punk attitude. Taking up the standup bass, Rubin joined the band along with a Texas banjoist named Danny Barnes. After a very brief tenure with Killbilly, the two moved to Austin where Barnes formed the Barnburners with J. D. Foster and Rich Brotherton. Later, he reunited with Rubin as the Danny Barnes Trio, employing a variety of Austin musicians before settling on accordionist/ fiddler Ralph White. Changing their name to the Bad Livers (the dumbest name they could think of), they began to mix bluegrass with a wide variety of styles ranging from jug music to punk, Tex-Mex to metal, Cajun to African, classical to country. Their first single was a bluegrass cover of Iggy Pop's "Lust for Life," and in 1991 they cut (in Barnes' house) a cassette of classic old-time/bluegrass gospel songs called **Dust on the Bible**. Distributed as a musical Christmas card to family and friends, the recording eventually reached a wider audience. It and regular live performances at Austin clubs turned lots of heads including that of the Butthole Surfers' Paul Leary who was so impressed he financed and produced their first full length recording, **Delusions of Banjer**, which came out in 1992 on Quarterstick. It solidified the Livers' unique take on traditional music intermixing banjo and fiddle with accordion and even tuba (courtesy of Rubin) to produce modern interpretations of standards ("I Know You're Married"), and novel originals ("Crow Black Chicken," "Shit Creek," and "The Adventures of Pee Pee the Sailor"). An import only LP, **The Golden Years** (highlighted by a Johnny Cash/Motorhead medley), a second CD, **Horse in the Mines** (including "Puke Grub" and "Chainsaw Therapy"), and extensive touring before both bluegrass and punk crowds brought them a great deal of notoriety which seemed to fall into two extremes. Bluegrass purists generally reviled them for daring to put Bill Monroe and Iggy Pop in the same room while praise came from more progressively minded reviewers and a few punkers who seemed to understand the connections the Livers were making. All in all, no one really knew what the heck to call their sound, but it was most often dubbed trashgrass or punkgrass. Unfortunately, this focus on the experimental aspects of their sound and branding as a "novelty" act tended to obscure their excellent musicianship and songwriting abilities. Through it all, the Bad Livers have been resolute in their determination to avoid labels and just play Bad Livers music or as one member put it, "Call us whatever you like, just don't call us late for dinner." A new album, **Hogs on the Highway**, was recorded in 1995 and shopped around for over a year and a half before the Livers signed with, somewhat surprisingly, Sugar Hill. On this record, the band toned down the punk/metal image in favor of a diversity of styles: bluegrass ("Corn Liquor Made Fool Out of Me"), ragtime, Appalachian Tex-Mex (corn-*junto*?). But, of course, it's all done with the Livers inimitable flair punctuated by the ever popular tuba and a very bizarre closing song, "Falling Down the Stairs with a Pistol in My Hand." On the eve of its release, Ralph White dropped out of the band and was replaced by multi-instrumentalist and long-time friend, Bob Grant, who joined them on their 1997 tour during which they did their 1,600+ show.

Over the years, Barnes and Rubin have worked on a variety of side projects. Rubin has played bass (*toloche*) for the great *conjunto* accordionist Santiago Jimenez, Jr. (also produced one of his albums), produced the Asylum Street Spankers' 1996 debut, and fronts an Eastern European/Jewish folk band, Rubinchik's Orkestyr. Barnes has performed occasionally as the Danny Barnes Experience, with Rubin as the Bluegrass Vampires, and with Texas fiddle phenom Erik Hokkanen as the Mad Cat Trio. Additionally, they have made frequent guest appearances on a variety of recordings by Austin based musicians. In 1997 and 1998, the Bad Livers did work on two films: a documentary about lead miners in Oklahoma and *The Newton Boys*, a Richard Linklater directed crime saga about a notorious gang of Texas outlaws in the early 1920s. For the latter, Rubin served as music supervisor, Barnes provided the score, and all the Livers appear in the film as musicians along with other notables including Kevin Smith (High Noon), Erik Hokkanen, Steve James, Stan Smith, and Carl Sonny Leyland. In spring of 1997, Barnes moved from Austin to Port Hadlock, Washington, but continued to reunite with Rubin (Grant dropped out in late 1997) to tour and to record **Industry and Thrift** which many consider their finest effort to date. Produced by Lloyd Maines, it has the usual signature BL old-time/bluegrass ("Lumpy, Beanpole & Dirt," "Brand New Hat," "I'm Going Back to Mom and Dad") plus a rock version of "Doin' My Time" (oh my Gid!, a drummer and electric guitar), 20s style blues, and even klezmer ("A Yid Ist Geboren Inz Oklahoma"). A truly amazing piece of Americana!

Into late 1998-early 1999, Barnes did some solo gigs, toured and recorded with the Bill Frissell quartet, and played banjo on a Disney children's CD. He also started Minner Bucket Records and began making customized, one of a kind, signed and numbered CDs. **The Pathos of Smyke**, **Live at McCabe's**, and **Minor Dings** plus instructional tapes and transcriptions of Bad Livers' songs were available through Danny's web page. His next CD, **Danny Barnes and His Oft Mended Raiment**, came out in March 1999.

Danny Barnes (bj,f,g,v); Bob Grant (g,md,tr.bj,1996- 1997); Ralph White III (f,acc,1990-1996); Mark Rubin (ub,tuba,v)

    "Lust for Life" b/w "Jeffro's Dream"/Fistpuppet/ 1991; Cargo/1996 (7")
    Dust on the Bible/BL/1991 (CS); Quarterstick/1998 (CD with bonus trk.)

Delusions of Banjer/Quarterstick/1992
The Golden Years/Quarterstick/1992 (12" EP LP)
Souvenir (Mad Cat Trio)/MCT/1993 (CS)
Horses in the Mines/Quarterstick/1994
"Wild Bill Jones" on **Cowpunks**/Vinyl Junkie/1996
Hogs on the Highway/Sugar Hill/1997
The Newton Boys/Sony Soundtrax/1998 (sdtrk.)
Industry and Thrift/Sugar Hill/1998
Flipnotics Freilachs (Rubinchik's Orkestyr)/ Rubinchik Recordings/1998
The Pathos of Smyke (Danny Barnes)/Minner Bucket/1998
Live at McCabe's (Danny Barnes)/Minner Bucket/1998
Minor Dings (Danny Barnes)/Minner Bucket/1998
Danny Barnes and His Oft Mended Raiment/ Minner Bucket/1999

Bad Livers/Mark Rubin, P.O. Box 49227, Austin, TX 78765-9227

mdrubin@bga.com

Official Bad Livers Home Page
//www.hyperweb.com/badlivers/

Bad Livers Fan Page
//blevins.cns.vt.edu/localhome/badliv.htm

Danny Barnes, P.O. 1054, Port Hadlock, WA 98339

DannyBarnes.com //www.dannybarnes.com

dbarnes@waypt.com

Rubinchik's Orkestyr //www.nonpareil.net/rubinchik/

See Erik Hokkanen; Killbilly

The Bagboys
New Old-Time; Bluegrass; Swing
Medford, Massachusetts; Mid 1980s-

In the mid-1980s, Bob Chabot and Paul Jost, who had grown up together in Attleboro, Massachusetts, teamed up in Boston to play "outdoor venues" (parks, subways, streets) as Bobby Bag and the Bagboys. Later adding a mandolin player, they began performing at local clubs and recorded the tape **Here and Now** which got good reviews and some airplay. Expanding their ranks to include Larry Hirschberg and Paul Burch, the Bagboys landed a regular spot at the Plough & Stars in 1989, and their "psychedelic country" sound earned them a second place finish in a local radio station's Country Music poll. However, after Burch and Hirschfield left, Chabot and Jost (Harvey Bag) gravitated toward an old-time string band style and recruited the current Bagboys—Arthur Weinstein (Otis Ray Bag), Michael Sortor (Spider Mike Bag), and Gretchen Bowder (Gretchen Bag). They continued their popular weekly shows at the Plough & Stars where they offered delighted audiences a mix of bluegrass, new old-time, and Western swing with super lead/harmony vocals and playing especially by Bowder on banjo and Sortor on fiddle. A self-described "down-to-earth and friendly band," the Bagboys certainly live up to it on their debut CD, **Sensible Music for Troubled Times**. It literally invites the listener to come on up on the porch, sit back, and enjoy excellent covers of "John Henry," "Someday You'll Want Me to Want

You," "Damn Yankee Lad," "Miss Molly," and "Wah-Hoo!" and original bluegrass ("Carry Me Back"; "Wine & Roses"), old-time ("Sweet Molly Brown"), Western swing ("That Song About Bob Wills"), and interesting novelties ("My Three Dogs"; "WBAG"; "Ditch Diggin' Man"; "Papish Cats"). **Sensible Music for Troubled Times** was nominated for Recording of the Year by the Massachusetts Country Music Awards Association, and in late 1998, the Bagboys returned to the studio to do an album for later in 1999. Meantime, they can still be found every Saturday night at the Plough & Stars in Harvard Square, Cambridge.

Bobby Bag aka Bob Chabot (a.g.,hm,v); Gretchen Bag aka Gretchen Bowder (acc,bj,v); Harvey Bag aka Paul Jost (b,v); Otis Ray Bag aka Arthur Weinstein (e.g.,md, v); Spider Mike Bag aka Mike Sortor (f,v)

Sensible Music for Troubled Times/Hairy Moon/1997

The Bagboys, P.O. Box 604, Medford, MA 02155; 781-393-8252, (fax) 781-729-0487

The Bagboys Home Page
//www.erols.com/arthor/BagHome.html

dandog@erols.com

See Paul Burch

The Balfa Brothers; Balfa Toujours

Cajun
Bayou Grand Louise, Louisiana

The current Cajun culture craze has its roots in the late 1960s when Cajun music experienced a world wide revival. At the forefront of this renaissance was Dewey Balfa and his brothers from the Bayou Grand Louise area of southern Louisiana. In 1964, Dewey appeared at the Newport Folk Festival with Louis Lejeune (fiddle) and Gladius Thibodeaux (accordion) to a very warm reception and returned to the same venue in 1967 with his brothers and Hadley Fontenot where they played for the first time as the Balfa Brothers. From there, they went on to spread the popularity of Cajun music to new generations at home and abroad through extensive tours and classic Cajun recordings. Even after Rodney and Will Balfa died in a car crash in 1979, Dewey carried on this mission with a new line up (included Marc Savoy) until his death in 1992. Today, the Balfa legacy is carried on by Dewey's daughter Christine who heads a band known as Balfa Toujours. Like a number of other contemporary Cajun bands, they pay respects to the traditional music of the Balfa Brothers while incorporating the sounds that reflect the experiences of a new generation of Cajun music lovers. At the heart of the band are Christine's strong vocals supplemented by the stellar accordion and fiddle work of her husband Dirk Powell (a fine old-time musician as well) and the fiddle playing of Kevin Wimmer who is also a member of the excellent California Cajun Orchestra. Their originals fit the traditional Cajun mold with just a bit of an overflow into the modern. **Deux**

Voyages (produced by Tim O'Brien) is a true family affair with three other Balfa's making guest appearances along with Peter Schwarz (of Steve Riley & the Mamou Playboys) on fiddle.

Throughout 1998, Balfa Toujours kept up a rigorous tour schedule playing major festivals all over the U.S. plus a special performance as part of the tribute to Americana musicologist Harry Smith. However, they took enough time out to make two recordings that effectively recapture the spirit of traditional music on the Bayou. **Allons Danser** with veteran Creole accordionist Alphonse "Bois Sec" Ardoin (82 years young) was followed by **La Pointe** which was recorded (on vintage equipment) at the Balfa home (La Pointe) which is the site of the first Acadian settlement (1765) along Bayou Teche. Christine also made a guest appearance on the D.L. Menard segment of the PBS documentary about music along the Mississippi called *River of Song*.

Balfa Brothers (1927-1992): Dewey (f,d,1992); Harry (acc); Rodney (g,d,1979); Tony (g,1979-1992); Will (f,d,1979); Hadley Fontenot (acc); Dick Richard (f,1979-1992); Marc Savoy (acc)
Balfa Toujours (1993-): Ganey Arsement (b); Christine Balfa (g,tri,v); Dirk Powell (acc,b,f); Kevin Wimmer (f,v)

Balfa Brothers Play Traditional Cajun Music/ Swallow/1965
The Cajuns (with Nathan Abshire)/Sonet/1972
Balfa Brothers Play More Traditional Cajun Music (with Marc Savoy)/Swallow/1974
The Good Times Are Killing Me (with Nathan Abshire)/Swallow/1975
J'ai Vu Le Loup, Le Renard et la Belette/Cezame Fr/1975; Rounder/1976, 1989
The New York Concerts/Swallow/; Ace UK/1991
Dewey Balfa, Marc Savoy, D. L. Menard: Under a Green Oak Tree/Arhoolie/1976, 1989
Cajun Legend: Dewey Balfa and Friends/ Swallow/1986, 1989
Souvenirs (Dewey solo)/Swallow/1987
Cajun Fait a la Main (Cajun Legend & Souvenirs)/ Swallow/1989
Play Traditional Cajun & More Traditional Cajun (Balfa Brothers)/Swallow/1987; Ace UK/1995
Pop Tu Me Parles Toujours (Balfa Toujours)/ Swallow/1993
A Vielle Terre Haute (Balfa Toujours)/Swallow/1995
New Cajun Tradition (Balfa Toujours)/Ace UK/1995 (**A Vielle Terre Haute** plus 7 trks. from **Pop Tu...**)
Deux Voyages (Balfa Toujours)/Rounder/1996
If I Go Ten Thousand Miles (Dirk Powell)/ Rounder/1996
Allons Danser (with Alphonse Ardoin)/ Rounder/1998
La Pointe/Rounder/1998
"Le Vieux Soulard et Sa Femme" on **The Harry Smith Connection: A Live Tribute**/Smithsonian Folkways/1998

Balfa Toujours, P.O. Box 389, Breaux Bridge, LA 70517; 318-845-5216, (fax) 318-845-5460

Balfa Toujours Home Page //members.aol.com/balfamusic/ BalfaTJ@aol.com

See The California Cajun Orchestra

The Balham Alligators
Cajun
London, England; 1983-

Along with the Bearcats and R. Cajun and the Zydeco Brothers, one of the earliest groups in the burgeoning British Cajun/zydeco music scene of the late 1970s and early 1980s was the Balham Alligators. Their original lineup was Pete Dennis, Robin McKidd, Kieran O'Connor, Gary Rickard, and Geraint Watkins. Tragically, O'Connor, one of the most respected drummers in London, died in the early 1990s. He was replaced by Bobby Irwin (Hank Wangford band) and when Dennis dropped out, Paul Riley (ex-Chilli Willi and the Red Hot Peppers) was hired to play bass. With this new ensemble in place, the Alligators became one of London's most popular Cajun/zydeco bands noted for a hard country rocking/Cajun style driven mainly by Geraint Watkins who had earned quite a reputation as one of the UK's finest rock 'n' roll pianists as a session player (Dave Edmunds, Shakin' Stevens) and fronting the Dominators and Red Beans & Rice. While individual members worked with various other bands (Watkins, Riley and Irwin as Nick Lowe's Impossible Birds and McKidd in The Companions of the Rosy Hour), the Alligators maintained a steady schedule of live performances and studio recordings in the 80s and 90s. What distinguishes their style is the blending of Cajun/zydeco with a variety of American roots including honky tonk and rockabilly. In addition to Cajun standards, the Alligators cover country and rock 'n' roll mainstays like "Honky Tonk," "Cash on the Barrellhead," "Six Days on the Road," "White Lightning," "Johnny B. Goode," and "Hot Rod."

Original Members: Pete Dennis (b); Robin McKidd (f,v); Kieran O'Connor (d); Gary Rickard (g,v); Geraint Watkins (acc,ky,v)
Current Members: Geraint Watkins (acc,ky,v); Bobby Irwin (d); Robin McKidd (f,v); Gary Rickard (g,v); Paul Riley (b)

The Balham Alligators/Special Delivery UK/1987
Life in A Bus Lane/Special Delivery UK/1988 (CS)
Live Alligators/Studio UK/1990
Gateway to the South/Proper UK/1996
A Po'boy 'n' Make It Snap/Proper UK/1997 or **Cajun Dance Party**/Emporio/1997

Geraint Watkins Fan Page //home6.swipnet.se/~w-69550/

The Band
Americana
Toronto, Ontario, Canada; 1960s-

The one name synonymous with contemporary Ameri- cana is The Band. Their unique mix of bluegrass, blues, Cajun, country, gospel, ragtime, and rockabilly on classic albums such as **Music From Big Pink**, **The Band**, **Stage Fright**, **Rock of Ages**, and **The Last Waltz** set a standard many have imitated but none have duplicated. They also participated in one of the defining moments in alternative country when they did **The Basement Tapes** with Bob Dylan in 1967. Recorded on a home tape recorder "just for fun," the sessions yielded a raw but inspiring collection of old-time, country, rock, blues etc. that has had an influence way beyond anyone's expectations. And though Dylan and The Band had no intention of releasing the tapes, Dylan's label, Columbia, did send out demos of some songs from these sessions to other artists. Two of these, "You Ain't Going Nowhere" and "Nothing Was Delivered" wound up on The Byrds' 1968 **Sweetheart of the Rodeo**. The Basement recordings were bootlegged many times before official release as a two record set in 1975. Subsequently, more material from the original sessions was discovered over the years and periodically issued as the five volumes of the **Genuine Basement Tapes**. These recordings present The Band and Dylan at their most laid back and playful on a variety of originals and covers including many country songs such as "Rock Salt and Nails" (Bruce Phillips), "A Fool Such as I," "I Don't Hurt Anymore," "Wild Wood Flower" (A. P. Carter), "I Forgot to Remember to Forget," "Stones That You Throw" (Hank Williams), and "You Win Again" (Hank too).

The Band broke up in the late 1970s with individual members going on to various solo projects and occasionally getting back together for special gigs. Their swan song, **The Last Waltz**, is a terrific concert movie/soundtrack bringing together some of the finest names in modern Americana to present a loving retrospective. In the early 1990s, the group returned with an altered line up (Danko, Hudson, Helm the only originals) and recorded two albums, **Jericho** and **High on the Hog**, which showed they were still near the top of their game. Several retrospective collections of The Band's work from their "golden years" have appeared, the best being **To Kingdom Come** and **Across the Great Divide**.

Two big events for The Band in 1998 were the release of a new album, **Jubilation**, and a historic recording with Dylan called **Bob Dylan Live 1966: The 'Royal Albert Hall' Concert (The Bootleg Series, Vol. 4)**. The former with originals and songs by John Hiatt, Tom Pacheco, and Bobby Charles comes closer than any of their more recent albums to reviving the vintage Americana sound of the late 60s and early 70s. The latter, recorded in 1966 (actually at the Free Music Hall in Manchester), had been widely bootlegged until Columbia put it together as a double CD package with a solo acoustic set and a rock set with Dylan and The Hawks (The Band minus Levon Helm) that brought howls of shock and derision from fans who felt betrayed by Dylan's decision to "plug in."

Original Members: Rick Danko (b,f,v); Levon Helm (d,md,v); Garth Hudson (acc,ky); Richard Manuel (p,v); Robbie Robertson (l.g.,v)
Current Members: Richard Bell (p); Randy Ciarlante (d,v); Rick Danko; Garth Hudson; Levon Helm; Jim Weider (l.g.)

  Music From Big Pink/Capitol/1968
  The Band/Capitol/1969
  Stage Fright/Capitol/1970
  Cahoots/Capitol/1971
  Rock of Ages/Capitol/1972
  Moondog Matinee/Capitol/1973
  Northern Lights-Southern Cross/Capitol/1974
  The Basement Tapes (with Bob Dylan)/Capitol/1975
  The Best of the Band/Capitol/1976
  Islands/Capitol/1977
  Anthology/Capitol/1978
  The Last Waltz/Warner Brothers/1978
  The Genuine Basement Tapes, Vols. 1-5/
    Genuine/1980s-1990s
  To Kingdom Come: The Definitive Collection/
    Capitol/1990
  Jericho/Pyramid/1993
  Live at Watkins Glen/Capitol/1994
  Across the Great Divide/Capitol/1994 (3 CD boxed set)
  High on the Hog/1994
  The Complete Last Waltz/Cool Daddy/1995
  Jubilation/River North/1998
  Bob Dylan Live 1966: The 'Royal Albert Hall'
    Concert/Columbia/1998

Jan Hoiberg's The Band Web Page //theband.hiof.no/

Rock Hall of Fame The Band Page //www.rockhall.com/induct/band.html

The Band Newsgroup alt.music.the-band

See Bob Dylan; Tom Pacheco

The Band of Blacky Ranchette

See Giant Sand

Banjo Dan and The Mid-Nite Plowboys

Progressive Bluegrass
Vermont; 1972-

A native of Baltimore/Washington, D.C., Dan Lindner's introduction to bluegrass came in the 1960s when that area was a major hub of bluegrass revival. Inspired to take up the banjo, he subsequently moved north to Vermont as part of the hippie "back to the land" movement. There, in 1972, Lindner formed the Mid-Nite Plowboys with brother Willy and Al Davis, and over the past 25+ years through various personnel changes, they've established themselves as the top bluegrass band in Vermont and one of the best in New England. Their numerous recordings pay respects to bluegrass traditions but also have a progressive bent with covers of a variety of artists (Ian Tyson, Richard Thompson, Jackie DeShannon, Michael Hurley, the O'Kanes, Eric Andersen) and styles (Cajun, honky tonk). However, the focus of most of their originals has been on their

host state, Vermont. Dan Lindner, in particular, has been a prolific songwriter penning hundreds of songs celebrating the natural beauty and rich cultural history of the Green Mountain State. In addition to his albums with the Mid-Nite Plowboys, he's done a duo recording (**With Friends Like These**) with Willy and several solos (**Sleepin' Under the Bridge**; **I'll Take the Hills**; **The Catamount is Back**) featuring Plowboy alumni. However, in Vermont, his name is most closely associated with Banjo Dan and the Mid-Nite Plowboys who made Vermonters proud in 1988 when they became the first American bluegrass band to tour the Soviet Union.

Banjo Dan Lindner (bj,l.v.); Sam Blagden (b,v, 1975); Alan Davis (g,v); David Gusakov (f); Willy Lindner (g,md,h.v.); Dan Mahoney (db,h.v.); Peter Riley (b,v,1984-); Pete Tourin (f,v)

  Snowfall/Philo/1974
  High Time/Philo/1977
  The Lindner Brothers: With Friends Like These/
    Philo/1981
  Sleepin' Under the Bridge (Dan Lindner solo)/
    Rabbit/1983
  Green Mountain Skyline/Revonah/1986
  I'll Take the Hills: Banjo Dan's Songs of Vermont/
    Vermont Songbag/1987
  Banjo Dan and the Mid-Nite Plowboys/Greener
    Pastures/1990
  The Catamount is Back: Banjo Dan's Songs of
    Vermont, Vol. II/Vermont Songbag/1994

Banjo Dan and the Mid-Nite Plowboys, P.O. Box 171, South Strafford, VT, 05070; 802-765-4341

Banjo Dan and the Mid-Nite Plowboys Home Page //www.sover.net/~daxtell/banjodan/

jdlind@together.net

Ricky Barnes and The Hoot Owls
(The Okra All-Stars)
Okra; Honky Tonk; Country Rock
Columbus, Ohio; 1983-1994

"The first time I saw them they gave me the heebie-jeebies, that sound of theirs was so lonesome and far away." So wrote Don Howland (the Gibson Brothers) about Ricky Barnes and the Hoot Owls, one of a number of fine alt. country bands that came out of the Columbus, Ohio music scene in the 1980s. Formed in 1983, Barnes and his Owls began as a rockabilly/punk band but soon mellowed into a honky tonk country sound dominated by Barnes' super nasally, twangy vocals. At a time when most mainstream country was "candyass" (Howland again), "High Sheriff" Ricky, as he came to be known, served up a healthy dose of real country on a debut album, **Lost Track of Time**, in 1988. Released on Columbus' Okra label (which also carried Hank McCoy, the Fellow Travelers, the Gibson Brothers, and the Schramms), the Hootowls debut shines on covers of Dallas Frazier songs ("California Cottonfields"; "Shoulder to Shoulder"; "Too Many Bridges"), Jimmy Skinner ("Try to Be

Good"), Wayne Raney ("Catfish Baby") as well as originals co-written by Barnes and local writer Jack Cupid (Howland?). This was succeeded by **Bone Country** which has some hilarious covers, "Who Throw Dat Rock?" (Ira Louvin), "I'm a People" (Dallas Frazier), "Waitin' in Your Welfare Line" (Nat Stuckey; Buck Owens) plus more tunes by Cupid/Barnes ("I Need a New Heart"; "Don't Rattle My Chain"), and one by Hank McCoy ("The Bottom of the Bottle"). In 1991, Barnes and a new nest of Hootowls (drawn mostly from the Dead Ringers) returned with **Ya Finally Said Something Good**, another great effort especially on numbers by Merle Haggard ("Every Fool Has a Rainbow"; "Runnin' Kind"), George Jones ("The House at 4033"), the Louvins ("I Take the Chance"), and Gram Parsons ("How Much I've Lied"). Meanwhile, Barnes joined with Okra stablemates, McCoy, Jeb Loy Nichols (the Fellow Travelers), and Dave Schramm to form the Okra All-Stars and record one eponymous album in 1993. This amazing twangfest stands out for its fine songwriting by Nichols ("Big Mistake"; "Falling Fast"; "Let's Build a Bridge"; "Blue Sides to Every Story"), winning pinch nosed harmonies, and able accompaniment by members of the Dead Ringers, the Fellow Travelers, and One Riot, One Ranger. For good measure, they throw in some interesting covers of Merle ("Shade Tree Fix-It Man"), Buck ("I Wouldn't Live in New York City"), and even Prince's "Purple Rain!" Unfortunately, the All-Stars didn't record together again perhaps due in part to the collapse of Okra in the mid-1990s. However, just before Okra's demise, the Hootowls managed to record a final album, **Welcome to...Hilltop USA**. Then, for still unexplained reasons, Barnes and his band had a very messy falling out on the eve of a scheduled tour of Germany. Disillusioned, Barnes quit the music business and today is a successful restaurateur in Columbus.

The Hoot Owls: Ricky Barnes (g,v); Paul Brown (f); Jim Casto (d); M. D. Der Bing (a.g.,e.g.,v); Brian Dunning (b); Tony Fischer (g, b.v.); Billy Hill (bj,s.g.,v); Kristen Jones (f); Mat Newman (b); John Sowder (d)
The Okra All-Stars: Ricky Barnes (g,v,b.v.); Hank McCoy (g,v,b.v.); Jeb Roy Nichols (g,v,b.v.); Dave Schramm (g,l.s.,v,b.v.) with James Castro (d); Al Greller (b); Bob Hite (p); Sandy Jones (f); James Mac Millan (b); Ron Metz (d); Lorraine Morley (b.v.); Jeff Passifiume (b,e.g.); Pete Remeny (db,hm)

> **Lost Track of Time**/Okra/1988
> **Bone Country**/Okra/1989 (LP)
> **Lost Track & Bone Country**/Amigo Swe./1990 (CD)
> "Who Throw Dat Rock" and "I Take a Chance" on
>   **Sample Some Okra**/Okra/1991
> **You Finally Said Something Good**/Okra/1991
> **The Okra All-Stars**/Okra/1993; Innerstate/1999
> **Welcome to...Hilltop USA**/Okra/1994

Okra Records Discography
//members.aol.com/tmivrecs/okra.html

See Hank McCoy; Jeb Loy Nichols; One Riot, One Ranger; The Schramms

The Barnshakers
Hillbilly Bop
Finland; c.1990-

The Barnshakers were started in the early 1990s as a side project by two members of the Finnish rockabilly band, Hal Peters & His Countrymen. Electric/pedal steel guitarist Jussi Huhtakangas and drummer Mike Salminen along with members of Whistle Bait and the Rhythm Hogs modeled their new band on the 1950s Sun-style but with a definite leaning toward hillbilly bop. Over the years, the Barnshakers have had a close association with members of High Noon, collaborated with Dave & Deke, and paid tribute to one of their big influences on the single "Big Sandy." Their prolific outpouring of 45s, 10"ers, and full-length LP/CDs on the Goofy/Goofin' are chock full of A-1 rockabilly with an appealing honky tonk, swing feel that has made them a popular backing band for the likes of Shaun Young and Darrell Higham. In 1998, On the Hill Records of Japan released a Barnshakers compilation called **Barnyard Stomp** which includes their first 10" (Cool Enough) and early out of print 45s.

Much of the effectiveness of the Barnshakers is due to the lead and steel guitar stylings of Huhtakangas who records under the pseudonym Lester Peabody. Further examples of his prowess (comparable to Deke Dickerson and Sean Mencher) can be found on his solo recordings including several singles and the full length **Focus on Guitars**, a top-notch album of electric and pedal steel guitar instrumentals with echoes of Merle Travis, Joe Maphis, Les Paul, Speedy West, and Jimmy Bryant.

Vesa Haaja (a.g.,v); Jussi Huhtakangas aka Lester Peabody (l.g.); Mika Liikari (b); Mike Salminen (d)

> "Country Jam" (Lester Peabody solo) on
>   **Fin-A-Billy**/Goofin' Fin./1990
> **Cool Enough**/Goofin' Fin./1992 (10")
> "She Done Quit Me" b/w "So Doggone Blue"/ Goofin'
>   Fin./1993 (7")
> **Complicated Fool**/Goofin' Fin./1993 (EP)
> **A Honky Tonk Session**/Goofin' Fin./1994
> "Big Sandy" b/w "Ooh Baby"/Rock-A-Billy/1995 (7")
> **Shakes the Barn**/Part Ger./1995 (10")
> "Chew Tobacco Rag" b/w "Twin Guitar Twist" (Dave &
>   Deke w/ Lester Peabody)/Goofin' Fin./1995 (7")
> "Chinatown" b/w "Caravan" (Lester Peabody solo) on
>   **Rock 'n' Roll Call**/Goofin' Fin./1995
> "Big River Rag" b/w "Navajo Rose" (Lester Peabody
>   solo)/Ecco-Fonic/1996 (7")
> **String-O-Rama**/Goofin' Fin./1996 (CD); On The Hill Jp./
>   (LP)
> "Desperate Santa" b/w "Santa's Got a Brand New Pedal
>   Steel"/Goofin' Fin./1996
> "Wiggle Like a Worm" b/w "Choo Choo's Coming
>   Back"/Goofin' Fin./1996 (7")
> **Sweethearts of Strangers** (Darrell Higham w/ The
>   Barnshakers)/Goofin' Fin./1997
> **Flattin'& Thumbin'** (Lester Peabody & Darrell
>   Higham)/Goofin'/1997 (EP)
> **Red Hot Daddy** (with Shaun Young)/Goofin'/1997

Focus on Guitars (Lester Peabody)/Goofin' Fin./1997
"Hocus Pocus" b/w "Gone A-Rockin'"/Goofin' Fin./1997
High Class Baby (Darrell Higham w/ The Barnshakers)/
    Goofin' Fin./1998
Barnyard Stomp/On the Hill Jp./1998

The Barnshakers/Lester Peabody Discography & Photos
//www.pcuf.fi/~tapiov/

tapiov@pcuf.fi or goofin.records@kolumbus.fi

See Hal Peters; Slap Sally Combo

The Barnstompers
"Swingbilly"
Lisse, Holland; 1991-

Those of you who follow the European rockabilly scene closely know that in recent years The Netherlands has produced a number of excellent groups including the Ranch Girls and the Hillbilly Boogiemen. Another name to add to the list is the Barnstompers who hail from Lisse in Holland. Kees, Erik, Jeroen, and Rutger (no last names provided) blend country boogie, Western swing and rockabilly into what they call "swingbilly" and like the Hillbilly Boogiemen and similar U.S. bands (Lucky Stars, Dalhart Imperials), they shoot for a thoroughly authentic late 1940s-early 1950s style and sound. Their press kit came with color photos showing the boys looking mighty dapper in vintage Western duds; likewise, their music sounds as if it could have come straight out of the old WLW Boone County Jamboree and Midwestern Hayride radio shows. Together since 1991, the Barnstompers toured Europe extensively (solo and backing Sonny Fisher and Sid King) and even did some dates in California with Big Sandy. However, until 1999, their recorded output was limited to two singles and two EPs, but all are well worth seeking out. The latest self-titled EP has three rocking, stomping covers of "49 Women" (with Arnold Lassuer of the Hillbilly Boogiemen on mandolin), "Dig Boy Dig," and "Big Dipper" plus an original instrumental called "Smelly's Bounce." A full-length CD was in the works at the end of 1998 with high hopes for release in early 1999. Keep your eyes open for this one and catch the Barnstompers at the Las Vegas Rock-A-Billy Weekender in 1999.

Kees (l.g.,v); Erik (r.g.,s.g.,v); Jan (d,v,1991-1997); Jeroen (ub,v); Rutger (d,1997-)

  Swingbilly/Barn Dut./1992 (EP)
  "What Am I Gonna Do" b/w "Waiting at the Station"/Mac
      Be./1993 (7")
  "Gonna Rock 'n' Roll" b/w "go Boy Go"/Barn Dut./1995
      (7")
  The Barnstompers/Barn Dut./1997 (EP)

The Barnstompers, Rembrandtplein 54, 2162 EC Lisse,
Holland; (0031) 252-417276

The Barnstompers Home Page
//www.ripe.net/home/john/barn/index.html

barnstompers@hotmail.com

See The Ranch Girls/Hillbilly Boogiemen

Larry Barrett
Singer/Songwriter; Grange Rock
Pocatello. Idaho; April 25, 1955-

You'd have to search pretty hard to find someone who has taken a more circuitous and interesting route to a career in music than Larry Barrett. Born in Idaho in the mid-1950s, he entered the military in the 1970s and while stationed in Germany served as a combat medic and then in the Army Ski Patrol. On leaving the service, Barrett relocated to Ft. Worth, Texas and began writing songs. However, his singer/songwriter aspirations were put on hold in 1978 when he moved back to Idaho and got a job with the Hacky Sack Company. For the next five years, Barrett was part of a touring group that did hacky sack demonstrations at public schools across the U.S. He emerged from the experience with lots of song material based on the people and places he had visited along the way, but Barrett wasn't quite ready to settle down. After a brief stay in Seattle, he returned to Germany where he worked on the ski patrol of a local resort. Barrett then went to Czechoslovakia in 1992 where, with girlfriend Lisa King, he busked on the Prague town square. Back in Seattle in the summer of 1992, Barrett recorded 11 songs at a local studio and self released them on a cassette called **Flowers** which was ultimately brought to the attention of Germany's Glitterhouse label by Bruce Wirth of Seattle's Walkabouts (they already had several records out on Glitterhouse). This resulted in a CD version of **Flowers** in 1993 after which Barrett played (lap steel, mandolin) in a number of Seattle bands (Gary Heffern, the Wigglin' Taters, the Walkabouts, the Picketts) and crafted lap steel guitars. Eventually, he formed the Barretts, with Larry handling guitar, harmonica, mandolin, and vocal duties backed by Andrew Hare on steel, Lisa King on acoustic and electric guitars, John Van Feldt (ex-Thin White Rope) on bass, and Larry Guldberg on drums. They recorded **Beyond the Mississippi** "live" in the studio in 1994. As a sideman or with different groups of musicians, Barrett did a number of European tours. His 1995, **Porch Song Singer**, is a combination of new and previously released material. Glitterhouse promo material describes Larry Barrett's music as "Dylan meets Merle," a combination of the songwriting style of Dylan with the country vocals of Haggard. He likes to call it "front porch swing."

  Beyond the Mississippi/Glitterhouse Ger./1994
  Flowers/Glitterhouse Ger./1994
  "The Ringing in My Ear" and "House of Sky" on **Speed of
      the Sound of Loneliness**/Glitterhouse Ger./1994
  "Old Black Car" on **Silos & Utility Sheds**/Glitterhouse
      Ger./1994
  "This Warm House" and "Twisted Roots of Trees" on
      Shotgun Barbeque/Bands We Like/1994
  Porch Song Singer/Glitterhouse Ger./1995

Larry Barrett/Glitterhouse Home Page
//www.ontide.de/glitterhouse/

Larry Barrett Home Page
//members.aol.com/porchsongs/LarryBarrett/

See Gary Heffern; The Walkabouts

Bayou Seco

Cajun; Conjunto; Cowboy/Western
Albuquerque, New Mexico; c.1980-

New Mexico is home to Bayou Seco, one of the most unique groups in the world of traditional American music. Ostensibly a Cajun band, their repertoire also includes music drawn from the Hispanic and Native American cultures of the Southwest. Founders Ken Keppeler and Jeanie McLerie first collaborated in the 1970s in Louisiana where they fell under the sway of Cajun music through sessions with Dewey Balfa, Canray Fontenot, Dennis McGee, Mark and Ann Savoy, and Beausoleil. Relocating to Northern New Mexico in 1980, the two were attracted to the traditional Hispanic music of the region through the influence of local musicians such as legendary fiddler Cleofes Ortiz. For a time, they played for folk dancing classes and then in 1981 moved to Albuquerque where as Bayou Seco, Keppeler and McLerie, along with an elastic collection of musician/friends, began working local dances and other occasions. Their performances were a novel merging of Cajun, Spanish colonial, cowboy/western, and "chicken scratch," a centuries old style of music native to the Tohono O'odham Indians of southern Arizona. They worked diligently to keep traditional music alive by backing some of the region's great but neglected musicians (Antonia Apodaca, Cleofes Ortiz) or recording the music of "chicken scratch" fiddler Elliott Johnson as Bayou Eclectico. As Bayou Seco they have made several memorable recordings, **Cactus Gumbo and Alligator Enchiladas**, **No Borders, Songs of New Mexico and Beyond**, and **Following in the Tuneprints**, all characterized as "desert stomps, Cajun romps, and songs for modern cowgirls and vaqueros." In addition, Bayou Seco recorded with the Delta Sisters and McLerie made two albums, **Harmony Pie** and **Second Helping**, with Alice Gerard and Irene Hermann as the Harmony Sisters. Keppeler was a member (in the late 1990s) of a highly experimental band called the Bubbadinos which local music journalist Stephen Terrell described as "avant-hillbilly." In 1997, Bayou Seco (Keppeler, McLerie, and Erik Hoffman, a California guitarist and contra/square dance caller) toured the United Kingdom where they played and taught traditional Cajun and Southwestern music and dances at folk clubs all across Great Britain. Bayou Seco returned to the British Isles in 1998 and extended their tour across The Channel to France, Germany, and Austria.

Ken Keppeler (acc,f,hm,tr,,v); Jeannie McLerie (f,g,v) with Chris Altenbach (e.g.); Linda Askew (g); Terry Bluhm (g,v); Erik Hoffman (f,g,sax,v); Frannie Leopold (g,v); Scott Mathis (md); Paul Rangell (guitarron,md); Karl Stalnaker (b); Jefferson Vorhees (d,wb,congas)

Harmony Pie (Jeanie McLerie and the Harmony Sisters)/Flying Fish/1980
Second Helping (Harmony Sisters)/Flying Fish/1983
Cactus, Gumbo, and Alligator Enchiladas/Blue Guitar/1983
No Borders/Ubik/1986
Violinista de Nuevo Mexico (McLerie, Cleofes Ortiz, Augustino Chavez)/Ubik/1987
Recuerdos de Rociada (backing Antonia Apodaca)/Ubik/1990 (CS)
Orquestra Cleofonica (backing Cleofes Ortiz)/Ubik/1990
Songs of New Mexico & Beyond/Ubik/1991 (CS)
Following in the Tuneprints/Ubik/1995
Memories of Cababi (Bayou Eclectico)/Ubik/1995 (CS)
"Squash Fields" (Bayou Eclectico) on **American Fogies, Vol. 1**/Rounder/1996
"Estas Lindas Flores" on **American Fogies, Vol. 1**/Rounder/1996
"Lonesome Cowgirl Blues" on **American Fogies, Vol. 2**/Rounder/1996
Ready As We'll Ever Be (Bubbadinos)/Zerx/1998
We're Really Making Music Now (Bubbadinos)/Zerx/1999

Bayou Seco, P. O. Box 1393, Silver City, NM 88062; 505-534-0298

Bayou Seco Home Page
//ourworld.compuserve.com/homepages/pete_shaw_3/bayousec.htm

Bubbadinos, 725 Van Buren Place S.E., Albuquerque, NM 87108; Zerxpress@aol.com

The Beacon Hillbillies

See The Blood Oranges

The Beat Farmers

Cowpunk; Country Rock
San Diego, California; 1983-1995

The Beat Farmers exploded out of the San Diego bar scene during the short lived cowpunk phenomenon of the mid-1980s. Like many bands playing this style of music, the BFers mixed country with straight ahead rock and punk but separated themselves from the pack through raucous and rowdy live performances highlighted by the manic persona of their drummer/leader Country Dick Montana aka Dan McClain. His big voice and impromptu rants and raves (*a la* Mojo Nixon with whom he worked on several projects) combined with some good, basic drunk 'n' roll (fueled by the guitar work of Buddy Blue and Jerry Raney) gained the band a loyal cult following. Their recordings achieved mixed results crossing and re-crossing the lines between country, blues, and rock threaded with a wicked irreverence on "Baby's Liquor'd Up," "Happy Boy," "Gun Sale at the Church," "Beer Ain't Drinkin'," and "Are You Drinking With Me Jesus?" Long after the cowpunk thing died out, the BFers stayed afloat signing on with a new label in the mid-1990s. However, their resurgence was cut short when Country Dick dropped dead from a heart attack in the middle of a performance (November 8, 1995) at a nightclub in

Vancouver, British Columbia. With their irreplaceable leader gone, the other Beat Farmers decided to call it quits but went on to various solo projects. In late 1996, Bar None Records issued a Country Dick solo, **The Devil Lied to Me**, recorded shortly before his death. But, perhaps the most fitting tribute is "Country Dick Montana's Rules of the Road" in the anthology *Alt-Rock-A-Rama* (Rolling Stone). This hilarious guide to touring is a succinct summation of a true wildman's philosophy of music and life.

Buddy Blue (l.g.,v,1983-1986); Joey Harris (l.g.,1986-); Rolle Dexter Love (b); Country Dick Montana (d,g,v); Jerry Raney (g,v)

> **Tales of the New West**/Rhino/1985; Demon UK/1986
> **Glad 'N' Greasy**/Demon UK/1985;Rhino/1985 (EP)
> **Van Go**/Curb/1986
> **Pursuit of Happiness**/Curb/1987
> **Poor and Famous**/Curb/1989
> **Live, Loud and Plowed**/Curb/1990
> **The Pleasure Barons** (Country Dick with Dave Alvin and Mojo Nixon)/Hightone/1993
> **Viking Lullabys**/Sector 2/1994
> **Best of the Beat Farmers**/Curb/1995
> **Manifold**/Sector 2/1995
> **The Devil Lied to Me** (Country Dick solo)/Bar None/1996

The Official Beat Farmers Home Page
//v-music.com/artists/bf/

Country Dick Montana Memorial Site
//www.hbo3.com/dick/

The Beat Farmers Mailing List kdrew@nd.edu
{Message Body: subscribe Bfer, your name}

Beats Walkin'
Western Swing
Philadelphia, Pennsylvania; 1994-

Hailing from The City of Brotherly Love, Beats Walkin' emulate the classic Western swing sound and style as revived by Asleep at the Wheel in the early 1970s. Several founding members of AATW had Philly connections including Ray Benson and steel player Lucky Oceans (born there as Rueben Gosfeld) who had a big influence on Beats Walkin' founder/ pedal steel player Jim Cohen (he also points to Junior Brown as a major inspiration). In 1994, Cohen contacted bassist Dan Gold (ex-Dukes of Destiny) about starting a Western swing group, and once they rounded up a fiddler (Mark Arrington), lead guitar (Jon Dichter), and drummer (Chuck Lindsay), Beats Walkin' began to take shape. However, they still needed a featured vocalist and chose New Zealand native Lindsay Gilmour, "The Kiwi Cowgirl." After several years of working venues around Philadelphia, Beats Walkin' cut a cassette and then in 1997 released their CD debut, **Western Omelette**. Philly's one and only Western swing band does the tradition proud on standards ("Don't Fence Me In"; "Hey Good Lookin'"; "In Care of the Blues") and several songs that were part of the AATW repertoire ("San Antonio Rose"; "Blues for

Dixie"; "Miles and Miles of Texas"; "The Last Meal"). They also chip in a couple of novelty originals, "Battered, Beaten Heart" and the very timely "On-Line Lover" ("she has reduced me to an icon, she can turn me on real quick, 'cause if she wants my lovin', she'll just point and double click"). Early in 1998, Beats Walkin' got a big boost when veteran musician Lew London became their fiddler but by the end of the year, he was replaced by Arty Artimiw.

Jay Ansill (f,1994-1997); Arty Artimiw (f,1998-); Jon Dichter (l.g.); Jim Cohen (p.s.); Lindsay Gilmour (l.v.); Dan Gold (b); Chuck Lindsay (d,v); Lew London (f,1998)

> **Western Omelette**/BW/1997

Beats Walkin', c/o Jim Cohen, 425 W. Upsal St., Philadelphia, PA 19119

Beats Walkin' Home Page //members.aol.com/jasaco/
Jasaco@aol.com

Beausoleil
Modern/Traditional Cajun
Lafayette, Louisiana; 1975-

Just as the Balfa Brothers were the leaders in the Cajun music revival of the late 1960s, Beausoleil was at the forefront of a similar resurgence in the 1970s. However, unlike the Balfas who adhered to a traditional sound, Beausoleil, led by fiddler Michael Doucet, never hesitated to expand on it by incorporating a wide diversity of musical styles. Their genesis goes back to the mid-1970s when fiddle player Michael Doucet, who had studied with Conray Fontenot and Dennis McGee, helped found two very different Cajun bands. Beausoleil initially stuck close to a traditional rendering while Coteau ventured into a more modern style which earned them the title of the "Cajun Grateful Dead." The latter eventually faded, but its spirit of experimentation lived on in Beausoleil which made a debut recording on a French label in 1976 then in the U.S. on Swallow in 1977 with **The Spirit of Cajun Music**. Combining traditional Cajun with a variety of American and world music, Beausoleil established themselves as the leaders of the Cajun music renaissance. Over the past two decades, they have become Cajun ambassadors to the world spreading their brand of contemporary Cajun through extensive touring, numerous band and individual recordings (with several Grammy nominations), radio and television, soundtracks (*Belizaire the Cajun*, *The Big Easy*), and sessions with other contemporary artists ranging from Richard Thompson to Mary Chapin Carpenter. Michael Doucet has collaborated with Marc Savoy as the Savoy-Doucet Cajun Band and hosted an NPR program, *South to Louisiana!*, a celebration of Cajun music and culture. In 1997, Beausoleil marked their 20th anniversary with the release of **L'Amour ou La Folie (Love or Folly)**, an eclectic retrospective with many guests including Augie Meyers, Richard Thompson, and Josh Graves. That year, Coteau reunited to record **Highly Seasoned Cajun Music** which recaptures their special blend of Cajun, blues, Southern rock, country, jazz, and reggae. Former Beausoleil accordionist, Errol Verret and Coteau/Beausoleil alumnus Tommy Comeaux went on to join another modern Cajun band, Al Berard & the Basin Brothers although, sadly, Comeaux died in a car accident in 1997.

Beausoleil scored two big triumphs in 1998 winning the Big Easy Award for Best Cajun Band (9th time) and after many previous nominations, a Grammy for Best Traditional Folk Record. They kept up a rigorous tour schedule but found time to record **Cajunization** which was released in mid-1999.

Beausoleil: Tommy Alesi (d, 1977-); Jimmy Breaux (acc,1988-); Tommy Comeaux (b,md,1975-1990); David Doucet (g,v); Michael Doucet (f,g,md,l.v.); Al Tharp (b,bj,f,g,v,1990-); Errol Verret (acc, 1975-1987); Robert Vignaud (b,1982-1984); Billy Ware (perc,vibra)
Coteau: Kenneth Blevins (d,perc); Tommy Comeaux (g,md); Michael Doucet (f,v); Bessyl Duhon (acc,f); Bruce MacDonald (g,v); Gary Newman (b,v)

The Spirit of Cajun Music/Swallow/1977
Michael Doucet with Beausoleil/Arhoolie/1981; 1994
Zydeco Gris-Gris/Swallow/1985
Belizaire the Cajun/Arhoolie/1986 (sdtrk.)
Bayou Boogie/Rounder/1986
Allons a Lafayette/Arhoolie/1986
Christmas Bayou/Swallow/1986
Michael Doucet and Cajun Brew/Rounder/1987
Hot Chili Mama/Arhoolie/1988
Bayou Cadillac/Rounder/1989
Beau Solo (Michael Doucet)/Arhoolie/1989
Live From the Left Coast/Rounder/1989
Deja Vu/Swallow/1990
Cajun Conja/Rhino/1991
Parlez-Nous a Boire & More/Arhoolie/1991
Quand J'ai Parti (David Doucet)/Rounder/1991
Le Hoogie Boogie: Louisiana French Music for Children (Michael Doucet)/Rounder/1992
Bayou Deluxe: The Best of Michael Doucet & Beausoleil/Rhino/1993
La Danse De La Vie/Rhino/1993
Cajun Jam Session (Michael Doucet with Poullard & Senuke)/Arhoolie/1994
L'Echo/Forward Rhino/1994
Vintage Beausoleil/Music of the World/1995
The Mad Reel (Michael Doucet)/Arhoolie/1995
Le Chemin que T'as Pris (Jimmy Breaux)/La Louisianne/1996
L'Amour ou La Folie (Love or Folly)/Rhino/1997
Arc de Triomphe Two Step/Hemisphere/1997
Highly Seasoned Cajun Music (Coteau)/ Rounder/1997
Cajunization/Rhino/1999

Beausoleil/Rhino Records Home Page //rhino.com

Beausoleil/Rosebud Agency Page //www.rosebudus.com/beausoleil/

See Al Berard & The Basin Brothers; The Savoy-Doucet Cajun Band

Beck
Roots Rock; Americana
Los Angeles, California; July 8, 1970-

Long before he broke through with his idiosyncratic fusions of folk, hip-hop, and rock in the mid-1990s, Beck Hansen was experimenting with American vernacular music in nightclubs from New York to L.A. He played improvised versions of songs by Leadbelly, the Carter Family, Mississippi John Hurt, and Woody Guthrie to punk rockers in the late 1980s and early 1990s and later added on the different musical styles and electronic effects that brought him fame on **Mellow Gold** and **Odelay**. However, Beck always had the idea in the back of his mind to do a more straight ahead, stripped down interpretation of traditional songs. His first halting steps in this direction actually came prior to his big hit "Loser" with **One Foot in the Grave**, a minimalist collection of folk, country, blues, and gospel with haunting songs like "He's A Mighty Good Leader," "I Get Lonesome," "Cyanide Breath Mint," and "I've Seen the Land Beyond." A planned sequel entitled **A Tombstone Every Mile** was not completed but several songs from it showed up on Beck's **Mutations**, a much more fully realized effort than **One Foot in the Grave** that gets right down into the very heart and soul of country/folk music but with a modern sensibility. Beck chose this title to reflect his realization that his songs were not "pure" folk or country but rather interpretations based on experiences from his own life and times. Interestingly, in December 1998, *Mojo* magazine made him the centerpiece of an article on the rise of alt. country/Americana called "The New Roots Explosion: The Lonesome Trail From Hank Williams to Beck." He was also invited by Emmylou Harris to do a duet ("Sin City") with her for the long-awaited 1999 Gram Parsons tribute, **Return of the Grievous Angel**.

One Foot in the Grave/K/1994
Odelay/Bong Load DGC/1996
Mutations/Bong Load DGC/1998
"Sin City" (with Emmylou Harris) on **Return of the Grievous Angel: A Tribute to Gram Parsons**/ Almo/1999

BECK! The Official Page //www.beck-web.com

Beck/Geffen Records Page //www.geffen.com/beck/

Bell & Shore
Singer/Songwriter; Country Rock
Riverside, Iowa; Late 1980s

Bell & Shore were a husband/wife duo from Eastern Iowa who, in the late 1980s, recorded two acclaimed albums with a dark but often times humorous perspective on life in America's heartland. Nathan Bell's songwriting on **Little Movies** and **L-Ranko Motel** focused on the has beens and never wases stumbling through a world of heartbreak, insanity, and violence. His songs are populated with real life bad men ("The

Outlaw Sam Bass"), post-modern losers ("He's Been Drunk Ever Since His Wife Went Punk"), an ex-prom queen and high school nobody ("L Ranko Motel"), a nutso race driver ("The Day Crazy Bobby Ran the Dirt Track in the Nude"), a washed up boxer ("Johnny 'El Gato' Miguel"), and a suicidal ex-soldier ("Radio VIETNAM"). His gritty solos trade off with Susan Shore's lustrous vocals on uncompromisingly realistic songs about women surviving in a man's world: "The Running Girl"; "Daddy Was No Good (But I Guess I Loved the Son of a Bitch"). They also harmonize well especially on the aching ballad "Blue is the Color of Regret," and the country mood is maintained throughout by able support from Dave McAnelly on dobro and Al Murphy on fiddle.

The Bell & Shore alliance ended in the early 1990s with Susan Shore going on to a solo career. Her debut album, **Old 218**, continued to examine the same rugged territory of desperation and abuse explored by Bell & Shore. Here, joined by Murphy on fiddle and mandolin, Shore covers "Dirty Old Town" (Ewan Macoll), "Poor Woman's Epitaph" (Holly Tashian), "Time" (Tom Waits), "The Devil's Right Hand" (Steve Earle) and contributes several originals, most notably, the powerful "Shouldn't You Know By Now." The follow-up, **Book of Days**, has an old-time Appalachian feel thanks to help from Murphy, James McCandless (who contributed several songs), Al Day, and Don Stiernberg (mandolin, fiddle).

Nathan Bell (g,v); Susan Shore (g,v,.md,mda); Dave McAnelly (db); Al Murphy (f)

Little Movies/Flying Fish/1988
L-Ranko Motel/ROM/1989
Old 218 (Susan Shore solo)/Buck Tone/1995
Book of Days (Susan Shore)/Waterbug/1998
Susan Shore Sushore@aol.com

Vince Bell
Singer/Songwriter
Texas

During the late 1970s and early 1980s, Vince Bell hob-knobbed with Texas' veteran and up-and-coming singer/songwriter elite including Guy Clark, Townes Van Zandt, Lyle Lovett, and Nanci Griffith. A regular on the circuit, he entered an Austin studio in 1982 to make his first demo (Stevie Ray Vaughan was one of the guest players). But, on one fateful December night after a session, a grinding wreck with a drunk driver changed all that putting Bell in a coma for more than a month. It also left him with a long recovery period during which he had to learn to do everything including singing and playing guitar all over again. Slowly, painfully, Vince returned first with new songs (two covered by Griffith), a 1989 album **Sun & Moon & Stars**, and then, in 1994, **Phoenix**, whose appealing mix of country/folk/blues behind Bell's knowing lyrics won widespread praise from reviewers and the Texas singer/songwriter community.

Back on the tour trail, he chronicled his long road back in the autobiographical *One Man's Music* and in 1998 recorded **Texas Plates** which Bell described as "rock 'n' western." His triumphant return was further underscored when Lyle Lovett covered Bell's "I've Had Enough" on his tribute to Texas songwriters, **Step Inside This House**.

Sun & Moon & Stars/Analog/1989 (LP); 1998 (CS)
Phoenix/Watermelon/1994
Texas Plates/One Man's Music/1998
Vince Bell Home Page //www.mindspring.com/~vincebell/

Belle Starr
Grain Belt Rock; Twangfest
St. Louis, Missouri; 1994-

Their name comes from the infamous late 19th century outlaw queen who came from Missouri but gained her reputation in Dallas where she was renowned as a bar room pianist. Belle Starr composed one of the most famous and bawdy of all cowboy songs, "Bucking Bronco"/"My Love Is a Rider" and once, so the legend goes, made a man who made fun of her kiss a horse's butt at gunpoint. But, this isn't to suggest that Belle Starr the band has a sound that is wild or raucous; rather, they combine Hank/Patsy era country, Western swing, rockabilly, and 1960s California country rock into a very appealing style that has made them one of St. Louis' top alt. country bands. Originally known as the Stonecutters, their debut as Belle Starr, **Far As the Wind Blows**, succeeds on all levels due to the literate songwriting of Kip Loui (long-time veteran of the St. Louis music scene), engaging solo and duet vocals by Loui and Lynne Reif, and top notch lap steel from John Horton. In addition, as a music reviewer, producer, and organizer, Loui has been one of the prime movers in St. Louis' rise to prominence in the alt. country community. He helped put together the St. Louis alt. country compilations, **Out of the Gate** and **Out of the Gate Again** and has been a driving force behind the annual Twangfest (see Festivals section). Belle Starr has been a featured performer at this event and contributed songs to several Twangfest compilations.

John Horton (l.g.,l.s.); Kip Loui (a.g.,v); Spencer Marquart (d); Lynne Reif (v); Fred Teutenberg (b)

Far as the Wind Blows/BJAM/1996
"Hook, Line, & Sinker" on **Out of the Gate Again**/
  BJAM/1996
"Far As the Wind Blows" on **Edges From the Postcard**/
  Semi-Tone/1997
"Fever Sleep"; "Stolen Glances"; "Out of the Mouths of
  Babes" on **Twangfest '97**/Twangfest/1997
"Nobody You'd Know" on **Edges From the Postcard2**/
  P2/1998
BJAM Records/Belle Starr, P.O. Box 13245,
St. Louis, MO 63157

Belle Starr/BJAM Home Page
//home.stlnet.com/~cdstelzer/bjam.html

Bjamrecord@aol.com
Twangfest //www.twangfest.com

Pinto Bennett

Honky Tonk; Country Rock
Mountain Home, Idaho; May 20, 1948-?

Burly, tattooed, mustachioed, hard core country, Pinto Bennett is everything the Nashville establishment hates. Raised on an Idaho ranch, Bennett was inspired by country's great honky tonk men to take up a career in music, but after arriving in Nashville twenty years too late for his raw style to be accepted, he took advice from Richard Dobson and headed for Great Britain. There, Bennett found more accepting audiences and record companies signing with PT Records in the 1980s. With his band, the Famous Motel Cowboys, Bennett recorded a series of albums, **Famous Motel Cowboy Songs**, **Big in Winnemucca**, and **Pure Quill** that made him one of Britain's most popular alt. country performers. One listen to **Pure Quill**, and it isn't hard to understand why; Bennett and his Famous Motel Cowboys are pure honky tonk/country rock with a solid beat behind Pinto's potent vocals and powerful originals ("You Cared Enough to Lie"; "Stranger in the Mirror"; "Prairie Blues"; "Pure Quill"; "No Sweat", co-written with Chris Wall). In 1995, his "Prairie Blues" was included on the **Country** compilation of American alt. country musicians put out by the British label Vinyl Junkie. At last, this sadly neglected performer was starting to get his due and an even more promising step in this direction came in 1998 when KOCH reissued **Pure Quill** on CD. However, I don't know if Bennett was able to enjoy it since I heard a rumor that after he returned to Idaho in the late 1990s, he died.

The Famous Motel Cowboys: Joe Dow (d,v); Jim Lemon (b,v); Rob Matson (g,v); Sergio Webb (g,v)

> **Famous Motel Cowboy Songs**/PT UK/1988
> **Big In Winnemucca**/PT UK/1988
> **Pure Quill**/PT UK/1989; KOCH/1998
> "Prairie Blues" on **Country**/Vinyl Junkie/1995

Al Berard & The Basin Brothers

Cajun
Lafayette, Louisiana; 1982-

One of the lesser known but liveliest of the modern Cajun bands is the Basin Brothers. They were founded in the early 1980s by fiddler Al Berard, a native of the Grand Anse region of Louisiana. Much of Berard's inspiration and training came from the great fiddler Hadley Castille who taught him to be proud of his French/Cajun heritage. In 1982, Berard began playing Cajun music with friends Keith Blanchard and Dwayne Brasseaux and later with Danny Collet and Barry Hebert. Basing themselves around Lafayette, they took their name from the local Atchafalaya Basin and built a following through the southern Louisiana dance circuit; at one dance, they held the winning raffle ticket and got enough money to buy all new equipment. Their energetic interpretation of Cajun music helped them get a contract with Flying Fish which released two albums, **Let's Get Cajun** (Grammy nominated) and **Stayin' Cajun**, in 1990 and 1991. When Hebert and Collet dropped out, they were replaced by Tommy Comeaux (ex-Coteau/Beausoleil) and Errol Verret who had previously been accordionist for Beausoleil. In 1994, Berard and Verret teamed up for **C'est dans le Sang Cadjin**, a fine collection of standards and originals that are tradition based but, through their innovation, signal the passing of the music to a new generation. This blend of classic Cajun songs with a modern sound drives the Basin Brothers as well and is most evident on **Dans la Louisiane**. Tragically, on November 9, 1997, Tommy Comeaux was killed in an automobile accident, but as far as I know, Berard and the Basin Brothers can still be found every Thursday night jamming at a Lafayette restaurant called Randol's.

Al Berard (a.g.,f,l.g.,md,v); Keith Blanchard (d,perc); Dwayne Brasseaux (b); Danny Collet (acc,v,1982- 1992); Tommy Comeaux (g,md,1993-d.1997); Barry Hebert (a.g.,v, 1982-1992), Errol Verret (acc,v,1993-)

> **Let's Get Cajun**/Flying Fish/1990
> **Stayin' Cajun**/Flying Fish/1991
> **C'est dans le Sang Cadjin: It's in the Cajun Blood**
> (Berard &Verret)/Swallow/1993
> **Dans la Louisiane**/Rounder/1996

Al Berard & Errol Verret,
P.O. Box 451, Cecilia, LA 70521

Al Berard & The Basin Brothers Web Page
//www.herschelfreemanagency.com/bb.html

See Beausoleil

Byron Berline

Fiddle; Country Rock; Progressive Bluegrass
Caldwell, Kansas; July 6, 1944-

Along with Vassar Clements and Johnny Gimble, Byron Berline was the most important and influential alternative country fiddler of the late 1960s and early 1970s. A fiddle champion at 10, he seemed destined for a career in music, but in high school and college leaned more toward one in athletics. However, while on football and track scholarship at the University of Oklahoma, Berline managed to stay musically active playing fiddle for several local groups. His full-time plunge into music came in 1963 when California country rock/bluegrass group, the Dillards, came through Norman on a tour. Berline was brought to the attention of their leader Doug Dillard who invited him to join them on stage during their concert. Such was the impression made by young Byron that, in 1964, he was hired to play on the Dillards' **Pickin' and Fiddlin'**. That year, Berline won his first National Fiddle Championship followed by another in 1965. He appeared at the

Newport Folk Festival (1965) where he met Bill Monroe, and two years later, just as Berline graduated from college and was about to take a coaching job in Texas, he was asked by Monroe to join his band. And although Berline accepted, his stint as a Blue Grass Boy was brief; he was drafted into the military after only six months with Monroe and replaced by Kenny Baker. But, he continued to play while in the army and on discharge in 1969 went to L.A. to join the Dillard/Clark Expedition. While recording and touring with them, Berline appeared on albums by other prominent California alt. country groups of the time including the Byrds, the Dillards, and the Flying Burrito Brothers. The latter group invited Berline, Kenny Wertz, Alan Munde, and Roger Bush to form a bluegrass group (initially the Hot Burrito Revue) and accompany them on tour. Out of this arose Country Gazette which did several progressive bluegrass albums including **A Traitor in Our Midst**, **Don't Give Up Your Day Job**, and **Bluegrass Special**. At the same time, Berline continued to do superb studio work for a variety of musicians. Most notably for alt. country fans, he was the featured fiddler on Gram Parsons' **GP** and **Grievous Angel** albums. After dropping out of Country Gazette in 1975, Berline formed another band, Sundance, with Dan Crary on guitar and John Hickman on banjo. The group recorded one album of California style country rock/bluegrass before disbanding in 1978. During the late 1970s and into the 1980s, Berline remained a much in demand session musician appearing on albums by Dillard and Clark, Emmylou Harris (**Pieces of the Sky**; **Elite Hotel**), and Chris Hillman. He cut a number of solo and collaborative recordings, fronted the L.A. Fiddle Band, and worked closely with Dan Crary and John Hickman. Berline, Crary, Hickman made several albums in the 1980s before adding more members in 1990 and becoming California (IBMA's Instrumental Group of the Year in 1992). Byron's 1995 release, **Fiddle & A Song**, is a mini-retrospective on the career of one of the most accomplished and versatile fiddlers of our time.

Currently, Berline heads a bluegrass/Western swing band (Byron Berline Band with John Hickman) and has become quite a music entrepreneur and promoter as owner of Byron's Music Hall and Double Stop Fiddle Shop in Guthrie, Oklahoma. In 1997, he organized and sponsored the first Oklahoma International Bluegrass Festival with some of the top names in contemporary bluegrass plus a reunion of Country Gazette and the L.A. Fiddle Band. It has now become one of the top events on the bluegrass calendar attracting the biggest names and huge crowds.

A Traitor in Our Midst (Country Gazette)/United Artists/1972
Don't Give Up Your Day Job (Country Gazette)/ United Artists/1973; Liberty/1983
Live in Amsterdam (Country Gazette)/Bumble Holland/1973

Bluegrass Special (Country Gazette)/Ariola Holland/1974
Berline, Sam Bush & Mark O'Connor/O'Connor/1976
Byron Berline and Sundance/MCA/1976
Dad's Favorites/Rounder/1977
Live at McCabe's (Country Gazette)/Takoma/1978
Outrageous/Flying Fish/1980
Byron Berline and the L.A. Fiddle Band/Sugar Hill/1980
Berline, Crary, Hickman/Sugar Hill/1981
Night Run (Berlin, Crary, Hickman)/Sugar Hill/1984
BCH/Sugar Hill/1986
Double Trouble (Berline & Hickman)/Sugar Hill/ 1986; 1995
Now They Are Four (Berline, Crary, Hickman)/Sugar Hill/1986
Jumpin' the Strings/Sugar Hill/1990
Traveler (California)/Sugar Hill/1992
Fiddle & A Song/Sugar Hill/1995

Byron Berline, 121 E. Oklahoma, Guthrie, OK 73044

Byron Berline Home Page //doublestop.com/byron.htm

bb1@flash.net

See Country Gazette

Steve Bice

Honky Tonk; Country Rock
Niagara Falls, New York; 1962-

"Nash Bashing" has become one of the favorite past times of performers rejected by Music Row and/or just disgusted with the excesses of New/Young Country; Dale Watson's "Nashville Rash," Mojo Nixon's "Let's Go Burn Old Nashville Down," and Robbie Fulks' "Fuck This Town" come most readily to mind. Falling in line with these sentiments is the attack by Steve Bice who, like so many others, was turned down and out by the Nashville establishment because in the words of Watson he was "too country now for country." Bice (born in upstate New York, now living in Michigan) channeled his bitterness into the scathing "Rubber Room" which is the showpiece of his debut recording, **The Sin Citizen Sessions: Vol. 1, Original Sins**. Wearing the outlaw mantle proudly, Bice surrounds himself with a fine cast of supporting musicians including fiddler Larry Franklin (ex-Cooder Browne; Asleep at the Wheel), ace steel player Al Perkins, and Andrea Zonn (lead vocal on two songs) on 16 originals dealing with subjects long anathema in Nashville. Sounding like a cross between Merle Haggard and Gary Stewart, Bice comes on strong with potent tearjerkers ("Colgate Wine/Whiskey Highway"; "Old Friend"; "Two Blue Teardrops"), classic honky tonk shuffles ("The Gates of Hell"; "Just the Way"), and rockers ("Detroit Saturday Night"). With this impressive debut, Bice had the last laugh on Music City.

The Sin Citizen Sessions: Vol. 1, Original Sins/ Sincitizen/1997

Steve Bice/Sin Citizen,
23005 Warner, Farmington, MI 48336

Steve Bice/Sin Citizen Home Page
//www.sincitizenmusic.com

Big Blue Hearts
Country Rock
San Francisco, California; 1996-

The first time I listened to the Big Blue Hearts self titled debut I thought I had put Chris Isaak in the CD player by mistake. And although none of the BBH promo material acknowledges it, there is no denying the resemblance; David Fisher's sensual Roy Orbisonesque vocals, slow, swingy tempos, reverb drenched guitars, and preoccupation with love lost and found and lost. Moreover, they are based in San Francisco, and they used Isaak's mixer. The good news is that like Isaak their sound is catchy and grows on you with each listening. Geffen was impressed enough to sign them after they had been together for less than a year. Fisher started the band in 1996 after stints with various hard rock bands left him wanting a more traditional, acoustic style such as that found in the Everly Brothers brand of country rock. He discovered the initial line-up for the Big Blue Hearts right in his own neighborhood and decked out in classic black suits, they began performing at local clubs. In search of a more "sensuous, reverby" sound, Fisher signed on lead guitarist Michael Donovan who stayed on long enough to complete their 1997 T-Bone Burnett produced **Big Blue Hearts**. Marriage took Donovan out of the picture, and he was replaced by Jamie Scott. The phenomenally rapid rise of BBH in the alt. country scene pegged them as the next "can't miss" act. That remained to be sawed, but in the meantime, the band set to work on their second recording in late 1998 testing out new material at Mick's Lounge where they were originally "discovered" by Geffen.

Michael Anderson (b,v); Michael Donovan (g,v,1996-1997); David Fisher (a.g.,l.v.); Jamie Scott (l.g.,1997-); Paul Zarich (d,v)

Big Blue Hearts/Geffen/1996

Big Blue Hearts/Geffen Home Page
//www.geffen.com/bigbluehearts/

Big Blue Hearts iMusic Showcase
//imusic.com/showcase/contemporary/

See Chris Isaak

Big Chicken (Born Naked)
Progressive Bluegrass; Roots Rock
Portsmouth, New Hampshire; 1994-1998

The most obvious reference point for New Hampshire's Big Chicken is The Band. Like them, they use a wide variety of traditional instruments and alternate between acoustic and electric originals running through folk, blues, bluegrass, country, and roots rock. They originated in 1994 when local musician David Marshall was recording a solo album and brought in Todd Jones (who was playing with his band, Born

Naked, at the time) and a friend Al Pratt to help out. This ensemble, known as A Little Big Chicken, grew into Big Chicken with the addition of Rob Kneeland on drums. Holding down day jobs, they performed in the Northeast region as time permitted. In 1996, Big Chicken recorded a self-titled debut CD on Marshall's Fat Cuz Records. Its 13 originals (contributed by all the members) with titles like "Asgaard Farm," "The Fairground," "Mountains Walking," and "Hogan's Barn" have a downhome but decidedly contemporary feel. After opening for none other than The Band at a concert in September 1996, Big Chicken reaped a number of Portsmouth music awards (Best New Band; Best Bluegrass Band; Best Folk Band) in early 1997. Still, Big Chicken had no pretensions about "making it big" and were content with just a little hometown recognition or as Al Pratt put it, "When they know you at the Dunkin' Donuts chain, that's success!" Unfortunately, they couldn't handle even that much fame and in late summer 1998 played their last official gig. However, Dave Marshall continued to perform and record on a regular basis (for Fat Cuz), and the sessions often included Big Chicken alumni.

Todd Jones (acc,a.g.,bj,e.g.,v); Rob Kneeland (d,perc,v); David Marshall (a.g.,e.g.,hm,md); Al Pratt (a.g.,bj,e.g., hmkz,v) with Jen Alexander (v); Rob Nelson (congas,v)

David Marshall With a Little Big Chicken/Fat Cuz/1994
Grow (Born Naked)/Fat Cuz/1994
Big Chicken/Fat Cuz/1996

Fat Cuz Records, P.O. Box 497, Durham, NH 03824; 603-749-0741

Fatcuzrec@aol.com

Big Chicken Home Page
//www.olmsted.com/fat-cuz-records/bcmain.html

Big In Iowa
Roots Rock
Hamilton, Ohio; 1996-

Actually based in Ohio, Big in Iowa evolved from informal jam sessions orgainzed by co-founders Bob Burns, Ken Glidewell, and Rick House. All were or had been in a variety of local bands and after adding two more members (Dusty Bryant; Jamie O'Keefe), they took the name Big in Iowa after a 1950s-1960s group Burns' uncle was in that was "big in Iowa." The sound they fashioned drew heavily on classic California country rock, Southern rock, Midwest alt. country, and roots rock/Americana icons such as Neil Young and The Band. All of these elements are readily apparent on their self-titled debut which is distinguished mostly by Burns' drawling vocals and witty originals. It plus strong live shows on their Mad Cow Tour and opening for groups like Dave Alvin, the Bottlerockets, Slobberbone, and the V-Roys earned them Best Rock Band (1997) honors from *CityBeat Magazine*'s Cincinnati Entertainment Awards. And while they were popular in the Upper Midwest, Big in Iowa also gained a following in Europe, and like many other American groups (Hazeldine, Go To Blazes), they ended up signing with an overseas label. Germany's Blue Rose Records released BII's **Twisted** in 1998. Once again, the group's influences are obvious, but **Twisted** also shows evidence of a band really coming into its own novel approach. Named Best Rock Band again in 1998, Big in Iowa remained big in their region but obscure in the rest of the U.S. However, their European star continued to rise in 1998 and 1999 with inclusion of songs on the **Sounds of the New West** alt. country CD (from England's *Uncut* magazines) and on the Dutch Neil Young tribute, **This Note's For You Too!**

Dusty Bryant (ky,1996); Bob Burns (a.g.,l.v.); Ken Glidewell (b,v); Rick House (g,md,s.g.,v); Mike McGuire (kys,v,1997-); Jamie O'Keefe (d,1996); Jeff Wilson (d,v,1997-)

> **Big In Iowa**/BII/1996
> **Twisted**/Blue Rose Ger./1998
> "Is This Love" on **The Blue Rose Collection, Vol. 4**/Blue Rose Ger./1998
> "September Song" on **Sounds of the New West**/Uncut UK/1998
> "Cinnamon Girl" on **This Note's for You, Too!: A Tribute to Neil Young**/Inbetweens Dut./1999

Big In Iowa, P.O. Box 13268, Hamilton, OH 45013; 513-868-8787

Big In Iowa Home Page //www.biginiowa.com

biginiowa@interserv.com

Big Sandy and The Fly-Rite Boys (Big Sandy and the Fly-Rite Trio; Country Cabin Boys)
Hillbilly Bop
Los Angeles, California; 1989-

Along with High Noon, the kings of the 1990s nouveaubilly scene are Big Sandy and the Fly-Rite Boys. The origins of the group date back to the mid-1980s rockabilly revival when lead singer Robert Williams (Big Sandy) got interested in the growing L.A. scene and put together the Fly-Rite Trio in 1989. The band's early recordings, **Fly Right** and **On the Go**, presented a frenetic rockabilly sound, but their growing interest in 1940s-1950s California country plus the addition of British born Lee Jeffriess on pedal steel led toward a smoother blend of rockabilly, honky tonk, and Western swing as the Fly-Rite Boys. When Dave Alvin helped them get a deal with Hightone Records in 1994, they were well on their way to becoming America's premier hillbilly boogie band. Their first album for Hightone, **Jumpin' From 6 to 6**, generally maintained the fast pace of the Trio days but also signaled a change in direction that came with **Swingin' West** in 1995. Here, Big Sandy and the Boys made a full transition to the classic California sound made famous by Spade Cooley, Tex Williams, West & Bryant, the Maddox Brothers and Rose, and Billy Jack Wills. They

continued in a hillbilly bop mode on the follow-up, **Feelin' Kinda Lucky**, which is anchored as always by Big Sandy's smooth as silk vocals and the solo and twin leads of Jefriess and lead guitarist Ashley Kingman. Late in 1997, they added the legendary pianist Carl Sonny Leyland whose heavier jump blues pounding adds yet another dimension to one of the tightest dance bands in the land.

Over the years, Big Sandy and his band members have done a number of interesting side projects. The Fly-Rite Boys sans Big Sandy have recorded as the Country Cabin Boys for Deke Dickerson's Ecco-Fonic label. Big Sandy and the Fly-Rite Boys cut a 78 rpm platter for Rockabilly Records, a split **Battle of the Bands** EP with High Noon, an all Spanish single with surf giants, Los Straightjackets, and a 45 with a "straight" and an X-rated version of "Back Door Dan." In 1998, **Big Sandy Presents The Fly-Rite Boys** allowed the band to strut their stuff on a collection of boogie woogie, swing, and hillbilly bop while Big Sandy cut **Dedicated to You**, his solo tribute to R&B and doo-wop.

Fly-Rite Trio: Wally Hersom (b); Ashley Kingman (l.g.); Bobby Trimble (d)
Fly-Rite Boys: Wally Hersom (b); Lee Jeffriess (p.s.); Ashley Kingman (l.g.); Carl Sonny Leyland (p,1997-); Bobby Trimble (d)
Country Cabin Boys: Wally Hersom (b); Lee Jeffriess (p.s.); Ashley Kingman (l.g.); Bobby Trimble (d)

> **Fly Right with Big Sandy and the Fly-Rite Trio**/ Dionysus/1990
> "Don't Desert Me" b/w "I'm Gonna Leave" (Fly-Rite Boys)/Dionysus/1990 (7")
> **On the Go** (Fly Rite Trio)/No Hit UK/1991
> **Jumpin' From Six to Six** (Fly-Rite Boys)/ Hightone/1994
> **Down at Jake's Barber Shop** (Fly-Rite Boys)/No Hit UK/1994 (EP)
> "Jake's Barber Shop" (Fly Rite Boys) on **Pushing the Norton**/Heyday/1994
> "Wounded Knee Polka" b/w "Lucky's Lullaby" (Country Cabin Boys)/Ecco-Fonic/1995 (7")
> **Swingin' West** (Fly-Rite Boys)/Hightone/1995
> **Battle of the Bands, Vol. One** (Big Sandy vs. High Noon)/Thunder Fr./1995 (EP)
> {"That Ain't It" & "Long Blonde Hair" (Big Sandy); "All Night Long" & "Havin' A Whole Lotta Fun" (High Noon)}
> "Que Mala!" b/w "La Plaga" (with Los Straightjackets)/ Spin Out/1997 (7")
> **Feelin' Kinda Lucky**/Hightone/1997
> "Back Door Dan" b/w "Back Door Dan" (X-Rated)/ Hightone/1997 (7")
> **Big Sandy Presents The Fly-Rite Boys**/ Hightone/1998
> **Dedicated to You** (Big Sandy solo)/Hightone/1998

Big Sandy and the Fly-Rite Boys/Hightone Page //www.hightone.com/bios/sandy.html

See Dave & Deke; High Noon

Big Wooden Radio

Americana
Iowa City, Iowa; 1994-

Iowa City's Big Wooden Radio play an eclectic mix of acoustic roots rock they characterize as "Good Tunes, Good Chops, Good Wood." From this radio you are as likely to hear the old-time sounds of gospel and Appalachian harmonies as zydeco, country, and modern rock. Formed in the mid-1990s, the band is made up of veterans who played with Cam Waters, Bell & Shore, and Al Murphy. Their self titled debut consists mostly of compositions from the pens of Dan Brown and Sam Thompson while their sophomore effort, **Along These Lines** presents a diversity of covers by Dave Alvin ("Fourth of July"), Doug Sahm ("Is Anybody Going to San Antone?"), Lowell George ("Truckstop Girl"), Robbie Robertson ("Caledonia Mission"), Jules Shear, and Zachary Richard. Into late 1996 and early 1997, Big Wooden Radio gradually received notoriety outside their home region through an appearance at the Telluride Bluegrass Festival and recording a soundtrack for the news show *20/20*. In 1997, they were voted #1 Band in an *Icon* magazine reader's poll and continued to be a popular draw in their home state.

Dan Brown (b,v); Paul Cunliffe (d,perc); Will Jennings (hm,h.v.,l.v.); Joe Peterson (md); Sam Thompson (g,v)

Big Wooden Radio/BWR/1995
Along These Lines/BWR/1996

Big Wooden Radio, 1154 Hotz Ave.,
Iowa City, IA 52245-3318

Big Wooden Radio Home Page
//www.poky.srv.net/~martyw/bwr.html

The Billy's

Grain Belt Rock
Minneapolis, Minnesota; 1991-

In concert, the Billy's, one of the most obscure of the Twin Cities' many fine roots rock bands, are known for rocking covers of John Denver, Gordon Lightfoot, Simon & Garfunkle, and Jim Croce, but they make an alt. country statement with their original material. Named after the lead character in Kurt Vonnegut's *Slaughterhouse Five*, their recordings, **Roses and Flowers and Plants**, **All American Lounge**, and **Another Winner**, combine roots rock/country with a good measure of wry humor ("Friends Like That," "Those Shoes," "Monitor Lizard," "Mr. Stipe") bearing a striking resemblance to Minneapolis' much beloved Gear Daddies (Martin Zellar appeared on their first two recordings).

Andy Christensen (b); Scott Ehrenberg (g,v); Eric Roberts (g,v); Rob Thompson (d)

Roses and Flowers and Plants/Oar Fin/1994
All American Lounge/Oar Fin/1996
Another Winner/Redshirt/1997

The Billy's c/o Redshirt Records, P.O. Box 300113, Minneapolis, MN 55403

The Billy's Home Page //www2.bitstream.net/~billys/

thebillys@juno.com

See The Gear Daddies

Birddog (aka Bill Santen)

Singer/Songwriter; Lo-Fi
Lexington, Kentucky

A native of Kentucky, Bill Santen moved to California at 18 to pursue a musical career and after wandering around the Golden State for a while settled in Portland, Oregon. Working primarily as a solo, Santen adopted the stage name Birddog and became known as a folk/country balladeer with considerable vocal, guitar playing, and songwriting skill. He made his recording debut on two singles and then began to get noticed with the release of a seven song EP, **The Trackhouse, The Valley, The Liquor Store Drive-Thru** in 1997. Recorded in three separate locales with three groups of musicians, it has a slightly rockier feel to it than Birddog's singles thanks mainly to contributions by producers Elliot Smith (bass, drums) and Paul K. But, overall, it creates a moody, lo-fi atmosphere made especially effective by the addition of Charlie Campbell on cello. Santen/Birddog's haunting tunes—"Killer," "Lights of Amarillo," "Last Song," "Parked Car Homestead"—wallow in the mire along side the best from the doom-and-gloom school of singer/songwriters. Late in 1997, Birddog got the chance to showcase his talents to a wider audience at the CMJ Music Fest in Chicago where he shared the stage with Edith Frost, Chris Mills, and Jon Langford's Skull Orchard. His 1998, **Ghost of the Salon**, presented more somber, acoustic based Americana that placed him in the same company as Richard Buckner, Will Oldham, and Tom House.

"Ten Later" b/w "Broken Lady Blues"/Casting Couch/199? (7")
"Killer"/Undercover/199? (7")
The Trackhouse, The Valley, The Liquor Store Drive-Thru/Sugar Free/1997 (CD EP)
Ghost of the Salon/Sugar Free/1998

Birddog/Sugar Free Records Page
//www.sugarfreerecords.com/birddogset.htm

The Black Boot Trio

Lo-Fi Country Rock
Ottawa, Ontario, Canada; 1994-

The music of the Black Boot Trio comes in three shades: black, blacker, and blackest. Dubbed by various critics as "acid and western" or "Johnny Cash meets Leonard Cohen on downers," they have also been likened to Lou Reed and Nick Cave gone country. Making maximum use of moody guitar and leader Steve Fai's growling vocals, the Black Boot Trio tell angst ridden stories about love, death, and depression on two albums, **A Pony Ride** and the ominously titled **Blood**.

Stef Bennett (d); Steve Fai (g,l.v.); Geoff Taylor (b,v)

A Pony Ride/Hassan's Rumpus Room Can./1995
Blood/Hassan's Rumpus Room Can./1996
"Angel" and "John's Song" on **Plug!: New Music From Ottawa**/1996
"The Last Days of Wine and Roses" on **Cowpunks**/Vinyl Junkie UK/1996

The Black Boot Trio Home Page
//www.globalx.net/cims/c3/blackbt.html

The Black Boot Trio/Primal Beat Web Page
//www.primalbeat.com/country/black/black.html

The Blackeyed Susans
Roots-Rock; Country Rock
Perth/Sydney/Melbourne, Australia; 1989-

For almost a decade, the Blackeyed Susans have been one of Australia's most popular bands. Their ever-evolving sound is similar to the formula that has become standard among 1990s alt. country roots rockers in the U.S.—begin with traditional blues, country, and folk then add a modern rock edge on originals and covers of standard tunes. And, like the best of their American counter-parts, the Blackeyed Susans' grand experiment has worked well in spite of a bewildering array of personnel changes since the band started in 1989 as a mostly part-time affair. Its earliest incarnations were drawn from other groups including another pioneering Australian roots rock band, the Triffids, with the steadiest members being lead vocalist Rob Snarski, David McComb, and Phil Kakulas. Feeling their way through several EPs, the Blackeyed Susans finally found what they were searching for on successive full-length recordings, **Welcome Stranger** (1992) and **All Souls Alive** (1993). Both are all over the musical map but of particular interest to alt. country fans are updated versions of traditional songs ("Cripple Creek"; "Spanish Is a Loving Tongue"; "Apartment #9") and melancholy originals like "In the Pines," "Every Gentle Soul," "Reveal Yourself," and "I Can See Now" with strong vocals from Snarski and engaging interplay between organ, accordion, and the lilting pedal steel of newcomer Lee Graham (ex-Triffids). In 1994 the group underwent another major line-up change with everyone replaced but Kakulas and Snarski. As a result, **Mouth to Mouth** and **Spin the Bottle** have a more pop rock orientation although a few snatches of the old Blackeyed Susans/Triffids rootsy rock remain. When **Mouth to Mouth** was picked up for distribution by American Recordings in 1996, they embarked on their first ever U.S. tour. Starting in New York City, the Susans' first show was opening for Johnny Cash who expressed his approval of their song, "Smokin' Johnny Cash" (in some parts of the world "Johnny Cash" is argot for good dope). They also opened for Wilco and though they failed to break through with

American audiences, the Blackeyed Susans are still going strong Down Under.

Past Members: Will Akers (perc,b.v.,1989); Ross Bolleter (acc,org, 1989); Martin Casey (b,1990); James Cruikshank (org,1991); Jim Elliott (d,1991); Warren Ellis (acc,org,1992-1993); Graham Lee (g,l.s.,p.s.,v, 1992-1993); David McComb (g,v,1989-1990,1992- 1993); Alsy McDonald (d,1989-1990); Timothy Rollinson (g,1991); Kim Salmon (g,v,1990); Jim White (d,1992-1993); Adrian Wood (ky, 1990)
Current Members: Kiernan Box (hm,org,p,1994-); Ken Davis (acc,ky,1991,1995-); Mark Dawson (d); Phil Kakulas (b,1989,1991-); Dan Luscombe (g,1994-); Rob Snarski (g,v)

Some Births Are Worse Than Murders/Waterfront Aust./1990 (EP)
Anchor Me/Waterfront Aust./1991 (EP)
Depends on What You Mean By Love/Waterfront Aust./1991 (EP)
Welcome Stranger/Shock Aust./1992
All Souls Alive/Shock Aust./1993; Frontier/1994
Mouth to Mouth/Hi-Gloss Aust./1995; American/1996
Spin the Bottle/Hi-Gloss Aust./1997
La Mascara/Hi-Gloss Aust./1998 (EP)

The Official Blackeyed Susans Web Site
//www.melbourne.net/susans/news.html

See Love Me; The Triffids

Blackie & The Rodeo Kings
Country Rock
Toronto, Ontario, Canada; 1996-

Willie P. Bennett is one of Canada's greatest songwriters. During the 1970s-1980s, through acclaimed recordings and frequent appearances on the Canadian folk circuit, he developed a cult following and in the late 1980s became a vital member of Fred Eaglesmith's backing band, the Flying Squirrels. In 1996, two of Bennett's most ardent fans, Stephen Fearing and Colin Linden, decided to pay tribute to Bennett by recording an album covering some of his finest songs. Both Fearing and Linden already had established musical careers; Fearing as a folk singer/songwriter with three albums to his credit and Linden as a blues guitarist and songwriter with five recordings and a Juno Award. They enlisted the help of another Canadian performer, Tom Wilson of Junkhouse and took the name Blackie & the Rodeo Kings (from the title of a Bennett album). With many Canadian guests including Bruce Cockburn, Colleen Peterson (Quartette), Russell De Carle (Prairie Oyster), and Willie P. himself on mandolin and background vocals, they laid down 14 songs in 5 days for the album **High or Hurtin'**. Bennett's fine country songs like "White Line," "Country Squall," "Driftin' Snow," "For the Sake of a Dollar" are given loving and energetic treatment primarily through the shared vocals of Fearing, Linden, and Wilson. Their work won a Juno nomination for Best Roots/Traditional album of 1996.

After touring for a time in 1997, the three principals of BRK returned to solo projects but still collaborated. With help from Linden (producer) and Wilson, Fearing recorded **Industrial Lullaby**, an acclaimed album of rock, pop, and folk. Also lending support were Margo Timmins, Bazil Donovan (Blue Rodeo), Richard Bell (The Band), and Willie P. Bennett who co-wrote "Coryanna," one of the recording's highlights, with Fearing.

Stephen Fearing (g,v); Colin Linden (g,v); Tom Wilson (g,v)

> **High or Hurtin'**/True North Can./1996
> **Industrial Lullaby** (Stephen Fearing)/Red House/1998

Blackie & The Rodeo Kings Home Page
//www.ccinet.ab.ca/cfmf/1996bios/Blackie
AndTheRodeoKings/

Stephen Fearing Information Page
//www.interlog.com/~samy/fearing.html

Colin Linden: The Raised by Wolves Website
//www.colinlinden.com

See Fred J. Eaglesmith

The Blacks

Insurgent Country
Chicago, Illinois; Late 1990s-

Danny Black (bj,g,l.s.,tp,v); Gina Black (hm,org,ub,v); James Emmenegger (d); Nora O'Connor (g,p,v)

Originally known as The Black Family (changed to avoid conflict with an Irish band of the same name), The Blacks are "second generation" insurgent country, and they do that tradition proud with a self-described "bastardized punk-inflected cowboy blues." Their CD debut, **Dolly Horrorshow** (produced by Eric Ambel), creates an ominous mood through subtle and not so subtle strategies; some songs like "Dolly," "New, New Waltzing Blues," "Horrorshow," and "He's Gone" just come right out and hit you over the head with loud fuzzy guitar, drunken trumpet, and/or angry vocals (Gina Black on "Horrorshow") but the most effective numbers ("Teresa Leaves Lonesome Town"; "Tortured Holiday"; "Crazy"; "Moan"; "Take Me Now"; "Dear Little Girl") take a mailed-fist-in-a-velvet-glove approach with traditional, even pleasant sounding country music and lead vocals by Danny Black combined with an ever-lurking dark edge and very disturbing lyrics. On stage, the Blacks go for maximum dramatic effect as well dressed in an array of bizarre costumes led by upright bass player Gina Black who is notorious for wearing ultra-gaudy dresses and wigs of varying colors. She also did the surreal, nightmarish artwork for **Dolly Horrorshow**.

The Blacks c/o Mary Jones Management, 2438 N. Greenview, Chicago, IL 60614; maryjonz@wwa.com

> **Dolly Horrorshow**/Bloodshot/1998

The Blacks/Bloodshot Page //www.bloodshotrecords.com

The Blacktop Rockets

Redneck Underground; Rockabilly
Atlanta, Georgia; 1995-

While many of the charter members (Delta Angels, Greg Smalley, Vidalias) of Redneck Underground have come and gone, the Blacktop Rockets have endured with a powerhouse sound that has made them one of Atlanta's top roots/rockabilly bands since they first came on the scene in the mid-1990s. Led by lead guitarist/vocalist Dave Weil, they became regulars at the R.U. mecca, the Star Community Bar. An early member of the group, Greg Dean Smalley, was the brain behind the annual Bubbapalooza showcases, and the Rockets appeared at the inaugural festival and subsequently on **Bubbapalooza, Vol. 1**. They've also performed at Sleazefest and currently sponsor their own annual event, the Dixie Rockabilly Rumble. Their two full-length CDs, **What'll Ya Have?** and **Make Mine a Double**, are brimming with straight-ahead 50s style rockabilly as well as some dead-on country ballads, honky tonk, and swing. In 1998, the Blacktop Rockets' "Ruby" (from 1996 with Greg Smalley on guitar) was included in **Bubbapalooza, Vol. 2**, and they did a rousing cover of "American Music" for a tribute to one of their main influences, the Blasters.

Johnny Knox (g,v); Matt Sickles (b); Gregory Dean Smalley (g,1996); Dave Watkins (d); Dave Weil (g,v)

> "Rockabilly Show" on **Bubbapalooza, Vol. 1**/Sky/1995
> **What'll Ya Have?**/Straight 8/1996
> "Yuletide Blues" b/w "El Rudolfo" (Thee Kustom Kings)/Straight 8/1996 (7")
> "Ruby" on **Bubbapalooza, Vol. 2**/Criminal/1998
> "American Music" on **Blastered: A Musical Tribute to the Blasters**/Run Wild/1998
> **Make Mine a Double**/Straight 8/1998

The Blacktop Rockets, 1072 Bouldercrest Dr. SE, Atlanta, GA 30316

The Blacktop Rockets Home Page
//www.mindspring.com/~blacktoprockets/

blacktoprockets@mindspring.com

See Gregory Dean Smalley

Norman Blake

New Old-Time; Progressive Bluegrass
Chattanooga, Tennessee; March 10, 1938-

Like another legendary multi-instrumentalist of his generation, David Bromberg, Norman Blake has been primarily known for his work as a super session/sideman. However, he has also made a plethora of fabulous albums as a soloist or with some of the great names in modern old-time/bluegrass. A native of Tennessee, Blake apprenticed with a number of groups in the late 1950s including the Dixieland Drifters, the Lonesome Travelers, Hylo Brown and the Timberliners, and the June Carter band. However, it was his association with Johnny Cash and Bob Dylan in the late 1960s that brought him to the attention of a new and larger audience. Blake was a member of Cash's band and also performed regularly on the Man in Black's television show; he and Cash appeared on Dylan's ground-breaking **Nashville Skyline** (1969). Throughout the 1970s-1980s, Blake was a much-in-demand session player mostly for his Doc Watson inspired flatpicking and worked on some of the key alt. country projects of the time including John Hartford's **Aereo-Plain** and the monumental **Will the Circle Be Unbroken**. In the 1990s, Norman passed on his experience to a new generation of performers, most prominently Steve Earle who used Blake along with alt. country veterans Peter Rowan, Roy Huskey, and Emmylou Harris on his acoustic gem, **Train a Comin'**. During this period, Blake recorded an impressive number of solo albums and top notch collaborations with Charlie Collins, Jethro Burns, Sam Bush, Tut Taylor, Red Rector, Tony Rice, and his multi-talented wife Nancy that are some of the finest examples of contemporary old-time/bluegrass.

> **Back Home in Sulphur Springs** (with Tut Taylor)/ Rounder/1972; 1995
> **Blackberry Blossom**/Flying Fish/1974
> **The Fields of November**/Flying Fish/1974
> **Norman Blake With Jethro Burns, Sam Bush, Tut Taylor**/Flying Fish/1975
> **Old & New**/Flying Fish/1975
> **Live at McCabe's**/Takoma/1976
> **Whiskey Before Breakfast**/Rounder/1976
> **Norman Blake and Red Rector**/County/1976
> **Directions**/Takoma/1978
> **Rising Fawn String Ensemble**/Rounder/1979
> **Full Moon on the Farm**/Rounder/1981
> **Original Underground Music From the Mysterious South**/Rounder/1982
> **Nashville Blues**/Rounder/1984
> **Lighthouse on the Shore**/Rounder/1985
> **The Norman and Nancy Blake Compact Disc**/ Rounder/1986
> **Grand Junction** (Nancy Blake)/Rounder/1986
> **Slow Train Through Georgia**/Rounder/1987
> **Natasha's Waltz** (with Nancy Blake)/Rounder/1987
> **Blake & Rice**/Rounder/1987
> **Blind Dog** (with Nancy Blake)/Rounder/1988
> **Blake & Rice 2**/Rounder/1990
> **Just Gimme Somethin' I'm Used To**/ Shanachie/1992
> **Live at McCabe's & Directions**/Takoma/1993
> **While Passing Along This Way** (with Nancy Blake)/ Shanachie/1994
> *Norman Blake & The Rising Fawn String Band*/ NTSC/1994 (60 min. Video)
> *My Dear Old Southern Home*/NTSC/1994 (60 min. video)
> **Flatpickin' In the Kitchen** (with Tut Taylor)/ Tutlee/1997
> **Chattanooga Sugar Babe**/Shanachie/1998

Norman Blake/Rounder Page // www.rounder.com

See Tony Rice; Tut Taylor

Clay Blaker & His Texas Honky-Tonk Band
Honky Tonk
New Braunfels/Austin, Texas; 1977-

For over 20 years, Clay Blaker and His Texas Honky-Tonk Band have been entertaining crowds throughout the Lone Star State, the U.S., and Europe. Born and raised along the Texas Gulf Coast, Blaker was drawn to country music early on but, ironically, he formed the THT Band in California after he moved there in the early 1970s. They were popular in venues from L.A. to San Diego but after a very successful run at Houston's Steamboat Springs in late 1976, Clay and company moved back to Texas where they became dance hall regulars, did a six week European tour, and cut several singles written by Blaker. One of these, "The Only Thing I Have Left," was picked up by George Strait who knew Blaker from the dance hall circuit and whose career was really beginning to blossom in the early 1980s. Blaker opened on several of Strait's early tours, and George subsequently covered six other Blaker originals on his mega-hit albums. Other HNC stars including Tim McGraw, Mark Chesnutt, Derryl Dodd, and Leann Rimes have also used Blaker's songs while Clay has stuck with playing his original honky tonk/Western swing/country rock sound in dancehalls and on several full-length CDs (**Laying It on the Line**; **Rumor Town**).

> "Goin' Home to Texas" b/w "I Don't Know What Sells the Records"/Diamondhead/1978 (7")
> "The Only Thing I Have Left" b/w "Texas Honky Tonk"/D/1980 (7")
> "My Drinkin' Made Me Stumble (But Her Leavin' Made Me Fall)" b/w "What a Way to Live"/Paid/1981 (7")
> **What a Way to Live**/Texas Musik/1981
> "Under the X in Texas" b/w "Darkness on the Face of the Earth"/Texas Musik/1982 (7")
> "South of the Border" b/w "Lonesome Rodeo Cowboy"/Texas Musik/1986 (7")
> **Sooner or Later**/Texas Musik/1986
> "A Honky Tonk Heart (And a Hillbilly Soul)" b/w "The Only Thing I Have Left"/Rain Forest/1988 (7")
> **Laying It All on the Line**/Neobilly/1993
> **Rumor Town**/Neobilly/1998

Clay Blaker, P.O. Box 310448, New Braunfels, TX 78131; 830-899-7090, (fax) 830-899-7094

Clay Blaker Home Page //www.clayblaker.com

cblaker@gvtc.com

The Blasters; Dave Alvin; Phil Alvin
Roots Rock; Americana
The Blasters: Los Angeles, California; 1980-1985; 1994-Present
Dave Alvin: Los Angeles, California; November 11, 1955-
Phil Alvin: Los Angeles, California; March 6, 1953-

A friend of mine once told me he took his leather jacket to a Blasters' concert and draped it underneath the microphone of lead singer Phil Alvin so his cascading sweat could christen it. Such is the fanaticism the Blasters have inspired in their followers since they burst on the L.A. music scene in the late

1970s. Brothers Dave and Phil Alvin (5th generation Californians) had been steeped in blues, country, r&b, rockabilly, and swing at an early age growing up in L.A. and when they added a dash of the punk sound that was sweeping the city, they had a potent and unbeatable combination. Initially a quartet (the Alvins plus John Bazz on bass and Bill Bateman on drums), the Blasters released their first album, **American Music**, on the obscure Rolling Rock label in 1980. It defined the band's direction, and they expanded on it with the addition of two sax players (Steve Berlin; Lee Allen) and keyboardist Gene Taylor. With a succession of fine albums for Slash (Warner Brothers), **The Blasters**, **Over There (Live)**, **Nonfiction**, and **Hardline** plus dynamic live performances, they became the consummate roots rock band of the early 1980s. At the heart of their dynamic and winning sound were the vocals of Phil and the sizzling guitar work of Dave who also penned a number of great songs including "Hollywood Bed," "Long White Cadillac," "Border Radio," and "Fourth of July." However, while they were riding high through 1984-1985 (appeared for two songs in the 1984 movie, *Streets of Fire*), tensions between the Alvin brothers were beginning to pull the band apart. While Dave was working with John Doe and Exene Cervenka on the Knitters' **Poor Little Critter On the Road**, he was invited to join their band X as lead guitarist (replacing Billy Zoom). He accepted and left the Blasters who went on with several new guitarists until the late 1980s when Phil put the band on hold so he could get his Masters in mathematics. Phil then put out an eclectic solo album in 1986, **Un "Sung Stories,"** with the Dirty Dozen Brass Band and Sun Ra; a year later, Dave released his first solo, **Romeo's Escape** and a soundtrack called **Border Radio** with cuts by the Divine Horsemen, Green on Red, Chris D, and Dave Alvin in duets with John Doe and Steve Berlin. Into the 1990s, Dave recorded a number of solo efforts, **Blue Blvd.**, **King of California**, **Museum of the Heart**, and **Interstate City**, recorded live at the Continental Club in Austin, Texas. They cover some familiar Blasters territory plus much more; he also did a very amusing and entertaining record with Country Dick and Mojo Nixon as the Pleasure Barons. At the same time, Dave branched out into producing primarily for Hightone and has production credits for Sonny Burgess, Tom Russell, and the Derailers. He is an accomplished poet with two books, *Any Rough Times Are Now Behind You* and *The Crazy Ones*, and inclusion in a collection of modern California poetry called *Scream When You Burn*. In 1997, Dave covered "Seeds" for **One Step Up, Two Steps Back: The Songs of Bruce Springsteen** and into 1998 was hard at work on a new recording, producing Red Meat's second CD, and touring with Tom Russell, Ramblin' Jack Elliott, and Chris Smither as the "Monsters of Folk." He also received a Grammy nomination for his contribution to the liner notes for a Ray Charles boxed set. His **Blackjack David** (released mid-1998) was a collection of compelling acoustic based folk, country, blues squarely in line with the best of the

American troubadour tradition. It received widespread acclaim, and Alvin's star continued to rise; he was invited to open a few shows for Bob Dylan late in 1998. Many fans and reviewers concurred with John Conquest, editor of *3rd Coast Music*, who named Dave "Artist of the Decade."

As for Phil, he finished his M.A., put out another recording in 1995 entitled **County Fair 2000**, and then earned a Ph.D. in set theory mathematics in 1996. Farther out than a Boolean equation, he can pontificate for hours on the furniture company/record sales conspiracy, music touring "quadrants," and many other interesting theories. And what of the Blasters? In the early 1990s, Phil revived them with only John Bazz remaining from the original line-up. They have gone through several lead guitarists including the multi-talented James Intveld, toured extensively, and recorded a live album, **At Home**, that has been scheduled for a number of release dates. In late 1997, their first album, **American Music**, (now a rare collectors' item fetching $100+) was re-released by Hightone on CD to the great delight of Blasters fans everywhere. In 1998, a sure sign of their continued cult status came in the form of **Blastered: A Musical Tribute to the Blasters** which featured covers of their classic songs by some of the best of the current crop of rockabillies and honky tonkers (Blacktop Rockets, Libbi Bosworth, Sloe Gin Joes, Joise Kreuzer, Last Train Home). The latest news on the band plus some hilarious stories about Phil can be found on the Blasters home page.

Dave Alvin (g,v,1980-1986); Phil Alvin (g,l. v); Lee Allen (sax,1981-1986); Jerry Angel (d,1995-); Bill Bateman (d,1980-1986); John Bazz (b); Steve Berlin (sax,1981-1986); David Carroll (d,1987-1994); James Intveld (g,v,1993-1995); Gene Taylor (ky,1981-1986); Keith Wyatt (g,1996-)

American Music/Rolling Rock/1980; Hightone/1997
The Blasters/Slash Warner Brothers/1981
Over There: Live at the Venue, London/Slash WB/1982
Non Fiction/Slash WB/1983
Streets of Fire: A Rock 'n' Roll Fable/MCA/1984 (sdtrk.; two cuts)
Hard Line/Slash WB/1985
The Age in Which We Live/UK/198? (picture disc promo with cuts from 1st four albums)
Un "Sung Stories" (Phil Alvin solo)/Slash WB/1986
Romeo's Escape (Dave Alvin solo)/Epic/1987 (released in England on Demon as **Every Night About This Time**)
Interchords (Dave Alvin solo)/Epic/1987 (promo LP with interview and cuts from **Romeo's Escape**)
Border Radio(Dave Alvin solo)/Enigma/1987
The Blasters Collection/Slash WB/1990
Blue Blvd. (Dave Alvin solo)/Hightone/1991
Tennessee Border (Sonny Burgess with Dave Alvin)/ Hightone/1992
The Pleasure Barons (Dave Alvin, Country Dick, Mojo Nixon)/Hightone/1993
King of California (Dave Alvin solo)/Hightone/1994
"Kern River" (Dave Alvin) on **Tulare Dust**/ Hightone/1994
Museum of the Heart (Dave Alvin solo)/ Hightone/1995

County Fair 2000 (Phil Alvin solo)/Hightone/1995
Interstate City: Live (Dave Alvin & The Guilty Men)/
    Hightone/1996
"Seeds" (Dave Alvin) on **One Step Up, Two Steps Back:
    The Songs of Bruce Springsteen**/1997
Blackjack David (Dave Alvin)/Hightone/1998
Blastered: A Musical Tribute to the Blasters/Run
    Wild/1998

American Music: The Blasters Newsletter, c/o Billy Davis,
80-16 64th Lane, Glendale, NY 11385 or
P. O. Box 210071, Woodhaven, NY 11421;
Davistb@aol.com

The Blasters Home Page
//bullwinkle.as.utexas.edu/scot/blasters.html

sjk@bullwinkle.as.utexas.edu

Dave Alvin Home Page
//bullwinkle.as.utexas.edu/scot/dave.html

Museum of the Heart: Dave Alvin Fan Page
//www.ntplx.net/~kiddk/dalvin.htm

The Blasters AOL Folder: Entertainment>Music>Chat &
Messages>Music Community>Jazz/BluesBlues Artists

Dave Alvin AOL Folder: Entertainment>Music>Chat &
Messages>Music Community>Folk/Acoustic

See James Intveld; The Knitters; Los Lobos

The Blazers

Roots Rock
Los Angeles, California; 1990-

Like fellow Angelenos, Los Lobos, the Blazers cook up blues,
country, rockabilly, and r&b heavily spiced with *cumbias,
norteno,* and other Latin styles. In 1971, Manuel Gonzales and
Ruben Guaderrama began playing music together in high
school, but the Blazers didn't become a full-fledged band until
1990 when Ruben Gonzalez (drums) and Lee Stuart (bass) were
brought in. After a few years of circulating through L.A. clubs,
they made their first recording, **Short Fuse,** in 1994. Produced
by Cesar Rosas of Los Lobos, it conjures up that band in some
places but, overall, rocks harder and has the Blazers special
brand on it. A follow-up, **East Side Soul**, mined the same
ground but their third outing, **Just for You** (produced by Pete
Anderson), adds a few more Latin and r&b touches with the
addition of a dynamic horn section.

Manuel Gonzales (l.g.,v); Ruben Gonzalez (d); Ruben
Guaderrama (l.g.,v); Lee Stuart (b)

   Short Fuse/Rounder/1994
   "Yeah, Yeah, Yeah" on **Country**/Vinyl Junkie UK/1995
   East Side Soul/Rounder/1996
   Just for You/Rounder/1997
   "If There Was a Way" on **Will Sing for Food: The Songs
      of Dwight Yoakam**/Lucky Dog/1998

The Blazers/Rounder Records Home Page
//www.rounder.com/rounder/artists/blazers/

See Los Lobos

Billy Block

Promoter; DJ; Drummer
Nashville, Tennessee

Billy Block has been one of the most important promoters of alt.
country/Americana in the 1990s. Born in Texas, he drummed
for a number of area performers (Billy Joe Shaver, Freddy
Fender) in the late 1970s before relocating to L.A. in 1985. He
got in on the ground floor of the rising Town South of
Bakersfield scene as drummer for the Palomino Club's house
band and over the next decade, shared the stage with the best of
Southern California's alt. country and participated in the pioneering alt. country showcase, Ronnie Mack's Barn Dance. It
inspired him to start a similar event called the Western Beat
Americana Showcase. Then, in 1992, Block decided to move to
Nashville where initailly he took a sales and marketing position
with a Music Row magazine. But, he longed to get back into the
action and began doing studio work and co-founded his own
band, the Bum Steers. His big project, however, was the
promotional organization Western Beat Entertainment from
which came Billy Block's Western Beat Roots Revival in 1996.
This popular weekly showcase, which started at The Sutler then
move to Zanie's before settling at the Exit/In, has featured over
400 alt. country/Americana performers (many of them unsigned acts) from Nashville and around the U.S. As part of
Western Beat Entertainment, Block hosted the weekly Western
Beat Radio show, "Five Hours of Underground Country
Music" including a two hour live broadcast of the Roots
Revival. In 1998, the radio program was expanded into a
worldwide online cybercast and plans were in the works to
syndicate it to country stations across the nation. In addition,
WBE, in collaboration with Cloudland Filmworks, planned to
do a TV series **Guitar Town** centered on the Western Beat
Roots Revival.

Western Beat Entertainment
P.O. Box 128105, Nashville, TN 37212;
615-383-5466, (fax) 615-383-6331

Western Beat Home Page //www.westernbeat.com

westernbeat@home.net

Blood on the Saddle

Cowpunk
Los Angeles, California; 1983-1987; 1990-

Blood on the Saddle was one of the best cowpunk bands to come
out of Los Angeles in the mid-1980s. The original group
included Annette Zilinskas, later of Bangles fame, and was
noted for a hard driving sound bolstered by leader/lead guitarist
Greg Davis' unique picking style (he lists Doc Watson as a
major influence). The 1987 edition of the *Trouser Press*
commented that "Blood on the Saddle's idea of country is Hank
Williams OD-ing in the back of his car; their Western that of
spaghetti flicks...a rodeo where even the horses are doing

speed...a post-adolescent barn dance." Their recordings from the 1980s, **Blood on the Saddle**, **Poison Love**, and **Fresh Blood**, are generally high energy romper stompers with rousing covers of "Folsom Prison Blues" and "Rawhide" and vintage cowpunk originals; at times, they slip back a notch or two into a toned down country sound. As cowpunk became *passé* in the late 1980s, Blood on the Saddle broke up, but in 1990, Davis returned with new blood. And though he lost one bass player to a drug overdose, Davis kept the band together and continued to record (**More Blood**) sporadically into the mid-1990s.

Original Members: Ron Botelho (b); Greg Davis (g,v); Hermann Senac (d,v); Annette Zilinskas (g,hm,v)
Current Members: Greg Davis (g,v); Dave Frappier (d); John Stephenson (b)

> **Blood on the Saddle**/New Alliance/1984
> **Poison Love**/Chameleon/1986
> **Fresh Blood**/SST/1987
> **More Blood**/1993
> "Please Quit Calling Me From Jail"; "I'm a Poor Lonesome Cowboy" b/w "I Wanna Ramble and Roam"; "Beer Drinking Man"/Kill Rock Stars/1994 (EP)

Blood Oranges

See Jimmy Ryan; Cheri Knight

The Blue Chieftains

See Tim Carroll

Blue Mountain (The Hilltops)

No Depression
Oxford, Mississippi; 1988-

Blue Mountain comes from the home state of Jimmie Rodgers, William Faulkner, and Elvis. The influences of all three clearly show in their music; slow acoustic ballads and country rockers all infused with vivid images of the South. Laurie Stirratt and Cary Hudson, the founders and driving force behind Blue Mountain, met in Oxford in the late 1980s and formed the Hilltops with Stirratt's brother John. They recorded one cassette, **Holler**, and an independently released album, **Big Black River**. For the most part, the Hilltops were a punk group but showed blues (Robert Johnson), folk (Woody Guthrie), and country influences as well. When they ended, with John Stirratt joining Uncle Tupelo (and later Wilco), Hudson and Laurie Stirratt moved to California to test the musical waters. Overall, their time in California was filled with one disheartening experience after another, but it did result in an early version of Blue Mountain (named for a small hamlet near Oxford) and renewed appreciation for their home state's music and culture. Returning there in early 1993, they teamed with drummer Matt Brennan and soon there after released **Blue Mountain** on their own 4 Barrel label. This recording has the punk edge held over

from the Hilltops days but shows evolution toward a rootsier sound inspired by blues, bluegrass, old-time, and early Neil Young country rock. Then, while performing at an Uncle Tupelo show in Missouri, Blue Mountain, with new drummer Frank Coutch, were "discovered" by Roadrunner's lead A/R guy Jeff Pachman (signed Uncle Tupelo to Rockville). The band inked a five record deal and in 1995 came **Dog Days** which mostly reworks material from previous recordings. With production and instrumental assistance from Eric Ambel, Blue Mountain turned in a stirring collection of blues/country/rock stories based primarily on experiences growing up in the South: "Mountain Girl," "Blue Canoe," "Epitaph," "Jimmy Carter." Alt. country and Americana fans warmly embraced it and looked forward to bigger things. In 1996, Blue Mountain opened for alt. country's leading lights (Jayhawks, Son Volt, Wilco), worked on a movie soundtrack, and started Black Dog Records. They reissued **Big Black River** (with three from **Holler**), an album of 1991-1992 demos by John Stirratt's old group, the Gimmecaps (with Hudson and Laurie Stirratt), and a single by the Continental Drifters. Blue Mountain's second, **Homegrown**, continued their exploration of Southern Americana using a distinctive amalgam of traditional acoustic and modern electric sounds, strong duets from Hudson and Stirratt, and poignant storytelling on "Bloody 98," "Black Dog," "Last Words of Midnight Clyde," and "Ira Magee."

Flush with success, Blue Mountain expanded the Black Dog roster in 1998 and released debuts from Philadelphia roots rockers Marah and finger-picking guitarist Noah Saterstrom. In turn, these performers joined Blue Mountain and John Stirratt for a week of r&r, drinking, and musical collaboration that resulted in **Rock & Roll Summer Camp '98**.

The Hilltops (1988-1991): Cary Hudson (bj,g,md,v); Hank Sossaman (d); John Stirratt (l.g.); Laurie Stirratt (b,v)
Blue Mountain (1993-): Frank Coutch (d,v); Cary Hudson (bj,g,md,v); Laurie Stirratt (b,v)

> **Holler** (Hilltops)/Hilltops/1989 (CS)
> **Big Black River** (Hilltops)/Hilltops/1992; Black Dog/1996
> **Blue Mountain**/Four Barrel/1993
> "Mary Jane" b/w "The Day They Tore Down the Happy Hotel"/Faye/1994 (7")
> **Dog Days**/Roadrunner/1995
> **The Gimmecaps**/Black Dog/1996
> **Homegrown**/Roadrunner/1997
> "Mountain Girl" on **Luxury Liner**/Glitterhouse Ger./1997
> "Mary Jane" on **Hempilation2: Free the Weed**/ Capricorn/1998
> **Rock & Roll Summer Camp '98**/Black Dog/1998

Blue Mountain/Black Dog Records, Route 1, Box 163A, Monticello, MS 39654; 601-587-2047

Blue Mountain/Black Dog Records Home Page //www.blackdogrecords.com

blackdog@telapex.com

Genericamerica: The Blue Mountain E-Mail List //www.onelist.com/subscribe.cgi/genericamerica/

Blue Mountain Unofficial Home Page
//www2.msstate.edu/~sgnl/blue.html

sgnl@ra.msstate.edu

Blue Mountain Biography
//www.roadrun.com/bands/bluemtn/bio.htm

See Marah

The Blue Rags

Tobacco Row; New Old-Time
Asheville, North Carolina; 1990-

The Blue Rags are a bit of an anomaly in the Tobacco Row alt. country community in that, rather than drawing on country rock or country punk, they go back several generations and tap into ragtime, jug band, old-time, country blues, bluegrass, and swing. At the same time, they color their interpretation of these traditional styles with a modern brush much in the same way as groups like the Holy Modal Rounders, Hypnotic Clambake, and the Bad Livers have done. Jack Hollifield and Scott Sharpe were the original nucleus of the band in 1990 and over time added more players from a variety of musical backgrounds. In 1997, the Blue Rags signed, somewhat surprisingly, with SubPop and did **Rag-N-Roll**, a composite of standards ("Salty Dog"; "Bourgeois Blues"; "Sister Kate"; "Dr. Jazz"; "I Got Rhythm") and originals that got good reviews all around. In early 1998, *No Depression* gave them a nice little write up, and they headed to New York City for a "Life During Ragtime" tour during which they were interviewed for MTV's *Indie Outing* show. The Blue Rags joined the Asylum Street Spankers and fellow Carolinians, the Squirrel Nut Zippers, as one of the top pre-WWII music revival bands.

Jack Hollifield (p,v); Bill Reynolds (b); Mike Rhodes (d); Scott Sharpe; Aaron Wood (l.g.)

Rag-N-Roll/SubPop/1997

The Blue Rags/SubPop Home Page
//www.subpop.com/bands/bluerags/

The Blue Rags Biography //www.billions.com/blue/bio.htm

Blurags@aol.com

See Asylum Street Spankers

Blue Rodeo

Country Rock; Roots Rock
Toronto, Canada; 1981-

For over fifteen years, Blue Rodeo has been Canada's undisputed champions of country/roots rock. Formed in 1981 by Jim Cuddy and Greg Keelor, they made their recording debut in 1987 with **Outskirts** (a major seller in Canada) and then into the 1990s did a series of albums, **Diamond Mine**, **Casino**, **Lost Together**, moving back and forth (sometimes smoothly, sometimes not) between pop and roots rock. When keyboard player Bob Wiseman left in 1992, he was replaced by steel player Kim

Duchamps who had been on the Cowboy Junkies early recordings. This led to the more easy going, country rock of **Five Days in July** which was followed by the brooding **Nowhere to Here**. Through it all, Blue Rodeo has continually tried to make in roads in the U.S., but their biggest following has remained in their home country. However, their latest and most consistent recording, **Tremolo**, showed signs of breaking that trend. Released on Sire, a major newcomer in the Americana market, it has guest appearances by Wilco's Jay Bennett and Jeff Tweedy. In between tours in 1998 to support the new album, Keelor and Cuddy cut their first ever solo recordings. Cuddy's **All in Time** (with Bennett and Tweedy) has a much twangier feel to it than his Blue Rodeo material due in large part to the presence of lots of good old country style fiddling.

Cleve Anderson (d,1981-1989); Jim Cuddy (g,v); Kim Deschamps (p.s.,1992-); Bazil Donovan (b); Mark French (d,1989-1992); James Gray (ky,1992-); Greg Keelor (g,v); Glenn Milchem (d,1992-); Bob Wiseman (hm,ky, 1981-1992)

Outskirts/Warner Music Can.; Atlantic/1987
Diamond Mine/ Warner Music Can.; Discovery/1989
Casino/Warner Music Can.; Atlantic/1990
Lost Together/Warner Music Can.; Discovery/1992
Five Days in July/Warner Music Can.; Discovery/1993
Nowhere to Here/Warner Music Can.; Discovery/1995
Tremelo/Warner Music Can.; Sire/1997
Gone (Greg Keelor)/Warner Music Can./1998
All in Time (Jim Cuddy)/Warner Music Can./1998

Blue Rodeo Fan Club, Box 185, Station C, Toronto, Ontario, Canada, M6J 3M9

Official Blue Rodeo Home Page //www.bluerodeo.com

home@bluerodeo.com

Warner Music Blue Rodeo Page //warnermusic.ca/bluerodeo/

The Blue Rodeo Music Database Home Page
//www.canoe.com/JamMusicBlueRodeo/home.html

Blue Rodeo Fan Page
/www.geocities.com/sunsetstrip/lounge/7824/bluerodeo.html
(contains fan club and mailing list information)

The Blue Shadows

Country Rock
Vancouver, British Columbia, Canada; 1990-1995

In the late 1960s when family singing groups were in vogue perhaps the most well known next to the Partridge Family were the Cowsills. They played jingly feel good tunes sung mostly by teenage heartthrob Billy Cowsill (I still remember a horde of nubile girls squealing and screeching with delight during a Cowsills performance at the State Fair of Texas). After the Cowsills faded, Billy tried his luck around the U.S. as a musician (with J. J. Cale and Joe Ely) and bar owner and failed at both. Finally, in the early 1990s, he went to Canada (Vancouver) where he formed the Billy Cowsill Band, a duo with Elmar Spanier specializing in Hank Williams and Roy Orbison. It evolved into Blue Northern and then the Blue

Shadows when Jeffrey Hatcher and Jay Johnson were added. Calling their sound "Hank Goes to the Cavern Club," Cowsill and Hatcher began writing originals, and this resulted in **On the Floor of Heaven** which delivers some fine 1960s-1970s country rock *a la* the Byrds, the Flying Burrito Brothers, the New Riders, et al. Cowsill and Hatcher trade off vocal duties on country rock ("If It Ain't Rockin'"), honky tonk ("The Fool is The Last One to Know"), and tender ballads ("Think On It," "Deliver Me," "Is Anybody Here"), and their Everly Brothers style harmonies are a real treat.

After Barry Muir replaced Spanier in 1993, the Blue Shadows recorded **Lucky to Me** which offered more of the same although at a more vibrant pace. They toured with a number of major acts (The Band, Crash Test Dummies), had a showcase at SXSW, and were building a following among fans and critics alike when suddenly with everything going their way, they broke up on December 25, 1995.

Billy Cowsill (g,v); Jeffrey Hatcher (l.g.,v); Jay Johnson (d); Barry Muir (b); Elmar Spanier (b,1990-1993)

> **On the Floor of Heaven**/Bumstead Sony Can./1994
> **Lucky to Me**/Sony/1995

The Blue Shadows Biography
//www.music.sony.com/Music/ArtistInfo/BlueShadows/biography.html

The Boat Band

Cajun
Norwich, Cheshire, England; 1989-

Started in 1989, the Boat Band was aptly named for its tours of the harbor bars along the English coast aboard a restored 50 ft. wooden navy service launch. They also played inland clubs and festivals and along the way polished their hard driving, exuberant take on southern Louisiana musical styles (Cajun, zydeco, Creole). Over the years, they have put out several solid recordings including two with J. C. Gallow (fiddler/washboard player from Mamou, Louisiana), sponsored a Grand Cajun Cruise in the summer of 1996, and toured in both the U.K. and the U.S. Like a number of modern American Cajun bands, the Boat Band starts from a traditional base but adds a more powerful beat and contemporary musical touches. After a brief hiatus in late 1996 and early 1997, they returned to action with a new album, **Burning the Water** and continued to tour the seaways, canals, and islands around the U.K. while working on a new one with J.C. Gallow called **Back Deck Blues**. This recording, a lively mix of Cajun/zydeco, was offered as a double CD release with **Fais Pas Ca**, the Boat Band's first recording with Gallow.

Carolyn Francis (f); Stefan Spitz (b,sax); Tony Wetherall (acc)

> **Back Up and Push** (as Fiddlin' Boots Barfield and the Boat Band)/Harbourtown/1991

> **Take Me Over the Tide**/Harbourtown/1993
> **Fais Pas Ca** (with J. C. Gallow)/Harbourtown/1995
> **Burning the Water**/Harbourtown/1997
> **Back Deck Blues**/Harbourtown/1998

The Boat Band c/o Harbourtown Records, P.O. Box 25, Ulverston, Cumbria, LA12 7UN, England

The Boat Band Page
//www.rootsworld.com/harbourtown/boatband.html

boat@hartown.demon.co.uk

Bodeco

See Wink O'Bannon

The Boiled Buzzards

New Old-Time
South Euclid, Ohio; 1988-

Like most every other type of music, old-time has gone through many cycles, constantly being rediscovered by successive generations. And while purists may cling to the way laid down by their predecessors, others like the Boiled Buzzards of Ohio opt for a more contemporary sound founded on a respect for tradition but layered with modern styles and themes. Dan and Ruth Levenson (husband/wife) started the group in 1988 and worked with a revolving line up of musicians until settling on two Pittsburgh natives, Annie Trimble and Mark Tamasula in the early 1990s. The Buzzards have since become favorites on the old-time circuit for their often humorous and always very danceable songs such as "Boys Them Buzzards are Flying" (by Gary Harrison), "Grey Haired Dancing Girl," and "The Engineers Don't Wave From Trains Anymore." They have three records to their credit, **Salt & Grease**, **Fine Dining**, and **Early Bird Special** and have been featured on the second volume of Rounder's **Old-Time Music on the Radio**.

Dan Levenson (bj,f,v); Ruth Levenson (b); Annie Trimble (g,v); Mark Tamsula (f)

> **Salt & Grease**/Merimac/1991
> **Fine Dining**/Merimac/1993
> **Early Bird Special**/Buzzard Productions/1994
> "Grey Haired Dancing Girl" on **Old-Time Music on the Radio, Vol. 2**/Rounder/1996

Buzzard Productions, P.O. Box 21712
South Euclid, OH 44121

Ponty Bone (The Squeezetones)

Accordion; Lubbock Mafia; Country Rock; Cajun; Tex-Mex
Dallas, Texas; October 9, 1939-

Check the credits for just about any recording from the 1980s-early 1990s by an Austin area musician and chances are that if it lists accordion the name next to it will be Ponty Bone. A fixture on the Austin music scene today, Bone first came to the city as part of the Joe Ely Band in 1980. He had been playing with Ely and fellow band mate Jesse Taylor in Lubbock since Jimmie Dale Gilmore introduced him to them way back in 1964.

Initially, they played local coffee houses, goat roasts and such but in 1976, Joe Ely and group hit it big with an MCA contract. This led to several excellent recordings of Texas style country/roots music, and a big part of the credit for the band's distinctive sound goes to the accordion playing of Ponty Bone. His tenure with Ely ended in the early 1980s and then Bone became a guest musician on numerous recordings and put together the Squeezetones. This band mixed up a pleasing gumbo of Cajun, Tex-Mex, and blues on two 1987 albums **Easy as Pie** and **My, My...Look at This!** Into the 1990s, Ponty and the Squeezetones maintained a rigorous tour schedule as reflected in the title of their 1995 effort **Dig Us on the Road Somewhere!** which compiles the best songs from the first two recordings. When in Austin, Bone is still in great demand for session work and performs with two other bands—Zydeco Loco (with Don Leady of the Tailgators) and the Keepers (with former Ely guitarist Jesse Taylor).

Current Squeezetones: Cliff Hargrove (b); Justin Hess (d); Spencer Jarmon (l.g.)

Easy as Pie/Amazing/1987
My, My...Look at This!/Amazing/1987
Dig Us on the Road Somewhere!/Real World/1995

Ponty Bone and the Squeezetones, P.O. Box 163421, Austin, TX 78716; 512-443-7952, (fax) 512-280-8558

See Joe Ely

The Bone Tones

Contemporary Cajun
Minneapolis-St. Paul, Minnesota; 1987-

Although southern Louisiana is the heart and soul of Cajun music, there are a number of very active scenes scattered throughout the U.S. and Europe. Perhaps the most surprising of these is the one located at the northern end of the Mississippi in the Upper Midwest. Centered mainly in the Minneapolis-St. Paul area, this Cajun music crowd meets regularly for dances, holds annual festivals, and even has a web page ("Louisiana Upriver") devoted to connecting an ever growing number of enthusiasts in the area. Among the many Cajun bands that are the backbone of this scene, one of the best and most popular is the Bone Tones (the name is a play on the famous Cajun phrase, "Laissez les bons temps rouler"). Inspired by Cajun artists (Balfa, Menard, Schwarz et al.) who toured the upper Mississippi, the band formed in 1987 in the Twin Cities; its members came from a variety of musical backgrounds (old-time, bluegrass, country, rock, jazz) the Bone Tones synthesized into an exuberant dance music that is at once authentic and contemporary. One element setting them off from most other contemporary Cajun bands is the use of pedal steel which generates a style like that of Walter Mouton and the Scott Playboys. They have three recordings, **Cajun Dance Tonight**, **Queue de Tortue**, **Chez Nonc Bob**, a track on **American Fogies, Vol. 2**, and numerous festival appearances on their resume.

Matt Haney (f,p.s.); Doug Lohman (b,g,v); Paul Loughridge (d,tri); Eric Mohring (f,v); Gary Powell (acc,g,v)

Cajun Dance Tonight/Marimac/1991 (CS)
Queue de Tortue/Bonetone/1992
Chez Nonc Bob/Bonetone/1996
"New Crowley Two Step" on **American Fogies, Vol. 2**/Rounder/1996

The Bone Tones, 3024 11th Ave. South, Minneapolis, MN 55407-1606; 612-721-8026

The Bone Tones Web Page
//www.blubird.com/upriver/band/bonetone.htm

Douglohman@aol.com

See Walter Mouton and The Scott Playboys

The Boneheads

Roots Rock; Americana
Portland, Maine; 1991-

As their name implies, the Boneheads don't take themselves too seriously. However, their Monty Pythonish spirit of fun doesn't mean they are cavalier or sloppy when it comes to the music. Each member brings years of experience and a variety of talents to the mix and, collectively, they generate a hybrid of American music that most often draws comparisons to The Band, the Grateful Dead, Little Feat, and Uncle Tupelo. Formed in 1991, the Boneheads released three albums in five years, **The Boneheads**, **Cranium**, and **Donkey**, and garnered lots of positive attention through articles in regional and national publications, energetic live shows (sometimes included the "Purple Haze" polka), and an appearance on NPR's *Mountain Stage*. In addition to their instrumental skills, part of the reason for the success of the Boneheads lay in the fact that the singing/songwriting chores are shared. The result is a pleasing variety of honky tonk ballads, country rock, blues, swamp pop, rock, and more that is never stale or monotonous. They defined their 1997, **Words-n-Things-n-Numbers-n-Stuff**, as an "attempt to return to their electric roots." They also branched out into soundtracks, scoring for the delightful series *HELLevator, HELLevator II*, and *HELLicatessan*.

Bob Colwell (acc,ky,md,v); Scott Elliott (b,kz,v); Stephen B. Jones (g,sl.g.,v); Richard Hollis (d,perc); Roger Sampson (db,g,sl.g,v)

The Boneheads/River/1991
Cranium/River/1993
Donkey/River/1995
Words-n-Things-n-Numbers-n-Stuff/River/1997

The Boneheads c/o Skyline Music, 32 Clayton St., Portland, ME 04103; 207-878-2330

The Boneheads Home Page
//www.biddeford.com/~bonehead/

jhjort@juno.com

Simon Bonney

Singer/Songwriter; Lo-Fi
Sydney, Australia; June 3, 1961-

Simon Bonney was the leader of the 1980s Australian band Crime & The City Solution. In 1990, when that group broke up, he found himself in Nashville where he was inspired to explore American country music. His first solo effort, **Forever**, featured Bonney's wispy voice, backed by haunting dobro and reverby guitar, speaking out for shattered lives scattered across America's hinterlands. A trip into the vastness of the American West compelled Bonney to expand on this theme with **Everyman**, a musical journal recounting one man's (aka "Everyman's") search for meaning in a world filled with hard work, love/pain, and trouble. Bonney's brooding originals and moody covers of "Goodtime Charlie's Got the Blues" and "Blue Eyes Crying in the Rain" are trenchant due in no small part to his spare but convincing vocals and atmospheric accompaniment by a large supporting cast including Chuck Prophet and Austin stalwarts, J.D. Foster, Jon Dee Graham, Freddy Krc, Chris O'Connell, and Maryann Price. Bonney has also contributed to the soundtracks of films (*Faraway, So Close*; *Wings of Desire*) by another interpreter of the contemporary American West, Wim Wenders.

> **Forever**/Mute/1992
> **Everyman**/Mute/1995
> **Don't Walk Away From Love**/Mute/1996 (EP)

Simon Bonney //gs.knave.co.uk/mute/bonney.html

Bill Booth & The Convertibles

Country Rock; Roots Rock
Oslo, Norway; 1992-

A native of Maine, Bill Booth began his musical career in the 1970s in New York City as a "freelance musician" specializing in fiddle and guitar and leaning toward country, rock, and Irish folk music. A tour in Norway convinced him to move to Oslo in the early 1980s where he became an in-demand session player, started his own record label (Wheeling), and formed his own group, the Convertibles. As a stuido musician, Booth has been on numerous recordings by Norwegian based artists (e.g. Steinar Albrigtsen; Trond Granlund; Tom Pacheco). Wheeling Records has released one fabulous album (**Can't Quit Now**) by the excellent singer/songwriter Trond Granlund and three by Bill Booth & The Convertibles. The latter includes some of Norway's most respected musicians including accordionist Geir Otnes who has played with Granlund and electric guitarist Nils Halleland whose stellar lead work can be found on recordings by Granlund and the wonderful Somebody's Darling. Booth and band have toured Scandinavia, Austria,

Germany, and the U.S., and their recordings offer a mix of styles that place them squarely in Texas' Third Coast music tradition. Their **Heart in Hand** is representative of the band's varied and very delightful sound: Cajun/zydeco groove ("Hot Lovin'"), country two step ("Heart in Hand" co-written with Erik Moll), country rock ("Anybody Out There"), rock 'n' roll ("Stand This Abuse"), Tex-Mex ("I Know What I Do Wrong"), honky tonk sadness ("One Night With Love"), Cajun two step ("Are You Leaving Me"), and slow ballad ("Looking Too Hard"). Booth's originals consistently hit the mark as do his lead vocals which have that folksy, Bobby Bare tone. And, no matter what style he's called on to cover, Geir Otnes' accordion is always just right.

Bill Booth (a.g.,f,v); Per Eriksen (d); Nils Halleland (a.g.,e.g.,md); Andy Nesblom (b); Geir Otnes (acc) with Morten Sand (p.s.)

> **Hard Times on Easy Street**/Wheeling Nor./1992
> **Round the Bend**/Wheeling Nor./1994
> **Heart in Hand**/Wheeling Nor./1998

Bill Booth, Fredensborgvn. 22, 0177 Oslo, Norway; +47 22 206623 (ph./fax)

Bill Booth/Wheeling Records Page
//www.nordi.no/music/wheeling/billbooth/

bilbooth@riksnett.no

See Trond Granlund; Somebody's Darling

Libbi Bosworth

Austin; Honky Tonk; Country Rock; Singer/Songwriter
Galveston, Texas; November 28, 1964-

Austin's alt. country history has primarily been male dominated, but there have been a few exceptions: Lucinda Williams, Kelly Willis, and Libbi Bosworth. The latter took a long and sometimes rough road to a musical career. Reared on country music by her truck driving daddy, Bosworth left home in her teens and dabbled in punk and jazz (Berklee School of Music) before settling in Austin and becoming a country singer. In the late 1980s and early 1990s, she played the local clubs, built a loyal following, had one of her songs ("Up All Night") covered by Willis but failed to make a big breakthrough. After marrying guitarist Bill Dwyer (ex-Kelly Willis band), they gave it a go in Nashville but found no takers and lost their marriage to boot. Bosworth returned to Austin at an auspicious moment as the city's latest cycle of alt. country was really beginning to heat up. She was included on two collections of Austin/Texas alt. country, **Austin Country Nights** and **True Sounds of the New West** and shortly thereafter made her full length debut with **Outskirts of You**. Her vocal and songwriting abilities brought flattering comparisons to country's best divas and placed her firmly in the forefront of the next wave of Austin alt. Country. This position was strengthened by inclusion on *Austin City Limits*' 1997 showcase of Austin's new wave of alt. country with Don Walser, Dale Watson, and the Derailers. In 1998, Libbi contributed a rocking version of "Hey Girl" (redone as "Hey Boy") to a Blasters tribute compilation, and she continued to perform in and around Austin.

> "It's Late" on **True Sounds of the New West**/ Freedom/1995
> "Baby, Maybe Then I'll Love You" on **Austin Country Nights**/Watermelon/1995
> **Outskirts of You**/Freedom/1996
> "Hey Boy" on **Blastered: A Musical Tribute to the Blasters**/Run Wild/1998

Official Libbi Bosworth Site //www.libbibosworth.com

libbi@libbibosworth.com

The Bottle Rockets

No Depression; Insurgent Country; Grain Belt Rock
Festus, Missouri; 1992-

The Uncle Tupelo family tree branches off in many directions. Festus, Missouri's favorite sons, the Bottle Rockets trace their UT lineage through their founder and leader Brian Henneman who toured with them and played banjo, guitar, mandolin, and slide guitar on **March 16-20, 1992**. Prior to this time, in the late 1970s, Henneman had fronted a variously named band (the Blue Moons, Waylon Van Halen and the Ernest Troubadours) which included the Parr brothers (Tom and Bob). They became popular in the St. Louis/Illinois area and along the way got acquainted with Uncle Tupelo's co-founders, Jay Farrar and Jeff Tweedy. By the mid-1980s, Henneman, the Parrs, and drummer Mark Ortmann were calling themselves Chicken Truck and refining their distinct country/roots rock sound which made it to one cassette recording (**Drag Myself**) before the group broke up and the members scattered. Henneman began his association with Uncle Tupelo and cut a demo and a single ("Indianapolis") with assistance from Farrar and Tweedy. He then decided to form his own group and reunited with Tom Parr and Ortmann. When they added Tom Ray on bass, the Bottle Rockets were born and released their first record in 1993 (Tweedy and Farrar contribute background vocals). **The Bottle Rockets** opens moderately with the banjo driven, old-timey "Early in the Morning" then launches abruptly into the rocking "Gas Girl" and "Trailer Mama"; this pattern sets the tone for the rest of the record which alternates between country ("Hey Moon"; "Kerosene"; "Lonely Cowboy"), country rock ("Wave the Flag"; "Every Kinda Everything"), and full blown rock ("Manhattan Countryside") *a la* Neil Young and Crazy Horse. Thematically, it emphatically displays the Bottle Rockets concern with the not-so-pretty sides of rural life such as poverty ("Kerosene") and chauvinism ("Wave That Flag") as well as lust ("Gas Girl") and love gone wrong ("Got What I Wanted"). With the inclusion of "Every Kinda Everything" on Bloodshot Records, **For a Life Sin**, the Bottle Rockets joined the first wave of insurgent country artists and got a deal with

ESD which led to **The Brooklyn Side** in 1994. Like their debut, this album (produced by Eric Ambel) continues to explore the territory between country and rock and reiterates their preoccupation with life's raw deals on "Welfare Music," "Radar Gun," "$1,000 Car," "I'll Be Coming Around," "What More Can I Do?" and "I Wanna Come Home." In 1995, Tag Records reissued **The Brooklyn Side**, and after some label limbo, the Bottle Rockets landed a record deal with Atlantic which released **24 Hours a Day** in 1997. Once again, the Bottle Rockets stick close to the formula that has put them in the front ranks of No Depression alt. country: solid Grain Belt rock and hard hitting songs about hard hit people—"Smokin' 100s Alone," "Slo Toms," "Waitin' on a Train," and "Turn For the Worse." Late in the year, bass player Tom Ray departed and was replaced by John "The Kid" O'Brian. Unfortunately, Atlantic did little if anything to promote **24 Hours**, and so the Bottle Rockets decided to get out of their contract. However, before they could act, Atlantic beat them to the punch, and they were dropped in early 1998. But, the BoRox landed on their feet moving on to Doolittle Records (Mount Pilot; Slobberbone) which released **Leftovers**, an eight track EP of songs recorded for but not included on **24 Hours**. The band was given a segment on the PBS/Smithsonian documentary *River of Song* about contemporary music along the Mississippi. Their "Get Down River" was included on the companion CD for the series, and in mid-December, the Bottlerockets played a promotional kickoff concert for the series at the Smithsonian.

Brian Henneman (g, bj, v); John O'Brian (b,1997-); Mark Ortmann (d); Tom Parr (g); Tom V. Ray (b,1992-1997)

> **Drag Myself** (as Chicken Truck)/Every Kind of Everything/1990 (CS)
> "Indianapolis"/"Get Down"/"Wave That Flag" (Brian Henneman solo)/Rockville/1992 (7")
> "Gravity" (Brian Henneman solo) on **St. Louis School House**/Hush Hush/1993
> "Every Kinda Everything" on **For a Life of Sin**/ Bloodshot/1993
> **The Bottle Rockets**/ESD/1993; Tag/1995
> **The Brooklyn Side**/ESD/1994; Tag/1995
> "Get Down" on **Hell-Bent: Insurgent Country, Volume 2**/Bloodshot/1995
> "Truck Driving Man (Give All I Can)" on **Rig Rock Deluxe**/Upstart Diesel Only/1996
> "Radar Gun" b/w "Always on the Outside" (Jim Lauderdale)/Diesel Only/1996 (7")
> **The Bottle Rockets & Dead Hot Workshop**/Mile High/Tag/1996 (Tag promo CD)
> **24 Hours a Day**/Atlantic/1997
> **Leftovers**/Doolittle/1998 (EP)
> "Get Down River" on **Mississippi: River of Song**/ Smithsonian Folkways/1998

The Bottle Rockets Web Site //www.bottlerockets.com

The Bottle Rockets iMusic Showcase //imusic.com/showcase/modern/

See Uncle Tupelo

BR5-49

Honky Tonk; Hillbilly Bop
Nashville, Tennessee; 1993-

Since at least the mid-1980s, alternative/underground country scenes have sprung up in major cities across the U.S. Not surprisingly, the last bastion of resistance to "real" country music has been Nashville. For years now, since the Las Vegas pop country mentality took over Music City, hillbilly, honky tonk music has been relegated to a small strip of dives along Lower Broadway. During this time, no one paid much attention to this scene but in the mid-1990s that attitude began to change due in large part to the success of one group, BR5-49 (named for a famous phone number on *Hee Haw*). In 1993, founders Chuck Mead and Gary Bennett were just two more among many musicians working the joints in downtown Nashville, but they shared a love of good old country music, formed the band, and landed a regular gig at Robert's Western Wear, a makeshift honky tonk just down the street from the famous Tootsie's lounge. Using the storefront window as a stage, they started out playing for tips to small audiences but within a short-time, their reputation for solid performances brought them overflow crowds. In 1995, they won Most Outstanding Group at the Nashville Music Awards, caught the attention of Music Row execs, and secured a recording contract from Arista. And while some critics have been suspicious, it seems clear the group is motivated by a sincere devotion to and respect for the traditions they represent. They got off to a somewhat shaky recording start with their EP CD debut **Live at Robert's**. The songs are pretty weak (and downright silly e.g. "Me & Opie"), and the album fails to capture the spirit of their dynamic live performances. However, their first full length studio recording, **BR5-49**, delivers the promised goods with some lively covers of country classics (from Ray Price to Gram Parsons) plus a number of fine originals all highlighted by the steel and fiddle of Don Herron.

On their next recording, **Big Backyard Beat Show**, BR5-49 wavered (sometimes uncomfortably) between the best of their honky tonk ("There Goes My Love"; "Out of Habit"; "Pain, Pain Go Away"; "My Name is Mudd"), HNC ("Hurtin' Song"), and some frenetic and forgetable rock numbers ("Wild One"; "Seven Nights to Rock"). A truer representation of their generally solid live performances was released in a boxed EP (**Bonus Beats**) of seven previous songs re-recorded by Steve Albini. And while performers like Big Sandy, the Derailers, and Junior Brown ultimately have a more solid twang, BR5-49 has the image and visibility to bring the hillbilly/honky tonk sound to an even wider audience.

Gary Bennett (a.g.,l.v.); Don Herron (db,f, md, s.g.); "Smilin'" Jay McDowell (b); Chuck Mead (a.g.,e.g.,l.v.); Shaw Wilson (d,b.v.).

Live From Robert's/Arista/1996
BR5-49/Arista/1996
"Mama Was a Rock, Daddy Was a Rolling Stone" (w/ Kay Adams) on **Rig Rock Deluxe**/Upstart Diesel Only/1996
"18 Wheels and a Crowbar" (live) on **American Songbook**/UK/1996
"Gathering Flowers for the Master's Bouquet" on **Clinch Mountain Country: Ralph Stanley & Friends**/Rebel/1998
Big Backyard Beat Show/Arista/1998
Bonus Beats/Arista/1998 (EP)

The Hayloft Gang: BR5-49 Fan Club 1-888-96-BR549

BR5-49 Home Page //www.br5-49.com

BR5-49 iMusic Showcase //imusic.com/showcase/country

BR5-49 AOL Folder: Entertainment>Music>Chat & Messages>Music Community>Country/Folk>Country & Western, A-K

Grace Braun

Singer/Songwriter; New Old-Time
Kentucky

In recent years, the number of pop/punk rock performers who have ventured into alternative country projects has steadily risen: the Supersuckers, Neko Case, The The, Stephen Fearing just to name a few. Grace Braun formed the garage/punk band DQE while still in high school and in the early 1990s guided it to considerable success and two acclaimed recordings, **Me I Fell Down** and **Jump on In**. Yet, all the while, lurking inside Braun was a backwoods, old-time country singer. A descendent of the famous Methodist hymnist Charles Wesley, she began to rediscover the traditional music of her native Kentucky singing with a church choir and performing standard as well as original old-timey folk, blues, and country as a solo. Her first recordings in this direction e.g. "Liftin' Me Up" on **Revival, Vol. 2: Kudzu and Hollerin' Contest** were country with a bit of a punk edge but her 1997 full length debut **It Won't Hurt** lost the edginess in favor of a more fully realized Appalachian sound. Here Braun relies on traditional instrumentation (fiddle, dobro, e-bow, pedal steel, wash board), simple but very moving storytelling, and twangy old-time vocals (she does both lead and harmony) that are consistently appealing whether rendering poignant ballads ("Jenny Wren"; "Mermaid and the Sailor") or an a capella hymn ("What Wondrous Love This Is"). The result is surprisingly fresh and uplifting.

"Liftin' Me Up" on **Revival, Vol. 2: Kudzu and Hollerin' Contest**/Yep Roc/1997
It Won't Hurt/Slow River/1997
"It Won't Hurt" on **Loose: New Sounds of the Old West**/Vinyl Junkie UK/1998

Grace Braun/DQE History
//www.geocities.com/~wolf-eyes/grace/grace-history.html

Grace Braun/Slow River Home Page //www.slowriver.com

Mockingbird@mindspring.com

Jeff Bright and the Sunshine Boys

Honky Tonk
San Francisco, California; 1995-

Jeff Bright makes no mystery about what he and the Sunshine Boys want to do: "Our notion is to take the classic Ray Price sound and give it a little more go-juice." Working in the highly competitive Bay Area alt. country scene since 1995, the band deals in honky tonk music *a la* Price, Jones, and the Bakersfield Sound but with a bit of a modern twist. Bright (originally from Dayton, Ohio) started the group after burning out on playing several rock acts (Darke County; Myself a Living Torch) in the late 1980s and early 1990s. He returned to country/western music with the Sunshine Boys whose make-up varies somewhat between live and recorded performances. Regulars now on the Northern California twang circuit, Jeff Bright and the Sunshine Boys keep avid dance crowds happy with a solid beat behind Bright's smooth crooning tenor. Their recording debut came on the **Pushing the Norton** compilation with "Let's Get Drunk (And Talk About Marriage)," and they've also done one EP, **She's a Nail in My Heart**, which has three Bright honky tonk originals.

Jeff Bright (r.g.,l.v.); David Antony (ub); Max Butler (l.g.,live); Christopher Fisher (d); Kevin Ink (l.g.,on record); David Phillips (p.s.,live); Michael Ross (l.g.,live); Eric Schulz (p.s.,b.v.,on record)

"Let's Get Drunk (And Talk About Marriage)" on
Pushing the Norton: The Ace Cafe Compilation/ Heyday/1995
She's a Nail in My Heart/Star Tone/1998 (EP)

Jeff Bright and the Sunshine Boys, P.O. Box 421627, San Francisco, CA 94142; 415-252-8607

Jeff Bright and the Sunshine Boys Home Page //www.dimlights.com/sunshine/bright.htm

Jabright@aol.com

Mark Brine

Singer/Songwriter; Jimmie Rodgers Country; Rig Rock
Cambridge, Massachusetts

Many country musicians have aspired to be like Jimmie Rodgers, but in recent years, no artist has done so with more sincere and heartfelt devotion than Mark Brine. This claim rests on a number of impressive awards and achievements: 1st Prize at the 1979 Jimmie Rodgers Memorial Festival talent contest, live performances with Roy Acuff on WSM in 1980 and with Hank Snow at the Grand Old Opry in 1992, a Jimmie Rodgers tribute album (**American Pieces**), Grammy nominations for Best Country Vocalist and Best Country Song in 1992 for "New Blue Yodel." This tune first showed up as a Diesel Only 45 and then as a cut on **Rig Rock Juke Box** and is the centerpiece for Brine's 1996 CD of the same name. Accompanying himself on guitar or backed by a fine corps of musicians including dobro

ace Stacy Phillips, Brine dips into the roots of country music (Stephen Foster's "Oh Susanna"), serves up bright originals in the tradition of the Singing Brakeman ("When You Love Me"; "New Blue Yodel"; "Jalopy Blues") and Hank, Sr. ("Blues in My Mind"), and fills in with a variety of bluesy country ("Wrong Side of Bourbon St. Blues"; "Ay'ee Louisiana"; "Country Music's Gone to the City") and ballads ("Shy Boys Always Dance with the Big Girls"; "Aggie"). Brine has also penned a folk musical *The Carol* available as an audio book. Early in 1999, Mark released an anthology of his personal Americana favorites plus a few new tunes as **American Bleak House**.

American Pieces/KJK/1990 (LP)
"New Blue Yodel (Blue Yodel #14)" b/w "Blues in My Mind"/Diesel Only/1991 (7")
"New Blue Yodel" on **Rig Rock Juke Box**/Diesel Only/1992
The Carol/North Star Publishing/1993 (audio book)
New Blue Yodel/Re:signed/1996
American Bleak House/Re:signed/1999

Mark Brine/KJK Productions, P.O. Box 9799, Baltimore, MD 21284-9799; 410-665-4061

Mark Brine–New Blue Yodeler //www.markbrine.com

info@markbrine.com

Marc Bristol

Americana; Musician; Writer; Editor
Muskegon, Michigan; 1950-

Marc Bristol is perhaps best known as the editor of the groundbreaking roots music magazine *Blue Suede News* but in a life dedicated to keeping good music alive, he's also excelled as a songwriter, musician, band leader, record producer, promoter, and DJ. From his early years growing up in Michigan, Bristol seemed destined for a musical career; his great grandfather and grandmother owned and entertained in a carnival, his grandmother was a vaudeville singer/contortionist known as Baby Nona, his father sang with a champion barbershop quartet, and his mom was a tap dancer. Like many other youngsters of the time, Marc first dabbled in rock 'n' roll but also absorbed folk, blues, and country influences. He played in a few bands in high school (the Moogaloonies; the Phog; the Aristocrats) and college (the Light Fantastic; the Screamin' Fetus Blues Band) before going solo as a folk act on the coffeehouse/cafe circuit in Michigan and then in Seattle when he moved to Washington State in the early 1970s. After living in a rustic cabin in the Cascades for a few years and commuting to Seattle, Bristol eventually settled in the suburb of Duvall where he formed the Okie Doke String Band with local residents Quentin Rhoton and Dan Kersten. In the late 1970s-early1980s, they worked the Puget Sound, did a brief California tour (opened one show for Cornell Hurd), and recorded a self-titled EP in 1981 that was best described as "Bob Wills and Elvis meet

Dan Hicks at a bar in the Twilight Zone." It was released on Bristol's own King Noodle Records (founded 1980) and was followed a year later by Marc's solo record (with Okie Doke backing), **This Feelin'**, a homey collection of folk/old-time country originals.

Continuing to perform solo and with Okie Doke and a jug band named Blisswater, Bristol branched out in the late 1980s and early 1990s. He recorded a rockabilly cassette, **Wam Bam Boom**, which contains the clever "Sucker for a Cheap Guitar" (later covered by Ronnie Dawson) and started a new group called the File Gumbo Zydeco Band which has done several very fine recordings filled with Cajun, zydeco, and swamp pop plus blues, country, R&B, and rock. Along the way, Bristol chalked up another well-received rockabilly tape, **Let's Shake It!**, with the Shack Shakers (actually members of File Gumbo). This recording has two especially memorable tunes: the socially responsible, "Condom In His Pocket (Gonna Get It On Tonight)" and a tribute to Elvis, "White Trash Millionaire." The latter along with "Sucker for a Cheap Guitar" is reprised on the high octane, **Rockabilly Rhythm & Blues** from 1997. In addition, Bristol's songs have appeared on several rockabilly compilations (**Turning the World Blue**; **All-American Hardcore Hillbillies**; **Rockabilly Hall of Fame, Vol. 1**).

Throughout his early musical career in the 1970s-1980s, Bristol also polished up his writing skills as freelancer, publisher of an underground newspaper (*Mondo Feces*), and then for six years with a music column in *The Mother Earth News* called "Homegrown Music." The latter, which covered making, collecting, and playing traditional instruments, was eventually assembled in both book form and as a video program for public schools. When Marc had some music articles rejected by *Rolling Stone* and *The Rocket* (Seattle) and friends complained about the lack of a magazine devoted to good, roots music, he decided to start his own publication. The first issue of *Blue Suede News* came out in 1986 and over the past decade and beyond, it has become recognized as a pioneering and important roots music forum with consistently entertaining editorials, interesting features on and interiews with many of the greats (past and present; well-known and obscure), and 100s of informative reviews.

The Okie Doke Band/King Noodle/1981(EP)
This Feelin' (with Okie Doke)/King Noodle/1982 (LP)
Wam Bam Boom/King Noodle/1987 (CS)
File Gumbo Zydeco Band/King Noodle/1988 (CS)
File Gumbo Live/King Noodle/1990 (CS)
Feel LikeFlying (wth Okie Doke)/King Noodle/1992 (CS)
Bon Ton Two Tone (File Gumbo)/King Noodle/1992
The Family Jewels: King Noodle's Best Weirdest, and
   Rarest/King Noodle/1993 (CS)
Sweet Misery Moan (with Blisswater)/King Noodle/1994
Big Big Love (File Gumbo)/King Noodle/1994 (CS, CD)
Let's Shake It! (with the Shack Shakers)/King
   Noodle/1995 (CS)
All-American Hardcore Hillbillies/BSC/1995

Mardi Gras in New Orleans (File Gumbo)/King
   Noodle/1996
"Five Feet of Lovin'" on Turning the World Blue: A
   Tribute to Gene Vincent/Skizmatic/1996
Rockabilly Rhythm & Blues/King Noodle/1997
"Sucker for a Cheap Guitar" (Marc Bristol) on Rockabilly
   Hall of Fame, Vol. 1/RABHOF/1998

Marc Bristol/Blue Suede News, P.O. Box 25, Duvall, WA 98019-0025; 425-788-2776
Blue Suede News Home Page //www.bluesuedenews.com
ShakinBoss@aol.com

Marti Brom
Austin; Hillbilly Bop
St. Louis, Missouri; June 12, 1962-

The success of High Noon was instrumental in the rise of a number of other Austin rockabilly performers including Marti Brom. When she and her husband Bob moved to Austin in 1991, he encouraged her to perform and with some very able assistance from her Jet-Tone Boys (Shaun Young and Kevin Smith of High Noon plus Todd Wulfmeyer), Brom (compared most often to legends like Wanda Jackson and Janis Martin) caught the attention of Austin's small but dedicated rockabilly crowd. Unfortunately due to the demands of touring, Young and Smith were only sporadically available and consequently, it was hard for Brom to maintain performance and recording consistency. In addition, Marti was preoccupied with having and raising a child. Still, she managed to put out several singles, one live cassette, and contributions to several compilations that helped spread the word about her talents to both national and international rockabilly audiences. Then, came another pregnancy pause for about a year and a half during which the stars of new rockabilly divas like Kim Lenz and Josie Kreuzer began to rise. However, in 1998, Brom came back with a vengeance releasing a unique box set, **Mean!** with an eight cut CD and four singles (same songs on both). Produced by Brent Wilson (ex-Wagoneers), it's equally divided between covers and Brom originals and shows her back in peak rockin'form. To promote the recording, Marti began to perform more regularly in Austin (with Lisa Pancrantz and Dave Biller) and on the road with Her Jet Tone Boys (Shaun Young, Todd Wulfmeyer, Billy Horton). Three of her songs were included on **Renegade Rockabilly**, the companion CD to Billy Poore's 1998 book *Rockabilly: A 40 Year Journey*. **Lassoed Live** was re-released on CD by Goofin' in 1999.

Her Jet-Tone Boys: Shaun Young (d); Todd Wulfmeyer (l.g.); Kevin Smith (b), Billy Horton (b,1998-) with Chris Miller (s.g.), Amy Tiven (f), and Brent Wilson (r.g.)

"Hiccups" b/w "Crazy Fever"/Renegade/1993 (7")
"Don't Stop" b/w "Dirty Dog"/Jet-Tone/1995 (7")
"Stop, Look, and Listen" on **Rock-A-Billy Record Co,
   Vol. 1**/Rock-A-Billy/1995

Marti Brom and Her Jet-Tone Boys Lassoed Live/
Square Bird/1995 (CS); Goofin' Fin./1999 (CD)
"Mean" on **True Sounds of the New West**/ Freedom/1995
"Kisses for Christmas" b/w "Sleigh Bell Rock"/Goofin'
Fin./1996 (7")
"All I Could Was Cry" on **Rock-A-Billy Record Co.,
Vol. 2**/Rock-A-Billy/1996
Mean!/Squarebird/1998 (box with CD & 4 singles)
"I Still Can't Forget You"; "Mean Streak"; "Feelin' Right
Tonight" on **Renegade Rockabilly**/Renegade/1998

Marti Brom/Squarebird Music,
P.O. Box 160011, Austin, TX 78716

rab@io.com

Marti Brom/Rockabilly Hall of Fame Page
//www.rockabillyhall.com/MartiBrom.html

Marti Brom Fan Page //marti.notrix.de/

See High Noon; Kim Lenz

David Bromberg

Multi-Instrumentalist; Old-Time; Bluegrass; Country Rock
Philadelphia, Pennsylvania; September 19, 1945-

David Bromberg's musical career is best summarized by the
title of his 1990 recording **Sideman Serenade**. A highly
respected multi-instrumentalist (banjo, dobro, fiddle, guitar,
mandolin), he has been the consummate session player with a
list of credits including many of the leading names in 1960s-
1970s alternative country. He was a key player on the pivotal
Hillbilly Jazz as well as its sequel, **Hillbilly Jazz Rides Again**.
Throughout this period, Bromberg found time to record a long
string of solo records covering the gamut of Americana (blues,
country, jazz, rock) with a liberal dose of humor and backed by a
string of musician/friends that among many others included
Emmylou Harris and the Grateful Dead. Into the 1990s,
Bromberg, who now resides in Chicago, has seriously cut back
on performances with only occasional solo appearances at
various clubs and festivals. His legacy was kept alive in 1998
with the reissue of several of his early LPs on CD and the release
of an appropriately titled anthology, **The Player: A Retrospective**.

David Bromberg/Columbia/1971
Demon in Disguise/Columbia/1972
Wanted Dead or Alive/Columbia/1974
Midnight on the Water/Columbia/1975
Hillbilly Jazz/Flying Fish/1975
How Late'll Ya Play 'Til/Fantasy/1976
Out of the Blues: The Best of David Bromberg/
Columbia/1977
Bandit in a Bathing Suit/Fantasy/1978
My Own House/Fantasy/1978
You Should See the Rest of the Band/Fantasy/1980
Long Way From Here/Fantasy/1986
Hillbilly Jazz Rides Again/Flying Fish/1986
Sideman Serenade/Rounder/1990
Reckless Abandon/Bandit in a Bathing Suit/
Fantasy/1998
The Player: A Retrospective/1998

David Bromberg, 5438 South Hyde Park Blvd.,
Chicago, IL 60615-5802; 773-493-4516

David Bromberg Page
//www.acorp.com/users/jms/bromberg.html

The Brother Boys

New Old-Time; Hillbilly Bop; Close Harmony
Johnson City, Tennessee; 1989-

The Brother Boys describe their sound as "new hillbilly music...
a backwoods fiddle on a two lane highway rolling into 1964
with Sam McGee, Johnny Cash and Jimmie Rodgers in the
backseat stringing up an old flat-top box with Black
Diamonds." What this means is that on their recordings you get
old-time country, rockabilly lite, Delta blues, and bluegrass
done in the style of the famous "brother" acts (Blue Sky Boys to
the Everlys) but with a modern feel. The driving force behind
the Boys is triple threat vocalist, songwriter, and multi-
instrumentalist Ed Snodderly with Eugene Wolf providing
harmony vocals and a varied supporting cast lending solid back
up. Their recordings, **The Brother Boys**, **Plow** (produced by
Jerry Douglas), and **Presley's Grocery,** pretty much cover the
same ground offering a generous number of covers by the
greats (Bill Monroe, Louvin Brothers, Wilburn Brothers,
Loretta Lynn, Wayne Raney, Elvis) plus Snodderly's originals
which are cut from the same mold. Snodderly is proprietor of
one of East Tennessee's best alt. country venues, The Down
Home, in the heart of Johnson City.

Eddie Lee Snodderly (db,f,g,hm,mda,v); Eugene Wolf (v)

The Brother Boys/New Hillbilly/1989
Plow/Sugar Hill/1991
Presley's Grocery/Sugar Hill/1995

The Brother Boys, P.O. Box 5326 EKS,
Johnson City, TN 37603; 615-753-5927

The Brother Boys/Moonlight Mercantile Page
//www.alternetcomm.com/mercantile/bb.html

Rick Broussard (Two Hoots and a Holler; The Shadowmen)

Austin; Roots Rock; Cowpunk
Austin, Texas; Early 1980s-

One of the most popular groups on the Austin scene in the late
1980s and early 1990s was a hot little trio called Two Hoots and
a Holler. They won *The Austin Chronicle* Best Roots Rock
Band award five times and had a loyal following among the
city's rabid dance crowd. Powering their sound was the hot lead
guitar, edgy/twangy tenor, and energetic showmanship of Rick
Broussard. Born and raised in Central Texas, he had early
exposure to music through his father and brothers who played in
various country and rock bands. However, Broussard caught
the punk bug while still in high school and headed for
California. There he was in a few new wave bands and

witnessed the emergence of the hybrid sound of cowpunk. When he returned to Texas in the early 1980s, Broussard formed Two Hoots and a Holler. The band fit right into the burgeoning country/rock/punk scene in Austin led by the likes of Rank & File, the Hickoids, Teddy and the Tall Tops, and the Wagoneers. Their style blended Texas style rock and country with just a dash of punk attitude. Through constant touring and one album, **No Man's Land**, Two Hoots gained a large fan base and good press but due to a variety of internal problems fell apart in 1994. Whereupon, Broussard headed to New York City and formed a new band. With money and time set aside, they were ready to record in Austin, but the members bailed on Broussard at the last minute leaving him scrambling to find new musicians. Fortunately, he was able to enlist locals Matt Eskey, Mike Middleton, and Pete Gordon (plus guests like Pony Bone, Erik Hokkanen, Bruce and Charlie Robison) to record **Shadowman** which has some echoes of Two Hoots but also draws more on country and Cajun influences. Additionally, it allows Broussard to showcase the fine singing and songwriting he previously displayed on a 1992 solo release called **Angels Cry & Counted Sorrows**. For most of 1996, Rick Broussard and the Shadowmen toured in support of the album. Then, in late 1996, Broussard reunited with Gerard (who had been with the Derailers) to reform Two Hoots. Into 1998 and 1999, they worked old haunts such as the Black Cat and Hole in the Wall to rekindle the spark that made them one of Austin's premier bands.

Two Hoots & A Holler: Rick Broussard (l.g.,l.v.); Vic Gerard (b); Chris Staples (d).
The Shadowmen: Matt Eskey (b); Pete Gordon (p); Mike Middleton (d)

> **No Man's Land** (Two Hoots and a Holler)/New Rose Fr./1992
> **Angels Cry & Counted Sorrows** (Rick Broussard)/ Dynamic/1992
> **Shadow Man** (with the Shadowmen)/Freedom/1996

Rick Broussard/Freedom Home Page //www.eden.com/~freedom/rick.html

Alison Brown
Banjo; Newgrass
Hartford, Connecticut; August 7, 1962-

In her late teens, New England native Alison Brown seemed destined for a future as a bluegrass banjoist. At 16, she was Canadian National Banjo Champion, recorded an album with Stuart Duncan at age 17, played in the Northern Lights bluegrass band while majoring in literature and history at Harvard, and hosted a bluegrass program on a Boston radio station. However, after graduation, Brown moved on to UCLA to pursue an MBA and then from there to an investment banking job with Smith Barney. Fortunately, for the bluegrass world, this romance with corporate finance only lasted a few years and

then Brown returned to her first love, the 5-string banjo. She became a member of Alison Krauss' Union Station from 1989-1991 and during that time became the only woman to win the IBMA's Banjo Player of the Year award. Brown later served as music director for Michelle Shocked and then moved on to a solo recording career. Like Bela Fleck and David Grisman (who produced her debut **Simple Pleasures**), Brown expands the boundaries of bluegrass by exploring the nether regions of the banjo incorporating many musical genres and instruments (from steel drums to didjeridu) for a worldly, jazzed up sound. In 1996, she created Compass Records with her bass player, Garry West, and continued experimenting in 1998 on **Out of the Blue** which pushes her banjo playing further into jazz as fashioned by Wes Montgomery and other guitar giants.

> **Simple Pleasures**/Vanguard/1990
> **Twilight Motel**/Vanguard/1992
> **Look Left**/Vanguard/1994
> **Quartet**/Vanguard/1996
> **Out of the Blue**/Compass/1998

Alison Brown/Compass Records Page //www.compassrecords.com/alison.htm

Alison Brown //users.quest-net.com/~camel/alisonb.htm

Alison Brown Folk Book Index Page //www.execpc.com/~henkle/fbindex/b/brown/brown_alison. html

Greg Brown
Singer/Songwriter
Iowa

At the beginning of his career, Greg Brown hoped to make it in the New York City folk scene. When that didn't happen, he returned to his native Iowa where during the past 20 years, he has become recognized as one of America's most prolific and perceptive singer/songwriters. Having a song covered by Willie Nelson and appearing on *Prairie Home Companion* several times brought some early attention, but he really began to get noticed after he founded his own Redhouse Records around 1980. From that base, Brown issued one acclaimed album after another focused mainly on life in the great American heartland. Part poet and part philosopher, Greg has a special knack for fleshing out the essence of his favorite subjects: the landscape ("Out in the Country"; "King Corn"; "A Little Place in the Country"; "Down at the Mill"), nature ("Where Do the Wild Geese Go?"; "Spring Wind"; "Laughing River"), cultural icons ("Jesus and Elvis"; "Brand New '64 Dodge"), disillusionment ("America Will Eat You"), and relationships ("Love is a Chain"; "In the Dark With You"; "One Cool Remove"; "You Drive Me Crazy"). His crusty vocals (often compared to Tom Waits) are a perfect companion to his lyrical insights.

Brown's first recordings were generally low-key acoustic folk/blues/country affairs, but in time, his albums (beginning with **One Big Town**) took on a sharper, electric edge with the addition of Kelly Joe Phelps on slide but especially through the production and guitar work of fellow Iowa singer/songwriter Bo Ramsey. Greg's efforts from the mid-late 1990s (**The Poet Game** and **Further In** in particular) were widely praised, placed high in the Gavin Americana charts, and were nominated or won awards from NAIRD. In addition, **Friend of Mine**, a 1993 collaboration with Bill Morrissey was nominated for a Grammy. Brown also showed his versatility by doing an album of William Blake poems called **Songs of Innocence and Experience**.

Hacklebarney (with Dick Pinney)/Mountain
    Railroad/1974
44 & 66/Brown Street/1980; Red House/1984
Iowa Waltz/Brown Street/1981; Red House/1984
In the Dark With You/Red House/1985
Songs of Innocence and Experience/Red House/1986
One More Goodnight Kiss/Red House/1988
One Big Town/Red House/1989
Down in There/Red House/1990
Dream Cafe/Red House/1992
Friend of Mine (with Bill Morrissey)/Philo/1993
Bathtub Blues/Red House/1993
The Poet Game/Red House/1994
The Live One/Red House/1995
Further In/Red House/1996
"Tell You a Story" on **Doublwide: Trailer Record**
    Compilation/Trailer/1997
Slant Six Mind/Red House/1997

Greg Brown Home Page //www.wing.net/gbrown/

See Bo Ramsey

Junior Brown

Austin; Steel/Lead Guitarist; Honky Tonk
Cottonwood, Arizona; June 12, 1952-

The story of Junior Brown begins with a dream. On a fateful night in 1984, sleep brought Junior a vision of a new kind of musical instrument, a fusion of electric and steel guitar that would remedy the awkwardness of having to switch back and forth between them during performances. Over the next year, he worked with guitar maker Michael Stevens to make the dream come true; they dubbed their creation the "guit-steel," and its birth marks the beginning of what has come to be known as the Junior Brown phenomenon. Prior to this time, Brown had worked for years in obscurity as a side/session man in bands throughout the Southwest. As Jamie Brown growing up in Santa Fe, New Mexico in the late 1960s, he played in psychedelic bands like Harmonious Discord and Humble Harvey but during the mid-1970s was a member of the area's most popular honky-tonk/Western swing group, the Last Mile Ramblers. A recording from that time features Junior's distinctive bass vocals that have become one of his trademarks.

From New Mexico, Brown moved on to Austin where in the early 1980s he played in many bands including Asleep at the Wheel, Alvin Crow's Pleasant Valley Boys, and even the cowpunk group Rank and File. After "the dream" and the development of the guit-steel, he recorded a single but then was off to Oklahoma where he taught guitar (under the direction of Leon McAuliffe) at the Hank Thompson School of Country Music. There he met and married one of his students, "the lovely Miss Tanya Rae." Not only did she become his wife but also his rhythm guitarist and main source of stability and support. After an abortive attempt at "making it" in Nashville, they returned to Austin where Junior became a regular performer (along with Don Walser, Cornell Hurd, and others) at a tiny but very popular bar called Henry's. In the late 1980s, Junior recorded a self-produced tape, **12 Shades of Brown** and developed a distinctive persona and sound. Ernest Tubb-like vocals, clever songwriting, and amazing guitar/steel playing (hot country picking with Hendrix and surf music thrown in) delivered by a bug-eyed guy in a straw hat and over-sized suit proved to be an irresistible combination. When Henry's closed in the early 1990s, Junior moved his band to the famous Continental Club where he really began to gather a loyal following, critical acclaim, and admiration from musicians as diverse as Ry Cooder, the Butthole Surfers, and Neil Young. After three more years of continuous praise from a growing list of fans and reviewers, Brown finally got a much deserved contract with Curb which simultaneously released **12 Shades** and **Guit With It**. From there, momentum carried Junior to tours all over the U.S. and Europe and even greater exposure through several hit videos on CMT; "Highway Patrol" and "My Wife Thinks You're Dead" each earned Grammy nominations. Through 1996-1997, Brown's star continued to rise with two more recordings **Junior High** and **Semi-Crazy** and a slew of nominations and awards from *Guitar Player*, *Performance Magazine*, and the CMA. He and his guit-steel showed up on numerous television shows (*Electrified, Amplified, and Deified*; *Austin City Limits*; *David Letterman*; *Conan O'Brien*; *Prime Time Country*), commercials, and magazines including the cover story for *Guitar Player* (March 1997).

In 1998-1999, between making Lipton Ice Tea commercials, appearing on a X-Files episode as a farmer, contributing to the Ralph Stanley anthology (**Clinch Mountain Country**), and guesting on a new Ray Price album, Junior promoted **Long Walk Home**. Once again he mixes quirky honky tonk two-steps and ballads ("Long Walk Back to San Antone"; "The Better Half"; "Just a Little Love") with songs that give his guitar prowess center stage ("Peelin' Taters"; "Freedom Machine"; "I'm All Fired Up"; "Stupid Blues"). But, this time out there's some new twists including a couple of 50s style songs: "Lookin' for Love" and a rousing remake of the old Elvis song, "Rock-A-Hula Baby." In June 1998, Brown returned to New

Mexico for a festive reunion concert with the Last Mile Ramblers (see *No Depression*, September-October, 1998, p. 10).

"Too Many Nights in a Road House" b/w "Gotta Get Up Every Morning"/Dynamic/1985 (7")
12 Shades of Brown/JRB/1989 (CS); Demon/1990; Curb/1993
Guit With It/Curb/1993
Junior High/Curb/1995
"Nitro Express" (with Red Simpson) on **Rig Rock Deluxe**/ Upstart/1996
Semi-Crazy/Curb/1996
"Stone Walls & Steel Bars" on **Clinch Mountain Country: Ralph Stanley & Friends**/Rebel/1998
Long Walk Back/Curb/1998

Junior Brown International Fan Club c/o Karen DuBois, P.O. Box 180763, Utica, MI 48318-0763

Junior Brown Home Page //www.juniorbrown.com

Junior Brown/Curb Home Page //www.curb.com/artists/jb.html

Junior Brown iMusic Showcase //imusic.com/showcase/country/

Tanya Rae Home Page //www.tanyarae.com

See The Last Mile Ramblers

Marty Brown

Honky Tonk
Maceo, Kentucky; July 25, 1965-

Marty Brown's life was "almost" a perfect fulfillment of one of the most popular tales in country music folklore: the rags-to-riches story of the hick-from-the-sticks musician who comes to the big city in search of fame and fortune and in the face of over-whelming hardships becomes a singing star. Almost because, yes, Brown did arrive in Nashville from the tobacco fields around Maceo, Kentucky with little more than his guitar; and yes, he did suffer through nights spent on the streets, repeated rejections, and derision for his rubeness. And in spite of all this, Brown secured a major record deal and in four years put out three albums, **High and Dry**, **Wild Kentucky Skies**, and **Cryin', Lovin', Leavin'**. However, the fame and fortune part just didn't happen. Unfortunately for Brown, he came along right in the middle of the singing hat gold-rush and with all the pretty boys, there was just no room on the radio for a genuine hillbilly with a real Jimmie/Hank type voice singing songs about honky tonks, heartache, and murder. Consequently, Brown's success was extremely limited, but the resurgence of hillbilly music and singers (e.g. Wayne Hancock) plus Brown's switch to Hightone Records held out greater promise. Based on Hightone's track record for quality honky tonk and country rock, Brown's debut **Here's To the Honky Tonks** should have been his best and possibly breakthrough recording. But, in-explicably, he strayed from the rootsy traditional sound of his previous recordings, and the result was a fence straddling clunker. Fans hoped they hadn't heard the last from Marty

Brown, and sure enough, they hadn't but were wishing it could have been under different circumstances. In late summer 1998, Brown was charged with felony theft of auto parts (1969 Plymouth Runner) in Indiana but pled guilty and had it reduced to a misdemeanor carrying a sentence of a $300 fine, a year's probation, and 24 hours of community service. Disturbing news, but isn't this the stuff country legends are made of e.g. Merle Haggard, Johnny Paycheck, David Allan Coe, et al.?

High and Dry/MCA/1991
Wild Kentucky Skies/MCA/1993
Cryin', Lovin', Leavin'/MCA/1994
Here's To the Honky Tonks/Hightone/1996

Marty Brown Fan Club, c/o Helena Williams, P.O. Box 70, Maceo, KY 42355

Marty Brown Web Page //www.bellnet.com/brown.html

Peter Stone Brown

Singer/Songwriter
Philadelphia, Pennsylvania; 1951-

Over the last 25+ years, Peter Stone Brown has been one of the most well-known members of the Philadelphia music scene. He's worked as a DJ (on WXPN), music journalist and editor (*East Coast Rocker*; *Welcomat/Philadelphia Weekly*), and band member/leader (the Crackers, the Fulminators, the Fumblers, the Others), but most of his energies have gone into carving out his own place as a singer/songwriter. With Dylan as his main influence, Brown honed his skills as a regular in Philly's nightclubs and seemed to be on his way until a mugging in 1990 left him with severe facial damage and put his singing on hold. However, while recuperating, he continued to write songs and steeled by the experience decided to go for broke in 1995 by self-financing his debut, **Up Against It**. Old childhood friend Ray Benson invited Brown to use his Bismeaux Studio in Austin and also loaned out Asleep at the Wheel members Tim Alexander (accordion, keyboards) and Cindy Cashdollar (dobro, lap steel) for the sessions. Joining them were Austin stalwarts, lead guitarist Casper Rawls (LeRoi Brothers; Toni Price) and fiddler Howard Kalish (Don Walser). They provide just the right folk/country/rock background for Brown's rough hewn vocals that can't help but be compared to Bobby D's. However, the lyrics are all Peter's own and while they tend to dwell on death, violence, and despair ("Matter of the Heart"; "You're Not There"; "Up Against It"; "Waiting for You"; "Insignificant"), Brown leaves some room for hope ("Here on Earth") and humor ("Rockabilly Guy"). Released by Tangible Music in 1996, **Up Against It** was well-received in the U.S. and Europe and made the Gavin chart by year's end. Since then, Brown has worked tirelessly performing in Philadelphia, the East Coast, and down South, waiting for that long overdue call.

Up Against It/Tangible Music/1996

Peter Stone Brown,
P.O. Box 31452, Phildaelphia, PA 19147

Peter Stone Brown/Tangible Page
//www.tangible-music.com/peterstonebrown/

peterb@erols.com

Jann Browne

TSOB
Anderson, Indiana; March 14, 1954-

As a teen angel just out of high school, Jann Browne toured the South with a country band and, with encouragement from her mother, moved to L.A. There, she played the local honky tonks and in 1981 was recruited by Ray Benson to be a vocalist with Asleep at the Wheel. After two years with them, Browne returned to Southern California and became part of the revitalized alt. country scene of the late 1980s. Her "Louisville" (co-written with Pat Gallagher) was included on the first volume of **A Town South of Bakersfield** in 1988 and a deal with Curb Records resulted in **Tell Me Why** which included an all star cadre of supporting musicians: Byron Berline, Albert Lee, New Grass Revival, Emmylou Harris, and Iris DeMent. It produced a #1 video award (for "Mexican Wind"), garnered rave reviews, and hope for Browne as "the next Emmylou." However, the promise was not fulfilled; Curb began pushing Browne in a direction she didn't want to go and after a disappointing second album, **It Only Hurts When I Laugh**, she relocated to Europe where she found very appreciative audiences. Browne reappeared on the American scene in 1995 when a new record **Count Me In** (first released on the Swiss Red Moon label) was put out by Cross Three. Its songs were all co-written by Browne who showed signs of a return to her glory days. And while she did appear at SXSW in 1995, she has been content to perform mostly in Europe where she has the freedom to go her own way.

"Louisville" on **Town South of Bakersfield, Vol. 1**/
 Restless/1988
Tell Me Why/Curb/1990
It Only Hurts When I Laugh/Curb/1991
Count Me In/Red Moon Switz./1995; Cross Three/1995

Jann Browne Fan Club, P.O. Box 3481,
Laguna Hills, CA 92654

Jann Browne/DasBro Home Page
//www.webcom.com/jhodgson/dasbro/jannbrowne.html

dasbro@pipeline.com

The Buckets

Country Rock; Honky Tonk
Boston, Massachusetts; 1988/San Francisco, California; c.1990-

The Buckets play traditional truck driving music with a modern attitude. It's Red Simpson and Gram Parsons flying down some highway in an eighteen wheeler; it's a trucker's jukebox where a single by Dave Dudley sits comfortably beside one by Jon Langford. And underlying it all is a generous sense of humor running from the band's *faux* hillbilly personae to witty songs with a twist on the usual country themes of heartbreak, over-indulgence, and the loneliness of the road. Lead singer Earl Butter (Ray Halliday) founded the Buckets in Boston along with fiddle player Wanda Taters (Carrie Bradley) who had been a member of such bands as the Breeders and Ed's Redeeming Qualities. In the early 1990s, they moved the band to San Francisco, and the Buckets became a fixture in the Bay Area's burgeoning alternative country scene along with Dieselhed, Tarnation, Buck Naked, and Richard Buckner and the Doubters. After several singles, the Buckets made their full length debut in 1996 with a self-titled recording for Slow River. Here, Butter provides just the right degree of twang on witty originals about alcoholism ("I'm Drunk"; "Beer Belly"), love-gone-wrong ("I Wrote This Song"; "Mistake #1"), and, of course, truck driving ("Empty Cage"; "Western Star"; "Song of the True Divided Highway"). He is admirably supported by the other Buckets, but the fiddling of Wanda Taters is the real highlight. Her driving fiddle keeps the up tempo numbers moving along, and she's equally effective in setting the tone on some of the more somber, tear-in-beer tunes. Late in 1996, the Buckets released their first single "Beer Belly" (on beer colored vinyl), but according to the band's web page, they decided to take some time off because of their poor showing at the 1997 Grammys. Hopefully, it wouldn't be a long hiatus.

Original Members: Ray Halliday aka Earl Butter (g,v); Carrie Bradley aka Wanda Taters (f,v); Corey Porter aka Kid Coyote (l.g.); Rob Bob (d); Slim Volume (b)
Current Members: Earl Butter (g,v); Kid Coyote (l.g.); John Pike aka Long John Gonzalez (b); Robert Davis aka Blue Jewel (d); Wanda Taters (f,v)

"Cowgirls" b/w "Western Star"/Hairy/1993 (7")
"The Dog" on **Ain't This Bliss With You and This**/Spin
 the Bottle/1994 (7" comp)
"El Caballero, El Viento, El Diablo" (Live) on ?/
 Kommotion/1995
The Buckets/Slow River/1996
"Beer Belly" b/w "Pony Express"/Slow River/1996

The Buckets c/o Ray Halliday, 611 Guerrero #16,
San Francisco, CA 94110

The Buckets Home Page //www.slip.net/~kateoc/

ebutter@ix.netcom.com

Richard Buckner (The Doubters)

Singer/Songwriter; Lo-Fi
Fresno, California; 1964-

If Richard Buckner was a painter his landscapes would depict terrains of unrelenting bleakness broken by few places of refuge. As a singer/songwriter, Buckner performs emotionally charged, deeply personal songs plumbing the darkest depths of relationships gone bad. Such an extreme view has naturally invited comments on his work that generally fall at opposite ends of the spectrum. Detractors have found his Kierkegaardian "sickness unto death" approach self indulgent and even monotonous while his ardent supporters have hailed Buckner as a major new poet whose songs accurately capture the anxieties of contemporary society. Either way, there is no doubt Buckner is a force to be reckoned with in alternative country. Born and raised in Northern California, Buckner did not develop a serious interest in music until his college days at Chico State University. After graduation, he settled in San Francisco for a while then moved on to Atlanta where he suddenly found his songwriting muse. Inspired by the music of REM and other Atlanta groups, Buckner returned to the Bay Area and worked as a solo before forming a band called the Doubters in 1993. They became a vital part of the Frisco alt. country scene and helped establish Buckner's reputation as a singer/songwriter. Many of the songs he wrote while with the Doubters ended up on Buckner's debut, **Bloomed,** which was first released on the German Glitterhouse label and then domestically on Dejadisc. Recorded in Lubbock, Texas and produced by Lloyd Maines, it has spare accompaniment (Ponty Bone on accordion, Butch Hancock on harmonica, Maines on steel) for Buckner's slow, somber explorations of heartbreak and self-destruction. The haunting tone of songs like "22," "Rainsquall," and "Gauzy Dress in the Sun" is accentuated by his gritty, susurrus vocals. Immediately after its release, **Bloomed** began to receive raves (and jeers) and quickly pushed Buckner into the limelight he subsequently shared on bills with Dave Alvin, Townes Van Zandt, Peter Case, and many others. As a follow-up, Buckner toyed with the idea of an album about his family, but it never gelled. Instead, Buckner (now with MCA) recorded **Devotion and Doubt** (produced by J. D. Foster) which continued his obsession with the meaning of love and loss on songs that take the listener to the edge of despair but never quite over. This time Buckner accompanies himself on acoustic guitar or is occasionally backed by Maines, Champ Hood (Toni Price), Rich Brotherton (Robert Earl Keen), and members of Giant Sand/Calexico. Once again, Buckner provoked reactions of, well, either devotion or doubt that see his work as a product of stunted emotional growth or the genius of a star brightening to maturity.

Considering Buckner's problems (record label hassles; divorce) and unusual living circumstance (he literally lives out of his pick-up), one might have doubted he could keep it together long enough to put out another record. But, channeling his troubles into his music once more, he did **Since**. It has a lot of the musical qualities of **Bloomed** and **Devotion and Doubt,** with soft spare arrangements and floating pedal steel (from Son Volt's Eric Heywood) accentuating Buckner's grimacing vocals. This time out, however, his unrelenting despair is more jarring with the addition of electric guitar from Dave Schramm

and Chris Cochrane. For a fist full of dollars, Buckner embarked on The Good, the Bad, and the Ugly Tour with Bruce Robison and Kelly Willis although no one could say which was which. And, appropriately enough, Richard covered "When Love Is Gone" on the long-awaited Tom T. Hall tribute, **Real**. **Bloomed** was reissued with bonus tracks by Slow River Records late in 1998.

"Gauzy Dress" (The Doubters) on **Ain't This Bliss With You & This**/Spin the Bottle/1994 (7" comp)
Unreleased/RB/1994 (CS sold at Buckner's early shows)
Bloomed/Glitterhouse Ger./1994; Dejadisc/1994; Slow River/1998 (with extra trks.)
Devotion and Doubt/MCA/1997 (ltd. ed. box was also released)
Since/MCA/1998
Live at Schuba's Tavern/MCA/1998 (promo with trks. From **Since**)
"When Love Is Gone" on **Real: The Tom T. Hall Project, Vol. 1**/Sire/1998

Richard Buckner Fan Page
//home.earthlink.net/~doubters/buckner.html

Richard Buckner/Doubters On-Line Mailing List
majordomo@world.std.com {subscribe doubters}

Richard Buckner/Dejadisc Page
//www.eden.com/~dejadisc/buckner.html

Buffalo Springfield
Country Rock
Los Angeles, California; 1966-1968

Buffalo Springfield arose from the same late 1960s milieu that produced the Byrds. They could have been a monster group like the Stones or Beatles, but internal dissension tore them apart after only a few years together. Still, they did manage to make a couple of records (self-titled debut and **Again**) that had a big impact on American popular music. And while Buffalo Springfield has often been credited as one of the pioneers of country rock, it's a point that needs some clarification. To borrow some terminology from Richard Peterson (*Creating Country Music*), Buffalo Springfield's country rock was generally split between the "soft shell" style of Richie Furay and Jim Messina and the "hard core" leanings of Neil Young. This was a part of the creative tension that eventually broke the band apart, and its legacy lived on long after Buffalo Springfield was history. Young joined Crosby, Stills, and Nash for a time but then expanded his take on country rock as a solo performer and, like the Byrds, Gram Parsons, and the Flying Burrito Brothers, had a major influence on contemporary alternative country. On the other hand, Furay and Messina went on to form Poco and Messina later joined with Kenny Loggins as the popular duo Loggins & Messina. Both groups churned out tepid country rock that was really neither; their emphasis on high harmonies, feel good lyrics, and highly polished presentations had reverberations that extended from the Eagles down to today's HNC.

Richie Furay (r.g.,v); Dewey Martin (d,v); Jim Messina (b,v,1967-1968); Bruce Palmer (b,1966-1967); Stephen Stills (l.g.,v); Neil Young (l.g.,v)

Buffalo Springfield/Atco/1966
Buffalo Springfield Again/Atco/1967
Last Time Around/Atco/1968
Best of Buffalo Springfield...Retrospective/Atco/1969
There's Something Happening Here: The Story of Buffalo Springfield, John Einarson and Richie Furay, Quarry Books, 1998.

The Buffalo Springfield Homepage
//home1.swipnet.se/~w-11020/buffalo/start.html

See The Byrds; Neil Young

Paul Burch & The WPA Ballclub
Honky Tonk; Insurgent Country
Nashville, Tennessee; 1995-

Paul Burch was one of the leading figures in the music revival along Nashville's Lower Broadway in the late 1990s. Growing up in Indiana, Burch initially took up the drums and was drawn to many styles of music. He settled on vintage 1940s-1950s country and switched to rhythm guitar while still in high school. After graduating from college, he headed to Boston and joined a country/bluegrass band called the Bag Boys. Burch played with them for a few years but then was encouraged by a former Indiana bandmate, Jay McDowell to come to Nashville. McDowell (BR5-49's bass player) introduced him to Music City's growing alt. country scene, and Burch dove right in drumming for McDowell's group Hellbilly, playing vibra-phone in Lambchop on occasion, and fronting his own band (known first as His Honky Tonk Orchestra and then as WPA Ballclub) with steel player Paul Niehaus and a rotating line up of musicians. Burch and WPA became fixtures at Lower Broad-way venues such as Robert's and especially Tootsie's where they treated growing audiences to "sensible music for troubled times" (translation: good old solid, country and western). Their easygoing honky tonk and swing anchored by Burch's friendly vocals made them local favorites, and eventually, they got wider attention through a cut ("Your Red Wagon") on Bloodshot's **Nashville: The Other Side of the Alley** and a spread in *No Depression*. 1996 saw the release of Burch and company's first full length CD, **Pan American Flash** on the French Dixie Frog label. Featuring guest fiddler Jason Carter of the Del McCoury Band, this excellent collection of Burch originals ("Monterey"; "Born to Wait"; "Loser's Way to Get Along"; "Sage Advice") was nominated for Americana Album of the Year by the Nashville Music Awards. It was followed in 1997 by the even finer **Wire to Wire**, which includes a a cover of Webb Pierce's "Drifting Texas Sand" but mostly just more great Burch country ("I Turned a Corner"; "When You Go Wrong"; "This Time Next Year") and western ("Long Tall Glass of Water"). Along for the ride are members of the Bag

Boys, Deanna Varagona of Lambchop, and Ranger Doug of Riders in the Sky with some fancy yodeling. Both recordings were given glowing endorsements by top reviewers (Chet Flippo, John Conquest, Don Yates), and Burch's long overdue recognition in the U.S. was given a great boost through a domestic distribution deal with Checkered Past which re-released **Pan American Flash** and **Wire to Wire** in 1998.

Paul Burch & The WPA Ballclub: Paul Burch (g,v); George Bradfute (r.g.); Dennis Crouch (ub); Ken Loggains (d); Paul Neihaus (l.s.,p.s.); Deanna Varagona (h.v.)

"Your Red Wagon" on **Nashville: The Other Side of the Alley**/Bloodshot/1996
Pan American Flash/Dixie Frog Fr./1996; Checkered Past/1998
Wire to Wire/Dixie Frog Fr./1997; Checkered Past/1998

Paul Burch & The WPA Ballclub Home Page
//www.paulburch.ml.org

pburch@usa.net

Paul Burch/Checkered Past Page //www.checkeredpast.com

See The Bag Boys; Lambchop

T-Bone Burnett aka John Henry Burnett
Country Rock; Roots Rock; Producer
St. Louis, Missouri; January 14, 1948-

T-Bone Burnett started out in the late 1960s primarily as a producer for his small record label in Ft. Worth. His most notable achievement during that time was recording and getting radio play for the Legendary Stardust Cowboy's infamous debut, the cult single "Paralyzed." In the 1970s, Burnett was a member of Dylan's Rolling Thunder Review and in the 1980s made several solo records including the country rockish **Truth Decay**, the rockabilly influenced **Trap Door**, and his straight-est and best country album, **T-Bone Burnett**. The latter has some memorable dobro by Jerry Douglas and is highlighted by a cover of "Poison Love" and the haunting original "River of Love." In the 1990s, Burnett established his rep as a "super-producer" whose hand guided recordings by many prominent alt. country musicians including Jimmie Dale Gilmore, Peter Case, Gillian Welch, Los Lobos, and the Big Blue Hearts.

Truth Decay/Takoma/1980
Trap Door/Warner Bros./1982 (EP)
Proof Through the Night/Warner Bros./1983
T Bone Burnett/Dot/1986

T-Bone Burnett Home Page //www.tmtm.com/sam/burnett/

The Burnley Brothers (The Jimmy Nations Combo)
Tobacco Row; Hillbilly Bop
Wilmington, North Carolina; 1996-

Although the lion's share of the buzz has gone to groups like the Backsliders, Whiskeytown and Jolene, North Carolina has produced a wide variety of excellent alt. country acts including hot hillbilly boppers like Wilmington's the Burnley Brothers. Three veterans of the area's punk scene, Mark Griffiths, Chad Heye, and James Sardone (aka Jimmy Nations) formed the group in 1996 and after luring pedal steel player Bill Ladd away from Jolene began to create a style called "Tarheel boogie." Ostensibly a "rockabilly combo," the Burnley Brothers are actually more akin to late 1940s-early 1950s hillbilly swing precursors such as Johnny Bond, Paul Howard, Johnny Hicks, Curley Williams, and Smiley Maxedon (see the excellent Columbia anthology, **Hillbilly Boogie**). Not that the Brothers don't rock, but Sardone's twangy vocals and jazzy guitar licks plus Ladd's steel give them a more country/swing feel found in Big Sandy, the Dalhart Imperials, and other contemporary hillbilly bop bands. And while they can handle a variety of material including surf ("Car Hop"), honky tonk ("Pick Me Up on Your Way Down"), and 50s pop ("Gonna Let You Down"), the Burnley Brothers are especially strong on country boogie covers ("Everybody's Rockin'"; "Mean Mama Boogie") and Sardone originals ("New Rock City"; "All Bark & No Bite"; "Tarheel Boogie"; "On Again, Off Again"). Their recorded output as of the end of 1997 consisted of an EP cassette and two cuts on the **Revival** compilations, but a full length CD was on the way in 1998. Unfortunately, constant touring was too much, and the Burnley Brothers split up. Sardone kept their spirit going with a new hillbilly boogie band called the Jimmy Nations Combo. Playing New York City and other East Coast cities, the JNC went to North Carolina in late 1998 to record a CD and wait for "the big offer."

Mark Griffiths (u.b.); Chad Heye (d); Bill Ladd (p.s.); James Sardone aka Johnny Nations (g,l.v.)

Tarheel Boogie/BB/1997 (CS)
"Mean Mama Boogie" on **Revival 1: Brunswick Stew & Pig Pickin'**/Yep Roc/1997
"All Bark & No Bite" on **Revival 2: Kudzu and Hollerin' Contest**/Yep Roc/1997

Jimmy Nations/Burnley Brothers, 58 E. 3rd St., Apt. 6, New York, NY 10003

james_sardone@citysearch.com

Charlie Burton (The Cutouts; The Hiccups; The Texas Twelve Steppers)

Honky Tonk; Country Rock; Humor
Lincoln, Nebraska; September 19, 1950-

During preparations for our wedding a few years back, I tried to convince my bride-to-be that at the reception we should dance our spotlight dance to Charlie Burton's romantic tribute to marriage, "Without My Woman, I'd Be a Hopeless Sack of Shit." She looked at me like I was crazy and, you know, maybe I was. That's the kind of effect the music of Charlie Burton can have on you. Like Cornell Hurd, Burton is a master punster and astute parodist of low life culture who, if you're in a certain mood, can easily lure you into his demented world. Growing up

in Nebraska in a family of harpsichord makers, Burton inherited the business at age 21. Before that, he went to Antioch College (Ohio) and then to school in Ann Arbor, Michigan where instead of going into classical music, Charlie turned in a little bit different direction inspired by the Stooges, MC5, Commander Cody, and other popular Ann Arbor bands. In the early 1970s, he became a music critic (country) for *Rolling Stone* but dropped out of that position to run the family business when his father died and willed it to him. However, the pull of music was too strong, and Burton threw himself into several roots rock bands in the 1970s. The most successful of these was Rock Therapy, a punkabilly outfit that got good national press especially for the Burton penned single, "Rock and Roll Behavior." In the 1980s, Burton fronted the Cutouts and the Hiccups who blended rock and country laced with a generous supply of wicked humor and mayhem. His wild stage reputation and twisted songs (e.g. "Without My Woman") won them a cult following. After two studio and one live (**Puke Point at the Juke Joint**) recording, the Hiccups disbanded, and Burton moved to Austin in 1992. There, he teamed with Evans Johns and went to Europe where they did a song with a Dutch rockabilly band (Tuxedo Buck) for a compilation called **Texas Twang**. At about the same time, Charlie made *The Catalog of Cool: Too Cool* and started a honky tonk, country rock band, the Texas Twelve Steppers. After a couple of singles, Burton and the TTS recorded a full-length CD, **Rustic Fixer Upper**, in 1997. With help from many of Austin's finest including Mark Rubin, John Ely, Champ Hood, and Lisa Pankratz, Burton deals out another heaping helping of hard core hijinks on "Rogue Cop," "She's Out of My Hair (But Not Out of My Mind)," "I'm the Guy Who Let Miss Universe Slip Through His Hands." More unwary music fans got a the chance to enter Charlie's twisted little world during his showcase at SXSW 1998, but Burton's biggest triumph came when, while on a tour to the Kansas/Nebraska area, the Omaha City Council declared August 23, 1998 as Charlie Burton Day. Later in the year, Bulldog Records released **One Man's Trash**, a compilation of his "greatest hits" including material from out-of-print singles and albums. Burton's old band, the Hiccups, under the name Shithook put out their own CD, **When a Boyscout Gets the Blues**, in 1999.

The Cutouts and The Hiccups: Charlie Burton (g,hm,v); David Boye (b,sax,b.v.); Dave Roebel (d,b.v.); Phil Shoemaker (g,b.v.)
The Texas Twelve Steppers: Charlie Burton (a.g., v); John Ely (p.s.); Champ Hood (f); Mark Korpi (e.g.); Lisa Pankratz (d); Mark Rubin (b,b.v.)

"Rock and Roll Behavior" b/w "That Boy & My Girl" (with Rock Therapy)/Wild/1977
"Guitar Case" b/w "Dolled Up Cutie" (with Rock Therapy)/Wild/1978
"Dead Giveaway" b/w "Mobile, Alabama" (with Rock Therapy)/Wild/1979

Is That Charlie Burton...Or What?!?! (with the
   Cutouts)/Wild/1982
Don't Fight the Band That Needs You!!! (with the
   Cutouts)/Wild/1983
I Heard That (with the Hiccups)/Wild/1985
"Wishful Thinking" & "I, 4 1, Don't Care" (with the
   Hiccups) on **Staged! A Live Lincoln Sampler/**
   Zoom/1988 (CS)
Green Cheese (with the Hiccups)/Wild Seedy/1990
Puke Point at the Juke Joint (Live with the
   Hiccups)/Wild Whoops/1991
"Love at First Sight" on **Texas Twang, Vol. 1**/ Munich
   Dut./1993
"Spare Me the Details" b/w "It Must Have Been Someone
   I Loved" (with the Texas Twelve Steppers)/Loss
   Leider/1994 (7")
"Spare Me the Details" on **True Sounds of the New West/**
   Freedom/1995
"Rogue Cop" on **Hit the Hay 2**/Sound Asleep Swe./1996
Rustic Fixer-Upper/Lazy SOB/1997
One Man's Trash/Bulldog/1998
When a Boyscout Gets the Blues
   (Hiccups/Shithook)/1999

Charlie Burton, P.O. Box 49405, Austin, TX 78765

The Charlie Burton Hype'r Space
//www.bulldogrecords.com/burton/home.htm

Charlie Burton/Lazy SOB Page
//www.io.com/lazysob/burton.html

The Bushbury Mountain Daredevils
"Urban Hillbilly Folk"
Birmingham, England; 1993-

As all good fans know, Celtic and English folk music were two
of the major foundations for the evolution of American country
music. Over the years, Americana of all types has been exported
back to the British Isles where it has been wildly popular. And
although, as in the U.S., HNC has been most successful in the
U.K., a number of bands have remained true to country's
Anglo/American roots. One of these, the Bushbury Mountain
Daredevils, hails from Birmingham, England. Formed in 1994
and originally known as the New Bushbury Mountain
Daredevils, they combine traditional country, bluegrass, Cajun,
and rock with a little bit of Celtic and English into what they call
"urban hillbilly folk." Relying on an array of acoustic
instruments (accordion, banjo, mandolin, dobro, harmonica,
guitar, whistle) and tight vocals, they specialize in highly
danceable music but also have a heightened social consciousness as they demonstrate on originals addressing homelessness
("Barefoot in the City"; "Man Who's Got No Name") and
inequality ("Peace and Justice").

Brian Bannister (bj,g,mda,wh,v); Mick Barker (d,1998-);
Eric Barlow (g,v1994-1995); Buzby Bywater (b); Richard
Heath (d,b.v.,1994-1997); Eddy Morton (g,md,v); Gerry
Smith (acc,p)

   Bushbury Mountain/New Mountain Music UK/1994
   Peace and Justice/New Mountain Music UK/1995
   Urban Hillbilly/New Mountain Music UK/1996

Bushbury Mountain Daredevils in Concert/New Mountain
   Music UK/1996 (video)
   The Bushburys Live/Enigma UK/1997
   Brand New Day/Enigma UK/1998

The Bushbury Mountain Daredevils, 1768 Pershore Rd.,
Kings Norton, Birmingham, B30 3BG, England

The Bushbury Mountain Dardevils Page
/ourworld.compuserve.com/homepages/bushbury/mount.htm

Buttercup
Country Rock; Roots Rock
Boston, Massachusetts; 1994-

It's pretty clear that somewhere along the way the Boston based
band Buttercup put in a few hours listening to early Jayhawks'
records. Each of the members had been in various rock bands
before getting together around 1994. As Buttercup, they played
around Bean Town for a few years before their 15 song demo
tape was released on CD in 1996 by Spirit of Orr. **Gold** is
perhaps most aptly described as pop with a pedal steel.
However, their sophomore effort, **Love**, takes a decidedly
country rock turn that inevitably brings to mind the Jayhawks'
Blue Earth and **Hollywood Town Hall**. Jangly, twangy guitar,
folky lead and harmony vocals, omnipresent steel guitar, and a
few pop touches are all there, but Buttercup emulates rather than
imitates, and the results will please fans of country rock from
the late 1960s and early 1990s. But, with the departure of steel
player Tim Obetz, Buttercup's self-titled third recording drops
the country rock flavor of **Love** for a more moody folk/rock/pop
sound (it was named Americana CD of the Month in the January
issue of *Mojo*). Slated for Buttercup's future were a hard rock
recording and an album covering some of the group's favorite
bands. Obetz remained active on the Boston alt. country scene
lending his steel guitar talents to the Fritters and leading a
Hawaiian country group called the Pineapple Ranch Hands.

Jim Buni (g,v); Mike Leahy (g,v); Dan Lech (d,v); Colleen
MacDonald (b,v); Tim Obetz (p.s.,1994-1997)

   Gold/Spirit of Orr/1996
   Love/Spirit of Orr/1997
   Buttercup/Spirit of Orr/1998

The Byrds
Country Rock
Los Angeles, California; 1964-1973

Formed in 1964 by Roger McGuinn and Gene Clark, the Byrds
started out as a folk rock band and had a string of hits that made
them one of the most popular groups of the day. In the late
1960s, mainly under the urging of Chris Hillman, they began to
join rock with country. Greatly influenced by another California country rock band, Nashville West, which included
Clarence White and Gene Parsons, the Byrds made their first
country rock record, **The Notorious Byrd Brothers,** in early
1968. When Gram Parsons came on board later that year, they

recorded **Sweetheart of the Rodeo** considered by many to be the greatest country rock album of all time. Not much more can be said about this seminal recording that hasn't already been said, but its influence on the development of alternative country has been enormous. Hillman and Parsons left shortly afterward to form the Flying Burrito Brothers, but the Byrds with Gene Parsons and the great guitarist Clarence White (joined in 1968) continued to explore country rock territory on subsequent albums, **Dr. Byrds and Mr. Hyde**, **The Ballad of Easy Rider**, **Untitled**, and **Farther Along** until they broke up in 1973. Byrds alumni went on to participate in key musical moments in the early history of alt. country: Gram Parsons as the acknowledged "father of country rock" working solo or with Hillman in the Flying Burrito Brothers; Gene Clark as a soloist and with the Dillard/Clark Expedition; Clarence White with Muleskinner and the Kentucky Colonels; Gene Parsons as a solo performer and inventor (created the "string bender" with Clarence White). Roger McGuinn cut a number of solo records in the 1970s and in the early 1980s teamed with Clark and Hillman as McGuinn, Clark, and Hillman. The results of this collaboration were spotty, but a good example of their sound can be found on the 1997 release **Three Byrds Land in London**, a live recording from 1977 that features them as a trio and individually. In 1996, after a five year layoff from recording, McGuinn released **Live From Mars** with live tracks from 1994-1996 including acoustic versions of the Byrds' best. It also has two studio bonus tracks, "Fireworks" and "May the Road Rise," on which McGuinn is backed by the Jayhawks. In 1998, McGuinn worked with two other prominent members of alt. country's new generation when he joined Jay Farrar and Jeff Tweedy to contribute several songs to a live performance honoring folk musicologist Harry Smith.

Over the last three decades, the Byrds have been a continuing source of inspiration for several generations of alternative country musicians from the Long Ryders in the mid-1980s to Uncle Tupelo and a host of current alt. country groups. In 1997, Columbia issued upgraded versions of the Byrds' four most important country rock albums, **Notorious**, **Sweetheart**, **Dr. Byrd**, and **Ballad** (each with previously unreleased material) that clearly show why they are the godfathers of alternative country. Additionally, material from the Byrds country rock days continues to emerge including the 1998 **Byrdoholics**, an import recording with Gram Parsons at the Piper Club.

Notorious Byrd Brothers/Columbia/1968; Columbia Legacy/1997 (with extra trks.)
Sweetheart of the Rodeo/Columbia/1968; Columbia Legacy/1997 (with extra trks.)
Dr. Byrd & Mr. Hyde/Columbia/1969; Columbia Legacy/1997 (with extra trks.)
Ballad of Easy Rider/Columbia/1970; Columbia Legacy/1997 (with extra trks.)
Untitled/Columbia/1970
Farther Along/Columbia/1971

Roger McGuinn/Columbia/1973
Peace on You (McGuinn)/Columbia/1974
Roger McGuinn and Band/Columbia/1975
Cardiff Rose (McGuinn)/Columbia/1976
Thunderbyrd (McGuinn)/Columbia/1977
McGuinn, Clark, Hillman/Capitol/1979
City (MCH)/Capitol/1980
McGuinn-Hillman/Capitol/1980
The Byrds Boxed Set/Columbia/1990
Back From Rio (McGuinn)/Arista/1991
Live From Mars (McGuinn)/Hollywood/1996
Three Byrds Land in London (McGuinn, Clark, Hillman)/Strange Fruit/1997
"East Virginia Blues"; "Sugar Baby"; "James Alley Blues" (Roger McGuinn, Jeff Tweedy, Jay Farrar) on **The Harry Smith Connection: A Live Tribute**/ Smithsonian Folkways/1998
Byrdoholics (Live at the Piper Club with Gram Parsons)/1998
Bryd Parts/Raven Aust./1998

Roger McGuinn's Home Page
//pw2.netcom.com/~mcguinn/
(includes McGuinn's "Folk Den")

mcguinn@ix.netcom.com

The Byrd Watcher //ebni.com/byrds/
(the most comprehensive Byrds and alumni site)

The Byrd's Nest //www.waxing-eloquent.com/byrds/
(contains the Byrdmaniax mailing list)

Kevin's Byrds Page
//www.geocities.com/HollywoodHills/3120/music.htm

Jonathan Bennett's Byrds Page
//www.geocities.com/SunsetStrip/palms/2522/byrds.html

Niklas's Byrds Page //orthanc.campus.luth.se/~niklas/byrds/

Byrds On-Line Appreciation Society
//members.aol.com/byrdsonline/byrdsstuff/byrds.htm

The Byrds On-Line Newsgroup alt.music.byrds

See Gene Clark; Sid Griffin; Chris Hillman; Nashville West; Gene Parsons; Gram Parsons; Clarence White

The Cache Valley Drifters (The Acousticats; Cyrus Clarke Band; Rincon Ramblers)
Progressive Bluegrass; New Old-Time
Santa Barbara, California; Late 1970s-Early 1980s and 1995-

In the 1970s and 1980s, some of the best progressive bluegrass came out of California. One of the most innovative groups was the Cache Valley Drifters who weren't afraid to mix traditional bluegrass with country, swing, and even rock. On three albums for Flying Fish, **New Cache Valley Drifters**, **Step up to Big Pay**, and **Tools of the Trade**, the Drifters covered standards but also transformed songs by the Grateful Dead ("Cumberland Blues"), John Prine ("Hello in There"), and other modern artists into bluegrass numbers. They were well known for their dynamic live performances and perennial favorites on the festival circuit. In the late 1980s, the group went on a long hiatus with individual members moving on to various projects. Cyrus Clarke joined the Acousticats who between 1990-1995 cut two records and had a solid reputation based on hot twin fiddles and inventive bluegrass/old-time style. Clarke currently heads the Cyrus Clarke Band which specializes in California folk, country rock, and honky tonk.

Occasionally, the Cache Valley Drifters have reunited and in 1993 recorded a live set on radio station KPFK. Later, when the Acousticats broke up, guitarist Mike Mullins teamed with Bill Griffin, David West, and new bass player Wally Barnick in a revamped Cache Valley Drifters. Their return debut was **White Room** (1996) which continued where they left off with classics ("I Thought I Heard You Calling"), covers of Cream ("White Room") and Paul Simon ("Boy in the Bubble") along with imaginative bluegrass originals such as "Opal Eyes" and "Yacht Crash." In late 1996, fiddler and former Acousticat Phil Salazar replaced West who later produced a tribute album called **Pickin' on the Grateful Dead** and made a solo recording of down home music (**Arcane**) with Byron Berline, Glen D. Hardin, Chris Hillman, and Drifters past and present. Salazar is also a member of the folk/bluegrass band, the Rincon Ramblers. Into 1999, the Cache Valley Drifters could be found every Wednesday night at the Cold Spring Tavern in Santa Barbara.

Original Members: Cyrus Clarke (g,v); Bill Griffin (md,v); Tom Lee (b); David West (g,v)
Current Members: Wally Barnick (b,v); Bill Griffin (g,md,v); Mike Mullins (g,md,v); Phil Salazar (f,v)
The Acousticats: Rick Borella (b); Cyrus Clarke (g,v); Tom Corbett (g,md); Charl Ann Gastineau (f); Mike Mullins (g,md); Phil Salazar (f,v)
The Cyrus Clarke Band: Cyrus Clarke (a.g.,v); Tom Corbett (md); Tom Lackner (d); Gary Sangenitto (b); Barney Tower (e.g.)
The Rincon Ramblers: Bill Flores (acc,db,p.s.); Phil Salazar (f,l.v.h.v.); Alan Thornhill (g,l.v.,h.v.); Jon Wilcox (md,l.v.h.v.); Dan Wilson (b,g)

  New Cache Valley Drifters/Flying Fish/1979
  Step Up to Big Pay/Flying Fish/1980
  Tools of the Trade (Live at McCabe's)/Flying Fish/1981
  Down at Evangelina's (Acousticats)/Flying Fish/1992
  Live on KPFK "Folkscene" 8-1-93/KPFK/1993
  The Cat's Meow (Acousticats)/Ranch Music/1994
  White Room/CMH/1996 (released in Europe as **Echoes and Reflections**/Taxim/1996)
  Arcane (David West)/Sage Arts/1997
  Sunrise on the Radio (Cyrus Clarke Band)/Ranch/1998
  The Green Rolling Hills of La Conchita (Rincon Ramblers)/Matilija/1998

Cache Valley Drifters Page
//www.mandozine.com/depatments/spotlight/spotlight.cvd.html

Bill Griffin: chuba@rain.org

Phil Salazar's "Om" Page
//www.west.net/~psalazar/cacheval.html

psalazar@west.net

The Cyrus Clarke Band
//www.sevensouth.com/recordshop/clarkecy/clarkecy.html

cyclarke@west.net

The Rincon Ramblers
//www.sevensouth.com/recordshop/rinconra/rinconra.html

Wilcoxfree@aol.com

The Cactus Brothers (David Schnaufer)
Country Rock
Nashville, Tennessee; 1993-1996

The Cactus Brothers grew out of roots band Walk the West which was founded in the late 1980s by Paul Kirby and John and Will Goleman. After adding dulcimer wiz David Schnaufer, steel player Sam Poland, and multi-instrumentalist Tramp in 1993, they changed their name to the Cactus Brothes. The group blended a variety of styles from old-time to honky tonk, country rock to punk and while such experimentation can be risky, they pulled it off through restraint and decent musicianship. After a self-titled debut and follow-up, **24 Hrs., 7 Days a Week**, failed to make any headway, the Cactus Brothers called it quits. Paul Kirby went on to a solo career while Tramp became a member of Bonepony.

David Schnaufer was only with the Cactus Brothers for their debut, then carved out a special niche in progressive old-time music on several solo recordings. Like other musicians who have taken traditional instruments in new directions, Schnaufer breathed new life into the lowly hammered dulcimer which was long associated with polite parlor or folk music. Joined by innovators like Jerry Douglas, Bela Fleck, Joe Goldmark, and Mark O'Connor and by his Cactus Brother mates, he works his dulcimer magic on country and folk standards as well as modern day pop music. Today, Schnaufer is a member of the String Faculty at Vanderbilt's Blair School of Music along with Butch Baldassari, Edgar Meyer, and Mark O'Connor.

Walk the West: John Golemon (b); Will Goleman (l.g.); Richard Ice (d); Paul Kirby (g,v)
The Cactus Brothers: Jim Fungaroli (s.g.,1994-); John Golemon (b); Will Golemon (bj,g); David Kennedy (d); Paul Kirby (g,l.v.); Sam Poland (db,p.s.); David Schnaufer (dulc., to 1994); Tramp (f,g,md,v); Johnny Tulucci (d)

  Walk the West/Capitol/1986
  Dulcimer Player (David Schnaufer)/Smithsonian Folkways/1989
  Dulcimer Deluxe (David Schnaufer)/SFL/1990
  Dulcimer Player Deluxe (David Schnaufer)/SFL/1991
  Dulcimer Sessions (David Schnaufer)/SFL/1992
  Cactus Brothers/Liberty/1993
  24 Hrs., 7 Days a Week/Liberty/1995

David Schnaufer Home Page //www.mlapulse.com/david schnaufer/davids.html

David@mlapulse.com

Jean Caffeine

Rig Rock; Honky Tonk; Singer/Songwriter
San Francisco, California; 1960-

Jean Caffeine began her musical career in California in the late 1970s as a drummer in the all girl punk band the Urge. Moving to New York City in 1980, she worked as a nightclub DJ and became drummer for another all girl band, Pulsallama. Noted primarily for theatrical stage shows and a fun loving approach, Pulsallama had one minor underground hit, "The Devil Lives in My Husband's Body" (about a guy with Tourette's Syndrome) and opened a few shows for the Clash. After the band's demise (their record company ran out of money), Caffeine assembled yet another all female band, Clambake. It was short lived but included several Austin, Texas natives who gave Caffeine the idea she might have better luck there. Relocating to Austin in the mid-1980s, Jean put together an alt. country unit, Jean Caffeine's All-Nite Truckstop, that played a self described mix of "electrified porch music and garage country." Over the years, the band had a rotating collection of Austin musicians including Brent Wilson (Wagoneers), Mark Rubin (Bad Livers), Champ Hood (Threadgill's Troubadours, Toni Price), Mike Buck (Fabulous Thunderbirds), Charlie Llewellin (Gourds), Lisa Pancratz, Amy Tiven, and many others. In 1990, the All-Nite Truckstop cut a self-titled, self-released cassette which was released the next year on the German label Blue Million Miles. It combined country/rock/punk highlighted by Caffeine's originals ranging from sentimental ("Tears Away" and "Hole in My Heart") to comical ("You're Like a Mosquito," "That Was the Liquor Talkin'," "What's So Happy About Happy Hour?," and "Jesus Is Coming To A Theater Near You"). They followed it up with another cassette **Hard Work and a Lot of Hair Spray** produced by Gurf Morlix. This recording drew attention from Diesel Only which put out a single of "Hard Work" (b/w "Hoe-down in the Sky") in 1992 and later included "Hoe-down" on **Rig Rock Truck Stop**. All-Nite Truckstop made four appearances at SXSW and toured both coasts and Europe but in the mid-1990s, Caffeine decided to drop the honky tonk persona in favor of a more folk/rock oriented style. In 1997, with a new supporting cast of Austin musicians she recorded **Knocked Down 7 Times, Got Up 8** and released it on her Joe Records. Unlike, Caffeine's previous work, this effort is much more personal and introspective. As the title suggests, it explores, sometimes humorously, sometimes bitterly, life's ups and downs.

> **All-Nite Truckstop**/Porch Music/1990 (CS); Blue Millions Ger./1991 (CD)
> **Hardwork and a Lot of Hairspray**/Porch Music/1992
> "Hardwork and a Lot of Hairspray" b/w "Hoe-down in the Sky"/Diesel Only/1992
> "Hoe-down in the Sky" on **Rig Rock Truck Stop**/Diesel Only/1992
> **Knocked Down 7 Times, Got Up 8**/Joe/1997

Jean Caffeine Home Page //www.io.com/~jeancaf/
jeancaf@io.com

Calexico

See Giant Sand

The California Cajun Orchestra

Modern/Traditional Cajun
San Francisco, California; 1980s-

By all accounts, the hottest and most popular Cajun dance band on the West Coast is the California Cajun Orchestra. They have been playing the Bay Area dance circuit since the 1980s, and it's easy to understand the reason for their success. First of all, the CCO is blessed with superior musicians. Their leader, accordionist Danny Poullard, hails from Eunice, Louisiana, the traditional hotbed of Cajun music, and his virtuosity has placed him in the front ranks of contemporary Cajun accordion players. Adding to the unique sound of the group is the twin fiddle work of Kevin Wimmer and Suzy Thompson. The former studied with Dewey Balfa and is a member of Balfa Toujours, the heir apparent to the Balfa Brothers tradition. Thompson likewise studied with Dewey Balfa in the 1980s and in the early 1990s met and studied accordion with Poullard. She has performed as a duo with CCO guitarist Eric Thompson whose credentials include work in bluegrass bands with Jerry Garcia (Black Mountain Boys) and David Grisman (New York Ramblers) in the early 1960s plus sessions with Dr. Humbead's New Tranquillity String Band and the Graineog Ceilidh Band. Suzy and Eric recorded **Adam and Eve Had the Blues**, a mix of Cajun, string band, hillbilly, and blues, and are the leaders of another fine progressive Cajun band, the Aux Cajunals. Rounding out the CCO is the first-rate rhythm section of Terry O'Dwyer on drums, Sam Siggins on bass, and Charlie St. Mary on rub board.

Next to musicianship, the key to the CCO is their selection of material. Their recordings, **Not Lonesome Anymore** and **Nonc Adam Two-Step**, offer spirited covers of standards by the greats of Cajun and zydeco (Amede Ardoin, Joe Falcon, Iry LeJeune, the Balfas, Boozoo Chavis, et al.) and inspired originals, many written by Danny Poullard's father John who was a renowned accordionist in the Eunice area. Finally, the CCO have an obvious joy in and love for the music. They know that, above all, Cajun music is there to make people happy and get them up dancing. The industry took notice too in 1996 when NAIRD awarded an Indie to **Nonc Adam Two-Step** for Best Cajun/Zydeco Album of the Year (co-winners with Steve Riley).

The California Cajun Orchestra: Terry O'Dwyer (d); Danny Poullard (acc,v); Charlie St. Mary (rb); Sam Siggins (b); Eric Thompson (g); Suzy Thompson (f,v); Kevin

Wimmer (f,v)

The Aux Cajunals: Agi Ban (f); Alan Senauke (g); Eric Thompson (f,g,v); Suzy Thompson (acc,f,v)

Not Lonesome Anywhere/Arhoolie/1993
Adam and Eve Had the Blues (Eric & Suzy Thompson)/Arhoolie/1994
Nonc Adam Two-Step/Arhoolie/1995
"Baby Please Don't Go" (Aux Cajunals) on **The American Fogies, Vol. 1**/Rounder/1996
"John Poullard Special" on **American Fogies, Vol. 2**/Rounder/1996

Suzy Thompson: Cleoma@aol.com

See Balfa Brothers/Balfa Toujours

The Calvins
"Original Alternative Hipbilly Americana"
Nashville, Tennessee; 1992-

In 1992, Royann and Jim Calvin married and moved to Nashville where they became popular regulars around Music City playing a mix of old-time, honky tonk, and country rock they like to call "original alternative hipbilly Americana." Along the way, the Calvins have made some solid musical friends (Bill Monroe, Jimmy Martin, Byron Berline, Peter Rowan, Josh Graves, BR5-49, Greg Garing) who played with them live and/or as guests on their three recordings: **A Little O'Dis A Little O' Dat**, **Original Acoustic Music**, and **Hillbilly Boogaroo**. After earning enough money working two seasons at Dollywood, in 1996, they purchased a farm outside Nashville where they discovered that one of their neighbors was none other than Townes Van Zandt. The multi-instrumental (banjo, dobro, fiddle, guitar, mandolin) talents of Jim and Royann impressed Townes, and he eventually hired them as his opening act as well as live back up and studio band. Their first performance was at the Ryman for the Walter Hyatt tribute show where Townes covered "The Early Days With You." Subsequently, the Calvins accompanied Van Zandt on his final tour, performed on **The Highway Kind**, and stayed with him until his death at the beginning of 1997. A year and half later, the Calvins were set to host a "TownesFest" in Nashville when Royann suffered severe facial damage in a bicycle accident. The show went on, but the Calvins didn't play and had to cancel their musical plans until Royann could recover. They incurred some hefty medical expenses, and their musical friends rallied around them with donations and benefits. You can help out too by sending what you can to the address below.

Jim Calvin (bj,db,f,g,md,v); Royann Calvin (spoons,v)

A Little O' Dis A Little O' Dat (Jim Calvin)/ Bouncing Bow/1994
Original Acoustic Music/Bouncing Bow/1995
Hillbilly Boogaroo/Bouncing Bow/1996
"Try It Again" on **Nashville: The Other Side of the Alley**/Bloodshot/1996

The Calvins, P.O. Box 24663, Nashville, TN 37202; 615-742-4050, (fax) 615-758-6186

The Calvins Page //www.recoveryroadmusic.com/calvins/
calvinsmusic@webtv.net

Kate Campbell
Singer/Songwriter
Sledge, Mississippi

The South figures prominently in the music of many alt. country performers. On one hand are groups like Southern Culture on the Skids or the Drive-By Truckers who parody/celebrate/denigrate (depending on your perspective) many of the stereotypes (rednecks; white trash) closely associated with the South; on the other hand, there are artists who take a more balanced approach. One of these is Kate Campbell who not only has a gorgeous voice but writes lyrics that show a lot of deep and perceptive thinking about the meanings of the Southern culture. Although based in Nashville for some time, she was raised in rural Mississippi, and it is that experience that dominates her work. In a revealing interview for the 1997 Southern Music issue of *Oxford American* magazine, Campbell expressed her affection for Southern musical styles and spelled out the themes she thinks are most important to an understanding of the South: land, race, religion. Each of her three albums contain numerous references to each of these and are built on a solid country/folk/blues/gospel foundation. Neither critic or apologist, Kate isn't afraid to tackle tough issues like racism ("Crazy in Alabama") and poverty ("Visions of Plenty"), and she has a wry take on some of the quirkier sides of Southern living ("Bowl-A-Rama"; "Moonpie Dreams"; "See Rock City"). And while generally con- sidered a "folk" artist in the U.S., Campbell's **Moonpie Dreams** was selected Best Country Album of the Year (1997) by England's *Mojo* magazine.

Songs From the Levee/Large River/1994; Compass/1997
Moonpie Dreams/Compass/1997
Visions of Plenty/Compass/1998
"Crazy in Alabama" on **Sounds of the New West: The Best of Alternative Country**/Uncut UK/1998

Kate Campbell c/o Large River Music,
P.O. Box 121743, Nashville, TN 37212

Kate Campbell Home Page
//www.ccn.cs.dal.ca/~ac490/kate.html

Kate Campbell/Compass Records Page
//www.compassrecords.com/campbell.htm

info@compassrecords.com

Sarah Elizabeth Campbell
Singer/Songwriter
Austin, Texas; May 13, 1953-

Over the past 25 years or so, Austin has been home to several generations of singer/songwriters. One whose career spans the whole period is Sarah Elizabeth Campbell. Although not as well known outside of Austin as some (Gilmore, Hancock, LaFave, et al.), she has, in her own way, been very influential in keeping the tradition alive. A native Austinite, Campbell came from a musical family and in her late teens entered the folk scene that was growing up around the University of Texas. Still, she felt the need for a greater challenge and headed to California where she was a member of the Fiddlestix bluegrass band for a dozen years. Shortly after parting from that group, Campbell started touring around folk festivals as a solo and in 1992 recorded her first record, **A Little Tenderness**, backed by musicians from the Good Ol' Persons and guitarist Nina Gerber who also served as producer. The album went out of circulation shortly thereafter but several songs from it were covered by members of The Band, Jim Messina, and the Blue Rose Band (with Laurie Lewis). Faced with a choice of remaining in the San Francisco area or moving back to Austin, Sarah chose the latter when the big earthquake hit in 1993. Her wonderful voice and exuberant personality quickly won her a following, and in 1994, she recorded **Running With You** on Dejadisc which re-released **A Little Tenderness** in 1995. For several years, Campbell hosted a weekly "Bummer Night" at La Zona Rosa and Artz Rib House. This weekly showcase for singer/songwriters was very beneficial to both established and emerging artists. Into the late 1990s, she was a staff writer for John Prine's Oh Boy! Records.

A Little Tenderness/Kaleidoscope/1992; Dejadisc/1995
Running With You/Dejadisc/1994

Sarah Elizabeth Campbell/Dejadisc Page
//www.eden.com/~dejadisc/campbell.html

Sayraliz@aol.com

Camper Van Beethoven

Roots Rock
Redlands, California; 1984-1990

In the late 1980s, this group of musical tricksters built a cult following by tweeking the nose of musical convention. They served up a glorious mess of rock, country, bluegrass, polka, Cajun, folk, Middle Eastern, Indian, and reggae on clever covers and wickedly witty originals by David Lowery: "ZZ Top Goes to Egypt," "Take the Skinheads Bowling," "Interstellar Overdrive," "The Day Lassie Went to the Moon," and "I Was Born In a Laundromat." In lesser hands, the mixing of traditional and not so traditional instruments and sounds could have spun hopelessly out of control, but CVB had the musicianship to pull it off. On their 1986 **Camper Van Beethoven**, they were joined by avant-gardist Eugene Chadbourne and later guested on **Camper Van Chadbourne** and **Eugene Van Beethoven's 69th Sin Funny**, two bizarre sessions of irreverent covers (Pink Floyd, Frank Zappa, Tim Hardin), post-modern country, and assorted weirdness. After CVB's break-up in 1990, Krummenacher, Lisher, and Pederson went on to form the Monks of Doom while Segal produced the debut of another Bay Area alt.

country group, Granfaloon Bus. Lowery started Cracker and became a producer working with "Bavarian hillbilly" band FSK and with Sparklehorse/Mark Linkous. As David Charles, Lowery played drums and guitar on the latter's 1995 debut **Vivadixiesubmarinetransmissionplot**.

Victor Krummenacher (b,v); Greg Lisher (g,v); David Lowery (g,v); Chris Molla (g,1984-1987); Chris Pederson (d,1986-); Jonathan Segal (g,vio,v,1984-1989)

> **Telephone Free Landslide Victory**/Independent Project
>   Rough Trade/1985
> **Take the Skinheads Bowling**/Pitch-A-Tent Rough
>   Trade/1986 (EP)
> **II&III**/Pitch-A-Tent Rough Trade/1986
> **Camper Van Beethoven**/Pitch-A-Tent Rough Trade/1986
> **Vampire Can Mating Oven**/Pitch-A-Tent Rough
>   Trade/1987 (EP)
> **Camper Van Chadbourne**/Fundamental/1987
> **Eugene Van Beethoven's 69th Sin Funny**/
>   Fundamental/1988
> **Our Beloved Revolutionary Sweetheart**/ Virgin/1988
> **Key Lime Pie**/Virgin/1989

Camper Van-Etc Central
//reality.sgi.com/relph/campervan-etc/

David Lowery Home Page //members.aol.com/mccrackered/

See Eugene Chadbourne; FSK; Granfaloon Bus; Sparklehorse

Ray Campi

Rockabilly; Hillbilly Bop
New York, New York; April 20, 1934-

Running almost a half century, Ray Campi's career as a rockabilly/country performer has been one wild roller coaster ride. Born in New York City, his family relocated to Central Texas during WWII where Campi, influenced by Western swing, formed Ramblin' Ray & the Ramblers. In the 1950s, Campi made the transition from Western swing to rockabilly but, enjoying limited success, quit music for teaching (in California) before Ron Weiser of Rollin' Rock Records convinced him to take it up once more. Campi's discs for that label are now considered classics and they, along with constant touring (often with the Rockabilly Rebels), made him a cult star in Europe. Renowned for his stage antics on slap bass, Campi had his ups and downs in the 1970s but got a big boost from the 1980s and 1990s rockabilly revivals. New recordings for Flying Fish and Rounder as well as various compilations (**Perpetual Stomp**) of his older material vividly demonstrate his adeptness not only at rockabilly but also straight country and Western swing. Ray's important body of work for Rollin' Rock was reissued on several import labels and in the U.S. by Hightone as **Rockabilly Rebellion: The Best of Ray Campi., Vol. 1** in 1997. His **Train Rhythm Blue** as the Ray Campi Quartet with D. J. Bonebrake, Skip Heller, and Rip Masters is a somewhat uneven collection of rockabilly, honky tonk, and country ballads. Throughout 1998-1999, Ray remained a hot ticket on the rockabilly circuit with appearances at Ronnie Mack's Barn Dance, Greaseball, and several European tours.

Gone, Gone, Gone/Rounder/1980
The Original Rockabilly Album/Magnum Force UK/1990
Ray Campi With Friends in Texas/Flying Fish/1991
Eager Beaver Boy/Rockabilly/Bear Family Ger./1993 (Rollin' Rock material)
Taylor, Texas 1988/Bear Family Ger./1993
Hollywood Cats/Part UK/1994 (reissue of Rollin' Rock material)
Rockabilly Rocket/Magnum Force UK/1994 (reissue of Rollin' Rock material)
Rockin' Around the House/Rockhouse Dut./1994
The History of D Records/Starday/1996
Perpetual Stomp: Anthology, 1951-1996/ Dionysus/1997
A Little Bit of Heartache (with Rosie Flores)/ Rounder 1997
Rockabilly Rebellion: The Best of Ray Campi/ HMG/1997
Train Rhythm Blue/Sci-Fi Western/1998

Ray Campi Home Page //www.electricearl.com/campi.html

Jim Campilongo & The Ten Gallon Cats (The Jim Campilongo Band)

Guitar and Pedal Steel Instrumentals; Country/Swing/Rock
San Francisco, California; 1995-

One of the musical highlights of 1995 was the release of **Stratosphere Boogie** which brought together the best instrumentals of the great 1950s duo Speedy West on pedal steel and Jimmy Bryant on electric guitar. This tradition of hot hillbilly picking which was expressed by other famous pairs including Leon McAuliffe/Eldon Shamblin, Jimmie Rivers/Vance Terry is currently being carried on by Jim Campilongo and Joe Goldmark. Campilongo formed the Ten Gallon Cats in 1995, and to compliment his lead work which reflects everyone from Joe Maphis to Scotty Moore to Jimi Hendrix, he chose Goldmark who had long been a presence on the local music scene noted for his highly experimental steel playing (for more on him, see Joe Goldmark). In less than a year, they nailed down a weekly gig at the Paradise Lounge and gathered an enthusiastic following. In late 1995 came a self-titled debut, an eclectic album of ten Campilongo instrumental originals that veers in many directions but is held together by the amazing duets and solos of Goldmark and Campilongo. For his stellar guitar work, Campilongo was nominated for the Best Bay Area Guitar Player award in 1996. And though he didn't win, Jim and his band earned a bigger prize when they won the 1996 BAMMIE for Best Alternative Band. Hot on the heels of this success, they released **Loose** (described by one reviewer as "Joe Maphis-on-acid") another great selection of hillbilly/swing/jazz/rock with two covers ("Mr. Sandman"; "Harlem Nocturne") and nine searing originals. In 1997, Jim Campilongo and the Cats served as the backing band for Peter Rowan at the High Sierra and Telluride music festivals. As a side project, in 1998, Jim

formed the Jim Campilongo Band and cut **Table for One**, another tasty dish of hot guitar (electric and acoustic) with more emphasis on blues and jazz than country.

Jim Campilongo & The Ten Gallon Cats: Jim Campilongo (l.g.); Joe Goldmark (p.s.); Chris Kee (b); Ken Owen (d)
The Jim Campilongo Band: Jim Campilongo (l.g.); Rob Burger (acc,org); Chris Kee (b); Jason Lewis (d)

Jim Campilongo & The Ten Gallon Cats/Blue Hen/1995
Loose/Blue Hen/1997
Table for One (Jim Campilongo Band)/Blue Hen/1998

Jim Campilongo/Blue Hen Records, 900 Chestnut St #302, San Francisco, CA 94109; 415-928-4704 (ph./fax)

Jim Campilongo/Blue Hen Home Page //www.bluehenrecords.com

info@bluehenrecords.com

See Joe Goldmark

Scott Carpenter & The Real McCoys

Roots Rock
Buffalo, New York; 1994-

By all accounts, the best roots rock venue in Buffalo, New York is Mohawk Place. It's been host to many of the top touring acts in the 1990s, but without doubt the most popular local act to play there in recent years has been Scott Carpenter & The Real McCoys. Their combination of 50s rock, honky tonk, country rock, punk, blues, and ballads has packed 'em in regularly although the initimate 100 year old pub scarcely seems able to contain their powerhouse sound as evidenced on the 1996, **Live From Mohawk Place**. Founder and lead vocalist Scott Carpenter has been performing in Buffalo's music clubs since age 16 and did his first recording as Scott Carpenter & The Orbits in 1988 with current lead guitarist Matt Smith. They made their debut as the Real McCoys in 1994 with a self-titled tape and followed that with the Buffalo Music Award winning **2 A.M. Tragedy**, the live album, and **Dedicated Stroll** which brings all the elements together. Helping out on fiddle is Doug Moody of another fine Buffalo area alt. country group, the Steam Donkeys.

Scott Carpenter (r.g.,l.v.); Brian Daddis (d); Little Joe (b); Matt Smith (l.g.,v)

Scott Carpenter & The Orbits/SC/1988 (LP)
Scott Carpenter & The Real McCoys/SC/1994 (CS)
2 A.M. Tragedy/SC/1995
Live From Mohawk Place/SC/1996
Dedicated Stroll/SC/1998

Scott Carpenter & The Real McCoys Home Page //www.wnywebshop.com/scotcarp.htm

See The Steam Donkeys

The Carpetbaggers

Honky Tonk; Rockabilly
Edina, Minnesota; 1991-

On the crabgrass frontier of Edina, Minnesota (outside of Minneapolis), the Carpetbaggers captured a little corner of one of alt. country's most significant scenes. Unlike the Jayhawks, Golden Smog, and other country/roots/rock bands from the area, the 'Baggers play an infectious blend of honky tonk and rockabilly full of quirky songs, hillbilly harmonies, and twangy picking. This trio couldn't look less like a hard-core country band, but **Country Miles Apart** and **Nowhere to Go But Down** are chock full of catchy honky tonk/hillbilly tunes like "My Reasons for Living Are Killing Me," "Always a Pall Bearer," "Empties at My Feet," and "I'm Not Long for This Girl." These early recordings produced a sizable local following and support from groups like Soul Asylum and Son Volt who asked them to open their 1996 tour. This and a move to the higher profile roots label Hightone widened the Carpetbaggers fan base. **Sin Now...Pray Later** is another fun house of hillbilly, honky tonk songs including the title tune, "I Guess I'm Crazy," "My Jeannie's in a Bottle," and "Suburban Boy," an amusing spin on John Denver's "Thank God, I'm a Country Boy."

Rich Copley (b,v); Mike Crabtree (g,v); John Magnuson (g,v)

Country Miles Apart/Clean Restless/1992
Nowhere to Go But Down/Clean Restless/1994
Sin Now...Pray Later/Hightone/1996

The Carpetbaggers //tt.net/clean/carpetbaggers.html

Tim Carroll (The Blue Chieftains)

Rig Rock; Insurgent Country

Along with Courtney & Western, Go To Blazes, Angel Dean, and the World Famous Blue Jays, the Blue Chieftains were a vital part of the alternative country scene that emerged in New York City in the late 1980s. They were very popular on the club circuit, and in 1990, their song "Punk Rockin' Honky Tonk Girl" was one of two inaugural singles (the other was "Good Morning Mr. Trucker" by the World Famous Blue Jays) for the Diesel Only label. It was followed by "I Think Hank Woulda Done It This Way" and both along with "After the Hurricane" were included on the Diesel Only compilations, **Rig Rock Juke Box** and **Rig Rock Truckstop**. A number of reviews of these collections selected the Chieftains contributions as the highlight for their hard driving country rock sound but mostly for the twangy vocals and witty songwriting of Tim Carroll e.g. "She thinks about Sid as much as thinkin' about Merle, she's a punk rockin' honky tonk girl" (compare with BR5-49's "Little Ramona's Gone Hillbilly Nuts") or the rockers answer to Waylon Jenning's Hank Williams song which insists that "rock 'n' roll is what he played, I think Hank woulda done it this way."

In 1993, the Blue Chieftains went on "leave" which allowed individual members to pursue other projects. Most notably, Antonakos joined Five Chinese Brothers while Carroll moved to Nashville to begin a solo career. He became part of Music City's alt. country underground doing session work with Lonesome Bob and contributing "Open Flame" to **Nashville: The Other Side of the Alley**. In 1996, Tim did an EP **Good Rock From Bad** on the Swedish Sound Asleep label that presents some new material and updated versions of Carroll's best from his Blue Chieftain days. A full-length solo recording, **Rock & Roll Band**, was delayed for a couple of years before finally coming out in 1999. This collection of reworked ("After the Hurricane"; "Good Cry") and new ("When She Wants to Cry"; "The House That Ruth Tore Down"; "Girl That's Hip") roots rock was one of the best of the year.

The Blue Chieftains: Tim Carroll (l.v, g); Steve Antonakos (e.g., sl.g.); Scott Yoder (b); Mark Horn (d) with Howie Wyeth (p); Gib Wharton (p.s.)

"Punk Rockin' Honky Tonk Girl" b/w "I Would If I Could" (Blue Chieftains)/Diesel Only/1990 (7")
"I Think Hank Woulda Done It This Way" b/w "After the Hurricane" (Blue Chieftains)/Diesel Only/1992 (7")
"Punk Rockin' Honky Tonk Girl" and "I Think Hank Woulda Done It This Way"(Blue Chieftains) on **Rig Rock Juke Box**/Diesel Only/1992
"Illegal Smile" (Blue Chieftains) on **Marijuana's Greatest Hits**/Re-Hash/1992
"After the Hurricane"(Blue Chieftains) on **Rig Rock Truck Stop**/Diesel Only/1993
Good Rock From Bad (Tim Carroll)/Sound Asleep Swe./1996 (7 trk.EP CD)
"Good Cry" (Tim Carroll) on **Hit the Hay 2**/Sound Asleep Swe./1996
"Open Flame" (Tim Carroll) on **Nashville: The Other Side of the Alley**/Bloodshot/1996
Rock & Roll Band/Sire/1999

Tim Carroll, 2003 Graybar Ln., Nashville, TN 37215-2111; 615-297-1825

The Cartwrights

See Donny Ray Ford

Neal Casal

Singer/Songwriter; Lo-Fi
Denville, New Jersey; November 2, 1968-

In the summer of 1995, Zoo Records released the debut recording of a young California musician named Neal Casal. **Fade Away Diamond Time** was a record which seemed to have everything going for it: an appealing selection of bitter sweet songs and vocals (early Jackson Browne comes to mind), fine, laid-back accompaniment highlighted by the organ of John Ginty and the pedal steel of Fooch Fischetti and Greg Leisz plus a "feel" that put it on an equal footing with some of the best lo-fi alt. country. As the title of the opening song suggested, Neal Casal's "Day in the Sun" was about to come. But then, on the eve of a supporting tour, his record company experienced a number of shakeups and suddenly, Casal was a man without a label. With the rug pulled out from under his fledgling career, he could have easily become just another casualty of the music business. Instead, after a brief grieving period, Casal returned to the studio and made **Rain, Wind, and Speed** for the independent Buy or Die label. Here, on this generally acoustic effort, he found a place to pour out the bitter experience of the past year. Casal's very moody, understated style (*a la* Richard Buckner, Gary Heffern) drew interest from that haven for under appreciated American artists, Glitterhouse. In late 1996, they re-released **Rain, Wind, and Speed** and in 1997 presented **Field Recordings**, a limited edition (1,000 copies) collection of Neal Casal demos and outtakes from 1994-1997. His next full length recording, **The Sun Rises Here**, which came out in early 1998 with Don Heffington and Greg Leisz on board compares very favorably with **Fade Away Diamond Time**.

1998 was a busy year for Neal on the road playing guitar for Parlor James and touring Europe as part of the Glitterhouse Records showcase (with Hazeldine) and as a solo acoustic act. He also contributed some guitar work to James Iha's solo debut and showed up on a number of prominent alt. country/Americana compilations including **Loose** and **Sounds of the New West**. Glitterhouse and Casal just kept the quality flowing with yet another generous (25 tracks) CD, **Basement Dreams**, featuring material from 1996-1998.

Fade Away Diamond Time/Zoo/1995
Rain, Wind, and Speed/Buy or Die/1996; Glitterhouse Ger./1996
"Black Honey" on **Piss & Vinegar: The Songs of Graham Parker**/Buy or Die/1996
"Reason" on **Have One**/Glitterhouse Ger./1996
Field Recordings/Glitterhouse Ger./1997
"Eddy & Diamonds" on **Luxury Liner**/Glitterhouse Ger./1997
The Sun Rises Here/Glitterhouse Ger./1998
"All the Luck in the World" on **Loose: New Sounds of the Old West**/Vinyl Junkie UK/1998
"Today I'm Gonna Bleed" on **Sounds of the New West: The Best of Alternative Country**/Uncut UK/1998
Basement Dreams/Glitterhouse Ger./1998

Neal Casal/Morebarn Music, P.O. Box 1233, Morristown, NJ 07962-1233

Official Neal Casal Page //www.kikomusic.com/nealcasal/

Morebarn@aol.com

Cincinnati Motel: A Neal Site //www.geocities.com/SunsetStrip/palladium/8651/

Neal Casal/Buy or Die Web Page //www.buy-or-die.com/artists/nealcasal/

Neal Casal Fan Page //home.allgaeu.org/brosa/casal.htm

Neko Case (The Corn Sisters)
Insurgent Country
Alexandria, Virginia; September 8, 1970-

Tim Carroll's song "Punk Rockin' Honky Tonk Girl" could have been written with Neko Case in mind. Sharing a birth date and birth state with Patsy Cline, Neko Case had primarily been known for her work as drummer in the Canadian punk trio MAOW. However, underneath her hard core exterior beat a country heart and in 1997, Case recorded **The Virginian** for Mint Records which had also released MAOW's recordings. Backed by a band (Her Boyfriends) made up of Canadian rockers plus American bluegrasser John Reischman (mandolin), she croons and twangs her way through a fine selection of honky tonk and country rock with just a hint of a punk edge. Case acknowledges her country influences with covers of Loretta Lynn ("Somebody Led Me Away"), Ernest Tubb ("Thanks A Lot"), the Everlys ("Bowling Green") and chips in some credible originals ("High on Cruel"; "Lonely Old Lies"; "Honky Tonk Hiccups"). Based in Vancouver, Case also shows her country side playing snare with Carolyn Mark on acoustic guitar as the old-time country duo, the Corn Sisters. **The Virginian** was re-released in 1998 by Bloodshot which also issued **The Murder Ballads**, a split single with Case and up and coming Canadian roots rockers, the Sadies. For the remainder of the year, Case toured extensively (backed by the Sadies and Local Rabbits) making appearances at Blue Rodeo's Stardust Picnic and several stops on the Lilith Fair tour. In addition, she contributed "Stay a Little Longer" to Bloodshot's Bob Wills tribute album, did a split 7" with Whiskeytown, and released a live recording by the Corn Sisters (**The Other Woman**). Neko also completed her side of a Loretta Lynn tribute single (b/w Kelly Hogan) and began work on the follow-up to **The Virginian**.

The Virginian/Mint Can./1997; Bloodshot/1998
The Murder Ballads (Neko Case "Make Your Bed" b/w The Sadies)/Bloodshot/1998 (7")
"Stay a Little Longer" on **Pine Valley Cosmonauts Salute the Majesty of Bob Wills**/Bloodshot/1998
Car Songs (Whiskeytown "Highway 145" b/w Neko Case & The Sadies "My '63")/Bloodshot/1998 (7")
The Other Woman (The Corn Sisters)/1998
"Rated X" (Neko Case & The Sadies) b/w "Hanky Panky Woman" (Kelly Hogan)/Bloodshot/1999 (7")

Neko Case/Mint Records Home Page //www.mintrecs.com/bands/speak/neko/neko.html

Neko Case/Bloodshot Page //www.bloodshotrecords.com

See The Sadies

Peter Case
Singer/Songwriter
Buffalo, New York

In his teens and early twenties, Peter Case worked as a solo acoustic act playing blues, folk, and country on the streets or in the clubs of Buffalo, New York and then San Francisco. After stints as a rocker with the Nerves and the Plimsouls, he revived his solo career and after many border to border tours inked a deal with Geffen. Produced by T-Bone Burnett, **Peter Case** set the tone for his style with stories centered on the down-and-outers of America's wastelands (guest performers included Roger McGuinn, John Hiatt, and Victoria Williams to whom he was married from 1985-1989). His frank social commentary carried over to his 1989 **The Man With the Blue Postmodernist Fragmented Neo-Traditionalist Guitar** which helped put Case on the new singer/songwriter map. For **Six Pack of Love**, Case added a more rocked up sound and brought in several song writing collaborators including John Prine, Fred Koller, and Tom Russell and Bob Neuwirth on the memorable "Beyond the Blues." Peter was a logical choice for the Merle Haggard songwriter's tribute **Tulare Dust** that also included Russell, Iris DeMent, Joe Ely, Dave Alvin, and Lucinda Williams. However, things didn't go so well with Geffen; Case parted company with them in 1993 but was picked up by the more sympathetic Vanguard label. In 1996 came **Sings Like Hell**, a set of traditional blues, country, and folk, and it was followed by two moving albums of intelligent observation and introspection, **Torn Again** and **Full Service, No Waiting**.

Peter Case/Geffen/1986
**The Man With the Blue Postmodernist Fragmented
   Neo-Traditionalist Guitar**/ Geffen/1989
Six Pack of Love/Geffen/1992
"A Working Man Can't Get Nowhere Today" on T**ulare
   Dust: A Songwriter's Tribute to Merle
   Haggard**/Hightone/1994
Peter Case Sings Like Hell/Vanguard/1996
Torn Again/Vanguard/1997
Full Service, No Waiting/Vanguard/1998

Peter Case Home Page //www.jetpack.com/petercase/

Johnny Cash
Singer/Songwriter
Kingsland, Arkansas; February 26, 1932-

One of the giants of American music in the past 50 years, Johnny Cash has had a major impact on several generations of alternative country. In the late 1960s, he did a duet with Bob Dylan ("Girl From the North Country") on **Nashville Skyline** and invited Bob to appear on his popular television show. During Dylan's sojourn in Nashville, Cash cut a number of traditional country songs with him and these (along with tracks from the *Johnny Cash Show* and quadmasters from **Nashville Skyline**) were released in 1995 on Red Robin Records as the **Dylan/Cash Sessions**. On these landmark recordings, Bob and Johnny trade off and harmonize on standards ("Mountain Dew"; "I Still Miss Someone"; "Careless Love"; "Matchbox"; "That's Alright Mama"; "Blue Yodel") and Cash classics ("Big River"; "I Walk the Line"; "Ring of Fire"; "I Guess Things

Happen That Way"). The informality of the sessions, signature Johnny Cash country sound, and playful exchanges make this a delight from start to finish. Throughout the 1970s and early 1980s, Cash's music exerted its influence on each new cycle of alternative country, but it became especially strong beginning in the late 1980s. In 1988, Jon Langford paid tribute to Cash on a collection of covers **'Til Things Are Brighter** with Michelle Shocked, Sally Timms, the Mekons, Brendan Croker, and others. When the latest alt. country wave hit in the 1990s, Cash became mentor to a new generation of fans and musicians through his **American Recordings.** Here, it's just Johnny and his guitar, but the effect is powerful and signaled a triumphant return. More material from these great sessions recorded in producer Rick Rubin's living room in 1993 are available on a bootleg entitled **American Outtakes**. In 1994, Cash performed during SXSW before an exuberant crowd of country and punk fans at the legendary Emo's and got the same reception from similar audiences throughout the U.S. His standing within the alt. country community was further cemented by **Unchained** which finds Cash backed by Tom Petty and the Heartbreakers. Unfortunately, in late 1997, just after the publication of his autobiography and while on tour, Cash announced he had been diagnosed with a form of Parkinson's ("Shy Drager Syndrome"). The debilitating effects of the disease cast a giant shadow of doubt over the Man in Black's performing and recording future. However, Cash did get some good news when **Unchained** won the Grammy for Best Country Album. He then took out a full page ad in Billboard "thanking" (shooting the finger) the Nashville establishment and country radio for their "support." American Recordings released the Johnny Cash/Willie Nelson summit **Storytellers** in mid-1998 but, by the end of the year, things were looking bleak for JC once again as bouts with pneumonia put him in and out of the hospital.

Dylan/Cash Sessions (1969)/Red Robin/1995
American Recordings/American/1994
American Outtakes/Empire/1995
Unchained/American/1996
Storytellers (with Willie Nelson)/American
   Recordings/1998
"Washed My Face in the Morning Dew" on **Real: The
   Tom T. Hall Project, Vol. 1**/ Watermelon/1998

The Official Johnny Cash Page //www.johnnycash.com

Johnny Cash/American Recordings Page
//american.recordings.com

Johnny Cash: An American Legend
//www.odysseygroup.com/cash/legend.html
(fan page with lots of details on "The Man in Black")

Johnny Cash Online Mailing List //www.onelist.com (under Country)

See Bob Dylan

Eugene Chadbourne

Avant-Garde
Mt. Vernon, New York; January 4, 1954-

Like many youngsters of his generation, Eugene Chadbourne was first inspired to pick up an electric guitar after exposure to the Beatles, Jimi Hendrix, et al., but unlike most of his peers, he was not content with this music and ventured off in a number of unexpected directions. In his late teens, while living in Colorado, Chadbourne first heard blues and jazz on an independent Boulder radio station and decided to switch to an acoustic guitar so he could learn bottleneck style. Then, in 1970 when he moved to Calgary, Canada to avoid the draft, Eugene found himself attracted to the local free jazz scene as exemplified in the works of Coltrane, Braxton, Sanders, and Coleman. Weaving together these various influences, he began performing and making home made recordings. When amnesty was declared in 1977, Chadbourne returned to America (New York) and became a full time musician. In the meantime, he branched out into other genres including country and western to which he brought avant-garde's improvisational spirit. His first foray into country, **There'll Be No Tears Tonight,** was variously described as "free improvised country & western bebop," "Hank Williams on LSD," or "Waylon Jennings meets the Sex Pistols." It has *very* experimental covers of Hank Williams, Ernest Tubb, David Allan Coe, Merle Haggard, Willie Nelson, and Bobby Bare and featured fellow musical innovators John Zorn and Tom Cora. And while they play it straight at times, most of the record stretches country to the outer limits and beyond. Over the years, in between a wide variety of projects including recordings with Camper Van Beethoven, Evan Johns, and Shockabilly, Chadbourne did a number of other "country" projects: **198666, Country Music in the World of Islam, Country Music of Southeastern Australia, I've Been Everywhere, LSD C&W** plus highly politicized folk recordings including one with the Red Clay Ramblers (**Country Protest**) and another covering the songs of folk legends Tim Buckley, Nick Drake, and Phil Ochs (**Songs**). He has also recorded a fairly traditional instrumental album (Eugene on banjo and guitar), **Strings**, dedicated to "one of the true giants of bluegrass...John Coltrane." All have Chadbourne's outrageous musical slant mixing recognizable elements with many jolting surprises (electrified rakes, bird cages, plungers, dog skull harmonica) on covers of Roger Miller, Johnny Cash, Buck Owens, Willie Nelson, Merle Haggard, Faron Young, Hank Snow, and other country legends. You haven't heard anything until you hear how Eugene "renders" songs like Gram Parsons "Luxury Liner," Buck Owen's "I Wouldn't Live in New York City," or Hank Snow's "I've Been Everywhere." In the mid-1990s, Chadbourne worked with former Mothers of Invention drummer Jimmy Carl Black as the psycho-folk duo Jack and Jim. In 1996, he recorded **Jesse Helms Busted With Pornography: A**

C&W Opera which presents more of Chadbourne's special socio-political commentary and country covers with help from Black, Don Helms, and the Legendary Stardust Cowboy. His immense recorded output (on labels and EC's home mail order) plus lots of details about him can be found on several web pages devoted to "Doctor" Chadbourne. For those of you intent on throwing your life away on a music career, Eugene has written a handy and hilarious little book, *I Hate The Man Who Runs This Bar: The Survival Guide for Real Musicians.*

> **There'll Be No Tears Tonight**/Fundamental/1980
> **Country Protest**/Fundamental/1986 (with the Red Clay Ramblers)
> **Country Music of Southeastern Australia**/RR/1986
> **198666**/Ralph/1986 (EP)
> **LSD C&W**/Fundamental/1987
> **Camper Van Chadbourne**/Fundamental/1987
> **Eugene Van Beethoven's 69th Sin Funny/** Fundamental/1988
> **I've Been Everywhere**/Fundamental/1988
> **Country Music in the Land of Islam**/ Fundamental/1990
> **Songs**/Intakt Switz./1992
> **Strings**/Intakt/1992
> **Jesse Helms Busted With Pornography: A C&W Opera**/Fire Ant/1996
> *I Hate The Man Who Runs This Bar: A Survival Guide for Real Musicians*/1998

Oh No, It's Eugene Chadbourne! (Official Home Page)
//www.ice.net.~ponk/chadbrne.htm

The Unofficial Fan Club of Dr. Eugene Chadbourne
//wymple.gs.nt/~aaswell/eugene.html

Eugene Chadbourne Discography
//www.math.duke.edu/~priley/chadbourne/

Cassette Mythos:
//www.halcyon.com/robinja/mythos/chadbourne.html

Eugene Chadbourne Home Mail Order Catalog
707 Longview St., Greensboro, NC 27403

See Camper Van Beethoven

Slim Chance and The Convicts

Redneck Underground
Atlanta, Georgia; 1986-

Atlanta's alternative country scene is affectionately referred to as the Redneck Underground. The acknowledged "spiritual godfather," the "single person responsible for sowing the seeds of this alternative country movement" (**Bubbapalooza** liner notes) is James Kelly. Raised in Nashville, where his father was an aspiring country singer, James carried on his dad's dream when he moved to Atlanta in the 1980s and formed Slim Chance and the Convicts. Their first jobs were at the Georgia Retardation Center where Kelly had a day job working with the mentally challenged. They also began performing on a regular basis at a hangout called the Austin Avenue Buffet which in time became a magnet for like minded individuals with a reverence for real country music. With lots of encouragement from James/Slim, it became the springboard for a number of

Atlanta alt. country bands (Diggers, Jennie B. & The Speed-billies, Vidalias, Delta Angels) and for the development of the alt. country scene which one of its charter members, Deacon Lunchbox, dubbed the Redneck Underground. In 1990, "Bubbapalooza," a showcase for the RU, was held at the Star Bar, and in 1995, Sky Records released **Bubbapalooza, Volume 1: Chronicle of the Redneck Underground**, a compilation of bands featured at the festival. Slim Chance and the Convicts contributed the clever "George Jones Has Never Sung About My Girl" which was taken from their 1993 self-released cassette, **Letters to Mama**. This recording presented more catchy Slim originals including honky tonkers ("Brand New Honky Tonk Angel"), tear jerkers ("Mama Sings Amazing Grace"), heartbreakers ("Can't Hold on Anymore"), and flat out rockers ("#43"; "Hell Isn't Big Enough"). As the Redneck Underground grew, James worked toward his Ph.D. in clinical psychology while Slim remained very active opening for Joe Ely, Guy Clark, Jim Lauderdale, and Buddy Miller. He began working on a new CD with fan input (via questionnaires passed out at performances), better production, and a stronger supporting cast (especially lead guitarist Cecil Lawrence and steel player Bill Fleming). The result was the much improved sound of **Twang Peaks** released on Evolutionary Records and dedicated to charter Underground member Greg Smalley who died in early 1996. Once again, Slim and the Convicts dip into honky tonk ("Pop a Top"), weep-in-your-wine ballads ("Now That Love is Gone"; "Crying Over You"), and rockers including an eerie version of "Just Dropped In" (yes, the old Kenny Rogers and the First Edition song). However, the highlight is Slim's clever songwriting on "My Baby Drives a Shopping Cart," "King of Loserville," and a tune about romance and cognitive dissonance *a la* Yogi Berra, "I'll Believe It When I Want To." In late 1996, the band won the critic's choice award for Best Atlanta Country Band, and the self-proclaimed "smartest band in America" held down a regular spot at the Star where it hosted a monthly theme night ("Ladies Night"; "Slimmy Awards"; "God Bless America"). Early in 1998, James received an internship at Austin (Texas) State Hospital and with Slim in tow, moved there in August after a rousing farewell show at the Austin Avenue Buffet.

Slim Chance (g,v); Phil Anderson (b); Cecil Lawrence (l.g.,h.v.); Earl Maddox (d)

> **Letters to Mama**/Jailbait Productions/1993 (CS)
> "George Jones Has Never Sung About My Girl" on
> **Bubbapalooza, Vol. 1**/Sky/1995
> **Twang Peaks**/Evolutionary/1996
> "Mr. Teardrop" and "Backyard Swing" on **14 x 7: Hand Picked Songs From Georgia**/Hexamusic/1996
> "Jesus, Elvis and Me" on **Bubbapalooza, Vol. 2: A Tribute to Greg Dean Smalley**/Criminal/1998

Slim Chance/Evolutionary Record Home Page
//www.evoman.com/scpg02.html

James Kelly JKellySC1@aol.com

Vic Chesnutt

Singer/Songwriter; Lo-Fi
Jacksonville, Florida; November 12, 1964-

Heartache? Depression? Pain? How do you spell relief? For Vic Chesnutt, the answer has often been pills, booze, and suicidal tendencies, but this artist of suffering has another medium of expression: songwriting and singing. Paralyzed from the waist down since an auto accident in high school, Chesnutt has faced his share of physical and emotional problems, but the songs he writes are not of the self-pitying or "life is hard and then you die" variety. On the contrary, Chesnutt crafts stories that battle life's slings and arrows with a surprising amount of humor (twisted to be sure) and beauty that touch and move the listener. Each of his albums uses spare accompaniment in favor of a focus on Chesnutt's droll vocals and lyrics which squeeze every ounce of poignancy from life's most banal experiences.

Chesnutt's musical career began in 1984 when he moved to Athens, Georgia and became part of its flourishing music scene. Over time, his performances drew attention most prominently from REM's Michael Stipe who at the time was branching out into production (Chickasaw Mud Puppies). Won over by Chesnutt's abilities, Stipe produced his first two albums, **Little** and **West of Rome** which are very modern but also steeped in blues, folk, and country traditions. After three more acclaimed recordings in the mid-1990s, Chesnutt was given perhaps the ultimate in recognition when a group of his peers (REM, Soul Asylum, Nanci Griffith, Sparklehorse, et al.) recorded **Gravity of the Situation: The Songs of Vic Chesnutt**, the proceeds of which went to the Sweet Relief Fund for musicians with major medical expenses. A further symbol of the respect accorded Chesnutt by his fellow musicians is the number of collaborations in which he has been involved: Jack Logan, Giant Sand, Sparklehorse, Lambchop, Bob Mould, the Dashboard Saviors, Widespread Panic, and many others. In early 1997, Chesnutt received more recognition through an appearance (as leader of a band called the Titty Twisters) in the popular movie *Sling Blade*. When he returned to the studio in early 1998, Vic took fellow eccentrics, Lambchop, with him as backup band to record **The Salesman and Bernadette** which keeps it lo-fi on a little bit o' soul, pop, rock, and country with Emmylou providing backup vocals on, "Woodrow Wilson"; the song "Aunt Axis" was made into a video with Billy Bob Thornton directing. Unlike Chesnutt's previous recordings, this one is more upbeat musically and lyrically due in part to the presence of Lambchop (12 piece band) who also backed him on his 1998 European tour. Meantime, Vic showed up on a variety of recordings including *The End of Violence* soundtrack ("Injured Bird," a duet with Michael Stipe), **Hempilation2**, **Sounds of the New West**, and the **Southern Sampler** from *Oxford Americana* magazine which also did a lengthy profile of

Chesnutt. A closer look at this intriguing character can be had in a documentary entitled *Speed Racer: Welcome to the World of Vic Chesnutt*.

Little/Texas Hotel/1990
West of Rome/Texas Hotel/1992
"Hickory Wind" (with Bob Mould) on
    Commerativo/Rhino/1993
Drunk/Texas Hotel/1994
Is the Actor Happy?/Texas Hotel/1995
Nine High A Pallet/Capricorn/1995
Sweet Relief II: Gravity of the Situation, The Songs of
    Vic Chesnutt/Columbia/1996
About to Choke/Capitol/1996
"Goodbye Sadness" on **Howl!**/Glitterhouse Ger./1996
Salesman and Bernadette/Capitol/1998
"Duty Free" (with Lambchop) on **Southern Sampler '98**/
    Oxford Americana/1998
"Weed to the Rescue" on **Hempilation2: Free the**
    Weed!/Capricorn/1998
"Until the Led" on **Sounds of the New West: The Best of**
    Alternative Country/Uncut UK/1998
Speed Racer: Welcome to the World of Vic Chesnutt
    (video documentary)

Vic Chesnutt Fan Club,
P.O. Box 6994, Athens, GA 30604

Vic Chesnutt/Wolfeyes Home Page
//www.geocities.com/~wolf-eyes/vic_main.html

wolfeyes@tcd.net

Charlie Chesterman (Scruffy the Cat)

Country Rock; Roots Rock
Des Moines, Iowa; February 8, 1960-

One of the best, albeit very obscure, rock bands to come out of the late 1980s was Boston's Scruffy the Cat. Known primarily for their witty and engaging pop style, they occasionally dabbled in countryish sounds (the science fiction cover art of their final record **Moons of Jupiter** features a line of corona crowned images of Hank). However, according to their lead singer, Charlie Chesterman not all of the legends of country music approved; Patsy Cline appeared to him in a dream and insisted they stop playing "Route 66." Be that as it may, Scruffy broke up in 1989 after four exceptional albums but limited commercial success. Out of the group, the one member who (despite warnings from Patsy) went further into country music was Charlie Chesterman. His first foray into a more countrified sound came with a band called the Harmony Rockets, then on his debut solo **From the Book of Flames** (with the Motorbikes), and most fully on the cleverly titled **Studebakersfield** (both on Slow River). On the latter, Chesterman carries on in the fun loving tradition of Scruffy the Cat but within the familiar musical and lyrical idioms of country music. Backed by accordion, fiddle, steel, Chesterman whines his way through original tearjerkers ("If I Had a Heart"; "The Confession"), country rockers ("Mr. Blue"; "Out of Nowheresville"), hillbilly bop ("Heart of a Fool"), a whistling ditty ("Missing Persons'

Waltz"), and even a western tune ("Cowboy's Lament"). Fans of Scruffy and/or alt. country will find much to enjoy. Switching to Slow River's parent company Rykodisc in 1997, Chesterman recorded **Dynamite Music Machine**, a muscular blend of rock 'n' roll roots from the 1950s-1990s. An anthology (**Hit This & Kick That**) of the career of the man whom Plato Records says "paved the way for the Jayhawks and Wilco" was released in 1998.

Scruffy the Cat: Charlie Chesterman (g,hm,v); Stephen Fredette (b,g,v); Randall Lee Gibson (d); Burns Stanfield (ky); Mac Paul Stanfield (b,g)

High Octane Revival (Scruffy the Cat)/ Relativity/1986
Tiny Days (Scruffy the Cat)/Relativity/1987
Boom Boom Boom Bingo (Scruffy the Cat)/
    Relativity/1987 (EP)
Moons of Jupiter (Scruffy the Cat)/Relativity/1988
From the Book of Flames/Slow River/1994
Studebakersfield/Slow River/1996
Dynamite Music Machine/Rykodisc/1997
Hit This & Kick That/Rykodisc/1998

Charlie Chesterman Home Page
//www1.usa1.com/jfaris/charlie.html

Charlie Chesterman/Rykodisc Page //www.rykodisc.com

Kathy Chiavola

Singer/Songwriter
Chicago, Illinois; March 7, 1952-

Although Kathy Chiavola (key ah' vo lah) sang blues, folk, and rock as a child, the strength of her voice initially pushed her toward a career in opera. But after receiving B.A. and M.A. degrees in voice from Oberlin Conservatory, singing with several professional opera companies, and entering a Ph.D. program at Indiana University, her life took a slight detour into country music. Several tours on the bluegrass and folk circuits in North America and Europe spread the word about her amazing vocal prowess and in a short time she was in great demand as a session musician for Emmylou Harris, Ricky Skaggs, and Vince Gill. At the same time she began working with many prominent bluegrass artists including Bill Monroe, Country Gazette, and with Bela Fleck and Jerry Douglas as a member of the Lucky Dogs. In addition, Chiavola recorded two bluegrass style albums of her own, **Labor of Love** and **The Harvest**, with many of these musicians returning the favor and supporting her (including Bill Monroe making his last vocal recording). Her reputation for captivating vocal performances won Chiavola many fans at home and abroad, rave reviews, and numerous awards including Best New Female Recorded Act of the Year from Australian Country Music Radio in 1993 and 1995 Backup Vocalist of the Year at the Nashville Music Awards. In 1997, Chiavola signed with Nashville based Eagle Records and, between recording and touring, served on the board of the International Bluegrass Music Museum and taught voice at Belmont University in Nashville. She was one of many guest performers on Steve Earle's 1999 bluegrass album, **The Mountain**.

Labor of Love/My Label/1990
The Harvest/My Label/1995
"A Fool Such as I" on **Country**/Vinyl Junkie UK/1996

Kathy Chiavola Web Page
//www.nashville.net/~kate/chiavola.html

The Chickasaw Mud Puppies

Roots Rock
Athens, Georgia; 1990-

Flush with success, John Keane and Michael Stipe of REM ventured into a number of side projects in the early 1990s. One of these involved producing an Athens duo by the name of the Chickasaw Mud Puppies. Ben Reynolds and Brant Slay specialized in romping, backwoods country songs filled with quirky sounds and disturbing images. Each played an instrument called a "stomp board" and Slay's sometimes driving, sometimes eerie harmonica set the tone for much of their music. Their twisted roots rock was further accentuated by Slay's lead vocals which sound like they were done in an echo chamber or while he had a wad of chewing tobacco in his mouth. Keane and an assortment of other musicians lent support on slide guitar, dobro, and haunting fiddle on melodies ranging from full tilt hoe-down to chuggling swamp.

Ben Reynolds (g, perc., v); Brant Slay (hm, perc, v)

White Dirt/Polygram/1990
8 Track Stomp/Polygram/1991

The Chicken Chokers

See The Hix

Eugene Chrysler

Honky Tonk; Hillbilly Bop
Connecticut; November 28, 1960-

Eugene Chrysler has spent most of his life back East, but his musical heart always resided below the Mason-Dixon. Taking up the big old dog-house bass at age 12, he was in a few different bands in Connecticut and New Jersey before creating his own style and persona in the early 1990s. Backed initially by the One World Posse Band, Chrysler fashioned a sound based on Sun style rockabilly, honky tonk, blues, and Western swing and an image built on immaculate Western attire and wild slap bass antics. In addition, Eugene had a smooth-as-silk baritone, and knew how to write clever, catchy songs like "Drinkin' My Dinner and Eatin' My Words," "Next to You (I Look Like a Rocket Scientist)," "Dog Gone," and "I Saw the Light...But It Was Neon." The latter became the title of his debut CD which yielded two videos that got exposure on TNN, CMT, and even an episode of *Law and Order*. **I Saw the Light...** has plenty of fine moments of rockabilly and honky tonk to recommend it including a romping version of "Viva Las Vegas" complete with background whip cracks. Still, Chrysler wasn't completely satisfied feeling that the record was "a little overproduced" and didn't reflect what he and his band (now called the Hillbilly Shakespeares) really sounded like in person. So, in 1998, they headed down to Austin to record a more hard core honky tonk swing album with help from local luminaries like Ray Benson, Jason Roberts, and Cindy Cashdollar of Asleep at the Wheel plus Toni Price and Brian Hofeldt (Derailers). **Hillbilly Shakespeare**, which was due out in 1999, is more straight ahead honky tonk, rockabilly, and Western swing than its predecessor with noteworthy songs such as "I Don't Drive a Truck (But I Live at a Truckstop)" and "Get Hip," a duet with Ray Benson. Chrysler's alter-ego is a music video maker whose clients have included the Derailers, Toni Price, and Asleep at the Wheel; in 1998, while down in Texas, he shot a documentary on the making of Asleep at the Wheel's second Bob Wills tribute, **Ride With Bob**.

The Hillybilly Shakespeares: Ed Iarusso (p.s.); Allan Sheinfeld (l.g.); Tom Smith (d)

I Saw the Light...But It Was Neon/Carlco/1994
Hillbilly Shakespeare/EC/1999

Eugene Chrysler, 395 Orange Rd.,
Montclair, NJ 07042; 973-783-7059

The Cigar Store Indians

Rockabilly; Country Rock
Atlanta, Georgia; 1993-

One group from Atlanta's 1990s alt. country scene which experienced a rapid rise in popularity was the Cigar Store Indians. Their sound is basically straight ahead rockabilly with a generous helping of honky tonk, country rock, and Southern boogie. Founder and lead vocalist Ben Friedman had previously been in the rock band IBM but became disillusioned with the alternative scene in the early 1990s. He then turned to the 1950s era country and rockabilly his parents had exposed him to when he was a child and, gathering together a group of friends/musicians, formed the Cigar Store Indians. Playing the popular clubs around Atlanta, they honed a sound that is a little bit Johnny Horton/Webb Pierce country, a little bit Bo Diddley boogie, and a whole lot of Sun style rockabilly with a distinctly modern edge. After a good showing by a debut cassette tape in 1994, the Cigar Store Indians were signed by Landslide Records and in 1995 came a full length self titled CD. With a rep for high energy performances highlighted by Friedman's strong vocals and the hot guitar of Jim Lavender, the band earned honors as Atlanta's best dance band (voted by *Creative Loafing*) and as best live show (*99 X*). They received national and international exposure rising to the number 3 position on Gavin's Americana chart and touring Europe in the fall of 1996.

Incidentally, like the Atlanta Braves, they took some heat from Native Americans for their name; one outdoor concert was canceled after several Native Americans performed a rain dance that brought a deluge. However, the Cigar Store Indians received positive feedback from other Native Americans and decided not to change their name. Their sophomore effort **El Baile De La Cobra** retains much of their original roots rockabilly sound but adds a big dose of swing (with horns) the band likes to call "hillbilly-martini drinking music." And swing (and rock) they do. If scorching tunes like "Fast Lane," "Get on the Throttle," "Yipin," "Big Girl Blouse," and "She Makes Me Come Undone" don't get you up on the dance floor, well then, Jack, you dead!

Frances Ferran (d,1994-1997); Ben Friedman (g,l.v.); Jim Lavender (l.g.,v); Keith Perissi (b,v); Pup Roberts (d,1997-)

The Cigar Store Indians/Aint/1994 (CS)
The Cigar Store Indians/Landslide/1995
El Baile De La Cobra/Deep South/1998

The Cigar Store Indians Home Page
//www.cigarstoreindians.com

Csi@cigarstoreindians.com

Cisco
TSOB
Fresno/Los Angeles, California; 1997-

Cisco seemed to come from out of nowhere in 1998. His debut CD, **Wishing You Well From the Pink Hotel**, was sent out to alt. country reviewers by a guy who works for Disney, and that alone was enough to raise some red flags. The cover, an up-close photo of a nice looking Cisco with tattoos, earrings, white undershirt, and cowboy hat (does have some sweat around the band) leaning back in a convertible, looked dubious as well. However, things got brighter when I looked at the liner notes and saw that the recording was done at Mad Dog Studios (co-owned by Dusty Wakeman) and co-produced by Mike Ness of Social Distortion. But, the proof is in the recording and when I put it on the player, what a nice surprise: high energy honky tonk and country rock in the best of the Town South of Bakersfield tradition! Jeff Wall, editor of the *Rural Route Twangzine*, who wrote one of the first reviews of **Wishing You Well**, described it best as sounding like a combination of Steve Earle with Dwight Yoakam. Cisco's vocals definitely range somewhere between Dwight and Steve and lead guitarist Chris Lawrence, who also plays pedal steel, is right up there with Pete Anderson. The latter and Dusty Wakeman have not only been big influnces but also provided lots of advice and encourage-ment to Cisco and his band, the Reasons Why. Born and raised in Fresno in the San Joaquin Valley, Cisco has obviously absorbed the local Bakersfield Sound and the more modern TSOB style as evidenced by his originals like "Mr. Wright," "The Bum You Say I Am," "Hard Times Again," and "Long

Way Home." As the word got out in 1998, accolades poured in from around the alt. country world and in February 1999, Cisco and the Reasons Why opened two shows for Willie Nelson at Tramps in New York City.

The Reasons Why: Bogie Bowles (d,1997-1998); Jimmy Christie (d,1998-); Chris Lawrence (e.g.,p.s.); Jeff Roberts (b)

Wishing You Well From the Pink Hotel/Propellant Transmissions/1998

Cisco/Propellant Transmissions, P.O. Box 2297, Redondo Beach, CA 90278

Gene Clark
Country Rock
Tipton, Missouri; November 17, 1941-May 24, 1991

Although not as well known as Chris Hillman, Roger McGuinn, or Gram Parsons, Gene Clark was one of the most important contributors to the development of the California country rock sound of the late 1960s and early 1970s. Moving to L.A. in the mid-1960s after a brief run as a folkie with the New Christy Minstrels, Clark met Roger McGuinn and with Chris Hillman, Michael Clark, and David Crosby formed the Byrds. Clark's singing and songwriting played a major role in the band's meteoric rise but shortly after their elevation to "rock and roll star" status, Clark left to pursue a solo career. In 1967, before the Byrds began to explore country rock, Clark put together his own bluegrass/country rock album, **Gene Clark With the Gosdin Brothers** with Hillman, Clarence White, and Doug Dillard. Clark teamed with the latter in 1968 and 1969 for several albums of pioneering country rock (**The Fantastic Expedition of Dillard & Clark; Through the Morning, Through the Night; Kansas City Southern**). Into the 1970s, Gene made a succession of solo efforts, **White Light, Road-master, No Other**, fully displaying his considerable singing/ songwriting talents. For a short time, he rejoined his old Byrd mates in the short lived McGuinn, Clark, Hillman band which yielded a couple of unexceptional albums. In the late 1980s, Clark worked with the Long Ryders and teamed with Carla Olson (Textones) for some duet recordings most notably, **So Rebellious a Lover**. Unfortunately, Clark's health began to decline and shortly after the Byrds were inducted into the Rock 'n' Roll Hall of Fame, he died of natural causes in L.A. in May, 1991. But, since that time his legacy and popularity has grown as new generations discover the roots of country rock. Until recently much of Clark's recorded output was available only on European or Australian imports, but 1997 brought a flurry of important releases in the U.S. including his early work with the Gosdin Brothers. Additionally, renewed interest in the Byrds resulted in greater recognition for Clark; in early 1997, Columbia issued repackaged versions of the Byrds country rock albums, and Strange Fruit released **Three Byrds Land in**

London which has live tracks by McGuinn, Clark, and Hillman together and solo from a concert in the late 1970s.

The definitive Gene Clark retrospective, **Flying High**, compiled by Sid Griffin finally came out in August 1998 after a series of delays. Included on the double CD are Clark's best songs along with lots of previously unreleased material (some solo, some with Dillard & Clark), remixes of familiar tunes, and rare recordings. Griffin also wrote the extensive liner notes and did a long article on Clark for *Mojo* magazine that was published at the same time as the anthology.

> **Gene Clark and the Gosdin Brothers**/Columbia/1967; Sony/1991
> **The Fantastic Expedition of Dillard & Clark**/ A&M/1968
> **Through the Morning, Through the Night** (Dillard & Clark)/A&M/1969
> **White Light**/A&M/1972
> **Roadmaster**/Ariola/1973; Edsel/1986
> **No Other**/Asylum/1974; Line Ger./1989
> **Kansas City Southern** (Dillard & Clark)/Ariola/1975
> **Gene Clark**/A&M/1975
> **Two Sides to Every Story**/RSO/1977
> **McGuinn, Clark, Hillman**/Columbia/1979
> **City** (McGuinn,Clark,Hillman)/Columbia/1980
> **Firebyrd**/Takoma/1984
> **This Byrd Has Flown** (with Carla Olson)/Edsel UK/1984; Monster Music/1995
> **So Rebellious a Lover** (with Carla Olson)/ Rhino/1987; Razor & Tie/1995
> **Echoes**/Columbia/1991 (recs. with Gosdin Brothers and Byrds including 3 p.u.)
> **Silhouetted in the Light: Live in Concert** (with Carla Olson)/Demon UK/1992
> **American Dreamer, 1964-1974**/Raven Austr./1995 (reissue with interview; includes recs. with Gosdin Brothers, Byrds, Dillard & Clark, Carla Olson, solo)
> **Three Byrds Land in London** (McGuinn, Clark, Hillman)/Strange Fruit/1997
> **Flyin' High: The Gene Clark Anthology**/Polygram UK/1998

Gene Clark Main Page //www.geneclark.com

Gene Clark Page //www.ps.ket.kth.se/gc/

ralf.narfield@ips.se

See The Byrds; The Dillards; Chris Hillman

Guy Clark

Singer/Songwriter
Monahans, Texas; November 6, 1941-

In 1995, Philo Records issued a collection of three early Guy Clark albums entitled **Craftsman**. More than any other term, this sums up what the career of one of America's most respected singer/songwriters has been all about. Clark traces his passion for craftsmanship back to a summer job he had as a teenager on the Texas Gulf Coast. Through the construction of wooden boats, he learned patience, attention to detail, and pride in your work. When he moved to Houston in the early 1960s, Clark began applying these lessons to his first attempts at songwriting. He gained experience and confidence through friendships with Mance Lipscomb and Townes Van Zandt and performances at local clubs. In the late 1960s, Clark decided to move to L.A. and become a full time musician. Eventually, he signed on as a writer for Sunbury Music and headed for Nashville to pursue his dream. His first big break came in the early 1970s when Jerry Jeff Walker recorded Clark's "L.A. Freeway" and "That Old-Time Feeling"; shortly thereafter, notables like Johnny Cash and David Allen Coe covered "Texas 1947" and "Desperadoes Waiting for a Train." In 1975, Clark's perseverance was rewarded with an RCA recording contract that led to **Old No.1** and **Texas Cookin'**. Then came three albums for Warner Brothers and although they were not commercial hits, Clark gained popularity especially with critics and other musicians. Many of his best songs are about growing up in West Texas or along the Gulf Coast, but whatever his theme, Clark's compositions are admired for the ways in which they vividly bring to life the common, everyday aspects of life. And while Clark retired from recording for a time in the mid-1980s, his songs continued to be recorded by, and often became hits for, other artists. In 1989, he returned to the studio with **Old Friends** and then in the early 1990s, **Boats to Build** and **Dublin Blues**, all of which further strengthened his claim as a preeminent American songsmith. Guy has been mentor (along with Van Zandt) to Texas' newest generations of singer/ songwriters including Robert Keen, Lyle Lovett, and Jack Ingram. The majestic sweep of Clark's career was captured on **Craftsman** (an anthology of his Warner Brothers albums), the Columbia "greatest hits" collection **Essentials**, and his first ever live recording, **Keepers** in 1997. A duet recording with fellow Texas singer/songwriter Terry Allen was reportedly on the way for 1999.

> **Old No. 1**/RCA Victor/1975; Sugar Hill/1996
> **Texas Cookin'**/RCA Victor/1976
> **Guy Clark**/Warner Brothers/1978
> **The South Coast of Texas**/Warner Brothers/1981
> **Greatest Hits**/RCA Victor/1983
> **Better Days**/Warner Brothers/1983
> **Old Friends**/Sugar Hill/1989
> **Boats to Build**/Asylum/1992
> **Dublin Blues**/Asylum/1995
> **Craftsman**/Philo/1995
> **Essentials**/BMG Arista/1997
> **Keepers: A Live Recording**/Sugar Hill/1997

Guy Clark Fan Club, 59 Music Square West, Nashville, TN 37203

Guy Clark Home Page //www.physitron.com/~topher/guyclark/

Guy Clark AOL Folder: Entertainment>Music>Chat & Messages>Music Community>Country & Western, A-K

Vassar Clements

Fiddle; Hillbilly Jazz
Kinard, Florida; April 25, 1928-

During the 1970s and early 1980s, the three most prominent session fiddlers were Byron Berline, Johnny Gimble, and Vassar Clements. And though it's a tough call, the top spot among them in terms of range and influence belongs to the latter. Self taught on the fiddle (he started playing at age 7), Clements absorbed a variety of influences (jazz, country, bluegrass) and launched his long professional career while still a teenager. His earliest jobs were recording with Bill Monroe (1949-1956) and playing as a member of Jim & Jesse's band (1957-1961). For a few years, alcoholism forced him into semi-retirement, but Clements overcame this problem and from 1969-1970 was a member of several bands including Faron Young's Country Deputies, Tut Taylor's Dobrolic Plectoral Society, and the Earl Scruggs Revue. In the 1970s, when the first and second waves of alternative country really took off, Clements' fortunes rose with it. Suddenly, he found his services as a session player in great demand and over the next decade and more, Clements appeared on scores of recordings released by artists experimenting with various forms of Americana as well as other musical styles; included on this very long list are the Grateful Dead, Gene Parsons, Doug Dillard, Steve Goodman, Jimmy Buffett, Kris Kristofferson, J. J. Cale, Mike Auldridge, Jerry Jeff Walker, John Hartford, Willie Nelson, Bela Fleck, Bruce Hornsby, and Paul McCartney to name only a few. He played a key role in the making of three classic alternative country albums: **Will the Circle Be Un- broken**, **Hillbilly Jazz**, and **Old and in the Way** (with David Grisman, Jerry Garcia, Peter Rowan, and John Kahn). Vassar's contributions to each of these projects was immense, but his name has most often been associated with "Hillbilly Jazz," a hybrid of swing and country which was most fully expressed on the 1975 album of the same name. This first rate recording presents twanging bouncy covers of swing masters East (Goodman; Ellington) and West (Wills; Cooley; McAuliffe), old-time, Cajun, and originals highlighted by the super picking and plucking of Clements, David Bromberg, and steel virtuoso Doug Jernigan (a nice sequel, **Hillbilly Jazz Rides Again**, was released in 1987). Throughout the 1980s and into the 1990s, Clements collaborated with many renowned performers (Stephane Grappelli among others) and fronted the Vassar Clements Band. His impeccable musicianship and enormous contribution to Americana earned him the nickname Superbow as well as five Grammy nominations. In the 1990s, he continued to do collaborative recordings (**A Celebration of Merle Travis** in 1993), session work, and solo recordings; in 1996, Clements celebrated fifty years in music with **Vassar's Jazz**. Sadly, Vassar's wife Millie died of lung cancer in July 1998, but he and his daughter Midge continued to operate Vassillie Productions which not only handled all of Vassar's music but also offered fiddle seminars and workshops with VC at various festivals and other events.

> **Crossing the Catskills**/Rounder/1972; 1987
> **Sweet Dreams and Quiet Desires**/Avalanche/1972
> **Vassar Clements**/Mercury/1975
> **Hillbilly Jazz**/Flying Fish/1975
> **Superbow**/Mercury/1975
> **The Vassar Clements Band**/MCA/1977
> **The Bluegrass Sessions**/Flying Fish/1977
> **Nashville Jam**/Flying Fish/1979
> **Vassar**/Flying Fish/1981
> **Westport Drive**/Mind Dust/1984
> **Hillbilly Jazz Rides Again**/Flying Fish/1987
> **Together At Last** (with Stephane Grappelli)/Flying Fish/1987
> **Grass Routes**/Rounder/1991
> **Once In a While**/Flying Fish/1992
> **Vassar's Jazz**/Winter Harvest/1996
> *Vassar Clements Fiddle Instruction Videos/* Homestead
> *Vassar Swings (In Concert)/*Shikata (video)
> *Ramblin' 810 (In Concert)/*Shanachie (video)

Vassar Clements/Vassillie Productions Home Page //mbus.com/vassar/index.htm

Vassar Clements Fan Forum vassarmu@ix.netcom.com

The Cluster Pluckers

Progressive Bluegrass
Nashville, Tennessee; 1988-

Sporting a name that always draws second looks, the Cluster Pluckers are one of the finest progressive bluegrass bands around. Their history begins in 1980 when Dale and Kris Ballinger sang informally with Margaret Bailey at a party, clicked and then decided to perform on a more permanent basis. In a few short years, the trio racked up an impressive resume of appearances including the Folklife Festival Exhibition at the Knoxville World's Fair in 1982 and the American Folk Roots Series at Carnegie Hall in 1984. Kris and Margaret recorded two albums and toured with the Vassar Clements Hillbilly Jazz Band in 1986. In 1987, they met multi-instrumentalist Mark Howard and started the Cluster Pluckers (name inspired by songwriter Billy Ed Wheeler). With the addition of Richard Bailey, Blaine Sprouse, and Brent Truitt, the group began to tour and record. In the 1990s, the Cluster Pluckers released four albums including a gospel recording. Stylistically, their sound is epitomized by their 1992 release **Just Pluck It!** which covers bluegrass standards plus bluegrass based versions of country classics (Jimmie Rodgers, Hank Williams, Merle Haggard), Eastern, and Western swing. It also shows off the Pluckers characteristic good sense of humor with "Ding Dong" (about the perils of addiction to cream filled cup cakes) and the satirical "Would Jesus Wear a Rolex" (co-written by Margaret Bailey with Chet Atkins). And while other bands might trod similar ground, what sets the Pluckers apart is ultra hot picking and the exquisite vocals and harmonies of Margaret Bailey and Kris

Ballinger. Into the 1990s, this winning combination has won them many fans, the highest of praise, and appearances on *Austin City Limits*, *American Music Shop*, *Riders in the Sky Radio Theater*, and inclusion in the Ken Burns produced *Songs of the Civil War* for PBS. Their 1996, **Unplucked**, offers refreshingly new takes on familiar tunes such as "Where the Soul Never Dies," "Mama Tried," "Family Bible," "Midnight on the Water," and "Weapon of Prayer." If you're ever in Nashville, the best place to catch the Cluster Pluckers is at the Station Inn where they perform on a regular basis.

Margaret Bailey (v); Richard Bailey (bj); Dale Ballinger (v); Kris Ballinger (v); Mark Howard (g,v); Blaine Sprouse (f); Brent Truitt (md)

The Cluster Pluckers/Cluster Pluckers/1991
Just Pluck It!/Cluster Pluckers/1992
Old-Time Gospel Favorites/Cluster Pluckers/1994
Unplucked/Cluster Pluckers/1996

The Cluster Pluckers,
P.O. Box 1235, Cookeville, TN 38503

The Cluster Pluckers Home Page
//mbus.com/vassar/cpdirect.htm

The Coal Porters

See Sid Griffin

David Allan Coe

Outlaw
Akron, Ohio; September 6, 1939-

Aspiring film directors, listen up!; have we got a story for you; call it *Invictus, The David Allan Coe Story*. No one could make up a script so fascinating and bizarre. In reform school by age 9, Coe spent the next twenty years off and on in various penal institutions until released from the Ohio State Penitentiary in 1967. From there he went to Nashville where, for a time, he lived in a hearse parked outside the Ryman and tried to get the attention of record executives. Plantation Records took a chance on him and released two recordings of his prison songs (**Penitentiary Blues, I &II**) which today are prized collectors items. Along about this time, Coe began to develop his image as the outlaw's outlaw (way beyond Waylon and Willie) by sporting long hair and beard (sometimes multi-colored), earrings, rhinestone suits, drag outfits, and even priests' vestments to go along with the 350+ body tattoos he had accumulated while in prison. He made public appearances as the "Mysterious Rhinestone Cowboy" (sometimes he wore a mask on stage) and often made an unprecedented use of explicit language. Coe became equally well known for his off stage theatrics claiming to be a Mormon priest with nine wives and hanging around with a Hell's Angels gang. However, while his image gained some attention, it was as a songwriter that he found greatest success. Beginning in 1972, Coe had a string of his songs turned into hits by other artists: "Would You Lay with Me in a Field of Stone?"

(Tanya Tucker), "Take This Job and Shove It" (Johnny Paycheck). In 1973, he began a 13-year relationship with CBS that led to 26 albums and many charted singles including "You Never Even Call Me By My Name" (the perfect country western song), "Longhaired Redneck," "Willie, Waylon & Me," and "Mona Lisa Lost Her Smile." During and after the CBS years, Coe produced his own albums many of which contained "blue" material (**Nothing Sacred**; **Underground**) and were available only through mail order until Bear Family reissued some of them in 1993. In addition to being a musician, Coe is an accomplished magician, novelist, and movie actor. Unfortunately, the years of success were marred by numerous problems including tax troubles (he lived in a Tennessee cave for a while after the IRS took his home), battles with Nashville, and even a nervous breakdown. Surprisingly, Coe was never a drinker or druggie and in time toned down his hard-core image becoming much more of a family man and even a practicing Mormon. During a 36 hour ordeal, Coe went so far as to have his unseemly prison tattoos replaced with uplifting Native American images. Still based in Nashville where it all started for him over two decades ago, Coe has authored several books, *Just for the Record*, *Ex-Convict*, and *The Book of David: Poems, Prose, and Stories*. In 1997, Coe did **David Allan Coe Live: If That Ain't Country** his first major label release in over a decade. Recorded live at Ft. Worth's legendary Billy Bob's and released on Sony's alt. country subsidiary Lucky Dog, the consummate outlaw treats a new generation of outlaw wannabes to rocking versions of his signature songs. Counted among Coe's younger admirers is the heavy metal band Pantera who collaborated with him on the outlaw country/headbanger recording **Rebel Meets Rebel** in late 1998. Meanwhile, DAC completed **Johnny Cash Is a Friend of Mine**, an album of Man in Black covers sold at concerts or through his fan club.

Penitentiary Blues, Vols. I & II/Plantation/1968
Requiem for a Harlequin/SSS/1969
Mysterious Rhinestone Cowboy/Columbia/1974
Once Upon a Rhyme/Columbia/1975
Longhaired Redneck/Columbia/1976
David Allan Coe Rides Again/Columbia/1977
Texas Moon/Plantation/1977
Tattoo/Columbia/1977
Family Album/Columbia/1978
Human Emotions/Columbia/1978
Greatest Hits/Columbia/1978
Spectrum VII/Columbia/1979
Buckstone County Prison/Coe/1979
Nothing Sacred/Coe/1979
Compass Point/1980
I've Got Something to Say/1980
Invictus (Means) Unconquered/1981
Encore/Columbia/1981
Tennessee Whiskey/Columbia/1981
D.A.C./Columbia/1982
Hello in There/Columbia/1983
Just Divorce/Columbia/1984
Unchained/Columbia/1985
I Love Country/CBS UK/1986

Son of the South/Columbia/1986
A Matter of Life...and Death/Columbia/1987
Crazy Daddy/Columbia/1989
1990 Songs for Sale/DAC/1990; Bear Family Ger./1993
Super Hits/Columbia/1993
Headed for the Count/Bear Family Ger./1993
Standing Too Close to the Flames/DAC/1994
Compass Point/I've Got Something to Say/Bear Family Ger./1995
Invictus/Tennessee Waltz/Bear Family Ger./1995
Super Hits, Vol. 2/Columbia/1996
For the Record/Columbia/1996 (2 CD)
David Allan Coe Live: If That Ain't Country/ Lucky Dog/1997
Johnny Cash is a Friend of Mine/DAC/1998
Rebel Meets Rebel (with Pantera)/1998

David Allan Coe Fan Club,
P.O. Box 270188, Nashville, TN 37227-0188 or
//www.infosysnet.com/dac/

The David Allan Coe Connection
//members.aol.com/ribico/dac.html

The David Allan Coe Web Page //users.aol.com/acushen/

David Allan Coe Page
//www.users.csbsju.edu/~njschwar/coe.html

Ohio Abe's David Allan Coe Page //www.ds.net/~ohioabe/

The Very Unofficial David Allan Coe Home Page
//www.geocities.com/nashville/1313/

B. J. Cole

Steel Guitar; Country Rock; Avant-Garde
North Enfield, Herfordshire, England; June 17, 1946-

In the late 1960s and early 1970s, the steel guitar began showing up in some of the most unlikely places. Rock musicians in particular employed the instrument not only in country rock but in other styles as well. Many of the young steel guitar players who came along at this time ventured into previously unexplored musical territories. In the U.S. the most outstanding artists were Sneaky Pete, Lucky Oceans, and Buddy Emmons; the latter was the most in demand session player and appeared on many key recordings of the period. His British equivalent was B. J. Cole who after a brief time with the rock band Cochise became the session player par excellence in his home country. In the late 1960s, Cole played in Country Fever, an early British country rock band with Albert Lee. During the 1970s, he appeared on recordings by Elton John, T. Rex, Procol Harum, Humble Pie, Matthews Southern Comfort, Alan Parsons, and scores of others. In the 1980s and 1990s, Cole began to push the pedal steel way beyond its usual boundaries by incorporating a computer interface and applying it to various world music sounds on **Transparent Music** and **Heart of the Moment**. In 1995, he was part of an avant-garde music tour with John Cale (Velvet Underground) and the Soldier String Quartet. At the same time, Cole kept contact with the musical styles traditionally associated with the steel as a member of the British Western swing group Marshall and the Shooting Stars and the roots rock band Los Pistoleros. Today, he remains the preeminent European practitioner of his instrument and is still in great demand for recording sessions (Sting, Depeche Mode, John Cale, Traci Lords) and tours. Toward the end of 1998, Cole was sitting in with the Verve and with REM on TV/radio performances during a UK tour to promote their new recording.

Cochise/United Artists UK/1970
Swallow Tales (Cochise)/United Artists UK/1971
So Far (Cochise)/United Artists UK/1972
New Hovering Dog/United Artists/1972
Transparent Music/Hannibal/1989
Black Claw & Country Fever (Country Fever with Albert Lee)/Line Ger./1991
Air Mail Special (Marshall & The Shooting Stars)/1994
Heart of the Moment/Resurgence/1995

B.J. Cole/Rykodisc Page //www.rykodisc.com

See Freddy Krc; Albert Lee

Commander Cody and His Lost Planet Airmen

Country Rock; Honky Tonk; Rockabilly; Western Swing
Ann Arbor, Michigan/San Francisco, California; 1967-

Commander Cody and His Lost Planet Airmen were the first and some would say the best of the hippie honky tonk, rockabilly, Western swing bands. Their origins go back to 1967 when two University of Michigan grad students, George Frayne (art) and John Tichy (engineering) formed a semi-vaudevillian stage show with the Galactic Twist Queens, Pat the Hippie Strippie, and a rock band called Commander Cody and the Lost Planet Airmen (named for an old serial movie character, Commando Cody). Frayne took a teaching job at Wisconsin State in 1968 but kept the band going and for a time commuted to Ann Arbor on weekends for gigs. During this time, they added a new lead singer, Billy C. Farlow, a steel player, the "West Virginia Creeper" (later replaced by Bobby Black), and gravitated toward a country/swing sound. Frayne quit his job at WSU, and in 1969 took the Airmen to San Francisco where they were soon joined by Bill Kirchen on lead guitar, Bruce Barlow on bass, Lance Dickerson on drums, and "Swingin'" Andy Stein on fiddle. Playing regularly at Berkeley nightclubs (especially Mandrake's), they built a loyal entourage and inked a deal with Paramount. Their debut recording, **Lost in the Ozone**, yielded a big hit with a remade version of "Hot Rod Lincoln" (Johnny Bond) and was followed by four more albums for Paramount, each loaded with energetic boogie woogie, honky tonk swing (lots of truck driving songs) highlighted by the lead guitar work of Kirchen. The "Good Commander" and band found a second home in Austin where they became regulars at the Armadillo World Headquarters. In 1974, they cut a classic live album at the 'Dillo, **Live From Deep in the Heart of Texas,** that captures them at their peak. Switching to Warner Brothers, CCLPA made several albums on that label, most notably another live album, **We've Got a Live One Here!**, before calling it quits in 1976. Commander Cody went on to make two solo records before reassembling the Airmen with only two of the original members (Barlow and Black) remaining. They put out three fairly mediocre recordings although one, **Lose It Tonight** (1980) did produce a Grammy winning video of the song "Two Triple Cheese, Side Order of Fries." In the mid-1980s, Kirchen returned to record **Let's Rock** which with songs like "Your Cash Ain't Nothin' But Trash" and "Truck Stop at the End of the World" represented a return to the band's old form. With many of the old Airmen still on board, they recorded **Sleazy Roadside Stories** and **Aces High** which won Indie Country Albums of the Year in 1990 and 1991. However, by 1992, Kirchen had departed once again to pursue a solo career and in 1992, Commander Cody put together a whole new line-up with a more hard rock than country/swing sound. The revamped Airmen released **Worst Case Scenario** in 1993. Several collections of material from the early 1970s version of CCLPA are available and previously unreleased recordings continue to surface periodically including, a live recording from 1973 called **The Tour From Hell**.

Outside of Commander Cody, Frayne developed into an acclaimed visual artist who specializes in semi-abstract watercolors of American musicians such as Robert Johnson, Louis Armstrong, and Janis Joplin. He kept the LPA going in the 1990s in various incarnations; in 1997, after moving to Saratoga Springs, New York, George assembled a completely new lineup to keep the tradition alive.

Original Members: Bruce Barlow (b,v,1968-1976); Bobby Black (s.g.,v, 1970-1976); Lance Dickerson (d,v,1968-1976); Billy C. Farlow (hm,v,1968- 1976;1995); George Frayne aka Commander Cody (p,v); Bill Kirchen (g,v,1969-1976; 1986-1992); Andy Stein (f,sax,1968-1976); John Tichy (g,1967-1977); West Virginia Creeper (s.g.,1970-1976)
Current Members: Steve Barbuta (d); Clyde Davies (b); Mark Emmerick (g); George Frayne (p,v); David Malachowski (g)

Lost in the Ozone/Paramount/1971; MCA/1984
Hot Licks, Cold Steel and Truckers' Favorites/
   Paramount/1972; MCA/1986
Country Casanova/Paramount/1973; MCA/1987
Live From Deep in the Heart of Texas/Paramount/1974;
   MCA/1988
Commander Cody and His Lost Planet Airmen/ Warner
   Brothers/1975
Tales From the Ozone/Warner Brothers/1975
We've Got a Live One Here!/Warner Brothers/1976
Midnight Man (Commander Cody solo)/Arista/1977
Rock 'n' Roll Again/Arista/1977
Flying Dreams (Commander Cody solo)/Arista/1978
Lose It Tonight/Peter Pan/1981
Let's Rock!/Blind Pig/1986; Topic UK/1986
Very Best of...Plus/See for Miles/1987
Commander Cody Returns From Outer Space/Edsel UK/1988
Sleazy Roadside Stories/Relix/1988
"Daddy's Drinking Up Our Christmas" on **Hillbilly
   Holiday**/Rhino/1988
Aces High/MCA/1990

Too Much Fun...Best of Commander Cody/MCA/1990
**The Very Best of (...Plus) Commander Cody & His Lost
   Planet Airmen**/See for Miles/1991
Lost in Space (1975 Radio Show)/Relix/1993; Aim Aust.
   & Rounder/1993
Worst Case Scenario/Aim Rounder/1993
Lose It Tonight/Let's Rock/Line Ger/1994
Bar Room Classics (1973)/Aim/1994
Relix's Best of Commander Cody/Relix/1995
**The Further Adventures of Commander Cody and His Lost
   Planet Airmen: The Tour From Hell, 1973**/Aim/1996

Commander Cody/Globe Records Home Page
//www.globerecords.com/cody.html

Commander Cody Austin Links Page
//www.austinlinks.com/music/cody.html

See Bill Kirchen

Ray Condo (The Hardrock Goners; The Ricochets; Jimmy Roy's Five Star Hillbillies)
Hillbilly Bop; Western Swing
Hull, Quebec, Canada; 1980s-

When Ray Condo belts out "I'm a long gone daddy and a hep cat papa all the way!," he ain't fooling! In fact, Condo (aka Ray Tremblay) is perhaps the wildest, swingingest cat to ever come out of Canada. But, it wasn't always so. Growing up in a working class family in the city of Hull (Quebec province), he listened to the radio, sang country songs with his mom, dabbled on the guitar, and fell under the spell of the British Invasion. However, Condo's main ambition as a young man was not to become a musician but an artist. And so, after high school, he went to art school to study painting, but dropped out when he got caught up in punk and then by gradual steps rockabilly, blues, country, and swing. Ray's final conversion to the latter came when he moved to Montreal in the early 1980s and met Clive Jackson, bass player and American roots music enthusiast. Eventually (c.1983/4), the two formed Ray Condo and the Hard Rock Goners (named for Hardrock Gunter) with Chris Dean and brothers Eric and Peter Sandmark (now leaders of the Crazy Rhythm Daddies). Specializing in rockabilly and swing, they played a few dates around Montreal and in 1986 made their first recording **Crazy Date** on Pipeline. But soon after making a second album, the label went bankrupt and when it refused to release the recording, the Hard Rock Goners bootlegged a cassette version which was ultimately put out as an LP (**Hot 'n' Cold**) by Crazy Rekkids in 1988. After several European tours and three excellent albums of rockabilly, hillbilly boogie, Western swing (**Condo Country**, **Come On**, and **Hillbilly Holiday**), Ray and Jackson quit and headed for Vancouver where they found a thriving music scene with a number of A-1 rockabilly bands (the Dots, Stinging Hornets, Nervous Fellas) and several exceptionally good hillbilly honky tonk/swing outfits such as the Yodells and the Five Star Hillbillies. The latter was led by steel guitar player Jimmy Roy who began the band in the 1980s as a tribute to country singers Johnny and Jack but then gradually pushed the group toward a mix of honky tonk, rockabilly, and swing. Their **Everybody's Talking** was done in 1991 for East Side Records which also released two compilation cassettes of Vancouver's 1980s rockabilly and country band (see Compilations/Soundtracks section for details). Jimmy Roy and company received nominations for "Midnight Ride" as best original song (1992 Genies) and Country Group of the Year by the West Coast Music Awards. Two songs from **Everybody's Talking** were included on a British compilation **Lordy Hoody** and in 1993 Fury Records released an expanded version of it as the incredible **Five Star Hop**. In 1994, Jimmy Roy joined forces with Condo and Jackson plus former members of the Five Star Hillbillies, Steve Nikleva and Steve Taylor to create Ray Condo and the Ricochets. Their debut, **Swing Brother Swing,** was released by East Side in 1995 and then picked up by the Joaquin label (named for steel guitar legend Joaquin Murphey of Spade Cooley/Tex Williams fame). Highlighted by Condo's bluesy whoop/growl/scream vocals and cool sax playing, Jimmy Roy's stellar steel, and excellent support from the rest of the Ricochets, **Swing** offers a potent blend of rockabilly, swing, blues, and jazz that cooks on record and absolutely boils in person. They followed it up with **Door to Door Maniac** which delves deep into Americana (Dorsey Burnette, Billie Holiday, Tex Williams, Glenn Barber, Lee Bonds, Rocky Bill Ford, Gene Vincent, Frankie Lee Sims) to deliver another superb set of jump blues/swing/rockabilly.

The Hard Rock Goners (Mid-1980s-1993): Ray Condo (g,sax,v); Chris Dean; Clive Jackson (b); Eric Sandmark (g); Peter Sandmark (g)
The Ricochets (1994-): Clive Jackson (b,uke); Stephen Nikleva (l.g.); Jimmy Roy (s.g.,v); Steve Taylor (d)
The Five Star Hillbillies (Mid-1980s-1993): Ronny Hayward (b); Steve Nikleva (l.g.); Jimmy Roy (s.g.); Paula Spurr (v); Steve Taylor (d); Cam Wagner (r.g.)

   Crazy Date (Hard Rock Goners)/Pipeline Can./1986
   Mondo Condo (Hard Rock Goners)/HRG/1988 (boot CS)
   Hot 'n' Cold (Hard Rock Goners)/Crazy Rekkids
      Can./1988 (originally **Mondo Condo**)
   Condo Country (Hard Rock Goners)/Crazy
      Rekkids/1990; Fury UK/1993
   Everybody's Talkin' (Five Star Hillbillies)/East Side
      Can./1991 (CS)
   "Pierre's Boogie" and "Railroad Bridge" (Five Star
      Hillbillies) on **Lordy Hoody**/Fury UK/1991
   Hillbilly Holiday (Hard Rock Goners)/Fury UK/1993
   5 Star Hop (Five Star Hillbillies)/Fury UK/1993
   Come On (Hard Rock Goners)/Fury UK/1994
   Swing Brother Swing (The Ricochets)/East Side
      Can./1995; Joaquin/1996
   Door to Door Maniac (The Ricochets)/Joaquin/1997

Ray Condo c/o Joaquin Records, 254 Scott St., San Francisco, CA 94117

Ray Condo Rockabilly Hall of Fame Page
//www.rockabillyhall.com/RayCondo.html

See The Crazy Rhythm Daddies

Stompin' Tom Connors
Singer/Songwriter
Ontario, Canada; 1936-

Although most Americans have absolutely no idea who he is, Stompin' Tom Connors (Thomas Charles Connors) is not only Canada's most famous country performer but also one of the most revered figures in Canadian history. For the better part of four decades, over 40 albums, and miles of touring (in Canada only), he has won a special place in Canadian hearts and minds by writing hundreds of inspiring and memorable songs about just about every aspect of Canada and its cultures. He's also secured a special place by being a character's character who had a rough upbringing in Northern Ontario and troubadoured across the country for many years before settling down to play at a local bar in Timmins, Ontario. From that modest beginning, Stompin' Tom (named for vociferously pounding out the beat with one leg) went on to parlay an outlaw image and one hit record after another into national acclaim and adoration. His songs are Canadian to the bone proudly hailing the country's natural wonders, history, obscure and well-known person-alities, and eccentricities. They've won Tom numerous Juno Awards and respect from a wide spectrum of musicians including a group of punk bands who did a tribute album called **Stomp on Wood** in 1997. In addition, Connors was awarded an Order of Canada in 1996 and the first volume of his auto-biography, *Before the Fame*, was a #1 bestseller. Still going strong in his 60's, Stompin' Tom continued to tour and in 1998-1999, EMI re-issued 10 of his best recordings as the **Man of the Land** Series.

   25 of the Best Stompin' Tom Souvenirs/EMI Can./1998
   Man of the Land Collection/EMI Can./1999 (re-release
      of 10 of Stompin' Tom's best recordings)

Stompin' Tom's Place
//www.emimusic.ca/tom/html/music.html

Construction Joe
Lo-Fi Roots Rock
Burlington, Vermont; 1996-

There are few bands whose members have more eclectic back-grounds than Construction Joe. Lead singer/banjoist David Kamm was raised in upstate New York, got an engineering degree, learned ragtime guitar on the side, and ended up in Burlington, Vermont playing "ragtimepunkjazz" guitar at local coffeehouses. Later, he was in an experimental music group called Famous Potato where he met bassist Nicole Valcour, a Vermonter "born with shit between her toes" (farm girl) who studied native cultures at Colgate. Along the way, they found drummer Trevor Crist who had come from Kansas to the Green Mountain State to study film at Middlebury College. Post-Famous Potato, Kamm took up the banjo, decided to do a solo record, and asked Valcour and Crist to assist, but when the sessions really clicked they became Construction Joe in 1995. A year later, they added electric cellist Nelson Caldwell and began weaving together lo-fi roots rock based on esoteric lyrics, unusual arrangements, and unexpected instrument combinations. **Construction Joe** and its follow-up **Cry Uncle** defy easy categorization and while traces of other lo-fi roots rockers can be heard, the group has a certain uniqueness as well. Some of the songs are fairly straightforward including the folk rock hoedown "Victimized," the countryish ballad "Reason," and several really nice (but lyrically strange) waltzes with Kamm's lap steel lurking just underneath. But the really interesting material comes when Kamm's plunking, sometimes bouncy clawhammer banjo joins with Caldwell's electric cello (which he plays more like an electric fiddle) or when the cello teams with a nervous slide guitar on the 16 Horsepower sounding instrumental "Rugburn." Vocal duties are shared mainly by Kamm and Valcour; she is reminiscent of Paula Frazer of Tarnation and when they duo the Albion Band or Richard and Linda Thompson come to mind. Songwriting is split between Kamm, Caldwell, and Valcour; their lyrics are challenging and all three tend to stay on the darker side. However, they've got a whimsical side too as they show on the modern rock satire "2062" and "Big Beat," an old-time/rap tune sung through a bull horn *a la* the Hix.

Nelson Caldwell (cello,g,v); Trevor Crist (d); David Kamm (bj,g,hm,l.s.,v); Nicole Valcour (b,v)

Construction Joe/Sonic Dirt/1997
Cry Uncle/Sonic Dirt/1997

Construction Joe, P.O. Box 8384,
Burlington, VT 05402; 802-658-1984

Construction Joe Home Page //www.cjoe.com

joe@joe.com

The Continental Drifters
Roots Rock
Los Angeles, California; 1992-1993/
New Orleans, Louisiana; 1993-

The Continental Drifters emerged quite by accident when members of established bands began playing together informally at a local L.A. nightspot called Raji's in the early 1990s. Susan Cowsill (Cowsills, Psycho Sisters), Peter Holsapple (dBs, REM), Carlo Nuccio (Tori Amos), Vicki Peterson (Bangles, Psycho Sisters), and Mark Walton (Dream Syndicate, Steve Wynn, Giant Sand) kept their performances deliberately low key and felt free to experiment with a combination of styles including country, rock, and soul. They adopted the name Continental Drifters to reflect their commitment to a free flowing arrangement. In 1993, they drifted to New Orleans, developed a following on the local scene, and made appearances at the New Orleans Jazz Festival and at SXSW in 1994. The core of the Drifters made their first recording as the Walkin'

Tacos contributing "A Song for You" to the Gram Parsons' tribute album **Commemorativo**. After adding lead guitarist (Robert Mach), the Drifters recorded a self-titled debut album for the fledgling New Orleans label Monkey Hill. **The Continental Drifters** reflects their early commitment to a loose interpretation of a variety of Americana. In 1996, the band's touring and recording schedule was disrupted somewhat when Nuccio departed and Holsapple joined Hootie and the Blowfish as their temporary keyboard player. However, they quickly found a new drummer, Russ Broussard (ex-Blue Runners) and gained wider exposure after opening a few concerts for Hootie. A live single, "Christopher Columbus Transcontinental Highway" b/w "Meet on the Ledge" (Richard Thompson) was released in July 1997 on Blue Mountain's Black Dog label and a new full-length, **Vermilion**, came out in 1998 on Germany's Blue Rose. Recorded in a studio in rural Louisiana and named after a river, **Vermilion** wraps up the Continental Drifters' trademark roots rock in one neat package. Ex-Drifter Carlo Nuccio made his country rock solo debut in 1998 with **Loose Strings**.

Russ Broussard (d,1997-); Susan Cowsill (a.g.,v); Peter Holsapple (b,g,ky,md,sl.g.,v); Rob Ladd (d, 1996-); Robert Mache (e.g.,sl.g.,1994-); Carlo Nuccio (a.g.,d,v, to 1996); Vicki Peterson (a.g.,e.g.,v); Mark Walton (a.g.,b)

"A Song for You" (as the Walkin' Tacos) on
Commemorativo: A Tribute to Gram Parsons/
Rhino/1993
"I Can't Let Go" on **Sing Hollies in Reverse: A Tribute to the Hollies**/eggBERT/1993
The Continental Drifters/Monkey Hill/1994
"Christopher Columbus Transcontinental Highway" b/w "Meet on the Ledge"/Black Dog/1997 (7")
"Christopher Columbus Transcontinetnal Highway" on **Revival2: Kudzu and Hollerin' Contest**/Yep Roc/1997
"Mixed Messages" on **The Blue Rose Collection, Vol. 2**/ Blue Rose Ger./1997
Vermilion/Blue Rose Ger./1998
Loose Strings (Carlo Nuccio)/Monkey Hill/1998
"When You Dance I Can Really Love" on **This Note's For You Too!: A Tribute to Neil Young**/Inbetweens Dut./1999

The Continental Drifters, P.O. Box 820434,
New Orleans, LA 70182-0434

The Continental Drifters Home Page
//members.aol.com/contdrift/

Contdrift@aol.com

The Continental Drifters/Blue Rose Page
//www.bluerose-records.com

Cordelia's Dad (Northampton Harmony; Io)
New Old-Time; Shape Note Singing
Amherst, Massachusetts; c.1990-

Some of the most interesting bands to come along in recent years have been those that ignore boundaries and search for the commonalties joining the most disparate styles of music.

Groups that immediately come to mind are the Bad Livers, Donna the Buffalo, the Horseflies, the Chicken Chokers/Hix, and Boston's Cordelia's Dad. In the case of the latter, the connection is between modern rock, traditional Appalachian old-time, and New England ballad singing. On one level, the punk side of the band members was attracted to the lyrics of the old-time songs; the dark themes of disease, death, and tragedy woven through so much rural American music transcend a particular time or place and speak with equal poignancy to each new generation. On another level, the vocal intensity of certain types of traditional singing drew them to the music. In particular, they incorporated the Sacred Harp "shape note" style of singing (characterized by strong rhythm, atypical harmony, extreme volume) as practiced by Lee Monroe Presnell, Roscoe Holcomb, and other old-time singers. This amazingly intense form of a capella dates back to the Renaissance and traces a continuous line in America since colonial days. In the initial stages of their career, Cordelia's Dad was a Janus-faced band with an electric side ("like life, only louder") that could match the best of alternative bands and an acoustic side ("extreme modal music") as they showed on a self-titled debut, **How Can I Sleep?**, and **Joy Fun Garden**. Lots of college radio air play and touring in the U.S. (with Nirvana) in the early 1990s showed much promise, but their label went bust and so Cordelia's Dad tried their luck in Europe where they enjoyed their greatest success. However, after 1995, their fortunes in the U.S. rose with lots of exposure (SXSW; Folk Alliance) and rave critical acclaim (from *Folk Roots* to *Rolling Stone*). That year also marked the beginning of Cordelia's Dad turn toward an all-acoustic sound when they recorded **Comet**, an album of traditional acoustic/modal music. After releasing one more recording of raw-edged rock (**Road Kill**), Cordelia's Dad played a final electric show in late 1996 before going fully acoustic and adding fiddler Laura Rusk in early 1997. Since then, they have become devoted students and practitioners of shape note singing either as Cordelia's Dad or with the group Northampton Harmony. The latter recorded two songs for a Tony Trischka Christmas album and one full length CD, **The Hookes' Regular Sing**, dynamically illustrating the awesome power of shape note. Cordelia's Dad has participated in a number of other interesting side projects including the John Cage inspired composition "Trio for Bands" in which three rock bands played simultaneously ("it was loud") and the Yugoslav popular music band (Zabe i Babe); they have even toyed with the idea of doing an acoustic album of Residents covers.

Occasionally, Cordelia's Dad still lets loose their rock side as Io which recorded an as yet unreleased project with Steve Albini producing and recording. However, their main focus as Cordelia's Dad has been on continued interpretations of North American traditional music. In 1998, with Albini as producer,

they recorded **Spine**, a highly experimental and wholly respectful collection of songs drawn from well-known and obscure songwriters of the 18th-20th centuries. The liner notes are filled with lots of interesting details about neglected but important figures in American folk like Lena Bourne Fish, Vance Randolph, Clyde Davenport, Louis Boudreault, William Sidney Mount, Lee Monroe Presnell, and their big hero, Dwight Diller, who invited them to help out on his 1998 release **New Plowed Ground**. At the same time, Eriksen and Oss further explored shape note singing with Northampton Harmony on **Hope**.

Cordelia's Dad/Io: Tim Eriksen (bj,g v); Peter Irvine (d,frame d.,v); Cath Oss (acc,b,v); Laura Rusk (f,v,1997-)
Northampton Harmony: Jeff Colby (bass); Tim Eriksen (lead); Kelly House (treble); Cath Oss (alto)

> **Cordelia's Dad**/Okra Normal Ger./1990; Omnium/1996
> "Her Bright Smile" and "San Francisco" on **Sample Some Okra**/Normal Okra/1991
> **How Can I Sleep?**/Normal Ger./1992; Omnium/1996
> **Four Songs: Acoustic EP**/Normal Ger./1992
> **The Joy Fun Garden**/Return to Sender Normal/1993
> **Comet**/Omnium/1995
> "Three Snake Leaves" b/w "Hush"/Scenescof/1995 (7")
> **Road Kill**/Scenescof/1996
> **The Hookes' Regular Sing** (Northampton Harmony)/ Hazmat/1996
> "Something Out There" b/w "Leave Your Light On" (Io)/Ferric Mordant/1998 (7")
> **Spine**/Appleseed/1998
> **Hope** (Northampton Harmony)/Bison/1998

Cordelia's Dad, P.O. Box 175, Northampton, MA 01061

Cordelia's Dad Home Page //world.std.com/~steeple/cordelia.html

Cordelia88@aol.com

Cornerstone

Progressive Bluegrass
Ithaca, New York; 1991-

Cornerstone describes itself as a band that plays "mainly original material in the bluegrass vein, but varied and adventurous in content." This modest but accurate synopsis pretty much sums up this exceptional group which in just a few short years climbed high in the ranks of progressive bluegrass. Based in Ithaca, New York (also home to The Horseflies and Donna the Buffalo), Cornerstone formed in 1991 and quickly made its presence felt by winning the best band award at the 1991 Winterhawk Bluegrass Festival, showcasing at the 1992 IBMA conference, and securing a 20th place ranking on the *Bluegrass Unlimited* chart for their debut self-release **Maggie's Daughter**. An appearance at the 1993 MerleFest, where banjoist and leader Chris Stuart won two songwriting awards, was followed by a second album **Out of the Valley** which encompasses bluegrass, swing, and even a little Cajun for good measure. **Lonesome Town** follows the same successful formula and like all their recordings, its strength lies in the inventive writing of Stuart (including the hilarious "Twenty Naked Pentecostals in a Pontiac") and the powerful lead vocals of Dee Specker.

Rick Manning (f,md); Dana Paul (b); Dee Specker (f,l.v.); Chris Stuart (bj); Tim Wallbridge (g)

Maggie's Daughter/Ind/1992
Out of the Valley/Folk Era/1994
Lonesome Town/Folk Era/1995

Cornerstone c/o Chris Stuart, 495 E. Lake Rd, Dryden, NY 13053; 607-844-4910

Cornerstone Home Page
//www.cfe.cornell.edu/cstone/cstone.html

cs10@cornell.edu

Elvis Costello

Country Rock
Liverpool, England, August 25, 1955-

One of the advantages of making it big as a musician is the freedom to indulge in pet side projects. A case in point is Elvis Costello who threw fans and critics a real curve in 1981 when he recorded **Almost Blue**, an album of classic country. However, if they had been paying closer attention, this move might not have come as quite such a surprise. In 1978, as Tex & the Attractions, Costello first showed his "good ol' boy" side on a single **Stranger in the House** with covers of Hank Sr.'s "Honky Tonkin'" and "Honky Tonk Blues"; a year later, he dueted with George Jones ("Stranger in the House") on The Possum's **My Very Special Guests**. During this period, Costello began to include country standards in his live shows and then took the final step in 1981 by entering a Nashville studio to make **Almost Blue**. With Billy Sherrill as producer, Costello was joined by the Attractions and steel player John McFee on covers of Jones ("Good Year for the Roses"; "Color of the Blues"), Haggard ("Tonight the Bottle Let Me Down"), Patsy ("Sweet Dreams"), Hank ("Why Don't You Love Me?"), Gram ("I'm Your Toy"; "How Much I Lied"), and even the demented "Psycho" (Leon Payne). Reaction to the album was mixed, but if nothing else, Costello brought country to New Wavers who might not have listened to it otherwise. Likewise, Costello was exposed to country audiences when Jones had him on a 1981 HBO Special to do "The Bottle Let Me Down" and Hank Cochran's "He's Got You." A number of bootleg recordings of Costello concerts from the early 1980s subsequently appeared (**Almost Blue, Almost 1982**; **New Year for the Roses**) and contain live versions of songs from **Almost Blue** plus covers of Loretta Lynn, Webb Pierce, and more. An album entitled **Nashville & More** has studio demos from **Almost Blue** including many standards not released on the album. There is also a video called "The Making of Almost Blue" in *The Elvis Costello TV Collection* and in 1997, Rykodisc issued two ex-

tended versions of **Almost Blue**, one with the **Elvis Costello and the Attractions** boxed set and another with country material recorded **Live in Aberdeen**. One final bootleg of interest is the 1995 Czechoslovakian release **Sweetwater** taken from a live performance in Mill Valley, California in 1989 featuring Costello solo and with a band made up of Jerry Garcia, Bob Weir, James Burton, and Nick Lowe on "Only Daddy That'll Walk the Line," "You Win Again," "The Bottle Let Me Down," and "Why Don't You Love Me Like You Used to Do?" In 1998, Costello contributed "Sleepless Nights" to the much ballyhooed Gram Parsons tribute album which was released in 1999.

Stranger in the House: "Honky Tonkin'" b/w "Honky Tonk Blues" (as Tex & The Attractions)/ Cowboy Discs/1978 (7")
Almost Blue/Rykodisc/1981; 1994
Almost Blue, Almost 1982 (Live at L.A. Sports Arena)/ 1981 (2 CS bootleg)
Nashville & More/Caucasian/198? (AB studio demos)
New Year for the Roses (as Lucky Stevens Sings)/ Note/1982 (live at The Palladium)
Sweetwater/Moonlight Czech./1995
Almost Blue With Live in Aberdeen/Rykodisc/1997
"Sleepless Nights" on **Return of the Grievous Angel: A Tribute to Gram Parsons**/Almo/1999

Elvis Costello Home Page //www.east.isx.com/~schnitzi/ec/ (the best EC page with lots of information on obscure recordings and many links)

The Country Bumpkins (The Stumbleweeds)

Old-Time; Novelty; Honky Tonk; Rockabilly
Boston, Massachusetts; 1986-

Vaudeville played a major role in the early days of country music. On stage, record, and/or radio, routines of various types were a common part of performances. In particular, comedy or novelty acts by individuals or whole bands were standard fare. In recent times, the most familiar expression of this tradition has been *Hee Haw,* but for the most part, it disappeared from modern country music. However, one band which revived it is the Country Bumpkins who contrary to their name are all city folk (from Boston) whose previous musical experiences included playing in numerous punk and hard rock bands (Human Sexual Response, The Lyres, Concussion Ensemble). The impetus for "goin' country" came from sister and brother, Lynnette Lenker and Allan Sheinfeld, who began fooling around with a few songs, got inspired (by Michael Nesmith, Wanda Jackson, the Collins Kids among others), added three more members, and formed the Bumpkins. After rehearsing, they began playing in Boston and while performing on a local radio station (WMBR) decided to introduce comedy into their repertoire. Initially, the humor was limited to a few jokes between songs, but in time, they began to work up skits ("Klutzy Comedy Corner With Lem 'n Clem"; "Roy & Th' Reakin' Deacon") and country novelty songs. On their self-titled CD, the Bumpkins included skits plus applause and laugh tracks to introduce originals "The Bull & the Beaver" ("the world's first pornographic trucking song"), "LSD" (about a drug induced murder), "Po' White Trash" and covers of "18 Wheels," Iggy Pop's "Funtime," and the country s&m tune "Hog Tied," all done with a 1950s-ish honky tonk/rockabilly beat. In 1998, the band went on an extended vacation with members drifting on to other projects. Lynnette Lenker stayed very active in Boston's thriving Hellcountry community as lead singer of the Stumbleweeds whose forte is high-energy classic honky tonk and rockabilly.

The Country Bumpkins: Rich "Peckerhead" Gilbert (p.s.); Lynnette "Mimsy Farmer" Lenker (g,v); Chris MacLachlin (b); Allan "Roy Sludge" Sheinfeld (g,v); Judd Williams (d) **The Stumbleweeds:** Mike Feudale (u.b.); D.W. Highway (p.s.,v); Dennis Kelly (l.g.); Lynnette Lenker (g,l.v.); Kimberly Rullo (d)

"Funtime" on **North By Northeast**/ Northeastern/1991
  The Country Bumpkins/CB/1995

The Country Bumpkins Feature
//www.owlnet.rice.edu/~briwahl/countrybumpkinsFeature.html

The Stumbleweeds
//www.hellcountry.com/stumbleweeds.htm

Lynnette Lenker: llenker@mit.edu

Country Gazette (Alan Munde & Joe Carr)
Progressive Bluegrass; Country Rock
Los Angeles, California; 1972-1991

Country Gazette arose in the early 1970s from seminal country rock group, the Flying Burrito Brothers. During their 1970-1971 tour, three of the Burrito's sidemen, Byron Berline, Roger Bush, and Billy Ray Lathum, were brought out to perform bluegrass as the Hot Burrito Revue. In 1972, after the demise of the FBB, Alan Munde replaced Lathum, Kenny Wertz was added on guitar, and the Hot Burrito Revue officially became Country Gazette. Mixing bluegrass with California style country rock, they recorded two albums, **Traitor in Our Midst** and **Don't Give Up Your Day Job** for United Artists and toured the U.S. with some big name acts of the day but just didn't click with American audiences. However, they were strangely popular in England and Holland; they recorded a number of albums on British and Dutch labels (most notably **Bluegrass Special**) and in 1974 were voted Top Country Band by the British CMA. With the departure of Berline and Bush in 1975, Dave Ferguson and Roland White came on board, and after signing with Flying Fish, Country Gazette recorded **Out to Lunch**. They also did two albums for Ridge Runner, **What a Way to Earn a Living** and **All This and Money Too** with Richard Greene and Berline on fiddle. Wertz left in 1976, Joe Carr joined in 1978, and Country Gazette carried on through several more notable recordings for Flying Fish before breaking up in 1983. Munde

and White started the group up again in 1984 but called it quits in 1988 with Munde going on to a successful solo banjo career and White joining the Nashville Bluegrass Band. In 1991, Flying Fish issued **Hello Operator...This is Country Gazette**, a compilation the best of their Flying Fish material which clearly demonstrates the important contributions the band made to the development of progressive bluegrass.

Post-Gazette, Alan Munde and Joe Carr joined the faculty of the unique Country/Bluegrass Music Department at South Plains College in Levelland, Texas. The "Pickin' Professors" taught a variety of courses and did numerous instructional books and videos for banjo, guitar, mandolin, and fiddle. They also teamed up to co-author the highly entertaining and informative *Prairie Nights to Neon Lights: The Story of Country Music in West Texas*. In addition, Munde and Carr performed as a duo and recorded two albums (**Windy Days and Dusty Skies**; **Welcome to West Texas**) full of good ol' bluegrass plus Texas style and original music.

Byron Berline (f, to 1975); Roger Bush (b); (Joe Carr (g,v,1978-1984); Alan Munde (bj,v); Kenny Wertz (g,v); Roland White (g,md,v, 1975-1988)

  A Traitor in Our Midst/United Artists/1972
  Live in Amsterdam/Bumble Dut./1972
  Don't Give Up Your Day Job/United Artists/1973
  Bluegrass Special/Ariola Dut./1973
  Banjo Sandwich (Joe Carr)/Ridge Runner/1975
  Out to Lunch/Flying Fish/1976 or **Sunnyside of the Mountain**/Transatlantic UK/1976
  Country Gazette Live/Antilles/1976
  What a Way to Earn a Living/Ridge Runner/1977
  Otter Nonsense (Joe Carr)/Ridge Runner/1978
  All This and Money Too/Ridge Runner/1979
  American and Clean/Flying Fish/1981
  Strictly Instrumental/Flying Fish/1981
  America's Bluegrass Band/Flying Fish/1982
  Hello Operator...This is Country Gazette/Flying Fish/1991
  Texas Fiddle Favorites for Banjo and Mandolin (Alan Munde)/AM/1991
  Festival Favorites Revisited (Alan Munde)/Rounder/1994
  Blue Ridge Express (Alan Munde)/Rounder/1994
  Windy Days and Dusty Skies (Alan Munde & Joe Carr)/Flying Fish/1995
  Prairie Nights to Neon Lights: The Story of Country Music in West Texas, Alan Munde & Joe Carr, Lubbock: Texas Tech University Press,1995
  Welcome to West Texas (Alan Munde & Joe Carr)/Rounder/1998

Alan Munde/Joe Carr Profile
//www.banjo.com/profiles/mundecarr.html

Music Education/South Plains College
//www.musicvideo.com/spcca.html

See Byron Berline

The Country Gentlemen

Progressive Bluegrass
Washington, DC; 1957-

The granddaddy of all progressive bluegrass groups, the Country Gentlemen's lengthy alumni list is a veritable who's who of modern bluegrass. Started in Washington, D.C. in 1957, they distinguished themselves not just by tight harmonies and solid picking but by an unprecedented mixing of bluegrass with straight country, R&B, folk, and rock. Riding the crest of the folk scare of the 1960s, the Country Gentlemen became mainstays on the folk circuits and recorded albums on several labels (Folkways, Starday, Mercury) before finding a permanent home with Rebel Records. Their unique (for that time) blending of genres appealed to a variety of audiences and spread bluegrass beyond its traditional musical and demographic boundaries. Through many personnel changes, with Charlie Waller as the stabilizing force, the Country Gents maintained a level of consistency and innovation from their early recordings, **Country Songs Old and New** (1960) and **Folk Songs and Bluegrass** (1961) through many excellent Rebel albums including **Award Winning Country Gentlemen** (1972) to their Sugar Hill material compiled as the **Sugar Hill Collection** (1995). Through their work together and through that of the many great musicians (John Duffey; Doyle Lawson) who have been alumni, the Country Gentlemen established themselves as *the* preeminent progressive bluegrass band. In 1996, they were rewarded with induction into the IBMA Hall of Fame, and in 1998, Rebel Records issued a box set of their material from 1962-1971. Alumni of the Country Gentlemen and the Seldom Scene assembled at the Birchmere (Arlington, Virginia) in mid-November of 1998 for a one-night tribute to one of their greats, John Duffey.

Original Members: John Duffey (md,v,); Bill Emerson (bj,v); Tom Morgan (b); Charlie Waller (g,v)
Distinguished Alumni: Eddie Adcock; Jimmy Gaudreau; Doyle Lawson; Ricky Skaggs

  Traveling Dobro Blues/Starday/1959
  Country Songs Old & New/Smithsonian Folkways/1960
  Folk Songs and Bluegrass/Smithsonian Folkways/1961; 1988
  Bluegrass at Carnegie Hall/Starday/1962; Gusto/1988
  The Country Gentlemen on the Road/Folkways/1963
  Going Back to the Blueridge Mountains/Folkways/1963
  Folk Session Inside/Mercury/1963
  Hootenanny/Design/1963
  Bringing Mary Home/Rebel/1966
  The Country Gentlemen Sing Bluegrass/Zap/1967
  The Traveler and Other Favorites/Rebel/1968
  The Country Gentlemen Play It Like It Is/ Rebel/1969
  New Look, New Sound/Rebel/1970
  One Wide River to Cross/Rebel/1971
  Sound Off/Rebel/1971
  Award Winning Country Gentlemen/Rebel/1972
  The Country Gentlemen/Vanguard/1973

  The Country Gentlemen, Yesterday and Today: Vol. 1/ Rebel/1973
  The Country Gentlemen, Yesterday and Today: Vol. 2/ Rebel/1973
  The Country Gentlemen Live in Japan/Seven Seas Jp./1975; Rebel/1988
  Joe's Last Train/Rebel/1976
  Calling My Children Home/Rebel/1978
  River Bottom/Sugar Hill/1981
  25 Years/Rebel/1982
  Sit Down Young Stranger/Sugar Hill/1988
  Let the Light Shine Down/Rebel/1991
  New Horizons/Rebel/1992
  Sugar Hill Collection/Sugar Hill/1995
  The Country Gentlemen Box Set/Rebel/1998

See The Seldom Scene

The Country Rockers

Hillbilly Bop; Honky Tonk
Memphis, Tennessee; 1989-1994

Compared to the Country Rockers, long time boppers like Ray Campi, Ronnie Dawson and Sleepy LaBeef are young pups. Formed in Memphis in the mid-1980s, the Rockers got a record deal with help from Alex Chilton. When they released their first album, **Free Range Chicken**, in 1989, drummer Gaius "Ringo" Farnham was 77, lead guitarist Sam Baird, 70 and bassist Durand Easley a youngster at 40. But, don't let their ages fool you; these guys can flat out play! They capably handle honky tonk ("Drivin' Nails," "There Stands the Glass"), country ballads ("Don't Worry"), Western swing ("Fan It"; "Steel Guitar Rag"), Eastern swing ("Stompin' at the Savoy"), rockabilly ("Arkansas Twist"; "Alley Boogie"; "Rockin' Daddy"), and even surf ("Wipe Out"). Best of all, they infuse a spirit of fun and exuberance that is highly contagious. A follow-up, **Cypress Hill**, covers much the same ground with a similar good time attitude. In 1993, the German label Veracity recorded the Country Rockers live at their home club in Memphis, but this session was not released. And, unfortunately, the Rockers went into semi-retirement in 1994 when Ringo moved away after the death of his sister. However, leader Easley hasn't completely ruled out a reunion although the hour is getting late.

Sam Baird (g, v); Durand Easley (b,v); Gaius "Ringo" Farnham (d, v)

  Free Range Chicken/New Rose Fr./1989; Telstar/1992
  "Rock Around with Ollie Vee" on **Everyday is a Holly Day**/New Rose Fr./1990
  Cypress Room/New Rose Fr./1991
  Live at the Antenna Club, Memphis, September 1993/ Veracity Music Ger. (unreleased)

Country Rockers c/o Easley Recording
3744 Marion Memphis, TN 38111

The Country Teasers

Country Punk; Psychocountry
Edinburgh, Scotland; c.1995-

A not so favorable review in *Magnet* called their music "some of the most shittily recorded misinterpretations of country/ western ever made" and noted that "nobody has yet to make a record that captures the angry, unprofessional rotten spirit of roots rock" like this group does. The Country Teasers would probably consider this high praise. Even their own label's promo characterized them as an "outrageously filthy crew of Scots" who "punch out a crude, rude, irreverent brand of (usually) misogynistic, hard-boiled country music and garage SLOP." On their self-titled debut, they manage not only to take swipes at women ("Stand by Your Man"; "Bitches Fuck Off") but also cowboys ("Anytime Cowboy"), truckers ("Drove a Truck") and religion ("Only My Saviour"). As an encore the Country Teasers churned out another batch of highly offensive psychocountry on **Satan is Real Again** with subtle songs like "The Wide Open Beaver of Nashville," "Panty Shots," "I Don't Like People," "Thank You for Making Me an Angel," and "Country Fag."

BRW (d,g,v); A. K. Crichton (g); S, W. Stephens (b)

"Anytime Cowboy" b/w "#1 Man"/Crypt/1995 (7")
The Country Teasers/Crypt/1995 (10" with 10 cuts; CD with 12 cuts)
Satan Is Real Again/Crypt/1996

The Country Teasers/Crypt Home Page
//www.matadorrecs.com/crypt/bios/country_teasers.html

The Countrypolitans

Honky Tonk; Hillbilly Bop
Portland, Oregon; 1996-

Judging from their name, you might think the Countrypolitans play music with lush strings and saccarine background choruses, but guess again. This Portland, Oregon quartet delivers genuine honky tonk/hillbilly boogie inspired by Bakersfield and Nashville country from the 1950s-60s. And although they've only been together a few years, the Countrypolitans have become popular favorites in the local alt. country scene. In early 1998, they recorded a six song demo that showed the promise of exciting things to come on their 1999 full- length debut, **Tired of Drowning**. Lead singer Elisabeth Ames, whose vocals compare very favorably to Kim Lenz, Libbi Bosworth, Marti Brom, et al., writes all of their tunes and is ably supported by Roger Conley on bass, lead guitarist Geoff Clarkson (lots of James Burton, Don Rich influences), and steel player Pete Barak who knows how to wrap his instrument around a honky tonk song. The trade-offs and interplays between Barak and Clarkson provide some shining moments on the recording which is highly enjoyable from end to end. Helping out are Rosie Flores on backup vocals and Dale Watson

who does a lead guitar duet with Clarkson and also a vocal duet with Ames.

Elisabeth Ames (r.g.,l.v.); Pete Burak (s.g.); Geoff Clarkson (l.g.); Roger Conley (u.b.)

"Redneck Riot" on **Full Tank, Vol. 1**/Jackass/1998
The Countrypolitans/The Countrypolitans/1998 (6 song demo)
Tired of Drowning/Ultrapolitan/1999

The Countrypolitans 503-736-9518

The Countrypolitans Web Page //www.countrypolitans.com

cpinfo@countrypolitans.com

Courtesy Move

See Sherry Rich; Wilco

Cowboy Jazz

Western Swing
Baltimore, Maryland/Washington, DC; 1980-1984

Cowboy Jazz was a Western swing band of the early 1980s fronted by a trio of multi-talented women: Kate Bennett, Deanna Bogart, Denise Carlson. Each was blessed with exceptional vocal talent and shared the leads; Bennett handled most of the slower ballads (many of which she also wrote) while the more spirited numbers were generally taken by Carlson and Bogart (who contributed several originals as well). In addition, Carlson played hot, swing fiddle and Bogart pounded out a steady boogie woogie beat on the 88s. But, what really made them dynamic was their Andrews Sisters like harmonies that ranged from the sublime to the saucy. The other members of Cowboy Jazz provided excellent accompaniment, the real stand out being Barry Sless whose electric guitar and pedal steel work was always first rate. They made two recordings for Rounder with a Western swing sound like a combination of their predecessors, Commander Cody, and their successors, Ranch Romance. The first, **That's What We Like About the West**, relied more on covers like the title tune (Tex Williams), "Sugar Moon" (Bob Wills), "Cow, Cow Boogie," "Too Much Fun" (Commander Cody), but also had some fine originals. The follow-up, **Swing Boogie**, included a rocking version of the Davis Sisters' "Rock-a-Bye Boogie" and a Dan Fogelberg tune but the remainder were new songs by Bennett, Bogart, and Sless. In concert, Cowboy Jazz put on a very energetic, very danceable show and were well received from coast to coast. However, by the mid-1980s, the party was over, and Cowboy Jazz went their separate ways. Bogart formed a jump blues band which recorded several albums, made numerous tours to Europe, and was one of the most popular groups in the D.C. area (winner of many Wammies). Carlson also went on to a solo career and became leader of a swing band called Denise and De Nephews while Sless joined another Maryland based swing group, The Lone Starlet Band, and was also in the David Nelson

Band. Drummer Alpert has a web page (Rhumba.com) with an amusing account of the adventures and midsadventures on a Cowboy Jazz tour to Alaska.

Kate Bennett (r.g.,h.v.,l.v.); Deanna Bogart (p,h.v.,l.v.); Denise Carlson (f,h.v.,l.v.); Brian Alpert (d); Charlie Crane (d); Tony DeFontes (b); Barry Sless (e.g.,p.s.)

That's What We Like About the West/Rounder/1981
Swing Boogie/Rounder/1982

Deanna Bogart Home Page //www.bayblues.org/db.html

Rhumba.Com: Stories of Life on the Road (Brian Alpert) //rhumba.com/

The Cowboy Junkies
Lo-Fi Country Rock
Toronto, Ontario, Canada; 1985-

Described by the *All Music Guide* as "country on Valium," the Cowboy Junkies were one of the originators of lof-fi country rock and have had a big impact on many alt. country bands. While on tour to promote their 1986 debut, **Whites Off Earth Now!!** (mellow blues covers), they traveled through the South/Southwest and got hooked on country music. On their next effort, **The Trinity Sessions,** the influence clearly showed. Using the lowest of low tech (one microphone), they recorded (in a Toronto church) laid back covers of Hank, Patsy, and Waylon, country infused originals, and a memorable version of the Velvet Underground's "Sweet Jane." This haunting combination of country and narcotic rock won them a following and a deal with RCA which resulted in a string of critically acclaimed records highlighted by the ethereal vocals of Margo Timmins, understated but effective lead guitar by her brother Michael, and judicious use of pedal steel. Over 12+ years and 3 million in record sales, they never strayed far from this formula. The Junkies 1996 recording, **Lay It Down**, re-kindled the stripped down approach of their early recordings, and their ultra lo-fi style pervades the music of such alt. country groups as the Scud Mountain Boys, the Handsome Family, and Palace. Their 1998 **Miles From Our Home** represented somewhat of a departure with uptempo, pop rock style songs intermixed with the signature Cowboy Junkies downtempo sound. The latter is most poignantly displayed on "Blue Guitar," a tribute to their friend Townes Van Zandt that includes lyrics from his unfinished song, "Screams From the Kitchen."

Alan Anton (b); Margo Timmins (v); Michael Timmins (g); Peter Timmins (d)

Whites Off Earth Now!!/Latent/1986; RCA/1991
The Trinity Sessions/Latent/1988; RCA/1988
The Caution Horses/RCA/1990
Black Eyed Man/RCA/1992
Pale Sun, Crescent Moon/RCA/1993
200 More Miles: Live Performances, 1985-1994/
  RCA/1995 (2 CDs)
Lay It Down/Geffen/1996

Miles From Our Home/Geffen/1998
"Ooh Las Vegas" on **Return of the Grievous Angel: A Tribute to Gram Parsons**/Almo/1999

The Cowboy Junkies Ring //www.bomis.com

The Cowboy Junkies/Geffen Page //www.geffen.com/cowboyjunkies/

Cowboy Junkies Unofficial Fan Club //www.geocities.com/SunsetStrip/palms/7573/

Cowboy Junkies //members.aol.com/vey/junkies.htm

iMusic Cowboy Junkies Showcase //imusic.com/showcase/contemporary/

Cowboy Nation
See Rank and File

Cowboys & Indians
Western Swing
Dallas, Texas; 1990-

Someone once asked me to describe the Dallas Western swing band Cowboys & Indians. Without hesitation I said, "Bob Wills on amphetamines!" After further review, I still think that's a pretty fair characterization. Their leader, Erik Swanson, who formed the band in 1990 has acknowledged that from the start Cowboys & Indians' aim was to infuse Western swing and jump blues with a higher, more modern energy. How well they have succeeded in this goal can be measured by their live per-formances. This six piece combo goes into maximum overdrive delivering an unrelenting, frenetic attack of blaring horns and driving guitar leaving dancers panting and begging for mercy. On record, Cowboys & Indians are only slightly more subdued than in person. With their first CD, **The Western Life**, they honor their main man, Bob Wills with revved up modernized versions of "Roly Poly" and "Ding Dong Daddy From Dumas," cover jump swing master Louis Jordan, and Swanson con-tributes pumped up originals such as "Indian Attack!" and "Big Man." The follow-up, **Big Night in Cowtown**, continues along the same path with a special nod to Texas swing and honky tonk on a cover of Wills' "Drunkard Blues" and bouncy originals like the title tune, "Takin' Out the Trash," "You Never Want the Water," and "Stompin' at the Sons," a tribute to their favorite local venue, the Sons of Hermann Hall. In addition to their full-length CDs, the band's songs have been included on **Dallas Scene and Heard, Honkey Tonk Holidays** (a collection of X-Mas songs by Dallas alt. country bands), **Live From the Barley House, Jukebox Cowboy**, and the *Texas Monthly Contemporary Texas Swing* compilation along with Asleep at the Wheel, Alvin Crow, Maryann Price, and Don Walser.

Billy King (e.g.,l.s.); Jim Lehnert (sax,tromb); Brandon Lusk (trp); Larry Reed (b); Erik Swanson (a.g.,trb,l.v.); Geoff Vinton (d)

"Roly Poly" on **Dallas Scene and Heard**/Dallas Observer/1995

The Western Life/Cowboys & Indians/1995
"Drivin' You Out of My Mind" on **Contemporary Texas Swing**/Texas Monthly/1995
"Santa, Santa" and "Merry Christmas, Miss Molly" on **Honkey Tonk Holidays**/1995
"That's What I Like About the South" and "Big Man" on **Live From the Barley House**/BH/1995
"Western Life" on **Jukebox Cowboy**/Vinyl Junkie UK/1997
Big Night in Cowtown/Cowboys & Indians/1998

Cowboys & Indians,
P.O. Box 180161, Dallas, TX 75218

The Cowslingers
Cowpunk
Cleveland, Ohio; 1991-

O.K., let's face it; the history of country/western music has been filled with raving alcoholics (musicians and fans alike). Hank, Lefty, and a host of others past and present have pretty near raised drinking to the level of an art form. Of course, in recent years, this side of country has been downplayed, but there are still some who believe that "gettin' drunk" is not only a sacred rite but also one of the fundamental themes of a perfect c/w song. Take, for instance, the Cowslingers who have characterized themselves as "men who still eat red meat, refuse to cover their mouth when they sneeze, and worship the porcelain god every now and then." Backed by a romping, stomping cowpunk beat, they sing "heart felt hymns about truck stop waitresses livin' in trailers, hell bent buckaroos rejoicing in the 'evils' of alcohol, and shit-faced raunch hands indulging in 'pleasures of the flesh,' no matter how distorted." Shoot, even the horses in their songs get drunk and throw up! But, they can play it fairly straight as on their homage to the heroes of America's highways, **That's Truck Drivin'** which covers standards (e.g. "Truck Drivin' Man";) and originals ("18 Wheels to Hell"; "Trucker's Last Dollar"). In 1996, the Spanish label Rock & Roll issued a 21 track retrospective, **A Fistful of Pesetas**, (produced by Eric Ambel) of the "best of" the Cowslingers including unique cowpunk originals and one-of-a-kind covers of Duane Eddy, Dick Dale, and Hank Williams. In 1997, they toured Spain, showcased at SXSW, did a rousing cover of the Stanley Brothers "If I Lose" for Bloodshot's, **Straight Outta Boone County**, and in late 1997 released **West Virginia Dog Track Boogie** featuring all new cowpunkabilly hits. Touring to support the new one throughout 1998, the Cowslingers played a number of festivals including the Steam Donkey's annual Americana-Rama in Buffalo, New York. They named their 1999 CD in honor of that event.

Bobby Latina (g); Leo P. Love (d); Greg Miller (v); Ken Miller (b,1996-); Tony Primiano (b, to 1996)

"Bad Booze Rodeo" b/w "The Burro Show"/Drink n Drive/1992 (7")
Hangover Hoe-down/Drink n Drive/1993 (7")
"Hogtied" b/w "One Piece at a Time"/Estrus/1994 (7")

"My Baby Don't Cum Aroun' Here No More" b/w "Movin' n Groovin'"/"Only One"/HomoHablis/1994
The Cowboy Way ("Cowboy Bob" b/w "Hey Good Lookin'")/Shake It/1994 (7")
Off the Wagon and Back in the Saddle/Drink n Drive/1994
That's Truck Drivin'/SFTRI/1995 (10"; CD)
"Shotgun" b/w "I Can Tell"/Get Hip/1995 (7")
"Old One Eye" b/w "Heyday"/Demolition Derby/1995 (7")
"Spine Snapper" b/w "Bossa Nova Baby"/SFTRI/1996
"Mexican Blackbird"/Man's Ruin/1996 (7")
"Strip Bars, Liquor and Fireworks" on **The Estrus Cocktail Companion**/Estrus/1996
A Fistful of Pesetas/Rock & Roll Inc. Sp./1996
"If I Lose" on **Straight Outta Boone County**/Bloodshot/1997
West Virginia Dog Track Boogie/Shake It/1997
"It's Gotta Kill My Baby" b/w "The Bottle Let Me Down"/Drink 'n' Drive/1998 (7")
Americana-Rama/1999

The Cowslingers, P.O. Box 771101,
Lakewood, OH 44107; 216-221-9764

The Cowslingers //wnywebshop.com/cowslingers/
cowslinger@hotmail.com

The Cox Family
Progressive Bluegrass
Cotton Valley, Louisiana; 1976-

Family bands have been a mainstay of country music from the beginning. Many of the great groups started simply with parents and children singing and playing in the living room or on the porch and evolved into public performances and sometimes stardom. Such is the case with the Cox Family from Cotton Valley, Louisiana. Father Willard, a life long country music lover, taught each of his kids (Evelyn, Suzanne, Sidney) to play an instrument and sing when they came of age, and together they learned the nuances of old-time and bluegrass music. Inspired by a bluegrass festival near their home, the Coxes decided to "go public" and began to perform at clubs and festivals in the states around Louisiana. A live tape of one of their shows fell into the hands of Alison Krauss who was very impressed by their incredible lead and harmony vocals, instrumental prowess, and songwriting skills. She picked up four of Sidney's songs for her next album, brought the Coxes to the attention of Rounder, and produced their 1993 debut, **Everybody's Reaching Out for Someone**. This grand collection of bluegrass, gospel, and country covers ("Pardon Me"; "Little White Washed Chimney"; "Standing By the Bedside of a Neighbor"; "My Favorite Memory"; "When God Dips His Pen") and originals ("I've Got That Old Feeling"; "Cry Baby Cry"; "Backroads") has goosebump raising lead vocals by Evelyn, Sidney, and Suzanne (who sounds amazingly like Krauss), heavenly harmonizing, and five star picking from the Coxes and a supporting cast including Rob Ickes on dobro, Ron Block on banjo, Adam Steffey on mandolin, and Andrea Zonn and Alison Krauss on fiddles. It announced the presence of a major new bluegrass talent, and the Cox Family was suddenly a fixture on the festival circuit. Their second recording, a gospel album with Alison Krauss, entitled **I Know Who Holds Tomorrow** won the 1994 Best Bluegrass/Gospel Grammy, and **Beyond the City** (produced by Krauss), was nominated for the 1995 Grammy for Best Bluegrass Album. On **Beyond the City**, they ventured away from a strictly traditional sound and began to draw on other musical sources. This trend was carried even further on their major label debut for Asylum, **Just When You're Thinking It's Over** (produced by Krauss). Their adventurousness has won them many fans among the bluegrass crowd and beyond. In 1994 and 1995, they toured as the opening act for Counting Crows and much to their surprise and delight were warmly received.

Evelyn (r.g.,h.v.l.v.); Sidney (bj,db,g,h.v.l.v.); Suzanne (md,h.v.,l.v.); Willard (f,h.v.,l.v.)

Quiet Storm/Wilcox/1990
Everybody's Reaching Out for Someone/Rounder/1993
I Know Who Holds Tomorrow (with Alison Krauss)/
   Rounder/1994
Beyond the City/Rounder/1995
Just When You're Thinking It's Over/Asylum/1996

The Cox Family Fan Club, P. O. Box 787,
Cotton Valley, LA 71018

The Cox Family Home Page
//www.banjo.com/bg/profiles/cox.html

See Alison Krauss

The Crazy Rhythm Daddies
Hillbilly Bop; Swing
Montreal, Quebec, Canada; 1988-

In the mid-1980s, Montreal brothers Eric and Peter Sandmark teamed with fellow Canadians Ray Condo and Clive Jackson to form Ray Condo & the Hard Rock Goners. They specialized in country and rockabilly, but the Sandmarks were also into swing/jazz (particularly Western swing) and with other members of the Goners created a sub-group to open for the Goners at their live performances. During the late 1980s, the Goners toured Canada and recorded several albums (**Crazy Date**; **Hot 'n' Cold**; **Condo Country**), but in 1991, Condo and Jackson split for Vancouver. However, the nucleus of the Goners (the Sandmarks, Chris Dean, Edgar Bridwell) continued on as the Crazy Rhythm Daddies. In 1991 and 1992, they released two cassette recordings, **Flat Foot Floogie** and **Swingcats' Ball**, covering Bob Wills, Smokey Woods, Slim & Slam, Louis Jordan, and Django Reinhardt. With a new bass and drummer, the CRD went to Hemsby in 1992 and 1993 and toured Europe in 1994 after which they recorded another tape, **One is Never Too Old to Swing**. It was re-released as a CD in 1996 on Igloo Records with reworked material from their previous recordings plus Western and Eastern swing originals.

In early 1997, a revamped version of this CD with a deluxe three-panel cardboard foldout sleeve and more information on the CRD was made available from Marc Coulavin (see below). Tours in 1997-1998 through Canada and Europe brought wider acclaim to the Daddies, and they found themselves in good company when two of their songs were included on Bob Timmers' **Rockabilly Hall of Fame, Volume 1**. During 1998, Peter Hay and Peter Mika were added on pedal steel and piano respectively to give the Crazy Rhythm Daddies a fuller and more balanced sound. In 1999, while finishing a new CD they contributed to **Hope You're Satisfied**, a salute to Western swing legend Hank Penny.

John Davis (b); Peter Hay (p.s.,1998-); Rob Kraft (d); Peter Mika (p,1998-); Eric Sandmark (e.g.,v); Peter Sandmark (a.g.,v)

Crazy Date (Hard Rock Goners)/Pipeline Can./1986
Hot 'n' Cold (HRG)/Crazy Rekkids Can./1988
Condo Country (HRG)/Crazy Rekkids/1990
Flat Foot Floogie (Crazy Rhythm Daddies)/Crazy
   Rekkids/1991 (CS)
Swingcats' Ball (CRD)/Crazy Rekkids/1992 (CS)
One is Never Too Old to Swing (CRD)/Crazy
   Rekkids/1995 (CS); Iglu Can./1996 (CD)
"Bip Bop Bip" on **All-American Hardcore Hillbillies**/1996
"Lost and I'll Never Find My Way" and "What's the
   Matter With the Mill" on **Rockabilly Hall of Fame,
   Vol. 1**/RHF/1998

For info on the deluxe version of **One is Never Too Old to Swing** contact Marc Coulavin, P.O. Box 122, Station P, Toronto, ON, M5S 2S7, Canada; 416-944-9624 or //www.aracnet.net/~iglu/; iglu@aracnet.net

The Crazy Rhythm Daddies, c/o Peter Sandmark, 4358 Beaconsfield, Montreal, Quebec H4A 2H6, Canada; 514-482-7143

psandmark@hotmail.com

The Crazy Rhythm Daddies/Iglu Page
//www.aracnet.net/~iglu/index.html

The Crazy Rhythm Daddies Rockabilly Hall of Fame Page
//www.rockabillyhall.com/CrazRhyDad.html

See Ray Condo

The Crop Circles
Grange Rock
Seattle, Washington; 1994-

The Crop Circles were the brainchild of Earl Brooks, long time member of the Seattle music scene. In the late 1980s and early 1990s, he was in several bands including The Blood of the Lamb Band and played rhythm guitar for local singer/ songwriter Gary Heffern. While with the latter performer, he met Carolyn Wennblom who sang backup vocals for Heffern and singer/songwriter Larry Barrett. After forming the Crop Circles in 1994, Brooks asked Wennblom to sing on their first recording **Born With a Bad Heart**. She became a regular member, and in time, the band's sound came to revolve around the twin vocals and harmonies of Brooks and Wennblom. Musically, the Crop Circles describe themselves as "Seattle's original grange rock band"; they blend rock and country with a healthy dose of twisted humor and score high on covers such as "When I Win the Lottery" (Camper Van Beethoven) and "Year of the Sofa" (Model Rockets) and Brooks penned originals like "Rain Town," "One Step Closer," and "Tumbleweed Fences." In 1996, the Crop Circles worked on a sequel while Wennblom recorded a solo effort (**Bees to the Honey**) for Glitterhouse with help from members of the Gary Heffern Band and the Walkabouts. Early in 1997 the Crop Circles second CD **Sing the Songs of Stinky Doolittle** hit the stores. According to Brooks, he came across the music of an obscure North Carolina songwriter named Stinky Doolittle (who is really a dog!) while doing some research on hill music and work songs. The songs on the album, "Brown Eyed Girl," "One Cold Lie," "In My Time of Dying," "Tex Ritter is Dead," et al. come from the pen of Doolittle (Brooks) and range from ballads to country rockers.

Mike Birenbaum (ky); Earl Brooks (a.g.,v); Lauren Deknatel (b); Sean Sippel (d); Arttu Tolonen (bj,e.g.,hm); Carolyn Wennblom (v) with Andrew Hare (p.s.); Christine Marie Larsen (acc)

> **Born With a Bad Heart**/Big Redd/1996
> **Bees to the Honey**/Glitterhouse Ger./1996
> **Sing the Songs of Stinky Doolittle**/Big Redd/1997

The Crop Circles c/o Earl Brooks,
6649 Flora Ave. S., Seattle, WA 98108

The Crop Circles Home Page
//netcatchers.com/crop/crop.htm

patti@netcatchers.com

Carolyn Wennblom/Glitterhouse Web Page
//www.ontide.de/glitterhouse/

Alvin Crow

Austin; Fiddle; Western Swing; Honky Tonk
Oklahoma; September 29, 1950-

One of the most welcomed outcomes of the progressive country movement that hit Austin, Texas in the late 1960s and early 1970s was the revival of Western swing. Among the bands carrying on the tradition set by Bob Wills, Milton Brown, Bill Boyd, and many others, the two most prominent and influential in Austin were Asleep at the Wheel and Alvin Crow. Crow, who hails from Oklahoma, started the Pleasant Valley Boys in Amarillo in 1968 before moving them to Central Texas in 1971. With their mix of Western swing, Texas honky tonk, and Buddy Holly style rockabilly, they became favorites at local dance halls especially the legendary Broken Spoke. Alvin, who bears a striking resemblance to Holly, handled lead vocals and played a mean fiddle inspired by the greats of Western swing. The original Pleasant Valley Boys included brother Rick on lead guitar, Bobby Earl Smith on rhythm guitar, Roger Crabtree on harmonica, and Herb Steiner on steel. Their self-titled record-

ing of 1976 featured a guest appearance by Jesse Ashlock (Texas Playboys) and covers of Bob Wills ("All Night Long") and Jesse Winchester ("That's the Touch I Like") plus originals like "Fiddler's Lady" (Crow) and the classic crowd pleaser, "Nyquil Blues" penned by Steiner. In 1977, Alvin and the Boys made their big label debut with **High Riding**, a more straight ahead Western swing/honky tonk recording with production by Tommy Allsup, guest appearances by Al Strickland and Leon Rausch (both Texas Playboys), and tunes like "Yes She Do, No She Don't" (originally done by Milton Brown), "Wine Me Up" (Faron Young), "Cotton Eyed Joe," and a tribute to the King of Western Swing, "Here in Turkey Texas (The Home of Bob Wills)" by Steiner. It also has two tunes "High Stepper" and "Retirement Run" (one last marijuana haul) by the original King of White Trash, D. K. Little.

Over the years, Crow and various incarnations of the Pleasant Valley Boys continued to record lots of excellent Western swing/honky tonk/rockabilly and nailed down a permanent spot at the Broken Spoke. They cut several albums on the Broken Spoke label including one of classic cowboy songs, **Cowboy 1**. In the early 1980s, Crow joined Doug Sahm's band and played fiddle and guitar on several recordings. He was a member of the Texas Mavericks, a side project with Sahm, Speedy Sparks, and John X. Reed that recorded one pseudonymous album of country, rockabilly, blues, and Tex-Mex called **Who are These Masked Men?** Into the late 1990s, Alvin Crow and the Pleasant Valley Boys could be found several times a month at the Broken Spoke, and as hosts to that venues' annual New Year's Eve party.

> **Alvin Crow and the Neon Angels**/Big Wheel/1973, 1979
> **Alvin Crow and the Pleasant Valley Boys**/Long Neck/1976
> **High Riding**/Polydor/1977
> **Big Wheel**/Longneck/1979
> **Welcome to Texas**/Austex/1984
> **Long Texas Nights**/Austex/1986
> **Pure Country**/Broken Spoke/1988
> **Cowboy 1**/Broken Spoke/1991
> **Honky Tonk Trail and Sings Pure Country**/Broken Spoke/1993
> **Texas Classic**/Broken Spoke/1996

The Broken Spoke Home Page //www.instar.com/bspoke/
(for info on Crow's recordings)

See Doug Sahm

J. D. Crowe

Banjo; Progressive Bluegrass
Georgia; August 27, 1937-

Influenced by 5-string master Earl Scruggs, J. D. Crowe took up banjo in his early teens. He apprenticed with several bluegrass bands in the 1950s (including Jimmy Martin's Sunny Mountain Boys), but in the early 1960s went solo. At that time (like

Scruggs), he began to push bluegrass beyond its traditional borders by blending in blues, folk, and rock. Crowe continued down this path with his band The Kentucky Mountain Boys who recorded a first-class album of progressive bluegrass gospel called **The Model Church** in 1969. This early experimentation came to full flower in the 1970s when Crowe formed a band called New South with future stars Jerry Douglas, Tony Rice, and Ricky Skaggs. Their self-titled debut in 1975 with its unique take on standards and incorporation of non-bluegrass songs and styles turned the traditional bluegrass world on its ear and helped set the standard for a new generation of progressive bluegrass. With several different line ups (including Keith Whitley, Jimmy Gaudreau, Sam Bush), J.D. Crowe and the New South continued to innovate into the 1980s on bluegrass (**Straight Ahead**), country (**Somewhere Between**; **My Home Ain't in the Hall of Fame**), and even country rock (**Blackjack**) recordings. Crowe worked on a number of progressive bluegrass projects, most notably the acclaimed **Bluegrass Album** series with Rice, Douglas, Doyle Lawson, Bobby Hicks, Todd Phillips, Vassar Clements, and Mark Schatz. He stopped touring in the late 1980s and worked primarily as a guest artist. However in the early 1990s, Crowe returned with a completely revamped New South. In 1994, Rounder released **Flashback** (Grammy nominated), the definitive retrospective of one of the greats in progressive bluegrass and that year Crowe was named Banjo Player of the Year by the IBMA. He and the New South continued to make the festival circuit in the late 1990s. **Live in Japan** was re-issued on CD in 1997, but a new recording didn't appear until **Come on Down to My World** (1999) which showed J.D. and company in top form.

New South Alumni: Jerry Douglas (db); Jimmy Gaudreau (md,v); Tony Rice (b,g,v); Ricky Skaggs (f,md,v); Keith Whitley (r.g.,v).
Current Members: Curt Chapman (b); Glenn Duncan (f); Phil Leadbetter (db,g); Greg Luck (g,l.v.); Dwight McCall (md,v)

> **J. D. Crowe & The New South**/Starday Gusto/
> **J. D. Crowe & The New South**/Rounder/1975
> **Holiday in Japan**/Towa Jp./1975
> **New South Live**/Trio/
> **You Can Share My Blanket**/Rounder/1977
> **My Home Ain't in the Hall of Fame**/Rounder/1978
> **Somewhere Between**/Rounder/1981
> **The Bluegrass Album, Vols. 1-5**/Rounder/1981-1989
> **Live in Japan**/Rounder/1982; 1997
> **Bluegrass—The World's Greatest Show**/Sugar Hill/
> **Straight Ahead**/Rounder/1986
> **Blackjack**/Rebel/1987
> **Flashback**/Rounder/1994
> **Come on Down to My World**/Rounder/1999

Official J.D. Crowe & The New South Page
//www.rhrun.com/jdcrowe/

J.D. Crowe & The New South Web Page
//www.banjo.com/profiles/jdcrowe.html

J.D. Crowe Discography
//www.cs.cmu.edu/~jcm/discog.html

Justin Curtis and His Rockabilly Co-op
Rockabilly; Honky Tonk
Winnipeg, Manitoba, Canada/Nashville/Seattle

Talk about taking the long way around! Justin Curtis started life in the wilds of central Canada where his earliest musical memories were of another JC (Johnny Cash) pumping out of the 8-track in his parents '69 T-Bird. With this inspiration, Curtis started playing music in high school and after graduation enjoyed some local success with a single ("Tell Me Why") and two cassettes (**Little Message** and **Let It Burn**). Then, he made the long trek to Nashville where wide-eyed enthusiasm turned into five years of struggling for gigs and money with his band Two Fast. However, there were a few bright spots; he met bassist Shades Jacoby who's been with him ever since, and Two Fast was named Most Promising Band by a local entertainment association. But, Justin decided to head back to Canada (Calgary) where he and Jacoby started a new group called Outerlimits. Their **Banned From Nashville** did well enough to interest Music City's independent Reptile label for which they recorded **Rockabilly in 3D**. The latter received fairly widespread radio play, and a video of "Nothing to Do" aired on CMT and the New Country Network in Canada. But, Curtis wasn't satisfied and after some years of vagabonding, he and Jacoby finally found a musical home in Seattle especially at the Tractor Tavern where with his new band, Rockabilly Co-op, he hosted regular Johnny Cash tributes. On their 1998 release, **Let Them Ride**, the Man in Black's imprint is unmistakeable in Curtis' rich baritone and originals, but Justin has his own honky tonk hillbilly thing going here plus he's got a good sense of humor whether dealing with cars, flying saucers, or romance and its aftershocks.

His Rockabilly Co-op: Marc Barnhardt (d); Adam Bratman (e.g.); Shades Jacoby (b)

> "Tell Me Why"/Boomtown/1986 (7")
> **Little Message**/Boomtown/1989 (CS)
> **Let It Burn**/Boomtown/1990 (CS)
> **Banned From Nashville**/1992 (CS)
> **Rockabilly in 3D**/Reptile/1995; Plutonium Hillbilly/1997
> **Let Them Ride**/Galaxy/1998

Justin Curtis, P.O. Box 17248, Seattle, WA 98107; 206-784-9785

bopstreet@bopstreet.com

Mary Cutrufello
Austin; Honky Tonk; Country Rock
Fairfield, Connecticut; 1970-

O.K., how many female, African-American/Italian, New England raised, Ivy League educated, lead guitar playing honky tonk singers can you name? Give up? Well, you can start your list with Mary Cutrufello. Raised in Fairfield, Connecticut, she majored in American Studies at Yale and played in several rock bands before a trip out West and exposure to Dwight Yoakam's music converted her to country. After researching and locking into country's traditions, Cutrufello decided to head for one of the only remaining real country meccas, Austin, Texas. Inspired by local alt. country acts like Chapparal, Chris Wall, and Dale Watson, she polished up her country lead guitar chops and vocals but developed a much rawer, rootsier brand of honky tonk. She formed a group called the Havoline Supremes, released one cassette, and played the clubs, but her growling vocals, raucous guitar licks, and thinly veiled androgyny were too much even for Austin's progressively minded music crowd. Still, Mary persisted, making the rounds of Texas joints and dives (country and rock) outside of Austin and in time was welcomed back with open arms. In 1995, her song "Tonight I Know" was included on the **Austin Country Nights** compilation and in 1996, Cutrufello recorded her first CD, **Who to Love & When to Leave**. Gradually, her persistence paid off as the ever-important buzz got attention from "all the right people." During 1996-1997, Jimmie Dale Gilmore signed her up to play baritone guitar for his Braver Newer World tour, she got a slot on an *Austin City Limits* show devoted to the city's new cadre of alt. country performers, and was invited to perform at Farm Aid. By mid-1997, especially after a spread in *USA Today*, Cutrufello was being eagerly pursued by at least a half-dozen big labels. Steve Earle, with whom she wrote the song "Love's to Blame," was interested in signing her to E-Squared, but Mary inked a six album deal with Mercury and prepared to make her major debut in 1998. **When the Night Is Through** was a straight-ahead, no-nonsense (and no country) rock and roll album that sorely disappointed Mary's twang fans but clicked with a new batch of fans and critics who hailed the coming of a major new rock voice.

Mary Cutrufello (with the Havoline Supremes)/ MC/1993

"The Long Red Line" on **Songs of Route 66**/Lazy
   SOB/1995
"Tonight I Know" on **Austin Country Nights**/
   Watermelon/1995
Who to Love & When to Leave/MC/1996
"Sworn to Pride" on **Jukebox Cowboy**/Vinyl Junkie
   UK/1997
When the Night is Through/Mercury/1998
"Candy In the Window" on **Real: The Tom T. Hall
   Project, Vol. 1**/Sire/1998

Mary Cutrufello, P.O. Box 33175, Austin, TX 78764

PrideSworn@aol.com

Mary Cutrufello/Mercury Records Page
//www.mercuryrecords.com

Bruce Daigrepont
Traditional and Modern Cajun
New Orleans, Louisiana; 1959-

Growing up in New Orleans, Bruce Daigrepont (day-cray-pont) first took up the banjo and leaned toward bluegrass. However, a visit to Lafayette's famed Festival Acadiens in 1978 gave him a new appreciation of Cajun culture and music. Switching to the accordion, he formed the Bouree Cajun Band in 1980. It became a regular at the Crescent City's Maple Leaf Club and eventually evolved into the Bruce Daigrepont Cajun Band. As part of the new generation of Cajun bands alongside Beausoleil, the Basin Brothers, File, and Steve Riley, the BDCB combine music of the past and present although Daigrepont is probably the most traditional of the lot. His three recordings to date mix Cajun with Creole and zydeco plus some country, rock, and R&B elements highlighted by Bruce's unique accordion style and Waylon Thibodeaux's stellar fiddling. **Stir Up the Roux** and **Couer des Cajuns** were both named Album of the Year by the Cajun French Music Assoication, and Daigrepont won the Best Accordionist award from the same organization in 1988 and 1990. For a number of years, the BDCB has hosted a Cajun music night on Sundays at the legendary Tipitina's and have been frequent Cajun music ambassadors at Acadian festivals in New Brunswick and Nova Scotia and on tours through South America and Europe.

Stir Up the Roux/Rounder/1988
Coeur des Cajuns/Rounder/1990
Petite Cadeau/Rounder/1997

Bruce Daigrepont Home Page
//members.aol.com/bdcb/bdcb.htm

bdcb@prodigy.com

Dakota Suite
Lo-Fi Roots Rock
Leeds, England; 1996-

They take their name from the place where John Lennon was murdered; they write songs like "Crippled World," "Everything is Wrong," "I Can Feel Your Disease," "Loss," "Colder," "Wintersong," "Just Like Jesus," "Mood Indigo" and play them achingly slow using weary vocals, sullen violin, brooding cello, and weepy lap steel for a sound one reviewer labeled "quiet, patient music suffused with a heady melancholy" and another "country 'n' suicide." The core of the group is the trio, Chris Hooson, Richard Formby (Spacemen 3, Telescopes, Jazz Butcher), and Andy Thrower, who in just a few years together managed to create quite a stir in the U.K. and Europe with several acclaimed singles and EPs (gathered together as **Alone With Everybody**). 1998 was Dakota Suite's "breakthrough" year with **Songs for a Barbed Wire Fence** and inclusion on the **Loose** alt. country/Americana collection. Based in Leeds,

England, their nearest U.S. relatives are Palace, Lambchop, Sparklehorse, and U.S. Saucer.

Just Like Jesus/Amos UK/1996 (EP)
Mood Indigo/Amos UK/1996 (EP)
Colder/Amos UK/1997 (EP)
Alone With Everybody/Star Star/1998; Glitterhouse Ger./1998
"Mood Indigo" on **Loose: New Sounds of the Old West**/ Vinyl Junkie UK/1998
Songs for a Barbed Wire Fence/Amos UK/1998

Dakota Suite, c/o Amos Recordings, Roker Lane, Pudsey, West Yorkshire LS27 4RR England

Dakota Suite Home Page
//www.hooson.demon.co.uk/page3.html

dakotasuite@hooson.demon.co.uk

Dakota Suite Page //www.sensei.co.uk/dakota/

The Dalhart Imperials
Hillbilly Bop; Western Swing
Denver, Colorado; 1993-

From their stylish vintage cowboy/western wardrobe to their classic instruments and authentic honky tonk/swing sound, the Dalhart Imperials follow respectfully in the tradition of great groups that emerged from California and Texas after WWII. Named for a city in the Texas Panhandle, the Imperials, who are actually based in Denver, were started in 1994 by Kurt Ohlen and Les Cooper. Like contemporaries Big Sandy and Dave & Deke, their forte is the hillbilly bop style made famous by Hank Thompson, Billy Jack Wills, West and Bryant, and the Maddox Brothers & Rose. Their initial output consisted of a single and EP of original material on their own Wormtone label, but from a modest beginning, the Dalhart Imperials moved quickly up the ranks of nouveaubilly bands. A 1996 appearance at the Denver Rock 'N' Rhythm Weekend was followed by inclusion on the Bloodshot Midwestern Hayride tribute **Straight Outta Boone County**. In May 1997, they embarked on a European tour capped off by a performance at the prestigious Hemsby Festival in England. Back in Denver, the Imperials remained the top hillbilly bop band in the area hosting and/or playing the weekly "Tore Up!" showcase at the 9th Ave. West club and becoming regulars at the popular Denver weekender. Ohlen wanted them to tour more, but outside committments kept the other members close to home. So, in late 1998, he left to form a more full time Western swing combo, and the Dalhart Imperials continued on with a new bass player.

Rodney Bowen (d); Les Cooper (g,v); Dave Devore (l.g. 1993-1996); Craig Gilbert (d,1993-1994); Pascal Gumbard (l.g.,1996-); Kurt Ohlen (b,1993-1998); Tim Whitlock (s.g.)

"Crocodile Tears"/"When I Think of You" b/w "Already Gone"/"Man on a Mission"/Wormtone/1995 (EP)
"There Ain't No Place Like the Panhandle" b/w "Me, Myself, and I"/Wormtone/1996 (7")
"Won't You Ride in My Little Red Wagon" on **Straight Outta Boone County**/Bloodshot/1997

"No Good for You"/"Fresh Haircut" b/w "Guess What"/"Tell Ya Baby"/Shake It!/1997 (EP)

The Dalhart Imperials Home Page
//www.bigk.com/dalhart/dalhart.html

Kurt Ohlen: info@bigk.com

The Damnations TX
No Depression
Austin, Texas; 1994-

Austin's contributions to alt. country have mostly come from its rich singer/songwriter and honky tonk traditions. Once in a while, however, a group comes along with a different sound like the Bad Livers, the Gourds or the Damnations. The latter is clearly cut from no depression/insurgent country cloth, the closest reference point being Freakwater. Like that band, the Damnations tap traditional country led by two women (sisters Amy Boone and Deborah Kelly from upstate New York) who harmonize *a la* the Carters and write credible originals honed to a sharp modern edge. Over the past couple of years, the group has become very active on the Austin scene and gained exposure to a wider alt. country audience at a very successful SXSW showcase in 1997. Later that year, the Damnations (name inspired by a Sylvia Plath poem) made an Austin musical rite of passage by recording a live album on KUT radio. **Live Set** pays homage to country's roots with standards ("John Hardy," "Walking Boss," "Copper Kettle," "Your Long Journey") and two Carter tunes ("Ain't Gonna Work Tomorrow"; "Lonesome for You"). They also honor one of their obvious contemporary influences with a rollicking cover of Lucinda Williams' "Happy Woman Blues." The remainder of the CD is rounded out by some very affecting Boone/Kelly com-positions with "Spit n' Tears," "Kansas," "Unholy Train," and "Commercial Zone Blues" the real stand outs. Rob Bernard's plunking banjo and Gary Newcomb's wailing lap and pedal steels provide adequate backing, but the highlight throughout is the vocals of Boone and Kelly who are good separately but absolutely shine when they blend their voices in close harmony. Sire Records thought so too and made the Damnations an offer in early 1998 which, after some hesitation, they accepted. To avoid potential legal problems and confusion with a similarly named band in California, they toyed with changing their name to The Molly Brigade but then decided to stick to the original and add TX. The Damnations TX debut was initially scheduled for release in late 1998 but didn't hit the stores until early the next year. **Half Mad Moon** is comprised of a mix of new songs and studio versions of songs from the **Live Set** and was one of the early contenders for 1999 alt. country album of the year. Drummer Keith Langford subsequently moved on to the Gourds with whom the Damnations TX share musical and personal connections (Rob Bernard's brother Claude co-founded the Gourds).

Rob Bernard (bj,g); Amy Boone (b,p,l.v.); Deborah Kelly (g,l.v.); Keith Langford (d,1994-1998); Gary Newcomb (g,l.s.,p.s.)

Live Set/Damnations/1997
Half Mad Moon/Sire/1999

The Damnations TX, P.O. Box 4399, Austin, TX 78765
The Damnations TX Home Page //dnations.home.texas.net
dnations@texas.net

See The Gourds

Danny and Dusty

See Green on Red

Dash Rip Rock (The Swingin' Haymakers)

Roots Rock
New Orleans, Louisiana; 1984-

Named for a character on *The Beverly Hillbillies*, Dash Rip Rock has been turning out a fiery blend of rock, blues, country, swamp, and punk since their formation by Bill Davis, Ned Hickel, and Clarke Martty in 1984. They began as a rockabilly/cowpunk/roots rock trio modeled on mid-1980s contemporaries like the LeRoi Brothers, Rank and File, and Jason and the Scorchers, but when Martty tried to push them more toward country, Davis, who wanted to go further into roots rock, brought in a new drummer, Fred LeBlanc. They soon became favorites on the Southern college circuit and at clubs such as Atlanta's 688 which had its own record label and put out Dash's first LP in 1986. Touring and gaining fans in ever widening circles in the U.S. and Europe, their breakthrough recording came on Mammoth Records in 1988 with **Ace of Clubs** which rose to #1 on the college charts and got lots of praise from national music magazines. However, right in the middle of this success, LeBlanc went solo (later on created Cowboy Mouth) and was replaced by Chris Luckette. Into the early 1990s, DRR bolstered its standing as "the world's greatest bar band." The key to their appeal and longevity lay in a reputation for outrageous live shows and a string of recordings with searing roots rock, irreverent covers of country classics ("Jambalaya"; "I Saw the Light"), lots of songs about drinking ("True Drunk Love"; "All Liquored Up"), stinging parodies ("Stairway to Freebird"), and generally offensive songs like "Shootin' Up Signs" and "Rich Little Bitch." In 1995, when their career had hit somewhat of a lull, Dash recorded **Get You Some of Me** which contains the satirical "Let's Go Smoke Some Pot" (to the tune of "At the Hop"). This song became an instant cult classic through lots of air play on underground radio and led to a Dash mini-revival. **Gold Record** is a collection of their "greatest hits" plus true-to-form new material like "Locked in a Liquor Store With You." Dash worked on a new CD in 1998, running a contest to have fans give it a name; possible titles included **Too Drunk to Fish**, **Bored on the Bayou**, and **Exile on Bourbon St.**,

but they settled on **Pay Dirt**. Produced by none other than Fred LeBlanc, it delivers more patented rock 'n' twang in the aisles ("String You Up"; "Clown Down") plus a loving tribute to Country Dick called "King Death."

In the early 1990s, Davis and his wife Kim started a honky tonk, Western swing side project called the Swingin' Haymakers with local musicians Harold Cavallero, Joey Torres (Wild Peyotes, Johnny J & the Hitmen), and Michael Rouillier. They began playing informally at the Howlin' Wolf club, but their growing popularity induced them to cut an album (**For Rent**) of country/swing standards with guest piano pounder, Carl "Sonny" Leyland. It won Best Country Album of 1995 from *Offbeat* magazine, and the band was nominated for a Big Easy Award as Best Country/Folk Band, 1996.

Dash Rip Rock: Bill Davis (g,v); Ned Hickel (b); Fred LeBlanc (d,1984-1990); Chris Luckette (d,1990-1996); Clarke Martty (d,1984-1985); Kyle Melancon (d,1996-)
The Swingin' Haymakers: Harold Cavallero (p.s.); Dave Clements (b); Bill Davis (r.g.); Kim Roberts-Davis (l.v.); Michael Rouillier (l.g.); Joey Torres (d) with Carl "Sonny" Leyland (p)

Dash Rip Rock/688/1986; Mammoth/1989
Ace of Clubs/Mammoth/1989
Not of This World/Mammoth/1990
Boiled Alive!/Mammoth/1991
Tiger Town/Doctor Dream/1993
Get You Some of Me/Sector 2/1995
For Rent (Swingin' Haymakers)/Circle/1995
Gold Record/Naked Language/1996
Pay Dirt/PC/1998

Rip Rock Muckraker,
4859 Laurel, New Orleans, LA 70015
Official Dash Rip Rock Home Page //www.dashriprock.com
Bill@dashriprock.com
Dash Rip Rock Site
//www.datasync.com/~painter/history.shmtl
Dash Imitation Page //users.magbelle.net/neil/
Dash Rip Rock Shrine //www.netcom.co/~whodat/kru.html
The Swingin' Haymakers Hootenanny Page
//pw1.netcom.com/~haymaker/hoot.html
haymaker@ix.netcom.com

The Dashboard Saviors

Roots Rock
Athens, Georgia; 1991-

The Dashboard Saviors came out of the Athens Underground in the early 1990s. Like other bands from that milieu, they mixed rock with a variety of roots styles, but what set them slightly apart was a tendency to dig a little deeper into Southern musical traditions including folk, blues, and country. Their first outing **Kitty** was launched with lots of help from members of REM; Mike Mills played organ on several tracks while Peter Buck produced and strummed the 12-string. The REM sound is apparent on some songs, but the Saviors charted their own course on original folky numbers ("Town"; "Tracy's Calendar"), country rock ("Drivin' Blind"), and backwoods cuts ("A Trailer Is a Trailer"; "Brother Shiloh Collins") whose country mood is set by the ethereal fiddle and pedal steel of David Blackmon and John Keane. Also lending support was Vic Chesnutt (back up vocals) who along with Keane reappeared on the Dashboard Savior's follow-up **Spinnin' on Down** which covers much the same ground as their debut. Their third recording **Love, Sorrow, Hatred, Madness** revealed the band's unplugged side on acoustic folk, rock, blues, and country. After a European tour and release of a live CD, **Take One for the Team**, on the German Blue Rose label in 1996, the Saviors took a break with various members working on solo projects or performing with Athens/Atlanta musicians including Jack Logan, the Hot Burritos, and Bloodkin. In 1997, they were poised to enter the studio for a new record but broke-up instead. John Crist moved on to work with Marlee McLeod while Todd McBride went on to a solo career recording **Sketchy**, a Dashboard Saviors style recording alternating between rocking numbers and ballads including a cover of Townes Van Zandt's "You Are Not Needed Now." Blue Rose reissued the Saviors first three albums in 1997.

John Crist (d); Michael Gibson (g); Todd McBride (g,v); Rob Veal (b,org,v).

Kitty/Medium Cool/1992; Blue Rose Ger./1997
Spinnin' On Down/Medium Cool/1993; Blue Rose Ger./1997
Love, Sorrow, Hatred, Madness/Medium Cool/1995; Blue Rose Ger./1997
Take One for the Team (Live)/Blue Rose Ger./1996
Sketchy (Todd McBride)/Blue Rose Ger./1997
"Just Like Geronimo" on **The Blue Rose Collection, Vol. 2**/Blue Rose Ger./1997
"Wounded Ltd." (Todd McBride) on **The Blue Rose Collection, Vol. 4**/Blue Rose Ger./1998

Alan P. Scott's Dashboard Saviors Page
//www.pacifier.com/~ascott/me/dashboard.htm

Dashboard Saviors/Blue Rose Home Page
//www.bluerose-records.com/

The Dave and Deke Combo (Dave Stuckey & His Hire Hands; Deke Dickerson & The Ecco-Fonics)
Hillbilly Bop
Los Angeles, California; 1992-1996

Dave & Deke was the creation of Dave Stuckey and Deke Dickerson, both from central Missouri, who relocated to L.A. in the late 1980s and came up with the idea for a band that would lovingly recreate the sights and sounds of the Golden Age of hillbilly bop. Adding Lucky Martin on bass and Lance Soliday on drums, they took the name Dave & Deke Combo and adopted a style characterized by snappy vintage attire, downhome humor, jumpin' beat, and hot picking. The latter was provided

mainly by the guitar work of Dickerson who began his musical career in Missouri in the 1980s with the legendary surf/garage band Untamed Youth. With the Dave & Deke Combo, he played a vintage Mosrite double neck guitar and drew on a wide variety of influences (Joe Maphis, Jimmy Bryant, et al.). Consequently, the band could cover a lot of musical territory including honky tonk, rockabilly, and swing and flavor it with a healthy dose of hillbilly comedy using a vocal interplay between Dave and Deke (*a la* Homer & Jethro) or a narrative style (Stuckey) on whimsical originals such as "You Ain't as Dumb as You Look," "Warm Lips, Big Trouble," "Did Anybody Mention My Name," and "Henpecked Peckerwood." Additional comic relief was provided by the Stump Jumper's Club newsletter which presented Dave & Deke info, reviews, and articles plus vintage ads and news items all done up in a 1950s hillbilly motif.

During the early 1990s, the Dave & Deke Combo became one of the most popular of the modern hillbilly bop bands in England where their first recordings including their debut, **Moonshine Melodies,** were released on No Hit. In the mid-1990s, Dave & Deke began to build a following in the U.S. through regular appearances at California rockabilly/alt. country venues and rockabilly festivals. They recorded a number of singles but really broke through with the highly touted **Hollywood Barn Dance** which put them right up there with Big Sandy and High Noon. However, while at the height of their popularity, Dave & Deke shocked the hillbilly bop scene by splitting up when Dickerson decided to move on to other things. While still with Dave & Deke, he had been engaged in a number of side projects including a Joe Maphis newsletter (*Flyin' Fingers*) and the creation of Ecco-Fonic Records which has released singles and albums by Sean Mencher (High Noon), the Country Cabin Boys (Fly-Rite Boys w/o Big Sandy), T.K.'s Smith Ranch Boys (ex-Big Sandy guitarist), Jimmy Bryant, the Krazy Kats (1950s Missouri band), the Hot Shots (Japanese rockabilly), and Billy Zoom as well as a number of Dickerson instrumentals. Deke reformed Untamed Youth in late 1996 for a European tour and accompanied the Sprague Brothers on a Texas tour in 1997. H e also formed two new bands, the Go Nuts and the Dekes of Hazzard which eventually became the Ecco-Fonics. With the latter and help from Larry Collins, Joey D'Ambrosia (Bill Haley & the Comest), Carl Sonny Leyland, and Jeremy Wakefield (Lucky Stars), Dickerson cut **Number One Hit Record** which has a few echoes of Dave & Deke hillbilly music but also ballads, swing, and rock 'n' roll centered on Deke's formidable guitar versatility.

From late 1998-early 1999, Dickerson worked on variety of projects: producing a country-jazz guitar recording by Dave Biller (ex-Dale Watson) and Jeremy Wakefield, a multi-CD retrospective of the 1950s Missouri hillbilly label Jan, a compilation of 60s Missouri garage bands (**Drink Beer! Yell! Dance!**), and an anthology entitled **The Ecco-Fonic Records Story**. Meanwhile, Dave Stuckey drummed for the Horton Brothers and then started his own group which goes by the name of Pappy & His Hired Hands or Dave Stuckey & His Hired Hands. In addition, he works as a cartoonist and video producer and does a regular column on the L.A. rockabilly scene that can be found on the Collins Kids home page.

"Carrying On" b/w "Chrome Dome"/Bucket Lid/1993 (7")
The Chrome Dome UK/Dionysus (EP)
Hey Cuzzin'/No Hit UK/ (EP)
Moonshine Melodies/No Hit UK/1993
"Wild Woman" on **Pushing the Norton**/Hey Day/1994
"Chew Tobacco Rag" b/w "Twin Guitar Twist"/Goofin' Fin./1995 (7")
"TJ Tuck and Roll" b/w "This is Ecco-Fonic" (Deke)/Ecco Fonic/1995 (7")
"Swingin' in Outerspace" b/w "Diggin' It" (Deke)/Ecco Fonic/1995 (7")
"Asphalt Aisle" b/w "Midnight Swell" (Deke)/Estrus/1995
Hollywood Barn Dance/Heyday/1996
"Mother's Worry" b/w "Samoa" (Deke)/Gas Fin./1996
Solid Sender (Deke)/Ecco-Fonic/1997 (EP)
"Your Love is Like a Faucet" (Deke) on **L.A. County Line**/Strawdog/1998
Number One Hit Record (Deke Dickerson & The Ecco-Fonics)/Hightone HMG/1998

Flyin' Fingers (Joe Maphis Newsletter) and Ecco-Fonic Records c/o Deke Dickerson, P. O. Box 304, Hollywood, CA 90078 ; 818-558-3360 or //www.ecco-fonic.loomisgroup.com/ecco-fonic/ecco-fonic.html eccofonic@earthlink.net

Dave Stuckey Rockabilly Column //www.collinskids.com

Dave Stuckey dstuck@concentric.net

See Big Sandy; The Horton Brothers

Ronnie Dawson

Rockabilly; Hillbilly Bop
Dallas, Texas; August 12, 1939-

In the 1950s, Ronnie Dawson was a teen rockabilly prodigy noted for his blonde crew cut and high energy style. Through highly successful appearances as Ronnie Dee & the D Men at Big D Jamboree talent contests and two singles, "Action Packed" and "Rockin' Bones," Dawson won a huge local following and his breakthrough into national stardom was imminent. However, the promise fizzled, and for the next three decades, he fell into obscurity playing in a Western swing band (The Lightcrust Doughboys), as a session drummer for folk and country rock bands, and recording pop and blues rock on small labels as Snake Monroe and Commonwealth Jones. Then, with the 1980s rockabilly revival, fans and collectors (especially in Europe) rediscovered and resuscitated Dawson's rockabilly career. His comeback recordings, **Still a Lot of Rhythm** and **Rockinitis**, showed he could still pick 'em up and set 'em down with the best. An exciting lead guitarist and dynamite stage

presence, "The Blonde Bomber" took the European rockabilly scene by storm and then did the same in the U.S. in the early 1990s. His No Hit recordings were reissued by Dallas based Crystal Clear (**Monkey Beat** contains **Still a Lot of Rhythm** in its entirety) which also released a 2 CD set of Dawson's material (unreleased cuts, demos, alternate takes) from 1957-1962. In early 1994, Dawson, backed by High Noon and drummer Lisa Pancratz, appeared at Carnegie Hall and in 1996 signed with Upstart which issued **Just Rockin' & Rollin'**. Early in 1998, Dawson used one of his favorite venues, Austin's Continental Club, to make an "action packed" live recording and later in the year signed with Yep Roc which released his new one, **More Bad Habits** in mid-1999.

Still A Lot of Rhythm/No Hit UK/1988
Rockinitis/No Hit UK/1989; Crystal Clear/1996
Rockin' Bones: The Legendary Masters/No Hit UK/1993; Crystal Clear/1996 (2 CDs)
Monkey Beat/Crystal Clear/1994; No Hit UK/1995
Just Rockin' & Rollin'/Upstart/1996
Live at the Continental Club/Continental/1998
More Bad Habits/Yep Roc/1999

Ronnie Dawson //www.ronniedawson.com

Ronnie Dawson Rockabilly Hall of Fame Page //www.rockabillyhall.com/RonnieD.htm

Jesse Dayton

Country Rock; Honky Tonk
Beaumont, Texas; May 27, 1966-

Along the Texas gulf coast, from Brownsville at the southern most tip of the state to Beaumont along the border with Louisiana, there is a strong musical tradition of blues, honky-tonk, Tex-Mex, Cajun/zydeco, Western swing, and rock 'n' roll. One musician who carries on this unique "Third Coast" legacy is Jesse Dayton. A native of Beaumont, his first foray into music was as front man for a rockabilly group known as the Roadkings. Later, Dayton moved to Austin and led the popular rockabilly/honky tonk band, the Alamo Jets. During this time of playing bars and tonks all over central Texas and the coastal plain, he refined his songwriting by drawing on haunting images of small town Texas life. At one point, Dayton almost went the way of a number of other south Texas singers (Chesnutt, Byrd) when he had a brief flirtation with the Nashville assembly line. However, Jesse remained true to his roots, and in the early 1990s signed with Houston based Justice Records. His first album, **Raisin' Cain**, showcased Dayton's singing, songwriting, and lead guitar backed by a splendid supporting cast of fellow Texans (Floyd Domino, Flaco Jimenez, Johnny Gimble, Doug Sahm); it clearly reflected Dayton's absorption of the "Third Coast" sound including honky tonk ("Raisin' Cain"; "Big City Blues"), country rock ("Train of Dreams"; "Boystown"), Tex-Mex ("Carmelita"), blues ("Gut Bucket Blues"), and swing ("Angel Like You"). In 1996, Dayton contributed "Sad Songs and Waltzes" to the

Twisted Willie tribute album and lent his lead guitar chops to Waylon Jenning's Justice recording **Right for the Time**. A follow-up to his promising debut was originally scheduled for release in 1997 but was delayed until late in 1998. Like its predecessor, **Wayward Soul** is rooted in the Third Coast musical traditions with help from Johnny Gimble, Flaco Jimenez, and Floyd Domino. Dayton's song "Panhanlde Jane" was selected for the soundtrack of the independent film, *Deep in the Heart of Texas*.

> **Raisin' Cain**/Justice/1995
> "Sad Songs and Waltzes" on **Twisted Willie**/ Justice/1995
> **Wayward Soul**/Justice/1998
> "Panhandle Jane" on **Deep in the Heart of Texas**/ Shananchie/1998

Jesse Dayton/Justice Records Page
//www.justicerecords.com/arp19.html

Angel Dean

See The Last Roundup

Tony De La Rosa

Accordion; Conjunto; Tex-Mex
Sarita, Texas; November 1, 1931-

Along with Valerio Longoria, Tony De La Rosa was the most innovative of the post WWII *conjunto* musicians. Like Longoria, he added drums to the traditional ensemble but went even further by being among the first to use electrified bass and bajo sexto. In part, this idea might have come from Western swing which was a big influence on De La Rosa or from his first job with an Anglo country band. At any rate, with the drums and amplified instruments supplying a solid rhythm, De La Rosa moved front and center and furnished the melody with his renowned accordion playing. In 1949, he founded Conjunto De La Rosa and began recording albums (75 to his credit) in the 1950s which yielded numerous hit polkas. Into the 1960s, De La Rosa was at the top of the *conjunto* world and was the special favorite of dance hall crowds in South Texas. Recognized as one of the great modernizers of *conjunto*, De La Rosa paved the way for the next generation of innovators and the current resurgence of Tejano music. In the 1990s, Tony cut back somewhat but still recorded and performed now and then.

> **Asi Se Baila En Tejas**/Rounder/1991
> **Atotonilco: Early Recordings, 1953-1964**/ Arhoolie/1993
> **Mejor Solo**/Hacienda/1993
> **No Quiero Lagrimas**/Hacienda/1994
> **Es Mi Derecho**/Rounder/1995

Tony De La Rosa/La Onda Network Page
//www.ondanet.com:1995/tejano/artists/Tony.De.La.Rosa/

The Delevantes

Country Rock; Close Harmony
Hoboken, New Jersey; c.1985-

As boys growing up in the wilds of North Jersey, brothers Bob and Mike Delevante liked to harmonize and in their teens formed a "bluegrass" band, Wreckless Abandon, that did Beatles and Monkees covers! Later, they formed Who's Your Daddy, a roots rock group with a sizable local and regional following in the late 1980s. When they got no record offers from the Eastern musical establishment, the brothers decided to try Nashville when a music exec at a New Music Seminar told them they might find a home in that city's burgeoning New Country. Moving there in 1993, they started playing as the Delevantes and imme- diately began packing nightclubs and receiving great press. Shortly thereafter, they met Garry Tallent (of E Street Band fame) at a Steve Earle concert, and he agreed to produce their debut album **Long About That Time** for Rounder. Although their harmonies inevitably brought comparisons to the Everly Brothers, their more rocked up sound resembles contemporary duos such as the O'Kanes and Foster & Lloyd. After a major label move to Capitol Nashville came the Tallent produced **Postcards Along the Way** with more engaging brotherly harmonies on original ballads, honky tonk, and easy going country rock.

Bob Delevante (a.g.,hm,perc,v); Mike Delevante (bj,b,e.g.,perc,v)

> **Long About That Time**/Rounder/1995
> **Postcards Along the Way**/Capitol/1997

The Delevantes Fan Club
P.O. Box 23221, Nashville, TN 37202

The Delevantes Home Page
//www.nashville.net/~mhm/delevantes.html

The Delevantes/Rounder Records Page
//www.rounder.com/rounder/artists/delevantes/profile.html

The Delevantes iMusic Showcase
//imusic.com/showcase/country/

The Delevantes AOL Folder: Entertainment>Music>Chat & Messages>Music Community>Country/Folk>Country & Western, A-K

The Deliberate Strangers

New Old-Time
Pittsburgh, Pennsylvania; 1994-

Grounded primarily in old-time and bluegrass, Pittsburgh's Deliberate Strangers give traditional music a modern slant by drawing on the individual members' backgrounds in classical, punk, and Celtic. Husband/wife team Tom Moran and Stephanie Vargo formed the group in 1994; Moran had been a fixture on the Iron City punk scene in the 1980s while Vargo was steeped in Appalachian music. Adding a bass player (Erin Snyder) and guitarist (Phil Caruso), they explored old-time/ bluegrass but gave it a hard driving edge. When Caruso and

Snyder left in spring of 1995, Moran and Vargo enlisted 5-string banjoist Jimmy Earl Delmore and classically trained violinist, Erin Hutter. Taking their name from a TV movie about mass murderer Ted Bundy, the Deliberate Strangers came on strong in early 1996 playing bluegrass jams and radio and opening for alt. country groups like the Volebeats and the Steam Donkeys. In late 1996, they recorded **Hog Wild and Pig Bitin' Mad**, a collection of classics ("Pretty Polly") and originals ("Dooms-day Doors"—"give me a kiss from your sweet apocalips"; "Willie"; "Preacher's Lament") built around the themes of murder and damnation/redemption. **Mood Music for Snake Handlers** continues this same dark descent into death ("Box of Pine"; "Peach Ridge"; "Mather's Mine"; "Dead Man's Hand") and deliverance from the devil's domain ("Can't Hide the Devil"; "Out Foul Demon Spirits"; "Satan Your Kingdom Must Come Down"). But, this time the mood is even more ominous due to the stark vocals of Moran and Vargo, somber fiddling of Erin "Scratchy" Hutter, and the use of sonic effects on a few numbers for a sound "like Dock Boggs meets Throbbing Gristle" (Moran). But, the bleakness is not unrelenting as a few upbeat and even humorous notes come through on the hoedown "Marcella" and the witty "Trippin' Trucker." Late in 1998, the Deliberate Strangers played host to the inaugural Twangburgh festival, performed at alt. country showcases in Boston (Hellcountry) and Richmond (Capitol City Barndance), and through radio play found fans from as far away as Serbia.

Erin "Scratchy" Hutter (f,theremin,v); Jon Manning (d,perc,v); Tom Moran (bj,g,md,v); Stephanie Vargo (b,v)

Hog Wild and Pig Bitin' Mad/Payday/1997
Mood Music for Snake Handlers/Payday/1998

The Deliberate Strangers, P.O. Box 8104, Pittsburgh, PA 15217; 412-421-5240

The Deliberate Strangers
//members.tripod.com/~deliberate_strangers/index.html

hogwild@gateway.net

The Delta Angels
Redneck Underground
Clarkston, Georgia; 1990-1998

The Delta Angels were charter members of Atlanta's Redneck Underground. They emerged from the same venue (Austin Avenue Buffet) that produced Slim Chance, the Vidalias, the Diggers, and many others and performed at the first Bubbapa-looza festivals. In addition to being one of the RU's longest running bands, the Delta Angels were one of its most versatile. Credit for this diversity was due to the skills of the wife/husband team (and founders), Karen Jo and Alan Vennes. Blessed with glamorous 1950s style good looks, they also possessed fine voices (think Loretta Lynn, Emmylou; Gene Clark, John Doe) equipped to handle a variety of styles including country, blues, country rock, and rockabilly. Live and on record, they were

known to cover George Jones, the Gear Daddies, Maria McKee, Stoller & Leiber ("Riot in Cell Block #9"), and Billy Lee Riley, but the Vennes also had a feel for crafting a good song. They first displayed these talents with their contribution ("Cabbage-town") to the **Bubbapalooza** compilation, but the Vennes' songwriting and singing gifts really came together on their 1996 self-titled EP (dedicated to Gram Parsons). It offered five originals including the country rocking "You Come Back to Me," the bluesy honky tonk of "Blue Hill," and a gorgeous duet "Forever & Yesterday" that's sure to bring a smile from Gram/Emmylou fans. There was also Karen Jo on "You'll Never Do It Again," a humorous country tune reminiscent of those defiant Loretta Lynn songs like "Don't Come Home A'Drinkin'." And for good measure, they tossed in a bit of Southern Gothic on the moody "Cordis Moon." Into the late 1990s, the Delta Angels continued to be regulars at Bubbapalooza and worked on a full length CD but when no record deals were forthcoming, they decided to move on to other things. Alan Vennes became a stonemason working on restoration projects while Karen Jo sang in some local bands, ran a children's entertainment business, and wrote children's songs and stories.

Paul Fallatt (d); Duncan James (e.g.); Jeff Passifiune (b); Alan Vennes (a.g.,v); Karen Jo Vennes (l.v.,b.v.)

"Trouble Bound" on **Billy C. Riley Tribute**/1994
Down on Blue Hill/Delta Angels/1995 (CS)
"Cabbagetown" on **Bubbapalooza**/Sky/1995
The Delta Angels/Delta Angels/1996 (5 trk. EP)
"Black-Eyed Susan"; "Renegade Lover" on **14 x7: Hand-Picked Songs From Georgia**/ Hexamusic/1996

Karen Jo's Jigs & Juleps Page //www.jigsnjuleps.com
Alan/Karen Jo Vennes: deltangl@mindspring.com

Iris DeMent
Singer/Songwriter
Paragould, Arkansas; 1961-

If you're a city kid and want a glimpse of what it's like to grow up in rural America, listen to Iris DeMent. Like all the really great female country singers of the past, her plaintive voice and perceptive songwriting capture the joys and sorrows, hopes and fears of generations of country folk from Appalachia to California. Born in the boot heel area of Arkansas, she spent her first years on her parents farm which they had to sell when times got hard. For a time, the family (all 16 of 'em!) lived in town and dad had a factory job, but a strike put him out of work; like so many before them, the DeMents migrated to California. They were sustained by music especially country and gospel. Iris sang with the family or at church, learned piano, and began making up her first songs (at age 4 or 5). Eventually, the family moved back to the Mid West when Iris was 17 but within a few years she left home with a boyfriend and went to Topeka. During this time, DeMent got her first guitar and began to seriously pursue singing and songwriting. Astute powers of observation and a vivid imagination produced songs about dying towns ("Our Town"), dying love ("When Love Was Young"), Arcadian pasts ("These Hills"), and, of course, family ("Mama's Opry"). She began performing these songs in public while living in Kansas City and encouraged by the response, DeMent scraped enough money together to make the move to Nashville. Homesick for Kansas City and her boyfriend Elmer, Iris only stayed in Music City a short time but it was long enough to write some more good songs and grab the attention of record producers. Her first album, **Infamous Angel**, was warmly received and led to a bigger record deal and a tour opening for Nanci Griffith. Her second, **My Life**, is a deeply personal look at childhood, in particular, her relationships with Mom and Dad DeMent e.g. "Sweet is The Melody," "Child-hood Memories," the title tune, and a cover of Lefty Frizzell's "Mom and Dad's Waltz." **The Way I Should** continued along this introspective path but also widened DeMent's musical range and demonstrated her intense concern with socio-political issues. Throughout 1997 and 1998, Iris continued to tour and play venues and festivals large and small. No full length was released during this period, but she did guest on recordings by Emmylou, Tom Russell, Jeff Black, and Randy Scruggs and showed up on a number of high profile compilations and soundtracks including **Uprooted**, **In The Country of Country**, **The Horse Whisperer**, and **Real: The Tom T. Hall Project**. Several EPs with rare and live cuts have been issued by WEA in Germany.

Infamous Angel/Philo/1992; Warner Brothers/1992
Words & Music/Warner Brothers/1993 (40 min. promo
    w/ interview)
Our Town/WEA Ger./1993 (EP)
"Big City" on **Tulare Dust: A Songwriters Tribute to
    Merle Haggard**/Hightone/1994
Sweet is The Melody/WEA Ger./1994 (EP)
My Life/Warner Brothers/1994
The Way I Should/Warner Brothers/1996
Wasteland of the Free/WEA Ger./1997 (EP)
"Easy's Gettin' Harder Every Day" on **In the Country of
    Country**/Compass/1997
"Let the Mystery Be (Live)" on **KGSR Broadcasts, Vol.
    5**/KGSR/1997
"Box of Visions" (with Tom Russell) on **Uprooted: The
    Best of Roots Country**/Shanachie/1998
"Whispering Pines" on **The Horse Whisperer**/
    MCA/1998
"I Miss A Lot of Trains" on **Real: The Tom T. Hall
    Project, Vol. 1**/Sire/1998

The Iris DeMent Fan Club, P.O. Box 28856, Gladstone, MO 64188

The Iris DeMent Home Page //www.irisdement.com

Iris De Ment/Warner Brothers Page //www.wbr.com

Official Unofficial Iris DeMent Page //www.geocities.com/nashville/7327/

Unofficial Iris DeMent Home Page //members.aol.com/jarmode/dement.html

Steve's Iris DeMent Page //members.aol.com/palesun/iris/iris.htm

Iris DeMent AOL Folder: Entertainment>Music>Chat & Messages>Music Community>Country/Folk>Country & Western, A-K

The Derailers
Honky Tonk; Bakersfield Sound
Austin, Texas; 1993-

The Derailers have been one of the hottest groups of the late 1990s. The driving force behind the band is Tony Villanueva and Brian Hofeldt who met in Portland, Oregon in the late 1980s and briefly collaborated as a performing/songwriting duo. In 1989, Villanueva moved to Austin and after several years of correspondence convinced Hofeldt it was the place to be. Shortly after he arrived in 1993, they added Vic Gerard (Two Hoots & a Holler) on bass, and the Derailers were born. The sound they developed with twangy harmonies and lead guitar is vintage Bakersfield most reminiscent of Buck Owens/Don Rich. As it turned out, they came along during the early 1990s transition to another generation of Austin alt. country that produced Junior Brown, Don Walser, and Dale Watson. Playing clubs and holes-in-the-wall all over town, the Derailers gradually inherited the large dance crowd that had followed groups like Two Hoots & a Holler and Chaparral. In 1994, they made an independently produced tape of a session on KUT radio (**Live Tracks**) which was subsequently released on CD by Freedom Records. After inclusion of cuts on two Austin alt. country compilations, the Derailers were signed by Water-melon Records which brought in Dave Alvin to produce their first studio album, **Jackpot**. Its twelve great Villanueva/Hofeldt originals including "This Big City," "My Heart's Ready," "Where Ya Been?," "I'm Your Man," and "Lies, Lies, Lies" propelled the Derailers not only into the forefront of the Austin scene but also into the front ranks of the national alt. country movement (the CD originally came with a comb and a pamphlet, *The Official Derailers' Guide to Style,* which gave hilarious tips on how to always look sharp). Riding a wave of critical claim for their new record, the Derailers spent a hectic summer of 1996 touring in Europe, appearing in an HBO movie, playing on TNN's *Prime Time Country*, and showcasing at the Olympic Games in Atlanta. In early 1997, Hofeldt contributed to the outstanding twang guitar summit, **Travis County Pickin'**, and in the summer of that year the Derailers recorded, **Reverb Deluxe**, which came out as an advanced tape on Watermelon and then as a CD on their new label, Sire. With Alvin once again at the helm, the Derailers turned out their best recording yet with outstanding assistance from some of Austin's finest including Dave Biller (ex-Dale Watson; ex-Wayne Hancock), Alvin Crow, Scott Walls (Don Walser), and Bradley Williams (Los Pinkys). They deliver more of that great Bakersfield sound on covers ("I Don't Believe I'll Fall in

Love Today"; "No One to Talk to But the Blues") and originals ("Just One More Time"; "Lovers Lie"; "It's Too Late"; "Painful Days"; "Come Back"). They also stretched out a bit on "California Angel" which has that hillbilly surf groove going complete with Beach Boys riffs. There's even an extra track covering Prince's "Raspberry Beret!" **Reverb Deluxe** made just about everyone's alt. country top ten for 1997, and in 1998, with a new drummer (Mark Horn), they were ready to ride their self-styled "heavy western" sound to the top. Early that year, the Derailers taped a pilot for an MTV alt. country show called *Cringe* on which they host, perform, and even cook (?). In March 1998, they made a triumphant return home headlining at the Austin Music Awards.

For the remainder of 1998 and into early 1999, the ubiquitous Derailers appeared on *Conan O'Brien*, NPR, *Prairie Home Companion,* had two videos on CMT, and Hofeldt's instrumental "Ellen" was selected for play on his favorite show *King of the Hill*. They even managed to cut a promotional deal with Doritos through which Derailers guitar picks were distributed in bags of chips; those lucky enough to find a platinum pick would have the band come and play a concert in their town. The only rough moment during this time was the departure of bass player Ethan Shaw who was replaced by James Dungan who quickly succumbed to the rigors of touring and left the Derailers once again looking for a bassist who was "road ready, professional and mature." They found their man in Ed Atkins (ex-Roundhouse Wranglers) who came on board in early 1999.

Ed Atkins (b,v,1999-); James Dungan (b,1998); Vic Gerard (b,1993-1996); Brian Hofeldt (l.g., v); Mark Horn (d,1997-); Terry Kuykendall (d,1995-1997); Ethan Shaw (b,1996-1998); Tony Villanueva (g, v)

> **Live Tracks**/Freedom/1995
> "Lies, Lies, Lies" on **True Sounds of the New West**/ Freedom/1995
> "Just One More Time" on **Austin Country Nights**/ Watermelon/1995
> **Jackpot**/Watermelon/1996
> **Reverb Deluxe**/Watermelon/1997 (CS); Sire/1997 (CD)

The Derailers/Sire Records Page //www.derailers.com

The Derailers //home.att.net/~jscully/thederailers/

The Derailers/Real Counry Site (Official) //www.Derailers.RealCountry.net

The Derailers Fan Page //www.mike.harmon.net/music/artists/derailers.html

The Derailers Bio Page //www.pressnetwork.com/bios/derailbi.htm

The Derailers iMusic Showcase //imusic.com/showcase/country/

The Derailers AOL Folder: Entertainments>Music>Chat & Messages>Music Community>Country/Folk>Country & Western, A-K

The Dew Daddies
Honky Tonk; Country Rock
Bloomington, Indiana; 1994-

The Dew Daddies were originally Andy and Joe Ruff sitting around their house picking out old-time/bluegrass tunes until one night when neighbor/pedal steel player Dennis Scoville happened by and introduced himself. They hit it off and after adding bass and drum in 1994, the Dew Daddies evolved into a honky tonk, country rock outfit combining the Bakersfield Sound with New Riders, Flying Burrito Brothers, and Byrds country rock. Over the next two years, the band was an on and off again affair with many personnel changes (including Joe Ruff) but in early 1996, they finally put together a permanent line up and cut **Makin' Good Time**. This recording is pretty much the Andy Ruff Show; the personable front man handles lead vocals (a quavering Steve Goodman type voice), and he penned all 13 tracks which range from the nostalgic ("Livin' It Over"; "The Vincennes Waltz") to tongue- in-cheek ("I'm Not Crazy, I'm Just Out of Her Mind") to classic honky tonk ("The Nearest Honky Tonk"; "Honky Tonk Time"). The other Daddies provide adequate support but the real stand out is Scoville (also of John Strohm & the Hello Strangers) whose steel work gives Ruff's songs just the right kick.

Andy Bruce (g,h.v.); Peter Conway (hm); Dave Johnloz (b); Mike Norris (d); Andy Ruff (md,l.v.); Dennis Scoville (p.s.)

> **Makin' Good Time**/DD/1996

The Dew Daddies c/o Andy Ruff, 1414 E. University St., Bloomington, IN 47401

See John P. Strohm

Hazel Dickens; Alice Gerrard
Old-Time; Bluegrass

Two of the most influential women in old-time/bluegrass music in the last thirty years are Hazel Dickens and Alice Gerrard. As singer/songwriters, organizers, publishers, producers, and pro-moters, they have helped revive traditional music and have continually drawn attention to the problems of working class people, in particular the plight of working women. Dickens was born and raised in a West Virginia coal mining community but found solace in the old-time country that came over the family radio. In her late teens, she moved to Maryland and became involved in the growing old-time/bluegrass scene in the Baltimore/D.C. area. While playing as a solo and in various bands at festivals in the region, she met two other traditional music enthusiasts, Mike Seeger and Alice Gerrard. She was especially drawn to Gerrard who had trained in classical music but while in college was "converted" into a traditional music fan. They became students of the music, seeking out veteran players, doing research at the Library of Congress, and performing. Their passion, beautiful high lonesome harmonies, and focus on working class and feminist issues made them favorites on the festival circuit. Gerrard and Dickens made several early albums for Folkways, but their classic recordings were on Rounder in the mid-1970s. **Hazel & Alice** and **Hazel Dickens and Alice Gerrard** were nothing short of sensational, full of reborn standards and moving originals. These two albums have had a major impact on several generations of alt. country performers from Emmylou Harris to Freakwater. In 1995, Folkways issued an important retrospective of their early work called **Hazel Dickens & Alice Gerrard, Pioneer Women of Bluegrass**.

In the late 1970s, Hazel and Alice went their separate ways, and individually made enormous contributions. Dickens recorded numerous old-time and country flavored albums (**Hard Hitting Songs for Hard Hit People**; **By the Sweat of My Brow**; **Hard to Tell the Singer From the Song**; **Heart of a Singer**) and contributed songs to compilations examining the lives and hard times of America's underdogs. She worked on two powerful films about coal mining, penning four songs for the documentary *Harlan County USA* (1976) and playing a singing preacher in John Sayles' *Matewan* (1987). In addition, Dickens has been a tireless advocate for human rights and union causes, participating in benefits and protest rallies around the world. Meanwhile, Gerrard worked mostly on collaborative old-time music projects including the Strange Creek Singers (with Mike Seeger and Hazel Dickens) and the Harmony Sisters with Irene Hermann and Jennie McLerie of Bayou Seco. She recorded a solo old-time/bluegrass/country album called **Pieces of My Heart** in 1995 and continued to tour worldwide. Gerrard has produced recordings (Red Clay Ramblers) and films (two documentaries on Appalachian music) and been a leader in many organizations devoted to folk culture and old-time music. In 1987, she started the old-time Music Group and became managing editor of its fine publication *The Old-Time Herald*.

Who's That Knocking? (Dickens & Gerrard)/
  Folkways/1965
Won't You Come Sing for Me? (Dickens & Gerrard)/
  Folkways/1967
Alice Gerrard & Mike Seeger in Japan/King/1971
Hazel & Alice/Rounder/1973
The Strange Creek Singers/Arhoolie/1975
Hazel Dickens & Alice Gerrard/Rounder/1976; 1995
Mike Seeger & Alice Gerrard/Greenhays/1978
Harmony Pie (Harmony Sisters)/Flying Fish/1980
Hard Hitting Songs for Hard Hit People (Hazel
  Dickens)/Rounder/1981
Second Helping (Harmony Sisters)/Flying Fish/1982
By the Sweat of My Brow (Hazel Dickens)/
  Rounder/1983
It's Hard to Tell the Singer From the Song (Hazel
  Dickens)/Rounder/1987
A Few Old Memories (Hazel Dickens)/ Rounder/1987
Pieces of My Heart (Alice Gerrard)/Copper Creek/1995
**Hazel Dickens & Alice Gerrard, Pioneer Women of
  Bluegrass**/Folkways/1995

Heart of a Singer (Hazel Dickens with Ginny Hawker &
  Carol Elizabeth Jones)/Rounder/1998
Alice Gerrard Web Page
//www.mindspring.com/~artmenius/prod03.htm
The Old-Time Herald,
P.O. Box 51812, Durham, NC 27717
The Old-Time Herald Home Page //www.hidwater.com/oth/
agerrad@nando.net

See Mike Seeger

Diesel Doug and the Long Haul Truckers
Country Rock
Portland, Maine; 1996-

One of the most famous truck driving songs, "Tombstone Every Mile," is about a particularly hazardous "stretch of road up north in Maine that's never, ever, ever seen a smile." Diesel Doug and the Long Haul Truckers, out of Portland, understand the danger, freedom, and loneliness experienced by the Knights of the Open Road from Maine to Mexico and express it with a sound combining the spirit of Commander Cody/Bill Kirchen but with the harder edge of the famous Diesel Only/Rig Rock collections and even a few touches of No Depression alt. country. Their rise in Northeastern alt. country circles has been swift since they were started in 1996 by Scott Link (Diesel Doug), John Davison, and Charlie Gaylord. Playing all over New England opening for the likes of Wayne Hancock, the Old 97s, and Mike Ireland, Diesel Doug and company polished up Link's originals that became the basis for their 1997 debut, **An Angel Not a Saint**. In addition to truck driving songs ("Never Lookin' Down"; "One Light"; "Gold Wing Mama"; "18 Wheels of Love"), there's honky tonk hurtin' ("Not Much to Say"; "All Over"; "An Angel Not a Saint," and some flat out country and roadhouse rockers ("Wicked Ways"; "A Girl Like You"). A sequel, **The Fine Art of Carousing** was delayed until mid-1999, but Diesel Doug and the Truckers gave a little foretaste on a **Winter '98 Promo** with two songs ("Thin White Line"; "I'd Like to Quit Drinking But I Live Over a Bar") from the upcoming release and two twisted country Christmas classics: "Merry Christmas From the Family" (Robert Earl Keen) and "Daddy's Drinkin' Up Our Christmas" (Commander Cody).

Scott Conley (b,1998-); John Davison (d); Charlie Gaylord (e.g.,l.g.); Scott "Diesel Doug" Link (a.g.,e.g.l.v.); Cartwright Thompson (p.s.,1997-); Chris Tuttle (b,1996-1997)

An Angel Not a Saint/Sad Bird/1997
Winter '98 Promo/DD/1998
The Fine Art of Carousing/Ripchord/1999

Diesel Doug/Sad Bird, P.O. Box 10558,
Portland, ME 04104; 207-773-0109
Diesel Doug Home Page //www.dieseldoug.com
Cgaylord@cybertours.com

Dieselhed

Roots Rock; Cowpunk
San Francisco, California; 1989-

Long time members of San Francisco's alternative country scene, Dieselhed plays "post-modern truck driving music." They started in 1989 and became Bay Area favorites for their blend of country with frenetic punk and energetic, humorous, and unpredictable live performances. Like another popular Frisco alt. country band, the Buckets, Dieselhed sings a lot about food ("Hash Browns"; "Happy Donut"; "Gravy Boat"; "Pizza Box"), alcohol ("Snowblind in the Liquor Store"; "Five Shots"; "Cold Duck"), the road ("Cloud of Diesel"; "Hot VWs"; "Wipe Down the Vinyl"; "Greyhound"; "Trucker's Alibi"), and hard luck ("Poodle's Ear"; "Macrame Xmas Cards"). Their recordings (**Dieselhed**; **Tales of the Brown Dragon**; **Shallow Water Blackout**; **Elephant Rest Home**) move freely from brooding ballads to full bore thrashabilly and back again.

Atom Ellis (b); Danny Heifetz (d,tp); Zach Holtzman (g,v); Shon McAlinn (l.g.); Virgil Shaw (r.g.,v)

> **Dieselhed**/Amarillo/1993
> "Forklift"/"Peelin' Out"/"A-1 Steak Sauce"/Amarillo/1993 (7" EP)
> **Tales of the Brown Dragon**/Amarillo/1995
> **Shallow Water Blackout**/Amarillo/1997
> **Elephant Rest Home**/Bong Load/1998

The Porcelain Elephant Club, 425 Irving St., San Francisco, CA 94122

Official Dieselhed Home Page //www.dieselhed.com

star@dieselhed.com

Dieselhed Page //www.droolboy.com/bands/dieselhed/

See Granfaloon Bus; U.S. Saucer

The Dillards

Country Rock; Progressive Bluegrass
Los Angeles, California; 1962-1980; 1989-

Let's get this part out of the way first. Yes, the Dillards did play the sons in the Darling Family on the 1960s TV series *The Andy Griffith Show*. And while their numbers on that show popularized bluegrass beyond traditional audiences, this was only part of their many contributions. Raised in a musical family, Doug and Rodney Dillard began playing bluegrass when they were youngsters and in the early 1960s put together a band that eventually became the Dillards. Starting out in their home state of Missouri, they moved on to California where they got a contract with Elektra and that famous spot on the *Griffith Show*. Their first albums were fairly traditional bluegrass, but gradually, the Dillards gravitated toward a more progressive style incorporating country and rock elements through the use of amplified instruments including steel guitar and drums. Some European music critics have proclaimed the Dillards as

the founders of country rock and with some justification. Their work during this period (late 60s-early70s) pre-dates and/or parallels similar projects by Nashville West, the Byrds, and the Flying Burrito Brothers. The Dillards signature sound was most fully realized on **Pickin' & Fiddlin'**, **Wheatstraw Suite**, and **Copperfields** which included new members Herb Pederson and Byron Berline.

When not performing as the Dillards, Doug and Rodney worked on several other important country rock/bluegrass projects. Doug joined with the great Gene Clark in 1968 to form the Dillard-Clark Expedition, and they made several albums, **Fantastic Expedition, Through the Morning, Through the Night, Gene Clark & Doug Dillard**, and **Kansas City Southern** that offer some of the best country rock of the era. Rodney and Doug teamed with John Hartford in the late 1970s and early 1980s as Dillard-Hartford-Dillard and cut a number of albums of fine progressive bluegrass for Flying Fish. In addition, both brothers recorded solo albums throughout the 1970s and 1980s and into the 1990s. The Dillards took periodic hiatuses from recording but had a very productive period in the late 1970s when they signed to Flying Fish and recorded **The Dillards vs. the Incredible L.A. Time Machine, Decade Waltz**, and **Homecoming & Family Reunion**. In 1991, Vanguard released a 29 track retrospective of the Dillards work on Elektra called **There is a Time** (reissued by Sierra in 1995) that is a good overview of their role in the development of country rock and progressive bluegrass.

The original Dillards (Doug, Rodney, Mitch Jayne, Dean Webb) reunited in the late 1990s and began to tour once again. Vanguard Records released **The Best of the Darlin' Boys** in 1997 and in 1998, they joined Arlo Guthrie to cut a Woody Guthrie tribute CD whose release was to correspond with the issuance of a commemorative postage stamp to the great folk troubadour in 1999.

The Dillards: Doug Dillard (bj,g,v); Rodney Dillard (db,g,v); Mitch Jayne (b,v); Billy Ray Lathum (bj,v, 1972-1979); Herb Pederson (bj,v,1969-1972); Dean Webb (md,v)
Dillard-Hartford-Dillard: Doug Dillard (bj,g,v); Rodney Dillard (db,g,v); John Hartford (bj,f,v)
The Dillard-Clark Expedition: Doug Dillard (bj,g,v); Gene Clark (g,v); Don Beck (db,md); Byron Berline (f); Jon Corneal (d); Chris Hillman (g); Sneaky Pete Kleinow (p.s.); Bernie Leadon (g); Donna Washburn (g)

> **Back Porch Bluegrass**/Elektra/1963
> **Live...Almost!**/Elektra/1964
> **Pickin' & Fiddlin'**/Elektra/1965
> **Wheatstraw Suite**/Elektra/1968
> **The Fantastic Expedition of Dillard & Clark**/ A&M/1968
> **Through the Morning, Through the Night** (Dillard & Clark)/A&M/1969
> **The Banjo Album** (Doug Dillard)/Together/1969

Copperfields/Elektra/1970
Roots and Branches/Anthem/1972
Tribute to the American Duck/Poppy/1973
Dueling Banjos (Doug Dillard)/20th Century/1973
**Douglas Flint Dillard: You Don't Need a Reason to
    Sing**/20th Century/1974
Gene Clark & Doug Dillard/Ariola/1975
Kansas City Southern (Dillard & Clark)/ Ariola/1975
Country Tracks: The Best of the Dillards/Elektra
    UK/1976
The Dillards vs. The Incredible L.A. Time Machine/
    Flying Fish/1977
Dillard-Hartford-Dillard/Sonet UK/1977
Glitter Grass From the Nashwood Hollyville Strings
    (Dillard-Hartford-Dillard)/Flying Fish/1977
Decade Waltz/Flying Fish/1979
Heaven (Doug Dillard)/Flying Fish/1979
Jackrabbit! (Doug Dillard)/Flying Fish/1980
Mountain Rock/Crystal Clear/1980
Homecoming and Family Reunion/Flying Fish/1980
Permanent Wave (Dillard-Hartford-Dillard)/Flying
    Fish/1980
What's That? (Doug Dillard)/Flying Fish/1986
At Silver Dollar City (Rodney Dillard)/Flying Fish/1988
The Fantastic Expedition/Through the Morning
    (Dillard & Clark)/Mobile Fidelity/1988
Let It Fly/Vanguard/1991
There Is A Time, 1963-1970/Vanguard/1991; Sierra/1995
Let the Rough Side Drag (Rodney Dillard)/Flying
    Fish/1992
Take Me Along for the Ride/Vanguard/1993
Heartbreak Hotel (Doug Dillard)/Flying Fish/1993
Heartbreak Hotel & What's That?/Flying Fish/1994
Roots & Branches/Tribute to the American Duck/Beat
    Goes On/1996
The Best of the Darlin' Boys/Vanguard/1997
A Night in the Ozarks With the Dillards/ (90 min. video
    doc. prod. by John McEuen)

The Dillards Old Home Place //www.the-dillards.com

See Gene Clark; John Hartford; Herb Pederson

Dirtball

"Hillbilly Soul"; White Trash Parody
Richmond, Virginia; c.1994-

Dirtball was the off-spring (more or less) of a mid-1990s punk
group called Mudd Helmut. The latter's lead singer, Wes Freed,
was joined by some local musicians (Jeff Liverman, Peter
Headley, Neal Furguson) to do some acoustic versions of Mudd
Helmet songs and Dirtball slowly evolved from those sessions.
With a line-up that has sometimes included as many as eight
members, the band, led by wildman Freed, used a variety of
instruments including mandolin, accordion, electric guitar, and
trombone to produce a hybrid of old-time, rockabilly, and blues
they called "hillbilly soul." Their debut of the same name
prompted *Option* magazine to characterize Dirtball as
"alternative holler music," a combination of Rufus Crisp, the
Red Clay Ramblers, and the Meat Puppets. **Hillbilly Soul**
actually did quite well in Germany with help from the
"Bavarian hillbilly" band, FSK. Like Southern Culture on the

Skids and the Drive By Truckers, Dirtball's focus is on the
"white trash" lifestyle, especially drinking, carousing, and
trouble as on "Hills, Whores, and Liquor Stores." Further
explorations of the darker sides of backwoods life were
forthcoming on **The Well** which, with production by Cracker's
Bob Rupe, is a hard-hitting collection of country rock, Southern
style. Into the late 1990s, the band performed at the
Bubbapalooza and Route 1 South festivals and in their home
town organized the Capital City Barn Dance, a regular
showcase for local and regional alt. country/Americana acts.
They also held down a regular Wednesday night spot at Lucy's.

Josh Camp (acc,g); Jill Freed (v); Wes Freed (l.v.); Neal
Furguson (b,v); Jimmy Garthoff (trb); Peter Headley (a.g.,d);
Jeff Liverman (g,md); John Moser (l.g.); Mareck
Schneyedurh (d)

Hillybilly Soul/Fundamental/1994
The Well/Planetary/1998

Dirtball, P.O. Box 4361, Richmond, VA 23220

The Official Dirtball Web Site
//www.geocities.com/hollywood/2130/

dirtball@geocities.com

Disciples of Agriculture

Cowpunk; Roots Rock
Brooklyn, New York; 1987-

D.O.A.'s origins date back to the cowpunk era (mid-1980s
when Jon Cunningham, Dan Finn, and Joe Pelletier met while
attending college in upstate New York. They played informally
there and later in Brooklyn where they evolved into cowpun-
kers in the Jason and the Scorchers, Rank and File mold. With
the addition of cellist Sibel Firat, the Disciples developed a very
distinctive sound. Using the cello as a fiddle, Firat can play
hoe-downs or generate a low-down mournful feel. After a tentative self-titled CS/CD in 1994/1996, Cunningham, Nichols,
and Pelletier departed and were replaced in time for **This Same
Fate**, produced by Eric Ambel with a guest appearance by the
World Famous Bluejay's Jeremy Tepper (on harmonica). Their
sound might best be described as "rural electrification", a cross-
breeding of rustic, small town themes ("In My Town"; "I Ride
Alone"; "Girl Up the Road"; "Cow Down"; "Dumb Shit-
kicker"; "Walk on By"; "Shavertown") with country tinged
guitar rock. Finn's gruff twang fits well, and Firat's cello work
adds some nice touches to both slow and up tempo numbers.

Mark Boquist (d,b.v.,1997-); Keith Christopher
(b,b.v.,1997-); Jon Cunningham (g,v,1987-1996); Dan Finn
(g,l.v.); Sibel Firat (b,cello,b.v.); Erik Kristiansen
(g,b.v.,1997-); Jake Nichols (d,b.v.,1987-1996); Joe Pelletier
(d,1987-1996)

"In My Town" b/w "See Through You"/Paint Chip/1994
Disciples of Agriculture/Paint Chip/1994 (CS);
    KranePool/1996 (CD)
This Same Fate/Kranepool/1997

Disciples of Agriculture, 27 Wycoff St., Brooklyn, NY 11201

Richard Dobson
Singer/Songwriter
Tyler, Texas; March 19, 1942-

Originally intent on a career as a prose writer, Richard Dobson worked as a Spanish teacher and Peace Corps volunteer in the 1960s ,but in between found time to write two novels, numerous short stories, and publish a newsletter (*Poor Richard's Newsletter*, later *Don Ricardo's Life and Times*). He also began writing songs and gradually moved farther in that direction. Dobson worked in the 1970s with other Texas singer/ songwriters like Clark and Van Zandt in Houston and later in Nashville. It was there he got his first break when David Allan Coe covered his song "Piece of Wood and Steel." After saving enough money from working on oil rigs and shrimp boats along the Texas Gulf Coast, Dobson put out his debut, **In Texas Last December**, in 1977. In succeeding years, more of his songs ("Baby Ride Easy," "Old Friends," "The Ballad of Robin Wintersmith") were recorded by established artists, and he released a steady stream of albums full of pithy commentary and acute insight into the human condition. However, he never attained the kind of following other Texas singer/songwriters did and so decided to try his fortunes in Europe. Like a number of other expatriate American artists, Dobson found success. He played to larger and more receptive audiences and was signed to Brambus Records in Switzerland. In 1993, Dobson, whom Nanci Griffith called "the Hemingway of country music," paid tribute to one of his biggest fans, Townes Van Zandt, on **Amigos** which covers 15 of Van Zandt's most well known songs. His 1994, **Mankind**, in addition to presenting a pretty stern critique of modern America, contains the best of his songs previously covered by other artists. **One Bar Town** (1995) and **Love Only Love** (1996) are Texas style honky tonk, singer/ songwriter recordings well worth seeking out. In 1998, Dobson's book *The Gulf Coast Boys* was published; it's "an irreverent backstage peek at the gonzo lifestyles of the Hemmer Ridge Mountain Boys (Rex Bell, Mickey White, and Townes Van Zandt) who asked for little more than gasoline, guitar strings, and a jug of whiskey to get them to the next show."

In Texas Last December/Buttermilk/1977
The Big Taste/Rinconada/1979
Save the World/RJDII/1983
True West/Productions/Salty Dog/1987
State of the Heart/1988; 1995
Hearts and Rivers/1989
Blue Collar Blues/Brambus Switz./1992 (20 trk. reissue of **Hearts and Rivers**)
Amigos: Richard Dobson Sings Townes Van Zandt/RJD/1993
That's Right/RJD/1994
Mankind/Sundown/1994
Back Tracks (Save the World; True West)/RJD/1995

One Bar Town/Brambus Switz./1995
Love Only Love/Brambus/1996
Salty Songs/Brambus/1998
The Gulf Coast Boys/1998

Don Ricardo's Life & Times (Richard Dobson Newsletter), P. O. Box 5183, Jamalla Beach, Galveston, TX 77554

Richard Dobson Home Page //nativetexas.com/dobson/

Ricardo319@aol.com

Richard Dobson/Brambus Home Page //www.songs.com/noma/brambus/rd/

Richard Dobson Archive //PersonalWebs.myriad.net/dduryea/archive.html (repository for *Don Ricardo's Life & Times*)

Dolly Varden
Roots Rock
Chicago, Illinois; 1993-

Named after a Charles Dickens character and/or a species of freshwater trout, Dolly Varden was founded in 1993 by wife/husband team Diane Christiansen and Steve Dawson who had previously been together in Stump the Host. The latter was a popular Windy City alt. country act with a high twang quotient, but Dolly Varden has more of a lo-fi roots rock groove grounded in folk, pop, and rock. The mood of both **Mouthful of Lies** and **The Thrill of Gravity** is generally Prozacian including the ultra-downer, "All I Deserve," but there are also a few guitar driven energized moments as well. Their ace card is A-1 songwriting and the combined vocal talents of Christiansen and Dawson.

Mark Balleto (l.g.); Mike Bradburn (b); Diane Christiansen (g,v); Steve Dawson (g,v); Matt Thobe (d)

Mouthful of Lies/Mid-Fi/1995
The Thrill of Gravity/Evil Teen/1998

Dolly Varden Home Page //www.dollyvarden.com

Dolly Varden/Evil Teen Page //www.evilteen.com/etweb/dv/

Donna the Buffalo (Agents of Terra; The Heartbeats)
Roots Rock; New Old-Time
Ithaca, New York; c. 1988-

Maybe it's something in the water but whatever the reason, the Finger Lakes region of western New York has produced some of the most innovative old-time/bluegrass groups of the past two decades (Highwoods String Band, the Horseflies, Cornerstone). One of the most versatile is Ithaca's Donna the Buffalo which plays old-time string band, blues, Cajun, country, rock, Tex-Mex, and reggae all mixed up with a modern attitude and a strong environmental/political consciousness. Their initial output was self-released including a series of "color" tapes (**Purple, White, Red**), a self-titled CD, and in 1995, **The Ones You Love**. Each one displays an adventurous style that makes you dance and think at the same time. This same spirit carried over into their 1998 Sugar Hill debut, **Rockin' in the Weary Land**.

Members of Donna the Buffalo play in other progressive old-time bands: Jim Miller, Tara Nevins, and Jeb Puryear have joined with the Horseflies' Richie Stearns to form Agents of Terra which like Donna joins old-time with contemporary as on their cover of The Police hit "Every Breath You Take." Meanwhile, Nevins has been involved with the Heartbeats, a combination of New York and Pennsylvania musicians who specialize in "cutting edge" old-timey with a decidedly Cajun flavor and beautiful harmonies. Their work brought them a good deal of acclaim including Best Old-Time Band at the Mt. Airy Fiddlers Convention. Tara also cut an old-time, bluegrass solo, **Mule to Ride**, in 1999.

Donna the Buffalo: Shane Lamphier (d,v); Jim Miller (e.g.,v); Tara Nevins (acc,f,rb,tmb,v); Jeb Puryear (e.g.,v); Jorclan Puryear (b); Joe Thrift (ky,v)
Agents of Terra: Jim Miller (g); Tara Nevins (f); Jeb Puryear (f); Richie Stearns (bj)
The Heartbeats: June Drucker (b); Tara Nevins (f); Rose Sinclair (bj); Beverly Smith (g)

> **White Tape**/DTB/1989
> **Red Tape**/DTB/1991
> **Spinning World** (Heartbeats)/Green Linnet/1992
> **Purple Tape**/DTB/1993
> **Donna the Buffalo**/DTB/1993
> "Every Breath You Take" (Agents of Terra) on **Young Fogies, Vol. 1**/Rounder/1994
> **Living Black & White (Heartbeats)**/Marimac/1994
> "Citigo" (Heartbeats) on **Old-Time Music on the Air, Vol. 1**/Rounder/1994
> **The Ones You Love**/DTB/1995
> **Rockin' in the Weary Land**/Sugar Hill/1998
> **Mule to Ride** (Tara Nevins)/Sugar Hill/1999

Donna the Buffalo, P.O. Box 287, Trumansburg, NY 14886; 607-277-6214

Donna the Buffalo Home Page //www.DonnatheBuffalo.com

Wildlife@DonnatheBuffalo.com

See Horseflies

Barb Donovan

Singer/Songwriter
Detroit, Michigan

Raised in Detroit, Barb Donovan found her musical home in Austin, Texas when she moved there in the late 1980s. With vocal and writing skills to match any of that city's notable singer/songwriter corps, Donovan became a fixture as a solo or with the Barb Donovan Trio at acoustic venues like Chicago House and built a small but devoted following. Blending country, blues, rock, and folk, she recorded several independent cassettes, **Love You Blind** and **Thin Line**, that drew rave reviews from local critics and from national publications such as *Dirty Linen*. In 1994, Donovan's debut CD **Restless Soul**,

which collected the best from her previous recordings, was released to more great press and yet Donovan's big break didn't come. She retired from music but in 1995 her "Factory Town" was included on the Vinyl Junkie **Country** compilation and in 1996, **Restless Soul** was reissued in a slightly different form on Gregor Records as **Angelina**. Collected here are Donovan's unflinching looks at broken dreams ("Angelina"; "Factory Town") and bad relationships ("When Hell Freezes Over"; "Imperfect Man"; "Drive Me Crazy"). Also included is a duet with Townes Van Zandt on his song "I'll Be Here in the Morning" which also showed up on the 1997 **Jukebox Cowboy** compilation.

> **Love You Blind**/Backbeat/1990 (CS)
> **Thin Line**/Backbeat/1991 (CS)
> **Restless Soul**/Sundown/1994
> "Factory Town" on **Country**/Vinyl Junkie/1995
> **Angelina**/Gregor/1996 (reissue of **Restless Soul**)
> "I'll Be There in the Morning" (with Townes Van Zandt) on **Jukebox Cowboy**/Vinyl Junkie UK/1997

Jerry Douglas

Dobro; Progressive Bluegrass; Newgrass
Warren, Ohio; May 28, 1956-

When Jerry Douglas was 8, his father (a bluegrass musician) took him to a Flatt & Scruggs concert. Young Jerry was so impressed with their dobro player Josh Graves that he went home and adapted his Silvertone guitar so that it could be played dobro style. After a few years, he was good enough to join his father's band and at 17 was invited to join the Country Gentlemen. In the 1970s, Douglas was a member of J.D. Crowe's New South and formed a bluegrass band, Boone Creek, along with Ricky Skaggs. Douglas' legendary dexterity and distinctive chromatic, finger picking (Tut Taylor) style earned him the nickname "Flux." Eventually, he moved on to a solo career recording two exceptional albums of progressive bluegrass, **Fluxology** and **Tennessee Fluxedo**, with help from Sam Bush, Bela Fleck, Tony Rice, Ricky Skaggs and other leading lights of new acoustic music. Many of these musicians helped out on Douglas' more experimental bluegrass albums for MCA (**Under the Wire**, **Changing Channels**, **Plant Early**), and Douglas returned the favor by appearing on their solo efforts. In fact, Douglas was the premier dobro session man of the 1980s and 1990s guesting on countless country and pop music recordings and was a part of the house band on the wonderful TNN series *American Music Shop*. He continued to push the boundaries of dobrology in projects such as Strength in Numbers and a collaboration with Indian musician Vishwa Mohan Bhatt. For this impressive body of work, Douglas received numerous awards including *Frets* magazine's Best Dobro Player five consecutive years, a Grammy for Best Instrumental Performance (1983), two more Grammy nominations in 1986 and 1987, five straight Specialty Instrument awards from the ACM (1989-1993), and five IBMA Dobro Player of the Year awards. In 1996, the Dobro guitar company honored him with a Jerry Douglas Signature Model.

Not slowing down for a minute in 1997-1999, Douglas continued to lend a hand on numerous recordings (including Bill Frissell's **Nashville**) and put out the eclectic **Restless on the Farm** with Tim O'Brien, John Cowan, Sam Bush, Steve Earle (lead vocal on Johnny Cash's "Don't Take Your Guns to Town"), Victor Krauss, and Maura O'Connell on bluegrass, Celtic, funk, country, and blues.

Fluxology/Rounder/1978
Tennessee Fluxedo/Rounder/1983
Everything Is Gonna Work Out Fine (Fluxology/Tenn. Fluxedo)/Rounder/1984
Under the Wire/MCA/1986
Changing Channels/MCA/1987
Plant Early/MCA/1989
Slide Rule/Sugar Hill/1992
Bourbon & Rosewater (with Visha Mohan Bhatt)/Water Lily Acoustics/1992
Skip, Hop & Wobble (with Russ Barrenberg, Edgar Meyer)/Sugar Hill/1993
Yonder (with Peter Rowan)/Sugar Hill/1996
Restless on the Farm/Sugar Hill/1998

Jerry Douglas Home Page
//www.well.com/user/welvis/douglas.html

Moonlight Mercantile: Jerry Douglas Home Page
//www.alternetcom.com/moonlight/doug.html

Johnny Dowd

Singer/Songwriter; Lo-Fi Gothic
Ft. Worth, Texas; 1948-

1997 might be remembered as the year of the troubled troubadours; Richard Buckner, Tom Leach, Edith Frost, Gary Heffern, Tom House, Will Oldham, Fred Eaglesmith, and Jim White all put out brooding lo-fi recordings that take the listener on a slow walk down the dark side of the street. Added to this list is Johnny Dowd, perhaps the gloomiest and scariest of them all. Born in Texas and raised in Oklahoma and Tennessee, he has lived in upstate New York for the last 25 years where his time has been split between running a trucking business and writing songs and performing in bars around Ithaca. Dowd's self-released debut CD, **Wrong Side of Memphis**, has been described as "country gothic" or a collection of "twisted lo-fi tales" but that might be putting it mildly. The closest analogy is Jim Thompson as singer/songwriter. Recorded by Dowd in his studio (adjacent to his moving company) with sparse accompaniment (in particular, spooky organ), his unblinking focus is on murder and/or death: "Murder" (double homicide); "One Way" (a story literally about Christ on the cross); "Just Like a Dog"; "Ft. Worth Texas" (death row); "First There Was" (mass murder); "Wages of Sin." Pretty disturbing stuff but most frightening of all is Dowd's claim that it "is about people I've

known, places I've been." He adds, "I hope you enjoy it" and if you're a fan of Thompson, Tarantino, et al., you certainly will. **Wrong Side** was re-released by Checkered Past Records in 1998.

Wrong Side of Memphis/JD/1997; Checkered Past/1998

Johnny Dowd, 111 Coy Glen Rd., Ithaca, NY 14850; 607-272-8927

dalton@clarityconnect.com

Johnny Dowd/Checkered Past Page
//www.checkeredpast.com

Johnny Dowd Biography
//www.pressnetwork.com/dowd.htm

Drive-By Truckers

Redneck Underground
Athens, Georgia; 1996-

The Drive-By Truckers are one of the most promising of the second generation of Redneck Underground bands. Like their predecessors, the Truckers deal in raw twang and topics dear to Southern hearts. Drawn from other up and coming groups including the Star Room Boys and the Hot Burritos (see Redneck Greece), they are anchored by the gravely vocals of Patterson Hood who formed the band in 1996 after performing solo for a time. His slightly demented, very clever country songs are given steady down home backing from Mike Cooley (banjo, guitar), Adam Howell (bass), Matt Lane (drums), John Neff (pedal steel), and Barry Sell (mandolin). The Truckers' debut single has two of the most memorable songs to ever come down the Redneck Underground pike. On "Nine Bullets," Hood counts down the victims destined for a slug from his roommate's gun: unfaithful girlfriend, butt riding boss, annoying woman at the laundromat, self, immediate family, and the roommate (after all, it's his gun!). "Bulldozers and Dirt," a waltzing homage to earth moving machinery, contains the very hummable refrain, "I don't mean no harm, I just like to flirt, but most of all, I like bulldozers and dirt." Both tunes are sure to become sing along favorites.

Increasingly popular on their home turf through appearances at Athfest and Bubbapaloza, the Drive-By Truckers gained wider recognition in Southern alt. country circles and beyond with a cut on **Revival 2**, a tour in the Carolinas and Virginia, and performances at numerous alt. country/Americana events and festivals including the Capital City Barn Dance (Richmond) and Twangcore (New York City). Their debut full length CD, **Gangstabilly**, was released in April 1998 and is Redneck/White Trash dee-luxe. From its cover art (Outside: Bubba and Bubbette stradling the hood of a car with his hand moving up her thigh; Inside: Bubba sitting at the wheel of his pick-up defiantly shooting the finger) to songs like "Wife Beater," "Panties in Your Purse," "Why Henry Drinks," "Demonic Possession," "18 Wheels of Love," "Buttholeville," and "The Living Bubba" (dedicated to Greg Dean Smalley), it's a record certain to make you squirm and laugh at the same time. A new one, **Pizza Deliverance**, was unleashed in 1999.

Mike Cooley (bj,g,v); Patterson Hood (bj,g,v); Adam Howell (ub,v); Matt Lane (d); John Neff (p.s.); Barry Sell (md,v)

> "Nine Bullets" b/w "Bulldozers and Dirt"/Soul
>   Dump/1997 (7")
> "Nine Bullets" on **Revival 2: Kudzu and Hollerin'**
>   **Contest**/Yep Roc/1997
> **Gangstabilly**/Soul Dump/1998
> "The Living Bubba" on **Bubbapalooza, Vol. 2**/
>   Criminal/1998
> **Pizza Deliverance**/Soul Dump/1999

Drive-By Truckers/Soul Dump Records, P. O. Box 667, Athens, GA 30603; 706-549-5808

The Drive-By Truckers Side O' the Super Hiway //www.drivebytruckers.com

drivebytruckers@hotmail.com

Dry Branch Fire Squad

Bluegrass; New Old-Time; Novelty
Springfield, Ohio; 1976-

For over two decades, the Dry Branch Fire Squad has been searching for the "lonesome," a sort of holy grail of old-time/bluegrass music. Sounds serious but founder and leader Ron Thomason puts it into humorous perspective by characterizing lonesome as "a car on blocks." Such a light hearted attitude underlies the DBFS's commitment to keeping traditional music alive and kicking. Thomason served with Frank Wakefield and Ralph Stanley before forming the DBFS in 1976. They made two self-released albums before signing with Rounder in the late 1970s. Since then, the DBFS has released a steady stream of top notch old-time/bluegrass recordings of traditional material (obscure and well known) and Thomason originals. In addition to their strong vocals, tight harmonies, and first rate picking, the DBFS developed a reputation for off kilter humor. Their recordings come with tongue-in-cheek liner notes (penned by Thomason) written by a horse, as a send up of Stevenson's "Song of Hiawatha," or to explain how the DBFS's originals were composed by Thomason's siblings, Mucho, Macho, Bongo, and Go Go. This off-the-wall approach extends to the band's live performances where Thomason introduces the songs with hilarious "rants" about history, housework, testosterone poisoning, and banjo jokes. In 1996, the DBFS's appealing mix of old-time country with highbilly comedy ("aggressively traditional music") was captured on **Live! At Last**. Over the years, the band has undergone several personnel changes; their current line-up which includes banjo wiz Bill Evans may be their strongest yet. In honor of their contribution to the "lonesome," the Library of Congress placed the Dry Branch Fire Squad on its list of significant American recordings.

Suzanne Thomas, who was formerly leader of the legendary Ohio band, the Hot Mud Family, got the chance to show off her considerable vocal talents on the 1998 release **Dear Friends & Gentle Hearts**. Joining her for a very nice set of bluegrass/country are the Lonesome River Band, Seldom Scene, Laurie Lewis, John Hartford, IIIrd Tyme Out, and the Dry Branch Fire Squad.

Original Members: Charles Leet (b,g,p,v); Mary Jo Leet (b,g,v); Dan Russell (bj,v); Ron Thomason (bj,d,f,g,md,v); Suzanne Thomas (ah,bj,g,p,v)
Current Members: Bill Evans (bj); Charles Leet (b); Mary Jo Leet (g); Suzanne Thomas (cl. bj,g); Ron Thomason (g,md)

> **The Mandolin & Other Stuff** (Ron Thomason)/
>   Kanawa/1975
> **Spiritual Songs From Dry Branch**/RT/1977
> **Dry Branch Fire Squad**/RT/1978
> **Dry Branch Fire Squad on Tour**/Gordo/1979
> **Born to Be Lonesome**/Rounder/1979
> **Antiques & Inventions**/Rounder/1981
> **Fannin' the Flames**/Rounder/1982
> **Branching Out** (Ron Thomason)/Gordo/1984
> **Good Neighbors & Friends**/Rounder/1985
> **Golgotha**/Rounder/1986
> **Tried and True**/Rounder/1987; 1995
> **Strong at Heart** (Ron Thomason)/Gordo/1987
> **Fertile Ground**/Rounder/1989
> **Long Journey**/Rounder/1991
> **Just for the Record**/Rounder/1993
> **Native & Fine** (Bill Evans)/Rounder/1995
> **Live, At Last**/Rounder/1996
> **Dear Friends and Gentle Hearts** (Suzanne Thomas
>   solo)/Rounder/1998

Dry Branch Fire Squad //www.fortissimo.org/artists/drybranch/

Dry Branch Fire Squad/Rounder Web Page //www.rounder.com/rounder/catalog/

Bill Evans bevans@occ-uky.campus.mci.net

Bob Dylan

Country Rock; Roots Rock
Duluth, Minnesota; 1941-

1968 was a momentous year for country rock and the future of alternative country music: the Byrds recorded **Sweetheart of the Rodeo**, the Flying Burrito Brothers formed, and Bob Dylan's **John Wesley Harding** was released. The latter was ostensibly Dylan's first foray into country, but he had, in fact, been exploring it for several years prior to this. In 1966, he recorded **Blonde on Blonde** in Nashville using veteran session players and while not strictly a country album, it was a harbinger of things to come. One year later, Dylan and The Band, using a home tape recorder, cut **The Basement Tapes**, an incredible blend of old-time, honky tonk, blues, gospel, and rock with lots of modern touches. These sessions, which were not meant to be released, yielded great songs like "Tears of Rage," "I Shall Be Released," "This Wheel's On Fire," and

"Nothing Was Delivered" (the latter wound up on **Sweetheart**). They were heavily bootlegged and didn't make it to the general public until 1975; the influence of this monumental Americana recording on several generations of musicians has been tremendous. In 1967, Dylan returned to Nashville and with stripped down accompaniment from Kenny Buttrey (drums), Pete Drake (pedal steel), and Charlie McCoy (bass) recorded **John Wesley Harding**. As the story goes, he wrote the songs for the album with the Bible, Kafka, Colin Wilson's *The Outsider*, and the songs of Hank Williams close at hand; this helps explain the album's preoccupation with outsiders ("John Wesley Harding"; "Drifter's Escape"; "I Am a Lonesome Hobo"; "I Pity the Poor Immigrant") and salvation ("I Dreamed I Saw Saint Augustine"; "All Along the Watchtower"; "The Wicked Messenger"; "Down Along the Cove"). All in all, it is a stunning panorama of American culture, fully within the country music tradition. Dylan followed it up with an even more country album, **Nashville Skyline**. Once again, he used session men and recorded some memorable tunes including "I Threw It All Away," "Lay Lady Lay," "Nashville Skyline Rag" and a duet, "Girl From the North Country," with Johnny Cash. During this time, Dylan and Cash recorded a number of country standards ("Mountain Dew"; "Careless Love"; "Blue Yodel"), Cash hits ("I Walk the Line"; "Big River"; "Ring of Fire"), and some Sun era rockabilly classics ("Matchbox"; "That's All Right Mama"). In 1995, these memorable recordings were issued as an import, **The Dylan/Cash Sessions**; in addition to the studio material, they contain Dylan's performance on the Johnny Cash TV show and quadmasters of **Nashville Skyline**. His impact on several generations of musicians including many alt. country performers has been enormous; in 1997, Dylan invited Steve Earle, Dwight Yoakam, and a host of other artists to contribute to **The Songs of Jimmie Rodgers**, a tribute album that was the first recorded on Dylan's Egyptian label.

The big news in 1998 was the long-awaited release by Columbia of the famous 1966 "Royal Albert Hall" concert. Recorded during the controversial period when, with the help of The Hawks (later The Band), Dylan was experimenting with electric folk, it angered many acoustic folk fans but presaged his country rock recordings of a few years later. **Bob Dylan With the Band, Bootleg Series, Volume 4** also known as **Live 1966-The "Royal Albert Hall" Concert** (actually done at Manchester's Free Trade Hall) is a much cleaned up version of perhaps the most bootlegged recording of all time with one CD featuring Dylan solo acoustic and the other electric with The Hawks. Given the nature of those times and the startling contrast between the music on the two discs, it's easy to understand why Dylan's decision to plug in caused such a stir. (*Incidentally, Garth Brooks covered Dylan's "Make You Feel My Love" in 1998 and took it to #1 on the HNC charts. The apocalypse is at hand!)

Blonde on Blonde/Columbia/1966
The Basement Tapes/Columbia/rec. 1967, rel. 1975
John Wesley Harding/Columbia/1968
Nashville Skyline/Columbia/1969
The Genuine Basement Tapes, Vols. 1-5/Genuine/
The Booleg Series, Vols 1-3/1991
The Dylan/Cash Sessions (1969)/Red Robin/Spank/1995
The Songs of Jimmie Rodgers: A Tribute/Egyptian
   Columbia/1997
"The Lonesome River" on **Clinch Mountain Country: Ralph Stanley & Friends**/Rebel/1998
Bob Dylan With the Band: The Bootleg Series Vol. 4 or **Bob Dylan Live 1966—The "Royal Albert Hall" Concert**/Columbia/1998

Official Bob Dylan Page //ww.bobdylan.com

Bob Links //www.execpc.com/~billp61/boblink.html (the ultimate connection to hundreds of Dylan pages)

HWY61-L: The Bob Dylan Discussion Group //listserv.acsu.buffalo.edu/hwy-61-l.htm

See The Band; Johnny Cash

Fred J. Eaglesmith (Willie P. Bennett)
Singer/Songwriter
Alberton, Ontario, Canada; July 9, 1957-

The crisis that hit America's heartland in the 1980s also struck hard at Canada's farming communities where the same scenario of heartbreaking auctions and foreclosures was repeated again and again. Fred Eaglesmith was there to see and write about it first hand. Raised as one of nine children on a southern Ontario farm, he worked and played hard and developed an early interest in music. When the Eaglesmiths lost their farm like so many others, Fred took off at age 15 to Vancouver where he hoped to make a career as a singer/songwriter. But, the pull of his roots eventually brought him back to his home and farming. However, he didn't give up on music and continued to write and perform songs painting an honest picture of the brutal realities of life in rural Ontario: farm foreclosures ("Thirty Years of Farming"); the death of small towns ("Sweaburg General Store"); violence ("Little Buffalo"). In the 1980s, he recorded several albums (**Fred Eaglesmith, The Boy Who Just Went Wrong, Indiana Road**) and toured incessantly. His constant companions on the journey were bass player Ralph Schipper and mandolin/harmonica player Willie P. Bennett who attained cult status in Canada in the 1970s with a string of respected albums. As they traveled in ever widening circles, Fred and the Flying Squirrels (Bennett and Schipper) gathered more fans and critical acclaim in Canada and the U.S. American commentators rightfully compared him to Texas' great songwriters (Canada's answer to Robert Earl Keen?), but Eaglesmith has his own style that must be heard in person to be appreciated. His dynamic live performances were captured in the early 1990s on **There Ain't No Easy Road** (a double cassette packaged in a homemade pine box) and **From the Paradise Motel** recorded in Michigan. In between, Eaglesmith and band recorded **Things is Changin'**, another sterling collection of songs not only about the perils of farm life ("Sharecroppin'"; "Things Is Changin'"; "Harold Wilson"; "Carmelita") but also love ("Summerlea"; "Cryin' Yet"). In 1995 and 1996, Eaglesmith began to make a big U.S. breakthrough with **Drive-In Movie**. The response to "Freight Train," "Wilder Than Her," "Crashin' and Burnin'," "Good Enough," and other great songs on the album was overwhelmingly positive; it appeared on many alt. country/Americana top ten lists and won Canada's Juno for Best Traditional/Roots Album. In late 1996, Eaglesmith toured with the Cowboy Junkies and was invited by Robert Earl Keen to open for him on his winter 1996/7 tour. While on tour, Eaglesmith kept a diary "On the Bus" and read excerpts from it on NPR's *World Cafe*. Late in 1997, he signed with Razor & Tie and recorded **Lipstick, Lies & Gasoline**. Originally conceived by Eaglesmith as an album about Hank Williams' final journey, it turned into a collection of Fred's most potent and compelling commentary to date. Once again, Eaglesmith is the champion of the disaffected and disappointed: a man fed up with being fed upon ("7 Shells in My Six Gun"; "Time to Get a Gun"); a desperate man ("Pontiac"); a suspicious lover ("Are You Drinking Too Much?"—a beautiful duet with Claire Lynch); a frightened man ("Spookin' the Horses"); a man saddened by the loss of his musical heroes (Hank, Elvis, Gram, Jimi, Janis) to "Alcohol & Pills." His usual black mood is darkened a few shades on this recording by the wailing and gnashing of slide and electric guitar on "105" and the jolting title track. Powerful stuff!

Willie P. Bennett's recordings from the 1970s, **Tryin' to Start Out Clean and Sober, Hobo's Taunt, and Blackie & The Rodeo Kings**, are sadly out of print, but a collection of the best from them is available through Dark Light Music. A trio of respected Canadian musicians (Steve Fearing, Colin Linden, Tom Wilson) teamed up in 1996 as Blackie & the Rodeo Kings to make a Juno nominated recording of Bennett covers called **High or Hurtin'**. In 1998, Willie P. returned to the studio to record his first solo in many years; **Heartstrings** received a Juno nomination for Best Solo Roots/Traditional recording.

The Flying Squirrels: Willie P. Bennett (hm,md,v); Ralph Schipper (b,v); Washboard Hank (perc)

Tryin' to Start Out Clean (Willie P. Bennett)/1975
Hobo's Taunt (Willie P. Bennett)/Woodshed/1977
Blackie and the Rodeo King (Willie P. Bennett)/1979
Fred J. Eaglesmith/Sweetwater/1980
The Boy That Just Went Wrong/New Woodshed/1983
Indiana Road/Sweetwater Music/1987
The Lucky Ones (Willie P. Bennett)/Duke Street/1989
Wooden Wheels in Hagersville/Sweetwater Music/1990
There Ain't No Easy Road/Sweetwater Music/1991
Collectibles (Willie P. Bennett)/Dark Light Denon/1992
Take My Own Advice (Willie P. Bennett)/Dark Light Denon/1993
Things Is Changin'/Sweetwater Music/1993
From the Paradise Motel/Barbed Wire/1994; 1998
Drive-In Movie/Vertical/1996

Lipstick, Lies, & Gasoline/Razor & Tie/1997
Heartstrings (Willie P. Bennett)/B Natural/1998

Fred Eaglesmith Web Page //www.eaglesmith.com

Fred Eaglesmith Discography //www.ucs.mun.ca/~schipper/eaglesmith.html

Willie P. Bennett c/o Dark Light Music, 51 Bulwer St., Toronto, Ontario, Canada, M5T 1A1

See Blackie & the Rodeo Kings

Steve Earle

Twangtrust; Country Rock; Roots Rock; Singer/Songwriter
Fort Monroe, Virginia; January 10, 1955-

Steve Earle was once quoted as saying that "Hank Williams' records have a lot more to do with the Sex Pistols than they have to do with Brooks & Dunn." In a very real sense, this statement not only sums up his musical philosophy but also the course of his life. Like Hank and Sid Vicious, Earle, with his rocked up, politically conscious style of country, challenged the musical establishment and along the way gained cult status and a fiercely loyal following. Unfortunately, he shared with them a propensity for addiction and self-destructive behavior. His trouble with drugs as well as his musical career began when he was a teenager growing up in San Antonio, Texas. By age 16, he had a habit and was touring the state in a country band. Two years later, he had a wife (the first of four) and was working in a car wash and playing clubs in Houston where he met Townes Van Zandt and Jerry Jeff Walker. At 19, he was off again, this time to Nashville where he connected with Guy Clark who gave him a job playing bass in his band. But, after two years of this, Earle decided he wanted his own thing. He tried Austin for a time but then moved back to Nashville in 1979 where he remarried (twice), sold a few songs, and began putting together a band that was the foundation for the Dukes. After a rockabillyish EP debut (**Pink & Black**), Earle and the Dukes got a deal with Epic which led to a couple of unsuccessful singles. After Epic dropped him, Earle moved over to MCA and recorded his breakthrough release, **Guitar Town**. At the end of the 1980s and into the early 1990s, his rise to stardom was meteoric as he won over rock and country fans with albums (**Exit O, Copperhead Road, The Hard Way**) that tested the boundaries of country music and addressed controversial social issues. However, underneath the success, there were signs that things were not all rosy: two more broken marriages were accompanied by arrests in 1988 (assaulting an officer) and 1992 (drug possession), the end of his MCA contract plus numerous automobile accidents. Finally, Earle's 20 year drug habit took him to the bottom when he began smoking crack. For a while, he lived in South Nashville to get away and be near the city's crack houses, but there was no escape from the law and in 1994, Earle went to jail and then into rehab. Released in late 1995, Earle made a triumphant comeback with two powerful albums; first came the downhome, acoustic **Train a Comin'** (with Norman

Blake, Emmylou Harris, Peter Rowan) and then the rocking **I Feel Alright** on which Earle publically exorcised his demons and announced his determination to return to the promise of the 1980s. Trying hard to stay straight, Earle threw himself whole-heartedly into the music business setting up E-Squared Records where he and "Twangtrust" partner Ray Kennedy began producing up and coming alt. country acts like the V-Roys, 6 String Drag, and Cheri Knight. He continued to record as well doing a couple of EPs with the V-Roys and the Supersuckers and contributing (with the V-Roys) a rousing "In the Jailhouse Now" to Dylan's tribute album, **The Songs of Jimmie Rodgers**. Earle's 1997, **El Corazon**, pays homage to his many musical influences: "The Other Side of Town" with Del McCoury is old-time music (even sounds like a scratchy old 78); "I Still Carry You Around" is straight ahead bluegrass (courtesy of backing by the Del McCoury Band); "Christmas in Washington" gives a nod to Woody Guthrie; "Ft. Worth Blues" honors the late, great Townes Van Zandt. Also along are Emmylou Harris on the country rocking "Taneytown" and the Supersuckers on the country punkish "N.Y.C." This superb recording finished #1 on most alt. country Best of 1997 lists and established Earle as perhaps alternative country's most visible and popular performer.

As befits the stature of a musician who reaches Steve Earle's level, a number of important things happened in 1998. First of all, he began showing up on many recordings either as a guest performer (Nanci Griffith; Jerry Douglas) or contributor to tribute albums (Kris Kristofferson) and soundtracks (*The Horse Whisperer*; *Psycho*). Second, traffic in bootleg recordings (on labels and in private collections) of his live performances increased dramatically. Thirdly, the number of web pages devoted or related to Earle continued to rise and his online mailing list (Exit O) became the largest of any alt. country performer. And finally, Steve used his high profile to support a number of causes including Farm Aid, the Campaign for a Land Mine Free World, the Poor People's Summit, and the anti-death penalty campaign; in regard to the latter, he joined a group of protestors for a fast/vigil at the Supreme Court and even witnessed the execution of convicted murderer Jonathan Nobles (Earle had previously contributed the song "Ellis Unit One" to the anti-death penalty film *Dead Man Walking*). In addition to all this, Earle lent his production skills to albums by Bap Kennedy and Lucinda Williams and finished off the year by recording **The Mountain**, a "high risk, low tech" (E-Squared) bluegrass album featuring Earle's interpretations (some traditional, some modern) of classics and originals backed by the Del McCoury Band and a stellar supporting cast including Iris DeMent, Jerry Douglas, Sam Bush, Emmylou Harris, Kathy Chiavola, Tim O'Brien, John Hartford, Gillian Welch, David Rawlings, Jack Clement, and Peter Rowan.

Steve's little sister Stacey got her own singer/songwriter career going in 1998 with the release of **Simple Gearle**.

Pink and Black/LSI/1982 (EP)
Guitar Town/MCA/1986
Early Tracks/Epic/1987; KOCH 1998
Exit O/MCA/1987
Copperhead Road/Uni MCA/1988
The Hard Way/MCA/1989
Shut Up and Die Like an Aviator (Live)/ MCA/1991(promo)
We Ain't Ever Satisfied—The Essential Collection/ MCA/1992 (comp. of previously released material)
The Road and the Sky/Great Dane/1992 (live boot)
BBC Radio 1: Live in Concert/BBC Windsong UK/1992
Essential Steve Earle/MCA/1993
This Highway's Mine/Pickwick/1993 (comp. of previously released material)
Uncut Gems (Steve Earle Demos)/Warner Bros./1994 (promo)
Fearless Heart/MCA Special Prods./1995
Train a Comin'/Winter Harvest/1995
"Ellis Unit One" on **Dead Man Walking**/1995
I Feel Alright/Warner Brothers/1996
Ain't Ever Satisfied/Hip-O/1996 (dbl. CD 1980s-early 1990s retrospective)
"White Freight Liner Blues" on **Rig Rock Deluxe**/ Upstart Diesel Only/1996
Johnny Too Bad (with The V-Roys)/E-Squared/1996
Rebels & Road Songs: Steve Earle/Austin Music Network/1996 (video collection)
Hard Core Troubadour/Doberman/1996 (live boot)
The Very Best of Steve Earle—Angry Young Man/ Nectar Masters/1996 (comp. of previously released material)
Steve Earle/The Supersuckers/SubPop/1997 (EP)
"In the Jailhouse Now" on **The Songs of Jimmie Rodgers: A Tribute**/Egyptian/1997
El Corazon/E-Squared/1997
Simple Gearle (Stacey Earle)/Gearle/1998
"Me and the Eagle" on **The Horse Whisperer**/ MCA/1998
Do Not Try This at Home/Doberman/1998 (live boot)
The Last of the Hardcore Troubadours/ Red&Blue/1998 (live boot)
Acoustic For WXRT Radio-Chicago/Highway Is Alive/1998 (live boot)
Park West-Chicago, IL/KAT/1998 (live boot)
Come Back Woody Guthrie/Copperhead/1998 (live boot)
"All My Life" on **Psycho**/Geffen/1998 (sdtrk.)
The Mountain/E-Squared/1999
"High Fashion Queen" (with Chris Hillman) on **Return of the Grievous Angel: A Tribute to Gram Parsons**/Almo/1999

SteveEarle.Net: The Original Unofficial Steve Earle Site //www.steveearle.net (the most complete with biography, discography, archive of articles and reviews, tabs, lyrics, song index, e-mail mailing list, and links to other Earle pages)

Exit O Digest: The Steve Earle Online Mailing List (very large, very active, very informative about all things Steve Earle; to subscribe e-mail paulab@istar.ca and put Subscribe Steve as the subject)

Steve Earle/E-Squared Records Page //www.e2records.com/searle.html

A Steve Earle Jump Station
//home.sol.no/~billy2/se-jump.htm (trade page and mailing list archive)

Unofficial Steve Earle Home Page
//www.geocities.com/nashville/8404/

Old Grey Cat—The Steve Earle Pages
//www.geocities.com/sunsetstrip/towers/9961/steve.htm

Copperhead Road //www.auburn.net/~exit0/tapetrade/ (mostly a site where you can find and trade for bootlegs by Earle and other alt. country performers)

Steve Earle iMusic Showcase
//imusic.com/showcase/country/

Steve Earle AOL Folder: Entertainment>Music>Chat & Messages>Music Community>Country/Folk>Country & Western, A-K or Folk/Acoustic

Steve Earle Message Board
//www.triviapursuit.com/main.shtml (click Message Forums Link to find Earle's board)

Steve Earle in Quotes (a limited edition volume of quotes and stories from and about Steve Earle; for details contact Joanna Serraris, Postbox 84255, 2508 AG The Hague, The Netherlands or //www.musemix.demon.nl; joanna.s@musemix.demon.nl)

Steve Earle Fan Club,
P.O. Box 1113, Gallatin, TN 37066

See Bap Kennedy; Cheri Knight; Del McCoury; Buddy Miller; The V-Roys

Don Edwards
Cowboy/Western
New Jersey; 1941-

Like many other boys and girls of his generation, Don Edwards' first exposure to cowboy music and culture came via movies, Western pulp fiction, and 78 records. But, unlike most, his fascination was not a passing fancy but rather became a life-long love affair. Leaving home while still a teen, Edwards worked on the East Coast as a folk/country singer for a while before heading out West to Texas and New Mexico where, for a time, he was a ranch hand and rodeo rider. However, in the early 60s, he was on the move again finally landing in the Dallas-Ft. Worth area where he held a number of jobs (amusement park performer, trucker) but continued to pursue his musical dream. After cutting his first cowboy song ("The Young Ranger") for a local label, Don was off to Nashville where he was rejected for being a "folk" not country singer and then went back to wandering before returning to Ft. Worth. There he got lucky landing a regular spot at the famed White Elephant Saloon and parrying his popularity as a cowboy singer into a string of cowboy/Western albums that were financially and critically successful (**Desert Nights and Cowtown Blues** and **Chant of the Wanderer** were honored by The National Cowboy Hall of Fame and Western Heritage Museum). Then, in the early 1990s, Edwards came to the attention of nascent cowboy singer Michael Martin Murphey who helped set up the Warner

Western label. Don was brought on board and with another run of excellent recordings became one of the premier "cowboy troubadours" regularly performing at cowboy gatherings like Elko and WestFest. With rich Marty Robbins style vocals, the "minstrel of the Range" lovingly interprets the classic songs of the West, but Edwards is much more than just a cowboy cover singer. His sincere interest in Western culture and history has made him into one of America's most avid and respected cowboy musicologists. Edwards' tireless research stands up there along with the great John Lomax and has undercovered many songs which might otherwise have been lost; moreover, his experience has taught him how to write authentic originals that keep the tradition fresh and alive.

In the late 1990s, Edwards jumped to Shanachie Records' Western Jubilee subsidiary where he did an all-acoustic collection (**Saddle Songs**) of cowboy standards and originals and a very nice tribute, **My Hero Gene Autry**, to celebrate the 90th birthday of the legendary singing cowboy. On the latter recording, Don is backed by Texas swing band Tom Morrell & the Time-Warp Top Hands, and the collaboration yields a truly wonderful and memorable homage. And though Edwards was already well-known in cowboy/Western circles, his profile with the larger public was dramatically increased in 1998 when he had a prominent role as, what else, a singing cowboy in Robert Redford's *The Horse Whisperer*.

Songs of the Cowboys/DE/1986
Guitars and Saddle Songs/DE/1987
Desert Nights & Cowtown Blues/DE/1989
Chant of the Wanderer/DE/1991
Songs of the Trail/Warner Western/1992
Goin' Back to Texas/Warner Western/1993
The Bard and the Balladeer/Warner Western/1994
West of Yesterday/Warner Western/1996
Saddle Songs/Western Jubilee Shanachie/1998
My Hero Gene Autry/Western Jubilee Shanachie/1998
"Cowboy Love Song" on **The Horse Whisperer**/ MCA/1998
The Best of Don Edwards/Warner Western/1999

Don Edwards //www.westernjubilee.com/donedwards.htm

Don Edwards/Warner Western Page
//www.wbr.com/nashville/warnerwestern/cmp/done.html

T. Tex Edwards
Psychcountry
Dallas, Texas; November 14, 1954-

When it comes to psychotic country, Tex Edwards is in a class by himself. As proof, one need look no further than his debut album, **Pardon Me, I've Got Someone to Kill**. The cartoon cover depicts a pot bellied cowboy in boxer shorts, cowboy hat, and boots cavorting and drinking with a half nekkid woman while behind them a huge, hairy redneck in overalls brandishing a club has just burst into the room. This rosy little picture is an apt introduction to the material on the album: covers of obscure country songs about murder, mayhem, and madness. In addition to the title tune written by Johnny Paycheck, there is "I'm A Gonna Kill You" (Wynn Stewart), "LSD Made a Wreck Out of Me" (W. Austin), "The Girl on Death Row" (Lee Hazelwood), "Psycho" (Leon Payne), "You Ain't Never Gonna Live to Love Saturday Night" (W. Buckner), "The Cold Hard Facts of Life" (Bill Anderson), "Beatin' on the Bars" (Jack Clement), "Strangler in the Night" (A. DeSalvo), and "Rubber Room" (Porter Wagoner). Lending twangy support to Tex on lead vocals, rants, and raves is Out on Parole, a band made up of Austin musicians Mike Buck (drums), Joe Dickens (guitars), Marty Muse (pedal steel), J.J. Barrera (bass), John X. Reed (lead guitar), and Howard Kalish (fiddle).

Edwards performed in his native Dallas in the early 1990s where he was especially popular at the Barley House. He did a number of twisted recordings including "Scatter," "Lee Harvey Was a Friend of Mine" (Homer Henderson), "Strange Movies," "Man From Mars" with bands such as Lithium X, the Big D Ramblers, and the Sickoids or his own groups, the Loafin' Hyenas, and the Swinging Cornflake Killers. In 1997, Edwards relocated to Austin and in 1998-1999, with his new band, the Toe Tags, recorded another round of dementia, **Up Against the Floor**, followed by a cassette called **Intexicated**.

Pardon Me, I've Got Someone to Kill (with Out on Parole)/SFTRI/1989
"Lee Harvey Was a Friend of Mine" (with the Sickoids) b/w "It's Gravity" (with the Big D Ramblers)/SFTRI/1992 (7")
"Scatter" b/w "Move It" (with the Loafin' Hyenas)/ SFTRI/1993 (7")
"Strange Movies" b/w "Love Power" (with Lithium X)/1993 (7")
"Jekyll & Hyde" b/w "Man From Mars"/Honey/1994
"LSD Made a Wreck Out of Me"; "Whiskey Trip" on **Live From the Barley House**/BH/1995
"You Are So Predictable"/Living/1997 (7")
Up Against the Floor/Honey/1998
Intexicated/TexHex/1999 (CS)

T. Texas Edwards, 512-416-7242

See Homer Henderson

Ana Egge

Austin; Singer/Songwriter
Estevan, Saskatchewan, Canada; 1977-

Born in Canada, Ana Egge spent her childhood trekking with her family back and forth between communes in North Dakota and New Mexico. Along the way, she picked up lots of experiences and an affection for music. When the Egges settled near Silver City, New Mexico in 1989, she began to craft her own story songs and at age 17 met renowned bass player Sarah Brown who convinced her to move to Austin to record a demo cassette. For the next couple of years, Egge became a regular in Austin clubs as a solo or with a trio (Thamusement) gathering

many admirers: winner of the 1995 Village Voice Songwriter Search sponsored by the *Austin American Statesman* and *Music City Texas'* Best New Artist of 1996. In 1997, Dave Sanger, Asleep at the Wheel drummer and head of Lazy SOB Records, agreed to produce her first CD, **River Under the Road**. It was an auspicious debut not only because of Egge's vocals and perceptive songwriting but also for the amazing supporting cast drawn from Austin's musical elite; joining Egge were Jimmie Dale Gilmore (co-wrote and dueted on title track), Mary Cutrufello, Danny Barnes (Bad Livers), Rich Brotherton (Robert Earl Keen), Steve James, Paul Glasse, Marvin Dykhuis (Tish Hinojosa), Casper Rawls, Sarah Brown, Cindy Cash-dollar (Asleep at the Wheel), and Lucky Oceans (ex-Asleep at the Wheel). In 1998, Egge finished a tour opening for Iris DeMent, showcased at the NEA Extravaganza in Nashville, and did 25 shows on the Shawn Colvin tour. Early in 1999, Ana started her own label, Grace Records, and released **Mile Marker** which she co-produced with Rich Brotherton (Robert Earl Keen).

Ana Egge/AE/1995 (CS)
River Under the Road/Lazy SOB/1997
Mile Marker/Grace/1999

Ana Egge //www.anaegge.com

ana@anaegge.com

Ana Egge/Lazy SOB Page //www.io.com/lazysob/ana.html

The Bramble & The Rose: An Ana Egge Fan Page //www.geocities.com/sunsetstrip/amphitheatre/9240/ana.html

Ernst Eggenberger (Funny Hill)

Singer/Songwriter
Switzerland

If a man is known by the company he keeps then Swiss singer/songwriter Ernst Eggenberger must be a heck of a guy! In his native country, he is primarily known as the leader of Funny Hill, one of Europe's best and most popular country rock groups. Over many years of touring with them, Eggenberger met and befriended many American artists, and when he decided to record his songs in the U.S. called on them to help out. For the 1993 **Endless Avenue: Direction Nashville**, he got Richard Dobson, Joe Sun, Townes Van Zandt and a host of other Nashville based singers to cover his originals which clearly show the influence of the Texas troubadour tradition. They range from moderate ballads ("Dust on Your Shelf") to country rockers ("P is Burning") and an especially nice Mexican flavored waltz "Sage" that owes a lot to Van Zandt's "Pancho & Lefty" and is done as a duet between Townes and Denise Benson. Two years later, Eggenberger drew on his "Austin connections" to record **Endless Avenue: Next Stop Austin**. Here, Pat Mears, David Rodriquez, Susan Lindfors, and Billy Paul sing Eggenberger's songs and get support from Tish Hinojosa, Marvin Dykhuis (Hinojosa's lead guitar),

Champ Hood (Toni Price; Threadgill Troubadors), Katy Moffatt, steel player Marty Muse, and drummer Paul Pearcy (Jerry Jeff Walker, Darden Smith). As a result, the recording has that Texas honky tonk swing feel. Both **Endless Avenue** recordings were originally released on the Swiss Brambus label and re-released in 1996 in the U.S. by BCN.

Live in Nashville (Funny Hill)/Brambus Switz./1989 (with Richard Dobson)
Endless Avenue: Direction Nashville/Brambus Switz./1993; BCN/1996
Cowboy Boots (Funny Hill)/Brambus Switz./1994
Endless Avenue: Next Stop Austin/Brambus Switz./1995; BCN/1996
Bordertown (Funny Hill)/Brambus Switz./1996

Ernst Eggenberger Web Page
//www.bcnmusic.com/endless/endless.htm

Funny Hill Home Page
//songs.com/brambus/fh/index-nf.html

E*I*E*I*O

Country Rock; Cowpunk; Roots Rock
Madison, Wisconsin; 1985-1988

Undoubtedly one of the most obscure alt. country groups of the late 1980s, Wisconsin based E*I*E*I*O made one dynamite country/roots rock album, switched direction, and then disappeared. Anchored by the amazingly clean lead vocals of Steve Summers, killer harmonies, and a twangy and sometimes stinging twin guitar attack from Rob Harding and Mike Hoffman, **Land of Opportunity** is a winner from beginning to end. Co-produced by Steve Berlin (Blasters; Los Lobos), the recording serves up a veritable smorgasbord of alt. country from the late 1960s-1980s: "This Time," "Get Back to Arkansas," "Every Word True," "Blue Mountaintop," "When the Stars Are Out" are pure Byrdsian folk/country rock with jangly, twangly guitar and soaring harmonies; "Hello Heartache" and "Tear It Down" capture the more energized country rock of the Long Ryders; "Me and Jesus Christ" shows cowpunk influences; "Go West Young Man" and "White Lines, Blue Skies, Black Top" have a Blasters roots rock feel. Unfortunately, **That Love Thang** (minus Hoffmann) didn't measure up to its predecessor and by the end of the 80s, E*I*E*I*O was history.

Tommy Ciaccio (d); Rob Harding (g,v); Mike Hoffman (g,v); Steve Summers (a.g.,l.v.); Richard Szeluga (b)

Land of Opportunity/Frontier/1986; 1992
That Love Thang/Frontier/1988

Jason Eklund

Singer/Songwriter

In the tradition of Jimmie Rodgers, Woody Guthrie, Ramblin' Jack Elliott, and other great American minstrels comes Jason Eklund. And make no mistake about it, he's no armchair troubadour but a genuine wanderer, traveling around in an old Chevy searching for songs to sing and stories to tell. He stopped long enough to record two albums, **Jason Eklund** and **Lost Causeway**, full of country, folk, and blues originals delivered in the half singing, half talking style made famous by Guthrie and Dylan. And like his predecessors on the road, Eklund dwells on lonesome highways, decaying landscapes, beat down people, and the never ending quest for...? "Lonesome Out There," "Walk One More Mile," "I Am the Road," "Sand in My Shoes," "Travelin' on That Lost Causeway," "What's Left of 66," "Motel Thin" give a discerning glimpse of the freedom and insecurity of life on the open road in a way that is both moving and funny. In 1997, Eklund collaborated with New Orleans singer/songwriter Roger Johnson on **A Streamliner's Duet**, a menagerie of blues, ragtime, folk, and spoken word songs. The following year, Jason took on a new identity as Captain Stringbean and recorded **Dead Heart Days**.

Jason Eklund/Flying Fish/1993
Lost Causeway/Flying Fish/1995
"What's Left of 66" on **The Songs of Route 66**/Lazy SOB/1995
A Streamliner's Duet (with Roger Johnson)/Gadfly/1997
Dead Heart Days (as Captian Stringbean)/1998
Jason Eklund/Gadfly Page //www.gadfly.com

Betty Elders

Austin; Singer/Songwriter
Greensboro, North Carolina; December 15, 1949-

Originally from North Carolina, Betty Elders was raised on gospel and old-time country, began composing songs at age 6, formed a folk group, Just Us, as a teenager, and made her first album (as Betty Nicley) in 1981. Three years later, she and husband, Gene, moved to Austin where she became a local favorite. In 1989, Betty released **Daddy's Coal** on her Whistling Pig label. A mix of traditional country ("Bed of Roses/Bed of Thorns"; "A Drifter's Prayer"; "I Never Think of You at All"), jazz ("Welcome Home Heart"), and pop ("Silver Wheels"; "The Pilgrim"), it won Elders a passel of singer/songwriter awards from *Music City Texas*. The follow-up, **Peaceful Existence**, brought national and even international acclaim. Elders was placed in the same company as Nanci Griffith and Lucinda Williams and reviewers gushed with the highest praise (one was moved to name **Peaceful Existence** one of "the top 5 albums of the decade"). However, the title belied Elders' life which was beset by numerous personal tragedies and problems during this period. She rode them out and used her next recording (and major roots label debut), **Crayons** to publically grapple with the fall out from her troubled times. The result was a very revealing and often moving piece of work but overall, not quite up to Elders' previous efforts. But, with the dark days behind her, she was free to fulfill the promise that once touted her as Austin's next big "breakout" singer/

songwriter. Betty's fortunes did indeed rise in 1997 with several artists covering her songs including Joan Baez who invited her along for a European tour. 1998 brought several well-deserved honors: inclusion in two new books (*Music Hound Folk—The Essential Album Guide*; *Music From the Heart*, Rod Kennedy's *Kerrville Folk Music anthology*) and selection to the faculty of the 26th Annual Kerrville Folk Festival Songwriting School. A fifth album was on its way by years' end.

After the Curtain/Whistling Pig/1981
Daddy's Coal/Whistling Pig/1989
Peaceful Existence/Whistling Pig/1993
Crayons/Flying Fish/1995
Betty Elders Home Page //www.bettyelders.com

Ronny Elliott

Roots Rock; Country Rock
Tampa, Florida

When Ronny Elliott reads about the 90s roots rock "explosion," he might smile and say, "been there, done that." He began playing roots rock/Americana in Tampa, Florida in the mid-1960s when he was bassist with a garage band called the Raveons. By 1967, Elliott was fronting Your Local Bear, one of the first bona fide country rock bands whose big moment was opening for Hendrix. Subsequently, Ronny was a member of many bands (the Soul Trippers, Noah's Ark, Duckbutter, the Outlaws) through whom he got lots of recording and touring/ concert experience opening for the Allman Brothers, Bill Haley, Canned Heat, Chuck Berry, Van Morrison, and many others. Unfortunately, none of these bands enjoyed much commercial success and after doing time in many more long forgotten groups, Elliott decided to just go it on his own backed by the Nationals. In the late 1990s, after almost three decades in the musical trenches, Elliott finally got to cut the record he'd always wanted to on his Blue Heart label. **Ronny Elliott and the Nationals** is basically a retrospective touching the key roots rock bases of the last 30 years but with a wry sense of humor needed to cope with the many ups and downs of the music 'biz. With a voice that's a cross between Butch Hancock and Tom Russell, Elliott serves up enjoyable and highly amusing originals like "Billy's First Ex-Wife," "Toulouse Lautrec on a Bad Night in Paris" ('life's too short and so are you'), "Tell the King the Killer is Here" (about a real life Jerry Lee Lewis incident outside Graceland), "Skid Row Hillbilly," and "Too Hip for the Radio." The sequel, **A Postcard From Jack**, is a little more laid back with the highlights being "Blue Dreams," "White Knuckle Flight," "Carlos Diego," and the moving follow-up to "Tell the King the Killer is Here" entitled "Tell the Killer the King is Dead." Taken together, these recordings present an insightful chronicle of one man's long, strange musical trip.

Ronny Elliott & The Nationals/Blue Heart/1997

A Postcard From Jack/Blue Heart/1998

Ronny Elliott, 179 Baltic Circle, Tampa, FL 33606; 813-254-5388
Ronny Elliott Home Page //www.ronnyelliott.com

Joe Ely

Lubbock Mafia; Country Rock; Roots Rock
Amarillo, Texas; February 9, 1947-

Simply put, Joe Ely is Texas' consummate alternative country artist of the past twenty five years. In the early 1970s, he was a member, along with Jimmie Dale Gilmore and Butch Hancock, of the ultra-legendary country rock band, The Flatlanders. After its demise, Ely was the first of that remarkable trio to make a major musical breakthrough when he formed the Joe Ely Band in the mid-1970s. With an incredible troupe of musicians (including Ponty Bone, Lloyd Maines, Jesse Taylor) and the consistently fine songs of Ely, Gilmore, and Hancock, they recorded a run of albums (**Joe Ely**, **Honky Tonk Masquerade**, **Down on the Drag**, **Live Shots**, **Musta Notta Gotta Lotta**) that were among the best alternative country recordings of the era. What set the Joe Ely Band apart was its ability to so effectively combine traditional and modern musical styles including country rock, honky tonk, rockabilly, Tex-Mex, and Cajun. Their albums and live performances won them a large following at home and overseas (The Clash were big admirers and appeared on **Live Shots**) and widespread critical acclaim. Alas, they failed to meet the bottom line for MCA (i.e. hits) so in 1983, the label pulled the plug. A year later, Ely recorded the experimental **Hi Res**, but it wasn't until 1987 that he made a triumphant return with a new band and a new record label. In successive years, Hightone released **Lord of the Highway** and **Dig All Night**, two great roots/rock albums with more excellent Ely songs and the blistering guitar work of David Grissom. Ely's straight ahead rock 'n' roll sound of this period is best captured on **Live at Liberty Lunch** (1990). Into the 1990s, Ely gradually toned down and reached out in new directions. **Love and Danger** is a moodier, more insightful effort with good songs by Ely, Robert Earl Keen ("The Road Goes on Forever"), and Dave Alvin ("Every Night About This Time"). In 1995, on **Letter to Laredo**, Ely explored his long time fascination with Spanish music and poetry in a way that echoes the old Ely sound but is distinctly different due to the presence of the flamenco guitar of European virtuoso Teye. Guest appearances by Bruce Springsteen and Raul Malo show the respect accorded Ely by fellow musicians. Compilations of his music have been issued on British import labels; **Milkshakes and Malts** and **Whatever Happened to Maria** collect Ely's covers of Butch Hancock songs while **No Bad or Loud Talk** and **Time for Travelin'** feature his best from the 1970s and early 1980s. In 1997, Ely was asked to contribute a song ("The South Wind of Summer") to the soundtrack of Robert Redford's *The Horse*

Whisperer and brought Gilmore and Hancock in as co-writers. They wrote three new songs, appeared together on Letterman, and sparked a wave of rumors about a Flatlanders reunion. Joe also recorded "Twistin' in the Wind" with Jesse Taylor, Lloyd Maines, and David Grissom for the film *Hope Floats*. This song was the title track for his 1998 album which marked somewhat of a return to vintage Joe Ely country/roots rock/Tex-Mex with help from old bandmates Jesse Taylor, Lloyd Maines, Mitch Watkins, and David Grissom. He also did a recording with Los Super Seven, a Tex-Mex supergroup consisting of Flaco Jimenez, Freddy Fender, David Hidalgo, Cesar Rosas, Rick Trevino, and Ruben Ramos. Like his pal Butch Hancock, Ely is a multi-media artist. In 1998, he had a show for his artwork at Austin's Wild About Music and a triology of books (*Ripened*, *Seasoned*, *Salted*) about his travels on the road were published. In 1999, Ely guested on Jesse Taylor's **Texas Tattoo** with Jimmie Dale Gilmore, Butch Hancock, Don McCalister, Toni Price, and Kimmie Rhodes.

Joe Ely/MCA/1977
Honky Tonk Masquerade/MCA/1978
Down on the Drag/MCA/1979
One More Road (Flatlanders)/Charly UK/1980
Live Shots/South Coast MCA/1981 (some copies came with a **Texas Special** EP)
Musta Notta Gotta Lotta/South Coast MCA/1981
Lord of the Highway/MCA/1987; Hightone/
Dig All Night/Demon/1988; Hightone/
Milkshakes and Malts/Sunstorm UK/1989
Whatever Happened to Maria/Sunstorm UK/1989
More a Legend Than a Band (Flatlanders)/ Rounder/1990
Live at Liberty Lunch/MCA/1990
Love and Danger/MCA/1992
Unplugged (Flatlanders)/Sun/1995 (reissue of **One More Road** with p.u. trks.)
No Bad or Loud Talk: Joe Ely, 1976-1981/Edsel UK/1995
Letter to Laredo/MCA/1995
Time For Travelin': The Best of Joe Ely, Volume Two/ Edsel UK/1996
"South Wind of Summer" (The Hill Country Flatlanders) on The Horse Whisperer/MCA/1998
Twistin' in the Wind/MCA/1998
Live at the Cambridge Folk Festival/BBC Strange Fruit/1998
Texas Tattoo (Jesse Taylor)/Appaloosa/1999

Joe Ely, 7107 Hwy. 71, West A9, Austin, TX 78735

Letter to Laredo: The Joe Ely Home Page //www.ely.com

Joe@ely.com

Bernhard's Joe Ely Page //home.allgaeu.org/brosa/homepage.htm

Joe Ely iMusic Showcase //imusic.com/showcase/country/

See Terry Allen; Ponty Bone; The Flatlanders; Jimmie Dale Gilmore; Butch Hancock

Jon Emery
Hillbilly Rock
Vermont; December 28, 1946-

A local music critic once called Jon Emery "the best country singer to come out of Austin since Willie Nelson"; the Austin City Council proclaimed a "Jon Emery Day" in his honor in 1993. And still, most Austinites would say "Jon *who*?" Born in Vermont, Emery's first country influences were groups like the Delmore Brothers. In the early 1960s, he was living in California where he formed the VIPs with Leroy Preston (Asleep at the Wheel co-founder). Later, Emery started a country swing group, the Missouri Valley Boys, and toured around the Midwest until finally settling in Austin in 1976 where the MVB became a Western swing band called Whiskey Drinkin' Music. This band eventually evolved into the Jon Emery Band which combined hillbilly, honky tonk, and rock. Playing Austin bars and clubs throughout the 1970s and early 1980s, Emery recorded **Hillbilly Rock & Roll** for Bear Family in 1985. His supporting cast included local Austin stalwarts Alvin Crow and Erik Hokkanen and steel great Jimmy Day on originals plus a Delmore Brothers medley. Emery recorded a live album at Austin's Cactus Cafe in 1987 and in 1995 made another record for Bear Family, **If You Don't Buy This, I'll Find Somebody Who Will**. In 1997, he reasserted his claim to being the "King of Hillbilly Rock" with the release of **Two Separate Highways**.

Hillbilly Rock & Roll/Bear Family/1985
Live at the Cactus Cafe/1987
If You Don't Buy This Record, I'll Find Somebody Who Will/Bear Family/1995
Two Separate Highways/Rib House/1997

Jon Emery Booking Information c/o David Armentino, 512-478-0807

Buddy Emmons
Pedal Steel; Honky Tonk; Western Swing
Mishawaka, Indiana; January 27, 1937-

For most steel guitar players as well as for most side/session men, it's usually a case of heard but not seen. Not so with Buddy Emmons. Over the last thirty years, no steel player has attained greater visibility and recognition. This is attributable partly to the signature derby he sports when he plays, but more importantly, it is due to his innovative style and invaluable musical contributions. Starting out on lap steel at age 11, Emmons switched to pedal as a teenager and became so proficient in his teens that by age 18 he was a member of the Little Jimmy Dickens band where he stayed until the end of the 1950s. In the early 1960s, he was briefly with the Texas Troubadours and then in 1963 began a five year stint with Ray Price and the Cherokee Cowboys. During this time, he collaborated with another steel guitar player, Shot Jackson, on an album and in a business venture, the Sho-Bud Company, that produced the first push rod pedal steels. In the late 1960s and early 1970s, Emmons was a side/session player for several country and non-country artists but in the mid-1970s began to chart his own course. He absorbed a diversity of influences including bebop. Signed by Flying Fish, Emmons brought together top Western swing musicians (old and new) to record a number of wonderful albums (**Sings Bob Wills, Buddies, Live From Austin City Limits, Minors Aloud**). Throughout the 1980s and 1990s, Emmons continued to tour (with Ray Price and the Everly Brothers), promote Western swing (in collaboration with Ray Pennington) and serve as a leading spokesman for the steel guitar. In 1997, Razor & Tie issued an excellent Emmons' retrospective appropriately titled **Amazing Steel Guitar**.

Steel Guitar Jazz/Mercury/1963
Steel Guitar & Dobro Sound (with Shot Jackson)/1965
Best of Western Swing/Cumberland/196?
Emmons Guitar Inc./Emmons/1972
Steel Guitar/Flying Fish/1975
Buddy & Lenny/Flying Fish/1975
Buddy Emmons Sings Bob Wills/Flying Fish/1976
Buddies (with Buddy Spicher)/Flying Fish/1977
Emmons Live, Vol. 1 (At the International Steel Guitar Convention)/Midland/1978
Emmons Live, Vol. 2/Midland/1978
Live From Austin City Limits (Nashville Super Pickers)/Flying Fish/1979
Minors Aloud/Flying Fish/1979
Swingin' From the 40's Thru the 80's/Step One/1984
In the Mood for Swingin'/Step One/1986
Swingin' Our Way/Step One/1990
Swingin' By Request/Step One/1992
Buddy Emmons/Step One/1994
It's All in the Swing/Step One/1996
Amazing Steel Guitar: The Buddy Emmons Collection/ Razor & Tie/1997
Goin' Out Swingin' (with Ray Pennington)/Step One/1998

Dirt Production's Buddy Emmons Page //www.brainerd.net/~dirtprod/

Randy Erwin

Cowboy/Western; Yodeling
Dallas, Texas

In my collection, I have an enchanting CD called **Yodeling Crazy** that has examples of yodeling from around the world. Its very informative liner notes indicate that there are two general types of yodels, "Naturjodel" used by rural people to communicate out in the field and "Jodellied" which is yodeling used in songs. Over the years, many variations have emerged in different regions so that today yodeling styles are amazingly complex. Americans are familiar with yodeling primarily through the many country and western vocalists who have incorporated it into their sound over the years. In homage to this long and varied tradition, Dallas singer Randy Erwin made several fine recordings (**'Til the Cows Come Home; Cowboy**

Rhythm) in the late 1980s on Brave Combo's Four Dots label. With backing from Brave Combo, Erwin covers a diversity of American yodeling styles: Jimmie Rodgers' "Blue Yodel" ("T for Texas"; "In the Jailhouse"), sus- tained falsetto *a la* Elton Britt and Slim Whitman, cowboy caterwauling ("Cattle Call"; "Nightherd Song"), Hank Williams ("Lovesick Blues"; "Long Gone Lonesome Blues"), Wilf Carter/Patsy Montana fast yodeling, and the unique trilling or burring yodel made famous by Goebel Reeves ("My Sweetheart's in Love with a Swiss Mountaineer"). In his live performances, Erwin took on a more complete cowboy persona not only through yodeling but also his fancy trick roping which won him a role in David Byrne's *True Stories*. Additionally, Erwin was featured on NPR and made several appearances in England on stage, radio, and television. In 1989, he followed up his yodeling albums with **Back Home** which once again presents a variety of yodels but also a number of other songs demonstrating his musical range. By the mid-1990s, Erwin was leading a band called Cafe Noir which specialized in cabaret style gypsy swing music but occasionally showcased Erwin's yodeling skills as on a break-neck version of "Back in the Saddle." In early 1997, Erwin left Cafe Noir and began singing with a 1930s-1940s Western swing band called the Rounders and a Sinatra cover trio. I'm sure he still yodels with the former but probably not the latter since Old Blue Eyes only did do-be-doo-be-doos and never let go with any oh-deelay-de-oos as far as I can remember.

'Til the Cows Come Home/Four Dots/1986
Cowboy Rhythm/Four Dots/1987
'Til the Cows Come Home & Cowboy Rhythm/ ROM/1989
Back Home/ROM/1989
"Back in the Saddle" (with Cafe Noir) on **Dallas Scene, Heard**/Dallas Observer/1994

Randy Erwin, 10421 Vinemont St., Dallas, TX 75218-2231

See Riders in the Sky; Sourdough Slim; Don Walser; Wylie & The Wild West Show

Alejandro Escovedo

Cowpunk; Roots Rock; Singer/Songwriter; Insurgent Country
San Antonio, Texas; January 10, 1951-

An important but often overlooked performer, Alejandro Escovedo has been through it all since he started his musical career with a San Francisco punk band, the Nuns, in 1976. Two years with them were followed by several with art rocker Judy Nylon in New York before, back in California, he teamed with Chip and Tony Kinman to form one of the earliest and most influential cowpunk bands, Rank and File. After settling in Austin, Texas, that band had a successful run in the early 1980s, and Escovedo stayed with them through their first (and best) album, **Sundown**. From there, he went on to co-found with brother Javier the roots rock True Believers who were popular in the Austin area and had one self-titled recording released in

1986 but never really took off and disbanded in 1987 (a second recording was later repackaged and released with **True Believers** as **Hard Road** in 1994). Into the 1990s, Escovedo developed as a solo performer backed by his Orchestra which fluctuated from a trio to over a dozen members. They did covers of the Stones, Iggy Pop, and the Velvet Underground, but the real highlight was Escovedo's dusky vocals and songwriting which drew comparisons with everyone from Townes Van Zandt to Leonard Cohen. The Alejandro Escovedo Orchestra, which became one of Austin's favorites, did several highly acclaimed albums, **Gravity**, **Thirteen Years**, **The End/Losing Your Touch**, that effectively combine gritty rock with poignant string-driven ballads ("Baby's Got New Plans"; "Five Hearts Breaking"; "She Doesn't Live Here Anymore") reflecting Alejandro's struggle with his ex-wife's suicide. In 1996, Escovedo did **With These Hands** which expanded his previous roots rock sound into Latin and country rock territory with guest appearances by members of his extended musical family and Willie Nelson. He also participated in a couple of side projects during this period, the garage rock band, Buick McKane and a folk/roots/rock trio, the Setters, with Michael Hall (the Wild Seeds) and Walter Salas-Humara (the Silos). In 1998, Escovedo became one of the most high profile performers in the alt. country community when Bloodshot released his **More Miles Than Money: Live 1994-1996** and *No Depression* named him Artist of the Decade. He rounded out the century/millennium with **Bourbonitis Blues** featuring cameos by fellow Bloodshoters Kelly Hogan and Jon Langford.

Sundown (Rank and File)/Slash/1982
True Believers/Rounder EMI/1986
Gravity/Watermelon/1992
Thirteen Years/Watermelon/1993
The Setters/Blue Million Miles Ger./1993;
    Watermelon/1994
Hard Road (True Believers)/Rykodisc/1994
The End/Losing Your Touch/Watermelon/1994
With These Hands/Rykodisc/1996
The Pawn Shop Years (Buick McKane)/Rykodisc/1997
More Miles Than Money: Live 1994-1996/
    Bloodshot/1998
"Pyramid of Tears" (Alejandro Escovedo live) on **Viva Americana**/Boka UK/1998
Bourbonitis Blues/Bloodshot/1999

Sounds Strange to Your Ears: Alejandro Escovedo Web Page //www.valuserve.com/~floor13/music/alejan.htm

Alejandro Escovedo/Rykodisc Page //www.rykodisc.com/1/features/escovedo.html

See Rank and File; The Silos

Ethyl and Methyl
(Chris O'Connell and Maryann Price)
Western Swing; Cowboy/Western
Austin, Texas; Mid-1990s

Along with Commander Cody, Asleep at the Wheel and Dan Hicks and the Hot Licks were the leading Western swing revival bands of the 1970s and 1980s. A big part of the success of these two was due to the contributions of their female vocalists; Chris O'Connell (Asleep) and Hick's Lickettes (including Maryann Price) gave memorable performances as lead and harmony singers on both country and jazz inflected songs. After Price was teamed briefly with O'Connell as a member of Asleep at the Wheel in the late 1970s and early 1980s, the two divas went their separate ways but reunited in Austin in the early 1990s as the duo, Ethyl & Methyl. Decked out in cowgirl outfits and backed by a band including former Asleep at the Wheeler Danny Levin, they performed Western swing, cowboy, and country numbers with exquisite harmonies and plenty of wry humor. They recorded a number of CDs, which are available only through E&M by mail order. Maryann has a number of solo efforts of mostly Eastern swing but with a little of the Western variety too; **Etched in Swing** guest stars Texas Playboy vocalist Leon Rausch, and **Hot 'N' Cole** covers some of the best of Cole Porter. O'Connell has been featured vocalist on several recordings by another Texas Western swing band, Tom Morrell & The Time Warp Top Hands. Price and O'Connell have a number of rare live performances by Dan Hicks and the Hot Licks from the 1970s-1990s but for legal reasons can only give them as gifts if you buy enough E&M or Maryann Price recordings.

Ethyl and Methyl in Toronto/Rare Prime Cuts/
Super Swing Review/Rare Prime Cuts/
Ethyl and Methyl With the Little Big Band/Rare Prime Cuts/
Ethyl & Methyl Do the Beatles/Rare Prime Cuts/
Ethyl & Methyl Meet the Crickets/Rare Prime Cuts/
Ethyl and Methyl at the Armadillo World Headquarters 20th Anniversary, 9/3/94/Rare Prime Cuts/
Diva of Swing (Maryann Price solo)/Rare Prime Cuts/
Maryann Price with Zero Shapiro's Mad Hipsters/Rare Prime Cuts/
Etched in Swing (Maryann Price solo)/Watermelon/1993
Hot 'N' Cole (Maryann Price solo)/1997

Rare Prime Cuts, P.O. Box 33185, Austin, TX 78764

Maryann Price Home Page //members.aol.com/mranprice/index.html

Maryann Price: reddrum@bga.com

See Asleep at the Wheel; Dan Hicks; Tom Morrell

The Everly Brothers

Country Rock; Close Harmony
Don: Brownie, Kentucky; February 1, 1937-
Phil: Brownie, Kentucky; January 19, 1939-

Primarily known as mega rock 'n' roll stars through a series of gigantic hit records in the 1950s and early 1960s, the Everly Brothers also played a role in the development of country rock and have continued to influence alt. country artists to the present day. Their first serious attempt to break into the music business was actually as a country act, but they failed miserably in Nashville before reemerging as rock 'n' rollers on Cadence Records. However, the Everly's were never far away from country; their twangy Appalachian style harmonies (*a la* Delmores, Louvins, Blue Sky Boys) shone through their major songs. In 1959, at the height of their popularity, they paid homage to their roots on **Songs Our Daddy Taught Us**, a straight ahead collection of country standards. When country rock hit in the late 1960s, the Everlys jumped in with **Roots**, a fine but underrated recording that stands with the best of the era. After their breakup, Phil made several country influenced solos while Don lent backing vocals to albums by Emmylou Harris and Albert Lee. And, one doesn't have to look too far to see the ongoing influence of the Everlys on alt. country in the 1980s and 1990s. Their exquisite close harmonies are echoed in groups such as the Lonesome Strangers, the O'Kanes, the Delevantes, the Spanic Boys, and the Blue Shadows. In 1998, the Ryman began staging a musical tribute to the Everly's early years called *Bye, Bye Love*, and Phil and Don returned to country's most sacred shrine (for the first time in 40 years) for a special reunion concert. They also returned to Kentucky for their 11th annual Homecoming and then embarked on a tour.

Songs Our Daddy Taught Us/Cadence/1958; Rhino/1988
Roots/Warner Brothers/1968
Cadence Classics: Their Twenty Greatest Hits/ Rhino/1986
Classic Everly Brothers/Bear Family/1992
Walk Right Back: The Everly Brothers on Warner Brothers, 1960-1969/Warner Archives/1993
The Everly Brothers Info Circle //www.xs4all.nl/~ebi/

The Ex-Husbands

Country Rock; Honky Tonk
Brooklyn, New York; 1993-

The Ex-Husbands play what they call "Heavy Western," a melding of the members' backgrounds in rock bands with a newly found interest in country. From deep in the heart of Brooklyn, these New Yorkers give the impression they are just misplaced good ol' boys or cowpokes who'd be more at home in a Texas honky tonk or somewhere out on the lone prairie. Led by lead singer and songwriter, Anders Thomsen, the Ex-Husbands have the honky tonk, country rock sound down pretty good for a bunch of Yankees. On their self-titled debut,

they present a slightly romanticized vision of a wild, wild West populated with hard drinking ("Johnny Walker Redneck"; "Tequila, Salt & Lime"; "I Have a Ball"), hard living ("Run Until I Die"; "Born to Wander") sons of the soil ("Ain't You Been a Cowboy for Too Long"; "Rodeo Man"). Yee-ha, youse guys! Throughout 1998-1999, the Ex-Husbands were one of the hardest working bands in alt. country land constantly touring in the U.S. and Europe with just enough time off to begin their sophomore recording which was to be produced by Dave Alvin.

Mark Miller (b); Mike Smith (d); Anders Thomsen (e.g.,l.v.)

The Ex-Husbands/Slow Ass/1996 (CS); Tar Hut/1997
The Ex-Husbands, c/o Anders Thomsen P.O. Box 442, Brooklyn, NY 10009 or Tar Hut Records, P.O. Box 441940, Somerville, MA 02144
The Ex-Husbands/Tarhut Page //www.tarhut.com
info@tarhut.com

Farmer Not So John

No Depression
Nashville, Tennessee; 1995-

Farmer Not So John trods the country/roots/rock road well worn by Uncle Tupelo-SonVolt-Wilco, the Jayhawks, the Bottle Rockets, et al.; like their predecessors, they alternate between laid back acoustic country and country rockers, and their lyrics show a definite social and political consciousness. Their songs (mostly from the pen of lead singer Mack Linebaugh) like "Fire in the Valley," "Rusty Weathervane," "Every Street in Nashville" or "This is Our House" might have come from **Still Feel Gone**, **Blue Earth**, **The Brooklyn Side**, or **Trace**. What ultimately makes Farmer Not So John successful is that on their very listenable debut, they emulate the best the No Depression school of alt. country has to offer highlighted by the musicianship of multi-instrumentalist, Richard McLaurin. The latter and Mack Linebaugh had to continue on as a duo in 1998 when drummer Sean Keith and bass player Brian Ray split for various reasons. In the wake of the breakup, they decided to go a little deeper into No Depression territory with **Receiver** which is moodier and takes more musical chances than its predecessor with assistance from Peter Rowan, Clive Gregson, and Matthew Ryan.

Sean R. Keith (d,1995-1998); Mack Linebaugh (a.g.,e.g.,l.v.); Richard McLaurin (a.g.,db,e.g., l.s.,md,org,perc,v); Brian Ray (b,v,1995-1998)

Farmer Not So John/Compass/1997
"Fire in the Valley" on **Luxury Liner, Vol. 2**/Glitterhouse Ger./1998
Receiver/Compass/1998
Farmer Not So John Home Page
//members.aol.com/FarmerNSJ/Farmer.html
Farmernsj@aol.com

Farmer Not So John/Compass Page
//www.compassrecords.com/farmer.htm

The Fellow Travelers

See Jeb Loy Nichols

The Felsons

Roots Rock
Edinburgh, Scotland; 1995-

The Felsons pride themselves in being a band "united by a collective devotion to American roots music" and while these influences echo throughout their music, they're updated and/or intermixed with contemporary pop and indie rock drawn from a wide array of British and American sources. Their history dates back to 1995 when Kevin McGuire and Dean Owens worked as a duo around Edinburgh specializing in country music. A subsequent recording session yielded the generally straight country album, **One Step Ahead of the Posse**. As the Felsons (as Owens and McGuire called themselves) grew in popularity, they added multi-instrumentalist Calais Brown and drummer Keith Burns (ex-Proclaimers) and by 1997 had earned a nomination as Best British Band from the British Country Music Awards (the U.K. establishment is generally more accepting of alt. country acts). After an EP, **Lasso the Moon**, the Felsons were picked up by Greentrax for their G2 subsidiary and recorded **Glad** in 1998. And though the album opens on a roots rock note with "Boomerang Boy," most of it consists of easygoing material with tinges of the Everly Brothers ("Heart is Home"), old-time ("Postcards"), California country rock ("Born to Lose You"), No Depression roots rock ("Joseph Black"), rockabilly ("What About Me?"), lo-fi country ("Belfast Blues"), and folk balladry ("Meet Me After the Show"). Owens' rich lead vocals and competent songwriting are the highlight with sturdy backing from the rest of the Felsons.

Calais Brown (bj,g,md,v); K.W. Burns (d,perc); Kev McGuire (b,v); Dean Owens (g,hm,l.v.)

> **One Step Ahead of the Posse**/1996
> **Lasso the Moon**/1997 (EP)
> **The Felsons**/G2 Scot./1998

The Felsons/Stoneyport Agency Page
//www.stoneyport.demon.co.uk/bio/felsonsbio.html

File

Progressive Cajun
Scott, Louisiana; 1983-

The dominance of Beausoleil in the Cajun music revival of the 1980s has overshadowed the contributions of other bands. One of these is File, formed in 1983 by accordionist and lead vocalist Ward Lormand (from Ossun near Lafayette) and bassist Kevin Shearin (born in the Catskills). Although they began somewhat as a reaction to the modernization of Cajun music (they called their style "regressive"), in time, File became one of the most adventurous of the new breed of Cajun groups. Like other modern Cajun bands, their interpretation honors tradition but compliments it with contemporary blues, r&b, and rock. As expressed in the titles of their first two records, **Cajun Dance Band** and **Two Left Feet**, File wanted, above all, to be known as a hot dance band. They did just that, consistently packing the dance halls of Southwest Louisiana. In the early 1990s, they underwent personnel changes but came back strong in 1996 with **La Vie Marron (The Runaway Life)**, a highly experimental recording cementing their place as one of the world's top progressive Cajun bands.

Original Members: Ward Lormand (acc,perc.,v); Faren Serrette (f,g,v); Kevin Shearin (a.g.,b,v); Peter Stevens (d,perc); Darren Wallace (f,g)
Current Members: D'Jalma 'Dee' Garnier (bj,f,g,v); David Egan (g,ky,v); Ward Lormand; Kevin Shearin; Peter Stevens

> **Live at Mulate's**/Skoweat Now/1985
> **Cajun Dance Band**/Flying Fish/1987
> **Two Left Feet**/Flying Fish/1990
> **La Vie Marron**/Green Linnet Xenophile/1996

File Home Page //cust.iamerica.net/bandfile/
bandfile@iamerica.net

Five Chinese Brothers

Country Rock; Roots Rock
New York City; 1987-1999 (?)

Five Chinese Brothers are named after a children's story by Claire Huchet Bishop in which five identical siblings outwit an executioner by drawing on their extraordinary individual talents. Like their namesakes, the band members pool their musical talents and produce a catchy country roots rock style layered with very humorous takes on love and life. Paul Foglino and lead singer/songwriter Tom Meltzer were in a cover band (the Special Guests) in college, but eventually joined forces with New York alt. country band, the Surreal McCoys. Influenced by Gram Parsons and the Flying Burrito Brothers, they moved toward a country rock sound and in 1987 became the Five Chinese Brothers. They were regulars on the vibrant New York City alt. country scene that included the World Famous Bluejays, Amy Allison, the Blue Chieftains, et al. and in the early 1990s cut several songs for Diesel Only released as singles and on the **Rig Rock** compilations. Their wry take on truck stop romance, "She's a Waitress (And I'm in Love)" plus the nostalgic "Baltimore" and the melancholy "If I Ain't Falling" effortlessly mix country, rock, folk, and other roots music and hold it all together with fine playing, intelligence and wit. These songs were included on their first full length CD **Singer, Songwriter, Beggarman, Thief** along with tunes about "Paul Cezanne," aging ("My Dad's Face"), and the ups and downs of romance ("Don't Regret"; "Alone Together").

The critical acclaim for their debut from *Dirty Linen* to *Rolling Stone* pushed them to the top of the Northeastern country rock pyramid. After recording a very different kind of X-mas EP **Santa Claustraphobia**, the Brothers did **Stone Soup** (also named after a children's story). Like its predecessor, this recording brims with smart lyrics and catchy music which examines the foibles of relationships ("The Avalanche Song") and the bizarre ("Amazing Dolores") but also exudes FCB's unquenchable if slightly skewed optimism ("You Are Where You Want to Be"; "Faith in Something Bigger"). And though it did not seem possible, in 1997, the Brothers out did themselves with **Let's Kill Saturday Night** which is top notch from the opening title track (by Robbie Fulks who also provides background vocals) through a variety of country, rock, Cajun, and pop punctuated with smart but never smart assed humor on "Three Cool Guys," "My Love for You Has Turned to Hate," "Product of Dysfunction," and "I Call My Pain By Your Name." Late in 1997, the Five Chinese Brothers released another "twisted" holiday recording, **A Window Shopper's Christmas**. Disappointed with the response to **Let's Kill Saturday Night**, the Brothers went on an "extended indefinite hiatus" beginning in early 1999.

Stephen Antonakos (a.g.,e.g.,l.v.,b.v.); Peter DeMeo (d,1997-); Paul Foglino (b,bj,b.v.); Tom Meltzer (a.g.,e.g.,md, l.v.,b.v.); Charlie Shaw (d); Neil Thomas (acc,org, p)

> "Baltimore" and "If I Ain't Falling" on **Rig Rock Juke Box**/Diesel Only/1992
> "She's a Waitress" and "Alone Together" on **Rig Rock Truck Stop**/Diesel Only/1993
> **Singer, Songwriter, Beggarman, Thief**/1-800-PRIME CD/1992
> **Santa Claustrophobia**/1-800-PRIME CD/1994
> **Stone Soup**/1-800-PRIME CD/1995
> **Let's Kill Saturday Night**/1-800-PRIME CD/1997
> **A Window Shopper's Christmas**/1-800-PRIME CD/1997
> "I'll Never Learn How to Stop Loving You" on **Edges From the Postcard2**/P2/1998

Five Chinese Brothers World Headquarters, P. O. Box 023507, Brooklyn, NY 11202-0035

Five Chinese Brothers Home Page //www.primecd.com/5cb.htm

fivecb@bway.net

Flathead

Rockabilly; Honky Tonk ; Country Rock
Phoenix, Arizona; 1994-

With respects to Diesel Only Records, Flathead plays what they like to call "rig rock": truck driving inspired music combining honky tonk, swing, and rockabilly with just a little bit of punk to give it that modern edge. Lead guitarist/vocalist, Greg Swanholm, started out playing banjo in bluegrass bands but later adapted the finger stylings of that instrument to electric guitar and developed a style heavily influenced by Joe Maphis and Merle Travis. He and drummer Vince Ramirez performed as a duo around Phoenix for a time before stand up bass player Ruth Wilson joined them. Initially, Flathead was a cover band (Johnny Cash to X), but Swanholm began to write songs, and in 1995, they recorded **Flathead**, a rocking hillbilly debut fueled by Swanholm's lead guitar on four covers ("Flash, Crash, Thunder"; "Old 97"; "Give Me 40 Acres"; "Tennessee Stud") and rollicking originals like "Alcohaulin'," "Buckshot," "Bad Roll," "'Til I Die," and "Highway." In just a few short years, Flathead became regulars at the Rhythm Room and the Rockin' Horse where they opened for BR5-49, Dave Alvin, Bad Livers, and the Carpetbaggers. In 1997, Flathead gained wider exposure through an appearance at SXSW and inclusion of their cover of J. E. Mainer's "Run Mountain" on the **Straight Outta Boone County**.

Vince Ramirez (d,h.v.); Greg Swanholm (l.g., l.v.); Ruth Wilson (ub)

> **Flathead**/Truxton/1995
> "Run Mountain" on **Straight Outta Boone County**/ Bloodshot/1997

Flathead, P. O. Box 1005, Tempe, AZ 85280-1005

Official Flathead Home Page //www.funpage.com/flathead/

flathead@funpage.com

The Flatlanders

Lubbock Mafia; Country Rock
Lubbock, Texas; 1970-1972

Late in 1997, alt. country hearts beat a little faster when it was announced that Joe Ely had been asked to contribute to Robert Redford's new movie, *The Horse Whisperer*, and brought Jimmie Dale Gilmore and Butch Hancock in as co-writers. This collaboration yielded several new songs and set the rumor mill whirring about a possible reunion of the Flatlanders, a band that has attained a status of near mythological proportions in alt. country circles. However, at the time the Flatlanders were formed in the early 1970s, they seemed like just another flash in the pan. Their experimentation with country rock paralleled California performers like Gram Parsons and the Flying Burrito Brothers, but the Flatlanders had a special sound born of the unique natural and cultural environments of West Texas. Gilmore's high, warbling vocals and Steve Wesson's haunting musical saw were most memorable, but Ely, Hancock, and the other Flatlanders made important contributions as well. Unfortunately, they tried to make a go of it in Nashville and only lasted through one recording which was issued as an 8 track tape in 1972. It resurfaced first in 1980 as an import LP, **One More Road**, then ten years later as a CD, **More a Legend Than a Band,** and five years after that in a slightly repackaged format as, **Unplugged**. And, in hindsight, what emerges from these modest recordings is the early development of a distinctive Texas alt. country style that came to full flower in the individual careers and frequent collaborations of Ely, Gilmore, and Hancock in the 1970s-1980s. Hancock's immense songwriting talent is already apparent, and there are hints of Jimmie Dale's subsequent path toward a mystical Om on the Range sound (i.e. "Bhagavan Decreed"). However, there are surprisingly few signs of the dynamic frontman Ely would later become. In 1998, the Ely/Gilmore/Hancock song "The South Wind of Summer" was included on *The Horse Whisperer* soundtrack, they performed together on Letterman, and the rumored reunion of The Flatlanders moved closer to reality (?).

Joe Ely (db,g,hm,v); Jimmie Dale Gilmore (g,v); Butch Hancock (g,v); Tommy Hancock (f); Tony Pearson (md); Syl Rice (b); Steve Wesson (saw)

One More Road/1972 (8 trk. tape); Charly/UK/1980
More a Legend Than a Band/Rounder/1990
Unplugged/Sun/1995
"The South Wind of Summer" (as the Hill Country Flatlanders) on **The Horse Whisperer**/MCA/1998

The Flatlanders //www.mods.demon.co.uk/flatland.htm

See Joe Ely; Jimmie Dale Gilmore; Butch Hancock

Rosie Flores
TSOB
San Antonio, Texas; September 10, 1950-

The Southern California alt. country scene of the 1980s produced a number of fine female artists, but preeminent among them was Rosie Flores. Born in San Antonio, her family moved to San Diego when she was 12, and Rosie got caught up in the varied musical sounds of California. By age 16, she was in the all girl Penelope's Children that toured with several prominent pop rock groups in the late 1960s. In 1978, Flores formed a hard core country/rockabilly band, Rosie and the Screamers, and a few years later, in the middle of the cowpunk craze became a member of the Screamin' Sirens, a popular all female band that did an HBO movie, *The Running Kind*. By 1987, Flores relocated to L.A. and became a full fledged member of the Town South of Bakersfield crowd. Signed to Warner Brothers, Flores put out a solid, self-titled collection of California style country rock and honky tonk backed by James Intveld, Billy Bremner, Greg Leisz, and Donald Lindley with guest appearances by Pete Anderson (producer) on lead guitar and David Hidalgo of Los Lobos on accordion. Although sometimes touted as the female equivalent to Dwight Yoakam, Flores career didn't take off. In 1988, she moved to Austin where she played local clubs and collaborated on writing and performing with Joe Ely, Jimmie Dale Gilmore, and Butch Hancock. A deal with Hightone eventually brought her out of the shadows in the early 1990s. Her two albums for that label, **After the Farm** and **Once More With Feeling**, displayed her songwriting and guitar playing talents and though not as dynamic as her debut still present some pleasant country/roots music. A severe hand injury in 1994 put her on hold for a time, but in 1995, she

returned to her rockabilly roots on **Rockabilly Filly** with guest appearances by legends Wanda Jackson and Janis Martin. Taking advantage of the resurgence of alt. country, Rounder Records reissued her 1987 debut with previously unreleased tracks, and in early 1997, Watermelon released **A Little Bit of Heartache,** a collection of country duets done with Texas rockabilly legend Ray Campi in 1990. In addition, Flores signed a long term contract with Rounder and surprised everyone by signing on as female lead singer with Asleep at the Wheel. Around the same time, Flores joined the Wandering Eyes, a studio group made up of Dale Watson, Kelly Willis, Ted Roddy, and David Sanger, to contribute several cuts to **Sing Songs of Forbidden Love**. Her version of the Butch Hancock classic "Boxcars" was included on the soundtrack of the 1998 independent film, *Deep in the Heart of Texas*. Rosie's Rounder debut, **Dance Hall Dreams**, continues the Wanda Jackson/ Rose Maddox tradition with backing from a great band including Sarah Brown, Cindy Cashdollar (Asleep at the Wheel), Donald Lindley (Lucinda Williams), and Kevin Smith (High Noon).

!Fiesta! (with the Screamin' Sirens)/Enigma/1984
Rosie Flores/Reprise/1987
"Heartbreak Train" (with Albert Lee) on **A Town South of Bakersfield, Vol. 1**/Restless/1987
After the Farm/Hightone/1992
Once More With Feeling/Hightone/1993
"My Own Kinda Hat" on **Tulare Dust**/Hightone/1994
Hillbilly Filly (with Wanda Jackson & Janis Martin)/ Hightone/1995
Honky Tonk Reprise/Rounder/1996 (**Rosie Flores** with additional trks.)
A Little Bit of Heartache (with Ray Campi)/ Rounder/1997
"In Some Room Above the Street"; "Even If I Have to Steal" on **Sing Songs of Forbidden Love** (with The Wandering Eyes)/Lazy SOB/1998
"Dream, Dream Blue" on **L.A. County Line**/ Starwdog/1998
"Boxcars" on **Deep in the Heart of Texas**/ Shanachie/1998
Dance Hall Dreams/Rounder/1999

Rosie Flores, P. O. Box 1168, Studio City, CA 91604-2600

The Rosie Flores Connection //lonestar.texas.net/~dqkidd/

Rosie Flores AOL Folder: Entertainment>Music>Chat & Messages>Music Community>Folk/Acoustic

See James Intveld; Dee Lannon

Florida Slim & The Hurricanes
See Neil Mooney

The Flying Burrito Brothers
See Chris Hillman; Gram Parsons

John Fogerty
Country Rock
Berkeley, California; May 28, 1945-

Although the Byrds, Gram Parsons, and the Flying Burrito Brothers are most often sighted as the "inventors" of country rock, one of their contemporaries deserving mention is Creedence Clearwater Revival. Their swampy, country rock not only made them huge stars in the late 1960s and early 1970s but also echoes in many of the current crop of alt. country acts. Leader John Fogerty, a gifted songwriter and musician, developed an affinity for hard core country music while still a member of CCR. After the band fell apart, Fogerty gave full vent to his country side on a solo project called **The Blue Ridge Rangers**. This "group" was actually just Fogerty playing all instruments (banjo, guitar, dobro, fiddle, piano, drums, bass) on covers of standards like "Blue Ridge Mountain Blues," "Jambalaya," "She Thinks I Still Care," "California Blues," "Working on a Building," "Today I Started Loving You Again," and many more. Commercially, it was miserable flop, but like similar efforts by Leon Russell and Elvis Costello, this recording helped spread traditional country awareness to rock audiences and still sounds good today. After it, Fogerty went on to pop rock stardom with songs like "Centerfield" but in 1997 returned somewhat to the CCR sound with **Blue Moon Swamp** (Grammy winner for Best Rock Album). At the same time, his contributions to the development of alt. country gained recognition through feature articles in *Addicted to Noise* and *No Depression*. A retrospective live album (**Premonition**) with songs from his Creedence and solo years was released in late 1998. An unofficial history of the triumphs and tribulations of CCR titled *Bad Moon Rising* by Hank Bordowitz was published around the same time by Schirmer Press.

> **Blue Ridge Rangers** (John Fogerty)/Fantasy/1973
> **Chronicle, Vol. 1** (CCR)/Fantasy/1976
> **Chronicle, Vol. 2** (CCR)/Fantasy/1986
> **Blue Moon Swamp** (John Fogerty)/Reprise/1997
> **Premonition (John Fogerty Live)**/Reprise/1998
> *Bad Moon Rising: The Unofficial History of Creedence Clearwater Revival* by Hank Bordowitz/Schirmer/1998

Official John Fogerty Site //www.johnfogerty.com

John Fogerty/Warner Brothers Page //www.wbr.com/johnfogerty/

John Fogerty Mailing List //www.xs4all.nl/~wdw/

Original CCR Home Page //www.jyu.fi/~petkasi/ccr.htm

Creedence.ca //www.escape.ca/~mloewen/ccr/

Steve Forbert
Singer/Songwriter
Meridian, Mississippi; 1955-

In 1978, writer Greil Marcus gave Steve Forbert what could have been the kiss of death when he named the young song-writer to his "New Dylans" list. Fortunately, Forbert was able to overcome this burden and stake out his own territory with a succession of acclaimed albums that moved gradually from folk rock to roots rock. Not too shabby for a Southern boy who started out in the 1970s playing the mean streets of New York City then holding down odd jobs while breaking in at folk and punk clubs. After several critical successes on the independent Nemperor label, Forbert became embroiled in a contract mess with Columbia that put his recording career on hold in the mid-80s. Meanwhile, he moved to Nashville but while doing a Buddy Holly tribute show back in the Big Apple in 1987, Gary Tallent saw him and got Forbert hooked up with Geffen. **Streets of This Town** and **The American in Me** (produced by Pete Anderson) marked a transition to a fuller roots rock sound and while well-received, Steve's relationship with Geffen was shaky, and he was set free in th early 1990s. Touring and making independent live recordings in the mid-90s, Forbert finally signed with newcomer Paladin and made a comeback especially among alt. country fans with **Rocking Horse Head** on which he was backed by multi-instrumentalist Max Johnston and Jay Bennett and Ken Commer of Wilco. His penetrating story songs, which have always leaned toward the desolate side of life, are nicely accentuated by banjo, fiddle, harmonica, mandolin, steel, and organ. **Here's Your Pizza** is a quirky live recording from 1987 with originals and covers of John Lennon, Ritchie Valens, and Tony Joe White. When Paladin Records folded in 1999, Forbert found himself looking once more for a label to take him in.

> **Alive on Arrival**/Nemperor/1978
> **Jackrabbit Slim**/Nemperor/1979
> **Little Stevie Orbit**/Nemperor/1980
> **Steve Forbert**/Nemperor/1982
> **Streets of This Town**/Geffen/1988
> **The American in Me**/Geffen/1991
> **What Kinda Guy?: The Best of Steve Forbert**/
>   Columbia Legacy/1993
> **Be Here Now** (Live solo)/SF/1994
> **Be Here Again** (Live solo)/SF/1995
> **Mission of the Crossroad Palms**/Giant/1995
> **Steve Forbert in Concert**/King Biscuit/1996
> **Rocking Horse Head**/Paladin Revolution/1996
> **Here's Your Pizza**/Paladin Revolution/1997

Steve Forbert Fan Page //www.dip.uct.ac.za/~brendt/music/forbert/

Donny Ray Ford (The Honky Tonkers; The Cartwrights; Liberty Valance; The Mutineers; The Widowmakers)
Honky Tonk; Insurgent Country
Dallas, Texas; Late 1980s-

For over a decade, Donny Ray Ford has been a major figure in Dallas' alternative country scene. Once described by the *Dallas Observer* as "a heartfelt honky tonk angel with a two-fisted attack," Ford, with a voice and songwriting style that draws comparisons to George Jones, served with several local bands (including bass player for Ted and the Talltops) before he began offering up his brand of country in the late 1980s with the Honky Tonkers (Bad Livers' bassist Mark Rubin was an early member). Through a regular gig at Dallas' local alt. country bar, the Hot Klub, they built a following and in 1989 released an independent cassette, **Lookin' for Grace** which showcases Ford's singing/songwriting and hot Albert Lee style country lead of Tony Black. Ford shows his understanding of what makes a good honky tonk song on "I Slipped on a Bottle of Gin," "The Darkside," "Nell's Place" (about saving a burning whorehouse), and the title tune "Looking for Grace"; the band, with guest help from Tim Alexander (Asleep at the Wheel) on accordion, keeps things rocking along throughout. When they went no further, the Honky Tonkers broke up, but Ford returned in the early 1990s with a new group, the Cartwrights. Like their predecessor, they specialized in honky tonk ("Crazy Broken Heart"; "Take Me Drunk, I'm Home"), but with the addition of Alan Wooley (ex-Killbilly) on banjo and mandolin and Kim Herriage on dobro, the Cartwrights could also handle "unplugged" numbers such as "Walking on My Grave." Along with the Old 97s, who emerged at about the same time, the Cartwrights were at the forefront of the Dallas alt. country scene in the mid-1990s. They recorded one album **Ponderosa Fabulosa** and like the Old 97s became part of the insurgent country movement with inclusion of "Walking on My Grave" on **Hell Bent**. And though the Cartwrights recorded a second album, internal dissension broke them apart in late 1995, and it was not released. Ford, who had already been performing with a country rock side project, Liberty Valance, soon enlisted ex-Cartwrights, Herriage and Barry Kooda, in forming a new alt. country group called the Mutineers. They recorded a couple of songs for local compilations, but in 1997 Ford left to create yet another band, the Widowmakers. That year, Ford's song "Cowboy Boots" was covered by the Backsliders on **Throwin' Rocks at the Moon,** and Kooda released a solo **Crossin' the Line**. The Cartwrights got back together for one night in May 1997 for a Skeletons CD release party and left open the prospect of a more permanent reunion.

The Honky Tonkers: Donny Ray Ford (g,l.v.); Tony Black (l.g.); Mark Fishback (b); Mark Hayes (d) with Tim Alexander (acc); Kent Coleman (d); Murray Conklin (g); Sam Swank (a.g.); T. Tex Waggoner (b)
The Cartwrights: Alan Wooley (a. g., bj, v); Barry Kooda (a. g); Donny Ray Ford (b); Kim Herriage (db); Richie Vasquez (d) with Howard Kalish (f); Lloyd Maines (p.s.); Ted Roddy (hm)
Liberty Valance: Tommy Brame (l.g.); Donny Ray Ford (b,v); Ron Gulley (d); Phillip Prince (r.g.)
The Mutineers: Donny Ray Ford (b,v); Kim Herriage (db,g,p.s.); Barry Kooda (g,v); Frank Pittinger (d)

Lookin' for Grace (Honky Tonkers)/DRF/1989
Ponderosa Fabulosa (Cartwrights)/Big Iron/1993

"Walking on My Grave" (Cartwrights) on **Hell Bent: Insurgent Country, Vol. 2**/Bloodshot/1995
"Miss You Babe" (Liberty Valance) on **Dallas Scene, Heard, Vol. 1**/Dallas Observer/1995
"1-900-GIRLS" and "Sleeping in the Doghouse" (Cartwrights) on **Live From the Barley House/ BH**/1995
"Honky Tonk Life" (Liberty Valance) on **Live From the Barley House/BH**/1995
"Santa Looked a Lot Like Daddy"(Donny Ray Ford & Liberty Valance) on **Honky Tonk Holidays**/1996
"Santa Claus is Coming to Town" (Mutineers) on **Honky Tonk Holidays**/1996
"Best of You & Me" (Mutineers) on **Dallas Scene, Heard, Vol. 2**/Dallas Observer/1996
Crossin' the Line (Barry Kooda)/Big Iron/1997
"Cowboy Boots" (Donny Ray Ford, Live 1987) on **Texas Renegade Radio**/KNON/1998

The Mutineers Home Page
//rampages.onramp.net/~mutineer/mutineer.htm

See Killbilly

Rex Foster
Outlaw; Singer/Songwriter
Comfort, Texas

While many Texas singer/songwriters have achieved legendary status (Clark, Van Zandt, Lovett), a great many others like Rex Foster, for instance, have labored in obscurity. Born and raised in Texas, Foster was really a child of California's psychedelic 60s. Urged by a friend, he migrated to the West Coast in his late teens and a few years later returned to his home state with a new outlook and a way to express it—music. Back in San Antonio, Foster joined Rachel's Children, one of a handful of psychedelic bands (along with the 13th Floor Elevators) in Central Texas. Their music gained a following and attention from Elektra Records which at the time was in the market for a psych band and was set to choose between Rachel's Children and the Doors. Unfortunately, the drug related messages of RC's music also drew attention from Federal narcotics agencies, and so, the band decided to break up and disappear. Foster returned to California where he renewed his interest in the psychedelic movement by joining the Medicine Ball Caravan which like Ken Kesey's Merry Pranksters traveled to remote areas of the U.S and Europe staging free "happenings" and generally blowing the minds of the local population. When this trip wound down, Foster found himself in France where, in 1970, he cut a debut album, **Roads of Tomorrow**, on Barclay Records. Although a hit in Europe, Foster still decided to go back to America. Once again in California, he reunited with some of his old band mates, rejected a solo contract from Geffen, and then headed back home to Texas at just about the time that the outlaw thing was starting to heat up. His background was tailored made for this marriage of redneck and hippie styles, and he soon found himself hanging around and playing in Luckenbach, the spiritual center of the movement. On the heals of the success of

Jerry Jeff Walker, Waylon and Willie and others, Foster did a progressive country album, but it was never released. At that point, Foster put music on the back burner and settled down in his home town of Comfort to concentrate on raising a family and making fine jewelry. In the latter regard, he has become a master craftsman whose exquisite pieces have been in demand by the likes of Johnny Cash, Emmylou Harris, and Rodney Crowell. In the 1990s, Foster renewed his interest in music through concerts and two independently released albums, **Artist** and **Believn'**. His sound both musically and lyrically is a unique blend of Texas and California that, like his jewelry, is finely crafted and thought provoking.

Roads of Tomorrow/Barclay/1970
Artist/Agarita/1991
Believn'/Agarita/1994

Rex Foster, P. O. Box 97, Comfort, TX 78013

Rex Foster/Agarita Page //www.arts-online.com/agarita/

Rex Foster/NOMA Web Page
//songs.com/noma/rexfhome.htm

perfessr@edge.net

Michael Fracasso

Austin; Singer/Songwriter
Stubbenville, Ohio; February 10, 1952-

At an early age, Michael Fracasso seemed destined to follow the family tradition and spend his life working in the steel mills of eastern Ohio. He did in fact work in a mill in Steubenville while in his late teens and early twenties, but two events altered his life course. First of all, one of his uncles gave him a guitar, and with practice and encouragement, Fracasso began performing at high school assemblies to very warm receptions. That seed planted, he went on to Ohio State then to Washington State to work as a surveyor but never lost the music bug. In 1978, he took the leap, moved to New York City, and became part of a burgeoning folk scene. His years there gave him invaluable experience but no real satisfaction, so in 1990, on not much more than a whim, he relocated to Austin. There, Fracasso found sympathetic venues and audiences. His effective blending of country, folk and rock, intelligent songwriting and above all ethereal voice were irresistible, and after only a year of performing, he was named Best New Artist in a poll conducted by *Music City Texas*. In 1992, he independently released **Love & Trust** on cassette. On the strength of its reception, it was re-released on CD one year later through Dejadisc. For the next two years, Fracasso toured as a solo and as part of the Austin Songwriters on the Road with David Halley, Jimmy LaFave, and Jo Carol Pierce. Meanwhile he worked with Ian Matthews on a side project, the roots based band known as Hamilton Pool (after a popular local swimming hole) and put out another critically acclaimed record, **When I Lived in the Woods** which remained in the Gavin Americana Top 10 for five weeks. In late

1997, Fracasso worked with a new band including local hero Charlie Sexton. Their debut at the Cactus Cafe was a great success and left fans eagerly anticipating **World in a Drop of Water** (produced by Sexton), which equals and in some ways surpasses Fracasso's previous work.

Love and Trust/Dejadisc/1993
Return to Zero (Hamilton Pool)/Watermelon/1994
When I Lived in the Woods/Bohemia Beat/1994
World in a Drop of Water/Bohemia Beat/1998

Michael Fracasso/Rounder Page
//www.rounder.com/bobeat/mfhome.htm

Michael Fracasso/Dejadisc Page
//www.eden.com/~dejadisc/fracasso.html

Freakwater (Jeff and Janet)

Insurgent Country
Louisville, Kentucky; 1989-

Of all the insurgent country groups that have mined the old-time, Appalachian tradition, none has done so more effectively than Freakwater whose heart and soul is the close harmony vocals of Janet Beveridge Bean and Catherine Irwin. In the late 1980s, Bean, who was drumming for garage band Eleventh Dream Day, decided to launch a traditional country side project and called on Irwin, an old teenage buddy from Louisville. With the addition of a rotating line up of musicians on dobro, fiddle, banjo, mandolin, and pedal steel, Freakwater was born. **Freakwater** and **Dancing Under Water** presented country and bluegrass standards ("Rank Strangers"; "You're Still on My Mind"; "Little Girl and The Dreadful Snake"; "Dark as a Dungeon") and potent Irwin originals ("A Song You Could Cry For"; "Blood and Fire"; "Your Goddam Mouth"). In 1993, Freakwater paid homage to one of their main influences with inclusion of three cuts on an off beat but appealing Carter Family tribute album, **Keep on the Sunny Side**. **Feels Like the Third Time** continued the band's fresh take on traditional country and uncompromising look at rural angst. One song from that album, "My Old Drunk Friend," was included on Bloodshot's first insurgent country compilation, but Freakwater's big breakthrough album in the U.S. came in 1995 with **Old Paint**. They were also well received in Europe due to a promotional tour and live record, **June 6, 1994**, sponsored by Glitterhouse. Bean did a side project (with Jeff Lescher), an obscure but worthy tribute to the Gram Parsons/Emmylou Harris collaborations entitled **Jesus Built a Ship to Sing a Song To**. To capitalize on their success, Freakwater hoped to reissue their early, long out of print Amoeba recordings, and although at first owner Keith Holland refused, late in 1996, he gave permission. The first re-release was **Dancing Under Water** in 1997. Riding high, Freakwater entered negotiations with Steve Earle's E Squared, but the deal went south due to a disagreement over "creative decisions." Earle's camp wanted a more polished sound using veterans like Norman Blake and Peter

Rowan, but this was unacceptable to Bean and Irwin who insisted on using their own band and sticking to their original formula. In late 1997, Freakwater continued to work a new recording and toured with a band including multi-instrumentalist Max Johnston (ex-Uncle Tupelo; ex-Wilco). They staked their claim for best alt. country album of 1998 early on with the January release of **Springtime** which more than vindicated Freakwater's decision to do it their way. Once again, they crafted a raw but beautiful collection of new old-time (lots of banjo, fiddle, mandolin) centered on death, salvation ("Washed in the Blood"), drinking, sex, labor unions ("Harlan"), and protest ("Louisville Lip"). Late in 1998, Johnston left to join Austin Americana band, the Gourds.

Janet Beveridge Bean (g,perc,v); Brian Dunn (l.g.,1993); Bob Egan (db,p.s.,1991-1995); Dave Gay (b); Catherine Ann Irwin (g,v); Max Johnston (bj,f,md,1997-1998); Lisa Marsicek (f,md,1993); Wink O'Bannon (sl.g.,1989); John Rice (f,md,p.s.,1991); Dan Scanlon (f,1989); John Alexander Spiegel (bj,db,p.s., s.g.,1989-1991)

> **Freakwater**/Amoeba/1989
> "Your Goddamned Mouth" b/w "War Pigs"/1 1/4 York/1990 (7")
> **Dancing Under Water & Freakwater**/Amoeba/1991; Thrill Jockey/1997
> **Feels Like the Third Time**/Thrill Jockey/1993
> "My Old Drunk Friend" b/w "Kentucky"/Thrill Jockey/1993 (7")
> "Broken Hearted Lover," "No Phone in Heaven," "Lover's Return" on **Keep on the Sunny Side: A Tribute to the Carter Family**/Amoeba/1993
> "My Old Drunk Friend" on **For a Life of Sin**/ Bloodshot/1994
> **Jesus Built a Ship to Sing a Song To** (Jeff & Janet)/ Kokopop/1995
> **Half Cocked**/Matador/1995 (EP)
> **Old Paint**/Thrill Jockey/1995
> "South of Cincinnati" b/w "Count Me Out"/Thrill Jockey/1995 (7")
> **June 6, 1994**/Glitterhouse Ger./1995 (through m.o. only from Glitterhouse)
> "Withered and Died" on **Cowpunks**/Vinyl Junkie UK/1996
> **Springtime**/Thrill Jockey/1998
> "Lorraine" on **Sounds of the New West: The Best of Alternative Country**/Uncut UK/1998

Freakwater c/o C. Irwin, 1703 Bonny Castle Ave., Louisville, KY 40205

Freakwater Web Page //iglo.cpedu.rug.nl/~evert/bands/ef/freakwat.htm

Freakwater Biography Page //www.billions.com/freakwater/bio.htm

The Freight Hoppers
New Old-Time
Bryson City, North Carolina; 1993-

The Freight Hoppers have been acclaimed as the most exciting old-time group since the Highwoods String Band. Like their predecessors, the Hoppers infused 1920s-1930s hillbilly string band music with a decidedly modern energy that made them festival favorites in a very short period of time. David Bass, Cary Fridley, and Frank Lee were all raised around music and were attracted to old-time country early on; Hanne Jorgensen (from Denmark) learned about old-time music while on an exchange program at the John C. Campbell Folk School in North Carolina. The four of them met at various festivals and finally got together in Bryson City, North Carolina in 1993 as the Freight Hoppers. Playing regularly at the Great Smoky Mountains Railway, they polished and tightened their style and then descended on fiddlers' conventions and old-time festivals where they won many awards including First Place Traditional Band at Clifftop in 1996. Their **Going Down the Track With a Chicken on My Back** and **Where'd You Come From, Where'd You Go?** are non-stop, full speed ahead train rides covering classics by the Skillet Lickers, Uncle Dave, famous and obscure fiddlers, and old-time revival bands like the Indian Creek Delta Boys. Through appearances on *Prairie Home Companion*, at SXSW (1997, 1998), and a variety of venues across the country, the Freight Hoppers, like the Highwoods String Band before them, won over a new generation to the joys of old-time music. A taste of their dynamic live performances can be sampled on the 1997 video, *Freight Hoppers Live at the Bearsville Barn*.

1998 was an incredibly busy year for the band who's mottos are "Get Right With Gid" and "Gid is My Co-Pilot." Non-stop touring included stops at small venues as well as the major festivals (Winterhawk, Merlefest, Telluride) to support a new recording, **Waiting on the Gravy Train,** which has more great mountain music done in the Freight Hoppers infectious new old-time way. Also released were instructional videos by Cary Fridley (*Singing Old-Time Mountain Music*) and Frank Lee (*Old-Time Banjo Clawhammer Style*).

David Bass (f); Cary Fridley (g,v); Hanne Jorgensen (b); Frank Lee (bj,v)

> **Going Down the Track With a Chicken on My Back**/ FH/1994 (CS)
> **Where'd You Come From, Where'd You Go?**/ Rounder/1996
> *Freight Hopper Live at the Bearsville Barn*/ Homespun Tapes/1997 (video)
> **Waiting on the Gravy Train**/Rounder/1998
> *Old-Time Banjo Clawhammer Style* (with Frank Lee)/ Homespun/1998 (video)
> *Singing Old-Time Mountain Music* (with Cary Fridley)/ Homespun/1998 (video)

The Freight Hoppers, P.O. Box 82, Bryson City, NC 28713; 704-488-0931

The Freight Hoppers Web Page //www.dnet.net/freighthoppers/

Cary Fridley: cfridley@swain.main.nc.us

Frank Lee: franklee@dnet.net

Homespun Tapes, 800-338-2737

See Highwoods String Band

Kinky Friedman
Outlaw; Satire
Chicago, Illinois; October 31, 1944-

Kinky Friedman isn't prejudiced, he offends everyone equally. For nearly twenty five years, "The Kinkster" has churned out a brand of country music and commentary that has won him many fans and perhaps as many enemies. A native of central Texas (born in Palestine, Texas...really!), he attended the University of Texas where he had a band called King Arthur and the Carrots. However, his musical career really took off during the outlaw movement when he formed Kinky Friedman and the Texas Jewboys and relocated to California. Kinky's appearance (frizzy hair under a big cowboy hat, cowboy boots with stars of David, ever present cigar, and shades) combined with his no-punches-pulled lyrics earned a rep, a following, and, eventually, a recording contract. **Sold American** was released in 1973, followed by a self titled LP on ABC (produced by Willie), and then **Lasso From El Paso** with Eric Clapton and Bob Dylan who had included the Jewboys in the Rolling Thunder Revue. These recordings contain the songs that made Friedman (in)famous: "Ride 'Em Jewboy," "Get Your Biscuits in the Oven, And Your Buns in the Bed," "Old Ben Lucas Had a Lot of Mucous," "The Ballad of Charles Whitman," "They Ain't Makin' Jews Like Jesus Anymore." In the early 1980s, Friedman went solo, taking up semi-permanent residence at New York City's famous Lone Star Cafe. He made two records, **Live From the Lone Star** and **Under the Double Ego** and while in the Big Apple got the idea for a book series built around a Jewish private detective. Subsequently, he launched a new career as a successful mystery writer producing nine critically acclaimed works including, *God Bless John Wayne* and *The Love Songs of J. Edgar Hoover*. Kinky's 1997, *Road Kill*, finds his fearless detective trying to save Willie Nelson from an old Indian curse. His recorded output in recent years has consisted of compilations (**Old Testaments and New Revelations**; **From One Good American to Another**) of older material although there were plans for new recordings. In the 1990s, Friedman lived in a trailer and in between writing mysteries and searching for the killers of Stringbean occasionally took the Jewboys out on the road. Toward the end of 1997, a stellar cast of admirers were assembled to record a Kinky tribute album called **Pearls in the Snow: The Songs of Kinky Friedman** which features Willie Nelson, Lyle Lovett, Asleep at the Wheel, Guy Clark, Kinky himself, and others doing the best of his unforgettable/unforgiveable tunes.

Sold American/Vanguard/1973; 1989 (CD)
Kinky Friedman and the Texas Jewboys/ABC/1974; Varese Sarabande/1994 (CD)
Lasso From El Paso/Epic/1976; Epic Fr./1993 (CD)
Live From the Lone Star Cafe/Bruno Dean Enterprises/1982
Under the Double Ego/Sunrise/1983
Old Testaments and New Revelations/Fruit of the Tune/1992
From One Good American to Another/Fruit of the Tune/1995
Pearls in the Snow: The Songs of Kinky Friedman/Kinkajou/1998
Kinky Friedman: Musician, Author, Cigar Smoker //www.kinkyfriedman.com

Bill Frisell
Americana; Guitar
Baltimore, Maryland; March 18, 1951-

Bill Frisell is in that long line of Americana innovators who begin with a classical, jazz, or rock base then seamlessly blend in familiar idioms and/or refrains from folk, blues, gospel, and country. Primarily a jazz guitarist, he has certainly stretched the boundaries in that genre as a solo or with fellow improvisors like Wayne Horvitz and John Zorn but has also done some very illuminating experiments (**This Land**; **Lookout for Hope**; **Have a Little Faith**; **Gone, Like a Train**) that show a unique appreciation of traditional Americana. His most accessible recording in this vein has been the highly touted **Nashville** from 1997. With a stellar backing band including the ever reliable Jerry Douglas on dobro and Ron Block (banjo; acoustic guitar), Viktor Krauss (bass), and Adam Steffey (mandolin) from Alison Krauss' Union Station, Frisell explores numerous branches (old-time, bluegrass, gospel, blues) of the country music family tree in a way that is familiar yet fresh. And while, many of his extended pieces ("Gimme a Holler"; "Brother"; "Family"; "Dogwood Acres"; "Shucks") have a David Grisman/Tony Rice New Acoustic Music feel, Bill and company keep things farily twangy and even play it straight on the chuggling hoedown "Go Jake," the bluegrass/gospel "Will Jesus Wash the Bloodstains From Your Hands," and the country-pop, "The End of the World." Another Americana innovator, Robin Holcomb, lends her distinctive vocals to the latter two songs and a cover of Neil Young's "One of These Days."

Lookout for Hope/ECM/1987
Have a Little Faith/Nonesuch/1993
This Land/Nonesuch/1994
Nashville/Nonesuch/1997
Gone, Like a Train/Nonesuch/1998
Bill Frissell Home Page //www.geocities.com/hollywood/2251/frisell.html

See Bad Livers; Robin Holcomb

Frog Holler

Roots Rock; Country Rock
Shoemakersville, Pennsylvania; 1996-

Inspired by Bill Monroe, the Stanley Brothers, and Norman Blake, Frog Holler began as a bluegrass trio in the summer of 1996. Darren Schlappich, Will Dennis, and Mike Lavdanski played local events such as the Camp Strauss Fire Company bluegrass night for a time but with the addition of John Kilgore on electric and lap steel guitar, Toby Martin on drums, and Josh Sceurman on bass, they evolved into an alt. country band influenced by the work of the Replacements and UncleTupelo. Lead singer Schlappich's songwriting skills began to blossom bringing a modern lyrical and musical interpretation to traditional country themes and styles. He sent me a copy of their self-released **Couldn't Get Along** right after the first edition of *Modern Twang* came out, and I was completely bowled over. In this one generous 19 track package, Frog Holler captures the very best elements of Uncle Tupelo/Jayhawks country/roots rock not through rote imitation but genuine emulation; lazy day lo-fi country with lilting lap steel, twangly guitar and/or plunking banjo ("One More"; "Liquor"; "Just Ahead"; "Supposed to Be Livin'"), straight and edgy old-time/bluegrass ("Farmer Schmidt"; "Never Gone Too Far"; "Hayden Wampler's Truck"), country rock ("The Brownsville Inn"), and crunchy roots rock ("Double-Edged Sword"; "Another Shoeless Joe") are all well-served. Schlappich's songs are consistently sophisticated even when he's taking good-natured pokes at rural life ("Possum"; "Bluebilly County"; "Worms Are Good Life"; "Sheep"). Frog Holler made their "big city debut" in early 1999 when they opened for *wunderkinder* Marah at the Tin Angel in Philadelphia.

Will Dennis (b,md,1996-1998); Ted Fenstermacher (f,md,1998-); John Kilgore (a.g.,e.g.,l.s.,v); Mike Lavdanski (bj,l.s.,b.v.,1996-1998); Toby Martin (d); Josh Sceurman (b); Darren Schlappich (a.g.,e.g.,l.v.)

Couldn't Get Along/Zobird/1998

Frog Holler, 521 Adams Hotel Rd.,
Shoemakersville, PA 19555

zobird@enter.net

See Marah

Edith Frost

Singer/Songwriter; Lo-Fi Country
San Antonio, Texas; August 18, 1964-

Born and raised in Texas (San Antonio/Austin), Edith Frost left the Lone Star State in 1990 for Brooklyn but carried with her a love for country music and cowgirls. In New York City, she fronted a country band, The Marfa Lights, a rockabilly group, Edith and Her Roadhouse Romeos, and dueted with friend Deborah Moore in the Louvin/Carter/Stanley inspired Harmony Sisters. Around the same time, Frost began collecting cowgirl memorabilia and in 1995 set up a web page, Cowgals Home on the Web, devoted to Patsy Montana, Dale Evans, et al. That site also contained a page dedicated to one of her favorite groups, Palace, which became a major influence on her development as a singer/songwriter. In 1996, Frost sent some demos to Drag City (Palace/Will Oldham), and that label released a four track EP, **Edith Frost**. Frost's haunting vocals, morose songs, and the instrumentation invited comparisons not only to Oldham but also to female singer/songwriters like Kendra Smith and Liz Phair. After moving to Chicago in November 1996, she recorded the full length, **Calling Over Time**, with low key country/folk/rock accompaniment from members of Gastro Del Sol (David Grubbs, Jim O'Rourke), Eleventh Dream Day (Rick Rizzo), Palace (Rian Murphy), and the High Llamas (Sean O'Hagan). It was hailed by a number of reviewers as the most promising debut since Richard Buckner who shares with Frost an unrelentingly somber obsession with heartbreak and the search for recovery. With a full time band consisting of Michael Krassner (Pinetop Seven), Braden King, Joe Ferguson, Glen Kotche (Paul K & The Weathermen), and Mike Daly (Swales), Frost embarked on a nation wide tour in late 1997. When not performing and recording, she designs web pages for various corporations and maintains her own home page where she provides many details about her life and, of course, cowgirls. With a completely new band, Frost entered the studio in 1998 to do **Telescopic**. She also remained closely associated with the Insurgent Country community contributing "My Window Faces the South" to the grand **Pine Valley Cosmonauts Salute the Majesty of Bob Wills**.

Edith Frost/Drag City/1997 (EP)
Calling Over Time/Drag City/1997
Ancestors/Trade2 Island UK/1997 (7")
Telescopic/Drag City/1998
"My Window Faces the South" on **The Pine Valley Cosmonauts Salue the Majesty of Bob Wills**/Bloodshot/1998

Edith Frost Home Page //members.tripod.com/~edithforst/

Edithfrost@yahoo.com

Cowgals Home on the Web
//www.cowgirls.com/dream/cowgals/ (not maintained by Frost but has most of her original information)

FSK

Bavarian Hillbilly
Munich, Bavaria, Germany; 1980-

There are two places I know of where you can find a sound combining traditional German music and hillbilly. One is Central Texas and the other is in the Bavarian based band FSK (named for the Freiwillige Selbstkontrolle, Germany's film ratings board). Their initial exposure to country music came through American GI bands and radio shows. Around 1980,

FSK began to fuse country with German folk music and a driving punk beat recording six albums in Germany during the 1980s-1990s. While traveling around the U.S. soaking up various American musical styles from Appalachia to Texas, the band met David Lowery (of Cracker, Camper Van Beethoven fame) who was raised in Schertz, a small Texas town established by German immigrants in the mid-19th century. He understood the country/German folk/rock connections FSK was trying to make and played on their 1991 German release **Son of Kraut**. Lowery then produced their U.S. debut **The Sound of Music** which joins oom-pah-pah, yodeling, and accordion with country and driving modern rock on songs like "The Transatlantic Feedback," "Diesel Oktoberfest," "Elke Sommer Territory Band," "Hobo Zwiefacher," and covers of "Unter Der Doppeladlre" (Under the Double Eagle) and "Distant Drums." The effect is very quirky but very catchy as well. Lowery also collaborated on FSK's 1996 **International** (German release).

Justin Hoffmann (g,p,v); Thomas Meinecke (d,g,v);; Michaela Melian (b,v); Carl Oesterhelt; Wilfred Petz (g,trb,v) with David Lowery

FSK: The Peel Sessions/Strange Fruit Dut./1991
Son of Kraut/Sub Up Ger./1991
The Sound of Music/Flying Fish/1995
International/Sub Up Ger./1996

FSK c/o Melian, Gotthardst. 127, 80689 Munich, Bavaria, Germany

David Lowery Home Page //members.aol.com/mccrackerd/index.html (will eventually have an FSK site with biographical, discographical, and other information)

Robbie Fulks

Insurgent Country
York, Pennsylvania; March 25, 1963-

The cover of Robbie Fulks' debut CD, **Country Love Songs**, is a photo of a man about to hit a woman in the head with an ax. That image juxtaposed with the title is a good summation of his skewed take not only on country music but life in general. Born in Pennsylvania and raised in North Carolina and Virginia, Fulks lived in New York City for a time (where he worked with 5 Chinese Brothers) but ended up in Chicago in 1983. At various times during the 1980s, Fulks played folk (background singer for Bob Gibson) and bluegrass (guitar player for Special Consensus), taught at the Old Town School of Folk Music, and performed in the musical *Woody Guthrie's American Song*. Inspired by Elvis Costello's **Almost Blue**, he formed the Trailer Trash Revue, a parodic country outfit complete with dancing girls in bikinis. They recorded a couple of Fulks originals ("Little King" b/w "Jean Arthur") and got some local radio play

but eventually broke up. Robbie labored on as a solo (and very disgruntled Nashville songwriter) in the early 1990s, and then, he caught the ears of Chicago's nascent insurgent country movement. His satirical indictment of the tobacco industry, "Cigarette State" (originally covered on the Sundowners' **Chicago Country**) was included on **For a Life of Sin**; the even more cynical, "She Took a Lot of Pills and Died," about an aging movie star's suicide, made it on Bloodshot's second insurgent installment, **Hell-Bent**. In 1996, the label released **Country Love Songs** on which Fulks' rich twangy vocals are backed by the Skeletons and steel player Tom Brumley (Buck Owens, Rick Nelson); they convincingly recapture the sound of the best of 1950s-1960s country on some really good hurting songs, "The Buck Starts Here (With Hank Sure to Follow)" and "Barely Human," one excellent loser tune "Rock Bottom, Pop. 1" plus the clever "Scrapple Song" and "Every Kind of Music But Country" (by Tim Carroll). With this release, Fulks rocketed into the upper ranks of new alt. country artists and earned a multi-disc deal with Geffen. However, before moving to the new label, Fulks finished up with Bloodshot by recording **South Mouth**, another album (again with the Skeletons) of Fulks' unmistakable brand of honky tonk and country rock including "I Told Her Lies," "Goodbye, Good Lookin'," "Forgotten But Not Gone," "What the Lord Hath Wrought (Any Fool Can Knock Down)," and the last word in Nashville dis songs, "Fuck This Town." For his major label debut on Geffen, Fulks came on with a new band and a new sound. **Let's Kill Saturday Night** retains some of his previous country leanings ("God Isn't Real"; "Can't Win for Losing You"; "Pretty Little Poison" with Lucinda Williams) but the real standout tunes ("Down in Her Arms"; "She Must Think I Like Poetry"; "Caroline"; "Take Me to the Paradise"; title cut) are straight-ahead guitar-driven pop-rock. Fans and critics seemed to be about evenly divided over whether they liked Fulks' departure or hoped he'd soon get back to the country.

"Little King" b/w "Jean Arthur"/RF/1992 (7")
"Cigarette State" on **For a Life of Sin**/Bloodshot/1992
"She Took a Lot of Pills and Died" on **Hell Bent**/ Bloodshot/1995
Country Love Songs/Bloodshot/1996
South Mouth/Bloodshot/1997
"Wedding of the Bugs" on **Straight Outta Boone County**/ Bloodshot/1997
Let's Kill Saturday Night/Geffen/1998
"Stone River" on **Edges From the Postcard2**/ P2/1998
"Across the Valley From the Alamo" on **The Pine Valley Cosmonauts Salute the Majesty of Bob Wills**/ Bloodshot/1998

RobbieFulks.Com: The Robbie Fulks World Wide Web Site //robbiefulks.com

See The Skeletons

Chris Gaffney
TSOB
Vienna, Austria; October 3, 1950-

In the late 1980s, Chris Gaffney was guest accordionist on numerous recordings by some of the best of Southern California's alt. country (Forbidden Pigs, the Lonesome Strangers), but in the 1990s, he emerged as a respected performer in his own right. Born in Austria, Gaffney was raised in Arizona and California, and his music reflects the influence of the varied styles and cultural experiences of the region. On **Road to Indio** (debut EP), **Chris Gaffney & The Cold Hard Facts**, and (his best, IMO) **Mi Vida Loca**, Gaffney and his band, the Cold Hard Facts (with help from Dave Alvin, Jim Lauderdale, the Lonesome Strangers) move comfortably from honky tonk ("King of the Blues"; "Six Nights a Week," co-written with Dave Alvin) to Tex-Mex ("Frank's Tavern"; "Get Off My Back Lucy") to rock ("Lift Up Your Leg"; "Not Tonight") and lots of styles in between (like a more countrified Blasters). Gaffney's singing brings to mind country Doug Sahm; his originals can be serious ("The Gardens"; "'68"), touching ("Daddy's Little Girl"), self-deprecating ("They Made a Mistake And They Called It Me"), or tongue-in-cheek ("As Far as I'm Concerned She Doesn't Live Here Anymore"; "Silent Partner"; "Not Tonight"; "Psychotic Girlfriend"). For his third outing, **Loser's Paradise**, (produced by Dave Alvin), Gaffney used a crack corps of musicians drawn from Austin's alternative country elite (Sarah Brown, Ted Roddy, Bradley Jaye Williams, Gene Elders, Dale Watson, Tony Villanueva, Scott Walls) for another round of honky tonk ("Loser's Paradise"; "See the Big Man Cry") and Tex-Mex ("Azulito") plus Cajun ("East of Houston, West of Baton Rouge"), R&B ("Cowboys to Girls"/ background vocals by Lucinda Williams), and blues ("Sugar Bee"). Gaffney's debut LP, **Road to Indio**, from 1986 was re-issued on CD in 1998 with live tracks added. He toured Europe in the summer of that year and did two songs for Neil Mooney's Southern California alt. country compilation, **L.A. County Line**. A new full-length from Chris was in the works in 1999.

The Cold Hard Facts: Chris Gaffney (acc,g,l.v.); Mike Barry (b, 1997-); Tucker Fleming (d); Doug Livingston (p.s.); Danny Ott (a.g.,e.g.,v); Wyman Reese (ky)

Road to Indio/Cactus Club/1986; 1998 (with live tracks)
Chris Gaffney and the Cold Hard Facts/ROM/1990
Mi Vida Loca/Hightone/1992
Loser's Paradise/Hightone/1995
"A Bridge Too Far"and "Faded Rose" (with Neil Mooney) on **L.A. County Line**/Strawdog/1998

Chris Gaffney & The Cold Hard Facts Home Page //home.earthlink.net/~amigoagogo/

amigoagogo@earthlink.net

Jerry Garcia
See The Grateful Dead; David Grisman; New Riders of the Purple Sage

Greg Garing
Insurgent Country
Erie, Pennsylvania; 1966-

With all the recent experimentation in alternative country, sooner or later someone was bound to join traditional country with trip hop and electronic pop. However, long time Nashville musician Greg Garing initially seemed like the least likely candidate for the task. Raised on rock, he had an epiphany as a teenager when he witnessed a live performance by Bill Monroe. Garing took up fiddle and headed to Music City in the late 1980s where he joined a folk rock outfit called the Shakers, sat in with Monroe and a variety of other Nashville musicians (Jerry Lee Lewis, Roy Duke, Wilma Lee Cooper) whenever he could, and played fiddle in bands led by Jimmy Martin and Peter Rowan. In the early 1990s, Garing led a honky tonk band at Tootsie's Orchid Lounge and became one of the leaders in the Lower Broadway renaissance that produced groups like BR5-49 and Paul Burch & the WPA Club. His contributions to this revival drew attention from Bloodshot Records which placed "Safe Within Your Arms" on **Nashville: The Other Side of the Alley**. Although tagged by some as a new Hank, Sr., Garing wanted to develop something unique and influenced by Garbage, Tricky, Portishead, and other modern pop/electronica began combining Appalachian old-time/bluegrass with contemporary urban music complete with drum machines, sampling, and even a disco whistle. Such a volatile mixture could have easily blown up in Garing's face, but he managed to pull it off tastefully and engagingly on his 1997 debut **Alone**. His high lonesome vocals, moody fiddle, and songwriting could stand on their own, but strangely enough, the country side of the equation is made even more effective by the trip hop enhancements courtesy of producer David Kahne's mixing and programming. Old colleague Peter Rowan even drops by to lend his mandolin and background vocals to the cyborgian proceedings on a tribute to Bill Monroe, "Where the Bluegrass Grows." Likened by one reviewer to "Bill Monroe and John Cage meeting at the end of the century," Garing's "Countronica" (Jon Langford's phrase) places him in rare company on the outer edges of the ever growing alt. country universe. Early in 1998, Garing relocated to New York City and played at Coney Island High/Roger's Juke Joint's weekly alt. country showcase ("Singin' a Beer, and Drinkin' a Country Song") before starting up his own at a club called 9C in the East Village. "Greg Garing's Alphabet City Opry" as it came to be called hosted a variety of local and regional alt. country performers with bluegrass and honky tonk music predominating. These Monday night sessions became quite popular with a cross section of New

Yorkers and was even the subject of a feature article by Peter Applebome in *The New York Times*.

"Safe Within Your Arms" on **Nashville: The Other Side of the Alley**/Bloodshot/1996
"No Such Thing as Sin" on **Cowpunks**/Vinyl Junkie UK/1996
Alone/Paladin Revolution/1997

Greg Garing/Paladin Records Page //www.paladin-records.com/garing2/

Greggaring@paladinrecords.com

Greg Garing iMusic Showcase //www.imusic.com/showcase/modern/greggaring.html

The Gear Daddies

See Martin Zellar

Sonny George (The Tennessee Sons; The Planet Rockers)

Honky Tonk; Rockabilly
Memphis, Tennessee; Early 1990s-

The Planet Rockers are a Memphis based neo-rockabilly outfit noted for their driving songs powered by the lead guitar of Eddie Angel (ex-Rubinovitz, Los Straightjackets). In 1996, their lead singer Sonny George made a diversion into a more traditional country/hillbilly sound with his band, the Tennessee Sons. Using Nashville session musicians, fiddle/pedal steel whiz, Fats Kaplin, and guest Eddie Angel, he recorded **Country Western Roundup, Vol. One** whose cover reminds us to "Keep a rockin' C&W style!" It more than lives up to this motto with some great hillbilly bop ("Hillbilly Beat"; "Hillbilly Train"; "King of Hillbilly Hill"; "Big Trouble"; "Look-a-Here"), honky tonk ("Lovesick Daddy"; "Gotta Travel On"), and western flavored songs including "Big Iron" (not the Marty Robbins hit) and a cover of Johnny Cash's "The Rebel Johnny Yuma." Kaplin's steel, Angel's lead, and George's twangy baritone make this one a standout. "Hillbilly Train" can be found on Bloodshot's **Nashville: The Other Side of the Alley** compilation. **26 Classic Tracks** is a sterling compilation of material from the Planet Rockers first two recordings and includes not only straight ahead rockabilly but also some righteous hillbilly boogie and honky tonk. Like Dale Watson, Sonny has always harbored a fondness for truckers and truck driving music and in 1998, he recorded **Truckin' Country**. George penned all the songs on this big rig bonanza ("Big Iron"; "The Lone Masked Trucker"; "Truck Driver Man #1 plus tunes about ghost and cross-dressing truckers and more) and is joined by Boz Boorer, Nick Kane (Mavericks), Darrel Higham, and Fats Kaplin.

Sonny George and the Tennessee Sons: Sonny George (g,v); Eddie Angel (l.g.); George Bradfute (g); Steve Ebe (d); Fats Kaplin (f,p.s.); Preston Rumbaugh (b); Kenny Vaughan (g)

The Planet Rockers: Eddie Angel (l.g.); Sonny George (g.v)

Coming in Person (Planet Rockers)/No Hit UK/1991
Invasion of the Planet Rockers/No Hit UK/1992
"Say When"; "Rampage" (Planet Rockers) on **Stateside Rockabillies**/NV/1994
Live: On The Rampage (Planet Rockers)/No Hit UK/1994
"Gotta Travel On" b/w "Batteroo" (Planet Rockers)/ Spinout/1995 (7")
Country & Western Roundup Volume One (Sonny George)/Hermitage/1996
"Hillbilly Train" (Sonny George) on **Nashville: The Other Side of the Alley**/Bloodshot/1996
26 Classics (Planet Rockers)/Spinout/1996
Truckin' Country (Sonny George)/Spinout/1998

Sonny George, c/o Hermitage Records, P. O. Box 8523, Memphis, TN 37076

Sonny George Web Site //webzone1.co.uk/www/cyderco/sonny.htm

The Geraldine Fibbers

Country Punk
Los Angeles, California; 1994-1998 (?)

When it comes to alternative country of the "twang & crunch" variety, the Geraldine Fibbers have few rivals. Formed in L.A. in early 1994, their first releases (**Get Thee Gone**; **The Geraldine Fibbers**) were heavy on country with covers of Bobbie Gentry ("Fancy"), George Jones ("The Grand Tour"), Dolly Parton ("Jolene") and originals like "Get Thee Gone." **Lost Somewhere Between the Earth and My Home** retained this country edge, but this is country played as if you were looking into the morphine/alcohol addicted soul of Hank Williams at its most tortured. In fact, it's a highly personal reflection of the harrowing life of the group's lead singer/ songwriter, Carla Bozulich. Growing up in San Pedro, she was a part of the 1980s punk scene (Neon Veins; Invisible Chains) but by her late teens was a full blown heroin addict resorting to hooking to support her habit. After cleaning up at age 21, Bozulich returned to music decked out in leather as lead "dominatrix" in the legendary techno/industrial band Ethyl Meatplow. When this project suddenly ended, Bozulich could have gone into a tailspin, but her commitment to music pulled her through, and she went on to start the Geraldine Fibbers. Her previous musical background is apparent in their sound but so is her connection to the dark side of country music. Losers, rejects, and all manner of wretched refuse have populated country from the beginning, and Bozulich's songs follow suit with vivid portraits drawn from personal experience. Through wrathful lyrics and a combination of twang (scorching fiddle by Jesy Green) with punk rage, she and the Fibbers seem to be casting out the demons of the past. This approach struck a responsive chord first among audiences in the L.A. club scene and then nationwide. **Lost Somewhere** made many top ten lists, and they were featured performers at SXSW and on the Lollapalooza tour. **Get Thee Gone** with several live and radio tracks was re-released as **What Part of Get Thee Gone Don't You Understand** in 1996. Later that year, the Fibbers lost fiddler Jessy Green (to the Jayhawks) and guitarist Daniel Keenan (to tendonitis), but in 1997, with avant-jazz guitar player Nels Cline and new violinist Jessica Moss, they recorded **Butch**, another dynamic collection of angry punk ("California Tuffy"; "Trashman in Furs"; "Toybox"), country waltzes ("Swim Back to Me"; "Pot Angel"), and backwoods twang ("Fools Like Me"). When not recording or performing, Bozulich wrote for underground 'zines like *Alternative Press* (a piece on Patti Smith) and *Ben Is Dead* (a story titled "Fuck You"). Citing disappointing sales totals, Virgin cut the Fibbers loose in mid-1998, and they decided to call it quits at least for the time being. Bozulich took a songwriting job with a music publishing company while Cline did a couple of jazz albums that rework, on the guitar, some the most experimental material of John Coltrane and Miles Davis. They also teamed up as the duo Scarnella and cut an avant-garde music album called **Smells Like Records**.

Carla Bozulich (g,l.v.); Nels Cline (l.g., 1997-); Kevin Fitzgerald (d); Jessy Green (violin,1994-1996); Daniel Keenan (l.g.,1994-1996); Leyna Marika (violin,1998); Jessica Moss (violin, 1997); William Tutton (b)

Get Thee Gone/SFTRI/1994(10")
"Fancy" b/w "They Suck"/Big Jesus/1994(7")
Geraldine Fibbers/Hut UK/1995 (compiles **Get Thee Gone** & "Fancy")
"Dragon Lady" b/w "Birthday Boys"/SFTRI/1995 (7")
Lost Somewhere Between the Earth and My Home/ Virgin/1995
Live From the Bottom of the Hill/Virgin/1996
What Part of Get Thee Gone Don't You Understand?/ Virgin/1997
Butch/Virgin/1997

The Geraldine Fibbers Shrine
//www.best.com/~djsq/fibbers.html

Geraldine Fibbers AOL Folder: Entertainment>Music>Chat & Messages>Music Community>Alternative>Alternative Bands, G-L

Mark Germino

Singer/Songwriter; Country Rock; Roots Rock
North Carolina

Like Steve Earle, with whom he is most often compared, Mark Germino spent much of his early musical career slugging it out in Nashville. Throughout the late 1970s and early 1980s, Germino worked as a company songwriter for Combine Music and played local venues before RCA signed him and released **London Town & Barnyard Remedies** in 1986. This was followed a few years later by **Radartown** (with the Sluggers), and both of these excellent but largely overlooked early albums have been aptly characterized as "hard-hitting heartland rock" (*AMG*). Switching to the independent label Winter Harvest in

1995 (as did Steve Earle for **Train' A Comin'**), Germino recorded **Rank & File** which was very well received and brought him long overdue recognition. Fancying himself "a folk writer, not a folk singer," Mark's vocals are of the raw Bob Dylan/Butch Hancock school and his songwriting style is a combination of John Prine, Steve Earle, and "Tom T. Hall with a big chip on his shoulder" (*New Country*). A veteran of both Vietnam and years of hard blue collar labor, Germino has a heightened political and social consciousness as he shows on the iconclastic "Felix Tucker's Biggest Lie" (trucking illicit guns) and "Fields of Man's New Order" (threats to freedom from the government and press); but, he can also be tender ("Always Be Your Man"; "Three Words, Two Hearts, One Night") and humorous as on "Lerdy and Bo' Totalitarian Showdown," "Rosemary's New Constitution," and the pointed satire "Rex Bob Lowenstein" about the battle of a DJ against the rampant spread of commercial radio.

London Moon & Barnyard Remedies/RCA/1986
Radartown/Zoo/1990
Rex Bob Lowenstein/Zoo/1991 (EP)
Rank & File/Winter Harvest/1995

Mark Germino Home Page
//songs.com/noma/wh/mg-home.html

Alice Gerrard

See Hazel Dickens

The Ghost Rockets

"Maximum Rhythm 'n' Bluegrass"
Hoboken, New Jersey; 1992-

In 1992, Californian Buddy Woodward and Canadian Gary Pig Gold met in New Jersey, discovered their disparate musical interests (Woodward: Buck Owens, Byrds, Burritos, Dillards; Gold: modern pop rock) blended well, and decided to create a band called the Ghost Rockets. They cut demos at Woodward's home studio, Spatula Ranch, recorded several singles and mini-cassettes for labels in England and New Zealand, and contributed cuts to several Canadian, European, and U.S. compilations. And while the Ghost Rockets can play good, straight country rock and bluegrass, it is "novelty" tunes that brought the most attention. In addition to witty originals about "hanging" on the "Family Tree," destroying Nashville, and the Brady Bunch ("Marcia, Marcia, Marcia"), the Ghost Rockets do a hilarious send up of "O Canada" (in German) and bluegrass versions of the Monkees' "What Am I Doin' Hanging Round?" and the Beach Boys' "In My Room." The latter and "Marcia, Marcia, Marcia" were big on several European radio show playlists. In the mid-late 1990s, these purveyors of "maximum rhythm 'n' bluegrass" bonded with the Postcard2 online alt. country mailing list crowd contributing songs to **Twangfest 1997** and **Edges From the Postcard, Vols 1 & 2** and appearing at the P2 sponsored Twangfest in St. Louis. Around the middle of 1998, The Ghost Rockets released a 10 song CD called **Bootlegs** and did a cut for a forthcoming Gene Clark tribute album. A 6 song EP on the French label Pop the Balloon! was due late in the year.

Gary Gold is involved in several side projects: his Pig Productions joined with To M'Lou Music to record compilations (The Unsound Series) of home demos solicited from bands via the Internet, and he writes insightful alt. country music articles ("Pigshit" he calls it) for print and online publications such as the *Rural Route Twangzine*.

Gary Pig Gold (g,v); Pete Green (d); Mick Hargreaves (b); Bob Hoffnar (p.s.); Buddy Woodward (bj,g,hm,md,v)

Ghost Rockets/Spatula Ranch/1994 (4 trk. CS)
"In My Room" on **Powerplay**/Roto Noto Can./1995
Ghost Rockets #2/Spatula Ranch/1995 (4 trk. CS)
"Marcia, Marcia, Marcia" on **Total Fun**/Roto Noto Can./1996
Ghost Rockets #3/Spatula Ranch/1996 (4 trk. CS)
"Try to Believe" on **Hit the Hay, Vol. 2**/Sound Asleep Swe./1996
"Roses to You" b/w "Marcia, Marcia, Marcia"/King NZ/1996 (7")
Never Been to Nashville/Acid Tapes UK/1996 (4 trk. CS)
Astral Weeks/Acid Tapes UK/1996 (4 trk. CS)
"Try to Believe" on **Pop!Productions, 1987-1997**/ Pop!/1997 (CS)
"My Guilty Pleasure" on **Edges From the Postcard**/ Semi-Tone/1997 (CS)
"Goodbye to Greatness" on **Fireworks**/Sound Asleep Swe./1997
"Hard to Get," "Sitting Alone in the Moonlight," "Juliet" on **Twangfest 1997**/Hookers and Blow/1997 (CS)
The Ghost Rockets, Astral Weeks/Acid Tapes UK/1997
"Under the Table" on **Edges From the Poastcard2**/ P2/1998
Bootlegs/1998

The Ghost Rockets, P. O. Box 1023, Hoboken, NJ 07030

Official Ghost Rockets Website
//www.hudsonet.com/~undertow/ghostrockets/

Gary Pig Gold: PigProd@aol.com

Buddy Woodward: budrocket@juno.com

Giant Sand (Howe Gelb; The Band of Blacky Ranchette; Calexico)
Desert Rock
Tucson, Arizona; 1980-

In the early 1980s, a new sound known as "desert rock" drifted out from the American Southwest. It combined rock and country influences, and among its leading practitioners were Green on Red and Giant Sand. The latter grew out of the Giant Sandworms which was formed by Howe Gelb after he moved to Tucson from Pennsylvania in the late 1970s. The Sandworms did only one EP and one tour before Gelb changed personnel, shortened the name to Giant Sand, and pushed the group toward

a unique Southwestern rock style. Country and western influences were obvious on their first release, **Valley of Rain** and then even more apparent on **Ballad of a Thin Line Man**. However, it was in the Giant Sand side project, the Band of Blacky Ranchette, that Gelb's love of real country music found full expression. Surprisingly, the albums of the BBR (**The Band of Blacky Ranchette**; **Heartland**; **Sage Advice**) are not covers but Gelb originals that suggest Hank and Jimmie but in a contemporary way. Down the years, Giant Sand's output (through a variety of personnel) has been prolific as they have continued to explore myriad combinations of rock, country, and even beat poetry. One of their more unusual recordings, **Backyard Barbecue**, done live at station WFMU (Montclair, New Jersey) comes complete with the sound of grilling, barking dogs, and pool splashing in the background. In 1996, Epiphany Records issued volume one of **The Official Bootleg Series** and a Giant Sand video documentary, *Drunken Bees*. When Giant Sand alumnus, Rainer Ptacek, was diagnosed with cancer, Gelb organized a benefit album called **The Inner Flame** to help pay medical expenses. Among those contributing to the cause were Emmylou, Victoria Williams, Jonathan Richman, Jimmy Page, and Robert Plant. Sadly, Ptacek succumbed to his illness in November 1997.

For the most part Giant Sand the group was on hold for most of 1998 although Gelb, Burns, and Convertino served as the backing band for Lisa Geramano's Op 8 project. Gelb recorded a solo album (**Hisser**) at home on a 4 track reel to reel and set up Ow Om Recordings with plans to organize and distribute material from the Giant Sand family tree past and present. He also regrouped Giant Sand in September 1998 to begin a new unnamed album which was described as "a mix of slow burning hot buttery Memphis moistness with the crispy quiet crackle of Tucson thirsty-ness."

Burns and Convertino guested on recordings by Vic Chesnutt, Victoria Williams, the Friends of Deam Martinez, Michael Hurley, Bill Janovitz, Barbara Manning, and Richard Buckner (**Devotion + Doubt**). In 1996, they began performing as the duo Spoke which eventually morphed into Calexico with Tasha Bundy added on drums. Calexico's recordings, **Spoke** and **The Black Light**, can best be described as Southwestern Americana. Each has a very moody but wondrous desert rock feel with many intriguing touches of Latin, spaghetti western, and other world music courtesy of accordion, pedal steel, cello, gitaron, Spanish guitar, marimba, mandolin, organ (Howe Gelb), trumpet, and vibes.

Giant Sand: Paula Jean Brown (v); Joey Burns (b); John Convertino (d); Howe Gelb; Scott Gerber (b); Neil Harry (p.s.); Al Perry (g); Rainer Ptacek (g); Dave Seger (b); Mark Walton (b)
The Band of Blacky Ranchette: Howe Gelb (b,g,v); Tom Larkin (d); Rainer Ptacek (g)

Calexico: Tasha Bundy (d,vox); Joey Burns (acc,b,cello, g,ky,md,s.g.,vox); John Convertino (acc,d,marimba,vibes)

Will Wallow and Roam After the Ruin (Giant Sandworms)/Boneless/1980 (EP)
An Evening at the Wildcat (Giant Sandworms)/Se-Mi-Round/1983 (EP)
Valley of Rain/Enigma/1985
The Band of Blacky Ranchette/New Rose Fr./1985
Heartland (Band of Blacky Ranchette)/Zippo UK/1986
Ballad of a Thin Line Man/Zippo UK/1986
Storm/What Goes On/1988
The Love Songs/Homestead/1988
Giant Songs: The Best of Giant Sand/Demon UK/1989
Giant Sandwich/Homestead/1989 (comp w/ 7 non-lp **Band of Blacky Ranchette** trks.)
Long Stem Rant/Homestead/1989
Sage Advice (Band of Blacky Ranchette)/Demon UK/1990
Dreaded Brown Recluse (Howe Gelb)/Amazing Black Sand Ger./1991; Restless/1993
Ramp/Amazing Black Sand/1992; Restless/1993
Center of the Universe/Amazing Black Sand Ger./1992; Restless/1992
Purge and Slouch/Amazing Black Sand, Restless/1993
Glum/Imago/1994
Giant Songs Two: The Best of Giant Sand, Vol. 2/Demon UK/1995
Backyard Barbecue Broadcast/KOCH/1995
Goods & Services/Glitterhouse Ger./1995
Stromausfall/Epiphany Ger./1995
Official Bootleg Series, Vol. 1/Epiphany Ger./1996
Drunken Bees/Epiphany/1996 (video)
"Spark" b/w "The Ride" (Calexico)/Wabana/1996 (7")
"Lost in Space" b/w "The Ride, Pt. 2" (Calexico)/All City/1996 (7")
Spoke (Calexico)/Hausmusik Ger./1996; Quarterstick/1997
Inner Flame:The Songs of Rainer Ptacek/Atlantic/1997
The Black Light (Claexico)/Quarterstick/1998
"Slag" (Calexico) on **Loose: New Sounds of the Old West**/Vinyl JunkieUK/1998
"Lester Lampshade" (Giant Sand) on **Loose: New Sounds of the Old West**/Vinyl JunkieUK/1998
"Trigger" (Calexico) on **Sounds of the New West: The Best of Alternative Country**/Uncut UK/1998
Hisser (Howe Gelb)/V2/1998
"Tulsa Telephone Book" (Calexico) on **Real: The Tom T. Hall Project**/Sire/1998

Howe Gelb/Ow Om, P.O. Box 2441, Tucson, AZ 85702; 502-620-1360

Official Giant Sand Home Page //www.giantsand.com

Unofficial Giant Sand Home Page //infosoc.informatik.uni-bremen.de/mad/giant.htm

Unofficial Calexico Page //infosoc.informatik.uni-bremen.de/mad/calexico/

Calexico Biograhy //www.billions.com/calexico/bio.htm

See Green on Red; Original Harmony Ridge Creek Dippers; Al Perry

The Gibson Brothers

Okra; Roots Rock; White Trash Parody
Columbus, Ohio; 1985-

Parodies of "lower class" white cultures otherwise known as hillbillies, white trash, crackers, Okies, rednecks, et al. have been a staple of mainstream country music from the early Grand Ol' Opry to *Hee-Haw* and beyond. Alternative country has had its share of such acts as well, and one of the earliest to explore (some might say exploit) this imagery was the Gibson Brothers of Columbus, Ohio. Formed in the mid-1980s, the initial line up included Dan Dow, Jeff Evans, Ellen Hoover, and Don Howland (ex-Great Plains). Their style, on **Build a Raft, Big Pine Boogie**, and **Dedicated Fool**, was basically country, country blues, and rockabilly with lots of lyrical and musical twists along the way; Howland's lead guitar, dripping with reverb or overgrown with fuzz, backed Evans' vocals which range from frenzied to backwoods mush mouth. Some songs were played in a "straight" but proudly amateurish way using only plunking banjo. Thematically, the Gibsons' focus was on life's uglier sides with covers of "Poor Me" (Charley Patton), "Coal Black Mare" (Richard Starling), "Skull & Crossbones," "Satanville," "Thy Burdens Are Greater Than Mine" (Pee Wee King) or originals like "Rovin' Dope Peddler," "Poor White Trash," "Dirt Preacher," "The Sperm Count," "Lost Track of Time," "Rubber Room," "Gonorrhea," and "White Nigger." In 1990, they teamed with the Workdogs (from Hoboken) to record a truck driver "tribute," **Punk Rock Drivin' Son of a Gun**. It has countryish covers of "Moody River" and "Amanda" plus an extended voodoobilly version of "Giddy Up Go" (Red Sovine) with a spoken dedication to all those "down to earth, pill poppin' working men (especially those who like punk rock)." Whether you see the Gibson Brothers as just fun loving parodists or mean spirited denigrators depends, of course, on your perspective, but there's no doubt they influenced other such acts, most notably, Southern Culture on the Skids. Howland (currently in the Bassholes) recorded a number of singles with SCOTS as "Los Falanas" while Evans led '68 Comeback, and Spencer was a member of Boss Hog and leader of the John Spencer Blues Explosion.

Dan Dow (a.g.); Jeff Evans (bj,g,v); Ellen Hoover (d,v); Don Howland (b,g,v); Jon Spencer (a.g.)

Keepers/Okra/1986 (EP)
Build a Raft/Old Age/1987 (CS)
Big Pine Boogie/Okra/1987; Homestead 1988 (LP)
Dedicated Fool/Homestead/1989 (LP)
Punk Rock Truck Drivin' Son of a Gun (with the Workdogs)/Homestead/1990
The Man Who Loved Couch Dancing/Homestead/1991
"Emulsified" b/w "Broke Down Engine"/Siltbreeze/1991 (7")
"My Huckleberry Friend" b/w "Old Devil"/Giant Claw/1991 (7")
Southbound/Glitterhouse Ger./1991 (EP)
"White Nigger" b/w "Minnie the Moocher"/SFTRI/1991

"Knock Down My Blues" b/w "I'm Driftin'"/In the
    Red/1992 (7")
Mean Mistreater/Homestead/1992 (EP)
Memphis Soul Today/SFTRI/1993 (LP)
Columbus Soul 1985/In the Red/1996

The Gibson Brothers Web Page
http://iglo.cpedu.rug.nl/~evert/bands/ef/gibsonbr.htm

See Southern Culture on the Skids

Wilson Gil

Honky Tonk; Country Rock
Bakersfield/San Francisco, California

Although Wilson Gil was raised in the Bakersfield, California area and was well-aware of its honky tonk tradition, his first forays into music were in San Francisco as leader of a power pop group called Sonic Brain Jam. Rooming with Blag Dahlia of the shock-rock group the Dwarves, Gil (full-blooded Esselin American Indian) was also drawn to Seattle and its burgeoning grunge rock scene in the early 1990s. Eventually, he went back to Bakersfield and the Bakersfield Sound but didn't completely leave behind his previous rock influences. In fact, Gil discovered that hard-core country music and the hard rock attitude dovetailed quite nicely. In 1995, with Buck Owens' Buckaroos behind him, Wilson recorded **Buck, Booze, and Bakersfield**, a fairly traditional homage to the Bakersfield Sound but with a bit more rock swagger as on "Drink," "Busted in Tucson," "Outlaw and the Loser," and Neil Young's "For the Turnstiles." A few years later he was back in San Francisco where he set up his own record label, Tinnitus (a buzzing, ringing or whistling in the ears) and assembled a new band, the Willful Sinners made up of Bay Area musicians including Stinky LePew who was formerly with Buck Naked & The Bare Bottom Boys. In 1998, Tinnitus released three CDs: **Sonic Brain Jam** ("100% Powertwang"), **Buck, Booze and Bakers-field**, and the self-titled debut of Wilson Gil and the Willful Sinners. The latter whose guests include Rick Derringer, Jim Campilongo, and the Oakland Interfaith Gospel Choir is undiluted, irreverent honky tonk/country rock; reportedly, Gil went to work in a mortuary during the album's recording to renew his flagging faith in the project. At any rate, **Wilson Gil and the Willful Sinners** is effective in no small measure due to Gil's despair ridden vocals and originals about teen strippers ("Stripped"), rock music hell ("18 Miles to Seattle"), poverty ("Get Through the Fall"), losers ("Gun Store Liquor Store Project"), infidelity ("Hell Yes I Lied, So What If I Did"), and the murder of Buck Naked, the King of Pornobilly ("Hey Greg").

Buck, Booze and Bakersfield/Tinnitus/1998
Sonic Brain Jam/Tinnitus/1998
Wilson Gil and the Willful Sinners/Tinnitus/1998
"Gunstore, Liquor Store Project"(Wilson Gil and the
    Willful Sinners) on **Full Tank, Vol. 1**/Jackass/1998

Wilson Gil //www.spydercide.com/tinnitus/wg.htm
tonygil@pacbell.net

Jimmie Dale Gilmore

Lubbock Mafia; Singer/Songwriter; "Zen Country"
Tulia, Texas; May 6, 1945-

Of all the greats (Allen, Ely, Hancock) to come out of the Texas Panhandle in the last 20 years, Jimmie Dale Gilmore is perhaps the most difficult to pin down. Growing up in Lubbock, Gilmore was exposed to country (father was in a honky tonk band) and rock (Buddy Holly's home town) like many other teens, but there was something else (perhaps the West Texas landscape?) that had a profound impact on him and came more and more to define his musical path. His earliest bands, the Rhythm Orchids, T. Nickel Hose Band, and Hub City Movers, were pretty traditional affairs, but with the Flatlanders in the early 1970s, he, Joe Ely, and Butch Hancock created something new and way too far ahead of its time to succeed. Their Texas style country rock showcased the trio's nascent writing skills and Gilmore's elegiac twang. One of Jimmie Dale's songs, the mystical "Bhagavan Decreed," hinted at things to come.

After the Flatlanders disbanded, Gilmore went on a personal quest in the late 1970s that took him to Colorado where he became a member of Guru Maharaji's community. Meanwhile, his songs ("Tonight I Think I'm Gonna Go Downtown"; "Treat Me Like a Saturday Night"; "Dallas") got exposure through the success of Joe Ely. In 1980, Gilmore decided to try music once more and moved to Austin. There, he read widely (*The Vedanta*, William Blake, Buckminster Fuller, Phillip Dick) and honed his singing/songwriting in the clubs, all the while seeking a way to combine his philosophy and music. In time, Gilmore's persistence led to three albums in the late 1980s and early 1990s (**Fair & Square**, **Jimmie Dale Gilmore**, and **After Awhile**) that feature Gilmore and Hancock originals done in a traditional yet decidedly modern style of country. Underlying it all is Gilmore's preoccupation with metaphysics, in particular, the four basic elements (earth, wind, fire, water). These concerns came more into focus on **Spinning Around the Sun** which pays tribute to Hank and Elvis, but openly bares his spiritual side as well ("Thinking About You"; "Another Colorado"). Critics were at a loss to label Gilmore's music ("Zen Country?," "Country & Eastern?," "New Age Country?") but warmly embraced him anyway. He won the respect of musicians from a variety of genres, opening for the Cowboy Junkies and recording with Mudhoney. During this period, Gilmore had some very fruitful collaborations with Butch Hancock especially a great live recording, **Two Roads**. He was also in the cast of the musical play *Chippy* with fellow Lubbock Mafiosos Terry Allen, Joe Ely, Jo Carol Pierce, and Butch Hancock. 1996's **Braver Newer World** (produced by T-Bone Burnett) took even more risks than Gilmore's previous efforts with mixed results and reviews. Shortly thereafter, Jimmie and Elektra Records parted company.

Sensing the potential of the Internet for bringing the world into closer communion, Jimmie Dale launched a web page designed for entertainment and greater understanding through links called "Inter Change" and "Mindstream." He became more involved in films playing Smokey, "a weird guy who hangs around the bowling alley" in the Coen Brothers *The Big Lebowski*, contributed "Just a Wave, Not the Water" to *Deep in the Heart of Texas*, and had two Lefty Frizzell covers included on the soundtrack of *Traveller* in 1998. That year also brought a collaboration with Ely and Hancock to write and record "The South Wind of Summer" for *The Horse Whisperer* soundtrack which sent rumors of a Flatlanders reunion flying. Butch and Jimmie Dale were inducted into the "Walk of Fame" that leads to Buddy Holly's memorial statue in Lubbock, Texas, and Gilmore returned to his roots when he and Dale Watson did a classic country music tour called "Two For the Road" in October 1998. By year's end, Gilmore found a new home with Rykodisc.

One More Road (Flatlanders)/Charly UK/1980
Fair and Square/Hightone/1988
Jimmie Dale Gilmore/Hightone/1989
Two Roads: Recorded Live in Australia (with Butch Hancock)/Virgin Australia/1990
More a Legend Than a Band (Flatlanders)/Rounder/1990
After Awhile/Nonesuch/1991
Spinning Around the Sun/Elektra/1993
Mudhoney/Jimmie Dale Gilmore/SubPop/1994 (EP)
Unplugged (Flatlanders)/Sun/1995 (reissue of **One More Road** w/ 2 p.u. songs, "Hello Stranger"; "Waiting for a Train")
Braver Newer World/Elektra/1996
"Black Snake Moan" (live) on **Viva Americana**/Boka UK/1998
"Just a Wave, Not the Water" on **Deep in the Heart of Texas**/Shanachie/1998

Jimmie Dale Gilmore Home Page
//www.monsteribt.com/jdg/

Jimmie Dale Gilmore iMusic Showcase
//imusic.com/showcase/country/

Jimmie Dale Gilmore AOL Folder:
Entertainment>Music>Chat & Messages>Music Community>Country/Folk>Country & Western, A-K or Folk/Acoustic

Jimmie Dale Gilmore Live Tapes through Teresa Jo Nolan:
tjnolan@ix.netcom.com

The Jimmie Dale Gilmore Fan Club, P.O. Box 128037, Nashville, TN 37212

See Joe Ely; The Flatlanders; Butch Hancock; Jo Carol Pierce

Johnny Gimble
Fiddle; Western Swing
Tyler, Texas; May 30, 1926-

Over the course of this century, Texas has produced some of the greatest of America's country fiddlers. While most of the early pioneer players have retired or "gone on," one of the best (some say *the* best) is still going strong at age 70+. Johnny Gimble began his professional career over 50 years ago when he played fiddle in a band made up of his four brothers. Soaking up the music of Milton Brown, Bob Wills, and other great Western swingsters of the day and gaining experience from performing at local functions in East Texas, Gimble was good enough by the end of high school to leave Tyler and find his musical destiny. His first job with the Shelton Brothers was followed by work with Jimmie Davis and then Bob Wills in 1949. For two years, Gimble handled fiddle and mandolin chores as a member of the Texas Playboys and continued to work with them off and on into the 1970s and 1980s. During the 1950s and early 1960s, he left music and worked as a barber in Waco, Texas, but when country music began to rise in popularity, Gimble returned and was suddenly in great demand. Over the next ten years, he was the undisputed king of country session fiddlers appearing on hundreds of records. Johnny found time to record his own albums and collaborate on several projects with the surviving legends of Western swing (he played a vital part in launching Western swing revivalists, Asleep at the Wheel). For his impressive body of work and contributions to the field, Gimble was honored with numerous awards: CMA Instrumentalist of the Year (1975, 1986, 1987, 1989, 1990), ACM Best Fiddle Player (1978, 1984, 1987), and two Grammy nominations for Best Country Instrumental Performance. Other highlights have included regular appearances on *Austin City Limits*, tours as part of Willie Nelson's band (1979-1981), and work with Chet Atkins, Mark O'Connor, and Asleep at the Wheel. In the 1990s, Gimble lived in Dripping Springs (near Austin) and had his own band (Texas Swing). And although a new generation of country fiddlers now did most of the session work, he still got frequent calls from musicians who wanted that incomparable Gimble sound. In 1996, Johnny and Bela Fleck won the Best Country Instrumental Grammy for "Hightower."

Fiddlin' Around/Capitol/1974
Johnny Gimble, Texas Dance Party/Lone Star/1975
Johnny Gimble's Texas Dance Party/Columbia/1976
Honky Tonk Hits/CMH/1976
My Kind of Music/Tejas/1979
Still Swingin': Johnny Gimble and the Texas Swing Pioneers/CMH/1980
More Texas Dance Hall Fovorites/Delta/1981
Honky Tonk Hurtin' Songs/Delta/
Swingin' the Standards/Delta/1981
Texas Fiddle Connection/CMH/1981
Still Fiddlin' Around/MCA/1988
Introduction to Gimble Fiddlin' (video)

Johnny Gimble Fan Club, P.O. Box 347,
Dripping Springs, TX 78620

Johnny Gimble //www.johnnygimble.com

See Asleep at the Wheel

Git Gone
Rockabilly; Honky Tonk
Austin, Texas; 1995-

Jim Stringer made his presence dramatically known in 1997 as the producer of **Travis County Pickin'**, a superb collection of country jazz originals from the cream of Austin's alt. country guitarists including Dave Biller (ex-Dale Watson; ex-Wayne Hancock; Panhandlers), Sean Mencher (High Noon), Brian Hofeldt (Derailers), Casper Rawls (LeRoi Brothers; Toni Price), Joel Hamilton (Clay Blaker), and Stringer himself. Around Austin, Jim has been known for years as the leader of one of the city's hardest working bands, Git Gone. Since 1995, they've served up rockabilly, honky tonk, rocking blues, and swing night after night at venues all around Austin but didn't make their first recording until **Gone Rockin'** in 1998. Stringer deftly handles all the styles (covers and originals) mentioned above on guitar as does Sharon Ward on bass and lead vocals while Lee Potter (ex-Dale Watson; ex-Derailers), who replaced Karen Biller (Cornell Hurd Band, Panhandlers), keeps it steady on the snare drum kit.

Karen Biller (d,1995-1997); Jim Stringer (l.g.,l.v.); Sharon Ward (b,l.v.); Lee Potter (d,1997-)

Travis County Pickin'/Hightone/1997
Gone Rockin'/Music Room/1998

Git Gone/The Music Room, 7301 Burnet Rd. #102-525, Austin, TX 78757; 512-302-0766

Git Gone //www.gitgone.com

Jim Stringer: jstrings@eden.com

Keith Glass
Singer/Songwriter
New South Wales, Australia

For almost a decade, Keith Glass has been a key figure in the evolution of alternative country in Australia. Based in Melbourne in the late 1980s and early 1990s, he recorded two pioneering contemorary country albums (**Going Over Old Ground**; **Living Down My Past**) with his band the Tumblers. Although critical successes, they went nowhere commercially, were dropped by Virgin Records, and Keith's solo career was temporarily on hold. However, Glass kept his hand in as a producer for Australian alt. country performers and of Jimmie Dale Gilmore and Butch Hancock's 1990 **Two Roads-Live in Australia**. He was also a DJ for a cutting edge country show, editor of *Rhythms on the Ether* ("Australia's premier roots magazine"), and a member of a rockabilly trio with Gary Young and Mick Hamilton. In 1997, Glass resumed his solo career with

Smoke & Mirrors which has a more hard-core honky tonk, country rock sound than his previous recordings.

Going Over Old Ground/Virgin Aust./1989
Living Down My Past/Virgin Aust./1991
Rocking Cowboy (with Mick Hamilton and Gary Young)/1992
Smoke & Mirrors/Shock Aust./1997

Keith Glass, P.O. Box 298, Marrickville, New South Wales 2204, Australia

Keith Glass Page
//www.ozemail.com.au/~shownet/glass.html

massive@mpx.com.au

Go To Blazes
Rig Rock; Cowpunk; Country Rock
Philadelphia, Pennsylvania; 1987-1997

Go To Blazes formed in D.C. in 1987 but soon moved to Philly where they combined electric blues, country rock, Stones, and Southern rock on **Any Time...Anywhere** (produced by Eric Ambel) and **Love Lust and Trouble**. Both were released on the French label Skyranch, and three songs from these early recordings were included on the landmark Diesel Only compilations, **Rig Rock Juke Box** and **Rig Rock Truck Stop**. Go To Blazes' brand of rig rock was, in the beginning, dominated by crunchy power guitar with a hint of twang; what they called "diesel fueled cowpunk steeped in hillbilly blues." However, they also geared down into a more acoustic country groove and eventually gravitated toward a slightly mellower style. Their most "unplugged" recording, **And Other Crimes,** was originally released on Glitterhouse and contained mostly low key country rock covers of Lou Reed, Gene Clark, Kinky Friedman, Blue Mountain, and even Hank Williams, Jr. ("OD'd in Denver"). **Waiting Around for the Crash** (produced by Eric Ambel) on ESD generally continued this toned down country rock vibe. When ESD moved away from producing roots rock, Go To Blazes moved on with Glitterhouse (re-issued **Love, Lust and Trouble**) and found the success in Germany that had eluded them in the U.S. They were well-received at venues and festivals all over Germany, and their recordings got good reviews in the local music press including an especially flattering write up in German *Rolling Stone*. In 1998, GTB celebrated ten years together with the release of **Almost a Decade**, a 21 track collection of live cuts, demos, and B-sides from 1988-1997.

Keith Donnellan (d,v); Thomas Heyman (l.g.); Aldo Jones (b, to 1993); Ted Pappadopoulos (b); Ted Warren (g,v) with Joe Flood (f,md)

Go To Blazes/Skyranch Fr./1988
"Blood Beach" on **It's Hard to Be Cool in An Uncool World**/I Wanna/1988
Love, Lust and Trouble/Skyranch Fr./1990; Glitterhouse Ger./1997
"Pagan Baby" b/w "Bad Cup of Coffee"/Get Hip/1990 (7")

"Why I Drink" b/w "97 Miles"/Diesel Only/1992 (7")
"Why I Drink" and "97 Miles" on **Rig Rock Juke Box**/Diesel Only/1992
"Billy Bardo" on **Marijuana's Greatest Hits**/Re-Hash/1992
"Messed Up Again" on **Rig Rock Truck Stop**/Diesel Only/1993
"Got It Made"/"I Let You Down" b/w "Because I Do"/Estrus/1993 (7")
Any Time...Anywhere/ESD/1993
"Any Time...Anywhere" b/w "Live at the Mercury Lounge"/ESD/1993 (7")
And Other Crimes/Glitterhouse Ger./1994; GTB/1995
Waiting Around for the Crash/ESD/1996; Glitterhouse Ger./1997
"Underneath the Bottle" on **Cowpunks**/Vinyl Junkie/1996
"Bad Cup of Coffee" on **Kill the Moonlight**/SFTRI/1997
Almost A Decade/Glitterhouse Ger./1998

Go To Blazes Home Page //home.att.net/~tpsquanto/

tpsquanto@worldnet.att.net

Golden Delicious (Pete Krebs; Bingo)

New Old-Time; No Depression
Portland, Oregon; 1996-

Golden Delicious combines the spirited new old-time style of groups like the Highwoods String Band or the Freight Hoppers with the madcap attitude of the Holy Modal Rounders. Founded in 1996, they came from a diversity of musical experiences: percussionist Jesse Spero from punk bands including Miss Red Flowers and the Frances Farmer Gals; banjoist Kevin Richey from old-time and ethnic folk; bassist David Reisch from the aforementioned Holy Modal Rounders; guitarist Peter Krebs from the rock band Hazel; and fiddler Marilee Hord by way of classical training. Their first recording was a live EP showing a flair for unpredictable, crowd pleasing performances. In 1997, Golden Delicious was included on **Used to Be**, a compilation showcasing Pacific Northwest alt. country and made their full length debut with **Old School**. Here, fueled by Hord's hot fiddle and Richey's bouncing banjo, they take liberties with rousing renditions of "Darling Corey," "Monday Morning," and "Hot Corn, Cold Corn," throw in a bit of whackiness ("Hoo Doo Bash"; "Low Down Dog") and whimsical old-time/bluegrass originals ("Cletus for the Very Last Time, Get the Hell Out of Your Sister's Dress, For the Very Last Time"; "White Knuckle Breakdown"; "Raven Maggie") plus covers of Ernest Tubb ("Waltz Across Texas") and a swingy version of Smokey Wood's slightly suggestive word play song "Truckin'." As a side project, Krebs did two folk/acoustic solo recordings (**Brigadier**; **Western Electric**) and then a split CD (**Cavity Search**) with Golden Delecious' rousing modern old-time/bluegrass on on side and his more laid back singer/songwriter approach on the other. In early 1998, Golden Delicious took their aggressive old-time to a wider audience at SXSW but by the end of the year had broken up. Krebs went on to front the Gossamer Wings while banjoist Richey formed Bingo which uniquely mixes old-time/bluegrass with lo-fi roots rock and East Indian music. While at the University of Kansas, Richey had studied Eastern music and the sitar and in time became interested in the connections between Western and Eastern musical styles. The result is **H om** which has some fairly traditional Americana from old-time to shape note ("Yonder Hill"; "Walking Boss"; Tea Song"; "Cuckoo") along side lo-fi grunge country ("Tornadoes") and songs merging Eastern (raga) and Western influences (bluegrass to psychedelia) with Richey's banjo and Marilee Hord's fiddle interlaced with sitar courtesy of Saffs from Cornershop. The standard "Same Old Man" takes on a whole new texture and "Sham Ba Q'Allah," "Halla'q Ab Mahs," and "Zenith Raga" will bring nirvana closer to fans of old-time, **Revolver**-era Beatles, and Ravi Shankar.

Golden Delicious: Marilee Hord (f,v); Pete Krebs (g,l.s.); David Reisch (b,v); Kevin Richey (bj,g,v); Jessie Spero (perc)
Bingo: Kevin Richey (bj,sitar); Peter Archer (perc); Forest Bloodgood (viola); Marilee Hord (f); Clayton Jones (d); Saffs (sitar); Julia Weisenbeck (b)

Live EP/Cavity Search/1996
"Little Sadie" on **Used to Be: Blues From the Pacific Delta**/Undercover/1997
"Lamentations" (Kevin Richey) on **Used to Be: Blues From the Pacific Delta**/Undercover/1997
Old School/Cavity Search/1997
Brigadier (Pete Krebs)/Cavity Search/1997
Western Electric (Pete Krebs)/Cavity Search/1998
Cavity Search (Golden Delicious/Pete Krebs)/Cavity Search/1998
H om (Bingo)/Undercover/1998
Sweet Ona Rose (Pete Krebs and the Gossamer Wings)/Cavity Search/1999

Kevin Richey/Bingo //www.undercover.net

Pete Krebs //www.cavitysearchrecords.com

Golden Rough

Country Rock
Sydney, Australia; 1995-

Dave Orwell started Golden Rough in 1995 as a side project to his band Oliver. In addition to Orwell on guitar, pedal steel, and lead vocals, the original line-up included Tracy Eliis on bass and Marty McDonald on drums. Their lo-fi country pop rock sound was first heard on the EP, **It's a Heck of a Machine**, which has Orwell originals alongside covers of Elvis Costello, Willie Nelson, and Gram Parsons. After Orwell played guitar and pedal steel with Melbourne's excellent country roots rock band Love Me from 1996-1997 and Oliver broke up, Golden Rough became a full-time thing. Adding an edgier guitar thrust to their previous lo-fi style, they took on a more Son Volt/Wilco kind of ambience on **Twin Firs** which was recorded partly in a regular studio and partly in their 16 track analogue studio in an old house in Sydney. It ambles nicely "from ragged swinging country rock to bittersweet, harmony driven pop to sparse acoustic minimalism" with slide and lead guitar help from Brad Shepherd of the Hoodoo Gurus. In 1998, Helen Meany took over bass chores from Ellis and Jason Walker was brought on to handle electric guitar and pedal steel duties.

Tracy Ellis (b,1995-1997); Marty McDonald (d); Helen Meany (b,v,1998-); Dave Orwell (g,p.s.,v); Jason Walker (e.g.,p,p.s.,1998-)

It's A Heck of a Machine/Summershine Aust./1995 (EP)
Twin Firs/Summershine Aust./1997

Golden Rough //www.geocities.com/sunsetstrip/stage/7113/
goldenrough@hotmail.com

See Love Me

Golden Smog
No Depression; Grain Belt Rock
Minneapolis, Minnesota; 1992-

Just when you thought all the fun had gone out of modern country rock along comes a merry band of pranksters by the name of Golden Smog. In the late 1980s, several members of some of Minneapolis' hottest bands—Dan Murphy (Soul Asylum), Gary Louris (the Jayhawks), Marc Perlman (the Jayhawks), Kraig Johnson (Run Westy Run)—got together just to mess with the minds of the local punk crowd by doing classic rock covers by the Stones, Eagles, Thin Lizzy, Bad Company, et al. For contractual reasons, they hid their real identities under pseudonyms (taken from the streets on which they were born)—Jarrett Deacatur (Kraig Johnson), Raymond Virginia (Marc Perlman), Michael Macklyn (Gary Louris), David Spear (Dan Murphy); they dubbed themselves Golden Smog and in 1992 recorded the cleverly titled EP **On Golden Smog**. Eventually, Noah Levy aka Leonardson Saratoga of the Honeydogs signed on as drummer and Wilco's Jeff Tweedy (aka Scott Summitt) was invited to join. Golden Smog's full length **Down By the Old Mainstream** turned out to be a solid mixture of country, folk, and rock with obvious affinities to the Byrds and Gram Parsons and infused with lots of good natured humor on such songs as "Pecan Pie" (Tweedy) and "He's a Dick." To further reinforce their general tongue-in-cheek attitude, they issued a phony promotional box set **35 Years of Golden Smog** containing two dummy CDs and a booklet profiling the "history" of the group (alas, two albums from their early years, **America's Newest Shitmakers** and **Swingin' Smog People**, have been "lost to the sands of time"). By the end of 1997, Levy was replaced by Jody Stephens (Big Star), but Golden Smog, which started out as a whim, continued on as an important player in the alt. country sweepstakes touring and recording a new CD, **Weird Tales** which has bits and pieces of the various members' influences (roots rock, acoustic ballads, power pop) but is perhaps most memorable for its catchy

Byrdsian country rock tunes "To Call My Own," "Looking Forward to Seeing You," "Until You Came Along," and "Fear of Falling." For first generation alt. country guys like me, these jingly-jangly morning songs are a very pleasant walk down memory lane.

Kraig Johnson (e.g.,v); Noah Levy (d,1992-1997); Chris Mars (d,v,1992); Gary Louris (g,v); Dan Murphy (g,v); Marc Perlman (b); Jody Stephens (d, 1997-); Jeff Tweedy (g,v,1994-)

On Golden Smog/Crackpot/1992; 1996 (EP)
Down By the Old Mainstream/Rykodisc/1996
35 Years of Golden Smog...The Box Set/Rykodisc/1996 (pseudo promo box)
"V" b/w "Backstreet Girl"/Rykodisc/1996 (7" promo)
"Glad & Sorry" (live) on **American Songbook**/Vinyl Junkie UK/1996
"He's a Dick" on **Cowpunks**/Vinyl Junkie UK/1996
Weird Tales/Rykodisc/1998

Golden Smog/Rykodisc Page //www.rykodisc.com

The Golden Smog Page
//www.netcomuk.co.uk/~wozza/golden_smog_page.html

A Golden Smog Page
//www.thomtech.com/mmedia/thorm/goldensm.htm

Jason's Golden Smog Page
//trantor.cse.psu.edu/~fournier/gs.html

Markun Ramone's Smog Page
//plaza21.mbn.or.jp/~pecanpie/

See The Honeydogs; The Jayhawks; Uncle Tupelo; Wilco

Joe Goldmark
Pedal Steel; "Honky Tonk Avant-Billy"
San Francisco, California

Like his English counterpart and contemporary B. J. Cole, Joe Goldmark is committed to expanding the boundaries of pedal steel guitar playing. As Goldmark said, "there's no use recording 'Mansion on the Hill' when twenty guys have already done it," so he opted instead for "reworked psychedelic honky-tonk avant-billy" reflecting the musical experiences of his generation. What this means is interpretations of songs by everyone from Hendrix to Zappa, the Beatles to Steely Dan unlike any other steel playing you've ever heard. Goldmark's eclectic stylings originated in 1970 when, influenced by early country rock bands such as the Byrds, Flying Burrito Brothers, and New Riders of the Purple Sage, he took up the steel. After several years of local performances, Goldmark became a member of a band headed by former Commander Cody lead singer, Billy C. Farlow (1977-1978). In 1979, Goldmark toured with Peter Rowan then returned to the Bay Area where, in the 1980s, he was with the Texas Chainsaw Band and then Osage. Sandwiched between his work with these bands, Goldmark recorded three solo albums, **Pickin' My Pleasures**, **Vertigo**, and **Rockin' It**, that chronicle the development of his unique sound. Into the 1990s, he became even more adventurous with

All Over the Road. In the mid-late 1990s, Goldmark was a member of the Ray Price Club (with wife Kathi), Mental Revenge (1950s-1960s honky tonk music), and a spin off from Mental Revenge known as Jim Campilongo and the 10 Gallon Cats. The latter is an all instrumental band specializing in lead guitar/steel guitar duets *a la* the great Jimmy Bryant and Speedy West. On top of all this, Goldmark guested on a variety of recordings and compiled and published *The International Steel Guitar and Dobro Discography,* a massive listing of every steel guitar instrumental ever recorded (in its 8th edition). In 1996, Goldmark issued a "greatest hits" compilation, **The Goldmark Roundup**, with 20 cuts from his first three albums and followed this up with a tribute to the Fab Four, **Steelin' the Beatles**.

Pickin' My Pleasures/Lo-Ball/1979
Vertigo/Lo-Ball/1981
Rockin' It/Lo-Ball/1982
All Over the Road: The Pedal Excursions of Joe Goldmark/Lo-Ball/1995
The Goldmark Roundup/Lo-Ball/1996
Steelin' the Beatles/Lo-Ball/1997
The International Steel Guitar and Dobro Discography

Joe Goldmark 2259 14th Ave., San Francisco, CA 94116

Joe Goldmark/Don't Quit Your Day Job Page
//www.dqydj.com/jgoldmar.htm

Globe Records/Joe Goldmark Home Page
http://www.globerecords.com/Goldmark_Bio.html

See Jim Campilongo

Goober & The Peas

Psychocountry
Detroit, Michigan; 1989-1995

Their name might make you think they were a cutesy, traditional country band. Sure they wore fringed shirts, string ties, and cowboy hats and projected an image of simple, sentimental hillbillies, but don't be fooled. Goober & the Peas were a riotous send up of country laced with overdoses of r&b, hip-hop, and hard rock. **The Complete Works of ...** begins innocently enough with the simple acoustic number "Dear Grandpa" then segues into the down and dirty disco of "Funky Cowboy." Occasional flourishes of twisted country come out on "Consider Me" and "Druthers," but most of the material ("Up the Stairs," "Hot Women, Cold Beer," "Garden," "Let's Go Hunt for Grandpa") is moody blues or guitar rock. Scattered throughout there is back porch dialogue between lead singer Goober Miller and lead guitarist Junior Hendrickson mainly about Goober's luckless love life. **The Jet Age Genius of ...** is a great big pile of musical styles: jolting ("Sentimental Tina"; "Killing is Bad"), bluesy ("Loose Lips"), grungy ("E-Flat"), swingy ("Jump Ship"), psychedelic ("Alienation") but little twang. Goober & The Peas gave up the ghost in 1995. RIP. However, in 1998, Dan Miller aka Goober showed renewed signs of life by forming a group called 2 Star Tabernacle with two former Peas. They recorded a single of "gospel fried country" for Bloodshot with Andre "Mr. Rhythm" Williams in 1999.

Goober Miller (cl,org,sax,v); Jim "Shorty" Currie (r.g.); Jack "Doc" Gillis (d,1994-); Tom "Junior" Hendrickson, Jr. (bj,f,l.g.,l.s.,org); Damian "Doc" Lang (d, 1989-1993); Michael "Hoss" Miller (b,b.v.,1989-1993)

"The Complete Works of Goober & The Peas"/ Fortune/1989 (7")
The Complete Works of Goober & The Peas/Detroit Municipal Recordings/1992
A Christmas Eve Get Together with Goober & The Peas/Detroit Municipal Recordings/1993 (EP)
The Jet-Age Genius of Goober & the Peas/Detroit Municipal Recordings/1994
"Lily White Mama, Jet Black Daddy" (Andre Williams & 2 Star Tabernacle)/Bloodshot/1999 (7")

Unofficial Goober & The Peas Home Page
//www-personal.umich.edu/~jmtuttle/goober.htm

Steve Goodman

Singer/Songwriter; Americana
Chicago, Illinois; July 25, 1948-September 20, 1984

Country music fans are familiar with Steve Goodman primarily through two classic songs from the early 1970s: "City of New Orleans" (covered by Arlo Guthrie, Johnny Cash, Willie Nelson) and "You Never Even Call Me By My Name" ('The Perfect Country Song' covered and embellished by David Allan Coe). Most often labeled a folk singer, Goodman did several solo recordings in the 1970s that cover a wide range of Americana. His status among his musical peers is reflected in the number who did session work or made guest appearances on these albums; the list includes John Hartford, David Bromberg, Arlo Guthrie, Byron Berline, Bonnie Raitt, Bob Dylan, Jethro Burns, and John Prine. These latter two were Goodman's closest collaborators during his career. The great country/jazz mandolinist, Jethro Burns, who had come to fame with the parody duo Homer & Jethro, figured prominently on **Jessie's Jigs and Other Favorites**, **Words We Can Dance To**, and **Say It in Private** and accompanied Goodman on several tours. Prine, an old friend from the early 70s folk circuit, co-wrote a number of songs with Steve including "The 20th Century is Almost Over," "If She Were You," "How Much Tequila (Did I Drink Last Night)," and the aforementioned, "You Never Even Call Me By My Name" (Prine wanted to be uncredited because the song made fun of country music). Goodman contributed electric guitar to many of Prine's early recordings and produced his 1978 **Bruised Orange**. Like Prine, Goodman is a keen observer of American culture who transforms some of its simplest fads and foibles into tales filled with pathos and humor: "Door Number Three" (a country spoof on *Let's Make a Deal*); "Watching Scotty Glow"; "Elvis Imitators"; "Chicken Cordon Blues"; "A Dying Cub Fan's Last Request." The latter song had special poignancy in that Goodman was a rabid Cub's fan and suffered from leukemia for the last 15 years of his life until it took him in 1984. A tribute album with Prine, Burns Hartford, Bromberg, Guthrie, and many others was released in 1985 and several retrospectives of Goodman's best work are available.

Steve Goodman/Buddha/1971
Somebody Else's Troubles/Buddah/1972
Jessie's Jigs and Other Favorites/Asylum/1975
Words We Can Dance To/Asylum/1976
Sat It In Private/Asylum/1977
High and Outside/Asylum/1979
Affordable Art/Red Pajamas/1983
Artistic Hair/Red Pajamas/1983
Santa Ana Winds/Red Pajamas/1984
Tribute to Steve Goodman/Red Pajamas/1985
The Best of the Asylum Years, Vol. 1/Red Pajamas/1988
The Best of the Asylum Years, Vol. 2/Red Pajamas/1989
No Big Surprise: The Steve Goodman Anthology/Red Pajamas/1994

Steve Goodman/Oh Boy Page //www.ohboy.com/sg1.htm

See John Prine

Kevin Gordon

Singer/Songwriter; Roots Rock
Louisiana/Iowa/Nashville

Kevin Gordon's evolution as one of the late 1990s most promising roots rock singer/songwriters came in three phases. Early on, his musical aspirations were born and nurtured through exposure to the musical styles indigenous to Louisiana and by performances in clubs and dives around his native home in West Monroe. Later, while studying and crafting poetry at the University of Iowa's Writers Workshop in the mid-1980s, Gordon fell in with local musicians including A-1 singer/ songwriter Bo Ramsey who had a big impact on his musical and lyrical style. Kevin became especially sensitive to the lives and hard times of the farmers and small town people of the Midwest as reflected in his songwriting. He also absorbed Heartland roots rock influences and in 1993 made his first recording **Carnival Time**, a lively blend of Cajun, honky tonk, blues, and rockabilly with Ramsey and other Iowa players including top fiddler Al Murphy (ex-Bell & Shore). Moving on to Nashville, Gordon began to break through in the late 1990s with an EP, **Illinois 5 a.m.**, and then in 1998 the full-length **Cadillac Jack's #1 Son** which brings together swamp rock, Jerry Lee Lewis rockabilly, and Mid-West roots rock on one of the most highly praised "debuts" of the year. Produced by Garry Tallent of E Street Band fame, it evokes some comparisons with The Boss, but Gordon is much closer in his singing and songwriting to Dave Alvin and John Hiatt with songs like "Dissatisfied," "Blue Collar Dollar," and "Lucy and Andy Drive to Arkansas." One other song from the recording, "Fast Train" was co-written with another very talented but over looked Nashville based songwriter, Gwil Owen. This tune was covered by rockabilly

veteran Sonny Burgess, and another Gordon/Owen song, "Deuce and a Quarter" was picked up for an album by All the King's Men (Scotty Moore, D. Fontana, Levon Helm, Keith Richard).

Carnival Time/Taxim/1993
Illinois 5 a.m./1997 (EP)
Cadillac Jack's #1 Son/Shanachie/1998

Kevin Gordon //www.nashville.net/~kate/kgordon.html

See Gwil Owen; Bo Ramsey

Roxy Gordon

Singer/Songwriter; Artist; Writer
Ballinger, Texas

My introduction to the work of Roxy Gordon came through his song "Indians" on the 1997 **Jukebox Cowboy** compilation. This remarkable song, spoken by Gordon in a soft drawl with mid-tempo country rock accompaniment, offers a humorous checklist of who/what is and is not Indian: Hank Williams, Chuck Berry, Willie Nelson, Los Angeles, Ft. Worth, Africa, baseball, poetry, Crazy Horse, circles/random lines are but JFK, Michael Jackson, the president of Baylor University, New York, Dallas, Europe, football, journalism, Custer, straight lines, expecting to live forever ain't. Intrigued, I delved deeper and found that Gordon, a Texas born Choctaw/Assiniboine Sioux, has had a long and varied career as writer, artist, and musician. In the mid-1970s, he edited and published *Picking Up the Tempo: A Country Western Journal* which mostly covered the Texas progressive/outlaw scene. Moving to Dallas in the late 1970s, Gordon worked on a musical career and also became an accomplished poet whose focus is Native American history and issues. Many of Gordon's poems were the basis for the songs he recorded on four albums. Unlike "Indians" (from his 1997 **Smaller Circles**, originally recorded in 1990), most of Roxy's compositions such as "Crazy Horse Is Alive," "Gods," "Joe Hill," and "Murder" are scathing indictments of continuing injustices against Native Americans and the poor and working classes in general. His understated but potent delivery and vivid imagery backed by the likes of Wes McGhee (who re-mastered **Smaller Circles**) and Max Johnston (Wilco; Freakwater) pack quite a wallop. Gordon has also expressed his outrage as a playwright (*Big Pow Wow; Indian Radio Days*) and author of several collections of essays and short stories (i.e. *Breeds*). He lived in Dallas running the Wowapi publishing company with his wife Judy until 1997 when he had to move to the tiny West Texas town, Talpa, to take care of his invalid mother and grandmother. Gordon's Assiniboine name is Toe Ga Juke Juke Gan Hok Sheena which means First Coyote Boy.

Crazy Horse Never Died/Sunstorm UK/199?
Smaller Circles/Road Goes on Forever UK/1997
"Indians" on **Jukebox Cowboy**/Vinyl Junkie UK/1997

Roxy Gordon/Wowapi, Route 1, Box 62, Talpa, TX 76882

See Geronimo Trevino III

Skip Gorman

Cowboy/Western
Providence, Rhode Island; May 18, 1949-

Most Americans' exposure to cowboy music has been through the singing cowboys of the Nashville or Hollywood variety. Skip Gorman acknowledges their contribution but believes it is important to present a more realistic portrait of the cowboy/cattle culture that thrived in the late 19th century. His dedication to authenticity is apparent in recordings of traditional cowboy music (**A Greener Prairie**; **Lonesome Prairie Love**) and frequent appearances before public school students where, dressed in period costume, he uses songs and stories to acquaint children with the "real" Old West. A native of Rhode Island, Gorman would seem an unlikely candidate for cowboy singer, but he was fortunate as a boy in having access to the records of Jimmie Rodgers whom he emulated in singing and guitar style. Gorman also had an early interest in bluegrass music and took up fiddle and mandolin in his teens. His skill on the latter instrument caught the attention of Bill Monroe who invited him to pick with him during a New England bluegrass festival. After graduation from Brown University, Gorman traveled to Ireland and Scotland to study traditional fiddling; in 1970, he moved to Utah where he became a member of the Deseret String Band and got first hand exposure to cowboy culture. It was at this time that Gorman was exposed to the recordings of Carl Sprague, Jack Lee, and other old-time cowboy singers. Gorman was hooked, threw himself whole hog into cowboy/western music, and began to develop his Old West persona. His interpretations blend cowboy music with bluegrass, Celtic, and even Native American styles. Each summer he spends time at a ranch near Cody, Wyoming working as a wrangler and guide by day and entertainer at night for "dudes" on vacation.

> **Land of Milk & Honey** (with the Deseret String
>   Band)/Okehdokee/1974
> **Powder River** (with Ron Kane)/Folk Legacy/1978
> **New Englander's Choice**/Folk Legacy/1983
> **Trail to Mexico**/Folk Legacy/1985
> **Feast Here Tonight** (with Rick Starkey)/Marimac/1988
> **Music of John Taggart** (as New Hampshire Fiddler's
>   Union)/1989
> **The Old Style Mandolin**/Marimac/1991
> **Late Last Night** (with Rick Starkey)/Marimac/1991
> **A Greener Prairie**/Rounder/1994
> **Lonesome Prairie Love**/Rounder/1996

The Gourds

Austin; Roots Rock
Austin, Texas; 1992-

Along with the Bad Livers, the Gourds have been the most successful at breaking out of the Austin alt. country mold that has leaned heavily toward honky tonkers and singer/songwriters. Most often compared to roots bands like The Band, their sound clearly shows "Third Coast" (Texas/Louisiana) influences absorbed by members Claude Bernard, Kevin Russell, and Jimmy Smith who were all raised in the region. Smith and Russell played together in the early 1990s in the popular Shreveport, Louisiana alternative band Picket Line Coyotes. When that group ended, they wound up in Austin where they met accordionist Bernard. With the addition of English drummer Charlie Llewellin, the Gourds were born and began moving into the Austin scene. They played clubs, appeared at the Austin Acoustic Music Festival, and like many another Austin band cut a live tape on KUT radio. Bolstered by an enthusiastic reception, the Gourds signed with Munich and recorded **Dem's Good Beeble** which was very favorably received by a growing list of fans and reviewers. What they all found so appealing was the winning combination of fine musicianship, top notch songwriting (by Russell and Smith), and glowing harmonies. On the heels of this success, the band toured Europe and the East Coast and were included in 1996 and 1997 on tribute albums to the Replacements and Fleetwood Mac. Late in 1997, Llewellin left on amicable terms, and the rest of the Gourds carried on throwing the first annual Beeble Fest at Stubb's in Austin with the Old 97s, Skeletons, Jon Dee Graham, and the Damnations. In 1998 the Gourds made a strong claim to the title of The Band of the 90s on **Stadium Blitzer**. With help from Amy Boone and Robert Bernard of the Damnations, they laid down a potent potpourri of Americana with several tips of the hat to The Band especially on tunes such as "Magnolia" and "Cold Bed." However, like fellow Austin experimenters the Bad Livers, the Gourds show they aren't afraid to mix old-time/bluegrass/country/folk with music/sounds from outside that tradition, and they like to throw in some high weirdness ("Stadium Blitzer"; "I Ate the Haggis") just to keep things really interesting. The Gourds enjoy reworking songs from other genres such as they did with David Bowie's "Ziggy Stardust" and Snoop Dogg's "Gin n' Juice" on their 1998 EP **Gogetyourshinebox** which also has some live cuts from **Stadium Blitzer**. They scored a major coup in late 1998 when multi-instrumentalist Max Johnston, who had been with Uncle Tupelo, Wilco, and Freakwater, hopped aboard the Gourds Americana merry-go-round; drummer Keith Langford moved over from the Damnations TX at about the same time. Both were on hand for the Gourds 1999 release **Ghosts of Hallelujah**.

Claude Bernard (acc,g,perc,v); Max Johnston (bj,f,md, 1998-); Keith Langford (d,1998-); Charlie Llewellin (d,1994-1997); Kevin Russell (bj,g,md,perc,v); Jimmy Smith (b,g,perc,v)

> **KUT Radio Live Set, 1995**/Munich/1995 (CS)
> **Dem's Good Beeble**/Munich/1996
> **Clear Night**/Munich/1996 (UK promo EP)
> "I Know I'm Not Wrong" on **Patron Saints of Pop**/ Undercover/1997
> "My Favorite Thing" on **So What!: An Austin Tribute to the Replacements**/1997
> **Stadium Blitzer**/Watermelon/1998
> **Gogitchyershinebox**/Watermelon/1998
> "Barstool Blues" on **Welcome to High Sierra**/High Sierra/1998
> "All the Labor" on **Loose: New Sounds of the Old West**/Vinyl Junkie UK/1998
> **Ghosts of Hallelujah**/Munich/1999

The Gourds Home Page //www.thegourds.com

Seagreen@eden.com

The Gourds Fan Page //members.aol.com/burned/gourds.html

Cucurbitaceae: The Gourds Mailing List //www.onelist.com/subscribe.cgi/cucurbitaceae/

The Max Johnston Homepage //www.trailerpark.com/moonwalk/bboy/johnston.htm

See Damnations TX

Earl Lee Grace
Aggressive Bluegrass
1995-

The Dwarves made their reputation in the 1990s as one of shock-rock's most outrageuos groups through blood-drenched concerts, controversial off-stage stunts, ungodly hardcore punk, and highly offensive albums. **Horror Stories**, **Blood**, **Guts & Pussy**, and **Lucifer's Crank** should give you a pretty good idea of where they're coming from. Their leader Blag Dahlia, who also goes by Blag Jesus or Julius Seizure, took on a completely unexpected new persona in 1995 when as Earl Lee Grace he recorded **Blackgrass**. Released by Sympathy for the Record Industry, it is basically a bluegrass album and does indeed feature some really fine old-time picking by Alan Bond (mandolin), Brian Godchaux (fiddle), Jim Mintun (dobro), Jonathan Schiele (banjo), P. Alan Wooton (guitar), and Grace's one-time roommate, honky tonk iconoclast, Wilson Gil (on "everything else"). The lead vocals are handled by Grace (except one number by Dee Lannon) who forsakes the high lonesome for a fairly dead-pan (but enjoyable) delivery with a defiant, almost angry edge. And with twisted and often disturbing song titles/lyrics like "Saturday Night" (Dwarves cover about hedonism and murder), "Every Girl in the World," "Sharon Needles," and "So Good" ("I'm young and I'm dumb

and I'm misunderstood but I fuck so good"), you know you've gone way beyond "Rocky Top." Grace revealed in personal correspondence that he did **Blackgrass** "because I got sick of rock 'n' roll, I couldn't do hip/hop, and new country music sucks," and he plans on a sequel. Meantime, as Blag Dahlia, he's leading the Dwarves into a second decade of "warping the minds of a generation."

> **Blackgrass**/Sympathy for the Record Industry/1995

The Dwarves //members.iquest.net/~teevie/dwarves.html

Blag Dahlia/Earl Lee Grace dwarves@sirius.com

See Wilson Gil

The Grandsons (of the Pioneers)
Americana
Arlington, Virginia; 1990-

Talk about versatility! A perusal of the Grandsons "song list" shows that at any given performance they can cover Thelonius Monk, Johnny Horton, Duke Ellington, Bob Wills, Elvis, Gene Vincent, Dr. John, Buck Owens, Hank Williams, Slim Harpo, Buddy Holly, Screamin' Jay Hawkins and a host of others. On record (**Howdy From. . .** and **It's Hip to Flip With**), they explore the same vast territory but mostly on originals such as "So Long" (country swing), "I Now Realize" (Tex-Mex), "Surf-O-Rama," "Zulu Queen" (mambo), "I'm Not Going to be Your Problem" (Cajun), and "The Road to No Good" (jump blues). Underlying the diversity is a lighthearted spirit and joy in the music as on "It Works for Me," "Silly Dilly," "Yodel Your Blues Away"; think of the Iguanas with a Marx Brothers attitude. The secret of their appeal lies in the exuberant lead vocals of Alan MacEwen and the double treat playing of Chris Watling who switches off on accordion and saxes. Because of their ability to wear many hats, the Grandsons (formerly known as the Grandsons of the Pioneers) have been invited to open for a wide variety of touring acts (Dirty Dozen Brass Band to Jimmie Dale Gilmore) and have appeared at a wide range of music festivals (SXSW, Wolf Trap, Black Mountain). They are also one of the most popular and acclaimed bands in the DC/Northern Virginia area; they were awarded a Wammie for Best Roots Rock Group in 1995 and 1996. In 1997 and 1998, "the hardest working band in DC" continued its frenetic performance schedule, contributed "Blue Shadows" to a Blasters tribute album, and finished another stirring collection of musical eclectica called **Pan-American Shindig**.

Jon Danforth (d,1990-1991); Bill Hansen (b,v,1990-1991); Rickey Jordan (b,v); Alan MacEwen (g,trp,v); Matthew Sedgley (d); Chris Watling (acc,sax)

> **Howdy From...The Grandsons of the Pioneers**/Whirling House/1991
> **It's Hip to Flip With**/Whirling House/1994
> "Pretty Bad Blues" on **Big D.C. Jamboree, Vol. 3**/Run Wild/1994

"Bethlehem Bound" (with Bill Kirchen) on **A Holiday Feast, Vol. 1**/HFM/ 1995
"The Day the World Turned Blue" and "Jezebel Had a Party" on **Turning the World Blue: A Tribute to Gene Vincent**/Skizmatic/1996
"Yorgi The Yodeling Reindeer" on **A Holiday Feast, Vol. 2**/HFM/1997
"Blue Shadows" on **Blastered: A Musical Tribute to the Blasters**/Run Wild/1998
Pan-American Shindig/Whirling House/1998

The Grandsons, P.O. Box 7622, Arlington, VA 22207; 703-243-WEST

The Grandsons Home Page
//www.clark.net/pub/wil/grandsons/index.htm

Grandsons@aol.com

Granfaloon Bus (The Lords of Howling)
Lo-Fi Country Roots Rock
San Francisco, California; c. 1990-

Granfaloon Bus follows in the tradition of late 1980s-early 1990s San Francisco bands such as American Music Club, Camper Van Beethoven, Tarnation, and Dieselhed who experimented to one degree or another with rock/country hybrids. Of all these groups, GB became the most improvisational as they developed a highly atmospheric, neo-country/Velvet Underground style. Their founder Todd Felix Costanza had previously led the Whitefronts who also dabbled in rock and country from 1985-1987. Several members of that band (Anne Costanza, David Costanza) later moved to New Mexico and started yet another alt. country experiment called the Lords of Howling. They established their own label (Discobolus) on which they released ten Lords cassettes plus the Granfaloon Bus CD debut, **A Love Restrained** which was produced by ex-Camper Van Beethoven violinist Jonathan Segal. And while GB became fairly well-known in the Bay Area, their destiny lay in Germany. Like Blue Rose and Glitterhouse, Trocadero Records had become a solid anchorage for ex-patriate alt. country acts from the States. They signed Granfaloon Bus who, in between making records, regularly toured Germany where they became quite popular with the music media for their melancholy country roots rock. They also returned to San Francisco peridocially, but in the late 1990s, Germany increasingly became their second home (*Many thanks to Carl Zimring of WRCT in Pittsburgh for providing most of my information on Granfaloon Bus).

Todd Felix Costanza (g,v); Alex Green (g); Jeff Palmer (d); Jeff Stevenson (b,v)

It's All Just Parlor Tricks/GB/1990 (CS)
A Love Restrained/Discobolus/1992
"Slip Away" b/w "Coffee Girl"/Hairy/1994 (7")
Rocket Noon/Trocadero Ger./1996
Sleeping Car/Trocadero Ger./1997
"OK" on **Luxury Liner, Vol. 1**/Glitterhouse Ger./1997
"The Mission Song" on **San Francisco: A Music City Compilation**/Trocadero Ger./1998

Good Funeral Weather/Trocadero Ger./1998

Granfaloon Bus, 418 Capp St., San Francisco, CA 94110

Granfaloon Bus //www.granfaloonbus.com

johnny.safety@eviltron.com

Granfaloon Bus/Trocadero: trocadero@bigfoot.de

Lords of Howling/Discobolus Records, HC 81 Box 629, Questa, NM 87556; 505-586-1429

Lords of Howling //www.sirius.com/~magnetic/lords.html

See American Music Club; Camper Van Beethoven

Trond Granlund
Singer/Songwriter
Norway

Although it might seem surprising, Norway is a major center for alternative country and Americana. Not only is it home to some of the music's most dedicated and knowledgeable fans (Tom Ekeberg, Frode Jensen, Tommy Nordeng, and Tom Skjeklesaether all have outstanding alt. country web sites) and one of the best Americana festivals (Down on the Farm), but it has also produced some excellent performers including Somebody's Darling and Trond Granlund. Most of my information about the latter comes from his 1993 CD, **I Can't Quit Now,** which I picked up for 50 cents at a rummage sale in Austin, Texas in 1995. Since that time, it has been one of my personal favorites. The recording has much of the classic Texas singer/songwriter feel to it with expansive story songs, Granlund's grainy vocals (Guy Clark, Townes Van Zandt), and nice and easy country/rock accompaniment (fiddle, dobro, pedal steel, electric guitar, accordion) provided by his all Norwegian band, the Hillbilly Cats. **I Can't Quit Now** is also greatly bolstered by the presence of veteran singer/songwriters Eric Andersen and Tom Pacheco. The former, who had a successful career as a folkie in the late 1960s and early 1970s and did several light country rock albums, penned three excellent numbers for this recording ("Today is the Highway"; "Close the Door Lightly"; "Hey Babe") and also chips in with support on acoustic guitar, harmonica, and shared vocals on Granlund's breezy "Driftin'." Pacheco contributes acoustic guitar, but his main contribution is "Blue Montana Sky" and the amusing historical revision "Nobody Ever Killed Billy the Kid." One other song deserving mention is "The Way I Feel" (by Kulseth & Kulseth) which contains the memorable line "I'm Hank Williams lonesome, Jimmy Rodgers blue, and I'll be George Jones drunk before the night is through." The band gets to strut its stuff on two rousing instrumentals, "Waitin' for the Federals" and "Old Joe Clark." Granlund has also collaborated with Bill Booth who heads the Norwegian band the Convertibles and runs Wheeling Records.

Hillbilly Cats: Jan Roger Fjeldberg (d); Trond Granlund (a.g.,l.v.); Niles Halleland (db,md); Rune Haukum (b); Tore Heggelund (e.g.); Gjermund Kolltveit (acc,f)

Promise the Moon/1989
Pleasure & Tears/1992
I Can't Quit Now/Wheeling/1993

Trond Granlund/Wheeling Records
//www.nordi.no/music/wheeling/

See Bill Booth; Tom Pacheco

The Grateful Dead; Jerry Garcia (Old and In the Way)

Country Rock
San Francisco, California; 1965-1995

Primarily known as the kings of psychedelic rock, the Grateful Dead were also for a brief time one of the best country rock bands of the early 1970s. Their affinity for country was the product of Jerry Garcia's early interest in old-time country and bluegrass which he expressed in the early 1960s as a member of the Bay Area Mother McCree's Uptown Jug Champions (included future Dead members Pigpen and Bob Weir). When the Grateful Dead first came together, they were pretty much an experimental jazz/rock group but eventually returned to their country roots on two albums in 1970, **Workingman's Dead** and **American Beauty**. Both featured Garcia on pedal steel and offer some by now classic tunes: "Truckin'," "Casey Jones," "Sugar Magnolia," "Friend of the Devil," "Ripple" (the latter two with David Grisman on mandolin). Around this same time, Garcia, Mickey Hart, and Phil Lesh launched a country side project that grew out of an informal session with John Dawson and David Nelson. The result was the New Riders of the Purple Sage which opened for several Dead performances. But, the stress of being in two bands at once proved too much for Garcia, Hart, and Lesh, and they dropped out although Garcia stayed on to play steel guitar on the NRPS debut. As a group, the Dead continued to record country songs (covers of Merle Haggard, Marty Robbins, Kris Kristofferson) over the years but would not record a full album of traditional music until the acoustic **Reckoning** which offered many old-time/bluegrass selections. However, Garcia as a solo or in collaboration with others returned time and again to country and participated in some key alt. country projects in the 1970s. In 1973, he and Grisman founded one of the most important progressive bluegrass bands of the day when they joined Peter Rowan, Vassar Clements, and John Kahn as Old and In the Way. Their 1975 self-titled release played a huge part in a major bluegrass revival by introducing a whole generation of rock raised kids to bluegrass; it is still the best selling bluegrass album of all time. And while the group was together less than a year, they recorded enough material for subsequent recordings, **That High Lonesome Sound** and **Breakdown**, released in the 1990s on Grisman's Acoustic Disc label. The Garcia/Grisman connection continued into the mid-1970s when Jerry played banjo in David's Great American Music Band. During this period, Garcia produced Frank Wakefield's excellent Good Ol' Boys bluegrass band for the Grateful Dead label. In 1987, Garcia assembled the Jerry Garcia Acoustic Band with David Nelson (ex-New Riders), John Kahn, David Kemper, Kenny Kosek, and Sandy Rothman. They toured and recorded **Almost Acoustic** which covers traditional country and country blues. He continued his long musical association with David Grisman doing **Garcia & Grisman** and **Not For Kids Only** in the early 1990s. After Garcia's death in 1995, Grisman issued the first installment of a series of recordings done with Garcia in 1990. **Shady Grove** consists mostly of folk material, but future discs would present the duo on country, jazz, bluegrass, and acoustic rock. 1998's **So What** features Garcia/Grisman interpretations of jazz tunes by Miles Davis and Milt Jackson.

The Grateful Dead: Jerry Garcia (l.g.,p.s.,v); Mickey (d); Bill Kreutzmann (d); Phil Lesh (b); Ron McKernan (org,v); Bob Weir (g,v).
Old And in The Way: Vassar Clements (f); Jerry Garcia (bj,g,v); David Grisman (md); John Kahn (b); Peter Rowan (g,v).
The Jerry Garcia Acoustic Band: Jerry Garcia (bj,g,v); John Kahn (b); David Kemper (d); Kenny Kosek (f); David Nelson (a.g.,v); Sandy Rothman (db,md)

> **Workingman's Dead**/Warner Brothers/1970
> **American Beauty**/Warner Brothers/1970
> **New Riders of the Purple Sage**/Columbia/1971
> **Old and in the Way**/Rounder/1973
> **Reckoning**/Arista/1981
> **Almost Acoustic** (Jerry Garcia Acoustic Band)/Grateful Dead/1988
> **Garcia & Grisman**/Acoustic Disc/1991
> **Not For Kids Only** (Garcia & Grisman)/Acoustic Disc/1993
> **Old and in the Way: That High Lonesome Sound**/Acoustic Disc/1996
> **Shady Grove** (Garcia & Grisman)/Acoustic Disc/1996
> **Old and In the Way: Breakdown**/Acoustic Disc/1997
> **So What** (Garcia & Grisman)/Acoustic Disc/1998

The Official Grateful Dead Homepage //www.dead.net (has connections to dozens of other GD web sites)

The Jerry Site http://www.deadlists.com/jerry/index.html

See David Grisman; The New Riders of the Purple Sage

The Great Western Orchestra

Cowboy Western
Turner Valley, Alberta, Canada; 1985-

Although the cowboy is most often associated with the American West, the Canadian West is home to an equally vibrant cowboy culture. One group which celebrates the old and new Canadian West is the Great Western Orchestra. Originally formed in 1985, GWO consisted of Cindy Church (now with Quartette and solo), Nathan Tinkham (Cindy Church; Ian Tyson), and San Franciscan Dave Wilkie. Their style was a contemporary blend of cowboy/western, swing, and Cajun which they put together on one eponymous LP before splitting up in 1989. A guest musician on GWO's debut, Stewart

MacDougall, then teamed with Wilkie to create a new Great Western Orchestra. Both had been members of Ian Tyson's Chinook Arch Riders (though not at the same time), but didn't meet until 1987 when they were in Katy Moffatt's swing band, the Cowtowns. In 1990, the MacDougall/Wilkie duo released **Wind in the Wire**, a collection of traditional and original cowboy songs, cowboy boogie, and swing. They paid tribute to the Native American experience in the Canadian/American West on this album and especially on its sequel, **Buffalo Ground**. Their song "Wind in the Wire" about the struggle of the Nez Perce was covered by Ian Tyson and Randy Travis. The GWO made regular appearances at Canadian folk and western festivals, performed with the Edmonton Symphony Orchestra, had several songs on *Northern Exposure*, and had "Wind in the Wire" included on a Canadian Cowboy tribute, **Word From the Ranch** (with Ian Tyson, Cindy Church, Nathan Tinkham, Quartette). In addition to his work with the Great Western Orchestra, Wilkie, who gained renown in the 1970s as "The Mandolin Kid," recorded several solo albums including **Cowboy Celtic** which acknowledges English, Irish, Scottish contributions to cowboy and western music. For the follow-up, **Cowboy Ceilidh**, Wilkie took his band to Ireland and Scotland to research the roots of classic cowboy songs and record with local musicians (e.g. Phil Cunningham). The result is an interesting conjoining of familiar songs of the Old West with their Celtic antecedents: "The Cowboy's Lament"/"The Brad of Armagh"; "Bucking Bronco"/"My Love Is a Rider"; "Buffalo Gals"/"The Old Chisholm Trail"/"The Blacksmith's Reel"; "Buffalo Skinners"/ "Clifford's Polka."

Original Great Western Orchestra: Cindy Church (g,v); Nathan Tinkham (l.g.); Dave Wilkie (md,v)
Current Great Western Orchestra: Stewart MacDougall (g,v); Dave Wilkie (md,v)
Cowboy Celtic: David Wilkie (g,md,mda,v); Wyatt Wilkie (md); Denise Whithnell (g,h.v.)

> **Great Western Orchestra**/1988
> **Wind in the Wire**/Centrefire Can./1990
> **Buffalo Ground**/Centrefire/1993
> **Shoebox** (David Wilkie)/Centrefire/1994
> **Cowboy Celtic** (David Wilkie)/Centrefire/1995
> **Cowboy Ceilidh** (David Wilkie)/Centrefire/1997
> "Wind in the Wire" (GWO) on **Word From the Range: A Canadian Cowboy Collection**/Glenbow Museum Can./1998

The Great Western Orchestra Home Page
//www.nucleus.com/~cowboy/gwonew.html

Dave Wilkie/Cowboy Celtic Home Page
//www.nucleus.com/~cowboy/davewilkie.html

See Quartette; Ian Tyson

The Great Western Squares
Country Rock
Dublin, Ireland; 1996-

In summer 1996, a pub in Dublin called The Hut began playing host to a music showcase put on by the local Johnny Cash Appreciation Society. Gary Fitzpatrick and Oona White of the punk group Pincher Martin became regulars at the event (later moved to the White Horse Pub) accompanied by mandolinist Gary O'Growney aka Gog and doing surprising country covers of the Bee Gees, Motorhead, Sonny Rollins, and Adam Ant. Eventually, what had started out as a lark became serious in 1997 after Fitzpatrick, White, and Gog invited some musical acquaintances to join them in the studio to record their unorthodox country songs (Pincher Martin was originally scheduled to use the studio but their equipment malfunctioned). These sessions yielded **Judas Steer**, a 13 song collection of country/roots rock covers including John Prine, Gram Parsons, and several originals. Taking the name Great Western Squares (from a street sign), the new band began playing local clubs/pubs and in 1998 recorded **Almost Sober** which this time had 11 originals and only two covers. The material (mostly from Fitzpatrick's pen) swings back and forth between friendly lo-fi country rock including a moody laid-back cover of Haggard's "Sing Me Back Home" and rollicking hoedown numbers including a cowpunkish "Luxury Liner" (Gram Parsons). Fitzpatrick and White trade off lead and harmony vocals and, overall, the Great Western Squares give a good account of themselves and a preview of what's sure to be better things to come.

Stan Erraught (dulc,e.g.,sl.g.); Gary Fitzpatrick (a.g.,v); Pat McGauley (b); Alan Murphy (d); Gary O'Growney (md); Tim Rogers (f,md); Oona White (v)

> **Judas Steer**/Blunt Independent Ire./1997
> **Almost Sober**/Blunt Independent Ire./1998

Great Western Squares c/o Blunt/Independent Records, 35A Barrow St., Dublin 4, Ireland; independent@tinet.ie

Great Western Squares/Blunt Page
//homepage.tinet.ie/~independentrecs/

Green on Red (Danny and Dusty; Chris Cacavas; Chuck Prophet; Dan Stuart)
Desert Rock
Tucson, Arizona; 1981-1987

For a brief period in the early 1980s, there was a movement in rock known as the "paisley underground." Mostly centered in L.A., it included bands such as Dream Syndicate and Rain Parade who played 1960s influenced psychedelic music. One non-California group that was part of this genre was Tucson's Green on Red. Unlike their counterparts, however, they blended psychedelia with country and blues much in the tradition of early Neil Young or Dylan's country recordings.

Green on Red evolved from a band formed in 1981 known as the Serfers with Van Christian, Dan Stuart, Jack Waterson. When Alex MacNicol took over drumming chores and Chris Cacavas came on board to play keyboards, the band became Green on Red and recorded an EP, **Two Bibles**, followed by a self-titled record, and **Gravity Talks**. These first efforts showed 1960s folk and rock influences but also hinted at things to come. In 1985, when Chuck Prophet joined as lead guitarist, Green on Red released **Gas Food Lodging** and **No Free Lunch** which were both more full blown country rock/roots rock recordings. Their sound, which was similar to fellow Arizona band Giant Sand, came to be known as Desert Rock for its blending of rock and roots music with a Southwestern flavor. As Danny & Dusty, Cacavas and Stuart further explored the territory where rock meets country on **The Lost Weekend** with Steve Wynn and members of the Long Ryders (this album was reissued in 1996 in the wake of alt. country's new wave). And while Green on Red had limited success in the U.S., they were fervently welcomed in Europe and toured there extensively in 1986. However, during this time tensions within the band began to surface and in 1987, after the issue of **The Killer Inside Me,** Cacavas and Waterson split. The remaining members continued to mine rock, country, and blues (with mixed results) into the early nineties before going on to solo careers. In general, the alumni of Green on Red continued on with the country rock/roots rock sound of their original band; Chuck Prophet as a solo artist, Dan Stuart as both soloist (retired in 1998) and with Al Perry, and Chris Cacavas with his band Junkyard Love.

Green on Red: Chris Cacavas (kybrds); Alex MacNichol (d); Chuck Prophet IV (l.g.); Dan Stuart (g,v); Jack Waterson (b) **Danny and Dusty:** Chris Cacavas (p) and Dan Stuart (l.v.) with Dennis Duck (d,v); Sid Griffin (db,g,v); Stephen McCarthy (g,l.s.,v); Tom Stevens (b); Steve Wynn (g,l.v.). **Chris Cacavas and Junkyard Love:** Chris Cacavas (g,v); Keith Mitchell (d); Tom Stevens (b); John Thoman (l.g.); Mark Walton (b)

Two Bibles/1981 (EP)
Green on Red/Down There/1982; Enigma/1984 (EP)
Gravity Talks/Slash/1983
Rhythm Roundup (Chuck Prophet & Wild Game)/ Dangerous Rhythm/1984
Gas Food Lodging/Enigma/1985
No Free Lunch/Mercury/1985 (EP)
The Lost Weekend (Danny and Dusty)/A&M/1985; Prima/1996
"Bend of the River" (Danny and Dusty) on **Don't Shoot**/Zong and **Acres for Cents**/Zippo/Demon/1985
The Killer Inside Me/Mercury/1987
You Can Run...But You Can't Hide/FFO boot/1988
Whose Dog? (Jack Waterson)/Heyday/1988
Here Come the Snakes /Restless/1989
Live at the Town and Country Club/1989 (EP)
Chris Cacavas and Junkyard Love/Heyday/1989
Brother Aldo (Chuck Prophet)/Fire/1990
Scapegoats /1991
Balinese Dancer (Chuck Prophet)/China/1993
Good Time (Chris Cacavas)/Heyday/1995
Can O'Worms (Dan Stuart)/Monkey Hill/1995

New Improved Pain (Chris Cacavas)/Normal Ger./1996
Feast of Hearts (Chuck Prophet)/China/1996
What Were We Thinking?/Corduroy Australia/1996 (demos and radio sessions 1980-1987)
Homemade Blood (Chuck Prophet)/Cooking Vinyl UK/1997
"Ooh Wee" (Chuck Prophet) on **San Francisco: A Music City Compilation**/Trocadero Ger./1998
"Tonight's the Night" (Chris Cacavas) on **This Note's For You Too!: A Tribute to Neil Young**/Inbetweens Dut./1998

Chuck Prophet/Green on Red Home Page
//home3.swipenet.se/~w-33845/cpgor/index.htm

Unofficial Green on Red Home Page
//www.csc.liv.ac.uk/users/micks/green/

Chris Cacavas Page //www.w2.com/heyday.html

The Lost Weekend Mailing List
//www.geofysik.aau.dk/~thomas/wynn/mailing-list.html (devoted to discussion of Green on Red and alumni; Danny & Dusty; the Long Ryders; the Coal Porters; the Continental Drifters). To subscribe e-mail mmorris@oeonline.com

See Giant Sand; Sid Griffin; Al Perry

Richard Greene

Fiddle; Progressive Bluegrass; Newgrass; Country Rock
Hollywood, California; November 9, 1942-

Like his contemporary David Grisman, Richard Greene is a virtuoso instrumentalist who as a session player, band member, and band leader has been involved in some of the most important country rock, progressive bluegrass, and newgrass projects of the past three decades. A Los Angeles native, Greene started out in various local bluegrass bands in the early 1960s before graduating to a two year stint with Bill Monroe. In the late 1960s and early 1970s, Greene branched out in a number of directions as a member of Jim Kweskin's Jug Band, the country/rock/fusion group Seatrain (with Peter Rowan), two very influential progressive bluegrass groups Old and In the Way (David Grisman, Peter Rowan, Jerry Garcia) and Muleskinner (Grisman, Rowan, Clarence White, Bill Keith), the Great American Music Band (Grisman; Taj Mahal), and Loggins and Messina. He also formed the Blue Velvet Band with Keith, Jim Rooney, and Eric Weissberg (of *Deliverance* fame), and they recorded one fine collection of classic country called **Sweet Moments**. Packaged on the inside as a board game based on the Grand Ole Opry ("The Mansion of Sweet Moments Game"), it has some memorable covers of "Little Sadie," "Sittin' on Top of the World," Hank Williams, Merle Haggard, and Bill Monroe. Never one to stay in one place for long, Greene moved on to become a highly prized session man, and leader of his own group, The Zone, with some of the best up and coming newgrass musicians. As a member of the Red Hot Pickers with Rowan, Tony Trischka, and Andy Statman, he toured Japan and cut two albums. Into the late 1980s and early 1990s, Greene experimented with a combination of bluegrass, classical, jazz, and rock called the Greene String Quartet but by the mid-1980s had returned to a new/bluegrass sound with The Grass is Greener, an all instrumental band with Butch Baldassari, Tony Trischka, Bill Keith, David Grier, and Buell Neidlinger. **The Greene Fiddler** offers a fairly concise retrospective of Greene's long career with unreleased and reissued material from his days as a Bluegrass Boy through his innovative style of the mid-1990s. And although Greene did not appear on Old and In The Way's debut recording (replaced by Vassar Clements), he can be heard on a 1996 reissue of a live recording by that group, **That High Lonesome Sound** and its sequel, **Breakdown**. Greene's **Sales Tax Toodle** received a Grammy nomination in 1998 for Best Bluegrass Album, and late into the year, he shared his skills as an instructor at Mark O'Connor's fiddle camp and as part of the Mancini Institute Fiddles Philharmonic.

Sweet Moments (Blue Velvet Band)/Warner Brothers/1969
Seatrain/Capitol/1971
Marblehead Messenger (Seatrain)/Capitol/1971
Muleskinner/Warner Brothers/1974; Sierra/1994
Duets/Rounder/1977
Ramblin'/Rounder/1979
Blue Rondo/Sierra/1980
Bluegrass Album (The Red Hot Pickers)/Nippon Columbia/1980
Hiroshima Mon Amour (The Red Hot Pickers)/Nippon Columbia/1980
Somebody's Gonna Love You/MCA/1983
Swingrass '83/Antilles/1983
Molly on the Shore (Greene String Quartet)/ Hannibal/1989
The String Machine (Greene String Quartet)/Virgin Classics/1991
Bluegreene (Greene String Quartet)/Virgin Classics/1993
Muleskinner Live/Sierra/1995
The Greene Fiddler/Sierra/1995
The Grass Is Greener/Rebel/1995
Wolves A' Howlin' (Grass Is Greener)/Rebel/1996
That High Lonesome Sound (Old & In the Way)/ Acoustic Disc/1996
Sales Tax Toodle (Grass Is Greener)/Rebel/1997
Old and In the Way: Breakdown/Acoustic Disc/1997

Greener Grass Productions, 6234 Rockcliff Dr., Los Angeles, CA 90068; 800-GRASS-93

Richard Greene and The Grass Is Greener Home Page //www.poky.srv.net/~martyw/greener.html

violiner@pacbell.net

See David Grisman; Bill Keith; Peter Rowan

The Grievous Angels—Canada (The Cajun Ramblers/Blackflies)
Country Rock; Roots Rock; Cajun
Timmins, Ontario, Canada; 1989-

As someone once said, "there is a town in North Ontario..."; in this case, it's the tiny hamlet of Timmins located in the heart of hard rock mining country. Chuck Angus grew up there soaking up the sights and sounds including the country music his

grandparents loved so much. His first foray into music was in Toronto punk band, L'Etranger, with Peter Duffin and Andrew Cash, but after that, he formed a folk/country duo with fellow Timmins native Michelle Rumball. They were later joined by Tim Hadley, Peter Jellard, and old band mate Duffin to form the Grievous Angels in 1987. By naming their band after a Gram Parsons album, the Grievous Angels may leave the impression that they are simply a California style country rock band, and while there are elements of this sound, there's a whole lot more including Canadian country, French Canadian, Cajun, Celtic, and swing. What really distinguishes the Grievous Angels is the songwriting of Chuck Angus who like fellow Canadian Fred Eaglesmith has a real feel for the ups and many downs of working class life. On their first recordings, **Tout Le Gang** and **One Job Town**, Rumball handled lead vocals but once she left, Angus assumed those duties on **Watershed**, and his growling country/Irish vocals give his songs added grittiness and a special poignancy. "Starting Over at Thirty," "Pot of Gold," "A Mile Outside of Kirkland," "The Pipeliner's Song," "We Don't Seem to Be Able to Love Anymore," "The Ballad of Red Dan," and "Six Hundred Dollars" pack a real punch, but Angus' concern with the historic problems of laboring people really comes out on the Angels' 1996 release **Waiting for the Cage**. Packaged as an interactive CD-ROM, it is really a documentary on hard rock mining in Northern Ontario with 10 country/ folk/rock originals interspersed with animation, interviews, and photographs (it also contains a library of songs from previous Grievous Angels albums). This innovative recording earned a first place award at the 1996 New York Exposition of Short Film and Video. Angus edits *HighGrader Magazine*, a bi-monthly which focuses on rural culture, environmental conflict, and resource extraction in Northern Canada.

To give fuller expression to their Cajun side, several members of the Grievous Angels have played in a side band originally called the Cajun Ramblers and then renamed the Blackflies. Conroy, Hadley, and Jellard, joined by local radio DJ Steve Fruitman ("Great North Wind" on CIUT) and Steve Copek, recorded **Couteau Jaune** (Cajun Ramblers) and **Poutine** (Blackflies), both of which are a merry mix of Cajun, Acadian, Celtic, and Tex-Mex.

The Grievous Angels: Chuck Angus (a.g.,e.g.,l.v.); Rick Conroy (acc,p,1993-1997); Peter Duffin (d,v); Tim Hadley (b); Peter Jellard (acc,e.g.,f,md,v); Michelle Rumball (v,1987-1992).
The Cajun Ramblers/Blackflies: Steve Copec (g); Rick Conroy (acc); Steve Fruitman (tri); Tim Hadley (b); Peter Jellard (acc,f).

Tout Le Gang/Moose Can./1989 (CS)
Couteau Jaune (Cajun Ramblers)/CR/1990 (CS)
One Job Town/Stony Plain Can./1991
Watershed/Jimmy Boyle Can./1993
Waiting for the Cage/Drog Can./1996
Poutine (Blackflies)/Self/1997

The Grievous Angels c/o Shelley Hines Creative, P.O. Box 65068, 358 Danforth, Toronto, Ontario M4K 3Z2, Canada

The Grievous Angels Home Page
//www.grievousangels.com

Steve Fruitman/Grievous Angels Web Page
//www.interlog.com/~gnwind/f-grievangels.html

The Cajun Ramblers/Blackflies c/o Steve Fruitman, 487 Markham, Toronto, Ontario M6G 2L1, Canada or

//www.interlog.com/~gnwind/

gnwind@bigfoot.com

HighGrader Magazine, P.O. Box 714, Cobalt Ontario, P0J 1C0 Canada; //www.ntl.net/highgrader/

higrade@ntl.sympatico.ca

The Grievous Angels—U.S. (The Inbreds)

Insurgent Country
Tempe, Arizona; c. 1993-

The Grievous Angels (originally known as Earl C. Whitehead and the Grievous Angels) build their sound around classic hillbilly, honky tonk with just a dab of Southwestern rock. With alter-ego band, Ned Beatty & The Inbreds (old-timey/ bluegrass flavored music), they hit the national alternative country scene in 1995 with two cuts (one by the Angels, one by the Inbreds) on the second insurgent country compilation, **Hell Bent** and an EP **Angels & Inbreds**. Any band that names itself for a Gram Parson's album sets up a daunting standard to measure up to but on their first full length CD **New City of Sin**, the Angels do their mentor proud thanks primarily to A-1 steel work by Jon Ranhouse, punchy lead guitar by Dan Hanzerling, and catchy originals by Russell Sepulveda (Earl C. Whitehead). Songs like "She's Lost Her Head," "Where Sinners Go," and "Going Once, Going Twice" from **Angels & Inbreds** and "Sleeping in the Bayou" and "My Life Story" from **New City of Sin** show the workings of a true honky tonk mind, but the Angels can really rock out when they want to as on "Full Moon Show," "Carolina Bound," and "Don't Die While I'm Alive." They can also pick old-time style ("Don't Bother to Cry") and even go a little south of the border ("Flowers"). Early in 1997, the Grievous Angels contributed a cover of Jimmie Rodgers' "In the Jailhouse Now" to **Straight Outta Boone County** on Bloodshot which also released the Angels' next disc **Miles on the Rail** in 1998. They hit the mark again with honky tonk/ country rock covers (Hank, Sr.; Tom Waits) and originals. Meanwhile, Jon Ranhouse particiapted in an atmospheric pedal steel project (as Sleepwalker) called **The Man in the Moon**.

The Grievous Angels: Mickey Ferrell (b,v); Dan Hanzerling (l.g.,v); Jon Ranhouse (bj,md,p.s.), Russell Sepulveda (a.g.,l.v.)
The Inbreds: Mickey Ferrell (b,v); Dan Hanzerling (g,v); Frank Mackey (bj); Jesse Navarro (d); Jon Ranhouse (p.s.); Russell Sepulveda (g,v)

"Get It While It's Hot" (Grievous Angels) on
    Hell-Bent/Bloodshot/1995

"Don't Die While I'm Alive" (Inbreds) on
    Hell-Bent/Bloodshot/1995
Angels & Inbreds/Bloodshot/1995 (7 trk. EP)
New City of Sin/Bloodshot/1997
"In the Jailhouse Now" on **Straight Outta Boone County**/
    Bloodshot/1997
"Dear John" on **Jukebox Cantina—Combo Platter**/
    Hayden's Ferry/1998
Miles on the Rail/Bloodshot/1998
The Man in the Moon (Sleepwalker)/Hayden's
    Ferry/1998

The Grievous Angels Home Page
//www.getnet.com/~grievous/

grievous@getnet.com

Sid Griffin (The Long Ryders; The Coal Porters)

Country Rock
The Long Ryders: Los Angeles, California; 1981-1987.
The Coal Porters: Los Angeles and London, 1989-

As a musician, writer, and promoter, Sid Griffin has devoted much of his life to the perpetuation of the classic California country rock sound. In the 1980s, he founded the Long Ryders who combined country/rock/pop/punk that showed lots of Byrds, Gram Parsons, Flying Burrito Brothers influences. Their recordings including **10-5-60**, **Native Sons** (with guest vocalist Gene Clark), **State of Our Union**, and **Two-Fisted Tales** were generally well received and helped establish them as the 1980s heirs to Parsons et al. Griffin, Stevens, and McCarthy also worked on one of the best country rock albums of the 1980s, **The Lost Weekend** by Danny and Dusty (Dan Stuart and Chris Cacavas of Green on Red). However, in 1988, due to the usual disagreements (leadership, musical direction) and lack of commercial success, the Long Ryders broke up. A decade later Polygram Records issued a double CD retro- spective, **The Long Ryders Anthology**, with live and pre- viously unreleased material. In the works for early 1999 was a live Long Ryders recording with material taken from their appearance on *The Whistle Test* TV show and a 1985 performance at the Mean Fiddler.

For a time after the Long Ryders' demise, a disillusioned Griffin dropped out of music. He resurfaced in London in the early 1990s with a new band, the Coal Porters, which continued to mine the same musical vein as the Long Ryders. Prima Records released two studio (**Land of Hope and Crosby**; **Los London**) and one live (**Whoah Big Fella!**) recording by the Porters plus reissues of the Long Ryders and Danny and Dusty. The Coal Porters had cuts included on many compilations including **Town South of Bakersfield, Vol. 3**, the Gram Parsons' tribute **Commemorativo**, **Viva Americana**, and **This Note's For You Too!: A Tribute to Neil Young**. As a preview to their 1999 **Western Electric**, they released an EP called **Roulette**.

In 1996, Griffin recorded a solo record of country/folk rock, **Little Victories**, with guests appearances by Wes McGhee, Billy Bragg, Steve Wynn, and members of the Coal Porters. Former Long Ryder, Tom Stevens pursued a solo career with several recordings, **Last Night**, **Another Room** and **Points Revisited**, which draw on the 1980s paisley underground as well as 1990s alt. country groups like Uncle Tupelo and the Jayhawks.

In between his work with the Long Ryders and Coal Porters, Griffin developed a second career as a writer. While still with the Ryders, he wrote *Gram Parsons: A Music Biography* for Sierra Books and has written liner notes for reissues of albums by Parsons, Clarence White, Gene Clark, the Byrds, and the Flying Burrito Brothers. In addition, he's a regular contributor to a variety of music and other magazines. Into the 1990s, Griffin continued to push for the release of previously unavailable material from the Byrds and Long Ryders periods. One particular pet project which (after many delays) finally saw the light of day in late 1998 was the Gene Clark anthology **Flying High** for which Griffin did the liner notes and an accompanying article for *Mojo* magazine.

The Long Ryders: Des Brewer (b); Sid Griffin (g,v); Stephen McCarthy (g); Matt Roberts (d); Barry Shank (b,v); Greg Sowders (d); Tom Stevens (b)
The Coal Porters: Rob Childs (l.g.,p.s.b.v.); Sid Griffin (g,hm,l.v.); Pat McGarvey (b,v); Dave Roberts (d); Bob Stone (ky,v)

> **The Long Ryders**/1983/ (EP)
> **10-5-60**/PVC/1983; Demon Zippo UK/1987 (EP)
> **Native Sons**/Frontier Zippo/1984
> **Sounds of an Empty Pint**/Pitchfork UK/1985 (boot LP)
> **A Conversation With the Long Ryders...State of Our Union**/Island/1985 (promo LP)
> **State of Our Union**/Island/1985; Prima/1995 (w/ 4 extra trks.)
> **Two Fisted Tales**/Island/1987; Prima UK/1996 (w/ 4 bonus trks.)
> **Metallic B.O.**/Overground UK/1989 (CS); Prima/1994 (CD)
> **Last Night** (Tom Stevens solo)/Devil in the Woods/1992
> "Crackin' at the Seams" (Coal Porters) on **Town South of Bakersfield, Vol. 3**/Restless/1992
> "November Nights" (Coal Porters) on **Commemorativo**/Rhino/1993
> **Rebels Without Applause** (Coal Porters)/Rubber Australia/19 (12" EP w/ 5 trks); Utility UK Zuma Ger./ (9trks)
> **Whoa, Big Fella!** (Coal Porters Live)/Prima/1994 (m.o. only)
> **In the Land of Hope and Crosby** (Coal Porters)/Prima UK/1994; Temple Bar/1994
> **BBC Radio One Live in Concert, 1985** (Long Ryders)/Windsong UK/1994
> **Another Room** (Tom Stevens)/Maia/1995
> **Los London** (Coal Porters)/Prima UK/1995; Temple Bar/1996
> **Little Victories** (Sid Griffin solo)/Prima UK/1996; Country-Town/1998

> "Six Days on the Road" (Coal Porters) on **Cowpunks**/Vinyl Junkie UK/1996
> **Points Revisited** (Tom Stevens)/Maia/1997
> "Sailors and Soldiers" (Sid Griffin) on **What's That I Hear: The Songs of Phil Ochs**/Sliced Bread/1998
> **The Long Ryders Anthology**/Polygram/1998
> "Cadillac Elvis" (Coal Porters) on **Viva Americana**/Boka UK/1998
> **Roulette** (Coal Porters)/Prima UK/1998 (EP)
> **Western Electric** (Coal Porters)/Prima UK/1999
> "Ohio" (Coal Porters) on **This Note's For You Too!: A Tribute to Neil Young**/Inbetweens Dut./1999
> "Everybody Knows This is Nowhere" (Tom Stevens) on **This Note's For You Too!: A Tribute to Neil Young**/Inbetweens Dut./1999

Rebels Without Applause: The Sid Griffin/Coal Porters Fanzine, c/o Grant Curley, ed., 37 Dean Close, High Wycombe, BUCKS, HP12 3NS, England

Sid Griffin Home Page
//interchem.chem.strath.ac.uk/pd/SidHome.html

The Long Ryders Home Page
//interchem.chem.strath.ac.uk/pd/LongRyders.html

The Coal Porters Home Page
//interchem.chem.strath.ac.uk/pd/CoalPorter.html

The Coal Porters Internet Mailing List
dennison@strath.ac.uk

Tom Stevens Home Page //www.skyenet.net/~stevens/

See The Byrds; Gene Clark; Green on Red; Gram Parsons

Gringo

Lo-Fi Country
Chicago, Illinois/Nashville, Tennessee; 1995-

Originally based in Chicago, this trio debuted in 1995 with a self titled recording of glum country rock with a hard electric edge. It failed to click with alt. country audiences, but a move to Nashville and a new sound changed that. Apparently, Gringo caught a bad case of Opry fever because their follow-up, **Combine**, was a spare acoustic collection of old-time, bluegrass, and country standards (Hank's "Long Gone Lonesome Blues"; Stanley Brothers' "In Heaven You'll Never Grow Old" and "How Mountain Girls Can Love") and traditional feeling originals. Leader and principal songwriter, just plain Jim and Leila Vartanian provide convincing high lonesome vocals and Martin O'Doherty lends credible accompaniment on both clawhammer and 5-string banjo. Their backwoods approach was much more appealing especially to fans of similar groups like Freakwater and the Damnations TX.

Jim (g,l.v.); Martin O'Doherty (bj); Leila Vartanian (b,v)

> **Gringo**/Pravda/1995
> **Combine**/Pravda/1997

Gringo/Pravda Page //www.pravdamusic.com

David Grisman

Mandolin; Progressive Bluegrass; Newgrass
Hackensack, New Jersey; March 17, 1945-

Although primarily known as one of the major innovators of what has become known as "new acoustic music," mandolinist David Grisman has been involved in many key moments in alternative country history. Starting out as a folkie in the early 1960s (with the Even Dozen Jug Band), Grisman eventually discovered bluegrass and became a member of Red Allen's Kentuckians. There, he met and learned some valuable lessons from Frank Wakefield, a pioneer in progressive mandolin playing. However, after only a few years of touring and recording with Allen, Grisman headed to San Francisco where like many other youngsters he fell under the spell of the Bay Area rock scene and joined a Peter Rowan created band, Earth Opera. Labeled a "rock-fusion" band, EO was musically and thematically a product of its time. Combining rock, jazz, country, and other styles, they recorded two albums in 1968 and disbanded leaving Grisman free to do session work for a variety of musicians including Tom Paxton, Judy Collins, the Grateful Dead (on **American Beauty**), Paul Siebel, Maria Muldaur, and Hazel Dickens. Then, in the mid-1970s, Grisman returned to bluegrass and became a part of two bands that were at the forefront of the development of progressive bluegrass: Old and In the Way and Muleskinner. The former was a Jerry Garcia/Grisman project with Rowan, Vassar Clements, Richard Greene, and John Kahn. And although the band was only together for nine months, they succeeded in recording one of the best selling and most influential bluegrass albums of all time. **Old and In the Way** acquainted a generation of kids raised on rock with bluegrass and helped prepare the way for "newgrass." In 1996, Grisman's Acoustic Disc label issued **That High Lonesome Sound**, a collection of 14 previously unreleased Old and In the Way songs; a third volume, **Breakdown**, with more new material came out in late 1997. Muleskinner included Grisman, Rowan, Bill Keith, Richard Greene, and Clarence White playing a hybrid of California style bluegrass/country on one studio album and one live performance later released by Sierra Records as a CD and video.

After these short lived projects, Grisman started to put together the rudiments of a musical vision combining bluegrass, jazz, and swing that became known as "Dawg Music." His first vehicle for this innovative style was the Great American Music Band with Jerry Garcia sometimes sitting in on banjo. It eventually evolved into the David Grisman Quintet. During the 1980s and 1990s, the top performers in new acoustic music (Tony Rice, Mark O'Connor, Darol Anger, Mike Mashall, Jerry Douglas) were in this group at one time or another. Grisman was also much in demand as producer and/or player for a variety of artists and did a number of collaborative albums (mostly on his own Acoustic Disc label) with Stephane Grappelli, Jerry Garcia, Tony Rice, and Andy Statman. In addition, he made several more traditional bluegrass/newgrass records: the excellent **Here Today** (with Herb Pederson, Vince Gill, Jim Buchanan), **Home is Where the Heart Is**, and **Blue Grass Reunion** with his old mentor Red Allen. In 1996, Grisman marked the 20th anniversary of the David Grisman Quintet with the release of **DGQ-20** and honored his old friend Jerry Garcia with the first in a series of recordings drawn from sessions they did together in 1990. The first volume, **Shady Grove**, presented the duo on traditional folk material while volume two, **So What**, featured Grisman/Gracia takes on jazz songs by Miles Davis and Milt Buckner. Future installments were to be divided into country, bluegrass, and acoustic rock. Meanwhile, Grisman issued **Doc & Dawg**, a selection of classic American tunes with flat pick legend Doc Watson from 1987-1991. He also participated in a quirky side-project called Joe Weed and the Vultures which features David, Norton Buffalo, Jim Boggio, Rob Ickes, Joe Craven, Todd Phillips, and Joe Weed on acoustic covers of surf and classic intrumentals like "Rebel Rouser," "Apache," Wipeout," "Last Date," and "Green Onions."

Even Dozen Jug Band/Elektra/1963
Jug Band Music & Rags (Even Dozen Jug Band)/
 Elektra/1963
Bluegrass & The Kentuckians (Red Allen)/
 Folkways/1964
Bluegrass Country (Red Allen)/County/1965
Red Allen/County/1965
Earth Opera/Elektra/1968; Edsel UK/1986
Great American Eagle Tragedy (Earth Opera)/
 Elektra/1968
Old and In The Way/Rounder/1973
Muleskinner/Warner Bros./1974
The David Grisman Rounder Album/Rounder/1976
The David Grisman Quintet/Rounder/1977
Hot Dawg/A&M/1979
Quintet '80/Wraner Bros./1980
Early Dawg/Sugar Hill/1981
Here Today/Rounder/1982
Mondo Mando/Warner Bros./1982
Dawg Jazz/Dawg Grass/Warner Bros./1983
Mandolin Abstractions/Rounder/1983
Acousticity/Zebra./1985
Swingin' With Svend/Zebra/1987
Home is Where the Heart Is/Rounder/1988
Dawg '90/Acoustic Disc/1990
Garcia & Grisman/Acoustic Disc/1991
Blue Grass Reunion (with Red Allen)/Acoustic Disc/1992
Dawgwood/Acoustic Disc/1993
Tone Poems/Acoustic Disc/1994
Dawganova/Acoustic Disc/1995
Tone Poems 2/Acoustic Disc/1995
Muleskinner Live/Sierra/1995
Old and In the Way: That High Lonesome
 Sound/Acoustic Disc/1996
DGQ-20: A Twenty Year Retrospective/Acoustic
 Disc/1996
Shady Grove (with Jerry Garcia)/Acoustic Disc/1996
Doc & Dawg/Acoustic Disc/1997
Old and In the Way: Breakdown/Acoustic Disc/1997

So What (with Jerry Garcia)/Acoustic Disc/1998

DawgNet: The David Grisman Home Page
//www.dawgnet.com

See The Grateful Dead; Richard Greene; Bill Keith; Tony Rice; Peter Rowan; Doc Watson; Clarence White

Arlo Guthrie

Americana
Brooklyn, New York; 1947-

Most closely identified with his hippie-dippy album/movie **Alice's Restaurant** and with his father Woody, Arlo Guthrie also established a place for himself as an interpreter of Americana through a long string of recordings. Not only did he consistently show great taste in material (folk, blues, country, jazz) but always surrounded himself with top-notch supporting musicians. In particular, his albums from the late 1960s-1970s included the cream of alt. country musicians such as Doc Watson, Ry Cooder, Gene Parsons, Doug Dillard, Gib Gilbeau, Don Rich, and Clarence White on Arlo's originals and a variety of traditional Americana including songs by Ernest Tubb, Hank Williams, Woody Guthrie, Bob Dylan, Steve Goodman, and many more. Most of these recordings were reissued in the late 1980s on Arlo's Rising Son label or in the 1990s by KOCH International. Like his pop and his compadres Cisco Houston and Ramblin' Jack Elliott, Arlo Guthrie has always had an affinity for songs about cowboys and the American West and in 1992 did **Son of the Wind**, a highly enjoyable collection of classics ("Buffalo Gals"; "Streets of Laredo"; "Ridin' Down the Canyon"; "I Ride An Old Paint"; "Red River Valley"). Over the years, Guthrie participated in many tribute albums to his father including a 1999 collaboration CD with the Dillards that coincided with the issuance of a Woody Guthrie memorial postage stamp.

> **Alice's Restaurant**/Reprise/1967; Rising Son/1986
> **Arlo**/Reprise/1968; Rising Son/1988; KOCH/
> **Running Down the Road**/Reprise/1968; Rising Son/1988; KOCH/1998
> **Washington County**/Reprise/1970; Rising Son/1988; KOCH/1998
> **Hobo's Lullaby**/Reprise/1972; Rising Son/1987
> **Last of the Brooklyn Cowboys**/Reprise/1973; Rising Son/1987; KOCH/
> **Arlo Guthrie**/Reprise/1974; Rising Son/1988; KOCH/1998
> **Amigo**/Reprise/1976; Rising Son/1988
> **The Best of Arlo Guthrie**/Warner Bros./1977
> **Outlasting the Blues**/Warner Bros./1979; Rising Son/1986
> **Son of the Wind**/Rising Son/1992

ArloNet—The Official Arlo Guthrie Home Page
//www.arlonet.net

The Hackberry Ramblers

Cajun
Lake Charles, Louisiana; 1933-1941; 1946-

Louisiana is primarily known as the home of Cajun music, but it has also produced a number of fine Western swing bands through the years. One group which has blended both styles is the Hackberry Ramblers. Named for a town near Lake Charles, they formed in 1933, quickly became a local favorite, and recorded many 78s (sometimes as the Riverside Ramblers). Disbanded during WWII, the Ramblers reunited in 1946 performing in the dance halls and making one album, **Jolie Blonde,** before taking a hiatus until the 1980s when the two founding members Luderin Darbone and Edwin Duhon reformed the Ramblers with new personnel. Their timing was perfect as it coincided with a major Cajun revival. In 1988, a collection of Ramblers' material from the 1930s and 1940s, **Early Recordings** was issued and then came a new recording for Flying Fish in 1993, **Cajun Boogie**. This was followed by numerous appearances at festivals, concerts, and on TV. After over 60 years together, the Hackberry Ramblers, the band that first brought electronic amplification to Southwest Louisiana dance halls (actually a PA hooked up to a car battery), was once again on the "cutting edge" with a virtual appearance on the New Orleans Jazz & Heritage Cyberfest. In 1996, the Ramblers won a Governor's Arts Award for their musical legacy and released a new album, **Deep Water**, recorded with Rodney Crowell, Michael Doucet, Jimmie Dale Gilmore, and Marcia Ball. Like all of their recordings, it is a wonderful mix of Cajun, Western swing, blues, and honky tonk. Unfortunately, in early 1997, long time member Johnny Farque died, but the Ramblers continued on as a quartet.

Luderin Darbone (f,v, 1933-); Edwin Duhon (acc,g,v,1933-); Glen Croker (l.g.,1993-); Johnny Faulk (b); Ben Samdel (d)

> **Jolie Blonde**/Arhoolie/1963
> **Early Recordings, 1935-1948**/Old-Timey/1988
> **Cajun Boogie**/Flying Fish/1993
> **Louisiana Cajun Music**/Arhoolie/1994 (CS)
> **Deep Water**/Hot Biscuits/1997

The Hackberry Ramblers Fan Page
//home.earthlink.net/~kcy/ramblers.htm

The Hackberry Ramblers iMusic Showcase
//imusic.com/showcase/country/

The Hackberry Ramblers Biography
//www.pressnet.com/bios/hackbio.htm

Hadacol

Grain Belt Rock; No Depression
Kansas City, Missouri; Early 1990s-

In early 1999, one of the fastest rising groups on the alt. country horizon was Hadacol from Kansas City. The founders of the group, brothers Fred and Greg Wickham, had actually been writing and making home recordings of country/roots rock material since the early 1990s. By the mid-1990s, they were performing at clubs and honky tonks in the area with Richard Burgess on bass and a succession of drummers. After finally securing a permanent drummer (Scottie McCuiston) in 1996, they took the name Big Iron (from a Marty Robbins song) and a year later became regulars at Kansas City's Hurricane where they opened for local (Bottlerockets; Skeletons) and touring (Todd Snider; Junior Brown) acts. Shortly thereafter, they went into the studio with producer Lou Whitney (Skeletons) to work on a debut and about the same time, changed their name to Hadacol (the popular patent medicine that was a sponsor of Hank Williams' 1940s radio show). Checkered Past signed them in 1998 and in 1999 released **Better Than This** which according to the band's promo page "combines strong roots-rock and country influences to explore the raucous and rambunctious side of the roots rock/alternative country scene, as well as the dark, sometimes lonesome aspects of life in the rural Midwest." Advanced reviews bore this out and promised good things for Hadacol's future.

Richard Burgess (b); Scott McCuiston (d); Fred Wickham (g,md,v); Greg Wickham (acc,g,p,v)

Better Than This/Checkered Past/1999

Hadacol Home Page //www.geocities.com/~hadacol/
hadacol@geocities.com
Hadacol/Checkered Past: //www.checkeredpast.com

Terry Lee Hale
Singer/Songwriter
Texas; 1954-

Terry Lee Hale is in that grand tradition of American troubadours who wander the length and breadth of the country absorbing musical influences where ever they find them. As a child in Texas, Hale was exposed to honky tonk and swing as well as pop music. After high school, he lit out to seek his musical fortune and in his many travels became familiar with a wide variety of Americana. At long last, Hale settled with his wife and child in Seattle in the early 1980s and began to synthesize the various musical influences into his own singing, songwriting and guitar playing style on 6 and 12 string and dobro. Fortunately, he hit Seattle at a time when Gary Heffern, Larry Barrett, and the Walkabouts were generating a musical environment receptive to performers such as Hale. Working as a bartender and booking agent, Hale formed The Ones, but it was short lived, and after that, he stuck to solo. Live performances and a series of independent releases won Hale the Northwest Area Music Association's Best Acoustic Guitarist (1988-1991) and Best Acoustic Artist (1991). Eventually, Hale made the German connection that launched many other Seattle artists (Larry Barrett, Heffern, the Walkabouts). He was picked up by Normal and then Glitterhouse which released **The**

Wilderness Years, a collection of material from his early recordings plus **Frontier Model**, **Tornado Alley**, and **Leaving West**. Each uses spare arrangements and instrumentation to highlight Hale's vocals and lyrics that are most often compared to Guy Clark and Townes Van Zandt. In 1997, Hale embarked on a German tour opening for the enigmatic Vic Chesnutt.

Fools Like Me/TLH/1988 (CS)
Little Wood Guitar/TLH/1989 (CS)
My Confession/TLH/1992 (CS)
Oh What a World/Normal Ger./1993
The Wilderness Years/Glitterhouse Ger./1993
Frontier Model/Glitterhouse Ger./1994
Tornado Alley/Glitterhouse Ger./1995
Leaving West/Glitterhouse Ger./1996

Terry Lee Hale, P.O. Box 45585, Seattle, WA 98145

Terry Lee Hale/Glitterhouse Home Page
//www.ontide.de/glitterhouse/

Bucky Halker (The Remainders; The Complete Unknowns)
Roots Rock
Beaver Dam, Wisconsin; 1954-

Most alt. country performers have received their musical education in the school of hard knocks and honky tonks. Bucky Halker's has come not only through bars and nightclubs but also from the University of Minnesota where he obtained a Ph.D. in American History. His main field of study was the American labor movement and from that interest came the book, *American Labor Protest Songs, 1865-1900* which came with a tape of Halker performing period songs. In between writing and teaching (rock history) at the College of Idaho, the "Singing Professor" honed up his skills as a singer/songwriter penning Woody Guthrie influenced songs reflecting his concern with the trials and tribulations of the working classes. These compositions were self-released on **A Sense of Place** and **Step 'N' Blue** which Halker recorded after he moved to Chicago in the late 1980s. Beginning in 1987, Bucky fronted a regionally popular roots/gumbo rock band called the Remainders, but they never clicked nationally and after one self-titled album broke up. Whereupon, Halker traveled around for a time, still teaching, performing and recording (**Human Geography**, 1993), before coming back to Chicago where he put together a new group, the Complete Unknowns. Their 1997, **Passion, Politics, Love**, is a blend of roots rock from Grain Belt to classic honky tonk ("I'll Be in Heaven in Milwaukee While You're Crying in St. Paul") with its country elements helped along by guests T.C. Furlong on pedal steel and Don Stiernberg on fiddle and mandolin. Halker's originals once again reflect his long time interest in socio-political issues ("Don't Let the Bastards Grind You Down," "Poverty's Lament," "Democratic Blues," and "Emma Goldman Says It's Fine").

The Remainders (1987-1993): Nick Forchione (perc); Rich Parenti (sax,v); Gordon Patriarca (b); Buddha Slim (acc,ky,v)
The Complete Unknowns: Brian Dunn (e.g.); Phil Levin (d); Gordon Patriarca (b)

   A Sense of Place/Revolting/1984
   "Nobody's Fool" & "High Steppin' Time" (The Remainders) on **Fresh Rockabilly**/Moon/1987
   Step 'N' Blue/Revolting/1986; 1993
   American Labor Protest Songs, 1865-1900/University of Illinois Press/1991 (book with cs)
   The Remainders/Revolting/1993
   Human Geography/Revolting/1993
   Passion, Politics, Love/Whitehouse/1997

Bucky Halker & The Complete Unknowns Home Page
//www.housedog.com/waterdog/whitehou/bucky/text/buckmain.html

George Hamilton V and The NashVegas Nomads (Hege V)

Country Rock; Honky Tonk
Nashville, Tennessee; Late 1980s-

George Hamilton IV was one of the most successful pop country singers of the 1960s and 1970s. He recorded over 50 albums, had a number of hit songs, and was known as the "International Ambassador of Country Music" for his incredible string of tours and great popularity abroad. The fifth George Hamilton is also a country singer, and while musically he couldn't be farther away from George IV, he has followed in his father's footsteps in one way by being named "Rebel Without a Pause" for his many world wide tours. Originally known as Hege V, he cut his first album, **House of Tears**, a collection of pop rock originals with a few tinges of country including "Burial Ground of the Broken Hearted." To promote it, Hege V embarked on a grueling 10,000 mile, 21 state, 27 day tour in a rustic Cadillac hearse, gaining fans and good reviews all along the way. In the 1990s, he made Nashville his home base, began going by George Hamilton V, formed a new backing band (the NashVegas Nomads), and moved toward a more country rocking honky tonk sound. True to their name, George and the Nomads became relentless tourers in the U.S. but especially overseas with eight tours in six years. In Great Britain, Hamilton V appeared at Wembley Arena (with guest George IV), the Cambridge Folk Festival, and had a seaside hotel in Brighton named for him. A successful tour of the Continent was topped off by a performance at the prestigious Festival De Lille in France, and George and the Nomads became the first American band to do a nationwide tour of Poland (20 years earlier George IV had been the first to tour behind the Iron Curtain). In addition, Hamilton made several trips "down under" for festivals and shows on Australian and New Zealand TV. And, everywhere they have gone, the Nomads, bolstered by Hamilton's raw edged vocals and intense delivery, have established themselves as one of the best country/roots/rock bands going. For the record, the band has done three ablums, **Roll With the Punches**, **Ghost Town**, and **Garden of Love** that, as their promo material says, are "guaranteed to kick your ass across the barnyard and back!" George V has also done an acoustic album with George IV called **Home Grown**. In 1997-1998, Hamilton continued his Spartan schedule with his ninth and tenth tours of the British Isles and a second tour of Poland. From Melbourne to Krakow, George V became renowned for his "gut wrenching...raw boned...pure hogwild...tuff twangin'."

Hege V: Hege V (g,v); Stephen Dubner (acc); Mitch Easter (bits & pieces); Tim Harper (b,b.v.); Rob Ragsdale (d); David Thrower (l.g.,p.s.)

   House of Tears (Hege V)/MGM/1987
   Roll With the Punches/Massive Australia/1995
   Ghost Town/Dixie Frog Fr./1996
   Home Grown (with George IV)/Loman/1996
   Garden of Love/Dixie Frog Fr./1998

George Hamilton V Home Page
//members.aol.com/hamiltonv/home.htm

HamiltonV@aol.com

Butch Hancock

Lubbock Mafia; Singer/Songwriter
Lubbock, Texas; July 12, 1945-

In late January and early February of 1990, Austin singer/songwriter Butch Hancock put on a show of epic proportions when for six consecutive nights, he took over the Cactus Cafe and with guests including Joe Ely, Jimmie Dale Gilmore, Townes Van Zandt, the Texana Dames, Kimmie Rhodes, Erik Hokkanen, Jesse Taylor and many more performed over 200 of his original compositions. These concerts yielded 14 one hour cassettes that were subsequently made available to the public through Hancock's "No 2 Alike" tape of the month club. All in all, it was a very fitting tribute to the career of one of Texas' best and most prolific songwriters of the 1970s and 1980s.

Born and raised in West Texas, Hancock was a member of the Flatlanders with Ely and Gilmore in the early 1970s, but while they went on to prominent solo careers, he remained in the shadows penning many of the songs that helped make them famous ("She Never Spoke Spanish to Me"; "If You Were a Bluebird"; "Boxcars"; "Just the Wave"; "My Mind's Gotta Mind of Its Own"; "West Texas Waltz"; "Nothing of the Kind"). Meanwhile, Hancock performed in Austin (where he relocated in 1976), started his own record company (Rainlight), and recorded a number of very low tech albums full of his clever word play and observations on the culture and environment of West Texas. He developed a second career as a painter and opened Lubbock or Leave It as a combination art gallery and performance space. In 1990, Hancock recorded a memorable live album, **Two Roads: Live in Australia** with old pal

Gilmore and in the early 1990s began to make more commercial albums for Sugar Hill (**Own the Way Over Here**; **Own and Own**; **Eats Away the Night**) mostly drawn from his old Rainlight material but with some new songs as well. He was also a member of the cast of the play *Chippy* along with Joe Ely, Terry Allen, Jimmie Dale Gilmore, and Jo Carol Pierce in the early 1990s. In 1996, Hancock tired of the Austin scene and relocated to the tiny town of Terlingua, Texas. Stretching out in a variety of directions (photographer, river rafting guide in the Southwest and Mexico, space age architect, painter, experimental physicist), Hancock still found time to write and record, **You Coulda Walked Around the World**, a stripped down collection of Hancockian ruminations that harken back to his earlier material. In 1998, **The Wind's Dominion** was re-released on CD, and Hancock worked with Ely and Gilmore (as the Hill Country Flatlanders) on a song for the soundtrack of *The Horse Whisperer*. Throughout 1998-1999, Butch re-issued his classic early albums on CD including **West Texas Waltzes**, **Firewater Seeks Its Own Level**, **The Wind's Dominion**, **Diamond Hill**, and **Yella Rose** with Marce Lacouture.

West Texas Waltzes and Dust Blown Tractor Tunes/
    Rainlight/1978; 1998
The Wind's Dominion/Rainlight/1979; 1998
Diamond Hill/Rainlight/1980; 1999
1981: A Spare Odyssey/Rainlight/1981
Firewater Seeks Its Own Level/Rainlight/1981; 1998
Yella Rose (with Marce Lacoutre)/Rainlight/1985; 1998
Split and Slide II (Apocalypse Now, Pay Later)/
    Rainlight/1986
Cause of the Cactus/Rainlight/1987
Two Roads: Recorded Live in Australia (with Jimmie
    Dale Gilmore)/Virgin Australia/1990
No 2 Alike/Rainlight/1990 (cassettes recorded 6
    consecutive nights beginning 1/31/90 at the Cactus
    Cafe in Austin and featuring 140 songs and over two
    dozen guests)
Own & Own/Sugar Hill/1991
Own the Way Over Here/Sugar Hill/1993
Songs From Chippy/Hollywood/1994 (sdtrk.)
Eats Away the Night/Sugar Hill/1995
You Coulda Walked Around the World/Rainlight/1997
"The South Wind of Summer" (the Hill Country
    Flatlanders) on **The Horse Whisperer**/MCA/1998

Butch Hancock c/o Rainlight Records,
P.O. Box 468, Terlingua, TX 79852

Butch Hancock Web Site
//www.angelfire.com/mi/jeffmiller/index.html

jeffmiller@mail.utexas.edu

Lubbock or Leave It/Rainlight,
2311 West North Loop, Austin, TX 78756

See Terry Allen; Joe Ely; The Flatlanders; Jimmie Dale Gilmore

Wayne "The Train" Hancock (The Ridgetop Westernaires)
Austin; Honky Tonk
Dallas, Texas; May 1, 1965-

Wayne Hancock has certainly lived the life of the classic rough and rowdy, rumble tumble honky tonker epitomized by Jimmie Rodgers and Hank Williams. Born and raised in Dallas and East Texas, he had early leanings toward music but first, after high school, came a half dozen years with the Marines. On his discharge, Hancock began wandering across the South picking up odd jobs (grease monkey, iron worker, garbage collector, Merry Maid Cleaner) and a major drinking habit along the way. He had his interest in a musical career reaffirmed through further exposure to Hank's music, but unfortunately, it also reinforced his propensity for drink and getting into trouble. In 1991, Hancock moved to Austin determined to make it as a musician, but his alcoholism and naïveté about the music business seriously hampered his plans. The former got him branded among club owners as difficult and unreliable while the latter led to a nightmarish management deal with Ray Benson and T. J. McFarland. Then, with the bottom in sight, things suddenly began to turn around. A new girlfriend, Sue Foley (local blues guitarist) helped him overcome his drinking and to get out of the Benson contract. Hancock put together a new band, the Honky Tonk Brakemen and began performing around Texas. They recorded a live set on KUT radio in 1992, and in 1994, Hancock was asked to join the cast (as a replacement for Jimmie Dale Gilmore) of the stage production of *Chippy* which starred Joe Ely, Terry Allen, and Jo Carol Pierce. His "Thunderstorms and Neon Signs" was included on the soundtrack from the play, and this exposure helped Hancock get a record deal with Dejadisc. This resulted in **Thunderstorms and Neon Signs** which was one of the most acclaimed alt. country albums of 1995. It's 1940s-1950s style honky tonk, swing, and country blues was a big hit with a growing body of fans and critics who drew the inevitable comparisons to Hank, Jimmie, and Gene O'Quinn. In 1997, with a number of labels in hot pursuit, Hancock signed with Ark 21 and recorded **That's What Daddy Wants** which once again showcases Hank style honky tonk and Jimmie Rodgers country blues and ragtime but branches out into rock ("Johnny Law") and even country lounge ("Lee Ann"). There's also a wild cover of The Clash song "Brand New Cadillac" which was included on a tribute to those British new wave legends. Another Hancock tune, "Hill Country Hillbilly Gal," made it to the soundtrack of the 1998 film *Deep in the Heart of Texas*. A 7" recording worth seeking out is the Ridgetop Westernaires which is Wayne with Kevin Smith and Shaun Young of High Noon plus Chris Miller and Todd Wulfmeyer doing some hot hillbilly honky tonk.

Live Set/Austex/1992 (CS)
"Thunderstorms and Neon Signs" **on Songs From
    Chippy**/Hollywood/1994 (sdtrk)

"Friday and Saturday Night" on **True Sounds of the New West**/Freedom/1995
Thunderstorms and Neon Signs/Dejadisc/1995
"Looking for Better Days" (as the Ridgetop Westernaires)/Jet Tone/1996 (7" w/ Chris Miller, Kevin Smith, Todd Wulfmeyer, Shaun Young)
"5 Dollars and a Heartache" (with Debra Peters) on **Jukebox Cowboy**/Vinyl Junkie UK/1997
That's What Daddy Wants/Ark 21/1997
"Hill Country Hillbilly Gal" on **Deep in the Heart of Texas**/Shanachie/1998

Wayne Hancock/Ark 21 Page
//www.ark21.com/artists/wayne_hancock/

Wayne Hancock/Dejadisc Page
//www.eden.com/~dejadisc/hancock.html

James Hand

Honky Tonk
Tokyo, Texas; 1953-

Like fellow Texas honky tonker, Don Walser, James Hand's day in the sun came late in life. In his mid-40s, after a quarter century of playing a honky tonk in his hometown of Tokyo, Texas (near Waco), Hand was suddenly "discovered" by hard-core country fans all over the Lone Star State and beyond. Again, like Walser, he became a favorite with the younger honky tonk crowd in Austin with regular appearances at the Broken Spoke and also received a write up in *No Depression*. Veteran Texas performer Tommy Alverson produced his first record, **Shadows Where the Magic Was**, which just overflows with honky tonk in the heart of Texas tradition. In contrast to Walser's smooth Johnny Bush/Ray Price croon, Hand's voice is more in the rough and tumble style of George Jones. In 1999, Austin's honky tonk contingent lent full support to his new record (no title at press time) on Chris Wall's Cold Spring label. Dave Biller, who has played lead guitar with Dale Watson and Wayne Hancock and fronted the Panhandlers, produced and was joined in the backing band by Watson, Wall, Jason Roberts (Wandering Eyes), Ethan Shaw (ex-Derailers), and Ricky Davis (Dale Watson).

> **Shadows Where the Magic Was**/Texas Independent/1997
> "Baby, Baby Don't Tell Me That" on **Texas Renegade Radio: A Country/Americana Collection**/ KNON/1998

Texas Independent Records, 817-446-8041
James Hand/Cold Spring music@cold-spring.com

The Handsome Family

Insurgent Country; Lo-Fi; Gothic
Chicago, Illinois; 1993-

Initially, one of the lesser known of Chicago's insurgent country bands, the Handsome Family found its own unique place through modern explorations of some of folk/country music's most time worn themes. Their promos note that they "worship" George Jones, Hank Williams, and Gram Parsons, but they are much more closely related to Palace and the Scud Mountain Boys. Like these artists, the Handsome Family use minimum instrumentation and ultra low key, slightly hickish vocals to set a somber tone on achingly slow two steps or waltzes that occasionally and unexpectedly veer off into a fuzzy, twang. Lead singer Brett Sparks, who was once committed to a mental hospital after a major melt-down at Christmas, formed the band in the early 1990s with drummer Mike Werner and wife Rennie Sparks who is the group's principle songwriter. **Odessa** and **Milk & Scissors** put the Handsomes into the "Gothic country" category due primarily to very bizarre lyrics (written mostly by Rennie) obsessed with death ("Drunk By Noon"; "Emily Shore"), depression ("Moving Furniture Around"), and mystery ("Water Into Wine"; "Lake Geneva"; "Winnebago Skeletons"). They also have a thing for strange animals: "Giant Ant"; "Gorilla"; "3-Legged Dog"; "Amelia Earhart vs. The Dancing Bear." In 1997, the Handsome Family covered the classic death song "Barbara Allen" on **Straight Outta Boone County** and included it on the **Invisible Hands** vinyl EP which continues their somber exploration of the meanings of death and the great beyond. For **Through the Trees**, they hoped to lighten up a little by focusing on the wonders and beauty of nature, but along the way, it turned into a thanatopsis. To achieve just the right mood for the recording, the Handsome Family used sound effects from nature, samples from old recordings, traditional instruments, and even a drum machine (Jon Langford dubbed it "countronica"). After a tour through the UK and The Netherlands in September-October 1998, the Handsome Family returned to the U.S. to do several dates in New York City with the Mekons. Their growing popularity abroad was signaled by inclusion on two UK alternative country compilations, **Loose: New Sounds of the Old West** from Vinyl Junkie Records and **Sounds of the New West: The Best of Alternative Country** from *Uncut* magazine.

Brett Sparks (g,v); Darrell Sparks (g,v); Rennie Sparks (b); Mike Werner (d)

> "Moving Furniture Around" on **For a Life of Sin**/ Bloodshot/1994
> **Odessa**/Carrot Top/1994
> **Milk & Scissors**/Carrot Top/1996
> "Barbara Allen" on **Straight Outta Boone County**/ Bloodshot/1997
> **Invisible Hands**/Carrot Top/1997 (EP)
> **Through the Trees**/Carrot Top/1998
> "Moving Furniture Around" on **Loose: New Sounds of the Old West**/Vinyl Junkie UK/1998
> "Weightless Again" on **Sounds of the New West: The Best of Alternative Country**/Uncut UK/1998

The Handsome Family, 1375 N. Milwaukee Ave., Chicago, IL 60622

Official Handsome Family Home Page
//handsomefamily.home.mindspring.com/

Handsomefamily@mindspring.com

The Hangdogs

Roots Rock
New York, New York; 1994-

Like many contemporary alt. country bands, the Hangdogs did hard time in various modern rock and punk amalgams before dissatisfaction sent them in search of their musical roots. Co-founders Matthew Grimm and Kevin Baier (friends at Syracuse University) looked for inspiration mainly from the golden ages of rock 'n' roll and country. Adding a like minded bassist and lead guitarist, they developed a rockabilly/honky tonk hybrid that earned them a place in New York City's growing alt. country scene through rousing performances at local clubs such as the Rodeo Bar. Their 1995 EP **Same Old Story** drew attention from *No Depression* which did a glowing piece on them in 1996. Late in 1997, the Hangdogs released their first full length CD, **East of Yesterday,** which they described as "songs of disenfranchisement, hopelessness, and love among our own ruins." They were a band on the go in 1998 promoting the new recording at the Hellcountry showcase in Boston, Twangcore in New York City, stops in Virginia, North Carolina, and Texas, and even a tour in Italy at the behest of an Italian music promoter who took a shine to them.

Automatic Slim (l.g.); Kevin Baier (d); JC Chmiel (b); Matthew Grimm (g,l.v.)

Same Old Story/Crazyhead/1995 (EP)
East of Yesterday/Crazyhead/1997

The Hangdogs/Crazyhead, P.O. Box 7602, JAF Station, New York, NY 10116-7602

The Hangdogs Home Page //www.walrus.com/~hangdogs/
hangdogs@walrus.com

Emmylou Harris

Country Rock
Birmingham, Alabama; April 2, 1947-

It is impossible to overemphasize the contributions made by Emmylou Harris to the development of alternative country. Protégé of Gram Parsons and member of the Fallen Angels, she recorded some memorable duets with Gram and carried on his legacy with a string of terrific albums (**Pieces of the Sky, Elite Hotel, Luxury Liner, Quarter Moon, Blue Kentucky Girl, Roses in the Snow**) that along with those by the Byrds and Flying Burrito Brothers set the country rock standard for the 1970s. Each one seamlessly blended traditional with contemporary music. Bluegrass and honky tonk melded with rock and pop; covers of songs by a variety of legendary artists (the Carter Family, Hank, Buck, George, Merle, Loretta, Dolly, the Louvin Brothers, the Beatles) played comfortably alongside tunes by

Gram Parsons and new singer/songwriters (Townes Van Zandt, Rodney Crowell); her Hot Band included seasoned musicians like James Burton, Albert Lee, Glen D. Hardin, and Herb Pederson and served as a springboard for up and comers like Ricky Skaggs; her commanding presence on stage helped break down barriers for several generations of female country performers (her autobiographical **The Ballad of Sally Rose**, though sadly overlooked was one of the finest country concept albums of the early 1980s). Gradually, the quality of her work with the Hot Band declined somewhat in the late 1980s, but in 1992, Harris emerged with a new band, the Nash Ramblers, that included Sam Bush, Roy Huskey, Jr., Al Perkins, and Jon Randall. Their live recording, **At the Ryman**, covered songs by Stephen Foster, Bill Monroe, Tex Owens as well as Steve Earle, Bruce Springsteen, and the O'Kanes and won the 1992 Grammy for Best Country Performance by a Duo or Group. Traditionalists and non-traditionalists alike loved **At the Ryman**, but in 1995, Harris surprised both with the very experimental, **Wrecking Ball**. Produced by Daniel Lanois, it was a radical departure from Harris' previous work, a very moody piece covering songs by Dylan, Hendrix, Springsteen, Young and newcomers like Gillian Welch. It garnered a number of awards including a Grammy for Best Contemporary Folk Album but alienated many fans of the "old Emmy." However, Elektra rewarded them with a real treat in 1996 when it released a retrospective boxed set, **Portraits**, an anthology of the best from her early albums plus those glorious duets with GP. In 1997, Harris was part of Lilith Fair along with many modern divas (Jewel, Sarah McLachlan, Madeleine Peyroux). Moving to a new label (Eminent) in 1998, Harris invited guitarist Buddy Miller, bass player Daryl Johnson (Neville Brothers), and jazz drummer Brian Blade to join for a new live recording called **Spyboy**. Produced by Miller, it distills the essence of her 25 years with slight reworkings of songs from her early days with Gram, the Hot Band years, her Nash Rambler period, and down through her association with Danile Lanois. That same year, she fulfilled a long time dream by becoming executive producer for a Gram Parsons tribute album. Modern heavyweights including Beck, Cowboy Junkies, Steve Earle, Lucinda Williams, Elvis Costello, Sheryl Crow, Wilco, Evan Dando, and Gillian Welch participated in **Return of the Grievous Angel: A Tribute to Gram Parsons** which was released in mid-1999.

Gliding Bird/Jubilee/1969
GP (Gram Parsons)/Reprise/1973
Grievous Angel (Gram Parsons)/Reprise/1974
Gram Parsons & The Fallen Angels, Live 1973/ Sierra/1982; 1994
More Gram Parsons & The Fallen Angels, Live 1973/Sierra/1983
Pieces of the Sky/Reprise/1975
Elite Hotel/Reprise/1976
Luxury Liner/Warner Brothers/1978

Quarter Moon in a Ten Cent Town/Warner Brothers/1978
Profile/Warner Brothers/1978
Blue Kentucky Girl/Warner Brothers/1979
Roses in the Snow/Warner Brothers/1980
Evangeline/Warner Brothers/1981
Cimarron/Warner Brothers/1981
Last Date (Live)/Warner Brothers/1982
White Shoes/Warner Brothers/1983
The Ballad of Sally Rose/Warner Brothers/1983
Duets/Warner Brothers/1984
Thirteen/Warner Brothers/1986
Trio (with Dolly Parton & Linda Ronstadt)/Warner Brothers/1987
Bluebird/Reprise/1989
Brand New Dance/Reprise/1990
Emmylou Harris and the Nash Ramblers at the Ryman/Reprise/1992
Nashville Country Duets (with Carl Jackson)/Sundown/1993 (rec. 1984-1985)
Cowgirl's Prayer/Asylum/1993
Wrecking Ball/Elektra/1995
Building the Wrecking Ball/Elektra/1995 (interactive CD with music and commentary on the making of "Wrecking Ball")
Portraits/Elektra/1996 (box set retrospective)
Spyboy/Eminent/1998
"Wrecking Ball"; "Boulder to Birmingham" (live) on **Sounds of the New West: The Best of Alternative Country**/Uncut UK/1998
Queen of the Silver Dollar: Live at the Boarding House, San Francisco, 9/29/76/1998 (import)
Trails End 1984/1998 (import)
Return of the Grievous Angel: A Tribute to Gram Parsons/Almo/1999

Emmylou Harris Fan Club, P.O. Box 99497, Louisville, KY 40299

Emmylou Harris Home Page //www.nashville.net/~kate/

Chris Baker's Emmylou Harris Page //www.utiadv.demon.co.uk/emmy.htm

Emmylou Harris Dutch Page //home.wxs.nl/~jsomers/

Emmylou Harris English/Catalan Page //www.redestb.es/personal/dcoll/index1.htm

Emmylou Harris iMusic Showcase //imusic.com/showcase/country/

Emmylou Harris Newsgroup: rec.music.artists.emmylou-harris

Emmylou Harris Discussion List //www.onelist.com/subscribe.cgi/emmylou/

AOL Emmylou Harris Folder: Entertainment>Music>Chat & Messages>Music Community>Country/Folk>Country & Western, A-K

See Albert Lee; Gram Parsons; Herb Pederson

John Hartford

Banjo; Fiddle; Bluegrass; Old-Time
New York, New York; December 30, 1937-

Bowler hat. Banjo. Fiddle. Womper-Stomper. Riverboat pilot's license. These are the trademarks of John Hartford, one of the most eccentric but influential of modern Americana musicians.

His name will forever be associated with the Grammy winning hit (for Glen Campbell in 1967) "Gentle on My Mind," but the real significance of this song was that it gave Hartford freedom to pursue his musical vision. From the late 1960s to the present, Hartford remained one of the most innovative and versatile of old-time/bluegrass performers. He appeared (as banjoist and fiddler) on recordings by the Byrds (**Sweetheart of the Rodeo**), Gene Clark, Bill Monroe, the Dillards and many others and made classic solo albums (**Aero-Plain, Mark Twang, The Walls We Bounce Off Of, Gum Tree Canoe**) full of Hartford's patented musical and lyrical idiosyncrasies. However, it is his dynamic live shows which have done more than anything to establish Hartford's reputation as a unique performer. Like some modern day minstrel, dressed in signature derby and vest, Hartford sings, plays fiddle or banjo, and dances on a wooden platform he calls a womper-stomper in a way that is thoroughly entertaining. In addition, Hartford is a certified riverboat pilot and expert on classic Old South culture; he has authored a book on an ill fated ship called *Steamboat in a Cornfield*, written a television program, *Banjos, Fiddles and Riverboats*, and provided narration for the epic *Civil War* documentary. In the 1990s, Hartford split his time between performing and recording (**Wild Hog in the Red Bush** which was nominated for a Grammy; **The Speed of the Long Bow**, a tribute to legendary old-time fiddler Ed Haley) and piloting riverboats on the Cumberland River near his home in Tennessee. In addition, John contributed fiddle tune transcriptions and other fiddle information to the Old-Time Fiddling Web Page and sponsored Fiddler's Retreats for aspiring banjoists, fiddlers, and songwriters.

Looks at Life/RCA/1967
Earthwords and Music/RCA/1967
The Love Album/RCA/1968
Housing Project/RCA/1968
Gentle On My Mind and Other Originals/RCA/1968
John Hartford/RCA/1968
Iron Mountain Depot/RCA/1970
Aero-Plain/Warner Bros./1971; Rounder/1997
Morning Bugle/Warner Bros./1972; Rounder/1995
Tennessee Jubilee/Flying Fish/1975
Mark Twang/Flying Fish/1976; 1989
Nobody Knows What You Do/Flying Fish/1976; 1992
Dillard-Hartford-Dillard/Flying Fish/1977; 1980; 1995
Glittergrass From the Nashwood Hollyville Strings (Dillard-Hartford-Dillard)/Flying Fish/1977
All in The Name of Love/Flying Fish/1977
Headin' Down Into the Mystery Below/Flying Fish/1978
Slumberin' On the Cumberland/Flying Fish/1979
Permanent Wave/Flying Fish/1980
Catalogue/Flying Fish/1981
Gum Tree Canoe/Flying Fish/1984
Clements, Hartford, Holland/Flying Fish/1984
Me Oh My, How the Time Does Fly: A John Hartford Anthology/Flying Fish/1987
Annual Waltz/Flying Fish/1987
Down on the River/Flying Fish/1989
Hartford & Hartford/Flying Fish/1991

Cadillac Rag/Flying Fish/1991
Banjoes, Fiddles and Riverboats/Opryland/1991 (video)
John Hartford in Concert/Shanachie/1992 (video)
Goin' Back to Dixie/Small Dog A Barkin'/1992
The Walls We Bounce Off Of/Small Dog A Barkin'/1994
Old Sport/Small Dog A Barkin'/1994
Live at the College Station Pennsylvania/Small Dog A Barkin'/1994
The Fun of Open Discussion (with Bob Carlin)/Rounder/1995
No End of Love/Small Dog A Barkin'/1996
Wild Hog in the Red Brush/Rounder/1996
The Speed of the Long Bow/Rounder/1998

John Hartford, P.O. Box 443, Madison, TN 37116

The John Hartford Home Page
//www.techpublishing.com/hartford/

Hartford@techpublishing.com

The Old-Time Fiddling Page
//www.techpublishing.com/hartford/fiddle/fiddle.html

See The Dillards; Tut Taylor

Hick'ry Hawkins & Sidemeat
Punkabilly
Columbia, South Carolina; 1996-

5'3" and 120 lbs., Hick'ry Hawkins admits that his music "ain't ya normal hillbilly." Instead, he plays a conglomeration of Hank, Johnny Cash, Buck Owens, the Ramones, and the Sex Pistols. While in a D.C. punk band some years ago, Hawkins began writing country songs and after moving to Columbia, South Carolina combined these musical influences into what he called punkabilly. Backed by his band, Sidemeat, ol' Hick'ry gained quite a reputation for his fiery performances, stage antics, and songs celebrating the best of the Hillbilly Nation: cars ("Hot Rod Ford"), good women ("My Girlfriend's Got Lizard Skin"), good lovin' ("Small Sweet Furry Things Made Out of Love"), porno ("Girlie Magazine"), and WWF ("Rasslin'"). Hawkins hoped that his initial CD EP, **Anarky, Tennessee**, would be the first step toward a future boxed set packed and preserved like Spam.

Sidemeat: T.W. Hawkins (l.g.); Sugar Tit Hawkins (d)

Anarky, Tennessee/Humminjones/1997 (CD EP)
Nobody Luvs You (Like Me)/Humminjones/1998 (CS EP)

Hick'ry Hawkins, P.O. Box 5615, Hootieville, SC 29250; 803-799-8062

Hick'ry Hawkins Home Page
//www.mindspring.com/~shait/hickry/index.html

humminjo@mindspring.com

Hayseed aka Christopher Wyant
New Old-Time
Western Kentucky; 1967-

Though his name conjures up lots of negative imagery, Hayseed (aka Christopher Wyant) isn't about denigrating or parodying rural Southern culture but rather unashamedly celebrates it through a respectful interpretation of its rich musical heritage. Born in backwoods Kentucky and raised by a hard-core Pentacostal family, he knows whereof he speaks. In the late 1990s, after moving to Nashville, Wyant reinvented himself as Clifford Eugene Mason aka Hayseed and at the 12th & Porter club began relating his "hillbilly" experiences in a cappella story/songs. His character caught on and eventually he assembled a band to do a self-released tape of old-time, gospel, bluegrass called **Homegrown** which became the basis for his 1998 full-length CD, **Melic** (Greek for "suitable for singing"). With help from Lucinda Williams and Joy Lynn White on several beautiful duets, Hayseed joins old-time/bluegrass with modern day themes in a way that enhances traditional music but at the same time dispels many stereotypes connected with it.

"God-Shaped Hole" on **Nashville: The Other Side of the Alley**/Bloodshot/1996
Homegrown/Big Stick/1998 (CS, EP)
Melic/Watermelon/1998

Hayseed: Hayseed98@yahoo.com

Hazeldine
Insurgent Country
Albuquerque, New Mexico; 1994-

In the current alt. country spectrum, Hazeldine falls roughly between the Geraldine Fibbers and Freakwater. Fronted by three "babes with axes," Shawn Barton, Tonya Lamm, and Anne Tkach, they generally have that "twang and crunch" sound of Carla Bozulich and company but sometimes, they delve into the mellower old-time groove laid down by Catherine Irwin and Janet Bean as on "I'm Lonesome Without You" on **Straight Outta Boone County**. Either way, Hazeldine managed to generate quite a stir in just a few short years since they began performing as Blister in 1994. Lamm and drummer Jeffrey Richards played music together in Athens, Georgia before they relocated to Albuquerque where they met Barton and Tkach. All were children of punk but also grew up on country and began to weld the two styles into a cohesive sound. Discovering two other bands were called Blister, they decided two's company and changed their name to Hazeldine after a street in Albuquerque. They made their debut at a Dia de Los Muertos (Day of the Dead) party in late 1994 and released their first single to great critical acclaim (from *No Depression*). After appearing at SXSW, in March 1997, they embarked on a Bloodshot/No Depression tour along with Whiskeytown, the Old 97s, and the Picketts. Meanwhile, signing with Glitterhouse, Hazeldine recorded their debut CD **How Bees Fly**. It's a honey of an album, waxing and waning through droning country tinged ballads and stinging garage rock highlighted by the harmonies of Hazeldine's three queens. The buzz was on especially in Germany where the group was voted Best New Band (1997) over Wilco, Jewel, and the Wallflowers in a German *Rolling Stone* reader's poll.

How Bees Fly was not officially released in the U.S., but four cuts from that recording along with seven new ones made it on to Hazeldine's 1998 record, **Digging You Up** which came out in Europe late in 1998 and the U.S early in 1999. An EP of covers (Thin Lizzy, Mekons, Gram Parsons, Radiohead, Hazel & Alice, Sparklehorse, John Doe and others) called **Orphans** (with Walter Salas-Humara on drums) was distributed as a limited edition first by Glitterhouse in Europe and later by E-Squared in the States. Taking advantage of their growing stature in Europe, Hazeldine toured Germany, Scandinavia, and the UK in 1998 but also did a few dates in North America.

Shawn Barton (g,v); Tonya Lamm (g,v); Jeffrey Richards (d); Anne Tkach (b)

"Tarmac" b/w "Apothecary"/Cherry Smash/1996 (7")
"I'm Lonesome Without You" on **Straight Outta Boone County**/Bloodshot/1997
"Apothecary" on **Luxury Liner**/Glitterhouse Ger./1997
How Bees Fly/Glitterhouse Ger./1997
Digging You Up/Polydor Euro./1998; U.S./1999
Orphans/Glitterhouse Ger./1998; E-Squared/1998
"Tarmac" on **Sounds of the New West: The Best of Alternative Country**/Uncut UK/1998

Official Hazeldine Home Page
//www.morebarn.com/hazeldine/

Old Official Hazeldine Home Page
//lahn.net/roots/hazeldine_homepage/

Unofficial Hazeldine Home Page
//staff-www.uni-marburg.de/~settler/hazeldine.htm

Hazeldine Web Page (German)
//home.allgaeu.org/brosa/hazel.htm

The Health & Happiness Show

Roots Rock
Hoboken, New Jersey; c.1992-

The Health & Happiness Show grew out of "kitchen table hootenannies" during which James Mastro (ex-Bongos; Strange Cave) and Vinny DeNunzio (ex-Feelies; Richard Hell) sat around with friends drinking beer and singing Hank, Sr. Eventually, these informal sessions gelled into a formal band named appropriately enough after the Hank Williams radio show of the late 1940s. **Tonic**, (derived from the alcohol based "medicine" Hadacol that sponsored Hank's Health & Happiness Show), used a variety of acoustic instruments to produce a contemporary backwoods, string band sound. While on tour to support **Tonic** in the summer of 1994, they were involved in an

auto wreck that left them and their equipment safe but destroyed their van. The tour abruptly ended but on the way home (in a rental van) a slogan on a trailer park ad reading "Instant Living" took on special meaning and became the title of their second release. This time out, the old-timey sound is present but has receded to the background in favor of a much more electric roots rock orientation thanks primarily to the guitar work of Mastro plus guests Richard Lloyd and Erik Della Penna. In the spring of 1995, the H & H Show with Lloyd on board went on tour with Texas' songwriter Butch Hancock for whom they served as opening act and backing band. In 1996, they did a cover of "Stupefacation" for a Graham Parker tribute album, **Piss & Vinegar**. Along with other American roots rockers like the Dashboard Saviors and the Continental Drifters, H & H Show got a boost in the late 1990s when they were signed by Germany's Blue Rose which re-issued **Instant Living** in 1998.

Dave de Castro (b,v, 1995-); St. Vincent DeNunzio (d,v); Sean Grissom (cello, 1990-1991); James Mastro (a.g.,e.g., bouz,hm,v); Erik Della Penna (l.g.,l.s.,md, 1995-); Todd Reynolds (f,1992-1994); Tony Shanahan (acc,b,org,v, 1992-1994); Kerryn Tolhurst (db,g,l.s.,md,tiple, 1992-1994)

Tonic/Bar None/1993
Instant Living/Bar None/1995; Blue Rose Ger./1998
"Stupefacation" on **Piss & Vinegar: A Tribute to Graham Parker**/Buy or Die/1996

The Health & Happiness Show, P. O. Box 5188, Hoboken, NJ 07030

The Health & Happiness Show
//www.hobokeni.com/hhs.html

The Health & Happiness Show/Blue Rose Page
//www.bluerose-records.com/d/www/health.html

Bill and Bonnie Hearne

Singer/Songwriter
Austin, Texas; 1968-1979; Northern New Mexico; 1979-

Back in the late 1960s and early 1970s, Bill and Bonnie Hearne were a vital part of Austin's fledgling progressive country movement. They met in 1968, married, and began performing together. Bill and Bonnie became regulars at Threadgill's and the Kerrville Folk Festival and were greatly respected not only for their musical skills but also for their perseverance in the face of serious "handicaps" (Bonnie has been blind since 9, and Bill is legally blind). In the early 1980s, they relocated to Northern New Mexico and became favorites in Red River, Santa Fe, Taos, and on the Colorado/New Mexico/Texas circuit. Over their thirty years together, Bill and Bonnie have made numerous recordings of Southwestern style music (honky tonk, bluegrass, cowboy, folk) highlighted by the duo's engaging harmonies. These were done on small labels, but 1997's **Diamonds in the Rough**, on Warner Western marked their major label debut and break into national prominence. It presents covers of "Invitation to the Blues," "I Had My Hopes Up High" (Joe Ely), "Walk Through the Bottomland" (Lyle Lovett), "Wild Geese" (Ian

Tyson), and a beautiful waltz, "New Mexico Rain" by Bill's nephew Michael with backing from Lloyd Maines, Roy Huskey, Jr., Stuart Duncan, and Al Perkins. Also along for the ride were a number of Bill and Bonnie's most ardent admirers including Lyle Lovett, Nanci Griffith, Tish Hinojosa, Christine Albert, and Jerry Jeff Walker who all contribute supporting vocals. It is a loving tribute to a couple whose dedication to each other and the music is truly inspiring. The Kerrville Folk Festival voted them duo of the year and inducted them into the Kerrville Hall of Fame in 1997.

Smilin'/B.F. Deal/1977
New Mexico Rain/BB/1982
"The Last Thing I Needed" on **Texas Folk & Outlaw Music: The Kerrville Folk Festival**/Adelphi/1983; Edsel UK/1992
Down the Road/BB/1985 (CS)
Navajo Rug/BB/1989 (CS)
Live at Poor David's/Poor David's/1991 (CS)
Most Requested Plus: The Best of Bill and Bonnie Hearne/Poor David's/1993
Saturday Night Girl (Bonnie Hearne)/BB/1995 (CS)
Diamonds in the Rough/Warner Western/1997

Bill and Bonnie Hearne Home Page
//bbhearne.adnetsol.com/

Bill and Bonnie/Warner Western Page
//www.wbr.com/nashville/warnerwestern/bbhearne.html

Gary Heffern

Grange Rock; Lo-Fi; Singer/Songwriter
Rovaniemmi, Finland; 1957-

In the late 1950s, a social worker named John Caldwell found a group of eight brothers and sisters abandoned in a barn in Finland. He wrote a book about the plight of these children called *Children of Calamity*. One of the infant boys, Gary Heffern, was adopted by a San Diego family and came to the U.S. in 1958. In his early twenties, Heffern formed a punk band with Dan McClain (Country Dick Montana) and Chris Sullivan known as the Penetrators. They recorded two albums and received some national recognition but broke up after five years. Heffern then began to chart his own course as a soloist doing spoken dialogue shows in San Diego before moving to Seattle (1984) where he was member of the Unwanted Christmas Orchestra and the Cunninghams. He completed a book, *Bald Tires in the Rain*, and was approached by Marty Jourard (ex-Motels) with an offer to produce a recorded version of it. Heffern added music to the words and attracted Terry Lee Hale, Chris and Carla (the Walkabouts), Country Dick, Mojo Nixon, John Doe, and Victoria Williams to participate in the project by contributing instrumental backing or original artwork. In 1990, Nocturnal Records out of San Diego agreed to release **Bald Tires in the Rain** as a combined album/booklet. With this behind him, Heffern took a new direction and became part of Seattle's growing alternative country movement. He

developed into a country influenced singer/songwriter noted for intensely gloomy songs exploring the darkest depths of the human condition. His work attracted the attention of Glitterhouse Records which had already signed a number of other Seattle alt. country performers including the Walkabouts, Larry Barrett, and Terry Lee Hale. For his first Glitterhouse recording, **Painful Days**, Heffern enlisted all star musicians including Chris and Carla, Hale, Scott McCaughey (Young Fresh Fellows), "Wes C. Addle" (Eddie Vedder), Peter Blackstock, Peter Buck (REM), Victoria Williams, Mark Olson (Jayhawks), and Carolyn Wennblom (Crop Circles). The album's title pretty much sums up its feel; "Torture Rack," "Out in the Streets (Junk is Still King)," "Big Thoughts," "Parisville," "When I Die," "Night of the Wolves," supported by lo-fi country accompaniment, are quite moving but without ever plunging into a slough of despondency or self pity. Heffern also recorded **Along Came a Ditch** available only through mail order from Glitterhouse. In 1999, Gary completed **Consolation** with guests Steve Berlin, Peter Case, Alejandro Escovedo, Mark Lannegan, and various Walkabouts and shopped it around to various labels.

Bald Tires in the Rain/Nocturnal/1991 (LP and booklet)
Painful Days/Glitterhouse Ger./1995; Y Records/1996
Along Came a Ditch/Glitterhouse/1996 (m.o. only)
Consolation/1999

Gar Heffern Page //www.musicscene.com/friends/hef.html

Gary Heffern Biography
//www.musicwest.com/Artists/H/Heffern/heffern.html

GHeffern@aol.com

See Larry Barrett

Roy Heinrich

Austin; Honky Tonk
Houston, Texas; 1953-

For a guy who started out his musical career as the founder of Houston's first punk rock band (Street Rage), Roy Heinrich has come a *long* way. After wandering in the wilderness as a punk rocker and bass player in rock, r&b, and Top 40 country groups in the late 1970s and early 1980s, Heinrich had a country epiphany through exposure to Dwight Yoakam's early recordings and a live performance in Houston by Jimmie Dale Gilmore. Through them, he began to "get" the connections between rock and country and inspired by Hank Williams and Johnny Cash developed as a honky tonker in his own right. Heinrich's initial experience was as a part of the Palomino Barn Dance in L.A., but his destiny lay in Austin. A trip there in the early 1990s to visit his musician girlfriend (Mandy Mercier) turned him on to Austin's vibrant alt. country scene and convinced him it was the place to be. Truck driving by day, Heinrich played the bars and dancehalls at night. In 1992, he recorded a cassette of first rate honky tonk originals called

After All This Time. Gurf Morlix, Billy Block, Doug Ateweel, and Rosie Flores lent support to Heinrich's Johnny Cash influenced baritone on gems such as "A Face in the Crowd," "Reap What You Owe," "Call Me Darlin'," and "Handle With Care." Unfortunately, the same thriving scene that gave Heinrich his opportunity also created some problems. In a place where groups vie for musicians the way sports teams compete for blue chip players, Heinrich frequently performed with the band *du jour* and consequently had trouble with maintaining a consistent performance schedule. Still, Heinrich persisted, and in the mid-1990s, his fortunes took an upward turn. In 1995, he had a song included on each of two compilations of Austin/ Texas alt. country and in 1996 recorded his first full length CD **Listen to Your Heart** for Stockade. With help from Chris Miller (steel) and members of the Derailers and High Noon, Heinrich once again showed his considerable skills as a honky tonker on more excellent tunes ("Sittin' in This Honky Tonk," "Mister Come Get Your Wife"). In 1997, two Heinrich originals were chosen for another collection of Austin alt. country called **The Edge of Country** and another song for an English compilation, **Jukebox Cowboy**. Roy kept plugging away in 1999 with another fine honky tonk collection called **Smokey Night in a Bar**.

> **After All This Time**/Fayette/1992 (CS)
> "Same Old Heartache" on **True Sounds of the New West**/Freedom/1995
> "A Face in the Crowd" on **Austin Country Nights/** Watermelon/1995
> **Listen to Your Heart**/Stockade/1996
> "Today I Taught Myself to Pray"; "You Walked Your Walk" on **The Edge of Country**/Stockade/1997
> "Listen to Your Heart" on **Jukebox Cowboy**/Vinyl Junkie UK/1997
> **Smokey Night in a Bar**/Stockade/1999

Roy Heinrich 512-263-7275

The Hellecasters
Electric Guitar; Country Rock; Roots Rock
Los Angeles, California; 1989-

Someday, someone should put together a compilation album of the great alternative country pickers who have used Strats, Teles, and other Fender instruments. Maybe, they could call it "Fender Benders." Anyway, one group that would deserve a cut or two would be the guitar supergroup known as the Hellecasters. This versatile trio (Jerry Donahue, John Jorgenson, Will Ray) call up images of the Ventures and other guitar bands of the past but also pay tribute to the best soloists of past and present. Donahue started out with English folk rock legends Fairport Convention and over the years, worked for a variety of prominent pop musicians including Ralph McTell, John Miles, and Gerry Rafferty. He recorded two guitar albums (**Telecasting**, **Neck of the Wood**) that helped earn his own signature model Telecaster. Jorgenson, a three time winner of Guitarist of the Year from the Academy of Country Music, was lead guitarist for the Desert Rose Band, featured guitarist on numerous recordings (John Prine, Michael Nesmith, Jann Browne), and made solo recordings including **After You've Gone** (Django style) and an album of duets with Rose Maddox, **The Moon is Rising**. Ray has long been a fixture in the L.A. alternative country scene. In the late 1980s, he produced two compilations of local alt. country artists: **Detour West** with Will Ray and the Gila Monsters, Kacey Jones, and the Doo Wah Riders and **Hollywood Roundup** with Candye Kane and the Armadillo Stampede, the Radio Ranch Straight Shooters, and the Super Pickers, an early version of the Hellecasters with Billy Bremner (both collections are available by m.o. from Camp Hellecaster). In addition, Ray performed on the pioneering Town South of Bakersfield compilations, did a lot of session work, and was lead guitarist for Wylie & the Wild West Show. Donahue, Jorgenson, and Ray have each done instructional books and videos on guitar playing techniques. As the Hellecasters, they have three recordings, **Return of the Hellecasters**, **Escape From Hollywood**, and **Hell III: New Axes to Grind** that give them plenty of room to show off their individual and collective talents on country rock inspired instrumentals plus swing, surf, and rockabilly. They have a special knack for three headed twang and whimsical originals such as "Help I've Fallen and I Can't Get Up," "Inspector Gadget," and "Mad for Mothra." Ray released a solo recording in 1996, **Invisible Birds** (variously described by him as "Farm Jazz," "Cow Thrash," "Range Rock," "Prairie Metal," "Nuke-a-Billy"), Joregensen toured with Elton John (1997-1998), and Donahue rejoined Fairport Convention and contributed to the tribute album, **To Roy Nichols With Love**.

> **Telecasting** (Jerry Donahue solo)/1986
> **After You've Gone** (John Jorgenson solo)/1988
> "Heartache Train" (Will Ray and Gila Monsters) on **Hollywood Roundup**/New Grange/1989
> "That's History"; "Wishful Thinking"; "Tumbleweed"; "Thinkin' 'Bout You" (Will Ray and the Gila Monsters) on **Detour West**/1989
> **Neck of the Wood** (Jerry Donahue solo)/1992
> "Rockin' the Dog" (Hellecasters) on **A Town South of Bakersfield, Volume 3**/Restless/1992
> **I've Got the Key to a Faster Car** (Will Ray)/F*W/1993
> **Return of the Hellecasters**/Pacific Arts/1993
> **Escape From Hollywood**/Rio/1994
> **Invisible Birds** (Will Ray)/1996
> **Hell III: New Axes to Grind**/Rio/1997

Camp Hellecaster Newsletter, P.O. Box 1150, Burbank, CA 91507

Twang De Modem: TheHellecasters Home Page //www.hellecasters.com

The Hellecasters Unofficial Home Page //www.flexquarters.com/casters.htm

Skip Heller

Singer/Songwriter; Guitarist; Producer; Music Journalist
Philadelphia, Pennsylvania; 1965-

During the 1980s and early 1990s, Skip Heller was working on a promising career as a singer/songwriter and guitarist in his native Philadelphia. However, after two pop roots-rock albums (**Fallen Hand of Love**; **Moon Country**) and seemingly endless gigging, he gave up performing and switched to the last refuge of a scoundrel, music journalism. Interviewing and writing articles about all types of musicians, Heller was especially drawn to the "godfather of exotica," Les Baxter, for whom he became chief publicist and score librarian. These duties induced Skip to move to L.A. (Baxter lived in Palm Springs) in 1995 where he became active in the resurgent lounge/exotica music scene as a producer of a Les Baxter live album and nuevo-lounge group Frenchy, contributor to a Henry Mancini tribute, touring guitarist for the incomparable Yma Sumac, and co-leader with D. J. Bonebrake (X; Knitters) of a jazz quartet. But, after getting his fill of lounge, Heller returned to roots rock in 1996 as producer of an anthology called **Ray Campi: Perpetual Stomp, 1951-1996** and subsequently as producer and guitarist on **Train Rhythm Blue**, a brand new collection of Campi honky tonk, rockabilly, and country ballads. Periodically returning to lounge with Sumac and as The Skip Heller Generation, he also continued working with roots rock performers. In 1997, he brought a California rockabilly legend, out of retirement to record **Everybody Digs Sammy Masters** with Heller, Campi, and Deke Dickerson, and he produced and played on Dee Lannon's EP **And the Angels Sing**. Topping off a busy year, Skip recorded his own album, **St. Christopher's Arms**, which features his understated vocals and sure-handed guitar on an eclectic selection of country, blues, Western swing, jazz, Latin, and more with support from Campi, Bonebrake, and Katy Moffatt. All the while, Heller continued writing about music including liner notes for the **Crimejazz** compilation and lengthy pieces about Jimmy Martin and John Hartford for Tower Records' *E-Pulse* magazine. As of the end of 1998, he was in the planning stages of a tribute album to the Louvin Brothers.

Fallen Hand of Love/Gladman/1992
Moon Country/Gladman/1993
One More Midnight (DJ Bonebrake-Skip Heller
    Quartet)/Dionysus/1995
Lonely Town (The Skip Heller Generation)/TRG/1997
St. Christopher's Arms/Mouthpiece/1998
Skip Heller //server.tt.net/ultramodern/skip/
Lonlytown@aol.com

Homer Henderson

Psychocountry; One Man Band
Ft. Worth, Texas; 1952-

Madison, West Virginia has Hasil Adkins; Dallas, Texas has Homer Henderson. Like Hasil, Homer takes great pride in his persona as a one man band and all around crazy person belting out very demented, very funny songs. In reality, Homer (aka Phil Bennison) has only been a solo act for about three years. Before that, he was involved in the Dallas music scene for several decades as a drummer in country (Teddy & the Talltops), blues, punk, and even noise bands. It was the hassles and headaches of those experiences that resolved him to go it alone as a new character, "Homer Henderson" (from the intersection of two Dallas streets) in the late 1980s. At his home "studio," Henderson recorded a number of self released singles "Picking Up Beer Cans on the Highway," "Lee Harvey Was a Friend of Mine," "Nightclub Cancer," and "I Want a Date With a Cowboy Cheerleader" and performed at local clubs with a band called the Dalworthian Garden Boys. However, in 1993, Homer decided to go solo playing guitar, harmonica, drum as a one man band. He tried Austin but found Dallas more hospitable to his zany style and with the resurgence of Dallas' old Deep Ellum district, Henderson became a fixture at places like the Barley House and Naomi's. He was also known to play at Dallas' legendary pro wrestling arena, The Sportatorium, where he seemed to be right at home. Honey Records reissued a number of Henderson's obscure singles and in 1997 released a CD of live performances by the "Amazing One-Man Band" that was originally going to be titled **Live From Hate City** (what Dallas was called by some after JFK's assassination), but was discreetly renamed **Live at The Sportatorium**. In 1998, Honey released, **Greatest Flops and Golden Filler**, a compilation of Homer's 45s ("Pickin' Up Beer Cans," "Lee Harvey," "Hillbilly Pecker," et al.) with liner notes penned by author Nick Toches who has written several books on the darker aspects of American pop music: *Unsung Heroes of Rock and Roll, Country—The Twisted Roots of Rock & Roll, Hellfire* (about Jerry Lee Lewis), and *Dino: Living High in the Dirty Business of Dreams* (bio of Dean Martin). And, as it turned out, Nick had a drawer full of lyrics for some really sick songs, and Henderson was only too happy to supply the music. A full-length recording from the demented duo was due out in 1999.

"Picking Up Beer Cans on the Highway" b/w "Lee Harvey
    Was a Friend of Mine"/HH/1984; Honey/1995
"Love on You" b/w "Dragstrip"/Honey/1994
"You Pretty Thing"; "Pickin' Up Beer Cans on the
    Highway" on **Live From the BarleyHouse**/Barley
    House/1995
"Nightclub Cancer" b/w "The Planets"/Honey/1994 (7")
**Homer Henderson: Live at The
    Sportatorium**/Honey/1997
Greatest Flops and Golden Filler/Honey/1998

Homer Henderson c/o Honey Records,
P.O. Box 141199-672, Dallas, TX 75214

See T. Texas Edwards

Terri Hendrix

Singer/Songwriter
San Antonio/San Marcos, Texas; 1969-

Terri Hendrix had the good fortune of having two generous mentor/collaborators in her lifetime. Early on when she worked on Marion Williamson's Wilory Farm near Stonewall, Texas, he gave her musical instruction and spiritual guidance in exchange for her tending to the farm animals and keeping the books. After Williamson passed on, Hendrix took up singing/songwriting around San Antonio becoming a darling with the reviewers there and in Austin and cutting an intial CD, **Two Dollar Shoes**. Then, after Lloyd Maines heard her music, he not only agreed to remix her first recording but also produce and play on her sophomore effort. **Wilory Farm** is an ultra-friendly collection of folk, pop, country originals sung by Hendrix in a way most often described as "charming" or "perky" by music critics. Bohemia Beat/Rounder was impressed enough to nationally reissue **Wilory Farm** and give her a contract for a new 1999 recording with Maines once more at the helm.

Two Dollar Shoes/Tycoon Cowgirl/1997; 1998
Wilory Farm/Tycoon Cowgirl/Bohemia
    Beat/Rounder1998

Terri Hendrix //www.terrihendrix.com
newsletter@terrihendrix.com

Joe Henry

Singer/Songwriter
Charlotte, North Carolina; December 2, 1960-

Since the early 1990s, Joe Henry has faded in and out of the alternative country picture. His first recordings, **Talk of Heaven, Murder of Crows**, and **Shuffletown**, were pretty standard singer/songwriter fare. However, when Henry switched to Mammoth Records in 1992, he move steadily in a more countryish direction due in large part to contributions by the Jayhawks' Marc Perlman and Gary Louris. **Short Man's Room** and **Kindness of the World** offered a range of styles from barroom ballads to country rock with the highlights being Louris' guitar and high harmonies on "Dead to the World" and "Buckdancer's Choice," a beautiful duet with Victoria Williams ("Kindness of the World"), and an interesting cover of Tom T. Hall's, "I Flew Over Our House Last Night." A follow-up EP, **Fireman's Wedding**, waded deeper into country waters with a cover of Merle Travis' "Dark as a Dungeon" with Billy Bragg on harmony vocals. Henry's 1996, **Trampoline**, took a sharp turn away from his previous acoustic material toward hard edged roots rock. He was tapped in 1998 to do "Home-

coming" for the Tom T. Hall tribute and later in the year recorded (for 1999 release) **Fuse**, an eclectic roots rocker co-produced by Henry, T-Bone Burnett, and Daniel Lanois with guest appearances by the Wallflowers and members of the Dirty Dozen Brass Band.

Talk of Heaven/Profile/1986
Murder of Crows/Coyote A&M/1989; Mammoth/1993
Shuffletown/Coyote A&M/1990; Mammoth/1993
Short Man's Room/Mammoth/1992
Kindness of the World/Mammoth/1993
Fireman's Wedding/Mammoth/1994 (EP)
Trampoline/Mammoth/1996
"Homecoming" on **Real: The Tom T. Hall Project**/
    Sire/1998
Fuse/Mammoth/1999

Joe Henry Home Page
//www.geocities.com/southbeach/palms/2992/joehenry.html
Joe Henry/Mammoth Records Page
//www.mammoth.com/mammoth/bands/jhenry/mr0096.htm

Kristin Hersh

Singer/Songwriter; Gothic Country
1967-

Throwing Muses were one of the most popular underground bands of the 1980s-1990s due in large measure to the powerful singing and songwriting of Kristin Hersh. While primarily a hard driving pop-rock group, the Muses, led by Hersh, sometimes delved into acoustic folk music as well. In 1994, she gave full vent to her acoustic side on the solo **Hips and Makers**, a spare lo-fi effort (guitar, cello) Kristin termed "very minor mountain girl"; as with the Muses, she cut to the bone with some very discomforting lyrics and eerie arrangements (with Michael Stipe's backing vocals on one song). After the demise of Throwing Muses in 1997, Hersh moved to the desert near Joshua Tree, California and a bit further into a lonesome country/folk sound on **Strange Angels** which alternates between raw and sensitive, gloomy and joyful. However, on her 1998, **Murder, Misery and Then Goodnight**, she fully immerses herself and the listener in a world of Appalachian Gothic with chilling renditions of traditional murder ballads/lullabies ("Banks of the Ohio"; "Three Days Drunk"; "What'll We Do With the Baby-O"; "Mama's Gonna Buy"; "Sweet Roseanna"). It was available only via the Internet or mail order from 4AD. **Murder, Misery and Then Goodnight** was voted December's Americana Album of the Month by the U.K.'s *Mojo* magazine, and Hersh was given a feature profile in the March-April 1999 issue of *No Depression*.

Hips and Makers/Sire/1994
Strange Angels/Rykodisc/1998
Murder, Misery and Then Goodnight/4AD/1998

Kristin Hersh //www.evo.org/html/group/hershkristin.html
Kristin Hersh/4AD Page //www.4ad.com
Kristin Hersh/Rykodisc Page //www.rykodisc.com

John Hiatt

Singer/Songwriter
Indianapolis, Indiana; 1952-

John Hiatt labored for many years as one of America's best but most under appreciated songwriters. His early albums were loaded with fine songs that were hits for other artists but brought Hiatt no commercial success. Moved around from label to label, he finally charted with three albums in the late 1980s: **Bring the Family**, **Slow Turning**, and **Stolen Moments**. These recordings, a mix of country, folk, rock, and blues, contain some of his best songs—"Drive South"; "Tennessee Plates"; "Have a Little Faith in Me"; "Bring Back Your Love to Me"—and helped spread the word about this major songwriting talent. **Bring the Family** with a strong backing band including Ry Cooder and Nick Lowe was an especially strong effort and considered by many not only as Hiatt's best but also one of the top country/roots/rock albums of the 1980s. In 1993, Hiatt's status as a top notch songwriter was honored with a tribute album, **Love Gets Strange**, by other s/s who covered him over the years. Into the 1990s, Hiatt gradually moved away from the rootsy feel of his early albums toward a harder rock sound (**Perfectly Good Guitar**), but in 1996, with help from the Jayhawks among others, he returned to acoustic territory with **Walk On**. A collection of Hiatt's material culled from 1974-1985, **Living a Little, Laughing a Little**, provides a good introduction to his formative years while 1998's **The Best of John Hiatt** covers the late 1980s-1990s.

Hangin' Around the Observatory/Epic/1974
Overcoats/Epic/1975
Slug Line/MCA/1979
Two Bit Monsters/MCA/1980
Riding With the King/Geffen/1983
Warming Up in the Ice Age/Geffen/1985
Riot With Hiatt/Geffen/1985 (live promo boot)
Bring the Family/A&M/1987
Slow Turning/A&M/1988
Ya'll Caught: The Ones That Got Away, 1979-1985/
   Geffen/1989
Stolen Moments/A&M/1990
Is Anybody There? (Live)/Great Dane Ita./1992
Love Gets Strange: The Songs of John Hiatt/
   Rhino/1993
Perfectly Good Guitar/A&M/1993
Comes Alive at Budokan/A&M/1994
Live at the Hiatt/A&M/1994
Walk On/Capitol/1995 (also available as CD-ROM
   interactive promo)
Living a Little, Loving a Little (*'74-'85*)/Raven
   Aus./1996 (18 trks. with rarities and interview.)
Masters Series/A&M/1996
Little Head/EMI/1997
The Best of John Hiatt/A&M/1998

Bring the Family/John Hiatt Fan Club, c/o Randy Hogan, Box 92944, Long Beach, CA 90809-2944

Shot Of Rhythm: The John Hiatt Home Page
//www.tiac.net/users/pfl/sor.htm (has John Hiatt mailing list)

Riot With Hiatt Fanzine
//ourworld.compuserve.com/homepages/kcwaller/ (listings for bootlegs, videos, and Hiatt covers)

Buffalo River: Unofficial John Hiatt Home Page
//hera.informatik.uni-bonn.de/patrick/bastard/Hiatt.html

Unofficial German John Hiatt Page
//www.hiatt.com.qtvr.com

The Hickoids

Cowpunk
Austin, Texas; Late 1980s-Early 1990s

A review by Richard Dorsett of *The Austin Chronicle* in 1985 had this to say about the one and only Hickoids: "a surreal country/heavy metal band with bluegrass sensibilities . . . they don't just run through their songs, they tear great gouges in them, leaving behind bloody remnants of old country clichés." Indeed, for a short time in the late 1980s, Austin's Hickoids eviscerated country music with a raucous double guitar attack and angry vocals by founder, Jeff Smith, "The Gay Hank Williams." One of the wildest cowpunk bands, they were notorious for rip roaring, high volume live shows (complete with cowboy cross dressing and hay bales on stage) and for shamelessly exploitative and downright demented originals like "Animal Husbandry," "Corntaminated," "O.A.F. (One Armed Farmers) Anthem," "Corn Foo Fighting," "He's the Queen of the BBQ," "Lampasas Monkey Boy," "Pennsylvania Mexican," "Driftwood 40-23," totally disrespectful covers of "There Stands the Glass," Elvis' "Burnin' Love," Jackson Browne's "Take It Easy," and punked up versions of the themes from *Hee Haw* and *Green Acres*. The most accessible Hickoids compilation is **Hickoid Heaven** which comprises **We're Only In It for the Corn**, **Waltz a Crossdress Texas**, and **Hard Corn**. Post-Hickoids, Dick Hays formed a band called the Country Giants. He ran into a spot of bad luck in late 1998 when his house burned (from a candle knocked over by his pet iguana), and he was pulled over and arrested for drunk driving while on the way to a benefit to help pay for the first mishap; the money raised from the benefit went to spring him from jail!

Arthur Hays (d); Richard Hays (b); Davey Jones (l.g.); Jukebox (l.g.); Jeff Smith (l.v.)

We're Only In It For the Corn/Matako Mazurki/1985
Hickoids New 15 Song LP/Matako Mazurki/1985
Hard Corn/Toxic Shock/1988 (EP)
Waltz a Crossdress Texas/Toxic Shock/1988
Hickoid Heaven/West World/1993 (includes **We're Only In It For the Corn**, **Waltz a Crossdress Texas**, and **Hard Corn**)

Dan Hicks (The Charlatans; The Hot Licks; The Acoustic Warriors; The Christmas Jug Band)
Swing; Country Rock
Little Rock, Arkansas; December 9, 1941-

As a teen growing up in the Northern California, Dan Hicks developed a love for swing jazz and country/western music. In high school and early college days (San Francisco State), Hicks took up the drums then after a brief infatuation with folk music returned to drumming as a member of the Charlatans. Among the most promising bands on the 1960s San Francisco scene, they were one of the earliest rock bands to blend old-time country, rock, and jazz. These "hippies" polished up their style during a successful three month gig at a redneck bar in Virginia City, Nevada and then became very popular in the Bay Area. Seemingly destined for big things, the Charlatans ran into constant contract troubles and eventually fell apart after only one album. In the meantime, Hicks began putting together the Hot Licks who incorporated 1920s-1930s jazz and old-time country highlighted by Sid Page's violin, the vocals of Maryann Price and Naomi Eisenberg, and Hicks witty songwriting. Their four albums included such gems as "I Scare Myself," "How Can I Miss You When You Won't Go Away?," "Moody Richard," "Waiting on the 103," and the standard "I'm an Old Cowhand." Along with Asleep at the Wheel and Commander Cody, they were at the forefront of 1960s-1970s bands that introduced a new generation to America's country swing heritage. However, just as they began to make it big, Hicks disbanded the group and went solo with **It Happened One Bite** (with support from some of the Hot Licks). After that, his career shifted into very low gear until the 1990s when he formed the Acoustic Warriors. Their **Shootin' Straight** offers some fine live swing jazz propelled once again by the very literate and alliterative lyrics of Dan Hicks on such numbers as "Up, Up, Up," "Bottom's Up," and the alien abduction song "Hell, I'd Go." Additionally, Hicks collaborated with some Commander Cody alumni as the Christmas Jug Band who released three collections of quirky holiday songs. An anthology of Dan Hicks and His Hot Licks' best from the early 1970s, **Return to Hicksville: The Blue Thumb Years**, was released in 1997. Former Lickette, Maryann Price now lives in Austin where she performs and records solo and with Chris O'Connell (ex-Asleep at the Wheel) as the Western swing duo Ethyl & Methyl. Their Rare Prime Cuts mail order offered an extensive catalogue of live and previously unreleased material from the Hot Licks and Dan Hicks solo until legal complications forced them to stop selling this material; now, it's available through Maryann Price as a "gift" when you purchase a quantity of her recordings (contact addresses below for details). In 1998, Big Beat Records issued **Early Muses**, 20 previously unreleased tracks from Dan Hicks & the Hot Licks formative years (1967-1968).

The Charalatans: Darrell DeVore (p); Michael Ferguson (p); Dan Hicks (d); George Hunter (auto,tamb,v); Richard Olson (b,cl,v); Mike Wilhelm (g,v); Terry Wilson (d)
The Hot Licks: Dan Hicks (g,v); Naomi Ruth Eisenberg (v); Tina Gancher (v); John Girton (g); Jaime Leopold (b); Sid Page (violin); Maryann Price (v); John Webber (g)
The Acoustic Warriors: Dan Hicks (g,v); Alex Baum (b); Stevie Blacke (f,md); Jim Boggio (acc); James Shupe (f,md)
The Christmas Jug Band: Bill DeKuiper; Lance Dickerson; Tim Eschliman; Dan Hicks; Austin de Lone; Nik Phelps; Blake Richardson

> **The Charlatans**/Kama Sutra/1969; Shark/1994
> **The Original Recordings** (Hot Licks)/Epic/1969
> **Where's the Money?** (Hot Licks)/Blue Thumb/1971
> **Striking It Rich** (Hot Licks)/Blue Thumb/1972
> **Last Train to Hicksville...The Home of Happy Feet** (Hot Licks)/Blue Thumb/1973
> **It Happened One Bite** (Dan Hicks)/Warner Brothers/1978
> **The Autumn Demos** (Charlatans)/1982
> **Moody Richard**/MCA/1986 (CS)
> **The Very Best of Dan Hicks and the Hot Licks**/See For Miles Fr./1991
> **Shootin' Straight** (Acoustic Warriors)/On the Spot/1993
> **Mistletoe Jam** (Christmas Jug Band)/Relix/1995
> **Tree Side Hoot** (Christmas Jug Band)/Globe/1995
> **The Amazing Charlatans**/BigBeat/1996 (60s recordings)
> **Return to Hicksville: The Best of Dan Hicks and His Hot Licks, The Blue Thumb Years**/MCA/1997
> **Rhythm On the Roof** (Christmas Jug Band)/Globe/1997
> **Early Muses** (Dan Hicks & The Hot Licks)/Big Beat/1998

Dan Hicks Home Page //www.ns.net/~chaler/hicks.html (includes online mailing list)

Unofficial Dan Hicks Home Page //www.primenet.com/~sramirez/dan.html

Maryann Price: reddrum@bga.com (for informaion on rare Dan Hicks and Hot Licks recordings)

The Christmas Jug Band Home Page //www.globerecords.com/cjb/index.html

See Ethyl and Methyl

High & Lonesome
Grain Belt Rock
Iowa City, Iowa; 1992-

Most of the contemporary alt. country bands from the great Midwest hail from Missouri, Illinois, and Minnesota, but Iowa has its share including Bo Ramsey and roots rockers High & Lonesome. The latter formed shortly after a chance meeting between David Zollo, Ruari Fennessy, and Dustin Conner at an Iowa City bar in 1992. Adding Darren Matthews and Jim Viner, High & Lonesome began to tour the western U.S. and Europe where in Italy, they received an especially congenial welcome from fans and critics. In the U.S., they opened for a diversity of groups from Widespread Panic to Joe Henry, Ramblin' Jack Elliott, the Jayhawks, and Uncle Tupelo. High & Lonesome layers country and blues on top of a solid Midwestern rock foundation with lead singer Zollo (often compared with Jay Farrar) sharing songwriting chores with guitarist Fennessey. In the studio, they rely heavily on Iowa City musicians including

Trailer Records stable mate Bo Ramsey who produced their debut **Alackaday** and co-produced **For Sale or Rent**. Zollo did one impressive solo recording, **The Morning Is a Long Way From Home**, in 1995 and another, **Uneasy Street**, in 1998 with Greg Brown, Bo Ramsey, and H&L members helping out. However, as of Septmnber 1998, High & Lonesome went into semi-retirement to pursue "personal interests."

Dustin Conner (b); Ruari Fennessy (g); Darren Matthews (g); Jim Viner (d); David Zollo (ky, l.v.)

> **Alackaday**/Trailer/1992
> **Livefromgabes**/Trailer/1994
> **The Morning is a Long Way From Home** (David Zollo)/
>   Trailer/1995
> **For Sale or Rent**/Trailer/1996
> "Strawberry Wine," "I Gave Up on You," "Shining Softly"
>   on **Doublewide**/Trailer/1997
> **Uneasy Street** (David Zollo)/Trailer/1998

High and Lonesome c/o Trailer Records, P.O. Box 3202, Iowa City, IA 52240-3202; 319-351-3683

High and Lonesome/Trailer Records Home Page //www.trailer-records.com

info@trailer-records.com

See Greg Brown; Bo Ramsey

High Noon

Hillbilly Bop
Austin, Texas; 1988-

Without question, High Noon has been one of the best (perhaps *the* best) hillbilly bop bands of the past decade. In the late 1980s, Kevin Smith and Shaun Young played in a Denver band (the Shifters) which they subsequently brought to Austin. When the Shifters disbanded in 1988, Smith prepared to go back to Denver while Young joined local band Chaparral as its bass player. Also in this band was lead guitarist Sean Mencher with whom Young and Smith (who decided to stay) began to play on an informal basis. Eventually, they decided to form their own group and named it after the classic Western movie. High Noon was a big hit in Austin and then began extensive touring in the U.S. and abroad. Some of their most enthusiastic receptions came from the rabid rockabilly fans of England and the Continent. Audiences all over were impressed by their effective blend of rockabilly with straight ahead honky tonk and swing on **The Rockabilly Trio**, **Rocks Me Right**, **Glory Bound**, and **Texas Style**. Young's smooth 'billy vocals, Smith's incomparable slap bass, and Mencher's hot finger picking won them special acclaim in their home town where they were voted best rockabilly band seven years running (1989-1996). They also attained greater national and international fame when they became the first American rockabilly band invited to play in Russia in 1993, performed at Carnegie Hall as back up band (along with Lisa Pancratz on drums) for Ronnie Dawson, and appeared on *Late Night With Conan O'Brien* in 1994. Oddly enough, High Noon's recordings of the late 1980s and early 1990s were all on import or small U.S. labels, and they didn't make their major domestic debut until Watermelon released **Stranger Things** and **Live in Texas and Japan** in 1996 and 1997 (both originally issued on import). Meanwhile, Finland's Goofin' Records reissued their 1990 debut **The Rockabilly Trio Show and Dance** on CD. Into the late 1990s, each member has worked on a number of side projects: Mencher, who moved to Maine, recorded 45s on a regular basis, contributed to various music magazines, performed locally as the Pine Tree Three with his lovely wife Leslie on bass, and was in Wayne Hancock's road band in late 1998; Smith played bass for the popular cabaret swing group 8½ Souvenirs, was a member of the Asylum Street Spankers and the Panhandlers, and did an instructional video with the Bad Liver's Mark Rubin called *Slap Bass: The Ungentle Art*; Young drummed with the Big Town Swingtet, the Horton Brothers, and his Texas Trio with whom he recorded **Red Hot Daddy** in 1997. Smith and Young backed Austin rockabilly diva Marti Brom for live gigs and on a number of her recordings. High Noon got together periodically to record and tour although certainly not as often as their fans around the world would have liked.

> **Sean Mencher and His Rockin' Guitar**/SM/1987 (CS)
> **The Rockabilly Trio Show and Dance**/Castle Fin./1990;
>   Goofin' Fin./1997; 1998 (with live tracks)
> **Train of Misery**/Rock-A-Billy/1990 (EP)
> "Baby, Let's Play House" b/w "Too Much
>   Trouble"/Rock-A-Billy/1991 (78 rpm)
> "Hold Me Baby" b/w "All Night
>   Long"/Rock-A-Billy/1991 (7")
> **Rocks Me Right**/Rock A Billy/1993 (10" LP)
> **Glory Bound**/Goofin' Fin./1993
> "Our Last Night" b/w "Heartache, Heartbreak" (Shaun
>   Young)/Goofin' Fin./1993 (7")
> **Baby Doll Boogie** (Shaun Young)/Goofin' Fin./1994
>   (10")
> **Texas Style**/Exile Ger./1995 (10" EP)
> "He Won, I Lost, She's Found" on **True Sounds of the
>   New West**/Freedom/1995
> **Stranger Things**/Goofin' Fin./1995; Watermelon/1996
> "When You Smile" b/w "Commanche Moon" (Sean
>   Mencher)/Goofin' Fin./1995 (7")
> **Battle of the Bands, Vol. 1**/Thunder Fr./1995 (7" EP split
>   with Big Sandy)
> *Slap Bass: The Ungentle Art* (Kevin Smith & Mark
>   Rubin)/Ridge Runner/1995 (video)
> "When She's Good" & "Rock Too Slow" on **American
>   Rumble, Vol. 1**/Rock-A-Billy/1996
> "Jumpin' Track" b/w "Your New Flame" (Sean Mencher)/
>   Ecco-Fonic/1996 (7")
> **Live in Japan**/On the Hill Jp./1997 (EP)
> **Live in Texas and Japan**/On the Hill Jp.;
>   Watermelon/1997
> **Red Hot Daddy** (Shaun Young)/Goofin' Fin./1997

High Noon, 2900 W. Anderson, Suite 20-215, Austin, TX 78757

High Noon Fan Page //highnoon.notrix.de/

High Noon/Outer Sound Page
//www.outersound.com/band/highnoon/home.htm

Sean Mencher c/o Freda Management, 90 Brockett Ave.,
Peaks Island, ME 04108 or MaineMench@aol.com

*See Asylum Street Spankers; Big Sandy; Marti Brom; The
Horton Brothers*

Highwoods String Band (Walt Koken)

New Old-Time
San Francisco, California; 1972-1978, 1993

Whatever you might think about the "hippy movement" of the
1960s, it did make a major contribution to the revival of interest
in all types of traditional music. In particular, old-time string
band music with its rural simplicity and joyful expression
dovetailed perfectly with the hippy ethic and lifestyle. As a
result, a great number of new old-timey groups emerged that
modeled themselves on the classic bands of the 1920s-1930s
but at the same time adopted a modern approach to the music.
Among these groups, one of the most important and influential
was the Highwoods String Band whose origins go back to 1967
when Mac Benford and Walt Koken met in North Carolina at
the Union Grove Fiddler's Convention. Like many others of
their generation, they were attracted to the counter culture in
Berkeley and with new friend Bob Potts played in several string
bands including the Busted Toe Mudthumpers, New
Tranquility String Band, Spare Change Boys and Fat City
String Band. In 1971, they attended fiddlers' conventions on the
East Coast and teamed up with Jenny Cleland and Doug
Dorschung to form the Highwoods String Band which became
one of the favorite string bands on the festival circuit. They
toured extensively and became especially famous for an annual
party near Trumansburg, New York that attracted legions of
fans and musicians. Wherever they played, the HSB had people
up dancing (called "hippy hopping!") and most of all, they
introduced a whole new generation of mostly city kids to
old-time string band music. In addition, they changed the way
the music was traditionally played by relying on the dynamic
twin fiddling of Koken and Potts. After six years together, the
band split up but reunited in 1993 at the Brandywine Festival. In
1994, Rounder issued **Feed Your Babies Onions**, a 23 track
compilation of the best from their first three albums. Their
inspiring example lives on in current new old-time bands like
the dynamic Freight Hoppers. The co-founders of the
Highwoods String Band went on to solo careers; Mac Benford
fronted the Woodshed All-Stars while Koken took up his
original instrument (clawhammer banjo) and released three
solo recordings, **Banjonique**, **Hei Wa Hoe-down**, and **Finger
Lakes Ramble** that push beyond the boundaries of traditional
banjo music.

Mac Benford (bj); Jenny Cleland (b); Doug Dorschung (g);
Walt Koken (f,v); Bob Potts (f)

Fire on the Mountain/Rounder/1972
Dance All Night/Rounder/1974
No. 3 Special/Rounder/1977
Feed Your Babies Onions: Fat City Favorites/
    Rounder/1978; 1994
"Sheep Shell Corn By the Rattling of His Horn" on **Young
    Fogies, Vol. 1**/Rounder/1994
Banjonique (Walt Koken)/Rounder/1993
Hei-wa Hoe-down (Walt Koken)/Rounder/1995
Willow (Mac Benford)/Rounder/1996
Finger Lakes Ramble (Walt Koken)/Mudthumper/1998

Walt Koken c/o Mudthumper Music, P. O. Box 853,
Trumansburg, NY 14886

//www.mudthumper.com

wkoken@epix.net

See The Freight Hoppers

The Hillbillies From Mars

New Old-Time
San Francisco, California; 1982-

The Hillbillies From Mars have been perennial favorites in the
Bay Area contra/square dancing scene since their formation in
1982. Their continued popularity is due mainly to their catchy
mix of traditional Appalachian and Celtic with rock, swing, and
world beats. Like the Hix or Hypnotic Clambake, the Hillbillies
often begin with a familiar old-time tune but then veer off into a
Latin or African mode and back again. The twin fiddles of Ray
Bierl and Kevin Carr (also in Open House) plus the sturdy
mandolin of Paul Kotapish are the driving force behind the
band with the modern touches provided by the keyboard/
synthesizer work of Daniel Steinberg. To date, the HFM have
one CD to their credit, but their real forte is energetic live shows,
and they are special favorites at contra, square, and other dance
events and festivals around San Francisco and throughout the
U.S. In addition to performing, the individual Hillbillies lead
festival workshops in dance, rhythm, vocal, and various
instruments.

Ray Bierl (f,g,v); Kevin Carr (acc,bgp,bj,f,v); Paul Kotapish
(g,md,perc); Daniel Steinberg (ky,perc)

The Hillbillies From Mars/MFM/1995

The Hillbillies From Mars, 285 Monroe Dr.,
Mountain View, CA 94040; 650-947-9669

The Hillbillies From Mars Home Page
//www.witw.com/hfm/main.html

Hillbilly Idol

Honky Tonk; Western Swing; Bluegrass
Chardon, Ohio; 1991-

Ohio's Hillbilly Idol call their music "town & country," a
reflection of the combination of 1940s-50s styles (honky tonk,
Western swing, bluegrass) with modern touches that make up
their sound. Co-founders Paul Kovac and Dave Huddleston
came from old-time/bluegrass and rock 'n' roll/Beatles back-

grounds respectively and after forming the group in 1991 added Scott Flowers (old-time/bluegrass), Al Moss (rock), and Bill Watson (roots). In 1998, they pooled their many experiences and talents on **Town & Country**, a top flight debut (in a very cool package) with enough variety to please fans of traditional and alternative country. Kovac, Huddleston, and Moss are triple threats on lead and soaring harmony vocals patterned on the Louvin, Wilburn, and Everly Brothers, and all three share songwriting honors as well. Huddleston contributes a honky tonk two step ("Straight to My Heart") and old-time feeling instrumental ("Half Empty"), Kovac chips in two excellent Western swingers ("It All Depends on You"; "When It Rains I Get Wet"), and Moss is credited with a bluegrassy polka ("Better Off Believin'"), two barroom ballads ("By Now"; "If It Were Only That Easy"), and a country groove ("Mind to Change"). There's also some fine country covers of the Louvins ("Blue From Now On"), Wilburns ("Someone Before Me"), Harry Stinson/Kevin Welch ("Those Shoes"), and Dirk Powell of Balfa Toujours ("There Ain't Nothin' in the World"). Kovac's mandolin and Moss's steel work are real standouts and supporting musicians Denny Jones on fiddle and Brad Smedley on accordion enhance the variety of an album that's a real treat from beginning to end. And, as good as they are on record, Hillbilly Idol is even better in person!

Scott Flowers (d); Dave Huddleston (l.g.,l.v.,h.v.); Paul Kovac (a.g.,md,l.v.,h.v.); Al Moss (l.g.,p.s.,l.v.h.v.); Bill Watson (ub)

Town & Country/Harmony House/1998

Hillbilly Idol, 10191 Kirtland Rd., Chardon, OH 44024; 440-285-3629 (ph./fax)

Paulkovac@aol.com

Chris Hillman (The Flying Burrito Brothers; The Desert Rose Band)
Country Rock
Los Angeles, California; December 4, 1944-

He has already been named to the Rock and Roll Hall of Fame as a member of the Byrds and someday if there is an Alternative Country Hall of Fame, he has a reserved place. Chris Hillman was "present at the creation" of country rock when it emerged in California in the late 1960s. Initially, while still in his teens, he was in several bluegrass bands including the Scottsville Squirrel Barkers and the Golden Gate Boys (later the Hillmen), with the Gosdin brothers and Don Parmley. In 1966, Hillman produced a Gosdin Brothers record and brought in Gib Gilbeau, Gene Parsons, and Clarence White to back them. These three later formed Nashville West, one of the earliest California country rock groups. They were a big influence on Hillman and the Byrds when that band began to experiment with blending rock and country in the late 1960s. Chris was instrumental in getting Gene Parsons and Clarence White to join the Byrds

during this period. Having earlier befriended Gram Parsons, Hillman brought him into the band and in 1968, they cut the seminal **Sweetheart of the Rodeo**. Due to differences with Roger McGuinn, Hillman and Parsons soon left the Byrds but continued exploring the boundaries of country and rock with a new band, the Flying Burrito Brothers. Joined by ex-Byrd Chris Ethridge and steel player Sneaky Pete Kleinow (also an animator for Gumby), they decked themselves out in Nudie suits decorated with sequined peacocks, pterodactyls, and marijuana leaves and proceeded to make several classic country rock albums. **Gilded Palace of Sin** (1968) highlighted great originals "Sin City," "Wheels," and "Christine's Tune" all co-written by Hillman and Parsons while the follow-up, **Burrito Deluxe,** covered Merle, Buck, Red Simpson, and Felice and Boudeleaux Bryant. Though not big sellers at the time, these recordings exerted a tremendous influence on subsequent generations of alternative country.

Parsons and Hillman left the Flying Burrito Brothers in 1971 with the former pursuing a solo career and the latter joining Manassas and the Souther, Hillman, Furay Band before reuniting with McGuinn and Gene Clark as McGuinn, Clark, Hillman in the late 1970s. Each of these projects continued in the country rock mode but with less spectacular results than in his Byrds and Flying Burrito Brothers days. Then, in the early 1980s, Hillman began collaborating with Byron Berline, Herb Pederson, Al Perkins, James Burton, and Jay Dee Maness. They recorded two albums including **Desert Rose** which became the basis for the Desert Rose Band with Pederson and Maness plus John Jorgenson, Bill Bryson and Steve Duncan. In the late 1980s, they released several albums of polished country rock that garnered them a number of top 10 and several #1 hits. After, the DRB broke up in 1994, Hillman continued to work with Pederson and in 1996, they put out a fine collection of 1950s-1960s style California country called **Bakersfield Bound**. Here they reprise several songs from the FBB era, "Close Up the Honky Tonks," "Brand New Heartache" plus covers of Hank Cochran and Buck Owens. The next year Hillman and Pederson reunited with Larry and Tony Rice with whom they had worked in the early 1960s on **Out of the Woodwork**, a collection of old-time and bluegrass. In mid-1997, Hillman toured with a trio in a show presenting material from each period of his 35+ year career; his solo records from the 1970s, **Slippin' Away** and **Clear Sailin'**, were reissued on a German import CD in 1997, and in 1998, he recorded **Like A Hurricane**, a very fine little solo album that reflects his years with the Byrds, Burrito Brothers, and Desert Rose Band.

As a side bar, it should be noted that the Flying Burrito Brothers went on for many years after Hillman and Parsons left but became an increasingly pale representation of the original band. However, over the years, material from the prime FBB period has seen the light of day in several retrospectives including the definitive **Out of the Blue**, a two CD import containing their very best with informative liner notes by Sid Griffin. In 1997, German A&M issued **Gilded Palace** and **Burrito Deluxe** on one CD and the British label Strange Fruit released **Three Byrds Land in London**, a concert recording by McGuinn, Clark, and Hillman from 1977 that features them as a trio and individually. And, each year, live material from the FBB's prime years continues to surface on various import labels (check *Goldmine* magazine).

The Flying Burrito Brothers: Byron Berline (f,1971-1972); Roger Bush (b,1971-1972); Michael Clarke (d,1969); Jon Corneal (d,1968); Chris Ethridge (b,1968); Chris Hillman (g,md,v); Sneaky Pete Kleinow (p.s.,v,1968-1970); Bernie Leadon (g,v,1969-1970); Alan Munde (g,v,1971-1972); Gram Parsons (l.v.,1968-1970); Al Perkins (p.s.,1971-1972); Popeye Phillips (d,1968); Rick Roberts (g,v,1971-1972); Joel Scott-Hill (g,v,1971-1972); Kenny Wertz (bj,g,v,1971-1972)
The Desert Rose Band: Bill Bryson (b,b.v.); Steve Duncan (d,b.v.); Chris Hillman (g,md,l.v.); John Jorgenson (e.g.,v); Jay Dee Maness (p.s.); Herb Pederson (g,bj,v); Tom Brumley (p.s.,1992-4); Tim Grogan (d,1992-4); Jeff Ross (g,1992-4)

    Bluegrass Favorites (Scottsville Squirrel Barkers)/Crown/1961
    The Hillmen/Together/1962; Sugar Hill/1980
    Sweetheart of the Rodeo (Byrds)/Columbia/1968
    The Gilded Palace of Sin (FBB)/A&M/1968; Demon UK/1994
    Burrito DeLuxe (FBB)/A&M/1970
    Flying Burrito Brothers/A&M/1971
    Last of the Red Hot Burritos (FBB)/A&M/1972
    Close Up the Honky Tonks: 1968-1972 (FBB)/A&M/1974
    Honky Tonk Heaven (FBB)/Ariola Dutch/1974 (dbl)
    Chris Hillman/TOG/1974
    Souther, Hillman, Furay Band/Asylum/1974; Line Ger./1994
    Hot Burrito (FBB)/Ariola/1975; UK/1996 (with 6 bonus trks.)
    Trouble in Paradise (S,H,F)/Asylum/1975; Line Ger./1994
    Sleepless Nights (FBB)/A&M/1976; Sierra/ (contains rare Gram Parsons)
    Slippin' Away (Chris Hillman)/Asylum/1976; A&M Ger./1997
    Clear Sailin' (Chris Hillman)/Asylum/1977; A&M Ger./1997
    McGuinn, Clark, Hillman/Columbia/1979
    City (M,C,H)/Columbia/1980
    Morning Sky (Chris Hillman)/Sugar Hill/1982
    Desert Rose (Chris Hillman)/Sugar Hill/1984
    Desert Rose Band/MCA Curb/1987
    Running (Desert Rose Band)/MCA Curb/1988
    Farther Along: The Best of the Flying Burrito Brothers/A&M/1988
    Pages of Love (Desert Rose Band)/MCA Curb/1989
    A Dozen Roses: Greatest Hits (Desert Rose Band)/MCA Curb/1990
    True Love (Desert Rose Band)/MCA Curb/1991
    McGuinn, Clark & Hillman: Return Flight I/Edsel UK/1992
    McGuinn, Clark & Hillman: Return Flight II/Edsel UK/1993

    Traditional (Desert Rose Band)/MCA Curb/1993
    Life Goes On (Desert Rose Band)/MCA Curb/1993
    The High Lonesome Sound of the Flying Burrito Brothers (Seattle Pop Fest 1969)/1995
    Relix's Best of the Flying Burrito Brothers/Relix/1995
    Out of the Blue: The Best of the Flying Burrito Brothers/A&M UK/1996 (42 trks.)
    Bakersfield Bound (Chris Hillman and Herb Pederson)/Sugar Hill/1996
    Out of the Woodwork/Rounder/1997
    Gilded Palace/Burrito Deluxe (FBB)/A&M Ger./1997
    Three Byrds Land in London (McGuinn, Clark, Hillman)/Strange Fruit UK/1997
    Like A Hurricane (Chris Hillman)/Sugar Hill/1998
    Saddle Up Palomino: Live L.A. 1969 (FBB)/Jp./1998 (import)
    "High Fashion Queen" (with Steve Earle) on **Return of the Grievous Angel: A Tribute to Gram Parsons**/Almo/1999

Byrdwatcher //ebni.com/ (lots of information on the Byrds and Flying Burrito Brothers including an extensive discography)

The Flying Burrito Brothers //ebni.com/byrds/spfbb1.html

Chris Hillman CHKick@aol.com

See The Byrds; Gene Clark; Nashville West; Gram Parsons; Herb Pederson; Clarence White

Tish Hinojosa

Singer/Songwriter
San Antonio, Texas; December 6, 1955-

The cult presence of Selena has tended to obscure the deeper and ultimately more enduring contributions of Chicana artists such as the legendary Lydia Mendoza and contemporary musicians like Tish Hinojosa who carry on her legacy. The youngest of 13 children in an immigrant family, Tish was influenced early on by the Mexican radio stations that were a constant in the Hinojosa household. She took up guitar and singing and made some recordings for a local Tejano label. In the late 1970s, Hinojosa moved to Northern New Mexico to pursue a career as a singer/songwriter, and after a brief try in Nashville returned to New Mexico where, in 1987, she recorded a promising debut cassette, **Taos to Tennessee,** with backing from local band South By Southwest. A year later her husband was accepted to the University of Texas Law School, and they moved to Austin where her fortunes began to rise. A deal with A&M produced one highly acclaimed album, **Homeland,** (produced by Steve Berlin of Los Lobos) highlighting her lovely voice on original compositions with a true Southwestern feel ("Amanecer") as well as a genuine concern over issues such as immigration ("Border Trilogy") and the hazards faced by migrant farmworkers ("Something in the Rain"). Her second recording (**Culture Swing**) for A&M stayed in the can, and Hinojosa was dropped when the label decided to go in a different musical direction. Sadder but wiser, Hinojosa released two albums, **Memorabilia Navidena** and **Aquella Noche** (*en Espanol*) on Watermelon and shortly thereafter got a deal with

Rounder that led to the release of **Culture Swing,** a bilingual blend of Spanish/English musical styles and social consciousness many consider Hinojosa's definitive effort. After a fine follow-up, **Destiny's Gate,** Hinojosa, backed by Santiago Jimenez and Mark Rubin (Bad Livers) embarked on an 11 city tour along the Tex-Mex border. Sponsored by Texas Folklife Resources, the Canciones y Corridos de la Frontera (Songs and Ballads of the Border) tour included concerts and public school performances designed to keep traditional music alive for adults and new generations alike. Continuing in this vein, Hinojosa recorded **Frontejas,** an all Spanish recording of *corridos* (border songs) with guest appearances by Ray Benson, Brave Combo, and *conjunto* greats Eva Ybarra, Flaco Jimenez, and Santiago Jimenez. In 1996, she made a children's record, **Cada Nino/Every Child** followed by a second album for Warner's, **Dreaming From the Labyrinth**, which finds Hinojosa probing deeper into her cultural and spiritual heritage with inspiration from Mexican literature (from Aztec poetry to Octavio Paz). That same year, Hinojosa performed at the White House and at the Olympics. In 1997, Watermelon issued **The Best of the Sandia** which packages Hinojosa's best material (including 4 previously unreleased songs) from 1991-1992; Warner and WEA International jointly released **Sonar del Labertino**, a Spanish version of **Dreaming** for distribution in Central America and Mexico. In 1998, Tish and Warner agreed to go for the gold by having her do several "radio friendly" songs that hopefully would propel her into the national limelight and lead to a new full-length recording.

Taos to Tennessee/1987; Watermelon/1992
Homeland/A&M/1989
Aquella Noche (That Certain Night)/Watermelon/1991
Memorabilia Navidena/Watermelon/1991
Culture Swing/Rounder/1992
Destiny's Gate/Warner Brothers/1994
Frontejas/Rounder/1995
Cada Nino, Every Child/Rounder/1996
Dreaming From the Labyrinth, Sonar del Laberinto/Rounder/1996
Tish Hinojosa, The Best of Sandia: Watermelon, 1991-1992/Watermelon/1997
Sonar del Labertino/Warner Brothers WEA/1997

Tish Hinojosa Mailing List/Newsletter,
P. O. Box 3304, Austin, TX 78764

Mundotish: The Tish Hinojosa Home Page
//www.mundotish.com

Tish Hinojosa/Warner Brothers Page
//www.wbr.com/tishhinojosa/index.html

Aquella Noche: Tish Hinojosa Web Page & Mailing List
//members.xoom.com/aquella/

Richard Hess Tish Main Page
//rlhess.home.mindspring.com/music/tish000.htm

Tish Hinojosa Resource Page
//www.io.com/~dsmith/tish/frames.html

Tish Hinojosa Fan Page
//www.silcom.com/~craig/tish/tish.html

The Hitchin' Post
Country Rock
Hann, Munden, Germany; 1993-

Like their countrymen FSK, Hitchin' Post link American rock and hillbilly music with the culture of their home region Sud-niedersachsen, Germany. They call it "handmade" American music, a mix of Johnny Cash, Neil Young, and German folk that's equally at home in the desert Southwest or the mountains of Munden. Their debut CD, **Death Valley Junction,**shows a decided Texas influence while their second **Roadmap** displays more of their German side. Both mix covers of Cash ("Folsom Prison"), Haggard ("Lonesome Fugitive"), Tom Russell ("One and One"), Bus Kurk ("Family Bible") and originals by Stefan Kletezka and Birgit Wiegandt full of Western references ("Lost Dutchman Mine"; "Dark Dressed Cowgirl"), gritty looks at love gone wrong ("No Snakes in Heaven"; "Poor Lonesome Boy"), the honky tonk life ("Naomi"; "Honky Tonkin' at the Hitchin' Post"), pain and suffering ("Kerosene"; "Weeping Willows"), wanderlust ("Today I'm Leaving Home"; "Ride"), and suicide ("Drown"; "River of No Return"). Recognized by critics as one of Germany's top alt. country bands, the trio has done a number of European tours with their label mates Larry Barrett, Terry Lee Hale, and the Walkabouts and been included on several roots compilations from Glitterhouse and twah! Records. **The Ballad of Cal & Cubi** from 1997 has songs by Neil Young, Tom T. Hall, Loretta Lynn, and Buck Owens plus more Kletezka/Wiegandt compositions including "Falling to the Ground," "Water/Hole/Trap," "A Prison He Called Home," and "The Dike." The Hitchin' Post was invited in 1998 to cover "Tell Me Why" for the much anticipated Neil Young tribute, **This Note's For You Too!**

Dirk Blume (d); Stefan Kletezka (g,v); Birgit Wiegandt (b,v)

Death Valley Junction/Glitterhouse Ger./1994
Roadmap/Glitterhouse Ger./1995
The Ballad of Cal & Cubi/Glitterhouse Ger./1997
"Tell Me Why" on **This Note's For You Too!: A Tribute to Neil Young**/Inbetweens Dut./1999

The Hitchin' Post, Beethovenstr. 7, 34346 Hann. Munden, Germany

The Hitchin' Post Home Page
//home.t-online.de/home/the.hitchin.post/index1.htm

the.hitchin.post@t-online.de

The Hitchin' Post/Glitterhouse Web Page
//www.ontide.de/glitterhouse/englisch/artists-h03.htm

The Hix (The Chicken Chokers)

New Old-Time
Philadelphia, Pennsylvania; 1993-

Two of the most experimental old-time string bands of the 1980s were the Horseflies and the Chicken Chokers. They each adapted traditional Appalachian song styles to a decidedly modern interpretation that went beyond previous innovations made by the Highwoods String Band and other such groups of the 1960s and 1970s. Both mixed old-time with rock and a wide variety of world music, but what separated the Flies from the Chokers was that while the former opted for a darker, more brooding sound, the latter loaded their music with lots of humor. They were paired on a half and half album, **Old-Time Music (Chokers & Flies)** in 1985, but the Chokers made only one full length recording, **Shoot Your Radio** in 1987. It presented "updated" versions of standards ("Shady Grove"; "Blackberry Blossom"; "Eef Got a Coon") along with synthesizer, a little Hawaiian music ("Singin' the Blues"), and even an Uncle Dave Macon "rap" song, "Worthy of Estimation." Their general spirit of adventure and wackiness was due in large part to Chad Crumm who while attending Ithaca College in the mid-1970s was really turned on to old-time music at a Highwoods String Band concert. For a time, Crumm trained as a classical violinist at the Berklee School of Music in Boston before venturing into old-time fiddle with help from David Molk. Moving to Virginia for a time, he joined Ace Weems and His Fat Meat Boys and at the same time began to delve into a variety of music from modern classical to electronic. Returning to Boston, Crumm co-founded the Chokers, playing fiddle (and synthesizer) and composing many of their more experimental tunes. When they split up, he moved to New York City in 1990 where he performed as a one man band presenting digitally processed fiddle and pretaped music for monologues shouted through a bullhorn. A few years later, Crumm found a more formal outlet for his unique approach when he joined a new band from Philadelphia called the Hix which was formed by local banjoist Keith Brand (long-time DJ on WXPN with the "Sleepy Hollow" old-time/bluegrass show) along with Alex Scala and Gary Wright. Like the Chicken Chokers, the Hix are based in old-time but add on a variety of cutting edge styles from Henry Cowell to Laurie Anderson, Tom Waits to the Talking Heads. On their eponymous CD debut, they do moody, modernist revisions of classics like "Careless Love," "Reuben," and "High on a Mountain" but under Crumm's influence go where few bands have gone before. His ethereal fiddle is prominent throughout (especially on "Waltz" and "People on the Go") as is his avant-garde approach on the quirky Appalachian "African Tune," the disturbing "Rollin' the Flesh," "Oh Holy Night" (vocals through a bullhorn), and the very strange, Chokers like "Teenage Danceland" (again spoken through a bullhorn). On their second recording, **Sweet Sunny South**, the Hix push the envelope even further with an alluring collection of originals and covers (title tune; Peggy Lee's "Is That All Their Is?") melding old-time elements, electronica, new acoustic, and world music.

The Hix: Keith Brand (bj,bj-uke,v); Chad Crumm (f,g,ky,v); Jim Roberts (d,perc); Alex Scala (b); Gary Wright (g)
The Chicken Chokers: Chad Crumm (f, synth); Jim Reidy (baritone-uke,bj-uke,md-uke); Stefan Senders (bj,g); Chip Taylor Smith (g,s.g.); Paul Strother (b); Mark Graham (harm)

> **Old-Time Music** (Chokers & Flies)/Rounder/1985
> "Chinkapin Hunting" (Chicken Chokers) on **Young Fogies, Vol. 1**/Rounder/1985; 1994
> **Shoot Your Radio** (Chicken Chokers)/Rounder/1987
> "Grey Eagle" (Chicken Chokers) on **Young Fogies, Vol. 2**/Rounder/1995
> **The Hix**/The Hix/1996
> "Walkaround"(Hix) on **The American Fogies, Vol. 1**/Rounder/1996
> **Sweet Sunny South**/Tritone/1998

The Hix c/o Keith Brand, 454 West Earlham Terrace, Philadelphia, PA 19144; 215-438-0223

The Hix Home Page //astro.ocis.temple.edu/~brand/hix.html

Kbphd@vm.temple.edu

See The Horseflies

Doug Hoekstra (Bucket No. 6)

Singer/Songwriter
Austin/Chicago/Nashville; Late 1980s-

In the late 1980s and early 1990s, Doug Hoekstra was the leader of a roots rock band called Bucket No. 6. Based in Austin and then Chicago, the group played a combination of country, blues, and rock drawn mainly from the pens of Hoekstra and bassist Bill Murphy. They lasted through two recordings, **Bucket No. 6** and **High on the Hog**, before splitting up in 1992 leaving Hoekstra free to pursue a solo career. Moving to Nashville, he started his own record company and debuted with a cassette, **Broken Rain** and then a CD, **When the Tubes Begin to Glow**, which include a number of Bucket No. 6 alumni and retain much of their sound. As a singer, Hoekstra's raspy, low key vocals place him in the same company with J.J. Cale, Lou Reed, or Nick Drake while as a songwriter, he falls into step with the corps of modern troubadours, wandering ("On the Interstate"; "The Way the Wind Blows"; "Driving to Georgia") and pondering the mysteries ("Grandad's Radio"; "Standing in the Station"; "Pieces of Man"), all the while maintaining a sense of hopefulness ("Dandelion Seeds") and humor ("Mama Was a Pinkerton"). **Rickety Stairs**, is a more straight ahead folk recording and was nominated Best Folk Album of the Year by the Nashville Music Awards. In 1996, Bucket No. 6 did a song for **Outstandingly Ignited**, a tribute to the poet Ernest Noyes Brookings. Hoekstra joined the new One Man Clapping label in 1998 and emerged with another round of country/folk with **Make Me Believe**.

Bucket No. 6: Mark Fornek (d,perc); Doug Hoekstra (g,org,v); Steve Meisner (e.g.,f,hm,md,b.v); Bill Murphy (b, e.g); Jeff Weber (d)

Bucket No. 6/Boat/1988
High on the Hog (Bucket No. 6)/Bucket Numbers/1991
Broken Rain/Back Porch/1993 (CS)
When the Tubes Begin to Glow/Back Porch/1994
Rickety Stairs/Back Porch/1996
Make Me Believe/One Man Clapping/1998

Doug Hoekstra/Back Porch Music, P.O. Box 110352, Nashville, TN 37222-0352

hoekstra@mcmail.vanderbilt.edu

Erik Hokkanen

Austin; Fiddle; Guitar; Mandolin; Swing
Maitland, Florida; February 23, 1963-

One of Austin's best kept musical secrets is multi-instrumentalist Erik Hokkanen. Growing up in Florida, his earliest inspiration came from his older brother Niles (editor of the *Mandocrucian Digest*) who not only encouraged him to take up mandolin, fiddle, and guitar but also introduced him to blue-grass, Western swing, country, and the swing jazz of Django Reinhardt. As a teenager, Hokkanen began to perform in public. One of his first jobs was as a fiddling bear at Disneyworld, but he also played with Diamond Teeth Mary Smith McClain (Bessie's half sister), jammed with Richard Thompson, appeared at local bluegrass and country events, and was a member of Niles' Flighted Ninth String Band. His interest in Texas country music was peaked in the 1970s when he heard Gary P. Nunn's "Home with the Armadillo." After moving to Austin, Erik met Nunn's fiddle player Danny Levin (ex-Asleep at the Wheel) and eventually replaced him when Levin dropped out. He performed with many other Austin musicians including Jon Emery, the Supernatural Family Band, Al Dressen (West-ern swing), Tex Thomas, and Alvin Crow; at the same time, Hokkanen started his own band, the Offbeats with old pal Levin. In 1986, they released a single ("Broken Spoke Song") and the following year recorded a self titled full length LP of Western swing, rockabilly, honky tonk, and Cajun. A second Offbeats recording, **Blue Corn**, showcased Hokkanen's prodigious fiddling and guitar talents on breakdowns, swing, reels, and polkas.

In the early 1990s, Hokkanen began to collaborate with local singer/songwriter Erik Moll, and they subsequently made an album, **Erik & Erik**, with help from Levin, Ponty Bone, and Ethyl & Methyl (Maryann Price and Chris O'Connell). It presents originals by both Eriks done with a swing and country flavor. Most memorable are Hokkanen's "Milky Way Jive" and "Blues for Brown" and two songs dear to Texas hearts "Tornado Warning" and "Fire Ant Dance." Hokkanen then gathered together a number of Austin musicians as the Snow

Wolves Orchestra for some more swing and even some newgrass flavored numbers on **Earth Swing**. In 1995, he visited Finland (his ancestral home) and assembled some Finnish musicians as Lumisudet to record **Kaustinen, Texas**, a collection of covers ("Ragtime Annie"; "Orange Blossom Special"; "Turkey in the Straw") and some beautiful originals. Into the late 1990s, the diminutive Hokkanen performed with various musicians around Austin including, at one time, an informal project with Danny Barnes and Mark Rubin of the Bad Livers by the name of the Mad Cat Trio. In 1997, they enlisted Hokkanen to play on their soundtrack for *The Newton Brothers* and throughout 1998, he did session work for a variety of performers including Candye Kane, Tommy Hancock, and Chief Jim Billie.

The Offbeats: Erik Hokkanen (f,g,v); Dale "Cowboy Dick" Dennis (b,g); Danny Levin (cello,vio,p); Wes Starr (d,rb) with Jon Blondell (trb); Serge Laine (acc,tri); L. E. McCullough (pw; bhn)
The Snow Wolves Orchestra: Erik Hokkanen (f,g,v); Joey DeLago (g); Jeff Haley (b); Charlene Hancock (b.v.); Elias Haslanger (sax); Freddie Mendoza (tmb); Rachel Rhodes (b.v.); Phil Richey (tp); Slim Richey (e.g.); Beckah Ross (b.v.); Mark Rubin (bj); Chris Searles (d)
Lumisudet: Erik Hokkanen (f,g,v); Petri Hakala (g,md); Arto Jarvela (f,g,md); Tapani Varis (b)

"I Miss the Train" b/w "Broken Spoke
   Song"(Offbeats)/Renaissance/1986 (7")
Erik & The Offbeats/Zippo UK/1987
Blue Corn (Offbeats)/EH/1989 (CS)
Erik & Erik (with Erik Moll)/Fire Ant/1992
Earth Swing (Snow Wolves Orchestra)/EH/1994
Kaustinen, Texas (Lumisudet)/Olarin Musikki Fin./1995
"2200 Miles" (The Mad Cat Trio) on **Songs of Route
   66**/Lazy SOB/1995
Swing the Night Away (Snow Wolves
   Orchestra)/EH/1996 (CS)

Erik Hokkanen, 39 Chalmers, Austin, TX 78702; 512-264-0101

See Bad Livers; Erik Moll

Robin Holcomb

Pianist; Singer/Songwriter; Americana
Georgia; 1954-

For most of her life, Robin Holcomb has mixed in some pretty long-haired musical company studying ethnomusicology (Indonesian gamelans) and composition in college, playing piano and writing songs as part of the experimental music scene in New York, giving poetry readings, and working in musical theater. But, along the way, growing up in Georgia, share-cropping for a time in North Carolina, and living in the mountains in California, she picked up an affinity for American folk culture and music. The melding of these seemingly disparate experiences and musical styles is at the heart of her recordings. Sometimes the rural, Appalachian influences are fairly overt especially when Holcomb uses her wavering slightly twangy vocals to good effect on gospel/old-time flavored songs like "Help A Man," "Deliver Me," "When I Stop Crying" or a straight cover of the cowboy classic, "The Goodnight-Loving Trail." More often, however, the folk, backwoods references are more subtle whether expressed in her arcadian lyrics and themes or in extended classical piano pieces which like those of her predecessors Charles Ives and Aaron Copland contain snippets of familiar folk songs such as "Oh Susanna." The cream of modern experimental musicians have worked with Holcomb including husband/producer Wayne Horvitz and guitarist extraordinaire Bill Frisell. She contributed her unique vocal skills to three songs on the latter's highly innovative and highly acclaimed "country" recording **Nashville** in 1998.

Robin Holcomb/Nonesuch/1990
Rockabye/Nonesuch/1992
Little Three/Nonesuch/1995

Robin Holcomb/Atlantic Page
//feature.atlantic-records.com/robin_holcomb/

See Bill Frisell

The Hollisters (The Rounders)

Honky Tonk
Houston, Texas; 1992-

The Rounders were a popular rocking Houston hillbilly band formed by a mutton chopped hunk of a man named Mike Barfield and guitarist Eric Danheim in the mid-1980s. Danheim left in the early 1990s (replaced by Danny Gardner) for Austin where he was briefly with the Wagoneers and then Chaparral. Meanwhile, the Rounders recorded one fine album of honky tonk bluesabilly (**Thrill-Billy Bop)** in 1993 but split up shortly afterwards. At about the same time, the "big things" planned for Chaparral failed to materialize, so Danheim returned to Houston where he teamed up with Barfield to write songs and form a new group. They added a drummer (Kevin Fitzpatrick) and bass (Denny Dale), called themselves the Hollisters (after a character on the *Andy Griffith Show*), and took up more or less where the Rounders left off playing hard core honky tonk/country/rockabilly fueled by Barfield's powerful baritone vocals and Danheim's ace lead guitar. For their recording debut, "Good for the Blues" on the **True Sounds of the New West** compilation, Barfield and Danheim enlisted Austin stalwarts John Ludwick, Lisa Pancratz, and Casper Rawls (all of whom had been in Chaparral). In 1997, the Hollisters, with Casper Rawls producing, recorded their debut CD, **The Land of Rhythm and Pleasure**. Released on Austin based Freedom Records, it is a potent blend of Texas musical styles from honky tonk to Tex-Mex including originals ("Good for The Blues"; "Tyler"; "Better Slow Down") and covers of Nick Lowe ("Without Love"), Tom Clifford ("Pike County Blues"), and Libbi Bosworth ("East Texas Pines").

The Rounders: Mike Barfield (g,hm,l.v.); Danny Gardner (l.g.,v); Rex Wherry (b); Steve Wood (d).
The Hollisters: Mike Barfield (g,hm,l.v.); Denny Dale (b); Eric Danheim (l.g.); Kevin Fitzpatrick (d)

Thrill-Billy Bop (Rounders)/Major/1993
"Good for the Blues" (Hollisters) on **True Sounds of the New West**/Freedom/1995
The Land of Rhythm and Pleasure/Freedom/1997

The Hollisters Home Page
//www.hollisters.com

Hollistex@aol.com

Donna Kay Honey & The Cowpokers

Cowboy/Western Parody
Seattle, Washington; 1995-

As legend has it, Donna Kay Honey was born and raised at the Bubblin' Vista Trailer Park near Enumclaw, Washington. Her parents, Claude and Bunny, had formerly been the musical troupe The Traveling Honeys (Sweetest Sound This Side of Heaven) before settling down at the Vista. Inspired by this background, Donna Kay made her singing debut at age 8 at a school talent show where she sang "There's a Little Bitty Spider Living in My Hair" and the ever popular "Uncle Teddy Loves My Brother." The stunned reaction of the audience that day convinced her that she had found her calling. Back at the trailer park, Donna Kay polished up her writing skills by setting her diary to music and performed with the Honeys at the Vista's barbecue "pig outs" and jam sessions. Eventually, she formed the Cowpokers from Bubblin' Vista residents and began her rise to stardom. In 1995, Donna Kay recorded **Queen of the Bubblin' Vista** with original songs based on real life experiences. Some of the titles tell you just what kind of life it has been: "My Boyfriend is a Convict," "Cowpokin'," "Tears in the Tanning Bed," "I Remember Your Member (But I Forgot Your Face)," "I Want to Watch You Hunt," and "Jesus, Jack Daniels & a Vibrator." As her promo material says, this is *reeeeal* alternative country, and it has won her scores of fans the world over (in Lithuania she's known as Princess Boobalina). In addition to her musical talents, Donna Kay has authored a self-help book for the 1990s called *Power Whining*. This plus T-shirts, a newsletter and other info is available through The International Pony Pullers Club.

Donna Kay Honey (l.v.); The Drifter (d); General Lee Nutts (g); Private "Earl Cootie" Parts (g); Dimples Vicious (b.v.); Emily Vicious (f); Willie R. Won'tee (b.v.)

Queen of the Bubblin' Vista/Weenie Dog/1995

International Pony Pullers Club/Northwest International Entertainment, 5503 Roosevelt Way N.E., Seattle, WA 98105-3630

Donnay Kay Honey Home Page
//www.musicscene.com/friends/don.html

nie@eskimo.com

The Honeydogs

No Depression; Grain Belt Rock
Minneapolis, Minnesota; 1994-

Over the past decade, the Twin Cities area has slowly but surely developed into one of the focal points of alternative country. The cavalcade of bands has been remarkable and continues to grow: the Gear Daddies, the Jayhawks, the Carpetbaggers, Golden Smog. To that list add the Honeydogs. The co-founders of the band, brothers Adam and Noah Levy, had been together in the Adam Levy Band (backing band for Martin Zellar, ex-Gear Daddies leader) and with Trailer Trash and the Picadors. By 1994, the Levys were ready to go with their own group and adding Trent Norton on bass and Tommy Borscheid on guitar formed the Honeydogs. Their first two releases, **The Honeydogs** and **Everything, I Bet You**, were solid Grain Belt roots. After a performance at SXSW in 1997, the Honeydogs signed with Debris (Mercury subsidary) and recorded **Seen a Ghost** which has three retreads ("I Miss You," "Those Things Are Hers," "Your Blue") plus new material that retains some of the band's previous style while breaking out in a more aggressively rock direction. When not playing in the Honeydogs, Noah Levy drummed for the alt. country "supergroup" Golden Smog from 1992 until mid-1997 when he left to devote himself full time to the Honeydogs.

Tommy Borscheid (g,v); Adam Levy (g,v); Noah Levy (d); Trent Norton (b,v)

The Honeydogs/October/1995
Everything, I Bet You/October/1996
Seen a Ghost/Debris/1997

The Honeydogs Home Page //www.honeydogs.com

The Honeydogs/October Page
//www.october-rec.com/honey.htm

The Honeydogs/Polygram Page
//www.polygram-us.com/mondo/honeydogs/honeydogs.htm

See Golden Smog; Martin Zellar

Honky Tonk Confidential

Honky Tonk; Western Swing
Washington, DC; 1996-

According to Honky Tonk Confidential, they play country music "the way it 'spoze to be," that is, honky tonk and Western swing from the Golden Age of the 1950s-1960s. And, obviously they do it well having been nominated for six Wammies the year after they formed (New Artist; Country Duo/Group; two for Country Instrumentalist; Country Male Vocalist; Country Female Vocalist) without even putting out a CD. In a region already brimming with alt. country talent (Ruthie & the Wranglers, the Grandsons, Bill Kirchen, the Wanktones, the Slim Jims), HTC managed to make an impressive breakthrough mainly because its members were expereinced veterans of local country, roots, and rock bands. Bassist Geff King had been in numerous bluegrass and honky tonk bands including the Slim Jims and the New Early Sunrise Band with whom he still plays; lead guitar, dobroist Mike Woods had not only done time with local alt. country pioneer Tex Rubinowitz but also with legends such as Kinky Friedman, Mac Wiseman, and Webb Pierce; man of steel Bobby Martin listed the Cold Steel Benders (with Evan Johns), Guitartown, and Ranjer Joe and the Buffalo Band on his long resume; singer Diana Quinn wore many musical hats as founder of Tru Fax & The Insaniacs, D.C.'s oldest continuing punk band, as well as two ongoing side projects, the Towering Bouffants (60s girl group) and Diana & the Moondogs (roots, R&B); drummer Rob Howe was also a member of the Bouffants and the Moondogs. Together, they served up a powerful honky tonk/swing cocktail anchored by dynamic lead and harmony vocals, very clever songwriting ("Honky Tonk 101"; "Barroom Tan"; "Lottery Tickets, Cigarettes & Booze"; "El Nino"; "The Cigarette Song"), and exceptional playing all around especially from Woods on lead guitar and Martin on pedal steel. In 1998, HTC's long-awaited eponymous debut took the D.C. alt. country scene by storm and once again, the Wammie nominations came rolling in: Country Duo/Group, Country Instrumentalist (Woods; King), Male Country Vocalist (King), Female Country Vocalist. Geff King's other honky tonk/swing band, the New Early Sunrise Band, also put out their first album, **Telephone**, in 1998. Meanwhile, Quinn and Woods assembled the cream of D.C.'s alt. country community for a compilation, **Greetings From the District of Country**, that is an excellent sequel to the **Big D.C. Jamboree** series of the early 1990s.

Honky Tonk Confidential: Rob Howe (d); Geff King (b,v); Bobby Martin (p.s.); Diana Quinn (g,v); Mike Woods (b,db,g,v)
New Early Sunrise Band: Dave Goodman (f,v); Dave Hadley (l.g.,p.s.); Geff King (b,v); George Ryder (d); Archie Warnock (g,v)

"Honky Tonk 101" on **Edges From the Postcard2**/
P2/1998
Honky Tonk Confidential/Muddypaws/1998
Telephone (New Early Sunrise Band)/NESB/1998
"Barroom Tan", "I Done It", "Fujiyama Mama" on
Greetings From the District of Country/Too Many Dogs/1998

Honky Tonk Confidential, 1203 East Capitol St. S.E., Washington, DC 20003; 202-544-7011

Honky Tonk Confidential Home Page
//www.muddypaws.com/honkytonk.html

diana@muddypaws.com

Geff King's Home Page //www2.ari.net/gking/

gking@ari.net

The Horseflies

New Old-Time
Ithaca, New York; Early 1980s-

The Horseflies once got a job playing a wedding reception, but things didn't go so well. At one point in the festivities, the mother of the bride turned to the groom (who had hired them) and said, "Billy, your band sucks and that's why everybody's going home." Which isn't a surprising reaction from a group of people who were expecting oldies, classic rock, or disco and instead got old-time string band music fused with world beat, modern rock, and even electronic music. Fact is, since their emergence in the mid-1980s, the Horseflies have caused no little bit of consternation among purists who look askance at their very contemporary take on traditional music. However, the Horseflies have never backed down from the challenge of breaking down boundaries and linking musical elements together in an unprecedented way. The first inkling of the direction they took came with their debut recording **Old-Time Music: Chokers & Flies**, a "half-and-half" with their friends and fellow eccentrics, the Chicken Chokers. On their side, the Tompkins County Horseflies, as they were then called, played traditional old-time with a few twists, but on their first two full length recordings, **Human Fly** ("Help me! Help me!") and **Gravity Dance**, they moved fully into what they called "neoprimitive bug music." Here, the sounds of old-time music, bolstered by Judy Hyman's rarefied violin and Rich Stearns' plunking clawhammer, are fully intermixed with African instruments, synthesizer, and computer programming on standards such as "Hush Little Baby" and "Cornbread" and on covers of the Cramps ("Human Fly") and the Residents ("It's a Man's, Man's, Man's Man's World"). Added to this is the Flies' exceedingly dark view of the world with "Jenny on the Railroad" (drug addiction), "Rub Alcohol Blues" (suicide), "Sally Ann" (prostitution), "I Live Where It's Gray," "Roadkill," and "Who Throwed Lye on My Dog." And although the Horseflies may drive away wedding guests and die hard traditionalists, these "electro-hillbillies" won many fans and acclaim from critics who applauded their daring and put them somewhere in the same league with Talking Heads, Camper Van Beethoven, and Laurie Anderson. Moreover, they influenced other progressive old-time bands like fellow Ithacans Donna the Buffalo.

The Horseflies scored two movie soundtracks: *Where the River Flows* (1994) and *A Stranger in the Kingdom* (1998) and planned to do more film projects in the future. In the late 1990s, they continued to appear at various festivals as either the electric Horseflies or in their original configuration as the Acoustic Flies or Cast Iron Lawn Dogs. However, after bass player John Hayward died in June 1997, the group decided to take a break from live performances. Stearns became a member of Agents of Terra (side project of Donna the Buffalo) and another contemporary old-time group, the Renegades. Claus and Hyman got involved in experimental world music as part of Ancient Hand.

Jeff Claus (g,v); Peter Dodge (ky); John Hayward (b,d. 1997); Judy Hyman (f,v); Richie Stearns (bj,v)

Old-Time Music: Chokers & Flies/Rounder/1985
Human Fly/Rounder/1987
Gravity Dance/MCA/1991
Where the Rivers Flow North/Alcazar/1994 (sdtrk.)
A Stranger in the Kingdom/1998 (sdtrk.)

The Horseflies Home Page
//www.simplenet.com/horse_flies/

See Donna the Buffalo; The Hix

Horseshoe

Country Rock; Roots Rock
Houston, Texas; 1994-

Horseshoe was pieced together from the remnants of three Houston rock bands: Pork Belly Picnic, Fleshmop, and Tab Jones. The latter was basically a psychedelic rock band but for fun played covers of Hank, Merle, George, Johnny Paycheck, and other country greats. Tab Jones alumni, Scott Daniels, Ed Hawkins, and Greg Wood, carried on this tradition with Horseshoe which they formed with Ben Collis and Cary Winscott in 1994. In fact, the country/folk/blues elements were even more pronounced leading local reviewers to describe Horseshoe's roots rock sound as "thrash 'n' twang" or "gulf coast gonzo country fried rock." In 1996, Horseshoe self released **King of the World**, a generous CD (70+ minutes) musically indebted to Buck Owens, the Rolling Stones, and Little Feat and lyrically inspired as much by Lester Bangs, Charles Bukowski, and William Yeats as Hank, Sr. and Johnny Cash. Openings for Davd Allen Coe and Steve Earle (among others), an appearance at SXSW 1997, and a profile in *No Depression* (late 1996) helped spread the word about one of Houston's finest alt. country bands. Founding member Eddie Hawkins departed in 1998 but was quickly replaced by new drummer Michael Fischer, and Horseshoe kept right on pitching.

Ben Collis (b); Scott Daniels (g); Michael Fisher (d,1998-); Eddie Hawkins (d,1994-1998); Cary Winscott (g); Greg Wood (l.v.)

King of the World/Horseshoe/1996

Horseshoe Home Page
//www.bizniz-web.com/horse/

gutoski@bizniz-web.com

The Horton Brothers

Hillbilly Bop
Austin, Texas; 1996-

In 1996, at the urging of High Noon's Shaun Young, two brothers from Beaumont, Texas moved to Austin to test the musical waters. Billy and Bobby Horton had been playing along the Gulf Coast and East Texas since their early teens as Big Roy's Jumpin' Cadillacs (r&b) and the Fender Benders (rockabilly) and immediately made their presence known in Austin. Billy plucked bass for the Asylum Street Spankers and Wayne Hancock, Bobby backed up Susanna Van Tassel and trumpeted for Shaun Young's Big Town Swingtet, while both served as the rhythm section for Young's Texas Trio. However, their biggest impact was through their own band the Horton Brothers with Shaun Young on drums and Derek Peterson (ex-Kid Pharaoh) on rhythm guitar. Their debut, **Hey! It's Bobby and Billy...**, with hot guitar licks, twangy harmonies, swingy, hillbilly bop beat, and hayseed humor clearly shows traditional (Merle Travis, Joe Maphis, Louvins, Delmores, Maddox Brothers and Rose) and contemporary (High Noon, Big Sandy, Dave & Deke) influences. Billy and Bobby share singing and songwriting duties and with help from locals Lisa Pancratz and Chris Miller plus Alberto Telo (Texas Trio) and Tjarko Jeen (Ronnie Dawson) fashioned a nice debut. In its wake, the Horton Brothers had a busy 1997 with appearances at the Big K Barndance in Denver, Austin's Rockabilly Romp, and a West Coast tour (with Dave Stuckey on drums). In early 1998, their EP **Jack in the Box Boogie** was released on Deke Dickerson's Ecco-Fonic label and later in the year, they followed it up with another solid hillbilly boogie recording, **Roll Back the Rug...It's the Horton Brothers**, on Jason Shields' new Texas Jamboree Records. Helping out were Dave Biller (ex-Dale Watson), Jeremy Wakefield (Lucky Stars), and Elena Fremerman of Hot Club of Cowtown. The latter, which in 1998 became the hottest new Western swing band, welcomed Billy Horton as their new bass player, but he and Bobby continued on as the Horton Brothers moving further up the hillbilly bop ladder with performances at the Denver Rock-N-Rhythm-Billy Weekend and the granddaddy of 'em all, Hemsby.

Billy Horton (u.b.,v); Bobby Horton (l.g.,v); Derek Peterson (r.g.); Shaun Young (d)

> **Hey! It's Bobby and Billy...**/Crazy Love Ger./1996
> "Did You Mean Jelly Bean?" on **Teenage Crime Wave**/Wild Youth/1997
> **Jack In the Box Boogie**/Ecoo-Fonic/1997 (EP)
> **Roll Back the Rug...It's the Horton Brothers**/Texas Jamboree/1998

The Horton Brothers, P.O. Box 143534,
Austin, TX 78714-3534; 512-467-1506

The Horton Brothers
//www.mindspring.com/~canner/hortbio.htm

fthorton@flash.net

See Asylum Street Spankers; The Dave & Deke Combo; High Noon; Hot Club of Cowtown

The Hot Club of Cowtown

Western/Eastern Swing
San Diego, California/Austin, Texas; Mid 1990s-

In the early 1990s, Whit Smith fronted a New York City Western swing group called Western Caravan that was popular at the Rodeo Bar. During this time he met fiddler Elana Fremerman, and eventually, they ended up in San Diego where they formed the Hot Club of Cowtown with T.C. Cyran. Their name reflects their blending of classic Western and Eastern swing fueled mainly by Fremerman's top notch fiddling. In 1997, HCC did a self-released cassette, **Western Clambake**, with covers of covers of Eastern and Western swing standards ("Chinatown," "Avalon," "After You've Gone," "Silver Dew," "I Laugh When I Think How I Cried Over You," "Milk Cow Blues," "Oklahoma Hills" etc.) and then, with lots of help and encouragement from California and Texas alt. country musicians (Dave Stuckey, Don Walser, Mark Rubin) moved to Austin. With new bass player, Billy Horton (Horton Brothers), they worked a variety of venues and events, built a following, and nailed down a weekly happy hour spot at the Continental Club. In early 1998, a number of labels began to court the Hot Club of Cowtown with Hightone eventually winning out. Their self-produced debut on that label, **Swingin' Stampede**, draws most heavily on the Milton Brown/Bob Wills Western swing tradition with covers of familiar standards, but there's also some "Le Jazz Hot" *a la* Reinhardt/Grappelli or Lang/Venuti, fiddle breakdowns, and even a little Tex-Mex. Veteran Johnny Gimble, Jeremy Wakefield (Lucky Stars), and Mike Maddux (accordion) help things along, but reviewers were generally agreed that **Swingin' Stampede** fell short of capturing the incredible dynamism of Hot Club of Cowtown live.

T.C. Cyran (ub,v, to 1997); Elana Fremerman (f); Billy Horton (u.b.,1997-); Whit Smith (a.g.,v)

> **Western Clambake**/HCC/1997
> **Swingin' Stampede**/Hightone/1998

The Hot Club of Cowtown/Hightone Page
//www.hightone.com/bios/hotclub.html

The Hot Club of Cowtown/Fly Agency Page
//www.flyagency.com/hotclub.html

See The Horton Brothers

Hot Rize

See Tim O'Brien

Tom House

Insurgent Country; Singer/Songwriter
Durham, North Carolina; 1950-

Tom House began publishing poetry while still in his teens and in the mid-1980s was editor/publisher of a jolting, slap in the face of a literary magazine called *raw bone*. In the early 1990s, House was commissioned to write a song cycle and opera based on William Faulkner's works (*As I Lay Dying*; *Light in August*), co-organized the Working Stiffs Jamboree (for s/s, poets, radicals) in Nashville, and recorded a self-released tape, **Inside These Walls**. In 1996, he became a member of the insurgent country community when two of his compositions were included on Bloodshot's **Nashville: The Other Side of the Alley**. His opening soliloquy, "The Hanks Williams Memorial Myth" sets the tone for the compilation to which he also contributed the song "Cole Durhew." With backing from members of local alt. country eccentrics, Lambchop, House made his CD debut in 1997 with **The Neighborhood is Changing**. His style and sense of humor are somewhat like John Prine's but with a much darker, hard hitting approach e.g. "I Got Neighbors," "Nuclear Winter," "A Woman and a Man," "I Had a Place," "The Deepest Part, The Deepest End." **This White Man's Burden** pretty much takes up where its predecessor left off with more tales about the bleak side of life in the land of rednecks, white socks and Blue Ribbon beer.

Inside These Walls/TH/1996
"The Hank Williams Memorial Myth" on **Nashville: The Other Side of the Alley**/Bloodshot/1996
The Neighborhood is Changing/Checkered Past/1997
This White Man's Burden/Checkered Past/1998

Tom House/Checkered Past Home Page
//www.checkeredpast.com

Ray Wylie Hubbard

Singer/Songwriter; Outlaw
Soper, Oklahoma; November 13, 1946-

Ray Wylie Hubbard's name will forever be associated with just one song: "Up Against the Wall Redneck Mother." And while, that song certainly helped launch his career, its immense popularity has tended to obscure the depth and complexity of Hubbard as a songwriter and musician. Considered one of the leading figures in progressive country of the early 1970s, Hubbard actually started out as a teen in the Dallas folk scene where he met another aspiring folkie, Jerry Jeff Walker. After high school, he entered college and began performing with the Coachmen (Rick Fowler, Wayne Kidd). During the summer, the group (later renamed Three Faces West) began playing at Red River, a resort town in Northern New Mexico. It was there in 1973 that Hubbard penned "Redneck Mother" which subsequently became a huge hit off Jerry Jeff's **Viva Terlingua**. Meanwhile, Hubbard formed another band in Red River, the Cowboy Twinkies, a proto-cowpunk band covering

Haggard *and* Led Zep. Relocating to Austin, Hubbard made a succession of albums in the late 1970s using a varied cast of musicians. First came **Off the Wall** for Willie Nelson's Lone Star label in 1978, then **Something About the Night** (with the Lost Gonzo Band) followed by **Caught in the Act** (live from Soap Creek Saloon). Each contained some fine songs by Hubbard ("Radio Song"; "Freeway Church of Christ"; "Hello Early Morning") including his version of "Redneck Mother" and "The Last Recording of Redneck Mother (Ever)." However, Hubbard's career went nowhere due in no small part to drug and alcohol abuse, and he more or less dropped out of sight. Then, in the early 1990s, he resurfaced clean and sober and reclaimed his spot as one of the best of the progressive country performers with **Lost Train of Thought**. In 1994 with able production from Lloyd Maines and help from old Twinkie lead guitarist Terry Ware, Hubbard showed his versatility on **Loco Gringo's Lament**, a stellar collection of country rock, blues, and folk representing his more introspective/spiritual side; it garnered a number of Texas album of the year awards. With Maines once again contributing his production and musical talents, in 1997, Ray recorded **Dangerous Spirits** for the Dutch label, Continental Song City. As strong as **Loco**, it shows Ray Wylie back in top form with help from Terry Ware, Lucinda Williams, Kevin Welch, Jimmy LaFave, Tish Hinojosa, Mike Henderson, Tony Joe White, and Kieran Kane. It was released domestically on Philo late in 1997. In mid-October 1998, the first annual Ray Wylie Hubbard Songwriters Workshop was held in Comfort, Texas. Fifteen lucky attendees were given first-hand lessons in country guitar picking and songwriting from Hubbard and other masters. Late in 1998, backed by a band made up of Lloyd Maines, Stephen Bruton, and Lisa Mednick among others, Ray recorded a live album at Cibolo Creek Country Club north of San Antonio with lengthy renditions of Hubbard's best and/or most well-known tunes including "The Obligatory Encore aka Redneck Mother."

Three Faces West/TFW/1971
Ray Wylie Hubbard and the Cowboy Twinkies/Warner Brothers/1975
Ray Wylie Hubbard/Lone Star/1978
Something About the Night/Renegade/1980
Caught in the Act/Misery Loves Company/1984
Lost Train of Thought/Misery Loves Company/1992; Dejadisc/1995
Loco Gringo's Lament/Dejadisc/1994
Dangerous Spirits/Continental Song City Dutch/1997; Philo/1997
Live at Cibolo Creek Country Club/Misery Loves Company/1998

Ray Wylie Hubbard, 13709 Ranch Rd., Ste. 210, Wimberley, TX 78676

Official Wylie World Headquarters //www.raywylie.com

Wylieworld@aol.com

Ray Wylie Hubbard/Dejadisc Page
//www.eden.com/~dejadisc/hubbard.html

Jeff Hughes and Chaparral

Austin; Honky Tonk; Country Rock
Austin, Texas; 1987-1993; 1995-

During the early 1990s, Chaparral was one of Austin's most popular and promising bands. Formed in 1987 by native Jeff Hughes, the group was firmly in the Austin honky tonk tradition, but Hughes had a background in punk, and it was this influence that helped set Chaparral apart and give them such a widespread appeal. Their ability to handle country standards and do honky tonk versions of songs like REM's "Rockville" gained them a uniquely diverse following especially among Austin's zealous dance crowd. It also helped that Hughes knew how to write first rate songs and was backed over the years by the cream of Austin's musical talent including Sean Mencher and Shaun Young (High Noon), Lisa Pancratz, Casper Rawls, John Ludwick, and Eric Danheim (the Hollisters). By 1991, Chaparral held down regular spots at the Black Cat and the legendary Henry's. In 1992, *The Austin Chronicle* readers voted them Best Country Band, and a writer for the paper labeled the latest round of Austin alt. country as "The Chaparral Generation." Chaparral and fans eagerly awaited the big label deal that was surely only a matter of time, but it never came. Late in the spring of 1993, Chaparral played their farewell gig (at the Broken Spoke). Hughes tried and failed in Nashville as a solo, then took time off to work a regular job and start a family. In 1995, he made his first steps toward a comeback by recording (as Jeff Hughes & Chaparral) "Choose Only Love" for the **Austin Country Nights** compilation. Over the next two years, Hughes and band returned to the clubs and in 1997 did two cuts for another collection called **The Edge of Country**. Then came the long overdue CD debut. **Chaparral** is as the liner notes say, a document encapsulating Hughes' decade long contributions to Austin's alternative country community. Supported by top notch musicians including Chaparral alumni and long time supporters (Bruce Robison and Kelly Willis on backing vocals), Hughes' and company do an admirable job on fine originals from country rocking ("Finer Lovin'"; "Locked in the Bighouse"; "Loneliest Tears") to honky tonk ("Same Old Magic") and engaging ballads ("All My Life"; "Bus Stop"; "Santa Fe Railroad").

Previous Members: Eric Danheim (l.g.); Sean Mencher (l.g.); Lisa Pancratz (d); Casper Rawls (l.g.); Shaun Young (d) **Current Members:** Merle Bregante (d); Mike Hardwick (e.g.,p.s.); John Ludwick (b,h.v.)

"Choose Only Love" on **Austin Country
    Nights**/Watermelon/1995
"Buildin' Me Up"; "Finer Lovin'" on **The Edge of
    Country**/Stockade/1997
Chaparral/Boar's Nest/1997

Two Roads Music, 4903 Finley Dr., Austin, TX 78731
Jeff Hughes Web Site //www.flash.net/~tworoads/
tworoads@flash.net

The Hula Monsters

Pedal Steel; Swing; Roots Rock
Los Angeles, California; 1994-

From the home of Baywatch comes a totally different beach experience brought to you courtesy of the Hula Monsters. They were the brainchild of longtime L.A. musician and steel guitarist Hank Mann. For a number of years, he had been designing and building non-pedal steel guitars out of koa wood from recycled Hawaiian surf boards. The resulting instruments (with 10, 12, or 14 strings) had a special quality of their own which Mann dubbed the "Hula Sound." With the addition of Jon Bare (of Killer Whales fame), Chet McCracken (ex-Doobie Bros.) on drums, and George Hawkins on bass, Mann started the Hula Monsters who played a unique hybrid of Hawaiian steel swing, surf, and southern blues rock; their live shows, complete with Hula girls, became a favorite on the beach party scene. The real star of the show, however, was Mann and his koa wood steel guitar which he played standing up; like Junior Brown and Joe Goldmark, Mann pushed traditional steel playing over the edge. The Hula Monsters debut, **Party Platter**, with its bold and fun loving attitude, received raves from many quarters including *Steel Guitar World Magazine*, *Music Connection*, *Electronic Musician*, and *The Beach Reporter*. (*There is also a D.C. area band called the Hula Monsters; see Ruthie & the Wranglers).

Jon Bare (l.g.); George Hawkins (b); Hank Mann (p.s.,l.v.); Chet McCracken (d)

Party Platter/Mega Truth/1995
The Hula Monsters c/o Hank Mann, Box 1105,
Pacific Palisades, CA 90272-1105
The Hula Monsters Home Page
//members.aol.com/hulamon/index.html

Dakota Dave Hull & Sean Blackburn
(Masterson & Blackburn)

Americana; Cowboy/Western
Minneapolis, Minnesota/Fargo, North Dakota

In the late 1970s, two old boys from way up north in Minnesota/ North Dakota were drawn together by their mutual love for Americana. Singer/guitarists Dakota Dave Hull and Sean Blackburn blended up hillbilly, Western swing, cowboy, folk, jazz, and more with an easy going, inviting feel. Their first two albums, **Ace Pickin' & Sweet Harmony** and **North By Southwest**, were on small, local labels, but **River of Swing** on Flying Fish brought them attention from a much wider audience in 1980. Its cartoon cover depicting a band of frogs "gigging" on lily pads and along a river bank are a clue to the light-hearted and joyful spirit that animates this recording. Hull and Blackburn pay homage to and thank their main influences on covers of "Deep Water" (Bob Wills), "Mississippi Shore" (Delmore Brothers), "What's the Use" (Bill Boyd), "Blue Shadows on the Trail" (Sons of the Pioneers), "Searchin' the Desert for the Blues" (Blind Willie McTell), and "Rollin' Along" (Prairie Ramblers). A large ensemble cast with Butch Tompson on clarinet and piano, Peter Ostroushko on fiddle and mandolin, Molly Mason on bass and harmony vocals, Mike Cass on dobro and pedal steel plus some tasty trombone and trumpet keep the swing tunes lively and add nice touches to slower songs like "I Don't Want to Set the World on Fire" and the beautiful Hull composition, "Annie's Waltz."

After Hull and Blackburn went their separate ways later in the 1980s, Dakota Dave did a recording (**Reunion Rag**) of originals and covers (from Stephen Foster to Leon McAuliffe) highlighted by his solo and duet guitar work with guests Cam Waters, Bill Hinkley, and Eric Peltoniemi. In the late 1990s, he hosted a country and Western swing show on radio station KFAI in Minneapolis. Blackburn moved to Colorado where he formed a cowboy/Western/swing duo with singer/yodeler, Liz Masterson. Specializing in singing cowboy era music as well as comedy and rope tricks, Masterson & Blackburn made several recordings and became regulars on the folk and cowboy poetry gathering circuits in the 1990s.

Ace Pickin' & Sweet Harmony/Train on the Island/1978
North By Southwest/Biscuit City/1979
River of Swing/Flying Fish/1980
Reunion Rag (Dakota Dave)/Flying Fish/1982
Swingtime Cowgirl (Masterson & Blackburn)
Tune Wranglin' (Masterson & Blackburn)
Swing With the Music (Masterson & Blackburn)
Born to the Saddle (Masterson & Blackburn)/1998

A Roundup of Cowboy Swing: Liz Masterson & Sean Blackburn //www.cowgirls.com/dream/liz-sean/

LizSean@aol.com

The Humpff Family
New Old-Time; Country Rock; Punkabilly
Glasgow, Scotland; 1987-

The Humpff Family mixes country, Cajun, rockabilly, and punk played at breakneck speed. Founder John Coletta and Dave Fitzpatrick write originals with quirky and disturbing lyrics ("Self Pity Waltz," "Conduct of Pigeons"; "Love, Death, Divorce, Prison, Alcohol, Rivers, Trains"), and the Humpffs are notorious for live shows filled with all sorts of lunacy. Since the late 1980s, they have toured Scotland extensively and made several recordings (**In the Family Way**; **Family Planning**; **Mothers**; **Fathers**) centered on "family values." Their extremely experimental approach to traditional music moved one reviewer to assert that the Humpff Family "would make a trappist monk yell 'yee-hah'." 'Nuf said?

Stuart Brown; John Coletta; Kat Evans; Dave "The Doc" Fitzpatrick; Malcolm Stevenson; Kevin Wilkinson

In the Family Way/HF/1989 (CS)
Family Planning/HF/1990 (6 trk. EP)
Mothers/Iona Gold/1992
Misty Again/Iona Gold/1993
Fathers/Iona Gold/1994
Hoo Haa/Hoo Haa Music/1995
"Henryetta" on **Indigenous Tribes**/Scottish Wildlife Trust/1997

The Humpff Family/Iona Home Page //www.lismor.co.uk/humpffs.html

Cornell Hurd
Austin; Honky Tonk; Swing
Berkeley, California/Austin, Texas; 1977-

At the beginning of every performance, Cornell Hurd, a hulking figure dressed in black from head to toe with an ever present cigar in one hand delivers this warning to the unwary: "Heads up you miserable drunks. It's show time. All the way from the bowels of south Austin. It's Garth Brooks' worst nightmare. Holy mackerel Andy, it's the Cornell Hurd Band!" Which is followed by what has become know as "honky tonk mayhem," a veritable carnival ride of jumping swing and honky tonk novelties, infamous Hurd monologues, and who knows what else. And, it has been this way from the beginning when Hurd and bass player Frank X. Roeber formed their first band (surf music) together near San Jose, California in 1964. While at Berkeley in the early 1970s, they fell under the sway of local favorites Commander Cody and Asleep at the Wheel and formed a similar type of band called the El Rancho Cowboys. Eventually, this evolved into the Mondo Hots Pants Orchestra, a cult band with a rep for over-the-top shows. Two of their singles, "Texas Behemoth" and "Bicentennial Boogie" got significant air play in California (the latter song reached #1 on Dr. Demento's Top 10) and after a few more singles and albums on El Rauncho Records, the MHPO became the Cornell Hurd Band with Paul Skelton on lead guitar. Though still based in California, they began to make regular treks to Austin in the late 1970s and early 1980s to appear at the Armadillo World Headquarters. Their single "That Unholy Roll" got good air play, and the album of the same title won a Bay Area award in 1980. However, by the mid-1980s, the group drifted apart.

After a disastrous marriage and drug habit caught up with him in 1986, Hurd relocated to Florida where he found his new wife/pianist Debra and reunited with Roeber and Skelton. They cut **Fever in the South** in 1987 and then two years later moved to Austin where in the early 1990s, they became one of the top acts at the late, lamented Henry's and later at the legendary Broken Spoke. After self-releasing **Honky Tonk Mayhem** in 1993, the Cornell Hurd Band became the first artists to record a live album at the Spoke. **Live! at the Broken Spoke** captures the Hurd show at its zany best with lots of honky tonk, swing novelty tunes "You Played on My Piano," "I Like 'Em Fat Like That," "I Bought the Shoes That Just Walked Out on Me," "Honky Tonk Has Been," "Paralyzed," peppered with Hurd's commentary on his "miserable ex-wife," show biz, and whatever else comes into his twisted mind. Close on the heels of this recording came inclusion of one cut on the **Hell-Bent** compilation and one ("I Cry, Then I Drink, Then I Cry") on the **Austin Country Nights** collection. Next up was **Cool and Unusual Punishment** which, with help from Johnny Bush, Chris O'Connell, Tom Morrell, and Lucky Oceans, bestows more prime Hurd on "Seven Cups of Coffee, Fourteen Cigarettes," "Your Ex-Husband Sent Me Flowers 'Cause He Feels Sorry for Me," "The Whiskey or the Wife" plus standards "Crazy 'Cause I Love You," "Drivin Nails in My Coffin," and "I'm Mad With You." Oh, and you also get to hear Cornell's humorous banter with the band about worst gigs, Hank Williams' death pact, manhood, Lalo Guerrero, and weirdest act. Late in 1997, Hurd returned with **Texas Fruit Shack**, another collection of Cornell's tongue-in-cheek originals ("It Wouldn't Be Hell Without You"; "I'm a Linda-holic"; "I Only Think About You Every Day") and covers of Johnny Bush, Jerry Lee Lewis, Moon Mullican, Ray Price, Tom T. Hall, and the Texas Playboys. Along for the joyride are Ponty Bone, Oceans, Bill Kirchen, the Texana Dames, Floyd Domino, and Howard Kalish. **At Large**, recoreded live at the Texicalli Grille, features guest artists Johnny Bush and Wayne Hancock.

Cornell Hurd (g,l.v.); Karen Biller (d,1997-); Debra Hurd (p,1986-1996); Terry Kirkendall (d,1993-1995); Frank X. Roeber (b,v); Paul Skelton (l.g.); Bobby "Scrap Iron" Snell (p.s.,1993-); Danny Roy Young (rb)

"Psychotic Love"/"Village of the Durned"/"Bicentennial Boogie"(Mondo Hot Pants Orchestra)/El Rauncho/1974 (EP)
"Texas Behemoth" b/w "Platinum Blondes"(MHPO)/El Rauncho/1974 (7")
"Under My Thumb" b/w "Is There a Lover in the House?" (MHPO)/El Rauncho/1975 (7")
"Cemetery Road"/"Marlena"/"Mountain of Love"/"Six Pack to Go"(MHPO)/El Rauncho/1975 (EP)
Here Come the Clones (MHPO)/El Rauncho/1973
Village of the Dumbed(MHPO)/El Rauncho/1974
Another Rock 'n' Roll Stage Plank(MHPO)/El Rauncho/1975
Plan 9 From San Jose (Cornell Hurd Band)/Behemoth/1978
That Unholy Roll (CHB)/Behemoth/1980
Fever in the South (CHB)/Behemoth/1987
Honky Tonk Mayhem (CHB)/Behemoth/1993
Live at the Broken Spoke (CHB)/Behemoth/1994
"Honky Tonk Has Been"(CHB) on **Hell-Bent**/ Bloodshot/1995
"I Cry, Then I Drink, Then I Cry" (CHB) on **Austin Country Nights**/Watermelon/1995
Cool & Unusual Punishment (CHB)/Behemoth/1996
"7 Cups of Coffee, 14 Cigarettes" (CHB) on **Jukebox Cowboy**/Vinyl Junkie UK/1997
Texas Fruit Shack (CHB)/Behemoth/1997

At Large (CHB)/Behemoth/1999

Cornell Hurd, P. O. Box 43532 Austin, TX 78745
Cornell Hurd Web Page
//www.intelliweb.com/cornell-hurd-band/
Cornell Hurd Gwolfcs@aol.com

Michael Hurley

New Old-Time; Snockgrass
Bucks Co., Pennsylvania; December 20, 1941-

When I think of Michael Hurley, the first thing that comes to mind is the crazy cartoon artwork that graces the covers of his recordings. Hurley likes to draw pictures of bird headed musical notes, oddly shaped naked men and women, and mischievous looking wolves in human clothing swilling liquor, driving cars, or playing in a band. The same zany spirit infuses his music but as with his paintings, there is much more here than meets the eye (or ear). Initially, Hurley was a Greenwich Village folkie in the early 1960s and was set to sign a record contract but was sidelined by a series of health problems (mono and hepatitis). When he recovered, Michael made his debut with **First Songs** (1964) which displayed his knack for eccentric singing and songwriting as on his signature tune "The Werewolf." Several years later, Hurley, who began to be known as Elwood Snock or Dr. Snock, recorded **Armchair Boogie** and **Hi-Fi Snock Uptown** for Raccoon Records. The former came with a Hurley comic book, *Boone and Jocko in the Barren Choking Land,* and both highlighted Hurley's eccentric, folksy vocals and droll songs ("Blue Driver"; "Open Up Eternal Lips"; "Sweedeedee") with minimal instrumental accompaniment that gives the recordings a laid back, old-time hillbilly feel. A subsequent deal with Rounder led to a collaboration with those merry pranksters, the Holy Modal Rounders and resulted in the contemporary folk/country classic **Have Moicy!** Hurley then did two more albums for Rounder most notably **Snockgrass** which is packaged in one of his bawdier covers and contains more of his wacky songs ("I Heard the Voice of a Porkchop"; "Automatic Slim & The Fat Boys") whose deceptive simplicity belie the workings of a complex and gleefully warped imagination. In 1989, Hurley recorded **Watertower** for Fundamental, but in the 1990s, started his own label, Bellemeade Phonics; his material from that time (**Excrusiasion, Growlin' Bo Bo, The Woodbill Brothers**) is only available through mail order. Hurley also did a number of "graphic novels" including *Uncle Gaspard Joins the Bograt Navy, Boone & Jocko in Heartbreak Hotel, The Honking Duck Marina* that can be ordered by mail along with the *Snocko News* which is full of Hurley's one of a kind insights (i.e. "Whenever you wish you were dead, you are dead"). **Wolfeyes** is a collection of his most popular tunes and was released first in Germany and then in the U.S. When not painting or fixing eight track tape players, Hurley continued to tour opening for Son

Volt in 1996 and doing his first ever performances in the U.K. in 1998. A compilation of some of Hurley's favorite country and blues tunes plus rare originals (**Bellemeade Sessions**) was issued on the Irish label Blue Navigator to coincide with the U.K. tour. Soon after returning, Dr. Snock (Hurley's alter ego) finished up a new album, **Weatherhole**, with assistance from David Reisch (ex-Holy Modal Rounders; ex-Golden Delicious), Paul Watson (Sparklehorse), John Hott (ex-Cracker), David Mansfield, and Kevin Maul. To promote it, Michael embarked on his first West Coast tour in twenty years. Throughout 1997-1998, Rounder steadily re-released Hurley's classics (**Have Moicy!**, **Long Journey**, **Snockgrass**) on CD, and a new generation gained respect for one of the under-appreciated greats in modern Americana.

> **First Songs**/Folkways/1964; Rounder/1997
> **Armchair Boogie**/Raccoon/1970; Bellmeade
>   Phonics/1995 (CS)
> **Hi-Fi Snock Uptown**/Raccoon/1972; Bellmeade
>   Phonics/1995 (CS)
> **Have Moicy!** (with the Holy Modal
>   Rounders)/Rounder/1976; 1992
> **Long Journey**/Rounder/1976; 1998
> **Snockgrass**/Rounder/1980; 1997
> **Blue Navigator**/Rooster/1984
> **Land of Lo-fi**/Bellmeade Phonics/1988 (CS)
> **Red Birds (Live 1976)**/Bellmeade Phonics/1988
> **Excrusiasion '86**/Bellmeade Phonics/1988 (CS)
> **Watertower**/Fundamental/1988
> **Growlin' Bo Bo**/Bellmeade Phonics/1991 (CS)
> "Wildgeeses" b/w "Coloured Birds"/SOL/1992 (7")
> "National Weed Growers Association" b/w "Slippery
>   Rag"/Snocko/1993 (7")
> **Wolfways**/Veracity Ger./1994; KOCH/1996
> **The Woodbill Brothers**/Bellmeade Phonics/1995
> **Parsnip Snips**/Veracity Ger./1996
> **Bellemeade Sessions: A Return to the Land of
>   Lo-Fi**/Blue Navigator Ire./1998
> **Weatherhole**/Field/1999

The Snocko News/Michael Hurley Web Site //sony.inergy.com/snocknews/ (Bellmeade Phonics products, Kornbred Cartoons, tour schedule and more)

Michael Hurley Fan Page //www.geocities.com/sunsetstrip/7262/snock.html

Michael Hurley/Holy Modal Rounders Fan Page //www.olywa.net/hilliard/hmr/

Michael Hurely Fanzine c/o Blue Navigator, 22 South Great Georges St., Dublin 2, Ireland or pcc@iol.ie

Walter Hyatt (Uncle Walt's Band)

Austin; Singer/Songwriter
Spartanburg, South Carolina; October 25, 1949-May 11, 1996

In early May 1996, Walter Hyatt died in the infamous ValuJet plane crash in the Florida Everglades; it was a dark day for the Austin music community. Hyatt had been a key figure in the early days of the Austin music scene and had many fans and friends there even though he left the city in the late 1980s. As news of the tragedy spread, a number of radio and club tributes were organized and the magnitude of Hyatt's achievements remembered. His greatest influence was exerted as leader of Uncle Walt's Band which included fellow South Carolinians David Ball and Champ Hood. In the early 1970s, their acoustic blend of folk and country seasoned with tight harmonies made them local favorites. After releasing two albums, Uncle Walt's Band broke up for a short time in the mid-1970s. Hyatt and Hood fronted another band called the Contenders in 1978, but that same year, UWB re-formed and began playing regularly at Waterloo Ice House and the Armadillo World Headquarters. The height of their success was a 1980 appearance on *Austin City Limits*, but in 1983, the band split up again. Each member went on to individual careers, but they occasionally reunited for reunion shows or in 1989 to sing back up for one tune on a Lyle Lovett album (two recordings of their best material, **The Girl on the Sunny Shore** and **An American in Texas Revisited**, were issued by Sugar Hill in 1991). Hood went on to host the Threadgill's Supper Sessions and work with Toni Price while Ball became a rising country star in the mid-1990s. Meanwhile, Hyatt moved to Nashville to do songwriting and solo work and received lots of help from Lovett. In the Uncle Walt days, Lyle had often opened up for them, and in the late 1980s, he reciprocated by letting Hyatt do the same. He produced and sang on Hyatt's first major solo effort **King Tears**. Walter's old band mates were featured on this record and on **Music Town**, a superb collection of swingy country. Over the years, Hyatt periodically returned to Austin and sat in with the Threadgill's Troubadours. His last recordings are on the second volume of **Threadgill's Supper Sessions** which was released in 1996. At the time of his death, Hyatt was completing work on a new record but no word as yet on when or if it will be issued. In 1997, *Austin City Limits* aired a special Walter Hyatt tribute show with performances of Hyatt's songs by Austin's musical elite. If you want to pay personal tribute to Walter, you can send a donation to his wife and three children in care of the Hyatt Family Fund, 3511 Belmont Blvd., Nashville, TN 37215. During 1998, Hyatt's legacy was revitalized by the reissue of **King Tears**, inclusion of two of his songs on the **Deep in the Heart of Texas** soundtrack, and most of all, by Lyle Lovett who covered a number of Walter's originals on his mammoth tribute to Texas songwriters, **Step Inside This House**.

Uncle Walt's Band: David Ball (b,snare,v); Deschamps Hood (f,l.g.,v); Walter Hyatt (r.g.,v)
The Contenders: Tommy Goldsmith (g,md,v); Walter Hyatt (g,v); Descamps Hood (f,g,p,v); Steve Runkle (b,v); Jimbeau Tabard Walsh (d,v).

> **Blame It on the Bossa Nova** (Uncle Walt's
>   Band)/Lapedeza/1973
> **Uncle Walt's Band**/Lespedeza/1975
> **The Contenders** (Hood; Hyatt)/Moonlight/1978
> **An American in Texas** (Uncle Walt's
>   Band)/Lespedeza/1980
> **Recorded Live** (Uncle Walt's Band)/Lapedeza/1982
> **Fall Thru to You** (Walter Hyatt)/Lespedeza/1985 (CS)

6-26-79 (Uncle Walt's Band)/Lespedeza/1988 (CS)
King Tears (Walter Hyatt)/MCA/1990; 1998
The Girl on the Sunny Shore (Uncle Walt's Band)/Sugar Hill/1991
An American in Texas Revisited (Uncle Walt's Band)/Sugar Hill/1991
Music Town (Walter Hyatt)/Sugar Hill/1993
Threadgill's Supper Sessions: Second Helpings/Watermelon/1996
"This Time Lucille" & "Last Call" on **Deep in the Heart of Texas**/Shanachie/1998

Walter Hyatt/NOMA Home Page //www.songs.com/walter/

Hypnotic Clambake
New Old-Time; ?
Boston, Massachusetts; 1990-

Boston's Hypnotic Clambake count themselves among a growing list of bands who take great pride in genre bending. HC joyously blends bluegrass, country, klezmer, jazz, rock, Latin, Cajun, and Slavic in a style that is really hard to pin down. Credit (or blame) for this smorgasbord of sound goes to accordionist and lead vocalist Maury Rosenberg, a Berklee College of Music graduate who started the band along with fellow Berklee student Mark Chenevert. They were joined by banjo/fiddle player Billy Constable who had performed old-time music in North Carolina, Chris Kew, a bassist with a rock/funk background, and drummer Dave Hamilton who studied music at the University of Connecticut. Over the years, they shared stages with a wide variety of acts from Bela Fleck to Burning Spear, Tripping Daisy to Nathan & the Zydeco Chas-Chas. Hypnotic Clambake's recordings including **Square Dance Messiah**, **Gondola to Heaven**, and **Ken the Zen Master** defy description but reviewers have tagged them as "psycho-klezmatic" or "like a bar mitzvah on acid." A sampling of the titles of their songs might give you some idea of what you are getting into: "Chef Mobie's Gator Gumbo," "Bisexual Military," "Scorched Earth Polly," "Trucking & Shucking," "Far Away Cows," "Arachnids Are Taking Over the Planet!" In 1997 and 1998, Hypnotic Clambake hosted the O.U.R. (Outrageous Universe Revival) Festival.

Mark Chenevert (cl.,sax); Billy Constable (bj,f); Dave Hamilton (d,b.v.); Chris Kew (b); Maury Rosenberg (acc,v)

Past Lives/HC/1990 (CS)
Square Dance Messiah/Blue Button/1991 (includes **Past Lives** plus 7 more)
General Turkey/HC/1992 (CS)
Gondola to Heaven/Blue Botton/1993 (**General Turkey** plus)
Arachnids/HC/1994 (CS)
Ken the Zen Master/Blue Botton/1995 (**Arachnids** plus)
Frozen Live, Vol. 1/Blue Botton/1995

Hypnotic Clambake c/o Maury Rosenberg, P.O. Box 121, Boston, MA 02131

Hypnotic Clambake Fan Correspondence, P.O. Box 91, Slippery Rock, PA 16057

Hypnotic Clambake Home Page
//www.hypnotic-clambake.com/

Ben Ieven
Accordionist; Music Editor
Neerpelt, Belgium

In general, I don't think Americans appreciate just how popular country music is overseas and especially in Europe. Relative to the size of its population and land base, The Netherlands/Belgium has one of the most energetic country music communities on the entire Continent. And while, like everywhere else, the majority of acts are of the HNC variety, the Low Countries are also home to a wide variety of alt. country styles including hillbilly, rockabilly, Western swing, country rock, Cajun, Tex-Mex, and singer/songwriters of all shades. Suporting them all is a large infrastructure of organizations, clubs, venues, radio, publications, promoters, studios, and much more. I know all of this because of the efforts of Ben Ieven from Neerpelt, Belgium who compiled and published *De Country Gids '98-'99*, a storehouse of information on all things country in The Netherlands and Belgium. Though mostly in Dutch, this remarkable guide and directory was an invaluable resource that provided me with many contacts and new additions (radio shows, magazines, etc.) for the 2nd edition of *Modern Twang*. It also came with a complimentary CD that gave me a good feel for the variety and quality of country music in the region. However, music editor is only one of the hats worn by Ben Ieven. In addition, he is a respected and much in demand accordionist as he demonstrates on his self-released **Folk Accordeon**. This highly appealing, all original collection covers the gamut including Irish jigs, Bavarian polkas, schottische, Cajun, Tex-Mex, and even some nice country touches (pedal steel, dobro, fiddle) courtesy of Belgium's Black Hills Country Band.

Folk Accordeon/BI/1997
De Country Gids '98-'99/Uitgeverij BIP/1998

Ben Ieven/De Country Gids, Wateringstraat 23, 3910 Neerpelt, Belgium; 0(032)11 648999, (fax) 0(032)11 803753
countrygids@online.be

Jack Ingram
Texas; Singer/Songwriter
Houston, Texas; 1970-

Jack Ingram was the first of the "next generation" of Texas singer/songwriters to break out of the pack in the mid-1990s. Raised on progressive country giants like Willie Nelson, Jerry Jeff Walker, Guy Clark, et al., Ingram began performing in Dallas when he was a college freshman. Starting as a solo at a bar called Adair's doing lots of covers (mostly Nelson) and a few originals, he slowly gathered a following and put together a cast of supporting musicians he called the Beat Up Ford Band.

Like Robert Earl Keen (with whom he is most often compared), Ingram became a favorite on the Central Texas college circuit, and his first recordings, **Jack Ingram**, **Lonesome Questions**, and **Live at Adair's** sold amazingly well for independent releases. On each, Ingram gives a nod to his early influences by covering their songs and presents originals ("Beat Up Ford," "Attitude and Driving," "Run Away With You," and "Things Get Cloudy"), placing him squarely in the Texas singer/songwriter tradition. However, Ingram also incorporated the edgier sound of modern alt. country found in musicians like Steve Earle who produced Ingram's major label debut **Livin' or Dyin'**. Once again, he pays homage to his Texas mentors with covers of Guy Clark ("Rita Ballou") and Jimmie Dale Gilmore ("Dallas") plus a duet with Jerry Jeff Walker ("Picture on My Wall"), and under Earle's guidance, Jack's "Nothing Wrong With That" and "Big Time" have that extra punch. "That's Not Me" (song and video) received lots of air play and in mid-1997, Ingram shared a double billing on *Austin City Limits* with none other than Robert Earl Keen. For his late 1997 tour (with Junior Brown), he scaled down the Beat Up Ford Band to a three piece including long time Dallas alt. country mainstay Alan Wooley (ex-Killbilly; the Cartwrights) on fiery lead guitar. As a warm up for a new full-length album (due in early 1999), Ingram contributed songs (one by Bruce Robison and one original) to the *Black Dog* and *Chasing the Dream* soundtracks in 1998.

The Beat Up Ford Band: Chris Claridy (e.g.,b.v.); Pete Coatney (d); Milo Dearing (f,md,p.s.); Reed Easterwood (bj,e.g.); Mitch Marine (b); Al Mouledoux (f); Jim Richmond (f,db,p.s.)

Jack Ingram/Rhythmic/1992; Crystal Clear/1993
Lonesome Questions/Rhythmic/1993; Crystal Clear/1994
Live At Adair's/Rising Tide/1996
Livin' or Dyin'/Rising Tide/1997
"Drivin' All Night Long" on **Black Dog**/1998 (sdtrk.)
"It's Just a Ride" on **Bull Riders: Chasing the Dream**/Cold Spring/1998 (sdtrk.)

Jack Ingram, P.O. Box 751035, Dallas, TX 75275

Jack Ingram & the Beat Up Ford Band Web Site //www.beatupford.com

Mark Insley
TSOB
Kansas/Los Angeles, California

Born in Kansas and raised in the Texas panhandle, Mark Insley attended Kansas State for a time, worked in the West Texas oil fields, and wandered through the Southwest before settling in L.A. in the 1980s. Having refined his singing and songwriting skills wherever he called home, Insley became part of the Town South of Bakersfield alt. country scene and a regular performer at the famous Palomino. In 1996, he signed with Country-Town Records and recorded **Good Country Junk** with support from TSOB luminaries Albert Lee, Greg Leisz, Skip Edwards, Pete

Anderson, Dwight Yoakam, Taras Prodaniuk (producer), Scott Joss, and Jann Browne. Its mix of honky tonk, country rock, and Tex-Mex, though not in the same league with the likes of Yoakam or James Intveld, is a welcomed addition to the TSOB tradition.

Good Country Junk/Country-Town/1996

Mark Insley/Country-Town Home Page //www.countrytown.com/insley/index.html

Mark Insley Page //www.electricearl.com/insley.html

James Intveld
TSOB
Compton, California

In 1990, Johnny Depp starred in the John Waters film *Cry Baby* in which he played a 1950s Elvis type roustabout who rode a motorcycle, sang, etc. The singing voice on the film's songs belongs not to Depp but to James Intveld who along with Dave Alvin was brought in to handle musical production. For Intveld, it was his biggest but by no means first film credit. Since he had moved to L.A. in the early 1980s, Intveld had balanced acting with a musical career. Inspiration for the latter came from his father who was into rockabilly when Intveld was a child and encouraged his son to take up drums and then guitar. In high school, Intveld sat in on hoot nights and talent shows at the Palomino and other clubs and, with his brother Rick, started a rockabilly band, the Rockin' Shadows, which played the local club circuit and recorded a few tracks. When his brother left to join the ill fated Rick Nelson band, Intveld moved to Pasadena and got a serious case of the acting bug. He entered acting school and got a steady stream of small parts in movies and TV: *Roadhouse 66* (with William Dafoe), *Private Eye* (TV series pilot), *Motown's Mustang*, *Sandman*, and *Cry Baby*. This last film got him a job playing in some musical scenes and coaching Nicholas Cage to sing like Elvis for *Wild at Heart*; this was followed by roles in *Shake, Rattle & Rock*, *A Thing Called Love* (he plays a band member and River Phoenix's friend), *Indian Runner* (as a killer killed off early in the film), and the *F.B.I Untold Stories* TV series in which he had a lead role as a real life rapist and murderer. Sandwiched in between acting jobs, Intveld continued to pursue his other love, music. He played in a few bands around L.A. and then in 1986 met Rosie Flores, wrote "Crying Over You" for her, and became bass player in her band. That was at the beginning of the whole Town South of Bakersfield thing, and Intveld landed a track, "Somewhere Down the Road," on **A Town South of Bakersfield, Vol. 2**. He also did a Christmas single with his good buddy Dale Watson called "Christmas Just Ain't Christmas Without You" which they put out on their own label (Penny-Ellen) and gave out as presents. In the early 1990s, Intveld joined the revamped Blasters, whom he'd known since 1981, as lead guitarist and also fronted a swing band called Jimmy & the Gigolos. In 1995,

Bear Family Records of Germany asked Intveld to contribute his song "Barely Hangin' On" to an anniversary compilation of songs that all have the word "bear" in them. The label's owner was so impressed he gave Intveld money to record a CD. For his full length self-titled debut, Intveld had total control of production and played all the instruments. Dedicated to his brother (who died in the plane crash that killed Rick Nelson), **James Intveld** is a super recording of easy going 1950s-style honky tonk country and ballads anchored by Intveld's smooth vocals and multi- instrumental talents. He covers Don Gibson's "Blue, Blue Day" and Huey Meaux's "I'm to Blame," but the rest of the material is Intveld originals including his version of "Crying Over You." (The LP **Introducing James Intveld** has four additional tracks with a more uptempo rockabilly feel). Critics rightly went wild over Intveld's debut, and it won 1996 Best Country/Roots CD from *Music Connection*. His star burned very brightly in Europe especially in Germany where he was the subject of a TV documentary, *James Intveld: Portrait of a Man and His Music*. Over the years, Intveld continued to work in movies and on a variety of musical projects including the Blasters, Kathy Mattea, and a tribute album to Merle Haggard's longtime guitarist, **To Roy Nichols With Love**. Toward the end of 1997, **James Intveld** was released domestically on the Innerworks label with two extra tracks, "Standin' On a Rock" (Rodney Crowell) and "My Heart is Achin' for You" (from his Rockin' Shadow days). In 1997-1998, Intveld worked on a Jimmy & The Gigolos CD and a new one for Bear Family on which he was once again given *carte blanche*. Meanwhile, he led a new group called the Swing Sinners and toured with Kim Richey as opening act and her bass player.

"Somewhere Down the Road" on **A Town South of Bakersfield, Vol. 2**/Restless/1988
"Christmas Just Ain't Christmas Without You" (with Dale Watson)/Penny-Ellen/1988
Introducing James Intveld/Bear Family Ger./1995 (10")
James Intveld/Bear Family Ger./1995
"Important Words" on **Turning the World Blue: A Tribute to Gene Vincent**/Skizmatic/199
"Cryin' Over You" on **Jukebox Cowboy**/Vinyl Junkie UK/1997
"Any Way Yo Want Me" on **Renegade Rockabilly**/Renegade/1998

James Intveld International Fan Club, P.O. Box 3601, Belmont Shore, CA 90803

James Intveld Fan Club Home Page
//members.aol.com/intveldfc/

IntveldFC@aol.com

James Intveld Web Page
//bullwinkle.as.utexas.edu/scot/bintveld.html

See The Blasters; Rosie Flores; Kathy Robertson; Dale Watson

Mike Ireland (Holler; The Starkweathers)
Grain Belt Rock
Kansas City, Missouri; 1961-

The Starkweathers were a short lived Kansas City based country rock band that "coulda been a contender" for the top spot in the alternative country movement of the late 1990s had it not been for intra-band squabbles that tore them apart. They started out as an REM-type group called And How in the mid-1980s but along the way opted for a new name and new sound. In the early 1990s, The Starkweathers, anchored by the singing and songwriting of Mike Ireland and Richard Smith, developed a reputation for hard driving rocking twang, tight harmonies, and songs that boldly addressed social and political issues: capital punishment ("Danny Taylor"), religious hypocrisy ("Do You Like to Be Lied To?"), patriotic chauvinism ("Burn the Flag"), bigotry ("Little White Trash Boy"), small town desperation ("Town of Shame"), and big city alienation ("Town I Hate"). Extremely popular around their hometown, they were also a hit with SubPop's president, and they cut a single for that label in 1995. That same year, Bloodshot Records adopted them into the insurgent country community with inclusion of one of their tunes ("Little White Trash Boy") on the **Hell-Bent** compilation. The Starkweathers were riding high, seemingly on their way to alternative country stardom, but then Ireland and Smith had a nasty falling out, and the group disbanded. Their official recorded output consisted of one self titled EP plus a couple of singles but in late 1996, super fan David Cantwell put together a cassette tape retrospective of the Starkweathers' career called **Learning the Hard Way**. It consists of outtakes, demos, radio shows, and live performances and for a while he made it available (for free) to members of the Postcard 2 alternative country Internet mailing list. In late 1996, former Starkweathers members Mike Ireland and Michael and Paul Lemon began to resurrect the spirit of their old band as Mike Ireland and Holler. A little more on the country side than their predecessor, their debut came on **Straight Outta Boone County** with a rendition of "No Vacancy." SubPop's president had maintained a steady interest in Ireland, signed him in 1997 and in 1998 came **Learning How to Live**, a pretty straight ahead country affair. The instrumental backing from Holler is first-rate, and producer Marvin Etzioni makes judicious use of strings to enhance the emotional impact of the slower songs. However, the real focus here is Ireland's strong tenor on covers of "Banks of the Ohio" and "Cry" and original cry-in-your-beer ballads and honky tonk including "Don't Call This Love," "Headed For a Fall," "House of Secrets," and "Worst of All." This recording and its supporting tour made Ireland and Holler one of the most publicized and sought-after alt. country groups of 1998. But, every silver lining has a dark cloud; Ireland and band grew disgruntled with SubPop's lack of support and worked to end their relationship with the label. Deciding they'd had enough, the Lemon brothers departed by year's end. Ireland and Mesh finished touring with fill-in musicians, but their recording future was very much up in the air.

The Starkweathers: Mike Ireland (b,v); Dennis Lang (g, to 1994); Michael Lemon (db); Paul "Smokey" Lemon (d); Richard Smith (g,v)
Mike Ireland and Holler: Mike Ireland (b,glock,v); Michael Lemon (l.g.,l.s.,md); Paul Lemon (d); Dan Mesh (l.g.,r.g.,h.v.)

> The Starkweathers/Faye/1994 (EP)
> "Do You Like to Be Lied To?" b/w "Town of Shame"/SubPop/1994 (7")
> "Greektown's in Flames" b/w "Took Me By Surprise"/Faye/1994 (7")
> "Little White Trash Boy" on **Hell-Bent: Insurgent Country, Vol. 2**/Bloodshot/1995
> **Learning the Hard Way** (Starkweathers)/1997 (cs retrospective)
> "No Vacancy" (Holler) on **Straight Outta Boone County**/Bloodshot/1997
> **Learning How to Live** (Holler)/SubPop)/1998
> "Pop A Top" on **Edges From the Postcard2**/P2/1998

Mike Ireland & Holler, P.O. Box 120186, Kansas City, MO 64112

Mile Ireland & Holler Page //www.empathetic.com/empathetic/mipage.htm (includes mailing list)

Mike Ireland/RealCountry Page //www.MikeIreland.RealCountry.net

Mike Ireland & Holler/SubPop Home Page //www.subpop.com

Mike Ireland & Holler Biography //www.billions.com/ireland/bio.htm

Chris Isaak (The Mysteries)
Lo-Fi Rockabilly
Stockton, California; June 26, 1956-

I may be going out on a limb, but I think Chris Isaak deserves a branch (or at least a twig) on the alt. country family tree. His early recordings (**Silvertone**, **Chris Isaak**, **Heart Shaped World**) are generally moody rockabilly and swingy country with a high twang quotient courtesy of James Calvin Wilsey's reverb soaked lead guitar and Isaak's mellow Elvis, Roy Orbison, Ricky Nelson inspired vocals. Added to this is Isaak's lyrics which can get down there and grovel in heartbreak and loneliness with country's best ("Funeral in the Rain"; "Tears"; "Wicked Game"; "Nothing's Changed"; "Lie to Me"; "Somebody's Crying")— in this regard, Isaak has often cited Hank Williams as a major influence. Finally, Isaak has done some nice steel guitar driven numbers including "Western Skies," "The New Girl," "The End of Everything," and "Dark Moon" from the *Perfect World* soundtrack. Convinced?

Isaak's 1998 release **Speak of the Devil** is a montage of his signature sound including the usual allotment of twang.

However, Chris was out-twanged by his former guitar player Wilsey who founded The Mysteries with Chuck Morris (drums), Bogie (bass), and Chris Lawrence (pedal steel) who is also a member of the country rock/honky tonk band Cisco. Variously described as "supercowboy western rock," "nitro-twang," "space-age hillbilly," and "little haunted house on the prairie music," The Mysteries had become an important new force in So-Cal alt. country and were working on a debut recording by the end of 1998.

> **Silvertone**/Warner Brothers/1985
> **Chris Isaak**/Warner Brothers/1987
> **Heart Shaped World**/Warner Brothers/1989
> **San Francisco Days**/Warner Brothers/1993
> **Forever Blue**/Warner Brothers/1995
> **The Baja Sessions**/Warner Brothers/1997
> **Speak of the Devil**/Warner Brothers/1998

Official Chris Isaak Home Page //www.repriserec.com/chrisisaak/

Unofficial Chris Isaak & Silvertone Home Page //fly.hiwaay.net/~mdlatham/isaak.html (information on bootlegs)

Heart Shaped Fanzine c/o Mara Fraser: Hypatia103@aol.com

The Mysteries //members.aol.com/nitrotwang/

NitroTwang@aol.com

See Big Blue Hearts; Cisco

Greg Jacobs
Singer/Songwriter
Choctaw, Oklahoma;

In the early 1980s, Stillwater, Oklahoma became a magnet for a group of rising singer/songwriters that included Jimmy LaFave, Tom Skinner, Bob Childers, and Garth Brooks. Joining the ranks of this "red dirt" sound as it was called was a young man named Greg Jacobs from the tiny town of Choctaw near Oklahoma City. He was initially inspired by Dylan but really got into singing/songwriting after he heard John Prine, and for the first few years after arriving in Stillwater was mostly a Prine cover artist. But he also collaborated with Tom Skinner and his brother on some country rock (Amazing Rhythm Aces; Gram Parsons) material and even worked (with the Skinners) in Garth Brooks' band. After spending some time in Kentucky, Jacobs followed the Skinners and Brooks to Nashville with aspirations of becoming a company songwriter. However, his songs were way to sophisticated and introspective for the Music City hit factory and so it was back to Oklahoma. In the late 1990s, he, Skinner, and Childers found a home with Binky Records out of Baton Rouge. On his 1997 debut, **South of Muskogee Town**, Jacobs shows he can write love/relationship songs with the best of them, but his main focus is on the darker side of recent Oklahoma history including the disgraceful "relocation" of the Creek Indian Nation ("South of Muskogee Town"), the hard times of the Depression/Dust Bowl ("A Little Rain Will Do"; "Okie Wind"), his great grandfather's struggles as a farmer/rancher ("River Run Dry"), and the sad passing of a happier time ("Used to Be"). Musically, **South of Muskogee Town** ranges from folk to swing to blues to light country rock with support from old friends like Jimmy LaFave and the Skinner brothers. Jacobs soft and smooth voice gives the recording an inviting quality and never fails to satisfy.

South of Muskogee Town/Binky/1997

Greg Jacobs, P.O. Box 776, Checotah, OK 74426; 918-473-2530

okewind@galstar.com

Duane Jarvis
Roots Rock
Astoria, Oregon; 1958-

Born and raised in the Pacific Northwest, Duane Jarvis cut his musical teeth with a couple of Portland, Oregon bands (the John Burroz Blues Band and the power pop Odds) before heading for L.A. in 1984 with high hopes of starting his own group. However, things didn't go quite as planned and for the next eight years, Jarvis became a solid guitar sideman for Marvin Etzioni (Lone Justice), Rosie Flores, Dwight Yoakam, John Prine, Lucinda Williams, and even the Divinyls from Australia. Then, in 1992, he got the chance to do his own songs fronting his own band, D. J.'s Front Porch which recorded an album of the same name in 1994. Its fervent mix of American roots with British Invasion rock fueled by Jarvis' keen lead guitar work and slightly twangy vocals helped him emerge from the shadows as a roots rock artist in his own right. Following a move to Nashville, Jarvis became part of Music City's underground/alt. country songwriting contingent (along with Gwil Owen, Lucinda Williams, Robbie Fulks, Buddy Miller, Greg Trooper) and had his "Cocktail Napkin" included on Bloodshot's 1995 insurgent compilation, **Nashville: The Other Side of the Alley**. He did a "No Hotels Tour" opening for Miller, Fulks, and Amy Rigby and then met Garry Tallent (E-Street Band) who co-produced Duane's 1998 release **Far From Perfect** which gives more latitude to his country roots side.

D.J.'s Front Porch/Medium Cool/1994
"Cocktail Napkin" on **Nashville: The Other Side of the Alley**/Bloodshot/1996
Far From Perfect/Watermelon/1998

Duane Jarvis Biography
//www.pressnetwork.com/bios/duanebio.htm

Jason & The Scorchers
Country Rock; Cowpunk
Nashville, Tennessee; 1981-1990; 1995-

The story of the rural boy/girl coming to the big city with hopes of being a big time singing star is a standard part of country music mythology. The history of Jason & the Scorchers gives this tale a very modern retelling. In 1981, Jason Ringenberg traveled from his family's Illinois pig farm to Nashville with high hopes for a musical career. There he met some good ol' Tennessee boys, Perry Baggs, Jeff Johnson, and Warner Hodges, who had been reared on country music but also infected by rock 'n' roll. As Jason & the Nashville Scorchers, they combined the two into a searing blend of honky tonk and thrash that was soon to become known as country punk or cow punk. Their first sessions (done on a 4-track) resulted in the **Reckless Country Soul** EP and were followed by lots of touring (now as just Jason & the Scorchers) where they became notorious for powerhouse shows. This was country and rock quite like no one had heard before, and it was contagious. Through another EP (**Fervor**) and three full recordings (**Lost and Found, Still Standing, Thunder and Fire**), they explored the connections between Hank Williams, Lefty Frizzell, Rolling Stones, Dylan, metal, and punk to great critical and fan acclaim becoming in the process the prototypical cowpunk band. They opened for a variety of acts from Willie Nelson to the Ramones and were riding high until the rigors of the road, alcohol, and bad record deals finally split the group up in 1990. Ringenberg put out a solo country effort **One Foot in a Honky Tonk** in 1992 and in the same year, **Essential Jason & The Scorchers** (**Fervor, Lost and Found** plus live and unreleased cuts) was released. In 1995, Jason & the Scorchers regrouped, went on tour, and recorded **A Blazing Grace**, a notable return with interesting covers of George Jones ("Why Baby Why") and John Denver ("Take Me Home Country Roads")! The triumphant resurgence of one of the pioneers in 1980s country rock was capped off in 1996 with **Clear Impetuous Morning**, a prime Scorchers recording that put them back into the thick of the alt. country movement. In the wake of their renewed popularity, EMI reissued **Fervor/Lost and Found** on one CD (**Both Sides of the Line**) as part of its "Acoustic Highway" collection. On November 7-8, 1997, Jason & The Scorchers (with new bassist Kenny Ames) took over Nashville's Exit/In to record their first ever live album, **Midnight Roads & Stages Seen**. This double CD retrospective was released in 1998 simultaneously with a full length video of these unforgettable live sessions.

Jason Ringenberg (g,hm,v); Kenny Ames (b, 1997-); Perry Baggs (d); Ken Fox (b,1989); Warner Hodges (l.g.,l.s.); Jeff Johnson (b, 1981-1988; 1994-1997); Andy York (g,1989)

Reckless Country Soul/Praxis/1982; Mammoth/1996 (EP)
Fervor/EMI/1983 (EP)
Lost and Found/EMI/1985
Still Standing/EMI/1986
Thunder and Fire/A&M/1989
One Foot in a Honky Tonk (Jason solo)/Liberty/1992
Essential Jason & The Scorchers, Vol. 1: Are You Ready for the Country?/EMI/1992
Blazing Grace/Mammoth/1995

Both Sides of the Line/EMI/1996 (**Fervor** and **Lost and Found**)
Clear Impetuous Morning/Mammoth/1996
"One Last Question" on **Nashville: The Other Side of the Alley**/Bloodshot/1996
Midnight Roads & Stages Seen (Live)/Mammoth/1998

Official Jason & The Scorchers Home Page & Fan Club //jasonandthescorchers.com

Jason & The Scorchers Original Unofficial Home Page //www.geocities.com/Nashville/3301/

Jason & The Scorchers //fly.hiwaay.net/~dderrick/scorchers/scorch.html

Jason & The Scorchers/Mammoth Page //www.mammoth.com/mammoth/bands/jscorch/

Rcsoup: Jason & The Scorchers Online Mailing List rcsoup@monroe.lib.mi.us

Jason & The Scorchers Message Board //imusic.com/cgi-bin/bbs/bbs.cgi?x=jasonthescorche

Jason & The Scorchers AOL Folder: Entertainment>Music>Chat & Messages>Music Community>Alternative>Alternative Bands, A-L

The Jayhawks
No Depression
Minneapolis, Minnesota; 1985-1995; 1996-

Along side Uncle Tupelo, the Jayhawks were the preeminent country rock band of the early 1990s. They traced their origins to the mid-1980s when a group of Minneapolis musicians led by country/folk songwriter Mark Olson and bassist Marc Perlman began performing Olson's songs at bars around town. In need of a lead guitarist, they secured Gary Louris (who was with a crack local rockabilly group called Safety Last) and took the name the Jayhawks. At the time, the Minneapolis scene was dominated by bands like Husker Du and the Replacements so the Jayhawks carved out their own space by opting for the country rock sound developed by the Byrds, Gram Parsons, Bob Dylan, Neil Young, the Flying Burrito Brothers and others in the late 1960s and early 1970s. In 1986, they recorded **The Jayhawks** for a small independent label (Bunkhouse), and its classic country rock feel with songs like "I'm Not in Prison," "The Liquor Store Came First," and "Six Pack on the Dashboard" led a number of reviewers to dub them the second coming of the Flying Burrito Brothers. However, when no major label deal materialized and several band members were hit with personal mishaps, the Jayhawks laid off for a while. Then, in 1988, Twin/Tone Records (the Replacements, Soul Asylum) agreed to re-record and remix accumulated Jayhawks demos and in 1988 released **Blue Earth**. From the opening strains of "Two Angels" to the final chords of "Martin's Song," the Jayhawks left no doubt that they (not the Eagles) were the true avian successors to the **Sweetheart of the Rodeo** era Byrds. The album's success allowed them to tour to places like SXSW and the New Music Seminar and along the way, they earned praise from a growing body of fans and critics; a writer for the *Village Voice* went so far as to call them "the only country rock band that matters" and in 1990, they got their big label contract with Def American (later American Recordings). **Hollywood Town Hall** put them at the pinnacle of the new generation of country rock (along with Uncle Tupelo whose full length debut came in 1990). After a very rewarding U.S. and European tour, they took a hiatus during which Olson, Perlman, and Louris worked on various side projects. Perlman and Louris contributed their talents to two Joe Henry albums and joined Jeff Tweedy (Uncle Tupelo), Noah Levy (Honeydogs), Dan Murphy (Soul Asylum), and Kraig Johnson (Run Westy Run) in the whimsical country rock group Golden Smog. Olson and Louris also worked on new material that became the basis for the 1994 **Tomorrow the Green Grass** which still had the Jayhawks distinctive country rock sound (including a romping version of Grand Funk's "Bad Time") but also more pop rock elements with the addition of Karen Grotberg on keyboards. In hindsight, the album may have been a sign of differences within the band over musical direction, and sure enough, in late 1995, Olson announced his departure so he could devote time to his family and work with his wife, singer/songwriter, Victoria Williams. The couple moved to Joshua Tree, California in 1997 and with Mike Russell formed the Original Harmony Ridge Creek Dippers (see separate profile).

The remaining Jayhawks shocked the alt. country world by calling it quits in early 1996. Louris and Perlman went back to performing and recording with Golden Smog, and Louris worked with members of Son Volt on Kelly Willis' EP **Fading Fast**. In time, the Jayhawks sans Olson began to regroup, adding Kraig Johnson and fiddler Jessy Greene (ex-Geraldine Fibbers) and returning to the studio in late 1996. Their new recording **Sound of Lies** was one of the most eagerly awaited albums of 1997, but the finished product caused quite a stir if not an outright split within the alt. country community. To the chagrin of some (but the delight of others), the signature Jayhawks country rock with lilting harmonies, steel guitar, harmonica, twangy guitar etc. was gone in favor of a more full blown pop rock sound. Just what direction they would take in the future remained to be seen. Grotberg departed in early 1999, and the Jayhawks carried on as a quartet, touring and recording a new album which was set to hit the shelves in mid-1999.

The Jayhawks: Ken Callahan (d;1990-1994); Jessy Greene (f,1996-); Karen Grotberg (ky,v;1991-1998); Kraig Johnson (l.g.,1996-); Gary Louris (e.g.,v); Mark Olson (a.g.,hm,v; 1985-1995); Tim O'Reagan (d,v;1995-); Marc Perlman (b); Norm Rogers (d); Thad Spencer (d,1985-1990)

The Jayhawks/Bunkhouse/1986
Blue Earth/Twin Tone/1989
Hollywood Town Hall/Def American/1992
Take Me With You/Def American/1993 (EP)
Tomorrow the Green Grass/American Recordings/1994

Modern Twang

Badtime ("Last Cigarette"/"Get the Lead Out")/American
Recordings UK/1995 (7")
Sweet Dreams (Live in Chicago 1993)/Ita./1995
Live, Minneapolis, 11-5-94; Live, St. Paul, 8-16 & 17-95
(DAT Masters available through Twin City Digital,
Dept. 1, 4215 Winnetka Ave. N. #195, Minneapolis,
MN 55428)
Poised for Stardom/1996 (bootleg)
Sound of Lies/American Recordings/1997

The Jayhawks/American Recordings Home Page

//American.recordings.com/American_Artists/Jayhawks/j

Jayhawks/Twin Tone Page //tt.net/twintone/jayhawks.html

Baltimore Sun: Unofficial Jayhawks Page
//www.tc.umn.edu/nlhome/g166/skog1004/blueearth/

Hollywood Town Hall: The Jayhawks Web Page
//www.geocities.com/SunsetStrip/palladium/8145/

The Jayhawks //www.ionet.net/~ramsey/jayhawks.htm

The Jayhawks //www.geocities.com/SunsetStrip/palms/5565/

The Jayhawks Page
//www.netcomuk.co.uk/~wozza/jayhawks.htm

Jason's Jayhawks Page
//www.geocities.com/SunsetStrip/studio/2389/jayhawks.html

Midwest Rooted Rock
//www.geocities.co.jp/hollywood-kouen/6823/ (Japanese fan
page for the Jayhawks, Golden Smog, Uncle Tupelo, et al.)

The Jayhawks iMusic Showcase //www.imusic.com

The Jayhawks Online Mailing List
jayhawks@listserv.servtech.com (Message: Subscribe; your
e-mail address)

The Jayhawks AOL Folder: Entertainment>Music>Chat &
Messages>Music Community>Alternative>Alternative
Bands, G-L

*See Golden Smog; The Original Harmony Ridge Creek
Dippers; Son Volt; Uncle Tupelo*

The Jazzabels

Singer/Songwriters; Americana
Buffalo, New York; 1990-

The Jazzabels take pride in being "Buffalo's favorite singing
and swinging, songwriting folk-country-blues-jazz-Tex-Mex-
Zydeco-rock and roll female duo." However, they are too
modest; the terrible twosome of Cathy Carfagna and Kilissa
McGoldrick with their effective genre blending, engaging
harmonies, and clever lyrics are crowd favorites wherever they
go. Both were from classical music backgrounds, but when they
met discovered they were also steeped in a variety of folk and
pop styles. Initially, the duo used guitar and electric piano and
covered mostly Everly Brothers and Michelle Shocked material
but in time Carfagna learned accordion, and this gave them
greater mobility and expanded their repertoire as well. In 1990,
they officially became the Jazzabels and began developing their
own material which resulted in an 8 song cassette **Come Hell or
High Harmonies**. It won them the Buffalo Music Award for
Best New Band and led to regional tours and a debut CD, **Cafe**

All Day, which earned them Outstanding Record of the Year
honors from *Buffalo Art Voice*. Live and on record, the
Jazzabels offer up a very appealing mix of good time music that
is perhaps best captured in their "I Wish That I Could Sing Like
Johnny Cash" which contains the memorable line, "it's hard to
sing like Johnny when you wear a dress." In 1996, the Jazzabels
released **Skyway**, another tempting buffet of rock, swing,
Cajun, folk, and rockabilly including a country rocking cover of
Neil Young's "Southern Pacific" and another witty tribute to
the Man in Black, "Whole Lotta Rhythm and a Little Twang." In
1996, they won Outstanding Original Acoustic Artists from the
Buffalo Nightlife Music Awards and made their first appearance at Kerrville in 1997.

Cathy Carfagna (acc,a.g.,e.g.,perc,v); Kilissa McGoldrick
(a.g.,fl,pw,perc,rec,sax,v)

> **Come Hell or High Harmonies**/Delmore/1993 (CS)
> "Should I Wait?"/Delmore/1993 (7")
> **Cafe All Day**/Delmore/1994
> "Little Harlem Hotel" on **No Illusions**/Hot Wings/1994
> **Skyway**/Delmore/1996

Jazzabel Central, P.O. Box 163, Buffalo, NY 14215-0163

Jazzabel Central Home Page
//www.wnywebshop.com/jazzabel.htm

Jzcentral@aol.com

Jivin' Jake Jern (Jake & The Spitfires)
Country Rock
Stockholm/Lund, Sweden; 1964-

Jakob Jern's start in music was about as far away from country
music as you could get. Growing up in Lund, Sweden he was a
featured soloist in the Boy's Cathedral Choir renowned for his
soaring soprano. Later, as a teenager he played in a Beatles
cover band, but in 1984 while serving in the military, some of
his platoon buddies introduced him to honky tonk and rockabilly via the music of Hank Williams and Johnny Burnett. Jern
was hooked and changing his name to Jivin' Jake, he fronted a
rockabilly group called the Wildcats and then another called the
Moonshiners. They had steady work for the remainder of the
80s, but Jake's real dream was to have a honky tonk country
band and in 1991, he made the switch as leader of the Spitfires.
Through endless touring (often opening for the likes of Dave
Alvin, Emmylou, and Joy Lynn White) around Scandinavia and
the U.S. (including SXSW) and two albums of honky tonk,
country rock, and country pop originals, Jivin' Jake & the
Spitfires established themselves as "the only Real Country band
in Sweden." In 1998, Jern signed with Ramblin' Records, a new
country and American roots label founded by his long-time
songwriting collaborator Marten Sanden. Their inaugural
recording was Jake's first solo **Songs From the 51st State**, a
five track EP of honky tonk and country ballads recorded partly
in Nashville and partly in Sweden with the Spitfires. It was a
prelude to a new Jake & the Spitfires album in 1999.

The Spitfires: Anders Birgersson (g); Jonas Bylund (b); Johan Ek (g); Marshall Karlsson (g); Ante Leven (d)

My Private Rodeo (Jake & The Spitfires)/Hawk
Swe./1993
Crazy Baby, Crazy Girl (Jake & The Spitfires)/Hawk
Swe./1995
Songs From the 51st State (Jivin' Jake Jern)/Ramblin'
Swe./1998

Jivin' Jake Jern c/o Ramblin' Records, Lilla Fiskaregatan 5, SE-222 22 Lund, Sweden; +46-46-37 22 73 or

Jivin' Jake/Ramblin' Records //www.ramblinrecords.com

info@ramblinrecords.com or marten@ramblinrecords.com

Tom Jessen

Grain Belt Rock
Iowa City, Iowa; 1994-

During one of the lowest points in his life, out of work and living in a wretched apartment in Portland, Oregon, Tom Jessen turned to songwriting to keep his sanity. He had played in a couple of rock/country bands (Peterbuilt; Devastation Wagon) in the late 1980s and early 1990s in his home state of Iowa, but left there in hopes of making it as a solo in Nashville. After a disillusioning detour to Branson, he got as far as Memphis before heading into a dead end in the Northwest. In the pit of depression, he turned to country music to express the loneliness and heartache of those bad times. In 1994, with a batch of songs and a new focus, Jessen returned to the Midwest where he teamed with former bandmates Jim Viner (Peterbuilt) and Steve Tyler (Devastation Wagon) plus Darren Matthews (High and Lonesome) to start Tom Jessen's Dimestore Outfit. Viner and Tyler were quickly replaced by Eric Griffin and Eric Staumanis and Marty Letz was brought on board to play pedal steel. After an independently released cassette in 1995, the band signed with Trailer Records which is also home to Bo Ramsey and High and Lonesome. Their debut, **Redemption**, is country/roots/rock originals from Jessen whose songs ("Shit Forsaken"; "Sanctuary"; "Blanket, Tombstone, Feather") are generally on the darker end of the spectrum.

Tom Jessen (g,hm,v); Eric Griffin (d,b.v.); Marty Letz (p.s.); Darren Matthews (bj,l.g.); Eric Staumanis (b)

Tom Jessen/TJ/1995
Redemption/Trailer/1996

Tom Jessen /Trailer Records Home Page
//www.trailer-records.com/profiles/tjpage.html

See High and Lonesome

Flaco Jimenez

Accordion; Tex-Mex; Conjunto
San Antonio, Texas; March 11, 1939-

No one has done more to popularize *conjunto* than accordionist extraordinaire Flaco Jimenez. In a career spanning over forty years as soloist and super session man, Jimenez has not only kept the music alive in his home town of San Antonio but also brought it to audiences around the world. His grandfather, Patricio, helped introduce the Texas/German dance hall accordion to the Tejano community and father, Don Santiago, was one of the first to make *conjunto* recordings back in the 1930s. "El Flaco" (the skinny one) as he came to be called, inherited and expanded on this rich tradition, first as a bajo sexto player for the Don and then as an accordionist with Los Caporales and later Los Caminantes in the 1950s. The latter featured a more contemporary *conjunto* sound and became one of the most popular groups in San Antonio. After a term in the service (Mingo Salvidar replaced him in Los Caminantes), Flaco returned to music and began making solo recordings for local labels and then Arhoolie. His innovative style was noticed by other American musicians and in the 1970s, he was invited to play on a number of classic albums including **Doug Sahm and Band** (1973), Ry Cooder's **Chicken Skin Music** (1976), and as a member of Peter Rowan's Free Mexican Air Force. Into the 1980s, Flaco was *the* accordion session player for a variety of artists from the Rolling Stones to Emmylou Harris. In addition, he continued to make one great solo album after another (including the 1994 Grammy winner **Flaco Jimenez**) and toured throughout the U.S. and Europe. In the 1990s, Jimenez became known primarily for his work with fellow San Antonians Doug Sahm and Augie Meyers plus Freddy Fender as the Texas Tornados. He also got a lot of exposure through a guest appearance on the video of the Maverick's "All You Ever Do is Bring Me Down." In 1995, Jimenez's recordings from the 1950s were made available by Arhoolie on an outstanding collection, **Flaco's First**. After a tour in Spain, in 1997, Flaco signed with BarbWire Records (subsidiary of EMI/Virgin) and in 1998 joined Los Super Seven, an all-star Tex-Mexican American band including David Hidalgo, Cesar Rosas, Ruben Ramos, Rick Trevino, Joe Ely, and Freddy Fender. His 1999, **Said and Done**, was a real change of pace with Tex-Mex making way for Spanish pop. As you will see in the next entry, Flaco's younger brother Santiago is also one of the great modern *conjunto* accordionists.

El Principe Del Acordeon/1977
Un Mojado Sin Licencia (Wetback Without a Green Card)/Arhoolie/1977; 1993
Flaco Jimenez y Su Conjunto/Arhoolie/1978
Ay Te Dejo En San Antonio/Arhoolie/1979; 1986; 1990
El Sonido De San Antonio (with Santiago Jimenez)/Arhoolie/1980
Flaco Jimenez and Peter Rowan Live Rockin' Tex-Mex/Waterfront/1982
Polka Favorites (Viva Seguin in UK)/1983
Tex-Mex Breakdown/1983
On the Move/1984
San Antonio Soul/Rounder/1985
Homenaje a Don Santiago Jimenez/1985
The Accordion Strikes Back/1987
Flaco's Amigos/Arhoolie/1988
Entre Humor Y Botellas/Rounder/1989

Arriba El Norte/Rounder/1989
San Antonio Soul/Rounder/1991
Partners/Reprise/1992
Flaco Jimenez/Arista Texas/1994
Flaco's First/Arhoolie/1995
Buena Suerta Senorita/Arista Texas/1996
Los Super Seven/RCA/1998
Said and Done/Barb Wire/1999

Flaco Jimenez/Border Fest Home Page
//ww.borderfest.com/flaco.htm

See Santiago Jimenez, Jr.; Peter Rowan; Doug Sahm

Santiago Jimenez, Jr.

Accordion; Tex-Mex; Conjunto
San Antonio, Texas; April 8, 1944-

The predominance of Flaco Jimenez in *conjunto* music has often overshadowed the contributions of his younger brother Santiago. While Flaco leans toward a more contemporary sound that incorporates other styles of music, Santiago has lovingly expanded on the traditions established by older generations of musicians. Playing a two button accordion, Jimenez utilizes the basic *conjunto* accompaniment of *bajo sexto* and *toloche* (string bass) pioneered by his father Don Santiago. "The Chief ," as Santiago, Jr. is affectionately known, began playing as a teenager and during his long career has made many wonderful recordings (two Grammy nominations; 1986, 1990), toured extensively in the U.S., Europe, and even the former Soviet Union. In 1990, Santiago's long time *toloche* player died and was replaced by the Bad Livers' Mark Rubin who got the job after a telephone call to Jimenez. Rubin also stepped in as producer most notably on **Canciones De Mi Padre**, a collection of traditional *conjunto* material and on **Musica De Tiempos Pasados, Del Presente, Y Futuro** which rejuvenates *orquestras tipicas*, an urban, pre-*conjunto* style featuring accordion, bass, and *bajo* along with harp, fiddle (Erik Hokkanen), trombone, clarinet, and tuba (Rubin). Jimenez also harkened back to a more traditonal style on his 1998 releases **Corridos de la Frontera** and **Purely Instrumental**.

Familia Y Tradicion/Rounder/1989
El Mero, Mero De San Antonio/Arhoolie/1990
El Gato Negro/Rounder/1990
Canciones de Mi Padre/Watermelon/1994
Santiago Strikes Again/Arhoolie/1994
Corazon de Piedra/Watermelon/1992
Live in Holland/Strictly Country Dutch/1995
Musica de Tiempos Pasados, del Presente y Futuro/Watermelon/1995
En Tu Dia/Chief/1996
Viva Seguin/Strictly Country Dutch/1996
Al Mirar Tu Cara/Hacienda/1997
Corridos de la Frontera/Watermelon/1998
Purely Instrumental/Arhoolie/1998

Santiago Jimenez, Jr. Home Page
//www.rootsworld.com/folklore/jimenez.html

See Flaco Jimenez

Kevin Johnson and the Linemen

Roots Rock
Washington, DC; 1992-

Arkansas born Kevin Johnson has most often been compared as a singer/songwriter to Marshall Crenshaw. His songs have been covered by Mary Chapin-Carpenter among others and he has fronted his own band the Linemen since 1992. They have played on the same bill with Dave Alvin, Lucinda Williams, Iris DeMent, Freedy Johnston, and Matthew Sweet to name only a few. Kevin and the band have been recipients of numerous awards for their recordings (**The Rest of Your Life** and **Memphis for Breakfast)** of appealing acoustic country/pop/rock—*Washington Post* Top Ten Records Critic's Poll 1992, *Offbeat* magazine's Top Ten Record Critic's Poll 1994, and Wammies for Best Rock/Pop Male Vocalist, 1994-1996 and Best Roots Rock Recording 1995. In 1996, they released their third album, **Parole Music**, which was produced by ex-Scruffy the Cat leader Charlie Chesterman. Its mix of covers (Townes Van Zandt's "Buckskin Stallion Blues") and Johnson's country/roots/rock originals ("She Changed the Country Station"; "Stay in Trouble"; "Don't Play the Mean One") pushed **Parole Music** rapidly up the Gavin charts. A compilation of Johnson's best, **The Purple CD**, was released in 1997 and a new recording, **A Hundred Years of Sundays**, was on the schedule for late in 1999.

Kevin Johnson (a.g.,v); Barbara Brousal (v); Tony Flagg (b); Dave Giegerich (db,l.s.,p.s.); James Key (md); Scott McKnight (l.g.); Antoine Sanfuentes (d)

The Rest of Your Life/Linemen Services/1992
Memphis for Breakfast/Linemen Services/1994
"Ave Nada" on **A Holiday Feast, Vol. 1**/Hungry for Music/1996
Parole Music/Linemen Services/1996
The Purple CD/Linemen Services/1997
"Lonely Christmas Call" on **A Holiday Feast, Vol. 2**/Hungry for Music/1997
"Look Over There" & "Helen" on **Fireworks, Vol. 2**/Sound Asleep Swe./1998
"Miss Lonelyhearts Out on the Town" on **Edges From the Postcard2**/P2/1998
"Takin' Care of Me" on **Greetings From the District of Country**/Too Many Dogs/1998
A Hundred Years of Sundays/Linemen Services/1999

Kevin Johnson Fan Club, Linemen Services, 5906 Dewey Dr., Alexandria, VA 22310

Kevin Johnson Home Page //www.kevinjohnson.com

linemen@clark.net

Jolene

Tobacco Row; No Depression
Chapel Hill/Charlotte, North Carolina; 1994-

During the early days of country music, the Tar Heel State produced some of the great pioneering bands like Charlie Poole and His Carolina Ramblers In the 1990s, North Carolina has become a focal point for alternative country with bands such as the Backsliders, Whiskeytown, and Jolene. The latter, like many current alt. country bands, is made up of city reared veterans of various regional punk bands (Veldt, Hardsoul Poets) who came late to country music. In Jolene's case, the nucleus of the band came together in 1994 in Wingate, North Carolina when cousins Dave Burris and John Crooke teamed with Mike Kenerley and Mike Mitschele to write songs and explore the (for them) new territory of country music. After moving to Charlotte, they added pedal steel player Bill Ladd and became Jolene, named after the famous Dolly Parton song. After signing with Ardent, they recorded an eponymous EP of originals plus a cover of Jimmie Dale Gilmore's "Tonight I Think I'm Gonna Go Downtown" followed by a full length CD **Hell's Half Acre** which got lots of attention from alt. country fans in North Carolina and around the U.S. A number of big labels, impressed by Jolene's fusion of No Depression style country rock with Tobacco Row alt. country, came courting, and in 1996, Jolene signed with Sire. Pedal steel player Ladd moved over to the hillbilly bop band, the Burnley Brothers in early 1997. Meanwhile, with help from members of the Continental Drifters, Jolene recorded **In the Gloaming** which, with the absence of Ladd's pedal steel, is a harder edged roots-rock album than its predecessor. An EP, **Feather, Film, Words**, with **In the Gloaming** outtakes, covers, and a new song was finished in 1998, but Jolene was undecided on whether to release it or wait until they completed their next full-length in 1999.

Dave Burris (g,md,v); John Crooke (bj,g,md,v); Mike Kenerley (d); Bill Ladd (p.s.,1995-1997); Mike Mitschele (b,v)

Jolene/Ardent/1995 (EP)
Hell's Half Acre/Ardent/1995
In the Gloaming/Sire/1998
Feather, Film, Words/ (completed but unreleased EP)
Jolene Home //www.jolenesite.com
Jolene Fan Page //www.freetown.com/soho/8th/1117/

Scott Joss

TSOB; Singer/Songwriter; Fiddle
Santa Monica, California; May 1, 1962-

Bakersfield, that grand Mecca of alternative country, is now entering its third generation of musicians continuing on the distinctive tradition of southern California honky tonk. One of the foremost of the new breed is Scott Joss. A champion fiddler, Joss received lots of encouragement from the great mandolinist Tiny Moore and made his professional debut as a member of Merle Haggard's Strangers. Leading his own band for a time after leaving The Hag, Joss was discovered by Pete Anderson who brought him to the attention of Dwight Yoakam. Joss officially became a member of Dwight's band in 1988. The

huge success of Yoakam allowed Anderson to form his own Little Dog Records and begin producing a number of new artists including Scott Joss. On **Souvenirs**, Joss gets the chance to display his many talents as a hot fiddler and strong vocalist (very clearly modeled on Haggard) on songs by Jim Lauderdale, Tom Russell, and Freddy Powers among others. On "Doin' Time In Bakersfield," "Mary Got a Baby," "I Never Got Anywhere With You," and "Stay Out of My Arms," Joss cleaves pretty closely to the sound made famous by Buck and Merle, but there's also some touches of modern country rock and pop country ballads. **Invite Scott Joss Into Your Living Room** (1998) is, as the title suggests, a more informal, intimate session with just Joss and his guitar playing some his favorite originals and songs by long-time Willie Nelson associate, Freddie Powers.

Souvenirs/Little Dog/1996
"Johnson's Love" on **Will Sing for Food: The Songs of Dwight Yoakam**/Little Dog/1998
Invite Scott Joss Into Your Living Room/Little Dog/1998
Scott Joss Fan Club, P.O. Box 6208, Santa Rosa, CA 95406
Scott Joss Home Page
//home.pacbell.net/bluejay/
bluejay@pacbell.net
Scott Joss/Little Dog Page
//www.littledogrecords.com/ScottJoss.html

See Dwight Yoakam

Jr. Gone Wild

Cowpunk
Edmonton, Alberta, Canada; 1982-1995

In their heyday, Jr. Gone Wild were characterized as "the Sex Pistols meet Hank Williams, the Clash meet George Jones" and had quite a following in Canada. They were founded by Mike McDonald who had been in a number of punk bands before falling under the influence of Neil Young and Byrds era country rock and the 1980s country/punk/rock of groups like Rank & File. Jr. Gone Wild's early recordings, **Less Art, More Pop** and **Too Dumb to Quit**, were highly praised and made them into the preeminent Canadian cowpunk band. Over the years, the band had some thirty members with McDonald the only constant. Toward the end of their run, critics and fans began complaining about Jr. Gone Wild's increasingly watered down sound and took to calling them "Jr. Gone Mild." Such criticism and the frequent personnel changes took their toll and after thirteen long years, the band broke up in 1995. However, they did reunite briefly to back the Three Dead Trolls in a Baggie comedy troupe for their performance of a slightly irreverent version of *The Messiah*. Lance Loree went on to become a member of the quirky hillbilly bop band the Alien Rebels.

Dave "Dove" Brown (b); Lance Loree (g); Mike McDonald (g,v); Paul Paetz (d,v); Larry Shelast (d) and many more.

Less Art, More Pop/Better Youth Can./1986
Folk You: The Guido Sessions/JGW/1989
Too Dumb to Quit/Stony Plain Can./1990
Pull the Goalie/Stony Plain Can./1992
Live at the Hyperbole/JGW/1993
Simple Little Wish/Stony Plain Can./1995

Jr. Gone Wild Web Page
//www.well.com.user/sjroby/jgw.html

Jr. Gone Wild Video //www.downrecs.com/jrgone2.asp

See The Alien Rebels

Emily Kaitz
Austin; Singer/Songwriter
Alexandria, Virginia

In 1976, a shy piano tuner and sometime singer/songwriter named Emily Kaitz moved to Austin from Baltimore when a group of Texan friends convinced her the Lone Star State was the place to be. Four years later, she began performing in local clubs and by 1984 was confident enough to start her own record label, Pingleblobber. Over the next decade, Kaitz issued a steady stream of cassettes that highlight her songwriting abilities. She is very perceptive on fairly straight songs about relationships, "Worn Out Getting Wise" (1980 Austin Music Umbrella songwriter award); "The Things He Doesn't Say," "So Afraid of Love," "When Your Best Friend Falls in Love," but her forte is very clever songs like "Jaywalkin'" (1984 Austin Music Umbrella songwriter award), "Shallow End of the Gene Pool," "The M Word Scares the F Word Out of Me," "Middle-Aged Rock & Rollers Are So Damn Cute," "The Day the Bass Players Took Over the World," and "Pico De Gallo." Many Austin performers have covered Kaitz's songs including the Austin Lounge Lizards, Trout Fishing in America, the Cow Pattys, and Christine Albert, and in 1994, a group of local musicians paid homage to her by holding an "Emilyfest" at La Zona Rosa (a CD of the night's music, **Live From the Emilyfest** was released later that year). Kaitz' first CD, **Terminally Trendy**, came out in 1996. It boasts a top notch supporting cast (Christine Albert, Danny Barnes, Paul Glasse, Ray Wylie Hubbard, Jimmy LaFave, Mark Rubin among others) and once again features poignant love songs but most especially more funny tunes including one about Bob Dylan going bowling ("Bob Dylan's 300 Game"). Over the years, Emily has toured in Texas and throughout the U.S. but seems most content with playing in small Austin venues and remaining what she calls an "obscure and happy person."

What You See Is What You Got/Pingleblobber/1984 (CS)
Purly Gates & Emily Kaitz/Pingleblobber/1987 (CS)
Emily's Christmas Tape, December 1989/EK/1989 (CS)
If It Wasn't for Her/Pingleblobber/1990 (CS)
Wild Careening Ways/Pingleblobber/1991 (CS)

Middle Aged Rock and Rollers Are So Damn Cute/Pingleblobber/1992 (CS); 1997 (CD)
A Household Word/Pingleblobber/1993 (CS)
Live at Emily Fest/Pingleblobber/1994
Terminally Trendy/Pingleblobber/1996

Emily Kaitz/NOMA Page //songs.com/noma/ek/

Candye Kane
TSOB
Los Angeles, California

As a single, teenage mother, Candye Kane supported her family as a topless dancer and model for nude photos. Fortunately, she also had a vast amount of singing talent and found another way to make a living. As a teenager, Kane got a scholarship to the USC Music Conservatory and studied opera (she has a five octave range) but found herself drawn more toward pop music including Broadway musicals (performed "Cabaret" on the *Gong Show*) and early country. In the late 1980s, Kane became part of the Los Angeles alt. country scene; as a solo she cut "Tell Me a Lie" for the second volume of **A Town South of Bakersfield** and as lead vocalist for the Armadillo Stampede did "Hey Nashville" for another L.A. alt. country compilation, **Hollywood Roundup**. In the 1990s, Kane made a name as a sultry, jump blues/swing artist backed by her band, the Swingin' Armadillos. Candye's potent sensuality is expressed in hot tunes and bawdy lyrics recalling the style of Julia Lee. She frequently included country tunes in her repertoire; her 1997 recording, **Diva La Grande**, was produced by Dave Alvin and has duets with Big Sandy on "I Left My Heart in Texas" and Toni Price on a hillbilly rendition of "These Boots Are Made for Walkin'." Guests on the album include Danny Barnes (Bad Livers), Erik Hokkanen, and Ted Roddy. Late in 1998, Kane made her contribution to the lounge/swing craze with **Swango**.

"Tell Me a Lie" on **Town South of Bakersfield, Vol. 2**/Restless/1988
"Hey Nashville" (as The Armadillo Stampede) on **Hollywood Roundup**/New Grange/1989
Burlesque Swing/Antone's/1993
Home Cookin'/Antone's/1994
Knockout/Antone's/1995
Diva La Grande/Discovery/1997
Swango/Discovery/1998

Candye Kane/Antone's Page
//www.antonesrec.com/candye.html

Candye Kane iMusic Showcase
/www.imusic.com/showcase/contemporary/candyekane.html

Kieran Kane (The O'Kanes)
Singer/Songwriter; Country Rock
Queens, New York; October 7, 1949-

In the mid-1980s, two Nashville songwriters, Kieran Kane and Jamie O'Hara, joined forces as the O'Kanes. Kane, from New York City, had cut his musical teeth playing folk, bluegrass, and honky tonk before coming to Music City in the late 1970s to go to work for Tree Publishing. He wrote for other artists but on the strength of his songs got a recording contract which led to a couple of minor hits. Meanwhile, O'Hara had gone from aspiring football star to music when an injury permanently sidelined him. Eventually, he too wound up working for Tree and penned "Grandpa," the Judds' #1 and Best Country Song of 1986. That year, informal recording sessions between Kane and O'Hara resulted in the O'Kanes and a deal with Columbia. Over the next few years, they crafted three very appealing albums with an old-time, bluegrass, low key rockabilly feel highlighted by the duo's Everlys influenced harmonies. But, as is too often the case, they went nowhere and broke up. However, the O'Kanes did prepare the way for later groups such as the Brother Boys and the Delevantes.

After the break up of the O'Kanes in 1990, both Kane and O'Hara went on to solo careers in the mid-1990s. The most successful has been Kane who along with Kevin Welch, Tammy Rogers, and Harry Stinson created Dead Reckoning Records in 1994. One of its first releases was Kane's **Dead Reckoning** which echoes the O'Kanes ("This Dirty Little Town"; "Cool Me Down") but also exhibits Kane's own touches ("Bell Ringing in an Empty Sky"; "Je Suis Tres Contendre"). In 1995, Kane and the other Dead Reckoning founders launched the Night of Reckoning Tour and in 1996 formed the Dead Reckoners. Their debut, **A Night of Reckoning**, showcases the DR cast collectively and individually on a variety of alt. country on the mild side. Kane was again joined by the Dead Reckoner crew in 1998 to record his solo, **Six Months, No Sun**, which true to its title looks at the darker side of life on songs about suicide ("To Whom It May Concern"), obsession ("Kill the Demon"; "Physical Thing"), possession ("Hysteria"), depression (title-tune), bad break-ups ("You're Just Takin' Up Space"), cheating ("In a Town This Size").

The O'Kanes/Columbia/1986
Tired of the Runnin' (O'Kanes)/Columbia/1988
Imagine That (O'Kanes)/Columbia/1990
Find My Way Home (Kieran Kane)/Atlantic/1993
Rise Above It (Jamie O'Hara)/RCA/1994
Dead Reckoning (Kieran Kane)/Dead Reckoning/1995
"I Cannot Give My Heart to You"(Kieran Kane) on **American Songbook**/Vinyl Junkie UK/1996
A Night of Reckoning (Dead Reckoners)/Dead Reckoning/1997
Six Months, No Sun/Dead Reckoning/1998
"Six Months, No Sun" on **Viva Americana**/Boka UK/1998

Kieran Kane Fan Club, 1111 16th Ave. Nashville, TN 37210

Kieran Kane/Dead Reckoning Home Page //www.songs.com/deadreck/kieran.html

Kieran Kane iMusic Showcase //imusic.com/showcase/country/

Kieran Kane Biography //www.pressnetwork.com/kieran.htm

See Kevin Welch

Robert Earl Keen, Jr. (Bryan Duckworth)

Texas; Singer/Songwriter
Houston, Texas; January 11, 1956-

In 1980, on the advice of Steve Earle, a promising young singer/songwriter named Robert Earl Keen moved from Austin to Nashville to try his luck. Earle, Lyle Lovett, and Nanci Griffith had preceded him down this route, but while they all found success, Keen's sojourn in Music City was pure hell. After two years of disappointment and humiliation, he hightailed it back to Texas and settled in Bandera near San Antonio. For a while Keen played as a solo at all types of dives but also got to open for the likes of Guy Clark and Townes Van Zandt. Then, with an old college pal, Bryan Duckworth, backing him on fiddle, he began to tour in and around the Lone Star State. His material was very popular with the college crowd especially at Texas A&M where Keen had received a B.A. in English and first began singing and writing songs (most notably "The Front Porch Song" with Lyle Lovett). Meanwhile, Keen was gaining a following among the cowboy and folk crowds as well and in 1984 recorded his first (self-released) album, **No Kinda Dancer**. In spite of a singing voice that he jokingly likened to "an 8th grader on quaaludes," Keen began a slow but steady ascent into the front ranks of Texas singer/songwriters with more fine recordings including **West Textures, A Bigger Piece of Sky, Gringo Honeymoon**, and **No. 2 Live Dinner**. His appeal lies in a special knack for telling stories about desperate characters ("Christabel," "The Road Goes on Forever," "Blow You Away," "Here in Arkansas"), the foibles of human relationships ("It's the Little Things"; "Merry Christmas From the Family"), and the peculiarities of life in Texas and the West ("The Armadillo Jackal," "No Kinda Dancer," "Copenhagen," "Corpus Christi Bay," "Jesse With the Long Hair"). The nature of Keen's material and its rousing delivery tended to attract a mixed throng of frat rats and rednecks that came to be known as the "Rowdy Crowd." However, Keen's base of popularity expanded, and in 1997, he recorded what was expected to be his major label breakthrough album. **Picnic** (named for a disastrous trip to Willie Nelson's 4th of July celebration where Keen lost his girlfriend and his car caught on fire all in the same day) retains some of Keen's boisterous image on covers of "4th of July" (Dave Alvin) and "Levelland" (James McMurtry) but shows his deeper side on "Over the Waterfall," "Shades of Gray," and "Then Came Lo Mein" (duet with Margo Timmins of the Cowboy Junkies). But, in spite of Keen's attempt to move beyond his bad boy reputation, his "Undone" became embroiled in controversy when a Florida state senator used some of the lyrics (whore; son of a bitch) to justify cutting off funds to a public radio station that played the tune. **Walking Distance** (co-produced by Gurf Morlix) finds Keen in a more introspective mode ("Feelin' Good Again"; "Travelin' Light"), but he also throws a couple of bones to the Rowdy Crowd on "That Buckin' Song" and "Happy Holidays, Y'All," a follow-up to the hilarious "Merry Christmas From the Family."

Keen's old compadre and fiddle player, Bryan Duckworth, has released an admirable collection of Western swing, honky tonk, Cajun, and *conjunto* called **Duckworth's Mood Swing**. Its supporting cast includes Keen, Ponty Bone, Bradley Williams, Mark Rubin, J. J. Barrera, Champ Hood, and the Robert Keen band on originals and standards ("Bonaparte's Retreat"; "La Calle Seis"; "Curly Headed Baby"; "Rancho Grande/Jesse Polka").

No Kinda Dancer/Keen Edge/1984; Philo/1990; Sugar Hill/1995
West Textures/Sugar Hill/1989
Live Album/Sugar Hill/1988
A Bigger Piece of Sky/Sugar Hill/1993
Gringo Honeymoon/Sugar Hill/1994
Duckworth's Mood Swing (Bryan Duckworth)/ Duckaway/1994
No. 2 Live Dinner/Sugar Hill/1996
Picnic/Arista Austin/1997
Walking Distance/Arista Austin/1998

The Robert Earl Show, P.O. Box 1734, Bandera, TX 78003; 830-796-SHOW

RobertEShw@aol.com

Robert Earl Keen Fan Club, 1026 16th Ave. S. Nashville, TN 37212

Official Robert Earl Keen Home Page //www.robertearlkeen.com

Unofficial Robert Earl Keen Home Page //www.cse.ucsc.edu/~darrell/keen/

The Robert Earl Page //www.io.com/~mshaw/keen/

My Robert Earl Keen Page //www.geocities.com/Nashville/3868/keen.html

Robert Earl Keen Fan Page //www.flash.net/~runge/#rek/

My Tiny Robert Earl Keen Page //www.baylor.edu/~william_mcdaniel/robert.htm

Robert Earl Keen AOL Folder: Entertainment>Music>Chat & Messages>Music Community>Country/Folk>Country & Western, A-K

Bryan Duckworth Fan Club, P.O. Box 1972, Sequin, TX 78155

Bryan Duckworth Home Page //www.cse.ucsc.edu/~darrell/duckworth/

Bill Keith (The Blue Velvet Band)

Banjo; Pedal Steel; Progressive Bluegrass; Country Rock
Boston, Massachusetts; December 20, 1939-

Bill Keith has been one of the most influential progressive bluegrass musicians of the last thirty years not only for his innovative banjo technique but also for some important contributions to banjo technology. Drawn early in life to the banjo, he was initially involved in folk music in the 1950s before moving into bluegrass in the 1960s when he began playing in the Kentuckians and for a brief period with Bill Monroe. During this time, Keith developed a banjo playing technique called the chromatic or "Keith" style (based on fiddle melodies) and invented a new tuning peg for the 5-string. After a four year stint with Jim Kweskin's Jug Band (1964-1968), Keith switched over to pedal steel and with Jim Rooney, Richard Greene, and Eric Weissberg formed the Blue Velvet Band. They recorded one album, **Sweet Moments**, with some commendable country rock, bluegrass originals, and covers of Hank Williams. Shortly after this, Keith (back on banjo once more) joined Greene, David Grisman, Clarence White, and Peter Rowan in Muleskinner which along with Old and In the Way was one of the most important of the early progressive bluegrass bands. Into the 1970s and 1980s, Keith worked for various performers (Judy Collins, Jonathan Edwards), toured as a duo with Jim Rooney, made several excellent solo recordings (especially **Something Auld, Something Newgrass, Something Borrowed** with Rooney, Grisman, Tony Rice, Vassar Clements), and wrote for *Frets* magazine. The 1990s found him working with a revived New Blue Velvet Band with Rooney, Weissberg, and Kenny Kosek and with Richard Greene in his The Grass is Greener newgrass ensemble.

The Blue Velvet Band: Richard Greene (f); Bill Keith (bj,p.s.); Jim Rooney (g,v); Eric Weissberg (g,v)

Livin' on the Mountain/Prestige Folklore/1963
Sweet Moments (Blue Velvet Band)/Warner/1969
Muleskinner/Warner Brothers/1973; Sierra/1995
Something Auld, Something Newgrass, Something Borrowed/Rounder/1976
Banjo (with Tony Trischka)/Bluegrass Masters/1978 (instructional book)
Fiddle Tunes for Banjo/Rounder/1981
Banjoistics/Rounder/1984
Beating Around the Bush/Green Linnet/
The Grass is Greener/Rebel/1995
Muleskinner Live/Sierra/1995

Bill Keith/Rounder Page //www.rounder.com

See Richard Greene; David Grisman

Bap Kennedy

Singer/Songwriter
Belfast, Northern Ireland; 1962-

In an interview done shortly after he completed **Domestic Blues**, Belfast native Martin "Bap" Kennedy subtly summed up his feelings about the recording: "Sure we (the Irish) invented fucking country music, and I'm just staking my claim." Growing up in Northern Ireland, he was drawn to American country music but playing it professionally wasn't much of an option at the time. Instead, Bap, nicknamed for a bread roll made by the famous Kennedy (no relation) bakery, turned to an ancient tradition (Celtic) and a modern one (punk rock). After moving to London in 1985, he formed Energy Orchard which mixed rock/blues and Celtic influences through five albums and ten years together. At one point in the late 1980s, Kennedy met Steve Earle while the latter was visiting London; the two hit it off but lost touch in the early 1990s as Earle went through his dark days and Energy Orchard slowly came to an end. However, when he heard Earle's 1995 "comeback" **Train A Comin'**, Kennedy decided this was the kind of basic acoustic country album he'd always wanted to do and that Steve was the man to help him do it. So, in 1996, Bap joined the Twangtrust and recorded **Domestic Blues**. Due to music industry red tape, it wasn't released until 1998 but turned out to be one of that year's most pleasant and highly praised surprises. Relying on many of the same musicians who played on **Train A Comin'** (Peter Rowan, Earle, Roy Huskey, Jr. plus Jerry Douglas and Nancy Blake), it has much the same feel but with sounds and images drawn from Kennedy's Irish background. Bap modestly labeled **Domestic Blues** "barroom philosophy with dobros" (some stellar steel by Douglas), but this doesn't really do justice to his impressive singing and songwriting. With a rough hewn voice tailor made for his subject matter, he movingly focuses on the ability of people to survive the daily grind as well as extreme circumstances such as those found in contemporary Belfast ("The Ghosts of Belfast"; "The Shankill and the Falls" with Nanci Griffith). Other highlights include a couple of drowsy love songs ("I Love Her So"; "I've Fallen in Love") and covers of Earle's "Angel is the Devil" and Ewan MacColl's "Dirty Old Town" (hidden track duet with Steve). In 1999, Kennedy, inspired by performers like Beck and Sparklehorse, hinted at doing a trip-hop country record perhaps with Steve Earle.

Domestic Blues/E-Squared/1998

Bap Kennedy/E-Squared Page
//www.e2records.com/bapken.html

Killbilly
Punkgrass
Dallas, Texas; 1987-1994

Although the Bad Livers have become known as the primary innovators of "punkgrass" or "thrashgrass," they were pre-dated by Killbilly which also probed the common boundaries between bluegrass and punk rock. Unfortunately, Killbilly lacked both the chops and the imagination needed to effectively make these connections, and although they had a few shining moments, more often than not the result was a hopeless mish mash. Strangely enough, Danny Barnes and Mark Rubin, the co-founders of the Bad Livers, were in an early incarnation Killbilly which cut a live cassette, **Alive From the City of Hate in the Lone Star State**. In 1992, Flying Fish took a chance and released, **Stranger in This Place**, which presents punk/metal/ bluegrass covers ("Maybelline") and originals that go for

maximum speed and yuks ("Wake Up and Smell the Coffee") but fall flat on their faces. A single for Diesel Only Records ("Diesel Dazey") slows down the pace and plays it straighter but on **Foggy Mountain Anarchy**, Killbilly kicked it back up a notch with "Mountain Dew or Die," "Jesse James," "Pass the Whisky Around," and an ill conceived cover of "Hare Krishna" by Husker Du. To be fair, in spite of their shortcomings, Killbilly did do a lot to prepare the way for the emergence of a strong alt. country scene in Dallas in the late 1990s. Moreover, in spite of their detractors, they continue to have a loyal cult following in Big D and beyond.

While still with Killbilly and after it broke up in 1994, guitar/mandolinist Alan Wooley became a member of the Cartwrights, a very promising but short lived country rock band fronted by Donny Ray Ford, and he produced the Old 97s debut, **Hitchhike to Rhome**. In the late 1990s, Wooley served as lead guitarist in Jack Ingram's touring Beat Up Ford Band. Murry Hammond became the Old 97s bassist and Michael Schwedler managed that popular band.

Danny Barnes (bj, 1989); Murry Hammond (b); Richard Hunter (b,v, 1990-1994); Harris Kirby (g); Steve Lutke (bj, 1993-1994); Mark Rubin (b, 1989); Michael Schwedler (d); Craig Taylor (hm,v); Stephen Trued (bj); Alan Wooley (g,md,v)

Alive From the City of Hate in the Lone Star State/Killbilly/1989
Stranger in This Place/Flying Fish/1992
"Don't Tread on Me" b/w "Diesel Dazey"/Diesel Only/1993
"Diesel Dazey" on **Rig Rock Truck Stop**/Diesel Only/1993
Foggy Mountain Anarchy/Crystal Clear/1994

Killbilly/Crystal Clear Page //www.crystalclearsound.com

See Bad Livers; Donny Ray Ford; Old 97s

Bill Kirchen (The Moonlighters; Too Much Fun)
Electric Guitar; Country Rock; Honky Tonk; Swing
Ann Arbor, Michigan; June 29, 1948-

As a kid growing up in Ann Arbor, Michigan, Bill Kirchen's first musical instrument was the trombone. Fortunately for us, he switched to guitar and in high school became active in the local folk scene where he was exposed to blues, country, and other roots music. While in college, Kirchen met George Frayne aka Commander Cody and became a charter member of the Lost Planet Airmen, the preeminent rockabilly, honky tonk, swing band of the late 1960s and early 1970s. From their home base in San Francisco, they established a huge national and international following on the strength of songs like "Too Much Fun," "Mama Hated Diesels," "Down to Seeds and Stems," and "Hot Rod Lincoln" which just missed being a million seller hit. A big part of their success was due to the lead guitar work of Kirchen who drew on all the greats from country and rock 'n' roll. He remained with the group through ten albums until they broke up in 1976. From there, Kirchen went on to form the semi-country rock, swing band, the Moonlighters, whose first record was produced by Nick Lowe. He rejoined a reformed Commander Cody for a few recordings (**Let's Rock**, **Sleazy Roadside Stories**, **Aces High**) but left once again in 1992. Moving to Washington, D.C., Kirchen became a popular local favorite with his band Too Much Fun. While Commander Cody went on to a more hard rocking style, Kirchen with his band Too Much Fun revitalized the classic Lost Planet Airmen style in two great recordings (**Tombstone Every Mile** and **Have Love, Will Travel**) of rockabilly, honky tonk, swing, Cajun, and, of course, lots of twanging truck driving tunes. For his work, Kirchen dominated the D.C. music awards in 1995 winning eight Wammies (Musician of the Year, Best Roots/Country Group, Best Debut Recording). Bill milks his vintage Telecaster for every iota of electric guitar history as exemplified in his knock out live performance of "Hot Rod Lincoln" in which the legends of blues, country, and rock guitar "pull over" to "let him by." This song, along with more great country/roots/rock, was included on his live Hightone debut aptly titled **Hot Rod Lincoln**: **Live!!** In addition to fronting Too Much Fun, Kirchen toured as guitarist and vocalist for Nick Lowe and his Impossible Birds. In 1997, Kirchen once again owned the Wammies winning Best Rock/Roots Rock Vocalist, Instrumentalist, and Group. *Guitar Player* magazine (May 1998) profiled Bill as one of its "Titans of the Tele" along with Roy Buchanan, Albert Collins, Danny Gatton, Keith Richards, Bruce Springsteen, and Muddy Waters.

The Moonlighters: Tim Eschliman (b,v); Tony Johnson (d,v); Bill Kirchen (l.g.,v); Austin de Lone (g,p,v); Nick Lowe (b.v.); Paul Bassman Riley (b.v.).
Too Much Fun: Bill Kirchen (l.g.,b,v); Johnny Castle (b, b.v.); Jack O'Dell (d,b.v.).

> **The Moonlighters**/Amhearst/1977
> **Rush Hour** (Moonlighters)/Demon UK/1983; 1994 (CD)
> **Tombstone Every Mile**/Black Top/1994
> "Santa! Don't Pass Me By" on **A Holiday Feast, Vol. 1**/ HFM/1995
> **Have Love, Will Travel**/Black Top/1996
> "Semi-Truck" on **Rig Rock Deluxe**/Upstart Diesel Only/1996
> **Hot Rod Lincoln: Live!!**/Hightone/1997
> "Truckin' Trees for Christmas" on **Holiday Feast, Vol. 2**/ HFM/1997

Bill Kirchen, P.O. Box 525, Owings, MD 20736

Bill Kirchen Home Page //www.crosstownarts.com/CrosstownArts/client_music/kirchen/kirchen.html

BKirchen@aol.com

Bill Kirchen Biography //www.hightone.com/bios/kirchenbio.html

See Commander Cody and His Lost Planet Airmen

Cheri Knight
Singer/Songwriter; Twangtrust
Western Massachusetts

In the early 1990s, Cheri Knight was a member of the seminal alt. country group Blood Oranges. Her singing and songwriting ("The Crying Tree"; "Shadow of You") were a vital part of their distinctive bluegrass/country/rock sound which has had a tremendous influence on roots rock alternative country. And although their two full-length recordings and EP were big with critics and an underground cadre of fans, Blood Oranges couldn't make it finanacially as a band and so decided to go their separate ways in 1995. Knight returned to the farming and commerical flower growing she had done for years but also prepared to make her first solo recording. **The Knitter**, produced by Eric Ambel, has vestiges of the Blood Oranges (Mark Spencer guests on organ) but also shows Knight moving toward her own roots rock style on originals and a cover of Brian Henneman's "Very Last Time." It garnered her considerable attention, but Cheri really broke through in 1998 with **The Northeast Kingdom** which was produced by Steve Earle's Twangtrust. This impressive roots rock pastiche features old bandmates Jimmy Ryan and Mark Spencer plus Will Rigby, Earle, Tammy Rogers, and Emmylou Harris (harmony on two songs) and ranges widely across Celtic ("Dar Glasgow"), Byrdsian folk/country rock ("Rose in the Vine"), Blood Oranges roots rock ("If Wishes Were Horses"; "Sweetheart"), grungy rock ("Black Eyed Susie"; "Dead Man's Curve"), honky tonk ("White Lies"), old-time ("The Hatfield Side"; "All Blue"). Thematically, **The Northeast Kingdom** reflects Knights' grounding in the land and culture of her home in rural Western Massachusetts with an accent on death and despair muted somewhat by the promise of rebirth and redemption.

> **The Knitter**/ESD/1996
> "Wagon of Clay" on **Rig Rock Deluxe**/Diesel Only Upstart/1996
> "The Knitter" on **Luxury Liner, Vol. 1**/Glitterhouse Ger./1997
> **The Northeast Kingdom**/E-Squared/1998

Cheri Knight/E-Squared Page //www.e2records.com/ck.html

See Jimmy Ryan/Blood Oranges

Chris Knight
Singer/Songwriter
Slaughters, Kentucky; 1961-

A disciple of both John Prine and Steve Earle, newcomer Chris Knight compares favorably with the current crop of songsmiths such as Tom House, R.B. Morris, and Fred Eaglesmith. Like them, he takes a hard look at unpopular subjects (child abuse, homelessness, rural hardships, losers, robbery, heartbreak, etc.) with a voice that leaves no doubt he knows what he's singing about. However, in his early years, a career in music didn't seem to be in the cards for Knight. A graduate of Western Kentucky University, he worked in the late 1980s and early 1990s enforcing surface mining laws for the state of Kentucky. Inspired by Earle and Prine, Chris noodled around with songwriting during this time before getting up the nerve to go to Nashville. There, an open mic spot at the Bluebird got him a staff writer position with Bluewater Music, and a four song demo, **The Trailer Tapes**, convinced Decca Records to take a chance. Early in 1998, they released Knight's self-titled debut which got lots of attention especially from the alt. country press. Whether or not powerful songs like "Love and a .45," "Framed," "William," "House and 90 Acres," and "If I Were You" (not on the CD) can separate Knight from the ever growing list of "gritty" singer/songwriters, only time will tell.

The Trailer Tapes/1997 (unrel. 4 trk. demo)
Chris Knight/Decca/1998

Chris Knight/Decca Records Home Page
//www.decca-nashville.com/ck/

Chris Knight iMusic Showcase
//imusic.com/showcase/country/

The Knitters (X)
Country Roots Rock
Los Angeles, California; 1985

X was one of the most important L.A. punk bands of the 1980s. Mostly known for their hard driving sound, they also played acoustic sets and occasionally threw some country into their recordings. In 1985, X gave full vent to their country side as the Knitters and made one recording, **Poor Little Critter on the Road**. For this session, their regular lead guitarist Billy Zoom was replaced by Dave Alvin of the much beloved Blasters. The recording itself has a fairly traditional country feel ranging from waltzes and ballads ("Someone Like You"; "Cryin' But My Tears Are Far Away") to wild stompers like the bizarre "Call of the Wrecking Ball" (about a professional poultry killer). Exene Cervenka and John Doe share lead vocals on covers of the Carters ("Poor Old Heartsick Me"), the Delmores ("Trail of Time"), Haggard ("Silver Wings"), and Leadbelly ("Rock Island Line") plus reworked versions of songs from the X files ("Love Shack"; "The New World"). Overall, for a one shot deal, **Poor Little Critter** is a splendid album well worth seeking out.

Post-Knitters, Alvin became a member of X for a very brief time, and the band stayed active until 1988. Cervenka went on to a career as a solo performer as did Doe whose **Meet John Doe** and **Kissingsohard** have a few country touches. In 1997, Doe made a cameo appearance in the movie *Boogie Nights* and in 1998 did an "unplugged" tour with Peter Droge, Glen Phillips (ex-Toad the Wet Sprocket), and Steve Poltz (Jewel). X reunited to record the live acoustic album **Unclogged**, and in 1997, Elektra released a double CD X retrospective, **Beyond &**

Back. To celebrate this event, X launched a reunion tour in early 1998.

The Knitters: Dave Alvin (a.g.,e.g.); Jonny Ray Bartel (ub); D. Bonebrake (d); Exene Cervenka (l.v.); John Doe (a.g.,l.v.) **X:** D. Bonebrake (d); Exene Cervenka (v); John Doe (g,v); Billy Zoom (l.g.)

Poor Little Critter on the Road (Knitters)/Slash Warner Brothers/1985; 1993
John Doe/Geffen/1990
Kissingsohard (John Doe)/Geffen/1994
Beyond & Back: The X Anthology/Elektra/1997

See The Blasters

Red Knuckles & The Trailblazers
See Tim O'Brien

Walt Koken
See The Highwoods String Band

Alison Krauss (Union Station)
Progressive Bluegrass
Decatur, Illinois; July 23, 1971-

One of the great popularizers of bluegrass in the 1990s, the secret of Alison Krauss' success is not hard to find: prodigious fiddling talent, gorgeous voice (like an early Dolly Parton), superb supporting musicians, and a willingness to do bluegrass versions of non-bluegrass material. An award winning fiddler as a pre-teen, Krauss cut her first album at 14 and then got a deal with Rounder. In the late 1980s, with her band Union Station, she recorded **Too Late to Cry** and the Grammy nominated, **Two Highways**, and then, in the 1990s really began to take off with the Grammy winner (Best Bluegrass Album) **I've Got That Old Feeling** and then **Every Time You Say Goodbye**. These recordings sold in record breaking numbers not only because of their impeccable musicianship and singing but also because they took chances with bluegrass covers of country, rock, and pop songs. Krauss further promoted progressive bluegrass by "discovering" and producing the terrific Cox Family who worked with her on **I Know Who Holds Tomorrow**. In 1995, Rounder issued a first class Krauss retrospective, **Now That I've Found You**, that showcases her best from the late 1980s-early 1990s. **So Long, So Wrong** earned more Grammys for Krauss and company in 1997 including Best Performance By A Duo/Group, Best Bluegrass Album, and Best Country Instrumental. She continued to work with the Cox Family in 1998 and prepared to do a solo which was reportedly going to be different but not too far out.

Union Station: Barry Bales (b,v); Ron Block (bj,g,v); Tim Stafford (g,v,1990-1992); Adam Steffey (md,v,1992-1997); Dan Tyminski (g,v,1994-)

Different Strokes/Fiddle Tunes/1985

Too Late to Cry/Rounder/1987
Two Highways/Rounder/1989
I've Got That Old Feeling/Rounder/1990
Every Time You Say Goodbye/Rounder/1992
I Know Who Holds Tomorrow/Rounder/1994
Now That I've Found You: A Collection/Rounder/1995
So Long, So Wrong/Rounder/1997
"Pretty Little Miss in the Garden" on **Clinch Mountain Country: Ralph Stanley & Friends**/Rebel/1998

Alison Krauss and Union Station Land,
P.O. Box 121711, Nashville, TN 37212

Alison Krauss and Union Station: The Unofficial Website
//members.aol.com/dstalnaker/akus/akus.html

Alison Krauss Profile
//www.banjo.com/profiles/AlisonKrauss.html

Alison Krauss iMusic Showcase
//imusic.com/showcase/country/

See The Cox Family

Freddy Krc (Wild Country; The Shakin' Apostles)

Country Rock; Honky Tonk
Houston, Texas; April 17, 1954-

Freddy Krc's ancestors first came to Texas from Moravia (later a province of Czechoslovakia) in the mid-19th century bringing with them a rich musical heritage. His earliest musical experiences came from his mother's side, the Krenek's, who produced several generations of respected polka bands. Later, growing up along the Gulf Coast in La Porte, he was influenced by the area's unique mix of country, blues, Cajun, and rock and took up drumming. After a short period preparing for the ministry at Lon Morris College, Freddy dropped out and headed for Austin's musical hotbed. He traveled to the West Coast and England for a few years, but in the late 1970s settled back in Austin where he drummed for B. W. Stevenson, Steve Fromholz, and Jerry Jeff Walker. From 1979-1982, Krc was a member of the punk band the Explosives along with Cam King and Waller Collie. Recording several singles and one LP and backing Roky Erickson on occasion, they enjoyed some success in Austin and L.A. However, in the 1980s, Krc returned to country music as a member of bands supporting Jimmie Dale Gilmore, Butch Hancock, and Wes McGhee and fronted his own group, Wild Country, which included McGhee and English pedal steel king, B. J. Cole. They made two albums (**Lucky 7** and **Neon Dreams**), of Texas style honky tonk, country rock, and blues in the late 1980s for Amazing Records (Austin) and were especially popular in the United Kingdom. During this time, Krc began to make pilgrimages to his ancestral home in Czechoslovakia, and in 1989, when the Communist regime fell, was inspired to write "When the Wall Came Down." In 1990, Krc was given a unique opportunity to go to Czechoslovakia to record an album with local band Karel Zich & FLOP. **When the Wall Came Down** was dedicated to Czech hero Vaclav Havel. Returning to the U.S., Freddy rejoined Jerry

Jeff Walker for a time before starting a new band, the Shakin' Apostles with John Inmon (Lost Gonzo Band) and old pal, Cam King. Their self-titled debut and **Tucson** have a real Texas/ Southwest flavor courtesy of guest appearances by Ponty Bone, Lloyd Maines, Jerry Jeff, and Champ Hood. In 1996, the Shakin' Apostles signed with Germany's fast rising Americana label Blue Rose which released **Austin, Texas**, a best of compilation (with four live cuts and one previously unreleased). In late 1997 came **Medicine Show** which carries on the patented Shakin' Apostle style which they describe as "Electric Western Folk-Rock." Krc lent a hand or two to Wes McGhee's 1997 recording **Backbeat**. **Medicine Show** was re-released domestically in 1998 on Big Tex Records.

Wild Country: Fred Krc (v); B. J. Cole (p.s.); John Gordon (b); Bob Loveday (f); Wes McGhee (b,g,p); Geraint Watkins (acc,p)
The Shakin' Apostles: John Inmon (bj,l.g.,r.g., perc); Ronnie Johnson (b); Freddy Steady Krc (r.g.,l.v.); Danny Thorpe (l.g.,r.g.)

Lucky 7 (Wild Country)/Amazing/1987
Neon Dreams (Wild Country)/Amazing/1989
When the Wall Came Down (with Karel Zich & FLOP)/Multisonic Czech./1990
The Shakin' Apostles/ESD/1993
Tucson/ESD/1995
"Dear Eloise" on **Sing Hollies in Reverse: A Tribute to the Hollies**/eggBERT/1996
Austin, Texas/Blue Rose Ger./1996
"Tucson" on **The Blue Rose Collection, Vol. 1**/Blue Rose Ger.1997
Medicine Show/Blue Rose Ger./1997; Big Tex/1998

Freddy Steady Krc/Shakin' Apostles Home Page
//www.nonerds.com/krc/

See B.J. Cole; Wes McGhee

Jimmy LaFave

Austin; Singer/Songwriter
Wills Point, Texas; July 12, 1945-

As a young man in Oklahoma, Jimmy LaFave worked for a time as a truck driver. Traveling across the West and Midwest, he listened to lots of music on the radio, closely observed the changing landscapes, and collected stories about the people he met on the way. Following in the footsteps of Guthrie, Kerouac, and other "road warriors," LaFave began to write about his experiences on the road when he became a singer/songwriter in the Stillwater music scene in the early 1980s. He recorded one self released cassette **Broken Line** and made many musical pilgrimages to Austin before relocating there in 1986. Following several years of playing the clubs and building a following, LaFave made an independent cassette, **Highway Angels...Full Moon Rain** which won *The Austin Chronicle*'s readers' poll award for best tape of 1989. Three years later came a deal with Tomato Records which turned out to be an absolute nightmare and put LaFave's recording career on hold until he finally extricated himself in 1992 and signed on with Rounder subsidiary Bohemia Beat. This resulted in a live recording, **Austin Skyline**, with his band Night Tribe which alternates between ballads and rockers on Dylan covers ("Girl From the North Country"; "Shelter From the Storm") and great originals ("Only One Angel," "Desperate Men," "Deep South 61 Delta Highway Blues"). It and the follow-up, **Highway Trance**, won a number of awards from *Music City Texas* and put LaFave in Austin's new singer/songwriter elite. Appropriately enough, in 1993 and 1994, he contributed "This Land is Your Land" and "Oklahoma Hills" to a Woody Guthrie tribute, **Pastures of Plenty** and an original "Route 66 Revisited" to **Songs of Route 66**, a collection of songs about America's fabled highway.

In the mid-1990s, LaFave's popularity as a major poet of the American highway extended across the U.S. and into Europe. 1995 and 1996 were especially successful years with two more albums, **Buffalo Return to the Plains** and **Road Novel**, an appearance on *Austin City Limits*, Kerrville Music Awards' Songwriter of the Year (1995) and the Austin Music Awards' Best Singer/Songwriter for 1996. Both recordings continue LaFave's preoccupation with the road ("The Open Space"; "Big Wheels"; "Vast Stretches of Broken Heart") and with Native Americans ("The Great Night"). Highlights for LaFave in 1997 included an appearance at the 16th American Music Festival in Chicago and a performance at a music conference sponsored by the Rock 'n' Roll Hall of Fame called "Hard Travelin': The Life and Legacy of Woody Guthrie." He was also a featured performer at the first annual Woody Guthrie Free Folk Festival held in Okemah, Oklahoma (Guthrie's home-town) in July 1998. By the end of the year, LaFave was in the early stages of putting together (with Woody's daughter Nora's blessing) a **Mermaid Avenue** type recording with Joe Ely, Butch Hancock, and Ray Wylie Hubbard giving musical life to some of Guthrie's unrecorded lyrics. Nothing definite was expected on this fascinating project until later in 1999, but, in the meantime, Jimmy was busy putting out a 30 song live CD, **Trail**, with material from radio shows, board tapes, and boot-legs including many covers of his other favorite troubadour, Bob Dylan.

Broken Line/?/1981 (LP)
Highway Angels...Full Moon Rain/JL/1989 (CS)
Austin Skyline/Bohemia Beat Rounder/1992
Highway Trance/Bohemia Beat Rounder/1993
"This Land is Your Land" & "Oklahoma Hills" on
    Pastures of Plenty/Dejadisc/1993
"Route 66 Revisited" on **Songs of Route 66**/Lazy
    SOB/1994
The Open Road Highway Trance Acoustic Mini
    Album/LizardDut./1995 (recorded for Dutch radio
    program "VPRO Sunday Morning Coming Down")
Burden to Bear/Lizard Dut./1995 (3 trk. CD)
Buffalo Return to the Plains/Bohemia Beat
    Rounder/1995
Road Novel/Bohemia Beat Rounder/1997

"You'll Never Know" on **The Blue Rose Collection, Vol. 1**/Blue Rose Ger./1997
"Only One Angel" (live) on **Viva Americana**/Boka
    UK/1998
Trail/Bohemia Beat/1999

Official Jimmy Lafave Home Page
//www.rounder.com/bobeat/JimmyLafaveHome.htm
(includes the *Zen Okie Gazette*)

The Jimmy Lafave Page
//web.inter.nl.net/hcc/jtm.janssen/jimmy_lafave.html

Lambchop
Lo-Fi Country
Nashville, Tennessee; 1986-

In size and style, Lambchop is one of the most alternative of country bands. What started out as a gathering of friends to play music just for the heck of it, in the course of a decade, grew into a band that has varied in size over the years (up to 14 in 1998). Led by lead vocalist/songwriter Kurt Wagner, who is also a sculptor with a masters in fine arts, Lambchop's founding spirit of informality also guided the group's choices about what to play and how to play it. From the start, the attitude was to take whatever instruments (wrenches to pedal steels; euphoniums to bongos) and influences (country, rock, pop, classical) each member brought, mix them up, and see what happens. What might have been expected is some kind of mess, but, instead, Lambchop delivers a surprisingly coherent collection that is a cross between country rock, country pop (the infamous "Nashville Sound"), avant-garde jazz, and big band music. Lilting steel, woodwinds, cello, muted brass, and Wagner's soft, more spoken than sung stories on **I Hope You're Sitting Down** and **How I Quit Smoking** establish a sort of Country-politan mood, but Jim Reeves and Eddy Arnold never did songs like "Soaky in the Pooper" (about suicide), "Hellmouth," "Cowboy on the Moon," "The Man Who Loved Beer," "The Scary Caroler," or "Your Life as a Sequel." Downright raw and disturbing tunes such as "Moody Fucker," "Loretta Lung," "Playboy, The Shit," and "Poor Bastard" (from the **Hank** 10") are hauntingly effective precisely because of their matter of fact, laid-back pop/rock/country feel. Lambchop's quirky and slightly demented edge with strings has placed them in a class of their own although they have been embraced by both the No Depression and Insurgent wings of alt. country. In 1996, they contributed a sarcastic paean to Anglo/ American heroes ("Whitey") to Bloodshot's **Nashville: The Other Side of the Alley** and in 1997 released **Thriller**, another collection of contemporary "Nashville Sound" including "The Old Fat Robin," the delightful "My Ass, Your Face," and the inspiring "Your Fucking Sunny Day."

1998 was one of Lambchop's busiest and most productive years yet. They served as backing band on Vic Chesnutt's **The Salesman & Bernadette**, toured with him in the U.S. and

Europe, and put out another new record, **What Another Man Spills**, which presents covers of Curtis Mayfield, Dump, East River Pipe, and Frederick Knight. Meanwhile, their status as one of the leading alt. country bands rose overseas with a number of glowing reviews and inclusion in several European compilations. Deanna Varagona (who cut a single of her own in 1998), Paul Niehaus, and Hank Tilbury are also members of Paul Burch & the WPA Ballclub, one of the prime leaders in Nashville's honky tonk revival.

Paul Burch (vibe); C. Scott Chase (perc); John Delworth (org); Mike Doster (b); Steve Goodhue (bj,d,harp,ky,md); Bill Killebrew (g); Allen Lowrey (d); Jonathan Marx (cl,sax,v); Paul Niehaus (l.s.,tromb,v); Hank Tillbury (glock, synth); Marc Trovillion (b); Deanna Varagona (bj,cello,sax,v); Kurt Wagner (g,v)

"Nine" b/w "Moody Fucker"/Merge/1992 (7")
"My Cliché" b/w "Loretta Lung"/Sunday Driver/1994 (7")
"Soaky in the Pooper" b/w "Two Kittens Don't Make a
    Puppy"/Merge/1994 (7")
I Hope You're Sitting Down/Merge/1994
"Your Life as a Sequel" b/w "Smuckers"/Mute/1995 (7")
How I Quit Smoking/Merge/1996
"The Man Who Loved Beer" b/w "Alumni Lawn" &
    "Burly and Johnson"/City Slang Ger./1996 (CD single)
Hank/Merge/1996 (10" EP)
"Playboy, the Shit" on **Cowpunks**/Vinyl Junkie UK/1996
"Whitey" on **Nashville: The Other of the Alley**/
    Bloodshot/1996
Thriller/Merge/1997
Cigarettiquette/Merge/1997 (dbl. 7" EP)
Your Sucking Funny Day/City Slang/1998 (10")
What Another Man Spills/City Slang/1998
"The Petrified Florist" on **Loose: New Sounds of the Old
    West**/Vinyl Junkie UK/1998
"I'm a Stranger Here" on **Luxury Liner, Vol. 2**/
    Glitterhouse Ger./1998
"Saturday Option" on **Sounds of the New West: The Best
    of Alternative Country**/Uncut UK/1998
"Hesitation" b/w "Secrets for Dusty" (Deanna
    Varagona)/Star Star Stereo/1998 (7")

The Official Lambchop Site //www.lambchop.ml.org

Lambchop/Merge Page
//merge.catalogue.com/biolamb.html

See Paul Burch & WPA Ballclub; Vic Chesnutt

Lancaster County Prison

Country Punk Rock
Brooklyn, New York; 1993-

My copy of Lancaster County Prison's self titled debut recording came with a paperback called *Lobster Boy*, a charming true life story about a guy with stunted claw like hands and feet who is brutally murdered by family members. Like the book, the CD dives head first into the macabre with lots of stories about drunkenness ("Poppers & Whiskey"; "Drunk on Whiskey"; "Village Idiot"; "I Don't Need It I Just Like It"), dysfunctionals ("I Had a Problem"; "Wedding Dress of Hell"), and of course, murder ("Cold, Cold Sun"; "Lookin' For a Way";

"Killin' Kin") all set to a country/punk/rock drive that LCP calls "Country and Western for the hard of hearing." For added effect, several tracks are introduced with actual dialogue from classic movies, *The Searchers*, *Touch of Evil*, and *The Wild Bunch*. There are also a couple of rowdy Johnny Horton covers, "Ol' Slewfoot" and "Battle of New Orleans." Their insurgent country sound is due to the backgrounds of the band's founders: John R. Carruthers and Roy Edroso. Both had formerly been in Brooklyn rock bands (Carruthers with the Gashounds, Edroso with the Reverb Motherfuckers) and both liked country music, so they began to combine them first as a duo and then as LCP when they added bassist Mark DeAngelis (ex-My Sick Friends) and fiddler Megan Karlen. Switching to newly formed Gregor Records in 1997, they recorded another twisted country punk concoction, **What I Like About America**, with "interesting" covers of the traditional "Darlin' Corey," "Free Man," "Go 'Long Mule," and Tom T. Hall's "I Got Lost" plus signature LCP originals like "Fat, Old, Drunk & Proud," "Beyond the Bottle," and "Go Cup in a Pickup." Later that year, the band signed with Coolidge Records to do a live album at New York City's Village Idiot. **LIVE!** captures LCP's raw and frenetic energy (kind of like the Hickoids) on favorites from their studio recordings, six new white trash classics, and covers of Roger Miller, Waylon Jennings, The Hag, and even "The Yellow Rose of Texas." Carruthers is the mastermind behind the semi-annual TwangCore NYC which showcases alt. country from the Big Apple and beyond.

John R. Carruthers (bj,hm,perc,v); Mark DeAngelis (b,g,v); Gerald Donnelly (g,v); Matt Dow (d); Roy Edroso (g,v); Megan Karlen (f,v); Joe Vazquez (g,p.s.)

Lancaster County Prison/One Drinky Winky/1995;
    Gregor/1997
What I Like About America/Gregor/1997
**Lancaster County Prison LIVE! At the Village Idiot,
    New York City**/Coolidge/1998

Lancaster County Prison, 564 Sackett St.,
Brooklyn, NY 11217

Lancaster County Prison Page //www.squirty.com/lcp/

Hardcorn@aol.com

Lancaster County Prison/Coolidge Page
//www.gis.net/~coolidge/lcppic.html

k. d. lang

Singer/Songwriter
Consort, Alberta, Canada; November 2, 1961-

There were few, if any, precedents to prepare the country music world for the dramatic emergence of k.d. lang in the late 1980s. Heavily influenced by Patsy Cline, lang took up country singing in the early 1980s in Canada and with her band the Reclines did several acclaimed albums (**Friday Dance Promenade, A Truly Western Experience, Angel With a Lariat**) combining honky tonk, Western swing, rockabilly, wild polkas, and country ballads with a certain modern edge. But, beside lang's powerful vocals, what really made her stand out was an androgynous persona that took liberties with some of country and western's most familiar images. Lang's gay *caballera* approach was a hit with country and rock audiences in Canada where she won a number of important awards. Then, in the late 1980s, she made a huge breakthrough in the U.S. After channeling Patsy Cline on **Shadowland** (done in Nashville with Owen Bradley producing), lang scored her biggest triumph with **Absolute Torch and Twang**, an amazingly dynamic recording that took both mainstream and alternative country by storm in 1989. It has several fine covers ("Three Days"; "Big, Big Love"), but the real highlight is the convincing originals co-written by k.d. and talented multi-instrumentalist Ben Mink. The album was good enough to win the Grammy for Best Female Vocal Performance, but ironically lang chose to move completely away from country toward full-blown pop in the 1990s. However, in her wake, she left avenues open for many excellent gay/lesbian alt. country performers including Ranch Romance, the Topp Twins, and Y'ALL.

The Reclines: Michael Creber (p); John Dymond (b); Gordie Matthews (e.g.); Ben Mink (f,g,mda); Michel Pouliot (d) with Greg Leisz (s.g.)

Friday Dance Promenade/Bumstead Can./1983
A Truly Western Experience/Bumstead/1984
Angel With a Lariat/Sire/1987
Shadowland/Sire/1988
Absolute Torch and Twang/Sire/1989

k. d. lang //www.wbr.com/kdlang

Obvious Gossip: The k.d. lang Fan Club Page //www.kdlang.com

Jon Langford (The Mekons; Hillbilly Lovechild; The Pine Valley Cosmonauts; The Waco Brothers; Skull Orchard; Sally Timms; Rico Bell)
Insurgent Country
England/Chicago, Illinois; Mid-1980s-

When the history of alternative country is written, Jon Langford will surely rate a chapter of his own. For over a decade, as a musician and promoter, he has made numerous invaluable contributions to the development of the genre. His first band, the Mekons, initially played politically oriented, rock noise but in the mid-1980s took a turn toward country on a series of releases, **Fear and Whiskey, Crime and Punishment, The Edge of the World, Slightly South of the Border**, and **Honky Tonkin'**. These albums retain much of the punk sound but also employ accordion, banjo, fiddle, and mandolin; they also have a sharp political sense as on the mine tragedy song, "Trimdon Grange Explosion" but also present straight ahead covers of Hank Williams ("Lost Highway") and Merle Haggard ("Deep End") plus a generous dose of songs about hurting, crying,

drinking etc. sung mostly by Langford in his distinctive growling voice. The Mekons experimentation with a countryesque sound was greatly aided by the addition of Sally Timms on vocals. In the late 1980s, she explored country territory on several acoustically oriented solo efforts with her band, the Drifting Cowgirls (including Langford and Brendan Croker). Over the years, Langford became ever more intensively involved in alternative country music. In 1988, he was the leading force behind a Johnny Cash tribute CD **'Til Things are Brighter** with Cash covers by the Mekons, Sally Timms, Brendan Croker, Michelle Shocked and others; the proceeds from the recording went to an AIDS trust fund. Relocating from Leeds to Chicago, Jon Boy became involved in and was a leading proponent of the Windy City's "insurgent country" movement that emerged in the early 1990s. Langford was instrumental in vitalizing that scene by promoting local bands and fronting his own groups. He was a most prominent figure in the three volumes of insurgent country (**For A Life of Sin, Hell Bent, Nashville**) issued by Bloodshot Records beginning in 1994. His band, Hillbilly Lovechild, contributed the rollicking "Over the Cliff" to volume 1 and for the second installment, Langford's group, the Waco Brothers, did "Bad Times Are Coming Round Again." This latter band grew out of Hillybilly Lovechild and another Langford brainchild, the Pine Valley Cosmonauts which recorded a Johnny Cash tribute album, **Misery Loves Company**, in 1995. With members drawn from the Mekons, Wreck, Poi Dog Pondering, and the Bottle Rockets, the Waco Brothers were in many ways a more fully realized version of the Mekons blend of country, punk, and politics. **To the Last Dead Cowboy**, and its follow-up, **Cowboy in Flames**, with their hardest of hard core country approach and radically political statements ("Plenty Tough, Union Made"; "Bad Times Are Comin' Round Again"; "See Willy Fly By"; "Dollar Dress"), established them as *the* consummate insurgent country band. Late in 1997, Bloodshot issued a collection of outtakes from the Waco's first two recordings called **Do You Think About Me?** Langford also fronted a Waco Brothers spin off, Skull Orchard, whose self titled debut offers hard driving country punk rock and biting socio-political commentary focused on the industrial waste-lands of South Wales.

Langford supported a number of other insurgent groups like the Handsome Family and also fellow Mekons Sally Timms and Rico Bell on solo records. **The Return of Rico Bell** showcased Bell's singing, songwriting, and playing talents (accordion) on country/roots/rock covers ("Dark End of the Street"; "I Am a Lonesome Fugitive") and originals while Timms' **Cowboy Sally** was a 5 track EP featuring members of the Mekons, Waco Brothers, and Handsome Family on covers of Lefty Frizzell ("Long Black Veil"), Pee Wee King ("Tennessee Waltz"), John Anderson ("Seminole Wind"), and the Handsome Family's bizarre "Drunk By Noon." In addition, to his musical talents, Langford is an accomplished visual artist whose one-of-a-kind depictions of country music legends (Williams, Wills, Cline, Cash, et al.) have graced the covers of Bloodshot's insurgent country compilations. Described by Langford as "ink drawings on paper...stuck down to hardboard then painted on with.. pastels, acrylics and white-out pens...glazed with scummy transparent nicotine varnishes, gouged, scratched, scraped and torn," these paintings were gathered into a New York exhibit in early 1998 called "Hard Country." Later in the year, Langford opened another exhibition of etchings, paintings and grave-stones he titled "The Death of Country Music." Running concurrently at the American Pop Culture Gallery in Nashville and the Eastwick Gallery in Chicago, the showpieces were the thirteen 135 lb. granite headstones carved with Langford's iconclastic portrayals of country musicians (especially Hank, Sr.) and the country music industry. And though he toyed with the idea of placing the gravestones outside Music Row's corporate offices, Langford contented himself with just the exhibit which got a fair amount of attention from the national press. Bloodshot Records issued a Langford EP, **Gravestone**, to coincide with the show; its highlight is "Nashville Radio," a scathing indictment of the current state of mainstream country music.

Langford's other big project in 1998 was the mammoth tribute, **The Pine Valley Cosmonauts Salute the Majesty of Bob Wills, The King of Western Swing**. Backed by the PCV, Chris Mills, Robbie Fulks, Jimmie Dale Gilmore, Edith Frost, Brett Sparks (Handsome Family), Jane Baxter-Miller (Texas Rubies), Neko Case, Alejandro Escovedo, Sally Timms, the Meat Purveyors, Kelly Hogan, and Jon Langford cover Bob's big songs. The two CD set was also issued as a limited edition double LP which includes an insert with liner notes on one side and a nifty Langford pen and ink drawing of "Bob Wills' Dream" on the other. In 1999, the Wacos returned with **Waco World**, "whiskey and datachip fueled anthems" that offer "a glimpse into the future of insurgent country...(if you just...open a bottle and open your mind."

The Mekons (1977-): Ross Allen (b); Rico Bell; Andy Carrigan (v); Sarah Corina (b); Tom Greenhalgh (g,v); Jon Langford (d); Kevin Lycett (g); Sally Timms (v); Mark White (v)
The Drifting Cowgirls: Sally Timms (l.v.); Rory Allan; Emma Bolland; Brendan Croker; Steve Goulding; Jon Langford; Marc Almond
Hillbilly Lovechild: Jon Langford (g,v); Tracy Dear (md); Brian Doherty (d,b.v.); Tony Maimone (b)
The Pine Valley Cosmonauts: Jon Langford (g,v); Dave Max Crawford (p,tp); Tracey Dear (md); Mark Durante (p.s.); Steve Goulding (d); Paul Mertens (cl,sax); Jane Baxter-Miller (v); Tom Ray (b); John Rice (bj,f,g,md)
The Waco Brothers: Deano (g,v); Tracy Dear (md,v); Marcus Durante (s.g.); Alan Doughty (b); Steve Goulding (d); Jon Langford (g,v); Tom Ray (b); Dean Schlabowske (g,v)

Skull Orchard: Alan Doughty (b); Mark Durante (l.g.); Steve Goulding (d); Jon Langford (g,v)

Fear and Whiskey (Mekons)/Sin/1985
Crime and Punishment (Mekons)/Sin/1986 (EP)
The Edge of the World (Mekons)/Sin/1986; Sin Quarterstick/1996
Slightly South of the Border (Mekons)/Sin/1986 (10")
The Butcher's Boy Extended Player (Sally Timms)/TIM UK/1986 (EP)
This House Is a House of Trouble (Sally Timms)/ TIM/1987 (EP; LP)
Long Black Veil (Sally Timms)/TIM/1987
The Mekons: Honky-Tonkin'(Mekons)/Twin Tone/1987
So Good It Hurts (Mekons)/Twin Tone/1988
Somebody's Rocking My Dreamboat (Sally Timms)/ Tim/1988
'Til Things Are Brighter: A Johnny Cash Tribute/Red Rhino Fr./1988
Original Sin/Twin Tone/1989 (remastered CD of **Fear and Whiskey**, **Slightly South**, parts of **Crime and Punishment**, and one trk. from **Edge of the World**)
"$1,000 Wedding" (Mekons) on **Commemorativo: A Tribute to Gram Parsons**/Rhino/1993
"Over the Cliff" (Hillbilly Lovechild) on **For a Life of Sin**/Bloodshot/1994
Misery Loves Company (Pine Valley Cosmonauts)/ Scout/1995; Bloodshot/1998
To the Land of Milk and Honey (Sally Timms)/ Scout/1995
"Bad Times" b/w "The Harder They Come" (Waco Brothers)/Bloodshot/1995 (7")
"Bad Times" (Waco Brothers) on **Hell-Bent**/ Bloodshot/1995
To the Last Dead Cowboy (Waco Brothers)/ Bloodshot/1995 (CD;LP)
The Return of Rico Bell/Bloodshot/1996
Cowboy in Flames (Waco Brothers)/Bloodshot/1997
Cowboy Sally (Sally Timms)/Bloodshot/1997 (EP)
"Nine Pound Hammer" (Waco Brothers) on **Straight Outta Boone County**/Bloodshot/1997
"Tennessee Waltz" (Sally Timms) on **Straight Outta Boone County**/Bloodshot/1997
Do You Think of Me? (Waco Brothers)/Bloodshot/1997
Skull Orchard/Sugar Free/1997
Me (Mekons)/Quarterstick/1998
Gravestone (Jon Langford)/Bloodshot/1998 (EP)
The Pine Valley Cosmonauts Salute the Majesty of Bob Wills, The King of Western Swing/Bloodshot/1998 (dbl. CD/LP)
Waco World (Waco Brothers)/Bloodshot/1999

Club Mekon
//home.t-online.de/home/Norbert.Knape/mekonhom.htm

The Wonderful World of the Mekons
//www.ellipsis.com/mekons/

The Waco Brothers Web Page
//home.t-online.de/home/norbert.knape/waco.htm

The Waco Brothers/Bloodshot Page
//www.bloodshotrecords.com

The Waco Brothers iMusic Showcase
//imusic.com/showcase/country/

The Waco Brothers/Pressnetwork Page
//www.pressnetwor.com/~pressnet/waco.htm

John Langford's Skull Orchard //www.sugarfreerecords.com

Jon Langford/Skull Orchard Page
//centerstage.net/music/whoswho/JonLangford.html

Jon Langford: Skull Orchard
//www.fortunecity.de/kraftwerk/can/6/skull.htm

Dee Lannon

TSOB; Honky Tonk; Rockabilly
San Francisco, California

Dee Lannon has been a regular on the California alternative country scene for almost a decade. Her musical career began in the late 1980s in her hometown San Francisco where she played clubs like the DNA and Paradise Lounge and had one of her songs "Hello Mr. Bottle" included on a compilation of Bay Area alt. country groups called **Lazy, Loud and Liquor'd Up**. Relocating to L.A. in the early 1990s, Lannon quickly hooked up with that city's leading alternative country musicians. She landed a weekly spot at the Blue Saloon, which also regularly billed Big Sandy, Dave & Deke, and Russell Scott, and made frequent appearances at the Palomino Barn Dance. Dee's first L.A. band, the Rhythm Rustlers, included Russell Scott and Randy Weeks (the Lonesome Strangers); they recorded the single **Lasso Your Heart** in 1993 and one song from it, "$3 Left" was included on the soundtrack of *Deadfall* with Nicolas Cage (Lannon even had a bit part in the film). That year, she made her first visit to Japan where she was very well received. Then for her next recording, **Honky Tonk Nighttime Gal**, Lannon assembled a great supporting cast that among others included Nick Kane (the Mavericks) on guitar, James Intveld on bass, and DJ Bonebrake (X, the Knitters) on drums. Recorded on red vinyl in "Superhypoluxo Stereophonic Fidelity," its four originals plus a reworking of Haggard's "Honky Tonk Nighttime Man" placed Lannon squarely in that long line of California female country singers that runs from Rose Maddox to Rosie Flores. The latter, a longtime friend of Lannon's, toured with Dee and co-wrote "Keep You a Dream" for Lannon's **Town Casino**. Produced by Nick Kane and described as "cocktail country," it offers more Lannon originals including honky tonk, rockabilly, r&b, and torch songs. To support it, Lannon made her second successful tour to Japan in late 1996 where she played with several local groups including local hillbilly boppers, the Rollin' Rocks. Her trips to the Land of Rising Sun paid off in 1998 when the Japanese label On the Hill released her 7" EP, **And the Angels Sing**, which has three rockabilly/swing originals plus a cover of Jean Shepard's "Jeopardy."

Lannon was involved in an interesting side-project when she sang backing vocals on the 1995 "bluegrass" recording, **Blackgrass**, by Earl Lee Grace (actually Blag Dahlia of the Dwarves).

"Hello Mr. Bottle" on **Lazy, Loud and Liquor'd Up**/ Shindig/1989

Lasso Your Heart ("Until You're Mine" b/w "$3 Left")/Iloki/1993 (7")
Honky Tonk Nighttime Gal/Iloki/1995 (10")
Town Casino/Blue Puffer/1996
And the Angels Sing/On the Hill Jp./1998 (EP)

Dee Lannon/Blue Puffer Records, 100 1st St., Ste. 100-228, San Francisco, CA 94105

Dee Lannon Home Page //home.earthlink.net/~hobp/

Deelannon@earthlink.net

See Earl Lee Grace

The Last Mile Ramblers

Honky Tonk; Western Swing
Northern New Mexico; c.1970-1983; 1988-

If there is any one group that really got me started down the long road to *Modern Twang*, it has to be the Last Mile Ramblers. Back in the 1970s, when I first moved to Albuquerque, they were the most popular honky tonk band in Northern New Mexico with a loyal following of dancers in bars and roadhouses throughout the region. I missed their early years (c.1970-1973) when they were led in Santa Fe by banjo player Steve Keith who, in those days, was joined by a rotating lineup of musicians including George Bullfrog (Bourque) on guitar and Spook (Nathaniel) James on bass. Their regular gig was at Claude's Bar on historic Canyon Road, but in 1973, with the addition of J.B. (Junior) Brown on electric lead guitar, Charlie Relleno (Jobes) on Drums, and Don Gale (to replace Keith) on banjo and pedal steel, the Last Mile Ramblers took up weekend residence at a classic roadhouse, the Golden Inn, which was located near a ghost town about half way between Santa Fe and Albuquerque. Like other musicians of their generation, they were truly inspired by both country legends (Hank Williams, George Jones, Ernest Tubb, Bill Monroe, Bob Wills) and by contemporary innovators such as Gram Parsons. Each Sunday afternoon, the Ramblers treated a unique mix of hippies, bikers, cowboys, Indians, Hispanics, college students, and professionals to a modern blend of honky tonk, Western swing, and bluegrass. Spurred by their popularity, they cut a single and went on a tour to Austin where they were warmly received; their single got airplay on KOKE, arguably the first alt. country radio station. Keith returned in time to record **While They Last** which was released in late 1974. Bullfrog, Brown, James, and Relleno share vocals on this fine, eclectic collection of honky tonk, bluegrass, outlaw, swing, and truck driving covers and originals (including "The Golden Inn Song").

After 1975, Bullfrog became leader of the Ramblers and was joined by all new personnel. J.B. Brown, who later went on to fame as Junior Brown, was replaced by Tommy Fenton, Daved Levine came in for James, and Relleno was followed by Waldo Latowsky and then Pete Amahl. Other new members were Sandy Mares on piano and vocals and Woody Vermeire, and then Ollie O'Shea on fiddle and vocals. This was about the time I first began to go see the Ramblers on a regular basis not only at the Golden Inn but also at an Albuquerque dive called the Headquarters (it later became a DWI school). In time, I fell in with the wonderful dance crowd that was the backbone of the Ramblers' following, and it's no exaggeration to say that my life was forever changed. Not only did I learn to dance, but the band, directly and indirectly, set me down a musical "garden of forking paths" that just got better and better. The Ramblers of the late 1970s-early 1980s evolved into a tight honky tonk, Western swing outfit as they demonstrated on their 1979 release **LMR**. With newcomer Jon Potrykus on pedal steel and vocals, they deliver an excellent set of great tunes including "The Girl of My Dreams Thinks I've Got a Hole in My Head" (Al Dean), "Sally's Got a Wooden Leg" (Sons of the West), "Blue Drag" (Django Reinhardt), "Play Me Some More George Jones Songs", and "Mess of Blues." In between tours to Kansas City and New York City, the Ramblers continued to play regularly in Northern New Mexico at places like the Line Camp, Golden Inn, and Big Valley Cattle Company . However, after changes in personnel and the local musical climate, they decided to go their separate ways in 1983. Then after a gala reunion party in 1988, the Ramblers got back together in 1990 to perform on a semi-regular basis. In June 1998, they opened for and backed Junior Brown at a special performance on the plaza in Cerrillos, New Mexico. The large and appreciative crowd, including many from the Ramblers' early years, was treated to Brown and the band doing three truck driving songs from **While They Last**, "Phantom 309," "The Hurrier I Go, The Behinder I Get," and "Diesel Smoke, Dangerous Curves." As local writer and DJ Stephen Terrell (who covered the event for *No Depression,* September-October 1998) noted, "The Last Miles Ramblers were Rig Rock when Rig Rock wasn't cool." I can heartily second that and say, thanks guys for giving so much to so many!

c. 1970-1975: J.B. Brown (db,l.g.,p.s.,v); George Bullfrog (r.g.,l.v.); Don Gale (bj,p.s.,v); Spook James (b,v); Charlie Jobes (d,v). Steve Keith (bj,f,v).
1976-1983: Pete Amahl (d); George Bullfrog; Tommy Fenton (l.g.); Waldo Latowsky (d); Daved Levine (b,v); Ollie O'Shea (f,v); Jon Potrykus (p.s.); Woody Vermeire (f).
Current Members: Pete Amahl; George Bullfrog; Tommy Fenton; Daved Levine; Jon Potrykus.

While They Last/Blue Canyon/1974
LMR/Windswept/1979

George Bullfrog, P.O. Box 82, Cerrillos, NM 87010; bllfrog@concentric.net

See Junior Brown

The Last Roundup (Angel Dean and The Zephyrs; Amy Rigby; Sue Garner)
Rig Rock
New York City; Mid 1980s-

The Last Roundup emerged from New York City's East Village during the cowpunk craze of the mid 1980s. Like their contemporaries, the Knitters and later groups such as Moonshine Willy and the Picketts, they played traditional country but with a slight edge to it and were favorites in local rock clubs. And although the Last Roundup only made one recording, **Twister** (produced by Lou Whitney), it was a fine one indeed! Angel Dean's rich, powerful lead vocals (anticipating Kim Docter; Kristi MacWilson) are the highlight, but the other members lend very capable support especially multi-instrumentalist Michael McMahon and sister Amy McMahon Rigby on harmony vocals. Amy also wrote or co-wrote (with Michael) all of the material on the album which includes haunting ballads ("At the Well"), shuffles ("Playin' the Fool"; "Mama's Last Stand"; "Walk in a Straight Line"), and downhome romps ("Cast Iron Girl"; "River of Red"). After the "last roundup," Dean went on to become a part of New York's Rig Rock alt. country in the early 1990s. Her band, the Zephyrs, which included Jay Sherman-Godfrey of the World Famous Bluejays on lead guitar, recorded a single for Diesel Only and had the A side of it ("Leaving") included on **Rig Rock Juke Box**. They also had two songs, "Life Preserver" and "Second Best" on **Rig Rock Truck Stop**. Amy Rigby later appeared on then husband Will Rigby's (ex-Dbs and Diesel Only alumnus) solo recording **Sidekick Phenomenon** and as a member of the "post-modern girl" trio, the Shams. In 1996 and 1998, she showed off her singing/songwriting talents on solo efforts, **Diary of a Mod Housewife** and **Middlesence**, which offer a variety of roots and rock. Hopefully, Rounder can be induced to re-release **Twister**, one of the best alt. country albums of the mid 1980s, on CD.

One short term alumnus of the Last Roundup who deserves mention is Sue Garner. One of the charter members of the group, she was later in Fish & Roses, the Shams, and Run On before going solo with **To Run More Smoothly**, a fairly twangy lo-fi affair with a very intriguing version of Haggard's "Silver Wings."

The Last Roundup: Angel Dean (g,l.v.); Sue Garner (d,v); Michael McMahon (db,e.g.,f,l.s.); Amy McMahon Rigby (g,md,h.v.); Garth Powell (bj,b,f)
The Zephyrs: Don Christensen (d, v); Bob Hoffnar (p.s.); Jay Sherman-Godfrey (g, v); Mike Weatherly (b, v); Syd Straw (b.v.)

Twister (Last Roundup)/Rounder/1987
"Leaving" b/w "Turned Around" (Angel Dean & the Zephyrs)/Diesel Only (7"); also on **Rig Rock Juke Box**/Diesel Only/1992

"Life Preserver" and "Second Best" (Angel Dean & the
   Zephyrs)on **Rig Rock Truck Stop**/Diesel Only/1993
Diary of a Mod Housewife (Amy Rigby)/KOCH/1996
Middlesence (Amy Rigby)/KOCH/1998
To Run More Smoothly (Sue Garner)/Thrill Jockey/1998

Amy Rigby Main Page //www.amyrigby.com

Amy Rigby/KOCH Page //www.kochint.com/

See Will Rigby

Last Train Home

Country Rock
Washington, D.C.; Mid 1990s-

When Last Train Home's self-titled debut was awarded a
WAMMIE (Washington Area Music Association) for Best
Country Recording of 1998, it came as no surprise to me. From
the first time it nestled into my CD player, all my instincts told
me its irresistible combination of smooth vocals, discerning
songwriting, deft accompaniment, and just overall accessible,
friendly feel were destined for big things. Lead singer/
songwriter Eric Brace had originally played in a bluegrass band
(Mystic Valley Mountaineers) in Boston before becoming a
regular in D.C. with numerous bands including bassist for
Kevin Johnson & the Linemen. In the late 1980s, he formed a
pop band called B-Time with his brother Alan who had also put
in lots of hours with a variety of local groups. Eventually, they
became the core of Last Train Home which went through
several incarnations before finding a steady line-up with Alan
Enderson on keyboards, Jim Gray (ex-Kelly Willis & the
Fireballs) on bass, Martin Lynds (Graverobbers) on drums, and
Bill Williams (ex-Kevin Johnson) on lead guitar. In between,
writing music reviews and articles as "Nightlife" columnist for
The Washington Post, Eric Brace polished up his growing
catalog of originals and the band got plenty of practice with
performances all around the Nation's Capital. Ironically, when
LTH went looking for a label to work with, they ended up
signing with Adult Swim which was run by local hardcore punk
legend Jeff Nelson (Minor Threat) who genuinely liked their
laid-back approach. **Last Train Home**'s disarming warmth
and simplicity work on all levels: instrumentally Alan Brace's
harmonica and mandolin, Bill Williams lead and slide, and
guest David Van Allen's pedal steel are always just right; Eric
Brace's subtly sophisticated songs dwell mostly on love and
sorrow and his amiable vocals fit them to a tee ("List of
Sorrows"; "Angelina"; "Tonight"; "Who Could Blame Me" are
real stand outs). Refreshingly, LTH keeps the pace at
mid-tempo or below, just another one of the many keys to their
appeal. Their mesmerizing, slowed down version of "So Long
Baby, Goodbye" was (IMO) the most effective cut on 1998's
Blastered: A Musical Tribute to the Blasters.

Alan Brace (hm,md,v); Eric Brace (r.g.,l.v.); Alan Enderson
(ky); Jim Gray (b); Martin Lynds (d); Bill Williams with
David Van Allen (p.s.)

"Home for Christmas" on **A Holiday Feast, Vol. 1**/
   HFM/1997
Last Train Home/Adult Swim/1998
"So Long Baby, Goodbye" on **Blastered: A Musical
   Tribute to the Blasters**/Run Wild/1998

Last Train Home c/o Adult Swim, P.O. Box 1535,
Arlington, VA 22210-0835

Last Train Home //www.lasttrainhome.com

Eric Brace: bracee@washpost.com or 202-334-7611;
703-812-8326

Dave Van Allen/Moose Music Page
//www.pond.com/~vanallen/ (site devoted to the pedal steel
with short profiles of the best honky tonk and country rock
players plus links to many steel related pages)

Jim Lauderdale

Singer/Songwriter
Statesville, North Carolina; April 11, 1957-

In the late 1980s, Jim Lauderdale was part of the Town South of
Bakersfield scene; over the years, he received lots of support
(musical and otherwise) from the likes of Emmylou Harris,
Dwight Yoakam, and Dusty Wakeman; he collaborated with
and his songs were covered by numerous alt. country performers; he had plans to do an album with Ralph Stanley and a
tribute to one of his main heroes, Gram Parsons. So, with all
these credentials, why isn't Lauderdale an alt. country icon?
Part of the problem lies in his recordings which tread a fine line
between new and alt. country without ever committing to either
one. Lauderdale has also been heavily identified with Nashville
as a Music Row songwriter whose songs have been covered by
George Strait, Vince Gill, Patty Loveless, Mark Chesnutt, et al.
On the other hand, he's still way too alternative to be accepted
by new country audiences. Fence riding is never easy.

"What Am I Waiting For?" on **A Town South of
   Bakersfield, Volume 2**/Restless/1988
Planet of Love/Reprise/1991
Pretty Close to the Truth/Atlantic/1994
Every Second Counts/Atlantic/1995
"Always on the Outside" b/w "Radar Gun" (Bottle
   Rockets)/Diesel Only/1996 (7")
Persimmons/Upstart/1996
Whisper/BNA/1998
"I'll Lead You Home" on **Clinch Mountain Country:
   Ralph Stanley & Friends**/Rebel/1998

Jim Lauderdale Fan Club, 1114 17th Ave. S., #202,
Nashville, TN 37212

Jim Lauderdale Home Page //www.jimlauderdale.com

jim@jimlauderdale.com

Jim Lauderdale/Pressnet Web Page
//www.pressnetwork.com/~pressnet/jim.htm

Eddy Lawrence

Singer/Songwriter
Birmingham, Alabama

He was raised in the South, lived in the Big Apple, and now resides in far upstate New York. And wherever, he has been, rural or urban, Eddy Lawrence has studied the common denominator that ties them together: masses of desperate people living mundane lives and working banal jobs with just a glimmer of hope and humor to get them by. Writing song stories about these individuals is Lawrence's forte. Musically, he was "a victim" of classical violin lessons as a child but at 17 quit school to teach guitar and play in local bars. In 1982, Lawrence migrated to New York City and co-founded the Lower East Side Rockers who released one EP in 1984. In 1986, Lawrence resurfaced as a country/folk singer/songwriter and released a string of albums full of poignant tales about the downs and very few ups of junk (trash) dealers, fish farmers, smugglers, pot growers, runaways, ex-Marines, and other curiosities. However, the picture he paints isn't one of unrelenting bleakness; Lawrence tempers his sadness with humor and with admiration for the resilience and persistence of his characters in the face of adversity. Each album uses a minimum of country instrumentation (mandolin, steel, fiddle) with the emphasis on Lawrence's lyrics which are delivered with an easy going Guthrieish twang. His 1998, **Guitars, Guns & Groceries**, contains some real gems including "The Man Who Was Hit By a Comet," "The Day the Humvee Came to Town," "Just Down the Road From Shania Twain," and the title tune which is dedicated to a one-stop shopping place in upstate New York called Dick's County Store, Music Oasis & Gun City.

Walker County/Snowplow/1986
Up the Road/Snowplow/1988
Whiskers and Scales and Other Tall Tales/
    Snowplow/1990
Used Parts/Snowplow/1992; 1-800-PRIME CD/1994
"Blues For Tomorrow" on **Hit the Hay**/Sound
    Asleep/1994
Locals/Snowplow/1997
Guitars, Guns & Groceries/Snowplow/1998

Eddy Lawrence/Snowplow Records, P. O. Box 27, Moira, NY 12957

Eddy Lawrence/Prime CD Page
//www.primecd.com/eddy.htm

Eddy Lawrence/Mabel's Music Page
//www.futuris.net/mabels/eddy_lawrence.html

Tom Leach

Singer/Songwriter; Lo-Fi Country
Georgia

The cover art of Tom Leach's self-titled debut CD tells the listener a lot about the music that waits inside. Primitive, grainy woodcut portraits (vaguely sad, vaguely whimsical) of people in a seedy bar portend this raw collection of songs about heartache, loneliness, and the slow struggle for emotional survival through faith and humor. Drawn from 100 tunes done by Leach alone in his apartment on a 4 track (he plays all instruments: guitar, harmonica, mandolin, and drum), the 15 cuts (remixed to eliminate hiss and to equalize) deal mostly with Leach's misery and sharing it with anyone who will listen: heartless ex-lovers ("Confidence is Gone"; "Ice Below You"; "If I Were You"; "Send in the Blues"), old acquaintances ("Hello Friend"), other miserable people ("Yesterday's News"; "Mr. Hang Up the Phone"). But lest you think **Tom Leach** is all doom and gloom, there are a couple of hopeful, up beat tunes ("Savior"; "Tomorrow Comes") and the sly cornerstone of the album, "The Doris Days" ("I was trapped in a domestic maze, so I gave up my Doris days") which first appeared as one side of a single along with fellow Georgian Vic Chesnutt. The ultra lo-fi sound and delivery (his voice is most often compared to Johnny Cash) along with Leach's lyrics make this recording totally believable; you can easily visualize a wretched guy in a seamy room pouring out his beleaguered soul into a tape recorder. Classic DIY. A limited edition live recording on WFMO radio was provided for a short time in 1997 to *No Depression* subscribers. A concert recording in 1999, **Live in Person With Band**, presents Leach and company on a sort set of rough and rowdy covers (Hank, Merle, Dolly) and originals. It was available only via the Internet and filled in the gap until Leach's full-length studio CD was released later in the year.

"The Doris Days" b/w "She's Coming of Age" (Vic
    Chesnutt)/Slow River/1996 (7")
Tom Leach/Slow River/1997
Live on WFMO/Slow River/1997 (ltd. ed. available to *No
    Depression* subscribers)
"Doris Days" on **Loose: New Sounds of the Old
    West**/Vinyl Junkie UK/1998
Live in Person With Band/Slow River/1999

Tom Leach/Slow River Home Page
//www.slowriver.com/slowriver/tom/

Albert Lee

Electric Guitar; Country Rock
Leominster, Herefordshire, England; December 21, 1943-

Alternative country fans are probably most familiar with Albert Lee through his hot lead guitar work on Emmylou Harris' classic country rock albums including **Luxury Liner** and **Quarter Moon in a Ten Cent Town**. However, this represents only one part of the long, productive career of a sideman, session player, and soloist who is one of the most influential guitar pickers of this era. Lee's fascination with electric guitar began in his pre-teen years under the influence of British and American greats such as Denny Wright (Lonnie Donegan Band), Buddy Holly, Cliff Gallup (Gene Vincent), James Burton, Scotty Moore, Jimmy Bryant, Johnny Burnette, Chet Atkins, and Hank Garland. During the 1960s, he played in a succession of rock and r&b bands and around 1968 joined an early British country rock/roots group called Country Fever (sometimes called Black Claw) with Chas Hodges and B.J. Cole. They released a few singles but a full length collection of material from their two years together did not appear until 1991's **Black Claw & Country Fever**. This impressive recording of roots/country rock is highlighted by Lee's burgeoning guitar skills and his not too shabby Everlys influenced vocals. From there, Lee went on to co-found another seminal British country rock outfit, Head, Hands, & Feet. They released three respectable albums between 1970-1973 distinguished mainly by Lee's stunning lead guitar; however, they never really got off the ground and disbanded (a retrospective of Lee's years with HHF can be found on the 1986 release **Country Guitar Man**). This left Albert free to become a much in demand side/session man, and in the early 1970s, he found continuous work with among others Jerry Lee Lewis, the Crickets, Don Everly, and Joe Cocker. Then, when another guitar legend, James Burton, left Emmylou's Hot Band in 1976, Lee joined up lending his special country rock stylings to some of her best recordings. When he decided to go solo in 1978, his debut, **Hiding**, was produced by Brian Ahern (Emmylou's then husband/producer) and had a backing band made up of Emmylou, the Hot Band, Buddy Emmons, and Don Everly. Lee and company serve up some fine country/roots rock including a super version of Lee's signature song from his HHF days, "Country Boy." This was followed up by a lackluster self-titled recording, but in the early 1980s, Lee really cemented his formidable reputation by doing side and session work for a variety of performers including Emmylou, Eric Clapton, Guy Clark, Rodney Crowell, and the Everlys. During this time, Lee consistently finished at or near the top of *Guitar Player* magazine's Best Country Guitarist balloting. In 1986 and 1987, Lee further proved why with two excellent instrumental albums, **Speechless** (Grammy winner) and **Gagged But Not Bound**. Both are amazing displays of Lee's legendary guitar prowess on traditional songs ("Salt Creek"; "Arkansas Traveler"; "Midnight Special"), covers of Chet Atkins and Duane Eddy, and Lee's fine originals. In the 1990s Albert was engaged in a number of projects: session work (Emmylou, Rosie Flores, Tish Hinojosa, John Prine, Mark Insley, Sylvia Tyson and many more), leading the country/roots rock band Hogan's Heroes (with Gerry Hogan on steel), touring with the Everly Brothers and Bill Wyman's Rhythm Kings, and conducting guitar clinics in Europe for Ernie Ball.

Country Fever: B. J. Cole (p.s.); Micky Burt (d); Matt Fisher (p); Harvey Hinsley (r.g.); Chas Hodges (b,g,v); Albert Lee (l.g.,v)
Head, Hands & Feet: B.J. Cole (p.s.); Tony Colton (v); Pete Gavin (d); Chas Hodges (b,f,g); Albert Lee (g,ky); Ray Smith (b)
Hogan's Heroes: Gerry Hogan (p.s.); Albert Lee (l.g.,v)

Head, Hands & Feet/Capitol/1971
Tracks (HHF)/Capitol/1972
Old Soldiers Never Die (HHF)/Atlantic/1973
Hiding/A&M/1979
Albert Lee/Polydor/1982
Country Guitar Man/Magnum/1986
Speechless/MCA Master/1987
Gagged But Not Bound/MCA Master/1988
Black Claw & Country Fever/Line Ger./1991
In Full Flight (with Hogan's Heroes)/Round Tower Ire./1994

Albert Lee Home Page
//homepage.tinet.ie/~johnwoconnor/albertlee/

Mike Warner's Albert Lee Page
//www.musik-treff.tia.de/html/bands.html

See B.J. Cole; Emmylou Harris

Leftover Salmon
"Slamgrass"
Boulder, Colorado; 1992-

Leftover Salmon was spawned by the merger of progressive bluegrassers, Left Hand String Band, and the modern Cajun band, Salmon Heads. The result was what the group calls "polyethnic Cajun slamgrass." These Salmon swim in familiar waters ("Whiskey Before Breakfast"; "Hot Corn/Cold Corn"; "Lonesome Road"), but they take tradition into the deep end with a combination of skill and playfulness ("Jokester"; "Pasta on the Mountain"; "Zombie Jamboree"; "Rodeo Geek"). The driving force behind the band is the energetic playing of Mark Vann on electric banjo, electric tree stump, waterphone (to make whale noises), and rubber fish and Drew Emmit on electric mandolin and fiddle. Add in drums, bass, rubboard, loud vocals, and you get "an unpretentious balls-to-the-wall" sound. Leftover Salmon's first studio album in 1993, **Bridges to Bert**, (produced by Charles Sawtelle of Hot Rize) was followed by **Ask the Fish** which captures the intensity of their live performances. To enhance, the carnival atmosphere of their concerts they enlisted circus type acts to warm up the crowd. Leftover Salmon has been featured at many prominent festivals including Telluride, Merle Fest, and most recently, the H.O.R.D.E. fest in 1997. **Euphoria**, on Hollywood Records, once again fused rock, bluegrass, Cajun, and traditional country and added to their already substantial cult following. In addition to entertaining their fans, Leftover Salmon seeks to educate by asking them to get involved with the Save Our Wild Salmon Coalition which works to preserve the salmon's natural habitat in the Pacific Northwest.

Drew Emmit (g,md); Vince Herman (a.g.,wb,v); Ty North (b); Mark Vann (bj); Michael Wooten (d)

Get Me Outta This City (Left Hand String Band)/Brewgrass/1991
Bridges to Bert/BERT/1993
Ask the Fish LIVE/BERT/1995
Euphoria/Hollywood/1997

Leftover Salmon Newsletter/Mailing List,
P. O. Box 393, Nederland, CO 80466

Leftover Salmon Home Page //leftoversalmon.com

bert@leftoversalmon.com

Leftover Salmon Fan Page
//www.his.com/~vann/LOSstuff/losfans.htm

Leftover Salmon Internet Mailing List
listproc@lists.colorado.edu {subscribe leftover; your first
and last name}

The Legendary Stardust Cowboy (aka Norman Carl Odam)
Psychocountry
Lubbock, Texas; September 5, 1947-

What do Terry Allen, Joe Ely, Jimmie Dale Gilmore, Butch Hancock, and Norman Carl Odam have in common? All grew up in Lubbock, Texas in the 1950s and 1960s; all were attracted to country and rock 'n' roll at an early age; and all used music as a way out of the Panhandle. However, Norman Carl went just a little bit farther out than the rest. As a teenager struggling to be popular with classmates, Odam found he could get lots of attention through singing. He began to write songs (his first was "Peach Orchards" to the tune of "Cottonfields") and sing them at school adding Indian war whoops, Rebel yells, and animal noises to his act. At about the same time, Odam developed a fascination with cowboys, outer space, and being famous and soon became the Legendary Stardust Cowboy. Throughout junior high and high school, Norman evolved as a musician, learning to play guitar (Chet Atkins style), bugle, drums, kazoo, buffalo horn, and harmonica; he began performing as the Legendary Stardust Cowboy for school assemblies, frat parties, and at local hangouts such as the Hi-Di-Ho Drive-In. After graduation, Odam attended college for a time, but then wrote his masterpiece of weirdness, "Paralyzed." He performed it for a local radio talent show, and the response convinced him he could make the big time. After disappointing tries in San Diego and L.A. and working numerous day jobs, Odam, at age 21, decided to go to New York City and get on the *Johnny Carson Show*. On the way, he stopped in Ft. Worth where he was "discovered" by two vacuum cleaner repairmen who took him to a recording studio where T Bone Burnett was in charge of production. Burnett went crazy over "Paralyzed" ("2½ minutes of unbridled chaos"), recorded it on the spot, and then had a local station promote and play the song all day. The overwhelming enthusiasm of callers prompted Burnett to cut a single of "Paralyzed" and in no time "The Ledge" had a contract with Mercury; he also finally made it to New York City where he performed on *Laugh-In*. In the middle of America's major push to the moon, the LSC began to play up his outer space buckaroo image to the hilt, but a number of factors combined to ground his blast off to stardom. Dropping out of music in the 1970s, Odam/LSC returned in the 1980s when he

recorded his debut album **Rock-It to Stardom** followed by **The Legendary Stardust Cowboy** then **Rides Again** and **Retro-Rocket Back to Earth**. All contain Odam's unique brand of musical strangeness such as "Standing in a Trashcan Thinking of You," "My Underwear Froze on the Clothesline," "I Took a Trip on a Space Shuttle," "I Hate CDs," and of course, the incomparable "Paralyzed." In 1996, filmmaker Tony Philputt released a documentary about "The Ledge," *Cotton Pickin' Smash: The Story of the Legendary Stardust Cowboy* which has clips of Odam live plus interviews with him, Burnett, Ely, Gilmore, and Butch Hancock. The LSC worked on Eugene Chadbourne's country/western opera, **Jesse Helms Busted With Pornography** in 1997.

"Paralyzed" b/w "Who's Knocking at My Door?"/
   Mercury/1969 (7")
"I Took a Trip on a Space Shuttle"/Mercury/1969 (7")
Rock-It to Stardom/Amazing/1984
Legendary Stardust Cowboy/Amazing/1984
"Standing in a Trashcan (Thinking of You)" b/w "My
   Underwear Froze on the Clothesline"/Spider/1987 (7")
Retro-Rocket Back to Earth/New Rose Fr./1987
The Legendary Stardust Cowboy Rides Again/New
   Rose Fr./1987
Retro-Rocket Back to Earth and **Rides Again**/
   Norton/1989
"Revelation" b/w "I Ride a Tractor"/Norton/1991 (7")
"I Hate CDs" b/w "Linda"/Norton/1992 (7")
*Cotton Pickin' Smash: The Story of the Legendary
   Stardust Cowboy!* (video documentary)

The Legendary Stardust Cowboy, P. O. Box 36305,
San Jose, CA

The Legendary Stardust Cowboy Home Page
//www.rootsworld.com/hollow/paralyzed/

Kim Lenz and Her Jaguars
Rockabilly; Hillbilly Bop
Dallas, Texas; 1995-

Kim Lenz's first experiences in the music business after graduating from U.C.L.A. back in the late 1980s was with a Los Angeles publishing company. Hard working employee by day, she cut loose at night making the rounds at clubs where she heard big band, jump blues, and her growing favorite, rockabilly/hillbilly bop as done by local bands like Big Sandy and Dave & Deke. In reality, the latter sound was not totally new to Lenz whose father was a big fan of Sun rockabilly. By 1994, Kim had had enough of music publishing and decided to go back to college this time at the University of North Texas near Dallas. She started a band called Rocket Rocket that did rockabilly and 1960s music, but they performed sporadically and disbanded after a short time. However, the stage bug had bitten Lenz and after relocating to Big D, she put together another band, Her Jaguars, in 1995. Influenced by Charlie Feathers, Gene Vincent, Carl Perkins, Wanda Jackson, and Janis Martin, Kim Lenz and Her Jaguars began to get noticed around Dallas and beyond. In 1997, they ventured into the prime rockabilly territory around L.A. and went into the studio with none other than Deke Dickerson to do an EP entitled **Shake A Leg**. That same year, Kim was voted Best Female Vocalist by the weekly independent *Dallas Observer*. Not long after, Hightone Records came calling and in 1998 released, **Kim Lenz and Her Jaguars**. Produced and recorded in Wally-phonic High Fidelity on all vintage equipment by Wally Hersom (Big Sandy's bassist), it's pretty much straight ahead 1950s rockabilly distinctive mostly for Lenz's credible originals and fiery delivery.

Kim Lenz (g,v); Jake Erwin (u.b.); Robert Hamilton (d); Mike Lester (l.g.)

> **Shake A Leg**/Wormtone/1997 (EP)
> **Kim Lenz and Her Jaguars**/Hightone HMG/1998

Kim Lenz and Her Jaguars, P.O. Box 190807, Dallas, TX 75219

Kim Lenz and Her Jaguars //www.kimlenz.com

kimlenz@kimlenz.com

Kim Lenz/Rockabilly Hall of Fame Page //www.rockabillyhall.com/KimLenz.html

The LeRoi Brothers

Austin; Roots Rock
Ft. Worth/Austin, Texas; 1981-

For almost two decades, the LeRoi Brothers have been one of Austin's leading roots rock bands. Their origins go back to 1970 in Cool Valley, Missouri when Steve Doerr and Don Leady met while auditioning for a band. They decided to perform as a duo and spent the next decade touring the East Coast, Midwest, and Texas. Settling in Ft. Worth, Doerr and Leady were asked to be part of the backing band for the Legendary Stardust Cowboy's **Rock-It to Stardom**. The drummer for those sessions was Mike Buck (ex-Fabulous Thunderbirds) who convinced them to come to Austin and form a band. Adding Lou Ann Barton on vocals and Alex Napier on bass, they began performing around town as Lou Ann and the Fliptops or as the Headhunters. After Barton left and Napier was dropped, Doerr, Leady, and Buck took the name the LeRoi Brothers and in 1982 recorded an EP, **Moon Twist** (Amazing), and an LP, **Check This Action**, for Jungle Records. This was Jungle's premier release, and they celebrated this now classic recording of rockabilly, country, rocking blues, and swamp with a parade down Congress Ave. with the LeRois playing from the back of a truck. On the heels of this acclaimed debut, the LeRoi Brothers went on tour and then brought Joe Doerr (Steve's brother) into the band along with bass player Jack Newhouse. By this time, major labels were beginning to show interest, and in 1984, they did an EP, **Forget About the Danger, Think of the Fun** for Columbia. However, that deal fizzled, and Leady departed to form another popular roots rock band, the Tailgators. The remaining LeRois picked up a new lead guitarist, Evan Johns followed by Casper Rawls

and reigned as *the* Austin roots rock band of the late 1980s and early 1990s winning *The Austin Chronicle's* Best Roots Rock Band on numerous occasions. They recorded a steady stream of impressive albums (domestic and import labels) and though not as active as in the 1980s, the LeRois performed in Austin in the 1990s and various members were in other bands as well. Buck drummed with the Naughty Ones for several years, Doerr played guitar with Bradley Jaye Williams' (Los Pinkys) Cajun/zydeco band, the Gulf Coast Playboys in 1997, and Rawls was guitarist for Toni Price.

Original Members: Mike Buck (d); Joe Doerr (v,1983-1985); Steve Doerr (l.g.,v); Evan Johns (g,1985-1986); Don Leady (l.g.,v,1981-1984); Alex Napier (b)
Current Members: Mike Buck (d); Pat Collins (b); Steve Doerr (l.g.,v); Casper Rawls (l.g.)

> **Moontwist**/Amazing/1982 (EP)
> **Check This Action**/Jungle/1983; Rounder/1994
> **Forget About the Danger Think of the Fun**/Columbia/1984 (EP)
> **Lucky, Lucky Me**/Profile/1985
> **Protection From Enemies**/Demon UK/1985
> **Open All Night**/Profile/1986
> **Viva LeRoi**/New Rose Fr./1989
> **Rhythm & Booze**/New Rose Fr./1990
> **Crown Royale**/Rounder/1992

The LeRoi Brothers Web Page //www.ddg.com/amw/artists/bands/lbros.index.html

Duke Levine

Electric Guitar; Americana
Boston, Massachusetts

Duke Levine's business card might well read, "Have Stratocaster, will travel." Over the years, on stage and in the studio, his ax has cut timbre for a wide variety of artists including Ellis Paul, the Story, the Del Fuegos, Otis Rush, Jimmy Dawkins, Carol Noonan, Sleepy LaBeef, Bob Moses, and Mary Chapin-Carpenter. It is obvious Levine has absorbed an assortment of guitar styles ranging from Danny Gatton to Chet Atkins, Don Rich, Duane Eddy, and Steve Cropper to name only a few. This diversity of influences gels on Levine's three solo instrumental recordings: **Country Soul Guitar**, **Nobody's Home**, and **Lava**. On each, The Duke lays out a rich smorgasbord of Americana including rockabilly, honky tonk ("Bud's Bounce"; "Buckaroo"), Western swing ("Remington Ride"), spaghetti Western ("Longhorn"), hoe-down ("Nashville Skyline Rag"), and more. Levine also plays a mean lap steel as he shows on his original "King Kamehameha Blues." He received additional praise for his guitar work on movie soundtracks for, *Troublesome Creek: A Midwestern* and *Lone Star*.

> **Country Soul Guitar**/Daring/1993
> **Nobody's Home**/Daring/1995
> **Troublesome Creek**/Daring/1996 (sdtrk.)
> **Lava**/Daring/1997

Lone Star/Daring/1997 (sdtrk.)

Duke Levine/Daring Records Home Page
//www.rounder.com

Laurie Lewis (Grant Street; The Good Ol' Persons; Blue Rose)

Progressive Bluegrass
San Francisco, California; 1950-

As a child growing up in Berkeley, Laurie Lewis took up the violin and as a teen was heavily involved in folk music. Eventually, she became part of the nascent Bay Area bluegrass scene in the early 1970s playing in pioneering bands such as the Phantoms of the Opry and the Arkansas Sheikhs. She also entered California fiddle competitions and won the women's division on several occasions. A co-founder of what would prove to be one of the area's most long lived bands, the Good Ol' Persons, she stayed with them long enough to record their debut album in 1976 but then went on to form her own group, the Grant Street String Band in 1979. Their first self-titled album in 1983, a collection of old-time, bluegrass, and country, highlighted Lewis' evocative vocals, impressive songwriting, and fine fiddle work. Into the late 1980s and early 1990s, Lewis continued to work with the Grant Street String Band but also as a soloist, duo (with Kathy Kallick of Good Ol' Persons), and with Blue Rose, an all woman bluegrass supergroup with Cathy Fink, Marcy Marxer, Molly Mason, and Sally Van Meter. Laurie's solo debut, **Restless Rambling Heart**, won the NAIRD Album of the Year in 1986 and in 1987 mandolinist Tom Rozum joined her band. In 1991, Lewis put together a new group, called simply Grant Street, with a more modern and diverse sound. Her star continued to rise with IBMA Female Vocalist of the Year awards in 1992 and 1994, IBMA Song of the Year for 1994 ("Who Will Watch the Home Place?"), a Grammy nomination in 1996 for her duet album, **The Oak and the Laurel**, with Rozum plus tours all across the U.S. and in Europe. In 1997, Rounder issued **Earth and Sky: The Songs of Laurie Lewis** which covers her first three Flying Fish recordings and four previously unreleased songs. Lewis's 1998 projects included a track on the Ralph Stanley tribute, **Clinch Mountain Country**, co-producing and performing on Tom Rozum's, **Jubilee**, and a new solo, **Seeing Things**.

Grant Street: Cary Black (b); Peter McLaughlin (g); Tom Rozum (md,v)
The Good Ol' Persons: Kathy Kallick (g,v); Laurie Lewis (f,v); Bethnay Raine (b); John Reischman (md); Paul Shelasky (f); Sally Van Meter (db); Kevin Wimmer (f)
Blue Rose: Cathy Fink (bj,h.v.); Laurie Lewis (f,l.v.,h.v.); Marcy Marxer (l.g.,md,l.v.,h.v.); Sally Van Meter (db,h.v.)

Good Ol' Persons/Bay/1976
I Can't Stand to Ramble (Good Ol' Persons)/ Kaleidoscope/1983
Grant Street String Band/Bonita/1983
Part of a Story (GOP)/Kaleidoscope/1986

Restless Rambling Heart (Laurie Lewis)/Flying Fish/1986
Live in Holland, Vol. 4 (GOP)/Strictly Country Dut./1987
Blue Rose/Sugar Hill/1988
Love Chooses You (Grant Street)/Flying Fish/1989
Any Way the Wind Blows (GOP)/Kaleidoscope/1989
Together (Laurie Lewis & Kathy Kallick)/ Kaleidoscope/1990
Singing My Troubles Away (Grant Street)/Flying Fish/1990
True Stories (Laurie Lewis)/Rounder/1993
The Oak and the Laurel (Laurie Lewis and Tom Rozum)/ Rounder/1995
Good 'N' Live (GOP)/Sugar Hill/1995
Good Ol' Persons: 20th Anniversary Collection/Sugar Hill/1996
Earth and Sky: The Songs of Laurie Lewis/ Rounder/1997
"Old Love Letters" on **Clinch Mountain Country: Ralph Stanley & Friends**/Rebel/1998
Jubilee (Tom Rozum)/Dog Boy/1998
Seeing Things/Sugar Hill/1998

Laurie Lewis Home Page //www.laurielewis.com

Laurie Lewis Profile
//www.banjo.com/bg/profiles/laurielewis.html

Steven Hull's Laurie Lewis Page
//www.sirius.com/~seadog/laurie_lewis.html

Little Sue

Country Rock; Honky Tonk
Portland, Oregon; 1995-

In the late 1990s, with the rise of bands like Richmond Fontaine, Golden Delicious, and Little Sue, Portland suddenly became the second most important (behind Seattle) focal point for alt. country in the Pacific Northwest. Little Sue was created in 1995 when West Virginia native Susannah Weaver became lead vocalist for a roots rock band called the Crackpots. With Weaver at the helm, they not only got a new name but a new sound combining lo-fi country rock (Cowboy Junkies, Damnations, Freakwater) with honky tonk and bluegrass. Weaver's vocals have most often been likened to Kitty Wells and her originals are steeped in traditional Americana. Little Sue's debut, **Chimneys & Fishes**, is a very friendly collection of country/folk/rock that twangs in all the right places thanks in large part to support from an array of Portland musicians including several members of Golden Delicious on banjo, fiddle, mandolin, accordion, and steel guitar. **Crow** continues along the same track but with a bit more polish and flair than its predecessor.

Dan Haley (md); John Lambert (d); Bill Rudolph (b); Susannah Weaver (g,l.v.)

Chimneys & Fishes/Cravedog/1997
"Passing Train" on **Can't Stand the Smell**/Cravedog/1997
Crow/Cravedog/1999

Little Sue c/o Cravedog Records, P.O. Box 1841, Portland, OR 97201

Little Sue/Cravedog Page
//www.teleport.com/~cravedog/littlesue.html

cravedog@teleport.com

See Golden Delicious

Lone Justice (Maria McKee; Marvin Etzioni)

Roots Rock
Los Angeles, California; 1983-1987

Lone Justice earned its reputation as one of the seminal country roots rock groups of the mid-1980s largely on the basis of their debut **Lone Justice**. Formed by Maria McKee and Ryan Hedgecock in 1983, the original line up also included Marvin Etzioni on bass, Don Heffington (ex-Hot Band) on drums, and Benmont Tench (ex-Tom Petty) on keyboards. McKee's dynamic vocals and songs like "Ways to Be Wicked" should have made Lone Justice a "can't miss," but it didn't happen. So, McKee assembled a new group of musicians, and the second incarnation of Lone Justice recorded **Shelter**, a straight ahead rock affair that went nowhere. Dissolving the band once and for all in 1987, McKee moved on to a successful career making several albums including **You've Got to Sin to Get Saved** which comes close to capturing the spirit of the original Lone Justice with help from Etzioni, Heffington, and Louris and Olson of the Jayhawks. Maria, known as the "Little Diva," has been very popular in Europe where she tours frequently; in 1997-98 she recorded **Life Is Sweet**, covered "Candy's Room" for a 1997 Bruce Springsteen tribute, and contributed backing vocals to recordings by Steve Earle and Dwight Yoakam.

Marvin Etzioni, who played bass with Lone Justice, became a producer (Peter Case, Voice of the Beehive, Toad the Wet Sprocket) and switched to mandolin after Lone Justice. Under the name Marvin the Mandolin Man or just Marvin, he made several recordings that combine country/folk/rock and new agey philosophy; he also worked as a producer (Mike Ireland and Holler). Heffington became prominent as a session player and member of many aggregations including the Dead Reckoners with Kevin Welch and Kieran Kane. He was also a member of the Gothic, lo-fi group Parlor James, co-founded by Ryan Hedgecock and twangteuse Amy Allison.

Lone Justice fans got a treat in early 1999 when a retrospective CD of the band's career, **The World Is Not My Home**, was released by Geffen. It has cuts from their two albums but of special interest are several songs (title tune; "Drugstore Cowboy"; "Working Man Blues"; "Cottonbelt") from their more countryish, pre-Geffen days plus a remix of "Go Away Little Boy," written for them by Dylan and featuring Bob and Ron Wood on the recording.

Bruce Brody (ky,1986-1987); Marvin Etzioni (b,v,1983-1986); Shayne Fontayne (g,1986-1987); Ryan Hedgecock (g,v,1983-1986); Don Heffington (d,1983-1986); Maria McKee (l.v.) Rudy Richman (d,1986-1987); Greg Sutton (b,1986-1987); Benmont Tench (ky, 1983-1986)

Lone Justice/Geffen/1985
Shelter (Lone Justice)/Geffen/1986
Maria McKee/Geffen/1989
Bone (Marvin)/Restless/1992
The Mandolin Man (Marvin)/Restless/1992
You Gotta Sin to Get Saved (Maria McKee)/Geffen/1993
Lone Justice Radio 1, Live in Concert/Windsong UK/1993
Weapons of the Spirit (Marvin)/Restless/1994
Life is Sweet (Maria McKee)/Geffen/1997
The World Is Not My Home/Geffen/1999 (Lone Justice retrospective)

Maria McKee: The Absolutely Barking Star
//hem1.passagen.se/brickbat/

Maria McKee/Little Diva Home Page
//www.ziplink.net/users/bourbeau/main.html

Old Grey Cat–Maria McKee //oldgreycat.com

Marvin/Restless Records Home Page
//www.restless.com/marvin.html

See Amy Allison

Lonesome Bob

Insurgent Country; Singer/Songwriter
Mount Ephraim, New Jersey/Nashville

Former drummer for the Ben Vaughan Combo, the Mekons (recording sessions), and the Ernest Noyes Brookings CD series, Lonesome Bob (aka Robert Gordon Chaney) stepped out from behind his drum kit in the mid-1990s to perform as a singer/songwriter. He made his recording debut on **Nashville: The Other Side of the Alley** with an original love and murder waltz "The Plans We Made" (as a duet with Elizabeth Lee). That song sets the tone for his full-length CD, **Things Fall Apart**, a moody affair that continues Bob's bleak exploration of love gone sour: "What Went Wrong"; "Point of No Return"; "Waltzing on the Titanic"; "My Mother's Husband." His lyrics are pretty rough at times, and the recording comes with a disclaimer. Lonesome Bob cautions the listener that he does not "recommend or advocate murder, suicide, or violence of any kind" and asks those with murderous or suicidal tendencies to put down their weapon of choice and seek professional help. Adding support on the album are insurgent country heavyweights, Jon Langford and Sally Timms (the Mekons and Waco Brothers have covered two of Bob's songs), Amy Rigby, lead guitarist Tim Carroll, and Allison Moorer who provides exceptional backing vocals.

"The Plans We Made" on **Nashville: The Other Side of the Alley**/Bloodshot/1996
Things Fall Apart/Checkered Past/1997

Lonesome Bob/Checkered Past Page
//www.checkeredpast.com

Lonesome Bob Biography
//www.pressnetwork.com/bob.htm

The Lonesome Strangers

TSOB
Los Angeles, California; 1984-

In their heyday, the Lonesome Strangers were an integral part of the alt. country scene that flourished in L.A. in the late 1980s-early 1990s. Co-founders, Jeff Rymes and Randy Weeks, migrated from Colorado and Minnesota respectively and met in the early 1980s. They discovered that not only did they share a love for early country music but could harmonize like the Blue Sky Boys, Delmores, Louvins, and other duos of country's "Golden Age." After finding a drummer and bass player, they started the Lonesome Strangers and became regulars at the Palomino Barn Dance where they rubbed shoulders with Dave Alvin, Rosie Flores, James Intveld, Dwight Yoakam, and other members of the Town South of Bakersfield generation. They made their recording debut on the first volume of **A Town South of Bakersfield** with a Rymes' "Lonesome Pine." A full length album of the same name followed a year later on Wrestler Records. Produced by Pete Anderson, it showcases the Lonesome Strangers early punkabilly style highlighted by Rymes/Weeks whiney (in the very best sense) harmonies on great originals including "Don't Cross the Bad Man," "Ton of Shame," "Hillbilly Music," "The One Who Wore My Ring" (with Chris Hillman on mandolin), and "Walkin' Over Hot Coals" plus a romping cover of "Here Comes the Night." Rymes and Weeks also provided excellent twanging guitar. In 1986 and 1987, the Lonesome Strangers got a big boost in exposure when they opened on tours for Dave Alvin and Dwight Yoakam whom Rymes and Weeks supported on **Buenas Noches From a Lonely Room**. With a new bass player (Lorne Rall), they switched to Hightone in 1988 and recorded **The Lonesome Strangers**. With Bruce Bromberg at the helm this time and support from Alvin, Chris Gaffney, Greg Leisz, and Stephen McCarthy (Long Ryders), they came up with a true gem. Less edgy than their debut, it is filled from beginning to end with the best in hillbilly/roots/rock. In addition to more first-rate Rymes/Weeks originals ("Clementine"; "Another Fool Like Me"; "Daddy's Gone Gray"; "Just Walk Away"; "We Use to Fuss"), it includes the Delmore's "Lay Down My Old Guitar" and a rocking version of Johnny Horton's "Goodbye Lonesome, Hello Baby Doll." The latter became a minor hit for the Strangers, but by 1990, they had topped out; McLean and Rall departed, and soon Rymes and Weeks called it quits. They remained active for the next few years as supporting musicians; Weeks was a member of Dee Lannon's Rhythm Rustlers, and Rymes and Weeks provided background vocals for Chris Gaffney's debut. In 1994, Rymes and Weeks hooked up again as the Lonesome Strangers, but it was three long years before they were able to put out a new record. Finding a home at Pete Anderson's Little Dog Records, they reentered the studio and in early 1997 came **Land of Opportunity** which showed the Strangers still in prime form after their long lay off. An updated version of "Ton of Shame," covers of "Tobacco Road" and "I Don't Believe You've Met My Baby" (Louvin Brothers) are surrounded by more excellent Rymes/Weeks tunes ("And It Hurts"; "Fine Way to Treat Me"; "Ramblin' Around") highlighted as always by those endearing backwoods harmonies. In support of their new release, the Strangers embarked on the Dogs in Heaven tour with Anderson and Jeff Finlin in the spring of 1997. In 1998, they toured Southern Cal, worked on a new album, and did a twangy rendition of "Takes a Lot to Rock You" for **Will Sing for Food: The Songs of Dwight Yoakam**.

Mike McClean (d,v); Nino Del Pesco (b,1986-1987); Greg Perry (d,1997-); Lorne Rall (b,v, 1987-1989); Jeff Roberts (b,1997-); Jeff Rymes (g,v); Randy Weeks (g,v)

"Lonesome Pine" on **A Town South of Bakersfield, Vol. 1**/Restless/1985
Lonesome Pine/Wrestler/1986
The Lonesome Strangers/Hightone/1989
Land of Opportunity/Little Dog/1997
"Takes a Lot to Rock You" on **Will Sing for Food: The Songs of Dwight Yoakam**/Little Dog/1998

The Lonesome Strangers Home Page
//www.concentric.net/~shaffers/smain.html

The Lonesome Strangers/Little Dog Home Page
//www.littledogrecords.com/

Shaffers@concentric.net

The Long Ryders

See Sid Griffin

Valerio Longoria, Sr.

Accordion; Tex-Mex; Conjunto
San Antonio, Texas; February 14, 1924-

Valerio Longoria, Sr. was one of the great innovators (along with Tony De La Rosa) of the post-WWII generation of *conjunto* players. His popularity on the South Texas dance circuit was due not only to his accordion work and great singing but also to his experimentation with traditional *conjunto* using drums, trying different types of accordions and keys, and introducing new musical styles. While still in his teens, Longoria began to play dances and made his first recordings in the mid 1940s. About this same time, he introduced two new sounds to *conjunto*: the spirited Spanish *bolero* and the *cancio ranchera*. During the 1960s, Longoria moved around the country from Chicago to Florida to California and wherever he could play for migrant workers. It was during these travels that he learned the *cumbia* from Puerto Ricans in Chicago and on Miami short wave radio from Columbia and soon incorporated it into *conjunto*. Not only did this introduce a new dance but also for the first time, the use of minor keys in *conjunto* accordion. Throughout, the 1960s and 1970s, Longoria recorded for numerous labels and continued his wanderings around the U.S.

Then, in the 1980s, he settled in San Antonio where he became a teacher at the Guadalupe Cultural Center. That organization named him to the Conjunto Hall of Fame and in 1986 the NEA recognized his accomplishments by giving him a National Heritage Award. Into his 50th+ year as a performer, Longoria appeared and recorded with his sons and grandsons; an updated recording of his material from the 1950s and 1960s, **Texas Conjunto Pioneer**, provides a good overview of his illustrious career and contributions.

Caballo Viejo/Arhoolie/1989
Texas Conjunto Pioneer/Arhoolie/1994
Vengo A Pedirte/Hacienda/1996
La Piragua/Hacienda/1997

Loose Diamonds (The Highwaymen)

Austin; Roots Rock
Loose Diamonds: Austin, Texas; 1990-
The Highwaymen: Dayton, Ohio; 1985-1989

In 1985, brothers Troy and Mike Campbell formed a roots rock band in Dayton, Ohio known as the Highwaymen. They cut a single and a mini LP (rockers and countryish ballads), but in 1989, under the influence of the True Believers and other Austin bands, the Campbells with drummer Mark Patterson in tow relocated to Central Texas. Shortly thereafter, they began to put together a new version of the Highwaymen and got a break when they found singer/guitarist Jud Newcomb one evening at an open mike session. With him on board, they began performing and in 1990 recorded an impressive live cassette, **Live Texas Radio**, (on KUT) for Jungle Records. Then, Patterson departed to be replaced by a succession of drummers. The big change, however, was a decision to switch names to avoid confusion with "the other" Highwaymen. They chose Loose Diamonds after a Jo Carol Pierce song, did some tracks with Stephen Bruton producing, and finally got a deal with Dos, a subsidiary of Antone's. This resulted in **Burning Daylight** which won Austin Music Awards Album of the Year and NAIRD's Rock Album of the Year for 1993. The particular strengths of the band were the guitar playing of Newcomb, the vocals of Troy Campbell, and the songwriting skills of both. They have sometimes been compared to the Jayhawks but more often to The Band with their combination of rock, blues, country, and folk. Loose Diamonds switched to Austin's new Americana label, Freedom, in 1996 and released a 7 track EP called **Fresco Fiasco**. It was their most acoustic effort since 1990 and featured guest artists Toni Price and Champ Hood. In 1997, Loose Diamonds took advantage of their popularity in Europe by doing some recordings for Glitterhouse. However, by the end of the century, the band was pretty much in limbo as its members went on to pursue individual projects.

The Highwaymen: Mike Campbell (b,b.v.); Troy Campbell (g,hm,v); Jimmy Davidson (a.g.,e.g.,v); Mark Patterson

(d,perc)
Loose Diamonds: Ian Bailey (d); Mike Campbell (b,v); Troy Campbell (g,v); Jud "Scrappy" Newcomb (g,v)

Highwaymen/I Wanna/1986 (4 song LP)
Revisited (Highwaymen)/Ind/1990 (CS)
Live Texas Radio (Highwaymen)/Jungle/1990 (CS)
Blue Days, Black Nights/Amazing/1991 (CS)
Burning Daylight/Dos/1993
New Location/Dos/1994
Fresco Fiasco/Freedom/1996
"You Keep Me Hanging On" on **Luxury Liner**/
    Glitterhouse Ger./1997
Man vs. Beast (Troy Campbell)/M-Ray; Blue Rose
    Ger./1999

Los Lobos

Roots Rock
East Los Angeles, California; 1974-

Contrary to the title of their first LP, Los Lobos have turned out to be *mucho* more than "just another band from East L.A." They started out in 1974 as an all acoustic quartet, Los Lobos Del Este de Los Angeles, playing traditional Mexican music at a local restaurant. In time, they added accordion and electric instruments for a modern Tex-Mex sound. Their debut record in 1978 was a collection of traditional Mexican music, but they soon began developing the synthesis of Latino, rock, country, blues, and r&b that became the basis of the Los Lobos sound. Their timing was fortunate as the L.A. roots rock scene was beginning to take off in the early 1980s with groups like the Blasters who played a major role in helping Los Lobos break through. They opened for a number of Blasters shows and added the band's sax player, Steve Berlin, to their line up. In 1983, they got a deal with Slash Records (the Blasters' label too) and cut **...And A Time to Dance**, a combination of *norteno* and roots rock that produced a Grammy winning *ranchera*, "Anselma." Two more great albums followed before Los Lobos made a national splash with their work on the *La Bamba* soundtrack in 1987. They followed up this success with a return to tradition on **La Pistola Y El Corazon** (second Grammy), but then began to expand their musical horizons with **The Neighborhood** and **Kiko**. In 1994, Slash issued a 2 CD retrospective, **Los Lobos: Just Another Band From East L.A.**, which dramatically captures the evolution of one of the most innovative and influential roots bands of the past twenty years. That same year they did a children's record **Papa's Dream** with one of the great innovators in Hispanic music in the U.S., Lalo Guerrero. Into the mid-late 1990s, Los Lobos have remained on the cutting edge through experimental side projects like the Latin Playboys (Hidalgo; Perez) and their most daring recording, **Colossal Head**, in 1996. In addition, they contributed to soundtracks for movies (*Feeling Minnesota* and *Desperado*) and were instrumental in helping similar groups like the Blazers get a break. After breaking with Warner Bros. and signing with Hollywood Records in 1998, Los Lobos started to work on a new one while individual members branched out. Rosas, Hidalgo, and Berlin joined Freddy Fender, Flaco Jimenez, Ricky Trevino, Joe Ely, and Ruben Ramos in the super side project Los Super Seven, and Rosas recorded (released early 1999) his solo debut **Soul Disguise**, a collection of blues rock, bar rock, and Tex-Mex with four songs co-written with LeRoy Preston (ex-Asleep at the Wheel).

Steve Berlin (sax); David Hidalgo (f,g,v); Conrad Lozano (b); Louie Perez (d); Cesar Rosas (l.g.,v)

Just Another Band From East L. A./New Vista/1978
...And a Time to Dance/Slash/1983
How Will the Wolf Survive?/Slash/1984
By the Light of the Moon/Slash/1987
La Pistola Y El Corazon/Slash/1988
The Neighborhood/Slash/1990
Kiko/Slash/1992
Just Another Band From East L.a.: A Collection/
   Slash/1993
Papa's Dream (Lalo Guerrero)/Warner Brothers/1994
The Latin Playboys/Slash Warner/1994
Colossal Head/Warner Brothers/1996
Los Super Seven (Rosas, Hidalgo, Berlin)/RCA/1998
   (with Joe Ely, Freddy Fender, Flaco Jimenez)
Soul Disguise (Cesar Rosas)/Rykodisc/1999

Los Lobos Home Page //www.wbr.com/loslobos/

Los Lobos iMusic Showcase
//imusic.com/showcase/contemporary/

See The Blasters; The Blazers

Los Pinkys (The Gulf Coast Playboys)
Conjunto; Tex-Mex; Cajun
San Francisco, California/Austin, Texas; Mid 1990s-

He was born in Saginaw, Michigan, and I don't know if he grew up in a house on Saginaw Bay. However, I do know that Bradley Jaye Williams grew up listening to Bavarian and Polish music and was introduced to a variety of other types through his father who was a juke box record distributor. Initially taking up the mandolin, Williams was also inspired by *conjunto* greats Don Santiago Jimenez and Narciso Martinez to learn the accordion. In the mid-1980s, he moved to San Francisco where he co-founded a band called the Movie Stars which covered everything from country to rock to Tex-Mex. They opened several shows for Flaco Jimenez who gave Williams lots of encouragement. With this inspiration, Williams decided to start his own *conjunto* band which he called Los Pinkys ostensibly after a pink Gabbanelli accordion but really because all of the members were *bolillos* ("whitebreads"). Eventually, Williams struck out on his own and moved to Austin where he hooked up with a number of *conjunto* musicians including accordion and *bajo sexto* player Isidro Samilpa who had been a part of the East Side *conjunto* scene for many years. The new Los Pinkys gained acceptance from the *conjunto* community, air play on Tex-Mex radio, and a recording contract with Rounder that produced two critically acclaimed recordings, **Sequro Que Si!** and **Esta Pasion**. In 1995 and 1997, Los Pinky's were named best Tejano/Conjunto band at the Austin Music Awards. Williams applied his accordion skills to Cajun/zydeco music starting the Gulf Coast Playboys with Steve Doerr (LeRoi Brothers) on guitar and ex-Bad Liver Ralph White on fiddle in 1997.

Los Pinkys: Augie Arreola; Javier Cruz; Chris Cruz; Isidro Samilpa (acc,bajo,v); Bradley Jaye Williams (acc,bajo,v)
The Gulf Coast Playboys: Steve Doerr (l.g.); Ralph White (f); Bradley Jaye Williams (acc,l.v.)

Heck-Ola(The Movie Stars)/Lucky Pierre/1989
Seguro Que Si!/Rounder/1994
Esta Pasion/Rounder/1996
Gulf Coast Playboys/GCP/1997 (CS)

Los Pinkys Fan Club, P.O. Box 3322,
Austin, TX 78764

Los Pinkys Web Page
//www.ondanet.com:1995/latinos/los.pinkys/lospinkys.html

Lou Ford
Tobacco Row; Country Rock; Roots Rock
Charlotte, North Carolina; 1996-

Named for the psycho sheriff in Jim Thompson's eerie classic, *The Killer Inside Me*, Lou Ford is one of the newest bands to come out of the ever expanding North Carolina alt. country milieu. Co-founders Mark Lynch and brothers Alan and Chad Edwards (originally from Athens, Georgia) had previously played in various pop and punk groups around the U.S. before getting together in the summer of 1996. Enduring a succession of drummers, Lou Ford fashioned modern rock with country influences ranging from Woody Guthrie to Gram Parsons. And though lumped with other Tobacco Row outfits like the Backsliders, Whiskeytown, and Mercury Dime, Lou Ford prefer to call what they do "Rural Pop" instead of alternative country. But, call it what you will, there is no denying they make effective use of the prototypical no depression/insurgent country formula layering countryish lyrics with twangy vocals over searing rock licks and power chords. Still, Lou Ford has distinguished itself somewhat from their predecessors as evidenced by their debut EP cassette, **I Am Not a Prize** and full length, **Sad, But Familiar**.

Alan Edwards (g,v); Chad Edwards (g,v); Mark Lynch (u.b.); Shawn Lynch (d)

I Am Not a Prize/Sorry Ass/1997 (EP CS)
"So Far Gone" on **Revival 2: Kudzu and Hollerin'**
   Contest/Yep Roc/1997
Sad, But Familiar/Sorry Ass/1998

Lou Ford, 7131 Dorn Circle, Charlotte, NC 28212

Lou Ford Home Page //www.mindspring.com/~louford/
louford@mindspring.com

Love Me

Lo-Fi Country Rock; Roots Rock
Sydney, Australia; 1992-

The Love Me story began in 1992 with a chance meeting between Madeleine King, Tom Kristensen, and Mandy Pearson while they were walking their dogs in a neighborhood park. Wife/husband, King and Kristensen had been playing music together since they were teenagers and found they shared similar musical interests with Pearson. Kristensen was particularly enamored with traditional country (i.e. Hank Williams), but all three had a feel for rock and pop from Australia and overseas. With King on bass and harmonica, Kristensen on guitar, Pearson on drum kit, and all three on vocals, they began to write songs as Love Me. With the addition of Dave Orwell on pedal steel and Barry Turnbull on electric guitar, they entered the studio to record their self-titled debut in 1996. It's opening track, "Buy Me a Drink", begins with a didjeridu fading into lilting pedal steel, dobro, and harmonica behind King's soft lead vocal and lush harmonies. This melancholy (slightly sarcastic) paen to life Down Under generally sets the tone for the album. King contributes several more achingly beautiful numbers ("Some Will, Some Won't"; "Something's Missing"; "Sticky"; "Rope Swing"; "I Can't Love You Enough"), but Love Me varies things up by letting Pearson and Kristensen have turns at lead vocals. Mandy's gruff, whispered voice ("Let Me Take You In"; "The Sitting Song"; "Slipping Asleep") and Tom's deep, half-spoken vocals (*a la* Nick Cave) make a nice couterpoint to King. Simply wonderful lo-fi country rock from beginning to end.

Violinist Amanda Brown (ex-Go-Betweens) guested on **Love Me** and was invited to join in 1997 while Orwell departed and headed Golden Rough. That year, the band toured down to Melbourne and opened shows in Sydney for the Blackeyed Susans, Jonathan Richman, the Dirty Three, and Richard Buckner. They also returned to the studio for their sophomore effort, **Fuel**, which pushes their previous sound in a poppier direction but with plenty of twangy touches (spaghetti western guitar and pedal steel by Turnbull). The overall mood is darker and edgier ("White Shirt"; "What Went Wrong"; "To Lose the Ball"; "Drink Too Much"; "Ashes"; "One Day Down"), but the great lead vocals and harmonies and wry sense of humor are still intact. Brown left shortly after the album came out, but into 1998-1999, Love Me continued performing (opened for Ben Harper; Will Oldham) and hoped to tour the states once King finished her PhD in medical statistics.

Amanda Brown (md,vio,1997-1998); Madeline King (b,hm,v); Tom Kristensen (db, g,v); Dave Orwell (b,p.s.,v, 1996-1997); Mandy Pearson (d,v); Barry Turnbull (e.g.,p.s.,sl.g.)

Britannia Hotel Live 1/LM/1995 (CS)
Love Me/Hi Gloss Aust./1996
Some Will, Some Won't/Hi Gloss Aust./1996 (EP CD)
Buy Me a Drink/Hi Gloss Aust./1997 (EP CD)
Fuel/Hi Gloss Aust./1997

Love Me, P.O. Box 40, Erskinville, N.S.W. 2043 Australia

Love Me Home Page //www.ebom.org/loveme/

Madeline King: madeline@dph1.health.usyd.edu.au

See The Blackeyed Susans; Golden Rough; The Triffids

Lyle Lovett

Texas; Singer/Songwriter
Klein, Texas; November 1, 1957-

Among the second generation of modern Texas singer/songwriters that includes Steve Earle and Robert Earl Keen, Lyle Lovett stands at the top. Like the best of his predecessors (Clark, Van Zandt, et al.), Lovett's songwriting combines superb narrative skills, literate presentation, and wry humor, but what sets him apart has been his eagerness to branch out into a variety of musical styles including swing jazz, rock, gospel, and r&b. His first recordings, **Lyle Lovett** and **Pontiac**, were two of the outstanding alternative country albums of the 1980s with excellent country songs including "Farther Down the Line," "This Old Porch" (co-written with Robert Earl Keen during their days at Texas A&M), "Lights of L.A. County," "Walk Through the Bottomland" (duet with Emmylou), and "If I had a Boat." Both contain portents ("An Acceptable Level of Ecstasy," for example) of what was to come on his third LP, **Lyle Lovett & His Large Band**, which has straight country ("I Married Her Just Because She Looks Like You"; "Stand By Your Man") on one side but big band swing and r&b on the other (made especially effective by the vocal contributions of Francine Reed). It won the Grammy for Best Country Record in 1989 and propelled Lovett into other avenues as a record producer (Walter Hyatt) and actor (*The Player*). Returning to the studio, Lyle recorded the cleverly titled **Joshua Judges Ruth** his most eclectic outing yet with gospel, folksy country, honky tonk, rock, and bluesy swing. Then, he entered his "Julia period" during which he released only one album, the fairly forgettable, **I Love Everybody**. As one of Lovett's early songs "Farther Down the Line" (equally applicable to rodeos or relationships) said, "this time he sure drew a bad one, one that nobody could ride," but after the demise of his marriage, Lyle made a laudable comeback with **The Road to Ensenada** which displays the old Lovett sense of humor ("Don't Touch My Hat") and insight ("Her First Mistake"; "Promises") and the usual variety including Western swing ("That's Right You're Not From Texas"), country weepers ("Who Loves You Better"; "I Can't Love You Any Better"), country rock ("Private Conversation"), Cajun ("Fiona"), and novelty ("Long Tall Texan"). With top notch backing from Stuart Duncan on fiddle, Paul Franklin on steel, and Herb Pederson and Chris Hillman on a couple of harmony vocals, Lyle took **The Road to Ensenada** to another Grammy. Lovett's 1998 recording **Step Inside This House** is a very personal tribute to the Texas singer/songwriter tradition. On this double CD set, Lyle covers songs by his mentors and contemporaries including Townes Van Zandt, Guy Clark, Walter Hyatt, Steve Fromholz, Willis Alan Ramsey, Eric Taylor, Vince Bell, Robert Earl Keen, and Michael Martin Murphey.

Lyle Lovett/Curb/1986
Pontiac/Curb/1987
Lyle Lovett and His Large Band/Curb/1989
Joshua Judges Ruth/Curb/1992
I Love Everybody/Curb/1994
The Best of Lyle Lovett/Curb Ita/1994 (import)
The Lights of L.A. County (Live in L.A., 1988)/ Curb Ita./1995 (import)
Here He Is/Curb/1995(15 trk. promo compilation)
The Road to Ensenada/MCA/1996
Step Inside This House/MCA/1998 (dbl. CD)

Lyle Lovett Fan Club c/o Chuck Morris, 4155 East Jewell, Ste. 412, Denver, CO 80222

Let Lyle Be Lyle/Curb Page //www.curb.com/artists/ll.html

lyle@curb.com

Lyle Lovett //www.geocities.com/soho/1192/lyle.html

Unofficial Lyle Lovett Home Page //www.io.com/~gcouger/

Lyle Lovett iMusic Showcase //imusic.com/showcase/country/

The Lucky Stars
Hillbilly Bop
Los Angeles, California; 1994-

The honky tonk/hillbilly/swing music that was so popular on the West Coast in the 1940s and 1950s experienced a phenomenal resurgence in the 1990s with Big Sandy, Dave & Deke, Radio Ranch Straight Shooters, and the Lucky Stars. Based in Hollywood, the Stars came out around 1994 by Sage Guyton and Chris Anderson who had previously been together in a local honky tonk band called the Toughskins. Adding lead and steel guitar, bass and drum, the Lucky Stars, revitalized the sound made famous by Bob Wills, Maddox Brothers and Rose, Spade Cooley, and Hank Thompson. Decked out in vintage cowboy band outfits, they became regulars at prominent L.A. hangouts (Jack's, the Palomino, Doll Hut) and opened for Dave Alvin, Big Sandy, the Derailers, the Mavericks, and Dave & Deke. The latter produced the Lucky Stars' first recording, a four track EP called **Look What the Cat Dragged.** In 1997, the Stars broke through on the national alt. country scene with a cut "No More Nuthin'" on **Straight Outta Boone County**. "Everybody's Fool" was released as a 45 in 1997 and also made it to Neil Mooney's **L.A. County Line** alt. country compilation in 1998. For 1999, the boys were penciled in for a Hank Penny tribute (**Hope You're Satisfied**) and a long-play CD of their own. Steel wizard Jeremy Wakefield has piled up quite a list of album credits as a session man and in 1998 was a member of Wayne

Hancock's band. There he met lead guitar sensation Dave Biller (ex-Dale Watson; the Panhandlers), and they subsequently collaborated on **The Hot Guitars of Biller and Wakefield**, an outstanding collection of instrumentals in the spirit of Speedy West and Jimmy Bryant.

Whitey Anderson (acc,md,p); Sage Guyton (r.g.,l.v.); Mooney Harding (ub,h.v.); Tim Magg (d); Jeremy Wakefield (s.g.,h.v.)

Look What the Cat Dragged In/Bucket Lid/1996 (EP)
"No More Nuthin'" on **Straight Outta Boone County**/Bloodshot/1997
"Everybody's Fool" b/w "Tennessee Tango"/Fate/1997
"Everybody's Fool" on **L.A. County Line**/Strawdog/1998
The Hot Guitars of Biller and Wakefield/High Tone/1999

The Lucky Stars Home Page //www.theluckystars.com

Lullaby For the Working Class
Lo-Fi Roots Rock
Lincoln, Nebraska; 1994-

Mike Mogis and Ted Stevens played together in various Lincoln, Nebraska pop rock bands in the early 1990s but in 1994 wanted a change of pace. Influenced especially by Uncle Tupelo's **March 16-20, 1992**, they worked up some acoustic material and gradually added more instruments and members. Mogis became proficient on banjo, mandolin, dulcimer, melodica, and even glockespiel and in addition to a bassist and percussionist, the newly named Lullaby for the Working Class added a cellist, violinist, and trumpet player. With this combination of instruments in place, they moved away from an Uncle Tupelo country rock sound toward a lo-fi roots rock style whose closest reference points are the Scud Mountain Boys, Dakota Suite, and Lambchop. Like these groups, Lullaby's recordings (**Blanket Warm; I Never Even Asked for Light**) are characterized by a deliberate pace, unusual takes on traditional music, unorthodox instrumental accompaniment, mournful vocals (Stevens), and esoteric, slightly disturbing lyrics. And, as with acts that tend toward a moody, avant-garde country edge, Lullaby for the Working Class has been eagerly received in Europe (perhaps more so than in the U.S) where labels such as Glitterhouse and Vinyl Junkie have included their songs on alt. country/Americana compilations.

John Anderson (d); Ben McMahan (cello); A.J. Mogis (b); Mike Mogis (bj,dulc,glock,md,melodica,s.g.); Ted Stevens (a.g.,uke,v); Tiffany (vio); Nate Walcott (trp)

Consolation/Lumberjack/1996 (EP)
Blanket Warm/Bar None/1996; Lumberjack/1996 (LP)
I Never Even Asked for Light/Bar None/1997; Lumberjack/1997 (LP)
"Boar's Nest" on **Luxury Liner, Vol. 2**/Glitterhouse Ger./1998
"Every Day is Like a Birthday Party" on **Loose: New Sounds of the Old West**/Vinyl Junkie UK/1998

Lullaby Web Page
//members.aol.com/creekrec/html/body_lullaby.html

Lullaby/Bar None Page
//www.bar-none.com/bios/lullabio.html

Ronnie Mack
TSOB
Baltimore, Maryland; April 18, 1954-

Hooked on rockabilly as a kid growing up in Baltimore, Ronnie Mack bucked all the musical trends of the 1960s and 1970s determined to hang on to the spirit of traditional American roots music. In the late 1970s and early 1980s, he found a musical home in the TSOB scene that produced the Lonesome Strangers, Rosie Flores, Dwight Yoakam, the Blasters, James Intveld, Dale Watson, and many other alt. country performers. Mack played L.A. clubs, recorded several singles for Rollin' Rock, and had a cut on the third volume of **A Town South of Bakersfield**, but his big contribution came in 1988, when he along with James Intveld began the weekly Barn Dance showcase. Initially held at the Little Nashville, it later moved to the Palomino where it became *the* center of California alternative country. In 1995, the Ronnie Mack Barn Dance, as it came to be called, was relocated to Jack's Sugar Shack. It was still going strong in the late 1990s thanks to Mack's incredible energy and sheer commitment to keeping the music alive. He was also a major force in the charity Elvis Birthday Bash that yearly showcases the cream of California's alt. country. A retrospective of Mack's recording career, **Born to Rock**, was released in 1996 on the Swedish Sunjay label. Its generous 27 cuts cover his output on the Rollin' Rock and Lonesome Town labels including early rockabilly/rock style numbers plus countryish material such as a duet, "Brand New Heartache," with Rosie Flores.

"Mama's Reward" on **Town South of Bakersfield, Vol. 3/** Restless/1992
"Lucky Star" (with Hot Rod Lincoln) on **Turning the World Blue: A Tribute to Gene Vincent/** Skizmatic/199
Born to Rock/Sun Jay Swe./1996

Ronnie Mack Home Page //www.electricearl.com/mack.html

Ronnie Mack's Barn Dance
//www.electricearl.com/bdance.html

Rose Maddox
Hillbilly Boogie; Bakersfield Sound
Boaz, Alabama; 1925-April 15, 1998

Rose Maddox is best known for her work as lead vocalist for the incredible 1940s-1950s California honky tonk/swing band Maddox Brothers & Rose ("America's Most Colorful Hillbilly Band"). Their free wheeling, fun loving performances, joyously captured on **Maddox Brothers & Rose, Vols. 1 & 2** and **On the Air**, come with the highest recommendation. In the late 1950s, when the band ended, Rose went on to a solo career most notably with Capitol where she had several hits including duets with Buck Owens ("Loose Talk"; "Mental Cruelty"). Her output on Capitol was issued as a Bear Family boxed set **The One Rose, The Capitol Years** in 1993; into the 1980s-1990s, Rose overcame serious health problems and personal tragedies and made a comeback. In 1983, she reasserted her stature in California country with **Queen of the West**, an album of Bakersfield style country with backing from Merle Haggard & the Strangers and Emmylou Harris ; she followed this in 1990 with **Rose of the West Coast Country** which features gospel, bluegrass, and some classics from her Maddox Brothers days. The rise of alternative country on the West Coast brought recognition and respect from a new generation of neo-hillbillies thrilled with the music of Maddox Brothers & Rose. In 1994, she recorded **$35 and a Dream** with Byron Berline, Herb Pederson, Jay Dee Manness, and John Jorgenson (the Hellecasters) on covers of Maddox Brothers & Rose, Buck, Merle, and the Flying Burrito Brothers. The same line-up supported Rose on her 1997, **The Moon is Rising**, a collection of honky tonk duets with Jorgenson. However, less than a year later, after battling numerous health problems Rose passed away. For a closer look at her extraordinary live and legacy see *Ramblin' Rose: The Life and Career of Rose Maddox.*

Rose Maddox Sings Bluegrass/Capitol/1962
Rockin' Rollin' Maddox Brothers & Rose/Bear Family Ger./1981
Queen of the West/Rounder/1983
Rose of the West Coast Country/Arhoolie/1990
Maddox Brothers & Rose, Vol. 1: 1946-1951/ Arhoolie/1993
The One Rose, The Capitol Years/Bear Family Ger./1993 (boxed set)
$35 and a Dream/Arhoolie/1994
Maddox Brothers & Rose, Vol. 2: 1946-1951/ Arhoolie/1994
Maddox Brothers & Rose On the Air/Arhoolie/1996
The Moon Is Rising (with John Jorgensen)/Country Town/1997
Ramblin' Rose: The Life and Career of Rose Maddox, Jonny Whiteside, Nashville: Vanderbilt University Press, 1997.

Rose Maddox/Country Town Home Page
//www.countrytown.com/

Lloyd Maines
Lubbock Mafia; Pedal Steel; Producer
Acuff, Texas; June 28, 1951-

Lloyd Maines was born into a country music family. In the 1950s and 1960s, his father and uncles were the Maines Brothers Band, one of the most popular in West Texas. As part of this act, Lloyd and his younger brothers learned to play instruments, dressed in cute cowboy outfits, and were billed as the Little Maines Brothers Band. Lloyd started out on lead guitar but in 1968 took up the steel guitar which would become his signature instrument. His career with the Little Maines Brothers lasted until graduation from high school when Lloyd and his siblings went on to other pursuits. Lloyd found a position as engineer and session man at the famous Caldwell Studios in Lubbock, and there, in 1973, met Joe Ely and became his steel guitarist. For the next seven years, Maines was a vital component of the great Joe Ely Band that recorded some of the best alt. country albums of the 1970s. At the same time, he rejoined his brothers who now became the Maines Brothers Band when the old group retired. They did several albums on their own label Texas Soul and charted a few songs in the early 1980s. After an unsatisfying two record deal with Mercury, they returned to Texas Soul and into the early 1990s remained as one of the area's favorite bands. In the late 1970s and early 1980s, they made up Terry Allen's Panhandle Mystery Band touring and backing him on his classic albums such as **Lubbock (On Everything)**.

Into the 1990s, Lloyd Maines was a member of the Jerry Jeff Walker band and established himself through his innovative steel (and dobro) work as one of the premier session players. He appeared on an incredible number of recordings for a variety of artists including Bruce and Charlie Robison, Dale Watson, Wilco, and Uncle Tupelo. In addition, his long years of experience with the Caldwell Studios helped him become a super producer. His production credits, which number almost 50, include recordings by many alt. country performers: Terry Allen, Bad Livers, Richard Buckner, Jimmie Dale Gilmore, Butch Hancock, Wayne Hancock, Terri Hendrix, Ray Wylie Hubbard, Robert Earl Keen, Bruce and Charlie Robison, Wagon, and Chris Wall. Maines' resume also lists work on the soundtrack for *End of the World*, a film by artist Bruce Nauman presented as part of the 5th Biennial of the Whitney Museum of American Art. After many miles and years of commuting, Lloyd finally made the move to Austin in 1998 so he could more easily pursue his production projects and be with his family. A number of Maines' pedal steel instructional videos are available through Texas Music & Video.

Anyone Can Play Honky Tonk Pedal Steel/Mel Bay/ (30 min. video)
Hot Pedal Steel With Lloyd Maines/TMV (video)
66 Hot Licks for Pedal Steel Guitar/Lick a Minute (video)

Lloyd Maines Music Production, P.O. Box 80225, Austin, TX 78708; (ph./fax) 512-832-0277

Mainesteel@aol.com

Texas Music & Video, P.O. Box 16248, Lubbock, TX 79490-6248; 1-800-261-3368; //www.musicvideo.com

See Terry Allen; Joe Ely

Doug Mansfield and The Dust Devils
Honky Tonk
Melbourne, Australia; 1991-

Doug Mansfield is from Melbourne, Australia, but his heart beats hard-core Texas honky tonk. His early exposure to country music came through his "mum" who loved Australian legends such as Smokey Dawson and Tex Morton. Later, he fell under the influence of the 1970s "outlaw movement" (Waylon, Willie, David Allan Coe, et al.) and for a number of years worked the pubs of inner city Melbourne as a country/blues solo act. In 1989, Doug put together his first band, the Bearbrass Ramblers, with bassist Jack Coleman. Two years later, Mansfield formed, the Dust Devils with Coleman, Adam Gare, Bruce Kane, and Gerard Rowan (ex-Starliners). At first, they played honky tonk music "mainly for our own amusement" but in time began to take it more seriously with encouragement from local producer Grahan Lee (ex-Blackeyed Susans) who produced their 1996 debut, **You Can Never Go Home**. Mansfield's songwriting and singing and the Dust Devils superb accompaniment would be right at home in honky tonks from Austin to Australia. Doug has frequently pointed out the influence of his Texas counterparts Junior Brown and Cornell Hurd, and like them, he knows how to capture the essence of bar life with great perceptiveness and humor ("One More Beer"; "Sticky Wicket"; "Messin Around" with Lisa Miller; "Buckle Bunny Bride"; "The Girl Who Cleans the Ashtrays"; "Little Details"; "My House Is Leavin' Home"; "One More Drinking Song"). His humor also pervades the achingly nostalgic title tune and "The Ballad of Steve Miller," a musical biography of a local punk rocker/music impresario with a very memorable refrain about his being "nothing but a Handsome Dude." The song "One More Beer" received considerable attention with video play on CMT plus inclusion on an Australian country compilation and on a motion picture soundtrack. Doug and the Dust Devils have been regulars at various hotel pubs around Melbourne for years and performed at a variety of venues including Pentridge Prison and the famous Tamworth Country Music Festival.

Doug Mansfield (a.g.,v); Jack Coleman (b); Adam Gare (f,md,h.v.); Bruce Kane (d); Gerard Rowan (e.g.,p.s.)

You Can Never Go Home/W. Minc Aust./1996
"One More Beer" on **Saturday Night Country Favorites**/ABC Aust./1998

Doug Mansfield and The Dust Devils, P.O. Box 54, Elsternwick, 3185; 6 13 9596 3258

Doug Mansfield and The Dust Devils //www.home.aone.net.au/jack/

ddevils@pop.alphalink.com.au

See The Starliners

Marah

Roots Rock
Philadelphia, Pennsylvania; 1993-

Of all the new bands to emerge in late 1998, none made a bigger splash than Marah. The South Philadelphia quartet's defiantly titled debut **Let's Cut the Crap and Hook Up Later on Tonight** took the music world almost completely by surprise although, in fact, the group had been together since 1993. Anchored by the Bielanko Brothers, Marah were Philly favorites and originally did **Let's Cut the Crap** on a local label. Then, they got a copy to Cary Hudson of Blue Mountain and the recording was re-released on their Black Dog label. Once the CD began to make the rounds, the accolades gushed forth. Its hodge-podge of urban/rural, modern/traditional country, rock, blues, and gospel with squalling guitars occupying the same aural space as banjo, horns, mandolin, bagpipes, steel, harmonica, piano, and bottle-blowing drew parallels to the Replacements' **Hootenanny**, Bruce's **Darkness on the Edge of Town**, the Stones **Exile on Main Street**, and Whiskeytown's **Faithless Street**. Hyperbole swarmed around Marah like a halo of crazed flies and by year's end it was not uncommon to hear predictions like "next big thing" and yes, even "the future of alternative country." (An interesting CD to seek out is **Rock and Roll Summer Camp '98**, informal sessions done with Blue Mountain and Marah at the Black Dog studios).

Dave Bielanko (bj,g,l.v.); Serge Bielanko (g,v); Danny Metz (b); Ronnie Vance (d)

**Let's Cut the Crap and Hook Up Later On
   Tonight**/Black Dog/1998
Rock and Roll Summer Camp '98/Black Dog/1998

Marah, 1014 Salter St., Philadelphia, PA 19147

Marah/Black Dog Page
//www.blackdogrecords.com/marah.htm

See Blue Mountain

The Mary Janes

Lo-Fi Country Rock
Bloomington, Indiana; 1993-

The Vulgar Boatmen are a lesser known but excellent pop rock band originally formed by Walter Salas-Humara (Silos) in the 1980s. In 1994, two members of the group, vocalist Janas Hoyt and violist Kathy Kolata started a side project which grew into a full-time concern called the Mary Janes (after a Vulgar Boatmen song). With a revolving door line-up of bassists, drummers, and violinists, they crafted melodic folk/country/rock with a lineage running from the Carter Family through the Velvet Underground and Cowboy Junkies. Hoyt's soft vocals and folksy songs are framed in mesmerizing tiers of electric violin and viola that one reviewer labeled "sort of country chamber music." In early 1998, the Mary Janes had an all-female cast with Hoyt and Kolata joined by Heather Craig, Freda Love, and Pam McLaughlin, but by year's end, Kolata, Love, and McLaughlin were out. They were replaced by Dan Hunt, Mark Minnick, Dennis Scoville, and Kevin Smith, and the Mary Janes soldiered on. Their stock made a major jump when they contributed a lilting "I'm Not Ready Yet" to the much anticipated **Real: The Tom T. Hall Project** and were profiled in *No Depression* (March-April 1999). After three years, fourteen musicians, and four studios, the Mary Janes' **Record No. 1** had its coming out party in March 1999.

Heather Craig (violin); Janas Hoyt (g,v); Dan Hunt (b); Kathy Kolata (viola,1993-1998); Mark Minnick (d); Dennis Scoville (p.s.); Kevin Smith (g,md)

"Telescope" b/w "Baby Honey"/MJ/1994 (7")
"Downtown" on **Howl!**/Glitterhouse Ger./1995
"Never Felt Better" on **Live From Bloomington 1997**/
   1997
"I'm Not Ready Yet" on **Real: The Tom T. Hall Project**/
   Sire/1998
Record No. 1/Delmore/1999

The Mary Janes //www.themaryjanes.com

Ray Mason Band (Lonesome Brothers)

Roots Rock; Country Rock
Northampton, Massachusetts; 1982-

Around Western Massachusetts, Ray Mason is known as "the godfather of Northampton music." In a career that's spanned over thirty years, he's taken on each new wave of rock (folk, country, punk, pop, post-punk) with a number of bands but most notably with his Ray Mason Band which he started in 1982. Vocally and stylistically, Ray compares most favorably to The Band and John Hiatt, but his versatility puts him close to NRBQ and Jack Logan. His recordings (**Missyouville**; **Old Souls Day**; **Castanets**) are a panorama of styles over the past three decades including mandolin driven folk/country, barroom rock, grunge, pop, blues, and more. Helping him out have been some of the elite of Massachusetts alt. country such as Cheri Knight and Stephen Desaulniers, Bruce Tull, and Tom Shea of the much-missed kings of lo-fi, the Scud Mountain Boys. In 1998, Mason, Matt Hebert, Keith Leverault (ex-Blood Oranges), Bob Hennessey (Angry Johnny), Matt Cullen, and some Scuds joined as the Ware River Club to record the roots rocking, **Bad Side of Otis Ave.** The following year, Tar Hut Records released a Ray Mason tribute album, **It's Heartbreak That Sells**, with covers by Eric Ambel, Angry Johnny, the Ass Ponys, Cheri Knight, and others.

In 1986, Mason teamed up with two other veterans of the local music scene, Jim Armenti and Bob Grant to form the Lonesome Brothers. Long before the current wave of alternative country came along, the Brothers were concocting a catchy blend of country, swing, pop, and roots rock. However, they didn't get around to making a record until they signed with Tar Hut (Angry Johnny; Ex-Husbands) which released their self-titled debut in 1997. It ranges freely across straight ahead country ("Need a Second Chance"; "Strictly Pavement"; "Eyes Wide Open"; "Down By the Water"—previously covered by Cheri Knight) and flat out rock, ("Warm Vinyl '59"; "Red House"; "Three Sisters"). The twangy side of the Lonesome Brothers is helped along by the contributions of local steel player Doug Beaumier. When not playing with the Lonesome Brothers, Armenti moonlights as a clarinetist in a klezmer group called Klezamir which has an album out called **Back in the Shtetl Again**!

Ray Mason Band: Ray Mason (g,l.v.); Stephen Desaulniers (b,v); Frank Marsh (d,v); Tom Shea (l.g.,md,v); Bruce Tull (l.g.,l.s.)
The Lonesome Brothers: Jim Armenti (g,v); Bob Grant (d); Ray Mason (b,v) with Doug Beaumier (l.s.,p.s.)

> **Between Blue and Okay**/Ocean Music/1995
> **Missyouville**/Chunk/1996
> **The Lonesome Brothers**/Tar Hut/1997
> **Old Souls Day**/Wormco/1998
> **Bad Side of Otis Ave.** (Ware River Club)/Natural Disaster/1998
> **Castanets**/Wormco/1999
> **It's Heartbreak That Sells** (Ray Mason Tribute)/Tar Hut/1999

Ray Mason Band, 9 Depot Rd., Haydenville, MA 01039; 413-268-7059

The Lonesome Brothers/Tar Hut, P.O. Box 441940, Somerville, MA 02144

The Lonesome Brothers/Tar Hut Page //www.tarhut.com

info@tarhut.com

Klezamir //www.klezamir.com

The Mavericks (Jerry Dale McFadden)
Country Rock
Miami, Florida; 1988-

The Mavericks arose quite unexpectedly out of Miami in the late 1980s on the strength of dynamic lead singer/songwriter, Raul Malo and a reputation for intense live performances. After a semi-demo debut in 1990, they signed with MCA and put out **From Hell to Paradise**. The album pays homage to tradition with covers of Hank and Buck (actually the weakest cuts), but the Mavericks are at their best on original honky tonkers, country rock, and ballads like the gorgeous "This Broken Heart" that show off Malo's formidable pipes. With a new lead guitarist (Nick Kane) on board, the Mavericks put together **What a Crying Shame**, an album that owed as much to Elvis and Roy Orbison as to Bakersfield. The sound is traditional yet modern on covers as diverse as Jesse Winchester and Bruce Springsteen but especially on Malo/Kostas originals like the title tune, "There Goes My Heart," and "Pretend." The album put them over the top, and, suddenly, the Mavs were popping up everywhere, *Austin City Limits, Letterman, TNN, CMT*. For the follow-up, the Mavericks caught the "lounge fever" sweeping the nation in the mid-1990s and recorded **Music For All Occasions** which ranges over shuffles, Tex-Mex ("All You Ever Do Is Bring Me Down" with Flaco Jimenez), and even the old Frank and Nancy Sinatra duet "Something Stupid" (Raul & Trisha Yearwood). After some time off, the Mavericks returned in 1998 with a cut on *The Horse Whisperer* soundtrack and a new album, **Trampoline**, which continues their experimentation, adding a horn section and reaching further into Tex-Mex and blues rock.

In 1994, the Mavericks added keyboardist Jerry Dale McFadden to their touring band. Born in Texas, the "fifth Maverick," originally came to Nashville to study at Belmont University but ended up with a budding country rock career. McFadden's *way, way* off center style was characterized by breakneck tempos, your not so usual country lyrics, and "stunning" vocals. Jerry Dale's voice was described by one reviewer as sounding like he was "gored by an angry bull on his 9th birthday" (sounds like David Bowie as Ziggy Stardust to me). His one and only album, **Stand and Cast a Shadow** (with Duane Eddy on guitars) had rocking covers of "Waiting in Your Welfare Line" and "B-I-Bickey, Bi, Bo-Bo-Go" and over-the-edge McFadden originals including "Sunset Died When the Whores Went Away" and one of country's only s&m songs "Country Music Beats the Hell Out of Me" in which he shrieks, "I like to listen to Hank, while I'm being spanked." Happily, Reptile records reissued this forgotten nugget in 1997. Meanwhile, McFadden (who has recorded with Jason & the Scorchers and toured with Jill Sobule) not only handles keyboards for the Mavericks but adds to their live shows with outlandish outfits and stage antics.

Paul Deakin (d);David Lee Holt (l.g.,1990-2); Nick Kane (l.g.,1992-); Raul Malo (g,p,l.v.); Ben Peeler (a.g.,bj,db, e.g.,l.s.,md); Robert Reynolds (b,g) with Jerry Dale McFadden (acc,ky)

> **The Mavericks**/Y&T/1990 (also came in ltd. boxed, autographed edition); Hip-O/1999
> **From Hell to Paradise**/MCA/1992
> **What a Crying Shame**/MCA/1994
> **Music For All Occasions**/MCA/1995
> **Stand and Cast a Shadow** (Jerry Dale McFadden)/Reptile/1986; 1997
> **It's Now, It's Live**/Universal Music Can./1997
> **Trampoline**/MCA/1998
> "Hot Burrito #1" on **Return of the Grievous Angel: A Tribute to Gram Parsons**/Almo/1999

The Official Mavericks Website //www.themavericks.com

Mavfanclub@aol.com

The Mavericks/MCA Nashville Home Page //www.mca-nashville.com/mav/mavalbum.htm

Dawn Wiley's Mavericks Page //www.personal.umich.edu/~dwiley/mavericks/

Don McCalister, Jr.
Western Swing; Honky Tonk
California; May, 28, 1955-

Because his father's work (university professor) never allowed the family to stay in one place very long, Don McCalister, Jr. saw a lot of the U.S. growing up. And, wherever he lived, from Maine to California, he soaked up the musical influences of each region. Moving to Austin in 1981, his first bands in the late 1980s were bluegrass groups including the Bluegrass Demons and Kerrville Folk Festival regulars, the Flakey Biscuit Boys. After they crumbled, McCalister recorded a country/folk record, **Silver Moon**, in 1990 but then developed an interest in Western swing and released another independent tape, **Brand New Ways.** His supporting band, named the Cowboy Jazz Revue, included Floyd Domino (ex-Asleep at the Wheel), Gene Elders, Johnny Gimble, Champ Hood (co-producer), Lynn Frazier (steel), Boomer Norman (lead guitar), and ex-Flakey Biscuit Boy clarinetist, Stan Smith. This recording got enough good reviews and air play to interest Dejadisc in issuing a completely reworked version in 1993 with originals and covers of Jimmie Dale Gilmore and the Louvins. Its appealing mix of country and Texas swing was particularly well received in Europe, and Don made several tours there where he was "strangely popular in Italy." He followed it up in 1996 with, **Love Gone Right**, another collection of honky tonk ("Somebody's Back in Town"), country ballads ("Red Rose of Morning"), and swing ("Swing Me Back to Texas"; "Radio Boogie") on his own Biscuit Boy label. Once again Don is supported by Domino and Gimble plus Kimmie Rhodes, Jesse Taylor and Buddy Emmons. In 1997, his **Down in Texas** was released in Europe on Appaloosa Records and offers more great Lone Star State honky tonk/swing with help from Ponty Bone, Champ Hood, Chris Gage, Floyd Domino, Stan Smith, and Doug Sahm.

Silver Moon/Biscuit Boy/1989 (CS)
Brand New Ways/Dejadisc/1992
"Brand New Ways" on **Country**/Vinyl Junkie UK/1994
Love Gone Right/Biscuit Boy/1996
"Ain't It Funny" on **Jukebox Cowboy**/Vinyl Junkie UK/1997
Down in Texas/Appaloosa It./1997

Biscuit Boy Music, P.O. Box 160942, Austin, TX 78716

Don McCalister, Jr. Home Page
//www.cris.com/~Donmccjr/

donmccjr@concentric.net

Mary McCaslin (Jim Ringer)
Singer/Songwriter
Indianapolis,Indiana; December 22, 1946-

Mary McCaslin has been making contributions to the "good kind" of country/folk music for over two decades. As a singer/songwriter, she rates with the best of her contemporaries although she hasn't had nearly the amount of recognition she deserves. Drawn to country music early in her life, McCaslin got a record deal at age 21 with Capitol and cut one single. Two years later, she made her full length debut with Barnaby Records and in the early 1970s began traveling the folk circuit where she met another up and coming singer/songwriter, Jim Ringer. They began living together, and both recorded several excellent records for Philo. McCaslin's **Way Out West**, **Prairie in the Sky**, and **Sunny California** celebrated the culture of the American West and led *Rolling Stone* magazine to dub her "a prairie songstress." Meanwhile, Ringer made several strong recordings exploring traditional country themes such as hard living, hard working, and hard drinking. In 1978, they married and teamed up to do **The Bramble and the Rose,** one of the finest country duet albums of the 1970s. Three years later, they were picked up by Flying Fish, and each released a terrific record—McCaslin did **A Life and a Time** while Ringer did **Endangered Species** with help from the Dillards and members of the Flying Burrito Brothers. As a duet act, McCaslin and Ringer toured throughout the 1980s but divorced in 1989. Three years later, Ringer died still generally unheralded for his excellent body of work, the best of which is available on the retrospective, **The Band of Jesse James**. McCaslin's prime material from the 1970s can be found on two collection's **The Best of Mary McCaslin** and **Things We Said Today.** In the 1990s, McCaslin made the festival rounds and hosted a radio show on KZSC in Santa Cruz, California. "The Fat Farm" with "off the wall country, folk, bluegrass, and beyond."

Goodnight Everybody/Barnaby/1969
Way Out West/Philo/1974; 1998
Prairie in the Sky/Philo/1975; 1995
Old Friends/Philo/1977
The Bramble and the Rose (with Jim Ringer)/Philo/1978
Sunny California/Mercury Philo/1979
A Life and Time/Flying Fish/1981
Endangered Species (Jim Ringer)/Flying Fish/1981
The Best of Mary McCaslin/Philo/1990
Things We Said Today/Philo/1992
Broken Promises/Philo/1993
The Band of Jesse James: The Best of Jim Ringer/ Philo/1996

Mary McCaslin, P.O. Box 3394, Santa Cruz, CA 95063

Mary McCaslin Home Page
//www.cruzio.com/~gpa/mary.html

marygreg@cruzio.com

Jim Ringer: Notes by Mary McCaslin
//www.freestone.com/ringer.html

Mose McCormack

Singer/Songwriter
Dophan, Alabama/Rio Arriba County, New Mexico; 1950-

Singer/songwriter, music journalist, DJ, and all-around wild man, Stephen Terrell deserves a hearty round of thanks for bringing attention to one of the all-time alt. country survivors, Mose McCormack. Born in Dixie, "Mosey Mack" had a run in with the law "out West" in his early 20s and ended up on probation in Arizona where he learned to make jewelry. In 1973, he relocated to Santa Fe so he could sell his wares, but he also continued to pursue his favorite pastime, singing and songwriting. At the time, Northern New Mexico was home to a small but thriving alt. country community with performers like the Last Miles Ramblers, Christine Albert, and Stephen Terrell playing bars, honky tonks, and roadside taverns scattered throughout the Sandia and Sangre De Cristo Mountains. McCormack's 1976 debut **Beans & Make Believe** is filled with images of the area's utterly unique landscape and cultural mix ("New Mexico Blues") and generally easy-going often humorous country stories about hard lessons ("Bustin' for the Door"; "Left Handed Man"), hard labor ("Anthem"), and hard times ("Five & Dime"; "Fatter Pickins"; and the classic title tune). Over the years, Mose went down a few dead end record deals and didn't do another album for over twenty years when he recorded **Santa Fe Trail**. Supported by some of New Mexico's best musicians, McCormack deals out some fine honky tonk and honest tales about the American Southwest. In late 1998, Mose was given long overdue recognition in the wider alt. country community when Terrell did a nice little profile of him for *No Depression* (November-December).

Beans & Make Believe/CMH/1976
Santa Fe Trail/1997

Mose McCormack/New Mexico Sound Page
//newmexicosound.com/sftrail.htm or 505-296-2766

See Last Mile Ramblers; Stephen Terrell

Del McCoury

Traditional/Progressive Bluegrass
Bakersville, North Carolina; February 1, 1930-

In the world of contemporary bluegrass, the name that is synonymous with "high lonesome" is Del McCoury. Born in North Carolina but raised in south central Pennsylvania, he first played banjo with a number of bluegrass bands in the 1940s-early 1960s before becoming lead vocalist and rhythm guitarist with Bill Monroe for one year (1963-1964). After stints in several more bluegrass outfits, McCoury formed his own Dixie Pals in 1967. That group, which went through many personnel changes over the next two decades, recorded for a number of small labels beginning in 1972. In 1987, McCoury changed its name to simply the Del McCoury Band and brought in a new line up including sons Rob (banjo) and Ronnie (mandolin). And though McCoury's Dixie Pals years turned out some fine music, it is with the DMB that he hit his stride as one of the top bluegrass performers of the 1990s. Central to this success has been Del's amazing bluesy vocals which have won numerous IBMA vocalist and entertainer of the year awards. The excellent support from Rob and Ronnie, fiddler Jason Carter, and bassist Mike Bub deserves much of the credit as well; all are multiple IBMA award winners on their respective instruments. What has also set McCoury and band apart has been their ability to deftly handle traditional bluegrass (i.e. **Classic Bluegrass**) along with an inclination to tackle bluegrass versions of songs drawn from country, blues, and rock sources (like Crowe and Krauss). **Don't Stop the Music**, **Blue Side of Town**, **Deeper Shade of Blue** (Grammy nominated), and **Cold Hard Facts** (Grammy nominated) are all fabulous recordings with excellent old-time bluegrass along side outstanding covers of a variety of performers including Lefty Frizzell, Ernest Tubb, George Jones, Jerry Lee Lewis, Robert Cray, Tom Petty, Kevin Welch, and Steve Earle. Not to be missed by fans of traditional and/or progressive bluegrass.

In 1997, Del joined with Doc Watson, Mac Wiseman and funk artists Bootsy Collins on two recordings, **The GrooveGrass Boyz** and **GrooveGrass 101** which were intended to "bring old-time and traditional American music into the 21st Century." If funkgrass versions of old-time/ bluegrass standards ain't your bag, dad then try the more traditional **Mac, Doc and Del** or **The Family**. McCoury and band participated in a major alt. country/ bluegrass event in 1998-1999 when they served as Steve Earle's backing band on **The Mountain**.

Del McCoury Band: Mike Bub (b); Jason Carter (f); Rob McCoury (md,v); Ronnie McCoury (bj)

I Wonder Where You Are Tonight/Arhoolie/1968
Del McCoury Sings Bluegrass/Arhoolie/1968 (re-issue of **I Wonder**)
Collector's Special/Grasshound/1971
Livin' on the Mountain/Rebel/1971
High on a Mountain/Rounder/1972; 1995
Del McCoury and His Dixie Pals/Revonah/1975
Our Kind of Grass/Rebel/1978
The Best of Del McCoury and the Dixie Pals/Rebel/1980
Del McCoury—Live in Japan/Copper Creek/1980
Take Me to the Mountains/Leather/1981
Sawmill/Rebel/1985
The McCoury Brothers/Rounder/1987; 1995
Don't Stop the Music/Rounder/1990
Classic Bluegrass/Rebel/1991
Blue Side of Town/Rounder/1992
Deeper Shade of Blue/Rounder/1993
Cold Hard Facts/Rounder/1996
The GrooveGrass Boyz/Sugar Hill Groovegrass/1997
GrooveGrass 101/Sugar Hill Groovegrass/1998
Mac, Doc, and Del/Sugar Hill Groovegrass/1998
The Mountain (Steve Earle)/E-Squared/1999
The Family/Ceili/1999

Bluegrass: The Del McCoury Band
//www.banjo.com/profiles/DelMcCoury.html

Del McCoury/Rounder Page //www,rounder.com

The Groovegrass Boyz //www.groovegrass.com

See Steve Earle; Doc Watson

Hank McCoy and The Dead Ringers (The Okra All-Stars)

Okra; Honky Tonk; Country Rock
Columbus, Ohio; Early 1990s

Hank McCoy and the Dead Ringers were part of the thriving Columbus, Ohio alternative country scene of the early 1990s that also produced Ricky Barnes & the Hoot Owls, the Gibson Brothers, One Riot, One Ranger, and the Schramms. Like Barnes, Hank specialized in raw, ultra nasally vocals on twangy honky tonk shuffles, country ballads, and country rockers. McCoy wrote most of the material including originals such as "Jealousy," "Back in the Front of My Mind," "The Bottom of the Bottle and the Long Lonely Night," and "The Last Teardrop." In 1994, McCoy and the Dead Ringers won most of the country awards in the *Columbus Guardian*'s 1st Columbus Music Awards. McCoy teamed with Barnes, Jeb Loy Nichols, and Dave Schramm in 1993 as The Okra All-Stars on one superb self-titled recording with a twang factor of 9 on a scale of 10; he also hosted a country radio program on WCBE in the mid-1990s. In 1995, after the release of **Mohawk St.**, perhaps their best, the Dead Ringers toured Germany but broke up shortly after their return. McCoy subsequently married a German girl and moved to her home country. The last heard from him was "Gonna Hang Out My Mind" for **Hit the Hay, Volume 2** in 1996.

Hank McCoy (g,v); Trent Arnold (b); Ricky Barnes (v); Pete Cary (b); James Castoe (d); Bob Hite (ky); Kristi Leigh Jendry (v); Jim Maneri (p); Matt Newman (g); Jeff Passifiume (g); Randy Stockwell (b); Brad Westall (s.g.)

"Lately My Luck" and "Laughing at the Ghost" on **Sample Some Okra**/Okra/1991
Hank McCoy and the Dead Ringers/Okra/1992
Still Feeling Blue & Lately My Luck Has Been Changing/Okra/1993
The Okra All-Stars/Okra/1993; Innerstate/1999
Mohawk St./Okra/1995
"Gonna Hang Out My Mind" on **Hit the Hay, Vol. 2**/Sound Asleep Swe./1996

See Ricky Barnes; Jeb Loy Nichols; The Schramms

Country Joe McDonald

Country Rock
Washington, D.C.; 1942-

Although recordings like the tribute **Pastures of Plenty** and Billy Bragg/Wilco's **Mermaid Avenue** sparked renewed interest in Woody Guthrie in the 1990s, this was not the first time that alt. country/Americana performers had paid homage to the great troubadour. Back in the late 60s and early 70s, a new generation of hippies and protestors "re-discovered" and celebrated Guthrie's life and music. One of the leaders of this revival was Country Joe McDonald who is mostly remembered as the leader of the acid rock/blues group Country Joe and the Fish; their anti-Vietnam War song "I Feel Like I'm Fixin' to Die" and the infamous "fish cheer" at Woodstock made them heroes to the "flower power" generation. In 1969, on the heels of a string of successful Country Joe and the Fish albums for Vanguard, McDonald inked a solo deal and like several of his contemporaries (Bob Dylan; Ian & Sylvia) went to Nashville to record. Backed by country session veterans such as Harold Bradley (guitar), Grady Martin (dobro, guitar, sitar), Hargus Robbins (piano), Norbert Putnam (bass), Buddy Harmon (drums), and even the Jordanaires, Joe did **Thinking of Woody Guthrie**, a truly excellent collection of covers including "Pastures of Plenty," "So Long It's Been Good to Know Yuh," "Tom Joad," "Roll on Columbia," "Pretty Boy Floyd," and "This Land is Your Land." It was a big hit with critics and earned McDonald an invitation to participate with Bob Dylan, Arlo Guthrie, Pete Seeger, Joan Baez, and others in a gala Woody Guthrie celebration at the Hollywood Bowl in 1970. He also contributed several songs to two subsequent tribute compilations featuring many of the same artists. Because **Thinking of Woody Guthrie** was recorded so quickly, Joe had extra studio time and decided to do a more straight-forward country album. The result was **Tonight I'm Singing Just for You** which presents credible versions of standards ("Ring of Fire"; "Tennessee Stud"; "Heartaches By the Number"; "Crazy Arms"; "Oklahoma Hills"; "Six Days on the Road") with an overall feel that anticipates Leon Russell's similar **Hank Wilson's Back** from 1973.

Thinking of Woody Guthrie/Vanguard/1969
Tonight I'm Singing Just for You/Vanguard/1970
"Roll on Columbia" & "When the Curfew Comes Around" on **The Greatest Songs of Woody Guthrie, Vol. 1**/Vanguard/1972
"Woman at Home" on **Tribute to Woody Guthrie Part 2**/Warner Brothers/1972

Country Joe McDonald //www.countryjoe.com

John McEuen

Newgrass; Multi-Instrumentalist
Garden Grove, California; December 19, 1945-

John McEuen is one of the most versatile performers in what has become known as the "new acoustic" music. Proficient on banjo, fiddle, and guitar, he was a member of the popular country rock lite group Nitty Gritty Dirt Band for twenty years (1967-1987). They recorded numerous albums during this period that yielded several hits ("Mr. Bojangles"; "House at Pooh Corner"), but their biggest contribution was the landmark **Will the Circle Be Unbroken** which paired old-time country royalty (Roy Acuff, Maybelle Carter, Jimmy Martin, Earle Scruggs, Merle Travis, Doc Watson) and a bunch of "hippie" musicians (NGDB, Vassar Clements, Norman Blake). The result was a mammoth 3 record set of choice traditional old-time, bluegrass, country that proved to be one of the most important albums in carrying the music to a new and more diverse generation of listeners. It also elevated the status of the NGDB, although they never again measured up to its high standard of excellence (the cream of their recordings has been collected on two volumes, **20 Years of Dirt** and **More Great Dirt**). John McEuen departed the NGDB in 1987 although he did return to participate in **Will the Circle Be Unbroken Vol. II**. From there, he went on to a diverse musical career as a producer, television and movie scorer, and solo performer. He produced a video in 1990 for the Dillards who were one of his biggest early influences; his most important soundtrack work was for the musical *Paint Your Wagon* and for the TV special *The Music of the Wild West*. McEuen guested on albums by a variety of musicians and recorded several acclaimed albums of acoustic music including **String Wizards I** and **II** (with Byron Berline, Vassar Clements, and Earl Scruggs). **Acoustic Traveler**, carries a double meaning as McEuen shows off impressive multi-instrumentality (banjo, fiddle, dulcimer, guitar, koto, lap steel, mandolin) on a wide range of genres ranging from Eastern European to Celtic, Spanish to Appalachian.

Will the Circle Be Unbroken/United Artists/1972
Will the Circle Be Unbroken, Vol. 2/Universal/1988
String Wizards I/Vanguard/1991
The Wild West/Aspen Recording Society/1993
String Wizards II/Vanguard/1994
Acoustic Traveler/Vanguard/1996
String Wizard Picks: The Best of John McEuen/Vanguard/1997
Moonlight Dancing/Vanguard/1998

John McEuen Fan Club, 6044 Deal Ave., Nashville, TN 37209

John McEuen: The Five String Marval //www.johnmceuen.com

Johnmceuen@aol.com

Bluegrass: John McEuen //www.banjo.com/profiles/JohnMcEuen.html

John McEuen AOL Folder: Entertainment>Music>Chat & Messages>Music Community>Folk/Acoustic

Wes McGhee

Singer/Songwriter
Lutterworth, Leicestershire, England; October 26, 1948-

An all too common scenario for American alt. country singer/songwriters has been rejection in their own country but success and even cult status in Europe e.g. Richard Dobson, Pinto Bennett, Calvin Russell, et al. A rare reversal of this pattern is represented in the career of British performer Wes McGhee who has not achieved much recognition in Great Britain but has been heartily accepted in the United States especially among Texas' alt. country music elite. During the 1960s, McGhee worked as a lead guitarist on the Merseybeat scene but in the 1970s in collaboration with another British musician, Arthur Anderson, switched toward pub rock and then country rock. In the early 1980s, McGhee began to visit Texas where he developed a working relationship with a number of Austin musicians including Ponty Bone, Alvin Crow, Jimmy Dale Gilmore, Freddy Krc, Lloyd Maines, and Kimmie Rhodes. They backed him on two albums recorded in Texas, **Landing Lights** and **Thanks for the Chicken**, a double live LP done at the legendary Soap Creek Saloon. Still unheralded in Britain, McGhee signed with Bug Music (U.S.) and recorded **Zacatecas** which included the beautiful epic ballad "Monterey" (he had become fond of Tex-Mex during his years in Texas). Wes finally got a deal with a British label in 1991, and this resulted in a compilation of songs from his previous records called **Neon and Dust**. Into the late 1980s and early 1990s, he maintained his Texas connections with Freddy Krc's Shakin' Apostles and as Kimmie Rhodes' lead guitarist for a time; on 1994's **Border Guitars,** he was assisted once again by Rhodes, Krc, and Bone. Many of the Texas artists with which McGhee has been affiliated were featured on a 1996 retrospective of his work, **Heartache Avenue: Classic Recordings**. This was followed up by **Backbeat** which presents more material from McGhee's early albums, a couple of outtakes from a TV documentary he worked on, some tunes by the Wes McGhee Band's alter ego, Vince & the Viletones, and two new songs. In 1997, Wes worked with Roxy Gordon, the Native American poet/musician from Texas, whose **Smaller Circles** (re-mastered by McGhee) is full of great country/rock songs with a focus on civil wrongs and rights.

Long Nights and Banjo Music/Terrapin UK/1978
Airmail/Terrapin/1980 (with B. J. Cole; Hank Wangford)
Landing Lights/TRP/1983
Thanks for the Chicken/TRP/1985 (live dbl. LP rec. in Texas)
Zacatecas/Bug/1986
Neon and Dust/Minidoka UK/1991
Border Guitars/Road Goes On Forever/1994
"Monterrey" on **Country**/Vinyl Junkie UK/1995

Heartache Avenue: Classic Recordings/Road Goes On
    Forever UK/1996
Backbeat/Road Goes on Forver UK/1998

Road Goes on Forever Web Site
//www.rgfrecords.demon.co.uk/

See Roxy Gordon; Freddy Krc; Kimmie Rhodes

Roger McGuinn

See The Byrds

Maria McKee

See Lone Justice

James McMurtry

Texas; Singer/Songwriter
Ft. Worth, Texas; March 18, 1962-

Singer/songwriter James McMurtry is the product of two venerable Texas storytelling traditions: novelists like his father Larry and the long line of troubadours from Guy Clark and Townes Van Zandt to Lyle Lovett and Robert Earl Keen. And although he spent most of his youth moving around from Virginia (boarding school) to Spain to Arizona and Alaska, it was in Texas where McMurtry found inspiration and increasing notoriety. He made his first public performances at a beer garden in Tucson and began writing songs (his first was "Talking at the Texaco") while in his late teens and, after a brief side trip to Alaska, moved to West Texas. Eventually, McMurtry ended up in San Antonio where he worked day jobs and played bars at night. His first break came in 1987 when he won a songwriting award in the New Folk category at Kerrville. Shortly thereafter, father Larry and John Mellencamp were working on a screen writing project (*Lonesome Dove*) and dad gave a demo of James' songs to John who was so impressed he agreed to produce his debut album, **Too Long in the Wasteland**. He also invited James to contribute to the soundtrack for the movie, *Falling From Grace*. In 1992, the younger McMurtry was part of the In Their Own Words songwriters tour and in the same year released his second recording, **Candyland**. McMurtry who is no slouch on electric guitar was helped on **Where'd You Hide the Body?** by several top pickers including Lloyd Maines, Stephen Bruton, and David Grissom (ex-Joe Ely Band). McMurtry's label, CBS, took the unusual step of asking a group of USC film majors to makes videos for all the songs on **Where'd You Hide the Body** and then releasing them as a special video promo. One tune from that collection, "Levelland" received a good deal of attention, and Robert Earl Keen covered it on his 1997 CD, **Picnic**. Unfortunately, sales of the recording were not great, and so McMurtry was dropped by CBS. He rebounded very well on Sugar Hill with **It Had to Happen** and **Walk Between the Raindrops** (produced by Lloyd Maines) which like his

previous efforts present gritty and insightful vignettes ("Sixty Acres"; "12 O'Clock"; "Every Little Bit Counts"; "Fast As I Can"; "Racing the Red Light"; "Airline Agent") drawn mainly from the underside of life.

Too Long in the Wasteland/CBS/1989
Interchords/CBS/1989 (promo LP with music and
    interview)
Candyland/CBS/1992
Where'd You Hide the Body/CBS/1995
It Had to Happen/Sugar Hill/1997
Walk Between the Raindrops/Sugar Hill/1998

Official James McMurtry Web Page
//www.sony.com/artists/jamesmcmurtry/

James McMurtry iMusic Showcase
//imusic.com/showcase/contemporary/jamesmcmurtry.html

Rob McNurlin

Singer/Songwriter
Kentucky; December 18, 1963-

Growing up listening to his parents 1950s rock 'n' roll and country albums, Rob McNurlin got his first guitar for Christmas at age 9 and decided he wanted to play like Johnny Cash. Then, after someone gave him a 45 of Dylan's "Gates of Eden," he added the harmonica and set his sights on becoming a singer/songwriter while still in high school. Drawing on a variety of other influences including Woody Guthrie, Jack Kerouac, and The Band, McNurlin devoted himself to a musical career full-time after graduation, performing solo until 1994 at which time he formed the Beatnik Cowboys to back him. Their first recording **Last of the Beatnik Cowboys** mixes blues, folk, country, gospel, and rock into a sound one reviewer called "smooth as barbed wire and as honest as the Bible." McNurlin's rough hewn vocals perfectly match his compositions such as "Lotta Good Men" ("I don't wanna die like Jack Kerouac"), "Ha, Ha, Ha (They're Laughin' at Me")," "Headin' Down the Valley," "Bottle of Yahoo," and the Guthrie/Dylanish "Strip Poker Waltz" and "Talkin' X-Communist Hoopla Blues."

In between several tours (one with Ramblin' Jack Elliott) around the U.S. in the late 1990s, McNurlin and the Cowboys did a couple of cassette recordings, **Jesus Was a Gypsy** and **Skinned Alive**. The latter is mostly covers of traditional songs ("Buffalo Skinners"; "Way Out There"; "Swing Low"; "Barbara Allen"; "In the Pines"; "Amazing Grace/The Weight") but also contains the original, "Cowboy Boot Heel" which became the title of his 1998 release of folk and country. In addition, McNurlin composed the music for two documentaries, *Kentucky, Land of Tomorrow* and *A Driving Tour*.

The Beatnik Cowboys: Bob Adkins (d); Daryl James (g);
Dave Prince (b,g); The BO Man (b)

Last of the Beatnik Cowboys/Buffalo Skinner/1995
Jesus Was a Gypsy/Buffalo Skinner/1996

Skinned Alive/Buffalo Skinner/1997
Cowboy Boot Heel/Buffalo Skinner/1998

Rob McNurlin/Buffalo Skinner Productions,
313 Prichard St., Ashland, KY 41102; 606-325-7178

jadkins@ramlink.net

Rob McNurlin/PoetMan Page //www.poetusa.com

The Meat Puppets

Cowpunk
Tempe, Arizona; 1981-

The exact time and place of the birth of that 1980s country rock hybrid known as "cowpunk" will always be open to debate, but one of the earliest out of the chute was the Meat Puppets. Their initial EP was straight noise rock, and a debut LP continued in this vein but contained some countryish undertones (most notably raging covers of "Walkin' Boss" and "Tumbling Tumbleweeds") that signaled things to come. **Meat Puppets II** took the punk world by surprise with its inspired merger of thrash, psychedelia, and twang. Over the next decade, the Meat Puppets veered erratically between a number of rock styles always finding a place for the desert country punk of **MPII** primarily on **Up on the Sun, Mirage,** and **Too High to Die.** And while other Arizona bands like Giant Sand and Green on Red explored similar territory none did it with quite the same manic flair as the Meat Puppets. However, the price of fame was high. In the late 1990s Cris Kirkwood became a full-blown junkie; his wife died of an overdose in August 1998, and Cris was careening further out of control or as brother Curt put it, "a suicide in progress." So, although technically still a band, the Meat Puppets' future was in very serious doubt. Then, at the beginning of 1999, things definitely began to get brighter as Cris entered treatment, and Curt hit the road with a completely new string of Meat Puppets. Moreover, Ryko released a live 1988 recording and planned to re-issue the Puppets entire SST catalog with extra tracks and extensive liner notes.

Cris Kirkwood (b,v); Curt Kirkwood (g,v); Derrick Bostrom (d)

In a Car/World Imitation/1981; SST/1985
Meat Puppets/SST/1983 (EP)
Meat Puppets II/SST/1984
Up on the Sun/SST/1985
"Magic Toy Missing" on **Leather Chaps and Lace Petticoats: Welcome to Alternative Country/** Anagram UK/1985
Out My Way/SST/1986 (EP)
Mirage/SST/1987
Huevos/SST/1987
Monsters/SST/1989
No Strings Attached/SST/1990
Forbidden Places/London/1991
Too High to Die/London/1994
No Joke/London/1995
Live in Montana 1988/Rykodisc/1999

Official Meat Puppets Home Page
//www.amug.org/~bsandig/puppets/ (links to many other MP sites)

The Meat Purveyors

Insurgent Country
Austin, Texas; 1996-

The first time I saw the Meat Purveyors was at a backyard BBQ they hosted during SXSW 1997 for members of Postcard 2, Bloodshot, *No Depression*, et al. They provided the musical entertainment (with help from Jon Langford), and their backporch/stage was a perfect venue for their style: old-time, bluegrass with an edge, a sort of combination of Freakwater, the Damnations, and the Bad Livers. At the time, I (and probably most everyone present) could see it was only a matter of time before the MPs landed a record deal and, sure enough, later in 1997, Bloodshot welcomed them into the insurgent country fold. Not bad for a group that had only begun playing together informally at a local coffeehouse less than a year and a half earlier. Originally known as the Texas Meat Purveyors (changed due to conflict of interest with a local organization of the same name), their debut, **Sweet in the Pants**, offers up some bizarre originals ("Go Out Smokin'"; "Biggest Mistake") by lead guitarist Bill Anderson and even stranger covers of "Burning Love" (Elvis), "The Bottle Let Me Down" (Merle), "Lady Muleskinner" (Jimmy Rodgers), and "Dempsey Nash" (Glass Eye). The playing (including ex-Bad Livers fiddler Ralph White) is raw and spirited, but the real standout is the lead singing of Jo Walston (ex-Joan of Arkansas) and her harmonies with bassist Cherilyn diMond. For the remainder of 1998, the MPs were on the go with a SXSW showcase (and backyard BBQ), a tour of the Midwest's top alt. country venues (many dates with label-mates Split Lip Rayfield), and covering "Take Me Back to Tulsa" for the Pinve Valley Cosmonauts/Bloodshot Records grand tribute to Bob Wills. In early 1999, Bloodshot released the Purveyors' single, **The Madonna Triology**, a tribute to "America's smutty pop iconoclast."

Bill Anderson (g,v); Cherilyn diMond (u.b.); Pete Styles (md); Jo Walston (l.v.)

Sweet in the Pants/Bloodshot/1998
"Take Me Back to Tulsa" on **The Pine Valley Cosmonauts Salute the Majesty of Bob Wills/** Bloodshot/1998
The Madonna Trilogy/Bloodshot/1999 (7")

The Meat Purveyors/Bloodshot Home Page
//www.bloodshotrecords.com

Cherilyn diMond/The Meat Purveyors
nakkoo@mail.utexas.edu

The Mekons

See Jon Langford

D. L. Menard (The Louisiana Aces)

Cajun Country
Erath, Louisiana; April 14, 1932-

D. L. Menard received his first guitar by mail order from Monkey Wards when he was 16 and just one year later was playing dances around his hometown of Erath, Louisiana. In 1951, a major turning point came for D. L. when he met Hank Williams who gave him advice about how to write a good country song. Menard took it to heart and in 1961 penned "The Back Door" which is now considered to be the second most famous Cajun song behind "Jolie Blonde." Blending traditional Cajun music with honky tonk, he became known as the "Cajun Hank Williams" for his songwriting and nasally Acadian twang. Over the years, he performed with Cajun legends (Dewey Balfa, Austin Pitre, Marc Savoy), with his band the Louisiana Aces, and as the Trio Cadien with Ken Smith and Eddie LeJeune. In 1989, Menard went to Nashville to record **Cajun Saturday Night**, one of the best all-time Cajun country albums. With backing from members of Hank, Sr.'s original band plus Jerry Douglas, Ricky Skaggs, Buck White and others, he recorded six of Williams songs plus six of his own. The NEA Folk Heritage Award winner continued to perform in the 1990s but when at home devoted his time to crafting fine traditional furniture (chairs and rockers mostly) in the one man factory next to his house. In 1998, PBS/Smithsonian Folkways tabbed D.L. for their documentary, *River of Song*, which showcases the various musical traditions along the Mississippi. Menard's segment finds him hosting a crawfish feast in his backyard and singing a few songs (on the **River of Song** CD) accompanied by the Louisiana Aces, Christine Balfa of Balfa Toujours, and accordionist Robert Jardell.

The Louisiana Aces: Blackie Forestier (acc,h.v.); Ken Smith (f).

D. L. Menard and the Louisiana Aces/Rounder/1974 (cs)
Under the Green Oak Tree (with Marc Savoy and Dewey Balfa)/Arhoolie/1977
The Back Door/Swallow/1980
Cajun Saturday Night/Rounder/1984
No Matter Where You At, There You Are/ Rounder/1988
Le Trio Cadein (with Ken Smith and Eddie LeJeune)/Rounder/1992
The Swallow Recordings (with Austin Pitre)/Ace UK/1993
Cajun Memories/Swallow/1996
River of Song/PBS Smithsonian Institution/1998 (documentary and CD)

D. L. Menard & The Louisiana Aces
//www.herschelfreemanagency.com/dlm.html

Mercury Dime

Tobacco Row; No Depression
Faith, North Carolina; c. 1994-

Mercury Dime is the embodiment of that rags to Rickenbackers story oft repeated in modern American music history; three high school buddies—Darryl Jones, Cliff Retallick, Eric Webster—from an obscure little hamlet (Faith, North Carolina) get together in a barn with a four track recorder to experiment with rock and traditional country, add a couple more members, form a band and before long, "Hey! Let's put on a show!" It happened just that way and playing at clubs in nearby Charlotte and other foci of the emerging North Carolina alt. country scene, Mercury Dime began to get noticed. In 1996 with Mitch Easter producing, they recorded **Baffled Ghosts**. Like another alt. country band from backroads America, the Bottle Rockets, they blend up roots rock with country (courtesy of moody pedal steel) and write about what they know best, the joys and sorrows of small town life. In addition to that Midwestern grain belt rock sound, Mercury Dime has touches of the distinctive Tobacco Row style of Jolene and Whiskeytown. With Easter once again at the helm, Mercury Dime recorded **Darkling** in 1997 (released 1998); it retains much of the somber roots rock feel of its predecessor but has a few late 1960s-early 1970s country rock touches as well.

Darryl Jones (p.s.); Jim Martin (d); Cliff Retallick (p,l.v.); Eric Webster (b); Alan Wyrick (g)

Baffled Ghosts/Opry Fired Hank/1996
"Dog Star" on **Revival 1: Brunswick Stew & Pig Pickin'**/Yep Roc/1997
"Are You Positive?" on **Revival 2: Kudzu & Hollerin' Contest**/Yep Roc/1997
Darkling/Yep Roc/1998

Mercury Dime, P.O. Box 27, Faith, NC 28041

Buddy Miller (Julie Miller)

Honky Tonk; Country Rock
Ohio; 1953-

Buddy Miller's 1995 debut, **Your Love and Other Lies,** seemed to signal the arrival of a newcomer to the ranks of alternative country, but he had actually been lurking around its fringes for years. In the 1960s and early 1970s, Miller kicked around the country playing in bluegrass, country rock, and even psychedelic bands before ending up in Austin where he joined a band called Rick Stein & the Alley Cats. He clicked immediately with their female singer, Julie Griffin, and after a few years, they moved to the Big Apple where the duo had a regular spot at the famous Lone Star Cafe. During this time, Julie suffered a mental breakdown and went back to Texas to join a Christian commune while Buddy stayed in New York working with Shawn Colvin for a while before rejoining and finally marrying Julie. Relocating to the West Coast, Julie made several recordings for the Christian label Word in Tacoma before the Millers made it to L.A. where Buddy hooked up with songwriter Jim Lauderdale who gave him a job in his band and connected him with Hightone Records. The result, **Your Love and Other Lies**, features Buddy's twangy lead guitar and vocals on originals (several co-written with Julie) and covers of the Louvins' "You're Running Wild" and Tom T. Hall's "That's How I Got to Memphis." Julie, Emmylou Harris, Lauderdale, Lucinda Williams, Gurf Morlix, and Donald Lindley lend support to the album which was one of the most highly praised of 1995. Basking in the spotlight after years behind the scenes, Miller kept very busy over the next two years as part of Hightone's Roadhouse Revival Tour (with Dale Watson, Dave Alvin, and Big Sandy), as guitarist for Emmylou's Wrecking Ball Tour, and as producer for Julie's Hightone debut **Blue Pony**. This recording echoes Julie's Christian music days on "All My Tears" (covered on **Wrecking Ball**) but has many country, rock, and pop elements as well. Meanwhile a number of Buddy's songs were picked up by Nashville artists, and his second, **Poison Love,** came out in the summer of 1997. Once again Julie, Emmylou, Lauderdale, Morlix, and Lindley are along as is Steve Earle (who called Buddy's debut "the country album of the decade") on a duet of the Johnny & Jack title track. Other highlights include the hillbilly romp "Love Snuck Up," the old Roger Miller/George Jones honky tonk hit "Nothing Can Stop Me," the Buddy/Julie penned "Don't Tell Me," and the timely "100 Million Little Bombs" about the danger of land mines. The Millers opened for Steve Earle during his early 1998 tour, and Buddy pulled double duty as Earle's lead guitarist. Later in the year, Emmylou Harris invited Buddy to be lead guitarist/harmony vocalist on her live recording, **Spyboy**.

Your Love and Other Lies/Hightone/1995
Blue Pony (Julie Miller)/Hightone/1997
Poison Love/Hightone/1997

Buddy Miller/Hightone Page
//www.hightone.com/bios/bmillerbio.html

Buddy Miller Web Page
//www.nashville.net/~kate/buddym.html

Julie Miller Web Page
//www.nashville.net/~kate/jmiller.html

See Steve Earle; Emmylou Harris

Chris Mills
Insurgent Country; Singer/Songwriter
Collinsville, Illinois; 1975-

Judging strictly by Chris Mills' innocent, almost cherubic face you wouldn't think of him as insurgent country. However, his grainy vocals (sometimes whispered, sometimes growled), dusky originals, and edgy sound (sometimes acoustic, sometimes electric) have made him one of the most rapidly rising talents in Chicago's prestigious alt. country community. His

debut CD, **Nobody's Favorite**, bears the unmistakable imprint of that little old band from southern Illinois, Uncle Tupelo. Mills' singing (a Farrar/Tweedy cross), bare instrumentation, and choice of themes ("Trouble Me No More"; "Stone Walls, Steel Bars"; "Killers"; "Nowhere Town"; "Keep the Corpse Beautiful") are reminiscent of UT's acoustic country/rock material. The follow-up, **Every Night Fight for Your Life**, while retaining remnants of this formula, shows a much more insurgent country influence with its electric guitar based fusion of country, folk, and punk. His high regard among Chicago's alt. country elite was evidenced by his inclusion (doing "Home in San Antone") on Jon Langford's Pine Valley Cosmonauts acclaimed **...Salute the Majesty of Bob Wills**.

"Nowhere Town" b/w "Stone Walls, Steel Bars"/Argyle Manor/1997 (7")
Nobody's Favorite/Sugar Free/1997
Every Night Fight for Your Life/Sugar Free/1998
"Home in San Antone" on **The Pine Valley Cosmonauts Salute the Majesty of Bob Wills**/Bloodshot/1998

Chris Mills/Sugar Free Records, P.O. Box 14166, Chicago, IL 60614; 312-528-7080

Chris Mills/Sugar Free Records Page
//www.sugarfreerecords.com/

Chris Mills/Centerstage Web Page
//centerstage.net/chicago/music/whoswho/Chris Mills.html

Miss Xanna Don't (The Wanted; The Willin')
Country Rock; Gay Country
Boston, Massachusetts; 1990-1993; Austin, Texas; 1993-

In the early 1990s, Boston was home to a thriving alternative country scene with bands like the Blood Oranges, Swingin' Steaks, and The Willin'. The latter was fronted by the dynamic Miss Xanna Don't who became famous not only for her incredible beehive hairdo (all natural) but also for her belt-it-out country vocals. Prior to this, Miss Xanna had a pretty full resume: professional jello wrestler, the role of Mary Magdalene in *Jesus Christ Superstar*, writer for a local arts magazine, avant-garde opera singer, host of her own radio show (Xanna's Corner) plus numerous appearances on Boston television programs. However, it was as an alt. country act that Miss Xanna had the greatest impact. Miss Xanna was honored by Boston fans and critics with various awards including nominations for Best Country Act, 1989-1993 (winner in 1990), Female Personality of the Year (1989), Best Female Vocalist (1993), and the title of The Country Queen of Boston. Surprisingly, the group never cut a full length recording but did appear on two local compilation CDs contributing "Dead Flowers" to the **Boston Gets Stoned** tribute to the Rolling Stones and "Midnight Blue" (about a NYC cable porno show) to the roots rock collection, **North By Northeast**. She made a video of her song "Train to Satanville" but decided that Boston was not the place to pursue a full time musical career. Miss

Xanna moved to Austin in 1993 and dove right in; she was selected as Austin's representative to SXSW in 1994 and with her new band, the Wanted, played the city's most important venues (opening for Lucinda Williams, Don Walser, Bottle Rockets, Southern Culture on the Skids). Interestingly enough, with her gender bending appearance and delivery, Miss Xanna may have been too alternative even for Austin so her bid to become The Country Queen of Austin was slow although the *American-Statesman* dubbed her Austin's Underground Country Queen. However, she remained undaunted and, in addition to performing, was very active in promoting local acts and in women's and gay/lesbian issues through her newsletter *Don't Label It*. Throughout 1998, Xanna continued opening for a variety of local and touring acts including Pansy Division, El Vez, Impotent Sea Snakes, and the Ex-Husbands. Known now as The Callas of Cowpunk (Don Walser's The Pavarotti of the Plains), she and the Wanted cut a new record **The Cowboy Chronicles** which features two songs, a reworking of Sonny & Cher's "A Cowboy's Work Is Never Done" and "Cowboy On a Railroad Track" aka "The Janet Reno Song." By the way, her name comes from an incident with a heckler who kept yelling "Do such and such song..." to which she replied "Miss Xanna Don't!"

The Willin': Jim Cuniff (d); Beth Grey (b); Tony Hecht (g); Dan Kellar (f)

"Dead Flowers" on **Boston Gets Stoned**/Botown/1990
"Midnight Blue" on **North by Northeast**/
    Northeastern/1991
Ode to Punk/Don't Label It/1992 (CS single); Triggerfish
    Ger./1996
"Death & Texas" on **L'Austin, Tx Space: The
    Triggerfish Music Compilation, #1**/
    Triggerfish Ger./1997
The Cowboy Chronicles/Don't Label It/1998 (7")

Miss Xanna, P.O. Box 3859, Austin, TX 78704; 512-973-9473, (fax) 512-973-9472

Missxanna@yahoo.com

Moby Grape

Roots Rock; Country Rock
San Francisco, California; 1966-

The story of the dramatic rise and fall of Moby Grape in the late 1960s is one of the most famous in rock mythology. Led by an erratic prodigy named Skip Spence, they had the complete package and for one year (1966-1967), it seemed they might live up to their billing as America's answer to the Stones and Beatles. Their self-titled debut is now acknowledged as one of the great roots rock recordings of all time with an irresistible blend of rock 'n' roll, folk, acid rock, blues, and even some early experiments with country rock. Then, beset by bad management decisions, legal hassles, drug excesses, and mental illness (Spence), Moby Grape began to slowly and inexorably disintegrate. They kept making albums in the late 1960s, but the

quality was spotty and never came even close to measuring up to **Moby Grape**. Still, as the terrific retrospective, **Vintage Grape**, shows there were some bright spots here and there. Of particular interest to the history of alt. country is the 1969 release **Truly Fine Citizen** which was a pioneering country rock recording right in there with work done by Buffalo Springfield, the Byrds, and Flying Burrito Brothers during the same era. Skip Spence also managed to make a memorable solo called **Oar** after he was released from Bellevue Hospital in 1968. In 1999, a group of musicians including Jay Farrar, the Bottlerockets, Wilco, Alejandro Escovedo, Tom Waits, and Mudhoney paid hoamge to him with **More Oar**, a tribute CD covering songs from **Oar**. And, believe it or not, after years of trials and tribulations, Moby Grape reunited in 1998 with a tour and plans for a new recording.

Peter Lewis (g,v); Jerry Miller (g); Bob Mosley (b,v); Skip Spence (g,v); Don Stevenson (d)

Moby Grape/Columbia/1967
Wow & Grape Jam/Columbia/1968
Moby Grape '69/Columbia/1969
Truly Fine Citizen/Columbia/1969
Oar (Skip Spence)/Columbia/1969
20 Granite Creek/Reprise/1971
Vintage: The Very Best of Moby Grape/Sony
    Legacy/1993
More Oar: A Tribute to Skip Spence/1999

The Ark: The Moby Grape Home Page
//www.geocities.com/sunsetstrip/1256/

Katy Moffatt

Singer/Songwriter
Ft. Worth, Texas; 1950-

Katy Moffatt is one of the great survivors in the alt. country singer/songwriter community. Back in the late 1970s, she was a promising country singer who cut three albums for Columbia (only two were released). The first, **Katy,** was on the country rock side, but the follow-up, **Kissin' in the California Sun,** was more pop oriented, and Moffatt found herself caught in the musical nether region between the two genres. When her Columbia recordings failed commercially, Moffatt moved on to an independent label where she had several hits and a nomination for ACM Best New Female Vocalist. However, contract and label problems plus her out of the mainstream style kept Katy's career from taking off. Then, in the early 1980s, after touring in the U.S. and worldwide as an opening act for a variety of performers, Moffatt settled in L.A. where she became part of the incipient alt. country scene. Her "Love Only Love" was included on the first installment of the **A Town South of Bakersfield** series. In 1987, she signed on with a label (Philo/Rounder) that could appreciate her style. Around the same time, Moffatt met Tom Russell at Kerrville, and this was the beginning of a long and fruitful songwriting collaboration. Her albums for Philo, **Walking on the Moon**, **Child Bride**, and

The Evangeline Hotel, contain numerous Moffatt/Russell compositions. Throughout the 1990s, Katy remained very active recording solo for Watermelon (**Hearts Gone Wild**; **Midnight Radio**), with her singer/songwriter brother Hugh, with Kate Brislin, for the Merle Haggard tribute album **Tulare Dust**, and as a guest on many albums. Along the way, she endured her share of problems including bouts with T.B. and back surgery, but the experiences served to enrich her writing and performing rather than deterring them. Moffatt appeared on two records by Tom Russell (**The Long Way Around**; **Song of the West**) and one by Dave Alvin (**Interstate City**) in 1997, and their label, Hightone, signed her in 1998. With Andrew Hardin on guitar she recorded **Angel Town** which offers covers of Cole Porter, Steve Goodman, Chris Smither, David Olney, and three tunes co-written with old friend Russell.

Katy/Columbia/1976
Kissin' in the California Sun/Columbia/1977
"Love and Only Love" on **A Town South of Bakersfield, Vol. 1**/Restless/1985
Walking on the Moon/Philo/1987; 1989
Child Bride/Philo/1989
Dance Me Outside (with Hugh Moffatt)/Philo/1992
Indoor Fireworks/Red Moon Switz./1992
The Greatest Show on Earth/Philo/1993
Evangeline Hotel/Philo/1993 (reissue of **Greatest Show on Earth**)
Hearts Gone Wild/Watermelon/1994
"I Can't Be Myself" on **Tulare Dust**/Hightone/1994
Sleepless Nights (with Kate Brislin)/Rounder/1996
Midnight Radio/Watermelon/1996
Angel Town/Hightone/1998

Katy Moffatt World Headquarters, P.O. Box 334, O'Fallon, IL 62269

Midnight Radio: The Katy Moffatt Home Page //members.aol.com/klmoffatt/index.html

kmwhq@mcleodusa.net

The Evangeline Hotel //www.phoenix.net/~nishimi/moffatt.html

Katy Moffatt/Hightone Page //www.hightone.com

See Tom Russell

Erik Moll
Austin; Singer/Songwriter
Wisconsin; September 7, 1948-

If you put all the Austin singer/songwriters in one room, Erik Moll would still be easy to pick out. Tall and lanky, his distinctive and ever present Mexican style straw hat stands out in any crowd. And, in a career that spans three decades, Moll has proven to be outstanding as a performer and songwriter as well. Traveling around California, Texas, and Scandinavia early on, he settled in Austin in the late 1980s. His first recording, **Wayward Ways**, was an engaging selection of country, blues, and swing originals; in 1990, Moll's Scandinavian connection paid off when Norwegian country artist Steinar Albrigtsen

chose six Moll songs for his double platinum, **Alone Too Long**. A year of touring with Albrigtsen followed and in the early 1990s, more Moll originals were covered by Albrigtsen and other Norwegian artists. Back in Texas, Moll began performing with multi-instrumental wizard Erik Hokkanen. They played a number of Kerrville Folk Festivals and in 1992 released **Erik & Erik,** an exceptional combination of Hokkanen's hot picking and Moll's first class writing. Hokkanen also appeared on Moll's second album, **In the Shadows**, along with Christine Albert, Ponty Bone, Steinar Albrigtsen, Paul Glasse, and Marty Muse. This recording helped reinforce Moll's reputation and following not only in Austin but also in Scandinavia. His stature in Europe was further enhanced by inclusion on the 1997 alt. country compilation (**Jukebox Cowboy**) from the U.K.'s Vinyl Junkie label. Back home in Wimberley in 1998, Moll recorded **Most of All**, an impressive montage of Cen-Tex musical traditions.

Wayward Ways/Armadillo/1988 (CS)
Erik & Erik (with Erik Hokkanen)/Fire Ant/1992
In the Shadows/Fire Ant/1994
"Let Me Mend Your Broken Heart" on **Jukebox Cowboy**/Vinyl Junkie UK/1997
Most of All/Fire Ant/1998

Erik Moll, P.O. Box 1253, Wimberley, TX 78676; 512-847-2633

Erik Moll Web Page //www.flash.net/~emoll/index.htm

emoll1@flash.net

See Erik Hokkanen

The Mollys
Celtic Tex-Mex Country
Tucson, Arizona; 1990-

Celtic Tex-Mex Country? Imagine equal parts Los Lobos and the Pogues/Black 47 with a splash of American folk/country, and you've got the richly unique flavor of the Mollys. This unlikely but surprisingly compatible mix comes from the band's co-founders, Nancy McCallion and Catherine Zavala. Friends since high school, they played in a punk band (Nadine & the MoPhonics) for a time, then went their separate ways for a time before reuniting in 1990 to form the Mollys. Drawing on their respective Irish and Mexican-American backgrounds, they began to piece together a Celtic Tex-Mex crazyquilt with help from Dan Sorenson (ex-MoPhonics) on bass, Kevin Schramm on accordion, and Gary Mackender on drums. Their first two recordings, **Tidings of Comfort and Joy** and **This is My Round**, leaned heavily in the Celtic direction with support from Irish musicians Eugene O'Donnell and Mick Moloney. However, the Mollys also integrated old-time country and Tex-Mex, sometimes on individual tunes or seamlessly interwoven with a Celtic song. **Hat Trick** added some endearing country elements ("Odessa"; "Came for a Dance"; "That's All You Do") with the addition of Steve English on pedal steel. The earthy, gruff vocals of McCallion and Zavala and the band's instrumental (especially Schramm) adaptability have the special ability to transport the listener across many locales: swaying or raucously jigging in a pub ("Jock in London/I Don't Wanna Go to Bed"; "Long is The Dark"), polkaing in a cantina ("La Llorona"; "La Filamena"), waltzing in a honky tonk ("Came for Dance"), or sitting on the front porch of a shack in the Appalachian coal fields ("I'll Be True to My Love"; "Prospector's Lament"). Such diversity has made the Mollys perennial favorites not only at home (Tammies for Best Ethnic/Traditional Band, 1993-1997 and Band of the Year, 1997) but also on the North American folk/Celtic festival circuit, and even on the world scene with inclusion of their song "On We Go" on Putamayo's **Celtic Women of the World**. 1998's **Moon Over the Interstate**, perhaps their strongest effort yet, has more catchy accordion-driven Tex-Mex/Celtic/country/rock which is most vividly presented on the medley "Holding On/I Want to Polka/Skoda Lasky (Beer Barrel Polka)/Carnival Mundo." There's even a *norteno* with yodeling called "Mi Casita."

Gary Mackender (d); Nancy McCallion (g,hm,wh,l.v.); Kevin Schramm (acc,bj,g,wh); Dan Sorenson (b); Catherine Zavala (f,g,md,l.v.)

Tidings of Comfort and Joy/The Mollys/1994
"Rosie" on **Occupational Hazard**/Transatlantic/1994
"La Llorona" on **Faces of the Sun**/SWSW1/1994
"All for Me Grog/Youngest Daughter" on **Manana: Tammies '94**/Epiphany/1994
This Is My Round/Apolkalips Now/1995
Welt The Floor/Apolkalips Now/1995
"All Around My Hat" on **Caramba!: Tammies '95**/Epiphany/1995
"On We Go" on **Women of the World: Celtic**/Putamayo/1995
Hat Trick/Apolkalips Now/1997
Wankin' Out West (Live)/Apolkalips Now/1997
Moon Over the Interstate/Apolkalips Now/1998

The Mollys, P.O. Box 40940, Tucson, AZ 85717

The Mollys Home Page //www.themollys.com

mollys@mollys.com

The Moonee Valley Drifters

Honky Tonk; Western Swing; Country Rock
Melbourne, Australia; Mid 1980s-Late 1990s

After WWII, Detroit was not only the major automotive center in the world but with its large working class population, a hotbed for country music. One young man who fell under its sway was Tom Forsell. He listened to the greats on record, caught Grand Old Opry acts when they visited the Motor City, and learned to play guitar, harmonica, accordion, and mandolin. After graduating from college, in 1973, Forsell moved to Melbourne, Australia to teach in the public schools never figuring he would find much of the country music he had grown

to love. However, he was pleasantly surprised to find that Australia had a rich tradition of country music and a pool of country music lovers with whom he could jam. Forsell and a group of his new friends formed the Moonee Valley Drifters in the 1980s and devoted themselves to playing vintage (1940s-1960s) country. Several personnel changes followed, but eventually a steady line up was assembled with pedal steel player Rick Dempster who had been with a very popular local western swing band, the Dancehall Racketeers. With sponsorship from the Brunswick City Council (!), the MVD recorded their first album, **Boogie Woogie Fever**, which covers Moon Mullican, Commander Cody, Gene Autry, and Marty Robbins as well as Forsell originals. Their follow-up, **Juke Joint Johnny**, showed greater diversity on more of Forsell's songs and tunes by Buck Owens, Hank Thompson, Merle Travis, Curtis Gordon, and Syd King plus Cajun and Tex-Mex. During this time, Forsell fronted an old-time country band called Hillbilly Fever that specialized in Delmore and Louvin Brothers style music. The Moonee Valley Drifters came to an end in the late 1990s when Forsell decided to move back to the U.S.

James Black (p); Ed Colbourne (d,v); Rick Dempster (hm,p.s.,v); Tom Forsell (g,md,v); Paul Pyle (b,v); Brendan Shearson (l.g.,v)

Boogie Woogie Fever/Brunswick Australia/1988
Juke Joint Johnny/Brunswick/1994

Brunswick Recordings, 10 Dawson St., Brunswick, Victoria 3056, Australia

See Lucky Oceans; Doug Mansfield; The Starliners

Neil Mooney (Florida Slim)

TSOB
Los Angeles, California; 1990s

Although a number of reviewers spoke of Neil Mooney's 1997 **Ranchstyle** as his debut, in reality, he had been part of California alt. country for a number of years in the guise of Florida Slim. His first musical training was on guitar at D. D. Yoakley's Banjo Ranch when he was growing up in Florida, and Mooney's first job as a professional musician came as leader of a New York City rockabilly band, the Drive-Ins. They were riding high until heroin addiction did in the rhythm section leaving Mooney disenchanted and about ready to give up on music. He was revived by mega-doses of Hank Williams' records and in the early 1990s relocated to L.A. where he took on a new identity as Florida Slim and the Hurricanes. They became regulars at the Palomino and the White Horse Tavern and cut the country rocking "Ain't Life Grand" for volume three of **A Town South of Bakersfield**. The Hurricanes, which at one time or other included Russell Scott and Slim Evans (ex-Rank & File), were notorious for high energy rockabilly/cowpunk highlighted by Slim's delivery of "white trash" rants stripped down to his boxer shorts. In time, Mooney grew tired of his Slim alter-ego and began writing more introspective, "heartfelt" songs in a straight ahead country rock, honky tonk vein. Dropping the Florida Slim moniker, he began performing and recording under his own name. Neil "Don't Call Me Florida Slim" Mooney's "debut" **Ranchstyle** which retains some echoes of his Hurricane days, is a potent mix of TSOB styles: honky tonk ("Start the Music Without Me"; "Back to the Wild Side"), teardrop shuffle ("Blue Moon Blue"), country rock ("Blue Train"; "Givin' Up"), Tex-Mex ("Fool's Gold" with Chris Gaffney on accordion), reverby Roy Orbison/Chris Isaak ballad ("Swanee"), redneck stomp ("Blazing Trailer of Love"), and rockabilly ("Hot Rod Women"). There are even covers of the old standard "Sea of Heartbreak" and f**k singer Phil Ochs,' "Chords of Fame." Mooney's powerful baritone handled it all with flair and announced the advent of an important "new" guy on the block. In 1998, Mooney produced a compilation to showcase the newest generation of alt. country in a town south of Bakersfield. **L.A. County Line** features an eclectic roster including raucous country roots-rock (The Groovy Rednecks; Trailer Park Casanovas), hillbilly boogie (Deke Dickerson; The Lucky Stars), honky tonk (Chris Gaffney; Rosie Flores, Little Miss Tammy Smith, Dan Janisch, Mooney), California country-rock (Thousand Dollar Wedding), ballad (Annie Harvey), old-timey (The Losin' Brothers), and Tex-Mex (Mooney & Gaffney).

"Ain't Life Grand" on **A Town South of Bakersfield, Vol. 3**/Restless/1992
Ranchstyle/Strawdog/1997
"Faded Rose" (with Chris Gaffney) on **L.A. County Line: A Country Compilation From the City of Angels**/Strawdog/1998

Neil Mooney c/o Strawdog Records, P.O. Box 26584, Los Angeles, CA 90026

Neil Mooney Home Page //members.aol.com/neilmooney/
NeilMooney@aol.com or Ranchoteca@aol.com

Moonshine Willy

Insurgent Country
Chicago, Illinois; 1993-

Moonshine Willy was one of the charter members of the insurgent country movement that emerged in Chicago in the early 1990s. Drawing on a diversity of styles, they created a hard driving bluegrass/rockabilly/punk sound. Lead singer and songwriter, Kim Docter grew up in Southern California where she honed her deep, honey rich vocals in the Holy Sisters of the Gaga Dada and a folkabilly outfit, Vavoleen. Multi-instrumentalist, Nancy Rideout, learned her freewheeling style on lead guitar, banjo, and mandolin with East Coast bands like the punkgrass group, the Monsignors. Stand up bassist and gut bucket vocalist Mike Luke (native Chicagoan) played in a Nashville country band, Longhorn, and then in Chicago with

Rockin' Billy and the Wild Coyotes, while fiddle player Rachel Ferro (also from Chicago) came from a background in classical music. These four and a drummer (the first of many) formed Moonshine Willy in 1993. Just two years later, their "Way Out West" was the opening shot on Bloodshot's **For a Life of Sin** compilation. With its brash hillbilly/punk style and bizarre twist on country themes, this song set the insurgent country tone. In 1995, Moonshine Willy's debut CD **Pecadores** showcased Docter's darkly humorous originals ("Baby Alive"; "Bare Bones"; "Red Cross"; "Daddy Cried") plus several covers including "Great Atomic Power" (Louvins) and two amusing Docter/Luke duets, "You're the Reason Our Kids Are Ugly" and "Jackson." A subsequent, grueling tour schedule that included many openings for Southern Culture on the Skids gave Moonshine Willy greater exposure outside Chicago as did more recordings. A track on the second insurgent anthology, **Hell-Bent**, and the single "George Set Me Straight," about a woman who is given a message by a vision of George Strait, were followed by their second full length recording, **Bold Displays of Imperfection**. Once again propelled by Docter's resonant vocals, Ferro's fiery sawing, and Rideout's no-holds-barred picking, Moonshine Willy delivers an exceptional collection of punkabilly, all drawn from Docter's vivid imagination. But, here, in addition to their straight ahead hoe-down tunes ("Eatin' Crow"; "Message From the Grave"; "Glorybone"; "Brady's Leap"), Moonshine Willy throw in some slower paced songs ("River"; "Gone Far Away") showing off the "delicate" side of Docter's vocal range. In early 1997, Rideout departed to join a punk band and drummer Chris Ganey moved on to play jazz. They were replaced by George Goehl a multi-instrumentalist with a bluegrass background and by a drummer named, believe it or not, Lance Willy. Chuck Uchida joined Moonshine Willy on guitar for their 1998 **Bastard Child**, a melange of "mutant bluegrass pop" with more clever Docter originals and covers of Human League, the Mekons, and Black Oak Arkansas. By year's end, Ferro, Goehl, and Willy were out, Jessica Billey (fiddle), Chris Estrada (mandolin), and Ganey were in, and Docter had given birth to her first child.

Jessica Billey (f,1998-); Kim Docter (g,v); Chris Estrada (md,1998-); Rachel Ferro (f,1993-1998); George Goehl (bj,l.g.,md,1997-1998); Chris Ganey (d,1995-1997;1998-); Mike Luke (b,v); Nancy Rideout (l.g.,1992-1997); Chuck Uchida (g,1998-); Lance Willy (d,1997-1998)

"Way Out West" on **For A Life of Sin**/Bloodshot/1994
"Baby Alive"/"Nevermore" b/w "Alone"/Bloodshot/1994
Pecadores/Bloodshot/1995
"Roulette Wheel" on **Hell-Bent**/Bloodshot/1995
"Complicated Game" b/w "George Set Me Straight"/Bloodshot/1996 (7")
Bold Displays of Imperfection/Bloodshot/1996
Bastard Child/Bloodshot/1998

Moonshine Willy, P.O. Box 577217, Chicago, IL 60657-7217

Alison Moorer

Singer/Songwriter
Frankville, Alabama; 1972-

She seemed to come out of nowhere in 1998 with an auspicious debut not only as a singer in Robert Redford's *The Horse Whisperer* but also with a highly acclaimed album, **Alabama Song**. In fact, Alison Moorer had been working in the shadows for a number of years in Nashville just waiting for the chance to show what she could do. Raised in southern Alabama, her sister Shelby saw her through the teenage years after their father murdered their mother and committed suicide. Upon graduation from the University of South Alabama in 1993, Alison moved to Nashville where her sister (now Shelby Lynne) had developed a moderately successful solo career. She sang harmony vocals for Lynne and also cut some demos with new songwriting partner and husband Doyle Primm. Meanwhile, Moorer was invited to do a song for an *Austin City Limits* tribute to Walter Hyatt in 1996 and that same year contributed stand-out harmonies to alt. country newcomer Lonesome Bob's **Things Fall Apart**. Eventually, she got the attention of MCA's Tony Brown who got her the role singing "A Soft Place to Fall" (co-written with Gwil Owen) in *The Horse Whisperer* and a contract to make **Alabama Song**, one of the most real country albums to come out of Music City in years. And though she has the image and voice the Nashville hit makers drool over, Moorer resisted their advances (at least in 1998), choosing instead to throw her hat into the alt. country ring with the likes of Steve Earle, Lucinda Williams, Buddy Miller, and Dave Alvin. "A Soft Place to Fall" received an Oscar nomination for Best Original Song, and Moorer performed it on the Academy Awards Show in 1999.

> "A Soft Place to Fall" on **The Horse Whisperer/**
> MCA/1998
> **Alabama Song**/MCA/1998

Alison Moorer/MCA Page //www.mca.com

Tom Morrell and The Time-Warp Tophands

Pedal Steel; Western Swing
Little Elm, Texas; Early 1990s-

Tom Morrell is without doubt the most prolific Western swing musician of the last ten years. Since the early 1990s, from his home base in the tiny Texas town of Little Elm, he has made nine recordings in what he calls the **How the West Was Swung** series. Each volume presents Morrell and his steel guitar (1953 pedalless Bigsby) supported by a varying cast of Time-Warp Top Hands (large band and small combo) plus guest musicians on Western swing standards (mostly Bob Wills), Eastern swing done Western swing style, and Morrell's instrumental originals. Inaugurating the series was **How the West Was Swung** with ex-Playboy Leon Rausch and cowboy singing great Don Edwards carrying the vocals on classics including "I Can't Go on This Way," "Honeysuckle Rose," and "Hang Your Head in Shame." This was followed by two volumes with a Western swing big band playing the music of Bob Wills and Tommy Duncan. **Let's Ride With Bob and Tommy** and **Let's Take Another Ride with Bob and Tommy** once again have Leon Rausch on lead vocals with Playboy alumni Bob Boatright and Tommy Allsup. Next came two recordings of "jazz oriented Western swing," the all instrumental **Pterodactyl Tales** and **Uptown**. The former employed a small ensemble on take-offs of "Mood Indigo" ("Moo-Indigo"), "Moten Swing" ("Mutton Swing"), "Bluesette" ("Moo-Sette") and Morrell's steel instrumentals with a Jurassic Park flavor, "Dinosaur Droppings," "Room Full of Reptiles," and "Brontasaur Breath." **Uptown** is Western and Eastern swing standards anchored by the vocals of Rausch and ex-Asleep at the Wheel diva, Chris O'Connell. After another album of Wills style Western swing, **Smoke a Little of This**, came an all instrumental recording, **No Peddlers Allowed** powered by five non-pedal steel players including Morrell, Herb Remington, and John Ely. In 1995, Morrell and the Top Hands had a cut, "Mississippi Delta Trilogy," included on the *Texas Monthly* produced **Contemporary Texas Swing** and in 1996 came two full length recordings, **On the Way** and **The Return of No Peddlers Allowed**. However, 1997 started out on a bad note when a fire ravaged Morrell's home and studio, but Tom announced his intention to rebuild and keep on swingin'. In 1998, he and the Top Hands backed Don Edwards on his excellent live tribute recording, **My Hero Gene Autry,** worked with Leon Rausch on his **Deep in the Heart of Texas** and **Close to You: A 20 Song Salute to the Music of Cindy Walker,** and prepared Volume 10 of the **How the West Was Swung** series.

The Time Warp-Top Hands: Mark Abbott (b,h.v.); Dave Alexander (trp); Bob Boatright (f); Rich O'Brien (l.g.)

> **How the West Was Swung, Vol. 1**/WR/1990 (CS)
> **How the West Was Swung, Vol. 2: Let's Ride With
> Bob and Tommy**/WR/1991 (CS)
> **How the West Was Swung, Vol. 3: Let's Take Another
> Ride With Bob and Tommy**/WR/1992 (CS)
> **How the West Was Swung, Vol. 4: Pterodactyl Ptales/**
> WR/1993
> **How the West Was Swung, Vol. 5: Uptown**/WR/1994
> **How the West Was Swung, Vol. 6: Smoke a Little of
> This**/WR/1995
> "Mississippi Delta Trilogy" on **Contemporary Texas
> Swing**/Texas Monthly/1995
> **How the West Was Swung, Vol. 7: No Peddlers
> Allowed**/WR/1995
> **How the West Was Swung, Vol. 8: On the Way/**
> WR/1996
> **How the West Was Swung, Vol. 9: The Return of No
> Peddlers Allowed**/WR/1996

My Hero Gene Autry (Don Edwards)/Western Jubilee
Shanachie/1998

Tom Morrell/WR Records, P.O. Box 248, Hunt, TX 78024;
830-238-4612

Tom Morrell/WR Records Page
//wr-records.com/tophands.htm

See Don Edwards; Ethyl and Methyl

R. B. Morris

Singer/Songwriter
Knoxville, Tennessee

R. B. Morris spent his early years knocking around Tennessee playing in a variety of bands from old-time Appalachian to rock, devouring the writings of novelists like James Joyce and Arthur Rimbaud, absorbing the poetry of both Bob Dylan and the Chinese bard, Han-Shan. After a period as a world traveler and hermit in the hills of Tennessee, Morris went to San Francisco where he was influenced by the Beats to turn to prose and poetry. Returning to Knoxville, he wrote poetry, edited an avant-garde magazine, *Hard Knox Review,* and wrote *The Man Who Lives Here is Loony*, a one person play about the life of Tennessee writer James Agee (he also took the lead role in a video version of the play). When Morris returned to music in the mid-1990s, his years as poet and actor showed clearly in his songs, recording (**Local Man**, 1992), and live performances in Nashville where he drew attention from the likes of Steve Earle, Lucinda Williams, and John Prine. The latter signed him to Oh Boy Records and in 1997 released Morris' **Take That Ride**. With guest appearances by Prine and Williams, it brews up blues, country, rock, and spoken word with many songs drawn from Morris' essays for the *Hard Knox Review* including "They Say There's a Time," "Bottom of the Big Black Hull," and "Hell on a Poor Boy" plus a cover of "The Ballad of Thunder Road." In between promoting his new recording, Morris worked with Iron John Webb on a new play called *The Poisoning of Robert Johnson*. He covered "Don't Forget the Coffee Billy Joe" on the 1998 tribute to one of country music's greatest poet/singers, Tom T. Hall and issued **The Knoxville Sessions**, a collection of avant-garde, beat poetry, funk, blues, polka, and country done with Hector Qirko and the Irregulars prior to **Take That Ride**. In early 1999, Morris jumped from Oh Boy to KOCH International.

Local Man/RBM/1992
"Roy" on **Nashville: The Other Side of the
   Alley**/Bloodshot/1996
Take That Ride/Oh Boy/1997
"Don't Forget the Coffee Billy Joe" on **Real: The Tom T.
   Hall Project**/Watermelon/1998
The Knoxville Sessions/RBM/1998
R. B. Morris/Oh Boy Home Page //www.ohboy.com/rb.html

Mount Pilot

Americana
Chicago, Illinois; 1994-

Although on the surface Mount Pilot might seem to be just another no depression knock off, a closer listen reveals a multifaceted band whose sound embraces the spectrum of Americana. The group originated in 1994 when two guitarists, Matt Weber and Jon Williams, began performing around the Windy City as an acoustic act. Weber's forte was Doc Watson flatpicking while Williams contributed a montage of styles drawn from Django Reinhardt, Merle Travis, Jerry Garcia, and Stevie Ray just to name a few. After two years as a duo, they teamed with two Northwestern University music majors, Chris Grady and Kevin O'Donnell, who brought a love for swing jazz to the mix. Taking the name Mount Pilot (think *Andy Griffith Show*), they cut a demo and sent it off to noted producer John Keane who volunteered to guide their first CD and helped them get a deal with Austin's Doolittle Records (he also plays pedal steel on their debut). **Help Wanted, Love Needed, Caretaker** which appeared in late summer 1997 is an impressive smorgasbord of traditional and contemporary Americana. There's old-timey/bluegrassy ("Rain"; "Arkansas Ambush"), mellow honky tonk ("Taken All I've Got"), jump blues ("I'm Gone"), 1960s-1970s country rock ("Gypsy Queen"), and several songs ("3 Years in October"; "Been Forgotten") that clearly fall into the no depression category. There are also several tunes ("Drop D Blues"; "County Swing"; "Cretin") that move back and forth across musical genres. Credit for this versatility is due mainly to Williams' guitar virtuosity, but Weber's vocals and traditional cum modern lyrics are no small part of Mount Pilot's appeal.

Christopher C. Grady (b,v); Kevin O'Donnell (d,perc); Matthew Weber (r.g.,l.v.); Jon Williams (l.g.,md,org,p,v) with John Keane (p.s.,b.v.)

Help Wanted, Love Needed, Caretaker/Doolittle/1997
Mount Pilot, P.O. Box 4700, Austin, TX 78765
Mount Pilot/Doolittle Home Page
//www.doolittle.com/bio_mount.html

Walter Mouton & The Scott Playboys

Cajun
Scott, Louisiana; 1952-

In 1952, at the age of 13, accordionist Walter Mouton started the Scott Playboys and nearly 50 years later, they're still going strong. Like many of the Cajun bands of the 1950s (Wandering Aces; Rambling Aces), Mouton and the Playboys combine traditional instruments (accordion; fiddle) with pedal steel for an energetic Cajun/country sound rarely found in modern Cajun bands (see The Bone Tones). But, don't expect these Cajun Music Hall of Fame members to come to your town any time soon; for over thirty years, they've played every Friday night at

La Poussiere in Breaux Bridge but due to day job commitments, they almost never tour except for the rare special event like the Accordion Kings (Round Rock, Texas) or Finger Lakes (New York) Grassroots Festivals. And, don't run out to your local record store searching for their CDs because they haven't made any. Surprisingly, in all these years, Mouton has only recorded one single (in 1973) and contributed two songs to the **J'ai Ete Au Bal** Cajun/zydeco compilation in 1990. Well, you always did want to visit the Bayou Country now didn't you?

"Lonely Girl's Waltz" b/w "Scott Playboys' Special"/Cajun Jamboree/1973 (7")
"J'ai Ete Au Bal" & "Convict Waltz" on **J'ai Ete Au Bal**/Arhoolie/1990

See The Bone Tones

Muleskinner

See David Grisman; Richard Greene; Bill Keith; Clarence White

Heather Myles

TSOB
Riverside, California

Heather Myles came out of the Southern California alt. country milieu in the early 1990s. The native Californian's feisty vocals and neo-Bakersfield sound caught the attention of Hightone Records which released her **Just Like Old-Times** in 1992. Produced by Bruce Bromberg, its supporting cast included Buddy Miller, Greg Leisz, Brantley Kearns, Dusty Wakemen, and Dick Fegy and was an exceptional debut of honky tonk ("Make a Fool Out of Me"; "Love Lyin' Down"; "Changes") and barroom ballads ("Rum & Rodeo"; "Just Like Old-Times") written mostly by Myles. Her sophomore effort, **Untamed**, had a few sparks but generally lacked the verve of her debut. And while Myles found limited success in the U.S., she fared considerably better in England where she built a loyal following. In 1996, Demon Records issued a live album, **Sweet Little Dangerous**, with Myles' best from her first two CDs plus covers of "When the Tingle Becomes a Chill," "Worried Life Blues," and "Walk Through This World With Me." Based in London, Myles switched labels in late 1996 and signed with Rounder. Her debut on that label was **Highways and Honky Tonks**, a decent collection of Bakersfield honky tonk and California country rock with Pete Anderson, Scott Joss, and even The Hag on a duet, "No One is Gonna Love You Better."

Just Like Old-Times/Hightone/1992
Untamed/Hightone/1995
Sweet Little Dangerous (Live at the Bottom Line)/Demon UK/1996
Highways and Honky Tonks/Rounder/1998

The Heather Myles Fan Club, P.O. Box 21107, Riverside, CA 92516

Heather Myles Home Page
//www.iac.net/~sharon/heather.html

Nadine

No Depression; Grain Belt Rock
St. Louis, Missouri; 1996-

Old college chums Adam Reichman and Todd Schnitzer founded an alt. country group in the early 1990s called Sourpatch that also included drummer Bill Reyland. In 1996, these three plus ex-Wagon multi-instrumentalist Steve Rauner started a new group and named it Nadine. They claimed influences ranging from David Bromberg and Gram Parsons through the Silos and Daniel Lanois, but they are clearly direct descendents from early Neil Young and Crazy Horse down through fellow Missourians Uncle Tupelo and their off-shoots. Their generally laid-back sound broken by the occasional guitar crunch behind high mournful vocals is certain to please fans of Son Volt and the Bottlerockets. In 1997, they recorded an EP, **Back To My Senses**, which was co-produced by ex-Uncle Tupelo/Wilco live sound producer Michael Praytor. Released domestically on Undertow, it didn't make much of a splash in American alt. country waters but was enthusiastically received across the Big Pond. Germany's top alt. country/Americana label, Glitterhouse, which had already made Hazeldine a hit in Europe, released **Back to My Senses** as a full-length CD in 1998. The European music press, especially in Great Britain, gave it two enthusiastic thumbs-up, and *Uncut* magazine included Nadine along with Hazeldine, Neal Casal, Willard Grant, and Lambchop in its September 1998 issue and CD dedicated to "The Best of Alternative Country." They also made it on to Vinyl Junkie's 1998 alt. country compilation **Loose** with Lullaby for the Working Class, Red Star Belgrade, the Handsome Family, and the Gourds.

Steve Rauner (acc,g,l.s.,mda,v); Adam Reichman (g,v); Bill Reyland (d); Todd Schnitzer (b,org,v)

Back to My Senses/Undertow/1997 (EP); Glitterhouse Ger./1998 (CD)
"Brother" on **Loose: New Sounds of the Old West**/Vinyl Junkie UK/1998
"Dark Light" on **Sounds of the New West: The Best of Alternative Country**/Uncut UK/1998

Nadine, 3714 Utah Pl., St. Louis, MO 63116; 314-771-1172

Nadine Page //www.delta-music.co.uk/nadine.html

Nadine23@aol.com

Nadine/Round Tower Page
//www.roundtower.com/html/artists/nadine.html

Buck Naked and The Bare Bottom Boys

"Pornobilly"
Omaha, Nebraska/San Francisco, California; Early 1990s-

If Elvis had performed without his pants and with a wider camera angle on the Sullivan Show or in a g-string in Vegas (ee-yah!!), he could have done it. But, the world just wasn't ready then, so it was up to Buck Naked (aka Philip Bury) to invent "pornobilly" in the early 1990s. Buck and his Bare Bottom Boys (Hector Naked and Stinky LePew) first revealed their combination of rockabilly with pornographic lyrics to the good people of Omaha, Nebraska, but quickly realized this was probably not the best environment in which to develop their art. They headed for the friendlier (and more sinful) confines of San Francisco and after a tour that gained them a national following became permanent residents of the City by the Bay. Playing a regular gig at the Paradise Lounge, Buck developed a reputation as the King of Kinky, the Lord of Lewd, the Prince of Passion; dressed only in a cowboy hat, pink cowboy boots and a toilet plunger cod piece, Buck led the Boys (also barely clad) through songs like "Teenage Pussy From Outerspace" which became their first single. Their antics brought a lot of fans but also the disfavor of a group of Frisco ministers who picketed one of their performances "to rid the city of demons and high-ranking evil spirits." Buck and the Bare Bottom Boys survived this blow and in 1994 entered the studio to begin recording (in Dynamic Highly Offensive Stereophonic Sound) a full length CD of classic tunes such as "Enema Party," "Hard On From Hell," and "Sit On My Face." Unfortunately, just prior to completion of the album, Buck was shot to death in Golden Gate Park. However, Hector and Stinky managed to do the final mixing and released it as a final tribute to Buck (re-released in 1998). All proceeds from sales of the record went to his family.

Buck Naked (g,v); Stinky LePew (d); Hector Naked (b)

"Teenage Pussy From Outer Space"/Scam/1990 (7")
Buck Naked and the Bare Bottom Boys/Heyday/1994; 1998

Buck Naked/IUMA Page
//www.iuma.com/IUMA/band_html/Buck_Naked_and_the_
Bare_Bottom_Boys.html

Orville Nash (aka Alan Wolfson)
Honky Tonk; Hillbilly Boogie
Atlantic City, New Jersey; August 3, 1947-

Alan Wolfson's musical odyssey began in Atlantic City, New Jersey, where his father, a featured vocalist at the famous 500 Club, taught him to sing and his French born mother gave him piano lessons. However, it was a performance by legend James Burton at the Steel Pier that got him interested as a teenager in rock guitar and early rock 'n' roll/rockabilly. Eventually, Alan took the stage name Orville Nash and migrated to Houston, Texas, where he got to know Huey P. Meaux (Crazy Cajun Records) and did some solo and duet (Warren Smith; Sleepy LaBeef) demos in the early 1960s. However, Orville's nascent musical aspirations fizzled and for the next twenty years, he was a good family man holding down a steady sales position with Texaco. But, the pull of the music was still there and Orville was reborn in the nightclubs of Paris, France, after Alan relocated

there in the late 1980s. Over the next decade, Nash became a regular at country and rockabilly festivals on the Continent and recorded for several Europeam labels. A rockabilly single on the French Bronco label in 1989 was followed by a string of LP/CDs in the 1990s: **Nashin' Around** (Swiss Rollin' Rock); **Fuckin' Formidable** (French Yep Yep); **Get Along** (UK Fury). All feature Orville's appealing country baritone (Dave Dudley style) on a top drawer mix of Texas/Louisiana honky tonk/rockabilly and Western tunes. Nash covers Buck Owens, Johnny Cash, Mac Curtis, Al Ferrier, Skeets McDonald, and others with *savoirfaire*, and his originals ("Tombstone Gun"; "Boogie Woogie Cajun Girl"; "Wells Fargo Train"; "Wide Open Highway") are *tres bien* as well. Orville/Alan has been backed by numerous bands including the Kentucky Two and the Crazy Ramblers but in the late 1990s performed with the French country rock group Coastline.

"Rebel Rousin' Days" b/w "Gator Boogie Man"/Bronco Fr./1989 (7")
Nashin' Around/Rollin' Rock Switz./1990
Lennerockers & Friends, Vol.2/Rockhouse Dut./1991
Fuckin' Formidable/Yep Yep Fr./1993
"Tombstone Gun" on **Country Collection**/Arcade Fr./1994
Get Along/Fury UK/1997

Orville Nash, 16 Rue Clairaut, 75017 Paris, France; 01-42-26-17-83

Orville Nash & Coastline
//perso.wanadoo.fr/coastline.fritz/page8.html

Nashville West
Country Rock
Los Angeles, California; 1967-1968

When the Byrds were beginning to make the transition toward country rock in the late 1960s, one of their main role models was fellow L.A. band Nashville West. Although not formally started until 1967, its co-founders, fiddler Gib Guilbeau and drummer Gene Parsons, had known each other since the early 1960s when they were members of a country group called the Castaways. In 1966, the Byrds' Chris Hillman was producing the Gosdin Brothers and hired Guilbeau, Parsons, and electirc guitarist Clarence White to back them on a single that was undeniably one of the first country rock recordings. Subsequently, Guilbeau, Parsons, and White became session players and recording artists for Gary Paxton's Bakersfield International Productions and Records. They each did singles and backed BIP labelmates including Paxton, the Gosdin Brothers, and Wayne Moore. Around this same time, Guilbeau and Parsons began performing as Cajun Gib and Gene with White at the Jack of Diamonds in Palmdale, California. Eventually, in 1967, they brought in bassist Wayne Moore and took the name Nashville West after a nightclub in El Monte where they had a regular gig. Honing what would later become known as California country rock, Nashville West were often joined by guest musicians including Gram Parsons , the Byrds, and the Flying Burrito Brothers. And though only one recording by Nashville West survived (recorded in 1968 but not issued until 1978; re-released on CD in 1997), its heavy influence on the development of early country rock is readily apparent. Recorded live on a Sony two-track, **Nashville West** is a bit rough in spots but has that merging of hard country and rock later refined by GP, the Byrds, FBB, and Rick Nelson. Of course, the standout feature on the album is the electric guitar wizardry of Clarence White which is stellar throughout but really shines on covers of "Mental Revenge," "Green, Green Grass of Home," "I Washed My Hands in Muddy Water," "Ode to Billy Joe," and the original instrumental "Nashville West" (later on **Dr. Byrds & Mr. Hyde**). During the time (late 1968) when Hillman and Gram Parsons were considering a split from the Byrds, they did some informal recordings with Guilbeau, White, and Gene Parsons who called them "prototype Burrito Brothers." Nothing came of this historic country rock summit as the Byrds soon went on tour. When they came back minus Gram Parsons, White, who had already done session work with them, joined the Byrds and was soon followed by Gene Parsons. Guilbeau and Moore were left to wonder what could have been, but Guilbeau did not remain idle long. He became a session player for a variety of performers including Arlo Guthire and Linda Ronstadt, formed his own respectable country/Cajun band, Swampwater, joined with Sneaky Pete in two early 70s bands, Cold Steel and the Docker Hill Boys, and has been a member of the post-Hillman/Gram Parsons Flying Burrito Brothers since 1974.

Gib Guilbeau (r.g.,l.v.); Wayne Moore (b,v); Gene Parsons (d,v); Clarence White (l.g.,v)

   Nashville West/Sierra/1979; 1997 (with p.u. trks.)
Nashville West //ebni.com/byrds/spnw1.html

See The Byrds; The Flying Burrito Brothers; Gene Parsons; Clarence White

Rick Nelson (The Stone Canyon Band)
Country Rock
Teaneck, New Jersey; May 8, 1940—DeKalb, Texas; December 31, 1985

When teen idol and pop singer Rick Nelson's popularity began to wane in the mid-1960s, he gravitated toward a country sound and, in fact, became one of the earliest practitioners of the country rock hybrid that was emerging in California. In reality, this was not a big stretch for Nelson who had always shown an affinity for country music during his low key rockabilly days (e.g. **Rockin' With Ricky**). In 1966 and 1967, he recorded **Bright Lights and Country Music** and **Country Fever** backed by a solid band including Glen D. Hardin, Clarence White, Glen Campbell, and his long-time guitarist James

Burton on slide dobro. Nelson covers country classics ("Truck Drivin' Man"; "No Vacancy"; "Night Train to Memphis"; "Take These Chains From My Heart"; "You Win Again"; "I Heard That Lonesome Whistle Blow"), contemporary country (Willie Nelson's "Hello Walls" and "How Time Slips Away"), and pop singers like Randy Newman and Nilsson with a rock feel, and was arguably one of the first to do so. In June 1967, Nelson, backed by Burton, White, Hardin, Leo Russell (bass), and Bob Watford (banjo) played a historic country rock concert at L.A.'s Shrine Auditorium. Two years later, Rick assembled the Stone Canyon Band with Tom Brumley of Buck Owens' Buckaroos on pedal steel. They had a minor hit in 1970 with a country rock version of Dylan's "She Belongs to Me" and did three commendable but often overlooked albums–**Rick Sings Nelson** (all originals), **Rick Nelson in Concert**, **Rudy the Fifth**–with a West Coast country rock groove. Unfortunately, Nelson's new sound was not well received by fans including an especially rude crowd at Madison Square Garden in 1971 who wanted to hear his teen idol hits. In rebuttal, Rick wrote "Garden Party" which was huge but also his last big record. Sadly, the Stone Canyon Band and Nelson's country rock phase faded away by 1974. Nelson went on to make some pretty tepid records and toured until claimed by a plane crash in 1985. However, his death elevated him to cult status and over the years numerous collections from his catalog have been issued including CD pairings of his best country rock material, **Bright Lights/Country Muisc & Country Fever** and **Rick Sings-Nelson/Rudy the 5th** in 1998.

The Stone Canyon Band: Tom Brumley (p.s.); Allen Kemp (g); Randy Meisner (b); Pat Shanahan (d)

   Bright Lights and Country Music/Decca/1966
   Country Fever/Decca/1967
   Rick Sings Nelson/Decca/1970
   Rudy the Fifth/Decca/1971
   Garden Party/Decca/1972
   Rockin' With Ricky/Ace/1984
   Rick Nelson Live, 1983-1985/Rhino/1989
   Rick Nelson and The Stone Canyon Band, Vols. 1-2/
      Edsel UK/1996-1997
   Bright Lights and Country Music & Country Fever/
      Ace/1998
   Rick Sings Nelson/Rudy the 5th/Ace UK/1998
Rick Nelson and The Stone Canyon Band--Legacy
//www.geocities.com/nashville/6082/

Willie Nelson
Outlaw
Ft. Worth, Texas; April 30, 1933-

In the 1960s, Willie Nelson was a Nashville singer/songwriter whose songs (e.g. "Hello Walls," "Nightlife," "How Time Slips Away") were major hits for other performers but whose laudable solo albums for RCA failed to break through. A member of the Grand Ole Opry, Nelson bridled when his label tried to market him as a "Countrypolitan" type performer and left Music City for Texas. He dropped out of music for a time before having a revelation that changed his career and the face of country and rock. Like Gram Parsons, Bob Dylan, and others before him, Nelson came to realize that all over the U.S. a whole generation of rockers were getting turned on to good old country music. He, along with Waylon Jennings, David Allan Coe, Billy Joe Shaver, and others, adopted a new country rock sound and look which came to be known as "Redneck Rock," "Progressive Country," or most familiarly, "Outlaw." With Atlantic and then Columbia, Nelson cut several landmark albums including **Shotgun Willie** and two innovative concept recordings, **Phases and Stages** and **Red Headed Stranger** that helped rocket him to stardom. The Outlaw movement culminated in an immensely successful collaborative session, **Wanted: The Outlaws**, with Nelson, Jennings, Jessi Colter, and Tompall Glaser which sold millions and was one factor in pushing Nashville toward its "urban cowboy" phase. Meanwhile, Nelson rode the Outlaw mythology to megastardom but increasingly gravitated toward a more pop country sound leaving the hard core stuff to Coe, Shaver, and other remaining outlaws. With a few exceptions, the quality of Willie's musical output took a serious dip in the 1980s and 1990s, and he became famous mostly for his work with FarmAid, as a movie actor, and for his IRS troubles. Still, Nelson was a very important bridge between musical genres and generations, and his work in the 1970s had a major impact on alternative country. His annual 4th of July picnic provided a showcase for Outlaws as well as contemporary alternative country musicians. In 1995, a variety of alt. rock and alt. country acts saluted Nelson's legacy on an eccentric collection of his songs entitled **Twisted Willie**. Taking the same plunge as Emmylou a few years before, Willie called on Daniel Lanois to produce his 1998 **Teatro**. Recorded in an old Mexican movie theater in Oxnard, California, it mostly features re-workings (with Emmylou on harmony) of Nelson classics such as "I've Just Destroyed the World I'm Living In," "Darkness on the Face of the Earth," "I Never Cared for You," "Pick Up the Pieces" using the moody electronics and noises associated with Lanois.

Yesterday's Wine/RCA/1971
Shotgun Willie/Atlantic/1973
Phases and Stages/Atlantic/1974
Red Headed Stranger/Columbia/1975
The Troublemaker/Columbia/1976
Wanted: The Outlaws/Columbia/1976
Nightlife: Greatest Hits and Rare Tracks, 1959-1971/Rhino/1989
The Early Years: The Complete Liberty Recordings Plus More/Liberty/1994
Revolutions of Time: The Journeys, 1975-1993/Columbia Legacy/1995
Twisted Willie/Justice/1995
Teatro/Island/1998
"Just One Love" (with Kimmie Rhodes) on **Deep in the Heart of Texas**/Shanachie/1998 (sdtrk.)

"Me & Paul" on **Hempilation 2**/Capricorn/1998
"Ride 'Em Jewboy" on **Pearls in the Snow: The Songs of Kinky Friedman**/1998
Willie Nelson/Sony Page
//www.music.sony.com/artists/WillieNelson
Willie Nelson iMusic Showcase
//imusic.com/showcase/country/

Michael Nesmith (Red Rhodes)
Singer/Songwriter; Country Rock
Houston, Texas; December 30, 1942-

1965; in L.A., auditions for a new TV series *The Monkees* are held, and Michael Nesmith beats out Charles Manson and Stephen Stills for one of four parts. The Monkees rolled on through four years of saccharine pop hits and a silly sitcom while Nesmith chafed under such a restricted role. Originally a mainstay on the L.A. folk scene, Nesmith eventually left the Monkees and returned to these roots. In 1968, he recorded **Wichita Train Whistle Sings** and in 1969 formed the country rock outfit, the First National Band. Most prominent among the members of the band was steel guitarist Red Rhodes who had a regular gig at the legendary Palomino Club, worked on **Sweetheart of the Rodeo**, and had won ACM's Steel Guitarist of the Year from 1965-1968. He was also a session man for many pop rock acts of the day including the Monkees. This association led him to Nesmith and three albums with the First National Band (**Magnetic South**; **Loose Salute**; **Nevada Fighter**) which began as straight ahead country but evolved toward a more adventurous country sound highlighted by Nesmith's literate lyrics and Rhodes' steel. After the demise of the First National Band, they collaborated as the Second National Band on **Tantamount to Treason** and on **And the Hits Keep on Coming** which compiled a number of Nesmith's songs ("Different Drum"; "Some of Shelley's Blues," etc.) that had been hits for other artists. In 1972, Nesmith formed the Countryside record label and produced works by Ian Matthews and Red Rhodes (**Velvet Hammer in a Cowboy Band**), but it was soon axed by parent label Elektra. So, Nesmith formed another label, Pacific Arts, in 1974 and released the controversial multi-media recording **The Prison** and then **From a Radio Engine to a Photon Wing** which yielded the Nesmith produced video *Rio*. Through his work in this medium, Nesmith began to see the possibilities of music video and became a pioneer with his show *Popclips* which later evolved into MTV. Spurred on by these early successes, Nesmith moved further into film with a full-length music video *Elephant Parts* (won the first ever video Grammy) and then with feature films such as *Square Dance*, *Repo Man*, and *Tapeheads*. Throughout the 1980s and 1990s, Nesmith explored video and expanded Pacific Arts into a major audio and film making force. "The Nez" occasionally put out compilations of his early work and a new album here and there, did a film version of *Hithchiker's*

Guide to the Galaxy, and a tour with the Hellecasters in the mid-1990s. His first novel, *The Long Sandy Hair of Neftoon Zamora*, was published in 1998 and recounts the spiritual journey of a musician in search of the voice of the title character. A follow-up, *The America Gene*, was reportedly centered on something he calls "The Elvis Paradigm."

Wichita Train Whistle Sings/Dot/1968; Pacific Arts/1978
Magnetic South/RCA/1970
Loose Salute/RCA/1970
Nevada Fighter/RCA/1971;1992
Tantamount to Treason/RCA/1972
Velvet Hammer in a Cowboy Band (Red
   Rhodes)/Countryside/1973
And the Hits Keep on Coming/RCA/1972; Pacific
   Arts/1979
Pretty Much Your Standard Stash/RCA/1973; Pacific
   Arts/1979
The Prison/Pacific Arts/1975
Michael Nesmith and the First National Band/Island
   UK/1976 (EP)
From the Radio Engine to the Photon Wing/Pacific
   Arts/1977
Live at the Palais/Pacific Arts/1978
Infinite Rider on the Big Dogma/Pacific Arts/1979
Michael Nesmith Radio Special/Pacific Arts/1979
The Newer Stuff/Awareness/1989
**The Older Stuff: The Best of Michael Nesmith
   (1970-1973)**/Rhino/1991
Nesmith Live/Pacific Arts/1992 (video)
Tropical Campfires/Pacific Arts/1992
First National Band: Complete/Pacific Arts/
   1993 (2 CDs)
The Garden/Rio/1994
The Solo Years, 1963-1965/Pacific Arts/1998
The Long Sandy Hair of Neftoon Zamora/St.
   Martin's/1998

Michael Nesmith's Video Ranch //www.videoranch.com

Nez@videoranch.com

The New Duncan Imperials

Insurgent Country
Chicago, Illinois; 1990-

Without doubt, the wildest and weirdest of Chicago's insurgent country bands is the New Duncan Imperials who were formed in 1990 as a side project by three members of the garage rock band Service. Goodtime, Pigtail Duck, and Skipper have worked hard to establish themselves as the self-styled "Kings of Trash Rock" majoring in rip roaring rockers with occasional swerves into country on twisted covers of Hank and Buck and send ups like "Jimmy Page Loves Country." Their recordings are wild rides into musical dementia and assorted mayhem populated with characters you'd go out of your way to avoid. True to their image, the NDI are especially fond of low life and losers as demonstrated on "Born to Be Hit," "Hamhocks," "White Trash Boogie," "Gizzards, Scrapple, Tripe," and "Home Sweet, Mobile Home." In 1994, they were welcomed into the insurgent country club when their whimsical dream car

song "If She Wasn't on Blocks" was included on the **For a Life of Sin** compilation. The New Duncan Imperials also developed quite a reputation for maniacal live shows and published their own comic book and mail order catalog from which you could order the usual plus peanut butter, pig parts, and custom toothpicks. In 1995, they did an album of Michael Jackson covers and in 1997 **In-A-Gadda-Da-Vegas** which has many charming tunes including "Pesticide," "Pathetica," "Potato Chicks (and Cheese Girls)," and "Making Out With My Dad."

Goodtime (d); Pigtail Dick (l.g.,v); Skipper (b,v)

"Feelin' Sexy"/"Hamhocks" b/w "Chicken Walk"/
   "Pensacola 99"/Pravda/1990 (7")
Hanky Panky Parley Voo!/Pravda/1990
The Hymns of Bucksnort/Pravda/1991
"The Queen of Venus"/Pravda/1992 (7")
Live, Rare and Bad/NDI/1992 (CS)
"I'm Drunk" b/w "Hey Brother, Pour the Wine" (with
   Mojo Nixon)/NDI/1993 (7")
Loserville/Pravda/1994
"If She Wasn't on Blocks" on **For a Life of Sin**/
   Bloodshot/1994
We're in a Band/Pravda/1994 (EP)
Fried (Live)/Pravda/1995 (27 trks.)
The Best of Michael Jackson/Gaga Goodies Fin./1995
In-A-Gadda-Da-Vegas/Pravda/1997
Video Trash/NDI (50 mins. of NDI videos)

The New Duncan Imperials Mail Order & Fan Club,
P. O. Box 268043, Chicago, IL 60626

The New Duncan Imperials Home Page
//members.aol.com/indirocks/index.htm

NDIrocks@aol.com

The New Duncan Imperials/Pravda Records Home Page
//pravdamusic.com/duncan.html

See Mojo Nixon

The New Grass Revival

Progressive Bluegrass; Newgrass
Louisville, Kentucky; 1972-1989

New Grass Revival was created in the early 1970s from the remains of the Bluegrass Alliance, an early progressive bluegrass band whose line-up included Sam Bush, Courtney Johnson, Ebo Walker, Tony Rice, and Dan Crary. At the time of their formation, the NGR was Bush, Johnson, Walker, and Curtis Burch. In keeping with their name, they took bluegrass way beyond its traditional boundaries by adding a diversity of musical elements. They recorded a debut album, **Arrival of the New Grass Revival**, in 1972, and then shortly after, Butch Robbins and then John Cowan, a bass player with a great set of pipes, joined in place of Walker. Several pioneering recordings for Flying Fish (**Fly Through the Country, Too Late to Turn Back Now, When the Storm is Over, Barren Country, Commonwealth**) were some of the best progressive bluegrass of the late 1970s. After Johnson and Burch departed, Pat Flynn and banjo wiz kid Bela Fleck were brought in. The latter had previously been a member of Tasty Licks and Spectrum and recorded a solo album, **Crossing the Tracks**. This incarnation of NGR (now on Sugar Hill) was much more widely acclaimed and popular due to a series of dynamic and very accessible releases (**On the Boulevard**, **New Grass Revival**, **Hold to a Dream**, **Friday Night in America**) in the late 1980s-early 1990s. During this time, Bush and Fleck branched out into other progressive bluegrass projects with Bush making solo records, Fleck forming the ultra newgrass Flecktones, and both joining the supergroup Strength in Numbers with Jerry Douglas, Edgar Meyer, and Mark O'Connor. Then, in 1989, the NGR, one of the most successful of all progressive bluegrass bands, called it quits. When founding member Courtney Johnson died in 1996, the surviving NGR alumni gathered for a tribute concert. The NGR's best material is available on two retrospective anthologies: **New Grass Anthology** and **Best of the New Grass Revival**.

Curtis Burch (db,g,v,1971-1981); Sam Bush (f,md,v); John Cowan (b,v,1974-1989); Bela Fleck (bj,v,1981-1989); Pat Flynn (g,v,1981-1989); Courtney Johnson (bj,v,1971-1981); Ebo Walker (b,v,1971-1974)

> **Arrival of the Newgrass Revival**/Starday/1972
> **Fly Through the Country**/Flying Fish/1975
> **Too Late to Turn Back Now (Live at Telluride)**/Flying Fish/1977
> **When the Storm is Over**/Flying Fish/1977
> **Barren County**/Flying Fish/1979
> **Commonwealth**/Flying Fish/1981
> **Live** (with Leon Russell)/Paradise/1981
> **On the Boulevard**/Sugar Hill/1984
> **Late as Usual** (Sam Bush)/Rounder/1984
> **New Grass Revival**/EMI/1986
> **Hold to a Dream**/Capitol/1987
> **Friday Night in America**/Capitol/1989
> **NGR Live**/Sugar Hill/1989
> **Anthology**/Capitol/1989
> **New Grass Revival**/Vintage Nashville Capitol/1996
> **Glamour and Grits** (Sam Bush)/Sugar Hill/1996
> **Howlin' At the Moon** (Sam Bush)/Sugar Hill/1998

Bela Fleck Home Page
//www.vuw.ac.nz/~gnat/bango/fleck-faq/

Bela Fleck On-Line Newsgroup alt.music.bela-fleck

The New Lost City Ramblers (Mike Seeger; The Tracy Schwarz Cajun Trio)
New Old-Time
New York, New York; 1958-

It is universally agreed that the most important new old-time band of the last forty years is the New Lost City Ramblers. Modeling themselves on classic string bands like the Skillet Lickers and the North Carolina Ramblers, Mike Seeger, John Cohen, and Tom Paley got together in New York City during the 1960s folk scare. Initially, the NLCR specialized in Appalachian style old-time, but when Cajun style fiddler/accordionist Tracy Schwarz replaced Paley in 1962, they

incorporated Cajun and early bluegrass elements as well. Through live performances and numerous recordings, they helped renew America's rich heritage of traditional music not only for their generation but for many to come. Happily, the best from their early studio albums and concerts is available on several anthologies. In the late 1970s, the Ramblers stopped performing together, but individual members went on to make invaluable contributions: John Cohen co-founded Friends of Old-Time Music, wrote for folk journals, annotated old-time albums for Folkways, and produced several films including the acclaimed bluegrass documentary, *The High Lonesome Sound*; Tracy Schwarz was active as leader of the excellent Tracy Schwarz Cajun Trio; and Mike Seeger worked as a film maker, field recorder, and performer recording solo and with the newest round of new old-time bands (the Horseflies, Agents of Terra). He was also a member of modern old-time groups like the Strange Creek Singers (with Schwarz, Alice Dickens, Alice Gerrard) and A. Roebic and the Exertions. For his many efforts on behalf of traditional music, Seeger earned a Ralph Gleason Lifetime Achievement Award. In 1997, the NLCR reunited for several performances and to make their first recording in 23 years. **There Ain't No Way Out** recaptures the band's vintage sound on reworked versions of some of their best known numbers plus fresh renditions of obscure songs drawn from old-time/bluegrass archives. They also performed together live at the Harry Smith tribute concert and had two songs included on the accompanying CD, **The Harry Smith Connection**. Only time will tell if this marks a permanent return of one of the era's most important and influential bands.

The New Lost City Ramblers: John Cohen; Tom Paley (g,v,1958-1962); Mike Seeger (bj, g,v); Tracy Schwarz (acc,f,g,v,1962-)

The Tracy Schwarz Cajun Trio: Lee Blackwell (g); Matt Haney (f); Tracy Schwarz (acc,v)

> **Old-Time Country Music** (Mike Seeger)/Folkways/1962
> **Music From the True Vine** (Mike Seeger)/Mercury/1971
> **Second Annual Farewell Reunion** (Mike Seeger)/ Mercury/1973
> **Twenty Years of Concert Performances**/Flying Fish/1978
> **New Lost City Ramblers 20th Anniversary Concert**/ Flying Fish/1978
> **Fresh Old-Time String Band Music** (Mike Seeger with Horseflies et al.)/Rounder/1988
> **Feel Bad Sometimes** (Tracy Schwarz Trio)/Merimac/1990
> **Solo: Old-Time Country Music** (Mike Seeger)/ Rounder/1991
> **The New Lost City Ramblers: The Early Years, 1958-1962**/Smithsonian Folkways/1991
> **The New Lost City Ramblers Vol. 2, 1963-1973: Outstanding in Their Field**/Smithsonian Folkways/1993
> **Tracy Schwarz**/Swallow/1993
> **The New Lost City Ramblers and Friends (Live)**/ Vanguard/1994
> **The Third Annual Farewell Reunion** (Mike Seeger)/ Rounder/1994

Mes Amis! (Tracy Schwarz Trio)/Swallow/1996
"Jai Pleure" (Tracy Schwarz Trio) on **American Fogies,
Vol. 2**/Rounder/1996
Collector's Choice (Mike Seeger)/Rounder/1997
There Ain't No Way Out/Smithsonian Folkways/1997
"Home Sweet Home" on **The Harry Smith
Connection**/Smithsonian Folkways/1998

Mike Seeger True Vine Page //www.mikeseeger.pair.com/

See Hazel Dickens

The New Patrons
Country Rock
St. Louis, Missouri; 1993-1998

One of the saddest events of 1998 was the demise of the New
Patrons. The band's members had grown up together in
Washington, Missouri, and played music together under a
variety of names before officially becoming the New Patrons of
Husbandry (later shortened to the New Patrons) in 1993. With
astute songwriting by Greg Lamb and Jeff Swift, effective violin and viola by Mary Dee Brown, savory lead guitar from John
Horton, and amazing lead vocals by Jenny Stuckenschneider,
they quickly pushed into the front ranks of St. Louis' flourishing
alt. country scene that included top-notch groups like the
Bottlerockets, Belle Starr, and One Fell Swoop. The New
Patrons regularly played to packed houses around town and
were voted Best Folk Group in the St. Louis Music Awards;
they finished second behind the Bottlerockets in the Best
Country Group category. In early 1998, they proudly released
their first CD, **The New Patrons** (produced by Lou Whitney)
and seemed poised to make an impact on the national alt.
country community. However, under the everything's-coming-
up-roses surface, there were thorny inter-band and inter-
personal problems that had built up from long years of
familiarity. These issues eventually became too much and the
New Patrons disbanded in December 1998 after a final show.

Mary Dee Brown (vio,viola); John Horton (l.g.); Greg Lamb
(b); Jenny Stuckenschneider (v); Jeff Swift (g)

"Too Busy Cryin'" on **Out of the Gate Again**/
BJAM/1996
The New Patrons/New Patrons/1998

The New Patrons, P.O. Box 430125, St. Louis, MO 63143;
417-886-6998

The New Patrons //www.usmo.com/~patrons/

patrons@usmo.com

New Riders of the Purple Sage (David Nelson Band)
Country Rock
San Francisco, California; 1969-1981; Early 1990s-

The New Riders of the Purple Sage grew out of a series of
informal sessions between Grateful Dead members, Jerry
Garcia, Phil Lesh, Mickey Hart and friends John Dawson and
David Nelson (who had started out in the early 60s with Garcia
and Robert Hunter as the Wildwood Boys). During one of those
pickin' parties, Dawson came up with the idea for a country
band and thus was born the New Riders of the Purple Sage
(named after Zane Grey's famous novel of the West). Garcia
had long been a bluegrass and country fan and had recently
taken up the pedal steel. For a while, the two groups toured
together as "An Evening With the Grateful Dead and New
Riders of the Purple Sage." Eventually, however, the strain of
being in two groups was too much for Hart and Lesh, and they
were replaced by Spencer Dryden and Dave Torbert. Garcia
stayed on as steel guitarist for the New Riders self titled debut
but was soon replaced by Ian and Sylvia's steel player Buddy
Cage. With a firm line up, the New Riders now played up the
"Cosmic/Psychedelic Cowboy" image that was popular in
Texas and California to the hilt. Their association with The
Dead with whom they frequently toured plus several decent
country rock albums gained them a sizable following in the
early 1970s. Their best songs such as "Glendale Train,"
"Lonesome L.A. Cowboy," "Kick in the Head," and "Panama
Red" (Peter Rowan) were on their first three recordings, the
most successful of which was **The Adventures of Panama
Red** which eventually went gold. The New Riders' influence on
a new generation of country enthusiasts was significant, but,
over time, the quality of their work dropped off considerably.
Disbanded in 1981, Dawson put a new New Riders together in
the 1990s, and they began touring and recording once again
(they even performed at the 1994 Armadillo World Headquarters reunion). In the late 1990s, the NRPS performed as a
trio consisting of Dawson, Rusty Gauthier, and Clarence White
style guitarist, Evan Morgan. Material from the New Riders
formative and most productive years can be found on **Before
Time Began** which contains four tracks by Gracia, Dawson,
Lesh, Hart, Nelson (side two is music played backwards?!) and
on several collections including **Wasted Tasters** and **Relix's
Best of the Early New Riders of the Purple Sage**.

After leaving the New Riders in 1981, David Nelson became a
member of the Jerry Garcia Acoustic Band and the bluegrass
group, the Good Ol' Boys (Don Reno, Frank Wakefield,
Chubby Wise), who recorded the wonderful **Pistol Packin'
Mama** which was produced by Garcia on Grateful Dead
Records. In the late 1990s, he put together the David Nelson
Band with former members of the New Riders, Cowboy Jazz,
and Bob Weir's Ratdog. Their albums, **Limited Edition** and
Keeper of the Key, are an amalgam of 1960s style progressive
bluegrass, New Riders country rock, and Grateful Dead
psychedelic roots rock.

Previous Members: Skip Battin (1974-1981); Buddy Cage
(p.s.,1972-1982); John Dawson (g,hm,v,1969-); Spencer
Dryden (d,1971-1978); Jerry Garcia (p.s.,1969-1971); Rusty

Gauthier (db,f,g,md,v,1982); Mickey Hart (d,1969-1970); Allen Kemp (g,1977-1985); Bill Laymon (b,1993-1997); Phil Lesh (b,1969-1970); Evan Morgan (g,1993-); David Nelson (g,v,1971-1981); Brent Rampone (d,1993-1997) Dave Torbert (b,1971-1975); Gary Vogensen (g,v,1985-1993)
Current Members: John Dawson (g,hm,v); Rusty Gauthier (db,f,g,md,v); Evan Morgan (a.g., e.g.)
The David Nelson Band: David Nelson (g,v); Bill Laymon (b); Mookie Siegel (acc,ky); Barry Sless (p.s.); Arthur Steinhorn (d)

New Riders of the Purple Sage/Columbia/1971
Powerglide/Columbia/1972
Gypsy Cowboy/CBS/1973
Adventures of Panama Red/Columbia/1973
Home, Home on the Road/Columbia/1974
Brujo/Columbia/1974
Oh What a Mighty Time/Columbia/1975
New Riders/Columbia/1976
Before Time Began/Columbia/1976; Relix/1995
Best of New Riders of the Purple Sage/Columbia/1976
Who Are These Guys?/Columbia/1977
Marin County Line/Columbia/1978
Feelin' Alright/Columbia/1981
Vintage NRPS/Columbia/1988
Friend of the Devil/Columbia/1991
Live in Japan/Relix/1994
Live (1982)/Avenue/1995
Keep on Keepin' On/Relix/1995
Wasted Tasters, 1971-1975/Raven Austr./1995
Limited Edition (David Nelson Band)/DNB/1995
Live on Stage/Relix/1996
Midnight Moonlight/Relix/1996
Relix's Best of the Early New Riders of the Purple Sage/Relix/1996
Keeper of the Key (David Nelson Band)/DNB/1997

New Riders //www.skylineonline.com/sage.htm

David Nelson Band, Freaks of Nature Official Home Page //www.nelsonband.com

dnb@nelsonband.com

New Riders of the Purple Sage Fanzine, c/o R. Harvey, 35 The Marles, Exmouth, EX8 4NE, England

See The Grateful Dead

Jeb Loy Nichols (The Fellow Travelers)
Okra; Roots Rock
Lander, Wyoming

The Fellow Travelers were part of the great stable of Okra Records alternative country groups in the late 1980s-early 1990s. They were founded in London by American Jeb Loy Nichols who had moved there to pursue art but got caught up in music and started a country band that often opened for the up and coming Pogues. In 1990, Nichols recorded a tape of his originals with Dave Schramm. It made its way to Okra which gave Nichols a contract. He put together a new band with his wife Lorraine Morley and called it the Fellow Travelers. The musical environment in London was conducive to the band's novel blend of styles. Unlike other Okra artists like Ricky Barnes and Hank McCoy who specialized in hardcore honky-tonk, the Fellow Travelers took traditional music and gave it a very unusual spin. They had all the elements of old-time country: Nichols' ultra twangy voice complemented by Lorraine Morley's old English style vocals, conventional instrumentation (accordion, banjo, fiddle, mandolin), and politically conscious lyrics (by Nichols) with a very down home feel. And while sometimes they played it fairly straight on ballads ("Promise of a Kiss") or waltzes ("Pecan Tree"), what distinguished them was that most of their songs were laid over a definite reggae beat. The subtitle of their 1990 debut, **Local Hits in a Brand New Country Style**, is a definite understatement; what you get is post-nasal vocals, lilting fiddle and accordion, plunking banjo with a righteously mellow groove. The Fellow Travelers' dub/country is hard to imagine and even harder to describe (*Spin* called them "the lonesome children of Merle, Marley, and Marx"), but the result is quite intriguing and strangely contagious. They lasted through several albums of rastabilly, **Just a Visitor**, **Things and Time**, and **A Few Good Dubs** before breaking up in 1993. Morley went on to make one solo recording, **A Face Drawn in the Sand** while Nichols collaborated with Barnes, McCoy, and Dave Schramm on a fine twangmeisters' summit called **The Okra All-Stars**. Many of its most memorable moments are provided by Nichols' vocals and great originals including "Big Mistake," "Falling Fast," and "Let's Build a Bridge." For several years, Nichols dropped out of sight in London but returned in 1997 with a new record, **Lovers Knot**. With assistance from members of Medeski, Martin & Wood, the Jazz Passengers, and the Holmes Brothers, Nichols revived the dub/country/r&b soul of the Fellow Travelers reprising several songs including "As the Rain" and "Yesterday's a Long Time Ago."

The Fellow Travelers (1990-1993): Aine Ni Bhraonain (acc); Martin Harrison (b,bj,ky); Tim Harrison (perc); Lorraine Morley (tb,v); Jeb Loy Nichols (f,g,md,v); Danny Sheals (d); Netti Zaandrager (f)

No Easy Way: Local Hits in a Brand New Country Style, Part One/Okra/1991
"GTO" and "As the Rain" (p.u.) on **Sample Some Okra**/Okra/1992
Just a Visitor/Okra/1992
Things and Time/Okra/1993
A Few Good Dubs/Okra/1993
The Okra All-Stars/Okra/1993; Innerstate/1999
A Face Drawn in the Sand (Lorraine Morley)/Okra/1994
Lovers Knot (Jeb Loy Nichols)/Capitol/1997

Starland Motel: Jeb Loy Nichols //hollywoodand vine.com/jebloynichols/index.shmtl

See Ricky Barnes; Hank McCoy; The Okra All-Stars; The Schramms

Nine Pound Hammer

Cowpunk
Lexington, Kentucky/Nashville, Tennessee; 1985-

The members of Nine Pound Hammer grew up on the suburban frontier of Lexington, Kentucky, where farm and city came together. There they were exposed to urban and rural musical influences and in 1985 joined them in a searing marriage of Cash/Haggard/Owens country to Motorhead/Ramones rock. The result was ultrawild cowpunk with lots of screaming guitars and yelling vocals extolling the virtues of the white trash, redneck lifestyle on "Redneck Romance" and "Turned Traitor for a Piece of Tail." Their debut **The Mud, the Blood, and the Beers** was hard core punk with country inflections, but on subsequent releases, Nine Pound Hammer adopted a more twanging sound most clearly heard on **Hayseed Timebomb**. However, the punk attitude remains as evidenced by the album's cover (a surreal drawing of a shotgun toting redneck protecting his mobile home) and on songs such as "Out of the Way Pig Fuckers," "Run Fat Boy Run," "Shotgun in a Chevy" plus revved up covers of Buck and Johnny tunes. On their web page, Nine Pound's label Crypt unashamedly calls their sound folk music but "without the acoustic guitars, thesaurus, university coffee house pseudo-intellectual bullshit and weepy sentimentality/sensitivity." (Watch out, Joan Baez!) In the late 1990s, Nine Pound Hammer has toured and recorded sporadically (singles and EPs) with Blaine Cartwright moving on to the band Nashville Pussy and Rob Hulsman to Taildragger.

Matt Bartholomy (b); Blaine Cartwright (g,1985-1997); Rob Hulsman (d,1985-1997); Scott Luallen (g,v); Bill Waldron (d)

The Mud, the Blood and the Beers/Wanghead/1988; Crypt/1993
"Cadillac Inn" b/w "Surfabilly"/Baylor/1991 (7")
Smokin' Taters/Crypt/1991; 1992 (CD includes **Mud**)
Hayseed Timebomb/Crypt/1995
"Teenage Head" b/w "Two Tub Man"/Scooch Pooch/1995
"Ain't Nothin' to Do" b/w "Radar Love"/Royal/1995 (7")
Nine Pound Hammer/Answer/1997 (EP)

Nine Pound Hammer, 909 20th Ave. South, #3, Nashville, TN 37212

Nine Pound Hammer Web Page
//www.cpedu.rug.nl/~evert/bands/mn/ninepond.htm

Mojo Nixon (Skid Roper; The Toad Liquors)

Country Rock; Roots Rock; Rant and Rave
Chapel Hill North Carolina; August 2, 1957-

In 1980, a young man named Kirby McMillan, Jr. graduated from college and moved to Denver where he took a job working for VISTA, singing Guthrie and Leadbelly songs in soup kitchens, and "organizing winos." Leaving VISTA, Kirby fronted a punk band, Zebra 123, for a time then went to San Diego where he was jilted by an old girlfriend. Heading back East on his motorcycle McMillan had what he called "The Mojo

Nixon Revelation," a vision in which he performed "front porch boogie woogie...to make your grandma buck dance...blush... and hit you in the head with her purse." Following his dream, McMillan, now Mojo, moved back to San Diego and in 1984 began berating the local music scene with his unique blend of demented hillbilly music and socio-political rants. Playing acoustic guitar and accompanied only by his trusty sidekick Skid Roper on washtub bass and washboard, Nixon sounded like an amphetamine crazed Southern televangelist but, in this case, praising the virtues of sin and degradation. Nixon and Roper got the attention of Restless Records which put out **Mojo Nixon and Skid Roper** in 1985, followed by several more albums (**Frenzy!**; **Get Out of My Way!**) on Restless and Enigma (**Bo-Day-Shus!!!**; **Root Hog or Die**). All are classic Mojomania including "Jesus at McDonald's," "Ain't Gonna Piss in No Jar," and "I'm Living with a Three Foot Anti-Christ." However, it was his "Burn Down the Malls" and two tributes to The King, "Elvis is Everywhere" and "619-239-KING" that brought him national attention when MTV aired the videos accompanying those songs (one of Nixon's early tunes was "Stuffin' Martha's Muffin," dedicated to MTV*s* Martha Quinn). A brief association with the network ended when MTV refused to show Nixon's "Debbie Gibson is Pregnant With My Two Headed Love Child." Shortly thereafter, Nixon and Roper parted company with Roper going on to make one very underrated country/rock album, **Trails Plowed Under**, with his band the Whirling Spurs. Meanwhile, Mojo enlisted the aid of Eric Ambel, Country Dick Montana (Mojo's "de-mentor"), John Doe, and Bill Davis (Dash Rip Rock) to record **Otis** which continues the fun with "Put a Sex Mo-Sheen in the White House," "Destroy All Lawyers," and everybody's favorite "Don Henley Must Die." Unfortunately, Enigma collapsed, and for a number of years, Nixon had to fight to get back control of the rights to his songs. However, during this period, he formed a new band, the Toad Liquors, and branched out into side projects with the New Duncan Imperials, the Pleasure Barons (with Dave Alvin and Country Dick), the World Famous Bluejays (for **Rig Rock Truckstop**), and, amazingly, Jello Biafra on a country album, **Prairie Home Invasion**. This outrageous album of twisted roots includes "Let's Go Burn Old Nashville Down," "Are You Drinking With Me Jesus?," and a most irreverent version of "Will the Circle Be Unbroken?" as "Will the Fetus Be Aborted?" Mojo's 1995 solo effort, **Whereabouts Unknown**, (produced by Ambel) finds the leader of the "fornication nation" in prime form with "Don't Ask Me Why I Drink," "Girlfriend in a Coma" (Morrissey), "Tie My Pecker to My Leg" (co-written with Country Dick), and a tender cover of Elvis' "If I Can Dream." In 1997, Needletime Records released **Gadzooks!!**, a collection of Mojo obscurities and previously unreleased material including "UFO's, Big Rigs, and BBQ" (from **Rig Rock Truckstop**), "The Poontango," "I Like Marijuana," "Winnebago Warrior," "Beer Ain't Drinkin'," and the highly controversial, "Bring Me the Head of David Geffen." In the late 1990s, Nixon toured with the Toad Liquors, worked in movies (*Raney*; *Butt Crack*), expanded *The Mojo Manifesto* (a pamphlet about "what's fucked up in America and how to fix it"), and finished a new solo, **Prisoner of the Tiki Room**, with classic Mojo songs about O.J. and a guy who crushed cars with a tank in San Diego plus the sure to be banned "Christians, I Hate 'Em!"

The Toad Liquors: Earl B. Freedom (b,b.v.); Pete Gordon (ky,b.v.); Mike Middleton (d)
Skid Roper and the Whirling Spurs: Jayne Robson (v); Lance Soliday (d); Danny Vasquez (b) with Tim Cook (p.s.,trb); Joe Lunga (org,p); Mike Martt (sl.g.)

Mojo Nixon and Skid Roper/RBI/1985; IRS/1989
Frenzy (with Skid Roper)/Restless/1986
Get Out of My Way (with Skid Roper)/Enigma/1986 (EP)
Bo-Day-Shus!!! (with Skid Roper)/Capitol/1987
Root Hog or Die (with Skid Roper)/Enigma/1989
Unlimited Everything (with Skid Roper)/Enigma/1990
Trails Plowed Under (Skid Roper & the Whirling Spurs)/Triple X/1989
Lydia's Cafe (Skid Roper solo)/Triple X/1991 (CS)
"I'm Drunk" b/w "Hey Brother, Pour the Wine" (with New Duncan Imperials)/Pravda/1991 (7")
Otis (with the Toad Liquors)/IRS/1991
Horny Holidays Christmas LP/Triple X/1992
The Pleasure Barons: Live in Las Vegas (with Dave Alvin & Country Dick)/Hightone/1993
"UFOs, Big Rigs & BBQ" & "Chug-a-Lug" (with World Famous Bluejays) on **Rig Rock Truckstop**/Diesel Only/1993
Prairie Home Invasion (with Jello Biafra)/Alternative Tentacles/1994
Whereabouts Unknown/Ripe & Ready/1995
Gadzooks! The Homemade Bootleg/Needle Time/1997
Prisoner of the Tiki Room/1998

Mojo Nixon: High Priest of the Fornication Nation //www.julianstargazer.com/mojo.htm

See The New Duncan Imperials; The World Famous Blue Jays

Northern Lights
Progressive Bluegrass
Boston, Massachusetts; 1975-

In 1972, Taylor Armerding, who cut his musical teeth on classical, rock, and folk, saw the light at the Union Grove Old-Time Fiddlers Convention and decided to switch to bluegrass. Three years later, he was playing mandolin with a Boston area bluegrass band called How Banks Fail. Influenced by progressive bluegrass, the group decided to develop a newgrass sound and changed their name to Northern Lights in 1975. Then, after an appearance at the Winterhawk Festival, they signed on with Renovah Records which released their self-titled debut in 1976. However, over the next five years, Northern Lights went through several personnel changes and even disbanded for a time but in 1982 assembled a stable line-up that included Armerding and Bob Emery from the old band plus

banjo prodigy Alison Brown and guitarist Bill Henry. They recorded **Before the Fire Comes Down** in 1983, and a year later, Brown departed to be replaced by Mike Kropp. Their third recording, **On the Edge**, won them an invitation to play at the 1987 IBMA World of Bluegrass festival. This performance plus the help of Peter Rowan got them a contract with Flying Fish which resulted in **Take You to the Sky** (with Rowan, Alison Krauss, Matt Glaser), **Can't Buy Your Way** (with Vassar Clements), and **Wrong Highway Blues**; all reached the top ten on the National Bluegrass Survey. Guided by the innovative spirit of Bill Monroe (whom Armerding calls a "revolutionary"), Northern Lights combines bluegrass with jazz, country, Cajun, blues, Western swing, pop, and classical, on a range of covers and evocative Armerding originals with glorious three part harmonies and high energy. With a line-up including Armerding's son Jake on fiddle and new bass player Chris Miles, the band switched to the Red House label in 1996 and recorded **Living in the City** which continued to push the traditional envelope in a fresh and exciting way and kept them at the top of New England's bluegrass community.

Jake Armerding (f,md,l.v.,h.v.,1992-); Taylor Armerding (md,l.v.,h.v.); Alison Brown (bj, 1982-1983); Bob Emery (f,v,1975-1986); Bill Henry (g,l.v.,h.v.); Jeff Horton (b,1993); Mike Kropp (bj,g,1983-); Chris Miles (b,l.v.h.v.,1996-)

Northern Lights/Revonah/1976
Before the Fire Comes Down/Revonah/1983
On the Edge/NL/1987
Take You to the Sky/Flying Fish/1990
Can't Buy Your Way/Flying Fish/1992
Wrong Highway Blues/Flying Fish/1994
Living in the City/Red House/1996

Northern Lights Home Page //www.super-charged.com/nlights/

Nlightsmgmt@aol.com

The Notting Hillbillies
Country Rock
Holbeck, Leeds, England; 1986-

A number of years before he formed Dire Straits, Mark Knopfler was half of a country/blues duo with Steve Phillips called the Duolian String Pickers. Later, after Dire Straits made it big, Knopfler enlisted Phillips, Brendan Croker (leader of the 5 O'Clock Shadows), Ed Bicknell, Guy Fletcher, Paul Franklin, and Marcus Cliff (5 O'Clock Shadows) for a country rock side project called the Notting Hillbillies. A one time performance at a small pub in Holbeck, Leeds turned into a tour and then a record, **Missing . . . Presumed Having a Good Time**. This low key set of traditional songs ("Run Me Down"; "Railroad Song"), covers of the Louvins ("Weapon of Prayer"), the Delmores ("Blues Stay Away From Me"), and Charlie Rich ("Feel Like Going Home"), and originals is a definite English take on American country music with lots of Dire Straits undertones. Strangely appealing, it hardly made a dent in the U.S. but did chart in Great Britain. This was supposed to be the Hillbillies one and only album, but there is a live bootleg, **A Funny Friendly Night**, floating around, and in 1993, the band got back together (sans Franklin and Fletcher) for a benefit to save the Swan Hunter Shipyard. A limited edition (750 copies) recording of that event, **Swan Hunter**, includes Dire Straits material and cuts from **Missing**. Knopfler also did a memorable album with Chet Atkins called **Neck & Neck**. As you might expect, it's full of plenty of great guitar licks as well as some humorous banter between Atkins and Knopfler.

Ed Bicknell (d); Marcus Cliff (b); Brendan Croker (r.g.,v); Guy Fletcher (ky); Paul Franklin (p.s.); Mark Knopfler (l.g.,v); Steve Phillips (g,v)

> **Missing . . . Presumed Having a Good Time**/Warner Brothers/1990
> **A Friendly Funny Night (Live)**/Backstage/1990 (boot)
> **Neck & Neck** (Knopfler & Chet Atkins)/Columbia/1990
> **Live in London**/Indian/1992 (boot)
> **Swan Hunter (Live)**/By Fans, For Fans/1995 (boot)

The Notting Hillbillies Web Page
//www-stud.unisg.ch/~tgygax/ds/biographies/nhb.html

Notting Hillbillies: Having a Good Time Online
//huizen.dds.nl/~lfb/home.htm

Gary P. Nunn (The Lost Gonzo Band)

Outlaw; Honky Tonk
Oklahoma

Back in the heady days of Outlaw country, a young Texas boy wrote a song, "London Homesick Blues (Home With the Armadillo)" that became the official anthem of the movement, the theme song for *Austin City Limits*, and one of the great unofficial state songs along with "Yellow Rose of Texas," "San Antonio Rose," and "Waltz Across Texas." Based on a true experience, the tune was penned by Gary P. Nunn in 1973 and was made into a mega hit by Jerry Jeff Walker on his hugely successful **Viva Terlingua!** At the time, Nunn was bass player for Walker, Willie Nelson, and Michael Murphey and fronted the Lost Gonzo Band which included other members of Jerry Jeff's group. The Gonzos developed their own brand of Texas progressive country on three albums in the 1970s and reunited in the 1990s with Nunn for the album **Rendezvous**. In the interim, Nunn pursued a solo career with his Sons of the Bunkhouse and became a big favorite on the Southwestern circuit. Nunn's albums (**Border States**; **Home With the Armadillo**; **Roadtrip**; **Totally Guacamole**; **Under My Hat**) celebrate the culture of the region including a new unofficial Texas anthem, "What I Like About Texas." His work in this regard led to his being named Texas' Official Ambassador to the World in 1985 by gubernatorial decree. Based in Oklahoma, Nunn hosts the annual Terlingua North music festival at his ranch near Hanna and regularly plays the Broken Spoke. Gary's

greatest hits from the last 25 years were released in 1998 on **What I Like About Texas**.

The Lost Gonzo Band: Donny Dolan (d,perc); Kelly Dunn (ky); John Inmon (g,v); Robert Livingston (b,ky,v); Gary Nunn (b,g,p,v)

> **Lost Gonzo Band**/MCA/1975
> **Thrills** (Lost Gonzo Band)/MCA/1976
> **Signs of Life** (Lost Gonzo Band)/Capitol/1978
> **Border States**/Campfire/1986
> **For Old-Times Sake**/Campfire/1989
> **Live at Poor David's Pub**/Poor David's/1991
> **Totally Guacamole**/Campfire/1992
> **Home With the Armadillo**/Campfire/1993
> **Roadtrip**/Campfire/1994
> **Rendezvous** (Lost Gonzo Band)/Vireo/1995
> **Hands of Time** (Lost Gonzo Band)/Vireo/1996
> **Under My Hat**/Campfire/1996
> **What I Like About Texas**/Campfire/1998

Gary P. Nunn, Route 1, Hanna, OK 74845; 918-657-2432, (Fax) 918-657-2438

Gary P. Nunn Home Page
//www.hepcat.com/campfire/gpnunn/index.html

Unofficial Gary P. Nunn Home Page
//rampages.onramp.net/~mitchel/gpn/gpn.html

German Home of the Bluebonnets Unofficial Gary P. Nunn Home Page
//www.oberland.net/homepages/remeth/GaryPNunn.htm

The Lost Gonzo Band Home Page
//www.lscn.com/music/gonzo.htm

Wink O' Bannon (Bodeco)

Insurgent Country
Louisville, Kentucky

Wink O'Bannon is best known for his work as a lead guitarist with the Louisville band Bodeco. Named for Bo Diddley and zydeco, this band was famous for its roots rocking raunch-o-rama style that places it in the same company as Southern Culture on the Skids and the Gibson Brothers. **Bone, Hair, and Hide** and **Calling All Dogs** are unrelenting aural attacks, complete with scorching guitars (O'Bannon and Ricky Feathers) and growling vocals (Feathers) on songs whose titles just about say it all: "Wicked, Mean, and Evil," "M. F. Tramp," "Crazy Wild," "Suicide Ride," "Nut Fuzz," "Spank Your Fanny." O'Bannon who also played guitar in Eleventh Dream Day (with Catherine Irwin of Freakwater) carved out a niche in alt. country as a soloist with "Cry Baby" on the inaugural insurgent country collection, **For a Life of Sin**. It was taken from his full-length **Matthew Wink O'Bannon**, a "big turd recorded between 1984-1983" with mostly just O'Bannon on lead and Brett Holsclaw on drums. Like Bodeco's recordings, it is a giant but glorious mess of blues, boogie woogie, rockabilly, country rock, swamp, surf, and Memphis r&b. In 1997, O'Bannon co-produced **Sourmash**, a compilation of Louisville alt. country/roots rock groups including the Palace Brothers (previously unreleased song), Starbilly, Bodeco, Chicken Hawk, and O'Bannon with his brother and sister as Nod.

Bodeco: Jimmy Brown (b); Brian Burkett (d); Ricky Feathers (l.g.,l.v.); Matthew "Wink" O'Bannon (l.g.,r.g.v); Gary Stillwell (ky,perc)

  Bone, Hair & Hide (Bodeco)/Homestead/1992
  "Suicide Ride" b/w "This Train" (Bodeco)/
    Homestead/1992 (7")
  "High Window" b/w "M. F. Tramp"
    (Bodeco)/Feedbag/1992 (7")
  "Cry Baby" (Wink O'Bannon) on **For a Life of Sin**/
    Bloodshot/1994
  Matthew Wink O'Bannon/Safe House/1995
  Callin' All Dogs (Bodeco)/Safe House/1995
  Sourmash: A Louisville Compilation/X-Static/1997

Tim O'Brien (Hot Rize; Red Knuckles and the Trailblazers; The O'Boys)

Bluegrass; Old-Time; Honky Tonk
Hot Rize/Red Knuckles: 1978-1992; 1998-

Growing up in Wheeling, West Virginia, Tim O'Brien sang folk style duets with his sister Mollie, learned fiddle and mandolin, and played in bluegrass, country, and rock bands. In the late 1970s, he moved to Boulder, Colorado where he met Charles Sawtelle and Pete Wernick. The latter, known as Dr. Banjo, had been a member of Country Cooking and in 1977 recorded a solo album, **Dr. Banjo Steps Out**, which showcases his signature "phase shifted" banjo. Among those helping out were Charles Sawtelle and Tim O'Brien on fiddle, mandolin, and vocals. A year later Wernick (along with Sawtelle) returned the favor by performing on O'Brien's debut solo, **Guess Who's in Town**. From these collaborations came a new bluegrass band called Hot Rize after the mystery ingredient in Martha White's Self Rising Flour. With the addition of Nick Forster on guitar, Hot Rize began recording for Flying Fish and, anchored by O'Brien's high lonesome vocals and hot picking by all, became one of the hottest new bluegrass bands of the 1980s. In 1982, they came up with the clever idea of a 1940s-1950s style alter-ego honky tonk/swing band, Red Knuckles and the Trailblazers, that would "tour" with Hot Rize and perform between their bluegrass sets. Combining humor with some very authentic country/western musicianship, Red and the Trailblazers (named for Martha White's brand of dog food) became a fan favorite and recorded several albums that cover Lefty, Hank, Bob Wills, George Jones, Hank Snow, and many other country greats. Sadly, Hot Rize/Red Knuckles broke up in 1992. Wernick went on to pursue a career as a progressive banjoist with his group, Live Five; Forster formed a band called the Whippets and hosted the popular syndicated public radio music program, E-Town; and Sawtelle became a guitarist in Peter Rowan's bluegrass project, the Panama Red Riders. Meanwhile, O'Brien moved on to a number of projects. He recorded several solo albums weaving together bluegrass,

old-time, honky tonk, rock, and Cajun. His most ambitious effort, **Red on Blonde** (Grammy nominated), presents bluegrass and old-timey versions of Dylan songs such as "Masters of War," "Oxford Town," "Farewell Angelina," and "Subterranean Homesick Blues." Several of Tim's originals ("Walk the Way the Wind Blows"; "Untold Stories") became top ten country hits for other artists. In addition, O'Brien reunited with his sister Mollie to record several collections of duets covering traditional old-time and bluegrass; he also toured and recorded with his band the O'Boys (Scott Nygaard; Mark Schatz). In early 1996, Hot Rize re-formed for a tour, but future plans were put in doubt when Sawtelle was diagnosed with leukemia. Fortunately, treatment was controlling the disease, but medical costs were high, and a fund was set up on his behalf (c/o Crow Recording Studio, 4000 Wallingford Ave. N, Seattle, WA 98013). By 1998, things were looking up , and Hot Rize was back out on the circuit. O'Brien continued his string of pleasant recordings with **When No One's Around** in 1997 and was invited to be on two prominent 1998 tributes, **Clinch Mountain Country** (Ralph Stanley) and **Will Sing for Food** (Dwight Yoakam).

Hot Rize: Nick Forster (g,l.v.,h.v.); Tim O'Brien (f,md,l.v.,h.v.); Charles Sawtelle (b,l.v.,h.v.); Pete Wernick (bj,h.v.)
Red Knuckles & The Trailblazers: Red Knuckles/Tim O'Brien (a.g.,l.v.); Wendell Mercantile/Nick Forster (e.g.); Elmo Otto/Tim O'Brien (f); Waldo Otto/Pete Wernick (s.g.); Slade/Charles Sawtelle (b).
The O'Boys: Mark Schatz (md,v); Scott Nygaard (g,v)

  Dr. Banjo Step's Out (Pete Wernick)/Flying Fish/1977
  Guess Who's in Town (Tim O'Brien)/Biscuit City/1978
  Hot Rize/Flying Fish/1979
  Radio Boogie (Hot Rize)/Flying Fish/1981
  Hot Rize Presents Red Knuckles and the Trailblazers/
    Flying Fish/1982
  **Red Knuckles and the Trailblazers/Hot Rize in
    Concert**/Flying Fish/1982; 1984
  The French Way (Red Knuckles)/1984
  Hot Rize in Concert (Hot Rize)/Flying Fish/1984
  Traditional Ties (Hot Rize)/Sugar Hill/1985
  Hard Year Blues (Tim O'Brien)/Flying Fish/1985
  Untold Stories (Hot Rize)/Sugar Hill/1987
  Take Me Back (Tim & Mollie O'Brien)/Sugar Hill/1988
  Odd Man In (Tim O'Brien)/Sugar Hill/1991
  Take It Home (Hot Rize)/Sugar Hill/1992
  Shades of the Past (Red Knuckles)/Sugar Hill/1992
  Remember Me (Tim & Mollie O'Brien)/Sugar Hill/1992
  Oh Boy! O'Boy! (with the O'Boys)/Sugar Hill/1993
  Pete Wernick's Live Five/Sugar Hill/1993
  Rock in My Shoe (Tim O'Brien)/Sugar Hill/1995
  Away Out on the Mountain (Tim & Mollie O'Brien)/
    Sugar Hill/1995
  Red on Blonde (Tim O'Brien)/Sugar Hill/1996
  I Tell You What!(Pete Wernick's Live Five)/Sugar
    Hill/1996
  When No One's Around (Tim O'Brien)/Sugar Hill/1997
  "Let Me Love You One More Time" on **Clinch Mountain
    Country: Ralph Stanley & Friends**/Rebel/1998

"Thousand Miles From Nowhere" on **Will Sing for Food: The Songs of Dwight Yoakam**/Little Dog/1998

Hot Rize Fan Club, P.O. Box 121134, Nashville, TN 37212

Tim O'Brien Fan Club, P.O. Box 4040, Duke Station, Durham, NC 27706

Hot Rize/Red Knuckles Web Page
//www.banjo.com/Profiles/HotRize.html

Tim O'Brien/Mollie O'Brien Web Page
//www.banjo.com/Profiles/Obrien.html

Bluegrass: Pete Wernick
//www.banjo.com/profiles/wernick.html

Tim O'Brien & Pete Wernick/Sugar Hill Pages
//www.sugarhillrecords.com

Lucky Oceans (Dude Ranch)

Steel Guitar; Western Swing; Honky Tonk
Philadelphia, Pennsylvania; April 22, 1951-

Born and raised in Philadelphia, Reuben Gosfield (aka Lucky Oceans) was greatly influenced by jazz which prepared him well for his work with the great modern Western swing band Asleep at the Wheel. Oceans was one of the founding members of the group in 1969. He remained with them through their best albums, the quality of which was due in no small part to his stellar steel work. Lucky O left Asleep in 1980 and moved to his wife's native home in Western Australia. In 1983, Oceans assembled a number of his former bandmates, Ray Benson, LeRoy Preston, Chris O'Connell, Danny Levin, and Floyd Domino (as the Asleep at the Wheel Review) to record **Lucky Steals the Wheel** which stayed true to the band's old sound on covers of "Deep Water," "Careless Love," "Playboy Rag," "Weary Blues" and instrumental originals ("Lucky Lopes In"). Back in Australia, Oceans worked as a session player for various artists and formed his own band, Dude Ranch. Their **Dude Ranch** is full of wonderful swing and honky tonk (reminiscent of vintage Asleep at the Wheel) highlighted by Oceans' innovative steel. In late 1995, Oceans briefly renewed his association with Asleep at the Wheel for their 25th anniversary reunion concert and 1997 live recording. Back in Australia, Lucky worked with a new group called Snakefoot and hosted "The Planet," a world music program on Radio National.

The Asleep at the Wheel Review: Ray Benson (r.g.); Fran Christina (d); Floyd Domino (p); Johnny Gimble (f); Danny Levin (f,p); John Nicholas (v); Chris O'Connell (v); Leroy Preston (v); Spencer Starnes (b)
Dude Ranch: Donal Baylor (f); Greg Bird (e.g.); Peter Busher (g, l.v.); Richard Danker (b); Jim Fisher (g,h.v.); Gary France (d); Tony Garnier (b); Roger Garood (saxes); Kent Hughes (e.g.); Sam LeMann (e.g.); Lucky Oceans (p.s.); Bob Patient (p)

> **Lucky Steals the Wheel**/Blind Pig/1983 (LP)
> **Dude Ranch**/Darling Rangers Australia/1992

Lucky Oceans c/o ABC Radio National, GPO Box 9994, Perth, W.A., 6001 Australia

The Planet //www.abc.net.au/rn/music/planet/planet.htm
See Asleep at the Wheel; The Starliners

The O'Kanes

See Kieran Kane

Oh Susanna (aka Suzie Ungerleider)

Singer/Songwriter; Old-Time
Amherst, Massachusetts/Vancouver, British Columbia, Canada; 1969-

Suzie Ungerleider first saw the light of day in Amherst, Massachusetss, but when she was just a year old, her father moved the family to Vancouver after he was hired by the University of British Columbia. Growing up in Canada, Suzie's taste in music was fairly atypical for her generation (rock, punk, etc.), but she credits the Rolling Stones with helping connect her with blues and country. Later, when she moved to Montreal to attend college (McGill and Concordia), Ungerleider became more deeply involved in traditional music. A roommate exposed her to Hank Williams and for a time, Suzie hosted a roots music radio show ("Great Works of Country & Western Civilization") that featured music and discussion of the history of folk, bluegrass, and Western swing. That experience really got her hooked on traditional music, and she began to noodle around with the guitar and singing and even composed a few "joke songs." However, Suzie didn't get serious about singing/songwriting until she met local musician Scott Chernoff who gave her encouragement, co-wrote several songs, and invited her into his band. But, eventually, Ungerleider decided to go it alone and moving back to Vancouver, immersed herself body, mind, and spirit into traditional country music. She was especially drawn to the genuineness and emotive power of old-time Appalachian ballads, particularly ones about violence, death, and sorrow. She crafted songs in this vein and in the summer of 1995, with just an $80 Stella mail order guitar, she premiered her new persona, Oh Susanna, at the Railway Club in Vancouver and created quite a sensation with her mournful vocals and spooky originals. After recording a self-produced cassette EP (**A Shot of Old Susanna**), Suzie/Susanna started her own Stella records and cut a seven song self-titled CD. A true student of the music, Oh Susanna has said she wants "to communicate some kind of eerie beauty" through "intense and terrifying music that evokes mystery." With intelligent and haunting songs like "Crooked Down the Road," "Deathyard," "Shame," and "All Eyes on Baby," she certainly reaches her goal. Comparisons with Gillian Welch, Iris DeMent, and early Michelle Shocked are accurate, but Oh Susanna can stand on her own among the growing number of modern day interpreters of traditional music. In 1999, with backing from a band including Bob Egan (Freakwater, Wilco) and Bazil Donovan of Blue Rodeo, she recorded **Johnstown** which gorgeously reworks songs from her 1996 cassette and adds seven new ones. An extensive tour of the U.S. in early 1999 included a memorable showcase at SXSW.

A Shot of Oh Susanna/SU/1996 (CS EP)
Oh Susanna/Stella/1997 (EP)
Johnstown/Stella/1999

Oh Susanna/Stella Records, 1363 Fountain Way, Vancouver, BC V6H 3TA Canada; (fax) 416-531-5879

Oh Susanna //www.swellinteractive.com/ohsusanna/

ohsusanna@sympatico.ca

The Okeh Wranglers
Hillbilly Bop
Southampton, England; 1989-

To borrow from an old adage, "the family that plays together, stays together!" Just ask the Kyme clan of Southampton, England, who play hillbilly and Western swing in the 1990s that you'd swear was recorded in the 1940s-1950s. Their vintage country sound is the product of parents and children pulling and picking together: father Pete, Sr. handles rhythm guitar and male leads (sounds like Onie Wheeler or early Billy Joe Shaver); mother Sheila slaps the stand-up bass; Pete, Jr. completes the rhythm section on drums and Irene provides steel guitar; but the real highlight is the work of daughters, Christine and Louise. Not only do they contribute beautiful lead vocals and harmonies, but Louise adds nice touches on accordion, and Christine plays hot fiddle and lead guitar. All the Kyme's participate in the songwriting process which results in some terrific honky tonk swing originals to go along with covers of standards like "I'll Never Be Free," "Don't Let the Stars Get in Your Eyes," and "Well Oh Well." As of 1996, the Okeh Wranglers had released a 10" LP, **Hop Skip Right Over That Stump,** an excellent CD, **Beneath the Western Skies**, and a Christine and Louise album of hillbilly bop duets called **Jukebox Hop**. In 1997 and again in 1998, they delivered their best yet, **Honky Tonk Crazy** and **Lonesome Vistas**, which display their incredible diversity on honky tonk, Western and Eastern swing, rockabilly, and Cajun. Absolutely not to be missed!

Christine (a.g.,l.g.,f,v); Irene (e.g.,s.g.); Louise (acc,v); Pete, Sr. (a.g.,v); Pete, Jr. (d); Sheila (u.b.)

Hop Skip Right Over That Stump/Faye UK/1994 (10")
Beneath the Western Skies/Fury UK/1996
Jukebox Hop (Christine & Lou Kyme)/Fury UK/1996
Honky Tonk Crazy/Blue Smoke UK/1997
Lonesome Vistas/Blue Smoke UK/1998

The Okeh Wranglers/Blue Smoke Records, P.O. Box 631, Southampton, England SO16 5ZG; +44 (0) 1703 770453

The Okeh Wranglers Web Site
//dialspace.dial.pipex.com/town/parkkcd11/

bluesmoke@dial.pipex.com

The Okra All-Stars
See Ricky Barnes; Hank McCoy; Jeb Loy Nichols; Dave Schramm

The Old 97s
Insurgent Country
Dallas, Texas; 1993-

Slightly mystified by their success and inclusion in insurgent country (they had to look the word up), the Old 97s quickly rose to the top of Dallas' burgeoning alt. country scene and became a presence on the national scene as well in the 1990s. The group's co-founders, Ken Bethea, Rhett Miller, and Murry Hammond, had been in various bands (Peyote Cowboys; Smeg Wentfields; Killbilly) in the Dallas area and made their first appearance as the Old 97s in early 1993 for a small group of friends at a local club. After recording an independently produced cassette EP, they entered the studio in the spring of 1994 to make their first full length CD. The result was **Hitchhike to Rhome** produced by Alan Wooley of Dallas' insurgent bluegrass band, Killbilly. On a supporting tour in the East and Midwest, the Old 97s opened for such alt. country bands as Blue Mountain and Freakwater. On returning to Big D, they released their album which quickly sold out its initial 1000 copies (as long time Dallas alt. country artist Donny Ray Ford noted, "It went plywood!"). The band got the attention of Bloodshot Records and signed a record deal. Their song "Por Favor" was included on the insurgent country compilation, **Hell-Bent** and was followed by **Wreck Your Life** which sold 2,500 copies in the first week. Through 1995 and into 1996, the Old 97s toured continually and were part of Bloodshot's Insurgent Country Showcase at SXSW (1996) along with the Waco Brothers, Slobberbone, Blue Mountain, and Whiskeytown. As for their sound, the band claims to be a rock band that only incidentally plays country and attribute the country influences to growing up in Texas. On **Hitchhike to Rhome**, the country is overt as on covers of Bob Wills' "Miss Molly," Merle Haggard's "Mama Tried" (and a great hidden track version of "Tupelo County Jail") or on originals such as "Dancing With Tears in My Eyes," but overall, it underlies the rock elements that dominate their sound. Their rocking side was full blown on **Wreck Your Life**; the insurgent country sound of the Bloodshot label was much more in evidence with Jon Langford making a guest appearance to yell "Asshole!" on their cover of his "Over the Cliff" (Don Walser even stops by to do a little yodeling). In late 1996, the Old 97s signed with Elektra, and 1997 proved to be the band's red letter year when they cut a single with Waylon Jennings, performed on the No Depression Tour and at Lollapalooza, and released **Too Far to Care**. This recording marked somewhat of a return to the Old 97s original country rock ("Northern Line"; "West Texas Tear Drops") sound but with plenty of hard edged, punky "strum and twang" ("Time Bomb"; "Four Leaf Clover" with Exene Cervenka) and their slightly cynical brand of humor ("Barrier Reef"). Happily, **Hitchhike** was re-released in 1998, and the band polished up a new recording, **Fight Songs**, for release in mid-1999. Afraid of being pigeonholed, the Old 97s have publicly tried to distance themselves from the alternative country movement, but, like it or not, they are one of its most popular and visible acts.

Ken Bethea (e.g.); Murry Hammond (b,bj,v); Rhett Miller (a.g.v); Philip Peeples (d)

> **Hitchhike to Rhome**/Big Iron/1994; 1998
> "Por Favor" on **Hell-Bent**/Bloodshot/1995
> "W-I-F-E" b/w "Eyes"/Bloodshot/1995
> **Wreck Your Life**/Bloodshot/1995
> "Victoria Lee" and "Doreen" on **Live at the Barley House**/BH/1995
> "I'll Be Home for Christmas" and "Have a Holly Jolly Christmas" on **Christmas in Deep Noellum**/Big Iron/1995
> "Stoned" (Funland Band) b/w "Garage Sale" (Old 97s)/Idol/1995 (10")
> "Cryin' Drunk" b/w "Let the Train Blow the Whistle"/Bloodshot/1996 (7")
> "The Other Side" b/w "Iron Road" (with Waylon Jennings)/Elektra/1997 (7")
> **Too Far to Care**/Elektra/1997
> **Fight Songs**/Elektra/1999

The Old 97s Home Page //www.old97s.com

The Old 97s Online Mailing List //www.onelist.com/subscribe.cgi/wrecked/

Old and In the Way

See The Grateful Dead/Jerry Garcia; David Grisman; Peter Rowan

The Old Joe Clarks

Lo-Fi Country Rock
San Francisco, California; c.1994-

The wife/husband team of Jill and Mike Coykendall began making beautiful music together in Kansas as members of the modern classical unit, the Wichita New Music Ensemble. In the early 1990s, they moved to San Francisco, switched to lo-fi country rock, and became known as the Old Joe Clarks. Going through several amalgamations, the Clarks finally met and clicked with dobro/lap steel player, Kurt Stevenson. In 1996, they recorded **Town of Ten** which *Dirty Linen* accurately described as a cross "between the Cowboy Junkies and the Scud Mountain Boys tanked up on espresso." Like those bands, the Clarks aim for a mellow, homey feel provided by a variety of acoustic instruments and Mike Coykendall's hushed vocals (sounding quite a bit like Dylan). His originals like "Breaking Ground," "Welfare Hotel," "Town of Ten," "Weekender," and "Too Late" have a familiar, traditional ring to them backed by spare but solid old-timey accompaniment. **Town of Ten**, which reached #23 on the Gavin Americana charts in 1996, was re-released by Checkered Past in 1997 and was followed by **Metal Shed Blues** in 1999.

Mike Coykendall (bj,g,hm,v); Jill McClelland-Coykendall (b,cl,melodica,v); Mark Orton (d); Kurt Stevenson (db,l.s.)

> **Town of Ten**/Open Mind/1996; Checkered Past/1997
> **Metal Shed Blues**/Checkered Past/1999

The Old Joe Clarks, P.O. Box 219710, San Francisco, CA 94121-0710

The Old Joe Clarks/Checkered Past Home Page //www.checkeredpast.com

Will Oldham (Palace; Palace Brothers; Palace Music; Palace Songs)

Lo-Fi Gothic
Louisville, Kentucky; 1972-

Will Oldham is, to put it mildly, an enigma. Notoriously reluctant to be interviewed, the few he has granted have driven interviewers mad with their mis- and disinformation. What we do know is that Oldham was born and raised in Louisville, Kentucky, and before he took up music was into acting. His first experiences as an actor were on the stages of theaters in Louisville, and he tried his luck in New York and L.A. before returning to his home town. In 1987, Oldham landed a role in John Sayles labor saga, *Matewan* and had minor parts in a few other films.

When it comes to dealing with Oldham's musical career, the mystery deepens. If Oldham is hesitant concerning the details of his life, he is even more reticent when discussing his music. Somewhere around 1989, he began playing music informally with friends and in 1990 recorded his first album, **Fearful Symmetry**, under the name Box of Chocolates. In 1992, Oldham came up with the Palace concept in which a rotating group of musicians or Oldham solo would record with little rehearsal and maximum spontaneity just to see what would happen. Over the years, this produced a plethora of singles and four full length CDs under the names Palace, Palace Brothers, Palace Music, Palace Songs, and sometimes the Sundowners. Just who is involved in each of these incarnations is hard to pin down due to meager or non existent liner notes, but the most consistent performers have been Will's brothers, and he has also recorded with members of Slint, Sebadoh, and Gastro Del Sol plus assorted guests including writers and university professors. The result is a brooding country music that by comparison makes Hank seem like a pretty happy go lucky guy. Oldham, accompanied very sparingly by acoustic or electric guitar, slide, drums, and banjo, sounds like a shell shocked hillbilly endlessly ruminating over drunkenness, sex and death, sin and salvation. **There Is No One That Will Take Care of You, Days in the Wake**, and **Arise Therefore** are all excruciatingly slow and sad in a way that alternately repels and attracts. The exception to this lethargy is the loud, cacophonous "country rock" of **Viva Last Blues**.

In late 1996, Oldham announced he would no longer perform under the various Palace names but only as a solo. Early in 1997, Drag City released a collection of Palace singles called **Lost Blues and Other Songs** and soon after, Oldham made his solo debut with a single "Patience"/"Take However Long You Want" and a split 7" (with Rising Shotgun) covering two David Allen Coe songs. In addition, he contributed to the soundtracks of independent films, *The Broken Giant* and *Dutch Harbor: Where the Sea Breaks Its Back*. On his first full length solo, **Joya**, Oldham delivered more languid jeremiads on "O Let It Be," "Antagonism,""Under What Was Oppression," "Be Still and Know God," "Apocalypse," "No!," and "I Am Still What I Meant to Be." Late in 1997, he collaborated with the Dirty 3 on an EP called **Western Music**, and they backed him on an Australian tour in early 1998. The bonus CD, **Songs Put Together for the Broken Giant**, originally issued with the 1st 1,000 copies of **Arise Therefore** was re-released as **Black/Rich Music** in late 1998. Then, at the beginning of 1999, the great alt. country chameleon changed colors once more and released lo-fi singles and one CD, **I See Darkness**, under the name Bonnie Prince Billy.

Fearful Symmetry (Box of Chocolates)/Mad Entropic Carnival/1990
"Ohio River Boat Song" b/w "Drinking Woman" (Palace Songs)/Drag City/1992 (7")
"For the Mekons"(Palace Brothers) on **Hey Drag City**/Drag City/1993
There is No One That Will Take Care of You (Palace Songs)/Drag City/1993
"Come In" b/w "Trudy Dies" (Palace)/Drag City/1993 (7")
"Goat Songs" (Sundowners)/Sea Note/1993 (7")
"Horses" b/w "Stable Will" (Palace Songs)/Drag City/1994 (7")
An Arrow Through the Bitch (Palace Brothers)/Domino UK/1994 (12" EP)
Days in the Wake (Palace Brothers)/Drag City/1994
Hope (Palace Songs)/Drag City/1994 (CD EP)
"O How I Enjoy the Light" b/w "Marriage" (Palace Songs)/Drag City/1994 (7")
"West Palm Beach" b/w "Gulf Shores" (Palace)/Drag City/1994 (7")
"The Mountain" b/w "End of Traveling" (Palace)/Drag City/1995 (7")
The Mountain (Palace)/Drag City/1995 (EP)
"Gezundheit" b/w "Let the Wires Ring" (Palace)/Hausmusik Ger./1995 (7")
Viva Last Blues (Palace Music)/Palace Records/1995
"Every Mother's Son" b/w "No More Rides" (Palace)/Drag City/1996 (7")
Arise, Therefore (Palace)/Drag City/1996 (1st 1,000 copies included the EP **Songs Put Together for The Broken Giant**)
"The Girl With the Thing in Her Hair" b/w "The Summer Song" (Sundowners)/Sea Note/1996 (7")
Palace Live/Drag City/1996 (7")
Lost Blues and Other Songs (Palace)/Drag City/1997
"Patience" b/w "Take However Long You Want" (Will Oldham)/Drag City/1997 (7")
"In My Mind" (Will Oldham) b/w "Spotlight" (Rising Shotgun)/Drag City/1997 (7")

Joya (Will Oldham)/Drag City/1997
"Big Balls" (Palace) b/w "Let There Be Rock" (Zeni Geva)/Skin Graft/1997 (7")
Western Music (with the Dirty 3)/Ovni Sp.1997 (CD EP)
Black/Rich Music/Drag City/1998 (originally issued with **Arise Therefore** as **Songs Put Together for The Broken Giant**)
"Apocalypse No!" (Will Oldham) on **Sounds of the New West**/Uncut UK/1998
"Black Dissimulation" b/w "No Such as What I Want" (Bonnie Prince Billy)/Nomad/1998 (7")
I See Darkness (Bonnie Prince Billy)/Domino/1999

The Pulpit: Unofficial Palace Home Page
//lookandfeel.thehub.com.au/thepulpit/

david@thehub.com.au

The Royal Stable/Will Oldham Site
//www.flakkee.net/~ljmeijer/oldham/index.htm

Official Palace Records Homepage
//www.palacerecords.com

The Billions Palace Web Page
//www.billions.com/palace/palace.html

Lost Blues: Palace Japanese Fan Page
//www.geocities.co.jp/hollywood/6951/

James Richard Oliver
Psychobilly
Blue Ridge, Georgia

For the better part of a decade, James Richard Oliver has been quietly churning out psychobilly gems at his rustic home studio near Blue Ridge, Georgia. In the late 1980s, he was lead guitarist for a punkabilly trio called the Boonies who were roughly modeled after Jason and the Nashville Scorchers. After a series of mishaps (suicide, robbery, etc.), they disbanded in 1991, and Oliver started his own Illbilly Records shortly thereafter. Influenced by Elvis, Johnny Cash, Sid King, the Ramones, the Cramps, Mojo Nixon, Cordell Jackson, Billy Poore, and the Flat Duo Jets to name just a few, he recorded a series of lo-fi tapes brimming with delectably demented rockabilly and psychobilly. **Blown Mad Baby**, **Psychobilly Joe Bob**, **Lo-Fi**, and **Hemi-Hayride** feature J.R. on all instruments (electric guitar, drums, bass) and vocals and though the production values are strictly bargain basement, his fiercely exuberant d.i.y. spirit (like a less frenzied Hasil Adkins) and crazy originals ("40 Ft. Elvis"; "Lord of the Flies"; "Juicehead Cracker"; "Rockin' With J.C."; "Belly Acres"; "Mona the Donut Queen"; "T.V.D.T.s") are irresistible. Oliver's "Hillbilly Monster From Arkansas" was included on the 1996 **Tribute to the Legendary Billy Lee Riley**.

Blown Mad Baby!/Illbilly/1992 (CS)
Psychobilly Joe Bob/Illbilly/1995 (CS)
"Hillbilly Monster in Arkansas" on **A Tribute to the Legendary Billy Lee Riley**/BSC Sanity Check/1995
Dr. Iguana Meets the Illbilly Monster (Ken Burke & J.R. Oliver)/Illbilly/1996 (CS)
Lo-Fi/Illbilly/1997 (CS)
Hemi Hayride/Illbilly/1998 (CS)

James Richard Oliver/Illbilly, P.O. Box 924, Blue Ridge, GA 30513-0924

One Fell Swoop

Acoustic Country Rock
St. Louis, Missouri; 1993-

As their self description ("folk country irish blues whatever") implies, the acoustically inclined band One Fell Swoop is a little hard to categorize. But, whatever you want to call their sound, there is no denying this group has all the ingredients that make up a real winner: old-time twang, savvy songwriting, skillful instrumentation, and knock out vocals. Formed in 1993, One Fell Swoop quickly became a vital part of St. Louis' active alt. country scene. They made their recording debut in 1996 with a cut on the **Out of the Gate Again** compilation and a self titled EP. Reviews in both local and national (*3rd Coast Music*; *Country Standard Time*; *No Depression*) publications were positively glowing; critics were rightfully impressed by the contributions of Steve Molitor on harmonica and Andy Ploof on dobro, fiddle, and mandolin, the astute originals by John Wendland ("$500 Funeral"; "Fences"; "Flesh & Blood"), strong vocals by Wendland, Dade Farrar, and the stunning Cheryl Stryker. Late in 1996, OFS was invited to play Farm Aid along side Steve Earle, Son Volt, and Neil Young. In 1997, they became part of the Twangfest contingent and released the full length **Look Out** which like its predecessor drew universal raves. With a multi-pronged attack that splits singing and songwriting duties, One Fell Swoop comes at you with many facets as they move through one winning tune after another. They give you sentiment ("Good Heart"), sorrow ("Sad State of Affairs"; "Good for You"), bitterness ("Entourage"), somberness ("Lone White House"), jubilance ("Crazy, Wild-Eyed Preacherman"), country heartache ("Bitter End"), and humor ("Seven Solid Days"; "Hairless Chihuahua"). Fans of groups like the Damnations TX, the New Patrons, and Freakwater will certainly feel right at home with One Fell Swoop.

Dade Farrar (b,v); Spencer Marquart (d,v); Steve Molitor (f,hm,wh); Andy Ploof (db,f,md,v); Cheryl Stryker (p,v); John Wendland (g,md,v)

"Fences" on **Out of the Gate Again**/BJAM/1996
One Fell Swoop/Magoo/1996 (EP)
"Fences" on **Edges From the Postcard**/Semi-Tone/1997
Look Out/Magoo/1997; Brambus Switz./1998
"One to Grow On" on **Edges From the Postcard 2**/
    P2/1998

One Fell Swoop Page //www.musicfolk.com/swoop

swoop@musicfolk.com; Magoorec@aol.com

One Riot, One Ranger

Bluegrass; Country Rock; Swing
Columbus, Ohio; 1990-

Of all the fine alt. country bands to emerge on the Columbus, Ohio, scene in the early 1990s, the only one left standing is One Riot, One Ranger. Named for a Texas Rangers' motto, 1R1R was the brainchild of Mark Wyatt who had previously been keyboardist with the local punk band Great Plains. It was during this time that Wyatt developed an interest in bluegrass music, and after Great Plains ended in 1989, he learned accordion and started 1R1R in 1990. But wait, hold on just a minute you're saying, "An accordion in a bluegrass band!" Well, as you might guess, this ain't no ordinary group. Starting from a bluegrass base (they have a banjo, dobro, and fiddle), 1R1R blends in blues, country/western, and swing plus an occasional tune by Pere Ubu or Roky Erikson. Their first self released, self titled cassette featured covers of bluegrass songs "Tennessee Coot," "The Memory of Your Smile" (Stanley Bros.), "The Old Home Place," a bluegrass version of Duke Ellington's "Caravan," and bluegrass and cowboy originals by all the Rangers. In 1995, they won the Columbus Music Awards Outstanding Country Band for their unique style and engaging harmonies. A year later, Fundamental Records released 1R1R's first CD called **Faces Made for Radio**, a mix of originals and covers of the Delmore's "Blues Stay Away from Me" plus "Drifting Texas Sand," "Hello City Limits," and "Cloud 149." In early 1997, 1R1R received greater exposure in the alt. country community when their cover of the Delmore's "Southern Moon" was included on Bloodshot Records' **Straight Outta Boone County**. They were also closely connected to the Postcard 2 community performing at the inaugural Twangfest in June 1997 and contributing to **Edges From the Postcard**. A new CD for Checkered Past Records was in the works for release in 1998, and 1R1R even played a SXSW Checkered Past showcase with soon to be labelmates Paul Burch, Tom House, Johnny Dowd, and Lonesome Bob. However, at the 11th hour, Checkered Past pulled out leaving the band searching for another label for their completed recording. After a no go with Bloodshot, One Riot finally found a home with the new alt. country/Americana label Hayden's Ferry which subsequently put out **Side Tracks**, a truly excellent album of bluegrass, gospel, and country highlighted by impeccable playing and beautiful three-part harmonies. 1R1R returned to Twangfest in Summer 1998 and in November participated in the first ever Twangburgh alt. country festival in Pittsburgh.

Mark Gaskill (g, l.v.); Peter Remenyi (b,db,hm); Chas Williams (f,md,); Mark Wyatt (acc,v); Carl Yaffey (bj)

One Riot, One Ranger/1R1R/1994 (CS)
Faces Made for Radio/Fundamental/1996
"Southern Moon" on **Straight Outta Boone County**/
    Bloodshot/1997

"Long and Slow Decline" on **Edges From the Postcard/** Semi-Tone/1997

"Allison Town"; "Cloud 149"; "Working On a Building" on **Twangfest '97**/Twangfest/1997

"It Must Be Heaven" on **Edges From the Postcard2/** P2/1998

Side Tracks/Hayden's Ferry/1998

One Riot, One Ranger c/o Mark Wyatt, 1267 City Park Ave., Columbus, OH 43206; 614-445-7288

One Riot, One Ranger: The Old Home Page //members.aol.com/oneriot/oneriot.html

OneRiot@aol.com

The Original Harmony Ridge Creek Dippers (Victoria Williams)

Country Rock
Joshua Tree, California; 1995-

Mark Olson shocked the alt. country world in 1995 when he announced his decision to leave the Jayhawks. In hindsight, he had good reasons: disappointment with big label machinations, doubt about the Jayhawks musical direction, and a strong desire to work more closely with his wife, Victoria Williams, who had established her own special place as a singer/songwriter. In 1996, the happy couple left the bright lights and big city for the solididute of the desert near Joshua Tree, California. With Mike Russell on fiddle, they became the Original Harmony Ridge Creek Dippers and began recording songs in a studio built into their cabin. Their first, self-titled CD, which Olson likened to the Jayhawks **Blue Earth**, is low-key country/folk rock originals (by Olson) full of natural imagery ("She Picks the Violets"; "Flowering Trees"; "Run With the Ponies"; "Hummingbird") and plenty of good feelings all around. Olson handled all the lead vocals (with Victoria on harmonies) on this recording but for the follow-up, **Pacific Coast Rambler**, they share songwriting and vocal credits. Here the sound is fuller and more uptempo with the addition of Marc Ford (ex-Black Crowes) on guitar, but the organicism and cheery feel are still present in songs built around the theme of someone wandering around California just trying to get in touch with nature and self ("Owens Valley Day"; "Bellflower"; "Prayer of the Changing Leaf"; "Golden State Locket"; "Call the Light In"). Forsaking the usual distribution networks, the OHRCD decided to self-release these CDs by mail order or at selected record stores. They also made available a number of Victoria Williams' solo recordings including her 1998 **Musings of a Creekdipper**, a very personal and introspective collection with help from Olson, Greg Leisz, Buddy Miller, Julie Miller, and Joey Burns and John Convertino from Calexico. The Creek Dippers have emerged from their arid hide-a-way now and then to tour in the U.S. and Europe, and Williams, who suffers from MS, runs the Sweet Relief foundation which raises money to pay medical bills for uninsured musicians; worth searching out are **Sweet**

Relief tributes to Williams and Vic Chesnutt which feature a variety of performers covering their songs.

Mark Olson (g,v); Mike Russell (f); Victoria Williams (b,v)

Happy Come Home (Victoria Williams)/Geffen/1987; 1994

Swing the Statue (Victoria Williams)/Rough Trade/1990; Mammoth/1994

Sweet Relief: The Songs of Victoria Williams/1992

Loose (Victoria Williams)/Mammoth/1994

This Moment in Toronto (Victoria Williams)/Mammoth/1995

The Original Harmony Ridge Creek Dippers/ OHRCD/1997

Musings of a Creekdipper (Victoria Williams)/ Atlantic/1998

Pacific Coast Rambler/OHRCD/1998

"It Sure Can Get Cold in Des Moines" (Mark Olson w/ Victoria Williams) on **Real: The Tom T. Hall Project**/Sire/1998

The Original Harmony Ridge Creek Dippers, P.O. Box 342, Joshua Tree, CA 92252

The Original Harmony Ridge Creek Dippers //www.thegrid.net/creekdipper/

creekdipper@thegrid.net

Victoria Williams Home Page //www.victoriawilliams.com

See Peter Case; Giant Sand; The Jayhawks

Gwil Owen

Rig Rock; Insurgent Country
Nashville, Tennessee

In the late 1980s and early 1990s, Gwil Owen fronted a band called the Thieves. They recorded two albums, **Seduced By Money** (produced by Marshall Crenshaw) and **Phoenix**, for Bug (Capitol) Records. Both drew favorable reviews and *Stereo Review* was moved to call Owen a "country-rock natural," but, in spite of this, the label dropped the band in 1991. So, Owen decided to go it alone in Nashville where he honed his singing/songwriting skills and recorded a few demos including a self-released cassette, **Near-Sighted Angel**. A magazine article about a new record company, Diesel Only, prompted Owen to contact them and as a result, they issued his country rocker "Messed Up Thing" (b/w "Tennessee Hi-Way Blues") as a single in 1991 and put the song on their 1992, **Rig Rock Juke Box** compilation. This was followed by another 7", the caffeine charged "Hot Black Coffee"/"Too Much Coffee" which was released on coffee and cream colored vinyl in 1993. Both tunes made it on to the second Diesel Only collection, **Rig Rock Truck Stop**, later that year. Meanwhile, Owen was getting attention from other quarters. Austin favorite Toni Price was impressed by his songs, and the bulk of her recordings **Swim Away** (1993), **Hey** (1995), and **Sol Power** (1997) are made up of Owen's originals including the title tunes plus "Hell on Love," "I Doubt If It Does to You," "Throw Me a Bone," "Tumbleweed," and "Too Much Coffee." Owen became a part of the insurgent country family in 1995 when he was included on Bloodshot's **Hell-Bent** compilation singing the rollicking "Tennessee Hi-Way Blues"; he also made the third volume of insurgent country, **Nashville: The Other Side of the Alley**, doing the rocking "No Ammunition" which was taken from his self-released, **Last Man on the Moon**. Further recognition for this sadly overlooked artist came in 1998 when Owen was included on the **Uprooted: The Best of Roots Country** along side Robbie Fulks, Kelly Willis, Tom Russell, Iris DeMent, Dale Watson, Paul Burch, Kevin Gordon, and Wayne Hancock. He also co-wrote "A Soft Place to Fall" with Alison Moorer for *The Horse Whisperer*; the song was nominated for an Academy Award as Best Original Song.

Seduced by Money (The Thieves)/Bug Capitol/1989
Phoenix (The Thieves)/Bug Capitol/1991
Near-Sighted Angel/Rambler/1991 (CS)
"Messed Up Thing" b/w "Tennessee Hi-Way Blues"/ Diesel Only/1991 (7")
"Messed Up Thing" on **Rig Rock Juke Box**/Diesel Only/1992
"Hot Black Coffee" b/w "Too Much Coffee"/Diesel Only/1993 (7")
"Hot Black Coffee" and "Too Much Coffee" on **Rig Rock Truck Stop**/Diesel Only/1993
Last Man on the Moon/Rambler/1993 (CS)
"Tennessee Hi-Way Blues" on **Hell-Bent**/Bloodshot/1995
"No Ammunition" on **Nashville: The Other Side of the Alley**/Bloodshot/1996
"Mother Nature" on **Uprooted: The Best of Roots Country**/Shanachie/1998

Gwil Owen/Rambler Records, P.O. Box 90685, Nashville, TN 37209

See Toni Price

Steve Owen (Bottomless Joe)

Country Rock; Bluegrass
San Francisco, California; 1994-

Take some old-time and bluegrass, add Johnny and Merle, a little bit of Texas singer/songwriter, folk rock, and a dash of punk, and there you have Steve Owen. Now, as to just what to call this concoction, nobody, not even Owen seems to know. His recordings (**Bottomless Joe**; **Quality Used Parts**) with his band, Bottomless Joe, have a somewhat traditional sound with fiddle, banjo, and mandolin, but they give it a different spin using coffee cans, jugs, bottles, and even a tuba which as Owen admits "pretty much knocks us straight off the country stations." Add to this a driving beat (*a la* the Pogues) and lyrics with a decidedly jaundiced view of life centered on murder, suicide, drunkenness, heartbreak, and the woes of the working classes, and it's pretty safe to say Steve Owen won't be showing up on HNC radio any time soon.

Steve Owen (g,v); Steve Braa (d,perc); Tom Lucas (bj,f); Greg Rodriguez (b,tuba,v)

Bottomless Joe/Cojema/1995

Quality Used Parts/Cojema/1997
Cojema Music, P.O. Box 874, Belmont, CA 94002
WendellT2@aol.com

Tom Pacheco

Singer/Songwriter

The consummate wandering minstrel, Tom Pacheco has spent over three decades searching for his due respect as a singer/songwriter. In the late 1960s, he was a member of the Texas "flower power" vocal quartet Euphoria who had one self-titled album on Heritage. After striking out on his own in the 70s, he recorded **Swallowed Up in the Great American Heartland** and **The Outsider** for RCA. They were country/folk gems and became underground favorites but took him nowhere professionally. The titles were prophetic as, over the years, he roamed across the U.S. from California to Woodstock, New York, New England, Greenwich Village, Austin, and Nashville, an obscure and alienated troubadour. In time, Pacheco migrated to Dublin, Ireland, in the 1980s and also spent a lot of time in Norway where he worked with Steinar Albrigtsen (**Big Storm Comin'**) and Trond Granlund (**I Can't Quit Now**). In Ireland, Round Tower Records gave Tom the chance to make the kind of records he had always wanted to: **Eagle in the Rain**, **Scarecrows and Sunflowers**, **Tales From the Red Lake**. His gravely voice gives special poignancy to his songs about long years of travel ("Lost Soul in the Middle of Nowhere"; "Home Is A Place Inside Me"), but Pacheco's real forte is biographical vignettes and commentaries on the quirky side of American culture. This is perhaps captured best on his 1997 **Woodstock Winter** which was recorded in upstate New York (where he had lived for a time) with members of The Band at Levon Helm's studio. Not surprisingly it often has the flavor of an album made by The Band, but the songs are all Pacheco including tributes to Robert Johnson ("Hey Hey Robert Johnson"), Jerry Garcia ("Jerry's Gone"), and Billy the Kid ("Nobody Ever Killed Billy the Kid") plus tunes about the 60s ("The Hills of Woodstock"), the Oklahoma City bombing ("Real Americans?"), and the Roswell UFO incident ("Four Angels"). A double CD anthology of Pacheco's material from the early 1990s called **Bare Bones & Barbed Wire** was released by Road Goes on Forever in 1997. They also issued his appropriately titled 1998 **The Lost American Song Writer** which was produced by The Band's current lead guitarist Jim Weider.

Swallowed Up in The Great American Heartland/ RCA/1976
The Outsider/RCA/1977
Eagle in the Rain/Ringsend Ire./1989
Sunflowers and Scarecrows/Round Tower Ire./1991
Tales From the Red Lake/Round Tower Ire./1993
Big Storm Comin' (w/ Steinar Albrigtsen)/Round Tower Ire./1996
Woodstock Winter (w/ The Band)/Mercury/1997

Bare Bones & Barbed Wire/Road Goes on Forever
UK/1997 (2 CDs)
The Lost American Song Writer/Road Goes on Forever
UK/1998

See The Band; Trond Granlund

Palace

See Will Oldham

Parlor James

See Amy Allison

Gene Parsons

Country Rock; Inventor
Los Angeles, California; September 4, 1944-

Though not nearly as well known as his contemporaries (Gram Parsons, Chris Hillman, Roger McGuinn, Clarence White), Gene Parsons nonetheless made important contributions to the development of country rock. In the 1960s, he was bass player in the rock band the Castaways with Gib Gilbeau (Swampwater) and then worked with the latter as Cajun Gib & Gene. Later, they were in one of the earliest and most influential country rock bands Nashville West with Clarence White. That band produced only one self titled album in 1968, but it was one of the best of the period and had a big impact on the Byrds' country rock sound. During this time, Parsons and Clarence White came up with a device called the "String Bender" which allowed White to get steel guitar sounds from his Telecaster. After Gram Parsons and Chris Hillman left the Byrds, Gene signed on as drummer for the group along with White on lead guitar. They were on several of the Byrds' lesser known (but still worth seeking out) country rock recordings including **Dr. Byrd & Mr. Hyde** and **The Ballad of Easy Rider**. Parsons remained with them until 1972 then went on to record the great solo country rocker, **Kindling**, with Gilbeau, White, Ralph Stanley, and Vassar Clements; he worked as a session drummer (including Sneaky Pete's 1979 solo) and as a member of the post-Parsons/Hillman Flying Burrito Brothers. In 1980, Parsons became a record executive with Sierra and recorded another country rock solo **Melodies** (with Albert Lee, Herb Pederson) for that label. Into the 1980s and 1990s, Parsons performed with the Gene Parsons trio and as a duo with his wife. He continued to make String Benders by hand for many years and put them into hundreds of guitars including some belonging to rock's giants but in the late 1980s went into partnership with a company that began to mass produce them. Parsons' best from the 1970s including **Kindling** and 11 songs from his years with the Byrds and the FBB have been issued as the **Kindling Collection**.

    Nashville West/Sierra/1968; CBS/1996
    Dr. Byrds & Mr. Hyde/CBS/1969; 1997

Ballad of Easy Rider (Byrds)/CBS/1970; 1997
Untitled (Byrds)/CBS/1970; 1997
Farther Along (Byrds)/CBS/1972
Kindling/Warner Brothers/1973
Melodies/Sierra/1980
The Kindling Collection/Sierra/1992
Birds of a Feather (Parsons/Green)/Sierra/1992

Gene Parsons Stringbender Home Page
//www.stringbender.com/

See The Byrds; Nashville West; Clarence White

Gram Parsons

Country Rock
Winter Haven Florida; November 5, 1946-d. Joshua Tree, California; September 19, 1973

What more can you say about Gram Parsons? The universally acknowledged "father of country rock" (apparently Gram hated the phrase opting for "Cosmic American Music" instead) has been the subject of two full length bios, **Gram Parsons** by Sid Griffin and **Hickory Wind** by Ben Fong-Torres, plus numerous profiles in rock and country music guides and many web sites devoted just to him. (There are also two insider, tell-all portraits of Parsons: *Road Mangler Deluxe* by road manager Phil Kaufman and *I'm With the Band: Confessions of a Groupie* by Pamela Des Barres). During his short and stormy life, Parsons fronted the path breaking country rock group, the International Submarine Band, contributed to the country rock magnum opus, **Sweetheart of the Rodeo** (although his vocals were deleted due to a contract dispute), co-founded (with Chris Hillman) the indispensable Flying Burrito Brothers, and recorded two monumental solo albums, **G.P.** and **Grievous Angel** with his protégé Emmylou Harris on harmony vocals. And although his records sold poorly at the time, since his premature but not unexpected death in 1973, he has attained cult status especially among the alternative country movements of the 1980s and 1990s. Everyone from the Long Ryders and Elvis Costello to the Jayhawks and Uncle Tupelo to Steve Earle and hundreds of current alt. country acts trace at least a part of their lineage to Parsons, and legions of fans cite his recordings with the Byrds, Flying Burrito Brothers, or solo as defining moments in their alt. country consciousness. Continued interest in the man and his music has resulted in a steady stream of posthumous releases including **Sleepless Nights** (previously unreleased FBB material), **Gram Parsons and the Fallen Angels** and **The Legendary Gram Parsons and the Fallen Angels** (both live from 1973), **Warm Evenings, Pale Mornings, Bottled Blues** (a retrospective of his entire career), **Cosmic American Music** (a very rough set of demos for completists only), **The Early Years** (Shilos), and **Yours Truly Anonymous** (previously unreleased live from 1968-1973). The Gram Parsons Home Page lists over a dozen known live bootlegs of Parsons with the Byrds, FBB, and Fallen Angels. Parsons can be found on an expanded version of **Sweetheart** that has "lost tracks" with

Gram on vocals and on several Flying Burrito Brothers retrospectives (released and p.u. material): **Close Up the Honky Tonks**; **Dim Lights, Thick Smoke and Loud, Loud Music**; **Farther Along: The Best of the Flying Burrito Brothers**; and the definitive, **Out of the Blue: The Best of Flying Burrito Brothers**. Gram's legacy has also been kept alive on several tribute albums including **Commemorativo** and a monster one (with Emmylou Harris as executive producer), **Return of the Grievous Angel**, with Evan Dando, Elvis Costello, Beck, Chrissie Hynde, Wilco, Steve Earle, Gillian Welch, and Lucinda Williams that was released in mid-1999. The Gram Parsons Foundation in Tampa, Florida, publishes *The Cosmic American Music News* and *The Gram Parsons Communique* (now online) and houses The Gram Parsons Music Museum. Its founder and owner, Mark Holland, has produced a video documentary, *Gram Parsons: The Legend of The Grievous Angel* and operates Gram's Place Bed & Breakfast! (Information on The GP Foundation and its publications can be found on The Gram Parsons Home Page.) Parsons' contributions and continuing presence are celebrated annually at the Cosmic American Music Festival aka Gram Fest held near the site of his death in Joshua Tree, California.

During 1998 several previously unavailable Gram related video and audio collections were released: from Sierra Home Video came *Live at Liberty Hall*, the only known live video performance of Gram and the Fallen Angels with guitar master Clarence White; **Byrd Parts**, a compilation of rarities and oddities, has one cut with Parsons and Fred Neil and another with the International Submarine Band; and **Byrdoholics** is a late 1960s recording of Gram with the Byrds live at the Piper Club. Sierra Records planned to release (in 1999) **Gram Parsons Live, Volume 2** and **Rare California Gold** with GP, the Byrds, Flying Burrito Brothers, Gene Clark, and Jerry Garcia. Late in 1998, Scorpio Records put out **Under Your Spell**, a double CD collection of obscure live and studio material from 1964-1973.

Safe at Home (International Submarine Band)/LHI/1968; Shiloh/1976,1987
Gilded Palace of Sin (Flying Burrito Brothers)/ A&M/1969
Burrito Deluxe (FBB)/A&M/1970
GP/Reprise/1972
Grievous Angel/Reprise/1973
Close Up the Honky Tonks (FBB)/A&M/1974
Sleepless Nights (FBB)/Reprise/1976
The Early Years/Sierra/1979
Gram Parsons and the Fallen Angels Live, 1973/ Sierra/1981; 1995
Gram Parsons/1982
Dim Lights, Thick Smoke, and Loud, Loud Music (FBB)/Edsel UK/1987
Farther Along: The Best of the Flying Burrito Brothers/A&M/1988
GP/Grievous Angel/Reprise/1990

Commemorativo: A Tribute to Gram Parsons/ Rhino/1993
Warm Evenings, Pale Mornings, Bottled Blues: 1963-1973/Raven Australia/1994
Cosmic American Music: The Rehearsal Tapes, 1972/ Sundown/1995
The Legendary Gram Parsons and the Fallen Angels, Live '73 (Boston)/Ita./1995
The Early Years, Vol. 1 & 2 (Shilos)/Sierra/1996
Out of the Blue: The Best of the Flying Burrito Brothers/A&M UK/1996
A Tribute to Gram Parsons & Clarence White/Magnum UK/1996 (live from 1988 with Bobby Bare and Swampwater)
Gilded Palace of Sin/Burrito Deluxe (FBB)/A&M Ger./1997
Live at Liberty Hall (The Fallen Angels w/ Clarence White)/Sierra Home Video/1998 (video)
Byrd Parts/Raven Aust./1998 (1 cut w/ GP; 1 w/ ISB)
Byrdoholics (Live at The Piper Club)/1998
Under Your Spell/Scorpio/1998
Gram Parsons Live, Vol. 2/Sierra/1999
Rare California Gold/Sierra/1999
Return of the Grievous Angel: A Tribute to Gram Parsons/Almo/1999

The Gram Parsons Home Page //www.gramparsons.com

The Grievous Angel: Gram Parsons //www.geocities.com/SunsetStrip/venue/4082

Gram Parsons' Room //belzebut.welcome.mech.nagasaki-u.ac.jp/~rain/gram/ (in Japanese)

Gram Parsons //ux01.so-net.or.jp/~m-sasaki/gramparsons.html (in Japanese)

Sid Griffin/Gram Parsons Connection //interchem.chem.strath.ac.uk/pd/gp.html

Gram Parsons Fan Page //www.nashville.net/~kate/gram.html

Gram Parsons Tape Trading Page //members.aol.com/veloce/gram.html

Gram Parsons AOL Folder: Entertainment>Music >Chat & Messages>Music Community>Folk/Acoustic

The Gram Parsons Foundation/*The Cosmic American Music News*/*Gram Parsons Communique* 3109 Ola Ave., Tampa, FL 33603; 813-221-0596 or The Gram Parsons Home Page //www.primenet.com/~klugl/gpf.html

GPFTampa@aol.com

See The Byrds; Sid Griffin; Emmylou Harris; Chris Hillman

Li'l Mo Passin & The Monicats (The Twanglers)
Rig Rock; Hillbilly Bop; Honky Tonk
New York City; 1992-

In the mid-1980s, Long Island native Monica Passin was playing in rockabilly/pop/rock bands, but an encounter with a cheap copy of **George Jones Salutes Hank Williams** changed all that. Sequestered in her apartment for two years, she studied country music intensively and then emerged in the early 90s leading a new group called the Twanglers. They became a vital component of New York City's alt. country scene that revolved around the World Famous Bluejays and Diesel Only Records. The Twanglers recorded a single for the label, and their "Two Hearts" was included on its **Rig Rock Juke Box** compilation. After they ended in 1994, Monica started Li'l Mo & the Monicats (with her old guitarist Doug Walker from the Twanglers). She quickly became a regular at two of the Big Apple's best alt. country/Americana nightclubs, the Louisiana Bar & Grill and the Rodeo Bar. Her 1997 debut, **Li'l Mo & The Monicats**, is an utterly delightful honky tonk and rockabilly recording with Passin (think Loretta Lynn; Wanda Jackson) moving easily through twangy romps ("Every Kind of Music But Country" by Tim Carroll), two-steps ("Two Hearts" reprise; "Paradise, Lost"), tough 'billy ("That Cat"; "Sideburn Daddy"; "She-Wolf"), and tender ballads ("Let's Invite Them Over," a duet of the old George Jones/Melba Montgomery hit with Tom Meltzer of 5 Chinese Brothers). As of the end of 1998, Li'l Mo and her Monicats had become frequent performers at two new alt. country showcases, Honky Tonk Thursday Nights at the Sidewalk Cafe and Greg Garing's famous Alphabet City Opry.

The Twanglers: Alan Lee Backer (bj,g); Rob Fahn (d); Ross Garnick (g); Monica Passin (l.v.); Sal Rappa (b); Doug Walker (g)
Li'l Mo & The Monicats: Monica Passin (a.g.,l.v.); Hank Bones (b,e.g.,l.s.,h.v.); Shannon Ford (d); Billy Troiani (b); Doug Walker (l.g.)

  "Two Hearts" on (The Twanglers) on **Rig Rock Juke Box**/Diesel Only/1992
  Li'l Mo & The Monicats/ Townhouse/1997; Motoons/1998

Passin Fancy Music, 350 East 52 St,. Ste 2F, New York, NY 10022; 212-750-5266

lilmo@earthlink.net

Li'l Mo & The Monicats //pages.prodigy.net/mike/monicats/

Herb Pederson (The Laurel Canyon Ramblers)
Country Rock; Progressive Bluegrass
Berkeley, California; April 27, 1944-

Put on some of those old classic Emmylou albums, **Pieces of the Sky, Elite Hotel, Luxury Liner**, and listen to the beautiful harmony vocals courtesy of California alt. country veteran Herb Pederson. Raised in the Bay Area, his first musical experiences were with local bluegrass bands such as the Pine Valley Boys (with Chris Hillman) and the Smokey Grass Boys (with David Grisman). Pederson's banjo and vocal skills won a spot with Vern and Ray and then a temporary job with Flatt & Scruggs when Earl was out for surgery in 1967. After this, Pederson moved on to record on two albums with alt. country pioneers the Dillards and in the 1970s played banjo or harmonized on recordings for a variety of pop (Linda Ronstadt, Johnny Rivers, James Taylor) and alternative country artists including Gram Parsons, Country Gazette, Flying Burrito

Brothers, Emmylou Harris, John Prine, and Doug Dillard. He recorded two solo albums, **Southwest** and **Sandman**, of country rock/bluegrass, toured with John Denver, and wrote music for movies and popular television series. Then, into the 1980s, while continuing to be in great demand for session work, Pederson participated in the excellent bluegrass album **Here Today** with Grisman and Vince Gill and did the solo **Lonesome Feeling** with old friend Hillman and steel guitarist Jay Dee Maness. This album of bluegrass/honky tonk material plus Hillman's own **Desert Rose** album with Pederson and Maness led to the formation of the Desert Rose Band in 1986. Specializing in easy going country rock, this band enjoyed considerable success in the late 1980s and early 1990s. When it disbanded in 1993, Pederson returned to his first love, bluegrass, and formed the Laurel Canyon Ramblers with veteran musicians from the Bluegrass Cardinals, Country Gazette, Byron Berline's L.A. Fiddle Band, The Grass is Greener, and the Desert Rose Band. Their recordings of contemporary bluegrass, **Ramblers Blues**, **Blue Rambler 2**, and **Back on the Street Again** received widespread acclaim from bluegrass fans and reviewers. In 1996, Pederson and Chris Hillman recorded a super collection of covers of 1940s-1950s country standards called **Bakersfield Bound** and in 1997 teamed with Tony and Larry Rice on the old-time/bluegrass CD, **Out of the Woodwork**.

The Laurel Canyon Ramblers: Kenny Blackwell (md,v); Bill Bryson (b,v); Herb Pederson (bj,v); Roger Reed (r.g.,v); Gabe Witcher (f)

  Southwest/Line/1976
  Sandman/Epic/1977
  Here Today (with David Grisman, Vince Gill, Jim Buchanan)/Rounder/1982
  Lonesome Feeling/Sugar Hill/1984; 1995
  Ramblers Blues (Laurel Canyon Ramblers)/Sugar Hill/1995
  Blue Rambler 2 (LCR)/Sugar Hill/1996
  Bakersfield Bound (with Chris Hillman)/Sugar Hill/1996
  Out of the Woodwork (with Hillman, Tony Rice, Larry Rice)/Rounder/1997
  Back on the Street Again (LCR)/Sugar Hill/1998

The Laurel Canyon Ramblers, P.O. Box 125, 11333 Moorpark St., Toluca Lake, CA 91682

The Laurel Canyon Ramblers Home Page //home.aol.com/LCRamblers/

LCRamblers@aol.com

See Country Gazette; The Dillards; Emmylou Harris; Chris Hillman

Al Perry (The Cattle)
Desert Rock; Cowpunk
Tucson, Arizona; 1986-

Al Perry is one of the strangest creatures to crawl out of the desert Southwest since the giant ants in *Them*. He and his band the Cattle were regulars in Tucson's "desert rock" scene in the 1980s. Their debut LP, **Cattle Crossing**, was pretty much rompin', stompin' cowpunk with plenty of Perry's skewed commentary on contemporary Southwestern lifestyles: "4WDORV," "Shopping Mall Baby," "Biblical Sense," "Die Like a Dog." In the late 1980s, Al and the Cattle recorded numerous singles with covers sporting weird drawings and bizarre cowpunk songs like "Escalator Stampede," "Lobotomy," "Good Life," "You're the Flake That Takes the Cake," and "Bitter Pill." Perry's off key, ruptured yodeling on the classic "Cattle Call" could send Elton Britt and Don Walser into therapy. Into the 1990s, Perry eased back on the throttle a bit toward a sound he defines as "a twisted, high-energy punk version of Buck Owens." **Losin' Hand** is toned down honky tonk/country rock although Al's vocals and lyrics ("Loserville"; "Twisted"; "Hit Over the Head"; "The Only Thing That Hurts Now is the Pain") remain as addled as ever. The Australian import of **Losin' Hand** comes with a mini CD of honky tonk covers called **Bakersfield, Arizona**. In 1996, Perry recorded an album of desert country rock, **RetroNuevo**, with Dan Stuart of Green on Red fame.

Original Cattle: Al Perry (g,jew harp,kybrds,v); Dave Roads (b); Dave Robey (d)
Current Cattle: Al Perry (a.g.,e.g.,v); Pete Catalanotte (d); Neil Harry (p.s.); Dave Roads (b)

> Cattle Crossing/Addled/1985
> Escalator Stampede ("El Dio"/"Magnets" b/w
>   "Lobotomy"/"Penstemon")/Addled/1987 (EP)
> Big Guy Dance Party/Addled/1988 (CS)
> "Cattle Call"/"On the Patio" b/w "You're the Flake, That
>   Takes the Cake"/Dionysus/1989 (EP)
> Good 'N' Bitter ("Good Life" b/w "Bitter Pill"/
>   "Gerbils")/ERL/1989 (EP)
> "It's Your Grave (Can You Dig It?)" b/w "Lower Sonoran
>   Desert"/SFTRI/1990 (7")
> Ol' What's Her Name/September Girls Ger./1995 (EP)
> Losin' Hand/Addled/1995
> Losin' Hand and Bakersfield, Arizona/Edme
>   Australia/1995
> Retro Nuevo (with Dan Stuart)/Normal/1996

See Giant Sand; Green on Red

Hal Peters

Hillbilly Bop; Western Swing
Finland; 1984-

Finland was hit hard by a rockabilly tidal wave in the late 1970s and early 1980s. Among the many bands that cropped up were the Rhythm Wheel Combo and the Ballroomers. Eino Rastas was lead guitarist in the former, Heikki Laakkonen lead singer in the latter, and in 1984, they joined with bassist Timo Uimonen to form a 1950s style rockabilly group. Laakkonen took the name Hal Peters (after early rockers Hal Harris and Janice Peters), and they became the Hal Peters Trio. Their first recordings were made for a compilation on Pete Hakonen's new Goofin' label, but their first LP, **Snatch and Grab It** came out on the Finnish Moondogs label in 1986. That same year, Jussi

Huhtakangas was added on lap steel and drums, and the renamed Hal Peters and His Trio now dealt in both rockabilly and honky tonk. Rising to the top of the Scandinavian rockabilly heap, they opened for and/or recorded with local stars like Jussi "Big John" Raittinen and Hank Edwards ("Sweden's Hank Williams") as well as U.S. legends like Mac Curtis, Ray Campi, Joe Clay, and Hayden Thompson. The Trio also recorded a string of solid hillbilly bop singles and LPs for Goofin'. By 1992, Huhtakangas had taken up pedal steel and when Heikki Kangasniemi joined on fiddle, they moved toward a Western swing sound first as Hal Peters & His Country Men and then in 1998 as Hal Peters & His String Dusters which did the terrific Western swing 10"/CD, **Lonesome Hearted Blues**. Later that year, one of Europe's top hillbilly bop/Western swing bands stormed the U.S.A. with a West Coast tour and headline performance at the Viva Las Vegas rockabilly festival.

Around 1990, Salminen and Huhtakangas, who also records under the named Lester Peabody, started a hillbilly bop side-project called the Barnshakers; for details, see their entry.

Hal Peters Trio (1984-1988)
Hal Peters & His Trio (1988-1994)
Hal Peters & His Countrymen (1994-1998)
Hal Peters & His String Dusters (1998-): Hal Peters aka Heikki Laakkonen (a.g.,l.v.); Jussi Huhtakangas (l.s.,p.s., r.g.,1986-); Heikki Kangasniemi (f,1993-); Eino Rastas (l.g.); Mike Salminene (d,1989-); Timo Uimonen (b).

> Snatch It and Grab It (Trio)/Moondogs Fin./1986
> Happy Again (Trio)/Goofin' Fin./1987 (7" EP)
> You Don't Have to Worry (Trio)/Goofin' Fin./1988 (EP)
> Follow Thru (Trio)/Rockhouse/1988 (LP)
> Rockin' The Country (Trio)/Goofin' Fin./1989
> Jussi "Big John" Raittinen w/ Hal Peters & His
>   Trio/Goofin' Fin./1991 (12" EP)
> "Rock Me Up" b/w "Blue Blue Day" (Trio)/Goofin'
>   Fin./1991 (7")
> Baby I'm Ready (Trio w/ Ray Campi)/Goofin' Fin./1991
> "In The Silence of the Night" b/w "I Wish I Had a Nickel"
>   (Hank Edwards w/ Hal Peters & His Trio)/Goofin'
>   Fin./1992 (7")
> "Chicken" b/w "Finlandia is Grandia" (Ray Campi w/ Hal
>   Peters & His Trio)/Goofin' Fin./1992 (7")
> "Heartbreakin' Love" b/w "Blue Blue Heartache"
>   (Trio)/Rock-A-Billy/1994 (7")
> "Hard Hearted Girl" b/w "Don't Cry Baby" (Trio)/Goofin'
>   Fin./1994 (7")
> Fireball Mail (Trio)/Goofin' Fin./1994
> *The First Ten Years, 1985-1995*/Goofin' Fin./1995 (video)
> Lonesome Hearted Blues (String Dusters)/Goofin'
>   Fin./1998

Hal Peters c/o Goofin' Records, P.O. Box 63, 01601 Vantaa, Finland

goofin.records@kolumbus.fi

Hal Peters Home Page //personal.inet.fi/cool/halpeters/
heikki.laakkonen@pp2.inet.fi

See The Barnshakers

The Picketts

Grange Rock
Seattle, Washington; 1990-

Wipe away the grungy surface layer covering the Seattle music scene and just underneath you will find a thriving alternative country community. One of its foremost bands, the Picketts, began to take shape in 1990 when rhythm guitarist/vocalist Christy McWilson met standup drummer Leroy "Blackie" Sleep. She came from a 60s pop background, he from rockabilly, but they shared a mutual love of country and formed the Power Mowers which in time became the Picketts (word play based on McWilson). With John Olufs and Jimmy Sangster (Young Fresh Fellows) on electric guitars plus Walt Singleman (Red Dress) on bass, they established a pattern with their first EP single which had something old (Buck Owen's "Fallin' for You"), something borrowed (The Clash's "Should I Stay or Should I Go"), and something new (McWilson's "Walkin' Talkin' Jukebox"). A second EP single **Pick It** con- tained all instrumentals (sans McWilson) including "Remington Ride" and "Sukiyaki." Their original blend of traditional and modern was given full expression on a debut CD **Paper Doll** with McWilson and Sleep sharing lead vocals and harmonizing on lots of good natured rock 'n' rolling, honky tonk like "Fool," "Rockpile," "Seeing Red," "Tornado," plus country ballads ("Bad Girl") and a cover of Tom Waits' "Heart of a Saturday Night." After a winning performance at the 1994 SXSW, the Picketts secured a contract with Rounder and returned for more of the same on **The Wicked Picketts** and **Euphonium**. The former takes on Yoko Ono's "Walking on Thin Ice" as a moody rockabilly number, reprises "Sukiyaki," covers "Still in Love" (Boudeleaux Bryant), and comes through with more witty, toe tapping originals such as "Just Because You Ain't Got," "If You Love Me," "Can't Take It With You," "Dyin' Ain't Much of a Living," and "The Grass May Be Greener." **Euphonium** rocks a little harder ("Good Good Wife"; "Seven"; "Same Town, Same Planet, Different World") but also offers nice shuffles ("Just Passin' Through"; "Overworked, Overloaded, Under-paid"), "Should I Stay Or Should I Go?" as a two step, and the Who's "Baba Riley" interpreted by McWilson/Sleep as a slow, down home country rock ballad.

Toward the close of the century, the Picketts, who play "Grange not Grunge!," slowed down a bit when their big break didn't come and Rounder declined to support another recording. Still, they stayed together and continued to perform occasionally around the Seattle area. McWilson began work on a solo album in late 1998 and at last word was trying to enlist Dave Alvin as producer.

Christy McWilson (g,v); John Olufs (l.g.,v); Jimmy Lloyd Sangster (a.g.,e.g.,v); Walt Singleman (b); Leroy "Blackie" Sleep (d,v)

"Should I Stay or Should I Go? " b/w "Walkin' Talkin' Jukebox"/"Fallin' for You"/PopLlama/1990 (EP)
Pick It ("Sukiyaki"/"Stella Stomp" b/w "Party Hat"/"Remington Ride")/Cruddy/1994 (EP)
Paper Doll/PopLlama/1994
"The Longer You Wait" on **Hit the Hay, Vol. 1**/Sound Asleep Swe./1995
The Wicked Picketts/Rounder/1995
Euphonium/Rounder/1996

The Picketts/Rounder Home Page //www.rounder.com

Jo Carol Pierce

Lubbock Mafia; Singer/Songwriter; Actress
Wellington, Texas; July 20, 1944-

Jo Carol Pierce comes from the same West Texas environment that produced Terry Allen, Joe Ely, Jimmie Dale Gilmore, Butch Hancock. Like her contemporaries, she spent most of her life trying to understand that unique place through writing and music. Married to Gilmore in the mid-1960s (divorced 1967), Pierce relocated to Austin in the early 1970s where she began writing songs and plays and polishing the acting skills she learned in high school. Her most successful plays were *In the West* (five year run in Austin; Kennedy Center in 1991) and the critically acclaimed *Bad Girls Upset By the Truth*. The latter, which was originally titled *Commit Suicide Every Morning And You'll Feel Better All Day*, highlighted Pierce's amusing but quite moving autobiographical ruminations on relationships ("Secret Dan"; "Buttons of Your Skin"), religion ("I Blame God"; "Does God Have Us By the Twat or What?"), and emotional breakdown with J. D. Foster and David Halley providing musical accompaniment. Pierce performed *Bad Girls* regularly at Austin's Chicago House in the early 1990s and began singing at other clubs around town. Her songwriting skills were greatly admired by Austin's musical community and in 1993, a group of them including Allen, Gilmore, Ely, Kris McKay, David Halley, and Loose Diamonds paid tribute to her on **Across the Great Divide: The Songs of Jo Carol Pierce**.

In 1994, Pierce and old friends Ely, Hancock, Gilmore acted in and sang original songs for a musical play called *Chippy* (written by Terry and Jo Harvey Allen). Based on the diary of a prostitute in the Texas Panhandle during the Great Depression, the play had a successful run in Philadelphia and New York. The music from the play was subsequently issued as a soundtrack, **Songs From Chippy**. In 1995, **Bad Girls Upset By the Truth** made it to CD on Monkey Hill records and into the late 1990s, Pierce was at work on a screenplay for 20th Century Fox.

Across the Great Divide: The Songs of Jo Carol Pierce/Dejadisc/1993
Songs From Chippy/Hollywood/1994 (sdtrk.)
Bad Girls Upset By the Truth/Monkey Hill/1995

Jo Carol Pierce/Davis McLarty Page
//www.davismclarty.com/jocarol.html

Jo Carol Pierce Biography
//www.eden.com/~dejadisc/piebio.html

See Terry Allen; Jimmie Dale Gilmore

The Pine Dogs
Roots Rock
Buffalo, New York; 1987-1998

For over a decade, the Pine Dogs were one of Buffalo's top bands. Formed in 1987, the original line up was Jim Celeste, Tom Fischer, Don Vincent, and Jim Whitford with vocalist Gretchen Schulz joining in 1988. Their first recordings, a cassette (**Jane...Stop This Crazy Thing**) and a single, were self released, but their CD debut, **Going Away Party** (produced by Gurf Morlix) was issued by Das Kapital complete with a corn chili recipe. From 1992-1994, the band toured the Northeast opening for a diversity of acts including Peter Case, Lucinda Williams, and Crash Test Dummies. In 1995, they recorded their sophomore album, **Mighty Engines of Love**. Reviewers from *Dirty Linen* to *No Depression* have noted that the Pine Dogs fall into that nebulous area lying somewhere between the Byrds and a host of current alt. country bands. But whatever you call it, the Pine Dogs' sound made them very popular at home where they won a slew of Buffalo music awards including Best New Band (1989), Best Female Vocalist (1989, 1990, 1992), Best Local Album (1992), and Outstanding Band (1994). However, in the late 1990s, as their momentum began to wane, the group called it a day with Whitford moving on to join another local favorite, the Steam Donkeys.

Jim Celeste (d); Tom Fischer (b); Gretchen Schulz (b.v.); Don Vincent (g,b.v.1987-1995); Jim Whitford (g,v,)

Jane...Stop This Crazy Thing/PD/1989 (CS)
"Give It Back" b/w "Do You Really Mean It?"/PD/1990
Going Away Party/Das Kapital/1992
"Naked Truth" on **Hit the Hay, Vol. 1**/Sound Asleep Swe./1994
Mighty Engines of Love/Das Kapital/1995

The Pine Dogs Home Page //www.pinedogs.com/central/

Dogmail: The Pine Dogs Electronic Newsletter & Mailing List //pinedogs.com/cgi/subscribe.cgi/

Info@pinedogs.com

See The Steam Donkeys

Pine State
Tobacco Row; Cowpunk
Chapel Hill, North Carolina; 1994-

Pine State plays what they call "pint of moonshine and accidental shotgun wound country." In concert, led by founder C. Wiley Riser, they move wildly from covers of Pussy Galore to songs by Hank and Haggard, start fires and smash things with crowbars and sledgehammers, and enjoy hurling stuff at and berating their audiences. In a region that's become known as one of the hottest in alt. country (Backsliders, Whiskeytown, Jolene), their "honkypunk" earned them the distinction of being "the loudest...ugliest, the messiest, the most depraved" country group in the Chapel Hill/Raleigh area. The title of their 1995 debut, **Smash Hits Opry**, literally says it all.

Lemuel Huffines (bj); A. C. Lee (g); Danny Partridge (p,tp); Nick Petti (s.g.); C. Wiley Riser (g,l.s.,p.s.v); Mike Shoffner (d); Charlie Speight (jh,wb,v)

"Hundredth Broken Heart"/"Moanin' the Blues" b/w (Trailer Bride)/Fiction Media/1995
"I'm Your Man" on **Who the Hell: A Tribute to Richard Hell**/Cred Factory/1995
"Bird Dog Blues" on **Cognitive Mapping, Vol. 2**/ FM/1995
Smash Hits Opry/Cred Factory/1995

Pine State c/o Friction Media, P. O. Box 373, Chapel Hill, NC 27514

Pine State Home Page //unc.edu/~riser/psmain.html

riser@email.unc.edu

Pinetop Seven
Insurgent Country; Avant-Garde
Chicago, Illinois; 1995-

Pinetop Seven is no respecter of musical boundaries. They have no compunction about freely mixing traditional country with Charles Mingus, Ennio Moriccone, Astor Piazzolla, classical, world music, and modern rock. This unabashed spirit of experimentation comes primarily from the group's co-founders Charles Kim and Darren Richard who began playing music together while students (both psychology majors) at Vanderbilt University. After relocating to Chicago, they found like minded musicians and formed Pinetop Seven. The avant-garde approach of their self titled debut placed them in a long line of American musical experimenters from Charles Ives, Virgil Thompson, and Harry Partch through Captain Beefheart, Tom Waits, and John Zorn. It also left reviewers scratching their heads and scrambling for the right words to describe their sound. However, alt. country/Americana fans and critics found enough twang in Pinetop Seven to place them in the ranks of insurgent country. 1997 brought them wider recognition through showcases at SXSW and the CMJ Music Fest in New York City, but 1998 was their breakthrough year with two acclaimed albums, **No Breath in the Bellows** and **Rigging the Toplights**. These strange-but-somehow-familiar recordings placed Pinetop Seven in good company with innovators such as Greg Garing and Lambchop.

Ryan Hembrey (b,1996-); Charles Kim (bj,g,hrm, sl.g); Mike John Peeler (b, 1995-1996); Darren Richard (g,p,v)

Pinetop Seven/PS/1996; Truckstop Atavistic/1997
No Breath in the Bellows/Truckstop Atavistic/1998 (EP)
Rigging the Toplights/Truckstop Atavistic/1998
"Money From Home" on **Luxury Liner, Vol. 2**/ Glitterhouse Ger./1998

Pinetop Seven/Truckstop Atavisitc, P.O. Box 578266, Chicago, IL 60657; 773-384-9626; (fax) 773-384-9677

info@atavistic.com

Pinetop Seven/Centerstage Page
//centerstage.net/chicago/music/whoswho/PinetopSeven.html

Pinetop Seven Biography
//www.billions.com/pinetop/bio.htm

The Pinetops

Tobacco Row; Roots Rock
Winston-Salem, North Carolina; 1995-

Poster child for the Music School of Hard Knocks, Jeffrey Dean Foster endured over a decade of ups and spirit crushing downs before his perserverance began to pay off in the late 1990s. During the late 1980s, he was with alternative rockers The Big Profile which got a contract with Arista and was a "can't miss" band that did mainly due to poor management. When that group disovled, Foster and some of its members became the Carneys but in time, Jeffrey Dean went solo. Then in the mid-1990s, he put together the Pinetops with ex-Big Profile drummer, Jon Wurster. His bassist (Danny Kurtz) and lead guitarist (Brad Rice) were also in the up-and-coming alt. country group, the Backsliders, who hit it big with Mammoth Records and left Foster scrambling for replacements which he found in John Chumbris (bass) and John Pfiffner (guitar). With a stable line-up, the Pinetops kept riding the music merry-go-round but the magic ring was always out of reach. Record companies teased and taunted, but Foster and the Pinetops finally decided to go the independent route and in 1997 signed with Monolyth out of Boston. With Don Dixon producing, they recorded **Above Ground and Vertical** with guests Rice and Kurtz. It has its share of guitar driven roots rock ("Evil Town"; "Underneath Your Wheels"; "Jesus Spoke"; "Birds of Prey"), but Foster's plaintive tenor and (understandably) dark originals ("So Lonesome I Could Fly"; "Lottery"; "Hello Down There"; "Good Luck Charm"; "Linger") accompanied dreamily by acoustic guitar, harmonica, swirling organ, and/or crying lap steel are the most moving and memorable. Maybe this time, Jeffrey Dean.

John Chumbris (b,g,v,1995-1998); Will Dyar (d,1998-); Jeffrey Dean Foster (b,g,hm,org,p,perc,v); Danny Kurtz (b,1995); Andy Mabe (b,1998-); John Pfiffner (g,l.s.,p.s.p,v); Brad Rice (g,1995); John Wurster (d,1995-1998)

"Birds of Prey" on **Revival, Vol. 1**/Yep Roc/1997
Above Ground and Vertical/Monolyth Soundproof/1998

The Pinetops //www.monolyth.com/pinetops/

The Polkats

Tex-Mex; Country Rock
Baltimore, Maryland; Mid-1990s

What little I know about the Polkats comes from a 1994 CD, **Low Man**. The grinning, multi-colored gremlins on its cover suggest a good time awaits within, and sure enough, the Polkats deliver. Driven by John Shock's accordion, they live up to their name on country romps through Woody Guthrie's "Do Re Mi," Kris Kristofferson's "For the Good Times," and Tom T. Hall's "Never Havin' You," the title song, and covers of Tex-Mex *conjunto* standards ("El Guero Polkas"; "Mi Negra Ausencia"; "Cotulla/La Piedra"). There are a number of other Latin flavored tunes (originals and covers) including a pretty cheesy take on "Tiny Bubbles." And while Shock's squeeze box versatility is the primary focus, the rest of the Polkats make strong contributions with special kudos to Paul Margolis for his songwriting, vocals, and multi-instrumental skill on electric guitar, lap steel, and mandolin.

Mike Barth (a.g.,hm,v); John Keith (b); Paul Margolis (a.g.,e.g.,l.s.,md,v); Steve Raskin (d); John Shock (acc,ky,v)

Low Man/The Polkats/1994

The Polkats c/o Paul Margolis, 6226 Woodcrest Ave., Baltimore, MD 21209-3935

Toni Price

Austin; Singer/Songwriter
Pennsylvania; March 13, 1961-

In the 1990s, the preeminent female performer on the Austin music scene was Toni Price. Her secret? Start with a fabulous bluesy/country voice that matches the best of yesterday and today, add great songs by Gwil Owen, and tie it all up with backing from the elite of Austin's rich pool of talented musicians. Originally, Price tried to make a breakthrough in commercial country in Nashville. Recording under the name of Luiese, she cut two singles before branching out musically with rock bands like Mel & the Party Hats and Toni Price & the Jam Wranglers. Gwil Owen sometimes filled in on guitar with the Wranglers, and Price discovered he was one of the best unknown songwriters in Nashville. After performing at SXSW in 1989, Price decided to move to Austin where she became a regular at Antone's nightclub and secured a deal with Antone's Records. The non-native captured the essence of "Texas music," mixing blues, country, rock, folk, and pop with help from a great band anchored by multi-instrumentalist Champ Hood and guitar stalwart Casper Rawls. Her other ace in the hole was the songwriting of old acquaintance Gwil Owen whose originals "Hell on Love," "I Doubt If It Does to You," "Throw Me a Bone," "Too Much Coffee," and many others were the bedrock of her first two releases, **Swim Away** and **Hey!** With these recordings and live performances, Price developed a tremendously loyal following; her weekly "Hippie Hour" at the

Continental Club was standing room only for years. She won the hearts of the critics with **Hey!** named Album of the Year (1996), and Price was voted Female Vocalist of the Year (1994-1996) at the Austin Music Awards. 1997's **Sol Power**, was recorded live at the Railroad Blues club in the West Texas town of Alpine. Accompanied by Hood, Rawls, and Jud New-comb (Loose Diamonds), Price unleashes her glorious voice on all previously unreleased material dominated once more by songs from the pen of Gwil Owen. To accompany **Sol Power**, Price made a four song video diary, *Howdy, Welcome to Alpine.*

Swim Away/Watermelon/1993
Hey!/Watermelon/1995
Toni Price Live/Ind/1996 (4 trk. CS rec. July 1992 at
 Pearl's Oyster Bar)
"Starry Lullaby" on **Rock-A-My Baby Cradle Songs**/
 1996
"Something" on **Cowpunks**/Vinyl Junkie UK/1996
Sol Power/Discovery/1997
Howdy, Welcome to Alpine/1997 (4 trk.video diary)

Toni Price P. O. Box 650080, Austin, TX 78765 (mailing list includes *The Dish Rag* newsletter)

Toni Price Home Page //www.valuu.net/toni

Toni Price/Discovery Records Page
//www.discoveryrec.com/artists/tonprice/

Toni Price AOL Folder: Entertainment>Music>Chat & Messages>Music Community>Folk/Acoustic

See Gwil Owen

John Prine

Singer/Songwriter
Maywood, Illinois; 1946-

Of the many great songs penned by John Prine, the one that comes closest to capturing his approach to songwriting and life in general is "It's a Big Ol' Goofy World." For going on three decades, his genius has resided in an ability to find the humor in the high and the low, the best and the worst and turn the ordinary into something quite extraordinary. From his legendary, self titled debut in 1971 down to **Lost Dogs & Mixed Blessings** in 1995, Prine, who was once tabbed "the next Dylan" occupied a unique place in America's songwriting tradition. And while he used a number of styles to express his vision, his most notable songs have been straight ahead country; "Angel From Montgomery," "Spanish Pipe Dream," "Paradise," "Christmas in Prison," "Aimless Love," "Come Back to Us Barbara Lewis Hare Krishna Beauregard," "Illegal Smile," "Grandpa Was a Carpenter," "Speed of the Sound of Loneliness" to name just a few. In terms of influence, Prine stands right alongside the other artists (like his very good friend and collaborator Steve Goodman) of the early 1970s who acquainted a new generation raised on rock with the pleasures of country. His Oh Boy! Records became home to a number of new artists including multi-talented singer/songwriter R.B. Morris; it also re-issued Steve Goodman's albums on its subsidiary Red Pajamas label.

Diagnosed with and treated for cancer in 1998, Prine made his major movie debut in Billy Bob Thornton's *Dad & Them* in which he played a member of a "white trash" family (Billy Bob as brother; Andy Griffith as father) who reunite to help an uncle on trial for murder.

John Prine/Atlantic/1971
Diamonds in the Rough/Atlantic/1972
Sweet Revenge/Atlantic/1973
Common Sense/Atlantic/1975
Prime Prine/Atlantic/1976
Bruised Orange/Asylum/1978
Pink Cadillac/Asylum/1979
Storm Windows/Asylum/1980
Aimless Love/Oh Boy/1984
German Afternoons/Oh Boy/1988
John Prine Live/Oh Boy/1988
The Missing Years/Oh Boy/1991
The John Prine Anthology: Great Days/Rhino/1993
Lost Dogs and Mixed Blessings/Oh Boy/1995
The John Prine Music Video Collection/Oh Boy/1996
Live on Tour/Oh Boy/1997

John Prine/Oh Boy Home Page //www.ohboy.com

The John Prine Back Page
//www.hepcat.com/goodman/prine.html

John Prine Shrine
//www.geocities.com/heartland/1985/prine.htm

Very Unofficial JP Home Page
//www.atw.fullfeed.com/~bix/prine.htm

John Prine //rylibweb.man.ac.uk/datal/sy/jw/prine.html

Space Monkey's John Prine Page
//www.geocities.com/Nashville/4351/prine.html

John Prine AOL Folder: Entertainment>Music>Chat & Messages>Music Community>Folk/Acoustic

See Steve Goodman; R.B. Morris

Quartette (Cindy Church; Sylvia Tyson)

Singer/Songwriters
Toronto, Ontario, Canada; 1993-

Quartette is a supergroup made up of four of Canada's best female performers. Canadian Music Hall of Fame Member, Sylvia Tyson, is the most well known of the group for her years with Ian Tyson as the famous folk/country duo Ian & Sylvia. Their album **The Great Speckled Bird** (1970) was one of the pioneering country rock recordings along with those of the Byrds, Gram Parsons, the Flying Burrito Brothers, Rick Nelson, and Steve Young. Her many solo albums are full of easy going country, country rock, Cajun, and more and are best sampled on the **You Were on My Mind** compilation. Cindy Church came to prominence as a background vocalist for Ian Tyson, as a member of the Great Western Orchestra, and as a soloist. American born, Caitlin Hanford led her own band, the Adobe Brothers, and recorded with her husband Chris Whiteley while Colleen Peterson performed with many of Canada's top musicians. Surprisingly, the group's formation was not the result of a carefully conceived plan but rather resulted from a chance appearance at a music festival in 1993. So favorable was the response to this performance, they decided to record an album, **Quartette**, in 1994. It lets each members' distinctive vocal talents shine on great songs (penned individually or collectively) that range through a capella ("The Circle"), country rock ("Unabashedly Blue"), swing ("Cowboys and Rodeos"), beautiful ballads ("Denim Blue Eyes"; "Hobo Girl"), gospel ("When God Deeps His Pen"), and Cajun/Acadian ("Papere's Mill"). However, it is their harmonizing which makes Quartette so utterly appealing. Added to this is A-1 accompaniment especially from guitarist Nathan Tinkham (Ian Tyson Band and Church's partner), Janet Munson on fiddle, and Whiteley on dobro and pedal steel. For their efforts, Quartette won a Canadian Country Music Award in 1994 and over the next two years appeared at the Edmonton Folk Festival, on *Prairie Home Companion*, and at SXSW. **Work of the Heart**, takes up where their debut left off with more top notch songs and superb vocals. Sadly, in late 1996, Peterson passed away, but the group decided to continue and brought in veteran singer/songwriter, Gwen Swick. Caitlin Hanford made her solo debut in 1997 on **Bluer Skies**, a mix of bluegrass, blues, Cajun, and jazz very much in the Quartette mold; Sylvia Tyson, who was awarded the Governor General's Order of Canada in 1995, acted in the stage play *The Piano Man's Daughter* which toured Canada in Spring 1997. A renewed Quartette returned in 1998 with **In the Beauty of the Day** which, like its predecessors, serves up tradition based country layered with swing, gospel, R&B and highlighted by superb arrangements and gorgeous harmonies.

Cindy Church (v); Caitlin Hanford (v); Colleen Peterson (v, 1993-1996); Gwen Swick (v,1997-); Sylvia Tyson (acc,v)

> **Woman's World** (Sylvia Tyson)/Stony Plain Can./1975
> **Cool Wind From the North** (Sylvia Tyson)/Capitol EMI/1975
> **Satin on Stone** (Sylvia Tyson)/Salt/1978
> **Sugar for Sugar, Salt for Salt** (Sylvia Tyson)/Salt/1979
> **Big Spotlight** (Sylvia Tyson)/Stony Plain Can./1986
> **You Were on My Mind** (Sylvia Tyson)/Stony Plain Can./1989
> **Gypsy Cadillac** (Sylvia Tyson)/Stony Plain Can./1993; Round Tower Ire./1994
> **Quartette**/Denon Can./1994
> **Love on the Range** (Cindy Church)/Stony Plain Can./1994
> **Just a Little Rain** (Cindy Church)/Stony Plain Can./1995
> **Work of the Heart**/Denon Can./1995
> **Cindy Church**/Stony Plain Can./1997
> **Bluer Skies** (Caitlin Hanford)/HYC Can./1997
> **In the Beauty of the Day**/1998
> "Cowgirl's Lullaby" (Cindy Church) on **Word From the Range: A Canadian Cowboy Collection**/Glenbow Museum Can./1998
> "Code of the West" (Colleen Peterson) on **Word From the Range: A Canadian Cowboy Collection**/Glenbow Museum Can./1998

> "Cowboys & Rodeos" & "Neon Cowboy" (Quartette) on **Word From the Range: A Canadian Cowboy Collection**/Glenbow Museum Can./1998

Quartette, P.O. Box 853, 31 Adelaide St. East, Toronto, Ontario M5C 2K1 Canada

Quartette Official Homepage //www.interlog.com/~quartett/home.html

Cindy Church, P. O. Box 698, Turner Valley, Alberta, T0L 2A0 Canada

See The Great Western Orchestra; Ian Tyson

R. Cajun and The Zydeco Brothers
Modern Cajun
Derby, England; 1979-

Some twenty years ago, a Cajun music craze hit London and spread like a bayou wild fire. At the front of the pack of Cajun bands (the Electric Bluebirds, the Balham Alligators, Zip Gun and the Bayou Big Shots) formed during this time were R. Cajun and the Zydeco Brothers. Accordionist Chris Hall created the band in 1979 and through club and festival appearances established them as the top Cajun band in the London area. In the early 1980s, R. Cajun made their home base in Derby the focal point of the Cajun scene by sponsoring an evening of Cajun films and music and by hosting weekly Gumbo Nights with a variety of Louisiana as well as world music. **Bayou Rhythms** went to #1 on the British folk charts in 1984, and in spite of numerous personnel changes, they managed to hold on and record five more albums for Bearcat. While paying homage to traditional Cajun music, R. Cajun added in zydeco, country, r&b, and rock in a way that made the music accessible to a wide audience.

Beeds (g,hm 1980-); Alf Billington (g,v 1984-); Dave Blant (b,v 1984-); Tony Dark (f ,1979-1989); Chris Hall (acc,v); Jan Hall (tri,perc); Clive Harvey (g,v 1986-); Trevor Hopkins (b, 1980); Neil "Freddy"Hopwood (d); Graham Jones (b, 1982-4); Veronica Matthews (tri); Dave "Mitch" Proctor (f, 1990); Derek Richardson (f, 1989-); John Squire (f,g,md, 1982-6)

> **Bayou Rhythms**/Bearcat UK/1984
> **Pig Sticking in Arcadia**/Bearcat UK/1987
> **Don't Leave the Floor**/Bearcat UK/1988
> **Out of the Swamp**/Bearcat UK/1990
> **That Cajun Thing**/Bearcat UK/1993
> **No Known Cure**/Bearcat UK/1994

Radio Ranch Straight Shooters
Western Swing
Los Angeles, California; 1981-

Long before the 1990s swing craze hit the West Coast, Paul Greenstein was inspired by Spade Cooley, Tex Williams, and Bob Wills to form his own Western swing band. In 1981, he created the Radio Ranch Straight Shooters who were named for a fictional place in a Gene Autry movie and for their no nonsense approach to the music. The only Western swing band on the scene at the time, the RRSS became a part of the growing L.A. alt. country movement and in 1989 cut a single, "The Next Big Thing," for Will Ray's **Hollywood Roundup** compilation. With the upsurge of interest in swing in the early 1990s, they became regulars at the Three of Clubs, the Derby, and Spaceland; their line-up at one time included the Blasters' former drummer, Bill Bateman. The Shooters hoped to do a CD, but in the mid-late 1990s, things slowed down for them due to outside committments. Greenstein was very involved in film work and through his connections managed to get some RRRS songs on the soundtrack of Roger Corman's *Alien Avengers II* and hoped to do some music for a David Lynch film.

Original Members: Bill Batemen (d); Paul Greenstein (r.g.,l.v.); Greg Hormel (l.g.); Laura Kass (f,v); B. Koskie (acc); Jerry Mascott (b); Tim Spain (l.s.)
Current Members: Paul Greenstein; Laura Kass; Chaz Smith (s.g.); David Strother (f); Hank Vansickle (b)

"The Next Big Thing" on **Hollywood Roundup**/New Grange/1989 (CS)

The Radio Ranch Straight Shooters: 323-225-2224

Radio Sweethearts

Country Rock
Glasgow, Scotland; Early 1990s-

Scotland's Radio Sweethearts are living proof that Americana knows no borders. The band was founded by John Miller and Frank MacDonald who met on a commuter train to Glasgow and found they shared common musical interests. Miller was raised on country while MacDonald, a drummer with pop rock bands (Teenage Fan Club, BMX Bandits, Pastels) was a late convert. Inspired mainly by Hank, Sr., and pioneer country rockers like the Byrds, Gram Parsons, and the Flying Burrito Brothers, they began to write songs and then put together Radio Sweethearts (after **Sweetheart of the Rodeo**) with John McCusker (Battlefield Band) on fiddle, Martin Hayward (Pastels) on bass, Brian Taylor (Pastels) on guitar, and Malcolm McMaster on pedal steel. In 1996, they enlisted Kim Fowley to produce **New Memories** for U.S. based St. Roch Records. Anchored by Miller's fine lead vocals, the Sweethearts do proficient honky tonk and country rock covers of Hank ("I Saw the Light"; "House of Gold"), Charlie Pride/Doug Sahm ("Is Anybody Going to San Antone?"), and Warren Smith ("Red Cadillac and a Black Mustache"). MacDonald and Miller also write credible originals including "Don't Make Me Wait," "Lonely Footsteps," and "Beer & Whisky" which was #1 on the Country Music Radio for Europe charts for several weeks. Radio Sweethearts' California country rock inspired sound has earned high praise from U.K. music publications (e.g. Sid Griffin for *Q Magazine*) as well as many of the top reviewers in the U.S. including Billy Block, Rob Bleetstein, and Jeffrey Remz. In 1998, MacDonald set up Shoeshine Records which

issued several RS singles as well as a re-release of the Sweethearts debut with extra songs as **New Memories Revisited**.

Martin Hayward (b); Frank MacDonald (d,b.v.); John McCusker (f,md); Malcolm McMaster (p.s.); John Miller (g,l.v.); Brian Taylor (l.g.)

New Memories/St. Roch/1997
"New Memories" b/w "Beer & Whisky"/Shoeshine Scot./1998 (7")
"Rambling Man" b/w "Found a New Love"/Shoeshine Scot./1998 (7")
New Memories Revisited/Shoeshine Scot./1998

Radio Sweethearts/Shoeshine Records, Box 15193, Glasgow G2 6LB, United Kingdom

Radio Sweethearts/Shoeshine Page //www.users.globalnet.co.uk/~shoeshine/

shoeshine@globalnet.co.uk

Rainravens

Country Rock
Austin, Texas; 1994-

In the late 1980s, a young music major (from North Texas State) and singer/songwriter named Andy Van Dyke arrived in Austin, Texas. He played local folk venues as a solo then formed the Andy Van Dyke Band which became the hard rock band, Drop the Gun. Eventually, Van Dyke and Drop the Gun's guitarist David Ducharme-Jones decided they wanted to do more acoustic based music. They performed as a duo for a time before expanding into the Rainravens in 1994 when they landed Dave Evertson on bass and veteran drummer Herb Belofsky (Gary P. Nunn, Ray Wylie Hubbard, Chris Wall). Tapping into the country rock line running from the Byrds and Burritos through the early Jayhawks, the Rainravens built a framework of mostly acoustic (sometimes electric) folk, country, rock, and pop with tight harmonies around Van Dyke's catchy originals and dynamic lead vocals. Flavored with dobro, fiddle, and pedal steel, their 1995 self-titled debut on Dejadisc was well-received by local, national, and European reviewers. After extensive touring in the States, in 1996, the Rainravens sent a demo tape off to the new German alt. country/Americana label Blue Rose which was fast becoming a haven for numerous U.S. performers old and new. They were impressed enough to give them a contract which led to **Diamond Blur** (1997) and **Rose of Jericho** (1999) which stick close to the formula that made **Rainravens** so appealing.

Herb Belofsky (d); David Ducharme-Jones (g); Dave Evertson (b); Andy Van Dyke (l.v.)

Rainravens/Dejadisc/1995; Blue Rose Ger./1996
Diamond Blur/Blue Rose Ger./1997
"What Did You Save Me For?" on **Luxury Liner, Vol. 1**/Glitterhouse Ger./1997
Rose of Jericho/Blue Rose Ger./1999

Bo Ramsey

Singer/Songwriter
Burlington, Iowa; 1952-

Never known as much of a music center, Iowa does have the advantage of being at the hub of a number of areas of musical influence; country/folk/bluegrass (Nashville), blues (Chicago, Memphis), rockabilly (Memphis). Out of these sources has been fashioned what locals call the "Iowa Sound," and one of its leading figures is Bo Ramsey. Born into a musical family (father a swing musician, mother always singing folk music around the house), Ramsey was initially drawn to blues while a student at the University of Iowa in the mid-1970s. He worked with Mother Blues, then in the 1980s formed the Third Street Sliders and began his career in earnest with tours and several albums. In 1987, Ramsey returned to college to finish up his degree and afterward returned to music but with a slightly different focus. He began working with fellow Iowan Kevin Gordon, an aspiring roots rocker and with folkie Greg Brown. Ramsey produced two albums for the latter and in the meantime recorded **Down to Bastrop**, a potpourri of blues, rock, and hard edged country. It drew attention from Lucinda Williams who did lots of promotional work on his behalf. In 1994, he did a songwriters-in-the-round tour in the South with Williams, R.B. Morris, and Steve Young. Ramsey's songwriting abilities caught the ears of Steve Earle and Guy Clark among others, and in 1995, Nashville began courting him to come there to make his next record. However, Ramsey was wary of such a move and continued to work in Iowa producing Greg Brown and roots rockers High and Lonesome and performing with his own band, the Sliders. In 1997, he played guitar and did some vocals on R.B Morris' **Take That Ride** and enhanced his reputation through **In the Weeds** which got high marks from alt. country/ Americana publications around the country; it was also well-received in Europe after the French label Dixie Frog released it there. Long-time admirer Lucinda Williams contributed vocals to one song ("Desert Flower") on the album and invited Ramsey to help out on her **Car Wheels on a Gravel Road** in 1998. And, that same year, he lent his considerable guitar and vocal skills to recordings by fellow singer/songwriters, Kate Campbell and Kevin Gordon.

Brand New Love/3rd Street/1980
Feelin's Gettin' Stronger (with the Sliders)/3rd
  Street/1983
Northwind (with the Sliders)/3rd Street/1986
Either Way/3rd Street/1988
Rockinitis (with the Sliders)/3rd Street/1989
Down to Bastrop/Shed/1991; Trailer/1996
Bo Ramsey and the Backsliders, Live/Trailer/1995
In the Weeds/Trailer/1997; Dixie Frog Fr./1997

Bo Ramsey Home Page //www.boramsey.com

See Greg Brown; Kevin Gordon; High and Lonesome; Lucinda Williams

The Ranch Girls (The Ragtime Wranglers; The Hillbilly Boogiemen)

Hillbilly Bop
Rotterdam, Holland; 1991-

Forgive me for saying it, but here's a real "Dutch treat!": The Ranch Girls (Caroline and Maryann) and their band the Ragtime Wranglers. Natives of Rotterdam, Caroline and Maryann got to know each other through the local music scene and in the late 1980s decided to form a harmony duo called the Half Pint Pigmies (for their diminutive size). They began to do hillbilly/Western swing music and modeled themselves after the country sister acts of the 1930s-1940s (Davis, Dinning, Girls of the Golden West). Accepting an invitation to a festival before they even secured a backing band led to a mad scramble for musicians, but in the nick of time, they put together a group including Joe Sixpack and Erwin Sietse who had previously been with Maryann in a band called the Greyhounds. After the festival, they assembled a more stable line up and took the name, the Drifting Texans which, after a few additions, became the Ranch Girls with the Ragtime Wranglers. Two years of European touring and a few personnel changes were followed by their first recordings for Longhorn Records. **Rhythm on the Ranch** showcases the Ranch Girls' wonderful twangy harmonies (with just a hint of a Dutch accent) and fine support from the Ragtime Wranglers on covers of the Collins Kids ("Go Away Don't Bother Me"; "Hot Rod"), Janis Martin ("I Gotta Know"), Shaun Young ("I'm Done, I'm Through") and the Carters ("Foggy Mountain Top"; "Wild- wood Flower"). 1993 saw their first of several appearances at the famous Hemsby Music Festival, and their selection as Favorite European Act. After that, the Ranch Girls became popular on the European club and festival circuit. Released in 1997 **Hillbilly Harmony** is another great album of honky tonk, swing, and rockabilly highlighted once again by the Ranch Girls' vocals on covers of "I Wanna Wanna," "Rock-a-Bye Baby," "Seven Lonely Days," "Mad at You," originals "Move Over Rover" (Maryann), and hot instrumentals by the Wranglers ("Traveling Blues"; "Roundup of Fun," both by Sixpack). In the spring of 1997, the Ranch Girls made a rare U.S. appearance at the Fairmount Rockabilly Weekender in Indianapolis and returned in 1998 for the Denver Rock 'N' Rhythm-Billy Weekend. However, after they returned home, Caroline announced she was leaving but was quickly replaced by Lil' Esther who had previously been in an Andrews Sisters style trio called the Bugaloos and a rockabilly group, Jess & Jill and the Sinners. Meanwhile, Mary Ann recorded a three track 45, **Mary Ann and Her Ragtime Wranglers**.

Performing as the Hillbilly Boogiemen, the Ragtime Wranglers established their own following with two excellent hillbilly boogie/bluegrass records, **Live at the Pumpkins** and **Rockin' and Cloggin'**. In Fall 1998, they ventured to the U.S. for their first ever tour that included stops in California, Texas, Arizona, and even an appearance at the International Bluegrass Festival in Guthrie, Oklahoma.

The Ragtime Wranglers/Hillbilly Boogiemen: Buzz (s.g.); Erwin (b); Erwin Sietse (d); Joe Sixpack (e.g.); Arnold (md)

"When I Hold You"/"I Forgot More"/"Fiddle Diddle Boogie"/"The Rockin' Gypsy" (with the Ragtime Wranglers)/Longhorn/1993 (EP)
Rhythm on the Ranch (with the Ragtime Wranglers)/Longhorn/1994
"Christmas Times A Coming" b/w "Christmas Boogie" (with the Hillbilly Boogiemen)/Homebrew/1994 (7")
"Kawliga" b/w "I'll Get Him Back" (with the Ragtime Wranglers)/Homebrew/1995 (7")
"Way Down Yonder"/"Brand New Sweetheart"/"Where D'Ya Go?"/"We Could" (with the Ragtime Wranglers)/Goofin' Fin./1995 (EP)
"I Gotta Know"/"Hey Doll Baby"/"Foggy Mountain Top"/"Hillbilly Gal" (with the Ragtime Wranglers)/On the Hill Jp./1995 (EP)
"The Rockin' Gypsy" b/w "Road Stop" (Ragtime Wranglers)/Homebrew/1995 (7")
Live at the Pumpkins (Hillbilly Boogiemen)/Longhorn/1995
Hillbilly Harmony (with the Ragtime Wranglers)/Goofin' Fin./1997
Mary Ann and Her Ragtime Wranglers/Goofin' Fin./1998 (EP)
Rockin' and Cloggin' (Hillbilly Boogiemen)/1998

The Ranch Girls and Their Ragtime Wranglers, P.O. Box 21685, 3001 AR Rotterdam, Netherlands (in May 1998, they began offering their own newsletter called *Lowdown Hoedown Magazine*)

The Ranch Girls and Their Ragtime Wranglers Website //www.xs4all.nl/~homebrew/

The Hillbilly Boogiemen Home Page //www.xs4all.nl/~hillbmen/

See The Barnstompers

Ranch Romance

Western Swing; Cowboy Western
Seattle, Washington; 1987-1995

In 1987, four Seattle women who shared a love for old-time Western swing and cowboy music got together on a whim and formed an "all star cowgirl revue" they called Ranch Romance. Nancy Katz, Barbara Lamb, Jo Miller, and Lisa Theo performed around the Seattle area for several years gaining a following built on their unique personae, energetic shows, and fabulous nouveau western outfits. In 1989, Ranch Romance recorded **Western Dream** on their Ranch Hand label. Their debut consisted of swing, cowboy/western, and torch covers of "When the Bloom is On the Sage," "Lovesick Blues," "St.

Louis Blues," "Ain't No Ash Will Burn," and "Why Don't You Love Me Like You Used to Do" held together by the band's hot playing and Miller's smooth lead vocals complete with goose bump raising yodels. A big career boost came when k.d. lang asked them to tour with her in 1989. This and frequent appearances on the women's festival circuit won Ranch Romance a larger following and a deal with Sugar Hill. With accordionist Nova Karina Devonie replacing Theo and a larger supporting cast including David Keenan on lead guitar, they recorded **Blue Blazes**, a sparkling blend of Western swing, honky tonk and sultry ballads all from the pen of Miller. Calling their sound "regressive country," Ranch Romance now brought in Keenan full time and recorded the Tim O'Brien produced **Flip City** which was a little more eclectic and jazzier than previous outings. After fiddler Lamb left in 1994 to become a member of Asleep at the Wheel and solo performer, the remaining members carried on for a while before throwing in the towel in 1995. Katz went on to play in the Seattle old-time band Lost Rosin and Keenan later joined a Buck Owens cover group called the Buck-A-Roosters. Jo Miller teamed with Laura Love (and Ranch Romance alumni) for some excellent high lonesome harmonizing on **...Sing Bluegrass and Old-Time Music**. Their covers of Flatt & Scruggs, Bill Monroe, Jimmie Rodgers, Hank Williams, the Delmores, Patsy Montana, and traditional standards are truly outstanding and with Devonie, Katz, and Keenan along on a few numbers, there's more than a little of the old Ranch Romance spark.

Nova Karina Devonie (acc,1991-1995); Nancy Katz (b,v,); David Keenan (e.g.,v,1992-1994); Barbara Lamb (f,v, 1987-1994); Jo Miller (g,l.v.); Lisa Theo (md,v,1987-1991)

Western Dream/Sugar Hill/1989
Blue Blazes/Sugar Hill/1991
Flip City/Sugar Hill/1993
Fiddle Fatal (Barbara Lamb)/Sugar Hill/1994
...Sing Bluegrass and Old-Time Music (Jo Miller & Laura Love)/RO/1995
Tonight I Feel Like Texas (Barbara Lamb)/Sugar Hill/1996

Rank and File (Cowboy Nation)

Cowpunk
Rank and File: Austin, Texas; 1981-1987
Cowboy Nation: Los Angeles, California; 1996-

In the cowpunk stampede of the 1980s, Rank and File were near the front of the herd. Not only were they one of the earliest bands in this genre but, for a brief shining moment, one of its best. The founders of the band had formerly played in California punk bands, Chip and Tony Kinman with the Dils and Alejandro Escovedo with the Nuns. Eventually, they all wound up in Austin in 1981 where they found fertile ground for their exploration of the connections between hard country and punk rock. The Kinmans' work with the Dils demonstrated a radical social and political consciousness, and they seemed to be especially attracted to the defiant working class aspects of country. Adding drummer Slim Evans, they took the name Rank and File and in 1982 recorded **Sundown** which is generally considered a consummate cowpunk record. Rank and File rode the strength of the album to an appearance on *Austin City Limits*, but shortly thereafter, both cowpunk and Rank and File fizzled. Escovedo and Evans departed in 1983 leaving the Kinmans to carry on using studio musicians for **Long Gone Dead** which had some country rock elements but was really more of a pop rock record than **Sundown**. **Rank and File**, moved even farther away from the band's cowpunk origins and showed it was time to hang up their spurs. In 1987, the Kinmans gave up on Rank and File and took an extreme musical turn when they formed the short lived and much maligned industrial rock band, the Blackbirds. Escovedo went on to front the roots rock True Believers before embarking on a solo career and making several recordings that earned him a very loyal following in Austin and beyond. The Kinmans dropped out of sight for a number of years but with the resurgence of alternative country in the 1990s reemerged with a new cowpunkish band, Cowboy Nation, with John Norman (ex-Taco) on drums. Their self titled debut is heavy on the cowboy/western with covers of traditional songs like "Cowboy's Lament," "Old Paint," "My Rifle, My Pony and Me," and "Remember the Alamo." But, contrary to what you might guess, this is not a cow-boy punk recording but rather a very restrained and moody lo-fi reading of the Old West.

Rank and File: Slim Evans (d); Alejandro Escovedo (g,v); Chip Kinman (g,v); Tony Kinman (b,v)
Cowboy Nation: Chip Kinman (g,hm,v); Tony Kinman (b,db b,v); John Norman (d)

   Sundown/Slash/1982
   Long Gone Dead/Slash/1984
   Rank and File/Rhino/1987
   "Cowboy Nation" on **Cowboy Jukebox**/Vinyl Junkie
      UK/1997
   Cowboy Nation/Demon UK/1997; Coconut Grove/1998

See Alejandro Escovedo

The Rank Outsiders

Tobacco Row; Country Rock
Charlotte, North Carolina; 1991-

North Carolina natives Gigi Dover and Bill Noonan began performing in Charlotte as an acoustic duo in 1989. For one show in particular, they needed a drummer and when that worked added a bass. The new foursome brought an assortment of influences to the mix (the Rolling Stones, Janis Joplin, Patsy Cline, Gram Parsons, and Lou Reed) which they developed into a country rock band, the Rank Outsiders (from a line in a Rolling Stones song). After playing local clubs for a few years, they put out an EP, **First Things First**, in 1993. Its six tracks included five by Noonan and a cover of "I Know You Rider." A year later

came a full length CD, **One Man's Trash is Another Man's Treasure** and then, **Checkpoint**, which reached as high as #11 on the Gavin Americana charts. The Outsiders' secret weapons are Noonan's songwriting ("Break a Heart & Pass It Along"; "Walkin' Institution of Heartache"; "Paradise Motel"; "You Don't Owe Me Nothin'") and Dover's potent lead vocals. Their sound was convincing enough to win them the Best Country Band in Charlotte award from *Creative Loafing* for three years running (1994-1996). They made numerous appearances outside North Carolina at the Western Beat Barndance in Nashville and many festivals in the Southeast. National exposure came through a positive write-up in *No Depression*.

Gigi Dover (a.g.,e.g.,v); Tom Kuhn (b,v); Ray Mitchell (d); Bill Noonan (a.g.,e.g.,v)

   First Things First/Rank/1993
   One Man's Trash Is Another Man's Treasure/
      Rank/1994
   Checkpoint/Rank/1996

The Rank Outsiders, P.O. Box 189100,
Charlotte, NC 28218-9100

The Rank Outsiders Backyard Home Page
//olacserv.com/ranks/

The Rank Outsiders/NOMA Web Page
//www.songs.com/rankos/ro-home.html

ranks@vnet.net

Reckless Kelly

"Hick Rock"
Austin, Texas; 1996-

The first thing about Reckless Kelly that jumps out at you is how much they sound like early Steve Earle. Lead singer Willy Braun sounds uncannily like Earle, and the band as a whole has the **Copperhead Road**, **Guitar Town**, etc. sound down to a tee. Still, they have weathered charges of being too derivative and developed a self described brand of "hick rock" that swiftly catapulted them into Austin's alt. country limelight. Originally based in Oregon, Reckless Kelly was named for an Australian film starring Yahoo Serious. Led by brothers Cody and Willy Braun, who had grown up playing in the family's cowboy/western band, Muzzie Braun and the Boys, they moved to Central Texas in 1996. After less than a year of continuous gigging, Reckless Kelly not only gained a huge number of fans and opening slots for Robert Earl Keen and Todd Snider but also a record contract with Chris Wall's Cold Spring Records. Their debut, **Millican**, moves nicely across bluegrass ("Black & White"), blues ("Waitin' on the Blues"), and country rock ("Baby's Gone"; "Hatax") bearing a definite early Earle imprint with hints of a band trying to chart its own course. Reviews were mixed (damning with faint praise or praising with faint damns), but the consensus held that Reckless Kelly possessed genuine talent and in time would carve out their own little alt. country niche. This was borne out in 1998 when they not only won Best New Band and Best Roots Rock Band at the Austin Music Awards but also showed up on several high profile compilations (**Will Sing for Food**; **Chasing the Dream**), performed on Robert Earl Keen's Texas Uprising tour, and backed Chris Wall on his **Tainted Angel**. They also showed off their in person dynamism on **Acoustic Live** from Austin's legendary Stubb's BBQ. By year's end, Reckless Kelly were poised and ready to take it to the next level.

Cody Braun (f,hm,md,v); Willy Braun (r.g.,v); Jay Nazz (d); Casey Pollock (l.g.,r.g.); Chris Schelske (d)

> **Millican**/Cold Spring/1997
> "Please, Please Baby" on **Will Sing for Food: The Songs of Dwight Yoakam**/Little Dog/1998
> "Rodeo Man" on **Bull Riders: Chasing the Dream**/Cold Spring/1998
> **Acoustic Live**/Reckless/1998

Reckless Kelly/Cold Spring Records, P.O. Box 162822, Austin, TX 78716; 512-320-9156; coldspring@ccsi.com

Reckless Kelly Home Page //www.recklesskelly.com

Reckless Kelly/Davis McLarty Page //www.davismclarty.com/reckless.html

See Chris Wall

The Red Clay Ramblers
New Old-Time
Chapel Hill, North Carolina; 1972-

For over a quarter of a century, the Red Clay Ramblers have been one of the most innovative of Americana bands. The founding members had previously played in various modern string bands, and although the Ramblers sound was based on this style, it incorporated music drawn from an incredible diversity of sources. Their many albums join blues, old-time, bluegrass, country, ragtime, swing jazz, classical, and rock, all given a playful twist and infused with plenty of whimsy. The Ramblers lent their inventive touches to a number of projects including sessions with Eugene Chadbourne (**Country Protest**) and Michelle Shocked (**Arkansas Traveler**) and several off-Broadway plays. Their first stage effort was with a musical called *Diamond Studs: The Story of Jesse James* and then Sam Shepard's *A Lie of the Mind* for which they supplied a variety of music including standards such as "Hard Times," "South of the Border," "In the Pines," "The Gal I Left Behind Me," and "Killing Floor" plus unique originals (soundtrack released in 1986). The Ramblers subsequently provided the soundtrack for Shepard's movie *Far North*, performed in his 1994 *Silent Tongue*, and worked on the musical, *Fool Moon* which had successful runs in L.A., New York City, and Europe. In the late 1990s, they were involved with a musical entitled *Kudzu: The Southern Musical*. Based on a comic strip by Doug Marlette, it depicts the curious goings on in the town of Bypass, North Carolina (sort of a combination *Greater Tuna* and *Li'l Abner)*. In 1997, the Ramblers self-released their first **Live** recording.

Clay Buckner (f,hm,v,1980-) Mike Craver (hm,p,v, 1973-1986); Chris Frank (acc,g,p,trp,v,1987-); Jack Herrick (b,hm,tp,wh,1976-); Bill Hicks (f,v,1972-1981); Bland Simpson (p,v,1986-); Tommy Thompson (bj,g,v,1972-1994); Jim Watson (g,md,v,1972-1986)

> **Red Clay Ramblers**/Folkways/1974
> **Stolen Love**/Flying Fish/1975
> **Twisted Laurel**/Flying Fish/1976
> **Merchant's Lunch**/Flying Fish/1977
> **Chuckin' the Frizz**/Flying Fish/1979
> **Meeting in the Air**/Flying Fish/1980
> **Hard Times**/Flying Fish/1981
> **A Lie of the Mind**/Rykodisc Sugar Hill/1986 (sdtrk.)
> **It Ain't Right**/Flying Fish/1986; 1992
> **The Merry Wives of Windsor, Texas**/Snappy/1988
> **Far North**/Sugar Hill/1989 (sdtrk.)
> **Twisted Laurel & Merchant's Lunch**/Flying Fish/1991
> **Rambler**/Sugar Hill/1992
> **Live**/RCR/1997

The Red Clay Ramblers //www.herschelfreemanagency.com/RCR.html

The Red Dirt Rangers
Country Rock; Western
Oklahoma City, Oklahoma; 1990-

The Red Dirt Rangers evolved from the living room picking sessions of a group of college friends at Oklahoma State University in the 1980s. By 1990, they were good enough to play local clubs, tour, and record **Cimarron Soul** and then **Red Dirt** in 1993. Named for the color of the soil in central Oklahoma, they blend traditional Southwestern styles (Western swing, honky tonk, cowboy, Tex-Mex) with contemporary influences ranging from Dylan to the Dead. The Rangers contributed to two fine tribute compilations, **Pastures of Plenty** (to Woody Guthrie) and **Songs of Route 66** (to America's venerable highway). Both were produced in Austin which became a second home for the Rangers. They were very kid conscious, recording **Blue Shoe** which came with a coloring book; they regularly included children's shows on their tour schedule. Most of the band's performances were in and around Oklahoma, but in 1997, they toured in Switzerland. The Red Dirt Rangers paid homage to their home state on **Oklahoma Territory**, which, aided by the always able production of Lloyd Maines, excels on honky tonk/country rock/swing covers and originals. The band participated in two major musical events in Oklahoma in 1998: Byron Berline's International Bluegrass Festival and the first annual Woody Guthrie Free Folk Festival in his home town of Okemah.

Scott Buxton (d); John Cooper (md,v); Benny Craig (hm,p.s.); Ben Han (e.g.,v); Brad Piccolo (a.g.,v); Bob Wiles (b,v)

> **Cimarron Soul**/RDR/1990
> **Red Dirt**/RDR/1993 (CS)
> "The Ranger's Command" on **Pastures of Plenty: An Austin Tribute to Woody Guthrie**/Dejadisc/1993
> **Blue Shoe**/RDR/1994 (with a coloring book)

"Used to Be" on **The Songs of Route 66**/Lazy SOB/1995
Oklahoma Territory/Ranger/1997
"Idabel Blues" on **Full Tank, Vol. 1**/Jackass/1998

The Red Dirt Rangers, 948 SW 24th, Oklahoma City, OK 73109; 405-525-DIRT, (fax) 405-634-9524

The Red Dirt Rangers Home Page
//moon.uokhsc.edu/mvaughan/rdr.html

The Red Dirt Rangers //www.okclive.com/reddirtranger/

The Red Dirt Rangers Fan Club
//www.wkkj.com/fanclubs/r/red.dirt.rangers.htm

Red Meat

Honky-Tonk; Swing
San Francisco, California; 1993-

k. d. lang's least favorite band, Red Meat developed from the Genuine Diamelles and the Movie Stars, a Bay Area country/roots/rock band that put out a couple of albums (**Heckola!**; **Head on a Platter**) in the late 1980s and early 1990s. Three members of that band (which also included Bradley Jaye Williams of Austin's Los Pinkys and the Gulf Coast Playboys), Steve Cornell, Michael Montalto, and "Wholesome" Jill Olson formed Red Meat in 1993 adding Scott Young on fiddle. After doing several years of hard time in Bay Area venues, in 1997, they released **Meet Red Meat**, a thoroughly enjoyable and sometimes side-splitting ablum of honky tonk music. Red Meat specializes in numbers (written by Young) with clever word play or updated takes on traditional country themes: "One Glass at a Time," "Highway of Heartaches," "Inner Redneck," "Phone Tag," "Nashville Fantasy," "The Girl With the Biggest Hair," and "12 Inch, 3 Speed Oscillating Fan" not only sound like the genu-whine article but will make you laugh out loud. Their debut reached the top 20 on the Gavin Americana report, and "Texas, Texas" reached #5 on the French country music charts. After a tour through the Southwest, Red Meat landed none other than Dave Alvin to produce **13** which has songs not only by Young but also Cornell, Montalto, and Olson. And though Alvin convinced them to alter their arrangements and vocal styles somewhat, the overall result is, once again, a nifty album of "high cholesterol honky tonk" that has made them one of the top acts of their kind on the West Coast.

Steve Cornell (bj,g,p.s.); Les James (d,v); Michael Montalto (l.g.,md,v); Jill Olson (b,v); Smelley Kelley (v); Steve Young (f,g,v)

Meet Red Meat/Ranchero/1997
13/Ranchero/1998

Red Meat/Ranchero Records, 4200 Park Blvd. Ste 227, Oakland, CA 94602

Red Meat's High Cholesterol Honky Tonk Page
//home.earthlink.net/~lesjames/index.htm

RanchRecs@aol.com

The Red Mules

New Old-Time
Central Ohio; 1982-

Back in the early heydays of old-time music family acts were as common as fleas on a hound dog. One modern group which carries on that tradition is the Red Mules. For over twenty years, brothers Jeff and Rick Goehring along with Jeff's wife Sue have diligently preserved and promoted the old-time music heritage of Ohio and also quietly become one of the best new old-time groups around. As youngsters, Rick and Jeff were fortunate to have a grandpa who taught them to play guitar and sing traditional songs and though both dabbled in rock and popular music in the late 1960s-early 1970s, they were eventually drawn back to their old-time roots. After Rick took up clawhammer banjo and Jeff the fiddle, they joined the Flat City String Band for a time but then started their own trio in 1978 with guitarist Pam Fisher. During a trip to play at the Kent State Folk Festival, Jeff met Sue Colpetzer, an aspiring old-time flat-picker whose biggest influence was the great David Molk. She joined the trio (and married Jeff) in 1979, and they became the Huckabuck Stringband. Later, Rick, Jeff, and Sue teamed with Judy and Howard Sacks as the Red Mule String Band which in 1982 became into the Red Mules. Along the way, all three had become avid collectors of old-time songs and made regular pilgrimages to see veteran old-time musicians like Wade Jarvis, Tommy Jarrell, and Dee and Delta Hicks. Jeff, in particular, was a tireless gatherer of tunes by Ohio fiddlers and in 1985, he and Sue produced **Seems Like Romance to Me**, an award winning collection of field recordings featuring nine traditional fiddlers from Ohio. Throughout the 1980s and 1990s, the Red Mules were popular favorites on the folk/old-time festival circuits and did (often with Beth Braden and Lynn Frederick) numerous recordings for local and national compilations including Rounder's **Young Fogies** and **Old-Time Music On the Radio** series. Like the Highwoods String Band and Freight Hoppers, their style is what might be called "innovative nostalgia," a close reading of the traditional old-time book with some modern chapters added on.

Jeff Goehring (f); Rick Goehring (bj); Sue Colpetzer Goehring (f)

"Blind Steer in a Mud Hole" on **The Young Fogies, Vol. 1**/Rounder/1985; 1994
The Red Mules: Old-Time Music/Marimac/1992 (CS)
"Tomahawk," "Possum on a Rail," & "Three Forks of Reedy" on **1993 Indiana Fiddlers' Gathering**/Log Cabin/1993 (CS)
"I Wouldn't Mind Dying If Dying Was All" on **1993 Augusta Concert Souvenirs, Vol. 4**/Augusta Heritage Center/1993 (CS)
"Icy Mountain" on **The Young Fogies, Vol. 2**/Rounder/1995
"Foggy Mountain Top" on **Old-Time Music On the Radio, Vol. 2**/Rounder/1996

The Red Mules, P.O. Box 566, Zoar, OH 44697

Red Star Belgrade

Tobacco Row; Roots Rock
Raleigh, North Carolina; Chicago, Illinois; Late 1990s-

Reviews and features in *Option, Magnet, No Depression, Puncture, Request,* and other music magazines consistently pointed out two things: Red Star Belgrade sound a lot like Neil Young in his **Ragged Glory** days and lyrically, lead singer/ songwriter Bill Curry is one bitter mo-fo. He and wife/drummer Graham Harris-Curry once had a quieter country rock band called the Uncrowned Nashville Kings, but Red Star Belgrade (named for an Eastern European soccer team) is a horse of a different color. A typical song offers a kind of call and response between grinding, searing guitars and Curry's nasally tirades about murder ("Favorite Thing"; "Union, SC"—about Susan Smith), revenge ("Under My Wheels"), suffering ("Lord's Prayer"; "Sour Juice"), and this veil of tears ("Age of Regret"). Occasionally, Red Star Belgrade takes a break from the aural assault, but the despair seldom subsides. "Saddest Girl" features an electric guitar strumming jauntily, but with lyrics like "sometimes it hurts just to see her smile" and "there's not a damn thing we can do," it's one big bummer. But, in a mad world careening out of control, that's ultimately the purpose of groups like Red Star Belgrade; sort of like professional mourners for a planet in its death throes. At any rate, RSB created somewhat of a stir not only in the U.S. but also in the United Kingdom where they were mentioned in *Uncut* magazine's September, 1998, special on alt. country and had a cut included on Vinyl Junkie's alt. country compilation **Loose**. RSB's **End of the Line** was released in late 1998 in the U.K. and Europe on Vinyl Junkie's sister label Loose; the U.S. version of it, **The Fractured Hymnal**, had yet to be released as of early 1999, but a Chicago based label (Bloodshot?; Checkered Past?) had expressed interest. Perhaps in anticipation of that deal, Red Star Belgrade relocated from Chapel Hill to The Windy City "where there is a real music scene."

Paul Cardillo (b); Bill Curry (l.v.); Graham Harris-Curry (d,h.v.); Bob Taylor (l.g.)

> **Lose a Temper, Gain an Injury**/Put It On a Cracker/1996
> **Union, South Carolina**/Put It On a Cracker/1996 (EP)
> **Polpot**/Put It on a Cracker/1996 (7")
> **Where the Sun Doesn't Shine**/Put It on a Cracker/1997
> "Under My Wheels" on **Revival, Vol. 1**/Yep Roc/1997
> "Favorite Thing" on **Revival, Vol. 2**/Yep Roc/1997
> "Saddest Girl" on **Loose: News Sounds of the Old West**/ Vinyl Junkie UK/1998
> **End of the Line**/Loose Ryko UK/1998 (set for U.S. Release in 1999 as **The Fractured Hymnal**)
> "Saddest Girl" on **Uncut Magazine's 1999 Compilation**/ Uncut UK/1999

Red Star Belgrade Home Page //www.redstarbelgrade.com
nyr@interpath.com

Redneck Greece Delux (The Hot Burritos)

Redneck Underground; White Trash Parody
Ellijay, Georgia; July 18, 1961-

One of the earliest members of the Atlanta/Athens Redneck Underground was Redneck Greece (aka Greg Reece). Born in northern Georgia (Ellijay), Reece worked his family's beef cattle farm then attended the University of Georgia where he received a B.A. in agriculture and developed a serious interest in country music. He returned to the farm, but the lure of a musical career was too great so Reece headed back to Athens and a new persona, Redneck Greece, was born. The legend of Redneck Greece told of a mountain boy drifting into town with only "a jug of corn liquor, a bag of songs, and a vision (blurred by massive amounts of drugs and alcohol)." After several years of struggle as a solo act in local dives and honky tonks, Greece assembled his Delux band in 1991. Redneck Greece Delux played good old hillbilly, country music *a la* Hank, George, Johnny, et al. but put a little different slant on the standard themes such as drinking ("Dixie Deadhead"—she chases LSD with Jack), cheating ("Don't Let Another Penis Come Between Us"), mother ("Momma Was a Dancer at the Claremont Lounge"), religion ("Jesus Was a Rebel"), car racing ("Redneck Demolition Derby Man"), and truck driving ("Rest Area Ruby"). On stage and on record, they played the Redneck Nation role to the hilt from phony names to wild outfits and stage props including motorcycles, tractors, and horses. Redneck Greece Delux performed at the inaugural Redneck Underground festival, Bubbapalooza and were on the widely disclaimed **Bubbapalooza** compilation. In the late 1990s, Greece/Reece performed solo and became a local cable celebrity with outrageous advertisements for his famous Redneck Burgers (available only at Loco's Deli). Still a leading figure in the Redneck Underground, Redneck Greece appeared at every Bubbapalooza and teamed with the Stump Broke Steers. Their cover of the Diggers "She's Breakin' My Heart While I'm Drinkin' Her Beer" was included on the Greg Dean Smalley tribute, **Bubbapalooza II**.

Two ex-Delux members, Barry Sell (Heartless) and William Tonks (Weasel) fronted the Hot Burritos (named for shared employment at the Taco Stand and love for Gram Parsons/ Flying Burrito Brothers). In the late 1990s, they had a regular Tuesday night gig at the High Hat where they played their own songs and backed frequent guests such as Redneck Greece, Vic Chesnutt, and other Atlanta/Athens music celebrities.

Redneck Greece Delux: Knuckles Beanblossom (p); Redneck Greece (g,v); Earl Grizzell (f); Wayne Heartless (b); Brahma Huertha (concertina, hm); Junior (d); Hooty Sugarlegs (b.v.); Johnny Weasel (g); Jo Lynn Wheeler (b.v.)
The Hot Burritos: Barry Sell; William Tonks

> **Good Eatin'**/SMBT/1992

"Redneck TV" on **Deep South, Vol. 1**/Spinning Mule/1992
Cold Hard Facts/SMBT/1994
"Mama Was a Dancer at the Claremont Lounge" on **Bubbapalooza**/Sky/1995
"Redneck Loves Redette" and "Dish Pan Boogie" on **14 x 7: Hand Picked Songs From Georgia**/Hexamusic/1996

Greg Reece, P.O. Box 935, Athens, GA 30603; 706-369-1486

The Hot Burritos, P.O. Box 42, Athens, Georgia 30603

The Hot Burritos Home Page //virtual.atlanta.com/burrito/

The Renderers

Lo-Fi Country Roots Rock
New Zealand; 1990-

When I think of New Zealand, sunny beaches and smiling faces come most easily to mind. But, one listen to the Renderers brooding country rock noise on songs like "A Touch of Evil," "Shrunken Heads," "It's Sad," "Timebomb," "Carnival of Souls," and "Unforgiven" blows that image all to hell and back; the names of their albums (**Trail of Tears**, **That Dog's Head in the Gutter Gives Off Vibrations**, **Surface of Jupiter**) are pretty disconcerting too. Formed in the early 1990s, the black heart and soul of the group is the husband/wife team of Brian and Maryrose Cook; she handles the lead vocals with an eerie grace, he adds some jolting exclamation marks with "effective diseased guitar work," and they combine on mournful old-timey harmonies. Rooted in traditional country music, the Renederers oscillate between Neil Young/Crazy Horse era rock and Velvet Underground lo-fi in much the same way as American counterparts like Sparklehorse, Palace, and U.S. Saucer.

Brian Cook (l.g.,v); Maryrose Cook (l.v.); Denise Roughan (b); Robbie Yeats (d)

Trail of Tears/Flying Nun NZ/1991
That Dog's Head in the Gutter Gives Off Vibrations/Ajax/1994
The Surface of Jupiter/Ajax/1996
Dream of the Sea/Siltbreeze/1998

J. J. Reneaux

Cajun Country; Singer/Songwriter/Storyteller
Louisiana/Atlanta, Georgia

A native of southern Louisiana's bayou country, J. J. Reneaux established herself as a highly respected interpreter of the region's rich culture through her work as a storyteller, author, and musician. With her band, the Mojos, she took the area's diverse musical influences—Cajun, Creole, zydeco, country, blues, New Orleans R&B—and melded them into a style that comfortably wed the traditional to the modern. On the self-released tape, **Bayou Girl,** and CD, **Cajun, Country, and Blue**, Reneaux's powerful yet smooth vocals deftly handle two steps and waltzes as well as sultry blues and touching ballads.

Her originals and rearrangements of standards are traditional and fresh at the same time. In addition, Reneaux authored and edited several award winning collections of Cajun folk, ghost, and fairy tales (*Cajun Folktales, Cajun Ghost Stories, Wake Snake, Haunted Bayou*, and *Why Alligator Hates Dog*) and is a renowned Cajun storyteller who delights all ages on audio cassettes and through personal appearances at schools and workshops. In 1997-1998, she was hard at work on an anthology of humorous short stories for adults called *GRITS: Girls Raised in the South* and toward the end of '98 released an album of country rock and blues (**If Only in Dreams**) with her daughter Zoe.

The Mojos: Andy Carlson (f,g,md); Matt Donaldson (d,perc,h.v.); Karen Ann Krieger (acc,p,h.v.); Mark Maxwell (b,g,md)

Bayou Girl/JJR/1991 (CS)
Cajun, Country and Blue/Brambus Switz./1995
If Only in Dreams (with Zoe Reneaux)/JJR/1998

J.J. Reneaux, P.O. Box 7782, Athens, GA 30604; 706-549-7212

J. J. Reneaux //www.jjreneaux.com

jj@jjreneaux.com

The Replacements

Roots Rock
Minneapolis, Minnesota; 1980-1991

Rude and crude, boisterous and belligerent, the Replacements were one of the greatest and most important rock bands of the 1980s. The imprint of their sound and style is readily apparent in modern alt. country especially in the plethora of roots rock bands that emerged in the 1990s. Check the press kits of these types of groups from the Midwest to North Carolina and chances are they'll cite the Replacements as a major influence. On record and live, the 'Mats were prone to rave-ups of classic tunes like "Jolene" (Dolly Parton) and "Hey Good Lookin'" (Hank, Sr.) and did an occasional country shuffle original ("Portland"; "I Will Dare"). Their albums, especially **Hootennany, Let It Be**, **Pleased to Meet Me**, and **All Shook Down**, gloriously jumbled blues, country, rock, and punk with a lot of attitude and helped pave the way for more fully realized alt. country/roots rock recordings by a host of other groups later on. Leader Paul Westerberg's sometimes wacky, sometimes tender songs exerted a powerful influence on many alt. country singer/songwriters; Jeff Tweedy/Wilco's "The Lonely 1" from **Being There** is dedicated to Westerberg. And though they ended in 1991, the Replacements' legacy lived on through solo albums by Dunlap and Westerberg and retrospectives such as the 1997 double CD, **All for Nothing, Nothing for All**. That same year a group of Austin musicians including the Gourds, the Damnations, the Asylum Street Spankers, and Buick MacKane (Alejandro Escovedo) recorded a tribute to the 'Mats called **So What?** Rock's beautiful losers still command a big and loyal following as witnessed by numerous web pages and a very active online mailing list devoted to them.

Slim Dunlap (l.g.,1988-); Chris Mars (d); Bob Stinson (l.g.,1980-1987); Tommy Stinson (b); Paul Westerberg (g,v)

Hootenanny/Twin Tone/1983
Let It Be/Twin Tone/1984
Pleased to Meet Me/Sire/1987
All for Nothing, Nothing for All/Sire/1997
So What?: An Austin Tribute to The Replacements/ Wretched/1997

The Replacements //www.tt.net/twintone/mats.html

The Realm of XrE //www.geocities.com/sunsetstrip/8292/

The Skyway: The Replacements Internet Mailing List //www.novia.net/~matt/sky/skyway.html

The Residents
Avant-Garde
San Francisco, California; Early 1970s-

There have been hundereds of tribute albums done to the greats of American music, but no one has done them like those San Francisco mysterians, the Residents. For over almost 25 years, the "World's Most Famous Unknown Band" has managed to maintain anonymity (they are often pictured with giant eyeball heads) while turning out dozens of recordings that present some of the strangest takes on popular music you're ever likely to hear. One of their most bizarre and ambitious projects was **The American Composer Series** in which the Residents paid homage to various songwriting legends with outrageous reworkings of their most famous songs. Volume one, **George & James**, was a split tribute to George Gershwin and James Brown while volume two, **Stars and Hank Forever!** feted John Phillip Sousa and Hank Williams. On the latter, five of Hank's songs ("Hey Good Lookin'", "Six More Miles," "Kaw-Liga," "Ramblin' Man," "Jambalaya") are presented in various settings (some humorous, some dark) using everything from startling slide to disco beat. Three other Hank songs ("Dear Brother"; "Pictures From Life's Other Side"; "I'm So Lonesome I Could Cry") from the **Stars and Hank** sessions were later released on the **Daydream B-Liver** CD as "The Hank Williams Death and Despair Trilogy in Waltz Time." Nine different versions of "Kaw-Liga" including "Nightmare," "Horror," "Prairie," and "Kaw-Live-Ga" were issued as singles between 1986-1994 and later compiled on **Poor Kaw-Liga's Pain**. Of related interest is **The King & Eye** which was part of the Residents' **History of American Music in 3-EZ Pieces**. Here their vocalist leads a group of children in an amusing discussion to discover "The King of what?" in between one-of-a-kind, highly entertaining renditions of Elvis' big hits.

The American Composers Series, Vol. 2: Stars and Hank Forever!/Ralph/1986
The History of American Music in 3 E-Z Pieces: The King & Eye/Enigma/1989

Daydream B-Liver/UWEB/1989
Poor Kaw-Liga's Pain/Torso/1990

RzWeb: The Residents //www.theresidents.com

Bob Reuter (Kamikaze Cowboy)
Singer/Songwsriter
St. Louis, Missouri; 1952-

Bob Reuter was a key figure in laying the foundations for the current generation of St. Louis alt. country. As a solo or with Kamikaze Cowboy, he has been putting down solid country/ roots rock since the late 1970s. Reuter draws on a variety of musical sources, but his most obvious influence is the Texas singer/songwriter tradition. Like Clark, Van Zandt, et al., his main strength lies in perceptive storytelling as on fine songs like "It Don't Matter." Throughout the 1980s and early 1990s, Reuter became a regular on the St. Louis scene but also performed frequently at the Bluebird Cafe in Nashville. Over the years his band, Kamikaze Cowboy, had more than two dozen alumni including members of St. Louis' current alt. country bands (e.g. Kip Loui and John Horton of Belle Starr). In the early 1990s, Reuter labored in relative obscurity, recording several self released cassettes but in 1995 and 1996 came successive CDs, **This Much I Know** and **Hurry Sundown**, that brought him greater recognition. In the wake of the current alt. country resurgence, Reuter was "rediscovered" and given his due as a musician and path breaker. Sadly, just as his star began to rise, Reuter was hit with a major medical problem that left him unable to perform. The St. Louis musical community quickly rallied to his aid to help defray medical expenses, and by late 1997, he was back in action.

Southern Exposure, Western Expansion/BR/1990 (CS)
Got in Some Trouble Writing Love Songs When I Should Have Been Just Strumming My Guitar/ BR/1991(CS)
Pray for the Repose of the Soul/BR/1993 (CS)
Confessions of a Kamikaze Cowboy/BR/1994 (CS)
"It Don't Matter" **on Hit the Hay, Vol. 1**/Sound Asleep Swe./1994
This Much I Know/BR/1995
Hurry Sundown (Kamikaze Cowboy)/Cowboy Angel/1996

Bob Reuter/Cowboy Angel Records, 2015 Alameda, St. Louis, MO 63143; 314-644-1660

Kamikaze Cowboy Home Page //www.mphase.com/reuter1.htm

kamikaze@mphase.com

The Revenants
Honky Tonk; Country Rock
Phoenix/Tempe, Arizona; 1996-

During the 1980s and early 1990s, Bruce Connole was a member of some of the most promising rock bands (Billy Clone and the Same, the Jetzons, the Strand) in the Phoenix/Tempe area.

However, each of these enterprises fell apart due in large part to Connole's well-publicized substance abuse problems. Eventually, Bruce retreated into the safety of his apartment for a couple of years, but during his seclusion developed an interest in hard-core country by the likes of Hank Williams, Buck Owens, Johnny Cash, et al. One evening in early 1996 at an acoustic night at a local spot called Nita's Hideaway, Connole and guitarist Deke Taylor (ex-Gin Blossoms) got on stage to do a few of Bruce's original country songs. From that modest beginning evolved the Suicide Kings with Connole and Taylor plus Bobby Domings on drums and Scott Kalkbrenner on bass. After only a year of playing area clubs, they were named Best Country/Americana Band by the Phoenix *New Times* magazine. In 1997, they recorded **The Suicide Kings**, an impressive set of hard line honky tonk (with a tinge of rock) and were once again voted Best Country/Americana Band. To avoid conflict with a California metal band of the same name, the Suicide Kings regrouped as the Revenants and in 1998 released **Artists & Whores** which reworks six songs (a little less rocked up) from **The Suicide Kings** and includes nine new tunes. In traditional honky tonk, Connole has found just the right vehicle for exercising and exorcising the demons of his past. Not surprisingly, most of his songs, delivered with a raspy desperation, deal with dysfunction ("That Girl's Insane"; "Light at the End of the Bottle"; "Bottle and a Gun"; "Prodigal Son"), disappointment ("Forever"; "She"; "Every Single Minute With You is Like a Minute Alone"), and death ("Flower on My Grave"; "Dead and Gone"; "Blood River"; "Cradle to the Grave"); but, in true honky tonk style, he allows room for some smiles between the tears. Supplemented admirably by local musicians on fiddle, dobro, and steel, the Revenants deftly work their way through shuffles, ballads, and romps and make it clear why they are such local favorites. A new CD, **"Live" at The Tempest** was recorded in late 1998 and due out sometime the next year.

Bruce Connole (a.g.,e.g.,l.v.); Bobby Domings (d); Paul Schneider (b); Deke Taylor (a.g.,e.g.,l.s.,b.v.)

Artists and Whores/Epiphany/1997
"Why Do You Love Me" on **Jukebox Cantina**/Hayden's
    Ferry/1998
The Revenants "Live" at The Tempest/1999

The Revenants: Honky Tonk Music //therevenants.com

revenants@therevenants.com

Official Revenants Web Page
//www.public.asu.edu/~mrklim/revenants.html

Kimmie Rhodes

Texas; Singer/Songwriter
Wichita Falls, Texas; March 6, 1956-

The Texas singer/songwriter tradition has been overwhelmingly male dominated, but one bright exception is Kimmie Rhodes. Raised in Lubbock, that great focal point of Texas music, her first musical experiences were with the Rhodes

family gospel trio, but she also absorbed a range of musical influences from West Texas and beyond. Rhodes' musical career really began to evolve when she moved to Austin in 1979. There she met Joe Gracey who was a major force in local music in the 1970s as a DJ at KOKE (it's eclectic format including blues, progressive country, rock, jazz, etc. made it arguably the first Americana station), music journalist, promoter, performer, and producer at his Electric Graceland Studios/Jackalope Records. Not only did he agree to produce the fledgling singer/songwriter's first album but married her too! Rhodes debut, **Kimmie Rhodes and the Jackalope Brothers**, firmly inducted her into the progressive country community and was followed by two albums recorded in England, **Man in the Moon** and **Angels Get the Blues**. Her heavenly vocals are given solid support on these recordings by a stellar cast of guest musicians including Gracey, Wes McGhee, Joe Ely, Butch Hancock, Jack Clement, Jimmy Day, Jesse Taylor, Chris O'Connell, and Maryann Price. Subsequent tours in Europe generated a large following for Rhodes and in 1993 a retrospective of her early work, **A Lot Like Texas**, was released on the Swiss Red Moon label. And although Rhodes worked with Willie Nelson and had her songs covered by Nelson ("Just One Love"), Wynonna Judd, Trisha Yearwood, and others, she remained virtually unknown in the U.S. until her breakthrough album, **West Texas Heaven**. First released on French New Rose, it was picked up in 1996 by Justice Records and brought Rhodes much deserved and overdue recognition. The album's duets with Nelson, Waylon Jennings, and Townes Van Zandt plus an appearance on a special *Austin City Limits* showcase with Nelson, Jennings, Kris Kristofferson, and Billy Joe Shaver helped cement her place in the Texas singer/songwriter pantheon. In the late 1990s, Rhodes toured with Gracey and son Gabe on guitar and worked on an autobiographical musical titled *Small Town Girl*. Another collection of Rhodes pre-**West Texas Heaven** material entitled **Jackalopes, Moons, and Angels** was released late in 1997. *Small Town Girl* had its gala premier in late September 1998 in Luck, Texas, Willie Nelson's Old West town/movie set. Co-starring Joe Ely and Joe Sears (of *Greater Tuna* fame) who also directed, it presents a fact/fiction portrait in story and song of Kimmie's early years growing up in West Texas. Initial reviews were good and hopes were high for taking the show on the road and perhaps all the way to Broadway. Meanwhile, Rhodes and Gracey worked on a follow-up to **West Texas Heaven** for release sometime in the new year.

Kimmie Rhodes and the Jackalope Brothers/
    Jackalope/1981
Man in the Moon/Heartland UK/1985
Angels Get the Blues/Heartland UK/1989
**The Kimmie Rhodes Collection: A Lot Like West
    Texas**/Red Moon Switz./1993
West Texas Heaven/New Rose/1995; Justice/1996
Jackalopes, Moons and Angels/Jackalope/1997

"Just One Love" (w/ Willie Nelson) on **Deep in the Heart of Texas**/Shanachie/1998
"Lines" on **Edges From the Postcard2**/P2/1998
"Just To Be Near You" (Live) on **Texas Renegade Radio: A Country/Americana Collection**/KNON/1998

Kimmie Rhodes, P.O. Box 90183, Austin, TX 78709-0183

West Texas Heaven: The Kimmie Rhodes Home Page
//www.kimmierhodes.com

jgracey@outer.net

See Wes McGhee

The Rhythm Sinners
Country Rock
Melbourne, Australia; 1997-

As a rule, I've tried to limit profiles in *Modern Twang* to artists who have at least one full-length CD under their belts. However, from time to time, I hear a demo tape on which a band shows so much promise that (with an eye toward the future) I feel compelled to include them. Such is the case with the Rhythm Sinners from Melbourne, Australia, who were brought to my attention by DJ and local alt. country expert Sophie Best. Their very amiable leader/lead singer, Keith Burt sent me a copy of their self-titled tape which transported me back to the late 1960s-early 1970s glory days of rough and rowdy country rock. Nothing fancy here, just drum, upright bass, electric guitar, and pedal steel but from this simplicity comes one raw but enjoyable recording. They pay homage to the "big three" (Rodgers, Monroe, Williams) with covers of "Dear Old Sunny South By the Sea," "Blue Ridge Mountain Blues," and "Lonesome Whistle," but their strongest numbers are Burt's originals ("Be Thankful"; "Kickin' With the Breeze"; "Melbourne Bitter"; "Ray of Hope") which he delivers with a whiny twang that fits his slightly cynical lyrics. James Lee's pedal steel work is fabulous throughout but particularly on the moody psychedelic jam "Solitaire." With growing support from fans and music reviewers, the Rhythm Sinners should, with a bit of luck, be headed for bigger things.

Richard Andrew (d); Keith Burt (g,v); Easy Andy (b); James Lee (g,p.s.,h.v.)

The Rhythm Sinners/RS/1998 (CS)

The Rhythm Sinners, 38 Woodside St., North Fitzroy 3068, Australia

The Rhythm Sinners Home Page
//www.ozemail.com.au/~rsnrs/

ckburt@ozemail.com.au

Tony Rice
Flat Pick Guitar; Progressive Bluegrass; Newgrass
Danville, Virginia; June 8, 1951-

Flat pick ace, Tony Rice was taught to play by his father Larry, but real inspiration came from modern masters like Norman Blake, Ry Cooder, and the inimitable Clarence White. He cut his musical teeth with early progressive bluegrass bands like Bluegrass Alliance and J. D. Crowe and The New South (with Ricky Skaggs and Jerry Douglas) in the early 1970s before moving into newgrass as a charter member of the David Grisman Quintet. Drawing on these experiences, Rice moved in a number of bluegrass/newgrass directions in the 1970s-1990s as a soloist, leader of the newgrass (what he called "space-grass") Tony Rice Unit, member of the stellar Bluegrass Album Band, collaborator (with Norman Blake, Ricky Skaggs, Larry and Wyatt Rice, John Carlin, Herb Pederson and Chris Hillman), and as an interpreter of contemporary songwriters. Rice won renown as one of the great modern day flat pickers winning *Guitar Player*'s Best Acoustic Pickstyle Guitarist in 1996.

California Autumn/Rebel/1975; 1990
Tony Rice/Rounder/1977
Guitar/Rebel/1978; 1991
Manzanita/Rounder/1979
Acoustics (Tony Rice Unit)/Kaleidoscope/1979; Rounder/1994
Mar West (Tony Rice Unit)/Rounder/1980
Skaggs & Rice/Sugar Hill/1980
Bluegrass Albums Band, Vol. 1-5/Rounder/1981-1989
Still Inside (Tony Rice Unit)/Rounder/1981
Backwaters (Tony Rice Unit)/Rounder/1982
Church Street Blues/Sugar Hill/1983
Cold on the Shoulder/Rounder/1984
Me and My Guitar/Rounder/1986
Blake & Rice/Rounder/1987
Native American/Rounder/1988
Devlin/Rounder/1988
Tony, Larry, Ron, & Wyatt Rice/Rounder/1989
Norman Blake and Tony Rice 2/Rounder/1990
Rice Brothers 2/Rounder/1994
River Suite for Two Guitars (with John Carlin)/ Rounder/1995
Tony Rice Sings Gordon Lightfoot/Rounder/1996
Tony Rice Plays and Sings Bluegrass/Rounder/1996
Out of the Woodwork (with Chris Hillman, Herb Pederson, Larry Rice)/Rounder/1997

Tony Rice/Rounder Home Page
//www.rounder.com/rounder/artists/rice_tony/profile.html

Acoustic Cafe Biography
//members.aol.com/acousticc/tony.html

See Norman Blake; David Grisman

Sherry Rich

Singer/Songwriter
Lismore, Australia; April 9, 1969-

Australia has a long country music history and while it has mostly been a good old boys club, there have been some notable women performers as well. One of the first "girl" singer/guitarists in Australian country was Noelene Rich who toured with legends like Slim Dusty and Reg Lindsay in the 1960s. After she became a mother in 1969, Noelene passed on the country tradition to her daughter Sherry by teaching her to play ukelele and sing, letting her listen to country records, and even bringing her up on stage to perform during shows around Queensland. Later, Sherry moved to Melbourne from her home on Bribie Island (off the coast of Queensland) to go to art school. She was in a country band (Cactus Fever) for a brief time in 1986 before starting an all girl rock band called Girl Monstar in 1988. Described by Rich as "the Runaways meet the Ramones," they did lots of touring and recorded two singles and an LP (**Monstereo Delicio**) before disbanding in 1994. Remembering what her mum had tried so hard to teach her, Sherry formed an alt. country band in 1995. Later in the year, Sherry Rich & The Grievous Angels made their recording debut with an eponymous five song mix of country, rock, and pop. Rich shows plenty of songwriting savvy, and her strong vocals match up well with country rockers ("Get Your Kicks"), murder ballad hoedown ("Wild Dogs"), swamp blues ("When Love Calls"), jangly pop ("Beautiful, Talented & Dead"—about Kurt Cobain), and rock 'n' roll ("You Can Have That Man"). For her first full-length, she was set to use an Australian band, but her publisher, knowing how much Rich liked American alt. country bands, got in touch with Jay Bennett, John Stirratt, and Ken Coomer of Wilco while he was on a trip to Nashville. After much long distance negotiating between Stirratt and Rich, they agreed to back her and so in early 1997 she headed for Nashville. With Kerryn Tolhurst of the Australian band, the Dingos, joining in on mandolin and lap steel, two weeks of sessions yielded **Sherry Rich & Courtesy Move** (the name Bennett, Coomer, and Stirratt record under when not with Wilco). This superb marriage of twang and pop made alt. country fans and reviewers from all over sit up and take notice of this impressive newcomer from "down under." Rich wowed them with her strong vocals on tough original ballads and rockers ("Polite Kisses"; "Little Miss Cool"; "Three Time Loser"; "Is That All You Wanted") and a romping cover of Bad Finger's "I'll Be the One." Returning to Australia, Sherry reunited with the Grievous Angels for a promotional run, but in 1998 returned to Nashville and through early 1999 was working with Bennett on a new recording. Noelene must be mighty proud!

The Current Grievous Angels: Steve Brown (d); Matt Heydon (ky); James McInnes (g); Nick Volk (b,p.s.)

Sherry Rich & The Grievous Angels/Rubber Aust./1995 (EP CD)
Trying to Write a Love Song/Rubber Aust./1995 (EP CD)
Sherry Rich & Courtesy Move/Rubber Aust./1997
Is That All You Wanted/Rubber Aust./1997 (EP CD)

Sherry Rich, 4916 Monterey Dr., Nashville, TN 37220

Sherry Rich //www.geocities.com/nashville/opry/1810/

richsherry@hotmail.com

Sherry Rich c/o Rubber Records, P.O. Box 32, Hawksburn, Victoria 3142 Australia

Rubber Records //www.rubberrecords.com.au

kerrie@rubberrecords.com.au

See Wilco/Courtesy Move

Kim Richey

Singer/Songwriter
Zanesville, Ohio; December 1, 1956-

Like fellow Nashville singer/songwriter Jim Lauderdale, Kim Richey stands in that uncertain territory between alternative and new country. After moving to Music City in 1988 (inspired by Steve Earle's first album), she penned several songs that became big hits for mainstream country artists (most notably the Grammy nominated "Believe Me Baby, I Lied" for Trisha Yearwood) but also co-wrote "Fallin'" with John Crooke of Jolene and contributed some vocals to **Hell's Half Acre**. Richey opened for Yearwood and Mary-Chapin Carpenter but also Wilco and Junior Brown and showcased at SXSW 1997 with the V-Roys. This split is reflected in her recordings, **Kim Richey** and **Bitter Sweet**, which are pretty much equal parts country, rock, and pop tilted a bit more toward the alt. country side due to her smart writing, help from Sam Bush, Joy Lynn White, and John Crooke, and production by Richard Bennett who worked with Earle and Emmylou Harris. **Bitter Sweet** was named Best Americana Album at the 1998 Nashville Music Awards. For the follow-up, Richey traveled to London to work with producer Hugh Padgham whose credits include Genesis, XTC, and Sting (uh-oh!).

Kim Richey/Mercury Nashville/1995
Bitter Sweet/Mercury Nashville/1997
"Near You" (with Mandy Barnett) on **Will Sing for Food: The Songs of Dwight Yoakam**/Little Dog/1998

Kim Richey Fan Club, 2910 Poston Ave., Nashville, TN 37203

Official Kim Richey Page
//www.geocities.com/nashville/3235/

Kim Richey/Polygram Home Page
//www.polygram.com/nashville/artists/richey_kim/richey_kim.html

Kim Richey iMusic Showcase
//www.imusic.com/showcase/country/krichey.html

Richmond Fontaine

No Depression
Portland, Oregon; 1995-

If imitation is the sincerest form of flattery, then Richmond Fontaine are the greatest Uncle Tupelo fans of all time. A friend of mine responded to their debut CD, **Safety**, by exclaiming, "Hey, where'd you get the Uncle Tupelo bootleg!" Lead singer Willy Vlautin is a dead ringer for Jay Farrar, and the band does move back and forth between frenetic rockers, country rockers, and country tinged ballads. But, to be fair, while Richmond Fontaine has the UT sound pegged, they don't apishly mimic them, and in fact, draw on many alt. country and rock influences. And what matters most is the end result which, like the best of Uncle Tupelo, is really pretty good. Vlautin has had a number of his original short stories published and puts his prose talents to good use on **Miles From** which continues along the UT road albeit with a more laid back sound this time around and some nice pedal steel by Paul Brainard. The band began to get noticed overseas in 1997-1998 when two of their songs were picked for alt. country/Americana compilations in Germany and the U.K.

Joe Davis (d,1998-); Stuart Gaston (d,1995-1997); Dave Harding (b); Willy Vlautin (g,v) with Paul Brainard (p.s.)

"Trailways" b/w "Whirlpool"/Cravedog/1995 (7")
Richmond Fontaine/Cravedog/1996
Safety/Cravedog/1996
"Whirlpool" on **Can't Stand the Smell**/Cravedog/1996
　　and on **Luxury Liner**/Glitterhouse Ger./1997
Miles From/Cavity Search/1997
"Calm" on **Loose: New Sounds of the Old West**/Vinyl
　　Junkie UK/1998

Richmond Fontaine, P.O. Box 15063, Portland, OR 97215

Richmond Fontaine Web Page
//www.cryptographics.com/richmond/fontaine.htm

rfontaine@cnnw.net

Richmond Fontaine/Cavity Search Page
//www.teleport.com/~csr/richmond.html

Riders in the Sky

Cowboy/Western
Nashville, Tennessee; 1977-

Combining fresh remakes of singing cowboy classics, authentic originals, excellent musicianship, tight harmonies, superb yodeling, snappy dressing, and hilarious skits, Riders in the Sky have been America's #1 cowboy band for over twenty years. Douglas B. Green, a respected country music writer and historian, Paul Chrisman, a PhD graduate from M.I.T. in theoretical physics, and Fred LaBour first got together in Nashville in 1977. All were accomplished musicians having played with Bill Monroe, Loggins & Messina, and Dickey Lee. After playing Music City venues for a few years, the Riders recorded the first in a long string of consistently fine cowboy/

western albums in 1979 for Rounder; they remained with that label until 1986. In 1983, Riders in the Sky landed their own TV show on TNN called *Tumbleweed Theater*; it ran until 1986, and in 1989, they began hosting the *Rider's Radio Theater* which still runs on NPR. After doing a self-titled children's TV program and several albums for MCA and Columbia, the Riders returned to top form in the 1990s with Rounder Records once again. One of their finest during this period was a tribute to Gene Autry, **Public Cowboy #1**. Prime material from their Rounder years can be found on **The Best of the West Rides Again**. Joey Miskulin, "The Cowpolka King," has often added his sterling accordion to the Riders records and live performances. Over the years, Riders in the Sky have rightfully earned many honors including several appearances on *Austin City Limits*, induction into the Grand Ole Opry and Western Music Association Hall of Fame, and numerous music awards for their albums. If you've never experienced Riders in the Sky, do yourself a favor because as they'd surely tell you, "It's the Cowboy way!"

Ranger Doug Green aka Douglas B. Green (r.g,,v); Too Slim aka Fred LaBour (b,v); Woody Paul aka Paul Chrisman (f,v) with Joey Miskulin (acc)

Three on the Trail/Rounder/1979
Cowboy Jubilee/Rounder/1981
Prairie Serenade/Rounder/1982
Weeds and Water/Rounder/1983
Saddle Pals/Rounder/1985
New Trails/Rounder/1986
The Cowboy Way/MCA/1987
The Best of the West Rides Again/Rounder/1987
Cowboys in Love/Epice/1994
Always Drink Upstream From the Herd/Rounder/1995
Public Cowboy #1: The Music of Gene Autry/
　　Rounder/1996
Songs of the Sage (Ranger Doug)/Rounder/1997
A Great Big Western Howdy.../Rounder/1998

Meet Riders in the Sky //www.ridersinthesky.com

Joey Muskulin //www.musicwagon.com

Amy Rigby

See The Last Roundup

Will Rigby

Rig Rock

Will Rigby was a member (drummer) of two legendary rock bands in the 1970s and 1980s. First he was with North Carolina's Sneakers along with Chris Stamey and Mitch Easter and then New York's dBs with Stamey and Peter Holsapple. The latter band sometimes strayed into countryesque territory, and Rigby gave full vent to this side on his 1985 solo record, **Sidekick Phenomenon**. Handling all the instruments and vocals, with occasional assistance from Holsapple and Amy McMahon (later Rigby), Will pays a somewhat warped homage to country music on originals ("Heart's Expired"; "I've Stopped My Dreaming About You"; "Let Me Show You How I Can Do") and quirky covers of Hank's "Settin' the Woods on Fire" and Merle's "I Can't Hold Myself in Line." His eccentric take on country later caught the attention of Diesel Only records which released three of his songs on an EP single in 1993. A look at the subject matter of these tunes gives a good summary of where Rigby is coming from when it comes to country music: "Red Bra & Panties," the hilarious "Ricky Skaggs Tonite" which imagines what happens when the country singer is kidnapped by terrorists while on a visit to the Middle East (it was also included on **Rig Rock Truck Stop**), and "Short Stubby Legs and Long Torso" expressing Rigby's preferred female body type. In the late 1990s, Rigby finished up a new album and drummed for Cheri Knight and Kelly Willis.

Sidekick Phenomenon/Egon/1985
"Red Bra & Panties" b/w "Ricky Skaggs Tonite"/"Short
    Stubby Legs, Long Torso"/Diesel Only/1993 (EP)
"Ricky Skaggs Tonite" on **Rig Rock Truck Stop**/Diesel
    Only/1993
"The Room's Still Spinnin'" b/w "Dave"/SOL/1993 (7")
"Red Bra"; "Ricky Skaggs"; "Long Torso"/Hello/1996
    (EP; subscription only)

DAVISRIG@aol.com

Steve Riley and The Mamou Playboys
Traditional and Modern Cajun
Lafayette, Louisiana; 1988-

From the heart of Cajun country, Steve Riley and the Mamou Playboys were among the leaders of Cajun music's new wave in the 1990s. Riley took up accordion as a youngster, was heavily influenced by the style of his cousin Marc Savoy, and learned fiddle under the tutelage of Dewey Balfa who invited him to join his band. Formed in 1988, the Playboys' first incarnation included Kevin Barzas, Christine Balfa, Mike Chapman, and David Greely. In 1993, Kevin Dugas replaced Chapman and Peter Schwarz, son of Tracy Schwarz, joined on fiddle. On their early recordings, Riley and band concentrated mostly on traditional songs but with time began to compose and play modern, original tunes that set them apart. This transition came to full flower on the experimental **La Touisannt** in 1995 with new guitarist Jimmy Domengeaux. As a strong link between past and present with an eye toward the future, Steve Riley and the Mamou Playboys won fans at clubs and festivals all over the world and accumulated numerous Best Cajun Band and Acadiana Music awards. Along with Riley, fiddle player David Greely deserves much of the credit for their success. A switch to the long time Louisiana label Swallow resulted in 1997's **Friday at Last** which marked a return to a more traditional sound. However, they threw fans a real curve the next year with **Bayou Rouler** which moves away from Cajun roots to a rousing mix of zydeco, R&B, and swamp pop. In early 1999, guitarist Jimmy Domengeaux was killed in a motorcycle accident in southwestern Louisiana.

Steve Riley (acc,f,l.v.); Christine Balfa (tri,1988-1992); Kevin Barzas (g,1988-1995); Mike Chapman (d,1988-1993); Jimmy Domengeaux (g, 1995-); Kevin Dugas (d,1993-); David Greely (f,sax,v); Peter Schwarz (b,f,v,1993-1997)

Steve Riley and the Mamou Playboys/Rounder/1990
Mamou Playboys/Rounder/
'Tit Galop Pour Mamou/Rounder/1992
Trace of Time/Rounder/1993
Live!/Rounder/1994
La Touissant/Rounder/1995
Friday at Last/Swallow/1997
Bayou Rouler/Rounder/1998

Steve Riley, P.O. Box 53926, Lafayette, LA 70505-3926

Steve Riley Home Page
//harp.rounder.com/mamouplayboys.html

Schwarzy@aol.com

Steve Riley Fan Page
//www.lafourche.k12.la.us/teymard/steveriley/

The Rimshots
Hillbilly Bop
Cardiff, Wales, United Kingdom; Late 1980s-

As evidenced by their initial self-titled release on Rockhouse, the Rimshots were pretty much a straight ahead rockabilly outfit when they started out in the late 1980s. Gradually, these Cardiff giants moved more into hillbilly boogie territory with 1996's **Everybody Bop...Let's Bop** which has lots of rockabilly but also, with guests on fiddle and pedal steel, a generous dose of honky tonk and swing. Lead singer John Lewis, who has been likened to Charlie Feathers or Narvel Felts, penned most of the songs on the recording, and there's some hum-dingers including the swinging "One More Beer." The Rimshots also do right by Hank Williams ("Ramblin' Man"), Jack Guthrie ("Oklahoma"), Johnny Cash ("Wide Open Road"), and Jim Reeves ("Yonder Comes a Sucker"), but whether covers or originals, they retain an authentic honky tonk hillbilly vibe throughout. Adding a permanent steel player (Paul Godden) in 1997, they went a little futher down this road with their third release **Sentimental Fools**. In addition, the Rimshots have backed Mac Curtis on a CD, did a split Hank Williams tribute with Rusti Steel & the Tin Tax, and had plans to do one with Narvel Felts. Appearances at all the top festivals in Europe and the U.S. as a solo act or supporting Curtis and Felts strengthened their rep as one of the best of the current hillbilly bopsters.

Tony Biggs (u.b.,b.v.); Paul Godden (s.g.); Mark Kemlo (d,b.v.); John Lewis (r.g.,l.v.); Robert Nedin (l.g.,b.v.)

The Rimshots/Rockhouse UK/1993
Everybody Bop...Let's Bop/Vinyl Japan UK/1996
"Planet Bop" b/w "Shut Up and Drink Your Beer"/Vinyl
    Japan UK/1997 (7")
Mac Curtis & The Rimshots/Vinyl Japan UK/1998
Sentimental Fools/Vinyl Japan UK/1998
**The Hank Williams Tribute: The Rimshots Meet Rusti
    Steel & The Tin Tax**/BeBe's Ger./1998

The Riptones

Insurgent Country
Chicago, Illinois; 1991-

When you think of insurgent country, the names that most often come to mind are Chicago groups like the Waco Brothers and Moonshine Willy who add a punk attitude to their musical mix. However, another Windy City band that falls under the insurgent umbrella but takes a bit more traditional roots rock approach is the Riptones. Beginning in 1991, they served up a fine brew of country, blues, and rockabilly much to the great pleasure of a growing number of fans in their home town. The Bonansinga brothers led the Riptones; "Ranger" Tod (second job was as a forest ranger) capably handled harmonica and rub-board and shared vocal duties with Jeb who contributed lead guitar along with Andon T. Davis. Rounding out the band was the rhythm section, Earl Carter on bass and Tom Harmon on drums. Their recording debut was on Bloodshot's **For a Life of Sin** with the rollicking "Suburbia." Their first CDs, **Cool Hand** and **World Renowned**, released on their Ruby label move easily through honky tonk ("In Ten Days It's Three Months"), country rock ("Lonely"), mandolin driven old-timey ("She Waits"), roadhouse rock ("Gas, Food, & Lodging"; "Hotel Coup De Ville"), and rockabilly ("Bubble City"). The band obviously has a great sense of humor as evidenced by satirical songs about the 'burbs ("Suburbia"), truck driving ("Feelin' Fine"), Don Juanism ("Middle Aged Lothario"), and ducktail vanity ("Don't Touch My Hair"). They also covered Homer & Jethro's whimsical "Hucklebuck" on **Straight Outta Boone County**. In 1997, the Riptones signed with Bloodshot and recorded **Extra Sauce** (produced by Ian Spanic), another sizzling country/roots/rock recording with miles of smiles guaranteed by "Good BBQ," "I Forgot to Cry," "Motorcycle Man," "Out All Night," and "The Meanest Man in the World." Spanic also produced their 1999 release **Cowboy's Inn** which hit on all cylinders once again.

Jeb Bonansinga (l.g.,v); Ranger Tod Bonansinga (hm,rub board,v); Earl Carter (b); Andon T. Davis (l.g.,g); Tom Harmon (d,1991-1997); Kurt Weisend (d,1998-)

"Suburbia" on **For a Life of Sin**/Bloodshot/1994
"World Renowned" on **Hell-Bent**/Bloodshot/1995
Cool Hand/Ruby/1995
World Renowned/Ruby/1996
"Hucklebuck" on **Straight Outta Boone County**/
  Bloodshot/1997
Extra Sauce/Bloodshot/1997
Cowboy's Inn/Bloodshot/1999

The Riptones Fan Club, P.O. Box 267843, Chicago, IL 60626 (includes the *Riptones Reveller Newsletter*)

The Riptones Official Website
//www.homestead.com/riptones/

Kathy Robertson

TSOB
Texas/Los Angeles, California

One of the more unheralded members of California's alt. country community, Kathy Robertson has been apart of it since the 1980s when she toured as a vocalist with Red Simpson. He and Bonnie Owens helped Robertson learn not only the Bakersfield style but also the ropes of the music biz. Later, as part of the Town South of Bakersfield crowd in L.A., she shared stages with Jerry Donahue (the Hellecasters), Rosie Flores, Chris Gaffney, James Intveld, Dale Watson, et al. and con-tributed "I'm Not Over You" to volume one of **A Town South of Bakersfield**. However, Robertson's full length debut was delayed until 1996 when she recorded and co-produced (with Donahue and David Vaught), **At the Cantina**. Backed by Donahue, Vaught, Brantley Kearns, Doug Livingston, Don Heffington, and Abe Manuel with Flores, Gaffney, Big Sandy, Katy Moffatt, and Bonnie Owens along on backing vocals, Robertson joyfully sings her way through honky tonk (Jean Shepard's hit "Twice the Lovin'"; "Leona" and "Startin' Today" by Bonnie Owens; "Queen of the Honky Tonks" by Robertson), country pop ("I'll Never Be Free," a duet with Gaffney), Tex-Mex ("La Locura"; "Paseando en Mazatlan" both by Robertson), and r&b ("It Came From Memphis" by Flores). In 1997, she was the driving force behind **To Roy Nichols With Love**, an ostensible tribute to Merle Haggard's long time lead guitarist but really more of a salute to Bonnie Owens and the Bakersfield sound as a whole. Owens, Flores, Gaffney, and Donahue are on hand once again along with James Intveld, Albert Lee, and the Derailers; Robertson takes lead vocals on songs written by Bonnie Owens, Buck Owens, Merle Haggard, Patsy Montana, and Jenny Lou Carson.

At the Cantina/Kitty LA Tour Music/1996
"I'll Never Be Free" (with Chris Gaffney) on **Jukebox Cowboy**/Vinyl Junkie UK/1997
To Roy Nichols With Love/Cowgirl/1997

Kathy Robertson c/o Cowgirl Records, 1977 Yale St., Ontario, CA 91764

Bruce Robison; Charlie Robison

Austin; Singer/Songwriters
Bandera, Texas; Bruce: June 11, 1966-;
Charlie: September 1, 1964-

Bruce and Charlie Robison arrived in Austin from Bandera, Texas, in the late 1980s and quickly became popular singer/songwriters in the alt. country crowd. At times, they performed with other bands or as a duo but mostly established separate careers. Younger brother Bruce developed a low-key style laced with tear jerking ballads sung in a soft Gram Parsons type voice. His songwriting talents came to the attention of local artists like Monte Warden and Kelly Willis who both recorded his songs. Meanwhile, Charlie adopted a more rough edged honky tonk sound born out of playing with Austin bands (Two Hoots and a Holler; Chaparral) and fronting his own group, the Millionaire Playboys. His songs delivered with a gruffer voice tend toward the dark side also but are often tempered with a good dose of cynical humor as on "Barlight," "I Don't Feel That Way Anymore," or on the excellent "Sunset Boulevard." In March 1995, Bruce and Charlie made solo debuts on the Vireo label and both had cuts on two Austin country compilations that appeared in the same year. Bruce's on and off again relationship with Kelly Willis finally stuck, and they married in late 1996. His "He Don't Care About Me" was included on her 1996 EP, **Fading Fast**. Charlie received a developmental deal with Warner Brothers and had all but finished working on a CD when company execs put pressure on him to include two songs with more "commercial potential." He withdrew from the deal and, sadder but wiser, began shopping his work to a more compatible label. In early 1997, Bruce released **Wrapped** on his Boar's Nest label and toured with his new bride. In 1998, **Wrapped** was picked up and re-released (with three extra songs) by Sony/Nashville which gave Bruce a new contract on its alt. country subsidiary Lucky Dog. In the later part of the year, **Wrapped** reached #1 on the Americana charts, the video of "Angry All the Time" (with Kelly) was being aired on CMT, and Bruce and Kelly embarked on The Good, the Bad, and the Ugly Tour with Richard Buckner. Brother Charlie also signed with Lucky Dog and did **Life of the Party** with co-producer Lloyd Maines. It includes previous material from **Bandera** ("Barlight") and compilations ("I Don't Feel That Way Anymore"; "Sunset Boulevard") plus new songs that range from the biting "You're Not the Best" (by Bruce) to the Tex-Mexish "Don't Call Me a Fool," Texas style ballads like "Indianola" (by Damon Bramlett), "Molly's Blues," and "Loving County." **Life of the Party** received lots of good attention and at long last, two brothers, who had been such a vital part of Austin's music scene in the early 1990s, began to get their due from alt. country fans across the nation.

Bruce Robison/Vireo/1995
"Angry All the Time" (Bruce) on **True Sounds of the New West**/Freedom/1995
"Poor Man's Son"(Bruce) on **Austin Country Nights**/Watermelon/1995
Bandera (Charlie)/Vireo/1995
"Sunset Boulevard" (Charlie) on **Austin Country Nights**/Watermelon/1995
"I Don't Feel That Way Anymore" (Charlie) on **Country**/Vinyl Junkie UK/1995
Wrapped (Bruce)/Boar's Nest/1997; Sony Lucky Dog/1998
Life of the Party (Charlie)/Sony Lucky Dog/1998
Official Bruce Robison Page //www.boarsnest.com
Bruce Robison Fan Page
//www.zoomnet.net/~michaelp/brobison.html

Charlie Robison Home Page
//www.texascountrymusic.com/charlierobison.html
Charlie Robison/Sony Music Page
//www.sonymusic.com/labels/nashville/CharlieRobison/
See Kelly Willis

Ted Roddy (The Talltops; The Tearjoint Troubadours)
Austin; Honky Tonk; Lounge
Corpus Christi, Texas

Growing up on the Texas Gulf Coast, Ted Roddy listened to honky tonk and rock music but after an Albert King concert he attended as a teenager was inspired to play the blues. He learned harmonica and when he moved to Dallas in the early 1980s formed a blues band called the Midnighters. By 1983, that group was history, and Roddy was becoming interested in rockabilly and honky tonk. In due course, he put together the Talltops with Jim Heath (later Rev. Horton Heat) and Phil Bennison (later Homer Henderson). From Dallas and later from Austin, where Roddy moved in 1985, Teddy & the Talltops (with constantly changing personnel) traveled the Texas/ Southwest circuit extensively, self released a single, "Christmas in the Congo," and cut an EP, **On the Line**. In 1987, the Tall Tops recorded **Rockin' Rollin' Honky Tonkin'** for French New Rose and toured Europe where they were heartily welcomed by avid rockabilly crowds. Back home, Roddy kept the Talltops alive through many more changes and established them as favorites among the Austin alt. country contingent in the early 1990s. They did a few independently released sessions most notably a dynamite live set on KUT radio called **Rockin' on the Radio**. During this period, Roddy made a number of video appearances on Billy Joe Shaver's "Hottest Thing in Town" and on several of Webb Wilder's feature length films. He got into lounge music, formed The Naughty Ones in 1994, and recorded **I Dig Your Voodoo**. In 1995, Roddy cut **Full Circle**, for Hightone Records. Produced by Bruce Bromberg, it presents an overview of the many styles Roddy experimented with over the years: blues, honky tonk, swing, rockabilly, lounge. In late 1996, Roddy fronted a revamped version of the Talltops known as the Teardrop Troubadours with a rotating line-up that included Dave Biller (ex-Dale Watson), Jim Stringer (Git Gone), Lisa Pancratz, and Terri Joyce who also fronts the Tag Alongs and has written some fine songs covered by Marti Brom and and Susanna Van Tassel. The Troubadours contributed three songs to **The Edge of Country** compilation. For a number of years, Roddy hosted the very popular Elvis Birthday extravaganza held annually at Austin's Continental Club. He continues in great demand as a harmonica player guesting on Dave Alvin's live **Interstate City** in 1997. In early 1998, he joined with Dale Watson, Rosie Flores, Kelly Willis, and Dave Sanger as the Wandering Eyes to record **Songs of Forbidden Love**. Roddy's honky tonk baritone is right at home on covers of "Devil in Mrs. Jones," "Cheatin' Traces," "Hell Yes, I Cheated," and "The Game of Triangles," a trio with Rosie Flores and Chris O'Connell.

Original Tall Tops: Ted Roddy (g,hm,v); Phil Bennison (b); Jim Heath (g); Jas Stephens (d)
The Tear Joint Troubadours: Dave Biller (l.g.); Teri Joyce (r.g.,v); Mas Palermo (d); Karen Poston (l.v.,b.v.); Dave Wasselowski (d)

> "Christmas in the Congo" b/w "Christmas Party"/ Talltop/1983
> **On the Line**/Amazing/1985 (4 trk EP)
> **Rock 'n' Rollin' Honky Tonkin' With Ted and the Talltops**/New Rose/1987
> **Rockin' on the Radio (Live on KUT Radio)**/1990
> "Stronger Than Dirt"; "Where Can She Be" on **Points West**/Hightone/1990
> **Ten Years of Talltops (1983-1993)**/Talltops/1993 (CS promo only)
> **C.C. Stomp** (Ted Roddy)/TR/1994
> "Honky Tonk Hell" on **Austin Country Nights**/ Watermelon/1995
> **Full Circle** (Ted Roddy)/Hightone/1995
> **I Dig Your Voodoo** (Naughty Ones)/Continental/1996
> "Time I Made My Presence Known"; "Tears on the Table"; "War Between Two Lovers" (Tear Joint Troubadours) on **The Edge of Country**/Stockade/1997
> "Devil in Mrs. Jones," "Cheatin' Traces," "Hell Yes, I Cheated," "The Game of Triangles" on **Songs of Forbidden Love** (The Wandering Eyes)/Lazy SOB/1998

Teddy Roddy Home Page
//www.actlab.utexas.edu/~spam/roddy/

Ted Roddy Biography
//www.hightone.com/bios/troddybio.html

Sandy Rogers
Singer/Songwriter
California

In April 1985, Sandy Rogers got a surprise phone call from her brother, the playwright, Sam Shepard, whose *Fool For Love* was being made into a movie. He had played a tape of her songs for director Robert Altman who was impressed and wanted her to write the soundtrack. **Fool For Love** appeared in 1986 to very favorable reviews; critics everywhere repeatedly focused in on Rogers two most outstanding qualities: astute songwriting and a highly distinctive voice (more on that later). Around this time, Sandy cut a four song demo ("Paint the Kitchen"; "Train Fare to Memphis"; "Fool for Love"; "Cowgirl Blues") in Nashville, and over the years, movie music supervisor Karyn Rachtman got them included in three films: *The Last Seduction*, *Motorcycle Gang*, and *Reservoir Dogs* ("Fool for Love"). Otherwise, Sandy was inactive for about ten years until she moved to Oakdale, California, in the Central Valley in 1995. The farming culture there gave her plenty of "song fodder," and in 1998, Rogers reemerged with **Green Moon**. Once again critics were impressed with her ability to capture the emotional essence of a situation (rural life) and movingly express it with

one-of-a-kind vocals; John Conquest of *3rd Coast Music,* who had given **Fool for Love** a big thumbs up back in 1986, noted quite rightly that she can evoke both Janis Joplin and Tammy Wynette. He and other reviewers most often used the words "haunting," "moving," "compelling" to describe her work, and I can't really improve on that. At any rate, **Green Moon** revitalized Rogers' career as she began to tour California, Texas, Tennessee, and the Midwest in 1998. For her dates in Austin in February 1998, Sandy (who is good friends with Susanna Van Tassel) was backed by a stellar pick-up band made up of Randy Glines (Jimmy LaFave), Donald Lindley (ex-Lucinda Williams; Joe Ely), Gurf Morlix (ex-Lucinda Williams), and Terry Ware (Ray Wylie Hubbard).

> **Fool for Love**/MCA/1986 (sdtrk.)
> **Green Moon**/Rattle/1998

Sandy Rogers/Rattle Records Page
//www.rattlerecords.com/artist.htm

Jim Roll
Singer/Songwriter
Chicago, Illinois; 1966-

A native of Chicago, Jim Roll was the leader of a band in the mid-1980s named the Bald Willies. Based in DeKalb, Illinois, they blended folk rock, blues, reggae, and rock and had a local following. However, band and personal problems forced Roll to move on to Ann Arbor, Michigan, in the early 1990s to study social work. As the music bug continued to bite, Jim kept up songwriting and did a few performances at folk venues around the area. He busked on the street for a while after relocating to Frankfurt, Germany, in 1993, but in 1996 was back in Ann Arbor where he became a regular performer at the Gypsy Cafe. Roll became quite a hit there and then began to venture out; he made an apperance at the Bluebird Cafe in Nashville for a Songwriter Night and also formed a band that opened for Mike Ireland, the Derailers, and the V-Roys, and headlined at clubs in Memphis and Chicago. In 1998, Jim recorded **Ready to Hang**, a heady brew of acoustic and electric folk, country, and rock. Vocally, he's been dubbed as a cross between Neil Young and Rick Danko. As a songwriter, Roll tends to dwell on relationships because as he once admitted, "I just really, really suck at them," and the ups and downs have given him a lot of food for thought and songs. And though, he tends to hang out on the dark side, he's no Bucknerian and lets in a few rays of sunshine now and then. Ultimately, **Ready to Hang** is an uplifting album for its hopeful messages and musical variety (country rock, rockabilly, blues funk, acoustic solo) that always keeps things interesting.

> **Ready to Hang**/One Man Clapping/1998

Jim Roll Page //www.lb.com/onemanclapping/jim.htm
jroll@umich.edu

The Rollin' Rocks

Hillybilly Bop
Osaka, Japan;1994-

Baseball isn't the only thing America has imported to Japan. Many Japanese also have a great love for American music including country —real, honest to goodness hillbilly music like that played by Osaka's Rollin' Rocks. Decked out in vintage western clothing, this sextet specializes in a blend of Western swing and rockabilly and have two singles to their credit, "Love Me" and "Sittin' on Top of the World" on the Japanese On the Hill label. Already popular in their home country, the Rocks made their American debut at the Denver Rockabilly Weekender in 1997.

Hirokazu Goto (d); Wataru Ishikawa (v); Jun Itabashi (s.g.); Masahiro Kasai (p); Hirotoshi Kawahara (l.g.); Yoshohiro Morita (b,d)

"Love Me"/On the Hill Jp./1995 (7")
"I'm Sittin' on Top of the World"/On the Hill Jp./1995

The Rollin' Rocks c/o On the Hill Records, Hayama Bldg. 2F, 1-92 Ekimae-Odori, Toyohashi, Aichi, Japan, 440

The Rolling Hayseeds

No Depression; Country Rock; Roots Rock
Philadelphia, Pennsylvania; 1990-

The Rolling Hayseeds were founded in 1990 by Rich Kaufmann and Kevin Karg. Both had been in local rock bands (Kaufmann: Electric Love Muffin; Karg: Fjord Rangers) and were looking to get more into country music. They began to collaborate, aiming for a sound that was a wedding of "hard" country (Hank, Merle, George, et al.) and the kind of 1980s roots rock pioneered by groups like the Replacements. Over the next few years, the Hayseeds were on a roller coaster ride personnel wise but did cut several demos (mostly of Kaufmann's originals) including a four song cassette in 1995 with Charlie Chesterman producing and a 1996 CD single with a cover of Kevin Welch's "I Came Straight to You." Later in 1996, they released a 10 song CD, **Tangled Up in You**, compiled from their disparate collection of previously recorded songs. Included on some of these songs on harmony vocals was Dorothea Haug (ex-Big Boots) who later became a permanent member along with Mike Frank (ex-Nixon's Head), John Kelsey (ex-BaBaLou), and Mark Tucker. **Tangled** is a pretty fine recording considering it is taken from so many scattered tapes and was done during a time of band turmoil. Kaufmann's fluid vocals are complemented by Karg's lead guitar on material ranging from slow country ballads to honky tonk, country rock, and roots rock. It hints at the good things yet to come from the Hayseeds with time and a consistent line-up.

Mike Frank (b); Dorthea Haug (b.v.); Kevin Karg (l.g.); Rich Kaufmann (g,l.v.); John Kelsey (d); Mark Tucker (p.s.)

Tangled Up in You/Record Cellar/1996

"Merry Christmas (This Makes One)" on **Seasons Greetings, Philadelphia**/Record Cellar/1997

The Rolling Hayseeds, 2122 Locust, Box 15, Philadelphia, PA 19103

Karg@pobox.upenn.edu

The Rolling Hayseeds Web Page
//philadelphia.digitalcity.com/music/hayseeds.htm

Peter Rowan

Progressive Bluegrass; Country Rock; Tex-Mex
Boston, Massachusetts; July 4, 1942-

Peter Rowan's musical resume reads like a synopsis of the history of Americana over the past thirty years. Grabbed by music at an early age (thanks in part to a musical family), he had his own Tex-Mex band, the Cupids, in high school and as part of the burgeoning Boston scene of the 1960s got lots of exposure to folk and bluegrass. He was briefly mandolinist for a local folk band, the Mother Bay State Entertainers, but it was toward bluegrass that he ultimately gravitated and for a short time (1967-1969), he toured and recorded with Bill Monroe and the Bluegrass Boys as rhythm guitarist and singer (Richard Greene and Bill Keith were also members). However, like many other young people in the restless 1960s, Rowan moved toward rock music and after relocating to Frisco formed a rock fusion band, Earth Opera, with David Grisman and Bill Keith. Their highly experimental style lasted through two albums after which Rowan joined another rock fusion group, Seatrain, which included Richard Greene. When that played out, Rowan joined forces with his younger brothers as the Rowan Brothers. They recorded one self titled album in 1972, and then, Peter became a part of the groundbreaking bluegrass band, Old and In the Way with Jerry Garcia, David Grisman, Vassar Clements, and John Kahn. He contributed his singing and songwriting talents to their recordings (**Old & In the Way**; **High Lonesome**) which proved to be some of the most influential and popular bluegrass of all time. After nine months with them, Rowan became a member of Muleskinner, another important early progressive bluegrass group with Grisman, Greene, Keith, and Clarence White. They were short lived as well but did manage two recordings, **A Potpourri of Bluegrass Jam** and **Muleskinner: Live**, that played a big role in bringing a modern bluegrass to new generations.

In the late 1970s, Rowan recorded with his brothers and then in the 1980s and 1990s worked as a songwriter, solo performer, and on a variety of collaborative efforts. His songs were covered by a variety of country musicians, and he displayed his depth and diversity on a number of interesting concept albums including **Land of the Navajo**, **Dust Bowl Children** (about the Great Depression), and **Awake Me in the New World** (interpretations of Central American music). Rowan's bluegrass/ rock band, Free Mexican Air Force, included accordion ace

Flaco Jimenez, and these two made several Tex-Mex albums instrumental in spreading *conjunto* to a wider audience than ever before. In addition, Rowan made a rockabilly album with the Wild Stallions and consistently returned to bluegrass with the Red Hot Pickers (with Richard Greene), the Nashville Bluegrass Band, Northern Lights, and Jerry Douglas. His 1996 bluegrass outing, aptly titled **Bluegrass Boy**, paid tribute to his old boss Bill Monroe with help from Rowan's new band the Panama Red Riders plus Del McCoury, Richard Greene, and Laurie Lewis. Rowan was also included on **True Life Blues: Songs of Bill Monroe** which Sugar Hill released in 1996. In addition, he was in demand by the new crop of alt. country artists contributing mandolin and vocals to one song on Farmer Not So John's **Receiver** and joining Norman Blake and Roy Huskey as part of the backing band on Steve Earle's **Train a Comin'** and on the E-Squared debut of Bap Kennedy. Rowan also worked in the late 90s with Don Edwards (Gene Autry tribute), Ramblin' Jack Elliott, and a Czechoslovakian group Druha Trava with banjoists Lubos Malina, Bela Fleck, and Tony Trischka. A Peter Rown songbook (print/CD-ROM) was in the works for early 1999.

> **The String Band Project** (with the Mother Bay State Entertainers)/Elektra/1965
> **Bluegrass Time** (with Bill Monroe)/Decca/1967
> **Earth Opera**/Elektra/1968
> **The Great American Eagle Tragedy** (Earth Opera)/Elektra/1969
> **Seatrain**/Capitol/1970
> **Marbelhead Messenger** (Seatrain)/Capitol/1971
> **The Rowan Brothers**/Columbia/1972
> **Old and In the Way**/Round/1973
> **A Potpourri of Bluegrass Jam** (Muleskinner)/Warner Bros./1974; Sierra/1994
> **Sibling Rivalry** (Rowan Brothers)/Asylum/1976
> **Jubilation** (Rowan Brothers)/Asylum/1977
> **Peter Rowan**/Flying Fish/1978; 1989
> **Medicine Trail**/Flying Fish/1980; 1992
> **Texican Badman**/Appaloosa Ita./1981; 1990
> **Peter Rowan & The Wild Stallions**/Appaloosa Ita./1982; 1994
> **The Walls of Time**/Sugar Hill/1982
> **Flaco Jimenez and Peter Rowan Live Rockin' Tex-Mex**/Waterfront UK/1982
> **Bluegrass Album** (with the Red Hot Pickers)/Better Days Jp./1983
> **Hiroshima Mon Amour** (with the Red Hot Pickers)/Better Days Jp./1983
> **San Antonio Sound** (with Flaco Jimenez)/Waterfront UK/1984
> **Peter Rowan With the Red Hot Pickers**/Sugar Hill/1984
> **T For Texas**/Waterfront UK/1984
> **Revelry**/Waterfront UK/1984
> **The First Whippoorwill**/Sugar Hill/1985; 1990
> **New Moon Rising** (with the Nashville Bluegrass Band)/Sugar Hill/1988
> **Dust Bowl Children**/Sugar Hill/1990
> **All On a Rising Day**/Sugar Hill/1991
> **Awake Me in the New World**/Sugar Hill/1993
> **Muleskinner: Live Original T.V. Soundtrack**/Sierra/1993

> **Tree On a Hill** (Rowan Brothers)/Sugar Hill/1994
> **Old And in The Way: That High Lonesome Sound**/Acoustic Disc/1996
> **Yonder** (with Jerry Douglas)/Sugar Hill/1996
> **Bluegrass Boy**/Sugar Hill/1996

Free Mexican Air Force Fan Club, P.O. Box 1918, Cleveland, TX 77328-1918

FreeMexAirForce@rocketmail.com

The Sacred Sombrero Newletter, P.O. Box 964, Blanco, TX 78606

Peter Rowan: The Official Web Site //BGR.ee/Rowan/ (includes online version of *The Sacred Sombrero*)

Peter Rowan AOL Folder: Entertainment>Music>Chat & Messages>Music Community>Folk/Acoustic

See Richard Greene; David Grisman; Flaco Jimenez

Jimmy Roy's 5 Star Hillbillies

See Ray Condo

Royer's Guitar Machine Band

Bluegrass; Old-Time; One Man Band
Boston, Massachusetts; 1994-

Eric Royer embodies the qualities that make up the best in Americana: ingenuity, innovation, and independence. In the mid-1980s, he was a guitarist in a Boston punk band called Junk but disgruntled by the whole experience headed West to Tucson where he underwent a radical change in musical direction. First of all, Royer discovered bluegrass music through a very active local scene and took up banjo. He became a solo act on the streets of Tucson and also played in a band but dissatisfaction with a bumbling rhythm guitarist led to his second revelation. He realized he could do a better job of accompanying himself and so, after gathering recycled materials, he designed and built his first "guitar machine." Initially, it consisted of a right foot pedal linked to a bicycle chain that stroked a pick across a horizontal guitar and several left foot pedals for making chords (he also constructed a drum machine from a washing machine). Later versions (compared to a Rude Goldberg contraption), added more strings, pulleys, and bars in a copper pipe frame so he could play (all with his foot pedals) bass and cowbell and make a little doll called Pretty Polly dance (Royer also plays lap steel). Initially, Royer performed on the streets and in the clubs in Tucson as "Pretty Polly and the Amazing Guitar Machine," and this bluegrass/old-time one-man band was a big hit. However, he moved back to Boston in 1996 where he became a popular attraction on Harvard Square in Cambridge and at local nightclubs. In 1998, Eric self-produced and self-released **Royer's Guitar Machine Band**, a collection of eighteen traditional and classic old-time and bluegrass tunes. On the surface, it seems like a simple enough recording; just a guy singing and playing banjo (quite well) accompanied by bass, guitar, harmonica, and lap steel, but when you really understand what's going on, you just shake your head and say "Amazing!"

Royer's Guitar Machine Band/ER/1998

Royer's Guitar Machine Band c/o Eric Royer, 327 Shawmut Ave., Boston, MA 02118

Royer's Guitar Machine Band //www.guitarmachine.com

ericroyer@msn.com

Calvin Russell

Austin; Singer/Songwriter
Austin, Texas; October 31, 1948-

Calvin Russell was fortunate enough to grow up in Austin, Texas, during the years when the city was establishing itself as a major music center. In the 1960s and early 1970s, Russell was heavily influenced by local radio station KOKE whose DJs (led by Joe Gracey) were given the freedom to play an unusually wide variety of music. At the same time, Austin was becoming a mecca for live music, and Russell decided to dive into the ever expanding pool of musicians and songwriters who were gathering there. His first public performance was in the late 1970s for an open mic night at a place called the Bag O' Chicken on the now legendary 6th Street. Through the 1970s and early 1980s, Russell honed up his s/s skills in Texas and California and also served time in jails in Texas and Mexico. After returning to Austin, he fronted the Characters who released one Joe Gracey (see Kimmie Rhodes) produced cassette in 1986. Shortly after this, Patrick Mathe of the French New Rose label offered Russell a record contract. This resulted in **A Crack in Time** (produced by Gracey) and then several more releases, **Sounds From the Fourth World** (produced by Gracey), **Soldier**, and **Le Voyageur**, which won Russell a big following in France. His grimly realistic portraits (in a blues/country/rock mode) from life's other side ("Behind the 8 Ball"; "This Is My Life"; "Rats and Roaches"; "Living at the End of a Gun") went over much better with European audiences while in his home country and even home town, he was virtually unknown except to a handful of fans and musicians. In 1995, New Rose went bankrupt, but Russell cut **Dream of the Dog** on Southern Union and then in 1997 moved over to Last Call which released an eponymous collection continuing his focus on the bleak side with "Nothing Can Save Me," "I Want to Change the World" and covers of John Kay ("Desperation") and Townes Van Zandt ("Mr. Mudd and Mr. Gold"). Late in 1997, Russell signed with Sony which issued a sampler, **This Is My Life**, in France and **Calvin Russell** in the U.S. The label planned to reissue Russell's New Rose recordings on its Columbia subsidiary, and this may finally bring Russell the recognition he deserves in the U.S. Unfortunately, Calvin's success was off-set by two big blows in 1998: a scheduled tour over seas to promote **This Is My Life** was cancelled when as a result of an arrest for marijuana possession, he was forbidden to leave the country;

No Plateau Productions sued Russell, Warner Chappell Music France, Sony Last Call, and Columbia for copyright infringement when it was discovered that three songs from Russell's previous recordings were actually the work of other songwriters ("Texas Song" by John Michael Blakemore; "9 Ball Song" and "White Rails" by Jubal Clark) but were not credited as such. The suit cast some doubt on Russell's credibility and integrity and cost Warner Chappell $5,000 in back royalties for "Texas Song" alone.

Act 1 (with The Characters)/NuWest/1986 (CS)
A Crack in Time/New Rose Fr./1990
Sounds From the Fourth World/New Rose Fr./1991
Soldier/New Rose Fr./1993
Le Voyageur (Live)/New Rose Fr./1994
Dream of the Dog/Southern Union Fr./1995
Calvin Russell/Last Call Fr./1997; Sony/1997
This Is My Life/Sony Fr./1997

Calvin Russell Home Page
//perso-info.enst-bretagne.fr/~aubert/calvin-en/

OlivierAubert@enst-bretagne.fr

Calvin Russell Page
//www.geocities.com/athens/forum/9962/cr1.html

Leon Russell

Country Rock; Bluegrass
Lawton, Oklahoma; April 2, 1941-

In the 1970s, Leon Russell was known mainly for his work as leader of the Asylum Choir and as a member of Joe Cocker's Mad Dogs and Englishmen. With long, flowing silver hair and beard, he was one of the more outlandish looking characters of the day and became popular for his piano pounding and scruffy vocals on a string of Southern boogie/blues/rock albums. However, in 1973, Russell indulged his good old boy side by recording **Hank Wilson's Back, Vol. 1**. Here, he assembled some of the best country session players of the day (Johnny Gimble, Harold Bradley, Pete Drake, Billy Byrd) for a rollicking collection of bluegrass and country covers by Bill Monroe, George Jones, Hank Williams, Hank Thompson, and others. Russell competently croaks and drawls his way through the material and though country purists stayed away, the recording was a big hit with rock and alt. country fans. Like Elvis Costello's **Almost Blue** a decade later, its importance was in bringing country to a new audience. In the late 1970s and into the 1980s, Leon mostly turned out folksy rock but occasionally dipped back into country, most notably, with Willie Nelson on the very popular live recording, **One for the Road** and another live album with the New Grass Revival in 1981. Two sequels, **Hank Wilson, Vol. 2** and **Legend in My Time: Hank Wilson, Vol. 3** were released in 1984 and 1998 respectively and both, like their predecessor, cover country classics by Hank, Sr., Willie, Ray, Ernest, Merle, George, and Lefty.

Hank Wilson's Back, Vol. 1/A&M/1973; DCC/1990

One For the Road (with Willie Nelson)/CBS/1979
**Leon Russell and the New Grass Revival, The Live
Album**/Warner Brothers/1981
Hank Wilson, Vol. 2/Paradise/1984
Leon Russell's Country Sampler/Virgin/1992 (promo
EP)
Gimme Shelter: The Best of Leon Russell/Capitol
EMI/1996
Hank Wilson, Vol. 3/Ark 21/1998

Leon Russell Home Page //www.mazeppa.com/leon.html

The Complete Leon Russell
//www.geocities.com/sunsetstrip/backstage/5646/

Leon Russell/Ark 21 Page //www.ark21.com

Tom Russell

Singer/Songwriter
Oklahoma City, Oklahoma; February 8, 1955-

While growing up in California in the 1950s and 1960s, Tom Russell was exposed to a variety of West Coast sounds including honky tonk, Western swing, cowboy, and folk. He was especially inspired by the singer/songwriters of the late 1960s (Dylan, Ian and Sylvia) and began his own musical journey. His first performances were in dives in Vancouver in the early 1970s where he encountered the types of characters who later came to populate his songs. When he got wind of the emerging Outlaw scene in Austin, Russell headed there in 1973 where he teamed up with a piano player named Patricia Hardin. They released two albums combining Southwestern style music with Beat poetry or what Russell called "cosmic folk" (this material was reissued in 1994 as **The Early Years, 1975-1979**). The duo later tried their luck in San Francisco but parted company in 1979 leaving Russell to pursue a new career as a novelist in New York City. To survive, Russell drove a cab and one night happened to pick up Robert Hunter of the Grateful Dead. Hunter was very taken with Russell's songwriting and invited him to play during a Dead concert in the Big Apple. Soon after, Russell met the sensational guitarist Andrew Hardin, and they began a very long and fruitful partnership. Initially, Russell and Hardin toured Europe and released several albums there in the mid-1980s. Into the late 1980s and early 1990s, Russell continued to record and tour with Hardin and collaborated with Ian Tyson on an album of cowboy songs (**Cowboy Real**) and with Barrence Whitfield on two eclectic recordings, **Hillbilly Voodoo** and **Cowboy Mambo**. In addition, Russell served as co-producer for a number of albums by Katy Moffatt, and Sylvia Tyson, as well as the Merle Haggard tribute **Tulare Dust** with Dave Alvin. His songs, recorded by numerous artists, are, of course, what make him special. Drawing on his many travels and experiences, Russell tells very literate and moving stories. There are tales about the famous cabaret diva Edith Piaf in "Chocolate Cigarettes," the world's first great African-American heavyweight in "Jack Johnson," an aging Bill Haley in "Haley's Comet" (co-written

with Alvin), the not so famous Inuit Indian who dies on skid row in "Blue Wing," and the lonely actress wannabe of "The Evangeline Hotel." There are also songs about cowboys ("Navajo Rug"; "The Sky Above, The Mud Below"), fighting cocks ("Gallo del Cielo"), lost love ("Heartaches Come Stealing"; "Outbound Plane"), and hope for better ("Beyond the Blues," co-written with Peter Case and Bob Neuwirth). Whatever the topic, Russell clearly stands as one of the great contemporary singer/songwriters. He has paid tribute to many of the best of these in a collection of songwriter quotes about songwriting he co-edited with Sylvia Tyson called *And Then I Wrote*. In addition, Russell has written a detective mystery published in German and Norwegian, and he hopes someday in English. A retrospective of Russell's output in the 1980s and early 1990s, **Beyond St. Olav's Gate** was released by Roundtower in 1992. In 1996, Russell's long time guitarist Andrew Hardin recorded an album of acoustic and electric instrumentals, **Coney Island Moon**, with help from Russell, Amos Garrett, and Albert Lee. 1997 proved to be one of Russell's most eventful years with a move from Brooklyn to a small ranch in Canutillo, Texas (near El Paso) and the release of both **Songs of the West** (cowboy material) and **The Long Way Around** which features duets with Katty Moffatt, Dave Alvin, Jimmie Dale Gilmore, Iris DeMent, Nanci Griffith and others on Russell's best songs.

Tom's big project in 1998-1999 was finishing and promoting **The Man From God Knows Where**, a "folk opera" based on the Russell family saga from immigration (Ireland; Norway) through his father whose life was a mirror image of Willie Lohman in *Death of a Salesman*. Musically, the recording has been described by Russell as a "bizarre soundscape" that mixes and matches various sounds and ethnic styles and even has a sampling of Walt Whitman. Recorded and initially released in Norway, the "cast" of **The Man From God Knows Where** includes Norwegian musicians as well as Iris DeMent and Irish folk singer Dolores Keene. Also along, as always, is side-kick Andrew Hardin whose second instrumental solo, **Lunchtime At An Alligator Farm**, hit the stores in Spring, 1998. Hightone released **The Man** in the U.S. in early 1999.

Ring of Bone (with Patricia Hardin)/1975
Wax Museum (with Patricia Hardin)/1979
Heart on a Sleeve/End of the Trail/1984; Bear
Family/1995
Road to Bayamon/Philo/1988
Poor Man's Dream/Philo/1990
Hurricane Season/Philo/1991
Cowboy Real(with Ian Tyson)/Philo/1992
Beyond St. Olaf's Gate: 1979-1992 Compilation/
Roundtower/1992
Hillbilly Voodoo (with Barrence Whitfield)/ESD/1993
Box of Visions/Philo/1993
Cowboy Mambo (with Barrence Whitfield)/ESD/1994
**Tom Russell & Patricia Hardin: 1975-1979, The Early
Years**/Philo/1994

Rose of the San Joaquin/Hightone/1995
Coney Island Moon (Andrew Hardin)/Round Tower/1996
Songs of the West/Dark Angel/1997
The Long Way Around/Hightone/1997
The Man From God Knows Where/Kirkelig
    Kulturverksted Nor./1998; Hightone/1999
Lunchtime At An Alligator Farm (Andrew
    Hardin)/Round Tower Ire./1998

Blood Shots: The Tom Russell Newsletter c/o Dark Angel,
P.O. Box 16083 Shawnee, KS 66203-6083;
1-800-DARKANGEL

Tom Russell Home Page
//www.musicvil.com/ (includes "Trampers and Hawkers:
The Tom Russell Home Shopping Network")

musicvil@idir.net

Tom Russell Biography
//www.hightone.com/bios/trussellbio.html

Andrew Hardin/Round Tower Page //www.roundtower.com

Andrew Hardin/Delta Music Page
//www.delta-music.co.uk/andyhardin.html

See Katy Moffatt; Ian Tyson

Ruthie & The Wranglers

D.C. Jamboree; Honky Tonk; Hillbilly Bop
Takoma Park, Maryland; c.1989-

Anyone familiar with the **Big D.C. Jamboree** compilations
knows that our nation's capitol is home to a lively alternative
country scene. Ruthie and the Wranglers have been part of it
since the late 1980s, and their dynamic honky tonk and rockabilly have made them one of the area's favorites. Front and
center of the band is Ruthie Logsdon's classic female country
vocals and perky stage presence. She and the original
Wranglers made their recording debut in 1993 on the third
volume of the D.C. Jamboree series with three rocking covers:
"Sparklin' Brown Eyes," "Straight A's In Love," and "Your
Good Girl's Gonna Go Bad." After a personnel change that
brought in a new lead guitarist (Billy Shelton) and a new bass
player (Ruthie's husband, Mark Noone), in 1995, they recorded
the Logsdon penned "Rockabilly Song #10" backed by a very
upbeat version of "Harper Valley PTA." The Wranglers had a
banner year in 1996 when they made their national TV debut on
TNN's *Prime Time Country*, performed on the *Ernest Tubb
Midnite Jamboree*, received a number of Wammie nominations
from the Washington Area Music Association, and released
their first full length album, **Wrangler City**. The latter, which
includes a guest appearance by another D.C. favorite, Bill
Kirchen, offers fine originals by Logsdon ("Hot Potato"; "My
Car Knows Where You Live"; "I'm a Little Confused") plus
covers of "Dirty, Dirty Feeling," "Paper Roses," and "Town
Without Pity." In early 1997, Ruthie & the Wranglers topped
off a great year with a showcase appearance at SXSW and
pulled off a major coup when they won four Wammies (13
nominations total) for Best Country Group, Country Album,

Debut Recording, and Country Male Vocalist (Noone). 1997
also brought a new lead guitarist, Phil Mathieu, an accomplished rock, jazz, and classical guitarist who also worked with
Charlie Byrd and was a member of the Washington Guitar
Quintet. New drummer Joel App came on board in 1998, and
Ruthie and the Wranglers released **Life's Savings**, another
winning combination of rockabilly, honky tonk shuffles,
weepers, and oddities including a cover of Loretta Lynn's "Fist
City" and the original sex change song "He's a Honky Tonk
Man (But He Wants to Be Honky Tonk Woman)." They toured
extensively in 1998 and scored big once again at the Wammies
with a second consecutive Best Country Group trophy and a
Best Female Country Vocalist award for Logsdon.

Logsdon and Noone have performed occasionally as the
hillbilly duo, Rip 'N' Ruby, and Noone is a member of two
other D.C. alt. country groups, the Wanktones and the Hula
Monsters whose repertoire includes swing, rockabilly, honky
tonk, and Hawaiian. They have been nominated for many
Wammies and in 1994 won for Best World Music Band.

Ruthie Logsdon (a.g.,l.v.); Joel App (d,1998-); Phil Mathieu
(l.g.,1997-); Mark Noone (b); Billy Shelton (l.g.,1994-1997);
John Shepherd (d, to 1997)

    "Sparklin' Brown Eyes"; "Straight A's in Love"; "Your
      Good Girl's Gonna Go Bad" on **Big D.C. Jamboree,
      Vol. 3**/Run Wild/1993
    "Rockabilly Song #10" b/w "Harper Valley PTA"/
      Spinout/1995 (7")
    "It'll Be a Rockin' Christmas This Year" on **Another
      Rockin' Christmas**/Run Wild/1995
    Wrangler City/Lasso/1996
    "Mele Kelikimaka" (The Hula Monsters) on **A Holiday
      Feast, Vol. 2**/HFM/1997
    Life's Savings/Lasso/1998
    "If It's the Last Thing I Do" on **Greetings From the
      District of Country**/Too Many Dogs/1998

Ruthie & the Wranglers, 7004 Westmoreland Ave.,
Takoma Park, MD 20912; 301-424-3754

Ruthie & the Wranglers //www.ruthieand thewranglers.com

Ted Smouse/Lasso Records: TedSmouse@aol.com

Ruthie & the Wranglers Tour Diary
//www.washcp.com/archives/indc/td/ruth/ruth1.html

See The Wanktones

Jimmy Ryan (Blood Oranges; Wooden Leg; Beacon Hillbillies)

Roots Rock; New Old-Time; Progressive Bluegrass
Binghampton, New York; 1957-

In 1987, Jimmy Ryan, a Boston mandolin player, founded the
Blood Oranges along with Cheri Knight, Mark Spencer, and
Keith Leverault. Ryan's earlier experience with traditional
music was the starting point of the band's sound which
combined bluegrass with rock, punk, and pop. In the early
1990s, the Blood Oranges made three strong recordings, **Corn**

River, **Lone Green Valley** (produced by Eric Ambel), and **The Crying Tree** (produced by Eric Ambel), offering refreshingly modern versions of standards ("Shady Grove"; "Dig A Hole"; "High on a Mountaintop") and very credible originals. Ryan handled the bulk of the lead singing, but Knight's vocal talent really stands out on ballads such as "Thief," "All the Way Down," and "Shadow of You."

When Spencer decided to move on, the Blood Oranges broke up in 1994 leaving Ryan and Knight free to pursue other projects. The latter showcased her talents on two very highly regarded recordings, **The Knitter** (produced by Eric Ambel) in 1996 and the 1997 release **Northeast Kingdom** produced by Steve Earle for his E-Squared label (for more on Cheri Knight, see her entry). While still with the Blood Oranges, Ryan had formed a bluegrass trio with John McGann and Jim Whitney called the Beacon Hillbillies. They did three fine recordings that are sure to satisfy fans of both traditional and contemporary. Whitney and McGann later went on to form the roots rock band Rust Farm. McGann was also a member of the Celtic band Sunday's Well with whom Ryan worked under the psuedonym, Seamus O'Riain. In addition, Ryan teamed with Mark Sandman of Morphine (as the Pale Brothers) now and then, but Ryan's next big project came in 1995 with the formation of Wooden Leg, a sort of Celtic Blood Oranges with ex-Oranges Mark Spencer and Keith Levereault plus Scott Yoder. They released one self-titled recording in 1996 but later that year, Ryan completely revamped the group which continued to play mostly in the Northeast but farther afield as well. And as if all this wasn't enough, Ryan served as mandolinist in Catie Curtis's band and made a guest appearance on Cheri Knight's **Northeast Kingdom**.

Blood Oranges: Cheri Knight (b,v); Keith Levereault (d); Jimmy Ryan (md,v); Mark Spencer (g)
Beacon Hillbillies: John McGann (g); Jimmy Ryan (md,v); Jim Whitney (b)
Wooden Leg (Original Members): Keith Levereault (d); Jimmy Ryan (md,l.v.); Mark Spencer (g); Scott Yoder (b)
Wooden Leg (Current Members): Jimmy Ryan (md,v); Mickey Bones (d); Brian Dunton (b); Joe Kessler (f,b.v.)

Corn River (Blood Oranges)/ESD/1990
Duffield Station (Beacon Hillbillies)/ESD/1992
More Songs of Love and Murder (Beacon Hillbillies)/ ESD/1994
Lone Green Valley (Blood Oranges)/ESD/1994 (EP)
The Crying Tree (Blood Oranges)/ESD/1994
A Better Place (Beacon Hillbillies)/ESD/1996
Wooden Leg/ESD/1996
"Wagon of Clay" (Cheri Knight) on **Rig Rock Deluxe**/ Upstart Diesel Only/1997
"Midnight Sun" (Beacon Hillbillies) on **Luxury Liner**/Glitterhouse Ger./1997
"Sweet Lies" (Wooden Leg) on **Blue Rose Collection, Vol. 1**/Blue Rose Ger./1997
Rust Farm (John McGann; Jim Whitney)/Daring/1998

"Little Sadie" (Wooden Leg) on **Edges From the Postcard2**/P2/1998

The Official Wooden Leg Home Page //www.hellcountry.com/woodenleg/
The Unofficial Wooden Leg Home Page //www.iwu.edu/~jsramek/wl.htm
Blue Rose Wooden Leg Page //www.bluerose-records.com/
John McGann/Rust Farm Home Page //world.std.com/~jmcgann/
jmcgann@world.std.com

See Cheri Knight

The Sadies
Roots Rock
Toronto, Ontario, Canada; 1995-

Canada's premier country group of the late 1970s and early 1980s was the Good Brothers who won eight Junos in a row for best band. This hot bluegrass outfit was founded by Bruce Good and his brothers but with time his sons Dallas and Travis became members. Dallas also developed quite a reputation around Toronto as a rock guitarist with Jughead and the Satanatras. Around 1995, he and Travis started a side project called the Sadies with Mike Belitsky (drums) and Sean Dean (bass) who were both in other groups at the time. Still, they managed to get together enough to develop a unique sound and style and move toward the front ranks of Canadian roots rock. Building on the Good's bluegrass background, they combined fiddle and harmonies with punk, Ennio Morricone twang, and surf. Thematically, they were drawn to "killing songs" or the murder ballads ("Little Sadie"; "Pretty Polly"; "Knoxville Girl") so prominent in old-time music. Their insurgent attitude attracted Bloodshot Records and in 1998, the Sadies did **The Murder Ballads** split single with Neko Case, the Canadian alt. country diva whose stock really rose that year with her acclaimed, **The Virginian**, on Bloodshot. They later backed Case on tour and on the **Car Songs** split single with Whiskeytown. Bloodshot also released their first full-length CD, **Precious Moments**, which was produced by Steve Albini and garnered them a growing audience in the States. That success was a major inducement for the Sadies to make a full-time go of it and all signs pointed in that direction in 1999.

Mike Belitsky (d); Sean Dean (b); Dallas Good (l.g.); Travis Good (f,g,md)

"Wagonwheel" b/w "Dying Is Easy"/1996 (7")
The Murder Ballads (Neko Case "Make Your Bed" b/w The Sadies "Litte Sadie")/Bloodshot/1998 (7")
Car Songs (Whiskeytown b/w Neko Case & The Sadies)/Bloodshot/1998 (7")
Precious Moments/Bloodshot/1998

The Sadies/Bloodshot Page //www.bloodshotrecords.com

Doug Sahm (Sir Douglas Quintet; The Texas Mavericks; The Texas Tornados)

Americana; Texana
San Antonio, Texas; November 6, 1941-

In the last thirty years, no one has embodied the spirit of Texas music better than Doug Sahm. Solo and with various bands, he skillfully handled all of its major elements including blues, Cajun, country, r&b, rock, Tex-Mex. His country roots go back to his early days as "Little Doug Sahm" when as a pre-teen, he performed on steel guitar around San Antonio and on the *Big D Jamboree* and *The Louisiana Hayride* (he even sat in with Hank on one occasion). Later, Sahm branched out into blues, r&b, Tex-Mex, and rock and played in several local bands. Along the way, Doug met organist/accordionist Augie Meyers, and they became the nucleus for the Sir Douglas Quintet which became most famous for its British invasion style song "She's About a Mover" in the late 1960s. However, Sahm and band were also one of a handful of bands experimenting with the fusion of rock and country at the time. **Mendocino**, **Together After Five**, and **1+1+1 = 4** were among the earliest examples of country rock with songs like "I Wanna Be Your Mama Again," "Texas Me," and "Be Real." Sahm showed his love for Tex-Mex during this period with "Nuevo Laredo," "Michoacan," and a cover of Freddy Fender's "Wasted Days and Wasted Nights." In the early 1970s, Sir Doug went solo and in 1973 recorded **Doug Sahm & Band** with guests Meyers, Bob Dylan, Dr. John, David Bromberg, Andy Statman, Ken Kosek, and *conjunto* accordion ace, Flaco Jimenez. It is a musical montage dominated by country material including covers of "Is Anybody Going to San Antone?," "Poison Love," "Faded Love," "Blues Stay Away From Me," "Me and Paul" (Willie Nelson), and a Dylan waltz, "Wallflower." Not all that well received at the time, this recording has since been recognized as one of the most influential of its kind. Into the 1970s, Sahm moved further into country rock on **Texas Tornado**, **Groover's Paradise** and **Texas Rock For Country Rollers**. His supporting musicians for these recordings included among others Stu Cook and Doug Clifford of Creedence; **Texas Rock** charted one song, "Cowboy Peyton Place," in 1976. During the 1980s, Doug worked on a number of solo and collaborative projects such as the Texas Mavericks, a group made up of Sahm, Alvin Crow, John Reed, and Speedy Sparks. Their **Who Are These Masked Men?** blended country, rockabilly, blues, and Tex-Mex e.g. "Rock and Roll Ruby" (Johnny Cash), "I Fought the Law" (Bobby Fuller), "Redneck Rock" (Crow), and "Hillbilly Soul and a Rockabilly Mind" (Sahm). In 1990, Sahm put together the Texas Tornados with Meyers, Flaco Jimenez, and Freddy Fender. Their marriage of country and Tex-Mex brought them considerable success in the country and Tejano markets, and although they broke up for a few years, in 1996, they came together once more to record **4 Aces** which yielded the hit single "A Little Bit Is Better Than Nada." Sahm has been a big influence on several generations of alt. country including current groups like Uncle Tupelo/Son Volt/Wilco, 6 String Drag, and many more. Austin upstarts, the Gourds, appeared on Sahm's blues/country/Tex-Mex/rock **S.D.Q. '98** and helped out on a few promotional dates. **S.D.Q. '98** is an excellent musical overview of sorts with honky tonk, blues, soul, Tex-Mex, Cajun, rock, a kooky cover of "The Ballad of Davy Crockett" and a funny critique of Austin, Texas, "Get A Life." Material from the early years of the Sir Douglas Quintet and Sahm's solo career continues to surface on import labels including most notably **Texas Fever: The Best of the Sir Douglas Quintet** and as Doug Sahm a.k.a. The Texas Tornado, **Get a Life** and **Goodbye San Francisco, Hello Amsterdam**.

The Sir Douglas Quintet: Harvey Kagan (b); Augie Meyers (ky); John Perez (d); George Rains (d); Wayne Talbert (p)
The Texas Mavericks: Samm Dogg (g,v); Rockin' Leon (f,v); Johnny X (l.g.); Viller V. Washington (b); Frosty (d); El Rocha (ky)
The Texas Tornados: Freddy Fender (v); Flaco Jimenez (acc,v); Augie Meyers (ky,v); Doug Sahm (g,v)

Best of the Sir Douglas Quintet/Smash/1967
Honkey Blues/Smash/1968
Mendocino (SDQ)/Smash/1969
Together After Five (SDQ)/Smash/1970
1+1+1 = 4 (SDQ)/Philips/1971
Doug Sahm and Band/Atlantic/1973; Edsel Demon/1985
Texas Tornado/Atlantic/1973
Groover's Paradise /Warner Bros./1974
Texas Rock for Country Rollers/Dot ABC/1976
Hell of a Spell/Takoma/1979
Border Wave/Takoma/1980
Live Texas Tornado/Takoma/1983
Who Are These Masked Men? (Texas Mavericks)/New Rose/1987; 1993
Juke Box Music/Antone's/1988
Sir Doug's Recording Trip/Edsel UK/1988
Return of the Formerly Brothers (with Amos Garrett; Gene Taylor)/Rykodisc/1988
The Best of Doug Sahm and the Sir Douglas Quintet: 1968-1975/Mercury/1990
Texas Tornados/Reprise/1990
Los Texas Tornados/Reprise/1990
Zone of Our Own (Texas Tornados)/Reprise/1991
Hangin' on By a Thread (Texas Tornados)/Reprise/1992
Doug Sahm and Friends/Rhino/1992
The Best of the Texas Tornados/Reprise/1994
The Early Years/1996 (pre-Sir Doug recs.)
4 Aces (Texas Tornados)/Reprise/1996
Texas Fever: The Best of the Sir Douglas Quintet/AIM Austr./1998
Get a Life (Doug Sahm a.k.a The Texas Tornado)/Munich Dut./1998
Goodbye San Francisco, Hello Amsterdam (Doug Sahm a.k.a The Texas Tornado)/Munich Dut./1998
S.D.Q. '98/Watermelon/1998

Amigos De Musica (Doug Sahm, SDQ, Augie Meyers, Texas Tornados) //www.toeset.com/texas/welkom.html

Unofficial Doug Sahm Home Page
//members.aol.com/sirdoug/index.html

SirDoug@aol.com

Doug Sahm & The Sir Douglas Quintet History & Discography //catalog.com/arts/sdg-disc.htm

Texas Tornados Fan Club, P.O. Box 530, Bellaire, OH 43906

The Texas Tornados on the Net //www.xanadu2.net/rrogers/tornados.html

Augie Meyers Home Page //www.borderfest.com/augie.htm

Freddy Fender Home Page //www.freddyfender.com

See Alvin Crow; Flaco Jimenez

Salamander Crossing
Progressive Bluegrass
Montague, Massachusetts; 1991-

Each spring, a salamander native to Massachusetts migrates as part of its mating ritual. The journey carries the little critters across a busy thoroughfare, and to prevent them from becoming road kill, local humanitarians installed tunnels to provide them safe passage. The dramatic sojourn of these salamanders has become an annual "event" drawing big crowds and heavy media coverage. In 1991, four Northampton residents formed a band and named it after this yearly "salamander crossing." Rani Arbo, Tim Farnham, Jeff Kelliher, and Andrew Kinsey were bonded by the desire "to bring back porch music into the twenty-first century" by giving an "edge" to bluegrass/old-time music. Calling their sound "amphibious bluegrass," Salamander Crossing became regulars on the festival circuit. Their self-titled debut (with Tony Furtado in to replace Farnham) has one oldie ("God Bless That Poor Moonshiner"), nice originals, and bluegrass versions of songs by Lennon/McCartney, Bruce Cockburn, Kate Wolf, and Shawn Colvin. SC's adept picking and tight harmonies can also be found on **Passion Train** (with Farnham back on board) which once again offers traditional ("Rocky Mountain Side"; "Walls of Time") and modern originals plus a bouncy version of Bruce Springsteen's "Two Faces Have I." In 1997, Farnham once again left the band and was replaced by World Banjo Champion Dave Dick (ex-Southern Rail). **Bottleneck Dreams** (produced by Colin Linden) expands on the usual tight harmonies, fine picking, and variety by bringing in steel guitar, organ, and accordion. Cameos by Tim O'Brien and The Band's Richard Bell plus strong originals and engaging covers (from Blue Rodeo to Tennyson) make this their finest outing to date.

Rani Arbo (f,v); Dave Dick (bj, 1997-); Tim Farmham (bj,1991-1997); Jeff Kelliher (g,hm,md); Andrew Kinsey (b,v)

Salamander Crossing/Signature Sounds/1995
Passion Train/Signature Sounds/1996
"Tear My Stillhouse Down" on **Live at the Iron Horse**/
  Signature Sounds/1997
Bottleneck Dreams/Signature Sounds/1998

Salamander Crossing c/o Jim Olsen, P.O. Box 106, Whatley, MA 01093; 1-800-694-5354

Salamander Crossing/Signature Sounds Page //www.signature-sounds.com

Ssrc2@aol.com

Salamander Crossing Profile //www.banjo.com/profiles/SalamanderCrossing.html

Mingo Saldivar
Accordion; Tejano Country; Conjunto
Marion, Texas; August 29, 1936-

The major labels would have us believe that Emilio, Rick Trevino, et al. are the best that the genre known as Tejano Country has to offer, but the real star of this music is Mingo Saldivar. For almost 50 years, he has performed his distinctive style of *conjunto* in the dance halls of his native San Antonio, in northern Mexico, and more recently for national and international audiences. What makes Saldivar special beside incredible accordion skills is his fusion of traditional Hispanic with other forms of music. While a young man in the service, he was drawn to country music and became one of the first, if not the first, to translate the songs of Williams, Cash, Owens and others into Spanish. He also began to incorporate R&B and rock 'n' roll with waltzes, *rancheras*, and *huapangos*. In addition, Saldivar has a remarkable stage presence and because of his animated style of accordion playing has been dubbed "The Dancing Cowboy." In 1975, he formed his band, Los Tremendos Cuatro Espadas, and in the 1970s and 1980s established himself as among the most innovative of *conjunto* artists. And while Saldivar became a big favorite in South Texas with many concerts and small label recordings, he received no national recognition until 1992 when his **I Love My Freedom, I Love My Texas** was nominated for a Grammy. After that came appearances at Carnegie Hall (teamed with Texas rockabilly veteran Ronnie Dawson), the Presidential Inaugural, Wolftrap, and an Africa/Middle East tour sponsored by the U. S. Information Agency. With the great upsurge in Tejano Country in the 1990s, Saldivar became more popular than ever especially in Texas and Mexico. One of the best introductions to Saldivar's work is **The Dancing Cowboy Sings Country** with Spanish/English covers of classic country including "I Walk the Line," "Ring of Fire" ("Rueda De Fuego"), "Swinging Doors," and "Streets of Bakersfield."

Conjunto Quatro Espadas de Mingo Saldivar/Joey/1976
I Love My Freedom, I Love My Texas/Rounder/1992
The Dancing Cowboy Sings Country/Hacienda/1994
Y Sus Tremendos Cuatro Espadas/Fonovision/1995
Rueda de Fuego/Hacienda/1995

Mingo Saldivar/La Onda Page //www.ondanet.com:1995/tejano/artists/Mingo.Saldivar/

Marc and Ann Savoy (Savoy-Doucet; The Magnolia Sisters; Savoy-Smith)

Cajun
Eunice, Louisiana

Two of the most important figures in the renaissance of Cajun culture and music have been the husband and wife team, Marc and Ann Savoy. The former has been an active ambassador for Cajun music since he began playing Louisiana dance halls as a pre-teen. As an adult, Marc Savoy carried on his work by touring worldwide and by becoming a master accordion maker ("Acadian" brand) at his workshop in Eunice. In addition, he used his factory as a place to promote Cajun music by holding a jam session there each Saturday morning. He recorded solo and for over a decade with Ann Savoy and Beausoleil's Michael Doucet as the Savoy-Doucet Cajun Band which harkens back to the old-time *fais do do* but with a very contemporary liveliness. When not playing in this band, Ann did her part as an author of two volumes of Cajun songs and interviews entitled *Cajun Music: A Reflection of a People*. She periodically performed with Jane Vidrine as the duo, the Magnolia Sisters. In 1991, Marc and Ann were the subject of a video (*A Visit to Cajun Country*) by noted documentary film maker Les Blank, and in 1992, Marc was honored with an NEA Heritage Award for his tireless efforts on behalf of Cajun culture. In the 1990s, the Savoys teamed with Louisiana State fiddle champ Ken Smith for tours and recording. The first from Savoy/Smith, **Now and Then**, dips deep into the Cajun music catalog with covers of masters like Amede Ardoin, Canray Fontenot, Austin Pitre, Cleoma Falcon, and the Hackberry Ramblers.

The Savoy-Doucet Cajun Band: Marc Savoy (acc,v); Ann Allen Savoy (g,v); Michael Doucet (f,v)
The Savoy-Smith Cajun Band: Marc Savoy (acc,v); Ann Allen Savoy (g,v); Ken Smith (f)
The Magnolia Sisters: Ann Savoy (g,v); Jane Vidrine (acc)

Oh What a Night (Marc Savoy)/Arhoolie/1981
Two Step D'Amede (Savoy-Doucet)/Arhoolie/1988
Home Music With Spirits (Savoy-Doucet)/Arhoolie/1992
Live! At the Dance (Savoy-Doucet)/Arhoolie/1995
Tramps (Savoy-Doucet)/Metrobeat/1995
Prends Courage (Magnolia Sisters)/Arhoolie/1995
Now and Then (Savoy-Smith)/Arhoolie/1996

The Savoy Cajun Band Bio
//www.rootsworld.com/folklore/savoy.html

Marc Savoy Biography
//www.orion-cs.com/eunice/marcsavoy.html

See Beausoleil

Say ZuZu

Roots Rock; Country Rock
Portsmouth, New Hampshire; 1988-

Say ZuZu actually began life in 1988 as a band called Flat Top then Hot Hose and C.O.D. before settling on ZuZu's Petals

(from *It's a Wonderful Life*). They made a couple of recordings under that name but in the meantime discovered several other groups (most notably one from Minneapolis) were operating under the same moniker. To avoid confusion, ZuZu's Petals became Say ZuZu. At the same time, the band changed its sound from rock to a country rock style in the Uncle Tupelo/Son Volt/Wilco mold. In 1994, a chance meeting with two members of Willie Nelson's band directed them to Brad Hartman who engineered their 1995 **Highway Signs & Driving Songs** in Nashville. Two years later, Say ZuZu returned to Music City to record **Take These Turns** which gained "New Hampshire's only purveyors of hick-rock" wider exposure in the alt. country community. Late in 1997, they had successful tours of the Southeast and Italy where a music critic with *Buscadero* magazine had given a big splash to their recordings. Say ZuZu's 1998 recording **Bull** is twangy, listener friendly country-rock that will definitely appeal to alt. country fans of the old and new schools. Cliff Murphy and Jon Nolan front a hard core honky tonk side project called Hog Mawl that covers everyone from the masters (Hank, Waylon/Willie, Johnny C.) down to Steve Earle and Wilco.

Cliff Murphy (r.g.,v); James Nolan (b); Jon Nolan (g,p.s.,v); Steve Ruhm (d)

Say ZuZu to The Grocer Man (as ZuZu's Petals)/ PP/1991
Tribal Moans (as ZuZu's Petals)/PP/1992
Highway Signs & Driving Songs/PP/1995
Say ZuZu/PP/1995 (EP); 1996 (CD reissue w/ extra trks.)
Take These Turns/PP/1997
Bull/Broken White/1998

Chez ZuZu Home Page //www.sayzuzu.com/~sayzuzu/
sayzuzu@sayzuzu.com

W. W. Schnipp

White Trash Parody
San Antonio, Texas; 1995-

At the start of recording sessions for W. W. Schnipp's debut recording, he gave the musicians a pep talk in which he told them: "All I ever wanted out of life is to be a nuisance and a headache to every wimp, feminist and pantywaist coward, who makes a hobby out of getting offended." The result was an album of "outrageous and unthinkable country music" entitled **Filthy Pictures**. In a masterpiece of understatement, Schnipp's web page promo notes "this music is unlike anything coming down from Nashville today." Not only does he use lots of fiddle and steel but also fills his songs with raw, "folkish type wisdom" that manages to step on just about everybody's toes. Like his counterparts, Kinky Friedman and Unknown Hinson, Schnipp has dedicated himself to taking political incorrectness "to a new high level that once was thought to be unreachable." However, ol' W. W. don't believe in using blue language so instead of dirty lyrics, he relies on some pretty pointed satire as in "My Doggie" (in which Old Shep is literally dog food), "Welfare Mothers (Make Better Lovers)," "Men Don't Shoot Their Wives (When They Cheat Anymore)," and "I Will Work for Food." Schnipp is always looking for material for a new recording so if you have some satirical, traditional country stuff send it along but remember, "we only use clean lyrics!"

Filthy Pictures/JMQ/1995

W. W. Schnipp/JMQ, 114 Shadow Hill, San Antonio, TX 78228; 800-786-6035

W. W. Schnipp/JMQ Home Page //cust.iamerica.net/quillian.net

Quillian@iamerica.net

The Schramms (The Okra All-Stars)

Okra; Country Rock; Roots Rock
Hoboken, New Jersey; 1988-

The Schramms were created in the late 1980s by Dave Schramm who was already renowned as an A-1 lead and pedal steel guitar session player with such bands as Human Switchboard and Yo La Tengo. He intended to call his band Walking Wounded, but the name was already taken so on a whim, he and his band mates decided on the Schramms. The initial group which included Terry Karydes, Mike Lewis (ex-Yo La Tengo), Pete Linzell, Ron Metz (ex-Human Switchboard), and Todd Novak cut **Walk to Delphi**, roots rock with a sweet country aftertaste anchored by Schramm's twangy guitar and vocals and intelligent songwriting. Karydes, Lewis, Linzell, and Novak soon departed but were quickly replaced by bassist Al Greller (ex-Beat Rodeo) and organist George Usher (ex-Beat Rodeo, Bongos, House of Usher) for a second roots rock recording, **Rock, Scissors, Paper, Dynamite**. In 1994, the group jumped to ESD which released **Little Apocalypse** (an EP, **Heart Not Within**, drawn from **Little Apocalypse**, came out in the same year) and reissued the Schramm's first two recordings. Meanwhile, Schramm worked on a number of side projects including sessions with the Replacements, Freedy Johnston, and Hank McCoy. The latter and Schramm joined fellow label mates Ricky Barnes and Jeb Loy Nichols for a memorable twang-a-rama entitled **The Okra All-Stars**: Schramm contributed several originals ("She's Taken My Toys Away"; "The Conqueror's Song"), lead and harmony vocals, and stellar lap steel to one of the 1990s finest alt. country albums. He also recorded a very nice solo acoustic effort, **Folk und die Folgen**, which was limited to a few thousand copies and available only through mail order from Normal in Germany. When ESD underwent a change in musical direction in the mid-1990s, the Schramms switched to another German label, Blue Rose, whose stable includes other U.S. alt. country artists (the Continental Drifters, Health & Happiness Show, and the Dashboard Saviors). The Schramms' debut for their new label, **Dizzy Spell**, continued to mine the country/roots/rock

vein. Its release domestically in 1998 by Checkered Past Records thrust the Schramms once more into the U.S. alt. country/Americana spotlight. Their back catalog on the now defunct ESD label is available from the Schramms' via snail mail or their Nasal Twang web page.

Al Greller (b); Ron Metz (d,perc); Dave Schramm (g,p.s.,v); George Usher (org,v)

Walk to Delphi/Okra/1990; ESD/1995
Rock, Paper, Scissors, Dynamite/Okra Normal Ger./1992; ESD/1995
Heart Not Within/Matador/1994 (EP CD)
The Okra All-Stars/Okra/1994
Folk und die Folgen(Dave Schramm)/Return to Sender/1994
Little Apocalypse/ESD/1994
"Heart Not Within" on **ESD Sampler 1995**/ESD/1995
"In Hell's Respite" on **East Side Story, Vol. 1**/ESD/1996
Dizzy Spell/Blue Rose Ger./1996
"Seven Horses" & "Sorrow on Sorrow" on **Blue Rose Collection, Vol. 1**/Blue Rose Ger./1997
"Can You Please Crawl Out Your Window" on **Fireworks, Vol. 2**/Sound Asleep Swe./1998

The Schramms/Nasal Twang, P.O. Box 1148, Hoboken, NJ 07030

The Schramms/Nasal Twang Home Page //members.aol.com/hotstove/

NasalTwang@aol.com

See Ricky Barnes; Hank McCoy; The Okra All-Stars

Scroat Belly

Insurgent Country; Cowpunk; Thrashgrass
Colwich, Kansas; 1993-

Scroat Belly is from the "can't slow down on the old hoe-down" school of cowpunk. In the words of a *Music Wichita* reviewer, they are "the roughest, toughest band of hard hittin', fast pickin', hellbound hayseeds to spew forth from the fiery bowels of the Midwest yet." They basically know three speeds (fast, faster, fastest), and their high velocity hillbilly, metal, and punk allows audiences to alternate between clogging, head banging, and slam dancing. Their singer/songwriter leaders, Roy Wayne Gottstine and Kirk Rundstrom, started Scroat Belly around 1993, built a following in Lawrence and Wichita, and recorded their debut, **The Great Alaskan Holiday**, in 1995. Their no-stops-along-the-way pace caught the attention of Bloodshot Records and in 1996, they released **Daddy's Farm** which from front to back "rock(s) you up one side and hillbilly down the other" (*Music Wichita*). Thematically, Gottstine and Lundstrom are obsessed with the darkest recesses of rural America—ignorance, violence, and especially, drunkenness ("Drinkin' & Flailin'"; "Drinkin' Around"; "Booze Won't Let Me Down"; "Whiskey's Gone"; "Whiskey Drinkin' SOB"). Occasionally, Scroat Belly indulges in a little more restrained country sound as on their contribution to the **Straight Outta Boone County** compilation, "Why Don't You Haul Off and

Love Me." If you like searing guitars punctuated by frenetic fiddle playing on songs about betrayal, murder, and drinking, check 'em out; you have nothing to lose but your sobriety (and maybe your hearing). In 1997, Lundstrom jumped ship to another Kansas insurgent bluegrass band Split Lip Rayfield who were also signed by Bloodshot.

Mitch Clay (b); John Ezell (d,v); Wayne Gottstine (g,v); Kirk Lundstrom (g,v,1993-1997)

> **The Great Alaskan Holiday**/Pig Skin Tunes/1995
> **Daddy's Farm**/Bloodshot/1996
> "Why Don't You Haul Off and Love Me" on **Straight Outta Boone County**/Bloodshot/1997

Scroat Belly, P. O. Box 323, Colwich, KA 67030

Scroat Belly Web Page //www.fn.net/music/scroatbelly.html

Scroat Belly/Bloodshot Page //www.bloodshotrecords.com

See Split Lip Rayfield

Earl Scruggs (Earl Scruggs Revue)
Banjo; Progressive Bluegrass
Flint Hill, North Carolina; January 6, 1924-

One of the biggest events in bluegrass history was the breakup of the legendary Flatt & Scruggs in 1969. Their differences over musical direction (Lester wanted to keep it traditional, Earl wanted to modernize) were much publicized and, in time, split them apart. Scruggs was especially drawn to the country rock and progressive bluegrass that were emerging in the late 1960s and early 1970s. He formed the Earl Scruggs Revue with his sons, Gary and Randy, and they developed a more rocked up bluegrass style on a steady stream of albums featuring guest appearances by many of the top alt. country artists of the day. Playing colleges and rock and folk venues, the ESR were one of a handful of groups who helped acquaint a new generation with the pleasures of progressive bluegrass. Edsel Records (U.K.) issued a retrospective of the band's work, **The Earl Scruggs Revue: Artist's Choice, The Best Tracks, 1970-1980** in 1998. In 1971, Scruggs recorded **Earl Scruggs—His Family and Friends** which included cuts with the Byrds and Bob Dylan. The interview introduction to the Byrds track has some telling insight into Earl's frustration with playing the same bluegrass song, the same way over and over and his attraction to modern alternatives. About that same time, he was an important bridge joining the old and new musicians who recorded the landmark, **Will the Circle Be Unbroken**, and he participated in its sequel in 1989. The latter was produced by Randy Scruggs who also played on **Circle Vol 1.**, did session work for many artists including Rosanne Cash and John Hartford, produced for Iris DeMent, and recorded solo, his most recent effort being the acclaimed **Crown of Jewels** with Roger McGuinn, Iris DeMent, Emmylou Harris, John Prine, Earl Scruggs, and Vince Gill. Gary Scruggs also went on to a successful career as producer and songwriter.

In the 1990s, Earl Scruggs pretty much retired from performing due to ill health, but his legacy with Flatt & Scruggs and contributions to progressive bluegrass have been remembered through numerous anthologies and re-issues. He gave a "Concert of a Lifetime" in 1998 at the Bluegrass Classic Festival when he reunited with Randy and Gary (first time in almost 20 years) with backing from Jerry Douglas, Glen Duncan, and Marty Stuart.

Earl Scruggs Revue: Earl Scruggs (bj,v); Vassar Clements (f); Josh Graves (db); Jody Maphis (d); Gary Scruggs (b); Randy Scruggs (b,g,v); Steve Scruggs (d)

> **Nashville Rock**/CBS/
> **Earl Scruggs—His Family & Friends**/CBS/1971
> **Live at Kansas State**/CBS/1972
> **Will the Circle Be Unbroken**/United Artists/1972
> **Dueling Banjos**/CBS/1973
> **The Earl Scruggs Revue**/CBS/1973
> **Where the Lilacs Bloom**/CBS/1974
> **Rockin' Across the Country**/CBS/1974
> **The Earl Scruggs Revue Anniversary Album, Vol. 1**/CBS/1975
> **The Earl Scruggs Revue Anniversary Album, Vol. 2**/CBS/1976
> **Live From Austin City Limits**/CBS/1977
> **Strike Anywhere**/CBS/1977
> **Bold & New**/CBS/1978
> **Today and Forever**/CBS/1979
> **The Story Teller (Tom T. Hall) & The Banjo Man**/CBS/1982
> **Will the Circle Be Unbroken, Vol. 2**/Universal/1988
> **The Earl Scruggs Revue: Artist's Choice, THE Best Tracks 1970-1980**/ Edsel UK/1998
> **Crown of Jewels** (Randy Scruggs)/Reprise/1998

Earl Scruggs Fan Club c/o Louise Scruggs, P.O. Box 66, Madison, Tennessee 37115

Earl Scruggs Page
//www.peermusic.com/country/earlscruggs.html

The Scud Mountain Boys (The Pernice Brothers; King Radio)
Lo-Fi
Northampton, Massachusetts; 1991-1997

In 1991, Steve Desaulniers, Joe Pernice, and Bruce Tull began jamming on an informal basis in Tull's kitchen. Desaulniers and Pernice were working in local Northampton coffee shops and Tull was attending UMass, but they found time to play some open mics around town and eventually added a drummer to form the rock oriented Scuds (think Gulf War). However, when they got tired of paying bands to open for them, they formed their own opener, the Scud Mountain Boys. This band reflected their love for the acoustic based country music they often played in Tull's kitchen. When the Scuds lost one drummer after another, they decided to scrap that group altogether and do the country thing full time. At their performances, they became noted for playing very quiet music while seated around Tull's kitchen table. When audiences didn't walk out, the SMB decided to stick with their new sound and began recording in late 1993-early 1994 on 4 and 8 track equipment in the place they felt most comfortable, Tull's kitchen. The results were a single and two full length recordings done very inexpensively and released on Chunk Records. **Dance the Night Away** appeared in the early part of 1995 and was followed up shortly by **Pine Box**. Both comprise very slow tempo originals (like Cowboy Junkies, Palace, Souled American) and interesting takes on "Gypsies, Tramps, and Thieves" (Sonny & Cher), "Please, Mr. Please" (Olivia Newton-John), "Where's the Playground Susie" (Jimmy Webb/Glen Campbell), and "Wichita Lineman" (Jimmy Webb/Glen Campbell). After adding a drummer once more, the Scud Mountain Boys were signed by SubPop which agreed to let them continue their kitchen recording but this time on a 16 track machine. This upgrade in technology proved to be a disaster, and they ended up with several weeks of worthless tapes. To complete their new record, they decided to enter the studio but to induce the proper feel, the SMB took along their signature kitchen table. **Massachusetts** retains their generally moody sound but includes a few uptempo songs as well. The Scud Mountain Boys toured extensively in 1996 and early 1997 and were riding pretty high when SubPop re-released **Pine Box** and **Dance the Night Away** as a 2 CD set called **The Early Year**. However, during this time Desaulniers left, and in late 1997, when Pernice decided to move on, the kings of "Slacker Country" called it quits. However, Pernice stayed with SubPop working with brother Bob as the Pernice Brothers. In 1997, they cut a single, "Jimmy Coma" b/w "Monkey Suit" and a year later the full-length **Overcome By Happiness** which drops all Scud traces for a full-blown pop rock sound. Tull and Desaulniers worked with the Ray Mason Band, and another SMB alumnus, Frank Padelloro formed King Radio whose **Mr. K is Dead, Go Home** encompasses 60s, 70s, and 80s rock and lots of styles in between.

The Scud Mountain Boys: Stephen Desaulniers (b,r.g.,v); Fran Padelloro (b,v); Joe Pernice (a.g.,e.g.,v); Tom Shea (d,e.g.,md); Bruce Tull (e.g.,l.s.,p.s.,v)
The Pernice Brothers: Bob Pernice (l.g.,b.v.); Joe Pernice (g,v); Michael Deming (p,v); Thom Monahan (b,v); Peyton Pinkerton (g,v); Aaron Sperske (d,perc)

Doom Pop (Scuds)/Scuds/1992 (CS)
"Television" b/w "Sittin' on the Bottom of the World" (Steve Westfield)/Chunk/1994 (7")
"Two Weeks Past" on **Hit the Hay, Vol. 1**/Sound Asleep Swe./1994
"Reservoir" on **Homegrown Harvest**/1994
Dance the Night Away/Chunk/1995
Pine Box/Chunk/1995 (LP)
"Knievel" b/w "1/2 Way"/SubPop/1995 (7")
Masschusetts/SubPop/1996
The Early Year/SubPop/1997 (**Dance the Night Away & Pine Box**)
"Jimmy Coma" b/w "Monkey Suit" (Pernice Brothers)/SubPop/1997 (7")

Overcome By Happiness (Pernice Brothers)/SubPop/1998
"Play the Greed" (SMB) on **Hempilation2**/Capricorn/1998
"Penthouse in the Woods" (SMB) on **Loose: New Soungs of the Old West**/Vinyl Junkie/1998
"Crestfallen" on **Sounds of the New West**/Uncut UK/1998
Mr. K is Dead, Go Home (King Radio)/Tar Hut/1998

The Scud Mountain Boys/Sub Pop Page //www.subpop.com/bands/scud/website/

The Scud Mountain Boys iMusic Showcase //imusic.com/showcase/contemporary/

Pernice Brothers/SubPop Page //www.subpop.com/bands/pernice/

See Ray Mason Band

Seconds Flat
Country Rock
Greenville, South Carolina; 1993-

South Carolina's Seconds Flat began hanging out on the fringes of alt. country in 1993. **Spittin' Cause We Like To** and **Temporary Fix** received minimal coverage, but in 1997, with **Seconds Flat**, they began to break into the limelight. Musically, the impeccable vocals by Larry Hoskinson and Anthony Tomlinson and the generally friendly pace drew refer ences to the best of late 1960s and early 1970s country rock. This was due in part, no doubt, to production by Brian Ahern, Emmylou's ex-producer/husband and veteran of that period of alt. country history. Hoskinson's and Tomlinson's songs range from the easy going ("In Your Arms") to light hearted ("Gone"), tongue-in-cheek honky tonk ("Me and My Friend Heartache"), ominous ("Walk Away"), cynical ("Murphy's Law"), and downright bitter ("Three O'Clock"—"I don't care who you've done, I just want my car"). Greatly helping things along were Jerry "Flux" Douglas on dobro and slide and Richard McLaurin of Farmer Not So John on lap steel and mandolin.

Jeff Hook (d,perc,1993-1997); Larry Hoskinson (a.g.,e.g.,l.v.,b.v.); Matt Morgan (e.g.); Martin Slater (d,1997-); Rick Stapleton (b,b.v.); David Stone (e.g.,b.v.); Anthony Tomlinson (a.g.,hm,ky,l.v.,b.v.)

Spittin' Cause We Like To/SF/1994
Temporary Fix/SF/1996 (EP)
Seconds Flat/Green Linnet/1997

Seconds Flat/Green Linnet Page //www.greenlinnet.com

Seconds Flat Fan Page //www.angelfire.com/nc/secondsflat/

Mike Seeger
See The New Lost City Ramblers

The Seldom Scene (Chesapeake)
Progressive Bluegrass
Washington, D.C.; 1971-

In late 1996, John Duffey, the man acknowledged by many as the "father of modern bluegrass," died suddenly from a massive heart attack. Subsequent tributes and obituaries reiterated his importance and influence to the development of progressive bluegrass. In the 1950s and 1960s, Duffey was a member of the Country Gentlemen, one of the pioneer groups in the transition from traditional to progressive bluegrass. He left the band in 1969 and began playing informally with a group of D.C. area musicians including Mike Auldridge, Ben Eldridge, Tom Gray, and John Starling. Eventually, they began performing as the Seldom Scene at area clubs (The Red Fox, The Birchmere) and partly on the basis of Duffey's reputation as a Country Gentleman soon built their own following. Like their predecessor, the Seldom Scene mixed traditional bluegrass with bluegrass versions of songs by a variety of musicians including Jimmie Rodgers, Benny Goodman, Hank Williams, Bob Wills, Gene Clark, Eric Clapton, and J. J. Cale. They were notable for their stunning three part harmonies (highlighted by Duffey's high roofed tenor) and strong instrumental playing featuring standout dobro picking by Mike Auldridge. Starling dropped out in 1977 to pursue a second career as an Army surgeon and was replaced by Phil Rosenthal who was later replaced by Lou Reid; Tom Gray departed in the late 1980s and was succeeded by long time Doc Watson bassist, T. Michael Coleman. In spite of these changes, the Seldom Scene consistently remained one of the most popular bluegrass bands of the 1970s-early 1990s and during this period cut many excellent recordings with guest appearances by Emmylou Harris, Ricky Skaggs, Tony Rice, Linda Ronstadt and many others. In addition, Auldridge worked on Emmylou Harris' classic **Elite Hotel** and **Luxury Liner** and recorded a number of highly recommended solo albums with members of the Seldom Scene. In 1992, the Scene held a twentieth anniversary concert later commemorated as a double CD, **Scene 20**, with appearances by the band's many admirers and collaborators. Starling returned briefly in 1993 but then went on to a solo career with a couple of acclaimed progressive bluegrass albums, **Long Time Gone** and **Waitin' on a Southern Train**. Lead guitarist and vocalist Moondi Klein joined the Seldom Scene in 1994 but only remained one year taking Auldridge and Coleman with him in 1995 to form a new band, Chesapeake. Auldridge started his own line of audio and video dobro instructional tapes and toured with Lyle Lovett in 1998. The remaining members of Seldom Scene (plus replacements) cut **Dream Scene** in 1996, and with the return of mandolinist Lou Reid carried on toward the new millenium. Current and past members of both the Seldom Scene and the Country Gentlemen came together in mid-November, 1998 at the Birchmere in Arlington, Virginia, for a gala tribute to the late, great John Duffey.

The Seldom Scene: Mike Auldridge (db,g,v); T. Michael Coleman (b,1986-1995); Dudley Connell (g,v,1996-); John Duffey (md,g,v,1971-1996); Ben Eldridge (bj,g,v,1971-); Tom Gray (b,v,1971-1986); Moondi Klein (g,l.v.,1994-1995); Lou Reid (g,l.v.,1986-1992; 1997-); Phil Rosenthal (g,l.v.,1977-1985); Ronnie Simpkins (b,v,1996-); John Starling (g,v,1971- 1977;1992-1994); Fred Travers (db,v, 1996-)
Chesapeake: Mike Auldridge (db); T. Michael Coleman (b); Moondi Klein (g,v)

Act I/Rebel/1972
Dobro (Mike Auldridge)/Takoma/1972
Act II/Rebel/1973
Act III/Rebel/1973
The Old Train/Rebel/1974
Blues & Bluegrass (Mike Auldridge)/Takoma/1974
Live at the Cellar Door/Rebel/1975
The New Seldom Scene Album/Rebel/1976
Mike Auldridge/Flying Fish/1976
Mike Auldridge & Old Dog/Flying Fish/1977
Baptizing/Rebel/1977
Bluegrass: The World's Greatest Show (Live)/Sugar Hill/1978
Act IV/Sugar Hill/1979
Critic's Choice (Mike Auldridge)/Takoma/1979
Slidin' Smoke (Mike Auldridge)/Flying Fish/1979
After Midnight/Sugar Hill/1980
Eight String Swing (Mike Auldridge)/Sugar Hill/1982
At The Scene/Sugar Hill/1983
Blue Ridge (with Jonathan Edwards)/Sugar Hill/1985
The Best of the Seldom Scene, Vol. 1/Rebel/1986
15th Anniversary Celebration/Sugar Hill/1987
A Change of Scenery/Sugar Hill/1988
Treasures Untold (Mike Auldridge)/Sugar Hill/1989
High Time (Auldridge, Reid & Coleman)/Sugar Hill/1989
Scenic Roots/Sugar Hill/1990
Scene 20: 20th Anniversary Concert/Sugar Hill/1992
Like We Used to Be/Sugar Hill/1994
Long Time Gone (John Starling)/Sugar Hill/
Waitin' on a Southern Train (John Starling)/Sugar Hill/1995
Rising Tide (Chesapeake)/Sugar Hill/1996
Dream Scene/Sugar Hill/1996
Full Sail (Chesapeake)/Sugar Hill/1997
Pier Pressure (Chesapeake)/Sugar Hill/1998

The Seldom Scene Home Page //www.seldomscene.com

The Seldom Scene Profile //www.banjo.com/profiles/seldomscene.html

Mike Auldridge Productions //www.mikeauldridge.com (highly informative dobro site plus the latest news about Chesapeake)

See The Country Gentlemen

The Shakin' Apostles

See Freddy Krc

Billy Joe Shaver (Shaver)

Outlaw; Honky Tonk; Country Rock
Corsicana, Texas; September 15, 1941-

In 1993, a "new" group called Shaver recorded one of the best albums of the year, **Tramp on Your Street**. In reality, the leader of the band, Billy Joe Shaver, already had twenty five years under his belt as a singer/songwriter, but the road to success had been long and sometimes very rocky. His first writing job in the late 1960s with the Bobby Bare company yielded "Willie the Wandering Gypsy and Me," "Old Five and Dimers," and "Ride Me Down Easy" which became a big hit for Bare in 1973. During this time, Shaver mingled with the song-writing community of Willie Nelson, Kris Kristofferson, and Waylon Jennings and became a member of the fledgling "outlaw" country movement when Waylon Jennings recorded an entire album of Shaver's songs entitled **Honky Tonk Heroes**. One of the landmarks of the period, this album helped secure Shaver a record contract and a chance to do his songs his way. Through the 1970s and 1980s, Shaver recorded six albums of progressive country with stellar support (Emmylou Harris, Ricky Skaggs, Pete Drake, Willie Nelson, Rodney Crowell) and great originals: "I Been To Georgia on a Fast Train," "You Asked Me To," "Black Rose," and "I'm Just an Old Chunk of Coal." However, while others (Bare, Elvis, Johnny Cash, John Anderson) made hay with Shaver's songs, his career, dogged by personal problems, languished. But, in 1993, Billy Joe made a triumphant return with his new band, Shaver. At his side was his son Eddie who had played lead guitar on Billy Joe's recordings in the late 1980s. Their debut, **Tramp on Your Street**, revisits "Georgia on a Fast Train" and "Old Chunk of Coal" and has two duets by Billy Joe and Waylon, the inspiring "Live Forever," and Eddie's blazing guitar work on "The Hottest Thing in Town" and "Tenntex Tear Down." Critics universally acclaimed this recording, and it made every top ten list. Two years later, the raw energy of Billy Joe's vocals and Eddie's lead was captured on the live recording **Unshaven**. Shaver's autobiographical **Highway of Life** slows the pace down considerably but also has some good honky tonkers like "You're as Old as the Woman You Feel." In addition to long overdue recognition, Shaver's resurgence brought the reissue of some of his albums including **Honky Tonk Heroes** (combines **When I Get My Wings** and **Gypsy Boy**) and **Restless Wind** that compiles his best from 1973-1987. Son Eddy showed off his formidable guitar chops on a 1997 solo recording, **Baptism of Fire**.

Billy Joe signed with the new Americana label, New West, in 1998, a year filled with personal ups and downs. He had a prominent role in Robert Duvall's hit movie *The Apostle* but during filming found out his ex-wife Brenda had cancer. Divorced since the late 1980s, they planned to remarry, and Shaver made it through their tough times with his faith which was potently expressed on **Victory**, a collection of acoustic gospel with Eddy. The full Shaver band also completed a new country/roots/rock album **Thunderbird** (produced by Ray Kennedy) which was released in 1999.

> **Old Five and Dimers Like Me**/Monument/1973;
>   KOCH/1996
> **When I Get My Wings**/Capricorn/1976 ·
> **Gypsy Boy**/Capricorn/1977
> **I'm Just an Old Chunk of Coal...But I'm Gonna Be a
>   Diamond Some Day**/Columbia/1981
> **Billy Joe Shaver**/Columbia/1982

> **Salt of the Earth**/Columbia/1987
> **Tramp on Your Street**/Zoo BMG/1993
> **Honky Tonk Heroes**/Bear Family/1994
> **Unshaven: Live at Smith's Old Bar**/Praxis Zoo/1995
> **Restless Wind: The Legendary Billy Joe Shaver,
>   1973-1987**/Razor & Tie/1995
> **Highway of Life**/Praxis Zoo/1996
> **Baptism of Fire** (Eddie Shaver)/Justice/1997
> **Victory**/New West/1998
> **Thunderbird**/New West/1999

Billy Joe Shaver Fan Club, 312 W. Alabama, Houston, TX 77098

Shaver Fan Club, 111 16th Ave. South, Ste. 202, Nashville, TN 37212

Shaver/New West Page
//www.bakernorthrop.com/artists/shaver/

Billy Joe Shaver Page
//www.justicerecords.com/~nancy/arp23.html

Unofficial Billy Joe Shaver Home Page
//watt.seas.virginia.edu/~gkm4d/shaver.html

Billy Joe Shaver AOL Folder: Entertainment>Music>Chat & Messages>Music Community>Country & Western, L-Z

Rick Shea
TSOB
Annapolis, Maryland; 1953-

Rick Shea made his first splash on the California alt. country scene in 1989 with his self-released **Outside of Nashville** (produced by Wyman Reese of Chris Gaffney's **Cold Hard Facts**). A disciple of Merle Haggard and other champions of the Bakersfield Sound, Shea demonstrated not only his singing and songwriting skills but also proficiency on electric and steel guitar. The latter put him much in demand by other members of the Town South of Bakersfield community, and Shea recorded with Dave Alvin, Chris Gaffney, Brantley Kearns, and Heather Myles. In 1992, his "Foot in the Fire" made the third installment of **A Town South of Bakersfield**, and in 1994, he was named Male Vocalist of the Year by the California Country Music Association. In between tours to Europe, session work, writing music reviews, and playing in bands like $1000 Wedding, Shea found time to record **The Buffalo Show** (once again produced by Reese) presenting more of his exemplary honky tonk, country rock, and Tex-Mex originals with help from TSOB alumni including Jann Browne, Skip Edwards, Gaffney, Kearns, Myles, Reese, and Randy Weeks (Lonesome Strangers). Into the late 90s, Shea remained in high demand as a side/session man touring with Dave Alvin in 1998 and playing mandolin, rhythm, and lead guitar.

> **Outside of Nashville**/RS/1989
> "Foot in the Fire" on **A Town South of Bakersfield, Vol.
>   3**/Restless/1995
> **The Buffalo Show**/Major Label/1995

The Shivers

Lo-Fi Country; Gothic Country
Austin, Texas/Portland, Oregon; 1988-

Wife/husband team, Kelly Bell and Carey Kemper started the Shivers in Austin, Texas, in 1988 but then began a zig zag journey across the country in an RV (with their drummer and children) between temporary homes in Tennessee, Minnesota, and Oregon. Like wandering troubadours of yore, they documented life along the highways and back roads in songs that look below the surface to reveal the dark underbelly of American life. Taking time out from their seemingly endless sojourn, the Shivers stopped long enough to commit their observations to two recordings: **The Shivers** and **The Buried Life**. Bell and Kemper share the singing and songwriting with spare instrumental backing; their earthy vocals (she somewhere between Lucinda and Exene; he between Johnny Cash and Jay Farrar) fit well with their somber, realistic songs ("Never Leave Nevada," "Red Cats," "House of the Spirits," "Dark of the Moon," "Rivers," "Cult 45," "Shade the Light," "Cannonball," "The Wind in Abilene") which have led a number of reviewers to label them "Gothic Country." However, occasionally, the Shivers step it up a notch as on the sprightly "Love Other Gone" and "Make a Wish" or the Son Volt sounding "Things Change." *New Country* magazine voted them one of the Top 10 Alt. Country acts in 1994.

In 1997, Bell and Kemper (and new drummer Rick Barry) decided to take up "permanent" residence in Portland. Bell began to freelance for Biohazard New Media as a graphic designer, but the Shivers remained active with performances and work on a new recording. Their profile overseas got a big boost when Glitterhouse began to distribute their records in 1998.

Kelly Bell (b,g,v); Carey Kemper (f,g,l.s.,v); Rick Barry (d,perc,1996-); Barry Haney (d,perc,1988-1996)

The Shivers/Restless/1994; Glitterhouse Ger./1998
The Buried Life/Restless/1996; Glitterhouse Ger./1998

The Shivers, 232 NE Monroe, Portland, OR 97212

The Shivers Online
//www.theshivers.com
KellyBell@aol.com

Michelle Shocked

Singer/Songwriter
Dallas, Texas; February 24, 1962-

Michelle Shocked is undoubtedly one of the most eccentric characters in modern popular music, but considering her harrowing early years it's not hard to understand why. Born in Dallas as Michelle Johnston her parents split up when she was about a year old and for the next sixteen years she was dragged around military bases in the U.S. and Europe by her mother and stepfather. Back in Texas, Michelle ran away from home to live with her father "Dollar" Bill Johnston who got her a guitar and encouraged her to practice and perform at country and blues festivals. In the early 80s, she gave songwriting and college a go in Austin but by 1983 was on the road in San Francisco and New York where she lived a life of homelessness and squatting. Her involvement in political causes got her in trouble with the law and landed her in mental hospitals in Frisco and Dallas where she was adminstered shock therapy for paranoid schizophrenia. That experience induced a change of name to Shocked and then she was off to New York City and Europe where she was raped. Still kicking, Michelle Shocked was a volunteer at the 1986 Kerrville Folk Festival where an English producer named Peter Lawrence recorded her (guitar and vocals) on a Sony Walkman. These tapes (with cricket noises and passing trucks in the background) were released in England and were a big hit in folk circles there. By 1987, Shocked was being courted by U.S. labels and in 1988 signed with Mercury. **Short Sharp Shocked** blended country, folk, and rock, **Captain Swing** (produced by Pete Anderson) had a big band sound, but her alt. country/ Americana showpiece was the 1992 Grammy winner, **Arkansas Traveler**. Shocked had become fascinated with the history of black minstrelsy and using a mobile studio traveled around to record a wide variety of American roots music with the Band (roots rock), the Red Clay Ramblers (old-time), the Hothouse Flowers (Celtic), Taj Mahal (blues), Clarence "Gatemouth" Brown (r&b), Jerry Douglas and Doc Watson (folk), Alison Krauss (bluegrass), Norman and Nancy Blake (old-time), and Pops Staples (gospel). One special treat is her rocking old-time song "Shaking Hands (Soldiers Joy)" with Uncle Tupelo which features Jay Farrar on lead vocals. Shocked also got to record with her father on the title tune (with Jimmy Driftwood) and a Woody Guthrie song ("Woody's Rag") with Max Johnston on guitar. All in all, an impressive if somewhat ragged outing that in light of the alt. country boom of the late 1990s came along a bit too early to be fully appreciated. Two years later, Shocked and Mercury had a major falling out, and they refused to release her **Kind Hearted Woman** album although she sold independent copies of it at concerts anyway. Eventually, Mercury let her out of her contract, and **Kind Hearted Woman** was officially issued by Private Music in 1996. This underrated album is perhaps Shock's most country flavored effort and compares favorably with Springsteen's **Nebraska** in its honest portrayal of the trials and tribulations of life in rural America. (*In 1988, Shocked did an inspired cover of "One Piece at a Time" for Jon Langford's Johnny Cash tribute, **'Til Things Are Brighter**).

The Texas Campfire Tapes/Cooking Vinyl UK/1986
"One Piece At a Time" on **'Til Things Are Brighter...A Tribute to Johnny Cash**/Rave UK/1988
Short Sharp Shocked/Mercury/1988
Captain Swing/Mercury/1989

Arkansas Traveler/Mercury/1992
"Holy Spirit" on **Sweet Relief: A Benefit for Victoria
   Williams**/Thirsty Ear Chaos Columbia/1993
Kind Hearted Woman/MS/1994; Private Music/1996
Artists Make Lousy Slaves (with Fiachna
   O'Braonain)/Mood Swing/1996
Mercury Poise: 1988-1995/Mercury/1996
"Quality of Mercy" on **Dead Man
   Walking**/Columbia/1996
Good News (Michelle Shocked & The Anointed
   Earls)/Mood Swing/1998

Official Michelle Shocked Page //www.shellshock.com

Graffiti Limbo: An Unofficial Michelle Shocked Site
//members.xoom.com/g_limbo/

The Silos
Roots Rock
New York City; 1984-

Of all the roots rock groups of the past fifteen years, there is
perhaps none harder to pin down than the Silos. Leader Walter
Salas-Humara started out as leader of the excellent Vulgar
Boatmen in Florida but later migrated to New York City where
he teamed with Bob Rupe to form the Silos. Their early efforts
(**About Her Steps**; **Cuba**; **The Silos**) has a definite country
rock ambience, but after Rupe moved on (to Gutterball then
Cracker), Salas-Humara surrounded himself with a fluctuating
collective of musicians, and they made several albums in the
early 1990s that combine rock, pop, roots, and more in a way
that really defies description. This isn't to say they aren't good
recordings with plenty of inspired moments (great Salas-
Humara originals), just that stylistically, they're a reviewer's
nightmare. Along the way, Salas-Humara did several solos and
a roots rock side project with Alejandro Escovedo, Gurf Morlix,
Lisa Mednick, Scott Garber (ex-Giant Sand), and Michael Hall
as the Setters. Dormant for a few years, the Silos re-emerged in
1998 with **Heater** which measures up well with their best from
the early 90s but with a few departures including some techno,
trip-hop grooves.

About Her Steps/Record Collect/1985
Cuba/Record Collect/1987; Watermelon/1994
Tennessee Fire/Record Collect/1987 (EP)
Lagartija (Walter Salas-Humara)/Recod Collect/1988
The Silos/RCA/1990
Hasta La Victoria!/Normal Ger./1992; Watermelon/1994
The Setters/Watermelon/1994
Diablo/Normal Ger./1994
Susan Across the Ocean/Watermelon/1994
Lean (Walter Salas-Humara)/Return to Sender Normal
   Ger./1994
Ask the Dust/Watermelon/1995
Radar (Walter Salas-Humara)/Watermelon/1995
Long Green Boat/Last Call Fr./1997
Heater/Checkered Past/1998

The Silos/Walter-Salas-Humara Homepage
//world.std.com/~silos/

TheSilos@aol.com

Jim Silvers
Honky Tonk; Rockabilly; Bluegrass
Chicago, Illinois

A jack-of-many-trades, Jim Silvers was at one time or another a
car salesman, truck driver, motorcycle racer, livestock auc-
tioneer, publicist for Universal Pictures, drama student,
professional photographer (pornography and the Grand Ole
Opry), and even had a highly rated gospel show down South
before it was discovered he was Jewish. However, his real love
was singing and after messing around in a few bluegrass and
country bands while in college, he ended up in L.A. where he
took guitar lessons from Richard Bennett (Neil Diamond band)
and convinced him to co-produce his first recording. Bennett,
who would later go on to produce Steve Earle, Emmylou Harris,
and Marty Stuart among others, played lead guitar, pedal and
lap steel, and mandolin and rounded up a supporting cast
including banjoist Fred Sokolow and fiddler Brantley Kearns in
his pre-Dwight Yoakam days. Released on CMH in 1978, **You
Gotta Let All the Girls Know You're a Cowboy** is a montage
of honky tonk, bluegrass, and country rock with covers of Elton
Britt ("Cannonball Yodel") and Ernest Tubb ("Waltz Across
Texas") and lots of clever originals by Silvers. But, the real
standout here is Jim's voice; he's one of those rare, pure country
singers like Webb Pierce or Don Walser whose singing can just
cut right through you. In 1981, Silvers recorded a second album
(**Colonel Jim Silvers**) with Bennett, but this time for Ronny
Weiser's Rollin' Rock label whose catalog included Mac
Curtis, Johnny Carroll, and Ray Campi. The latter played
stand-up bass on Silvers' sessions which, not surprisingly, have
a definite rockabilly/hillbilly feel with songs by the Louvin
Brothers ("Cash on the Barrell Head") and more great originals
including "I Ate the Whole Damn Hog" and the stunning "Blue
Night." A number of years later Bear Family gathered Silvers'
total output of 25 songs on one recording as **Music Makin'
Mama From Memphis**. Then, in 1997-1998, Hightone
reissued material from Rollin' Rock on two compilations, **Got
the Sock, Vol. 1-2**. Four of Silvers' songs were included and
hopefully, this was a prelude to a "best of" CD for a great but
sadly neglected country singer.

**You Gotta Let All the Girls Know You're a
   Cowboy**/CMH/1978
Colonel Jim Silvers/Rollin' Rock/1981
Music Makin' Mama From Memphis/Bear Family
   Ger./1992
"The Last to Get the News" and "Ain't It Strange" on **Got
   the Sock, Vol. 1**/Rollin' Rock HMG/1997
"Blue Night" and "Julie" on **Got the Sock, Vol. 2**/Rollin'
   Rock HMG/1998

Rockin' Ronny Weiser: Rockinron@aol.com

6 String Drag

Tobacco Row; Twangtrust; Roots Rock; Country Rock
Clemson, South Carolina/Raleigh, North Carolina; 1993-1998

Yet another in the apparently endless stream of quality alt. country bands to come out of the Carolinas in the past few years, 6 String Drag was co-founded in the early 1990s in Clemson, South Carolina, by Kenneth Roby and Rob Keller. The former had been leader of a punk group called the Lubricators for six years while the latter (through his mom and dad's record store) had been steeped in traditional country and bluegrass. Their first band, the Welfare Liners, eventually evolved into 6 String Drag which they relocated to Raleigh, North Carolina, the heart of the region's expanding alt. country scene. They started out with a sound much like the Backsliders, Jolene, Whiskeytown, and other similar bands from the Triangle area, but influenced by The Band, Elvis Costello, and Doug Sahm, 6 String Drag added a part time horn section and incorporated a variety of Americana. In 1995, they recorded a self-titled debut of fairly straight on country rock, but as a trombone and sax were brought into the mix, the band began to experiment with r&b (covers of James Brown), Dixieland, and even Tex-Mex. A 1996 performance at Bubbapalooza in Atlanta brought Steve Earle and E-Squared calling. Earle and the other half of the Twangtrust, Jack Emerson, produced their 1997 release, **High Hat**, whose spirited combination of country rock, Southern rock, swamp, jazz, old-time, and honky tonk, made it one of the best and most entertaining alt. country albums of the year. But, as is so often the case, success often breeds instability and in late 1998 when internal tensions over direction, etc., became too great, 6 String Drag played out their last string and broke up.

Ray Duffey (d,b.v.); Rob Keller (b,h.v.); Scott Miller (e.g.,md,b.v.); Kenneth Roby (g,l.v.); William Tonks (l.g.,1993-1997) with David Wright (ky,tmb); Steve Grothman (sax)

> **Six String Drag**/Fundamental/1995
> "Off With Your Head" on **Revival: Brunswick Stew & Pig Pickin'**/Yep Roc/1996
> "Bottle of Blues" b/w "Lorene"/E-Squared/1997 (7")
> **High Hat**/E-Squared/1997

Unofficial 6 String Drag Web Page //www.6stringdrag.com

ThomasDrake@6stringdrag.com

16 Horsepower

Gothic Country
Denver, Colorado; 1993-

Of the many alternative country acts whose sound has been labeled gothic, perhaps none is more enshrouded in that tradition than Denver's 16 Horsepower. Every aspect of this band oozes darkness, desolation, grotesqueness: the disturbing, grainy tin type images of their CD cover art; the scruffy, sullen appearance of David Eugene Edwards, Keven Soll, and Jean-Yves Tola; the creepy lap steel, haunting fiddle, plunking banjo, and wheezing bandoneon (antique push button accordion); Edwards lead vocals rendered as an eerie cry of warning; and most of all, the songs about ever present evil ("I Seen What I Saw"; "Shametown"; "Black Soul Choir"), death ("Heel on the Shovel"; "Neck on the New Blade"), and only one hope for salvation– "So I set my face to the Lord God to seek him by prayer and supplications with fasting, sackcloth and ashes" (Daniel 9:3). Even their exuberant reels and jigs are born more out of madness than joy. Overall, the effect is very disturbing as if the band had transported the listener back to the despair of 19th century mining camps, run down farms, and urban slums. In the late 1990s, 16 Horsepower backed Kelly Willis ("Aren't I True" on **Fading Fast**) and recorded CD, **Low Estate**, again named for a Bible verse. Its brooding compositions ("Coal Black Horses," "Brimstone Rock," "Black Lung," "Dead Run," "Hang My Teeth on Your Door") and creepy atmospherics sealed 16 Horsepower's place as the kings of gothic country. Moderately successful at home, Sixteen Horsepower enjoyed their greatest success (record sales and live performances) in Europe where audiences were more open to what they were trying to say. Throughout 1998, while still doing some dates in the U.S., their most extensive touring was on the Continent. Still, all was not so rosy as Jeffrey-Paul left in May (either due to burn out or "belt tightening"), but the big problem for 16 Horsepower was the sale of A&M to MCA which cut back on the band's publicity and tour budgets.

David Eugene Edwards (bj,bandoneon,g,v); Pascal Humbert (b); Jeffrey-Paul (cello,g,f,org,1993-1998); Keven Soll (b,1993-1996); Steve Taylor (g;1998-); Jean-Yves Tola (d)

> "Shame Town" b/w "Slow Guilt Trot"/A&M/1995 (7")
> **16 Horsepower**/A&M/1995 (6 trk CD)
> **Sackcloth 'n' Ashes**/A&M/1996
> **Low Estate**/A&M Euro./1997; A&M/1998

16 Horsepower, Idledale, P. O. Box 285, Denver, CO 80453-0285

Scrawled in Sap: The 16 Horsepower Home Page //www.paonline.com/heatherm/16hp/news.htm

16 Horsepower/A&M Records Home Page //amrecords.com/artists/16horsepower/

Skeeter and the Skidmarks

New Old-Time; Progressive Bluegrass
Galax/Wytheville, Virginia; Mid-1990s-

The mountains and hollows of Southwest Virginia have long been a fertile breeding ground for outstanding old-time and bluegrass musicians (Tommy Jarrell, Ted Lundy, Scotty Stoneman). Carrying on this tradition is a Galax/Wytheville based group with the very intriguing name, Skeeter and the Skidmarks. Their style is rooted in Appalachian and bluegrass but has a very contemporary feel due to the intermingling of jazz, folk, and even classical music. They employ the standard old-time/bluegrass instruments led by Edwin Lacy on claw-hammer banjo and Scott Freeman on fiddle and mandolin with a very upbeat, driving rhythm on classics ("Whiskey Before Breakfast"; "Been All Around the World") and originals ("Squawkin' Weasal Bait"; "Groundhog Shuffle"). Skeeter and the Skidmarks are also notable for their tight vocals and har-monies. As of 1997 they had recorded two albums, **Alternate Roots** and **Hubbin' It**, and have played many prominent events including Rocky Gap Bluegrass Festival, California Bluegrass Association's Father's Day Festival, and Merlefest (3 years running).

Scott Freeman (f,md,v); Willard Gayheart (g,v); Sandy Grover (b,v); Edwin Lacy (cl. bj,v)

> **Alternate Roots**/Hay Holler/1995
> **Hubbin' It**/Hay Holler/1996

Skeeter and the Skidmarks, 230 West Lee Hwy., Ste. C, Wytheville, VA 24382; 540-223-1171

Skeeter and Skidmarks Home Page //www.bev.net/community/nrac/perform/skeeter.html

The Skeletons (The Morells)
Roots Rock
Springfield, Missouri; 1979-

Randle Chowning (ex-Ozark Mountain Daredevils), Lou Whitney (ex-Original Symptoms), and D. Clinton Thompson (ex-Original Symptoms) founded the first incarnation of the Skeletons in Springfield, Missouri, in 1979. After Chowning was replaced by Nick Sibley, the band toured around the Midwest and cut singles on Whitney's Borrowed Records. After serving as backing band for Steve Forbert on his 1979 tour, the Skeletons drifted apart with Whitney and Thompson starting the Morells with Joe Terry. They recorded one terrific roots rock album, **Shake and Push**, before breaking up in 1984. Meanwhile, the Skeletons reactivated. They made two recordings for the Scottish label The Next Big Thing in the late 1980s; **Rockin' Bones** collected early singles and other material while **In the Flesh** displayed the Skeletons' versatility on original rock, r&b, funk, and pop plus covers of Sonny Bono ("Laugh at Me"), Little Jimmy Dickens ("I'm Little But I'm Loud"), the Flying Burrito Brothers ("Older Guys"), and "Take Me Out to the Ballgame." Demon (UK) later released both of these albums and in the U.S., ESD issued them as a package, **In the Flesh**, in 1991. In the early 1990s, the Skeletons added Kelly Brown, played SXSW (1992), got a record deal with Alias, recorded **Waiting**, and served as support band on recordings by Jonathan Richman (**Jonathan Goes Country**), Scott Kempner (**Tenement Angels**), and Boxcar Willie (**Rocky Box**). They also toured behind Kempner and Dave Alvin, then took some time off before getting back to work in 1995. After sessions with Syd Straw, the Skeletons signed on as backing band for Robbie Fulks debut, **Country Love Songs**,

which turned out to be one of the top 10 alt. country recordings of 1996 due in no small part to the Skeletons' superb accompaniment. In 1997, after signing with Hightone, the Skeletons recorded what many consider to be their finest, **Nothing to Lose**. Once again, they cover a wide spectrum of styles all tied together by exuberance and a quirky sense of humor ("On Your Way Down the Drain"; "I Ain't Lyin'"; "Mad Old Lady"; "Country Boys Don't Cry"; "Teardrop City"). The Skeletons backed Fulks on **South Mouth** and Oklahoma musician Bob Collum on **More Tragic Songs of Life** in 1997. During 1998, the Skeletons participated in two disparate projects, backing rockabilly Rudy "Tutti" Grazell on his recording and doing the music for the *Toons a GoGo* show on the Cartoon Network. Thompson worked with the rock/roots trio, the Park Central Squares and Hicks and Terry were part of Dave Alvin's touring band.

The Skeletons: Kelly Brown (ky,v,1990-); Randle Chowning (g,hm,v,1979); Bobby Lloyd Hicks (d,v); Nick Sibley (g,ky,v,1979,1988); Joe Terry (ky,v,1988, 1990-); D. Clinton Thompson (g,v); Lou Whitney (b,v)
The Morells: Maralie (ky,v); Ron Gremp (d,v); Joe Terry (ky,v); D. Clinton Thompson (g,v); Lou Whitney (b,v)

> "Very Last Day" b/w "Sour Snow"/Borrowed/1979
> "Trans Am" b/w "Tell Her I'm Gone"/Borrowed/1980
> **Shake and Push** (Morells)/Borrowed/1982; ESD/1989
> **Rockin' Bones**/Next Big Thing Scot./1987; Demon UK/1989
> "Do You Hear What I Hear?" b/w "Jingle Bell Rock"/ Borrowed/1988
> **In the Flesh**/Next Big Thing Scot/1989; Demon UK/1989; ESD/1991
> **Waiting**/Alias/1993
> **Nothing to Lose**/Hightone/1997

The Skeletons/Morells Web Site //members.aol.com/muzzi/morell.html

The Skeletons/Hightone Home Page //www.hightone.com/bios/skeletonsbio.html

See Robbie Fulks

Skull Orchard

See Jon Langford

Skydiggers
Country Rock; Roots Rock
Toronto, Ontario, Canada; 1988-

Influenced by country rock pioneers (Gram Parsons, the Byrds, Neil Young) and contemporary Canadian roots rockers (Blue Rodeo; Cowboy Junkies), the Skydiggers pooled their resources after laboring individually in various 80s rock bands. Josh Finlayson and Andy Maize had been members of the Ramblers (punk) and Direktive 17 (indie rock) and performed briefly as the acoustic tandem West Montrose in 1987. With help from singer/songwriter Andrew Cash, a year later, they added Peter Cash, Ron Macey, and Ronny Von Johnny to become the Skydiggers. Playing with or filling in for Andrew Cash at the Spindina Hotel, the newcomers rose quickly on the Toronto music scene and by 1989 had signed on with Enigma Canada. **Skydiggers** is Byrdsian country rock at its best with twangly guitar, pedal steel, and bright lead and harmony vocals, but there's also plenty of smooth, jangly countrified 80s rock with the same fine vocal consistency. Through innumerable drummer changes, the Skydiggers turned out albums in the 90s that stuck close to the winning formula of their debut but also gradually added on some different touches and textures. Their excellent recordings and live performances were honored with awards in 1993 from Juno (Most Promising Group) and COCA (Entertainers of the Year) and with a growing following in Canada and then the U.S.

Peter Cash (g,v,1988-1996); Josh Finlayson (l.g.); Ron Macey (d); Andy Maize (v)

Skydiggers/Enigma Capitol/1989
Restless/fre Capitol/1992
Just Over This Mountain/fre Capitol/1993
Road Radio/Warner/1995
Desmond's Hip City/Hip City/1997

Skydiggers //www.skydiggers.com

Elena Skye & The Demolition String Band

Honky Tonk; Country Rock; Bluegrass
New York City; 1993-

In the late 1980s and early 1990s, the focus of alt. country in New York City was the "Rig Rock" scene built around groups like the World Famous Bluejays, the Blue Chieftains, and Amy Allison & the Maudlins. During the late 1990s, that center shifted somewhat to new weekly showcases such as Greg Garing's Alphabet City Opry. Among the regular performers at these events, one of the most popular was Elena Skye & the Demolition String Band. Leader and co-founder Skye had already been a force in Northeast twang for a number of years as a promoter, organizer, musician, and DJ. She formed the Demolition String Band in 1993 with guitarist Boo Reiners, and after five years of working every conceivable type of venue and media, they released their first CD, **One Dog Town**, in 1998. Produced by Greg Garing, it is quite simply a first-rate offering of honky tonk, bluegrass, country rock, and more. Elena handles lead vocals (soft and sensuous), co-wrote seven of the album's eleven songs (with writing partner Caren Belle), and she plays a mean mandolin having once studied with the great Jethro Burns. Things get rolling with "Biggest Piece of Nothing," a naughty little shuffle about disappointment with a certain overrated organ (and I don't mean Hammond B-3!); then follow a variety of tasty numbers from the tender "Walk Away" to the Tex-Mex "I'll Try Not to Cry Tonight," the amusing honky tonker "It Still Hurts," the country rocking "Up

Close," the twangy instrumental "Are You Armed?," and the rowdy "Get Whtacha Got and Go," live at the Alphabet City Opry. There's even a few snatches of bluegrass on brief covers of "Shuckin' the Corn," Jethro Burns' "Rip Off," and a plunking banjo reprise of "Walk Away." All in all, a highly recommendable debut.

Elena Skye (g,md,l.v.); John Abbey (u.b.); Phil Cimino (d); Boo Reiners (bj,g,l.s.,v);

"Biggest Piece of Nothing" on **Edges From the Postcard2**/P2/1998
One Dog Town/North Hollow/1998

Elena Skye & The DSB c/o North Hollow Records, Box 47 North Hollow Road, Rochester, VT 05767; 802-767-4255; nhollow@sover.net

Elena Skye: MandoSkye@aol.com

Slap Sally Combo

Hillbilly Bop
Helsinki, Finland; 1991-

No, not a sado-masochistic punk group, but rather, a Finnish band that plays traditional boppin' hillbilly music from the 40s and early 50s. Slap Sally refers to their knock-out bass player Katarina Blomqvist's vigorous technique on her poor old upright (she's only broken it once). Her rock solid rhythm anchors the dead on hillbilly picking of guitarist Olli Holopainen and singing of lead vocalist Pasi Nyman. Together since 1991, Slap Sally Combo has only recorded a few singles, an EP, and contributed several songs to Rock-A-Billy Records compilations, but any and all would fit comfortably in Bear Family's **That'll Flat Git It!** collections of classic hillbilly bop and rockabilly. With hot bands like the Barnshakers, Hal Peters, and Slap Sally Combo, Finland must be one hoppin' place on a Saturday night.

Katarina Blomqvist (b); Olli Holopainen (l.g.); Pasi Nyman (r.g.,l.v.)

"Music Makin' Mama" on **The Rock-A-Billy Record Company Compilation, Vol. 1**/Rock-A-Billy/1995
Cotton Patch Hop/Goofin' Fin./1996 (EP)
"Daisy Darling"/Dynamite Magazine #10 Ger./1996
"Barking Up the Wrong Tree" on **The Rock-A-Billy Record Company Compilation, Vol. 2**/Rock-A-Billy/1997
"Somebody Lied" b/w "Three Alley Cats"/Goofin' Fin./1997 (7")

Slap Sally Combo, Mayratie 9 A 5, 00800 Helsinki, Finland

Slap Sally Combo--Hillbilly & Rockabilly Band //www.helsinki.fi/~kblomqvi/slapsallycombo/index.html

katarina.blomqvist@helsinki.fi

See The Barnshakers; Hal Peters

Slim Cessna's Auto Club

Country Rock; Honky Tonk
Denver, Colorado; 1994-

I freely admit I'm a sucker for the accordion, but when you combine it with honky tonk music, well, life just doesn't get any better. Such is the sentiment that seems to underlie Slim Cessna's Auto Club from Denver, Colorado. Formed in 1994, the band is led by none other than Slim Cessna whose vocals have that quavering despair found in Gary Stewart and Jerry Dale McFadden. He's ably backed by Glen Taylor on pedal steel, Jon Killough on drums, and John Rumley on bass and banjo, but what sets them apart from the run of other honky tonk bar bands is Frank Hauser's accordion which gives their music a distinctive Southwestern ambiance. Their 1996 debut, **Slim Cessna's Auto Club**, leads off with the rousing spaghetti western inspired "Hold On" and includes two steppers, polkas, and waltzes sweetened by Hauser's tasteful "stomach Steinway" and Taylor's dreamy steel. **American Country Music Changed Her Life** ("The Soundtrack"), recorded live at Denver's Bluebird Theater in 1997, gets the crowd riled up with the rip snortin' "Lethal Injection" and then things really get weird with a strange Ennio Morricone inspired cover of the traditional "Wade in the Water" and the truly bizarre Middle Eastern/Western "Come Along." From there Slim and company careen through a tender love waltz ("Sometimes I Wonder"), honky tonk ("Never Too Late"; "Lonely in Hell"), hoedown ("Barrel of My Gun"), rock ("Hotter"), the indescribable ("Raven"; "Counting Steps"), and a cover of Kris Kristofferson's "Help Me Make It Through the Night." It all teeters on the edge and is just a whole hell of a lot of fun!

Slim Cessna (g,l.v.); Frank Hauser, Jr. (acc,bj,g); Jon Killough (d); John Rumley (b,bj); Glen Taylor (p.s.,v)

Slim Cessna's Auto Club/SCAC/1996
American Country Music Changed Her Life/
SCAC/1998

Slim Cessna's Auto Club, P.O. Box 103212, Denver, CO 80250; SLIMCESSNA@aol.com

Slim's Cyder Co.

Cajun; Country Rock; Western Swing
London, England; 1994-

One of the mainstays of the very lively Cajun/zydeco scene in London is Slim's Cyder Co. Although their name is based on a very poor play on the word zydeco, the band actually likes to refer to their sound as "rockin' swamp country swing." Their leader, Slim, aka Clive Pain, was a seasoned veteran of the English punk and cowpunk scenes. His musical odyssey began in the late 1970s when he won the Champion Blockhead music competition held in support of Ian Drury's **New Boots and Panties**. First prize led to gigs playing piano with the Blockheads and the Clash on their London Calling tour. Pain

was given the additional duty of serving as guide for the Joe Ely Band who were on the same bill with the Clash. Ely's Texas style country roots music (and perhaps the virtuosity of Ely's accordionist Ponty Bone?) inspired Slim to take up the squeeze-box and throw himself into country influenced music. His first venture in this area was with the country/rockabilly/ska band, Roddy Radiation & the Tearjerkers and then came the cowpunk movement in the mid-1980s. During this time, Slim was a member of the Boothill Foot Tappers, Blubbery Hellbellies ("mostly large chaps playing boisterous music for oversized people"), and the Forest Hillbillies (ska/skiffle/ rockabilly). The Foot Tappers, formed by banjoist Chris Thompson (later leader of Bigjig), were fairly successful with several albums and a hit single "Get Your Feet Out of My Shoes" but were done in by record label politics. After cowpunk went out, Slim did session work with Billy Bragg, Primal Scream, and the Rockingbirds and maintained his Texas connection backing Ely, Butch Hancock, Jimmie Dale Gilmore, Robert Earl Keen , and Jesse Taylor whenever tours brought them to England. Slim also found time to form his Cyder Co. band with members of various country/rockabilly/Cajun bands including the Hackney Ramblers (Chrissie Lane, James Morrison, Jeff Mead); the Rhythm Wranglers (Chrissie Lane, Jeff Mead); the Prairies (Patrick Hogan). Slim's Cyder Co. did one self-released tape with covers of "Crazy," "Who Walks In?," "Jukebox of Your Heart," "Walk on By," "So Long Baby" (Dave Alvin), "Bare Necessities" (the Disney song) plus classics from the Blubbery Hellbellies, "My Baby She's as Fat as Me" and "Is It Love or Food Poisoning?" In addition to regular club dates on the local Cajun/zydeco circuit, Slim's Cyder Co. has been on the same bill with touring groups such as the Neville Brothers and the Texas Tornados. And, Slim also managed to find time to make periodic pilgrimages to Austin, Texas, where he could renew his old musical acquaintances.

Slim aka Clive Pain (acc,v); Paul Hookham (d); Patrick Horgan (b); Chrissie Lane (v); Jeff Mead (b,g,l.s.); James Morrison (f,md); Paul Seacroft (g)

Slim's Cyder Co./SCC/1995 (CS)
Slim's Cyder Space
//webzone1.co.uk/www/cyderco/slim.htm

slim@cyder.demon.co.uk

Slobberbone

Insurgent Country
Denton, Texas; 1992-

It seems appropriate that a band which began in the back room of a liquor store and plays intense rock/country/punk focused on disturbing themes like boozing, wrenching heartache, and brutal death should be named for an object well chewed by a dog. Slobberbone was started in 1992 in Denton, Texas, by a group of friends bonded by a fondness for music and drinking.

All had dabbled in a succession of musical trends, but it was the cowpunk and roots rock of the 1980s that hooked them. Led by lead singer and songwriter Brent Best, the band played around the North Texas area for a number of years before cutting the self released **Crow Pot Pie** in 1995. Shortly thereafter, charter members, Lee Pearson and Ed Alderson, split just as Slobberbone was about to sign a deal with Doolittle Records out of Austin. With a new bassist (Brian Lane), lead guitarist (Michael Hill), and fiddler (Scott Danbom), the group did a revamped version of **Crow Pot Pie**. This recording plus a showcase at SXSW 1996 with the Hangdogs and Whiskeytown gained them second looks from the alt. country community including a short profile in *No Depression*. And while often labeled country roots rock, Slobberbone made it clear that the emphasis should be on ROCK. Thematically, the band covers familiar country ground especially drinking ("Whiskey Glass Eye"; "Sober Song"; "Stumblin'" and numerous other alcohol related songs), and there are occasional twangy undertones (fiddle, guitar), but for the most part, Slobberbone cranks it up into high gear and never looks back. This is particularly true of **Barrel Chested** which, in the credits, tells the listener, "Remember: It's Rock." The recording (with Lloyd Maines and Susan Voelz) has a couple of countryish ballads ("Little Drunk Fists"; "One Rung") and a bit of bluegrass ("Engine Joe"), but the majority is flat out nose bleeding, ear ringing "twang-thrash" ("Haze of Drink"; "I'll Be Damned"; "Lame"). Slobberbone got to express their traditional country side with a cover of "Dark as a Dungeon" on 1997's **Straight Outta Boone County**. **Barrel Chested** sold well especially in The Netherlands, and the band toured there in late 1998. A special EP, **Your Excuse**, with "Dark As a Dungeon," acoustic versions of "Little Drunk Fists" and "Barrel Chested" plus the previously unreleased instrumental "Boy Howdy" was issued by the Dutch label Sonic Rendezvous to coincide with the tour.

Ed Alderson (b,1992-1995); Jess Barr (l.g.,1997-); Brent Best (a.g.,e.g.,hm,md,sl.g,l.v.); Scott Danbom (f,1995-1997); Michael Hill (l.g.,1995-1997); Tony Harper (d); Brian Lane (b,1995-); Lee Pearson (l.g,1992-1995)

> **Crow Pot Pie**/Slobberbone/1995; Doolittle/1996
> "Get Gone With You" on **Dallas Scene, Heard, Vol. 2**/
>   Dallas Observer/1996
> **Barrel Chested**/Doolittle/1997
> "Dark as a Dungeon" on **Straight Outta Boone County**/
>   Blodshot/1997
> **Your Excuse**/Sonic Rendezvous Dut./1998 (EP)
> "Engine Joe" on **New Highway**/Boka Discs/1999

Slobberbone, 712 W. Sycamore, Denton, TX 76201; 817-382-0185

Slobberbone/Doolittle Page
//www.doolittle.com/bio_slobber.html

slobber@doolittle.com

The Sloe Gin Joes
Roots Rock; Rockabilly
San Francisco, California; 1995-

According to their leader Frank Novicki, the Sloe Gin Joes live by three simple rules: twangy guitar is cool; songs about food, dancing, and girls are very profound; and rockin' like crazy is the only reason to step on stage. For several years, the Joes have been practicing what they preach in clubs all over San Francisco. Prior to founding the group, Novicki was lead guitarist in a wild instrumental surf rock combo called the Shockwaves which cut the highly praised **Primal Twang** in 1991. In the early 1990s, Novicki toured with the Forbidden Pigs and Rosie Flores, and produced the Legendary Stardust Cowboy before forming the Sloe Gin Joes with Mike Burns and Dez Mab. Though most often called a rockabilly band, the Joes are really much more of a roots rock outfit mixing up hillbilly, rock 'n' roll, swing, blues, and r&b. Their debut was recorded live at the Ivy Room before an audience of exactly 39 who were treated to a fun filled set of covers (Ray Price's "I Can't Go Home Like This" and Terry Clement's "She's My Baby Doll") and Novicki originals including "Fryin' Pan," "Gettin' a Dog," "Chicken Stew," and "Hot Link," a tribute to Link Wray, one of the band's major influences. In early 1997, the Sloe Gin Joes were named one of the top bands in the Bay Area, and in 1998, they contributed a rousing cover of "This Is It" to **Blastered: A Musical Tribute to the Blasters**.

Mike Burns (d); Dez Mab (b); Frank Novicki (l.g.,l.v.)

> **The Sloe Gin Joes**/Ever Cool/1997
> "This Is It" on **Blastered: A Musical Tribute to The Blasters**/Run Wild/1998

The Sloe Gin Joes, 2966 Diamond St., Box 169, San Francisco, CA 94131; 415-469-8487

The Sloe Gin Joes Home Page
//members.aol.com/sloginjoes/sgj.html

SloGinJoes@aol.com

Greg Dean Smalley
Redneck Underground
Cedartown, Georgia; September 3, 1964-March 25, 1996

Every alternative country scene has an individual who embodies its unique spirit. In the case of Atlanta's Redneck Underground, that person is Greg Dean Smalley who gained legendary status within the RU community as a musician, promoter, and all around flamboyant hillbilly character. Like many RU performers, Smalley emerged from the scene created by Slim Chance & the Convicts at the local Austin Avenue Buffet in the late 1980s. It became a magnet for individuals like Smalley who were tired of rock and pop country and wanted a taste of good old honky tonk, swing, and rockabilly. Over the next ten years, Smalley became a central figure in what came to be known as the Redneck Underground. Short and lean, decked out in work/bowling shirts, greasy pompadour, and dangling an ever present cigarette, Smalley fronted or was a member of over two dozen bands. His own groups included the Diggers, Gregory Dean and the Hicktones, and Gregory Dean and the Bubbamatics; he played with many others including the Crackers, Screaming Winnebagos of Love, Them Fresh Pig Knuckles, Slim Chance & the Convicts, Jennie B. & the Speedbillies, Redneck Greece Delux, and the Blacktop Rockets. However, Smalley's most enduring contribution was his idea to put on a music festival that would serve as a showcase for the Redneck Underground. Dubbed Bubbapalooza, the inaugural festival was held at the Star Community Bar in 1990 and featured the Diggers, Southern Culture on the Skids, Slim Chance, the Delta Angels, the Vidalias, and other charter members of the RU. It soon became an annual three day event and in 1995 led to the release of **Bubbapalooza**, a collection of songs by Redneck Underground bands that helped spread the word to a wider audience. Smalley was the chief compiler of this recording and became the leading RU spokesman ever ready to state in his blunt, down home way just what is wrong with Nashville and so right about the RU. Unfortunately, during this period, Smalley, although not in a high risk group, was diagnosed as HIV positive. However, even as his condition steadily deteriorated, Smalley continued to perform sometimes in a wheelchair and sometimes until he had to be carried from the stage. Yet, in spite of his open defiance of death, Smalley finally succumbed on March 25, 1996 with friends and family around his bed and Elvis' "How Great Thou Art" playing softly in the background. Two days later, the RU community held a musical celebration of the man and his legacy at Atlanta's High Hat. They built a more permanent memorial in 1998 with **Bubbapalooza Two: A Tribute to Gregory Dean Smalley** which includes his originals done by Smalley with Kelly Hogan, the Diggers, the Bubbamatics, and the Chant or by Redneck Undergound bands (Redneck Greece & The Stump Broke Steers; Slim Chance; Lost Continentals; Truckadelic). Also along are the Drive-By Truckers with the ultimate Gregory Dean tirbute, "The Living Bubba."

"She's Breakin' My Heart, While I'm Drinkin' Her Beer" (The Diggers) on **Bubbapalooza, Vol. 1**/Sky/1995
Bubbapalooza Two: Tribute to Gregory Dean Smalley/Criminal/1998

Greg Dean Smalley Memorial Page
//www.mindspring.com/~estuck/greg.htm

Darden Smith
Austin; Singer/Songwriter
Brenham, Texas; March 11, 1962-

Darden Smith got into writing songs while attending the University of Texas at Austin in the early 1980s. There, he mingled with other aspiring musicians including Lyle Lovett and Nanci Griffith who provided guest vocals on Smith's debut **Native Soil**. They also appeared on his stunning major label debut **Darden Smith** which came out in 1988. With backing from Asleep at the Wheel (Ray Benson, Chris O'Connell, John Ely, Floyd Domino, Larry Franklin, Tim Alexander, David Sanger) plus Roland Denny, Paul Pearcy, and zydeco artists C. J. and Cleveland Chenier, Smith comes into his own on a variety of original Texas/Third Coast music including poignant story ballads ("Two Dollar Novels"; "Love Me Like a Soldier"), old-timey ("Little Maggie"), r&b ("Day After Tomorrow"), country rock ("Want You By My Side"; "Talk to Me"), and zydecoish ("God's Will"). After another recording of country/folk/rock material, **Trouble No More**, Smith went in a different direction collaborating with Boo Hewerdine and moving into folky pop that was well received but a long way from his roots. Still, his early recordings are well worth seeking out.

Native Soil/Watermelon/1986
Darden Smith/Epic/1988
Trouble No More/Columbia/1990

Darden Smith/Plump Records Home Page
//www.plump.com/plump/dardart.html
Folk Book Index for Darden Smith
//www.execpc.com/~henkle/fbindex/s/smith/smith_darden.html

Todd Snider
Roots Rock
Portland, Oregon; October 11, 1966-

Born in Portland, Oregon, Todd Snider moved to Austin, Texas in his late teens and inspired by Billy Joe Shaver, Jerry Jeff Walker, and other members of the outlaw movement began writing songs. Relocating to Memphis, Snider set up shop at a local club called The Daily Planet absorbing more influences (Dylan, John Prine) and polishing up his act. Eventually, he was signed by Jimmy Buffett's Margaritaville label which released **Songs for the Daily Planet**. On it, Snider spins his signature social satire taking on child abuse ("You Think You Know Somebody"), imperialism ("This Land is Our Land"), the record business ("Easy Money"), and generally poking fun at his contemporaries ("My Generation, Part 2"; "Alright Guy"; "Talking Seattle Grunge Rock Blues"). Among those providing the country/roots/rock backing are lead guitarist Eddie Shaver (Billy Joe penned the liner notes). For his second recording, **Step Right Up**, Snider assembled the Nervous Wrecks for a session that rocks a little harder than its predecessor but once again offers pithy commentary on the ills of contemporary society ("T.V. Guide"; "Side Show Blues"; "24 Hours a Day"; "Prison Walls"; "I Believe You"). In addition Snider worked on various side projects including a part in the radio play production of *Fear and Loathing in Las Vegas*, co-writing with Jack Ingram ("Airways Motel"), dueting with Joe Ely on a Buddy Holly tribute record, and putting on the What the Folk Fest in Memphis (1997 featured Steve Earle, Jack Ingram, and Joe Ely). **Viva Satellite From Memphis, Tennessee**, released in early 1998, covers Neil Young ("Roll Another Number"), Jimmy Buffett ("Margaritaville"), and Hank, Jr. ("Whiskey Bent and Hell Bound") with guest appearances by Ingram, Kevin Kinney, and a bunch of Memphis musicians. However, within a few months Snider had falling outs with his record label and band and parted with both. Performing as a solo for the remainder of the year, he signed with John Prine's Oh Boy Records and workd on a new album of "gospel songs, anarchy songs, and drinking songs" with the tentative title, **Happy To Be Here**.

The Nervous Wrecks: Will Kimbrough (bj,db,l.g.,h.v.); Joe Mariencheck (b); Joe McLeary (d)

    Songs for the Daily Planet/Margaritaville MCA/1994
    Step Right Up/Margaritaville MCA/1996
    Viva Satellite From Memphis, Tennessee/Margaritaville
      MCA/1998
    Happy To Be Here/Oh Boy/1999

Todd Snider Home Page
//www.todd-snider.com

Solid Air
Country Rock
Sonoma, California; 1990-

Sonoma County, California's, Allegra Broughton and Sam Page have been performing together since 1983. Originally a duo, they expanded their act in 1990 to include a full band which they named Solid Air. **Love and Desire** and **Heartbreak Town** present originals by Broughton (sometimes in collaboration with bassist Page) about love and heartbreak but without the schmaltz and goo of new country. Solid Air rises above the usual Nashville fare by relying on a solid line up of supporting musicians including pedal steel marvel Joe Goldmark, Evan Marshall on fiddle and mandolin, and long time Bay Area dobro champ Sally Van Meter. Their sound has often invited comparisons to the country rock of the Flying Burrito Brothers and the folk rock of Gregson & Collister; their performances earned feature articles in *Acoustic Guitar* and *Performing Songwriter* plus a 1992 nomination for the *San Francisco Weekly*'s Alternative Music Awards.

Allegra Broughton (g); Sam Page (b) with Rick Cutler (d); Joe Goldmark (p.s.); Evan Marshall (f,md); Sally Van Meter (db,s.g.)

    Songs From the Heart (Broughton and Page)/1981
    Slow Fire (Broughton and Page)/1984
    Across the River (Broughton and Page)/1988
    Stand Up for Love (Broughton and Page)/1990
    Love and Desire/Solid Air/1992
    Heartbreak Town/Globe/1996

Solid Air, P. O. Box 733, Penngrove, CA 94951

Solid Air/Globe Records Home Page
//www.globerecords.com/solidair/

Somebody's Darling (Tine Valand)
Singer/Songwriters
Oslo, Norway; 1992-

Tine Valand and Liz Tove Vespestad began their musical collaboration while attending school in England and first performed in their native Norway as a trio along with guitarist Geir Sundstol (later with Jimmie Dale Gilmore). As Somebody's Darling, Valand and Vespestad made their recording debut in 1993 on a self titled release that has all the elements of greatness: Tine and Tove share exquisite lead and harmony vocals rivaling the best of Emmylou or Quartette; they are supported by a stellar international cast of musicians highlighted by the lead guitar, mandolin, and dobro of Sundstol and the fiddle and pedal steel of Fats Kaplin (Tom Russell Band); their song selection includes clever, literate originals by both plus a wide variety of covers (Los Lobos, Steve Wynn, Tom Russell/Katy Moffatt, Maria McKee). In Norway alone, this album sold upwards of 70,000 copies (only 4 million total population), earned a nomination for best Norwegian country/roots record, reached number 1 on England's import chart, and two videos from the album ("That's Why I Wear Black"; "You'll Remember Me") won the CMT International Video-artist of the Year. However, in the U.S., Somebody's Darling was generally ignored except by alt. country critics, insiders, and musicians. One of the latter who took notice was Kieran Kane who invited them to sing harmony vocals on two tracks of his **Dead Reckoning**. After **Forever From Now On**, which continues the quality performances of their debut, the duo decided to pursue individual singing careers. Valand was first to put out a solo effort in late 1996 with **She's Just Leavin'** (recorded in Austin). In the finest tradition of Somebody's Darling, she used Norwegian and American musicians (Kaplin, Sundstol) on a fine collection of her own compositions and songs by Guy Clark, Tom Russell, David Halley, Iain Matthews, and Russell Smith. Produced by Tom Russell's guitarist Andrew Hardin, one of its many high points is a duet with Guy Clark on Russell's, "Mineral Wells, Texas."

Tine Valand (l.v.,h.v.); Liz Tove Vespestad (l.v.,h.v.)

    Somebody's Darling/Sonet Nor./1993
    Forever For Now/Sonet Nor./1994
    She's Just Leavin' (Tine Valand)/Sony Nor./1996

Tine Valand Home //www.union.no/tinevaland

Son Volt
No Depression
St. Louis, Missouri; 1995-

Out of the much lamented break up of Uncle Tupelo, two groups emerged: Wilco and Son Volt. The latter, founded in 1995 by Jay Farrar, stuck closest to UT's original country/roots/rock formula alternating hard edged rock with somber country songs exploring the darker aspects of life in the rural

Midwest. Rounding out Son Volt was former UT drummer Mike Heidorn, Jim Boquist on bass, mutli-instrumentalist Dave Boquist, and part timer Eric Heywood on pedal steel. Their first recording, **Trace**, was hailed as one of the great all-time alt. country albums for moving songs like "Windfall" and "Tear Stained in Eye." On tour throughout 1996 and early 1997, Son Volt tried out its new material on audiences across the U.S. and Europe but seemed to draw the most enthusiastic response for reprising "Postcard," "Grindstone," "Chickamauga," and other popular songs from Uncle Tupelo days. As direct heirs to the UT tradition, Son Volt (and Wilco) became one of the major focal points of the current alternative country movement inspiring numerous Internet mailing lists and a host of imitators. Ironically, Farrar (Tweedy too) generally ignored or even rejected the whole alt. country phenomenon from fear of being pigeonholed and misunderstood. But, like it or not, Son Volt undoubtedly remained at the forefront of the no depression school of alt. country. That uncomfortable position was further cemented by **Straightaways** which rocks hard in places but really clicks on the quartet of closing acoustic numbers which, for better or worse, inevitably conjure up the spirit of Uncle Tupelo. In addition to a 1997 performance on *Austin City Limits*, Son Volt was involved in a number of alt. country side projects including a track ("Looking at the World Through a Windshield") on **Rig Rock Deluxe** and backing Kelly Willis on her EP **Fading Fast**. In 1998, Warner Brothers released a four track EP, **Switchback**, with non-album and live material and later that year came the new full-length, **Wide Swing Tremolo,** which has a more rocked-up-tempo than Son Volt's previous offerings. An electric tour to support it was preceded by an interesting all-acoustic tour covering smaller venues around the country. Farrar, brother Dade, Heidorn, and Brian Henneman and Tom Parr of the Bottlerockets, recording under the name Sir Omaha Quintet, contributed "Weighted Down" to the 1998 Skip Spence (Moby Grape) tribute **More Oar**.

Jay Farrar (g,l.v.); Dave Boquist (bj,db,f,l.g.,l.s.); Jim Boquist (b,b.v.); Mike Heidorn (d) with Eric Heywood (p.s.)

Trace/Warner Brothers/1995
Live (Minneapolis, 10-16-95)/Twin City Digital/1996
Live (Minneapolis, 12-21-95)/Twin City Digital/1996
Live (Minneapolis, 12-22-95)/Twin City Digital/1996
"Looking at the World Through a Windshield" on
   Rig Rock Deluxe/Upstart Diesel Only/1996
Straightaways/Warner Brothers/1997
Route 35/Strider/1997 (boot)
Switchback/Warner Brothers/1998 (EP)
Wide Swing Tremolo/Warner Brothers/1998
"Weighted Down" (as Sir Omaha Quintet) on **More Oar:**
   A Tribute To the Alexander "Skip" Spence
   Album/1998

Official Son Volt Page
//www.wbr.com/SonVolt

Unofficial Son Volt Home Page
//www.gumbopages.com/son-volt.html

Brad Lumley's Son Volt Page
//chattanooga.net/~mlumley/son_volt/son_volt.htm

Living Free: Son Volt Page
//www.geocities.com/SunsetStrip/towers/6433

Ten Second News: Son Volt
//www.geocities.com/sunsetstrip/towers/2218/

Son Volt Links Archive
//www.geocities.com/sunsetstrip/towers/5656/sonvolt.html

Son Volt/iMusic Modern Rock Showcase Page
//imusic.com/showcase/sonvolt.html

Son Volt, Wilco, Uncle Tupelo Lyrics
//www.usinternet.com/users/yoflute/index.html

Jay Farrar Ascetic Lifestyle Home Page
//darkwing.uoregon.edu/~dougr/index.html

Postcard: The Uncle Tupelo, Wilco, Son Volt On Line
Mailing List //www.servtech.com/ddewey/postcard/

Passenger Side (Postcard2): The Alternative/Insurgent
Country Music On Line Mailing List
//www.gumbopages.com/music/pass-side.html

Son Volt AOL Folder: Entertainment>Music>Chat & Messages>Music Community>Alternative>Alternative Bands, S-Z

No Depression AOL Folder: Entertainment>Music>Chat & Messages>Music Community>Alternative>Alternative Topics

See Uncle Tupelo; Wilco

Songs: Ohia

Lo-Fi Roots Rock
Cleveland, Ohio; 1995-

Songs: Ohia has most often been compared with Palace and for a number of good reasons. They both revolve around the persona and vision of one individual; what Will Oldham is to Palace, Jason Molina is to Songs: Ohia. Each dreams up all their own songs and record alone or with minimal accompaniment from an ever-changing cast of characters (although Molina doesn't perpetually change the name he records under as Oldham is prone to do). Like Will, Jason is moody and introspective, likes to keep it lo-fi, has a whispery, whiny voice, and is fascinated with biblical topics ("Nor Cease Thou Never Now.."; "Sin & Death"; "One Pronunciation of Glory") and rural landscapes ("Crab Orchard"; "Cotton Hill"; "Dogwood Gap"; "White Sulphur"). Songs: Ohia has also paralleled Oldham/Palace by putting out a bewildering array of singles, EPs, CDs, etc. on obscure labels in the U.S. and Europe. Fittingly, **Songs: Ohia**/Jason Molina's first single was issued by Oldham's Palace Records in 1995 and while the Palace similarities general hold true, Songs: Ohia has at times ventured away from the shadowy Appalachian country feel toward a sound that still drags but also picks it up a bit on a wider variety of material. Songs: Ohia's 1999 **Axxess and Ace** features lo-fi cowgirl Edith Frost guesting on several cuts including "Love Leaves Its Abuser" and "Capt. Badass."

"Boys"/Wingnut Magazine/1995 (7")
Nor Cease Thou Never Now.../Palace/1995 (7")
One Pronunciation of Glory/Secretly Canadian/1996 (7")
Songs: Ohia/Secretly Canadian/1997
"For the Neighbors of Our Age" on **Sounds of the Geographically Challenged**/Temporary Residence/1997
Hecla & Griper/Secretly Canadian/1997 (CD EP)
Impala/Secretly Canadian/1998
"Vanquisher"/Hatfever Magazine Ger./1998 (7")
"Still Around" on **Songs From the Loosing End**/Krank No./1998
"Nay, 'Tis Not Death"/Liquefication UK/1998
Axxess and Ace/Secretly Canadian/1999
"Sin & Death" on **Zum Compilation**/Zum/1999

Songs: Ohia //php.indiana.edu/~bjswanso/ohia/

Songs: Ohia Fan Page
//www.si-net.com/~kiz/songs_news.htm

See Edith Frost; Will Oldham

Souled American

Lo-Fi Country
Chicago, Illinois; 1987-

Souled American are the original practitioners of lo-fi country (*Trouser Press Guide* called their sound "country 'n' strychnine"). Formed in the late 1980s in Chicago by Joe Adducci and Chris Grigoroff, the band made a particularly strong showing at SXSW in 1988 and got a deal with Rough Trade. Their early recordings (**Fe, Flubber**, and **Around the Horn**) mixed country with rock, reggae, and New Orleans but with a very slow tempo accentuated by Adducci and Grigoroff's droning, twangy vocals. Souled American decelerated even more on **Sonny**, a snails' pace tribute to traditional country covering the likes of the Louvin Brothers and Merle Travis. After Rough Trade suddenly evaporated, Souled American seemingly dropped off the map, but rumors of their demise were greatly exaggerated. Adducci and Grigoroff kept the band together and, still based in Chicago, began to tour heavily in Europe. In 1994, they found a musical home with the German Moll Records where they became the "masters of abstract slow motion country-folk." On **Frozen** and **Notes Campfire**, Souled American scale traditional music down to single tones, long guitar chords, intermittent drumdots, and mournful singing. This is minimalism bordering on nominalism that makes groups like Palace, the Handsome Family, and the Cowboy Junkies seem like speeding bullets. In 1998, Souled American was "rediscovered" by American audiences when they got a spread in *No Depression*, and their first four albums were reissued by Tumult Records on two double discs and Checkered Past rereleased **Frozen** and **Notes Campfire**. Rock journalist Camden Joy has written a book about the band that is available through Tract Home Publications.

Original Members: Joe Adducci (b,g,v); Jamey Barnard (d); Chris Grigoroff (g,v); Scott Tuma (g)

Current Members: Joe Adducci; Chris Grigoroff; Scott Lucas (d); Brian Smith (tp); Scott Tuma

Fe/Rough Trade/1988
Flubber/Rough Trade/1989
Around the Horn/Rough Trade/1990
Sonny/Rough Trade/1992
Frozen/Moll Ger./1994; Checkered Past/1998
Notes Campfire/Moll Ger./1997; Checkered Past/1999
Fe & Flubber/Tumult/1998
Around the Horn & Sonny/Tumult/1998

Souled American/Moll Records Home Page
//www.spontan.de/moll

Tumult Records, P.O. Box 642371, San Francisco, CA 94164-2371; tumult666@hotmail.com

Tract Home Publications, P.O. Box 14806, Portland, OR 97293

Sourdough Slim aka Rick Crowder

Cowboy/Western; Accordion; Yodeling
Hollywood, California; 1950-

When Rick Crowder was growing up in Hollywood and on his family's ranch near the Sierra Mountains, little did he dream that one day he would become an acclaimed Western performer like something straight out of old singing cowboy movies. In the 1970s and early 1980s, he worked for a logging company in Oregon and UPS in Chico, California, where he was also in some country bands and acquired the nickname "Slim." Somewhere along this time, Crowder donned wool pants tucked into ornate cowboy boots, big white hat, cotton shirt, scarf, and vest and was transformed into Sourdough Slim. He learned accordion and taught himself to yodel in the attic of his house (much to his neighbors' delight, I'm sure), and in 1988 decided to let 'er buck full-time as Sourdough Slim. Fascinated with both cowboy music and vaudeville, Slim created a stage show *a la* Riders in the Sky complete with music, jokes, and stories. He has since become a favorite on the cowboy/Western festival circuit and did several satisfying recordings of classic and original cowboy music as a solo and with the Saddle Pals (Cactus Bob Cole and Chris "Prairie Flower" Stevenson) on Roundup Records. In 1997, Sourdough Slim performed at Carnegie Hall as part of a special Singing Cowboys program.

Yodeling Cowboy/Roundup/1995
True West/Roundup/1996
Goin' To the West (with the Saddle Pals)/Roundup/1997
Ridin' High, Singin' a Song/Roundup/1998

Sourdough Slim, P.O. Box 2021, Paradise, CA 95967; 916-872-1187

Sourdough Slim Online
//www.twc-online.com/custom/sourdough-slim/

See Randy Erwin; Skip Gorman; Riders in the Sky; Wylie & The Wild West

Southern Culture on the Skids

Hillbilly/Rockabilly; Surf; White Trash Parody
Chapel Hill, North Carolina; 1985-

Southern Culture on the Skids combine swamp rock and boogie blues with country, surf, and rockabilly in songs whose themes touch the hearts of rednecks everywhere. They are especially big on cars ("Voodoo Cadillac"; "Dirt Track Date") and food ("8 Piece Box"; "Biscuit Eater"; "Fried Chicken and Gasoline"). Hell, they even pass out fried chicken at their live performances to the women who come up on stage to cavort and gyrate to the "Camel Walk," "New Cooter Boogie," and "Cicada Rock." Masterminding this good time craziness is Rick Miller who formed SCOTS in 1985 with fellow University of North Carolina student Stan Lewis. In two years together, they released an EP (**Voodoo Beach Party**) and the full length **Southern Culture on the Skids** but parted company in 1987. Shortly after that, Rick met Virginia native Mary Huff who was playing bass in a rockabilly band, the Phantoms. She joined Rick and then enlisted drummer friend Dave Hartman, and the current version of SCOTS was born. For a time, they lived in an isolated backwoods house affectionately called Kudzu Ranch. Here, they developed a swamp rock sound ("Surruralism") highlighted not only by Miller's lead guitar work and twangy vocals but also by Huff's straight rockabilly singing that do Wanda Jackson proud and wailing that puts Yma Sumac to shame. In 1990, SCOTS began a mind boggling string of compilation cuts, singles, EP, 10", and LP/CDs. Their first full length was **Too Much Pork for Just One Fork**, released by Moist Records. When that label went under, SCOTS were picked up by Safe House which put out **For Lovers Only** in 1992. By this time, the band was committed to music full time and began to tour incessantly playing not only clubs but also porn movie houses, prisons, and proms. In addition to another album for SafeHouse (**Ditch Diggin'**) in 1994, SCOTS did a number of side projects including an EP, **Santo Sings!**, dedicated to the Mexican wrestler/movie star, and several singles as Los Falanas with Gibson Brother, Don Howland. In 1995, the band broke through to national attention with their major album debut **Dirt Track Date** and its very catchy tune "Soul City." And although some critics have accused them of demeaning certain segments of Southern society, their act (much, much hipper than Jeff Foxworthy) isn't mean spirited and seems to be well received by "redneck"/"white trash" audiences at events like Bubbapalooza and Sleazefest. In 1997, **Plastic Seat Sweat** (named for a recliner) continued the ribald, backwoods merrymaking with "Shotgun," "Earthmover," "Love-A-Rama," "Deja Varoom," and "Carve That Possum." For 1998, SCOTS left Geffen (with no hard feelings), did their second Australian tour, and recorded **Zombified!**, an eight song EP of horror movie theme songs just in time for Halloween. The only black mark on an otherwise successful year was the theft of two vintage guitars (1958 Gibson Les Paul; 1956 Gretsch Country Club) and two vintage basses (1971 Fender Precision; Jerry Jones Four-String) after shows in Salt Lake City and San Francisco. Rewards were offered for their return.

Dave Hartman (d); Mary Huff (b,v); Rich Miller (g,v)

Voodoo Beach Party/SCOTS/1984 (EP)
Southern Culture on the Skids/Lloyd St./1985 (LP)
"O-O Spy"; "Cicada Rock"; "Suede Pussycat" on
 Bible Belt Warbling/Blast/1990
"Clyde's Lament" b/w "C. W. James"/Moist/1990 (7")
Too Much Pork for One Fork/Moist/1991
"Roll Another for the Road" (as Uncle Dave Bacon & The
 Toxic Pig Fucks) on **Marijuana's Greatest Hits
 Revisited**/ReHash/1992
Santo Sings/Zontar/1992; Estrus/1996 (EP)
For Lovers Only/Safehouse/1992
"Come and Get It" b/w "Cicada Rock"/Giant Claw/1993
Girlfight/SFTRI/1993 (10")
"Nakema" b/w "Johnny B. Badd" (with Don Howland as
 Los Falanas)/SFTRI/1993 (7")
"Cockroach Blues" b/w "Bird Nest Blues" (with Don
 Howland as Los Falanas)/SFTRI/1994 (7")
Peckin' Party/Feedbag/1993 (10", CD)
Ditch Diggin'/Safehouse/1994 (CD; LP picture disc)
"White Trash" b/w "I'm Branded"/Demolition Derby/1994
"The Swag" on **Think Link!**/Drink 'n' Drive/1994 (10")
"Tantrum" b/w "Tantrum" (with Don Howland as Los
 Falanas)/SFTRI/1995 (7")
"Hell Blues" b/w "Taxman Blues" (with Don Howland as
 Los Falanas)/SFTRI/1995 (7")
"2 Pigs in a Blanket/She's My Little Biscuit Eater" on
 Bubbapalooza/Sky/1995
"Moonshine Martinis" on **Estrus Cocktail
 Companion**/Estrus/1995 (3 x 7")
Dirt Track Date/Geffen/1995; Telstar/1995 (LP, CD)
"Mudbuggy" & "Hubcap Hunch (with Hasil Adkins) on
 Sleazefest/Sleazy Spoon/1995
Plastic Seat Sweat/DGC/1997
Zombified!/SCOTS/1998 (EP)

SCOTS Home Page //www.scots.com

SCOTS iMusic Showcase //imusic.com/showcase/modern/

See Hasil Adkins; The Gibson Brothers

The Spanic Boys (The Spanic Family)

Electric Guitar; Roots Rock; Close Harmony
Milwaukee, Wisconsin; 1987-

Music can divide generations or bring them together. The Spanic Boys are a lucky example of the latter. Father Tom was into country and rock 'n' roll way back in 1956 when at the tender age of twelve his parents bought him a Stratocaster and then a steel guitar. Over the years, he played in a number of groups in Milwaukee and was even a classical guitar teacher for a time at the Wisconsin Conservatory of Music. Later, after he gave his son Ian a Strat, the two began jamming at home and then in public as Oh Those Spanic Boys. They developed their signature sound of twangy Everly Brothers type harmonies and hot guitar playing borrowed from Merle Travis, Les Paul, Chet Atkins, and Gene Vincent but also displayed their own special touches. A debut recording of original songs in 1988 led to an invitation to SXSW in 1988 where the Spanic Boys were rewarded with a contract from Rounder Records. This led to a series of fine albums (most notably **Strange World**), lots of touring, and an appearance on *Saturday Night Live* (in place of Sinead O'Connor who wouldn't appear on the show when it was hosted by Andrew Dicc Clay). In 1994, the Spanic Boys switched labels, added cousin Butch on guitar, and changed their name to the Spanic Family. The result was the **Spanic Family Album**, another impressive collection of honky tonk, country rock, and rockabilly. In 1997, Ian Spanic produced the Riptones' **Extra Sauce**, and the Spanic Boys recorded **Walk Through Fire**, 12 originals filled with twangy guitar and harmonies but available through mail order only.

Ian Spanic (e.g.,v); Tom Spanic (e.g.,v); Butch Spanic (e.g.,v)

Strange World/Rounder/1991
Early Spanic Boys/Rounder/1992
Dream Your Life Away/Rounder/1993
Spanic Family Album/ESD/1994
Walk Through Fire/SB/1998

Don't Panic! It's The Spanics! //www.spanicboys.com
info@spanicboys.com

Sparklehorse
Roots Rock
Richmond, Virginia; 1995-

Like the Silos, Palace, and Songs: Ohia, Sparklehorse is basically a one-man operation surrounded by a rotating community of musicians. Growing up in Virginia, Mark Linkous listened to bluegrass, country, punk, and pop, and in the late 1980s was in the Dancing Hoods, a rock band that tried hard but couldn't. So, Linkous returned to Richmond to recuperate from a mental breakdown and did some tapes at home that got channeled to Capitol Records by an old acquantaince, David Lowery (Camper Van Beethoven; Cracker). A contract was forth coming and led to **Vivadixiesubmarinetransmissionplot** whose odd title came from a dream Linkous had about swimming toward General Lee's submarine from which was emanating old-time music. Co-produced by Lowery (as David Charles), it features Linkous on vocals, guitar, organ, mellotron, echoharp, banjo, and more backed by Charles (drums, guitar), Bob Rupe (ex-Silos; Cracker) on bass, Johnny Hott on drums, and Mike Lucas on pedal steel. Its vascillation between languid country ballads, harder electric rock, and a variety of pop sounds hooked a growing underground of fans in the U.S. but especially in England. During a Sparklehorse tour stop in London in early 1997, an accidental combination of Valium and anti-depressants left Linkous unconscious on a hotel bathroom floor. He had a heart attack and was clinically dead for several moments, but even worse was the loss of circulation in his legs (trapped under him for over 12 hours) which led to multiple operations to save one of them. Subsequent confinement to a

wheel chair brought him closer to old friend Vic Chesnutt who has been paralyzed and wheel chair bound for most of his life; Linkous, Chesnutt, Lowery, and Kurt Wagner and Paul Niehaus of Lambchop had previously teamed up as A Loose Confederation of Saturday City States to cut a single of lo-fi Southern gothic. Vic helped Mark with his recovery, and Sparklehorse later contributed a cover of "West of Rome" to **Sweet Relief II: The Songs of Vic Chesnutt**. In 1998, Sparklehorse recorded **Good Morning Spider** with Linkous (who still had to use leg braces) once again showing remarkable dexterity on mulitple instruments (optigan?) with support from a new group of musicians with guest appearances by Lowery, Chesnutt, and Stephen McCarthy (ex-Long Ryders) on pedal steel. As of the end of 1998, it was only available in the U.K. but alt. country/roots rock fans were clamoring for its release in the U.S. in 1999.

"Spirit Ditch"/Slow River/1995 (7")
Vivadixiesubmarinetransmissionplot/Capitol/1995
"West of Rome" on **Sweet Relief II, Gravity of the
    Situation: The Songs of Vic Chesnutt**/Atlantic/1995
Chords I've Known/Slow River/1996 (EP)
"Heart of Darkness" on **Cowpunks**/Vinyl Junkie UK/1996
Good Morning Spider/Parlophone UK/1998

Eric's Sparklehorse Page
//www.parlophone.co.uk/sparklehorse/main.html

Derrick's Sparklehorse Page
//www.geocities.com/bourbonstreet/2174/

Sparklehorse Rules
//www.geocities.com/~wolf-eyes/sparkly1.html

Split Lip Rayfield
Insurgent Country
Wichita, Kansas; 1996-

Take an old Ford truck gas tank, bolt on a bull fiddle neck, and add one long nylon string and, you've got the Stitchgiver, a homemade standup bass whose distinctive thump underlies Split Lip Rayfield's get the hell out of my way approach to bluegrass music. Kirk Rundstrom, who had formerly been guitarist in the breakneck punkgrass band Scroat Belly, started the band in 1996 with David Lawrence (ex-Bottom Feeder) on banjo and Jeffrey Eaton on the aforementioned "bass." Eric Mardis replaced Lawrence in 1997 just as SLR was signing with Bloodshot and in time for their self-titled debut CD in 1998. This is bluegrass music for truck drivers who've popped a few bennies, put the hammer all the way down, and need heart racing songs like "Coffee," "Pinball Machine," "Long Haul Weekend," "Outlaw," and "Tiger in My Tank" to speed them down that endless black ribbon.

Jeffrey Eaton (b,v); David Lawrence (bj,v,1996-1997); Eric Mardis (bj,v,1997-); Kirk Rundstrom (g,v)

Split Lip Rayfield/Bloodshot/1998
Split Lip Rayfield //www.fiest.com/~mindy/splitlip.htm

See Scroat Belly

Bruce Springsteen
Singer/Songwriter
Freehold, New Jersey; September 23, 1949-

The Boss's impact on modern popular music is undeniable and alternative country is no exception. Echoes of Bruce the Rocker are unmistakeable in the sound of many roots-rockers from the 1980s-1990s, but Bruce the Troubadour has perhaps been just as influential. In 1982, Springsteen threw his fans for a loop with the stark and relentlessly grim acoustic album, **Nebraska**. Like Woody Guthrie and Ramblin' Jack Elliott, his focus was on the lives of people, rural and urban, at the bottom or even under the social pyramid, but unlike his predecessors, Bruce maintains a bleak mood throughout. His harrowing tales of murder, poverty, fear, and desperation, expressed dramatically by Springsteen's brooding vocals and mournful harmonica, offer few signs of hope. Directly or indirectly, **Nebraska** set a standard for future singer/songwriter champions of the down and out from Steve Earle to Michelle Shocked. Thirteen years later, Bruce returned to this theme with **The Ghost of Tom Joad** which was his answer to the "New World Order" where the characters in his songs find "no home, no job, no peace, no rest." Inspired by Steinbeck's *Grapes of Wrath*, it, like **Nebraska**, is a stripped-down affair with more harsh depictions of life in 1990s America. In 1997, a number of singer/songwriters including Dave Alvin, Maria McKee, and Martin Zellar paid homage to The Boss on **One Step Up, Two Steps Back: The Songs of Bruce Springsteen**.

Nebraska/Columbia/1982
"Vigilante Man" on **Folkways: A Vision Shared, A Tribute to Woody Guthrie and Leadbelly**/CBS/1988 (CD/video)
The Ghost of Tom Joad/Columbia/1995
One Step Up, Two Steps Back: The Songs of Bruce Springsteen/The Right Stuff/1997

Greasy Lake: The Ultimate Bruce Springsteen Tribute Page //www.greasylake.springsteen.com

The Starkweathers
See Mike Ireland and Holler

The Starliners
"Hillbilly Re-Bop"
Melbourne, Victoria, Australia; 1991-

The Starliners bill themselves as "Australia's #1 Hillbilly Bop & Western Swing Band," and that's no brag, just fact! Based in Melbourne, they've been together for about seven years under the leadership of Hank Ferguson whose lead vocals are modeled after hillbilly boogie crooners like Jack Bradshaw, Skeets McDonald, and Redd Stewart. He's supported by a veteran crew including Mike Miller on bass, Andrew Lindsay (ex-Moonee Valley Drifters) on drums, Phil Jones (replaced by Peter Baylor in 1998) on lead guitar, Adam Gare (ex-Dude Ranch; Doug Mansfield) on fiddle and mandolin, and steel man Dave Cantrell (ex-Straight Eights and Stringbusters) whose stylings have the rough and rowdy feel of legends like Noel Boggs and Vance Terry. Their 1997 CD debut **Re*Bop** is a top-drawer set of jumping, crazy hillbilly and swing in the spirit of Billy Jack Wills, Leon McAuliffe, Johnny Hicks, and other acts from the 40s and 50s. Covers of "Careful Baby" (Groovey Joe Poovey), "Cadillac in Model" (Billy Jack Wills), "Crazy Blues" (J.P. Richardson), "I Had Someone Else" (Harris/ Darcey/Stanley), "Hide and Seek" (Winley/Byrd), "Baby I'll Be Gone" (Lattie Moore) and others are dead solid on the mark, and originals such as "Well Oh Well" by Ferguson and Jones do the tradition proud. Put it on your jukebox and just try to stay still!

Peter Baylor (l.g.,1998-); Dave Cantrell (s.g.,b.v.); Hank Ferguson (a.g.,l.v.); Adam Gare (f,md,b.v.); Phil Jones (l.g.,1991-1997); Andrew Lindsay (d); Mike Miller (u.b.,b.v.)

Re*Bop/Aloha/1997

The Starliners, P.O. Box 436, Cheltenham, Victoria 3192, Australia

See Doug Mansfield; Lucky Oceans; Moonee Valley Drifters

The Steam Donkeys
Country Rock; Roots Rock; Redneck Underground
Buffalo, New York; 1992-

As the title of their 1994 release **Cosmic Americana** suggests, Buffalo's Steam Donkeys are mainly inspired by early 1970s California country rock groups like the Byrds, Gram Parsons, and the Flying Burrito Brothers. However, these Yanks also draw on a variety of musical influences from below the Mason-Dixon including bluegrass, old-time, Western swing, and Southern rock. Lead singer and songwriter Buck Quigley (ex-Jack Lords) pens honky tonk ("I'm the One You Love"), tear jerkers ("Silly Clown"), bluesy ballads ("Treat You Like a Child"), and novelty tunes ("I Wanna Be With You When the Big One Hits") in the grand spirit of country songwriting. Doug Moody's (ex-French Ticklers) fiddle weaves effectively through slow, moody tunes and hoe-downs and Charley Quill (ex-Meinzer's Dry Bones; French Ticklers) adds twangy licks on guitar, banjo, and lap steel. In 1994, the Donkey received a high compliment when they became the only non-Southern band to be invited to the inaugural Bubbapalooza in Atlanta. Their "Can't Find a Place to Stay" was later included in the first Redneck Underground compilation, and the Steam Donkeys were regulars at subsequent Bubbapalooza festivals. **Cosmic Americana** was reissued in 1997 on Atlanta's Landslide Records which also released the Donkeys' **Little Honky Tonks** in 1998. The latter, as the title implies, creates an aural atmosphere transporting the listener back to that golden age when hardcore country music could be found in dives and holes-in-the-wall from Bangor to Bakersfield. Late in the year, Jim Whitford joined the Steam Donkeys after his band, the Pine Dogs, called it quits. Since 1997, the Steam Donkeys have hosted the annual Americanarama festival which has featured the Cowslingers, Pine Dogs, Scott Carpenter, the Red Gills, and many other local and regional alt. country performers.

John Brady (d,v,1992-1995); Kyle Brock (b,1992-1995); Joe Kross (d, 1996-); Doug Moody (f,v); Frank Quebral (b, 1995-1997); Buck Quigley (g,v); Charlie Quill (g); John Weber (b,1997-); Jim Whitford (g,v,1998-)

Songs From a Stolen Guitar/SD/1993 (CS EP)
Cosmic Americana/SD/1994; Landslide/1997
"Can't Find a Place to Stay" on **Bubbapalooza, Vol. 1**/ Sky/1995
Little Honky Tonks/Landslide/1998

The Steam Donkeys, P.O. Box 1241, Buffalo, NY 14213; 716-884-8142

The Steam Donkeys Home Page
//www.wnywebshop.com/donkey1.htm

Doug Stevens & The Outband

Gay Country Rock
New York, New York; Early 1990s-

Of the handful of gay/lesbian country bands (David Diamond, Y'All, Topp Twins) in the 1990s, none has come farther out than Doug Stevens and the Outband. Born and raised in the heart of Elvis Country (Tupelo, Mississippi), his songs reflect the problems of growing up gay (or straight) in the South ("Born in Mississippi"; "White Trash"). He also writes about first loves and lost loves ("Out in the Country"; "I Can't Bear It"), the horror of aids ("HIV Blues"), and coming out boldly ("Act Up"). Stylistically, the Outband ranges from tender ballads to country rock and on **When Love is Right** do several appealing Cajun style numbers as well. Based in Manhattan, Doug Stevens and group have played many dances and concerts (gay and straight) in the East and Midwest and received national news attention with features on CNN and NBC.

Doug Stevens (g,v); John Cordes (f); Houston Davenport (b); Richard Dworkin (d); Marjorie Fein (g); Rachelle Gaurniez (acc,v); Dori Rhodes (v)

Out in the Country/Longhorn/1993
When Love Is Right/Red Hill/1995

Doug Stevens & the Outband Web Page
//www.escape.com/~bpsl/

Doug Stevens/GayWeb Home Page
//www.gayweb.com/404/stevens.html

See Y'All

Mack Stevens

Hillbilly Bop; Rockabilly
Corsicana, Texas; 1961-

Mild mannered mailman by day, Mack Stevens is one rocking hillbilly bopper by night. Based in Corsicana, Texas (about 50 miles south of Dallas), Stevens burst onto the rockabilly scene in the mid-1990s with a flurry of extended play singles. His first, two recordings, the **Bop Stop Rockabilly** LP and the **Killin' Spree** EP, were on German labels and are a mix of rockabilly and country including an up tempo title tune about a murderous postal worker. Stevens also recorded a series of singles and EPs on his own Freedonia label using rockabilly and country musicians from the Dallas area (Malcolm Yelvington, Rebel Rouser, and the Great Plainsmen). These delivered more great hillbilly bop and rockabilly on covers and Stevens' originals, "Cruisin' With Susan" and "There's a Little Life Left in This Old Boy Yet." In 1996, Mack really came into his own when he put together a new band, the Slapback Rhythmaires, and recorded an EP, **Rockin' Guitar Gal**, and a full length album, **Dangerous Man**, for the Japanese rockabilly label On the Hill. Stevens is at his hillbilly rocking best on **Dangerous Man** which covers "I'm Movin' On" (Hank Snow) and "Mean Eyed Cat" (Johnny Cash) but really shines on his own "From the Dead," "You Took a Man," "Blues Is Waitin' at My Door," "Dangerous Man," and "Head West on 66." Compared in looks to Warren Smith and stylistically to Johnny Carroll, Stevens is distinctly contemporary and through his recordings and appearances at important festivals such as the Denver Rockabilly Weekender and Austin's Rockabilly Romp plus several European tours quickly pushed to the top of the modern rockabilly hill. In late 1997 came a flurry of new recordings from Mack; a single, a cassette (**Cruisin' Down the Highway**), and a CD of **Dangerous Man** (with nine songs not on the LP) for On the Hill plus a collection of 20 new songs called **Home-made Tattoo** with more of his hard-edged rocking style. When veteran rockabilly producer Ron Weiser started a new series of recordings on his Rollin' Rock label (in conjunction with Hightone/HMG) in 1998, the first CD released was **Mack Stevens at Rollin' Rock: The Las Vegas Stomp!** Recorded in just two days, it presents Mack at his rawest both musically and lyrically. His long-time affinity for the macabre and violent comes on full bore here on "Don't Start a War Daddy," "Woodpecker Rock," "Diet Pill Boogie," "It's Armaggedon Time," "Only the Good Die Young," "The Scream," "Momma Stop Me Before I Kill Again," and "Daddy's Goin' Mad." And, make no mistake about it, this sucker will rock you up one side and down the other.

Bop Stop Rockabilly/Eagle Ger./1993 (LP)
Killin' Spree/Waterhole Ger./1995 (EP)
"It's Over Now" b/w "Just a Little Bit of Crawling"/ Freedonia/1995 (7")

Rockin' in Memphis (with Malcolm Yelvington)/
Freedonia/1995 (EP)
Rockabilly Insanity (with Rebel Rouser and the Great
Plainsmen)/Freedonia/1995 (EP)
Rockin' Guitar Gal/On the Hill Jp./1996 (EP)
"Daddy" b/w "Holy Roll"/On the Hill Jp./1997 (7")
Cruisin' Down the Highway/On the Hill Jp./1997 (CS)
Dangerous Man/On the Hill Jp./1996 (LP); 1997 (CD)
Homemade Tattoo/Freedonia/1997
**Mack Stevens at Rollin' Rock: The Las Vegas
Stomp**/Rollin' Rock HMG/1998

Mack Stevens, 128 N. Suttonwood,
Ft. Worth, TX 76108-4102

Mack Stevens Home Page
//members.aol.com/msslapback/index1.html

Msslapback@aol.com

Mack Stevens/Southern & Rocking Profile
//www.sci.fi/~srmusic/profile1.htm

Gary Stewart

Honky Tonk
Jenkins, Kentucky; May 28, 1945-

In the late 1960s, Gary Stewart was working in an airplane factory by day and singing country music in local nightclubs by night in Ft. Pierce, Florida. He teamed up with a local cop named Bill Eldridge to write songs and after a few tries pitching in Nashville got them covered by stars like Cal Smith, Nat Stuckey, Del Reeves, and Billy Walker for whom they became top ten hits. Relocating to Nashville, Stewart worked at Bradley's Barn studio and while there cut a few demos which eventually caught the attention of RCA execs in 1974. He had previously recorded an album for Kapp but with RCA came into his own with several strong recordings (**Out of Hand**; **Your Place or Mine**), scoring hits with "Ramblin' Man," "She's Acting Single (I'm Drinking Doubles)," and "Out of Hand." During this time, he became known as a hard core honky tonker distinguished by warbling vocals (grating for some) and propensity for alcohol and hard living. In the late 1970s, Stewart toured as pianist for Charley Pride and made several duet albums with Dean Dillon in the early 1980s, but due to substance abuse and other personal problems, his career began to decline. However, in the late 1980s, he found new life through the roots revival label Hightone which re-released some his older material as well as several new recordings (**Brand New**; **Battleground**; **I'm a Texan**). In 1996, Hightone cut Stewart loose, but he continued to be popular especially on the Texas honky tonk/dance hall circuit. A retrospective of Stewart's best, **The Essential Gary Stewart**, was issued by RCA in 1997.

You're Not the Woman You Used to Be/Kapp/1973
Out of Hand/RCA/1975; Hightone/1991
Steppin' Out/RCA/1976
Your Place or Mine/RCA/1977; 1981

Little Junior/RCA/1978
Gary/RCA/1979
Cactus & A Rose/RCA/1980
Gary Stewart's Greatest Hits/RCA/1981
Brotherly Love (with Dean Dillon)/RCA/1982
Those Were the Days (with Dean Dillon)/RCA/1983
Twenty of the Best/RCA International UK/1984
Collector's Series/RCA/1985
Brand New/Hightone/1988
Battleground/Hightone/1990
Gary's Greatest/Hightone/1991
I'm a Texan/Hightone/1993
The Essential Gary Stewart/RCA/1997

Gary Stewart Fan Club, 903 18th Ave. South,
Nashville, TN 37212

Gary Stewart Page //www.bellenet.com/stewartgary.html

John P. Strohm and the Hello Strangers

Roots Rock
Indianapolis, Indiana; 1995-

Indiana native John P. Strohm has certainly paid his indie-pop dues over the course of the last fifteen years. In the mid-1980s, while attending the Berklee School of Music in Boston, he founded the Blake Babies with Freda Boner and Juliana Hatfield; after the latter departed to join the Lemonheads, Boner and Strohm went back to Bloomington and formed Antenna, but John P. soon moved on to start Velo-Deluxe in 1994. Along the way, he was also a member of the on-and-off Lemonheads. In 1995, Strohm ventured into a country roots rock side-project with the Hello Strangers, a loose confederation of Indiana musicians including Mitchell Harris (Velo-Deluxe) and steel player Dennis Scoville who had also done time with the Dew Daddies. Their self-produced **Caledonia** (1996), a blend of country, rock, and pop, has more than a passing resemblance to the Jayhawks, Uncle Tupelo, Wilco, Son Volt, and other Grain Belt roots rockers. It made a small blip on the alt. country screen when it first came out then was revived overseas when John P. Strohm and the Hello Strangers were included on two Americana compilations in Europe in 1998. Strohm's 1999 solo **Vestavia** is best described as twangy pop rock.

John P. Strohm (g,v); Mitchell Harris (d); Glenn Hicks (b);
Dennis Scoville (f,p.s.); Steve Woods (g,v)

Caledonia/Flat Earth/1996
"Thelma" on **Loose: New Sounds of the Old West**/Vinyl
Junkie UK/1998
"Slip Away" on **Luxury Liner, Vol. 2**/Glitterhouse
Ger./1998
Vestavia (John P. Strohm)/Flat Earth/1999

John P. Strohm/Flat Earth Page
//www.infostrm.com/flatearth/

flatearth@surf-ici.com

The Supersuckers
Grange Rock
Seattle, Washington (by way of Tucson); 1989-

Originally formed in Tucson as the Black Supersuckers, the Supersuckers relocated to the Northwest in the early 1990s where they got a deal with SubPop and recorded several albums of hyperactive garage-grunge-rockabilly (**The Smoe of Hell**, **La Mano Cornuda**, **Sacricilious**) with such catchy ditties as "Hell City, Hell," "Like a Big Fuckin' Train," "She's My Bitch," "Born With a Tail," "Born Without a Spine," and "Creepy Jackalope Eye." On stage, they wore cowboy hats, although the Suckers' music had little to do with Gene Autry or George Strait. But, deep inside those hard rock breasts beat country hearts and as the Junkyard Dogs, they cut an album of country covers. The Supersuckers had a special fondness for Willie Nelson and in concert often covered his "Whiskey River." In 1995, their manager approached Justice Records with the idea for an unorthodox tribute to Willie. The result was **Twisted Willie**, an album of Nelson classics done by an unlikely collection of performers including L7, Jello Biafra, Horton Heat, X, and Tenderloin. The Supersuckers contributed "Bloody Mary Morning" and later played at Farm Aid and Willie's famous Fourth of July Picnic in 1996. They then decided to take a bunch of original rock songs and rearrange them into a country album, **Must Have Been High**. Produced by Justice Records owner Randall Jamail, it gets support from country rocker Jesse Dayton (with whom the Suckers toured), Brantley Kearns (former fiddler for Dwight Yoakam), Willie's harmonica player Mickey Raphael, steel guitarist Brian Thomas, and the Breeders' Kelley Deal. The songs which run the gamut from honky tonk to country rock to ballads are all laced with the Supersuckers characteristic twisted humor ("Hangover Together"; "Nonaddictive Marijuana"), and the sound is like a cross between punk, spaghetti western soundtrack, Merle Haggard, and Marty Robbins from his gunfighter period. To prove their foray into alt. country was not a fluke, in late 1996, the Supersuckers recorded several cuts with Steve Earle for **El Corazon** and for the EP **Steve Earle/Supersuckers** which has one Earle tune ("Angel is the Devil"), the Supersuckers' "Creepy Jackalope Eye," and the Rolling Stones' "Before They Make Me Run."

Dan Bolton (g); Edward Carlyle Daly III aka Eddie Spaghetti (b,v); Ron Heathman (g); Dan Seigal aka Dancing Eagle (d)

"Bloody Mary Morning" on **Twisted Willie**/Justice/1995
Must Have Been High/SubPop/1997
Steve Earle/Supersuckers/SubPop/1997 (EP)
"Must Have Been High" on **Loose: New Sounds of the Old West**/Vinyl Junkie UK/1998
The Supersuckers/SubPop Home Page
//www.subpop.com/bands/supersuckers/supersuckers.html
Headin' to Hell With a Beer & A Sneer
//jackalope.simplenet.com/supersuckers/menu.html

The Swine
"Grunge Bluegrass"; Political Satire
Seattle, Washington; 1989-

Billed as "the world's only 'grunge bluegrass' band and politically ambiguous 'public excess' comedy troupe," the Swine see themselves as a cross between Bill Monroe, Frank Zappa, Elvis, and Nirvana. Begun in 1989, the band's rock-abilly, bluegrass, blues, "acoustic thrash," and country with political satire made them a favorite at the Northwest Folk Life Festival and landed them a spot on Public Access TV doing *Swine Before Pearls*, a comedy show with music and sketches lampooning current trends and personalities. An album by the same name takes shots at fads ("Politically Correct"), pompous politicians ("I Didn't Inhale"), specious spirituality ("Shirley's Song"), sacred icons ("I Saw Elvis"), rock excesses ("Smells Like Pork Rinds"), and even alt. country ("Pseudo Country Boy"). With their TV co-host, Tanny Pendershott, the Swine could be found wallowing every second Tuesday on Channel 29 and were at work on another CD in the late 1990s. Real Audio and Video samples of their songs and skits could be viewed (with caution) at their web site.

Deidre Brownlow (b,v); Paul Brownlow (g,mlda,p); Duff X. Drew (d,perc); Glenn Phillips (bj,g,md,v); Randy Schulman (f,g,hm,md,v)

Swine Before Pearls/Backwash/1996
The Swine: A Seattle Alternative of a Different Odor
//www.serv.net/~swine/
swine@rezone.com

The Swingin' Doors
Honky Tonk; Country Punk
San Francisco, California; 1993-

The debut recording by San Francisco's Swingin' Doors is appropriately titled **Unhinged**. This is country music played *way* out on the edge of town in a honky tonk where hillbillies and modern rockers mingle quite comfortably. The explanation for this curious blend lies in the backgrounds of the group's members; while they were attending Kent State University, Diane Glaub and Jennifer McKitrick were in an all girl punk band (the Bettys) and met Dwight Been, an art student who cites Merle Haggard as his favorite country artist. Back in Frisco, where they all grew up, the three joined with violinist Stephanie Lee (direct descendant of Confucius) to form the Swingin' Doors (named for the classic Hag song). **Unhinged** weaves back and forth between Been's quirky honky tonk originals ("So Pretty So Fast"; "You're Just Her Tattoo"; "One Eye Love"; "On and On"; "Your Word Against Mine") and lead guitarist McKitrick's new wave influences on "Jaco," "Homeless," and "Offer Me the World." The two sides come together on the finale, a country tinged remake of the old Blondie song "Dreaming."

Dwight Been (a.g.v); Diane Glaub (d); Stephanie Lee (b,f); Jennifer McKitrick (e.g.,v)

Unhinged/SD/1996

The Swingin' Doors, 4104 24th St. #132, San Francisco, CA 94114

The Swingin' Doors Home Page //www.noevalley.com/swing.htm

maybaby@earthlink.net

The Swinging Steaks (The Steaks)

Roots Rock
Boston, Massachusetts; Late 1980s-

The Swinging Steaks were founded in the late 1980s in Boston by Jamie Walker and Paul Kochanski who had been in the popular rock band, the Drive. With Joe Donnelly (ex-Del Fuegos), Jim Gambino, and Tim Giovanniello, they forged a roots rock style fusing elements of rock, country, folk, soul, and pop on three recordings, **Suicide at the Wishing Well**, **Southside of the Sky**, and **Shiner**. And though they never played much straight country, the Swinging Steaks often found themselves named as Bean Town's Best Country Band. In 1997, inspired by Steve Earle's **Train A'Comin'**, the band recorded an unplugged album, **Bare**, as simply the Steaks at the Old Vienna Kaffeehaus. In addition to reworked versions of material from previous recordings, it covers George Jones ("He Stopped Loving Her Today") and Townes Van Zandt ("White Freight Liner Blues"). Toward the end of 1998, the Swinging Steaks played a one week engagement at the Cafe Deco in Hong Kong and had plans to do a more extensive tour of the Far East in 1999.

Joe Donnelly (perc,v,late 1980s-1995); Jim Gambino (ky,v); Tin Giovaniello (g,v); Paul Kochanski (b,v); Scott Mitchel (d,1995-); Jamie Walker (g,sl.g.,v)

"Live With Me" on **Boston Gets Stoned**/Botown/1990
"Beg, Steal or Borrow" on **North By Northeast**/
   Northeastern/1991
Suicide at the Wishing Well/Thrust/1992
Southside of the Sky/Capricorn/1993
Shiner/Thrust/1995
Bare (The Steaks)/Thrust/1997

The Swinging Steaks Home Page //www.swingingsteaks.com

steaks@xensei.com

The Sycamores

No Depression; Roots Rock; Country Rock
Minneapolis, Minnesota; 1990-

The Sycamores synthesize the best parts of the Twin Cities' impressive roster of alt. country bands into an intelligent lo-fi country and roots rock that moved *Rolling Stone* to call their sound "thinking twang." Since Frank Randall and Dave Downey started the group in 1989, the Sycamores frequently

received performance and recording support from alumni of the Gear Daddies (Dominic Ciola), the Honeydogs (Adam and Noah Levy), the Replacements (Slim Dunlap), and Golden Smog (Adam Levy) but unlike those bands remained virtually unknown outside their home town (they've never even toured the rest of Minnesota). Still, that didn't seem to bother the Sycamores who went quietly about their business building a loyal following in Minneapolis and making modest but very fine alt. country recordings anchored by Downey, Randall, and pedal steel player, Jim Johnson (they endured a succession of bass players). **Listening Skills Program** caught the ear of *No Depression* which gave the Sycamores a bit more notoriety through a write-up in the "Town and Country" section (March-April 1997).

Dave Downey (d); Heath Henjum (b,1996-); Jim Johnson (p.s.); Frank Randall (g,l.v.)

The Sycamores/Crackpot/1995 (EP)
The Sycamores/Rag and Bone Shop/1995
Listening Skills Program/Veto/1997

The Sycamores, 808 West 28th St., Minneapolis, MN 55408

The Sycamores Home Page //www.sycamores.com

frank@sycamores.com

See The Billy's; Golden Smog; the Honeydogs; Martin Zellar

T Bones

Country Rock; Roots Rock
Robinvale, Victoria, Australia; 1985-

The T Bones operate in that shadowy juncture between rural and urban life where they express the hopes and fears, dreams and disappointments of each in a fusion of country and rock. Like American counterparts such as Uncle Tupelo or the Bottlerockets, they grew up in a small town (Robinvale) but were deeply affected by the big city (Melbourne), and their songs deal with both the inner workings of and clashes between these cultures. Known as the pioneers of the "Sunraysia Sound," this quartet of friends first began playing together in 1985 while still in high school. The T Bones developed a high energy country punk that eventually evolved into the more sedate country rock (similar to early Jayhawks) found on their 1998 **5 Days Gone**. Their rural/urban dichotomy is revealed on the one hand in stories about living in the city and longing for the country (and vice versa). "I Don't Mind" is pure nostalgia; "Country Boy" is about a rock and roller living in the city, thinking about the land, and crying to Hank Williams; "Stainless Steel" is a funny tale of a small town teenager's rock star dreams. The T Bones also have an eye for problems common to country and city folks, namely, alienation ("16th Storey"), murder ("Blood Simple"), betrayal ("One Day"), and binge drinking ("5 Days Gone").

Jim Carden (d,perc,v); Hugh Martin (b,v); Andrew Pupillo (a.g.,v); Charlie Wilde (a.g.,e.g.sl.g.)

Cannot Settle Down/Corduroy Austr./1995
5 Days Gone/Corduroy Austr./1998

T Bones/Corduroy Records, Factory 4, 20 Advantage Rd., Highett 3190, Australia; corduroy@onthe.net.au

Tarnation
Lo Fi Country Rock
San Francisco, California;1992-

Growing up in the South (Sautee Nacoochee, Georgia; Eureka Springs, Arkansas), Paula Frazer was surrounded by country and gospel music and in high school sang in several jazz bands. When she moved to the Bay Area in the 1980s, Frazer carried these influences, but her initial musical outings in San Francisco were with a Bulgarian women's choir and local punk bands (Frightwig, Trial, Pleasant Day). Eventually, she began to re-explore the music of her roots and in 1992 started Tarnation. Its first incarnation consisting of Frazer, ex-SF Seals Lincoln Allen and Michelle Cernuto, and Matt Sullivan recorded **I'll Give You Something to Cry About** in 1994. Their laid back (like Cowboy Junkies, Scuds, Palace) country and rock is highlighted by Frazer's vocals which range somewhere between Joan Baez and Tammy Wynette but also show the influence of Patsy Cline and Roy Orbison among others. Frazer writes most of the material for the band drawing stories from personal experiences that reflect life's gloomier realms. In 1994, Tarnation were on an EP compilation of San Francisco alt. country acts (Buckets, Dieselhed, et al.) and a year later, Bloodshot Records put "Yellow Birds" on the second volume of insurgent country (**Hell Bent**). Then, 4AD Records signed them up, and Tarnation did **Gentle Creatures** which reworked a number of songs from **Something to Cry About** but also included haunting new songs like "Halfway to Madness" and "Stranger in the Mirror." Seemingly on their way to a big breakthrough, the band had actually been experiencing internal squabbles while doing **Gentle Creatures**. Creative differences led to the departure of Allen, Cernuto, and Sullivan, but, within a short time, Frazer assembled a new group of supporting musicians and secured a deal with Reprise. The revamped Tarnation's first release came in 1997 with **Mirador** ("Spectator"). It moved away from the brooding sound of the past toward a more upbeat sound inspired by spaghetti western soundtracks, Hispanic music, and modern pop rock.

Lincoln Allen (g,1992-1995); Joe Byrnes (d, 1996-); Michelle Cernuto (b,d,v,1992-1995); Paula Frazer (l.v.); Jamie Meagan (b,1996-); Alex Oropeza (l.g.,1996-); Matt "Wendell" Sullivan (p.s.,1992-1995)

I'll Give You Something to Cry About/Nuf Sed/1994
"Yellow Birds" on **Hell-Bent**/Bloodshot/1995

"The Hand"/"Is She Lonesome Now?"/"Two Wrongs, Don't Make a Right" (Paula Frazer)/Sunday Driver/1995 (EP)
Gentle Creatures/4 AD/1995
Live/Fr./1995 (import promo)
Your Thoughts & Mine/4AD/1996 (EP)
Mirador/Reprise/1997

Tarnation/4AD Page
//www.4ad.com

Tarnation iMusic Showcase
//imusic.com/showcase/modern/tarnation.html

Tut Taylor
Dobro
Baldwin Co., Georgia; November 20, 1923-

Born into a musical family, Robert "Tut" Taylor's first instruments were banjo and mandolin. In the 1940s, he switched to dobro but learned to play it using a flat-picking rather than the usual finger-picking technique. During the 1950s, Taylor did session work on Porter Wagoner's **Bluegrass Story** and in the 1960s was in the Folkswingers with the Dillards and Glen Campbell. His first solo recording was **Dobro Country** (1964) with Bill Keith, Chris Hillman, and Clarence and Roland White. Later, Tut was a member of the Dixie Gentlemen before moving to Nashville in 1970 where he teamed with Norman Blake, John Hartford, and Vassar Clements in 1971 to record Hartford's classic **Aero Plain**. During this time, Taylor joined with George Gruhn in a musical instrument sales company called GTR but after a short time split off to set up the old-time Pickin' Parlor which became a favorite Nashville hangout. Throughout the 1970s, Taylor developed his unique dobro style as a session player on albums by David Bromberg and Leon Russell (**Hank's Back**) and on Norman Blake's terrific but sadly neglected **Super Jam Session** which included Clements, Butch Robins, Jethro Burns, and Sam Bush. Blake accompanied Taylor on a string of superb solo recordings, **The Old Post Office**, **Dobrolic Plectoral Society**, **Friar Tut**, that sealed his place as one of the great modern dobroists. In turn, Tut produced Blake's albums and also co-produced (with Jerry Douglas) the Grammy and IBMA Award winning **Great Dobro Sessions**. Over the years, Taylor recorded numerous informal jam sessions with his favorite old-time/bluegrass musicians. In 1997, he decided to release a series of three CDs called the **Tut Taylor Archival Recordings**; the first issued was **Flatpickin' in the Kitchen** with old friend Norman Blake and the second, **Flash Flood**, with Mac Puckett, Hughie Wylie, Curtis Burch, Beppe Gambetta, Herschel Sizemore, and Vassar Clements.

Dobro Country/World Pacific/1964
Friar Tut/Rounder/1972; 1998
The Old Post Office/Flying Fish/1975
Norman Blake Super Jam Session/Flying Fish/1975
Dobrolic Plectoral Society/Takoma/1976
The Great Dobro Sessions/Sugar Hill/1994

Tut Taylor Archival Recordings, Vol. 1: Flatpickin' in the Kitchen (with Norman Blake)/TT/1997
Tut Taylor Archival Recordings, Vol. 2: Flash Flood/TT/1998

Tut Taylor's Official Home Page
//www.vicksburg.com/~tut/tutintro.html

tutlee@pop.usit.net

See Norman Blake; John Hartford

Tennessee Rhythm Riders

Hillbilly Bop
England; 1994-

One look at lead singer Lynette Morgan and the Tennessee Rhythm Riders in their fancy, embroidered cowboy oufits, and one listen to their hot combination of hillbilly, Western swing, rockabilly, and gospel with playful banter makes it clear their main source of influence is the Maddox Brothers and Rose. They often cover songs by Rose Maddox, and Morgan's voice is a dead ringer for Rose's hillbilly twang. She, Willy Briggs, and Phil Morgan founded the Riders back in 1994, then added more members and expanded their repertoire in the late 1990s. The London based combo cut a 10" LP, **Step It Up & Go** in 1996 which was later released as an expanded CD in 1997. **Headin' West** (1998) and **Little Red Wagon** (1999) are a real treat with very faithful covers of Ray Price, T. Texas Tyler, Webb Pierce, Hank Williams, Hank Snow, Marvin Rainwater, and, of course, Rose Maddox. TRR have performed on Country Music Radio for Europe many times and appeared at major festivals throughout Europe and the U.S.

Gary Boller (b); Willy Briggs (l.g.,md); Gregor Henz (f,b.v.); Dave Madgewick (g,p,v); Lynette Morgan (r.g.,l.v.); Phil Morgan (s.g.); Mark Richards (d)

Step It Up & Go/Fury UK/1996 (10"); 1997 (CD)
Headin' West/Rundell Ger./1998
"Viva Las Vegas" b/w "Pistol Boogie"/Studio 28 UK/1998
Little Red Wagon/1999

Tennessee Rhythm Riders Page //www.studio28.net/tennrr/

trr@studio28.net

Tennessee Rhythm Riders/Saradon Page
//users.powernet.co.uk/saradon/trr.htm

Stephen W. Terrell

Singer/Songwriter; Satirist; DJ; Music Journalist
Oklahoma City, Oklahoma

Northern New Mexico is a unique place where Pueblo Indians, Chicanos, and cowboys interact with artists, New Agers, and atomic scientists. In the early 1980s, Santa Fe born singer/songwriter Stephen Terrell captured, with great intelligence and humor, the essence of this strange scene on two fine albums. **Picnic Time for Potatoeheads** featured backing from a group of local musicians including ex-Mothers of Invention drummer

Jimmy Carl (I'm the Indian of the Group) Black. Terrell's songs, "Cajun Clones," "Green Weenie," "Solar Broken Home," and "I Lost My Baby to a Satan Cult," got lots of attention in New Mexico and beyond (*The Dr. Demento Show* and KFAT in California). Meanwhile, Terrell became a fixture at local Santa Fe hangouts and in 1984 released **Pandemonium Jukebox**. Recorded in a bedroom on a 4 track cassette, it is lo-fi to say the least but has some gems like "Huggin' the John," "The Mushroom Sweet," and "The Jackalope Chant." However, it was limited to a few hundred copies, and when it received little air play, Terrell gave up performing to become a crime reporter and music reviewer ("Terrell's Tune-Up") for the *Santa Fe New Mexican* into the late 1980s and 1990s. Into the 21st century, Terrell hosted two alt. country/ roots show on KSFR in Santa Fe: The Santa Fe Opry featured "country music as God intended it to sound" while Terrell's Sound World was "freeform weirdo radio." He also wrote insightful alt. country/Americana reviews ("Terrell's Tune Up") for *Reverb On-Line* and revived his musical career by reissuing **Picnic Time for Potatoeheads** on a CD with nine cuts from **Pandemonium Jukebox**; in 1996, Terrell co-wrote "Danger Peligro: South of the Border Detective" with Erik Ness and maintained a fascinating web site with details about his career, original music articles, and links to alt. country artists and web pages plus "miscellaneous weirdities" from Masked Wrestlers to the Three Stooges.

Picnic Time for Potatoeheads/BlueElf/1981; 1996
Pandemonium Jukebox/Blue Elf/1983

Stephen Terrell, c/o Blue Elf Records, 500 N. Guadalupe, Ste. G-48, Santa Fe, NM 87501

Stephen Terrell Home Page
//members.aol.com/bluespud/index.htm

ROBOTCLAW@aol.com

The Texana Dames (Tommy X. Hancock)

Tex-Mex; Honky Tonk; Western Swing; Country Rock
Austin, Texas; Late 1980s-

From the 1950s to the early 1970s, Tommy and Charlene Hancock were a vital part of the Lubbock music scene. They played together in a Western swing band, owned a prominent nightclub, and were friends with an emerging generation of musicians including Jimmie Dale Gilmore and Joe Ely. Then, quite suddenly, the Hancocks gave it all up and moved to the mountains of New Mexico where they lived under primitive conditions and searched for spiritual enlightenment. However, they didn't give up on music. After teaching their children to play various instruments and sing, they formed the Supernatural Family Band (Texas progressive country) and began performing at local bars. Eventually, they moved to Austin and with help from the cream of Lubbock/Austin musicians recorded several self-produced albums in the late 1970s and early

1980s. Daughters Conni and Traci Lamar cut solo records in the late 1980s and then joined their mother to form the Texana Dames who built a following by performing every Sunday afternoon at a local club/restaurant called La Zona Rosa. In 1990, the Hancock women showed off their vocal and instrumental versatility on **Texana Dames**. Just like their Sunday matinees, it offered a lively set of honky tonk, Tex-Mex, swing, ballads, and blues with support from Doug Sahm on bajo sexto, Erik Hokkanen on fiddle, Lloyd Maines and Jimmy Day on steel, Pony Bone on accordion, and Marcia Ball on piano. Touring nation and world wide in the early 1990s, they continued their Sunday show whenever they were in town but moved it to another venue, Guero's, in 1993. A collection of dynamic live performances was released in 1996 on two CDs, **Months of Sundays** and **Months & Months of Sundays**; they present the same enchanting Texas roots music that made the Dames local favorites. They also played on recordings by patriarch Tommy X. Hancock who after a long hiatus from music returned with a vengeance on no less than four albums of original and sometimes very bizarre material in 1996: **Outback** and **Dancers Do It on the Floor**, both by Tommy Hancock & The Phantom Dance Band, contain music meant for two-steppers, waltzers, and swingers everywhere; **Lost in North Austin** (Tom X & The Supernatural Family Band) is a collection of Hancock's more humorous material ("Six Roads in a Daze"; "Don't Ask Me Questions When I'm Stoned") from his days with groups like the Vulgar Indulgers and Born Again Zenners); **True Stories & Strange Romances** (as Tom X) is mostly adults only material plus numerous songs from **Dancers** done as karaoke instrumentals. In addition to the Texana Dames, each recording includes a veritable who's who of Austin musicians such as Alvin Crow, Keith Ferguson, Ponty Bone, Jesse Taylor, Mark Rubin, Erik Hokkanen, the East Side Flash, and many more.

The Texana Dames: Charlene Hancock (b,ky,v); Conni Hancock (p.s.,r.g.,v); Traci Lamar (acc,ky,v)

Traci Lamar/Akashic/1986
Split Personality (Conni Hancock)/Akashic/1986
Texana Dames/Amazing/1990
Months of Sundays/TD/1996
Months & Months of Sundays/TD/1996
Dancers Do It on the Floor (Tommy Hancock & The Phantom Dance Band)/Akashic/1996
Outback (Tommy Hancock & The Phantom Dance Band)/Akashic/1996
Lost in North Austin (Tom X & The Supernatural Family Band)/Akashic/1996
True Stories & Strange Romances (Tom X)/Akashic/1996

Traci Lamar 512-448-1820

Tom X/Akashic Page //txmusic.com/akashic/tomout.htm

The Texas Rubies
Insurgent Country; Honky Tonk; Country Rock
Chicago, Illinois; 1990-

The Texas Rubies were charter members of Chicago's budding alternative country community of the early 1990s. Jane Baxter Miller grew up in Kentucky and attended college in West Virginia. Later, she went to Chicago to get into theater and met Kelly Kessler who had gone to school in the BlueGrass State. Inspired by old-time, bluegrass, honky tonk, country rock, etc., they began singing together, first in subways for beer money, then in clubs for beer money as the Texas Rubies. In 1990, they cut a self-released, self-titled cassette of Kessler originals (one by Miller) with Jane on lead vocals and Kelly on acoustic guitar and harmony. Their moving ballads of love and heartbreak compare quite favorably with Hazel & Alice or Freakwater. Three years later, the Rubies made their CD debut with **Working Girl Blues** which re-works songs from their 1990 tape using supporting musicians on dobro, fiddle, harmonica, accordion, and pedal steel. They retain and enhance the previous old-time country feel and also allow Kessler and Miller to stretch out a bit on the Tex-Mex "Texas Jalapenos," the funny honky tonk weeper "Hank Drank" (Bobby Lee Springfield), and a very nice cover of the Hazel Dickens' title tune. Chicgo's emerging insurgent country movement embraced the Texas Rubies whose bad girl song "That Truck" was included on Bloodshot's landmark **For a Life of Sin** compilation in 1994. Shortly thereafter, the Texas Rubies parted company but remained connected through family (sisters-in-law) and music. Miller and her husband (Kessler's brother) formed a jump jive/R&B group called Baxter, but she also continued to write Appalachian style murder ballads. In 1998, Jane became a Pine Valley Cosmonaut and contributed lead vocals to "Time Changes Everything" and "Faded Love" for **The Pine Valley Cosmonauts Salute the Majesty of Bob Wills**. Kessler stayed very active in the local alt. country community and in mid-1998 created and launched the Honky Tonk Living Room, a regular showcase at the Hideout for Chicago and out of town alt. country of all types. In just its first few months, the event featured Jon Langford, Dolly Varden, Deanna Varagona (Lambchop), Jimmy LaFave, and Jane Baxter Miller as well as a reunion of the Texas Rubies who then became active once again working on an album of "Jesus songs" (bluegrass gospel and shape note hymns).

Kelly Kessler (g,h.v.); Jane Baxter Miller (g,l.v.)

The Texas Rubies/TR/1990 (CS)
Working Girl Blues/TR/1993
"That Truck" on **For a Life of Sin**/Bloodshot/1994
"Time Changes Everything" & "Faded Love" (Jane Baxter Miller) On **The Pine Valley Cosmonauts Salute the Majesty of Bob Wills**/Bloodshot/1998

The Texas Rubies c/o Kelly Kessler, 5607 N. Newcastle, Chicago, IL 60631; kykr@hotmail.com or kkessler@enteract.com

Honky Tonk Living Room //www.bcity.com/honkytonk/

Jane Baxter Miller: anchovy@mcs.net

The The

Country Rock
London, England; 1982-

A number of modern rock acts have taken a swing at reinterpreting the legends of country music: **'Til Things Are Brighter** (Jon Langford's tribute to Johnny Cash); **Keep on the Sunny Side: A Tribute to the Carter Family** (with Freakwater); **Twisted Willie: The Songs of Willie Nelson** (with the Supersuckers, L7, Jello Biafra, et al.); the Resident's **Stars & Hank Forever**. Add to the list the Hank Williams tribute, **Hanky Panky** by Matt Johnson otherwise known as The The. Noted primarily for moody power pop, Johnson sank himself into Williams' recordings and found a kindred spirit "articulate in the language of the heart" who "transformed pure undiluted pain into simple songs of... profound truth." By-passing many of Hank's most famous songs, Johnson went for the ones that touched him on the most visceral level. Using an unusual but effective array of instruments including harmonium, melodica, and slide guitar, Johnson fashioned a very modern take celebrating the "emotional essence" of Williams' work ("Honky Tonkin'," "My Heart Would Know," "I'm a Long Gone Daddy," "Weary Blues," "I Saw the Light," "Your Cheatin Heart") without ever being exploitive or patronizing. In addition to the **Hanky Panky** CD, Epic released a 10" and a limited edition CD, **The The vs. Hank**, (now a collector's item) alternating Williams' recordings with Johnson's interpretations.

D. C. Collard (hrm,org,p,teated mlda,vox); Hollywood Dorsey (b); Gentleman Jim Fitting (b,hm); Nick Hunt (tamb); Matt Johnson (b,e.g.tm,l.v.); Bruce Lampcov (tamb); Reverend MacLeod (d); Eric Schermerhorn (a.g.,e.g.,s.g.)

Hanky Panky/Epic/1995
The The vs. Hank/Epic/1995 (CD promo)
I Saw the Light/Epic/1995 (2x10" vinyl 4 trk. EP)

Official The The Page //www.thethe.com

The Threadgill's Troubadours

Austin; Singers/Songwriters
Austin, Texas; 1990-

In 1933, a part time businessman and country yodeler named Kenneth Threadgill opened a gas station on the outskirts of Austin, Texas. Over the years, Threadgill's became a honky tonk and restaurant and in the late 1960s and early 1970s, a popular college hangout and home to Austin's nascent progressive country movement. This tradition carried on into the late 1980s when Jimmie Dale Gilmore began hosting a regular Wednesday night music session with many of Austin's premier singers and songwriters. Backing them was a band made up of Champ Hood, Marvin Denton, Dave Heath, Ron Irwin, Steve Williams, Gary Primich, and Tex Sweeney (mandolin) which, in time, came to be known as the Treadgill's Troubadours. In 1991, they recorded the **Threadgill's Supper Sessions** with the Troubadours joined by Gilmore, Butch Hancock, Christine Albert, and Sarah Elizabeth Campbell on classics ("Deep Elum Blues," "Brown's Ferry Blues," "Sittin' on Top of the World," "Travelin' Blues," "Waitin' for a Train," "Sweet Dreams") and a great duet of "Bluebird" by Gilmore and Hancock. Gilmore eventually gave up his MC position and was replaced by Hood who kept the Troubadours going at the popular Wednesday nights' "Singing for My Supper." In 1996, Watermelon Records released another compilation of live performances, **Second Helpings**, with a little wider variety of music and guests including Tish Hinojosa, Toni Price, and the late, great Walter Hyatt. Early in 1997, Threadgill's finalized a deal with the City of Austin and Time/Warner for a series of live music telecasts hosted by the Threadgill's Troubadours. Meantime, they carried on the Sittin', Singin' & Supper tradition each Wednesday evening at the new, roomier Threadgill's in South Austin.

Threadgill's Supper Sessions/Buddy/1991;
Watermelon/1993
Threadgill's, Volume 2: Second Helpings/
Watermelon/1996

Threadgill's, Barton Springs & Riverside, Austin, TX; 512-472-9304

Threadgill's Troubadours Page //www.threadgills.com/troubdrs.htm

Sally Timms

See Jon Langford

The Topp Twins

Singer/Songwriter; Gay Country; Yodeling
North Island, New Zealand

In the summer of 1995, I read a review of the Topp Twins' **Two Timing** that raved about its engaging country harmonies, exquisite yodeling, and wry humor. All of my favorites in one package but only available on import, so what were my chances of finding a copy in Austin, Texas? One week later, I found it in the cut out bin of a local bookstore for $1. The liner notes told me precious little except that Lynda and Jools Topp are identical twins from New Zealand. However, after a little more searching, I found a brief bio in the *All Music Guide* that filled in some of the details; raised on a dairy farm, they were encouraged by their family to take up music and relocated to Christchurch, New Zealand where they worked day jobs, honed their musical skills, and built a local following. After they landed their own TV show, *Do Not Adjust Your Twin-Set*, they became celebrities in their home country and then gradually carried their music to wider audiences in Australia, Europe, and North America. Their self produced debut, **No War in My Heart**, defined their characteristic mix of country music with social satire on "The Queen," "Throw Down Your Guns," and the riotous "Dolly Parton." Most of all, it showcased their utterly fantastic vocals. Their live performances included hilarious skits and in 1987, they were named New Zealand's Entertainers of the Year. Another recording, **Hightime**, was followed by **Two Timing**, a wonderful romp through parodies of urban cowboys ("Horse") and lesbian lovers ("Martina"), moving songs of rural nostalgia ("Calf Club Day"; "Get on Back"; "History"), and, of course, Lynda's shimmering yodels (influenced by Australia's yodeling sweetheart, Shirley Tomms) on "Rockin' Over" and the beautiful "Yodeling Accordion Gal." One listen to this record and my wife and I were in love with the Topp Twins, but what were the chances of ever seeing them in person? Two days later, we read in *The Austin Chronicle* they were coming to the Cactus Cafe in a couple of weeks. Their strong reputation as musicians and politically active lesbians preceded them, and the night of their performance the Twins drew a packed and very enthusiastic audience. They were everything and more than we expected; exquisite harmonies, yodeling, and a take off on hillbilly culture that makes *Hee Haw* seem like pretty sophisticated stuff. In 1997, Jools and Lynda took their variety show which features send-ups of Kiwi characters (the Ginghams, Ken and Ken, Camp Mother and Camp Leader, the Friday Night Get Up Girls) on the road for a two week engagement at the Drill Hall in London. It was the basis for the Topp Twins' second TV comedy series which began airing in New Zealand in late 1997.

No War in My Heart/TT/1987
Hightime/TT/1992
Two Timing/TT/1994

Topp Twins Profile
//www.tntmag.co.uk/feature/1997/733/fea_2.html

Trailer Bride

Tobacco Row; Lo-Fi Country
Chapel Hill, North Carolina; 1995-

Bloodshot Records aptly describes Trailer Bride as "somnambulistic country." Like the Shivers, Cowboy Junkies, Scud Mountain Boys, Tarnation, et al., they specialize in a very laid back style. However, they have a much rawer edge than most due to the spooky slide guitar work and Lucinda Williams like vocals of leader Melissa Swingle who had formerly played bass in an all girl band she founded called Pussy Teeth. Taking up guitar, Swingle began to write songs and with bass player Robert Michener started Trailer Bride around 1995. They went through a succession of drummers (finally settled on Brad

Goolsby) and then added Bryon Settle on lead guitar before going into the studio; first came a split single with Pine State followed by an eponymous CD on Walt Records. As mentioned, Trailer Bride likes to maintain a lazy, backwoods pace, and Swingle's originals vacillate between the dark ("Graveyard"; "Trailer Bride"; "Sorry Times") and more pleasant aspects of life ("Arrowheads") along Tobacco Road. In 1997, Trailer Bride began to position itself firmly in the imposing North Carolina alt. country world through inclusion on the **Revival** compilations and an appearance at Honky-Tonk-a-Rama. **Smelling Salts**, with its generally eerie, dreary mood drew comparisons to other lo-fi, gothic bands such as Parlor James and 16 Horsepower and widened Trailer Bride's audience.

Brad Goolsby (d); Robert Michener (b,1995-1997); Bryon Settle (l.g.); Melissa Swingle (bj,g,hm,md,sl.g,l.v.); Daryl White (b)

"Hundredth Broken Heart" (Pine State) b/w "Moanin' the Blues" (Trailer Bride)/Fiction Media/1995 (7")
Trailer Bride/Walt/1996
"Mardi Gras" on **Revival, Vol. 1: Brunswick Stew & Pig Pickin'**/Yep Roc/1996
"Graveyard" on **Revival Vol. 2: Kudzu & Hollerin' Contest**/Yep Roc/1997
Smelling Salts/Bloodshot/1998

Trailer Bride, P.O. Box 5204, Chapel Hill, NC 27514

Trailer Bride Home Page
//sunsite.unc.edu/chbands/trailer.html

Geronimo Trevino, III

Country Rock; Honky Tonk
San Antonio, Texas

One of the great album titles in the history of country music has to be **My Heroes Have Always Killed Cowboys** by Geronimo Trevino, III. A product of San Antonio, Trevino's musical education was shaped by exposure to the unique mixture of *ranchera* and honky tonk in South-Central Texas. His style was also heavily influenced by his Native American heritage as evidenced by the aforementioned album. Produced by songwriting legend Hank Cochran, **My Heroes** is a blend of traditional country ("Train Back to Texas"; "You're Playing Hard to Forget"; "Honky Tonk, USA"; "Buy Me a Honky Tonk") and songs centered on Native American themes ("Cherokee Rose"; "Oklahoma Wind"; "Before You Think You're An Indian"). Though recorded in Nashville, it's pure Texas honky tonk that gets a big boost from the presence of veterans Vassar Clements, Roy Huskey, Jr., Chris Ethridge (Flying Burrito Brothers), and Buddy Emmons. In 1998, Trevino released a very interesting CD-ROM titled **Honky Tonk, USA** that not only comes with a full-length CD of **Live From Kendalia Halle** but also a generous compendium of information on Texas honky tonk music. You can find out about honky tonk greats of the past (e.g. Ted Daffan, Milton Brown,

Johnny Bush) and present (e.g. Don Walser, Alvin Crow, Chris Wall) through biographies, photographs, and sound clips, or you can make cyber-visits to Texas' venerable dance halls where you'll again find plenty of excellent photos and historical background. It's the next best thing to being there!

My Heroes Have Always Killed
    Cowboys/Campfire/1996
Live From Kendalia Halle/Campfire/1997
Honky Tonk Texas, USA/3B Information Systems/1998
    (CD-ROM)

Geronimo Trevino, III, P.O. Box 203, Geronimo, TX 78115

Geronimo Trevino, III/Campfire Page //www.texas.net/users/g/geronimo/campfire.htm (complete with the *Smoke Signal* newsletter; you can also order a t-shirt with an image of the real Geronimo over the logo "My Heroes Have Always Killed Cowboys")

geronimo@texas.net

See Roxy Gordon

Justin Trevino

Honky Tonk
Texas; 1974-

With the emergence of youngsters like Justin Trevino, it's safe to say that the classic Texas honky tonk tradition will continue for many years to come. This Cen-Tex native began performing professionally at 13 and by 17 had recorded his first album, **King of Clubs**. At 21, Justin was included in a segment of the Smithsonian/Folkways video *Anthology of American Folk Musics*. Along the way, he worked with local Austin and San Antonio performers such as Don Walser, Cornell Hurd, and Susanna Van Tassel and with veteran artists Justin Tubb, Kitty Wells, and Leona Williams (Merle Haggard's ex-wife). In 1998, Trevino showed that he's cut from the same mold as Johnny Bush or Ray Price with **Texas Honky Tonk** which was lauded far and wide. With assistance from Bush (drums and two duets) plus Howard Kalish and Scott Walls of Don Walser's Pure Texas Band, he soars through honky tonk covers and originals with a voice often compared with the likes of Marty Robbins, Johnny Rodriguez, and Wynne Stewart. Justin's #1 fan, Dr. Aaron A. Fox, a Texas music fanatic and ethno-musicologist at Columbia University, maintains a web site devoted to Trevino, had him as a guest performer at a Spring 1998 Ethnomusiciology Series, and prominently features the young honky tonker in his 1999 book *Out the Country: Speech, Song, and Feeling in American Rural, Working Class Culture.*

King of Clubs/1991
Texas Honky Tonk/Neon Nightmare/1998
    "As Long as There is a Sunday" and "We Must Have Been
    Out of Our Minds" (with Leona Williams) on **The**
    Heart of Texas Country/HHFC/1998

Justin Trevino c/o Neon Nightmare Records, 208 Skycrest, Maxwell, TX 78656-9622; 512-357-6498

Justin Trevino: Texas Honky Tonk //roar.music.columbia.edu/~cecenter/justin.html

Aaron Fox: aaf19@columbia.edu or hhfc1@airmail.net

The Triffids

Lo-Fi Country Rock; Roots Rock
Perth, Australia; 1980-1989

If the Triffids were around today, they would be in good company with the many lo-fi country roots rock bands that sprang up in the 1990s. Back in the 80s, this Perth, Australia band developed a generally languorous style that often included understated country ballads and country roots rock accentuated with pedal and lap steel by "Evil" Graham Lee. They also did a side-project of traditional folk/country as Lawson Square Infirmary. Named for the alien killer plants in John Wyndham's sci-fi classic, *Day of the Triffids*, they were led by David McComb through ten years and many EPs and CDs before calling it quits in 1989. Graham and McComb went on to become members of another Australian alt. country band, the Blackeyed Susans, in the early 1990s. McComb was killed in a car wreck near Melbourne in early 1999.

Jill Birt (k,v); Martin Casey (b,v); Phil Kakulas (ky); Graham Lee (l.s.,p.s.); David McComb (g,p,v); Robert McComb (g,ky,vio,v); Alsy McDonald (d,v)

Treeless Plain/Hot Rough Trade UK/1983
Raining Pleasure/Hot Rough Trade UK/1984
Lawson Square Infirmary/Hot Austr./1984 (EP)
Field of Glass/Hot Rough Trade UK/1985
Love in Bright Landscapes/Hot Megadisc Dut./1986
Born Sandy Devotional/Hot Rough Trade UK/1986
In The Pines/Hot Rough Trade UK/1986
Calenture/Island/1987
Holy Water/Island UK/1988 (EP)
The Black Swan/Island UK/1989
Goodbye Little Boy/Island UK/1989 (EP)
Falling Over You/Island UK/1989 (EP)
Stockholm (Live)/MNW Swe./1990
Love of Will (David McComb)/1994
Australian Melodrama: The Best of the Triffids/
    Mushroom/1994

The Triffids //users.skynet.be/bs131594/dphome.html

The Triffids Database //hem2.passagen.se/honga/database/t/triffids.html

See The Blackeyed Susans; Love Me

Greg Trooper

Singer/Songwriter
New Jersey/Nashville

Greg Trooper spent many years flirting with singer/songwriter stardom. In his late teens, he wandered around the country playing in various places and then labored fifteen long years among New York City's singer/songwriter contingent. He put in many miles touring as a warm-up for Joe Ely and Rosanne Cash, and recorded three solid albums from 1986-1996 that had reviewers placing him in the same league as Steve Earle and John Hiatt. His songs were covered by Eric Ambel, Billy Bragg, Sarah Elizabeth Campbell, Steve Earle, Robert Earl Keen, Tom Russell, and Salamander Crossing, and he co-wrote with Ambel, Earle, Sid Griffin, Duane Jarvis, and Tom Russell. Still, it took a fortuitous move to Nashville in 1996 to bring Trooper out of the shadows and into the limelight. With a new publishing deal and record contract in hand, Greg was eagerly adopted by Music City's alt. country upper crust. His **Popular Demons** was produced by Buddy Miller and attracted big time guests including Earle, Emmylou Harris, Jarvis, Buddy and Julie Miller, Al Perkins, and Tammy Rogers. This fine collection of country/roots rock originals brought Trooper long overdue noteriety and prompted KOCH Records to re-issue **Everywhere** and **Noises in the Hallway** in 1999.

We Won't Dance/Wild Twin/1986
Everywhere/Ripe and Ready/1992; KOCH/1999
Noises in the Hallway/D'Ville/1996; KOCH/1999
Popular Demons/KOCH/1998
"I'll Keep It With Mine" on **A Tribute to The Times They Are A Changin'/Bob Dylan, Vol. 3**/Sister Ruby/1998

Greg Trooper, 217 Bonnalynn Dr., Hermitage, TN 37076

Greg Trooper The Official Site
//earth.vol.com/~jessi11/index.htm

Two Dollar Pistols
Tobacco Row; Honky Tonk; Country Rock
Carrboro, North Carolina; 1995-

Modeled after good ol' boy country, North Carolina's Two Dollar Pistols owe their hard core sound mainly to founder/leader John Howie's classic honky tonk baritone and barroom ballads. His first acquaintance with country music came when he was a drummer with the punk band Finger which did Gram Parsons covers including "Still Feeling Blue" for **Commemorativo**. After messing around with "art rock" in his band, June, Howie, inspired by local groups like the Backsliders, got back to the country with the Two Dollar Pistols. Using a back up band assembled from a variety of North Carolina bands (from Jolene to Squirrel Nut Zippers), Howie and the Pistols began to break into the thriving Carolina alt. country scene in 1996. In 1997, with a more stable line-up, Two Dollar Pistols recorded **On Down the Track** for Howie's Scrimshaw label. With guest appearances by Steve Watson on pedal steel, Jon Kamppainen on fiddle, and Steve Howell of the Backsliders on mandolin, the band covers three master country songwriters, Roger Miller ("A World So Full of Love"), Lefty Frizzell ("She's Gone, Gone, Gone"), Tom T. Hall ("I Flew Over Our House Last Night"), and does a decent job of emulating them on Howie's "Bring the Heartache," "Let Me Be Your Fool," "I'll Tell the Bottle," and "Your Place in the Sun."

Beset by a series of problems in 1998 (lost his label, manager, and day job), Howie battled to keep Two Dollar Pistols going through many personnel changes. One bright spot was the permanent addition of Kemppainen, Newton, and Steve Howell who was free after the Backsliders' "reorganization." Eventually all the other spots in the band were filled in time to do a live album at Local 506. The energized **Step Right Up!** offers songs from the Pistols first album, many classic country covers, and some new tunes ("Me, Myself, and Whine"; "Serious Heart Condition") as well. It was regarded by reviewers and fans alike as one of the best honky tonk recordings of 1998.

Jack Campbell (b,1995-1997); Ellen Gray (b,b.v.,1998-); Greg Hawks (a.g.,b.v.,1995-1997); Steve Howell (l.g.,md); John Howie (r.g.,l.v.); Jon Kamppainen (f,b.v.,1998-); Chris Phillips (d, 1995-1997) John Price (l.g.,1995-1997)

"Let Me Be Your Fool" on **Revival: Brunswick Stew & Pig Pickin'**/Yep Roc/1996
On Down the Track/Scrimshaw/1997
Step Right Up (Live)/Yep Roc/1998

Two Dollar Pistols Web Page
//www.mindspring.com/~dtnewton/home.html

twodollars@mindspring.com

Laura Tyler
TSOB; Redneck Underground; Honky Tonk
Southern California/Atlanta, Georgia

A Southern California native, Laura Tyler's early musical influences included classical, rock and roll, and honky tonk. She eventually decided on the latter and worked nightclubs up and down the length of the West Coast in her teens and twenties before becoming a member of Canadian country singer Nadine Autry's band in the early 1990s. In 1993, Tyler met pedal steel player Jim Novak (ex-the Plowboys) after he joined Autry's group, and they began writing songs and singing together. By 1994, they had their own band, the Usual Suspects and debuted at the famous Palomino Club in L.A. early that year. Over the next several years, Tyler and company ran with the Town South of Bakersfield crowd and in 1995 released **Honky Tonk Heaven**, a strong outing of Southern California honky tonk originals (by Tyler and Novak) highlighted by Tyler's room-filling vocals that are right up there with Heather Myles, Rosie Flores, and Joy Lynn White. After their first European tour, Laura and Jim got hitched and then came **Everything But the Blame**, another commendable honky tonk recording but with a fuller and more diverse sound (swing, country rock, Tex-Mex) due to guests like Brantley Kearns (ex-Dwight Yoakam) on fiddle and Whitey Anderson on accordion. Following a second successful European tour, Tyler and Novak grew disenchanted with the L.A. scene especially after the Palomino closed and decided to move to Nashville to try their luck. However, they got sidetracked to Atlanta where they were hooked into the Redneck Underground by Slim Chance and started a new band, the Rebel Hearts, with local musicians including former Vidalias guitarist PageWaldrup.

Honky Tonk Heaven/Banyan/1995
Everything But the Blame/Banyan/1996

The Official Laura Tyler Web Site
//members.tripod.com/~lauratyler_2/
LTANDJN@aol.com

Ian Tyson

Singer/Songwriter; Cowboy/Western
Victoria, British Columbia, Canada; September 25, 1933-

During the 1960s "folk scare," one of the most popular duos was Ian and Sylvia. Ian Tyson grew up in the Alberta, Canada, ranching country and did the local rodeo circuit as a bronc rider and calf roper until side lined by a serious leg injury in 1956. While convalescing, he took up the guitar and in 1958 was confident enough to move to Toronto to seek his musical fortune. There, Tyson met and teamed up with fellow Canadian Sylvia Fricker. In 1964, they married and moved to New York City to become a part of the Greenwich Village folk scene. As Ian and Sylvia, they recorded numerous albums on the Vanguard label including original (later to be classic) songs like his "Four Strong Winds," "Someday Soon," and "You Were on My Mind." They also effectively covered songs by Dylan ("This Wheel's on Fire"), Lightfoot ("Early Morning Rain") and others. In the late 1960s and early 1970s, Ian and Sylvia followed the lead of other folk artists and went to Nashville to record a couple of country albums (**Nashville**; **Great Speckled Bird**). However, by 1974 their relationship had gone sour, and they divorced. Sylvia went on to record several solo albums and with fellow Canadians Cindy Church, Colleen Peterson, and Caitlin Hanford as the excellent Quartette. Meanwhile, Ian went back to Alberta to renew his cowboy dreams on his 160 acre T-Bar-Y ranch. He continued to perform in local bars and in the early 1980s began releasing a series of albums of standards and originals exploring the cowboy/western way of life. The best of these are **Ian Tyson**, **Eighteen Inches of Rain**, and **Cowboyography** with the exceptional songs "Summer Wages" and "Navajo Rug" (co-written with Tom Russell) and great guitar by Nathan Tinkham who also performed with the Great Western Orchestra, Cindy Church, and Quarttete. These records established Tyson as the modern cowboy singer par excellence. He kept touch with Sylvia by producing her debut solo, **Woman's World** and reunited with her periodically for Ian and Sylvia revivals. Much of the material from their early partnership was reissued on CD including most recently Bear Family's **The End of the Beginning**. In 1996, Stony Plain released Ian's "greatest hits," **All the Good 'Uns**, and Tyson had knee replacement surgery to repair the damage done so many years ago. This made tours in North America throughout 1997-1998 easier, and in 1999, a new album of cowboy music,

Lost Herd, was released in Canada and then the U.S. More details about Ian's life can be found in his fascinating autobiography, *I Never Sold My Saddle*.

Nashville (Ian & Sylvia)/Vanguard/1968
Great Speckled Bird (Ian & Sylvia)/Bearsville/1970; Stony Plain Can./1994
Ol' Eon/Stony Plain Can./1974
One Jump Ahead of the Devil/Stony Plain Can./1978
Old Corrals & Sagebrush/Stony Plain Can./1983
Ian Tyson/Stony Plain Can./1984
Cowboyography/Stony Plain Can./1986; Sugar Hill/1987
Old Corrals & Sagebrush and Other Cowboy Culture Classics/Bear Family Ger./1988
I Outgrew the Wagon/Stony Plain Can./1989
And Stood There Amazed/Stony Plain Can./1991
Eighteen Inches of Rain/Vanguard/1994
The Working Cowboy: In Search of a Cowboy Song with Ian Tyson/1995 (video)
The Good 'Uns/Stony Plain Can./1996
The End of the Beginning (Ian & Sylvia)/Bear Family Ger./1997
"Cowboy Pride"; "Half a Mile of Hell"; "Summer Wages" on **Word From the Range: A Canadian Cowboy Collection**/Glenbow Museum Can./1998
Lost Herd/Stony Plain Can./1999; Vanguard/1999

Ian Tyson: The Legend
//www.nucleus.com/~cowboy/IanTyson.html

Nathan Tinkham
//www.nucleus.com/~cowboy/NathanTinkham.html

See The Great Western Orchestra; Quartette; Tom Russell

U.S. Saucer

Lo-Fi Country Rock
San Francisco, California; 1991-

If you like your country sad, sad, sad and need a good wallow in self-pity, grab a bottle, a pack of cigs, and put U.S. Saucer on the player. The Bay Area trio of Brian Hageman (Thinking Fellers Union), Margaret Murray (San Francisco Seals, ex-Caroliner), and David Tholfsen do sorrowful, heartbreaking songs raising misery to the level of an art form. Like fellow slacker country performers (the Handsome Family, Palace, Souled American, and the Scuds), U.S. Saucer relies on the barest of instrumentation and unusual twists on traditional music to achieve the desired mood on **My Misery Is Company**, **Tender Places Come From Nothing**, and **Hell, Yes!** Minor chords, distortion, Hageman's viola, and Tholfsen's somber vocals set the tone on originals and covers of Merle ("Today I Started Loving Her Again"), Lowell George ("Willin'"), Tom T. Hall ("I Love..."), Nino Rota ("Paseo Mio"), and even Bette Midler's "The Rose!" Any band that can move critics to dig deep into their thesauri for words like piquant, pulchrude, and lachrymose must really have something going.

Brian Hageman (g,viola,v); Margaret Murray (l.g.,v); David Tholfsen (b,v)

My Company is Misery/Amarillo/1992 (LP)

"Size It Up" b/w "Consuela"/Amarillo/1993/ (7")
Tender Places Come From Nothing/Amarillo/1994
United States Saucer/Return to Sender Normal Ger./1996
"The Plasma Is Still Now" on Howl!/Glitterhouse
   Ger./1996
Hell, Yes!/Amarillo/1997
San Francisco—A Music City Compilation/ Trocadero
   Ger./1998

U. S. Saucer/Amarillo Page
//members.aol.com/starleigh7/saucer.html

Uncle Tupelo

No Depression
Belleville, Illinois; 1987-1994

When three friends in the tiny town of Belleville, Illinois, began playing music together in the late 1980s, they couldn't have dreamed of the impact they would have on American music. Jay Farrar, Mike Heidorn, and Jeff Tweedy (along with Wade Farrar) started out in high school as a Black Flag type punk group called the Primitives. After several years, Farrar, Heidorn, and Tweedy formed a new group which they named Uncle Tupelo. While retaining contemporary punk influences, Uncle Tupelo combined these with a long tradition of country music from old-time through honky tonk, the Bakersfield sound, and Gram Parsons, Neil Young, and Doug Sahm country rock. Honing their fusion of country and rock at venues in nearby Columbia and St. Louis, Missouri, they recorded several self produced demo tapes before signing with Rockville Records in early 1990. Later that year came **No Depression**, named after an A.P. Carter song and one of the key albums in alt. country history. Drawing on punk, country rock, old-time country, and blues, Uncle Tupelo developed what has become known as the "No Depression" sound: alternation between or joining of grinding punk, country rock, and acoustic country; a focus on the darker side of small town life; and a heightened social/political consciousness. This style was even more fully realized on **Still Feel Gone**. For their third effort, **March 16-20, 1992**, Uncle Tupelo brought in Peter Buck to produce and got able help from Brian Henneman (the Bottle Rockets) on banjo and guitar and John Keane on pedal steel and banjo. The result was an all-acoustic recording of traditional covers ("Coalminers"; "Satan Your Kingdom Must Come Down"; "Atomic Power"; "Warfare") and Farrar/Tweedy social commentaries ("Grindstone"; "Shaky Ground"; "Black Eye"; "Moonshiner"; "I Wish My Baby Was Born"; "Fatal Wound"). Shortly after, drummer Heidorn departed and was replaced by Bill Belzer who was in turn replaced by Ken Coomer late in 1992. Along about the same time, Max Johnston (dobro, fiddle, mandolin) joined the band as they toured extensively in the U.S. and Europe in 1992-1993. Switching to Sire/Reprise, Uncle Tupelo recorded **Anondyne**, a return to the blend of country and rock that made them so unique and ultimately so influential. And though the quality of this recording seemed to indicate all was rosy with Uncle Tupelo, behind the scenes, Farrar and Tweedy were pulling in different directions. Eventually, the strain became too much, and after Farrar announced his decision to leave, Uncle Tupelo finished its early 1994 tour with a May Day finale at Mississippi Nights in St. Louis. However, neither Farrar or Tweedy stayed inactive for long; Tweedy (along with Coomer, Stirrat, and Johnston) went on to start Wilco and Farrar and Heidorn formed Son Volt. While Tweedy/Wilco gradually distanced themselves from the classic UT sound, Farrar/Son Volt carried on that tradition. Meanwhile, Uncle Tupelo's legend and legacy grew dramatically. Like it or not, they became the fathers of the No Depression generation of alternative country, spawning two magazines (*No Depression*; *Grindstone*), generating numerous on-line mailing lists and newsgroups, and influencing a host of new bands including the Bottle Rockets, Blue Mountain, Richmond Fontaine, Farmer Not So John, Whiskeytown, and many more. In 1998, Uncle Tupelo fans were treated to a rash of bootlegs, the most interesting of the lot being **Cover Story, 1989-1993**, (also known as **No Regression**) on which the band takes requests during live performances and does their versions of songs by Woody Guthrie, the Byrds, Bob Dylan, Creedence, Johnny Cash, Buck Owens, the Stooges, and more. In 1999, a double CD boot of Uncle Tupelo's last gig plus other live material and outtakes was issued as **Not Forever, Just For Now**.

Bill Belzer (d,1992); Ken Coomer (d,1992-1994); Jay Farrar (bj,f,g,hm,md,v); Mike Heidorn (d,1987-1992); Max Johnston (bj,f,md,s.g.,1993-1994); John Stirratt (b); Jeff Tweedy (b,g,v)

Colorblind & Rhymeless/UT/1987 (CS)
Live and Otherwise/UT/1988 (CS)
Not Forever, Just For Now/UT/1988 (CS)
"I Got Drunk" b/w "Sin City"/Rockville/1990 (7")
"Before I Break" on **Out of the Gate**/Go Fish/1990
"Gun" b/w "I Wanna Destroy You"/Rockville/ 1991 (7")
No Depression/Rockville/1990
Still Feel Gone/Rockville/1991
"Sauget Wind" (+2)/Rockville/1992 (EP)
March 16-20, 1992/Rockville/1992
Still Feel Gone & March 16-20, 1992/Rockville/1992
"Movin' On" on **20 More Explosive Fantastic Rockin'
   Mega Smash Hit Explosions**!/Pravda/1992
Anodyne/Sire/1993
The Long Cut/Sire/1993 (promo 6 trk, 5 live 10-15-93)
"Blue Eyes" on **Commemorativo: A Tribute to Gram
   Parsons**/Rhino/1993
"Effigy" on **No Alternative**/Arista/1993
"Moonshiner" on **Best of Mountain Stage, Vol. 7**/Blue
   Plate/1994
Live (Minneapolis, 3-20-94)/Twin City Digital/1996
Live (St. Louis, 5-1-94)/Twin City Digital/1996 (last live
   performance)
Cover Story, 1989-1993/Piggy Puss/; **No Regression**/
   Strider/1998 (boot)
The Rare Essence of Uncle Tupelo/Strider/1998 (boot)
Right There: Live in the Midwest/1998 (boot)
Not Forever, Just For Now/1999 (boot)

Uncle Tupelo Fan Page
//www.servtech.com/ddewey/index.html (this is the place to subscribe to Postcard, the on line UT mailing list; also has a discography and faq)

Uncle Tupelo/ Gumbo Pages Page
//www.gumbopages.com/uncle-tupelo.html (includes history, complete discography, links to on line mailing lists: Postcard and Passenger Side plus the "Insurgent Country Roundup" with UT/SV/Wilco articles, songs, chords, tabs)

The Men From U.N.C.L.E.
//home.sol.no/~hekleive/uncletupelo.html (discography, links, reviews)

Uncle Tupelo: Oh My God They're Good!
//theory.physics.missouri.edu/~georges/josh/pages/ut.html

Dave Richeson's Uncle Tupelo, Son Volt, Wilco Page
//math.nwu.edu/~richeson/tweedfar.html

High Water: Uncle Tupelo, Son Volt, Wilco Page
//www.duke.edu/~cjr2/

Uncle Tupelo Fan Page
//www.city.ac.uk/~er583/music/uncle_tupelo/

Uncle Tupelo/Wilco/Son Volt Discography
//www.ask.or.jp/~saki/discography/ut/

Uncle Tupelo FAQ //gdbdoc.gdb.org/~sue/ut.faq

Uncle Tupelo UWP Info Archive
//anonymous:-WWWuser@ftp.uwp.edu/pub/music/artists/u/uncle.tupelo

Son Volt, Wilco, Uncle Tupelo Lyrics
//www.usinternet.com/users/yoflute/index.html

Uncle Tupelo On-Line Mailing List
mailserv@lyman.stanford.edu

Postcard: The Uncle Tupelo, Son Volt, Wilco Mailing List
//www.servtech.com/ddewey/postcard/

Passenger Side/Postcard 2 Mailing List
//www.gumbopages.com/music/pass-side.html

No Depression/Alt. Country AOL Folder:
Entertainment>Music>Chat & Messages>Music Community>Alternative>Alternative Topics

See The Bottle Rockets; Golden Smog; Son Volt; Wilco

Uncle Walt's Band

See Walter Hyatt

Unknown Hinson

Tobacco Row; White Trash Parody
Albemarle, North Carolina; 1993-

In spite of (or perhaps because of) political correctness, interest in Redneck culture has come on strong in the 1990s. Humorists, in particular, have had a field day. At one end of the spectrum is the popular "You might be a redneck if..." routine of Jeff Foxworthy which tends to gloss over some of the darker spaces in Southern society. However, several satirists have dealt with them head on: Southern Culture on the Skids, Redneck Greece Delux, Drive-By Truckers, W. W. Schnipp, and perhaps the most outrageous of all, Unknown Hinson. The latter is the alter ego of Danny Baker who had long been known as one of the

great guitarists in the Carolinas. He created Unknown Hinson in 1993 when he and a friend (Don Swan) put together a show for local cable TV called *Wild, Wild South*. It starred Baker as Unknown (think of a grown up Eddie Munster with huge side burns and bad teeth) and Swan as Rebel Helms in totally crazed out send ups of Redneck stereotypes: sexism, incest, child molesting, hunting, etc. Hinson, who fashions himself as a vampire, played originals on the show extolling the virtues of romance, Redneck style; "Love on Command" ("I want your love on command, it's communism if you don't"), "It Don't Bother Me" ("It don't bother me when you cuss me when I try to kiss you, or scream for help when I come home"). *Wild, Wild South* was picked up by the nationally broadcast satellite network, Weird TV, and in 1994, Hinson was voted Charlotte's Best Local TV Personality. In addition, Hinson established himself as a popular musical act, "The King of Country & Western Troubadours," who invented country music but had the idea ripped off by Nashville. The "Thomas Edison of Western Folk Music" recorded an independent tape (**21 Chart Toppers**) with his band, the Lost Combo, and did a cut ("Baby Let's Play Rough") for a compilation of wild North Carolina alt. country, **Bubbahey Mud Truck**. There's also a video collection from the *Wild, Wild South* aka *The Unknown Hinson Show*. To balance out the sociopathic Hinson, Baker had another personae, Veg McArtful, the embodiment of Political Correctness. However, it is his redneck character that drew national attention. *The Unknown Hinson Show* continued in the late 1990s as one of the most popular local shows, and as Hinson's promo material says, "Stay tuned...the future is UNKNOWN!"

21 Chart Toppers/UH/1995 (CS)
"Baby Let's Play Rough" on **Bubbahey Mud Truck**/Fire Ant/1996
The Unknown Hinson Show, Vol. 1/1998 (video)

Unknown Hinson Fan Club, 7810 Whitmere Ln., Charlotte, NC 28227

The Unknown Hinson Show
//www.silverhammer.com/unknown.html

Unhinson@aol.com

The V-Roys

Twangtrust; Roots Rock
Knoxville, Tennessee; c. 1994-

When Steve Earle and Jack Emerson established E Squared Records in 1995, the first band they signed was the V-Roys. They were impressed not only by the group's appearance (suits and ties) and sound (a mix of country with 1960s-1980s pop rock) but also with the fact that, just a year after their formation, the V-Roys had become one of the most popular acts in Western Tennessee. The leader of the group, Scott Miller, had previously played in a bluegrass band, pitched songs in Nashville, and was part of Atlanta's Redneck Underground before settling in Knoxville in 1990. There, he met drummer

Jeff Bills, and they began to jam informally. Inspired by the songwriting skills of Roger Miller, the duo crafted songs, added a guitarist, John Paul Keith, and bassist, Paxton Sellers, and took the name the Viceroys. Playing regularly in Knoxville and then Nashville, they caught a good buzz and interest from independent labels. Their initial deal was with Jack Emerson who had managed the Georgia Satellites and Jason & the Scorchers and whose Praxis label had recorded albums by Shaver and Webb Wilder. Unfortunately, Praxis folded shortly after the Viceroys signed on, but, luckily, Emerson and Earle formed E Squared soon thereafter, and the Viceroys got a new home. After getting a new guitar player (Mic Harrsion) to replace Keith and a new name, the V-Roys (to avoid conflict with another band), they entered the studio. With Earle producing, they recorded **Just Add Ice**. The album shows definite signs of Earle's influence but retains the V-Roys unique qualities: infectious energy, catchy melodies, and Miller's humorous and intelligent songwriting. Their debut created a major hoopla within the alternative country community and won them inclusion in several prominent alt. country compilations. In late 1996, they toured England with Earle and cut an EP with him, **Johnny Too Bad,** which has Earle doing his prison song "Ellis Unit One," the V-Roys on "Straight Highway," and Earle/V-Roys with two versions of the reggae influenced title track. In 1997, the V-Roys backed Earle on "In the Jailhouse Now" for Dylan's Jimmie Rodgers tribute album and toured the U.S. and Europe with him. The release of their second recording, **All About Town**, was delayed by a battle between Warner Brothers and E-Squared, but the latter finally issued it in October 1998. Once again, the V-Roys shoot for maximum pop/rock/country hooks although in a much more subdued manner than on **Just Add Ice**. Their own tour plus numerous TV and radio performances in 1998-1999 moved them further out of Earle's shadow and into their own little alt. country spot.

Jeff Bills (d); Mic Harrison (l.g.); Scott Miller (g,v); Paxton Sellers (b)

Just Add Ice/E-Squared/1996
"What She's Found" on **American Songbook**/Demon UK/1996
"Long Time Leavin'" on **Cowpunks**/Vinyl Junkie UK/1996
Johnny Too Bad (with Steve Earle)/E Squared/1996 (EP)
"In the Jailhouse Now" (with Steve Earle) on **The Songs of Jimmie Rodgers: A Tribute**/Egyptian/1997
All About Town/E-Squared/1998

The V-Roys Home Page
//www.vroys.com

V-Roys/E-Squared Page //www.e2records.com/vroys.html

The V-Roys AOL Folder: Entertainment>Music>Chat & Messages.>Music Community>Alternative>Alternative Bands, S-Z

See Steve Earle

Susanna Van Tassel
Austin; Honky Tonk
California/Austin

My introduction to Susanna Van Tassel was through Ace Cafe's compilation, **Pushing the Norton** (1995). Her version of "I've Got My Pride" really knocked me out, and I searched, in vain, for more information about her. Shortly after this, however, I learned Susanna had moved from California to Austin (where I was living at the time), and I got to know her when she became part of the Broken Spoke/Continental Club alt. country crowd. And, the one word which seemed to fit her was stunning; looks, stage presence, vocals. Plus, Susanna is one of the nicest people you'll ever meet and has remained that way in spite of a slow, two year climb up Austin's musical ladder playing whenever and wherever with the *band du jour*. Her endurance paid off in 1997 when she secured a stable supporting band with David Carroll on bass, the legendary John X. Reed on guitar, and the incomparable Lisa Pancratz on drums. Soon, Susanna and company nailed down a monthly spot at the Broken Spoke and were opening for Austin's alt. country elite (the Derailers, Jeff Hughes, Dale Watson, et al.). She made her Texas recording debut on **The Edge of Country** compilation with two songs ("I Remember You"; "Something Blue") which highlight her fine honky tonk voice. After a showcase at SXSW 1998 and a trip to Norway for the Down on the Farm Festival, Susanna took time off in late 1998-1999 to experience the joys of mommyhood.

"I've Got My Pride" on **Pushing the Norton**/Heyday/1995
"I Remember You" and "Something Blue" on **The Edge of Country**/Stockade/1997
"Something Blue" on **Down on the Farm XI**/DOTF Nor./1998

Susanna Van Tassel vojo@msn.com; 512-302-0605

Townes Van Zandt
Texas; Singer/Songwriter
Ft. Worth, Texas; March 7, 1944-d.
January 1, 1997; Nashville, Tennessee

Townes Van Zandt is one of the great (some would say the greatest) American songwriters of the last half century. The details of his life, which have been chronicled many times before, need not be recounted here and would only scratch the surface of this complex man. To really understand Van Zandt, you must look at his music; not just the individual songs ("If I Needed You"; "Pancho & Lefty"; "Waitin' Around to Die"; "To Live is To Fly"; "No Place to Fall"), which could stand on their own as testament, but his work in its entirety; an autobiography in the discography of a poet who seemed to be made of equal parts inspiration and desperation. After his untimely (but not unexpected) death from a heart attack on the last day of 1996, Van Zandt's music became more accessible due to a flurry of re-releases of material out of print for some time and the appearance of previously unreleased recordings. Sugar Hill reissued **Rear View Mirror** and **The Highway Kind** in 1997, and two slightly different versions of a recording with songs and interview from 1992-1993 (with Larry Monroe of KUT) were released in Europe and the U.S. In 1998, Charly Records issued the double CD **Anthology, 1968-1979**. However, the most anticipated posthumous collection was the 4 CD/60 track box (**Newology**) featuring 47 duets with Van Zandt's impressive list of friends and admirers (Johnny Cash, Bob Dylan, Joe Ely, Jimmie Dale Gilmore, Emmylou Harris, Lyle Lovett, Willie Nelson, John Prine, Doug Sahm, Neil Young, Steve Earle). Completed just prior to Van Zandt's death, its release date was delayed by a dispute about "overproduction" between Tomato and Townes' estate. Many of the artists who participated in this project were involved in several major tribute shows held in early 1997 in Los Angeles, New York, and Austin. Such events brought renewed interest in and appreciation for the enormous contributions made by the man who literally lived "for the sake of the song." In 1998, the Austin Music Network broadcast *Building His Houseboat in Heaven*, a taped tribute held in 1997 at the Cactus Cafe. Fans expressed their adulation by establishing impressive web pages devoted to Van Zandt. These sites not only contain extensive biographical and discographical information but also memorial pages, Internet mailing lists, and a "juke box" playing full length versions of Van Zandt's songs.

For the Sake of the Song/Poppy/1968; Tomato Rhino/1994
Our Mother the Mountain/Poppy/1969
Townes Van Zandt/Poppy/1970; Tomato/1989
Delta Mama Blues/Poppy/1971; Tomato/1989
High, Low and In Between/Poppy/1972; Tomato/1989; Rhino/1994; EMI/1996 (with **The Late, Great Townes Van Zandt**)
The Late, Great Townes Van Zandt/Poppy/1972; Tomato/1989
Live at the Old Quarter, Houston/Tomato/1977; Charly Ger./1998
Flyin' Shoes/Tomato/1978; Rhino/1994
At My Window/Sugar Hill/1987
Live and Obscure/Sugar Hill/1989
Rain on a Conga Drum, Live in Berlin/Exile Ger./1991
Rear View Mirror (Live)/Sundown/1993; Sugar Hill/1997
Nashville Sessions/Tomato Rhino/1993
Roadsongs/Sugar Hill/1994
No Deeper Blue/Sugar Hill/1995
The Best of Townes Van Zandt/Charly Ger./1996
Abnormal (Live)/Return to Sender Ger./1996 (only 2000 printed); Normal Ger./1998 (w/ extra trks.)
"The Hole (Live)" on **Cowpunks**/Vinyl Junkie/1996
The Highway Kind (Live)/Sugar Hill/1997
Last Rights: The Life and Times of Townes Van Zandt/ Gregor/1997 or **Documentary**/Normal Euro./1997
Anthology, 1968-1979/Charly Ger./1998
A Far Cry From Dead/Arista Austin/1999
Newology (Townes Van Zandt Box Set)/Tomato/?

Townes Van Zandt Central (Official)
//www.townesvanzandt.com (Jeanene Van Zandt's site w/ TVZ Catalog)

Jeanene.vanzandt@nashville.com

Townes Van Zandt/Lone Star Web Station Site
//www.lonestarwebstation.com/townesdex/ (lots of TVZ info and links)

Townes Van Zandt: Blue Sky Home Page
//www.orst.edu/dept/entomology/coopl/tvzindex.htm (with Juke Box and Memorial Page)

Townes Van Zandt Lyrics Page
//home3.swipnet.se/~w-36794/tvz/albums.html

Austin 360 Townes Van Zandt Web Page
//www.Austin360.com/enter/music/profiles/vanzandt/vanzandt.htm

Townes Van Zandt AOL Folder:
Entertainment>Music>Chat & Messages>Music Community>Folk/Acoustic

The Vidalias
Redneck Underground
Atlanta, Georgia; 1993-1997

In the early 1990s, Charles Walston was kicking around Atlanta, working as a journalist for a local newspaper, writing songs, and recording an occasional demo. He gave one of these to local musician, Page Waldrop, who was very impressed and encouraged Walston to start a band. With Walston on lead vocals and Waldrop on lead guitar, they added bassist Jim Johnson, drummer David Michaelson (ex-Georgia Satellites), and became the Vidalias (named for a local variety of sweet onion). While playing a gig one night, pedal steel player Henry Bruns sat in and was invited to become a permanent member. Soon, the Vidalias joined the Redneck Underground, playing several Bubbapalooza festivals and contributing "Falkin' It" to the **Bubbapalooza** compilation in 1995. That year, **Melodyland** was released to very favorable reviews and was followed in 1997 by another winner, **Stayin' in the Doghouse**. Like all Redneck Underground bands, the Vidalias deliver maximum twang for the buck with honky tonk, country rock, and wail-in-your-ale ballads by lead songwriter and singer Walston who was greatly influenced by Gram Parsons. Like most classic country songs, his originals employ catchy lyrics combining just the right amounts of humor and pathos. Walston possesses a deliciously nasal twang (most often compared to Gram) that is especially effective on moderate and slow tempo tunes about lovin' ("Carry Me"; "What a Nice Surprise"; "Such a Mystery") and losin' ("Tokens of Affliction"; "Loser Leave Town"; "Whole Lotta Doin' Without"; "All Over Me"). The other Vidalias provide very able support. Waldrop handles rockers and ballads with equal skill and Bruns, whether on pedal or lap steel, never fails to set just the right background mood. In 1997, the band welcomed a new drummer, Kat Cunningham, and toured extensively in support of their second album, but in a surprise move, announced their break-up late in the year. Page Waldrop went on in 1998 to play lead guitar with Atlanta newcomer Laura Tyler.

Randy Arrant (d,1995-1996); Henry Bruns (p.s.); Kat Cunningham (d, 1997-); Jim Johnson (b); David Michaelson (d,1993-1995); Page Waldrop (e.g.); Charles Walston (a.g.,e.g.hm,l.v.)

"Innocent Bystander" b/w "Misery Loves Company"/ Safety Net/1994 (7")
"Fakin' It" on **Bubbapalooza, Vol. 1**/Sky/1995
Melodyland/Upstart/1995
"Something She Said" b/w "Questioningly"/Diesel Only Upstart/1995 (7")
"Misery Loves Company" on **Revival: Brunswick Stew & Pig Pickin'**/Yep Roc/1996
Stayin' in the Doghouse/Upstart/1997

The Volebeats
Insurgent Country
Royal Oak (Detroit), Michigan; 1988-

There aren't too many bands who could take songs by Abba, Barry White, Slayer, and P-Funk and successfully transform them into engaging country/roots/rock numbers. However, this is the forte of the Volebeats who for almost a decade have skillfully combined traditional American music (country, folk, blues) with modern sounds ranging from the Byrds to the Violent Femmes. Created in Detroit in 1988 from an early Bob McCreedy/Jeff Oakes duo (the Frames), the band played street gigs for a time before getting established on the local scene; in 1989, the Volebeats were named Band of the Year by a group of Motor City music writers. Their debut album of that year, **Ain't No Joke**, was a collection of originals blending Gram/ Byrds/Flying Burrito Brothers country rock, honky tonk, surf/spaghetti western, and folkish ballads. It was well received by fans and critics, but over the next few years, the Volebeats drifted apart with McCreedy moving to San Francisco for a time. Upon his return in 1992, a reunited Volebeats cut a single of Abba's "Knowing You, Knowing Me" reworked into a jangly, Byrdsian style tune, but their next recording didn't come until 1994 with **Up North**. This album finds the Volebeats settling comfortably into their signature sound one critic called "cosmic backwoods bebop" but the band simply called "middle Western." In 1995, the Volebeats became Detroit's insurgent country representative when their song "One I Love" made the **Hell-Bent** compilation; before releasing their next full length CD they did an EP, **Bittersweet**, which has a haunting rendition of Barry White's "I'm Gonna Love You Just a Little More, Baby." Then, in 1997 came **Sky and the Ocean** and songs for two eclectic compilations. They cut "Hamtramck Mama" for the **Straight Outta Boone County** collection, and at the other end of the spectrum, an acoustic version of "Die By the Sword" for a tribute to heavy metal band, Slayer. Late in 1997, the Volebeats joined members of the Grievous Angels (Arizona)

and Thornetta Davis for a single of P-Funk's "Maggot Brain" further enhancing their reputation as one of the most unique and versatile of alt. country bands. They got a chance to bring their sound to a wider audience when they opened for Whiskeytown during a three month tour in 1998. European fans became more aware of the Volebeats as well when two of their songs were included on German and Swedish alt. country/Americana compilations in 1997 and 1998 and German Blue Rose began distributing the band's recordings.

Erika Hoffmann (b.v.,1988-1992); Russell Ledford (b); Bob McCreedy (g,b.v.); Scott Michalski (d); Keir McDonald (d); Brian Oakes (b); Jeff Oakes (v); Bill Peterson (d,1988-1994); Matthew Smith (g,l.v.)

Ain't No Joke/Relapse/1989
"Knowing Me, Knowing You" b/w "The First Time Next Time"/Icon/1992 (7")
Up North/Safe House/1994
"One I Love" on **Hell-Bent**/Bloodshot/1995
Bittersweet/Third Gear/1995 (6 trk. EP CD)
Sky and the Ocean/Safe House/1997
"Hamtramck Mama" on **Straight Outta Boone County**/Bloodshot/1997
"Die By the Sword" on **5 Out of 5 Kids Who Kill Love Slayer**/1997 (7")
"Maggot Brain, Parts 1 &2"/Bloodshot/1997 (7")
"Sky & The Ocean" on **Blue Rose Collection, Vol. 1**/Blue Rose Ger./1997
"What a Lonely Way to Go" on **Fireworks2**/Sound Asleep Swe./1998

The Volebeats c/o Safehouse Records, P.O. Box 214, Poultney, VT 05764

Safehouse@aol.com

The Volebeats //www.thirdgear.com/vole_m.html

The Volebeats Biography //www.bluerose-records.com/d/www/volebeat.html

The Volo Bogtrotters
New Old-Time
Chicago, Illinois; 1985-

The Volo Bogtrotters have been a vital part of the Upper Midwest's thriving old-time music community since the mid-1980s when they were founded by Chirps Smith, Steve Rosen, and Fred Campeau. All had been with a variety of local bands (Indian Creek Delta Boys, the Polecats, Hot Tamale and the Red Hots) and were especially active in the Chicago Barn Dance Co. dances of the 1970s and early 1980s. Taking their name from a geological anomaly near Volo, Illinois, they dipped into traditional old-time material from both Midwestern and Appalachian sources but like their contemporaries, the Boiled Buzzards, Skeeter & the Skidmarks, et al., infused it with a modern energy and plenty of humor. Bassist Tony Scarimbolo joined in the late 1980s, followed by guitarist Paul Tyler in 1993. The Bogtrotters recorded three cassettes (**The Volo Bogtrotters; Backside of Buncombe; Tough Luck**) on Marimac and were on two Rounder collections of new old-time before releasing their first full-length CD in 1997. Chirps Smith also did some solo recordings including **Prairie Dog** and **Midwestern Harvest**. Into the late 1990s, the Volo Bogtrotters were regulars on the old-time fiddler and dance circuits in northern Illinois. The tongue-in-cheek title of their 1998, **Old-Time String Band With Accompaniment**, is an apt summary of their attitude and style.

Fred Campeau (f,v); Steve Rosen (bj); Tony Scarimbolo (b); Lynn "Chirps" Smith (f); Paul Tyler (g)

> **The Volo Bogtrotters**/Marimac/198?
> **Backside of Buncombe**/Marimac/199?
> **Tough Luck**/Marimac/199?
> "Quit That Ticklin' Me" on **Old-Time Music on the Radio, Vol. 1**/Rounder/1994
> "The Crow Song" on **The Young Fogies, Vol. 2**/Rounder/1995
> **Prairie Dog** (Chirps Smith)/Marimac/1993
> **Midwestern Harvest** (Chirps Smith)/Marimac/1994
> **Old-Time String Band With Vocal Accompaniment**/Marimac/1998

The Volo Bogtrotters c/o Chirps Smith, 141 N. Lake St., Grayslake, IL 60030-1520 or smithl@hpd.abbott.com

The Volo Bogtrotters
//members.tripod.com/~nailthatcatfish/volo.html

The Waco Brothers

See Jon Langford

Wagon

No Depression; Grain Belt Rock
St. Louis. Missouri; 1992-

Although falling squarely within the no depression wing of alt. country along with other Midwestern bands like Uncle Tupelo/Son Volt/Wilco, the Jayhawks, and the Bottle Rockets, Wagon tended to tone down the rock in favor of a mellower take on traditional country. Adding a little grit now and then, they generally eschewed electric in favor of acoustic instruments and unvarnished vocals. Wagon was driven primarily by multi-instrumentalist Steve Rauner (accordion, mandola, organ) and the soaring fiddle of former Arkansas State champion, Chris Peterson. **No Kinder Room** (produced by Lloyd Maines) presented a variety of acoustic/electric material reminiscent (with a few original twists) of several other alt. country groups; "No Kinder Room," "Too Long Here," "Wishful Thinking" (early Jayhawks); "Downtown Larry Brown," "Yesterday's Coffee" (5 Chinese Brothers); "Crumble" (Bottle Rockets). In the summer of 1996, Wagon opened up on tours with Kelly Willis and Billy Pilgrim and in early 1997 began work (without Rauner who joined Nadine) on a follow-up recording, **Anniversary**. Released first in Europe by Glitterhouse and then the U.S. through the band in 1998, it was actually recorded in an old barn in rural Illinois and sticks close to the formula of **No Kinder Room**. England's *Uncut* magazine thought enough of

Wagon to include them in their special September 1998 Alternative Country issue and on its accompanying CD, **Sounds of the New West: The Best of Alternative Country**.

Ben Davis (g,v); Danny Kathriner (d,v); Chris Peterson (bj,dulc,f,md); Steve Rauner (acc, mda,org,1992-1996); Len Small (b,v)

> **Soon**/Station Music/1993
> **No Kinder Room**/Hightone/1996
> "Slack Key Blues" on **Out of the Gate Again**/BJAM/1996
> **Anniversary**/Glitterhouse Ger./1998; Wagon/1998
> "Slack Key Blues" on **Luxury Liner2**/Glitterhouse Ger./1998
> "Two Hours Alone" on **Sounds of the New West**/Uncut UK/1998

Wagon Home Page //www.wagon1.com

wagon@wagon1.com

See Nadine

The Wagoneers

See Monte Warden

Wake (The Flyin' Mice)

Tobacco Road; Country Rock; Roots Rock
Chapel Hill, North Carolina; 1989-

Wake grew out of the roots rock band Flyin' Mice which from 1989-1996 released three fine recordings (**So Hi Drive**; **Brighter Day**; **So Long**) with a wide variety of Americana from blues to bluegrass, ragtime to rock. Their sound was often tagged as "psychedelic hillbilly." Shortly after the Mice broke up, alumni Jon Shain and Mark Simonsen regrouped with Darrell Dixon, John Currie, and Kirsten Simonsen as Wake. And while they retained some vestiges of the roots rock that made the Flyin' Mice a local favorite, the new band shifted toward a more straight forward country rock sound. The songwriting ("Buttons of Gold"; "Weight of Time") and vocal interchange between Shain and Kirsten Simonsen on **Wake** evoke the classic pairings of Gram and Emmylou.

The Flyin' Mice (1989-1996): Stu Cole (a.g.,db,v); Aaron Oliva (b); Ben Saffer (bj,g,v); Jon Shain (g,md,v); Mark Simonsen (d,v) **Wake (1996-):** John Currie (a.g.,e.g.); Darrell Dixon (b,v); John Shain (a.g.,e.g.,v); Kirsten Simonsen (md,v); Mark Simonsen (d,v)

> **So Hi Drive** (Flyin' Mice)/Dr. Lime/1991
> **Brighter Day** (Flyin' Mice)/Dr. Lime/1994
> **So Long** (Flyin' Mice)/Dr. Lime/1996 (CS)
> **Wake**/Wake/1997

Wake/Flyin' Mice, P.O. Box 5215,
Chapel Hill, NC 27514-5002; 919-967-3596

The Official Wake Page //www.flash.net/~flyinrex/wake/

Flyinrex@aol.com

Dusty Wakeman

TSOB; Producer; Engineer; Bass
Texas/Los Angeles, California

Working quietly behind the scenes, Dusty Wakeman has been a key figure in Southern California alt. country for nearly two decades. The native Texan arrived in L.A. in the late 1970s and with Michael Dumas established Mad Dog Studios which became an important recording center. Throughout the 1980s and 1990s, Wakeman played bass for a variety of local musicians including Rosie Flores, Jim Lauderdale, Michelle Shocked, Lucinda Williams, and Dwight Yoakam, but his major contribution was as an engineer and producer. He guided/engineered recordings of many types, but the bulk of his work was with TSOB and other alt. country musicians: engineer for **A Town South of Bakersfield, Vols. 1 & 2**; engineer/producer for Lucinda Williams' **Lucinda Williams** and **Sweet Old World**, engineer/producer for Jim Lauderdale's **Pretty Close to the Truth** and **Every Second Counts**; engineer/producer for Rosie Flores' Hightone recordings; engineer for Dwight Yoakam's **Buenas Noches From a Lonely Room** and **This Time**. He produced or co-produced recordings by Tom Russell (**Box of Visions**), Somebody's Darling, Giant Sand, and Anthony Crawford. In 1996, Wakeman helped Pete Anderson set up Little Dog Records where he lent his production expertise to projects by Scott Joss and the Lonesome Strangers (**Land of Opportunity**). Dusty also helped TSOB's "next generation" in 1998 when he produced the debut of the Bakersfield style honky tonk band, Billy Tulsa and the Psycho Crawdads.

Dusty Wakeman c/o Little Dog Records, 223 W. Alameda #201, Burbank, CA 91502 or LilDogRecs@aol.com

The Walkabouts

Grange Rock
Seattle, Washington; 1984-

Although the Walkabouts have been around since the early 1980s and have over a dozen LPs and numerous EPs to their credit, they have remained one of America's most obscure and under-appreciated (in the U.S. at least) alt. country bands. Started in 1984, their original line up consisted of Chris Eckman and his brothers Grant and Kurt who all came from punk backgrounds plus Carla Torgerson whose roots were in folk music. On several small labels and then with famous grunge label, SubPop, they sought the commonalties between traditional folk and country and modern rock. With Chris Eckman's gruff, whispered vocals providing counterpoint to Torgerson's lush soprano, the Walkabouts showed a steady musical evolution on **Cataract** and **Scavenger** but found little success in their home country. But, with a new supporting band (the Eckman brothers left in 1991), Chris and Carla found more receptive audiences in Europe where their genre bending didn't seem so alien. Recording on SubPop's European labels and on Glitterhouse in Germany, the Walkabouts really blossomed on three successive albums, **New West Motel**, **Satisfied Mind**, and **Setting the Woods on Fire**. Each weaves together acoustic and electric sounds on Eckman originals plus covers ranging from the Carter Family and Hank Williams to Charlie Rich, Bob Dylan, Nick Cave, John Cale, and Patti Smith. These recordings and tours to support them helped win the Walkabouts an extensive following throughout Europe. Chris and Carla reinforced this popularity by touring as a duo and recording material (**Shelter for an Evening**; **Life Full of Holes**) with a decidedly Walkabouts flavor. Unfortunately, the Walkabouts continued to be virtually unknown in the U.S. although three of their best recordings were released in the States by Creativeman in 1995. In 1996, Glitterhouse issued **Death Valley Days**, a collection of demos, out takes, and contributions to various compilations that presents an overview of the Walkabouts' development between 1985 and 1995. That same year, the band signed with Virgin Europe signaling a slight detour in the Walkabouts' musical odyssey. **Devil's Road** keeps much of the signature Walkabouts' style while branching out using strings courtesy of the Warsaw Philharmonic; **Nighttown**, on the other hand, recorded with new bass player Baker Saunders (blues, r&b background), represents a fairly radical departure from the Walkabouts previous rural leanings toward a more contemporary urban sound complete with strings and synthesizers.

During an eight month Walkabouts "sabbatical" (February-September 1998), Chris & Carla recorded **Swinger 500**, a lo-fi affair (including Willie's "How Time Slips Away") with help from current and former Walkabouts. Eckman also produced an album for the Norwegian band Midnight Choir and then the Walkabouts reassembled to do a cover of "Albuquerque" for the Neil Young tribute, **This Note's for You Too!** and recorded their new CD, both of which were due in 1999.

Chris Eckman (a.g.,e.g.v); Kurt Eckman (b,1984-1991); Grant Eckman (d,1984-1991); Terri Moeller (d,b.v.,1991-); Baker Saunders (b,1997-1998); Glenn Slater (acc, ky); Carla Torgerson (a.g.,cello,e.g.,v), Mike Wells (b,1991-1996)

The Walkabouts/Necessity/1984 (EP CS)
22 Disasters/Necessity/1985
See Beautiful Rattlesnake Gardens/Pop Llama/1987
Cataract/SubPop/1989
Rag & Bone/SubPop/1990
Where the Deep Water Goes/SubPop/1991 (EP)
Scavenger/SubPop/1991
Rag & Bone & Cataract/Glitterhouse Ger./1992
Dead Man Rise/SubPop/1992 (EP)
Jack Candy/SubPop/1993 (EP)
New West Motel/SubPop UK/1993; Creativeman/1995
Your Hope Shines/SubPop Ger./1993 (EP)
Satisfied Mind/SubPop UK/1993; Creativeman/1995
Shelter for an Evening (Chris and Carla)/SubPop Ger./1993

Setting the Woods on Fire/SubPop UK/1994;
   Creativeman/1995
Good Luck Morning/SubPop Ger./1994 (EP)
Life Full of Holes (Chris and Carla)/Glitterhouse
   Ger./1995
Nights Between Stations: Live in Thessaloniki (Chris
   and Carla Live with The Mylos All Stars)/Glitterhouse
   Ger./1995
To Hell & Back, Live in Europe 1994/Glitterhouse
   Ger./1995
Devil's Road/Virgin Schallplatten/1996
Death Valley Days: Lost Songs and Rarities,
   1985-1995/Glitterhouse Ger./1996
Nighttown/Virgin Schallplatten/1997
"Runaround" (Chris and Carla) b/w "Archy's Lullaby"
   (Willard Grant Conspiracy)/Dahlia/1997 (7")
Swinger 500 (Chris and Carla)/Glitterhouse Ger./1998
"On the Beach" on **Sounds of the New West**/Uncut
   UK/1998
"Albuquerque" on **This Note's for You Too!: A Tribute**
   to Neil Young/Inbetweens Dut./1999

The Walkabouts, 4739 University Way NE, Ste. 1100,
Seattle, WA 98105

Walka777@aol.com

The Walkabouts Home Page
//www.hooked.net/~cbhall/walk.html

The Walkabouts/Glitterhouse Page
//www.ontide.de/glitterhouse/

See Larry Barrett

Chris Wall

Austin; Honky Tonk; Singer/Songwriter
Hollywood, California; February 26, 1952-

Chris Wall was born in the heart of Los Angeles, but as a kid he
had the rare privilege of spending summers on an uncle's cattle
ranch in Montana. There, he became familiar with country
music and cowboy culture and after graduating from Whittier
College toured around the West working part time as a movie
actor, bartender, and cowboy. Eventually, Wall landed in
Bozeman, Montana, where, in the mid-1980s, he began to learn
guitar and took up country songwriting. In 1987, Wall, at the
insistence of friends, made his first public performance at a bar
in Jackson Hole, Wyoming. Later that year at an Idaho music
festival, he met Guy Clark who was impressed by Wall's songs
and passed the word on to Jerry Jeff Walker. The "Scamp" came
to see Wall play, induced him to move to Austin, and covered
two of his songs on **Live at Gruene Hall** (1989). One of these,
"Trashy Women," subsequently became a mega-hit for the
group Confederate Railroad, but the other, "I Feel Like Hank
Williams Tonight," showed Wall's depth as a country songwriter. Meanwhile, Wall became a favorite on the Texas dance
hall circuit and developed a following known as his "entourage," a boisterous collection of cowboys/cowgirls, frat rats,
sorority sisters, and assorted hell raisers. They were lured by his
good time live shows (with his band, the Rhythm Wranglers)

and acclaimed recordings, **Honky Tonk Heart**, **No Sweat**, and
Cowboy Nation. Wall's songwriting skills (part honky tonk,
part cowboy poetry), which shine on "Rodeo Wind," "I Wish
John Stetson Made a Heart," "I'll Take the Whiskey (You Take
the Wheel)," "Way Out West," "I Drink Therefore I Am," and
many others, were honored in 1995 with an outstanding
achievement award from the Nashville Songwriters Association International. He appeared on television through TNN,
CMT, and on a BBC documentary. Wall took over historic
Gruene Hall on Texas Independence Day, 1996 to make a live
recording, **Any Saturday Night in Texas**, with many guests
including Dale Watson, Kelly Willis, Bruce Robison, and Mary
Cutrufello. His Cold Spring label signed local sensations
Reckless Kelly and put out their debut in 1997. They, in turn,
backed Chris on his 1998 **Tainted Angel** which as a result has a
different sound than his previous Texas honky tonk recordings
but retains Wall's usual high level of songwriting. Cold Spring
and Wall released the soundtrack for the 1998 documentary
Bull Riders: Chasing the Dream which has songs by Chris
and the elite of Austin alt. country including Don Walser, the
Derailers, and Reckless Kelly.

Honky Tonk Heart/Rykodisc/1989
No Sweat/Rykodisc/1991
Cowboy Nation/Cold Spring/1994
Any Saturday Night in Texas/Cold Spring/1996
Tainted Angel/Cold Spring/1998
"Cowboy Nation"; "Let 'Er Buck"; "Rodeo Wind" on **Bull**
   Riders: Chasing the Dream/Cold Spring/1998
"The Poet Is Not in Today" on **Edges From the**
   Postcard2/P2/1998

Rhythm Wrangler Music, P. O. Box 161943,
Austin, TX 78716; 512-320-9156

Chris Wall Home Page
//www.cold-spring.com

coldspring@ccsi.com

See Reckless Kelly

Don Walser

Austin; Honky Tonk; Yodeling
Brownfield, Texas; September 14, 1934-

Of the many honky tonk artists to come out of Austin in the past
ten years, none has been more beloved than Don Walser.
Country, rock, punk, and even classical fans and musicians
from the world over have found his classic honky tonk vocals
and yodeling (*a la* Jimmie Rodgers, Elton Britt, Slim Whitman)
irresistible. Even more remarkable is the fact that Walser's
success came so late in his life. Raised in West Texas, he worked
in the oil fields as a teen, married at 17, and in the early 1950s
began working as an accountant for the National Guard with
whom he would remain for over forty years. During this period,
Walser raised and supported his children and, on the side,
played and recorded with several country bands in West Texas
(most notably the Texas Plainsmen). After relocating to Austin

in 1984, he continued to support his family and pursue music part time but, in the late 1980s, began to assemble the band that would help propel him to his dream of a full time musical career. Named the Pure Texas Band, charter members included the great Jimmy Day or Bert Rivera on steel, Gil De Los Santos on drums, "Skinny" Don Keeling on bass, and Howard Kalish on fiddle. In the early 1990s, Walser and the PTB became regulars at the legendary Henry's honky tonk which also served as a springboard for such artists as Junior Brown and Cornell Hurd. Through this and other popular venues and a number of self released recordings combining covers of honky tonk and Western swing standards with Walser originals, the group built the all important buzz that spread through Austin and beyond like a prairie wildfire. With accolades like "greatest living country singer" and "Pavarotti of the Plains" (*Playboy*) pouring in, it was only a matter of time before Walser secured a record contract. In 1994, local label Watermelon signed him up, and Don finally gave up his day job. Soon thereafter, Watermelon released **Rolling Stone From Texas** to a legion of fans awaiting in breathless anticipation. However, the album, co-produced by Asleep at the Wheel leader Ray Benson and Walser's manager T. J. McFarland, was, to say the least, a bit of a disappointment. Although enthusiastically received outside of Austin, long time followers of Walser and the PTB were upset that the raw but genuine sound of Walser's live performances and self issued tapes had been sacrificed for a polished studio sound. Equally galling was the under or non-use of PTB members on the recording in favor of current and former Asleep at the Wheel musicians. Fans directed their invective at Benson and McFarland and were somewhat appeased when Watermelon issued **The Archive Series, Vol. 1 & 2** which contains 34 re-mastered selections from Walser's early recordings. And, in the long run, the controversy proved to be a tempest in a teacup as Walser's star continued to rise with induction into the Texas Music Hall of Fame, numerous appearances on national television, and a performance at the 1996 Olympics. His second studio recording, **Texas Top Hand**, again produced by Benson/McFarland and using mostly Asleep at the Wheel alumni, was also a pretty lackluster affair but by this time nothing could stop the "Rolling Stone From Texas." In early 1997, Walser won NAIRD's Best Country Band for **Texas Top Hand** and had one of his strangest gigs yet, a concert performance with the classical group, the Kronos Quartet. Later in the year, Don began work on his new recording, **Down at the Sky-Vue Drive-In** which marked his major label debut. Produced once again by Benson, the songs (picked mostly by Don) cover everyone from Jimmy Rodgers and the Louvins to Irving Berlin, the Sons of the Pioneers, and Johnny Bush; there's even a curious rendition of Oscar Hammerstein's "Rose Marie" with the Kronos Quartet. Highly regarded by fans and reviewers outside Austin, critics in Walser's hometown were as cool to

Down at the Sky-Vue ("overproduced"; "embellished") as they were to **Rolling Stone From Texas** and **Texas Top Hand**. However, none of this criticism seemed to bother the Big One. He showed up in publications and on radio and TV shows across the nation, made his movie debut with a part in the dance hall scene of *Hi-Lo Country* with Woody Harrelson, and contributed to the soundtracks for *The Horse Whisperer, Deep in the Heart of Texas,* and *Bull Riders: Chasing the Dream.* As first reported by John Conquest in *3rd Coast Music* (October 1998), Mark Rubin of the Bad Livers had attained the masters of some 1960s radio recordings of Walser with the Texas Plainsmen and hoped to put them out on CD sometime in the future.

Singing Pure Texas/DW/1991
More Pure Texas/DW/1991
100% Pure Texas/DW/1992
Official Souvenir of Pure Texas Music/DW/1993
Rolling Stone From Texas/Watermelon/1994
The Archive Series, Vols. 1 & 2/Watermelon/1995
"Love Song of the Waterfall" on **Austin Country Nights**/
    Watermelon/1995
Texas Top Hand/Watermelon/1996
Down At the Sky-Vue Drive-In/Sire Watermelon/1998
"Big Ball's in Cowtown" on **The Horse Whisperer**/
    MCA/1998
"Rolling Stone From Texas" on **Deep in the Heart of
    Texas**/Shanachie/1998
"Bullrider's Last Ride" on **Bull Riders: Chasing the
    Dream**/Cold Spring/1998

Don Walser Fan Club, P.O. Box 49056, Austin, TX 78765

Don Walser Home Page //www.donwalser.com

puretexas@donwalser.com

Don Walser/iMusic Showcase
//imusic.com/showcase/country/

Don Walser Chat Page
//www.austin360.com/interact/chat/donchat.htm

Hank Wangford

Country Rock; Cowboy/Western; Novelty
Wangford, Suffolk, England; November 15, 1940-

In March 1970, Gram Parsons traveled to England to work on musical projects with the Rolling Stones and Rick Grech. During his time there, Parsons met a Cambridge educated doctor named Sam Hutt who treated Gram for a minor complaint. One day while at his office, Parsons sang "You're Still on My Mind" from **Sweetheart of the Rodeo** and turned the good doctor on to the joys of country music. Hutt fell hard and began to divide his time between his gynecological practice (why did Gram consult *him*?) and performing country. Later, after his girlfriend dumped him, Hutt found catharsis by developing a separate identity, "Hank Wangford" (named for Hutts' hometown). He conceived of this character as a send up of the classic cry-in-your-beer country singer and in 1976 began playing London pubs. Singing comical originals ("Chicken Rhythm"; "Cowboys Stay on Longer") from the "Wangford

Hall of Pain" and capitalizing on his gynecologist/country singer split personality, Wangford built a cult following. With his band, which always included fine musicians (Martin Delmont, Bobby Valentino, Andy Roberts), he recorded several albums, put on a stage show called "Radio Wang," and did two country series for local television. In 1989, he published his autobiography *Hank Wangford, Vol. III The Middle Years* which discusses his musical career including his relationship with Gram Parsons. In the 1990s, Dr. Hutt was senior medical officer at a London family planning clinic while Hank Wangford and His New Lost Cowboys regularly put on their own version of the old Hank Williams "Health and Happiness Show" with the Lone Yodeler and the Hank Kerchiefs. Wangford wrote two books on cowboy culture: *Lost Cowboys From Patagonia to The Alamo* (part autobiography, part travelogue) and *The History of the Cowboy*. In 1997, he recorded **Wake Up Dead** (produced by Billy Bragg) which keeps the memory of GP alive with some pleasant late 1960s-early 1970s country rock along with Hank's ever present sense of humor.

Live: **Hank Wangford**/HW/1982
Hank Wangford/HW/1985
Rodeo Radio/HW/1985
Stormy Horizons/HW/1990
Hard Shoulder to Cry On/HW/1993
Wake Up Dead/Way Out West UK/1997

Hank Wangford c/o Way Out West Recording Co., 9 Wadley Rd., Leytonstone, London E11 1JF, England or gonecountry@mail.bogo.co.uk

The Wanktones

Big D.C. Jamboree; Honky Tonk; Rockabilly
Washington, DC; 1984-

The Wanktones are in reality the alter ego band of the Slickee Boys, a punk band that was popular in the D.C. area during the late 1970s-early 1990s. In the mid-1980s, the Wanktones cut an EP (**Have a Ball Y'all**) and one self-titled album of honky tonk and rockabilly. Like a similar alter ego group, Red Knuckles & the Trailblazers (Hot Rize), the Wankers adopted a faux hillbilly image complete with gaudy Western wear, hick pseudonyms (Ersel Wank, Hooter McFeeley, Mo Sloe, and Del Marva), and a pure corn history of the band. In 1991, they contributed two cool covers ("Hillbilly Fever"; "Forty Miles of Bad Road") to the first installment of Mike Lynam's **Big D.C. Jamboree** and did the rockabillyish "Little Pig" for volume 3. The latter song is also on the Wanktones' 1997 CD, **Live at the Fontana Bowlarama**, which covers hillbilly, honky tonk standards punctuated by the sound of falling pins and other bowling alley noises. Ersel Wank (Mark Noone) also played guitar with his wife Ruthie Logsdon in Ruthie & the Wranglers and as a member of the swing, Hawaiian, honky tonk, rockabilly trio, the Hula Monsters (not to be confused with the West Coast band of the same name).

Del Marva (g,v); Hooter McFeely (b,v); Mo Sloe (d,v); Ersel Wank (g,v)

Have a Ball Y'all/Wanktones/1984 (EP)
The Wanktones/Midnight/1985
"Hillbilly Fever" and "Forty Miles of Bad Road" on **The Big D.C. Jamboree, Vol. 1**/Run Wild/1991
"Little Pig" on **The Big D.C. Jamboree, Vol. 3**/Run Wild/1993
Live at the Fontana Bowlarama/Run Wild/1997

The Wanktones c/o Run Wild Records, P.O. Box 58, Sea Girt, NJ 08750

Run Wild Records //members.aol.com/blutwang/index.html

See Ruthie & The Wranglers

Monte Warden (The Wagoneers; The Loan Sharks)

Austin; Singer/Songwriter
Houston, Texas; April 26, 1967-

The Wagoneers were one of the most promising alt. country bands to come out of Austin in the late 1980s. Their Texas style rocking country earned them Band of the Year honors at the 1988 Austin Music Awards and a record contract with A&M which resulted in **Stout and High** and **Good Fortune**. The ostensible leader of the group was lead singer and songwriter Monte Warden who in 1983, at age 15, won Best New Band (Austin Music Awards) with a rockabilly group called Whoa, Trigger! His dreamy Buddy Hollyesque vocals and skill at writing ballads ("So Many Mistakes"), honky tonk ("I Wanna Know Her Again"), rockers ("All Nite"), and historical sagas about the battle of the Alamo and the burning of Atlanta made him the heart of the Wagoneers, but it also helped that he had a good band including A-1 lead guitarist Brent Wilson backing him up. Unfortunately, differences over leadership and direction eventually led to the untimely demise of the Wagoneers in 1990, but Warden was quickly snapped up by RCA which gave him a lucrative recording contract. However, the goose that laid the golden egg turned out to be a wolf in sheep's clothing, and Warden's career was mangled by the Nashville hit or else mentality. And though he got out of the contract, Warden was marked as a musical pariah in the Nashville community. Back in Austin, he concentrated on family (Downs syndrome baby born during this time) and songwriting. The latter produced songs covered by Patty Loveless and Kelly Willis, but Warden chafed at sitting on the sideline and in 1992 re-emerged as Monte Warden and the Loan Sharks. This new band, which initially included old pal Brent Wilson, played some Wagoneers ma- terial but generally dropped the country influence in favor of 1950s-1960s pop rock centered on Warden's impassioned vocals and songs like "'Til She Walked In," "All I Want is You," "Dyin' Inside," and "Teardrops." His "Just to Hear Your Voice" was covered by Toni Price and in 1994 was named Song of the Year at the Austin Music Awards. In 1995, the Wagoneers reunited briefly to record a rollicking version of Buddy Holly's "Down the Line" for the **Austin Country Nights** compilation. Monte contributed "Take Me With U" (backed by Jack Ingram's Beat Up Ford Band) to the curious **Do Me Baby: Austin Does Prince** in 1996. Weathering a divorce in 1997, Warden had several songs picked up by Nashville mega-stars like Billy Ray Virus and LeAnn "A Child Shall Lead Us" Rimes and in 1998, put the finishing touches on **A Stranger to Me Now**.

The Wagoneers (1986-1990;1995): Thomas A. Lewis (d); Craig Allan Pettigrew (b); Monte Warden (r.g.,l.v.); Brent Wilson (l.g.,v)
The Loan Sharks (1992-1996): Monte Warden (g,v); Brad Fordham (b,v); David Murray (l.g.,1994-1995); Mas Palermo (d,v); Brent Wilson (l.g.,v)

    Stout & High(Wagoneers)/A&M/1988
    Good Fortune (Wagoneers)/A&M/1989
    Monte Warden (with the Loan Sharks)/Watermelon/1993
    Here I Am (with the Loan Sharks)/Watermelon/1995
    "Down the Line" (Wagoneers) on **Austin Country Nights**/Watermelon/1995
    "Take Me With U" (Monte Warden) on **Do Me Baby: Austin Does Prince**/Fume/1996
    A Stranger to Me Now/Asylum Nashville/1999

Monte Warden Mwarden007@aol.com

See Kelly Willis

Dale Watson

TSOB; Austin; Honky Tonk
Birmingham, Alabama; October 7, 1963-

Dale Watson is one of the hardest of hard core honky tonkers. Since he began playing professionally at the age of 15, his life has been devoted to keeping alive the real country tradition pioneered by Tubb, Price, Owens, and Haggard. Watson's first job was in a honky tonk band with his brothers in Pasadena, Texas, but after seven years, he left to pursue his own career. First stop was Los Angeles, where the alternative country scene had been experiencing a serious resurgence through the Town South of Bakersfield movement. Watson became house guitarist for the Barn Dances at the legendary Palomino, did one song for the third **A Town South of Bakersfield** compilation, and got a contract with Curb. This yielded one video and two singles but, overall, the deal was very discouraging. An auto accident severely damaged Watson's right hand and almost ended his performing days, but new manager Mitch Cohen put him back on his feet physically and emotionally. Then, Dale struck out for Nashville to try his luck. He pitched some songs to record companies, but his hard country sound was rejected. With a new family to support, Watson became a staff songwriter out of desperation and was instantly miserable. He longed to get back to performing and for about 10 months gave L.A. a second chance. This time he appeared in a movie, *A Thing Called Love*, with River Phoenix; Watson and long time friend James Intveld played members of a country band that backed Phoenix's

character. However, Watson's musical fortunes didn't improve, and when the big California quake of '92 hit, he was convinced to return to Music City and his hellacious writing job. But, Dale got wind of the honky tonk revival in Austin, Texas and in early 1993 went there to take his best shot. For the next two years, Watson played every dive and honky tonk from Ginny's Little Longhorn to the Black Cat assembling his band (the Lone Stars) and building a following. In 1995, he got a big break when lead guitarist Dave Biller joined the Lone Stars and Hightone Records gave him the contract he had worked so hard for. Given a free hand to do it his way, Watson cut **Cheatin' Heart Attack**, a good old fashioned honky tonk record dedicated to his father Donald who played in a country band and was a big inspiration (his face is tattooed on Dale's arm). It is full of great originals about drinking, sour relationships, and suicide supported by a fine cast of musicians including the Lone Stars and guests Jimmy Day, Scott Walls, Gene Elders, and Floyd Domino. Watson even managed to take a shot at Music City ("Nashville Rash") and pay homage to Austin ("South of Round Rock, Texas"). A year later came another superb hard country recording, **Blessed or Damned**, on which Watson pays tribute to truckers ("Truckin' Man") and Ginny's Little Longhorn ("Honkiest Tonkiest Beer Joint") and fulfilled a dream by dueting with honky tonk legend Johnny Bush on "That's What I Like About Texas." Both recordings drew raves in U.S. and international circles, and propelled Watson into alt. country's new honky tonk elite along with the Derailers and Don Walser.

In 1996, Dale embarked on a grueling road schedule that included a unique tour on which he played truck stops around the USA. During the middle of a subsequent tour in Europe, the rigors and stresses of non-stop travel boiled over, and Watson and the Lone Stars parted company; Biller later appeared on the excellent guitar album, **Travis County Pickin'**, toured with Wayne Hancock, played with Ted Roddy's Tear Joint Troubadours, co-founded the Panhandlers, and collaborated with Jeremy Wakefield on the **Hot Guitars of Biller and Wakefield**. Undaunted, Watson put together a new band and went back into the studio to record another album, **I Hate These Songs**. In early 1997, a special ceremony was held at the Broken Spoke in Austin to honor Watson for his contributions. He was named Mr. Honky Tonk Gold, and his award was presented by none other than Johnny Bush. Added to this honor was 1997 Songwriter of the Year from the Austin Music Awards. Overseas, Watson was honored to receive four nominations in the International category of the British Country Music Awards for Best Male Vocalist (with Brooks, Jackson, and Strait!!), Best Album (**I Hate These Songs**), Rising Star (with BR5-49 and LeAnn Rimes), and Best Independent Artist (he won in this category). Later that year, Watson finished a pet project by making a recording of original trucking songs, **Good Luck 'N'**

Good Truckin'. Initially available only on cassette, it was released in mid-1998 on CD as **The Truckin' Sessions** in Europe and a short time later in the U.S.

Rather than pulling off the road for a little rest in 1998, Watson put the pedal further to the metal with continued touring at home and overseas. He was a vital part of the cheating song album, **Songs of Forbidden Love** (with Ted Roddy, Rosie Flores, Kelly Willis), made the cover of *Country Music People* (July), and was the focus of a segment, "My Heroes Have Always Been Cowboys," in *Naked Nashville*, a TV documentary about the country music industry that ran on Bravo. Dale also penned the shows' theme song, "Naked Nashville."

The Lone Stars: Dave Biller (l.g., 1994-1996); Ricky Davis p.s.,1997-); Scott Matthews (d,1998-); Craig Pettigrew (b,1994-1996); Preston Rumbaugh (b,1997-); Dennis Vanderhoof (d,1993-1995); Redd Volkaert (l.g.,1997-)

"You Pour It On"/Curb/1990 (7")
"One Tear At a time"/Curb/1990 (7")
"One Memory at a Time" **on A Town South of Bakersfield, Vol. 3**/Restless/1992
Cheatin Heart Attack/Hightone/1995
"Girl, I Hope You're Having Fun" on **Austin Country Nights**/Watermelon/1995
Blessed or Damned/Hightone/1996
I Hate These Songs/Hightone/1997
Good Luck 'N' Good Truckin'/DW/1997 (CS)
"List of Reasons" (live) on **Viva Americana**/Boka UK/1998
"Lovin' on Backstreets, Livin' on Main"; "Unspoken Kind" on **Songs of Forbidden Love**/Lazy SOB/1998
The Truckin' Sessions/Continental Song City Euro./1998; KOCH/1998 (**Good Luck 'N' Good Truckin'** with extra trks.)
"Good Truckin' Tonight" b/w "Flat Tire"/Shamrock/1998

Dale Watson International Fan Club, 508 Bennett Dr., Pasadena, TX 77504

Honkiest Tonkiest Hotline in Town 1-512-459-5517

Hard-Core Country: Official Dale Watson Web Site //www.dalewatson.realcountry.net/

WatsonTx3@aol.com

Unofficial Dale Watson Home Page //www.actlab.utexas.edu/~spam/watson/

Dale Watson Web Site //www.geocities.com/nashville/5690/

Dale Watson AOL Folder: Entertainment>Music>Chat & Messages>Music Community>Country/Folk>Country & Western, L-Z

See James Intveld

Doc Watson
Old-Time; Bluegrass; Flat Pick Guitar
Deep Gap, North Carolina; March 23, 1923-

I don't know how much more can be said about Doc Watson that hasn't been said many times before. To put it simply, the greatest flatpick guitarist of the last 50 years has exerted an

immense musical influence (in many directions) decade after decade. His early recordings in the 1960s for Vanguard helped introduce old-time music to a new audience from outside of the music's traditional centers and inspired countless individuals to take up the guitar; a very young Clarence White worked with Watson on **Treasures Untold** (the best of the Vanguard material is available in short form on **The Essential Doc Watson** or in the boxed **Vanguard Years**). In the 1970s, Doc worked closely with a new generation of old-time and bluegrass enthusiasts making a seminal contribution to the landmark **Will the Cirlce Be Unbroken** and following it up with **Memories**, a superb mini-country music history, with younger players like Sam Bush, Courtney Johnson, T. Michael Coleman, and his son and long-time collaborator, Merle Watson. Sadly, Merle died in a farming accident in 1985, but the annual Merlefest established in his memory became one of the major Americana events in the world. Into the 1990s, Watson worked his magic on alt. country performers and fans old and new recording with Junior Brown on **Docabilly** and David Grisman on **Doc & Dawg** and performing in concert with Tony Rice, Norman Blake, and Del McCoury. Feature write-ups in magazines like *No Depression* (Jan./Feb. 1998) assured that yet another generation would experience the healing powers of "the Appalachian Doctor of Flatpick."

Will the Circle Be Unbroken/United Artists/1972
Two Days in November/Poppy/1974
Doc Watson—Memories/United Artists/1975; Sugar Hill/1995
Red Rocking Chair (with Merle Watson)/Flying Fish/1981
Down South (with Merle Watson)/Flying Fish/1984
Riding the Midnight Train/Sugar Hill/1984
The Essential Doc Watson/Vanguard/1986
Docabilly/Sugar Hill/1995
The Vanguard Years/Vanguard/1996 (4 CDs)

Doc Watson Multimedia Site //sunsite.unc.edu/doug/docwat/docwat.html

Jon Wayne
Psychocountry
Los Angeles, California; Mid-1980s-

By any standards, Jon Wayne is responsible for some of the most warped country rock of all time. No, not The Duke, but a mysterious figure who in 1986 gained a permanent place in the country music hall of shame with the outrageous **Texas Funeral**, a raw country/rock/punk album full of nasty and offensive songs. Details on the history of Jon Wayne are sketchy, but by all accounts, "he" was the idea of L.A. studio owner/musician David Naught and drummer Jimbo aka Jim Goodall. These two did all the music on the recording, but Ernest Beauvine aka Doug Livingston and Billy Bob were brought in for some live gigs around L.A. in the mid-1980s. In the late 1980s, Jon Wayne played sporadically with Tommy

Spurlock aka Tommy Turlock replacing Billy Bob on bass and had all but dropped out until 1995 when **Texas Funeral** was re-issued on Fistpuppet (along with a single "Mr. Egyptian"). They were given a further boost the next year when they had a song included on the soundtrack of Quentin Tarantino's vampire flick *From Dusk 'Til Dawn*. They did a couple more live shows in 1996, but future plans remained up in the air as Turlock moved to Nashville where he worked as a pedal steel session player.

Jon Wayne aka David Naught (g,v); Ernest Beauvine aka Doug Livingston (g); Billy Bob (b); Jimbo aka Jim Goodall (d,v); Tommy Spurlock aka Tommy Turlock (b)

> **Texas Funeral**/Hybrid Cargo/1986; Fistpuppet/1995
> "Mr. Egyptian" b/w "Orange"/Fistpuppet/1995 (7")
> "Texas Funeral" on **From Dusk 'Til Dawn**/Epic/1996 (sdtrk.)

Jon Wayne, P.O. Box 218122, Nashville, TN 37221

Ernest Beauvine Ebovine@aol.com

Gillian Welch

Singer/Songwriter; Old-Time/Bluegrass
Los Angeles, California; October 2, 1968-

One of the biggest surprises of 1996 was the dramatic rise of singer/songwriter Gillian Welch. For several years, she had been familiar to Nashville audiences who saw her perform at local open mic sessions and to the musicians who covered her songs, but otherwise, Welch was generally unknown. Her debut album, **Revival**, changed that in a hurry. Its authentic old-timey feel, driven by Welch's mournful songs and sorrowful vocals, bowled over unsuspecting listeners and reviewers. Suddenly, Welch and her musical partner David Rawlings were popping up everywhere in features, interviews, and performances, and the details of her story began to unfold; born in the backwoods of Los Angeles, Welch grew up listening to a variety of music from folk to show tunes, but it wasn't until she attended the University of California at Santa Cruz in 1984 that she found her true musical love. While there, Welch fell in with a local bluegrass crowd who introduced her to the Stanleys, Flatt & Scruggs, Bill Monroe, et al. In the simple but powerful emotive qualities of bluegrass, Welch found the model for what she wanted to do as a singer/songwriter. Later, while attending the Berklee School of Music in Boston to polish up her composing skills, Welch met a guitar player named David Rawlings who shared her passion for traditional country music. In 1992, they moved to Nashville and began writing and playing local venues. Welch's vocals plus Rawlings great flatpicking and harmonizing were a winning combination. Word of the new duo's talents slowly spread and good things began to happen. Emmylou Harris included Gillian's "Orphan Girl" on her **Wrecking Ball**; Kathy Mattea covered her "455 Rocket"; Tim O'Brien and the Nashville Bluegrass Band recorded her songs;

and, in 1995, after a performance at The Station Inn, T-Bone Burnett agreed to produce her first album. Recorded largely in mono and with minimal accompaniment (including James Burton and Roy Huskey, Jr.), **Revival** conjures up somber recollections of rural tragedy and redemption ("Acony Bell"; "Pass You By"; "Tear My Stillhouse Down"; "By the Mark") tracing a direct line of ascent from the Carters through Hazel & Alice, Emmylou, Lucinda Williams, Freakwater, and Iris DeMent. In 1996, the *Gavin Report* tapped Welch as its Americana Artist of the Year, and **Revival** was nominated as the Grammy's Best Contemporary Folk Album.

During 1998, Welch was featured on several key alt. country/Americana compilations, but her big contribution was a new full-length recording, **Hell Among the Yearlings**. Even more stripped back (mostly with just Rawlings on guitar) and darker than **Revival**, it was one of most widely reviewed and discussed albums of the year. Songs like "My Morphine," "Caleb Meyer," "The Devil Had a Hold of Me," "Whiskey Girl," "One Morning," "I'm Not Afraid to Die," and "Miner's Refrain" brought consistent comments such as "stark," "bleak," "austere," "ascetic," "haunting." And while reviews of **Hell Among the Yearlings** were overwhelmingly positive, Welch's "modern Appalachian" sound generated a mini-controversy about authenticity: what does a Hollywood raised singer/songwriter know about backwoods/mountain music and culture (*Los Angeles Times* reviewer) versus artifice or "the ability of an artist to humbly immerse herself into a totally different frame of reference (as) perhaps the most highly evolved form of artistic expression" (Mark Kemp, *The New York Times*).

> **Revival**/Almo Geffen/1996
> **Hell Among the Yearlings**/Almo Geffen/1998
> "Gold Watch and Chain" on **Clinch Mountain Country: Ralph Stanly & Friends**/Rebel/1998
> "Leaving Train" on **The Horse Whisperer**/MCA/1998
> "Miner's Prayer" on **Will Sing for Food: The Songs of Dwight Yoakam**/Little Dog/1998
> "Hickory Wind" on **Return of the Grievous Angel: A Tribute to Gram Parsons**/1999

Gillian Welch/Geffen Home Page
//www.almosounds.com/gillian/

Gillian Welch iMusic Showcase
//imusic.com/showcase/contemporary/gillianwelc/

Gillian Welch AOL Folder: Entertainment>Music>Chat & Messages>Music Community>Folk/Acoustic

Kevin Welch (The Dead Reckoners; Mike Henderson)

"Western Beat"; Dead Reckoner
Long Beach, California; August 17, 1955-

Kevin Welch's musical career began in 1978 when, at the tender age of 22, he moved to Nashville and became a songwriter for the Sony Tree company. He labored there for a number of years penning songs for a variety of country artists. In the late 1980s, Welch played in a local roots/rock band called the Roosters along with Harry Stinson, Glenn Worf, and Mike Henderson. The latter had been in Music City since 1985 and developed quite a reputation as songwriter and much in demand multi-instrumental session player. Later, when Welch launched his own s/s career, Henderson joined his band the Overtones. They developed a sound Welch called Western Beat (combination of cowboys and Beats) and recorded two albums of intelligent country/folk/rock, **Kevin Welch** (1990) and **Western Beat** (1991) that vaulted Welch into the top echelons of early 1990s alternative country. On the heels of this success, Henderson released his own critically acclaimed solo debut, **Country Music Made Me Do It**. Things seemed to be going well for Welch and company but, underneath, the stress of dealing with corporate Nashville began to take its toll. Rather than caving in or quitting, Welch and Henderson joined with Kieran Kane, Tammy Rogers, and Harry Stinson to set up an independent record company called Dead Reckoning. Under their unique, cooperative agreement each artist was an owner in the company linked by a commitment to put out high quality music. Each member would put out solo recordings accompanied by the other members, and, in turn, they would perform collectively. After an inaugural release by Kane came Welch's **Life Down Here on Earth** which continues his Western Beat sound but expands on it due to the presence of the other Dead Reckoning partners. Henderson was given the freedom to showcase his versatility on **Edge of Night** and the blues album **First Blood** as Mike Henderson & the Bluebloods. In 1996, the Dead Reckoning crew which now included Fats Kaplin began touring as the Dead Reckoners in a show they called A Night of Reckoning. Their roots, country, rock, and blues based on the collective contribution of each musician was released as **A Night of Reckoning** in 1997. The Reckoners were branded as outlaws in Nashville for their "radical" experiment but also praised there and elsewhere for their courage and innovation. Welch's first two recordings on Reprise were reissued by Dead Reckoning in 1998.

The Dead Reckoners: Mike Henderson (l.g.,v); Kieran Kane (md,v); Fats Kaplin (f,v); Tammy Rogers (f,v); Harry Stinson (b,v); Kevin Welch (g,v)

  Kevin Welch/Reprise/1990; Dead Reckoning/1998
  Western Beat/Reprise/1991; Dead Reckoning/1998
  Country Music Made Me Do It (Mike Henderson)/
    RCA/1994
  Life Down Here on Earth/Dead Reckoning/1995
  In the Red (Tammy Rogers & Don Heffington)/
    Dead Reckoning/1995
  Edge of Night (Mike Henderson)/Dead Reckoning/1996
  First Blood (Mike Henderson & the Bluebloods)/
    Dead Reckoning/1996
  "One Way Rider" (Kevin Welch) on **American
    Songbook**/Demon UK/1996
  Another Day (Tammy Rogers)/Dead Reckoning/1996

  A Night of Reckoning (Dead Reckoners)/
    Dead Reckoning/1997
  Thicker Than Water (Mike Henderson & the
    Bluebloods)/Dead Reckoning/1998

Kevin Welch Home Page
//songs.com/noma/deadreck/kevin.html

Kevin Welch iMusic Showcase
//imusic.com/showcase/country/

Mike Henderson Home Page
//songs.com/deareck/hendo.html

The Dead Recknoners Home Page
//songs.com/deadreck/

The Dead Reckoners AOL Folder:
Entertainment>Music>Chat & Messages>Music
Community>Folk/Acoustic

See Kieran Kane

The Well Oiled Sisters

Cowpunk; Lesbian
Edinburgh, Scotland; London, England; 1995-

In the mid-1980s, England was home to a vital cowpunk scene with groups like Helen & the Horns, the Boothill Foot Tappers, and the Orson Family. A decade later, the Well Oiled Sisters carried on that tradition with a vengeance. Formed in Edinburgh, Scotland but quickly relocating to London in the mid-1990s, the group combined early k.d. lang country/western androgyny and Poguesque swagger into an uncompromising merger of hillbilly and punk. Heart and soul of the band was lead singer and songwriter Lucy Edwards whose material ranged from moving declarations of love ("Strange Elation"; "Homeward Bound") to bitter breakups ("Blood Turns to Ice"; "Why I'm Alone"), aching heartbreak ("Alcohol & Tears"; "I Miss You"), hard core drinking ("Drinking Song"), freedom ("Dancing in the Dubs"; "Miles Away"), and sex songs that are sometimes sensuous ("Mouth") and sometimes downright nasty ("Scratch"; "E Song"; "Hold on Tight"; "Dirty Cowgirls"; "Mad Girls Do Sex Better"). Backing her was a driving rhythm section (Alics and Sam), a Mohawk coifed accordionist (Angie Dypso), and a fiery fiddler (Miss Jones) whose over-the-top reels, breakdowns, and hoe-downs were one of the highlights of their intense live performances. The group billed as "holligan hillbilly honeys putting the cow grrl back into country" recorded two CDs, **Alcohol & Tears** and **Mad Girls Do Sex Better**. In addition, the Well Oiled Sisters served as Morrissey's backing band and had successful tours in the UK and Australia.

Alics (b,b.v.); Angie Dypso (acc,g,b.v.); Lucy (acc,l.g.,l.v.);
Miss Jones (f); Sam (d)

  Alcohol & Tears/Cycle/1995
  Mad Girls Do Better/WOS/1997

The Well Oiled Sisters Home Page
//drum.gduncan.com/wos/hello.html

drum@gduncan.com

Mike West and Myshkin

"New Orleans Hillbilly"
New Orleans, Louisiana; 1993-

Born in Australia but raised in England, Mike West was in a Manchester punk band called Man From Delmonte in the 1980s before taking up banjo and immigrating to New Orleans in 1993. There he found his muse and musical life partner Myshkin. Mike played lead guitar in her alternative rock band band Impossible, but he became most well-known around the Crescent City as a solo or duo (with Myshkin) playing a rag tag of old-time, bluegrass, blues, folk, early New Orleans jazz, rock, Cajun, Celtic, calypso, and Latin they took to calling "New Orleans Hillbilly" or "badass mountain music with a European sensibility." With West on banjo, lead acoustic guitar, mandolin and lead vocals and Myshkin on snare drum, washboard, mandolin, and harmony, they became regulars on the local folk scene and the ultimate wandering minstrels criss-crossing the U.S. and touring three continents in three years. Through 1998, Mike West had recorded three albums (**Interstate 10**; **Redneck Riviera**; **Race That Train**) under his name with Myshkin on harmony vocals and one, **Econoline**, as Mike West & Myshkin. All offer an eclectic variety of sounds provided by guests on fiddle, dobro, bass, tuba, congas, and accordion behind West's friendly vocals and story songs that take a generally satiric look at life in Louisiana and along the Gulf Coast. *Off Beat Magazine* named him Best Folk Artist of 1995 and 1996 and tapped **Redneck Riviera** as Best Folk Album of 1996. As West is fond of saying, "I try to write country music, but I keep getting it wrong...and folks seem to like it that way."

Interstate 10/Hillbilly for Your Head/1994; Binky/1995
Redneck Riviera/Binky/1996
Econoline (with Myshkin)/Binky/1997
Race That Train/Binky/1998

Mike West, 940 Royal St. #244, New Orleans, LA 70116; 504-945-6488

Mike West c/o Binky Records, 9656 Burbank Dr, Ste. F, Baton Rouge, LA 70810; 504-767-4361; cmaxwell@premier.net

Whiskeytown

Tobacco Road; No Depression; Insurgent Country
Raleigh, North Carolina/Austin, Texas; 1993-

Depending on who you ask, Whiskeytown is either: (a) the second coming of Uncle Tupelo, or (b) a bunch of ill behaved pseudo-redneck pretenders. Part of this disparity is attributable to the group's reputation for sometimes showing up like world beaters and sometimes showing up like drunken punks. Most of the comments (positive/negative) have been aimed at Whiskeytown's lead singer and songwriter, Ryan Adams. Already a veteran of Raleigh's 1980s punk scene (with the Patty Duke Syndrome) at age 20, Adams, tiring of the punk thing, pushed off in a more countryesque direction. In 1993, he founded Whiskeytown which concocted a volatile mix of country rock and punk ranging over countrified covers of Black Flag and Richard Hell to original ballads like "Angels Are Messengers From God." An initial EP, **Angels**, on Mood Food preceded the much ballyhooed full length debut **Faithless Street** which announced a major new alt. country presence. After a now legendary SXSW showcase in 1996, Whiskeytown was feverishly courted by numerous labels but decided to go with Geffen's Outpost subsidiary. However, there was a dark cloud in the silver lining. The furor surrounding the band's sudden success led to internal conflicts and the departure of bassist Steve Grothman. Whiskeytown regrouped and became the most talked about alt. country band of 1997. Favorites of both the insurgent and no depression crowds, Whiskeytown did a slew of recordings: cuts on tribute compilations (**Straight Outta Boone County**, Big Star) an EP, **Rural Free Delivery** (out takes from **Faithless Street**), and a double 45 whose "Theme for a Trucker" was included on the soundtrack of Wim Wenders' *The End of Violence*. However, it was their major label debut **Stranger's Almanac** that pushed them onto the alt. country center stage. Supporters hailed it as *the* alt. country recording of the 1990s and Whiskeytown as *the* future of alternative country. Adams vocals and songwriting (obviously indebted to Gram Parsons as well as Uncle Tupelo and the Stones) won high praise from reviewers and fans alike who were also generous with kudos for Caitlin Cary's fiddle and vocals which helped define Whiskeytown's distinct style. Other critics and fans, however, were not so kind; some viewed the band as "condescending" play actors using country as a "shock device" while others saw Adams versatility as "aimlessness." The pro and con judgments about Whiskeytown were due not just to their recordings but also to their live performances which drew wildly varying reactions from raves to raspberries. When Adams' undeniable charisma was in focus, Whiskeytown simply blew audiences away but when, at times, fueled by alcohol, it turned into arrogance, he (and band) put on miserable shows that had club owners threatening to pull the plug and patrons heading for the doors. Rumored confrontations with Dave Alvin and Keith Richards only added to their erratic reputation. Ultimately, each story (good/bad) enhanced Whiskeytown's visibility and increased the hype, and it was clear that, come what may, they would have a major impact on alt. country for years to come. That is, if they could survive the major band shake-up that came in the wake of conflict and even physical confrontations between Adams and guitarist Phil Wandscher. At the tail end of a summer/fall 1997 tour, Wandscher, Steve Terry, and Chris Laney were all dismissed from the band with Adams and Caitlin performing as a duo until they could find replacements in Ed "From Ohio"

Crawford, Mike Daly, Skillet Gilmore, and Jennifer Snyder. Ultimately, Whiskeytown's success or failure depended on Adams (now living in Austin) whose star could burn brightly for a long time or burn out in one big super-ego nova.

Throughout 1998, Ryan continued to be hard on himself, band members, equipment, and nightclubs. After yet another personnel shake-up, Whiskeytown embarked on a summer tour where on the West Coast, in three separate incidents, Adams sealed his place as alt. country's bad boy poster child. Vancouver: destroyed a guitar on stage; San Francisco: pushed monitors off the stage and set off a mini-brawl at the Fillmore and at the Whisky A Go Go left in mid-performance to throw up in his dressing room. Of course, these antics got Adams a lot of attention but left many like reviewer Neal Weiss wondering "is he self-destructive or just a good actor?" Either way, fans didn't get anything very positive from Whiskeytown in 1998 except the reissue of 1995's **Faithless Street** with "sonic enhancements" and additional tracks. A press release from Outpost in early 1999 revealed that Adams, Cary, Mike Daly, and James Iha (Smashing Pumpkins) were working on a new recording, **Go Bye Bye Music** (working title) at Dreamland Studios in Woodstock, New York. Fans didn't know whether to laugh or cry as Adams made it known that he had been learning piano and composition and, on this album, was going to let the music "convey the emotions I used to depend on the lyrics to spell out."

Ryan Adams (a.g.,bj,e.g.,p,l.v.); Caitlin Cary (f,v); Ed Crawford (g,v,1997-1998); Mike Daly (g,ky,l.s.,1997-); Skillet Gilmore (d,1997-); Steve Grothman (b,1993-1996); Danny Kurtz (b,1998-); Chris Laney (b,1996-1997); Brad Rice (g,1998-); Jeff Rice (b,1996); Jennifer Snyder (b,v,1997-); Steve Terry (d,v,1996-1997;1998-); Phil Wandscher (g,v,1993-1997); Jon Wurster (d,1997)

> **Angels**/Mood Food/1995 (7" EP)
> "Blank Generation" on **Who the Hell: The Richard Hell Tribute Album**/Cred Factory/1995
> **Faithless Street**/Mood Food/1995; 1998 (w/extra trks.)
> "Guns to Town" on **Revival, Vol. 1: Brunswick Stew & Pig Pickin'**/Yep Roc/1996
> "Bottom of the Glass" on **Straight Outta Boone County**/ Bloodshot/1997
> **Rural Free Delivery**/Mood Food/1997 (EP)
> "Theme for a Trucker"/Bloodshot/1997 (7" dbl) and on **The End of Violence**/Outpost/1997(sdtrk.)
> **Stranger's Almanac**/Outpost /1997
> **In Your Wildest Dreams**/Outpost/1997 (EP with 4 p.u. trks.)
> "Busted" on **Revival, Vol. 2: Kudzu and Hollerin' Contest**/Yep Roc/1997
> **Car Songs** ("Highway 145" b/w "My 63" by Neko Case & The Sadies)/Bloodshot/1998 (7")
> **Go Bye Bye Music**/Outpost/1999

Whiskeytown, P.O. Box 33370, Austin, TX 78764

Whiskeytown Unofficial Home Page
//www.mindspring.com/~bdjackson/whiskeytown/

Whiskeytown/Outpost Records Page
//www.outpostrec.com/whiskeytown/

Whiskeytown/iMusic Modern Rock Showcase Page
//imusic.com/showcase/modern/whisk.html

Whiskeytownavenues: Whiskeytown Online Mailing List
//www.onelist.com/welcome.cgi?listname=whiskeytownavenues

Clarence White
(The Kentucky Colonels; Nashville West)
Flat Pick and Electric Guitar; Country Rock; Progressive Bluegrass
Lewiston, Maine; June 7, 1944-July 14, 1973; Lancaster, California

Clarence White was only 29 years old when he died, but he lived a musically full life and made long lasting contributions to the creation and development of country rock as well as progressive bluegrass. At age 10, White began playing with his brothers in a bluegrass band, Three Little Country Boys. They were popular in the late 1950s and early 1960s in the L.A. area making television appearances and cutting several singles. In time, after a few personnel changes, this band became the Kentucky Colonels in 1963. Fueled by Clarence's innovative flat-picking guitar, they became one of the most progressive bluegrass bands of the day, but Clarence only stayed with them for two years. In 1965, White picked up the electric guitar and began experimenting with a new sound. He co-invented (with Gene Parsons) the Stringbender which made an electric guitar sound like a steel. Leaving the Colonels, he worked as a session player (for Gene Clark among others) and joined with Gib Gilbeau and Gene Parsons to form the house band for Gary Paxton's Bakersfield International Productions which released several low budget albums including **Guitar Country** by Bakersfield's Big Guitars. White collaborated with Guilbeau and Parsons on a number of musical projects and then, with them, formed a pioneering country rock band called Nashville West. Named for a local L.A. club, their shows drew many guest performers including Glenn D. Hardin (later with the Hot Band), Sneaky Pete Kleinow, and sometimes Gram Parsons. They did one self-titled album in 1966 (not released until 1978) and were a big influence on the Byrds' evolving country rock sound. While still with Nashville West, White did key session work in 1968 for **The Notorious Byrd Brothers** and the incomparable **Sweetheart of the Rodeo**. When Gram Parsons left the Byrds later that year, Clarence replaced him and contributed memorable lead guitar to **Dr. Byrds and Mr. Hyde, The Ballad of Easy Rider, Untitled, Byrdmaniax**, and **Farther Along**. Once the Byrds ended in 1973, White guested on albums for Country Gazette, the Everly Brothers, Roger McGuinn, Gene Parsons and many others. He also returned to performing bluegrass. First, he did two albums with one of the earliest newgrass bands, Muleskinner, which included David Grisman, Peter Rowan, Bill Keith, and Richard Greene. Then, he toured and recorded with his brothers as the White Brothers and the New Kentucky Colonels. Additionally, White got a deal with Warner Brothers for a solo album and was scheduled to go on a super country rock tour with label mates Gram Parsons, Emmylou Harris, Gene Parsons, the Kentucky Colonels, and Country Gazette. Tragically, just as his star was rising, White was killed by a drunken driver after a Kentucky Colonels show in Lancaster, California in July 1973. Happily, renewed interest in the originators of country rock led to a greater appreciation of White's importance through the reissue of many of his recordings. **Nashville West** was re-released along with **Muleskinner Live** and several collections of Kentucky Colonels material in the mid-1990s. The definitive Clarence White retrospective, **From Bakersfield to Byrdland**, came out on Sierra in 1996 and covers his work with the Kentucky Colonels and Byrds plus four solo recordings made just prior to his death. In 1998, around the 25th anniversary of White's untimely death, tributes to and articles on this guitar legend appeared in numerous magazines (*Acoustic Guitar*; *Flatpicking Guitar*) and on an ever growing number of web pages devoted to him.

The Kentucky Colonels (1963-1967): Roger Bush (b,v); Billy Ray Lathum (bj); LeRoy Mack (db); Bobby Sloane (f); Clarence White (l.g.,v); Roland White (bj,md,v)
Bakersfield's Big Guitars: Gib Guilbeau; Gene Parsons; Clarence White
Nashville West: Gib Guilbeau (f,v,); Wayne Moore (b,g,v); Gene Parsons (d,v,); Clarence White (g,v)
Muleskinner: Richard Greene (f); David Grisman (md,v); Bill Keith (bj); Peter Rowan (g,v); Clarence White (l.g,v)

  Appalachian Swing! (Kentucky Colonels)/World
    Pacific/1964
  Guitar Country (Bakersfield's Big Guitars)/Bakersfield
    Int. Prods./1966
  Nashville West/Sierra/rec. 1966, rel. 1978; Sierra/1996
  Muleskinner/Warner Brothers/1974
  The Kentucky Colonels 1965-1967/Rounder/1979
  Live in Sweden (Kentucky Colonels)/Rounder/1979
  Clarence White and the Kentucky Colonels/
    Rounder/1980
  The Kentucky Colonels Featuring Clarence White/1988
  Muleskinner Live/Sierra/1995
  From Bakersfield to Byrdland: The Clarence White
    Anthology/Sierra/1996 (2 CDs)

Clarence White Discography Page
//www.urban.or.jp/home/koa7/byrds.htm (includes biography, the *Clarence White Chronicles* on-line newsletter, and mailing list)

The Clarence White Tribute Page
//www.geocities.com/SunsetStrip/venue/4082/clarence.html

Jonathan's Clarence White Page
//www.geocities.com/nashville/palms/2522/white.html

Clarence White (Annotated) Discography
//ebni.com/byrds/refdiscogcw.html

Clarence White/Byrd's Nest Page
//www.waxing-eloquent.com/byrds/cwhite.html

See The Byrds; David Grisman; Nashville West; Gene Parsons

Jim White
Singer/Songwriter; Gothic Lo-Fi Country
Pensacola, Florida; ?

Jim White once told an interviewer his goal was "to merge white trash hillbilly with Sufi music." Huh?, you say. Well, actually everything about White is pretty much a head scratcher. Born Mike Pratt (won't tell when), he grew up in Pensacola, Florida but left there in his late teens. In the 1980s and early 1990s, Pratt was a pro surfer, fashion model in Italy, taxi driver, and film student at NYU (did *The Beautiful World* for his senior project). Along the way, he experimented with drugs, religion (fundamentalist Christian to Sufism), and music taking up an acoustic guitar (while convalescing from a surfing accident) and learning to play in spite of a maimed left hand (from a 1985 power saw mishap). Changing his name to Jim White (a compound of two friends' names), he began writing songs reflecting Southern influences including Appalachian music, William Faulkner, and Flannery O'Connor as well as contemporary musicians like Tom Waits, Neil Young, and the Cowboy Junkies. By a circuitous route, some of White's demos found their way to David Byrne who signed him to Luka Bop in 1996. From this came White's first recording, **Wrong Eyed Jesus**, a low key affair very much in the lo-fi, gothic mold of Palace, Tom Leach, and Parlor James. Like Will Oldham, White is obsessed with hillbilly ("white trash") culture and its preoccupation with religion, superstition, death, and salvation. The moodiness of White's songs is enhanced by his croaky voice, swamp noises, and vapory instrumentation including a wailing musical saw. From the disturbing cover art and bizarre liner notes relating "The Mysterious Tale of How I Shouted Wrong Eyed Jesus" to twisted songs like "Burn the River Dry," "When Jesus Gets a Brand New Name," "A Perfect Day to Chase Tornados," or "Stabbed in the Heart," White's debut is a haunting look into one life of quiet desperation. **No Such Place**, set for release in 1999, promised more of the same with songs like "Handcuffed to a Fence in Mississippi," "10 Miles to Go on a 9 Mile Road," and "The Wound That Never Heals."

Gimme 5/Luka Bop/1996 (EP)
Wrong Eyed Jesus/Luka Bop/1997
No Such Place/Luka Bop/1999

Jim White.Net //www.jimwhite.net

ry@jimwhite.net

Jim White iMusic Showcase
//www.imusic.com/showcase/indie/jimwhite.html

Joy Lynn White
TSOB
Turrell, Arkansas

In the early 1990s, Joy Lynn White danced around the edges of alternative country with two recordings, **Between Midnight and Hindsight** and **Wild Love**, for Columbia. Influenced by her father Nathan "Gene" White, she did her musical apprenticeship in Arkansas as Little Lynn White in the White Family Band which played local events and radio shows. At 19, Joy went to Nashville and, relying on her attention grabbing country vocals, worked her way up the ladder as session and demo singer. Eventually, Columbia came through with a deal, and (with lots of help from Marty Stuart), White made the previously mentioned recordings. They received very positive ratings, and White earned an ACM nomination for Best New Female Vocalist. But, she was just too hard core to succeed in Music City, and before White could make a third album for Columbia, they dropped her. This blow plus the delayed effects of her revered father's death a few years before put White into a tailspin for a time, but she came out of it through therapy and a new collaboration with Pete Anderson. Previously, in 1995, Joy had done some harmony vocals on Dwight Yoakam's **Gone** and in 1997, she was signed to Anderson's new Little Dog Records. Her debut with that label, **The Lucky Few**, signaled her full promotion into alt. country. Her no-holds-barred honky tonk and country rock on originals ("Life's Just Too Short"; "Too Big for This Town"), covers of Jim Lauderdale, Lucinda Williams ("Just Wanna See You So Bad"; "I Lost It"), and Gwil Owen ("I Doubt If It Does to You"), and a duet with Yoakam ("It's Better This Way") consistently registered 4-5 star reviews from music publications all across the USA.

> **Between Midnight and Hindsight**/Columbia/1995
> **Wild Love**/Columbia/1996
> **The Lucky Few**/Little Dog/1997

Joy Lynn White Fan Club c/o Wanda Knight, P.O. Box 128335, Nashville, TN 37212

Joy Lynn White/Little Dog Page //www.littledogrecords.com

Joy Lynn White/iMusic Showcase //imusic.com/showcase/country/

Joy Lynn White Biography //www.pressnet.com/joy.htm

Wilco (Courtesy Move)

No Depression
Chicago, Illinois; 1995-

After the conflict between Jay Farrar and Jeff Tweedy dissolved Uncle Tupelo in 1994, Tweedy was the first to emerge with a new band in 1995. Joining him in Wilco (as in "roger, wilco, over and out") were UT alumni Ken Coomer, Max Johnston, and John Stirratt along with Jay Bennett on guitar. Their debut recording **A.M.** has some UT vestiges but also demonstrated Tweedy's desire to move in his own direction. In 1996, the mammoth double CD/LP, **Being There**, moved further into pop rock territory inhabited by the Beach Boys, Beatles, and Rolling Stones but still had plenty of country grooves ("Far"; "Flowers"; "Say You"; "Someday"; "Dreamer") at times recalling the country rock of the Flying Burrito Brothers, the Grateful Dead, and New Riders. The alt. country community embraced it as one of its landmark recordings, and in spite of Tweedy's frequent protestations, Uncle Tupelo and now Wilco were permanently enshrined in the alt. country pantheon. However, as time went on, Wilco continued to put distance between themselves and their past image. Their 1999 **Summer Teeth** was described by Tweedy as a "dark pop record (with) nothing country or twangy about it." Yet, Wilco did return, for at least one more time, to their folk/country roots by joining with Billy Bragg on a collection of previously unpublished Woody Guthrie lyrics which they put to song on **Mermaid Avenue**. It featured Guthrie ballads, protest songs, and novelties done either Bragg style ("Way Over Yonder in a Minor Key") or Wilco style ("California Stars") with Tweedy on vocals. This was undoubtedly the most eagerly anticipated and widely reviewed recording (along with Lucinda's **Car Wheels**) of 1998 with major articles in publications in Europe and North America plus a BBC documentary on the project. It was also at the forefront of a major Woody Guthrie revival that continued unabated into 1999. Wilco also paid homage to Gram Parsons by contributing a cover of "100 Years" to the tribute CD, **Return of the Grievous Angel**.

When not touring and recording with Wilco, Tweedy ran (with his wife Sue Miller) Chicago's Lounge Ax nightclub and played in the alt. country "supergroup" Golden Smog (see their entry). In 1998, he and Farrar joined with Roger McGuinn to contribute three songs to the Harry Smith tribute show and CD. The other members of Wilco along with Bob Egan (ex-Freakwater) formed the side project Courtesy Move which did a cut for **Nashville: The Other Side of the Alley** in 1996 plus a single and some recordings backing Jeff Black, Steve Forbert, and Australian singer/songwriter Sherry Rich in 1997 and 1998.

Wilco: Jay Bennett (g,ky); Ken Coomer (d); Max Johnston (f,md,1995-1996); John Stirratt (b,v); Jeff Tweedy (g,v)
Courtesy Move: Jay Bennett (g); Ken Coomer (d); Max Robert Logue (b); John Stirratt (g,v) with Bob Egan (s.g.) and Max Johnston

> **A.M.**/SireReprise/1995
> **Box Full of Letters**/Sire Reprise Fr./1995 (mini-single)
> **Soil Samples**/Reprise/1995 (7")
> **Live (Minneapolis, 11-21-94)**/Twin City Digital/1996
> **Live (Minneapolis, 5-25&26-95)**/Twin City Digital/1996
> "Those I'll Provide" (Courtesy Move) on **Nashville: The Other Side of the Alley**/Bloodshot/1996
> **Being There**/Reprise Sire/1996
> "California" (Courtesy Move)/RockaMundo/1997 (7")
> **All Over the Place**/Reprise/1997 (10" promo EP)
> **Mermaid Avenue** (with Billy Bragg)/Reprise/1998
> "East Virginia Blues"; "Sugar Baby"; "James Alley Blues" (Tweedy, Farrar, Roger McGuinn) on **The Harry Smith Connection**/Smithsonian Folkways/1998
> **Summer Teeth**/Reprise/1999
> "100 Years" on **Return of the Grievous Angel: A Tribute to Gram Parsons**/Almo/1999

Official Wilco Home Page //www.wilcoweb.com

Wilcoweb@aol.com (Wilco Mailing newsletter)

Wilco/Reprise Home Page //www.repriserec.com/Wilco

Wilco/Gumbo Home Page
//www.gumbopages.com/wilco.html

Wilco Fan Page //members.aol.com/ocliw/wilco.html

Henning Kleiven's Wilco Page
//home.sol.no/~hekleive/wilco.html

Wilco/iMusic Showcase //imusic.com/showcase/modern/

Postcard: The Uncle Tupelo, Wilco, & Son Volt Mailing
List //www.servtech.com/ddewey/postcard/

Passenger Side/Postcard 2: The Alternative/Insurgent
Country Music Mailing List
//www.gumbopages.com/music/pass-side.html

Son Volt, Wilco, Uncle Tupelo Lyrics
//www.usinternet.com/users/yoflute/index.html

Wilco AOL Folder: Entertainment>Music>Chat &
Messages>Music Community>Alternative>Alternative
Bands, A-Z and Alternative Topics>No Depression/Alt.
Country

Billy Bragg Home Page //www.billybragg.co.uk/

Bob Egan Home Page //www.bobegan.com

*See Steve Forbert; Golden Smog; Sherry Rich; Son Volt;
Uncle Tupelo*

Webb Wilder (The Beatnecks; The Nashvegans)
Roots Rock
Hattiesburg, Mississippi; May 19, 1954-

In the late 1970s, John Webb McMurry was working as a
country DJ at a radio station in Hattiesburg, Mississippi. While
there, he collaborated with R. S. Field and Steve Mims on a film
entitled *The Saucer's Reign.* Inspired by both Raymond
Chandler and Andy Griffith, they invented a Southern private
eye named Webb Wilder (McMurry) to play the lead role. The
film, a bizarre blend of mystery and sci-fi, won numerous
awards, was picked up by the Campus Network, and made it to
the USA Network and A&E in the 1980s. At about the same
time, Wilder emerged as a musician who billed himself as "the
last of the full grown men" living by the motto "work hard, rock
hard, eat hard, sleep hard, grow big, wear glasses if you need
'em!" A combination of Buddy Holly, Jerry Lee Lewis, and low
key Mojo Nixon, Wilder first performed with a band called the
Beatnecks. They recorded three albums (**It Came From
Nashville, Hybrid Vigor, Doo Dad**) combining roots, rock,
country, and a good dose of humor on covers of "The Devil's
Right Hand," "Rock 'N' Roll Ruby," "Baby Please Don't Go,"
"I Had Too Much to Dream Last Night" and originals "Human
Cannonball," "Horror Hayride," "How Long Can She Last
(Going That Fast)." In 1995, Wilder renamed his band the
Nashvegans, and they released **Town and Country** with some
of their favorite road songs, "Goldfinger," "Streets of Laredo,"
"Stay Out of Automobiles," "Honky Tonk Hell," and "Nash-
ville Bum." Wilder's 1996 offering with the Nashvegans,
Acres of Suede, was all original roots/rock material plus a

speaking track called "Webb Wilder's Motivational Tips for
Teens and Rock 'N' Roll Pamphlet." His hillbilly private eye
character can be seen on semi-music videos, *Corn Flicks* and
Horror Hayride, featuring an unforgettable version of "I Had
Too Much to Dream Last Night" and a duet with friend Ted
Roddy on "If You Don't Think Elvis is Number One (You're
Full of Number Two)."

The Beatnecks: Denny Blakely (b,v); Bobby Field (d,g,v);
Jimmy Lester (d); Donnie Roberts (g,v)
The Nashvegans: George Bradfute (g,org,v); James Lester
(d,v); Kelley Looney (b,v)

  It Came From Nashville (with the Beatnecks)/
    Landslide/1986; Watermelon/1993
  Hybrid Vigor (with the Beatnecks)/Island/1989
  DooDad (with the Beatnecks)/Zoo/1991
  Town & Country (with the Nashvegans)/
    Watermelon/1995
  Acres of Suede (with the Nashvegans)/Watermelon/1996

Webbco, P.O. Box 49897, Austin, TX 78765

Official Webb Wilder Home Page
//www.webbwilder.com

Webb Wilder's Last of the Full Grown Men Music Site
//www.geocities.com/sunsetstrip/palms/5540/

Webb Wilder: The Original Web Site //www.nd.edu/~kdrew/

Willard Grant Conspiracy
Lo-Fi Roots Rock
Boston, Massachusetts; 1996-

Like their labelmates Sparklehorse, the Willard Grant Conspiracy is a loose conglomeration of musicians who specialize
in a very strange but alluring lo-fi roots rock that's a little bit of
Nick Cave, Vic Chesnutt, Velvet Underground, and Neil
Young all rolled up into one. Robert Fisher's husky lead vocals
and dark subject matter are wrapped in multiple layers of
acoustic guitar, organ, mandolin, banjo, violin, cello, and
electric guitar. Their first informal sessions in 1996 led to **3
A.M. Sunday @ Fortune Otto's** which was picked up by
Glitterhouse and impelled a brief tour in The Netherlands.
Meanwhile, back in the U.S. in 1997, WGC signed with Slow
River which released **Flying Low** in 1998. It received
considerable notice from the alt. country community in the
States, but their "slo-core campfire folk" was really a hit in
Europe where WGC was given spreads in German, French, and
English music magazines and had their songs placed on several
European compilations including *Uncut*'s **Sounds of the New
West: The Best of Alternative Country**. Late in 1998, Slow
River issued a limited edition live radio broadcast (WMBR) EP
called **Weevils in the Captain's Biscuit** and re-released **3
A.M.** plus the full-length **Mojave** (Europe only) with Edith
Frost in 1999.

  3 A.M. Sunday @ Fortune Otto's/Dahlia/1997; Slow
    River/1999

"The Ostrich Song" on **Luxury Liner**/Glitterhouse
   Ger./1997
Wake Me When I'm Under ("Archy's Lullabye" (WGC)
   b/w "Runaround" (Chris & Carla)/Hobo UK/1998
Flying Low/Slow River/1998
"Evening Mass" on **Sounds of the New West**/Uncut
   UK/1998
Weevils in the Captain's Biscuit/Slow River/1998 (ltd.
   ed. EP)
Mojave/Slow River UK/1999

Willard Grant Conspiracy Pix 'n' Fax
//world.std.com/~dahlia/willard.html

Willard Grant Conspiracy Page:
//www.popnews.com/wgc/

Lucinda Williams

Singer/Songwriter
Lake Charles, Louisiana; January 26, 1953-

In 1997, Miller Williams was selected as poet for President Clinton's second inauguration. Among those present to hear Williams deliver his poem for the occasion was his proud daughter, Lucinda. Her father was one of the earliest and most important influences in leading her toward a career in music. Not only did he instill in her a love for literature but also for country music (he is a huge Hank Williams fan). As an English literature professor, Miller had appointments with many different schools in the South and Latin America, and through this, Lucinda was exposed to a variety of cultures and musical styles. In the late 1960s, she fell under the sway of folk music, and after the Williams settled in Arkansas in 1971, she became acquainted with the blues. When country music heated up in Austin, Texas in the early 1970s, Lucinda headed there but ended up in Houston where she became part of the singer/songwriter clique with Lyle Lovett and Nanci Griffith. She paid for her first two recordings for Smithsonian Folkways out of her own pocket. **Ramblin'** is a collection of blues and country covers such as "Malted Milk Blues," "Jambalaya," "Great Speckled Bird," and "Satisfied Mind," but **Happy Woman Blues** is all original material running from traditional country to blues to Cajun and folk. It should have been the predecessor of big things for Williams but for the next eight years, she roamed around Texas and California writing songs, singing, and hoping. Finally, in 1988, she cut **Lucinda Williams** for Rough Trade records. Without question, it is one of *the* best alternative country albums displaying Williams' maturity and depth as a singer/songwriter on country rockers ("I Just Want to See You So Bad," "The Night's Too Long," "Passionate Kisses"), tender ballads ("Like a Rose," "Am I Too Blue"), Cajun ("Crescent City"), and roadhouse blues ("Changed the Locks," "I Asked for Water, He Gave Me Gasoline"). Much of the credit for the success of this recording goes to her incredible band: multi-instrumentalist Gurf Morlix, drummer Donald Lindley, and bassist Dr. John Ciambotti. The album generated several hits ("The Night's Too Long," "Passionate Kisses") for other artists, but most importantly, it spread the word about a major new talent. Basing herself in Austin, Williams built a big following in the early 1990s and in 1992 recorded her first major label album, **Sweet Old World**. It once again winningly combines country, rock, and blues on some very personal and moving songs, "He Never Got Enough Love," "Little Angel, Little Brother," and "Something About What Happens When We Talk." Williams was definitely at the top of her form, but then, for the next six years, fans waited and waited and waited for her next recording. Williams laid down tracks several times only to reject them and begin again. Steve Earle was brought in to finish production, but the experience left him saying, "I'll never work with a woman again!" Most seriously, the strain took a toll on Williams' band, and in 1996, long time associate Gurf Morlix departed. In early 1997, the rumor persisted that her new album, **Car Wheels on a Gravel Road**, was finished and would be coming out any time on American Recordings, but there were also some very public reports (*New York Times Magazine*) on her painful inability to complete the album. Late in 1997, Williams embarked on a tour to promote **Car Wheels** announcing it would be released "soon." That promise moved closer to being fulfilled in early 1998 when Mercury picked up Williams and brought in Roy Bittan to finish production on the wayward recording. They set a new release date for sometime in the summer and, lo and behold, it *finally* happened. But, after so many re-dos and re-trys and so many years, could it be any good? Suffice it to say that **Car Wheels** catapulted Lucinda back to the forefront and then some. Periodicals and newspapers that didn't have gushing feature length stories on her and the album were few and far between, and she was on music and talk shows galore. **Car Wheels on a Gravel Road** finished #1 on almost every Best of 1998 alt. country/Americana list.

Ramblin'/Smithsonian Folkways/1979; 1991
Happy Woman Blues/Smithsonian Folkways/1980; 1990
Lucinda Williams/Rough Trade/1988; Chameleon/1992;
   KOCH/1998 (with 6 extra trks.)
Passionate Kisses/Chameleon/1990 (EP CD)
Sweet Old World/Chameleon/1992
"Still Long for Your Kiss" on **The Horse
   Whisperer**/MCA/1998
Car Wheels on a Gravel Road/Mercury/1998
"Return of the Grievous Angel" (with David Crosby) on
   **Return of the Grievous Angel: A Tribute to Gram
   Parsons**/Almo/1999

Lucinda Williams Unofficial Home Page
//www.lonestarwebstation.com/lucinda.html

Lucinda Williams/Mercury Page
//www.mercuryrecords.com/music/

Lucinda Williams Guitar Chords & Tabs
//pobox.com/~schneider/music/lw/

Lucinda Williams AOL Folder: Entertainment>Music>Chat
& Messages>Music Community>Folk/Acoustic

Kelly Willis

Austin; Singer/Songwriter
Lawton, Oklahoma; October 2, 1968-

One memorable night in 1984, a painfully shy teenager named Kelly Willis made her singing debut with a D.C. area rockabilly band, the Fireballs. Prior to this her performing had been of the imaginary kind in cars and showers, but her boyfriend, Mas Palermo, was the leader of the Fireballs and was convinced to give her a shot. The dynamic voice (compared to Wanda Jackson, Janis Martin, Patsy Cline) coming from this demure young woman surprised and delighted fans, and Willis became a permanent member of the group. Renamed Kelly and the Fireballs, the band became popular on the D.C. scene and was nominated for a Wammie in 1987. Later that year, they decided to try Austin and renamed Radio Ranch began to make their presence known. MCA recording star Nanci Griffith brought Kelly to the attention of her label, and in 1990, MCA came through with a lavish contract and big plans for Willis. First came two successive albums, **Well Traveled Love** and **Bang, Bang**, each a melange of country, Texas honky tonk, rockabilly, and blues on songs by Steve Earle, John Hiatt, Jim Lauderdale, Joe Ely and Austin writers including Palermo and Monte Warden. At the same time, MCA spent lots of money trying to remake Willis' image and market her as a Nashville type country star through spreads in fashion magazines and *People* (she was named one of the 50 most beautiful people of 1993). She had a song included in the soundtrack of *Thelma & Louise* and appeared as a folk singer in the film *Bob Roberts*. However, Willis was unwilling to go in the direction MCA had in mind though they kept applying the pressure. When her first two recordings succeeded with the critics but failed on the charts, MCA gave her one more chance. **Kelly Willis** was a more pop country oriented album with songs by Kevin Welch, Willis, Libbi Dwyer/Bosworth, and new boyfriend Bruce Robison. When it too failed to live up to MCA's expectations, Willis was dropped in 1993. Ironically, she was nominated Top New Female Vocalist of 1994 by the Academy of Country Music. Back in Austin, Willis pulled herself together and charted a new course. Breaking somewhat from the mold of the "Austin sound," she tied herself closer to the new breed of alternative country musicians. In 1994, she did a duet with Jay Farrar (Uncle Tupelo/Son Volt), a version of Townes Van Zandt's "Rex's Blues" for the compilation, **Red, Hot + Bothered**. In 1995, Willis signed with A&M records and chose to record a four song EP, **Fading Fast**. Son Volt served as her backing band on three songs and one of these "What World Are You Living In?" she co-wrote with the Jayhawks' Gary Louris who also provided harmony vocals. The fourth song on the EP, "Aren't I True," featured another new alt. country band, 16 Horsepower. Overall, the harder, moodier country sound of the recording was a significant departure from Willis' previous

work. However, it was a big hit with fans and critics and was named Best EP of 1996 at the Austin Music Awards. It raised high expectations of things to come, but Willis' bad luck with big labels continued, and in early 1997, she and A&M parted company. Still, 1996 and 1997 were positive for Willis; she married long time boyfriend, singer/songwriter Bruce Robison, and assembled a new band with Jon Dee Graham (ex-True Believers) on steel, Tony Maimone (ex-Pere Ubu/Golden Palominos) on bass, Will Rigby (ex-DBs) on drums, and Mark Spencer (ex-Blood Oranges) on guitar. Early in 1997, they appeared at SXSW and began a tour to preview new songs. Willis was also part of the Lilith Fair and in late 1997 went to San Francisco to begin work on a new recording even though she wasn't signed to any label.

While waiting for the right record contract, in early 1998, Willis busied herself with a number of projects including contributions to noteworthy tributes to Big Star and Tom T. Hall and to the **Uprooted** and **Songs of Forbidden Love** compilations. After finally getting a secure deal with Rykodisc, Kelly spent the remainder of the year touring either solo or with Bruce Robison and Richard Buckner (The Good, The Bad, and The Ugly tour) and finishing her new album **What I Deserve** which came out in early 1999. It proved well worth the wait with an excellent variety of material by Bruce Robison, Willis/Gary Louris, Willis/John Leventhal, Damon Bramblett, Paul Kelly, Nick Drake, Dan Penn/Chuck Prophet, and Paul Westerberg. One additional treat for Willis' fans in 1998 was the inclusion of Kelly and the Fireballs' cover of "Your Cheatin' Heart" on Billy Poore's **Renegade Rockabilly** collection.

Radio Ranch: Brad Fordham (b); Mike Hardwick (r.g.,s.g.); David Murray (e.g.); Mas Palermo (d) Jon Dee Graham (s.g.); Tony Maimone (b); Will Rigby (d); Mark Spencer (l.g.)

> **Well-Traveled Love**/MCA/1990
> **Bang Bang**/MCA/1991
> "Little Honey" on **Thelma & Louise**/MCA/1992
> **Kelly Willis**/MCA/1993
> "Rex's Blues" (with Jay Farrar) on **Red, Hot + Bothered**/Red Hot Kinetic/1994
> **Fading Fast**/A&M/1996 (EP)
> "Not Long for This World" on **KGSR, Broadcasts Vol. 4/** KGSR/1996
> "Truckstop Girl" on **Rig Rock Deluxe**/Upstart Diesel Only/1996
> "When My Baby's Beside Me" on **The Big Star Tribute**/Small World/1998
> "He Don't Care About Me" on **Uprooted: The Best of Roots Country**/Shanachie/1998
> "Me and Mrs. Jones"; "It's a Cheatin' Situation" (w/ Dale Watson) on **Songs of Forbidden Love**/Lazy SOB/1998
> "That's How I Got to Memphis" on **Real: The Tom T. Hall Project**/Sire/1998
> "What I Deserve" (Live w/ Bruce Robison) on **Rykodisc's 15th Anniversary Acoustic Cafe Sampler/** Rykodisc/1998

"Your Cheatin' Heart" (Kelly Willis and the Fireballs) on
Renegade Rockabilly/Renegade/1998
What I Deserve/Rykodisc/1999

Official Kelly Willis Page
//www.kellywillis.com

See Bruce Robison; Monte Warden

Tommy Womack

Singer/Songwriter
Sturgis, Kentucky; November 20, 1962-

From 1985-1992, Tommy Womack was a member of Government Cheese, a rock band from Bowling Green, Kentucky, that toured a lot, made some records, and was even on MTV a few times. After their break-up, they united for a brief tour to promote *Cheese Chronicles: The Story of a Rock 'n' Roll Band You Never Heard Of*, Womack's astute and hysterically funny account of his years with Government Cheese. In 1992, Tommy joined a roots rock band called the bisquits who recorded an album for John Prine's Oh Boy! label. When they ended in 1994, he vowed "to never be in another band named after a food product." Instead, Womack pursued a solo career and made his recording debut in 1998 with **Positively Na Na** on Checkered Past. It covers a lot of musical ground (roots rock, pop, honky tonk, rockabilly, soul) with style to burn, but the real highlight is Womack's way with words as he skillfully takes on some pretty dark material—unwed mothers, spousal abuse, sex addiction, getting even, rejection, bingeing—and comes up swinging with humor and hope. **Positively Na Na** was nominated as Independent Album of the Year by the Nashville Music Awards.

Cheese Chronicles: The Story of a Rock 'n' Roll Band You Never Heard Of, Dowling Press,1997
Positively Na Na/Checkered Past/1998
"You're Not Made for This World" on **Fireworks, Vol. 2**/
Sound Asleep Swe./1998

Tommy Womack's Homepage
//www.pubwire.com/tommy/welcome.html

firebug@nc5.infi.net

The World Famous Bluejays

Rig Rock; Insurgent Country
Brooklyn, New York; 1983-

Founded in 1983 by Jay Sherman-Godfrey and Jeremy Tepper, the World Famous Bluejays were one of the pioneer groups in the New York City alt. country scene of the 1980s and early 1990s. After releasing several singles of country rock in the 1980s on Hideout Records, Sherman-Godfrey, Tepper, and Bluejays drummer (and owner of Coyote Studios) Albert Caiati decided to start their own record label. In January 1990, they set up Diesel Only Records which was devoted to keeping alive the 45 vinyl single and the type of hard country music traditionally found on truckstop jukeboxes. They named this sound "Rig Rock" and for the first DO singles chose bands from the New York City area. The two inaugural releases, "Good Morning Mr. Trucker" by the World Famous Bluejays and "Punk Rockin' Honky Tonk Girl" by the Blue Chieftains, set the DO standard for cutting edge country rock/honky tonk and were followed by singles from other New York alt. country groups. To promote the music, Diesel Only staged Rig Rock Revue showcases at various local clubs and did interviews and articles for a variety of nationally distributed magazines. This resulted not only in the recruitment of more New York City acts (Angel Dean, Five Chinese Brothers, Amy Allison) but also artists from all over the country including Mark Brine, Gwil Owen, Killbilly, and Jean Caffeine. Over the next few years, DO released over 25 singles, collecting the best of them on a compilation entitled **Rig Rock Juke Box** followed by **Rig Rock Truck Stop**. Both were widely acclaimed and very influential in launching individual artists and furthering the cause of alt. country in general. The World Famous Bluejays' contributions to these compilations were the "Diesel Only Theme," "Do It For Hank," and two duets with wild man Mojo Nixon, the rousing and hilarious "UFOs, Big Rigs, & BBQ" and a raucous cover of Roger Miller's "Chug-a-Lug." In 1995, the Bluejays entered the insurgent country fold when their "Mud Flap Boogie" was put on **Hell-Bent**. As a follow-up to the Rig Rock collections, Tepper and Caiati assembled non-DO performers to record **Rig Rock Deluxe: A Musical Salute to the American Truck Driver**. Released in 1996, it has cuts by Junior Brown, Steve Earle, Don Walser, BR5-49, Son Volt, the Bottle Rockets, Kelly Willis, Buck Owens, and Bill Kirchen and was one of the top alt. country albums of the year. As for the World Famous Bluejays, they continued to perform on occasion in New York City and did some original music for Michael Moorer's 1998 documentary *The Big One*. Tepper edited and published a jukebox trade magazine, *Streetbeat* and compiled a history of truck driving music from the 1930s-present for a Country Music Foundation CD.

Albert Caiati (d); Marc Fagelson (b); Jay Sherman-Godfrey (l.g.); Jeremy Tepper (a.g.)

"Annie is a Granny" b/w "Is a Bluebird Blue?"/Hideout
"10 Pin Boogie" b/w "Hush"/Hideout (7")
"Good Morning Mr. Trucker" b/w "Motor City"/Diesel
Only/1990 (7")
"Do It for Hank" b/w "Mud Flap Boogie"/Diesel
Only/1990 (7")
"Diesel Only Theme"; "Do It for Hank"; "Good Morning
Mr. Trucker" on **Rig Rock Juke Box**/Diesel
Only/1992
"Cookin' With Jay"; "Chug-a-Lug" (with Mojo Nixon);
"UFOs, Big Rigs & BBQ" (with Mojo Nixon) on **Rig
Rock Truck Stop**/Diesel Only/1993
"Mud Flap Boogie" on **Hell-Bent**/Bloodshot/1995
**Rig Rock Deluxe: A Musical Salute to the American
Truck Driver**/Upstart Diesel Only/1996

Diesel Only Records, 100 N. 6th St., Brooklyn, NY 11211

DieselOnly@aol.com

See Mojo Nixon

Wylie and The Wild West Show
Country Rock; Cowboy/Western; Yodeling
Los Angeles, California; 1990-

Raised on a cattle ranch in Montana, Wylie Gustafson was introduced to country music by his father who had a special love for cowboy songs. He taught his son a few guitar chords, and over the years, after playing in a number of bands, the younger Gustafson began performing in L.A. in the early 1990s as Wylie & the Wild West Show. Looking like a combination of Elvis Costello, Buddy Holly, and Lyle Lovett, Wylie specialized in Bakersfield country and Marty Robbins influenced Western music ("All Hat, No Cattle"; "I'm Gonna Be a Cowboy"; "Give Me a Pinto Pal"; "Jingle, Jangle, Jingle"). Blessed with a rich baritone, Wylie can handle honky tonk, country rock, and rockabilly but has a special talent for yodeling ("Yodeling Fool"; "Cattle Call"). The band's videos ("Hey Maria"; "Black Boots & Blue Jeans") were played regularly on CMT and TNN and brought Wylie & the Wild West Show to the attention of a wider country audience in the early 1990s. In 1997, they signed a deal with Rounder which re-released **Way Out West** (produced by Ray Benson). This album was named Best Country Album of the Year by The Association for Independent Music (formerly NAIRD) and was followed up by **Total Yodel!** on which Wylie covers all the classic cowboy/country yodels and yodelers from Jimmie Rodgers to Elton Britt, Slim Whitman, and Patsy Montana (see Randy Erwin, Sourdough, Slim, Riders, and Don Walser for comparisons). In the late 1990s, Wylie lived in a small town in Washington state where in addition to playing music he collected Western Americana.

Wylie & The Wild West Show: Wylie Gustafson (a.g.,b,l.v.); Duane Becker (db,l.s.,p.s.,1997-); Ray Doyle (a.g.,e.g.,h.v.,1991-); Mike Fried (a.g.,db,e.g.,s.g., 1992-1997); Kenny Griffin (d,perc,1992-1996); Larry Mitchell (d,1990-1992); Jon Shelley (d,1996-1997); Mark Thornton (a.g.,e.g.,1996-); Garth Whitson (d,1997-)

> **Wylie and The Wild West Show**/Oh Boy/1992
> "Since I Found You" on **A Town South of Bakersfield, Vol. 3**/Restless/1992
> **Get Wild**/Cross Three/1994
> **Way Out West**/Two Medicine/1996; Rounder/1997
> **Total Yodel!**/Rounder/1998

Wylie & the Wild West Show Fan Club 513 Wilshire Blvd., Suite 222, Santa Monica, CA 90401

Wylie & the Wild West Show Official Home Page //www.wylieww.com

Wynona Sue and The Turnpikes
Cowgirl/Western Parody
Calgary, Alberta, Canada; 1994-1998

From the home of the famous Calgary Stampede and Rodeo came a horse of a different color. Wynona Sue (aka Barbara Chamberlin) and the Turnpikes took a combination of early k.d. lang, Miss Xanna Don't big hair and overt sexuality, and bovine humor and turned it into a riotous parody of country and western music and lifestyles. In 1994, they starred in the independent film *Highway of Heartache*, a country/western melodrama by Gregory Wild that would make John Waters mighty happy. The soundtrack by the same name came out a year later and mixes fairly straight forward songs ("Blue Jeans"; "Ring on My Finger"; "Lonely Tears"; "Cowboy Moon") with some truly bizarre tunes e.g. "Bye Brown Baby, Bye" ("...Mama and the KKK forced me to give you away"), "Gutterbound," "Cow Cow Strut," "Burnin' Beaver Blues," "Filly Fry," and "Fightin' Time." What raises it above kitschy camp is the fact that the musicianship is exemplary, and Wynona/Barbara can belt it out with the best of 'em on ballads, honky tonk, and country rock. A reworked version of **Highway** with new songs was released as **Wynona Sue and the Turnpikes** in 1997. Rumor had it that Wynona Sue retired in 1998.

> **Highway of Heartaches**/WST/1995
> **Wynona Sue And The Turnpikes**/Tom Cat Can./1997

Wynona Sue and the Turnpikes Home Page //www.candisc.com/wynona_sue/

Y'ALL
Singer/Songwriter; Gay Country
New York City; 1992-

Y'ALL is a gay country duo from New York City. As legend has it, James Dean Jay Byrd (born in Okey Dokey, Texas, October 28, 1967) and Steven Cheslik-DeMeyer (born in Kornflake, Indiana, March 24, 1968) met during a violent thunderstorm near Circleville, Ohio. Byrd was trapped in a pumpkin field but light flashing off the rhinestones on his "lucky green dress" alerted Cheslik-DeMeyer who went to his rescue. The two fell in love, began harmonizing and writing songs, and in 1992 went to New York City. In August of that year, they debuted during an open mic session at a club on the Lower East Side. Since their names were too long and hard to remember, the owner had them sign up as Y'ALL, and after a successful premier, they began performing at nightspots all over, as they call it, "The Big Apple Pie." They developed a cabaret show in which they sang original songs and told stories about their lives. In 1993, the show became the basis for **An Evening of Stories and Songs**; in 1994, they won a Back Stage Bistro Award and were finalists in *Musician Magazine's* Best Unsigned Band Contest. Eventually, Y'ALL evolved into a country duo and began making the rounds of acoustic venues. They modeled themselves after groups like the Louvin, Everly or even the Smothers Brothers, but in this case, a more apt comparison would be George and Tammy or Dolly and Porter. Like their lesbian counterparts, the Topp Twins, Y'ALL specializes in tight country harmonies and original songs mixing rural nostalgia with an honest look at the gay lifestyle. They are satirical without ever being mean spirited, sentimental without being maudlin, and self-parodying without being campy. **The Next Big Thing**, is a good illustration of their underlying attitude especially on songs like the moving "Mamaw," the hilarious "Are You on the Top 40 of Your Lord?," and the witty Western send up "My Man, Our Horses, and Me." That recording has just Byrd and Cheslik-DeMeyer with occasional backing by the eight member Cow Girl Chorus (includes Amy Allison), but **Big Apple Pie** has a fuller sound using a band complete with banjos, mandolins, and fiddles. However, the spirit is the same on "Paradise," "God Bless New York City (My Big Apple Pie)," and a cover of Loretta Lynn's "You Ain't Woman Enough to Take My Man." Y'ALL's other projects include a Christmas EP, **Christmastime In the Trailerpark** and a sequence of cassette singles entitled **Chicken 'n' Dumplin's** to be issued throughout 1997-1998 and eventually gathered into a full length CD. They penned their autobiography, *The Good Book: The True Story of Y'ALL* which they sold by the chapter for $7.50 (to finance a new RV). For the long term, Y'ALL wanted to do a 1930s-1940s style country radio show and someday their own national TV program. They made a start toward TV stardom with several appearances on MTV and did a showcase at SXSW in 1998. On their way to Texas, they stopped off in Nashville and after a promising performance and encouragement from a few music promoters, Y'ALL decided to move to Music City in September. Move over Brooks & Dunn!

An Evening of Stories and Songs/Y'ALL/1993
The Next Big Thing/Y'ALL/1995
Big Apple Pie/Y'ALL/1995
Christmas Time in the Trailer Park/Y'ALL/1996
Chicken 'n' Dumplin's: Live With the Low Road/
    Y'ALL/1996 (CS single)
Chicken 'n' Dumplin's: Live From the Twin Pines/
    Y'ALL/1997 (CS single)
Chicken 'n' Dumplin's: Live at L'il Mo's/Y'ALL/1997
    (CS single)
Chicken 'n' Dumplin's: Live From the Rhythm Ranch/
    Y'ALL/1997 (CS single)
Best of the Family Reunion/Y'ALL/1997 (CS)

P. O. Box 24903, Nashville, TN 37202-4903; 615-460-9386
Y'ALL Home Page //songs.com/moo
y'all@songs.com

Eva Ybarra y su Conjunto
Accordion; Conjunto; Tex-Mex
San Antonio, Texas

From its beginnings, *conjunto* has been mostly an all male province; all of the great pioneers who developed the music in the San Antonio and South Texas region were men, and while women were not discouraged from taking up the accordion, it was understood within the community that being a *conjunto* accordionist was not really a suitable avocation for a woman.

Fortunately, Eva Ybarra had parents who not only gave her her first accordion (at age 4) but also encouraged her to pursue a musical career. They chaperoned Eva at her first performances (at age 6) with her brothers at local restaurants and dance halls and continued to support her over the years. Like other innovative players of her generation (Flaco Jimenez, Santiago Jimenez. Jr., Mingo Saldivar), Ybarra mastered the techniques of the great *conjunto* accordionists while absorbing and integrating musical influences from a variety of sources. Well versed in the traditional *rancheras*, *valses*, and *baladas*, she developed a very unique style incorporating *cumbias*, *huapangos*, tango, and country music. In addition to her versatile accordion playing, Ybarra was an adept composer of achingly beautiful songs about love and loss, "Triste Adios" (Sad Goodbye), "En Esta Cantina" (In This Cantina), "Dora," and "Las Palmeras"(The Palms). Her long time singing partners Gloria Garcia Abadia and Guadalupe Betancourt have contributed some gorgeously romantic songs as well including "Carino Bueno" (Good Love), "Lloro Por Ti" (Cry for You), and "Preferible Morir" (It is Better to Die). Ybarra has been famous in South Texas for almost three decades and made many recordings (mostly on Hacienda), but only in the 1990s did she gain wider recognition through events sponsored by Texas Folklife Resources and through two albums for Rounder Records, **A Mi San Antonio** and **Romance Involidable**. She can also be heard on the dynamite accordion music box set **Planet Squeezebox**. Ybarra has been very generous with her knowledge serving as master accordion instructor at the Guadalupe Cultural Arts Center in San Antonio and in 1998 became an Artist-in-Residence in the Ethnomusicology Department at the University of Washington where she taught accordion, guitarron, and bajo sexto.

A Mi San Antonio/Rounder/1994
Romance Involidable/Rounder/1996
"A Mi San Antonio" on **Planet Squeezebox**/Ellipsis/1997

Eva Ybarra/Womad Page
//www.womadusa.org/artists/8.html

Eva Ybarra/Rounder Page //www.rounder.com

Dwight Yoakam (Pete Anderson)
TSOB
Pikeville, Kentucky; October 23, 1956-

Of the many fine musicians to come out of the Town South of Bakersfield community, none has attained a higher profile than Dwight Yoakam. Raised in Kentucky, Yoakam went to Nashville in the early 1970s as an aspiring singer/songwriter, but his style was about 30 years too late, and he was spurned by the Nashville establishment. Relocating to L.A., Dwight was welcomed with open arms into the blossoming Southern California alt. country scene. He assembled a top notch band (the Babylonian Cowboys) with a talented lead guitar player Pete Anderson who produced Yoakam's 1984 debut recording, an EP on tiny Oak records entitled **Guitars, Cadillacs, Etc. Etc.** One of its songs, "I'll Be Gone," was on the first volume of **A Town South of Bakersfield** (produced by Anderson). In 1986, Yoakam got a big break when he was signed to Warner Reprise which issued an expanded version of **Guitar, Cadillacs, Etc. Etc.** It was the beginning of a fruitful relationship producing a string of highly successful albums (all produced by Anderson), **Hillbilly Deluxe**, **Buenas Noches From a Lonely Room**, **If There Was a Way**, **This Time**, **Gone**, and corresponding hit singles. Beside a classic voice and an ability to write believable country songs, the keys to Yoakum's meteoric rise were his effective melding of classic honky tonk with rock in a way that appealed to a broad spectrum of music fans. Each of his albums paid homage to tradition with updated versions of songs by Hank Williams, Johnny Horton, Lefty Frizzell, Buck Owens, Johnny Cash, Merle Haggard, et al. plus authentic sounding hard country rock originals. In the early 1990s, Yoakam parlayed his musical success into a second career as an actor making his debut in *Red Rock West* with Nicholas Cage and playing a menacing redneck in Billy Bob Thornton's *Slingblade*. He also had roles in 1998 in (as the "nitro man") in Richard Linklater's outlaw saga, *The Newton Brothers* and (as a reckless army officer) in the HBO World War II film, *When Trumpets Fade*. Pete Anderson expanded his horizons as a producer and performer in the 1990s guiding the Backsliders debut and setting up Little Dog Records (with Dusty Wakeman) where he produced recordings by fellow Babylonian Cowboy Scott Joss, the Lonesome Strangers, and Joe Lynn White. He recorded two solo albums, **Working Class** and **Dogs in Heaven**, showcasing his guitar versatility. A live bootleg from Pete's 1997 "Dogs in Heaven" tour was available from Little Dog. In late 1997, Yoakam released **Come on Christmas** and **Under the Covers** which presented his versions of songs by Roy Orbison, Johnny Horton, the Beatles, the Clash, and a variety of others. He, along with Anderson, contributed "T for Texas" to the Dylan produced **The Songs of Jimmie Rodgers** in 1997, and in 1998, Yoakam did songs for Ralph Stanley and Kinky Friedman tributes. Dwight was honored by his peers with a tribute album of his own. **Will Sing for Food** has covers of some of his most famous songs by the Backsliders, Lonesome Strangers, Gillian Welch, Scott Joss, Tim O'Brien, and others. Late in 1998, Yoakam returned to the prime form with the heralded, **A Long Way Home**.

The Original Babylonian Cowboys: Pete Anderson (l.g.); Jeff Donovan (d); J. D. Foster (b); Brantley Kearns (f) **Current Babylonian Cowboys:** Pete Anderson; Jim E. Christie (d); Anthony Crawford (a.g.,md,b.v.); Skip Edwards (acc,ky); Scott Joss (f,md,b.v.); Taras Prodaniuk (b)

Guitars, Cadillacs, Etc. Etc./Oak/1984 (EP)
"I'll Be Gone" on **A Town South of Bakersfield, Vol. 1/** Restless/1985
Guitars, Cadillacs, Etc. Etc./Reprise/1986
Hillbilly Deluxe/Reprise/1987

Buenas Noches From a Lonely Room/Warner/1988
Live Deluxe: Guitars, Cadillacs & Hillbilly Music, Live in Kentucky, 1988/RSM/1988
Just Lookin' For a Hit/Reprise/1989
This Is Dwight Yoakum/Rerpise Jp./1990
If There Was a Way/Reprise/1990
"Truckin'" on **Deadicated: A Tribute to the Grateful Dead**/1991
La Croix D'Amour/Reprise Eur./1993
This Time/Reprise/1993
"Holding Things Together" on **Tulare Dust: A Songwriter's Tribute to Merle Haggard/** Hightone/1994
Dwight Live/Reprise/1995
Gone/Reprise/1995
"Guitars, Cadillacs" (Live 1988) on **The Best of Austin City Limits, Vol. 1**/Columbia Legacy/1996 (CD/video)
Under the Covers/Reprise/1997
Come On Christmas/Reprise/1997
"T For Texas" on **The Songs of Jimmie Rodgers: A Tribute**/Egyptian/1997
"I Got Wise"; "The Darkest Hour is Before the Dawn" on **Clinch Mountain Country: Ralph Stanley & Friends**/Rebel/1998
"Cattle Call" on **The Horse Whisperer**/MCA/1998
"Rapid City, South Dakota" on **Pearls in the Snow: The Songs of Kinky Friedman**/1998
Will Sing for Food: The Songs of Dwight Yoakam/LittleDog/1998
A Long Way Home/Reprise/1998
Live at Ohio University (Pete Anderson)/Little Dog/1998

The Dwight Site //dwightsite.com (the most complete web page with biography, discography, on line mailing list, etc.)

The Dwight Yoakum/iMusic Showcase //imusic.com/showcase/country/

Dwight Yoakum AOL Folder: Entertainment>Music>Chat & Messages>Music Community>Country/Folk>Country & Western, L-Z

See Scott Joss

Neil Young
Country Rock; Roots Rock
Toronto, Ontario, Canada; November 12, 1945-

Neil Young has been one of the most important figures in popular music in the last 30 years. Along the way, he has had a major influence on several generations of alternative country. In the late 1960s and early 1970s, Young was a vital part of the seminal folk/country/rock band Buffalo Springfield but, at the same time, was pursuing his own country rock vision that came together on a series of recognized classics: **Neil Young**, **Everybody Knows This is Nowhere**, **After the Goldrush**, **Harvest**, **On the Beach**, **Tonight's the Night**, **Zuma**, **American Stars and Bars**, and **Comes a Time**. On each of these, Young developed a country rock style that was a little bit rawer and more wide open than that of contemporaries like the Grateful Dead, the Byrds and the Flying Burrito Brothers. Throughout the 1980s-1990s, he was a persistent experimenter and didn't flinch when the punk rock "revolution" hit. Rather,

Neil met it head on and in time became the acknowledged "grandfather of grunge" with potent albums from **Rust Never Sleeps** to **Ragged Glory**. He occasionally showed his softer country roots on **Old Ways**, **Harvest Moon**, and **Unplugged**. As a pioneer of both country rock and grunge, Young had an enormous influence on the evolution of alternative country. Echoes of his early recordings are apparent in a wide variety of acts, and his songs have been covered by many of alt. country performers. His oscillation between country, country rock, and grunge is clearly mirrored in Uncle Tupelo (Son Volt; Wilco), the Jayhawks, the Bottle Rockets, and many other No Depression bands. In early 1999 came confirmation of a massive Neil Young 32 CD archival set to be released in four volumes totaling seven CDs with over 70 previously unissued songs plus three bonus live CDs. As if that weren't enough, Young was set to record an acoustic album that was reported to be much like **Harvest Moon**.

In mid-1999, a tribute CD, **This Note's for You Too!**, sponsored by the Dutch Neil Young fan club and the Dutch Inbetweens label was released with a number of alt. country/Americana performers including Eric Ambel, the Walkabouts, Chris Burroughs, Continental Drifters, Big In Iowa, the Coal Porters, and Tom Stevens covering Young's songs.

Neil Young/Reprise/1969
Everybody Knows This Is Nowhere/Reprise/1969
After the Gold Rush/Reprise/1970
Harvest/Reprise/1972
Time Fades Away/Reprise/1973
On the Beach/Reprise/1974
Tonight's the Night/Reprise/1975
Zuma/Reprise/1975
American Stars 'n Bars/Reprise/1977
Decade/Reprise/1977 (anthology)
Comes a Time/Reprise/1978
Rust Never Sleeps/Reprise/1979
Hawks & Doves/Reprise/1980
Old Ways/Geffen/1985
Ragged Glory/Reprise/1990
Harvest Moon/Reprise/1992
Unplugged/Reprise/1993
This Note's For You Too!: A Tribute to Neil Young/
    Inbetweens Dut./1999

HyperRust Never Sleeps //HyperRust.org/ (the most complete Neil Young web site with on-line mailing list and lots of links to the *many* Young web pages)

reactor@hyperrust.org

Steve Young

Singer/Songwriter; Country Rock
Noonan, Georgia; July 12, 1942-

One of Steve Young's most famous songs "Lonesome, On'ry, and Mean" could easily be the title of his autobiography. For much of his long career as a singer/songwriter, Young was in open battle against social prejudice, the music business, and/or his own personal demons. During most of his childhood, he was without a father and his mother moved the family around from Georgia to Alabama to Texas in search of employment. Along the way, Young was exposed to blues and country and learned to play guitar; after high school, he ended up in Montgomery, Alabama for a while before heading for the folk scene in Greenwich Village. Fueled by the radical fires of protest, he returned to Montgomery where he openly lived a Bohemian lifestyle and sang out against Southern intolerance. When the residents made it clear he was unwelcome, Young moved to L.A. where he worked as a session player and became a member of an early country rock band, Stone Country. They recorded one album in 1968 before disbanding. Young got a deal with A&M and recorded his debut, **Rock Salt and Nails**, one of the defining moments in the development of California country rock. Its supporting cast included James Burton, Gene Clark, Chris Hillman, and Gram Parsons, and it yielded one of Young's most successful (for others but not him) songs, "Seven Bridges Road." It also seemed to portend big things for Young, but A&M dropped him. His next label, Reprise, released **Seven Bridges Road** in 1971 but made the process so unpleasant Young decided to leave California for Nashville. His "Lonesome, On'ry, and Mean" had been a hit for RCA star Waylon Jennings so the label decided to give Young a try. However, he balked when they tried to make him over in the image of a Nashville country singer, and RCA let him go after two recordings. To make matters worse, Young was in the throes of alcoholism and marital problems and for a time dropped into a bleak period of musical inactivity. Then, in the early 1980s, Young was rescued by a combination of AA and Zen and returned to writing and recording. However, his new deal with Rounder was shaky at best and resulted in several fairly lackluster albums. The best thing to come out of this period was Young's great tribute song to Hank Williams, "Montgomery in the Rain" (shame on you, Alan Jackson!). At this point, Young decided to try his luck in Europe where he toured and made recordings into the late 1980s. He did a number of tours around the world on behalf of the U.S. State Department. In 1991, Young made a triumphant return when he moved to Austin, signed with Watermelon, and did **Solo, Live** and then **Switchblades of Love** which was nominated for a Nashville Music Award for Best Folk Album in 1995. His contributions have been accorded greater appreciation through the re-issue of many of his early albums and the release a retrospective collection fittingly titled **Lonesone, On'ry, and Mean: Steve Young, 1968-1978**.

Stone Country/RCA/1968
Rock Salt and Nails/A&M/1969; Demon UK/1986
Seven Bridges Road/Reprise/1972; Blue Canyon/1973;
    Rounder/1981

Honky Tonk Man/Mountain Railroad/1975;
  Rounder/1984; Drive/1995
Renegade Picker/RCA/1976
No Place to Fall/RCA/1978
Old Memories/Country Road UK/1980
To Satisfy You/Rounder/1982
Look Homeward Angel/Mill Euro./1986
Long Time Rider/Golden Chain/1987; Voodoo
  Euro./1991
Solo, Live/Watermelon; Demon UK/1991
Switchblades of Love/Watermelon/1993
Lonesome, On'ry and Mean: Steve Young, 1968-1978/
  Raven Austra./1994

Steve Young, 1 All American singer/songwriter
//KyWebs.com/SteveYoungOnline/door.htm

Budayoung@aol.com

Steve Young/NOMA Home Page //songs.com/noma/sy/

The Zeftrons

Roots Rock
Portland, Maine; 1996-

Maine's entrant into the Americana derby is the Zeftrons, a roots rock band from the tiny town of Kittery outside of Portland. The group took shape in 1996 under the leadership of Michael Landgarten who had been in a number of local bands including the Doc Johnson Blues Band. After the group went through several incarnations, it settled into its current line up with Jon Haas, Ned Chase, and Brian Coleman. Landgarten, who is the group's main songwriter, points to a variety of inspirations. Hank, Sr., Bob Dylan, Dave Alvin, Bruce Springsteen, and Steve Earle have all been instrumental in forming the Zeftrons roots rock style. Those influences and more are evident on their self titled debut on the local Rockingham label. Already a hit in the far Northeast, the Zeftrons ("Southern Maine's premier roots rockers") achieved wider recognition through write ups in *Country Standard Time* and *No Depression* in 1997.

Ned Chase (l.g.); Brian Coleman (b); Jon Haas (d); Michael Landgarten (g,v)

  The Zeftrons/Rockingham/1997

The Zeftrons c/o Jennifer O'Neal, P.O. Box 432,
Eliot, ME 03903; 800-293-5030

The Zeftrons Home Page //www.spwa.com/zeftrons/

Zeftrons@aol.com

Martin Zellar (The Gear Daddies; The Hard Ways)

Roots Rock; Country Rock
Austin, Minnesota

One of the most popular alt. country groups of the late 1980s was the Gear Daddies. They formed in "the other Austin" (home of Hormel Meat Co. and Spam) but eventually moved to Minneapolis where they developed a local following. Their country inflected rock sound found expression on two recordings, **Let's Go Scare Al** and **Billy's Live Bait**, and brought them to the attention of a wider audience. What mainly distinguished the Gear Daddies was the singing and songwriting of Martin Zellar. His unique, raspy vocals lent a special poignancy to his songs about the frustration and desperation of life in small town America: "Statue of Jesus"; "She's Happy"; "Heavy Metal Boys." The country elements were mainly provided by the pedal steel of Randy Broughton who set the background for Zellar's moody songs. But, the Gear Daddies also rocked hard on occasion as they demonstrated on **Can't Have Nothing Nice**, a collection of rare live sessions and out takes released after the Gear Daddies disappointing but amicable break up in 1992. What they started was carried on by groups (the Billy's, Golden Smog, and the Honeydogs) in Minneapolis' thriving alt. country scene. Their spirit also lived on through Zellar who, post-Gear Daddies, dropped out of music for a time before returning with a solo album, **Born Under**, in 1995. Here he was supported by Ciola and Broughton (now with Trailer Trash) plus other local musicians including Adam and Noah Levy (now with the Honeydogs). In many ways, the recording could be called "Gear Daddies Part 2," due to the presence of GD alumni, Zellar's distinctive voice, and his continued exploration of teenage wastelands ("East Side Boys") and the dark side of love and life ("Lie to Me"; "Falling Sky"; "Summer Kind of Sad"; "Force a Smile"). In 1996, Zellar formed a new band and recorded **Martin Zellar & The Hard Ways** which has faint traces of the Gear Daddies but moves in a harder roots rock direction. In 1997, he contributed "Darkness on the Edge of Town" to the Bruce Springsteen tribute, **One Step Up, Two Steps Back**. Growing tired of the big label run-a-round, Zellar split from Rykodisc but kept the Hard-Ways together and independently recorded **The Many Moods of Martin Zellar**. As the title suggests it's a sort of "retrospective" that nicely weaves together the various styles Martin has explored in over the years.

The Gear Daddies: Randy Broughton (g,p.s.); Nick Ciola (b); Billy Dankert (d); Martin Zellar (g,l.v.)
The Hard Ways: Nick Ciola (b); Dan Neale (l.g.); Marc Retish (d); Patrick Tanner (l.g.,v)

  "She's Happy" b/w "2x18"/Gark/1987 (7")
  Let's Go Scare Al/Gark/1988; Polydor/1989
  Billy's Live Bait/Polydor/1990
  Can't Have Nothin' Nice/Crackpot/1992
  Born Under (Martin Zellar)/Rykodisc/1995
  Martin Zellar & The Hardways/Rykodisc/1996
  "Darkness on the Edge of Town" on **One Step Up, Two
    Step Back**/1997
  The Many Moods of Martin Zellar/Owen Lee/1998

Martin Zellar Fan Club, Crack in the Sidewalk, P.O. Box 50694, Minneapolis, MN 55403 or Cksidewalk@aol.com

Martin Zellar Web Zone //www.martinzellar.com

See The Billys; The Honeydogs

OTHER ARTISTS OF INTEREST

The Barkers
Country Rock; Roots Rock
Austin, Texas
grib@cs.utexas.edu

Big Smith
Hillbilly
Springfield, Missouri
205 Park Central East #214, Springfield, MO 65806
bigsmith@juno.com

The Billy Goats
Lounge-A-Billy
Nashville, Tennessee
//www.billygoats.com
info@billygoats.com

Jeff Black
Singer/Songwriter
Nashville, Tennessee
//www.jeffblack.com

Blazing Rains aka Tim Hanford
Singer/Songwriter
Upstate New York
//www.sugarfreerecords.com/blazing.htm

Bluetick
Country Rock; Roots Rock
brxtn@hotmail.com

Boondogs
Roots Rock
Little Rock, Arkansas
//www.boondogs.com
info@boondogs.com

Buckeye
Country Roots Rock
San Francisco, California
//www.rootsrock.com/buckeye.htm

Chris Burroughs
Singer/Songwriter
Tucson, Arizona
//www.bluerose-records.com

The Bystanders
Country Roots Rock
Johnson City, Tennessee

//www.geocities.com/nashville/9437/
russell@bnoc.net

Cadillac Angels
Roots Rockabilly
Santa Barbara, California
//members.aol.com/cadangels1/
cadangels1@aol.com

The Carbines
Honky Tonk
Chapel Hill, North Carolina
yeproc@redeyeusa.com
tift@email.unc.edu

Cash Hollow
Lo-Fi Country Rock
San Francisco, California
salamong@socrates.berkeley.edu

Clem Snide
Roots Rock
New York City
//www.users.interport.net/~tractorb
tractorb@interport.net

Coal Palace Kings
Roots Rock
Albany, New York
/www.rpi.edu/~tichyj/coal_palace_kings.html
PowerMower@aol.com

Bob Collum
Singer/Songwriter
Tulsa, Oklahoma
bobc@webzone.net

Deadnecks
New Old-Time
Bowling Green, Kentucky
bethunes@webtv.net

Johnny Dilks and His Visitacion Valley Boys
Hillbilly Boogie; Yodeling
San Francisco, California
//www.sfbg.com/music/32/32/yodel.html

Ditch Bank Okies
Redneck Parody
Clovis, California
//www.newmusic.net/ditchbank/
ditchp@net999.com

The Ditchdiggers
Cowpunk
Atlanta, Georgia
//ditchdiggers.com
ditchdiggers@mindspring.com

Arthur Dodge and The Horsefeathers
Country Rock; Roots Rock
Lawrence, Kansas
//www.barbersitch.com/arthur_dodge.html

Tim Easton/Haynes Boys
Roots Rock
Columbus, Ohio
blake@promo-west.com

Farmer Tan
Roots Rock
Southern California
//home.earthlink.net/~jhuber/index4.html
Farmertan@aol.com

The Flatirons
Roots Rock
Portland, Oregon
//www.checkeredpast.com

Fragile Jack
Grange Rock
Seattle, Washington
//www.fragilejack.com

The Fritters
"Regressive Country"
Boston, Massachusetts
//www.hellcountry.com/fritters.htm
pipesmo@ix.netcom.com

Frum the Hills
New Old-Time
Westminster, Maryland
//kwality.com/frumthehills/
frumthehills@kwality.com

Mary Gauthier
Singer/Songwriter
New England
//www.folkzone.com/marygauthier/
marygauthier@folkzone.com

Gladys
"Country Fried Rock"
Lexington, Kentucky
//www.musictrough.com/gladys.html
coolidge@gis.net

The Good Sons
Country Roots Rock
Lancashire, England
//www.roundtower.com

Grasshopper Highway
Country Rock
Chapel Hill, North Carolina
//www.grasshopperhighway.com
rafael@grasshopperhighway.com

Pat Green
Singer/Songwriter
Texas
//www.patgreen.com
webmaster@patgreen.com

Gretna Green
Country Rock; Roots Rock
Red Bank, New Jersey
//members.aol.com/ggreene4/
ggreene4@aol.com

The Groobees
Country Rock
Lubbock, Texas
//www.groobees.com
Thegroobee@aol.com

Gypsy Wranglers
Western Swing
Western Massachusetts
//www.tiac.net/users/treed/gypsywranglers/
chollingsworth@umext.umass.edu

The Haystack Hi-Tones
Hillbilly Boogie
The Netherlands
//www.xs4all.nl/~mzwaan/jive55/bands/haystacke.htm
hitones@dds.nl

The Henrys
Americana
Toronto, Canada
//www.irus.rri.on.ca/~henry/

The Hillbilly Iguanas
Redneck Parody
North Carolina
//www4.ncsu.edu/eos/users/s/sajackso/www/iguanas_pages/

The Hillbilly Trio
Hillbilly Jazz
Nashville, Tennessee
Box 52, Whites Creek, TN 37189
615/812-1973

The Hired Guns
Country Rock
Fitzroy, Victoria, Australia
Adam Kyle, 78 Moor St., Fitzroy, Victoria, Australia 3065

Hogleg
Cowpunk
Columbia, Missouri
//www.relaxonline.com/onidisc/hhogleg.html
Hoglegmail@aol.com

Home Groan
Roots Rock
Norway
//www.nordi.no/music/homegroan/
martinh@nordi.no

Hominy
Country Rock; Roots Rock
Seattle, Washington
//www.ivyrecords.com/hominy.htm

The Honky Tonk 5
Hillbilly Boogie
Germany
//f7alpha1.informatik.fh-muenchen.de/~ifw93074/ht5.html

Ignitors
Roots Rock
Tempe, Arizona
//www.goodnet.com/~ignitor/
ignitor@goodnet.com

Dan Israel and The Cultivators
Lo-Fi Roots Rock
Minneapolis, Minnesota
//www.haydensferry.com/israel.htm

info@haydensferry.com

Jasper Stone
Roots Rock
Dallas/Ft. Worth, Texas
//www.flash.net/~meyco/jasper.htm
meyco@flash.net

Greg Klyma
Singer/Songwriter
Buffalo, New York
//klyma.com
klyma@buffnet.net

The Konnarock Critters
New Old-Time
Independence, Virginia
//www.vektors.com/critters/critters.htm

Josie Kreuzer
Rockabilly
San Diego, California
//members.aol.com/bopgirl/josiekreuzer.html
BopGirl@aol.com

Kudzu Kings
Country Rock
Oxford, Mississippi
//www.kudzukings.com

Greta Lee
Singer/Songwriter
Atlanta, Georgia
//www.mindspring.com/~gretalee/

The Lilybandits
Country Rock
Columbus, Ohio
162 West Selby Blvd., Columbus, OH 43085; 614-781-0599

The Lonesome Trailers
Country Rock; Roots Rock
Kent City, Michigan
//www.globalstage.com/lonesometrailers.html
ltrailer@wmis.net

The Magadalenes
Roots Rock
Jamaica Plain, Massachusetts
//www.hellcountry.com/magdalenes.htm

Kevin Maul
Dobro
Saratoga, New York
//netsite.dn.net/williams/kevinmaul.html

Kevin Meisel
Singer/Songwriter
Belleville, Michigan
//www.lb.com/onemanclapping/
onemanclapping@lb.com

Lisa Miller
Singer/Songwriter
Melbourne, Australia
//www.ozemail.com.au/~wminc/lisa.htm

Lisa Miller & The Trailer Park Honeys
Country Rock; Blues; Rockabilly
Portland, Oregon
//www.rivergraphics.com/lisamill/
tphoney@habit.com

The MoJo Deans
 "Hardcore Hillbilly Speed Twang"
Carbondale, Illinois
//www.midamer.net/users/swankman/modex.html
swankman@midamer.net

Mr. Henry
Roots Rock
New York City
//mrhenry.com
hank@mrhenry.com

Mulehead
Country Rock; Roots Rock
Little Rock, Arkansas
//www.ho-hum.com

David Munyon
Singer/Songwriter
Nashville, Tennessee
//web.inter.nl.net/hcc/jtm.janssen/david_munyon.html

The Oklahoma Twisters
Western Swing
Washington, D.C.
//www.pressroom.com/~okt/
okt@pressroom.com

Luke Olson
Singer/Songwriter
San Antonio, Texas

P.O. Box 6125, San Antonio, TX 78209
210-826-3950

Paddlefoot
Americana
San Francisco, California
//www.paddlefoot.com
joel@paddlefoot.com

Pale Riders
Country Rock
Tasmania, Australia
//www.paleriders.com.au/
paleride@integrity.com.au

The Pawtuckets
Roots Rock
Memphis, Tennessee
//www.pawtuckets.com

Peatmoss
Roots Rock
Chicago, Illinois
//peatmoss.net
playrec@loop.com

Ed Pettersen and The High Line Riders
Country Rock; Roots Rock
New York City
//www.tangible-music.com
info@tangible-music.com

The Piners
New Old-Time; Progressive Bluegrass
Portland, Maine
//www.piners.com
Piners@aol.com

Hank Plank and The 2x4s
"Postmodern Roots Country"
Portland, Oregon
//www.rootsrock.com/hankplank.htm
myokoyama@earthlink.net

The Polish Hillbillies
Honky Tonk
Pittsburgh, Pennsylvania
rhirsch@pittsburgh.usweb.com

Poor Little Fools
"Honky Tonkin' Swing-A-Billy"
Atlanta, Georgia
//www.mindspring.com/~poorlittlefools/
poorlittlefools@mindspring.com

Steve Pride
Singer/Songwriter
North Carolina
//www.parasol.com

The Quinsonics (D. Braxton Harris)
Country Rock; Roots Rock; Singer/Songwriter
Birmingham, Alabama
//www.musictrough.com/quinsonics.html
dbrax@yahoo.com

The Red Gills
"Thrashabilly"
Western New York
greiertj@moran.com

Red Mountain White Trash
New Old-Time
Northern Alabama
//fly.hiwaay.net/~eabaggot/rmwt1.htm

River Bluff Clan
Country Rock
Memphis, Tennessee
//www.riverbluffclan.com
rbc@riverbluffclan.com

Alan Rogers
Singer/Songwriter
Santa Fe, New Mexico
P. O. Box 8364, Santa Fe, NM 87504
505/989-3690

Josh Rouse
Singer/Sonwriter
Nashville, Tennessee
//www.rykodisc.com

Saltgrass aka Max Rollo
Singer/Songwriter
Trinity, Texas
//www.saltgrassweb.com
max@saltgrassweb.com

Noah Saterstrom
Finger-Pick Guitar
Mississippi
//www.blackdogrecords.com

The Sorentinos
Country Rock
London, England
//www.twirlme.com/bands/sorentinos/
tinomania@compuserve.com

The Star Room Boys
Honky Tonk
Athens, Georgia
//www.arches.uga.edu/~mandrake/starroo
m.html
mandrake@arches.uga.edu

Stillwater
No Depression
St. Louis, Missouri
//walden.mo.net/~grabaucr/stillwater
grabaucr@mo.net

The Straightaways
Roots Rock
Tampa, Florida
//members.aol.com/strtaways/
straightaways@writeme.com

Thrillbilly
Roots Rock
Portland, Oregon
//www.cyberhighway.net/~kilman/thrillbilly
billies@cyberhighway.net

Trailhead
Country Rock
Columbia, Missouri
C587620@showme.missouri.edu

Truckadelic
Redneck Underground
Atlanta, Georgia
//www.mindspring.com/~truckadelic/
truckadelic@mindspring.com

Billy Tulsa & the Psycho Crawdads
Honky Tonk; Country Rock
Sherman Oaks, California
//www.billytulsa.com

Urban Hillbilly Quartet
"Hillbilly Roots Rock"
Minneapolis/St. Paul, Minnesota
//www.nmsr.labmed.umn.edu/students/bale
s/hillbill.htm
Ejbrandt@aol.com

Urban Twang
Country Rock
Chicago, Illinois
//www.globalstage.com/urbantwang.html
urbantwang@globalstage.com

Used Carlotta
Honky Tonk; Country Rock
Richmond, Virginia
Ucarlotta@aol.com

Varnaline
Roots Rock
Poughkeepsie, New York
//www.zerohour.com/varnaline/

Virginia Dare
New Old-Time
San Francisco, California
//dare.hypermart.net/

Shawn Waggoner
Singer/Songwriter
Austin, Texas
royale@flash.net

Western Omelet
Western Swing
Boston, Massachusetts
//home.sprynet.com/interserv/infofam/o2.h
tml
Westerno@aol.com

Dusty Wright
"Progressive Country"
New York City
//www.dustywright.com
petrock@dustywright.com

The Yonders
"Maximum Country & Western Swing"
Lexington, Kentucky
//www.lexmusic.com/yonders/
mpatter@pop.uky.edu

14x7: Hand-Picked Songs From Georgia/Hexamusic/1996

Collection of Redneck Underground acts compiled and produced by steel player Bill Fleming.

Includes: **Slim Chance & The Convicts** "Mr. Teardrop," "Backyard Swing"; **The Delta Angels** "Black-Eyed Susan," "Renegade Lover"; **Redneck Greece & The Stump Broke Steers** "Redneck Loves Redette," "Dish Pan Boogie"

Acres for Cents/Zippo Demon/1987

Desert Rock from the land of dry heat.

Includes: **The Band of Blacky Ranchette** "Heartland"; **Danny & Dusty** "Bend in the Road"; **Giant Sand** "Thin Line Man"; **The Long Ryders** "10-5-60"

Across the Great Divide: The Songs of Jo Carol Pierce/Dejadisc/1993

Tribute to Texas singer/songwriter.

Includes: **Terry Allen** "I Blame God"; **Joe Ely** "Queen of Heaven"; **Jimmie Dale Gilmore** "Reunion"; **Loose Diamonds** "Ruby"; **Darden Smith** "Scratch on My Windowpane"

All-American Hardcore Hillbillies/ BSN/1995

Rockabilly from *Blue Suede News* magazine.

Alligator Stomp, Vol. 5: The Next Generation/Rhino/1995

Modern Cajun

Includes: **The Basin Brothers** "Un Mariage Casse"; **Beausoleil** "Zydeco X"; **Bruce Daigrepont** "Les Mains Du Bon Dieu"; **David Doucet** "J'Etais Au Bal"; **Steve Riley** "La Valse Du Regret"

Alt. Country/Simitar/1998

Sampler of previously released material by Steve Earle, Emmylou Harris, Gram Parsons, Son Volt, Derailers, Junior Brown, Mavericks, Lucinda Williams, and more.

American Fogies, Volume 1/ Rounder/1996

A variety of traditional American music by contemporary acts.

Includes: **Balfa Toujours** "Duson Two Step"; **Aux Cajunals** "Baby Please Don't Go"; **The Hix** "Walkaround"; **Bayou Seco** "Estas Lindas Flores"

American Fogies, Volume 2/ Rounder/1996

Second installment of contemporary Americana.

Includes: **Bayou Seco** "Lonesome Cowgirl Blues"; **The Bone Tones** "New Crowley Two Step"; **The California Cajun Orchestra** "John Pullard Special"; **The Heartbeats** "Hollywood Dreams"; **Tracy Schwarz Cajun Trio** "J'Ai Pleure"; **Mike Seeger** "Down the Road"

American Rumble, Volume 1/ Skizmatic/1995

Rockabilly/Hillbilly Bop

Includes: **The Barnshakers** "Please Help Me"; **Ray Condo** "Something I Said"; **The Crazy Rhythm Daddies** "Bip Bop Bip"; **High Noon** "When She's Good," "Rock Too Slow"

American Songbook/ Demon UK/1996

UK collection of U.S. alt. country with p.u. material and 120 page booklet.

BR5-49 "18 Wheels and a Crowbar (Live)"; **Steve Earle** "Copperhead Road (Acoustic)"; **Freakwater** "Lonesome Sound"; **Golden Smog** "Glad & Sorry (Live)"; **The Hello Strangers** "Geronimo's Cadillac"; **Mike Henderson & The Blue Bloods** "Play Bo Diddly"; **Joe Henry** "Parade"; **Kieran Kane** "I Cannot Give My Heart to You"; **The V Roys** "What She's Found"; **Kevin Welch** "One Way Rider (Live)"

Americana: A Tribute to Johnny Cash/Irregular/1998

Interpretations of the Man in Black by 20 underground rock bands from Seattle.

Another Rockin' Christmas/ Run Wild/1995

X-mas album with many alt. country acts from the Big D.C. Jamboree collections.

Austin Country Nights/ Watermelon/1995

Alt. country from the "Live Music Capital of the World."

Area Code 512 "Waltz Across Texas"; **Libbi Bosworth** "Baby, Maybe Then I'll Love You"; **Mary Cutrufello** "Tonight I Know"; **The Derailers** "Just One More Time"; **Roy Heinrich** "A Face in the Crowd"; **The Cornell Hurd Band** "I Cry, Then I Drink, Then I Cry"; **Jeff Hughes & Chaparral** "Choose Only Love"; **Bruce Robison** "Poor Man's Son"; **Charlie Robison** "Sunset Boulevard"; **Ted Roddy** "Honky Tonk Hell"; **The Wagoneers** "Down the Line"; **Don Walser and the Pure Texas Band** "Love Song of the Waterfall"; **Dale Watson** "Girl, I Hope You're Having Fun"

Big D. C. Jamboree, Vol. 1/ Run Wild/1991

Great three volume series of 1990s honky tonk, rockabilly, hillbilly bop, Western swing from the D.C. area produced by Mike Lynam.

The Atomics "Pink Peg Slacks," "Cincinnati Fireball"; **The Capitol Hillbillies** "Go Down Swingin'"; **Goin', Goin', Gone** "Honky Tonk Mind," "Gone Dead Train"; **Dennis Jay and the Confidentials** "Let's Go, Let's Go, Let's Go"; **The Redeemers** "Lost Highway"; **The Thangs** "Heartaches and Hangovers"; **The Wanktones** "Hillbilly Fever," "Forty Miles of Bad Road"

Big D. C. Jamboree, Vol. 2/ Run Wild/1992

The Atomics "Lady Luck"; **The Capitol Hillbillies** "Lucky Guy," "One More Heartache"; **Go Cat Go** "I've Got My Eyes on You," "Other Side of Town"; **Goin' Goin' Gone** "Beauty is a Bluff," "No Dice," "Warm Beer, Cold Women and a Broken Heart"; **Dennis Jay and the Confidentials** "There's You," "What Kind of Sweetness"; **The Slim Jims** "I'm a Mistake (You're Gonna Have to Make)"; **Bobby Smith Band** "Cadillac Road," "Short Pretty Blue Eyes"; **The Thangs** "Blow My Stack," "Neon Highway"; **Joe Triplett and the Frednecks** "Hey Hey (Do You Think You Can Take My Love?)"

Big D. C. Jamboree, Vol. 3/ Run Wild/1993

The Atomics "Friday Night," "My Way," "Sweet Goodbye"; **The Blue Chunks** "Let 'Er Roll," "Tore Up Over You"; **Johnny Castle & the Hard Knights** "Hey Miss Hay," "Hot Seated Woman"; **Kid Davis &**

the Cowpokes "I Believe You Darlin'," "Let's Pass This Guy"; **Goin', Goin', Gone** "I'm Shakin'," "Lights Out"; **Grandsons of the Pioneers** "Pretty Bad Blues"; **David Kitchen & Red Eye Gravy** "Mystery to Me"; **The Maxitones** "Nervous Breakdown"; **The Novenas** "Cryin' Over You"; **The Redeemers** "Goin' Back to Texas"; **The Rubes** "Sweet Rachel"; **Ruthie & the Wranglers** "Sparklin' Brown Eyes," "Straight A's in Love," "Your Good Girl's Gonna Go Bad"; **Bobby Smith Band** "Honky Tonk Hardwood Floor," "Justine," "Someday When It's Over"; **Richard Taylor & the Ravers** "Like Water's Wet"; **The Wanktones** "Little Pig"

Blastered: A Musical Tribute to the Blasters/Run Wild/1998

The Barn Burners "I Don't Want To"; **The Blacktop Rockets** "American Music"; **Libbi Bosworth** "Hey Boy"; **Tom Clifford** "Trouble Bound"; **The Crescent City Maulers** "One More Dance"; **The Grandsons** "Blue Shadows"; **Billy Hancock** "Marie Marie"; **Highway 13** "Flat Top Joint"; **Hot Rod Lincoln** "Border Radio"; **Jumpin' Jupiter** "Rock and Roll Will Stand"; **King Kerosene** "Help You Dream"; **Josie Kreuzer** "Red Rose"; **Last Train Home** "So Long Baby Goodbye"; **Lucky 7** "So Long Baby Goodbye"; **The Original Sinners** "No Other Girl"; **The Sabrejets** "Barn Burning"; **The Sloe Gin Joes** "This Is It"; **The Tone Popes** "Long White Cadillac"

Blaze Foley: In Tribute and Loving Memory, Vol. 1/Deep South/1999

Kimmie Rhodes, Calvin Russell, Texana Dames, Townes Van Zandt, and others pay homage to one of Austin's lesser known but beloved singer/songwriters who was murdered in February 1989.

Blue Rose Collection, Vols. 1-5/ Blue Rose Ger./1997-1998

Samplers from German alt. country/Americana label that has become a haven for a number of lesser known but important acts including Big in Iowa, the Continental Drifters, the Dashboard Saviors, Health & Happiness Show, Jimmy LaFave, the Rainravens, the Schramms, the Shakin' Apostles, the Volebeats, Wooden Leg.

Boppin' in Canada/ Nervous UK/1991

Canadian rockabilly from the late 1980s-early 1900s with Ray Condo, The Dots, Rocking Fools, Stinging Hornets, Yodells and others.

Border Radio/ Enigma/1987 (sdtrk)

Soundtrack for movie starring Chris D. (Divine Horsemen) and John Doe (X, the Knitters) with music provided by Dave Alvin, Steve Berlin (the Blasters, Los Lobos), David Hidalgo (Los Lobos), D. J. Bonebrake (X, the Knitters), John Bazz (the Blasters), Bill Bateman (the Blasters), Chip and Tony Kinman (Rank & File), Steve McCarthy (the Long Ryders), and Green on Red.

The Tonys "Border Radio" (written by Alvin); **Dave Alvin** "La Frontera"; **The Lazy Cowgirls** "Drugs"; **Dave Alvin and Steve Berlin** "Burning Guitar"; **Dave Alvin** "Mi Vida Loca"; **John Doe and Dave Alvin** "Little Honey"; **The Divine Horsemen** "Mother's Worry"; **Green on Red** "Sixteen Ways"; **Chris D.** "Lily White Hands"; **Dave Alvin and Steve Berlin** "Driving to Mexico"

Bubbahey Mud Truck/ Fire Ant/1996

Demented alt. country from North Carolina

The Backsliders "Cowboy Boots," "Aloha Steve and Dano"; **Eugene Chadbourne** "Mi, Mi, Mi," "This Newt Was Made for Squawking"; **Tom Montefusco** "Blackberry Blossom," "Who Broke the Lock?"; **Mr. Peters Boom & Chime** "Loving Her Was Easier"; **Unknown Hinson** "Baby, Let's Play Rough"; **Zen Frisbee** "Alabama," "Baxter Jones & the Headless Horseman"

Bubbapalooza: Volume One, Chronicle of the Redneck Underground/Sky/1995

Fantastically crazy collection from members of Atlanta/Athens fabled alt. country community.

The Blacktop Rockets "Rockabilly Show"; **Slim Chance and the Convicts** "George Jones (Has Never Sung About My Girl)"; **Deacon Lunchbox** "Loweena, the Urban Redneck Queen"; **The Delta Angels** "Cabbagetown"; **The Diggers** "She's Breakin' My Heart (While I'm Drinkin' Her Beer)"; **Greasetrap** "Candy Kisses"; **Jennie B. and the Speedbillies** "Outta Town"; **Scott Miller** "Napoleon"; **Redneck Greece Delux** "Mama Was a Dancer at the Claremont Lounge"; **Southern Culture on the Skids** "2 Pigs in a Blanket/She's My Little Bisquit Eater"; **The Steam Donkeys** "Can't Find a Place to Stay"; **The Vidalias** "Fakin' It"

Bubbapalooza, Volume Two: A Tribute to Gregory Dean Smalley/Criminal/1998

Second installment from Atlanta's Redneck Underground dedicated to one of its founders and creator of the Bubbapalooza Festival.

The Blacktop Rockets "Ruby"; **The Chant** "Wonderin' Outloud"; **Slim Chance Experience** "Jesus, Elvis and Me"; **The Diggers** "Sorriest Christmas"; **The Drive-By Truckers** "The Living Bubba"; **Kelly Hogan & Gregory Dean Smalley** "A Lie I Believe"; **The Lost Continentals** "Spraypaint Your Name (On the Overpass of My Heart)"; **Redneck Greece & The Stump Broke Steers** "She's Breakin' My Heart (While I'm Drinkin' Her Beer); **Gregory Dean Smalley & The Bubbamatics** "State of Co-Dependency"; **Truckadelic** "Viva Valdosta"

Bull Riders: Chasing the Dream/ Cold Spring/1998

Soundtrack for film about rodeo.

Includes: **The Derailers** "The Glory Will Never Get Old"; **Jack Ingram** "Just a Ride"; **Reckless Kelly** "Rodeo Man"; **Chris Wall** "Cowboy Nation," "Let 'Er Buck"; **Don Walser** "Bull Rider's Last Ride"

Byrd Parts/Raven Aust./1998

Eclectic collection of country rock from performers associated with the Byrds.

Includes: **Dillard & Clark Expedition** "Why Not Your Baby," "Lyin' Down in the Middle," "Don't Be Cruel"; **Doug Dillard Expedition** "Runaway Country"; **International Submarine Band** "Sum Up Broke," "One Day Week"; **McGuinn, Clark & Hillman** "Don't You Write Her Off," "Won't Let You Down"; **McGuinn & Hillman** "Turn Your Radio On"; **Fred Neil with Gram Parsons** "You Don't Miss Your Water"; **Gene Parsons** "Melodies for a Bird in Flyght", "Hot Burrito #1"; **Clarence White & Ry Cooder** "Why You Been Gone So Long"; **Clarence White & Nashville West** "Ode to Billie Joe"

Cajun Dance Hall Special/ Rounder/1992

Sampler of some of the best in contemporary Cajun.

Beausoleil "Rolling Pin," "Valse Bebe"; **Bruce Daigrepont** "Coeur des Cajuns," "Arc en ciel"; **David Doucet** "Balfa Waltz," "T'en as au," "Ton papa"; **Michael Doucet** "Like a Real Cajun," "J'ai passe devant ta porte"; **D. L. Menard** "Little Black Eyes," "The Water Pump"; **Steve Riley** "La pointe aux pins," "High Point Two-Step"

Clinch Mountain Country: Ralph Stanley & Friends/Rebel/1998

Two CD tribute to one of the giants of bluegrass featuring Ralph and his Clinch Mountain Boys backing a variety of Alt. Country and HNC performers.

Includes: **BR5-49** "Gathering Flowers for the Master's Bouquet"; **Junior Brown** "Stone Walls and Steel Bars"; **Bob Dylan**

"The Lonesome River"; **Alison Krauss** "Pretty Little Miss in the Garden"; **Jim Lauderdale** "If I Lose"; **Laurie Lewis** "Old Love Letters"; **Tim O'Brien** "Let Me Love You One More Time"; **Ricky Skaggs** "Shouting on the Hills of Glory," "Nobody's Love is Like Mine"; **Gillian Welch** "Gold Watch and Chain"; **Dwight Yoakam** ""I Just Got Wise," "The Darkest Hour is Just Before the Dawn"

Commemorativo: A Tribute to Gram Parsons/Rhino/1993

Mixed bag of GP songs covered by a variety of alt. country and other performers. (*See return of the **Grievous Angel** compilation.)

Joey Burns & Victoria Williams "Return of the Grievous Angel"; **Pet Clarke** "Hot Burrito #2"; **The Coal Porters** "November Nights"; **Finger** "Still Feelin' Blue"; **Flor de Mal** "Juanita"; **Clive Gregson & Boo Hewerdine** "Sin City"; **Peter Holsapple & Susan Cowsill with the Walkin' Tacos** "A Song for You"; **Stephen McCarthy** "One Hundred Years From Now"; **The Mekons** "$1,000 Wedding"; **Bob Mould & Vic Chestnutt** "Hickory Wind"; **The Musical Kings** "Cody, Cody"; **Carla Olson** "Do You Know How It Feels to Be Lonesome"; **Polly Parsons & Eden** "The New Soft Shoe"; **Something Happens** "Brass Buttons"; **Uncle Tupelo** "Blue Eyes"; **Steve Wynn** "Christine's Tune"; **Wellsprings of Hope** "Big Mouth Blues"

Concert For Manglerdesh/1998

Two cassette collection drawn from a benefit concert held at the Ryman on October 6, 1996, for Phil Kaufman aka The Road Mangler (Gram Parsons' former road manager.) Order from Phil Kaufman:

9 Music Square South,
Nashville, TN 37203;
rdmangler@aol.com;
//www.nashville.net/~kate/phil.html

Includes: **BR5-49** "Big Mouth Blues"; **Sam Bush** "Put on Your Sailing Shoes"/ "Crossroads"; **Guy Clark** "Out in The Parking Lot"; **The Delevantes** "Drivin' at Night"; **Steve Earle** "More Than I Can Do," "Goodbye" (with **Emmylou**), "Guitar Town"; **Emmylou Harris** "Love Hurts" (with **Buddy Miller**), "Walls of Time," "Luxury Liner," "Wheels"; **John Prine** "I Ain't Hurtin' No One," "That's the Way the World Goes Round," "Speed of the Sound of Loneliness" (with **Nanci Griffith**); **Riders in the Sky** "Gene Autry Medley"; **Bob Woodruff/Sweethearts of the Rodeo** "So Sad to Watch Good Love Go Bad"

Country/Vinyl Junkie UK/1995

Diverse selection of the famous and not so famous in alt. country compiled by one of Britain's leading Americana authorities, Mary Costello. Came out as a CD and double LP with extra tracks. Followed by **Cowpunks**; **Jukebox Cowboy**; **Loose**.

Dave Alvin (LP only); **Pinto Bennett & His Famous Motel Cowboys** "Prairie Blues"; **The Blazers** "Yeah, Yeah Yeah"; **Rick Broussard** "She Makes the Angels Cry"; **Kathy Chiavola** "A Fool Such As I"; **Barb Donovan** "Factory Town"; **Rosie Flores** (LP only); **Michael Fracasso & Lucinda Williams** "Door Number One"; **Dirk Hamilton** "Ain't Licked Yet"; **Butch Hancock** "If You Were a Bluebird"; **Tish Hinojosa** "Corazon Viajero"; **The Lost Gonzo Band** "Friends"; **Don McCalister** "Brand New Ways"; **Wes McGhee** "Monterey"; **Katy Moffatt** "Walkin' on the Moon"; **Willie Nelson & Curtis Potter** "Turn Me Loose & Let Me Swing"; **The Picketts** "Fool"; **Celinda Pink** "Pack Up Your Lies"; **Toni Price** "Just to Hear Your Voice"; **Rattlesnake Annie** "I Gotta Have My Baby Back"; **Charlie Robison** "I Don't Feel That Way Anymore"; **Jimmy Roy's Five Star Hillbillies** "Midnight Ride"; **Billy Swan & Van Duren** "Undying Love"; **Townes Van Zandt** "No Place to Fall"

Cowpunks/Vinyl Junkie UK/1996

Another fine selection of alt. country from the folks who brought us the **Country** compilation; includes songs exclusive (*) to this recording; see **Jukebox Cowboy**; **Loose**.

*The Bad Livers** "Wild Bill Jones"; **The Beat Farmers** "Country Western Song"; ***The Black Boot Trio** "The Last Days of Wine and Roses"; **Bonepony** "Feast of Life"; **Cake** "Jesus Wrote a Blank Check"; **Chris Cacavas** "Bellyful of Bullets"; ***The Coal Porters** "Six Days on the Road"; **Ray Condo & His Hardrock Goners** "Something I Said"; ***The Flaming Stars** "Back of My Mind"; ***Freakwater** "Withered and Died"; ***Furnaceface** "We Love You, Tipper Gore"; ***Greg Garing** "No Such Thing as Sin"; **Go To Blazes** "Underneath the Bottle"; **Golden Smog** "He's a Dick"; ***Lambchop** "Playboy, The Shit"; ***Medicine Hat** "C'Mon Here"; **Mojo Nixon & Jello Biafra** "Let's Go Burn Ole Nashville Down"; ***Toni Price** "Something"; **The Shivers** "Gentle"; **Sparklehorse** "Heart of Darkness"; **Uncle Tupelo** "Still Be Around"; ***The V-Roys** "Long Time Leavin'"; ***Townes Van Zandt** "The Hole (Live)"; **The Vidalias** "Questioningly"

Deep in the Heart (Of Texas)/ Shanachie/1998

Soundtrack for independent film presenting some of the best in Texas/Americana music.

Includes: **Jesse Dayton** "Panhandle Jane"; **Rosie Flores** "Boxcars"; **Jimme Dale Gilmore** "Just a Wave, Not the Water"; **Wayne Hancock** "Hill Country Hillbilly Gal"; **Walter Hyatt** "This Time Lucille," "Last Call"; **Willie Nelson and Kimmie**

Rhodes "Just One Love"; **Don Walser** "Rolling Stone From Texas"

Detour West/Will Ray/1989 (CS)

1980s alt. country from L.A. produced by Will Ray of the Hellecasters (see **Hollywood Roundup**).

The Doo Wah Riders "Glowing in the Ashes," "Delta Star," "Dinah Might," "A Part of Me is Missing"; **Kacey Jones** "No Fault Love," "You Can't Make Someone Love You," "Watch Me Fly," "Give Me the Chance"; **Will Ray & the Gila Monsters** "That's History," "Wishful Thinking," "Tumbleweed," "Thinkin' 'Bout You"

Double Wide: The Trailer Compilation/Trailer/1997

Music from Iowa's alt. country elite.

Includes: **High and Lonesome** "Strawberry Wine," "I Gave Up on You," "Shining Softly"; **Bo Ramsey** "555x2", "I Don't Know," "In the Weeds"; **Tom Jessen's Dimestore Outfit** "Sanctuary"; **David Zollo** "Elizabeth Smiles"; **Greg Brown & the Trailer Records All Stars** "Tell You a Story"

Down On The Farm, XI/ DOTF/1998

Selection of studio tracks from Norwegian and American performers who appeared at Down on the Farm, "Europe's Definitive Twangfest," July 22-25, 1998, at Halden, Norway (see Festivals section for more details).

Includes: **Bonkers** "When Life Comes Crashing Down"; **Damon Bramlett** "Falling Apart"; **Guy Clark** "Homegrown Tomatoes"; **Johnny Dowd** "Ft. Worth, Texas"; **Ex-Husbands** "All the Way From Abilene"; **Robbie Fulks** "I Told Her Lies"; **The Good Sons** "Fade Away"; **Li'l Mo & The Monicats** "Every Kind of Music But Country"; **Tine Valand & Guy Clark** "Mineral Wells"; **Susanna Van Tassel** "Something Blue"; **Roger Wallace** "Runaround"

Dueling Banjos: Soundtrack From the Movie Deliverance/ Warner/1997

Not a soundtrack at all but rather a repackaged instrumental LP from 1962 by Eric Weissberg and Marshall Brickman with the hit "Dueling Banjos" added on. Nevertheless, a significant album because the super flat-picking is provided by Clarence White (uncredited) and the recording helped spread bluegrass to a much wider audience in the 1960s-1970s.

East Side Sampler 1995/ESD/1995

First of two collections from East Side Digital in Minneapolis.

Includes: **Eric Ambel** "Miles From the Machine"; **The Beacon Hillbillies** "Cold Light of Dawn"; **The Blood Oranges** "Miss It All"; **The Bottle Rockets** "$1,000 Car," "Truck Drivin' Man"; **Go To Blazes** "Why I Drink"; **The Morells** "The Man Who Has Everything"; **Jimmy Ryan** "Nothing But Time"; **Tom Russell & Barrence Whitfield** "Jack Johnson"; **The Shakin' Apostles** "Tucson"; **The Schramms** "Heart Not Within"; **The Skeletons** "Older Guys"; **The Spanic Family** "Billy"

East Side Story, Vol. 1/ ESD/1996

Sampler from what was once a leading alt. country/roots label.

Includes: **Eric Ambel** "From a Better Place"; **The Beacon Hillbillies** "Never Bad"; **The Blood Oranges** "Gone and Went"; **The Bottle Rockets** "Get Down"; **Go To Blazes** "Stone Mountain"; **Cheri Knight** "Last Barn Dance"; **The Schramms** "In Hell's Despite"; **The Shakin' Apostles** "Tucson"; **Wooden Leg** "Champaign"

The Edge of Country/
Stockade/1997

Some of Austin's veteran and up and coming alt. country acts.

Roy Heinrich "Today I Taught Myself to Pray," "You Walked Your Walk"; **Jeff Hughes** "Buildin' Me Up," "Finer Lovin'"; **Chris Miller** "Houndoggin'," "Big Blue"; **Ted Roddy's Tearjoint Troubadours** "Time I Made My Presence Known," "Tears on the Table," "War Between Two Loves"; **Susanna Van Tassel** "I Remember You," "Something Blue"

Edges From the Postcard/
Twangfest/1997 (CS)

Alt. country performers associated with the Postcard2 on-line mailing list and Twangfest (see **Twangfest Live, Edges From the Postcard 2,** and the **Online Mailing Lists** and **Festivals** sections for more details).

Belle Starr "Far As the Wind Blows"; **Cash Hollow** "Western Line"; **dim Bulb** "Long Haired Country Boy"; **Fear & Whiskey** "Burnin' Teardrops"; **Edith Frost** "Hide Out"; **Gasoline** "Before It's Gone"; **The Ghost Rockets** "My Guilty Pleasure"; **Roy Kasten** "Sweeter Ground"; **The Mystery Dates** "This Charmed Life"; **One Fell Swoop** "Fences"; **One Riot, One Ranger** "Long and Slow Decline"; **Pine State** "Heart on the Line"; **Raw Deal** "Tired of Drivin' Tractor"; **The Sovines** "Bitter Root"; **Jim Stringer** "Opposite Attraction"; **The Texas Meat Purveyors** "You Better Leave That Man Alone"; **Union Springs** "Little Bessie"

Edges From the Postcard 2/
P2/1998

Two CD set courtesy of the P2 online discussion list and Twangfest (see **Edges From the Postcard, Twangfest Live,** and the **Online Mailing Lists** and **Festivals** sections for more details).

The Barkers "Baytown"; **Belle Starr** "Nobody You'd Know"; **Bluetick** "Broken Hearted Born"; **Cash Hollow** "Rachel's Wedding"; **Walter Clevenger** "Only You"; **Buck Diaz** "Sincerity"; **Fear and Whiskey** "You Taught Me a Lesson"; **Five Chinese Brothers** "I'll Never Learn How to Stop Loving You"; **Robbie Fulks** "Stone River"; **The Ghost Rockets** "Under the Table"; **Honky Tonk Confidential** "Honky Tonk 101"; **Hudson Super Six** "Baltimore"; **Mike Ireland and Holler** "Pop a Top"; **Kevin Johnson and the Linemen** "Miss Lonelyhearts Out on the Town"; **Roy Kasten** "Blue Island, Illinois"; **Bill Lloyd** "I Can't Tell My Heart What to Do"; **The Meat Purveyors** "Morning After Song"; **Naked Omaha** "Stronghold"; **One Fell Swoop** "One to Grow On"; **One Riot, One Ranger** "It Must Be Heaven"; **Ed Pettersen and the High Line Riders** "If I Tell You"; **Quick and Dirty** "Smoke Rings"; **Kimmie Rhodes** "Lines"; **Elena Skye** "Biggest Piece of Nothing"; **The Sovines** "Jesus Dionysus"; **Jim Stringer** "Love a Little More (of the Way I Am)"; **Union Springs** "In My Dreams"; **Chris Wall** "The Poet is Not In Today"; **Wooden Leg** "Little Sadie"; **Bob Woodruff and Kerosene** "Angel at the Cafe Risque"

Fireworks, Vols. 1 & 2/Sound Asleep Swe./1998

Two more solid collections of roots-rock/alt. country (much of it previously unreleased) from Jerker Emanuelson who gave us the excellent **Hit the Hay** compilations.

Vol. 1 includes:—**The Ghost Rockets** "Goodbye to Greatness"; **Greg Scott Reeves** "California Moon"; **Tracy Santa** "Beatle Boots of Chinese Leather"; **Tommy Womack** "Whatever Happened to Cheetah Chrome?," "Christabella Wilson."

Vol. 2 includes:—**Buttercup** "The Hideout"; **Walter Clevenger** "Back to You," "Kimberly"; **Kevin Johnson & The Linemen** "Look Over There," "Helen"; **Bill Lloyd** "Work in Progress," "Ring Around the Moon"; **The Quinsonics** "Your Sweet Dreams"; **The Schramms** "Can You Please Crawl Out Your Window"; **The Volebeats** "What a Lonely Way to Go"; **Tommy Womack** "You're Not Made for This World"

For a Life of Sin: A Compilation of Insurgent Chicago Country/
Bloodshot/1994

Opening salvo of the acclaimed and very influential Insurgent Country series; focused mainly on Chicago acts (see **Hell Bent, Nashville: The Other Side of the Alley,** and **Straight Outta Boone County**).

The Bottle Rockets "Every Kinda Everything"; **Church Key** "Doghouse"; **The Flannel Tubs** "Flannel Boogie"; **Freakwater** "Drunk Friend"; **Robbie Fulks** "Cigarette State"; **The Handsome Family** "Moving Furniture Around"; **Jon Langford's Hillbilly Lovechild** "Over the Cliff"; **Milly & the Sequins** "Sucker for a Trucker"; **Moonshine Willy** "Way Out West"; **The New Duncan Imperials** "If She Wasn't on Blocks"; **Wink O'Bannon** "Cry Baby"; **The Riptones** "Suburbia"; **The Sundowners** "Rockin' Spot," "You Don't Know What Lonesome Is"; **The Swollen Spleens** "Tragic Woman"; **The Texas Rubies** "That Truck"; **Iggy Yoakum & His Famous Pogo Ponies** "Hole in the Ground"

Full Tank, Vol. 1/Jackass/1998

Diversity of alternative country/Americana by locally and regionally popular acts from around the U.S.

Blazing Haley "Back For No Good Reason"; **Boondogs** "Wishful Thinkin'"; **The Countrypolitans** "Redneck Riot"; **Creosote** "Trouble"; **Tim Easton** "All the Pretty Girls Are Leaving Town"; **Foggy Mountain F*ckers** "Always Country"; **Wilson Gil and the Willful Sinners** "Gunstore, Liquorstore Project"; **D. Braxton Harris** "Scarlet Red"; **Mulehead** "King of the Minimum Wage"; **Steve Pride** "River Red"; **Red Dirt Rangers** "Idabel Blues"; **Slim Cessna's Auto Club** "That's Why I'm Unhappy"; **Gregory Joe Spradlin** "Preacherman"; **Supperbell Round-Up** "Springfield"; **Trailer Park Casanovas** "Where You Belong"; **Ventilator** "Jericho's Pool"

Greetings From the District of Country/Too Many Dogs/1998

Gathering of alt. country from the nation's capital assembled by Diana Quinn and Mike Woods of Honky Tonk Confidential. (see **Big D.C. Jamboree, Vols. 1-3**)

Dallas Dudley and the Atomic Hillbillies "Lie to Me Heart," "Sunday Morning and I'm Going to Hell"; **Honky Tonk Confidential** "Barrom Tan," "I Done It," "Fujiyama Mama"; **Kevin Johnson and the Linemen** "Takin' Care of Me"; **Louise Kirchen** "Capital 'G'," "Dreamworld"; **The Local Yokels** "Too Much Me," "Right Attitude"; **The Oklahoma Twisters** "Leaving Today," "Did You Ever Hear of Tulsa, Oklahoma?"; **The Ornery Brothers** "Heavens Knows," "Nothing's Wrong"; **Tex Rubinowitz** "That Old

Patchwork Quilt"; **Ruthie and the Wranglers** "If It's the Last Thing I Do"

The Harry Smith Connection: A Live Tribute/S-F/1998

Performances from an October, 1997, concert at Wolf Trap to honor Harry Smith who compiled the monumental **Anthology of American Folk Music** in 1952 (reissued as handsome six CD boxed set in 1997). The collection presents interpretations of songs from the **Anthology** or otherwise associated with Harry Smith.

Includes: **Balfa Toujours** "Le Vieux Soulard et Sa Femme"; **Roger McGuinn, Jeff Tweedy, Jay Bennett** "East Virginia Blues," "Sugar Baby," "James Alley Blues"; **The New Lost City Ramblers** "Home Sweet Home"

Hell-Bent: Insurgent Country, Voldume 2/Bloodshot/1995

Second, equally excellent Insurgent Country collection; more geographically diverse than its predecessor (see **For a Life of Sin, Nashville: The Other Side of the Alley**, and **Straight Outta Boone County**)

The Bottle Rockets "Get Down"; **Richard Buckner** "22"; **The Cartwrights** "Walking on My Grave"; **Eleanor Roosevelt** "Espoontoon"; **Robbie Fulks** "She Took a Lot of Pills (and Died)"; **The Cornell Hurd Band** "Honky-Tonk Has-Been"; **Inbreds** "Don't Die While I'm Alive"; **Moonshine Willy** "Roulette"; **The Old 97s** "Por Favor"; **Gwil Owen** "Tennessee Hi-Way Blues"; **The Riptones** "World Renowned"; **The Starkweathers** "Little White Trash Boy"; **Tarnation** "Yellow Birds"; **The Volebeats** "One I Love"; **The Waco Brothers** "Bad Times Are Coming Round Again"; **Earl C. Whitehead & The Grievous Angels** "Get It While It's Hot"; **The World Famous Blue Jays** "Mud Flap Boogie"

Hempilation 2: Free The Weed!/Capricorn/1998

Recording of marijuana related songs to benefit NORML, the National Organization for the Reform of Marijuana Laws.

Includes: **Blue Mountain** "Mary Jane"; **Vic Chesnutt** "Weed to the Rescue"; **Hank Flamingo** "The Dope Smoking Song"; **Willie Nelson** "Me & Paul"; **Dar Williams & The Scud Mountain Boys** "Play the Greed"

Hillbilly Fever, Volume 5: Legends of Country-Rock/Rhino/1995

Uneven anthology featuring light weight (Poco; Pure Prairie League; Marshall Tucker; Linda Ronstadt; Nitty Gritty) and heavy duty (Bob Dylan; Flying Burrito Brothers; Gram Parsons; Commander Cody; Byrds; Michael Nesmith) pioneers of late 1960s-early 1970s country rock.

Hit the Hay, Vol. 1/Sound Asleep Swe./1995

First of two (so far) fabulous collections of American roots/alt. country masterminded by Jerker Emanuelson.

Includes: **Tim Carroll** "Good Cry"; **Eddy Lawrence** "Blues for Tomorrow"; **Ray Mason Band** "We Don't Get Along Anymore"; **The Picketts** "The Longer You Wait" (p.u.); **The Pine Dogs** "Naked Truth"; **Bob Reuter & Kamikaze Cowboy** "It Don't Matter"; **The Scud Mountain Boys** "Two Weeks Past"

Hit the Hay, Vol. 2/Sound Asleep Swe./1996

The Buckets "Coffee and Beer"; **Charlie Burton & the Texas Twelve Steppers** "Rogue Cop"; **Charlie Chesterman & the Firecrackers** "All By Myself"; **5 Chinese Brothers** "Walk Away"; **Robbie Fulks** "Tears Only Run One Way" (alt. version); **The Ghost Rockets** "Try to Believe"; **Hank McCoy & the Dead Ringers** "Gonna Hang Out My Mind"; **Nineteen Wheels** "Country Girl"; **Peck Of Snide** "Desparate Heart"; **Shades of Al Davis** "Older and Heavier"

A Holiday Feast, Vols. 1 & 2/HFM/1996 & 1997

Recordings to benefit the homeless in the D.C. Area with a variety of local performers lending a hand.

Vol. 1 includes:— **The Grandsons** "Bethlehem Bound"; **Kevin Johnson** "Ave Nada"; **Bill Kirchen** "Santa! Don't Pass Me By!"; **Out Behind the Barn** "New Year's Resolution." Vol. 2 includes:— **The Grandsons** "Yorgi the Yodeling Reindeer"; **The Hula Monsters** "Mele Kelikimaka"; **Kevin Johnson** "Lonely Christmas Call"; **Bill Kirchen** "Truckin' Trees for Christmas"; **Last Train Home** "Home for Christmas"

Hollywood Roundup/Will Ray/1988 (CS)

More late 1980s L.A. alt. country from Will Ray of The Hellecasters (see **Detour West**)

Billie Burner "My Baby's Eyes"; **Judy Chadwick** "Red and Pink Roses"; **P.J. Clark** "Two Eyes, Two Lips But No Heart"; **Candye Kane & the Armadillo Stampede** "Hey Nashville"; **The Mustangs** "Famous Last Words"; **The Radio Ranch Straight Shooters** "The Next Big Thing"; **Will Ray & the Gila Monsters** "Heartache Train"; **Jeffrey Steele** "Little White Lies"; **The Superpickers** "Picker's Brawl"; **Rusty Vail** "Photo Finish"; **Rick Vincent** "Someone Else's Baby"

Honed on the Range, Volume II: Contemporary Texas Swing /Texas Monthly/1995/

Menagerie of modern Western swing artists produced by *Texas Monthly* magazine.

Includes: **Asleep at the Wheel** "Fat Boy Rag"; **Cowboys & Indians** "Drivin' You Out of My Mind"; **Alvin Crow** "Fiddler's Lady"; **Johnny Gimble** "Under the X in Texas"; **Tom Morrell & the Time Warp Top Hands** "Mississippi Delta Trilogy"; **Willie Nelson & Asleep at the Wheel** "The Kind of Love I Can't Forget"; **Mary-ann Price** "Oilwell, Texas"; **Don Walser** "Cowpoke"

Honkey Tonk Holidays/Big Iron/1996

X-mas record produced by the Barley House pub with some of the best in Dallas alt. country (see **Live From the Barley House**)

Includes: **Cowboys & Indians** "Santa, Santa," "Merry Christmas, Miss Molly"; **Donny Ray Ford & Liberty Valance** "Santa Looked a Lot Like Daddy"; **The Mutineers** "Santa Claus Is Coming to Town"; **The Old 97s** "I'll Be Home for Christmas," "Holly, Jolly Christmas"

Hootenanny/Hootenanny Foil/1998

From the annual festival at Oak Canyon Ranch, California.

Includes: **Hasil Adkins** "Ugly Woman"; **Big Sandy** "If I Knew Now"; **The Blasters** "It's All Your Fault"; **Southern Culture on the Skids** "Love-A-Rama"

Hope You're Satisfied: A Tribute to Hank Penny/Shake It/1999

Dedicated to one of the great, overlooked hillbilly boogie artists of the 1940s-1950s with covers by Big Sandy, the Dalhart Imperials, the Lucky Stars, the Ranch Girls, the Riptones, and more.

The Horse Whisperer/ MCA/1998

Soundtrack for Robert Redford movie with many prominent alt. country performers. However, only the songs by Edwards and Moorer are actually heard during the film.

Includes: **Iris DeMent** "Whispering Pines"; **Steve Earle** "Me and the Eagle"; **Don Edwards** "Cowboy Love Song"; **Emmylou Harris** "Slow Surprise"; **The Hill Country Flatlanders** (Ely, Gilmore, Hancock) "South Wind of Summer"; **The Mavericks** "Dream River"; **Alison Moorer** "A Soft Place to Fall"; **Don Walser** "Big Ball's in Cowtown"; **Gillian Welch** "Leaving Train"; **Lucinda Williams** "Still Long for Your Kiss"; **Dwight Yoakam** "Cattle Call"

HOWL!/Glitterhouse Ger./1996

Sampler from one of Europe's most alt. country/Americana friendly labels.

Includes: **Vic Chesnutt** "Goodbye Sadness"; **Freakwater** "Lullaby"; **Giant Sand** "Route 66"; **Sid Griffin** "The Man Who Invented the Blues"; **Terry Lee Hale** "Too Much Life"; **Joe Henry** "Honky Tonk Masquerade"; **The Silos** "Nobody But You"; **Souled American** "Suitors Bridge"; **The Setters** "You're Gonna Miss Me"; **U.S. Saucer** "The Plasma is Still Now"; **Victoria Williams** "Feed the Birds"

The Inner Flame: The Songs of Rainer Ptacek/Atlantic/1997

Giant Sand initiated project to benefit long-time friend/bandmate who was stricken with and later succumbed to brain cancer. Impressive roster of performers covering Ptacek penned songs includes Emmylou Harris, P.J. Harvey, Evan Dando, Victoria Williams & Mark Olson, Vic & Tina Chesnutt, Robert Plant & Jimmy Page, and Giant Sand.

International Songwriters' Festival, Frutigan, Switzerland, 1987/Bear Family Ger./1988

Live sessions from one of the most prestigious of singer/songwriters' events.

Includes: **Katy Moffatt and the Tom Russell Band** "Walking After Midnight"; **Tom Russell** "Alkalai," "Mezcal," "Navajo Rug"; **Ian Tyson and Andrew Hardin** "Someday Soon," "Summer Wages"; **Steve Young and the Tom Russell Band** "Lonesome, On'ry and Mean"

It Lives! Vancouver Rockabilly, 1980-1988/East Side Can./1988 (CS)

Historic anthology of 1980s rockabilly from British Columbia with several bands (Rocking Fools, Dots, Stinging Hornets) that included Jimmy Roy.

It's So Hard to Be Cool In An Uncool World/I Wanna/1988

Includes: **The True Believers** "Foggy Notion"; **The Highwaymen** "Shine a Light"; **The Tall Lonesome Pines** "Prison Correspondence"; **The Schramms** "Walk to Delphi"; **Go To Blazes** "Blood Beach"

Jukebox Cantina-Combo Platter/Hayden's Ferry/1998

Alt. country/Americana mostly from Arizona based performers.

Beau "Untitled"; **David Beaudry** "Psychedelic Tom T. Hall"; **The Burnlackers** "Long Lonely Time"; **CAVU** "Rain"; **Norman Collins** "Loving Kind"; **Ronnie Glover** "On to Somethin' Good";

Grievous Angels "Dear John"; **Ignitors** "Fun and Games"; **Dan Israel and the Cultivators** "Before We Met"; **Kenny Love and the Rockerfellas** "Hands of Time"; **Out of the Blue** "Heartbrake"; **The Revenants** "Why Do You Love Me"; **H. Robertson** "Indian Mile"; **Stickman Jones** "Simple"; **Andy Tanas** "You Gotta Love Her"

Jukebox Cowboy/ Vinyl Junkie UK/1997

Third effort from the producers of **Country**, **Cowpunks**, and **Loose**.

Phil Burdett "Careless Coin"; **Simon Chardiet** "The Good, The Bad, and The Ugly"; **Cowboy Nation** "Cowboy Nation"; **Cowboys and Indians** "Western Life"; **Kevin Coyne** "Take Me Back in Your Arms"; **Mary Cutrufello** "Sworn to Pride"; **Roxy Gordon** "Indians"; **The Haoles** "Hillbilly Hula Gal"; **Roy Heinrich** "Listen to Your Heart"; **Mike Henderson** "One Foot in the Honky Tonk"; **Cornell Hurd** "7 Cups of Coffee"; **James Intveld** "Cryin' Over You"; **Don McCalister** "Ain't It Funny"; **Dan Penn** "Tearjoint"; **Debra Peters and Wayne Hancock** "5 Dollars and a Heartache"; **Duffy Power** "Till We Meet Again"; **LeRoy Preston** "Fool on a Stool"; **Stan Ridgway** "Luther Played Guitar"; **Kathy Robertson & Chris Gaffney** "I'll Never Be Free"; **Townes Van Zandt and Barb Donovan** "I'll Be Here in the Morning"

KGSR Broadcasts, Vols. 1- 6/ KSGR/1993-1998

Annual series of on-air performances from Austin radio station that has included songs by Dave Alvin, Richard Buckner, T Bone Burnett, Peter Case, Cowboy Junkies, Iris DeMent, The Derailers, Steve Earle, Joe Ely, Jimmie Dale Gilmore, Wayne Hancock, Emmylou Harris, Robin Holcomb, The Jayhawks, Robert Earl Keen, Lyle Lovett, Maria McKee, Jeb Loy Nichols, Son Volt, Townes Van Zandt, Whiskeytown, Wilco, Kelly Willis, and many more alt. country performers.

(//www.austin360.com/kgsr/music/)

Keep on the Sunny Side: A Tribute to the Carter Family/ Amoeba/1993

Off-beat but appealing tribute to the Carter Family from Freakwater and a variety of obscure alternative bands.

Blood "I've Been Gathering Flowers on the Hill"; **Les Bohem** "My Heavenly Home is Bright and Fair"; **Fifth Column** "Chewing Gum"; **Bob Forrest & the Melrose Hillbillies** "Last Move for Me"; **Freakwater** "Broken Hearted Lover," "No Phone in Heaven," "Lover's Return"; **The Lonesome Whippoorwills** "Keep on the Sunnyside," "Wildwood Flower"; **Glen Meadmore** "There's No One Like

Mother to Me," "My Honey Lou"; **The O'Bannons** "LuLu Walls"; **Pleasure Box** "Single Girl, Married Girl"; **Rick & Janet** "Lonesome for You"; **Shrimpboat** "Hello Stranger," "You Are My Flower"

Kerrvile Folk Festival: The Early Years, 1972-1981/Silverwolf/1995

Ten CD musical chronicle of the frst decade of the legendary Kerrville with "live" recordings by hundreds of performers including Willie Nelson, Townes Van Zandt, Guy Clark, Flaco Jimenez, Asleep at the Wheel, Joe Ely & Butch Hancock, Hardin & Russell, Gary P. Nunn, Peter Rowan, Lucinda Williams, Mary McCaslin & Jim Ringer.

Kerrville Folk Festival: Ten Great Years, 1982-1991/Silverwolf/1995

Mammoth 10 CD set containing 180 "live" performances by 150 artists who have played the venerable festival over the years including many alt. country personalities: Christine Albert, Terry Allen, Austin Lounge Lizards, Clay Blaker, Ponty Bone, Ray Campi, Guy Clark, Alvin Crow, Steve Earle, Rosie Flores, Jimmie Dale Gilmore, Butch Hancock, Bill & Bonnie Hearne, Ray Wylie Hubbard, Robert Earl Keen, Lyle Lovett, Tom Russell, Uncle Walt's Band and many more.

L.A. County Line: A Country Compilation From the City of Angels/Strawdog/1998

In the spirit of **A Town South of Bakersfield**, a variety of Southern California alt. country conceived and compiled by Neil Mooney (aka Florida Slim).

Billy Bacon and the Forbidden Pigs "You Don't Know"; **The Cousin Lovers** "Night of the Hunter"; **Deke Dickerson** "Your Love's Like a Faucet"; **Rosie Flores** "Dream Dream Blue"; **Chris Gaffney** "A Bridge Too Far"; **The Groovy Rednecks** "Born That Way"; **Annie Harvey** "Wallflower"; **Dan Janisch** "If You Say That You Love Me"; **The Losin' Brothers** "There Oughta Be a Law"; **The Lucky Stars** "Everybody's Fool"; **Neil Mooney with Chris Gaffney** "Faded Rose"; **P.J. Pesce & The Chile Rellenos** "Wish You Were Here"; **Jennifer Quinn** "Girlie"; **Russell Scott and His Red Hots** "Let's Start Over"; **Christopher Sprague** "Right or Wrong"; **Little Miss Tammy Smith** "Lucky Girl"; **Thousand Dollar Wedding** "Real Sad"; **Trailer Park Casanovas** "Drunk"

Last Honky Tonk: Live at Henry's, Vol. 2/Tex-Tex/1992 (CS)

Second of two tapes from the legendary bar that was the launching pad for many of Austin's current alt. country elite (see **Live at Henry's**)

Austin Lounge Lizards "The Car Hank Died In"; **Sarah Elizabeth Campbell** "You Win Again"; **The Hays County Gals** "Headed for Texas"; **The Pure Texas Band** "Faded Love," "The Wild Side of Life," "C Jam"; **Don Walser** "Curtains in the Window," "Cinderella," "The Key's in the Mailbox," "Rollin' Stone From Texas," "Heart Over Mind"; **Shaun Young** "Please Release Me"

Lazy, Loud, and Liquored Up/
Shindig/c.1990

Early collection of San Francisco alt. country with Dee Lannon, Buck Naked, Sloe Gin Joes and more.

Leather Chaps and Lace Petticoats: Welcome to Alternative Country/
Anagram UK/1985

Interesting anthology of mostly British cowpunk groups but also some American acts; the subtitle is one of the earliest uses of the term "alternative country."

Bad Mad Missouri Buffalo and the Everglade Alligators "Kickin' Som'"; **The Blubbery Hellbillies** "Hootin' and a Howlin'"; **The Boothill Foot Tappers** "Get Your Feet Out of My Shoes"; **Helen and the Horns** "Freight Train"; **The Meat Puppets** "Magic Toy Missing"; **The Mighty Lights of Paradise** "Foundations of Love"; **The Orson Family** "Pointed Bra"; **Dolly Parton** "Two Little Orphans"; **The Raunch Hands** "Stomp It"; **The Riverside Trio** "I've Only Just Turned 21"; **Peter Rowan with Flaco Jimenez and the San Antonio Tex-Mex Band** "Free Mexican Air Force"; **The Screamin' Sirens** "Your Good Girl's Gonna Go Bad"; **Ned Sublette** "Rye Whiskey"; **Way Out West** "Mystery Blonde"

Live at Henry's: The Last Honky Tonk, Vol.1/ Tex-Tex/1992 (CS)

First of two tapes from legendary bar that was the launching pad for many of Austin's current alt. country elite (see **Last Honky Tonk**).

Cornell Hurd "I Bought the Shoes That Just Walked Out on Me," "Time Changes Everything"; **Don Walser** "Big Ball's in Cowtown," "Casting My Lasso," "One More Drink," "Columbus, Georgia," "Dear Old Southern Home," "Mister Steel Guitar," "Still a Lot of Love"

Live at The Iron Horse, Vol. 1/
Signature Sounds/1997

In concert performances by Fred Eaglesmith, Jimmie Dale Gilmore, Tish Hinojosa, Salamander Crossing, and others from long established Massachusetts music hall.

Live From the Barley House/
BH/1996

From one of Dallas' leading alt. country venues, a set of 1995 live performances by the cream of Dallas' alt. country.

Includes: **The Cartwrights** "1-900-GIRLS," "Sleeping in the Doghouse"; **Cowboys & Indians** "That's What I Like About the South," "Big Man"; **T. Texas Edwards & the Swingin' Cornflake Killers** "Whiskey Trip," "LSD Madé a Wreck Out of Me"; **Homer Henderson** "You Pretty Thing," "Pickin' Up Cans on the Highway"; **Liberty Valance** "Honky Tonk Life"; **The Old 97s** "Doreen," "Victoria Lee"

LOOSE: New Sounds of the Old West/Vinyl Junkie UK/1998

Yet another top-notch gathering of cutting edge alt. country/Americana from the folks who gave us **Country, Cowpunks**, and **Jukebox Cowboy**. * Indicates previously unreleased.

*The Bonnevilles** "Tilt-a-Whirl"; **Grace Braun** "It Won't Hurt"; *Peter Bruntnell** "Handful of Stars"; *Calexico** "Slag"; **Neal Casal** "All the Luck in the World"; **Dakota Suite** "Mood Indigo"; **Fuck** "Ballet High"; **Giant Sand** "Lester Lampshade"; **The Gourds** "All the Labor"; **The Handsome Family** "Moving Furniture Around"; *Lambchop** "The Petrified Forest"; **Tom Leach** "Doris Days"; *Lincoln '65** "Dreams"; *Lullaby for the Working Class** "Every Day is Like a Birthday Party"; **Nadine** "Brother"; *Red Star Belgrade** "Saddest Girl"; *Richmond Fontaine** "Calm"; **Scud Mountain Boys** "Penthouse in the Woods"; **John P. Strohm** "Thelma"; **Supersuckers** "Must Have Been High"

Luxury Liner, Vol. 1 & 2/
Glitterhouse Ger./1997; 1998

Still more from the champs of samplers and one of Europe's best alt. country/Americana labels.

Vol. 1: **The Beacon Hillbillies** "Midnight Sun"; **Big Back Forty** "Lot's Song"; **Blue Mountain** "Mountain Girl"; **Chris Burroughs** "Pray for Rain"; **Neal Casal** "Eddy & Diamonds"; **Granfaloon Bus** "OK"; **Willard Grant Conspiracy** "The Ostrich Song"; **Hazeldine** "Apothecary"; **The Haynes Boys** "Guardian Angel"; **Cheri Knight** "The Knitter"; **Loose Diamonds** "You Keep Me Hanging On"; **Rainravens** "What Did You Save for Me?"; **Richmond Fontaine** "Whirlpool"; **Whiskeytown** "Midway Park"

Vol. 2: **The Conquistadors** "When I'm Drunk I Like to Drink"; **Farmer Not So John** "Fire in the Valley"; **Grandpa's Ghost** "Cheater"; **The Hooblers** "Waiting for a Real Rain"; **Lambchop** "I'm a Stranger Here"; **Lullabye for the**

Working Class "Boar's Nest"; **Nadine** "Machines"; **Pinetop Seven** "Money From Home"; **Quinsonics** "Ocean Floor"; **Sackville** "Tie Back Your Hair"; **Stillwater** "Porchlight"; **John P. Strohm & The Hello Strangers** "Slip Away"; **Volebeats** "Somewhere in My Heart"; **Wagon** "Slack Key Blues"

Marijuana's Greatest Hits/
Re-Hash/1992

Covers of songs about marijuana and gettin' high originally done by everyone from Bob Marley to Bob Dylan, Black Sabbath to Johnny Paycheck.

Includes: **The Blue Chieftains** "Illegal Smile"; **Go To Blazes** "Billy Bardo"; **The New Duncan Imperials** "Seeds and Stems (Again)"; **Mojo Nixon** "I Like Marijuana"; **Uncle Dave Bacon & the Toxic Pig Fucks** (Southern Culture on the Skids) "Roll Another Number"

More Oar/1999

Reworking of songs from **Oar**, an influential album by Skip Spence the mad genius of Moby Grape. Among those participating were Jay Farrar, the Bottlerockets, Alejandro Escovedo, Tom Waits, Mudhoney and more.

Nashville: The Other Side of the Alley, Insurgent Country Volume 3/Bloodshot/1996

Third Insurgent Country installment focusing on acts in the belly of the Beast!(see **For a Life of Sin** and **Hell-Bent**)

Dan Baird "Lonely at the Top"; **Paul Burch & his Honky Tonk Orchestra** "Your Red Wagon"; **Royann Calvin** "Try It Again"; **Tim Carroll** "Open Flame"; **Courtesy Move** "Those I'll Provide"; **Greg Garing** "Safe Within Your Arms"; **Sonny George & the Tennessee Sons** "Hillbilly Train"; **Hayseed** "God-Shaped Hole"; **Tom House** "Cole Durhew"; **Jason & the Scorchers** "One Last Quetion"; **Duane Jarvis** "Cocktail Napkin"; **Phil Lee & the Sly Dogs** "Daddy's Jail"; **Lonesome Bob** "The Plans We Made"; **R. B. Morris** "Roy"; **Gwil Owen** "No Ammunition"; **Kristi Rose & the Handsome Strangers** "Rise & Shine"

New Highway/Boka Discs/1999

Follow up to **Viva Americana** roots anthology includes songs by Neko Case, Neal Casal, Nadine, Slobberbone, Kevin Welch, and others.

The Newton Boys/Sony Soundtrax/1998

Soundtrack for Richard Linklater's 1920s Texas crime saga provided by Mark Rubin (music supervisor) and Danny Barnes (score) of the Bad Livers with a stellar line-up of supporting musicians (Erik Hokkanen, Steve James, Carl Sonny

Leyland, Kevin Smith, Stan Smith) playing old-time, ragtime, and other music of the period.

North By Northeast: Roots, Rock &c/Northeastern/1991

Alt. country/roots rock from the Beantown region in the early 1990s.

The Blood Oranges "High on a Mountaintop"; The Country Bumpkins "Funtime"; The Cowlicks "Joe Feraille"; The Derangers "Rio Sangre"; Hypnotic Clambake "Fate"; The Immortals "Two Sisters"; Miss Xanna Don't and the Willin' "Midnight Blue"; Chris Murphy "Heathen Hornpipe"; The Swinging Steaks "Beg, Steal or Borrow"; Treat Her Right "Early Man"; We Saw the Wolf "The Farmer of Chester's Daughter"

Norwegian Wood: A Selection of Contemporary Roots and Rock/ Samkultur No./1995

Norwegian (Somebody's Darling) and American artists (Erik Moll, Rick Danko, Tom Pacheco).

Old-Time Music on the Radio, Vols. 1 & 2/Rounder/1994; 1996

Another eclectic Rounder anthology offering a variety of new old-time performers.

Vol. 1 includes: Hazel Dickens "Pretty Bird"; The Heartbeats "Citigo"; Tracy Schwarz "Sioux Indians"; Mike Seeger "Candy Girl"; Mac Benford "Hangman's Reel";

Vol. 2 includes: Skip Gorman "Where the Old Red River Flows"; The Renegades "Highlander's Farewell"; Walt Koken "Jaybird's Town"; Bayou Seco "First Choice Two Step"

One Step Up, Two Steps Back: The Songs of Bruce Springsteen/ The Right Stuff/1997

Boss covers by a variety of artists including Dave Alvin and Martin Zellar.

Out of the Blue, Vols 1-5/ Glitterhouse Ger./1995-1998

Impressive series of European and U.S. alt. country/Americana from the king of compilations with tracks by Nadine, Hazeldine, the Hitchin' Post, Terry Lee Hale, the Walkabouts, Neal Casal, the Good Sons, Larry Barrett, Go To Blazes, and many more.

Out of the Gate/BJAM/1990

Volume one of St. Louis area alt. country.

Includes: Chicken Truck (The Bottle Rockets) "Headin' for the Ditch"; Bob Reuter "59 Cadillac"; Uncle Tupelo "Before I Break" (demo version)

Out of the Gate Again: Sixteen More From the Grain Belt/ BJAM/1996

Second volume of alt. country from the St. Louis region.

Includes: Belle Starr "Hook, Line, & Sinker"; The Kamikaze Cowboys "Your Sweet Face"; The New Patrons of Husbandry "Too Busy Cryin'"; One Fell Swoop "Fences"; Wagon "Slack Key Blues"

Pastures of Plenty: A Celebration of Woody Guthrie/ Dejadisc/1993

Tribute recorded live at La Zona Rosa, Austin, Texas, July 18, 1993.

Includes: Christine Albert "Pastures of Plenty"; Sarah Elizabeth Campbell "Ramblin' Round," "Hobo's Lullaby"; Michael Fracasso "1913 Massacre," "Dead or Alive"; Butch Hancock "Belle Starr"; Ray Wylie Hubbard "Jesus Christ/Vigilante Man"; Jimmy LaFave "Oklahoma Hills," "This Land is Your Land"; The Red Dirt Rangers "The Ranger's Command"; Steve Young "Do Re Mi"

Pearls in the Snow: The Songs of Kinky Friedman/Kinkajou/1998

Tribute to the one and only (thank god!) Kinkster.

Includes: Asleep at the Wheel "Before All Hell Breaks Loose"; Guy Clark "Wild Man From Borneo"; The Geezinslaws "Twirl"; Kinky Friedman "Marilyn and Joe," "Silver Eagle Express," "They Ain't Making Jews Like Jesus Anymore"; Lyle Lovett "Sold American"; Willie Nelson "Ride 'Em Jewboy"; Tom Waits "Highway Cafe"; Dwight Yoakam "Rapid City, South Dakota"

The Pine Valley Cosmonauts Salute The Majesty Of Bob Wills, The King of WesternSwing/ Bloodshot/1998

Gala tribute from Chicago's Insurgent Country community and beyond backed by Jon Langford and his Pine Valley Cosmonauts.

Includes: Neko Case & Bob Boyd "Stay a Little Longer"; Alejandro Escovedo & Jon Langford "San Antonio Rose"; Edith Frost "My Window Faces the South"; Robbie Fulks "Across the Alley From the Alamo"; Jimmie Dale Gilmore "Trouble in Mind"; Jon Langford "Sweet Kind of Love"; Jane Baxter-Miller "Time Changes Everything"; Jane Baxter-Miller, Rico Bell & Brendan Croker "Faded Love"; The Meat Purveyors "Take Me Back to Tulsa"; Chris Mills "Home in San Antone"; Brett Sparks "Roly Poly"; Sally Timms "Right Or Wrong"

Points West/Hightone/1990

Label sampler with a number of songs (*) done exclusively for this recording.

Joe Ely "Row of Dominoes"; Jimmie Dale Gilmore "Red Chevrolet," "Fair & Square"; The Lonesome Strangers "Goodbye Lonesome," "Another Fool Like Me"; Buddy Miller *"The Garage Sale," *"Feels Like I'm Falling in Love"; Heather Myles *"Rum & Rodeo", *"Lovin' The Bottle"; Ted Roddy & the Talltops *"Stronger Than Dirt," *"Where Can She Be?"; Gary Stewart "Rainin'," "Nothin' But a Woman"

Pushing the Norton: The Ace Cafe Compilation/Heyday/1995

Benefit recording with an assortment of Bay Area/L.A. acts including many alt. country who have played this popular venue.

Includes: Big Sandy and His Fly-Rite Boys "Jake's Barber Shop"; Jeff Bright and the Sunshine Boys "Let's Get Drunk (And Talk About Marriage)"; Gary Wayne Claxton "Poor Boy"; Dave and Deke Combo "Wild Woman"; Susanna Van Tassel and the Golden West Playboys "I've Got My Pride"; The Tombstones "No Sympathy"; Jimbo Trout and the Fish People "Columbus Stockade"

Real: The Tom T. Hall Project/ Sire/1998

Salute to one of country's great troubadours.

Includes: Richard Buckner "When Love is Gone"; Calexico "Tulsa Telephone Book"; Johnny Cash "I Washed My Face in the Morning Dew"; Mary Cutrufello "Candy in the Window"; Iris DeMent "I Miss A Lot of Trains"; Joe Henry "Homecoming"; The Mary Janes "I'm Not Ready Yet"; R. B. Morris "Don't Forget the Coffee Billy Joe"; Mark Olson with Victoria Williams "It Sure Can Get Cold in Des Moines"; Syd Straw with The Skeletons "Harper Valley PTA"; Whiskeytown "I Hope It Rains At My Funeral"; Kelly Willis "That's How I Got to Memphis"

Renegade Rockabilly/ Renegade/1998

CD accompanying the book *Rockabilly: A 40 Year Journey* by musician, producer, promoter Billy Poore. The previously unreleased material on the recording is by artists profiled in the book.

Includes: Marti Brom "I Still Can't Forget About You," "Mean Streak," "Feelin' Right Tonight"; Charlie Feathers "I'm Walkin' the Dog"; Robert Gordon with Danny Gatton "Gonna Romp and Stomp"; James Intveld "Anyway You Want Me"; Billy Lee Riley "Rockin' Man"; Kelly Willis and the Fireballs "Your Cheatin' Heart"

Return of the Grievous Angel: A Tribute to Gram Parsons/
Almo/1999

Realization of Emmylou Harris' long-time desire to honor her mentor. As executive producer, she assembled a cast of top-notch alt. country and rock musicians to cover GP's best songs (see the 1993 **Commemorativo** tribute).

Beck and Emmylou "Sin City"; **Elvis Costello** "Sleepless Nights"; **Cowboy Junkies** "Ooh Las Vegas"; **Sheryl Crow and Emmylou** "Juanita"; **Evan Dando and Juliana Hatfield** "$1,000 Wedding"; **Chris Hillman and Steve Earle** "High Fashion Queen"; **The Mavericks** "Hot Burrito #1"; **The Pretenders with Emmylou** "She"; **The Rolling Creekdippers** "In My Hour of Darkness"; **Gillian Welch** "Hickory Wind"; **Wilco** "100 Years"; **Lucinda Williams and David Crosby** "Return of the Grievous Angel"

Revival, Vol. 1: Brunswick Stew & Pig Pickin'/YepRoc/1997

First installment of alt. country drawn mostly from the North Carolina Triangle (Raleigh/Durham/Chapel Hill) but also from South Carolina, Florida, Georgia, and Virginia.

The Backsliders "Yep!"; **The Burnley Brothers** "Mean Mama Boogie"; **Chigger** "Hotwire"; **The Hootowls** "Depart From Me"; **Mercury Dime** "Dog Star"; **The Pinetops** "Birds of Prey"; **Six String Drag** "Off With You Head"; **Trailer Bride** "Mardi Gras"; **Two Dollar Pistols** "Let Me Be Your Fool"; **The Vidalias** "Misery Loves Company"; **Whiskeytown** "Guns to Town"

Revival, Vol. 2: Kudzu and Hollerin' Contest/Yep Roc/1997

Second volume of "southeastern backroads sounds".

Grace Braun "Liftin' Me Up"; **The Burnley Brothers** "All Bark and No Bite"; **The Continental Drifters** "Christopher Columbus Transcontinental Highway"; **Dirtball** "Ends of the Earth"; **Larry Sloane Doggett & the Alembic** "December 99"; **Drive By Truckers** "Nine Bullets"; **Gladys** "Her House"; **Grand National** "Money and Love"; **Lou Ford** "So Far Gone"; **Mercury Dime** "Are You Positive?"; **Noah** "Skillet"; **The Quinsonics** "Out of Town"; **Red Star Belgrade** "Favorite Thing"; **Star Room Boys** "The Daydreamer"; **Trailer Bride** "Graveyard"; **The Tremblers** "Get Back in the Car"; **Whiskeytown** "Busted"

Rig Rock Deluxe: A Musical Salute to the American Truck Driver/ Upstart Diesel Only/1996

All-star tribute to the Knights of the Open Road from the producers of the renowned **Rig Rock Juke Box** and **Rig Rock Truck Stop.**

Kay Adams & BR5-49 "Mama Was a Rock (Daddy Was a Rolling Stone)"; **The Bottle Rockets** "Truck Drivin' Man (Give All I Can)"; **Steve Earle** "White Freight Liner Blues"; **Bill Kirchen & Too Much Fun** "Semi-Truck"; **Cheri Knight** "Wagon of Clay"; **Nick Lowe** "I'm Coming Home"; **Buck Owens** "Will There Be Big Rigs in Heaven"; **Del Reeves & Jim Lauderdale** "Diesel, Diesel, Diesel"; **Shaver** "Mother Trucker"; **Red Simpson & Junior Brown** "Nitro Express"; **Marty Stuart** "Miss Marie & The Bedford Blaze"; **Don Walser** "Truck Driving Man"; **Kelly Willis** "Truckstop Girl"; **The Yayhoos** "Highway Junkie"

Rig Rock Juke Box/
Diesel Only/1992

Groundbreaking anthology of singles by mostly New York City alt. country ("Rig Rock") acts on the independent label founded by World Famous Bluejays founders Jeremy Tepper, Jay Sherman-Godfrey, and Albert Caiati in 1990.

The Blue Chieftains "I Think Hank Woulda Done It This Way," "Punk Rockin' Honky Tonk Girl"; **Mark Brine** "New Blue Yodel (Blue Yodel #14)"; **Courtney & Western** "Diplomat" and "Hands Off"; **Angel Dean & the Zephyrs** "Leaving"; **Five Chinese Brothers** "Baltimore"; **Go To Blazes** "97 Miles," "Why I Drink"; **Mumbo Gumbo** "Good Morning Mr. Afternoon," "Miss Fabulous"; **Gwil Owen** "Messed Up Thing"; **The Twanglers** "Two Hearts"; **The World Famous Blue Jays** "Diesel Only Theme," "Good Morning Mr.Trucker"

Rig Rock Truck Stop/
Diesel Only/1993

Second Diesel Only collection that widened the "Rig Rock" circle.

Amy Allison & the Maudlins "Cheater's World"; **Blue Chieftains** "After the Hurricane"; **Courtney & Western** "Am I In Love," "Lovin' You Is Killing Me"; **Angel Dean & the Zephyrs** "Life Preserver," "Second Best"; **Five Chinese Brothers** "She's a Waitress (And I'm In Love)"; **Joe Flood** "Hotel Albert"; **Go To Blazes** "Messed Up Again"; **Jean Caffeine's All-Nite Truckstop** "Hoe-down in the Sky"; **Killbilly** "Diesel Dazey"; **Mojo Nixon & the World Famous Blue Jays** "Chug-A-Lug," "UFOs, Big Rigs & BBQ"; **Gwil Owen** "Hot Black Coffee," "Too Much Coffee"; **Will Rigby** "Ricky Skaggs Tonite"; **The Surreal McCoys** "Woke Up"; **The World Famous Blue Jays** "Cheeseburger Deluxe," "Cookin' With Jay"

River of Song/
Smithsonian-Folkways/1998

CD drawn from documentary on the various musical cultures found along the Mississippi River. Among others featured on the video and recording are the Bottlerockets, Greg Brown, D.L. Menard with Christine Balfa, John Hartford, John Hiatt, and Levon Helm.

Rockabilly Hall of Fame, Vol. 1/
RABHOF/1998

Historic collection of spanning from the Maddox Brothers & Rose through Mac Curtis, Narvel Felts, Bill Haley, Glen Glenn to King Kerosene, the Crazy Rhythm Daddies and many more 'billies old and new. Produced by Bob Timmers, one of rockabilly's most dedicated promoters and creator of the impressive Rockabilly Hall of Fame on the Internet (www.rockabillyhall.com).

Rudy's Rockin' Kiddie Caravan/TNT/1998

Companion to the *Rudy & GoGo Show* with updated versions of children's classics. Proceeds to benefit the National Center for Family Literacy.

Includes: **Blacktop Rockets** "Froggie Went a Courtin'"; **Calexico** "The Man on the Flying Trapeze"; **Vic Chesnutt** "Home on the Range"; **Giant Sand** "Blow the Man Down"; **Mekons** "Oranges & Lemons"; **D.L. Menard** "J'ai Passe Devant Ta Porte"; **Moonshine Willy** "Skip to My Lou"; **Sally Timms** "Hush Little Baby"; **Waco Brothers** "Them Bones"

Sample Some Okra/
Okra Normal/1991

Sampler from the label that once was home to Columbus, Ohio's outstanding stable of alt. country performers; includes one p.u. song (*) by each act.

The Ass Ponys "Laughing at the Ghost," *"Peanut"; **Cordelia's Dad** "Her Bright Smile," *"San Francisco"; **The Fellow Travelers** *"As The Rain," "GTO"; **Ricky Barnes & the Hootowls** *"I Take a Chance," "Who Throw Dat Rock"; **Hank McCoy & the Dead Ringers** "Jealousy," *"Lately My Luck"; **The Schramms** "Out Of The Earth," *"Pet Sounds"; **The Wolverton Brothers** "Posse Comiatus," *"Vampyre"

San Francisco: A Music City Compilation/Trocadero Ger./1998

Two CD set presenting a variety of pop and roots styles including alt. country performers Granfaloon Bus, the Old Joe Clarks, Tarnation, U.S. Saucer, and Virginia Dare.

San Francisco Song Cycle/
Innerstate/1998

Live celebration of Bay Area songwriters including many from alt. country bands.

Includes: **Chris Cacavas** (Green on Red) "Anonymous"; **Mike Coykendall** (Old Joe Clarks) "Metal Shed Blue"; **Melanie DiGiovanni** (Buckets) "Will Ye No Come Back Again"; **Tom Heyman** (Go To Blazes) "Bottle Full of Wishes"; **Victor Krummenacher** (Camper Van Beethoven) "Angel Tattoo"; **Daniel Pearson** (American Music Club, Clodhopper) "1000 Days of Shame"; **Chuck Prophet** (Green on Red); "Burn This Firetrap Down"; **Sally Timms with Jon Langford** (Mekons) "Nighttime"

Silos & Utility Sheds: A Glitterhouse Compilation/
Glitterhouse Ger./1995

Label sampler with songs by Larry Barrett, Richard Buckner, Terry Lee Hale, Butch Hancock, Gary Heffern, Kitchen Radio, and others.

Silver Meteor: An Anthology of the Best of Country
Rock/Sierra/1997

Re-pressed re-release of rare album that includes the previously unreleased final recordings of Clarence White plus two cuts by the Everly Brothers with Clarence White and Gene Parsons, and songs by the Blue Velvet Band (Richard Greene, Bill Keith, Jim Rooney, Eric Weissberg) along with some obscure early country-rockers.

Sleazefest!/Sleazy Spoon/1995

Music from annual hillbilly/psychobilly event in Raleigh, North Carolina that promises "Two Nights of Bands, B Movies, BBQ & Beer"

Includes: **Hasil Adkins** "Boo Boo the Cat," "Head on the Wall," "Leaves of Autumn"; **Hillbilly Frankenstein** "Class With a Capital K," "High Class to Trailer Trash"; **Southern Culture on the Skids** "Mudbuggy," "Hubcap Hunch" (with Hasil Adkins)

So What?: An Austin Tribute to the Replacements/Wrteched/1997

Salute from deep in the heart of Texas to one of the greatest rock bands of the 1980s. Performers include the Asylum Street Spankers, the Damnations, the Gourds, and Buick MacKane (Alejandro Escovedo).

Songs From Chippy/
Hollywood/1994 (sdtrk)

Soundtrack from the Terry/Jo Harvey Allen play drawn from the diary of a Depression era prostitute in the Texas Panhandle. Original music was written and performed by the elite of West Texas singer/songwriters who also acted in the play during its successful run off Broadway.

Terry Allen "Gonna California," "Angels of the Wind"; **Joe Ely** "Goodnight Dear Diary," "Buildin' More Fires," "Cup of

Tea" (with Jo Harvey Allen), "Cold Black Hammer," "Whiskey and Women and Money to Burn," "Goodnight"; **Butch Hancock** "Wind's Gonna Blow You Away," "Low Lights of Town," "Boomtown Boogie," "Roll Around"; **Wayne Hancock** "Thunderstorms & Neon Signs," "Back to Black"; **Robert Earl Keen (with Butch Hancock)** "Morning Goodness"; **Jo Carol Pierce** "Across the Great Divide," "I Blame God"

Songs of Forbidden Love by The Wandering Eyes/Lazy SOB/1998

"Tribute to Indiscretion" dreamed up by Asleep at the Wheel bandmates Jason Roberts and Dave Sanger who brought together the cream of Austin's honky tonk pickers and singers (as The Wandering Eyes) to cover classic cheatin' songs.

Rosie Flores "In Some Room Above the Street"; **Rosie Flores, Chris O'Connell, Ted Roddy** "The Game of Triangles"; **Rosie Flores** "Even If I Have to Steal"; **Jason Roberts** "Forbidden Angel," "When She Does Me Right, She Does You Wrong"; **Ted Roddy** "Devil in Mrs. Jones," "Hell Yes, I Cheated," "Cheatin' Traces"; **Dale Watson** "Lovin' on Backstreets, Livin' on Main," "Unspoken Kind"; **Kelly Willis** "Me and Mrs. Jones"; **Kelly Willis and Dale Watson** "It's a Cheatin' Situation"

The Songs of Jimmie Rodgers: A Tribute/Egyptian Columbia/1997

Bob Dylan's first project on his own record label.

Includes: **Bob Dylan** "My Blue Eyed Jane"; **Steve Earle & the V-Roys** "In the Jailhouse Now"; **Jerry Garcia** (last recording), **David Grisman, John Kahn** "Blue Yodel #9"; **Willie Nelson** "Peach Pickin' Time in Georgia"; **Dwight Yoakam** "T for Texas"

Songs of Route 66: Music From the All-American Highway/
Lazy SOB/1995

Salute to America's Mother Road.

Mary Cutrufello "The Long Red Line"; **The Dusty Chaps** "Don't Haul Bricks on 66"; **Jason Eklund** "What's Left of 66"; **Jimmy LaFave** "Route 66 Revisited"; **The Mad Cat Trio with Cindy Cashdollar and Barbara Lamb** "2200 Miles"; **The Red Dirt Rangers** "Used to Be"; **Bobby Troup** "Route 66"; **Kevin Welch** "The Mother Road"

Sounds of the New West: The Best of Alternative Country/Uncut
UK/1998

CD included with the September 1998 issue of *Uncut* magazine which featured a special 10 page guide called "How the West Was Won: Everything You Need to Know about

Alternative Country" with profiles of artists, 'zines, labels, etc.

Calexico "Trigger"; **Kate Campbell** "Crazy in Alabama"; **Neal Casal** "Today I'm Gonna Bleed"; **Vic Chesnutt** "Until the Led"; **The Flying Burrito Brothers** "Sin City"; **Freakwater** "Lorraine"; **Willard Grant Conspiracy** "Evening Mass"; **The Handsome Family** "Weightless Again"; **Emmylou Harris** "Wrecking Ball," "Boulder to Birmingham (Live)"; **Hazeldine** "Tarmac"; **Lambchop** "Saturday Option"; **Nadine** "Dark Light"; **Will Oldham** "Apocalypse, No!"; **The Pernice Brothers** "Crestfallen"; **Josh Rouse** "Suburban Sweetheart"; **Silver Jews** "How to Rent a Room"; **Sixteen Horsepower** "Coal Black Horses"; **Wagon** "Two Hours Alone"; **The Walkabouts** "On the Beach"

Sourmash: A Louisville Compilation/X-Static/1997

Kentucky alt. country including the Palace Brothers, Starbilly, Chickenhawk, and Bodeco put together by Wink O'Bannon.

Stateside Rockabillies/
NV UK/1994

Hillbilly bop with Big Sandy, Dave & Deke, Ronnie Dawson, High Noon and more.

Straight Outta Boone County/
Bloodshot/1997

Insurgent Country tribute to WLW's 1940s-1960s Boone County Jamboree and Midwestern Hayride radio programs; covers songs by regulars on those shows: Merle Travis, Moon Mullican, Delmore Brothers, Webb Pierce, Stanley Brothers, Reno & Smiley, Hank Penny, Homer & Jethro and many others.

Caution Horse "Hangman's Boogie"; **The Cowslingers** "If I Lose"; **Flathead** "Run Mountain"; **Robbie Fulks** "Wedding of the Bugs"; **The Grievous Angels** "In the Jailhouse"; **Hardrock Gunter & the Dalhart Imperials** "Won't Your Ride in My Little Red Wagon"; **The Handsome Family** "Barbara Allen"; **Hazeldine** "I'm Lonesome Without You"; **Holler** "No Vacancy"; **The Lucky Stars** "No More Nuthin'"; **One Riot, One Ranger** "Southern Moon"; **The Riptones** "The Hucklebuck"; **Scroatbelly** "Why Don't You Haul Off and Love Me"; **The Showoffs** "Big, Big City"; **Slobberbone** "Dark as a Dungeon"; **Sally Timms** "Tennessee Waltz"; **The Volebeats** "Hamtramck Mama"; **The Waco Brothers** "Nine Pound Hammer"; **Waycross** "I Wanna Be Hugged to Death By You"; **Whiskeytown** "Bottom of the Glass"

Sunday Morning Sessions/ Munich Ger./1995

Includes: **Dave Alvin** "Every Night About This Time"; **Larry Barrett** "This Warm House"; **The Coal Porters** "The Light That Shines Within"; **Terry Lee Hale** "Boys Are Waiting"; **Butch Hancock** "Pumpkineater"; **Jimmy LaFave** "Minstrel Boy"; **Loose Diamonds** "Luck Runs Out"; **Calvin Russell** "Crack in Time"

Sweet Relief 1: A Benefit for Victoria Williams & Sweet Relief 2: Gravity of the Situation, The Songs of Vic Chesnutt/Sony/1993 & 1995

All-star collections celebrating and helping out two highly respected singer/songwriters. Volume 1 includes Soul Asylum, Lucinda Williams, Maria McKee, the Jayhawks, Giant Sand, Michelle Shocked, Lou Reed, Pearl Jam, and Evan Dando while Volume 2 has REM, Garbage, Kristin Hersh, Cracker, Sparklehorse, Joe Henry, Vic Chesnutt, Victoria Williams, and Madonna among others.

Texans: Live From Mountain Stage/Blue Plate/1995

Live performances by many of the best alt. country acts from the Lone Star State.

Includes: **Asleep at the Wheel** "Miles and Miles of Texas"; **Guy Clark** "She Ain't Goin' Nowhere"; **Joe Ely** "I Had My Hopes Up High"; **Jimmie Dale Gilmore** "You're Just a Wave, You're Not the Water"; **Tish Hinojosa** "Esperata"; **Ray Wylie Hubbard** "Portales"; **Billy Joe Shaver** "I've Been to Georgia on a Fast Train"; **The Texas Tornados** "Is Anybody Goin' to San Antone?"; **Townes Van Zandt** "Buckskin Stallion Blues"; **Kelly Willis** "Which Ever Way the Wind Blows"

Texas Folk & Outlaw Music : The Kerrville Folk Festival/ Adelphi/1983; Edsel UK/1992

Focus on Texas singer/songwriters from 1972-1976 originally on vinyl then re-released on CD.

Includes: **Guy Clark** "Anyhow I Love You"; **Steve Fromholz** "Birds & Wolverines," "Dear Darcy"; **Bill & Bonnie Hearne** "The Last Thing I Needed"; **Augie Meyer** "Down to Mexico"; **Willie Nelson** "The Party's Over"; **Threadgill's** "I'm a Drifter"; **Townes Van Zandt** "Tecumseh Valley," "Poncho & Lefty"; **Jerry Jeff Walker** "Charlie Dunn"

Texas Renegade Radio: A Country Americana Music Collection/KNON/1998

Singer/songwriter, honky tonk, and Western swing from KNON, a fine Americana station in Dallas.

Includes: **Cowboys & Indians** "Western Life"; **Donny Ray Ford** "Cowboy Boots"; **James Hand** "Baby, Baby Don't Tell Me That"; **Ray Wylie Hubbard** "Hey That's All Right"; **Kimmie Rhodes** "Just To Be Near You" (live in KNON studios)

Texas Twang, Vol. 1/Munich/1993

Dutch collection, but the only artist I know who's on it for sure is Charlie Burton doing "Love at First Sight."

Thirty Nine Steps to Seattle: An Alternative American History/ Diablo UK/1994

Cuts from a variety of 1980s alternative groups including the Band of Blacky Ranchette, Giant Sand, Green on Red, the Long Ryders.

This Note's for You Too!: A Tribute to Neil Young/Inbetweens Dut./1999

Eagerly anticipated double CD project initiated by Jos Starmans (Inbetweens Records) and the Dutch Neil Young Fan Club with proceeds going to one of Neil's favorite causes, the Bridge School. Contributors include a wide variety of European and North American alternative.

Includes: **Eric Ambel** "Revolution Blues"; **Big in Iowa** "Cinammon Girl"; **Chris Burroughs** "Powderfinger"; **Chris Cacavas** "Tonight's the Night"; **Coal Porters** "Ohio"; **Continental Drifters** "When You Dance I Can Really Love"; **Hitchin' Post** "Tell Me Why"; **Slobberbone** "Big Time"; **Tom Stevens** "Everybody Knows This is Nowhere"; **Ad Vanderveen** "Days That Used to Be"; **The Walkabouts** "Albuquerque"; **Steve Wynn** "Time Fades Away"

'Til Things Are Brighter...A Tribute to Johnny Cash/Rave UK/1988

Jon Langford produced this salute to the Man in Black with an eclectic line up of British and American musicians.

Marc Almond "Man in Black"; **Tracey and Melissa Beehive** "Five Feet and Risin'"; **Cathal Coughlan** "Ring of Fire"; **Brendan Croker** "Home of the Blues"; **Steve Mack** "Rosanna's Goin' Wild"; **Stephen Mallinder** "I Walk the Line"; **Mary Mary** "Boy Named Sue"; **David McComb** "Country Boy"; **The Mekons** "Folsom Prison Blues"; **Marc Riley** "Wanted Man"; **Peter Shelley** "Straight 'A's in Love"; **Michelle Shocked** "One Piece at a Time"; **Sally Timms** "Cry, Cry, Cry"

The Times They Are A Changin': A Tribute to Bob Dylan, Vols. 1-3/Sister Ruby/1998

Eclectic collection of covers by singer/songwriters and alternative acts.

Includes: **Charlie Chesterman** "Tonight I'll Be Staying Here With You"; **Greg Trooper** "I'll Keep It With Mine"; **The Vidalias** "Most Likely You'll Go Your Way"

Tombstone After Dark: A West Texas Compilation/Fury UK/1996

Mostly Texas performers with a few from California.

Dave Alvin "Border Radio"; **Asleep at the Wheel** "Big Beaver"; **Junior Brown** "My Baby Don't Listen to Nothin' But Ernest Tubb," "Don't Sell the Farm"; **Gene Clark & Carla Olson** "Gypsy Rider"; **Joe Ely** "Me & Billy the Kid"; **Jimmie Dale Gilmore** "Dallas," "Honky Tonk Masquerade"; **Butch Hancock** "Fools Fall in Love"

A Town South of Bakersfield, Vol. 1/ Restless/1988

First in a path breaking and highly influential series of L.A. alt. country collections; it and its sequels introduced some of the performers who have since become among the biggest names in alt. country (produced by Pete Anderson)

The Eddys "Big Big Love"; **Rosie Flores & Albert Lee** "Heartbreak Train"; **George Highfill** "Waitin' Up"; **The Lonesome Strangers** "Lonesome Pine"; **Katy Moffatt** "Love and Only Love"; **Reach for the Sky** "Same Old Fool"; **Kathy Robertson** "I'm Not Over You"; **Billy Swan** "Baby, I'll Show You"; **Tin Star** "Happy Hour"; **Dwight Yoakam** "I'll Be Gone"

A Town South of Bakersfield, Vol. 2/Restless/1988

Also produced by Pete Anderson; Vols. 1 & 2 have since been issued as a single CD.

Jann Browne "Louisville"; **Crazy Hearts** "We Get Along Just Fine (When We're Apart)"; **Dave Durham** "Let There Be Love"; **James Intveld** "Somewhere Down the Road"; **Candye Kane** "Tell Me a Lie"; **Jim Lauderdale** "What Am I Waiting For"; **Pete & the Bigshots** "Venice Skyline Rag"; **Jeffrey Steele** "Driftin' Man"; **Lucinda Williams** "Dark Side of Life"; **Re Winkler, Anne Harvey and Ree Van Vleck** "Mister Love"

A Town South of Bakersfield, Vol. 3/Restless/1992

Patty Booker "99"; **Calvin Davidson** "Hot 'N' Bothered"; **Mary Lyn Dias** "River of Love"; **Pam Dwinell** "In Your Room"; **Florida Slim & the Hurricanes**

"Ain't Life Grand"; **Sid Griffin & the Coal Porters** "Crackin' At The Seams"; **The Hellecasters** "Rockin' the Dog"; **Steve Kolander** "She's So Bad "; **Ronnie Mack** "Mama's Reward"; **The Neon Angels** "He's Breakin' My Heart"; **The Plowboys** "Nowhere Isn't Lonely"; **The Ruby Trees** "Hey (What Are You Doing?)"; **Rick Shea** "Foot in the Fire"; **Harry Dean Stanton** "I Hope I Never Get Too Old (To Rock 'n' Roll)"; **Dale Watson & the Lone Stars** "One Memory at a Time"; **Wylie & the Wild West Show** "Since I Found You"

Travis County Pickin'
/Hightone/1997

Hot collection of "country jazz guitar, Austin, Texas style"with an ensemble of ace string benders: Dave Biller, Joel Hamilton, Brian Hofeldt, Sean Mencher, Boomer Norman, Casper Rawls, Paul Skeleton, and Jim Stringer (producer) with support from Scott Walls Lloyd Maines, Lisa Pancratz, Kevin Smith, Erik Hokkanen, Donald Lindley, Terry Kuykendall, and Karen Biller.)

Tribute to Gram Parsons & Clarence White/Magnum UK/1996

Recorded live in Nashville and Dayton, Ohio in 1988 & 1989 by an ensemble including Bobby Bare, Swampwater, and members of the Flying Burrito Brothers; they cover Gram and Clarence's best songs.

True Life Blues: The Songs of Bill Monroe/Sugar Hill/1996

Tribute to The Father of Bluegrass by an all-star line up of musicians who performed with and/or were influenced by him.

True Sounds of the New West/
Freedom/1995

Austin (and region) alt. country, see **Austin Country Nights**

Includes: **Libbi Bosworth** "It's Late"; **Marti Brom** "Mean"; **Charlie Burton and the Texas Twelve Steppers** "Spare Me the Details"; **Tom Clifford** "Sometimes Saturday Night"; **The Derailers** "Lies, Lies, Lies"; **Wayne Hancock** "Friday and Saturday Night"; **Roy Heinrich** "Same Old Heartache"; **High Noon** "He Won, I Lost, She's Found"; **The Hollisters** "Good for the Blues"; **Sean Mencher** "Comanche Moon"; **Chris Miller** "Everybody's Lovin' (But Me)"; **Bruce Robison** "Angry All the Time"

Tulare Dust: A Songwriter's Tribute to Merle Haggard
/Hightone/1994

Dave Alvin/Tom Russell produced salute from some of The Hags' most ardent admirers.

Dave Alvin "Kern River"; **Peter Case** "A Working Man Can't Get Nowhere Today"; **Marshall Crenshaw** "Silver Wings"; **Iris Dement** "Big City"; **John Doe** "I Can't Hold Myself in Line"; **Joe Ely** "White Line Fever"; **Rosie Flores** "My Own Kind of Hat"; **Robert Earl Keen and the Sunshine Boys** "Daddy Frank"; **Katy Moffatt** "I Can't Be Myself"; **Tom Russell** "Tulare Dust/They're Tearin' the Labor Camps Down"; **Billy Joe Shaver** "Ramblin' Fever"; **Barrence Whitfield** "Irma Jackson"; **Lucinda Williams** "You Don't Have Very Far to Go"; **Dwight Yoakam** "Holding Things Together"; **Steve Young** "Shopping for Dresses"

Turning the World Blue: A Tribute to Gene Vincent/
Skizmatic/1996

Includes: **Marc Bristol** "Five Feet of Lovin'"; **Ray Campi** "Lotta Lovin'"; **Ray Condo** "Jump Back, Honey Jump Back"; **The Grandsons** "The Day the World Turned Blue"; **James Intveld** "Important Words"; **Ronnie Mack with Hot Rod Lincoln** "Lucky Star"

Twangfest Live Tape/
Twangfest/1997 (CS)

Two tape set of live performances from the inaugural of alt. country festival held annually in St. Louis (see the Twangfest web site for more details); also see **Edges From the Postcard**.

Belle Starr "Fever Sleep," "Stolen Glances," "Out of the Mouths of Babes"; **Cash Hollow** "Breathing Hole," "Land of Enchantment," "Suzanne's Lullaby"; **Fear & Whiskey** "Fireball," "Love Hurts Later," "8 Miles to the Gallon"; **Edith Frost** "Wayfaring Stranger Hideout," "Temporary Loan"; **Gasoline** "5/17," "Train," "Waiting Around to Die"; **The Ghost Rockets** "Hard to Get," "Sitting Alone in the Moonlight," "Juliette"; **Roy Kasten & the Sons of Perdition** "Halfway to Virginia," "The Tennessee River Waits for Me," "Hickory Wind," "Land"; **One Riot, One Ranger** "Allison Town," "Cloud 149," "Working on a Building"; **The Sovines** "Owner Operator," "Drinks After Church," "Truck Driving Man"; **The Waco Brothers** "Death of Country Music," "Plenty Tough and Union Made," "Wreck on the Highway," "White Lightning," "Big River"

25 Greatest Hits By Your Favorite Stars/East Side Can./1990 (CS)

Vancouver rockabilly/hillbilly bop from the 1980s with Jimmy Roy's 5 Star Hillbillies, the Yodells, the Dots, and others.

Twisted Willie/Justice/1995

Skewed but loving tribute to Willie Nelson from a surprising line-up of alternative performers.

Best Kissers in the World "Pick Up the Tempo"; **Jello Biafra with Life After Life** "Still is Still Moving to Me"; **Jerry Cantrell** "I've Seen All This World I Care to See"; **Johnny Cash** "Time of the Preacher"; **Jesse Dayton** "Sad Songs and Waltzes"; **Kelley Deal with Kris Kristofferson** "Angel Flying Too Close to the Ground"; **Gas Huffer** "I Gotta Get Drunk"; **The Reverend Horton Heat** "Hello Walls"; **Waylon Jennings** "I Never Cared for You"; **L7 with Waylon Jennings** "Three Days"; **Mark Lanegan** "She's Not for You"; **The Presidents of the United States** "Devil in a Sleeping Bag"; **Steel Pole Bathtub** "The Ghost"; **The Supersuckers** "Bloody Merry Morning"; **X** "Home Motel"

Uprooted: The Best of Roots Country/Shanachie/1998

Singer/songwriter focus with heavy emphasis on the Austin contingent.

Libbi Bosworth "East Texas Pines"; **Paul Burch** "Jackson, TN"; **Ana Egge** "River Under the Road"; **Robbie Fulks** "The Buck Starts Here"; **Kevin Gordon** "Dissatisfied"; **Wayne Hancock** "Thunderstorms and Neon Signs"; **R. B. Morris** "Take That Ride"; **Trish Murphy** "Boiling Water"; **Gwil Owen** "Mother Nature"; **Tom Russell with Iris DeMent** "Box of Visions"; **Don Walser** "John Deere Tractor Song"; **Dale Watson** "Pity Party"; **Kelly Willis** "He Don't Care About Me"

Used to Be: Blues From the Pacific Delta/Undercover/1997

Covers and originals in the spirit of Bill Monroe, Merle Travis, and other traditional country giants from Pacific Northwest alt. country performers.

Includes: **The Dickel Brothers** "Nine Pound Hammer"; **Golden Delicious** "Little Sadie"; **The Prairie Dogs** "Hussar's Dance"; **Kevin Richey** (Golden Delicious) "Lamentations"; **Richmond Fontaine** "Blackout."

Viva Americana/Boka UK/1998

British collection of U.S. Americana and alt. country performers inlcuding live and previously unreleased (*) material plus a 48 page guide book featuring interviews with the artists (see **New Highway**)

*Terry Allen** "Ourland"; ***The Derailers** "Painful Days & Sleepless Nights"; ***Alejandro Escovedo** "Pyramid of Tears"; ***Jimmie Dale Gilmore** "Black Snake Moan"; ***Sid Griffin & the Coal Porters** "Cadillac Elvis"; ***The Gourds** "Tearbox"; ***Jason & the Scorchers** "One Last Question"; **Kieran Kane** "Table Top

Dancer"; *Jimmy LaFave "Only One Angel"

Will Sing for Food: The Songs of Dwight Yoakam/Little Dog/1998

Tribute with proceeds donated to benefit the homeless.

Includes: **The Backsliders** "Doin' What I Did"; **The Blazers** "If There Was a Way"; **Scott Joss** "Johnson's Love"; **The Lonesome Strangers** "Takes a Lot to Rock You"; **Tim O'Brien** "Thousand Miles From Nowhere"; **Reckless Kelly** "Please, Please Baby"; **Kim Richey and Mandy Barnett** "Near You"; **Gillian Welch** "Miner's Prayer"

Will the Circle Be Unbroken, Vol. 1/ United Artists/1972

Landmark meeting of the masters of old-time/bluegrass (Roy Acuff, Mother Maybelle, Doc Watson, Earl Scruggs, Merle Travis, Jimmy Martin) and a new generation of fans(Nitty Gritty Dirt Band, Vassar Clements, Norman Blake, Randy Scruggs) resulting in a stellar collection of classic covers that turned out to be one of the most important and influential recordings of the 1970s and beyond.

Will the Circle Be Unbroken, Vol. 2/ Universal/1989

Originally intended as a sequel to WCBU1 with Michael Nesmith, Gram Parsons, Clarence White, and other alt. country artists of the early 1970s but it just didn't happen. However, the line-up assembled by the Dirt Band for WCBU2 isn't too shabby although the results were not nearly as impressive or influential as Vol. 1.

Includes: **Emmylou Harris** "Mary Danced With Soldiers"; **Levon Helm** "When I Get My Reward"; **John Hiatt & Rosanne Cash** "One Step Over the Line"; **Roger McGuinn & Chris Hillman** "You Ain't Goin' Nowhere"; **New Grass Revival** "Hear Jerusalem Moan"; **John Prine** "Grandpa Was a Carpenter"

Word From the Range: A Canadian Cowboy Collection/ Glenbow Museum Can./1998

Includes: **Cindy Church** "Cowgirls Lullaby"; **Great Western Orchestra** "Wind in the Wire"; **Colleen Peterson** "Code of the West"; **Quartette** "Cowboys and Rodeos," "Neon Cowboy"; **Nathan Tinkham** "Curly Bob"; **Ian Tyson** "Cowboy Pride," "Half a Mile of Hell," "Summer Wages"

Young Fogies, Vol. 1 & 2/ Rounder/1994; 1995

Contemporary old-time music.

Vol. 1 includes: **The Agents of Terra** "Every Breath You Take"; **The Chicken Chokers** "Chinkapin Hunting"; **The Highwoods String Band** "Sheep Shell Corn"; **The Horseflies** "Oh Death"; **The New Lost City Ramblers** "Then It Won't Hurt No More";

Vol. 2 includes: **The Chicken Chokers** "Grey Eagle"; **Lost Rosin** "John Robertson/Daisy Miller"; **The Volo Bogtrotters** "The Crow Song"

RESOURCES

IUMA's List of Labels
//www.iuma.com

Musician's Guide to Touring and Promotion, 13th edition, 1999 (available at Borders, Barnes & Noble, et al. in the music magazine section)

Record Labels on the Web
//www.arancidamoeba.com/labels.html

Ultimate Record Label List
//www.ubl.com/label/

Yahoo's List of Labels
//www.yahoo.com/business_and_economy/
companies/music/labels/

LABELS

A&M
P. O. Box 118
Hollywood, CA 90078
213-469-2411
//amrecords.com
16 Horsepower

Acoustic Disc
P. O. Box 4143
San Rafael, CA 94913
800-221-DISC
Dawgnet //www.dawgnet.com
David Grisman; Jerry Garcia; Tony Rice;
Old and In the Way

Addled
P. O. Box 40421
Tucson, AZ 85717
Al Perry

Adult Swim
P. O. Box 1535
Arlington, VA 22210-0835
Last Train Home

Agarita
P. O. Box 97
Comfort, TX 78013
830-995-3094
//songs.com/rex/
Rex Foster

Akashic
5704 Parkview Tr.
Austin, TX 78734
512-266-2892
//txmusic.com/akashic/
webmaster@txmusic.com
Texana Dames; Tommy Hancock

Amarillo
5714 Folsom Blvd., Ste. 300
San Francisco, CA 95819-4608
//members.aol.com/starleigh7/amarillo.html
amarillo@earthlink.net
Dieselhed, U. S. Saucer

Apolkalips Now
P. O. Box 43664
Tucson, AZ 85733
//www.themollys.com
The Mollys

Ardent
2000 Madison Ave.
Memphis, TN 38104
901-725-0855
//www.ardentrecords.com
info@ardentrecords.com
Jolene

Arhoolie
10341 San Pablo Ave.
El Cerrito, CA 94530
510-525-7471
//www.arhoolie.com
mail@arhoolie.com
California Cajun Orchestra; Maddox Brothers & Rose; Savoy-Doucet

Arista/Nashville
7 Music Circle N.
Nashville, TN 37203
615-780-9100
//www.twangthis.com
BR5-49

Arista/Texas
7447 Bee Caves Rd., Ste. 208
Austin, TX 78746
512-329-9910
Flaco Jimenez; Robert Earl Keen

Ark 21
14724 Ventura Blvd.
Sherman Oaks, CA 91403
818-461-1700
//www.ark21.com
Wayne Hancock; Leon Russell

Back Porch Music
P. O. Box 803702
Chicago, Il 60680-3702
Doug Hoekstra

Banyan
P. O. Box 4796
Chatsworth, CA 91313
818-700-0165
Laura Tyler

Bar/None
P. O. Box 1704
Hoboken, NJ 07030
201-795-9424
//www.bar-none.com/
info@bar-none.com
Country Dick Montana; The Health & Happiness Show; Lullaby for the Working Class

Barbed Wire
248-540-9031
barbedwirerecords@yahoo.com
Fred Eaglesmith (live CD)

Barley House
2916 N. Henderson
Dallas, TX
214-824-0306
//www.barleyhouse.com
jbarley@computek.com
Live From the Barley House

Bear Family
Box 1154
D-27727
Hambergen
Germany
49-4797-9300-0
//www.bear-family.de/
bear@bear-family.de
James Intveld; Jim Silvers; Ian & Sylvia;
Box sets of classic country

Behemoth Records
P. O. Box 43532
Austin, TX 78745
//www.intelliweb.com/cornell-hurd-band
Gwolfcs@aol.com
Cornell Hurd

Bellmeade Phonics
312 S. Cherry St.
Richmond, VA 23220
//sony.inergy.com/snockonews
Michael Hurley

Big Iron
Dallas, TX
The Cartwrights; The Old 97s; Honkey Tonk Holidays

Binky
9656 Burbank Dr., Ste. E
Baton Rouge, LA 70810
504-767-0209
cmaxwell@premier.net
Greg Jacobs; Mike West

Biscuit Boy
P. O. Box 160942
Austin, TX 78716
Don McCalister

BJAM
P. O. Box 13245
St. Louis, MO 63157
314-963-5231
//home.stlnet.com/~cdstelzer/bjam.html
Bjamrecord@aol.com
Belle Starr; Out of the Gate compilations

Black Boot
5503 Roosevelt Way NE
Seattle, WA 98105
206-524-1020
//www.w2.com/boot.html
nie@halycon.com
Black Boot Trio

Black Dog
Route 1, Box 163-A
Monticello, MS 39654
601-587-7966
//www.blackdogrecords.com
blackdog@telapex.com
Blue Mountain; The Continental Drifters; The Gimmecaps; The Hilltops; Marah; Noah Saterstrom

Bloodshot
912 W. Addison
Chicago, Ill 60613
773-248-8709
//www.bloodshotrecords.com
bludshot@mcs.com
Insurgent Country: The Blacks; Neko Case; Robbie Fulks; The Grievous Angels; Jon Langford; The Meat Purveyors; Moonshine Willy; The Old 97s; Pine Valley Cosmonauts; The Riptones; The Sadies; Split Lip Rayfield; Sally Timms; The Waco Brothers; Whiskeytown; For a Life of Sin; Hell Bent; Nashville: The Other Side of the Alley; Straight Outta Boone County

Blue Button
P. O. Box 121
Roslindale, MA 02131
//www.hypnotic-clambake.com
Hypnotic Clambake

Blue Elf
500 N. Guadalupe, Ste. G-48,
Santa Fe, NM 87501
//members.aol.com/bluespud/index.htm
Robotclaw@aol.com
Stephen Terrell

Blue Heart
179 Baltic Cr.
Tampa, FL 33606
Ronny Elliott & The Nationals

Blue Hen
900 Chestnut St., #302
San Francisco, CA 94109
415-928-4704
//www.bluehenrecords.com
info@bluehenrecords.com
Jim Campilongo

Blue Plate Music
//www.ohboy.com/bpm_artists.html
Live From Mountain Stage series

Blue Puffer
100 1st St., Ste. 100-228
San Francisco, CA 94105
//home.earthlink.net/~hobp/
deelannon@earthlink.net
Dee Lannon

Blue Rose
Rauheckstr. 10
74232 Abstatt
Germany
//www.bluerose-records.com
bluerose@t-online.de
Chris Burroughs; The Continental Drifters; The Dashboard Saviors; Health & Happiness Show; Rainravens; The Schramms; The Shakin' Apostles; Volebeats

Blue Smoke
P. O. Box 631
Southampton
England
SO16 5ZG
+44(0)1703 770453
//dialspace.dial.pipex.com/town/park/kcd11/
bluesmoke@dial.pipex.com
The Okeh Wranglers

Boar's Nest
P. O. Box 4635
Austin, TX 78765
//www.boarsnest.com
info@boarsnest.com
Jeff Hughes, Bruce Robison

Bohemia Beat (Rounder)
1001 South Josephine St.
Denver, CO 80209
303-744-1782
//www.rounder.com/bobeat/
shubobeat@earthlink.net

Michael Fracasso; Jimmy Lafave

Brambus
Box 44
CH-7000 Chur
Switzerland
CH+55614 10 77
//songs.com/brambus/index-nf.html
brambus@access.ch
Richard Dobson; Ernst Eggenberger; Funny Hill

Broken Spoke
3201 S. Lamar
Austin, TX 78704
512-442-6189
//www.instar.com/mall/brokenspoke/
Alvin Crow; Gary P. Nunn; Kimmie Rhodes

Brunswick Recordings
10 Dawson St.
Brunswick, Victoria 3056
Australia
The Moonee Valley Drifters

Buffalo Skinner
313 Prichard St.
Ashland, KY 41102
606-325-7178
//www.poetusa.com
Rob McNurlin

Campfire
1410 Ridge Creek Ln.
Bulverde, TX 78613
San Antonio, TX
830-885-2488
//www.hepcat.com/campfire/
campfire@hepcat.com
Gary P. Nunn; Geronimo Trevino

Capitol
1750 Vine St.
Hollywood, CA 90029
//www.hollywoodandvine.com
Vic Chesnutt; Jeb Loy Nichols

Capitol/Nashville
3322 W. End Ave.
Nashville, TN 37203
615-269-2000
//www.capitol-nashville.com
The Delevantes

Cargo
3058 N. Claybourn
Chicago, ILL 60618
//www.cargorecords.com
Jon Wayne

Carrot Top
935 W. Chestnut, Ste. LL15
Chicago, ILL 60622
312-432-1194
patrickm@mcs.com

The Handsome Family

Cavity Search
P. O. Box 42246
Portland, OR 97242
//www.teleport.com/~csr/
csr@teleport.com
Golden Delicious; Pete Krebs

Checkered Past
3940 North Francisco
Chicago, IL 60618
773-463-8103
//www.checkeredpast.com
eric@checkeredpast.com
Paul Burch; Johnny Dowd; Tom House;
Lonesome Bob; Old Joe Clarks; Tommy
Womack

Chunk
P. O. Box 244
Easthampton, MA 01027
The Scud Mountain Boys

Coconut Grove
940 Licoln, Ste. 308
South Beach, FL 33139
305-531-6080
Cgrecords@aol.com
Cowboy Nation

Cojema
P. O. Box 874
Belmont, CA 94002
650-591-6857
Cojema@aol.com
Steve Owen

Cold Spring
P. O. Box 161943
Austin, TX 78716
//www.coldspring.com
music@cold-spring.com
James Hand; Reckless Kelly; Chris Wall

Columbia/Sony
2100 Colorado Ave.
Santa Monica, CA 90404
310-449-2100
http://www.music.sony.com
Tine Valand; Bob Dylan; Byrds Legacy reissues

Compass
117 30th Ave. South
Nashville, TN 37212
615-320-7672
//www.compassrecords.com
info@compassrecords.com
Alison Brown; Kate Campbell; Farmer Not
So John

Continental
P. O. Box 1443
Austin, TX 78767
512-478-1414
Ronnie Dawson Live at the Continental Club

Coolidge
157 Coolidge Terrace
Wyckoff, NJ 07481
//www.gis.net/~coolidge/
coolidge@gis.net
Gladys; Lancaster County Prison

Corduroy
41 Fellows St.
Kew
Victoria 3101
Australia
T-Bones

Country-Town
P. O. Box 2649
Palos Verdes, CA 90274
//www.countrytown.com
info@countrytown.com
Mark Insley; Rose Maddox; Will Ray; Sid
Griffin

Cowgirl
1977 Yale St.
Ontario, CA 91764
Kathy Robertson; To Roy Nichols With
Love

Cravedog
P. O. Box 1841
Portland, OR 97201
503-233-7284
//www.teleport.com/cravedog/
cravedog@teleport.com
Little Sue; Richmond Fontaine

Criminal
466 Moreland Ave.
Atlanta, GA 30307
404-215-9511
//www.criminal.com
eric@criminal.com
Bubbapalooza, Vol. 2

Crypt
1250 Long Beach Ave., #101
Los Angeles, CA 90021
213-622-0173
//www.crypt.de/index.html
cryptrec@concentric.net
The Country Teasers; Nine Pound Hammer

Crystal Clear Sound
10486 Brockwood Rd.
Dallas, TX 75238
214-349-5057
//www.crystalclearsound.com
ccs@crystalclearsound.com
Ronnie Dawson; Jack Ingram; Killbilly

Curb
47 Music Square East
Nashville, TN 37203
615-321-5080
//www.curb.com
Junior Brown; Lyle Lovett

Daring
P. O. Box 793
Marblehead, MA 01945
1-800-44-DISCS
//www.rounder.com/daring/
Duke Levine

Das Kapital
P. O. Box 564
Buffalo, NY 14225-0564
The Pine Dogs

Dead Reckoning
P. O. Box 22152
Nashville, TN 37202
800-442-DEAD
//songs.com/deadreck/
DeadReck@aol.com
The Dead Reckoners; Mike Henderson;
Kiernan Kane; Tammy Rogers; Kevin
Welch

Deep South
P. O. Box 764
Manchaca, TX 78652
512-441-3045
//home.earthlink.net/~stewells/
Blaze Foley Tribute

Dejadisc
821 Porter Rd.
Nashville, TN 37206
615-226-1801
615-650-2957 (fax)
//www.eden.com/~dejadisc/
dejadisc@home.com
swilkison@home.com
Richard Buckner; Sarah Elizabeth Campbell; Michael Fracasso; Wayne Hancock;
Rainravens

Demon/Edsel
//www.fbeat.demon.co.uk/
Commander Cody; Joe Ely anthologies

Denon Canada
17 Denison St.
Markham, Ontario
L3R 1B5
Canada
Quartette

Diesel Only
100 N. 6th St.
Brooklyn, NY 11211
718-388-4370
www.dieselonly.com
DieselOnly@aol.com

Rig Rock compilations and singles by the World Famous Bluejays, Five Chinese Brothers, Go To Blazes and more.

Discovery

2034 Broadway
Santa Monica, CA 90404
310-828-1033
//www.discoveryrec.com

Blue Rodeo; Candye Kane; Parlor James; Toni Price

Dixie Frog

France
Fax 011-33-53-20-37-31

Paul Burch; George Hamilton V

Dog Patch

P. O. Box 882944
San Francisco, CA 94188-2944
//www.dog-patch.com

Wilson Gil

Doolittle

P. O. Box 4700
Austin, TX 78765
//www.doolittle.com
theherst@doolittle.com

Bottlerockets; Slobberbone; Mount Pilot

DOS

609-B W. 6th St.
Austin, TX 78701

Loose Diamonds

Drag City

P. O. Box 476867
Chicago, IL 60647
312-455-1015
//www.mcs.com/~apharris/dragcity/
gene@dragcity.com

Edith Frost; Will Oldham; Palace

E-Squared

1815 Division St., Ste. 101
Nashville, TN 37203
//www.e2records.com
E2rex2@aol.com

Steve Earle; Bap Kennedy; Cheri Knight; Six String Drag; V-Roys

East Side Records

2076 East 3rd Ave.
Vancouver, B.C.
V5N 1H7
Canada

Jimmy Roy, Ray Condo, Vancouver rockabilly compilations

Ecco-Fonic

P. O. Box 304
Hollywood CA 90078
818-558-3360
//web.ecco-fonic.lomisgroup.com/ecco-fonic/
eccofonic@earthlink.net

Deke Dickerson; Sean Mencher, Lester Peabody; Smith Ranch Boys

Elektra

345 N. Maple Dr., Ste. 123
Beverly Hills, CA 90210
310-288-3800
http://www.elektra.com

The Cox Family; The Derailers; Jimmie Dale Gilmore; Emmylou Harris; The Old 97s

Epiphany

1303 W. 21st St., Dept. ND
Tempe, AZ 85282
602-804-0992
epirec@getnet.com

Giant Sand; The Revenants; Tom Stevens

ESD

Great label went out of business in 1998.

The Beacon Hillbilles; The Blood Oranges; The Bottle Rockets; Go to Blazes; The Schramms; The Spanic Family

Estrus

P. O. Box 2125
Bellington, WA 98227
//www.estrus.com
info@estrus.com

The Cowslingers; Go To Blazes

Evolutionary

226 S. Jefferson St.
Frederick, MD 21701
1-888-Y-EVOLVE
http://www.evoman.com
eman@evoman.com

Slim Chance & The Convicts

Fat Cuz

//www.olmsted.com/fat-cuz-records/
Fatcuzrec@aol.com

Big Chicken

Fire Ant (North Carolina)

//www.futuris.net/mabels/fireant.html
mabels@futuris.net

Eugene Chadbourne; Bubba Hey Mudtruck compilation

Fire Ant (Texas)

P. O. Box 1253
Wimberley, TX 78676
512-847-2633
//www.flash.net/~emoll1/index.htm
emoll1@flash.net

Erik Hokkanen; Erik Moll

Flying Fish

1304 W. Schubert
Chicago, IL 60614
//www.rounder.com

Mike Auldridge; The Austin Lounge Lizards; Balfa Toujours; The Basin

Brothers; Norman Blake; John Hartford; D.L. Menard; Mingo Saldivar; Mike Seeger

Folk Era

705 S. Washington St.
Naperville, IL 60540-0782
800-232-7328
//www.cfe.cornell.edu/cstone/folkera.html
folkera@aol.com

Cornerstone

Freedom

P. O. Box 650032
Austin, TX 78765
512-302-3398
//www.eden.com/~freedom/
freedom@eden.com

Asylum Street Spankers; Libbi Bosworth; Rick Broussard; The Derailers; The Hollisters; True Sounds of the New West compilation; Texas Music Roundup catalog

Fundamental

P. O. Box 118
Pass Christian, MS 39571
228-822-2869

Eugene Chadbourne; Dirtball; The Johnsons; Lilybandits; One Riot, One Ranger; Six String Drag; Urban Hillbilly Quartet; Used Carlotta

Fury

7-11
Minerva Road
London
NW10 6HJ
England
0181 963 0352
//www.nervous.co.uk/

Ray Condo; The Okeh Wranglers; Jimmy Roy

Geffen

9130 Sunset Blvd.
Los Angeles, CA 90069
//geffen.com

Big Blue Hearts; The Cowboy Junkies; Robbie Fulks; Maria McKee; Southern Culture on the Skids; Gillian Welch (Almo)

Glitterhouse

Gruner Weg 25
D-37688
Beverungen
Germany
//www.glitterhouse.com
reinhard@glitterhouse.de

Larry Barrett; Terry Lee Hale; Hazeldine; Gary Heffern; The Walkabouts

Globe

P. O. Box 5523
Mill Valley, CA 94942
//www.globerecords.com
globe@microweb.com

Commander Cody; Joe Goldmark; Dan Hicks; Solid Air

Goofin'/Goofy

P. O. Box 63
01601 Vantaa
Finland
+358-9-7733 113
//www.pcuf.fi/~tapiov/
goofin.records@kolumbus.fi

The Barnshakers; High Noon; Hal Peters; The Ranch Girls; Slap Sally Combo; Mack Stevens; Shaun Young

Green Linnet

43 Beaver Brook Rd.
Danbury, CT 06810
203-730-0333
//www.greenlinnet.com
Grnlinnet@aol.com

Seconds Flat

Gregor

P. O. Box 1397
Montclair, NJ 07042
201-746-6437

Lancaster County Prison; Townes Van Zandt (Last Rights)

Hairy Moon

P. O. Box 604
Medford, MA 02155
781-393-8252
dandog@erols.com

The Bagboys

Harbourtown

//www.rootsworld.com/harbourtown/
boat@hartown.demon.co.uk

The Boat Band

Hay Holler

P. O. Box 868
Blacksburg, VA 24063

Skeeter & the Skidmarks

Hayden's Ferry

P. O. Box 27747
Tempe, AZ 85285
602-831-7233
//www.haydensferry.com
info@haydensferry.com

The Ignitors; Dan Israel & The Cultivators; One Riot, One Ranger; Jukebox Cantina: Combo Platter

Hermitage

P. O. Box 8523
Memphis, TN 37076

Sonny George

Hey Day

2325 Third St. #339
San Francisco, CA 94107
415-252-5590
//www.heyday.com
heyday@heyday.com

Pushing the Norton compilation

Hightone

220 4th St. #101
Oakland, CA 94607
510-763-8500
//www.hightone.com
htrecords@aol.com

Dave Alvin; Phil Alvin; Big Sandy; The Blasters; The Carpetbaggers; Rosie Flores; Chris Gaffney; Hot Club of Cowtown; Bill Kirchen; Kim Lenz; Buddy & Julie Miller; Ted Roddy; The Skeletons; Dale Watson

Hollywood

500 S. Buena Vista St., Team Bldg. 77
Burbank, CA 91521
//www.hollywoodrec.com

Leftover Salmon; Roger McGuinn

Honey

P. O. Box 141199-672
Dallas, TX 75214

Homer Henderson

Hot Biscuits

221 Metairie Ct.
Metairie, LA 70001
504-828-0461

The Hackberry Ramblers

Ichiban/Sky

P. O. Box 724677
Atlanta, GA 31139
770-419-1414

Bubbapalooza, Vol. 1

Iglu

P. O. Box 122, Station P
Toronto, Ontario
M5S 2S7
Canada
416-944-9624
//www.aracnet.net/~iglu/index.html
iglu@aracnet.net

The Crazy Rhythm Daddies

Inbetweens

P. O. Box 1431
5004 BK Tilburg
The Netherlands
//home.wxs.nl/~bborgman/jos/homejos.htm
starman1@hvision.nl

This Note's For You Too: A Tribute to Neil Young

Innerstate

P. O. Box 411241, Dept. N
San Francisco, CA 94144-1241
//www.innerstate.com

Okra All-Stars; San Francisco Song Cycle

Jackalope

P. O. Box 90183
Austin, TX 78709-0183
//www.kimmierhodes.com
jgracey@outer.net

Kimmie Rhodes

Jackass

P. O. Box 30488
Santa Barbara, CA 93130
1-888-798-4773 (U.S.)
1-805-898-0852
//www.jackassrecords.com

Full Tank, Vol. 1

Joaquin

254 Scott St.
San Francisco, CA 94117

Ray Condo

Joe Records

P. O. Box 3806
Austin, TX 78764-3806
//www.io.com/~jeancaf/

Jean Caffeine

Justice

P. O. Box 980369
Houston, TX 77098
800-533-5878
//www.justicerecords.com
justice@justicerecords.com

Jesse Dayton; Kimmie Rhodes; Shaver; Twisted Willie compilation

KJK

1341 Taylor Ave.
Baltimore, MD 21234
//www.markbrine.com

Mark Brine

KOCH International

2 Tri-Harbor Court
Port Washington, NY 11050
800-688-3482
//kochint.com/
koch@kochint.com

Amy Allison; Pinto Bennett; Steve Earle (Early Tracks); Dale Watson (Truckin' Sessions); Lucinda Williams (reissue)

Krane/Pool

P. O. Box 7164
Capitol Station
Albany, NY 12208
518-475-1293
Powermower@aol.com

Coal Palace Kings; Disciples of Agriculture

Landslide

1800 Peachtree St. NW, Suite 333
Atlanta, GA 30309
404-355-5580
//www.landsliderecords.com
mrland@mindspring.com

Cigar Store Indians; The Steam Donkeys

Lasso

7004 Westmoreland Ave.
Takoma Park, MD 20912
1-800-391-1854
TedSmouse@aol.com

Ruthie & The Wranglers

Lazy SOB

P. O. Box 49884
Austin, TX 78765-9884
512-480-0765
//www.io.com/lazysob/
LazySOB1@aol.com

Charlie Burton; Anna Egge; The Wandering Eyes; Songs of Route 66 compilation

Linemen Services

5906 Dewey Dr.
Alexandria, VA 22310
//www.kevinjohnson.com
linemen@clark.net

Kevin Johnson

Little Dog

223 W. Alameda #201
Burbank, CA 91502
800-603-5454
//www.littledogrecords.com
LilDogRecs@aol.com

Pete Anderson; Scott Joss; The Lonesome Strangers; Joy Lynn White; Will Sing for Food

Lo-Ball

2259 14th Ave.
San Francisco, CA 94116

Joe Goldmark

Longhorn

31-65 29th St. #A-6
Astoria, NY 11106

Doug Stevens & Outbound

Lucky Dog (Sony/Columbia)

//www.music.sony.com

Asleep at the Wheel; David Allan Coe; Bruce Robison; Charlie Robison

Magoo

7536 Forsyth, Ste. 166
St. Louis. MO
314-727-5153
//musicfolk.com/swoop
swoop@musicfolk.com

One Fell Swoop

Mammoth

1290 Ave. of the Americas
New York, NY 10104
212-707-2600
//www.mammoth.com/mammoth
Mammothpr@aol.com

The Backsliders; Joe Henry; Jason & The Scorchers

Marimac

P. O. Box 447
Crown Point, IN 46307
800-628-4507
marimac@netnitco.net

Boiled Buzzards; Volo Bogtrotters

MCA/Nashville

60 Music Square East
Nashville, TN 37203
615-244-8944
//www.mcarecords.com

Richard Buckner; Joe Ely; The Mavericks; Todd Snider

Mercury/Nashville

66 Music Sq. West
Nashville, TN 37203
615-320-0110
//www.mercuryrecords.com/mercury/

Mary Cutrufello; Lucinda Williams

Merge

P. O. Box 1235
Chapel Hill, NC 27514
//merge.catalogue.com
merge@mrg2000.com

Lambchop

Moll

Mittelweg 114b
20149 Hamburg
Germany
//www.spontan.de/moll/index.html
szlovak@metronet.de

Souled American

Monkey Hill

804 Spain St.
New Orleans, LA 70117
Monkeyhill@aol.com

The Continental Drifters; Jo Carol Pierce; Dan Stuart

Mood Food

1381 Kildaire Farms Rd., Ste. 246
Cary, NC 27511
919-557-8311
//www.moodfood.com
Moodfoodnc@aol.com

Whiskeytown (Rural Free Delivery)

Munich

P. O. Box 2242
Austin, TX 78768
512-476-8067
munich@munich.com

The Gourds

My Own Planet

P. O.Box 95921
Seattle, WA 98145
//www.imusic.com/labels/myownplanet/
michelev@earthlink.net

Clodhopper

New West

13351-D Riverside Dr.
Box 611
Sherman Oaks, CA 91423
818-501-0056
//www.newwestrecords.com
cary@bakernorthrop.com

Shaver

Norton

P. O. Box 646
Cooper Station
New York, NY 10003
//members.aol.com/nortonrec/norton.html
Nortonrec@aol.com

Hasil Adkins; The Legendary Stardust Cowboy

Nuf Sed

P. O. Box 591075
San Francisco, CA 91459

Tarnation

OBT

P. O. Box 41271
Plymouth, MN 55441-0271
612-374-5171 or 612-425-4784
//www.accidentclearinghouse.com
jtranberry@accidentclearinghouse.com

Accident Clearinghouse

October

6410 Wayzata Blvd.
Minneapolis, MN 55426
612-545-9266
//www.october-rec.com
info@october-rec.com

The Honeydogs

Oh Boy!

33 Music Square West, Suite 102A
Nashville, TN 37203
800-521-2112
//www.ohboy.com/~ohboy/
ohboy@ohboy.com

R. B. Morris; John Prine

Okra

1992 N. High St.
Columbus, OH 43201
614-421-9455
Okra Discography & Links to Artists
//members.aol.com/tmivrecs/okra.html

The Assponys; Ricky Barnes; Cordelia's Dad; Hank McCoy; The Fellow Travelers; Schramms; The Okra All-Stars

On the Hill

Hayama Bldg. 2F
1-92, Ekimae-Odori
Toyohashi
Aichi, Japan
Zip: 440

Dee Lannon; The Rollin' Rocks; Mack Stevens

One Man Clapping

2032 North Racine
Chicago, IL 60614
773-935-3537
//www.lb.com/onemanclapping/
gc@lb.com

Doug Hoekstra; Jim Roll

Outpost

//www.outpostrec.com

Whiskeytown

P2/Twangfest

c/o Junior Barnard
808 West 27th Terrace
Lawrence, KS 66046
//www.twangfest.com

Edges From the Postcard 1 & 2; Twangfest Live

Paladin

1514 South St., Ste. 200
Nashville, TN 37212
615-255-7191
//www.paladinrecords.com

Steve Forbert; Greg Garing

Part

c/o Andy Widder
Waldstr. 10
69234 Dielheim
Germany
//www.rockabillyhall.com/PARTrecords.ht
ml
Rrp-AndyWidder@t-online.de

The Barnshakers; Ray Campi; Doc Thomas
& His Honky Tonk Music Lovers

Pingleblobber

P. O. Box 49414
Austin, TX 78765

Christine Albert; Emily Kaitz

Planetary

2614 W. Cary St.
Richmond, VA 23220
804-353-2627
//users.aol.com/planetaryr/home.html
kwilkes@plan9music.com

Dirtball

Pravda/Bughouse

3823 N. Southport
Chicago, IL 60613
773-549-3776
//www.pravdamusic.com
pravda@pravdamusic.com

Hasil Adkins (Bughouse); Gringo; The New
Duncan Imperials

Prima

Box 2539
London
NW3 6DF
England
//interchem.chem.strath.ac.uk/pd/PrimaCat.h
tml

The Coal Porters; The Long Ryders

PRIME CD (1-800 CD Prime)

111 East 14th St., Ste. 300
New York, NY 10003
212-366-5982
//www.primecd.com
mail@primecd.com

The Boneheads; Five Chinese Brothers;
Eddy Lawrence

Propellant Transmissions

P. O. Box 2297
Redondo Beach, CA 90278
310-772-8130

Cisco

Quarterstick

P. O. Box 25520
Chicago, IL 60625
773-388-8888
//www.southern.com/southern/label/qua/mi
ndex.html

Bad Livers; Calexico; The Mekons

Rainlight

P. O. Box 468
Terlingua, TX 79852

Butch Hancock

Ramblin'

Lilla Fiskaregaten 5
SE-222 22 Lund
Sweden
+46-4´-37 22 73
//www.ramblinrecords.com
info@ramblinrecords.com

Jivin' Jake Jern

Ranchero Records

4200 Park Blvd., Ste. 227
Oakland, CA 94602
//home.earthlink.net/~lesjames/index.htm

Red Meat

Razor & Tie

214 Sullivan St., Ste. 4A
New York, NY 10012
800-633-9577
//www.razorandtie.com
info@razorandtie.com

Fred Eaglesmith; Dave Alvin & Billy Joe
Shaver reissues; Buddy Emmons anthology

Rebel

P. O. Box 3057
Roanoke, VA 24015
//www.rebelrecords.com

Country Gentlemen; Richard Greene; Bluegrass

Record Cellar

367 Trevor Ln.
Bala Cynwyd, PA 19004
karg@pobox.upenn.edu

The Rolling Hayseeds

Red House

P. O. Box 4044
St. Paul, MN 55104
800-695-4687
//www.redhouserecords.com

Greg Brown; Northern Lights; J.J. Reneaux

Redshirt

P. O. Box 300113
Minneapolis, MN 55403
//www2.bitstream.net/~billys/
billys@bitstream.net

The Billy's

Relapse

P. O. Box 611
Plymouth, MI 48170
//www.relapse.com

The Volebeats

Relix

P. O. Box 92
Brooklyn, NY 11229
718-258-0009
//www.relix.com/records/
Relixrec@aol.com

Commander Cody; The Flying Burrito
Brothers; The New Riders of the Purple Sage

Reptile

P. O. Box 121213
Nashville, TN 37212
reptile@chelseamusic.com

Jerry Dale McFadden

Restless/Twin Tone/Medium Cool

1616 Vista Del Mar Ave.
Hollywood, CA 90028
800-573-7853
//www.restless.com

The Shivers; The Carpetbaggers; The Dashboard Saviors; The Jayhawks

Rhino

10635 Santa Monica Blvd.
Los Angeles, CA 90025-4900
310-474-4778
//www.rhino.com

Beausoleil; Commemorativo; Hillbilly
Fever compilations

Road Goes on Forever

P. O. Box 12
Barnet
Herts
EN4 8PT

United Kingdom
//www.rgfrecords.demon.co.uk/
info@rgfrecords.demon.co.uk
Roxy Gordon; Wes McGhee

Roadhouse

P. O. Box 2257 Postterminalen
N-3103 Tonsberg
Norway
+47 33 31 18 80
roadrec@online.no

Norwegian acts.

Roadrunner

536 Broadway, 4th Floor
New York, NY 10012
//www.roadrun.com

Blue Mountain

Round Tower

48 Downside Heights
Skerries, County Dublin
Ireland
//www.roundtower.com
ronan@roundtower.com

Tom Pacheco

Rounder

1 Camp St.
Cambridge, MA 02140
617-354-0700
//www.rounder.com

Bruce Daigrepont; The Dry Branch Fire Squad; Rosie Flores; Skip Gorman; The Freight Hoppers; James Intveld; Steve Riley; Wylie & The Wild West Show; Eva Ybarra

Rubber

P. O. Box 32
Hawksburn 3142
441 Spencer St.
West Melbourne 3003
Australia
info@rubberrecords.com.au

Sherry Rich

Ruby

P. O. Box 267843
Chicago, IL 60626
riptones@mc.net

The Riptones

Run Wild

c/o Mike Lynam
P. O. Box 123
Lebanon, NJ 08833
908-534-8694
//members.aol.com/BluTwang/index.html
BluTwang@aol.com
mike@blast.net

The Wanktones; Big D.C. Jamboree Vols. 1-3; Blastered: A Musical Tribute to the Blasters

Rykodisc

Pickering Wharf, Bldg. C
Salem, MA 01970
800-232-7385
//www.rykodisc.com

Golden Smog; Martin Zellar

Saddle Creek

P. O. Box 8554
Omaha, NE 68108-0554
//members.aol.com/creekrec/
CreekRec@aol.com

Lullaby for the Working Class

Safehouse

P. O. Box 5349
W. Lebanon, NH 03874
//the webslinger.com/safehouse.com
safehouse@k2nesoft.com

Bodeco; Wink O'Bannon; Southern Culture on the Skids; The Volebeats

Secretly Canadian

1703 North Maple St.
Bloomington, IN 47404
//php.indiana.edu/~bjswanso/sc.html
erweddle@indiana.edu

Songs: Ohia

Shanachie

37 E. Clinton St.
Newton, NJ 07860
201-579-7763
//www.shanachie.com

Norman Blake; Don Edwards; Deep in the Heart of Texas; Kevin Gordon; Seconds Flat; Uprooted

Sierra

P. O. Box 5853
Pasadena, CA 91117-0853
626-355-4065 (fax)
//sierra-records.com/
sierra1@jps.net

Doug Dillard; Richard Greene; Muleskinner; Gene Parsons; Gram Parsons (records and Sid Griffin biography); The Flying Burrito Brothers; Clarence White

Signature Sounds

P. O. Box 106
Whately, MA 01093
800-694-5354
//www.signature-sounds.com
info@signature-sounds.com

Salamander Crossing

Sin Citizen

23005 Warner
Farmington, MI 48336
//www.sincitizenmusic.com

Steve Bice

Sire

936 Broadway
New York, NY 10010-2034

Jolene; Parlor James

Slow River

Shetland Park, 27 Congress St.
Salem, MA 01970
888-2-Earful
//www.slowriver.com/slowriver/
earful@rykodisc.com

Charlie Chesterman; Grace Braun; Tom Leach; Sparklehorse

Smithsonian/Folkways

Ctr. for Folklife Programs & Cultural Studies
955 L'Enfant Plaza, Suite 2600
Smithsonian Institution
Washington, DC 20560
202-287-3657
//www.si.gi.sgi.com/products/folkway/start.htm

The New Lost City Ramblers; The Harry Smith Connection; River of Song

Snowplow

309 11th Street, C-1
Union City, NJ 07087

Eddy Lawrence

Sonet

PJP
Boks 163
5051 Nesstun
Norway

Somebody's Darling

Soul Dump

P. O. Box 667
Athens, GA 30603
706-549-5808
//www.drivebytruckers.com
drivebytruckers@hotmail.com

Drive By Truckers

Sound Asleep

c/o Jerker Emanuelson
Storgatan 1
534 31 Vara, Sweden
jerker.emanuelson@mailbox.swipnet.se

Tim Carroll; Hit the Hay and Fireworks compilations

Spatula Ranch

P. O. Box 123
Hoboken, NJ 07030
//www.hudsonet.com/~undertow/ghostrockets/
PigProd@aol.com or budrocket@juno.com

The Ghost Rockets

Square Bird

P. O. Box 160011
Austin, TX 78716
rab@io.com

//www.rockabillyhall.com/MartiBrom.html

Marti Brom; The Ridgetop Westernaires (Wayne Hancock)

Stockade

P. O. Box 946
Georgetown, TX 78620
512-930-9032
Stkerec@aol.com

Roy Heinrich; The Edge of Country compilation

Stony Plain

P. O. Box 861
Edmonton
Alberta, Canada
T5J 2L8
//www.axionet.com/stonyplain/

Cindy Church; The (Canadian) Grievous Angels; Jr. Gone Wild

Strawdog

P. O. Box 26584
Los Angeles, CA 90026
213-662-5730
//members.aol.com/strawdogrx/
NeilMooney@aol.com

Neil Mooney; L.A. County Line: A Country Compilation

SubPop

P. O. Box 20645
Seattle, WA 98102
800-SUBPOP1
//www.subpop.com
press@subpop.com

Mike Ireland & Holler; The Scud Mountain Boys; The Supersuckers; The Walkabouts

Sugar Free

P. O. Box 14166
Chicago, IL 60614
312-528-7080
//www.sugarfreerecords.com
info@sugarfreerecords.com

Birddog; Chris Mills; Skull Orchard

Sugar Hill

P. O. Box 55300
Durham, NC 27717-5300
800-996-4455
//www.sugarhillrecords.com

Bad Livers; The Brother Boys; Guy Clark; Walter Hyatt; James McMurtry

Sunjay

Box 139
52422 Herrljunga
Sweden
+46/0513-12345
+46/0513-12510 (fax)
//www.sunjay.se
sunjay@sunjay.se

Ronnie Mack

Swallow

Drawer 10
Ville Platte, LA 70586

Steve Riley; Cajun

Sympathy for the Record Industry

4450 California Pl., #303
Long Beach, CA 90807
310-989-9387
www.cpedu.rug.nl/~evert/label/st/sftri.htm
Sympathy13@aol.com

The Cowslingers; The Geraldine Fibbers; Southern Culture on the Skids

Tangible Music

P.O. Box 340
Merrick, NY 11566-0340
888-800-8228
//www.tangible-music.com
info@tangible-music.com

Peter Stone Brown; Ed Pettersen; Andy Scheinman

Tar Hut

P. O. Box 441940
Somerville, MA 02144
617-776-5106
//www.tarhut.com
info@tarhut.com

Angry Johnny & The Killbillies; The Ex-Husbands; The Lonesome Brothers

Temple Bar

2118 Wilshire Blvd., #405
Los Angeles, CA 90403
//interchem.chem.strath.ac.uk/pd/Tbar.htm

The Coal Porters

Tex-Tex Music

1116 Terjo
Austin, TX 78732

Live at Henry's and The Last Honky Tonk compilation cassettes

Texas Hotel

P. O. Box 72449
Davis, CA 95617

Vic Chesnutt

Texas Jamboree

P. O. Box 161405
Austin, TX 78716
512-263-4178
//home.earthlink.net/~texjamboree/
sheriff@texas.net

The Horton Brothers

Third Gear

P. O. Box 1886
Royal Oak, MI 48068
//www.thirdgear.com
info@thirdgear.com

The Volebeats

Thrill Jockey

P. O. Box 476794
Chicago, IL 60647
traverse@mcs.net

Freakwater

Too Many Dogs

1203 East Capitol St., S.E.
Washington, D.C. 20003
800-893-7254
diana@muddypaws.com

Honky Tonk Confidential; Greetings From the District of Country

Trailer

P. O. Box 3202
Iowa City, IA 52240
319-351-3683
//www.trailer-records.com
trailer@avalon.net

High and Lonesome; Tom Jessen; Bo Ramsey

Triple X

P. O. Box 862529, Dept. BSN
Los Angeles, CA 90086-2529
//www.triple-x.com
xxx@triple-x.com

Billy Bacon & the Forbidden Pigs; Mojo Nixon

Truckstop

P. O. Box 578266
Chicago, IL 60057-8266

Pinetop Seven

Tumult

P. O. Box 642371
San Francisco, CA 94164-2371
tumult666@hotmail.com
aminor@dnai.com

Souled American (1st four recordings)

Ubik

P. O. Box 4771
Albuquerque, NM 87196
//www.nmia.com/~jmar/ubik.html
ubik@nmia.com

Bayou Seco

Undercover, Inc.

P. O. Box 14561
Portland. OR 97293
503-230-7728
//www.mnkyshine.com
Mnkyshine@aol.com

Bingo; Used To Be compilation

Upstart

1 Camp Street
Cambridge, MA 02140
//www.rounder.com/upstart/
upstart@rounder.com
617-661-6308

Ronnie Dawson; Jim Lauderdale; Rig Rock Deluxe compilation; The Vidalias

Vanguard

1299 Ocean Ave., Ste.800
Santa Monica, CA 90401
800-59-SONGS
//vanguardrecords.com
info@vanguardrecords.com

Alison Brown; The Dillards; John McEuen;
Ian Tyson

Vapor

2644 30th St.
Santa Monica, CA 90405
//www.vaporrecords.com
webstar@vaporrecords.com

Acetone

Vinyl Japan UK

98 Camden Rd.
London NW1 9EA
England
//www.vinyljapan.demon.co.uk/
info@vinyljapan.demon.co.uk

Marshall & The Shooting Stars; The Rimshots

Vinyl Junkie

//www.ftech.co.uk/~vinyl-j

Country, Cowpunks, Jukebox Cowboy, Loose
compilations

Virgin

338 N. Foothill Rd.
Beverly Hills, CA 90210
//www.virginrecords.com

The Geraldine Fibbers

Walt Records

341 Lafayette St., #585
New York, NY 10012

Trailer Bride

Warner/Reprise

20 Music Sq. East
Nashville, TN 37203
615-748-8000
//www.wbr.com

Tish Hinojosa; Los Lobos; Son Volt;
Tarnation; Wilco; Dwight Yoakam; Neil
Young

Warner Western

800-760-9965
//www.wbr.com/nashville/warnerwestern/

Don Edwards; Bill & Bonnie Hearne;
Ranger Doug

Watermelon/Sire

P. O. Box 49056
Austin, TX 78765
512-472-6192

The Derailers; Katy Moffatt; Threadgill's
Supper Sessions; Don Walser; Monty
Warden; Austin Country Nights compilation

Western Beat (California)

1738 Bay View Dr.
Hermosa Beach, CA 90254

Will Ray

Western Beat (Tennessee)

P. O. Box 128105
Nashville, TN 37212
615-383-5466
//www.westernbeat.com
westernbeat@home.net

Billy Block

Wheeling

c/o Bill Booth
Fredensborgvn.22
0177 Oslo
Norway
//www.nordi.no/music/wheeling/index.htmlb
bilbooth@riksnett.no

Bill Booth & The Convertibles; Trond Granlund

Whirling House

P. O. Box 7622
Arlington, VA 22207

The Grandsons (of the Pioneers)

Wormco

P. O. Box 266
Northampton, MA 01061
413-586-6657
wormco@javanet.com

Ray Mason

Wormtone

3339 W. Moncrieff Pl.
Denver, CO 80211

The Dalhart Imperials

WR

P. O. Box 248
Hunt, TX 78024
830-238-4612
//wr-records.com/tophands.htm

Tom Morrell

Yep Roc

P. O. Box 4821
Chapel Hill, NC 27515-4821
919-929-7648
//www.yeproc.com
Redeye202@aol.com

Mercury Dime; Two Dollar Pistols; Revival
compilations

MAIL ORDER

Ace Records

Traditional Cajun; Takoma; Vanguard

Bus Stop Mail Order
46-50 Steele Rd.
London NW10 7AS
England
//www.acerecords.co.uk/
info@AceRecords.co.uk

Blackmail/Demon

Country, Cajun, Rockabilly 1960s-1990s

Freepost (TK974)
P. O. Box 9
Brentford, Middlesex
TW8 8BR
England
//www.blackmail.co.uk/
support@blackmail.demon.co.uk

BlueGrassRoots Music

Humongous online catalog of bluegrass and
old-time from around the world from Jaanus
Vainu of Estonia!

//bgr.ee/
Bgr@bgr.ee

Bruce the Cat

Often have the latest in hard-to-find imports
by the likes of the Byrds, Bob Dylan, Steve
Earle, Emmylou Harris, Gram Parsons, and
more.

23 Cumberland Dr.
Yonkers, NY 10704
//www.brucethecat.com

Camsco

"The best in traditional music by mail."
//www.camsco.com

Columbarium

Rockabilly, roots, singer/songwriter.
//www.columbariumrecords.com/home.htm

Country Rock Specialisten

Well-stocked Swedish mail order house for a
variety of alternative country.

Box 4171
400 40 Goteberg
031-24 03 31
//www.algonet.se/~c_r_s/omoss.html

County

One of the best for bluegrass and old-time
(traditional/modern).

P. O. Box 191
Floyd, VA 24091
540-745-2001
//www.countysales.com
bhurd@rev.net

Derailed

"For alternative trains of thought"; specializing in "undiscovered, underrated, & hard-to-find artists.".

4108 Highland Ave., Suite 130
Manhattan Beach, CA 90266
//www.primenet.com/~rthomas/
rthomas@primenet.com

Elderly Instruments

Huge catalog offering traditional and contemporary Americana and music from around the world; they also have a large stock of instruments, instruction, books, and videos.

1100 N. Washington
P. O. Box 14249
Lansing, MI 48901
517-372-7890
//www.elderly.com
web@elderly.com

Flipsville

Rockabilly, rock 'n' roll, surf, blues, punk, garage from the co-organizers of the Viva Las Vegas Rockabilly weekender.

46 Inverness St.
Camden Town
London
NW1 7HB
+44 171 267 4682
//www.flipsville.com

Floyd's Record Store

Cajun, zydeco, swamp from Louisiana's oldest record store.

P. O. Drawer 10
434 East Main
Vine Platte, LA 70586
800-738-8668

FoF Music By Mail

Source for Australian music

P. O. Box 321
Alexandria, NSW
2015
Australia
fofmbm@geko.com.au

Frontiers

"The best selection of Americana, bluegrass, contemporary folk, blues, all kinds of country, rockabilly, cowboy, newgrass, Cajun, hillbilly, jazz, old-timey, Hawaiian, Tex-Mex and more"

888-863-8335 (toll free)
//www.frontiersmusic.com
frontier@goldrush.com

Gocattin'

'Billy Mail Order including rockabilly, hillbilly, psychobilly CDs

P. O. Box 123
Yellow Springs, WV 26865
304-874-3752

Good as Any...Better 'n Some

"The world's mom & pop record store" specializing in underground music including lots of alternative country artists

P. O. Box 220
Willoughby, OH 44096
GoodAsAny@lightstream.net

Hepcat

Rockabilly, swing, r&b, jump blues, country, psychobilly, jump jive, Western swing, hillbilly.

P. O. Box 1108
Orange, CA 92856
800-404-4117
714-532-2095
714-532-1474 (fax)
//www.hepcat.com/records/
HepCatReco@aol.com

Hillbilly Records

CD store run by Larry Roose and Rich Allen that is based in Grand Rapids, Michigan but has a mobile unit that travels to festivals and other musical events. They have a wide variety of alt. country including lots of independent and unsigned acts.

1813 Turner N.W.
Grand Rapids, MI 49504
616-361-0934

Indie Ocean

Best of the independent labels in roots rock and alternative country.

//www.ishops.com/ocean/

June Appal

Specialists in traditional and contemporary Appalachian music plus bluegrass, old-time, and blues; part of the Appalshop organization.

//www.uky.edu/projects/appal/junappal/jun
appal.htm

La Louisianne

Big selection of traditional and contemporary Cajun.

P. O. Box 52131
Lafayette, LA 70505
//cust.imaerica.net/laloumus/
laloumus@iamerica.net

Local Flavor

Great place to get hard-to-find recordings by Texas, independent, and small label artists especially from the Austin area.

305B East 5th St.
Austin, TX 78701
512-472-7773
//austinmetro.com/localflav.html
localflavor@austinmetro.com

Mental Disorder

What else? Psychobilly!!

c/o Marcus Coenen
Friedrich-Ebert-Str. 127

41236 Monchengladbach
Germany

Miles of Music

The alternative country/Americana catalog.

c/o Jeff Weiss
20929-47 Ventura Blvd., Suite 286
Woodland Hills, CA 91364
888-766-8742 (toll free U.S.)
818-883-9975; 818-992-8302 (fax)
//www.milesofmusic.com
MilesOMusc@aol.com

Nervous Records

"The future of Rock 'n' Roll!"; large assortment of American and Euro-Billy including Fury Records.

7-11 Minerva Rd.
London
NW10 6HJ
England
//www.nervous.co.uk/ (has lots of links to 'zines, radio, bands, etc.)

Oakhill Music

Specializing in hard to find material with a large alt. country/Americana inventory including recordings (CDs, CS, LPs, 8 trk.), videos, books, 'zines, collectibles.

P. O. Box 55832
Little Rock, AR 72215
501-312-1064
//www.oakhillmusic.com
oakmusic@flash.net
Oakhillcd@aol.com

Pinecastle/Webco

Big bluegrass catalog.

Dept. SO
5108 S. Orange Ave.
Orlando, Fl. 32809
800-473-7773 (catalog)
//pinecastle.com

Plato Records

Large array of alt. country/Americana from around the world.

Schoolstraat 22
2511 AX Den Haag
The Netherlands
(070) 365 1451
//mars.plato.nl
orders@plato.nl

Raucous Records

Vintage and modern rockabilly, swing, hillbilly bop.

Shakespeare House, 37-39
Shakespeare St.
Southport, Merseyside
PR8 5AB
England
//www.foobar.co.uk/dialin/hamm/rst.html
rauc@globalnet.co.uk

Redeye Distribution

Carrying Cigar Store Indians, Drive By Truckers, Greta Lee, Poor Little Fools, and other Southeastern, U.S. area roots/Americana.

P. O. Box 4821
Chapel Hill, NC 27515-4821
919-929-7648; 919-942-7224 (fax)
info@redeyeusa.com

Rockhouse Records Music Mail Express

Huge catalog of country, neo-rockabilly, psychobilly, etc.

Nieuwveensweg 23
2421 LA
Nieuwhoop
Holland
//www.musicmailexpress.com
(on-line catalog search; lots of links)
rockhous@cistron.nl

Roots & Rhythm

A variety of vintage and contemporary Americana and roots since 1974

P. O. Box 2216
San Leandro, CA 94577
888-ROOTS-66
//www.bluesworld.com/roots.html
roots@hooked.net

Roots Music (Sunderland)

Recordings, videos, books, mags for all types of country (new, old, alt.) including bluegrass, old-time, and other roots music.

RootsMusic@dial.pipex.com

Rounder

Includes Flying Fish, Philo, Bohemia Beat, Upstart labels

1 Camp St.
Cambridge, MA 02140
//www.rounder.com

Swamp: Cajun & Zydeco Trading Post

Cajun/zydeco from the U.S. and UK.

P. O. Box 94
Derby DE22 1XA
England
//www.netlink.co.uk/users/direct/swamp/tradpost.htm
john@swampcaj.demon.co.uk

Texas Music Catalog

Compiled by Waterloo Records, it lists their huge stock of Texas artists past and present.

600-A North Lamar
Austin, TX 78703
512-474-2500
(Fax) 512-474-2522
//www.eden.com/~waterloo/texas_music.html

The Texas Music Round-Up

Part of Lazy SOB and Freedom Records, and they mean it when they say "bringing you the finest in Independent Texas Music."

P. O. Box 49884
Austin, TX 78765-9884
512-480-0765; (fax) 512-499-0207
//www.eden.com/~freedom/roundup.html
LazySOB1@aol.com

Time Warp Records

Specializing in vintage vinyl including 1960s-1970s country rock.

P. O. Box 5296
Petaluma, CA 94955-5296
707-766-9757 (ph/fax)
//www.vintage.com/record/
mallstaff@vintage.com

Turnipseed Music: WWW Resource for New Orleans Music

All types of southern Louisiana music.

//www.turnipseed.com/record.html
turnip@turnipseed.com

Twin City Digital

DAT masters of live performances by the Jayhawks, Uncle Tupelo, Son Volt, Wilco.

Dept. 1, 4215 Winnetka Ave. N #195
Minneapolis, MN 55428

Village Records

"The best selection of folk music, Americana, country, roots rock, and reissues."

12156 W. 63 St.
Shawnee Mission, KS 66216
800-327-5264 (U.S. & Canada)
913-631-4199
(fax) 913-631-6369
//villagerecords.com
info@villagerecords.com

Wax Trax

"The best selection of rockabilly anywhere."

638 E. 13th Ave.
Denver, CO 80203
800-484-4165, sec. code 1358 (free catalog)

GENERAL ALTERNATIVE COUNTRY & AMERICANA

{Alternative country magazines; Americana and general roots music publications with frequent alt. country coverage; music and other periodicals with regular alt. country columns, articles, and/or reviews. Most print publications with web sites have online archives and independent weeklies are archived at:

Weekly Wire (//weeklywire.com)
DesertNet (//desert.net)
CLN: Newstand (//www.cln.com/newstand/)

@Country

Part of the Music Boulevard home page; under "Newstand," it has monthly alternative country reviews (by Ed Hewitt) from September 1995-Present.

//www.musicblvd.com/@country
alt.country@musicblvd.com

3rd Coast Music (formerly Music City Texas)

Insightful and informative commentary, articles, and reviews on Texas and all kinds of American roots music by the irascible, inimitable John Conquest; maintains the 3rd Coast Accordion Network.

John Conquest, ed.
620 Circle Ave.
Round Rock, TX 78664
512-218-8055 (& fax)
//www.3rdCoastMusic.RealCountry.net
ThirdCM@aol.com

9 Times

Online publication of Plan 9 Music Store (Virginia) with frequent articles on and reviews of alt. country and Americana musicians and events, 1994-Present; also has a monthly concert calendar (print copy available at Plan 9 stores).

2614 West Cary St.
Richmond, VA 23220
804-353-2627
(Fax) 804-355-0893
//www.plan9music.com/ninetimes.html
9times@plan9music.com

Addicted to Noise

Online 'zine with regular, high quality alt. country features and reviews.

//www.addict.com/atn/

American Music

The Blasters Newsletter and more.

c/o Billy Davis
80-16 64th Lane
Glendale, NY 11385
The Blasters Home Page
//bullwinkle.as.utexas.edu/scott/blasters.html
sjk@bullwinkle.as.utexas.edu

Amplifier

Covers the Pop spectrum with print/online features, columns, and reviews. "Root Beer" column looks at "The Best in 'Roots' Pop" i.e. alt. country.

5 Calista Terrace
Westford, MA 01886
//www.twomp.com/amplifier/
amplifier@twomp.com

Austin-American Statesman

Regular coverage of local and national alt. country/Americana especially in Thursday's "XLent" section which also has weekly club listings.

P. O. Box 670
Austin, TX 78767
512-445-3500
//www.austin360.com

The Austin Chronicle

Music section frequently has articles on and reviews of local and national alt. country plus Austin Musicians Register and links to Texas music, SXSW, etc.

P. O. Box 49066
Austin, TX 78765
//www.auschron.com
512-454-5766
mail@auschron.com

Beat Magazine

Norwegian roots magazine that often includes American and European alt. country material.

Rostedsgaten
12-C
N-0178
Oslo 1
Norway

Blue Juice

Roots/Rock

14 Spencer Ave.
Earlsdon, Coventry
CV5 6NP
UK

Blue Suede News

ALL American roots styles: one of the best with articles on pioneer and contemporary artists and lots of reviews.

Marc Bristol, ed.
P. O. Box 25E
Duvall, WA 98109
206-788-2776
//www.bluesuedenews.com

or

//members.aol.com/shakinboss/index.html
ShakinBoss@aol.com

Bucketfull of Brains

Rock & roll, pop, psych, garage, punk, r&b, country, folk.

P. O. Box 11301
London
WC1H 8HF
England
//www.users.dircon.co.uk/~spacedog/bobindex.htm

Buscadero

Italian roots magazine with lots of articles on and reviews of alt. country performers.

//www.logic.it/busca2.htm

The Chicago Reader

Insurgent and other types of alt. country get plenty of attention in this independent weekly through features, reviews, and weekly club listings.

//www.chireader.com

Cornfed

Modest 'zine (looks like the old Farmer's Almanacs) with entertaining alt. country features and reviews interspersed with humorous articles and ads.; on vacation in 1999.

Susan M. Clarke, ed.
P. O. Box 220135
Brooklyn, NY 11222
718-349-3398 (fax)

Cosmic Americana Music News

Part of The Gram Parsons Foundation, it publishes anything & everything related to Gram Parsons.

3109 Ola Ave.
Tampa, FL 33603
813-221-0596 or
The Gram Parsons Home Page
//www.primenet.com/~klugl/gramhome.html

Country.Com

Mostly HNC but under "Music News" there's a bi-weekly alt. country column called "Here's the Twang" (by Michael Gray) and another called "Bluegrass Breakdown."

//www.country.com

Country Gazette

Dutch roots music magazine specializing in HNC, hillbilly, country-rock, Tex-Mex, folk, bluegrass, rock 'n' roll, Cajun, and more. One of its regular columns is "Border Affairs" by the very knowledgeable Paul Jonker who focuses on the best in Third Coast Music from Austin and Louisiana. All in Dutch but you can correspond with Jonker in English via snail or e-mail.

Hans & Janny van Dam, eds.
Zwanenwater 25
NL-2771 KL Boskoop
The Netherlands
0172-214775; 0172-230577 (fax)

Paul Jonker
Toscaninstraat 34
2551 LX Den Haag
The Netherlands
31 70 3252695
gertjonker@wxs.nl

The Country Music Gazette

"The Ultimate Country Music Newspaper," it covers all varieties.

//www.homeusers.breathe.co.uk/jdenterprises/gazette.html
jdenterprises@breathe.co.uk

Country Music International

Glossy fanzine covering new & alt. country.

Link House Magazine Ltd.
Link House
9 Dingwell Ave., Croydon
Surrey CR9 2TA
England

Country Music Magazine

Huge distribution; covers all kinds of country.

329 Riverside Ave.
Westport, CT 06880
203-221-4950

Country Music People

"The world of country music" including new country, honky tonk, roots, traditional, acoustic, country-rock, old-time, bluegrass, rockabilly.

225A Lewisham Way
London SE4 1UY
England
//www.musicfarm.demon.co.uk/frmain.htm

Country Standard Time

A-1 publication with in depth articles and reviews on lots of alt. country in both print and online versions.

Jeffrey B. Remz, ed.

54 Ballard St.
Newton Centre, MA 02159-1251
617-969-0331
//www.countrystandardtime.com
Countryst@aol.com

Creative Loafing

Weekly independent covering Atlanta often has articles/reviews of the Redneck Underground plus local "Musician's Guide" and calendar.

//www.creativeloafing.com

Cringe

Covers Columbus, Ohio, music scene; includes music directory with info/links to area alt. country bands; sponsors the Cringe Community Music Fest.

133 W. 6th Ave.
Columbus, OH 43201
//www.cringe.com

Crossroads

"The folk, roots and world music resource for radio, retail, labels, and artists"; regular columns focus on bluegrass, Cajun, and other roots. In mid-1999, they began distributing the *Crossroads Music Industry Directory*, "the most comprehensive collection of music industry contacts for acoustic, folk, roots, and world music ever assembled."

P. O. Box 41491
Tucson, AZ 85717-1491
520-792-9891
//www.xrm.com
crossroads@theriver.com

Dallas Morning News

Thor Christensen and Mario Tarradell do regular, in-depth pieces on local and national alt. country.

//www.dallasnews.com

Dallas Observer

Independent weekly with frequent coverage of Big D's thriving alt. country scene.

//www.dallasobserver.com

Detour: Country, Folk, and Blues Magazine

A British version of Dirty Linen focusing on American roots music.

3 Lockwood Street
Driffield, N. Humberside
YO25 7RU
England

Dirty Linen

One of the best overall roots magazines covering all types with articles, reviews, and more; each issue has an extensive calendar of concerts and festivals.

Paul Hartman, ed.
P. O. Box 66600
Baltimore, MD 21239-66600
410-583-7973

//www.dirtynelson.com/linen/dirty.html
editor@dirtylinen.com

Down Home & Far Away

Syndicated monthly online American roots music column by Lansing, Michigan, journalist Brian Libbey.

/www.angelfire.com/pgl/twang/downhome.html
libbey@pilot.msu.edu

Exclaim (!*@#)

Alternative music magazine with alt. country reviews under its "Honky Tonkin'" section.

7-B Pleasant Blvd., Unit #966
Toronto, Ontario
M4T 1K2
Canada
416-535-9735
//www.shmooze.net/pwcasual/zines/exclaim/nfindex.htm

Express Magazine

Edited by DJ Doug Sherrard who hosts "Twang!," an alt. country show on WEGL in Auburn, Alabama; has frequent alt. country related material and a live music guide.

P. O. Box 2086
Auburn, AL 36831-2086
334-826-1559
//www.expressmagazine.com
editor@expressmagazine.com

Fast Folk Musical Magazine

Formerly *The Coop*, it is part of the Fast Folk Cafe and devoted to the new breed in singer/songwriters; each issue comes with a CD.

P. O. Box 938, Village Station
New York, NY 10014
//www.users.interport.net
stevena@teleport.com

Fatea

Roots & rock from the 1960s through the present.

372a Wallisdown Rd.
Bournemouth, Dorset
BH11 8PS
UK
//www.paragon.co.uk/junkkulture/

The Feedlot: The Journal of Real Country Music

Early alt. country 'zine published by Lee Nichols in late 1993 & early 1994; only made it through three issues but was important in spreading the word about alt. country and honing the writing skills of one its leading authorities.

Lee Nichols lnichols@auschron.com

Flagpole

Covers the Athens, Georgia, scene with events calendar and music directory too; frequent alt. country e.g. Redneck Underground coverage.

P. O. Box 1027
Athens, GA 30603
706-549-9523
//www.flagpole.com

Folk & Acoustic Music Exchange

Project of the Peterborough Folk Music Society that presents hundreds of reviews of folk & acoustic music including many alt. country performers.

//www.acousticmusic.com/fame/famehome.htm

Folk Roots

"The world's leading roots, folk, and world music magazine"; articles, reviews, and concert calendar.

Southern Rag, Ltd.
P. O. Box 337
London
N4 1TW
England
//www.froots.demon.co.uk/
Froots@froots.demon.co.uk

Folker!—Das Musikmagazin

In German and covering all kinds of roots music (bluegrass, Cajun, singer/songwriter, etc.) through articles, interviews, and reviews.

//members.aol.com/folkerwww/

Gavin Americana

Clearinghouse for Gavin Americana radio stations with Americana/alt. country articles, news, charts, links, etc.

//www.gavin.com

Gnashville Quarterly

Online newsletter by Vinyl Junkie which has produced an outstanding series of alt. country/Americana compilations (**Country Cowpunks, Jukebox Cowboy, Loose**). GQ provides brief notes on alt. country bands and doings in the UK.

//www.ftech.net/~vinyl-j/news.htm

Graham Weekly Album Review

George Graham has hosted "Mixed Bag" on WVIA in Pittston, PA, since 1973. Part of the show is devoted to in depth music reviews, and over the years, Graham has done thousands of Americana including many alt. country. His on air reviews are archived at his web site.

//www.scranton.com/~graham/

Grindstone

"The best in roots rockabilly alternative"

11288 Ventura Blvd. #450
Studio City, CA 91604

818-509-1957
//members.aol.com/grind55/
Grind55@aol.com

Happenstance

A British version of No Depression magazine but with a more jocular format and style; each issue offers fine features on and many, mini-reviews of alt. country/Americana worldwide.

Dave Henderson, ed.
Cooks House
Knowle, Pewsey
SN9 5JH
Wiltshire
England
dave.henderson@ecm.emap.com

Hearsay Magazine

"A forum for informed discussion of edgy, left-field songwriting talent, primarily from the Americas and Australasia" including many alt. country style s/s.

P. O. Box 11262
London
SW5 9ZQ
United Kingdom
//www.hearsaymagazine.demon.co.uk/
hq@hearsaymagazine.demon.co.uk

The Hillbilly Researcher

Scholarly type journal on the history of traditional country music.

c/o Al Turner & Philip J. Tucker, eds.
20 Silkstream Rd.
Burnt Oak, Edgware
Middlesex
HA8 0DA
England

Hogtown News

Extensive alt. country/Americana coverage for Europe and the U.S.

Melsbroek
Belgium

Jelly Music Magazine

"The Real Music Newsletter: Mostly All-American Blues Funk Jazz Country Soul Rock 'n' Roll"; published by a collective of local fans, it has lots of articles and reviews.

Glen Brooks, ed.
P. O. Box 24924
Seattle, WA 98124-0924
//www.jellyroll.com/
editor@jellyroll.com

Jem Online

Japanese fanzine by Mutsuo Watanabe about guitar pop and neo-roots rock which is his term for alternative country. Lots of reviews of everyone from Blue Mountain and the Bottlerockets to Whiskeytown and Wilco plus links to various related sites. Alas, all in Japanese except index titles and discography.

//www.asahi-net.or.jp/~aw5m-wtnb/

pxp06050@niftyserve.or.jp

The Journal of Country Music

Long running, glossy publication with excellent articles and interviews on vintage, new, and alternative country.

Paul Kingsbury, ed.
4 Music Square East
Nashville, TN 37203
615-256-1639
(fax) 615-255-2245

Leak CD-Magazine

"The Source for Contemporary Acoustic & Rock Music."

P. O. Box 131415
Birmingham, AL 35213
800-901-LEAK
//www.daenet.com/leak/

Lonesome Highway: The Broadsheet of Country Music and Americana

Features and reviews from Ireland's Round Tower Records.

14 Sir John Rogersons Quay
Dublin 2
Ireland
//www.roundtower.com/lonesome_highway/

Maybelle

Modest but informative alternative country 'zine that began publishing in the early 1990s.

735 Harrison St.
San Francisco, CA 94107

Mojo: The Music Magazine

Important British publication that in the late 1990s began to give lots of coverage to alternative country/Americana with full length features on Gram Parsons and "The New Roots Explosion: The Lonesome Trail From Hank Williams to Beck" plus Americana reviews and a section on "What's Happening in Americana."

mojo@ecm.emap.com

MoMZine

Alt. Country/Americana reviews, features, interviews, Jon Weisberger's "Bluegrass Breakdown" and more courtesy of Miles of Music mail order. Edited by Neal Weiss.

//www.milesofmusic.com/reviewmain.html
Milesomusc@aol.com

Music Matters Review

Quarterly print publication with articles, reviews, interviews on Americana and "Eclecticana."

P. O. Box 425
Smithtown, NY 11787
//www.mmreview.com
thefolks@mmreview.com

Music Monitor

General coverage of modern Americana with frequent reviews, interviews, and articles on alt. country performers.

107 E. Aycock St.
Raleigh, NC 27608
//www.penduluminc.com/mm/main.htm

Nash!: American Roots Music E-Magazine

"The Internet's 1st American Roots Music Magazine" with lots of articles, reviews, and links.

Paul Erwin, ed.
//www.nashmag.com/home.html
nashmag@aol.com

Nashville Scene

Music City independent weekly with regular features (by Bill Friskics-Warren; Michael McCall) on local alt. country.

//www.nashscene.com

Needle in a Haystack

Monthly cybercolumn published by Yvette Cadeaux 1995-1996 covering country, bluegrass, roots rock & more (still online).

P. O. Box 7495
Santa Cruz, CA 95061
//www.infopoint.com/pubs/needle/index.html

The New Rock 'n' Roll Calendar

Reviews, stories, news, performance lists for r 'n' r, rockabilly, hillbilly, bluegrass, Tex-Mex, Cajun.

Molstraat 7
3000 Leuven
Belgium or
c/o Mighty Sam Dams
j.v. Rijswijcklaan 247/4
2020 Antwerpen
Belgium
dekie@glo.be

No Depression

The first major alt. country publication, it grew out of the AOL No Depression/Alt. Country newsgroup. First published in a modest format with limited distribution in the Fall of 1995, it has grown dramatically into a widely circulated bi-monthly with articles on established performers, features on up-and-coming acts, live and recorded music reviews; the most recognized and cited alt. country publication.

Peter Blackstock; Grant Alden, eds.
P. O. Box 31332
Seattle, WA 98103
206-706-7342
//www.nodepression.net
NoDepress@aol.com

Peter Blackstock: Zeitgolf@aol.com

Grant Alden: Shocko@aol.com

Purr

Has column, "Pigshit" by Gary Pig Gold of the Ghost Rockets with frequent reviews of alt. country/Americana.

//www.purrmagazine.com

Red Hot Country Magazine

Mix of HNC and Alt. Country news, reviews, and features.

//redhotcountry.co.uk

Reverb On-Line

Insightful alt. country/Americana reviews ("Terrell's Tune-Up") by singer/songwriter and DJ Stephen Terrell (see his entry); his reviews are also available at:

//members.aol.com/bluespud/index.html
//www.reverb.com/

Rhythms on the Ether Magazine

"Australia's premier roots mag" featuring country, blues, Cajun/zydeco.

Keith Glass, ed.
P. O. Box 5060
Hughesdale, Melbourne
Victoria 3166, Australia
//www.aussiemusic.com.au/rhythms/rhyinfo.html
bwise@ozemail.com.au

Roadhouse Fever

American roots 'zine published by Chip Lamey who hosts a show by the same name on WLFR in Pomona, New Jersey

Chip Lamey, ed.
P. O. Box 54
Stone Harbour, NJ 08247
609-368-4051 (ph. & fax)

Rock-n-Reel

"The best in Folk & Roots & Rock & Blues & Beyond" (a British Dirty Linen)

Sean McGhee, ed.
8 Dent Place, Cleator Moor
Cumbria
CA25 5EE
UK
//www.phoenix.net.co.uk/rockreel/rnr.htm
phoenix@phoenix.co.uk

Rooted Magazine

Alt. Country, Americana, roots with the Lone Star State in mind.

//www.rooted.com

Rootin' Around

"A ragtag roots music review" by Kevin Roe for New York City's *Sound Views* with lots on alt. country and other Americana.

//www.rootinaround.com
Kevrave@aol.com

RootsTown Music Magazine

"Belgium's Leading American Roots Magazine"

Marc Nolis, ed.
Verbovenlei 79
B-2100
Deurne
Belgium
++32/(0)3-36602336
(fax) ++32/(0)3-321-8257
Roots.Town@glo.be

Rootsworld/Hollow Ear

"Online magazine of world music, roots, folk; the music made by people for people" edited by Cliff Furnald.

//www.rootsworld.com/rw/rw.html
cliff@rootsworld.com

Rural Route Twangzine

Jeff Wall's entertaining online mag full of articles, reviews, interviews, rants, raves, and lots of chuckles plus the "World Famous Buttload of Links."

//www.twangzine.com
whome@livenet.net

Saradon: Country & Western UK

E-zine with "news, reviews, and all things Country" including groups like the Okeh Wranglers and Tennese Rhythm Riders plus club, festival, and radio information.

Don Rudd, ed.
76 Wilton Rd., Handsworth
Birmingham B20 3SE
England
//users.powernet.co.uk/saradon/saradon.htm

Sing Out!

The longest running folk/roots quarterly with consistently fine articles, reviews, and more.

P. O. Box 5253
Bethlehem, PA 18015-0253
800-4-WE-SING
//www.singout.org
singout@libertynet.org

Southern & Rocking Music

International coverage of Southern roots, rock 'n' roll, rockabilly, hillbilly, swing with in depth articles on bands past and present plus reviews, music calendar, and scene reports from around the globe. In 1998, it moved from the UK to Finland and became part of a larger promotional organization of the same name (see "Alt. Country/Americana Web Pages" and "Promotion" sections).

Marc Fenech, ed.
PL 41
33721 Tampere
Finland
//www.sci.fi/~srmusic/
srmusic@sci.fi

Stomp and Stammer

Alternative 'zine with fairly generous coverage of alt. country.

//monsterbit.com/stammer/

Tales From L.A. County & Roots Music

Monthly update on the latest from the L.A. alt. country/roots scene for 1996 only by Jana Pendragon; articles still available online.

//www.diamondhard.com/mag/

Texas Jamboree

Rockabilly and honky tonk, past and present from Texas and beyond published by a real cool dude.

Jason Shields, ed.
P. O. Box 161405
Austin, TX 78716
512-263-4178; (fax) 512-477-9352
//home.earthlink.net/~texjamboree/
sheriff@texas.net

Texas Music News

Published by *Texas Monthly* magazine, it has news and reviews of all types of Texas music including alt. country by Jason Cohen, John Morthland, and Jordan Mackay.

//www.texasmonthly.com/events/texmus/

Texas Tears: La Fanzine di Musica Rock di Blue

Italian e-zine covering American roots rock through articles, interviews, reviews. Edited by Blue Bottazzi.

//www.agonet.it/texas/tears.htm
rock@agonet.it

Tower of Babel

Online international journal of arts and ideas which in early 1999 began running a column, "The Dragon's Roar," by long-time West Coast Americana historian and journalist, Jana Pendragon. In addition to lots of features on California honky tonk past and present it also covered bluegrass, cowboy, Western swing, and many other types of American roots music.

//www.towerofbabel.com/selections/music/honkytonk/dragonsroar/

Twangin'

Pioneering, highly influential alternative country publication started in 1993 by the irrepressible Cheryl Cline.

Cheryl Cline, editrix.
2230 Huron Dr.
Concord, CA 94519
510-687-6404
//www.steamiron.com
twangin@steamiron.com
Online version has "Twangin's Who's Who," an ever-growing directory of alt. country artists and lots of links to alt. country resources, "Country Grrl," a sub-site to promote women in country, especially alt. country performers, through articles, pro-

files, reviews, etc., and "Pay Day: Working Class Life & Art."

Uncut

British equivalent to *Spin* that like *Mojo* extended its coverage of alternative country in 1998 culminating in September issue devoted to "Sounds of the New West: The Best of Alternative Country" (with CD) including a 10 page guide called "How the West Was Won: Everything You Need to Know About Alternative Country."

//www.uncut.net/index.html

Uno Mas

A variety of music including alternative country through articles and reviews

P. O. Box 1832
Silver Spring, MD 20915
//www.unomas.com/
Unomasmag@aol.com

Western Beat Monthly

Part of Billy Block's Western Beat Entertainment (Nashville) which includes the Western Beat Roots Revival and Western Beat radio show.

Billy Block, ed.
P. O. Box 128105
Nashville, TN 37212
615-383-5466; (fax) 615-383-6331
//www.westernbeat.com
westernbeat@home.net

Y'ALL: The Webzine of the South

Has alt. country music features on artists from below the Mason-Dixon like Hasil Adkins, Blue Mountain, Six String Drag, et al. Their motto: "We Cover the South Like Kudzu."

//www.yall.com

ROCKABILLY

*Many of the publications listed in the previous "Alternative Country & Americana" (e.g. *Blue Suede News*, *The Grindstone*, *Roadhouse Review*, *RootsTown*, *Texas Jamboree*) have rockabilly coverage as well. Those listed below are specifically devoted to rockabilly.

American Music Magazine

Published in Sweden with features, reviews, etc. on rockabillies old and new. CD reviews can be found online at the Rockabilly Hall of Fame site.

Erik Petersson, ed.
Stangebergsv. 3
426 68 Vastra Frolunda
Sweden
//www.rockabillyhall.com/AmerMusicMag.html

Big Beat Magazine

"Rockin' News for Rockin' People!" from Finland with focus on rockabilly and hillbilly bop old and new (in Finnish).

P. O. Box 25
33710 Tampere
Finland
+358-50-597 9293
(fax) +358-3-318 0715

Continental Restyling

1950s culture mag including lots of music.

Jerome Desvaux, ed.
9 Rue de la Liberation
88360 Ferdrupt
France

Custom Built Magazine

"For Your Rock and Roll Pleasure": rock and roll, rockabilly, psychobilly, punkabilly, swing.

Markku Salo, ed.
Laksinkatu 2 As. 3
29200 Harjavalta
Finland
//www.sci.fi/~mjsalo/index.htm
mjsalo@sci.fi

Deathrow Database

Glossy but good psychobilly, rockabilly fanzine.

P. O. Box 1672
Frome, Somerset
BA11 1FQ
England
Deathrow@ndirect.co.uk

Dynamite!

"The World of Rock 'n' Roll" with nice coverage of rockabilly bands, weekenders, etc. Originally only in German but in 1998 an English version became available through the U.S. booking agency Kats Like Us. Editor Andy Widder also operates Part Records and the Rockin' Rollin' booking agency.

Andy Widder, ed.
Waldstr. 10
69234 Dielheim
Germany
//rockin-rollin.com or
//www.rockabillyhall.com/PARTrecords.html
rrp-andywidder@t-online.de

or

Kats Like Us
c/o May Elizabeth Crouse
1797 Winterwood Blvd.
Las Vegas, NV 89101
702-657-2958
//sony.inergy.com/katslikeus/
Maybeebabe@webtv.net

Greased Up!

"Your Guide to the Rockabilly Scene"

709 E. Juneau, #709
Milwaukee, WI 53202

Jamboree Magazine

Italian publication covering European and North American rockabilly, hillbilly, and swing (in Italian).

Maurizio Maiotti, ed.
Milano
Italy

Lo-Fi: The Magazine of Kool Kulture!

Slick little mag with articles, interviews, and reviews on the hottest names in contemporary swing, jump blues, rockabilly, and roots rock. "Easy Living for Cool Moderns."

Lee Sobel, ed.
123 W. 93rd St., #2C
New York, NY 10025
//www.postfun.com/lofi/
LeeSobel@aol.com

Now Dig This

"The Ultimate 1950s Rock 'n' Roll Magazine."

19 South Hill Road
Bensham
Gateshead, Tyne & Wear
NE8 2XR
UK

Original Cool

Rockabilly, swing, rock 'n' roll.

Sue VanHecke, ed.
4700 Colonial Ave.
Norfolk, VA 23508
//members.aol.com/OrigCool/
Sweetgene@aol.com

Rhythm & Roots Review

"The Newsletter of Rockabilly & Real Rock 'n' Roll."

Gregg & Joanne Van Vranken, ed.
360-A W. Merrick Rd., Box 296
Valley Stream, NY 11580

Rocket J's Rockabilly Riot Page:
//members.aol.com/rocketj66/rocketj.htm
Rocketj66@aol.com

Rock Therapy

About rockabilly, r&r, blue rhythm, and blues and their roots. En Espanol only.

Carlos Diaz, ed.
P. O. Box 122
Badalona
08910
Barcelona
Spain
carlos@active.es

Rockabilly Revue

Reviews of over 90 rockabilly CDs from four decades.

//www.daveandandrew.com/rockabilly/index.html
sopp@slip.net

Rockin' Fifties Magazine

German quarterly dedicated to American roots music especially rockabilly, R&B, hillbilly, blues, Western swing, and rock 'n' roll (in German only).

Bernd Kratochwil, ed.
Stoeberlstr. 18
80687 Munich
Germany
bernd@kratochwil.de

or in the U.S. contact:

Gabriele Maag/Marc Bristol
c/o Blue Suede News,
425-788-2776;
ShakinBoss@aol.com

The Rockin' Times

c/o The Rockin' Society
14 Salvington Gardens
Worthing
West Sussex
BN13 2BH
England

Screamin'

Covering American rockabilly and roots old and new since 1995.

rockababy@screamin-zine.com

WESTERN SWING

Swing Time Magazine

Focus mainly on Eastern style swing revival but occasional articles on new Western Swing groups like the Radio Ranch Straight Shooters and the Lucky Stars.

30 Baker, Suite B
San Francisco, CA 94117
415-255-8306
//www.hooked.net/~jlindsay
jlindsay@hooked.net

Western Swing Journal

Mostly has articles on groups from the Golden Age of Western swing (1920s-1940s) but some coverage of modern bands like Tom Morrell.

Jesse A. Morris, ed.
120 West Van Buren #4
Colorado Springs, CO 80907-6773
719-471-8053
//members.aol.com/westletter/western.htm
Tiffanytra@aol.com

Western Swing Newsletter

Published about twice/year by Stompin' Steve Hathaway who hosts "The Cupertino Barndance" radio show on KKUP. It presents biographies, discographies, reviews and news on past and current Western swing.

Steve Hathaway, ed.
1733 Cheney Dr.
San Jose, CA 95128-3605
//www.westernswing.com/wsn.html
steve@westernswing.com

BLUEGRASS/OLD-TIME

Bluegrass Buhne Online News

Old-time & bluegrass magazine covering the scene in Germany (in Deutsch).

Eberhard Finke, ed.
Eberhardstrasse 14/4
89073 Ulm
Germany
0731/213939 (ph./fax)
//141.40.140.3/bluena/bb.htm
bbfinke.ulm@t-online.de

Bluegrass Canada Newletter

Canadian & American bluegrass.

#106-147 Victoria St.
Kamloops, British Columbia
V2C 1Z4
Canada

Bluegrass Chronicle

Long running bi-monthly newspaper with articles, reviews, events/festivals calendar, and catalog.

P. O. Box 31557
San Francisco, CA 94131
800-746-TUNE
//www.slip.net/~bgchron/
bgchron@slip.net

Bluegrass Legacy

Published by the International Bluegrass Museum.

207 E. Second St.
Owensboro, KY 42303

Bluegrass Now!

Traditional and progressive.

Wayne Bledsoe, ed.
P. O. Box 2020
Rolla, MO 65401
800-736-0125
//www.bluegrassnow.com

Bluegrass Telegraph

News, profiles, reviews, and links.

//www.bluegrasstelegraph.com
lowellj@bluegrasstelegraph.com

Bluegrass Unlimited

Oldest & most respected bluegrass magazine.

Peter V. Kuykendall, ed.
P. O. Box 111
Broad Run, VA 20137
800-BLU-GRASS
//www.bluegrassmusic.com
info@bluegrassmusic.com

The Burr: The Backpocket Bluegrass 'Zine

Nifty little publication covering traditional and contemporary bluegrass (and more) in the New York City region and beyond.

Robin Wagner, ed.
Box 443, Cooper Station
New York, NY 10276
718-783-0549
lmmms@inch.com

Cybergrass: The Internet Bluegrass Music Magazine

The online publication for bluegrass with a massive collection of articles, reviews, artist profile, associations, events, etc. plus a huge number of links.

//www.banjo.com
cybergrass@banjo.com

Daily Clog

Monthly newsletter devoted to old-time clogging and Appalachian string band music.

Julie Mangin, ed.
1611 Dennis Ave.
Silver Spring, MD 20902
//www.access.digex.net/~jmangin/dlyclg.html

Folk Book Index of Periodicals

Huge, descriptive listing of print and/or online folk, bluegrass, old-time, acoustic blues, and finger style guitar publications.

//www.folkmusic.org

iMusic Bluegrass Magazine

"Your #1 Source for Bluegrass" with all kinds of information on bands, recordings, events, radio, organizations, and much more. Their motto is "Never Underestimate the Power of Bluegrass."

//www.iBluegrass.com

Moonshiner: Bluegrass Journal

Japanese magazine that looks good even if you can't read a word of it. Photographs and general layout demonstrate a high level of dedication to the music.

//www.kh.rim.or.jp/~bluegras/moonshiner/Moonshiner.html
bluegras@kh.rim.or.jp

The Old-Time Herald

Great magazine covering traditional & modern old-time through articles, reviews, etc.

Alice Gerrard, ed.
P. O. Box 51812
Durham, NC 27717
//www.mindspring.com/~oth/
oth@mindspring.com

Old-Time Radio Newsletter

A project of the old-time Music Group (Elkins, West Virgina) dedicated to preserving and promoting broadcasting of music drawn from Southern Appalachian tradition and other related styles

Old-Time Music Group
P. O. Box 3014
Elkins, WV 26251
//www.hidwater.com/OTR/otrhome.html
jfl@euclid.dne.wnet.edu

Pickers in a Jam: The Newsletter of Banjo in the Hollow

Publication of the Acoustic Instruments Musicians Association.

//www.rtpnet.org/~bith/newlet.html

Pine Cone Traditional Review

Published by the Piedmont Council of Traditional Music; dances, sessions, reviews, fetivals schedule.

P. O. Box 28534
Raleigh, NC 27611
919-990-1900

Reel Times: Austin Friends of Traditional Music

Old-time and bluegrass scene in Central Texas.

P. O. Box 49608
Austin, TX 78765
512-454-9481; 928-3632

Who's Where in Bluegrass

Monthly telling where bluegrass can be found in the northeast from Canada to Virginia.

137 Quinebaug Rd.
North Grovsvenordale, CT 06255-1133
bgatwwib@neca.com

Women in Bluegrass Bulletin

Stories about old and new artists plus database of women players.

P. O. Box 2498
Winchester, VA 22604
800-227-2357
//www.visuallink.net/murphy/wib.htm

SINGER/SONGWRITER

American Songwriter Magazine

All types of modern songwriters with frequent articles and reviews of alt. country performers.

121 17th Ave. South
Nashville, TN 37203
800-739-8712
//www.songnet.com/asongmag/
Asongmag@aol.com

Kerrville Kronikle

Arthur Wood's fanzine with special focus on the many great singer/songwriters who have performed at the Kerrville Folk Festival over the years. His many interviews and features have also appeared in Country Music People.

//wavespace.waverider.co.uk/~kerrkron/index.htm
kerrkron@waverider.co.uk

Performing Songwriter

A variety of genres represented including alt. country.

Lydia L. Hutchinson, ed
P. O. Box 158159
Nashville, TN 37215-9998
800-883-7664
//www.songs.com/noma/perfhome.html
PerfSong@aol.com

CAJUN

Cajun Country Newsletter

Cajun/Zydeco music scene in Europe; maintained by Peter de Vos.

pfox@pi.net

Cajun Times

Devoted to the UK scene with articles, reviews, events calendar, links

Ron Knowles, ed.
128 Basingstoke Rd.
Reading, Berks
2G2 0ET
UK
//www.multimag.demon.co.uk/Cajun/
cajun@multimag.demon.co.uk

Cajun/Zydeco Connections: A Regional Guide to Music & Dance

Monthly newsletter for California.

//www.slip.net/~arubinst/czdetail.shtml/

Northwest Zydeco Newsletter

Web page for Cajun/zydeco in N. California, Oregon, and Washington with links to other California sites.

//www.zydecomusic.com/zydeco/nwz.html

OffBeat

"Dirty Rice" column by Todd Mouton has lots of information on Cajun music.

> 333 St. Charles Ave., Ste. 614
> New Orleans, LA 70130
> //www.neosoft.com/~offbeat/

Passe Partout: West Coast Cajun & Zydeco Music & Dance Association Newsletter

Cajun/zydeco scene in Northern California

> Louisiana Sue, ed.
> 9226 Parfait Dr.
> Sacramento, CA 95826
> 916-361-1309

Zyde.com: The Internet Magazine for Louisiana Music

Plenty of Cajun coverage.

> //members.aol.com/zydecom/page1.htm

ZydE-zine

Gary Hayman's on-line mag for Cajun/Zydeco with beaucoup links.

> //www.erols.com/ghayman/
> ghayman@erols.com

INSTRUMENTS

Acoustic Musician: The Magazine for Acoustic String Instruments

The full range of acoustic instruments with comprehensive articles, interviews, and reviews.

> P. O. Box 1349, 1065 River Rd.
> New Market, VA 22844
> 540-740-4005; 540-740-4006 (fax)
> acoustic@shentel.net

Frets: The Magazine of Acoustic String Instruments

Another fine resource with consistently good features, reviews, etc.

> GPI Publications
> 20085 Stevens Creek Blvd.
> Cupertino, CA 95014

Accordion

Concertina & Squeezebox

Articles, interviews, news, reviews of interest to players of free reed instruments of all types.

> P. O. Box 6706
> Ithaca, NY 14851

RootsWorld's FreeReed

E-zine of accordion music from around the world with articles, reviews, and a free CD now and then. Part of the *RootsWorld* magazine edited by Cliff Furnald.

> //www.rootsworld.com/rw/freereed/
> cliff@rootsworld.com

Banjo

Banjo Newsletter: The 5-String Banjo Magazine

In print since 1973 and devoted to all aspects of the 5-string including players, techniques, tabs, etc.

> P. O. Box 3418
> Annapolis, MD 21403-0418
> 800-759-7425
> (fax) 410-263-6503
> //www.tiac.net/users/bnl/
> bnl@annap.infi..net

Banjovia

Sponsored by Nechville Musical Products, it has technical articles plus features and interviews on Heli-Mount banjo players e.g. Alison Brown, Bela Fleck, Pete Wernick et al.

> c/o Nechville Musical Products
> 10021 Third Ave. South
> Bloomington, MN 55420
> 612-888-9710

5 String Quarterly

"In depth quarterly for 5 string banjo players who play 3 finger style"; published 1995-1996, all eight issues were available through 1997; on-line version has reprints of feature articles and banjo resources.

> John Hood, ed.
> 8407 Loralinda
> Austin, TX 78753-5844
> 512-836-8255; Fax 512-346-2599
> //www.zilker.net/~5sq/
> 5sq@zilker.net

Fiddle

Bluegrass & Swing Music Magazine: The Web Magazine for Bluegrass, Country & Swing Fiddle

News, interviews, tabs, etc.

> //www.mossware.com/music.html
> jhmoss@mossware.com

Fiddler Magazine

"An information, education, and entertainment resource for fiddlers, accompanists, and appreciative listeners."

> Mary Larsen, ed.
> P. O. Box 125
> Los Altos, CA 94022
> //www.fiddle.com
> fiddlermag@aol.com

National Old-Time Fiddler

Monthly newsletter of the National Old-Time Fiddlers Association.

> P. O. Box 1056
> Cochise, AZ 85606

Texas Fiddler

Newsletter of the Texas Old-Time Fiddlers Association.

> Jim Day, ed.
> 10124 Stoneleigh Dr.
> Benbrook, TX 76126

Guitar

Acoustic Guitar Magazine

By and for musicians covering many styles, players, and techniques.

> String Letter Press
> P. O. Box 767
> San Anselmo, CA 94960
> 415-485-6946
> //www.acousticguitar.com
> editors.ag@stringletter.com

Cowpie News Bunkhouse

Stands for Country & Western Pickers of the Internet Electronic Newsletter; intended mostly for country (and its substyles) guitar players. Has a newsletter and archives with tabs, chords, and lyrics plus song search.

> //www.roughstock.com/cowpie/
> Cowpie@olga.net

Fingerstyle Guitar Magazine

Informational and instructional publication covering the widest range of styles and players.

> 800-718-7606
> //fingerstyleguitar.com

Flat Picking Guitar Magazine

Bi-monthly "dedicated to presenting all aspects of the art of flatpicking the acoustic guitar" with interviews and a variety of columns on styles and techniques.

> P. O. Box 2160
> Pulaski, VA 24301
> 800-413-8296
> //www.flatpick.com/
> highview@flatpick.com

Flyin' Fingers

Newletter devoted to guitar legend Joe Maphis published by Deke Dickerson formerly of Dave & Deke and now head of Ecco-Fonic Records.

> Deke Dickerson, ed.
> P. O. Box 304
> Hollywood, CA 90078
> 818-558-3360
> /www.ecco-fonic.loomisgroup.com/ecco-fonic
> eccofonic@earthlink.net

Harmonica

American Harmonica Newsmagazine

Most prolific and regular of the harmonica publications.

Al Eichler, ed.
104 Highland Ave.
Battle Creek, MI 49015-3227
616-962-2989

Harmonica Educator

For educators and players at all levels; since 1994.

Richard Martin, ed.
P. O. Box 340
North Hampton, OH 45349-0340
//members.aol.com/heducator2/index.html
ri58066217@aol.com

Harmonica Happenings: The Newsletter of the Society for the Preservation and Advancement of the Harmonica

Mostly information for club members.

Susan Williams, ed.
P. O. Box 865
Troy, MI 48099-0865
//members.aol.com/harmonica/
HarpSPAH@aol.com

HIP: Harmonica Information Publication

Packed with information on technique, theory, history plus interviews and reviews

Winslow Yerxa, ed.
203 14th Ave.
San Francisco, CA 94118-1007
76450.3230@compuserve.com

Mandolin

The Mandocrucian's Digest

Highly informative periodical from ace mandolin player and brother of Erik Hokkanen.

Niles Hokkanen, ed.
P. O. Box 3585
Winchester, VA 22064

Mandolin World News

Pioneering mandolin magazine started in 1976 by David Grisman, Darol Anger, and Todd Phillips; back issues can be obtained through e-mail or mail order.

Dix Bruce, ed.
P. O. Box 231005
Pleasant Hill, CA 94523
Musix1@aol.com

MandoZine

Online journal for mandolinists with articles on famous players, types of mandolins, etc. plus a resource guide and mandolinists directory.

//www.mandozine.com
jbaxter@mandozine.com

Steel Guitar

Steel Guitar World Magazine

Largest and most widely distributed steel guitar periodical.

P. O. Box 9297
Spokane, WA 99209-9297
509-487-5658
//pedalsteel.com/sgwmag/
rask@ior.com

GENERAL MUSIC RESOURCES

The American Music Information Source Guide

Large resource with heavy emphasis on music business sites (promotions, publishing houses, studios, agencies, etc.) but also huge unsigned/ independent band and label archives.

//www.auction-web.com/

Artists at the Edge of Obscurity Database

Maintained by radio station KFJC in Los Altos Hills, California with profiles and reviews of those hard to find performers.

//www.spies.com/misc/kfjc/md/db/

Austin Music Home Page

Everything you could want to know about the "live music capital of the world."

//www.austinlinks.com/music/

Austin Music Scene

Pretty comprehensive listing of bands, clubs, and radio from the *Austin-American Statesman*.

//www.austin360.com

Complete Music: Country Western Music Guide & Directory

Part of the Handilinks web site, this is a gigantic repository of links to artists, labels, publications, web pages, and much more for all types of country.

//www.handilinks.com/cat1/m/21757.htm

Driftweb

Clearinghouse for info on folk and roots music worldwide maintained by station WNUR at Northwestern Univesity.

//www.nwu.edu/wnur/drift/
j-germuska@nwu.edu

Folk Book: An Online Acoustic Music Establishment

Major resource with biographies, discographies, and links to all types of folk music; also has an extensive folk periodicals index.

//www.folkmusic.org

Folk Music Resources on the WWW

Gigantic site dedicated to all things related to folk music.

//www.sover.net/~gillette/sites.html

iMusic

Articles, BBS, and bookmarks for hundreds of performers including many alt. country under Country, Contemporary, and Modern.

//imusic.com

Internet Guide to Texas Music

Maintained by the Texas Music Office which also publishes the yearly *Texas Music Industry Directory*; web page has over 1,000 links to Texas music related sites

//www.governor.state.tx.us/music/igtm.htm

IUMA

Internet Underground Music Archive: huge site with connections to all types of alternative music and resources all over the globe.

//www.iuma.com/

Mammoth Music Meta-List

What it says.

//www.vibe.com/vibe/mmm/music.html

Microsoft Music Center

Nexus for Bill Gates' favorite music. No kidding!

//pi.microsoft.com

Music Resources on the Internet

Enormous archive.

//www.music.indiana.edu/music-resources/

North Carolina MEME Music Index

Links to bands, city scenes etc. with connections to Carolina alt. country.

//sunsite.unc.edu/ncmeme/music/

Texas Music

Almost as big as the state itself!

//www.txmusic.com

Texas Music Hotlist

Major hub for the Lone Star State from the *Austin Chronicle*.

//www.auschron.com/txmusic.html

Ultimate Band List

Gigantic resource for bands, venues, labels, zines.

//www.ubl.com

Yahoo

Huge music resource broken down into many useful categories and sub categories.

//www.yahoo.com/entertainment/music/

ALTERNATIVE COUNTRY & AMERICANA

Aaron A. Fox's Home Page

Professor of ethnomusicology at Columbia University who is also a Texas music devotee (PhD from UT, Austin). In addition to links to information on his high falootin' books and papers on country music, this site also has a page for his favorite project, Texas honky tonker, Justin Trevino. Dr. Fox has a book coming out in 1999 for Duke University Press called *Out the Country: Speech, Song, and Feeling in American Rural, Working-Class Culture.*

//roar.music.columbia.edu/~cecenter/
aaf19@columbia.edu

Akers Mic Online: Country & Western

History of and insightful commentary on classic and alt. country by one of Norway's leading authorities, Tom Skjeklesaether (in Norwegian and English); also has information on Norwegian alt. country artists.

//www.sol.no/akersmic/country.htm
tomskje@online.no

All Music Guide

A complete online database of recorded music based on the print books of the same name; searchable by artist, style, albums, essays. Both print and online versions have specific sections for "Alternative Country," "Americana," "Roots-Rock," "Rockabilly," "Country-Rock," et al. with historical essays, artist profiles, and recommended recordings for each category.

//www.allmusic.com/amg/

The Alt-Country Page

"Your Guide to Alt-Country" with musings by John Brandon on the music plus band info, chords, links, and top 10 lists.

//www.lubbock.demon.co.uk/~altc.html
jbrandon@wavefront.com

AlternativeCountry.Com

Extensive clearinghouse maintained by Chris Marino of *Gavin Americana* with bios, charts, reviews and lots of links to bands, radio, and many other resources (set up in early 1999).

//www.alternativecountry.com
chris@alternativecountry.com

Alternative Country Community Cookbook

"Music for your mouth...food for your soul"; ad site for cookbook offering recipes by alt. country/No Depression artists, writers, promoters, fans, etc.; also has lots of links to alt. country resources {P. O. Box 6432, Evanston, IL 60204}

//members.aol.com/altcooking/

Alternative Country Tape List

Boots of live performances (trade only) by Blue Mountain, Junior Brown, Steve Earle, Freakwater, the Jayhawks, Son Volt, Uncle Tupelo, and many more.

//www.tcd.net/~wolfeyes/country.html

Amazon.Com

Web site for Amazon Books and Music has a "Country" section divided into subjects including "Alt. Country," "Americana," "Bluegrass," "Outlaw," "Honky Tonk," and more with articles, interviews, reviews, and essentials for each section.

//www.amazon.com

American Music Archives

Large repository of biographies, discographies, photos, and other information on traditional American music.

//www.eyeneer.com/America/index.html
eyeneer@eyeneer.com

Americana, A-Z

Maintained by station WFUV in New York City, it has connections to hundreds of performers including many alt. country plus "Top 50 Americana Classics."

//www.wfuv.org/americana.html

Americana Archives

Hundreds of brief reviews including many alt. country by the DJs at station KCMU in Seattle; also has links to labels and the "Americana Top 40."

//www.kcmu.org

Americana Music

Central music source for artists, labels, magazines, venues, record stores, retailers, etc.

//www.americana-music.com
info@americana-music

Americana Music

German page with a Lone Star State focus through connections to Texas/Austin music, artists, and radio plus other Americana pages.

//www.geocities.com/athens.forum/9962/americana.html

Americana Music Resource

Good assortment of bookmarks for artists, clubs, discussion groups, labels, publications, radio.

//userwww.service.emory.edu/~lpeters/amr
lpeters@emory.edu

Americana Music Spotlight

Under the Country section, there is a separate No Depression heading with pointers to alt. country artists and other major web sites.

//www.geocities.com/~highway61/index.html
highway61@geocities.com

Arden's Garden

Page for alt. country show on KAZU (Pacific Grove, California) with archived playlists and a variety of links e.g. No Depression, Gavin, Strawberry Music Festival, Frontiers mail order.

//www.kazu.org/garden.html
arden@kazu.org

Bakersfield Sound

Site devoted to California honky tonk style and its practitioners, past and present; profiles and time line included.

//www.bakersfield.com/homich/baksound/

Bernhard's Homepage

Bernhard Rosa's fan page for Joe Ely, Hazeldine, Neal Casal, and the Rainravens with links to the Blue Rose and Glitterhouse labels and the annual Singer/Songwriter Festival in Thun, Switzerland.

//home.allgaeu.org/brosa/
bernhard.rosa@allgaeu.org

Big Mike Destiny Web Page

Station KFJC disc jockey page ("The Big Guitar Show") with reviews of all types of American roots music.

//www.kfjc.org/bigmike/

Bob Paterson's Home Page

Promoter and DJ on Country Music Radio (UK) whose site has an extensive set of links to the European and North American alt. country/Americana bands he promotes and enjoys.

//www.ursasoft.com/bob/
bob@windbob.demon.co.uk

Burn's Cowpunk Homepage

London cowpunk band site with links to cowpunk, alt. country, insurgent country, no depression, roots.

//www.combust.demon.co.uk/

Chicago Country Artists Who' Who

Brief profiles of Moonshine Willy, The Waco Brothers, Robbie Fulks, The Handsome Family, Wilco, The New Duncan Imperials, et al.

//centerstage.net/chicago/music/whoswho/styles/countryartists.html

ChillWebCo

Club, band, radio, and label information for the Chapel Hill and North Carolina with much related to alt. country in the area e.g. Local 506, Sleazefest, etc.

//www.chapel-hill.nc.us/

Copperhead Road

Steve Earle web site mainly for trading bootlegs of live performances by Earle but also by a wide variety of other alt. country artists including Emmylou, Jack Ingram, Leftover Salmon, Peter Rowan, Seconds Flat, Todd Snider, Son Volt, Wilco, Uncle Tupelo, Townes Van Zandt, Guy Clark, The V-Roys.

//www.auburn.net/~exit0/tapetrade/
Exit0@auburn.net

Country & Western Friends Koetz

From Southern Germany with emphasis on and links to European (e.g. Hillbilly Boogiemen; Tennessee Rhythm Riders) and American (e.g. Clay Blaker, Jann Browne, Derailers, Ray Wylie Hubbard) alt. country plus information on the International Kotzer Country Music Festival.

//www.bnv-gz.baynet.de/~bwiesner/cm/index.html

Country Music UK & Europe

"The definitive guide to country music in the UK and Western Europe"; includes links to bands, radio, publications, clubs, etc.

//dspace.dial.pipex.com/town/square/aat96/index.htm
pbryant@dial.pipex.com

Cowgals Home on the Web

Started by singer/songwriter Edith Frost and devoted to singing cowgirls past and present; it has cowgirl biographies and lots of alt. country & roots music connections.

//www.cowgirls.com/dream/cowgals/

The Cowpunk Corral

Caroline McDonald's page for groups like Wilco, Son Volt, Whiskeytown, the Jayhawks, et al. plus artists on "the bleeding edge of folk" (e.g. Sara Hickman).

//www.geocities.com/nashville/7669/
credhe@juno.com

Craven's Alternative Country Page

Fan/opinion page with pointers to artists, Gavin, Twangin', Miles of Music, Down on the Farm.

//www.webcom.com/jac/cravens/altcntry.html
jcravens@coyote.com

Cybercountry

Page maintained by Frode Jensen has many links to Norwegian and North American alt. country sites (Beware: there is a new country page by the same name).

//gaupe.hin.no/~fuzzy/cyber.html

Down Home and Free Roots Home Page

Maintained by DJ Chad Williams who hosts the Down Home and Free Roots shows on WCBN, Ann Arbor, Michigan; these programs offer lots of alt. country and the web site has pointers to alt. country resources.

//www.wcbn.org/downhome/
downhomeshow@wcbn.org

or

babooski@umich.edu

Electric L.A.

Loads of connections to the best in TSOB alt. country including big events like the famous Barn Dance and the more recent Sacred Honk.

//www.electricearl.com/index.html
ELAweb@aol.com

Freight Train Boogie

Bill Frater's American roots music information page for "Alternative Country" or "Americana" with a list of "definitive" artists, news, CD reviews, CD of the week, "humble list" of the best of '98, and various alt. country bookmarks. Also linked to the Freight Train Boogie radio show.

//www.freighttrainboogie.com
frater@freighttrainboogie.com

Great Lakes Twang

Dedicated to informing and promoting alt. country bands, venues, and happenings in the Great Lakes region.

//www.geocities.com/nashville/stage/9596/
gltwang.html
gltwang@hotmail.com

Gumbo Pages

Mainly devoted to New Orleans and Acadian culture but also has the "Insurgent Country Roundup" with articles, reviews, discographies, song/chord transcriptions etc. and lots of links to alternative/insurgent country sites especially Passenger Side (Postcard 2): The Alternative/Insurgent Country Music Mailing List and Postcard: The Uncle Tupelo, Wilco, & Son Volt Mailing List.

//www.gumbopages.com/
gumbo@webcom.com

Happy Trails

Web page for show on KXLU (L.A.) specializing in local alt. country and Americana with links to The Late Night Radio Edition (live performances by L.A. area alt. country artists) and the famous Barn Dance.

//www-scf.usc.edu/~leondani/happytrails.ht
ml

Hellcountry

Created by Stacey Taylor to support the Boston area twang scene and the Hellcountry showcase held monthly at the Kendall Cafe in Cambridge (see Venues). Site has an ever-growing guide to local (and beyond) bands, gigs, and venues plus links to mailing lists and lots of other alt. country information.

//www.hellcountry.com
stacey@hellcountry.com

Hepcat Corner

Connections to Campfire Records, Hepcat Records, *Blue Suede News*, and more.

//www.hepcat.com
chris@hepcat.com

The Hillbilly Music Page

Fine source of information on old and new hillbilly maintained by Stephen Lee Canner who also started the Hillbilly Music online mailing list in 1998.

www.mindspring.com/~canner/canner.htm
canner@mindspring.com

Hillbilly World

Tongue-in-cheek site by Jeff Jackowlew dedicated to "the forgotten segment of America's population" with links to hillbilly music including redneck/hillbilly bands like Southern Culture on the Skids, et al.

//www.hillbilly.pair.com
haywire6@ix.netcom.com

Honky Tonk Roundup

Key site for information on and links to TSOB events and acts. Also home page for the Happy Trails radio show on KXLU which has connections to Jana Pendragon's Late Night Radio Edition.

//www.thegrid.net/leondaniels/roundup.html

Hoot Hut: Western Outlaw Music Site

For alt. country radio show on KTHX with links to artists, labels, tabs, and playlists.

//www.fmedia.com/hoot/index.html

Independent Country Reviews

Part of the Country Music Review Pages offering insightful reviews of current alt. country releases by Steve Reid, "Sydney's only country music specialist" and owner of Yesterday & Today Records.

//www.ozemail.com.au/~fiddling/indie.html
fiddling@ozemail.com.au

Insurgent Country Home Page

Major site by Hans Settler with an amazing number and variety of alt. country resources including history, real audio, songbook, and many, many other bookmarks. The most comprehensive collection of alternative country information on the Web!

//staff-www.uni-marburg.de/~settler/news.
htm
settler@mailer.uni-marburg.de

Joe Ed Web Page

Home page for KFJC (Los Altos, California) DJ (Lubbock or Leave It) with reviews of all types of American roots music.

//www.kfjc.org/joeed/

Juan Geracaris Bootlegs

Site offering bootlegs (for trade) by many alt. country acts.

//skew2.kellogg.nwu.edu/~geracari/bootleg
s.html
j-geracaris@nwu.edu

Juke Joint

Large collection of resources for American roots music including bands, clubs, radio, books and mags, newsgroups, record collectors.

//www.jukejoint.com
Info@jukejoint.com

Melissa's KRSF Alt. Country Page

Site for DJ Melissa Garland's Bay Area radio show has links to bands (especially those associated with Postcard 2) and other important alt. country pages.

//members.aol.com/~radiosf/
magarland@earthlink.com

Midwest Rooted Rock

Japanese fan page for alt. country groups from America's heartland including Uncle Tupelo, Wilco, Son Volt, the Jayhawks, Golden Smog, and the Honey Dogs (in Japanese).

//www.geocities.co.jp/hollywood-kouen/68
23/

Mike's Alternative Country Links

Connections to well-known and obscure alt. country acts.

//www.zoomnet.net/~michaelp/links.html
michaelp@zoomnet.net

Mike's Music Pages

Maintains pages for Amy Rigby and L'il Mo Passin with links to other alt. country sites.

//pages.prodigy.net/mike/

Music

Fan page with special emphasis on alt. country (Uncle Tupelo, Son Volt, the Bottle Rockets, the Old 97s) and schedule of upcoming alt. country concerts in the D.C. Area.

//www.jegconsulting.com/users/brobertson/
home.htm
brobertson@jegconsulting.com

The Music Corner

Alternative reviews and interviews including many alt. country.

//members.aol.com/musccorn/index.html
Musccorn@aol.com

Newport/Cincinnati Roots Music Page

Home for roots music info in the Northern Kentucky/Greater Cincinnati area.

//w3.one.net/~newport/
newport@one.net

NOMA: National Online Music Alliance Page

Site for many artists pages including Richard Dobson, Rex Foster, Funny Hill, Emily Kaitz, David Olney, One Fell Swoop, Kevin Welch, Steve Young.

//songs.com/noma/nomahome.htm
perfessrr@songs.com

Northern Journey Online

Canadian folk music website with connections to many artists (alt. Country types included), clubs, festivals, etc. plus two e-zines: *Northern Journey Journal* and *Maple Roots.*

//www.interlog.com/~njo/

Peder's Page

Peder Brevik's fan site that is "truly dedicated to great music" e.g. The Handsome Family, Palace, Songs: Ohio, Edith Frost, Wilco, and other alternative with bookmarks for labels, radio, tabs and chords.

//home4.swipnet.se/~w-49077/index.html
peder.brevik@mbox200.swipnet.se

Pinch of Joy, Dash of Misery Home Page

Alt. country/roots music show (hosted by Jonathan Kriege) on WHPK in Chicago with a "big ass list of bands" and a smaller list of independent labels.

//student-www.uchicago.edu/users/jdkriege/radio.htm
jdkriege@midway.uchicago.edu

Porch Songs Music Links

Connections to Larry Barrett, Richard Buckner, Giant Sand, Neal Casal, Vic Chesnutt, The Coal Porters, Freakwater, Butch Hancock, Terry Lee Hale, Gary Heffern, Tarnation, Townes Van Zandt plus labels including Blue Rose, Glitterhouse, Watermelon, and Temple Bar.

//members.aol.com/porchsongs/musiclinx/index.html
Porchsongs@aol.com

Postcard MP3s

Place where you can hear music by Uncle Tupelo, Son Volt, Wilco, Whiskeytown, and the Jayhawks; if you have an MP3 player, that is.

//syru95-119.syr.edu
adhooker@syr.edu

Postcard2

This very active, informative, and entertaining alt. country mailing list has two separate web pages.

(1) Laura Levy's has subscription information and links to bands and labels, TwangCast, and member web sites such as Twangin', Twangzine, Hellcountry, and Miles of Music.

//www.drizzle.com/~lal/postcard2.htm
lal@drizzle.com

(2) Steve Gardner's has list background, subscription information, and P2's CDs of the Year Lists, 1996-1998.

//www.topsoil.net/postcard2.htm
steve@topsoil.net

The Press Network

Promotional site for many alt. country and Americana artists (Don Walser, Toni Price, et al.) with bios, features, reviews, and bookmarks.

//www.pressnetwork.com/index.html
lisa@pressnetwork.com

Progressive Torch & Twang

Web page for radio show on WDBM in East Lansing, Michigan hosted by Jamie DePolo and Doug Neal; has many links to artists and other key alt. country sites plus information on the annual Torch & Twang festival.

//www.msu.edu/user/depolo/
depolo@msue.msu.edu

Rancho De Nada

Contains "Jukebox Deluxe" (alt. country reviews), "Roundup" (links to folk/roots/alt. country pages), and "Songwriter's Network."

//www.newsome.org
newsome@accesscomm.net

RealCountry.net

"A spot on the web for those working in Real Country," that is, a clearinghouse for all "twang" related sites; one of their first collaborators was Mike Hay's Twanger's Home Page and first client, Dale Watson.

//www.realcountry.net
glm@realcountry.net

Real Roots Favorites

From The Netherlands, a select list of performers (Jimmy LaFave, David Munyon, Neal Casal Go To Blazes, Ray Wylie Hubbard, James McMurtry, and others) with brief descriptions and links to their web pages.

//web.inter.nl.net/jtm.janssen/real_roots_favorites.html

Renegade Texas

"All about real country music, singer-songwriters, and good times" Tejas style with links to artists, venues, reviews, Texas Renegade Radio, and even some "Twang North of the Salsa Line."

//users.why.net/RenegadeTexas/index.html
renegade@airmail.net

Rockin' Roots, Country Casanovas and Southern Sliders

Impressive Swedish contribution with links o'plenty from early country rockers through the current crop of alt. country elite with a special leaning toward Austin, Texas. Also pointers to labels, magazines, and other key web pages.

//home5.swipnet.se/~w-53855/roots.html

Rodney's Essential Music Page

"Dedicated to the music of Willie Nelson, Bob Dylan, Guy Clark, Gram Parsosn, Townes Van Zandt, Neil Young, Steve Earle, Steve Young, Uncle Tupelo, Johnny Cash, Terry Allen, The Byrds, Butch Hancock, Tom Russell, Jimmy LaFave, Tom Pacheco and other like-minded free-spirited writers and performers." Links to these artists, miscellaneous alt. country sites, and a tape trade list.

//www.lubbock.demon.co.uk/music.html
rodney@lubbock.demon.co.uk

Roots 66

Information on American roots music with reviews and links to artists and scenes by city.

//www.roots.com
Erika@roots66.com

RootsRock

"A labor of love for roots rock (alt. country, Americana, insurgent country, y'allternative, no depression...take your pick) music" with latest news, bookmarks for "Good Alt. Country Reading" (articles and magazines), schedule of related music on TV, and links to some local and other bands.

//www.rootsrock.com
music@rootsrock.com

Roots Rock MP3 Archive

"Online source for rare and bootleg MP3 audio files of artists (generically) categorized as 'roots rock'" e.g. Uncle Tupelo, Wilco, Son Volt, Jayhawks, and Blue Mountain.

//www.inxpress.net/~dn/
djnaab@students.wisc.edu

Roots Roundup

"Respectfully dedicated to Howlin' and Hank," it provides live music and radio show information plus thumbnail CD reviews for all types of Americana music in the Bay Area.

//sadieo.ucsf.edu/roots.html
sadieo@itsa.ucsf.edu

Roots Unlimited

Home page for roots performers based in Western New York state with links to Scott Carpenter, the Cowslingers, the Jazzabels, and the Steam Donkeys.

//www.wnywebshop.com
webmaster@wnywebshop.com

The Rural Route to Insurgent Country

Henning Kleiven's excellent project with many pointers to no depression and insurgent country musicians, magazines, and web pages.

//home.sol.no/~hekleive/insurgent.html
hekleive@online.no

Sleazefest

Promotional site for the annual musical event has lots of connections to clubs, bands, radio, record stores, press, and labels plus a very helpful "Ultimate Band Address Book" listing many alt. country performers.

//www.sleazefest.com/sleaze/whatis.html

Southbound Train

Jim Moran's page for his alt. country show on station WNUR in Chicago; includes playlists, band links, and photos of recent local shows.

//www.nwu.edu/wnur/southbound/

Southern & Rocking Music

Huge domain for European entertainment agency directed by Marc Fenech and handling over 400 "rocking" and "Southern roots" bands; it has a mammoth database of reviews, news, gigs, profiles, and fan clubs for rockabilly, rock 'n' roll, hillbilly, swing, and other Southern roots worldwide. Spinoff of the magazine of the same name which is now housed on this site.

//www.sci.fi/~srmusic/
srmusic@sci.fi

Spaceboy's No Depression Jukebox

Song samples from and links to Blue Mountain, the Honeydogs, the Bottle Rockets, Whiskeytown, the Old 97s, Bad Livers, Son Volt.

//www.artnet.net/~spaceboy/jukebox/alt.co
untry/alt-country.html
spaceboy@artnet.net

Stephen Terrell's Web Page

Cyberspace domain of outrageous singer/songwriter (**Picnic Time for Potatoeheads**), DJ, music journalist (*Reverb On Line*) with connections to his alt. country/Americana/roots articles and reviews, radio show, many alt. country related pages, and assorted wackiness from Masked Wrestlers to Zippy the Pinhead.

//members.aol.com/bluespud/
ROBOTCLAW@aol.com

Tape Trader Network

High quality recordings of live musical performances for over 2,000 different artists including Steve Earle, Uncle Tupelo, the Walkabouts, Dale Watson, Gillian Welch, Whiskeytown, Wilco, and Lucinda Williams.

//tapetracker.com/traderindex/

TapeTrading.Com

Jonathan Haynes's DAT list with many artists of interest including Dave Alvin, Greg Brown, The Byrds, Johnny Cash, the Gear Daddies, John Prine, the Replacements, Neil Young, and more.

//www.tapetrading.com
kc7fys@sa2.so-net.or.jp

Texas Country/Texas Punk

Twang! & Rawk! with a Texas focus.

//ccwf.cc.texas.edu/~simp/
simp@mail.utexas.edu

Texas Music Kitchen

Bookmarks for all types of Texas music

//www.lonestarwebstation.com
marq@lonestarwebstation.com

Texas Music Web Site

Fan page with links to Guy Clark, Steve Earle, Robert Earl Keen, Gary P. Nunn, Jerry Jeff Walker, and others.

//glueball.phys.unm.edu/~chris/texasmusic.h
tml
chris@cornelius.cc.vanderbilt.edu

Third Coast Music Network

Home page for station KSYM in San Antonio which has outstanding programming. Here you can get connected to many, many artists and all the major alt. country/Americana web sites.

//www.accd.edu/tcmn/
Joe Horn: RMould5417@aol.com

Tommy Nordeng's Good Music: No Depression Page

"A forum for no depression, alternative country, country rock..." featuring history, essential recordings, labels, etc.

//www.uio.no/~tommywn/music/goodstuff
98.html
Tommywn@bio.uio.no

Twang Thang: Burnt Dog Rodeo Home Page

Site for Gary Wells' radio show on KCPR in San Luis Obispo, California, it offers a generous number of bookmarks for alt. country artists.

//www.calpoly.edu/~sdalcerr/twang.html
Gwells@polymail.calpoly.edu

Twang's Thangs

Lots of links to Texas alt. country.

//web2.airmail.net/txtwang/
txtwang@airmail.net

The Twanger's Home Page

Mike Hays' page with a "Twang Zone" providing connections to various alt. country destinations including the TwangCast online music site.

//www.mikehays.realcountry.net
mike@mikehays.realcountry.net

Urbane Cowboys: Alt. Country in the 1990s

John Molinaro's interesting 1998 Master's Thesis from the University of Virginia which argues that alt. country music links the present with the 1920s-1930s when country first emerged in the mass media. Has Real Audio examples.

//xroads.virginia.edu/~ma98/molinaro/alt.c
ountry/front.html
asgrp@virginia.edu

Viktoria Park/Western Mail Online

These two sites aim at building an information network of country music for all of Germany and Europe; has links to alt. and new country pages (accessible through Wayne's Country Music Page).

//avus.de/viktoria/musik/country/index.htm
shroeder@avus.de

Wayne's Country Music Page

Perhaps the most connections to both new and alternative country sites

//www.tpoint.net//wallen/country/country.h
tml
wallen@tpoint.net

WHOAAH!!: The Home of Hot Rockabilly and Cool Twang

Yet another fine Norwegian alt. country web page, this one comes from Tom Ekeberg who provides perceptive reviews of and information on Norwegian and American acts and events in both Norwegian and English.

//home.sol.no/~tekeberg/home.htm
tom.ekeberg@online.no

World Famous Buttload of Twangin' Links

Jeff Wall's large catalog of alt. country plus connections to the major "Hillbilly" sites. Part of his *Rural Route Twangzine*.

//www.twangzine.com
whome@livenet.net

Y'alternaboy's Alternative Country Music Web Site

"A Tribute to Some Incredible No Depression Style Bands": Uncle Tupelo, Son Volt, Wilco, Blue Mountain, Whiskeytown.

//www.geocities.com/SunsetStrip/studio/40
59
Uncl2pelo@aol.com

Yodel Central

Yes, that's right, an entire web site for everybody's favorite caterwauling with lots of information and links to country & western yodelers past and present (Randy Erwin, Don Walser, Ranger Doug, Wylie).

//www.bayscenes.com/ind/spidra/yodel.html

ROCKABILLY PAGES

The Austrobilly Site

Connections to all things related to rockabilly and psychobilly in Austria.

//www.geocities.com/SunsetStrip/venue/9292/
austrobilly@geocities.com

Bop Central

"One-stop Billy Music Networking" with Bopbands, Bopdates, Bopboard, Bopchat, and the Boplicity Rockabilly database, a free promo tional registry and discussion list for musicians, DJs, club owners, et al. Maintained by Rockabilly Rose who also handles Josie Kreuzer's home page.

//members.aol.com/giltyrrell/BopCentral.html
GilTyrrell@aol.com

Doggone Cat's Rockabilly Page

Fan page with links and comprehensive list of rockabilly weekenders.

//members.aol.com/DoggoneCat/hogwild.html
DoggoneCat@aol.com

German Rock 'n' Roll

For the rockabilly scene in Deutschland with gig guide and links.

//members.aol.com/cthome001/rnr/1stgerman.htm
Cthome001@aol.com

Good Rockin' in Cyberspace

Australian DJ (6RTR, Western Australia) Bob Hope-Hume's site with lots of bookmarks and an online mailing list; also home of "The Rockabilly Ring," a clearinghouse for over 150 related web pages.

//kali.murdoch.edu.au/~hopehume/rockin.html
r.hope-hume@murdoch.edu.au

Jive 55

Homepage for rock & roll, hillbilly, country, and swing bands in the Netherlands with links to groups like the Barnstompers and the Hillbilly Boogiemen plus U.S. rockabilly/hillbilly artists old and new.

//www.xs4all.nl/~mzwaan/jive55/
jive55@bigfoot.com

Little Somethin' Rockabilly

Fun page with mailing list, chat, and links to High Noon, Wayne Hancock, and others.

//www.teleport.com/~oricet/rockabilly
oricet@teleport.com

Maybe...

Information site for rockabilly, hillbilly bop, and swing in the San Francisco area. Has Rockabilly chat page.

//www.maybe.com/index.html
marian@maybe.com

Net Cat Page

"The psychobilly and rockabilly page."

//swampy.rydnet.lysator.liu.se/netcat/
rebel@lysator.liu.se

Psychobilly Home Page

Big list of bands and releases past and present.

//www.wreckingpit.com
Roy@wreckingpit.com

Rockabilly Central

Mostly for the Chicago scene with band, concert, and other links plus a swing page.

//www.rockabilly.net
rob@rockabilly.net

Rockabilly Hall of Fame Home Page

Maintained by Bob Timmers, it has a whole bunch of information on and links to 'billies old and new, radio, labels, clubs, festivals, and much more; very comprehensive and entertain- ing. P. O. Box 70, Kimberly, WI 54136; 920-739-2503.

//www.rockabillyhall.com
bob@rockabillyhall.com

Rockabilly Home Page

Big site with tons of connections to bands, labels, magazines, radio, other rockabilly pages, and a calendar of events.

//www.rockabilly.com/
elvis01@rockabilly.com

Rockabilly-O-Rama

Pittsburgh band Highway 13's page with connections to other groups, labels, publications etc.

//www.pitt.edu/~blair1/rockabilly.html

Rockabilly Town

Fan site for Linz, Austria, with band, club, and radio info.

//www.geocities.com/nashville/9679/runten.html

Rocket J's Rockabilly Riot Page

Maintained by the publishers of *Rhythm & Roots Review* with lots of information on the current scene.

//members.aol.com/rocketj66/rocketj.htm
Rocketj66@aol.com

Rosey's RABworld

Global hub for information on rockabilly scenes in Austria, Australia, Finland, France, Holland, Spain, Sweden, the UK, the Ukraine, and the U.S.

//www.geocities.com/sunsetstrip/backstage/6273/world.html

Roy's Psychobilly Page

"The wrecking pit!": bands, news, concerts, chat plus "The Psychobilly Web Ring" of related pages.

//home.pi.net/~roy/psycho.html

Tapio's Fin-A-Billy Page

Tapio Vaisanen site with bookmarks for artists on the Goofin and other Finnish labels, gig guide, and an online Rockin' Records mailing list.

//www.pcuf.fi/~tapiov/
tapiov@pcuf.fi

WESTERN SWING

Western Swing

Lots of information on key books and recordings old and new.

//www.geocities.com/~jimlowe/western/westdex/
JimLowe@dumboozle.com

WesternSwing.com

Calendar of events and index of societies plus lots of other information maintained by Stompin' Steve Hathaway who also publishes the *Western Swing Newsletter* and hosts the "Cupertino Barn Dance" show on KKUP, California.

//www.westernswing.com
steve@westernswing.com

BLUEGRASS & OLD-TIME PAGES

Acoustic Roots

Fan page devoted to "any type of music that can be played without benefit of electricity" e.g. old-time, bluegrass, Celtic, etc.

//camalott.com/~jchaynes/
jchaynes@camalott.com

Banjo in the Hollow: The Acoustic Instruments Musicians Association

Dedicated to preserving and promoting bluegrass and old-time music with information on festivals, picking sessions, and workshops (see *Pickers in a Jam* newsletter).

//www.rtpnet.org/~bith/index.html
cornick@email.unc.edu

Barb Diederich's Handy Bluegrass Links

Another massive databse with over 1,750 links to bands, concerts, publications, associations, radio, and much more.

//www.tiac.net/users/familiar/

Bill's Bluegrass Music Page

Well connected site by "a proud member of the Southeastern Bluegrass Association."

//bcbrown.simplenet.com/bluegrass/

Blevin's Picks

Hook ups to many bluegrass and old-time pages.

//www.cns.vt.edu/localhome/music.html

Bluegrass/Acoustic Music Web Ring

Big connecting point for bluegrass and acoustic music pages.

/www.geocities.com/SunsetStrip/3406/ring.htm

Bluegrass Connection Home Page

"A world of bluegrass glorification" with links to musicians, instruments, festivals, and more.

//www.gotech.com
pmilano@gotech.com

Bluegrass Downunder

Covers the Australian scene; sponsored by the Queensland Bluegrass Assn.

//www.gil.com.au/~thurley/qbgrass.html

Bluegrass in Australia

Links to societies, venues, events, radio, etc. by state.

//www.healey.com.au/~mkear/bgaust.html

Bluegrass-Music.Com

"The premier resource for bluegrass music" with huge number of links to clubs, bands, radio, magazines and other bluegrass sites worldwide.

//www.bluegrass-music.com

The Bluegrass Music Page

Formerly Karen's Quick Bluegrass Page, it connects with many other pages, newsgroups, etc.

//www.best.com/~kquick/bg.html

BlueGrassRoots Links

Mega-connections to the gamut in bluegrass & old-time: artists, labels, publications, radio, etc. maintained by Jaanus from Estonia (over 500 links!)

//BGR.ee/
BGR@BGR.ee

Bluegrass World

"The comprehensive Bluegrass music connection to the electronic Internet index of world wide information."

//www.bluegrassworld.com
editor@bluegrassworld.com

Brandywine Friends of Old-Time Music

Loads of bluegrass & folk links maintained by John Lupton who hosts "Rural Free Delivery" on WVUD in Delaware.

//www.sas.upenn.edu/~jlupton/bfotm.html
jlupton@sas.upenn.edu

Cybergrass

Stupendous bluegrass nexus with loads of information and tons of pointers

//www.banjo.com

Dr. Smith's Acoustic Music Page

Maintained by Gary Smith with many links to other old-time sites.

//shoga.wwa.com/~flatpick/old_time.html

Early Country Home Page

Part of the Southern Folklife Collection Home Page maintained by the Wilson Library at the University of North Carolina which houses one of the largest collections of Southeastern tradition derived music including old-time string band or "hillbilly music."

//ils.unc.edu/dolma/country.html
Aschb@ils.unc.edu

Folk & Acoustic Music Exchange

Large collection of reviews of contemporary folk, Celtic, bluegrass, traditional, and a variety of ethnic styles. Ongoing project of the Peterborough, New Hampshire, Folk Music Society.

//www.acousticmusic.com
dnpyles@acousticmusic.com

FolkLib Index

Huge reference tool that tells you where to find information on the WWW about a wide variety of traditional and contemporary bluegrass and old-time artists.

//www.execpc.com/~henkle/fbindex/bluegrass.html

Grass Roots Pickers

Organization dedicated to preserving and promoting traditional acoustic music. This site was set up for members "as a gathering place, information library, place to promote their band or tapes, and networking or booking tool."

//www.grassrootspickers.com
sysop@rumpo.win.net

International Bluegrass Music Association (IBMA)

Web space for members of IBMA featuring news, events, etc.

//www.ibma.org

KiwiFolk

Folk and acoustic music around New Zealand.

//kiwifolk.org.nz/
mikem@earthlight.co.nz

The Newgrass Site

Only web page "dedicated to the furtherance and discussion of New Acoustic Music."

//www.cashiers.com/woodward/
wmckee@cashiers.com

Old-Time Music Home Page

Provided by David Lynch (not the *Twin Peaks* guy!) with many bridges to other sites including the old-time Fiddlers Hall of Fame, archives, museums, and organizations.

//www.geocities.com/~oldtimefiddler/
dlynch@mindspring.com

Old-Time Music Links

Pretty much what it says.

//funnelweb.utcc.utk.edu/~tkoosman/jca/oldtime.html

Old-Time Music on the Web

Selective list of links to resources, organizations, mailing lists, artists, and publications.

//www.korrnet.org/jca/oldtime.htm
jubilee@korrnet.org

Old-Time String Bands

//ils.unc.edu/barba/string/stringband.html

Pacific Bluegrass Network

Connections to bluegrass in Australia, New Zealand, and East Asia Part of the IBMA.

//www.healey.com.au/~mkear/pbn.htm
mkear@healey.com.au

Phil Salazar's "Om" Page

Cache Valley Drifters and old-time music links.

//www.west.net/~psalazar/
psalazar@west.net

Sam A. Funk Bluegrass Page

Many local and national connections.

//www2.southwind.net/~sfunk/#bam

SINGER/SONGWRITER

Harmony Ridge Music

Specializes in female singer songwriters from a variety of genres including Laurie Lewis, Iris DeMent, Josie Kreuzer, and many more.

//www.rahul.net/hrmusic/index.html
hrmusic@rahul.net

Singer/Songwriter Directory

Database divided into searchable categories such as Alternative, Country, Blues, Folk, Pop & Rock.

//singer-songwriter.com
info@singer-songwriter.com

CAJUN PAGES

Atlanta Cajun Dance Association
//userwww.service.emory.edu/~labst/acda/

Bay Area Cajun/Zydeco Club Calendar
//util.ucsf.edu/public/Cajun

Bon Temps Social Club of San Diego
//dances.com/dance/bonstemps.html

Cajun/Zydeco Music & Dance Page
Covers mostly Baltimore, D.C., & NYC but also other U.S. and U.K.; where to dance, schedules, etc.
//www.bme.jhu.edu/~jrice/cz.html
jrice@bme.jhu.edu

Cajun/Zydeco Resources
Anna Rubinstein's page for the Bay Area with bridges to national scenes as well.
//www.slip.net/~arubinst/index.html
arubinst@slip.net

Gumbo Pages
Very useful musical, cultural, & culinary information source for New Orleans & Acadiana.
//www.gumbopages.com
gumbo@webcom.com

Los Angeles Cajun/Zydeco Web Site
//home.aol.com/zydecobrad

Louisiana Upriver Home Page
Cajun/zydeco resources in the Upper Midwest
//www.bluebird.com/upriver/index.html

UK Cajun/Zydeco Resource
Covers Great Britain.
//www.alba.co.uk/ukCajun.htm
steve@alba.co.uk

Webfeet Database/Dance Data: Cajun
Information on Cajun bands and dance dates in the U.K.
//www.ftech.co.uk/~webfeet/Cajun/index.html
mgk@csu.npl.co.uk

Zydeco Underground
Cajun/Zydeco site for Southern California.
http://www.zydecomusic.com

TEJANO PAGES

BorderFest Box Office
Links to Tex-Mex, conjunto, and Latin artists including Flaco Jimenez, Augie Meyers, and the Texas Tornados.

//www.borderfest.com

Tejano Home Page
Major information source connected to many of the "New" Tejano stars as well as luminaries like Tony De La Rosa, Mingo Saldivar, Los Lobos, Santiago Jimenez.
//www.ondanet.com:1995/tejano/tejano.html

INSTRUMENT PAGES

All Kinds of Instruments on the Net!
Connections to pages on eveything from accordions to harps, bagpipes to bouzouki.
//www.csquare.com/1110/arts/music/instru/

Elderly Instruments
Music store/mail order service with huge stock of traditional instruments, instruction books and videos, and recordings.
//www.elderly.com
web@elderly.com

Lick a Minute
Series of one hour instructional videos from Texas Video for country related instruments/styles including bluegrass banjo (Alan Munde), pedal steel (Lloyd Maines), Western swing guitar (Joe Carr) plus dobro, fiddle, mandolin, harmonica, bass, and piano.
//applecity.com/music/hotlicks.html

Yahoo's Musical Instrument Links
Comprehensive listings broken down into many helpful indices and categories.
//www.yahoo.com/entertainment/music/instruments

Accordion

Accordion Home Page
Archive of information on all aspects of accordions and concertinas; includes Accordion FAQ
//www.cs.cmu.edu/afs/cs/user/phoebe/mosiac/accordion/html

Accordion Links
Jeroen Nijhof's on-going project with a wide variety of information on everything accordion plus many links to diversity of musical genres and bands using accordions (Cajun/zydeco, conjunto, country, rock, punk, etc.).
//www.th.rug.nl/~nijhof/accordions.html
nijhof@th.rug.nl

Accordion Music Appreciation Page
//www.hardlink.com/~mkozak/accordion/
mkozak@ualberta.ca

Accordions Worldwide Home Page
Largest site devoted to squeezeboxes (over 3,000 pages!) Includes articles, history, breakdown of types, and an accordion Yellow Pages.
//www.accordions.com

Hans Palm's Accordion Page
Technology and technique oriented site.
//accordion.simplenet.com

Jim Meloche's Cajun Accordion Page
History of the Cajun accordion and Meloche accordion plus many Cajun bookmarks
//www.meloche.net/accordio.htm

Linda C's Accordion Music Page
Part of Linda Candello's Totally Self-Centered Home Page featuring thoughts on the accordion and links.
//www.teleport.com/~lindac/accord.htm
lindac@teleport.com

Mr. Smarty Pants Knows
Lots of interesting accordion facts plus history and profiles of accordionists of all stripes.
//www.auschron.com/mrpants/
mrpants@auschron.com

Roots World/The Big Squeeze
Reviews of all types of music utilizing accordions.
//www.rootsworld.com/rw/feature/freereed.html

Banjo

Banjo Lounge
Resource for all 4-string banjo players with history, pictures, ads, and links.
//www.santhony.com/banjo/banjo.html
santhony@ix.netcom.com

Banjo Revolution
"A unique group of banjo related sites" provided by Nechville Musical Products.
//www.nechville.com/banjorev/

Banjo Tabs & Bluegrass Information
//bluegrassbanjo.com
phil@bluegrassbanjo.com

5-String Banjo
History, tabs, tunes, links, and more.
//www2.gol.com/users/f_banj.html
steve@gol.com

Four String Banjo Links
Bookmarks for players personal pages, resources, dealers, organizations, other banjo pages, hall of fame, and more.
//homepages.together.net/~induni/4string.htm

Dobro

Dobro or Resonator Guitar Website

History, players, resources, types, online discussion list, links.

//www.resoguit.com

The Dobro Pages

"The internet resource for resophonic players" with sound files, pictures, instructions, bookmarks.

//ourworld.compuserve.com/homepages/g
maass/
71043.2345@compuserve.com

Mike Auldridge Home Page

Highly informative dobro site by one of the greats.

//www.mikeauldridge.com

Planet Dobro

Loads of links to dobro and other steel guitar sites.

//www.mphase.com/planet2.htm

Transplanted Bluegrass Dobro Players Anonymous

Lots of information and connections to other dobro pages.

//members.tripod.com/~dobro/index.html

Fiddle

The Fiddle Web

Bridges to all things fiddle including artists, reviews, sheet music, camps, publications.

//www.gpfn.sk.ca/culture/arts/fiddle/
gfisch@gpfn.sk.ca

Fiddler's Home Page

"This site is about the world of the fiddle and its music."

//www.west.net/~psalazar/fiddlepage.html

Fiddlers on the Web

Stated purpose is "collecting and providing information to the internet public regarding fiddles, fiddle music, and other information relating to fiddles and fiddle music"; with many links to fiddlers and general violin/fiddle related sites.

//www.lad.bbn.com/users/gkeith/fiddles/fid
dler.html

NAFA: Fiddle-Related Web Sites

Bulletin boards, databases, styles, artists, resources, publications, instruction, tunes, etc.

//www.internetland.net/~bshull/NAFA/web
sites.html

Old-Time Fiddle Music

John Hartford's site sponsored by *Fiddler Magazine.*

//www.techpublishing.com/hartford/fiddle/f
iddle.html

Guitar

Alt-Country Tab Page

Clearinghouse of tab pages for Golden Smog, the Jayhawks, Lone Justice, Gram, Son Volt, Pistoleros, Sparklehorse, Uncle tupelo, the Walkabouts, Whiskeytown, and Wilco.

//www.netcomuk.co.uk/~wozza/altcountry_
tab_page.htm

Guitar Music Archive

Tabs, instruction, and more for a wide variety of artists and styles including alt. country.

//www.wildfire.com/~ag/gma/

OLGA: Online Guitar Archive

Immense repository for tabs, chords, and lots of other guitar information with many alt. country performers listed. Closed down (temporarily?) due to a threatened lawsuit by the U.S. National Music Publishers' association for copyright infringement.

//www.olga.net

Online Archive of Guitar Links

Big resource of pages for all types of guitar.

//www.oagl.com

Online Guitar College

"Comprehensive resource for guitar players" with connections to tabs, lessons, books, and repairs.

//www.eskimo.com/~ogre/

The Telecaster Appreciation Page

History, discussion, pictures, players, reading list, etc.

//www.geocities.com/sunsetstrip/studio/910
9/

Mandolin

Butch Baldassari's Nashville Mandolin Network

//www.idir.net/~mandonet/

Dan Beimborn's Mandolin Pages

Page "devoted to the collection of all things dealing with mandolins including construction, history, recordings and links to related sites"; also has info on how to get back issues of *Mandolin World News.*

//execpc.com/danb/mandolin.html
danb@execpc.com

Mandolin Cafe

Maintained by Scott Tichenor, this site contains a wide range of material on mandolins and players from all styles of mandolin music plus calendars, tabs, chords, etc.

//www.mandolincafe.com
stich@mandolincafe.com

Mandolin Mark's Mondo Mando Page

Mandolinists, Mandocharts, Mandolinks, etc.

//www.geoc@ities.com/bourbonstreet/3648/
mandomarkworldnet.att.net

Steel Guitars

Access Pedal Online

Links to players, builders, suppliers with players directory.

//www.dol.net/~harodl.liles/apedal2.htm
avalee@dol.net

The Pedal Steel Pages

Formerly the Bobby Lee/Quasar Steel Guitar Page, this is a major site with lots of information and a Steel Guitar Forum.

//b0b.com/index.html
quasar@b0b.com

Brad's Page of Steel

Huge location with data on all types of steel guitars including history, artist profiles, etc.

//www.well.com/user/wellvis/steel.html

Homemade Steel

"The Lap Steel Guitar Page" with information on how to build a guitar and links to related sites.

//www.geocities.com/sunsetstrip/studio/846
2/

Joe Wright's Pedal Steel Guitar Page

//www.pedalsteel.com

Moose Muse Music

Musings on all makes and styles of steel guitars by David Van Allen who developed the V-Steel or "Virtual" Steel Guitar Emulator Software both of which can be ordered by e-mail.

//www.pond.com/~vanallen/
vanallen@pond.com

Online Steelers

"The Worldwide Steel Guitarist Directory" for contacting amateur and professional players everywhere.

//www3.sk.sympatico.ca/waltd/
waltd@sk.sympatico.ca

The Pedal Steel Guitar Associaion

//www.psga.org

Pedal Steel Guitar Resources

Connections to non-pedal, dobro, and lap steel sites.

//steelguitar.com/resource/websioth.htm

The Steel Guitar Information Resource

Technical site with information on tuning, adjustments, strings, et al.

//www.steelguitarinfo.com
Sginfo@steelguitarinfo.com

ARTISTS

See Alternative Country Artists A-Z for separate lists.

MAILING LIST RESOURCES

Alt. Music Group List

For Usenet newsgroups.
//www.cs.ubc.ca/spider/edmonds/music/alt-music.html

CTI Music: List of Musical Mailing Lists

Divided and serachable by category.
//www.lancs.ac.uk/users/music/music/research/musicallists.html

Deja News: The Discussion Network

Searchable mailing list digest.
//www.dejanews.com

List of Musical Mailing Lists

Huge database.
//www.shadow.net/~mwaas/lomml.html

Liszt: Intro to Mailing Lists

Mailing lists, newsgroups, chat.
//www.liszt.com

Mailing Lists@Soundz

//www.soundz.com/netresources/mailinglist.html

INDIVIDUAL LISTS

ACCORDION

For players and builders of pianos, button accordions, and concertinas.
accordion-request@cs.cmu.edu

AustRoots

A discussion group for Australian roots music: blues, rockabilly, hillbilly.
//www.onelist.com/subscribe.cgi/austroots/

BANJO-L

"The Banjo Discussion List" with players' directory, archives, and more.
//idt.net/~zepp29/homepage.htm

BGRASS-L

One of the most active and lively music mailing lists; digest setting recommended
Listserv@lsv.uky.edu
(leave subject line blank, type Subscribe BGRASS-L followed by your name)

or through:

//www.mandolincafe.com/lists.html

BLUEGRASSDJ-L

"For bluegrass DJs, record labels, and performers who want to communicate."
//www.onelist.com/subscribe.cgi/bluegrassdj/
bluegrassdj@onelist.com

CoMando Mailing List

For mandolin players, those interested in learning to play, or those who simply enjoy mandolin music.
listserv@vmi.no.dak.edu
(type Subscribe Comando) or through
//www.mandolincafe.com/lists.html

Cool Guitar

Dedicated to great axe slingers like Jimmy Bryant, Danny Gatton, Scotty Moore, Link Wray, et al.
longhorn@worldonline.nl

COUNTRY-L

Members discuss traditional, new, and sometimes alt. country.
maiser@rmgate.pop.indiana.edu
(leave subject line blank, type Sub Country-L)

FIDDLE-L

For fiddle players and fans.
listserv@brownnvm.brown.edu
(type subscribe F-L, your name)

FLATPICK-L

Provided for flatpickers everywhere.
listserv@listserv.nodak.edu
(type Subscribe F-L, first and last name)
or go through:

//www.mandolincafe.com/lists/

FOLKDJ-L

Listserv mailing list for bluegrass, folk, roots disc jockeys AM/FM worldwide.
listserv@psuvm.psu.edu
with command "SUBSCRIBE FOLKDJ-L"

or through:

//folkradio.org

FOLK_MUSIC

Pertaining to new American folk music including reviews, schedules, releases etc.
Listserv@nysernet.org
(type Subscribe Folk-Music, your name)

Free Reed Mailing List

For accordion lovers everywhere.
GJackson@bradford.ac.uk

HARP-L Archives

Accordion & harmonica.
//www.wku.edu/~pierccm/harp_home.html
pierccm@wkuvx1.wku.edu

Hillbilly Music Mailing List

Created in May 1998 by Stephen Lee Canner "to provide a forum for intelligent discussion of traditional country, bluegrass, rockabilly, honky-tonk, and other related forms of culturally Southern music."

//www.mindspring.com/~canner/list.htm

NEWGRASS-L

"For discussion of newgrass and new acoustic music."
listserver@dte.net
(subscribe newgrass-l as message)

The No Depression Country Club

"No Nashville Junk" on this alt. Country list found in Yahoo's "Clubs" section.
//clubs.yahoo.com/clubs/thenodepressioncountryclub

Old-Time Music Discussion Group

listserv@listserv.vt.edu
(Subscribe old-time Music Discussion Group, your name as message)

Old-Time WWW Bulletin Board

For all areas of American old-time music.
//140.190.128.190/oldtime/oldtime.html

Passenger Side/Postcard 2: The Alternative/Insurgent Country Music Mailing List

Spin off of the Postcard mailing list for Uncle Tupelo, Wilco, Son Volt fans. P2 discussions are lively and cover a wide variety of alternative and related subjects (just mention "hookers & blow," and you're in!). The annual Twangfest in St. Louis grew out of this list.

Automated subscription through:

//www.gumbopages.com/music/pass-side.html

Subscription information also at:

//www.drizzle.com/~lal/postcard2.htm
//www.topsoil.net/postcard2.htm

Postcard: The Uncle Tupelo, Wilco, & Son Volt Mailing List

One of the first major alt. country mailing lists, it was initially devoted to Uncle Tupelo and its off shoots but later became more general in scope and spawned Passenger Side/Postcard 2: The Alternative/Insurgent Country Music Mailing List.

Automated Subscription through:
//www.servtech.com/ddewey/postcard/

or

//www.gumbopages.com/music/postcard.html

Archives:
//www.servtech.com/public/dave/postcard/date.html

Postcard Tape Traders

To set up trades, circulate tape lists, discuss trades, request shows for alt. country acts from The Bottlerockets to Wilco.

dpjsly@netnitco.net
(Subscribe Trade as subject)

Resoguit

For lap style players of Dobro/dobro/resonator guitars.

majordomo@intr.net (subscribe Resoguit, your e-mail as message)

or through

//www.resoguit.com

Rockabilly Discussion Group

One of the biggest and most active of rockabilly lists.

majordomo@teleport.com
(subscribe rockabilly-l as message)

or through:

//www.rockabillyhall.com/discusgrouppr.html

Rockabilly Hall of Fame Interactive Message Board

//www.rockabillyhall.com/index07.html

Rockabilly Mailing List

"Free wheeeling conversation about anything of interest among the rockabilly community"

//www.onelist.com
rab@onelist.com

Rockin' in Cyberspace Mailing List

Rockabilly forum maintained by Australian DJ Bob Hope-Hume

//kali.murdoch.edu.au/~hopehume/rockin.html

Rockin' Records

"For everyone who loves rockabilly, rock and roll, doowop, rhythm and blues, surf records."

//www.pcuf.fi/~tapiov/index.html#rockinrecordslist

Rootin' Around

"Chattin' & chewin' about roots music and roadtrips."

//clubs.yahoo.com/clubs/rootinaround/

Roots Music Gathering

"For professionals in the roots music field to stay in touch with each other and discuss issues and resources of concern to them."

//www.ikoiko.com/cuttingedge/rootsmail.html

Songwriters Mailing List

Listserv@peach.ease.lsoft.com
(subscribe Songtalk, your name)

Squeezeboxes Mailing List

Devoted to playing and repairing of all free reeds except harmonica.

Majordomo-squeezebox@cs.cmu.edu
{Message Body: subscribe squeezebox}

The Steel Guitar Forum

Part of the Pedal Steel Pages, it is a place to post messages broken down into categories: General, No Peddlers (lap steel, dobro, Hawaiian), Events, Technical, Humor, etc.

//b0b.com/forum/

Tapio's Fin-A-Billy Page

Another active rockabilly list.

//www.pcuf.fi/~tapiov/index.html

TRADITIONAL-L

A mailing list for discussion of traditional music i.e. bluegrass and old-time maintained by *iBluegrass Magazine*.

Automated subscription through:
//www.ibluegrass.com

or

listserver@dte.net
(subscribe traditional-l as message)

Twangfest List

Off-shoot of the Postcard2 list for discussion of "all fluff all the time."

twangfest@nashvegas.com
(subscribe twangfest in message body)

AOL MAILING LISTS

(follow Entertainment to Music to Chat & Messages to Music Community)

Banjo Folder

Under Country/Folk>Folk/Acoustic

Bluegrass/Old-Time Music Folder

Under Country/Folk

Cajun/Zydeco Music

Under Country/Folk Topics or World Music

Cool Texas/Roots Music Folder

Under Country/Folk>Country/Folk Topics

Dobro Folder

Under Country/Folk>Folk/Acoustic

Folk/Acoustic Folder

Hard Country Folder

Under Country/Folk>Country/Folk Topics

Mandolin Folder

Under Country/Folk>Folk/Acoustic

No Depression/Alternative Country Folder

"For the music of Gram Parsons, Uncle Tupelo, Blue Mountain, Jayhawks, and other practitioners of their craft", generated *No Depression* magazine.

Under Alternative>Alternative Topics

Old-Time Music Folder

Under Country/Folk>Country/Folk Topics

Progressive Bluegrass Folder

Under Country/Folk>Folk/Acoustic

Rockabilly Folder

Under Alternative>Alternative Topics

Steel Guitar Folder

Under Music Professionals>Musicians & Techniques

USENET NEWSGROUPS

rec.music.country

rec.music.country.western

rec.music.country.old-time

rec.music.makers.squeezebox

rec.music.western

alt.banjo

alt.banjo.clawhammer

alt.banjo.newsgroups
//vic.com/news/groups/alt.banjo.html

alt.culture.Cajun

alt.guitar.lap-pedal

alt.music.austin

alt.music.bootlegs
Lively trade in Uncle Tupelo, Son Volt, Wilco, the Jayhawks and other alt. country boots.

alt.music.chapel-hill

alt.music.harmonica

alt.music.rockabilly

alt.music.texas

CHAT GROUPS

#Bluegrass: Bluegrass Internet Relay Chat
//www.geocities.com/nashville/5386/

#Bluegrass: Chatroom on Chatnet
//members.xoom.com/bluegrassirc/

Bluegrass Chat Room
//www.bluegrass.com/bgchat.html

Rockabilly Chat Page
//www.maybe.com/chat/chat.cgi

Salty Dog Bluegrass Chat on AOL

Steel Guitar Cyberchat
//www.onlineinstitute.com/guitar/chat.cgi

**V
E
N
U
E
S**

Venue Guides
(Print and Online)

Acoustic London
Most comprehensive listing on the Internet of unplugged music in the London area.

//www.csed.demon.co.uk/ac_lon.htm

Acoustic Venue Database
Extensive listing for North America.

//www.indra.com/~radhardcd/

BarbCal: Boston Area and Regional Bluegrass Calendar
Mostly NE bluegrass events but also other types of alt. country/Americana by date, band, state, venue.

//www.tiac.net/users/jmmiller/barbcal/

Centerstage
Database for Chicago nightclubs.

//centerstage.net/chicago/music/clubs/

The Concert Web
Large listing of current tour dates and venues by state and country with many links to other venue resources

//www.the concertweb.com

Crosstown Arts
Venue resource for Maryland, D.C., Virginia.

//www.crosstownarts.com/crosstownarts/ct own_html/venues.html

Dirty Linen Tour Schedules
Large pull out of upcoming dates for folk, bluegrass, old-time, Cajun, etc. included with each print issue and available online (see Publications)

//www.dirtynelson.com/linen/

Folk Book Online: Folk Venues
The ultimate resource for folk venues.

//www.folkmusic.org

Folk Club Zueri
Listing of European venues for folk and roots.

//www.access.ch/folkclubzueri/

House Concerts
Directory for very intimate, informal (and often unpublicized) acoustic events held in various indoor and outdoor settings around the U.S.

//www.houseconcerts.com

Indie Web
Independent label site that has "Scene Pages."

//www.indieweb.com/index.html

Magic Bus Music Forum
Nationwide list of clubs with description, addresses, genres, dates.

//mbus.com/clubs/

Musi-Cal
Big site searchable by venue, city, artist, event.

//concerts.calendar.com/concerts/

Music Alive!
Connections to acoustic music venues in the U.S.

//www.acousticmusic.com/venupgs.htm

The Musician's Guide to Touring and Promotion
Published yearly by *Musician* magazine, it has detailed descriptions of all types of clubs in North America by state/city.

1515 Broadway, 11th Floor
New York, NY 10036
212-536-5248
//www.billboard-online.com/musician/

P2OnTour
Outgrowth of the Postcard2 alt. country mailing list where members who are in bands, manage bands, act as booking agents or venue representatives can post tour related information. Created by Stacey Taylor who also maintains the Hellcountry music showcase and web page to promote twang in the Boston area and beyond.

p2-ontour@nashvegas.com
(subscribe as message)

Performance Magazine
Giant venue/event database by state and country.

//www.performancemag.com

Planet Sound
European club guide
//clubs.de

Pollstar

Billed as "the most accurate, comprehensive, up to date concert tour database" with listings for over 2,000 artists plus search option by city and venue.

//www.pollstar.com

Puddlestomp Acoustic Venue Directory

Published by Puddlestomp Records with over 3,100 listings for every state in the U.S. including venues large and small, public and private plus open-mics and more.

P. O. Box 11110
Portland, ME 04104
//www.ime.net/~pdlstomp/directory.html

RAB: World-Wide Gig Guide

Large listing for psychobilly and rockabilly events.

//lowdown.psycho.org.au/gigs.html

River Sounds

Acoustic, folk, bluegrass venues in New York and New Jersey metro area.

//www.rivint.com/music/

Rockabilly Central

Lots of listings by band/performer.

//www.rockabill.net/tours.htm

Tourdates

Large list of live music events searchable by artist.

//www.tourdates.com/dates.html

Wild Bop Marlon's Hillbilly, Rockabilly, Bluegrass Western Swing, and Old-Time Country Music Events

Excellent listing for concerts and festivals in Europe and North America.

//www.geocities.com/SunsetStrip/alley/5938/events.html

WILMA: The Internet Guide to Live Music

Gigantic, user friendly site for finding venues and performers (over 8,000) world-wide.

//www.wilma.com

WWW Live Music

European database.

//www.live-music.com

UNITED STATES

ALABAMA

Birmingham

Five Points Music Hall

Wide range of alternative and Americana

1016 20th St. South
205-322-BAND
//www.5pointsmusichall.com

The Nick

Alternative variety with groups like the Bad Livers and Ex-Husbands on occasion.

2514 10th Ave. South
205-252-3831

Hayden

Acoustic Cafe

House concert north of Birmingham presenting bluegrass, old-time, singer/ songwriter in an outdoor, hillside setting (pp: Norman Blake, John Hartford, Tony Rice, Tut Taylor).

205-647-3237
//www.houseconcerts.com
AcousticC@aol.com

Tuscaloosa

The Chukker

Oldest (since 1956) and most popular alt. club in town; motto is "everything goes all the time" which means acoustic, bluegrass, blues, ethnic, kitchen sink.

2121 6th St.
205-391-0708
//www.thechukker.com

ARIZONA

Phoenix

*The *Phoenix New Times* has a weekly music calendar.

//www.phoenixnewtimes.com

Fiddler's Dream

Folk, bluegrass, country, Cajun, alternative

1702 E. Cactus Wren
602-997-9795
//www.primenet.com/~fiddler/

Rhythm Room

Mostly blues but also rockabilly, Cajun/ zydeco, etc. (pp: Big Sandy, Dave & Deke, the Forbidden Pigs, and many more)

1019 E. Indian School
602-265-4842
//www.rhythmroom.com

Rockin' Horse (Scottsdale)

Burned down in summer 1996 but rebuilt and still a prime venue for alt. country acts (pp: Junior Brown, Dale Watson, the Derailers)

7316 E. Stetson
602-949-0992

Tucson

Luna Loca

546 N. Stone
520-882-4488

The Rialto Theater

Located in historic theater built in 1919 and offering a wide variety of roots music (pp: Son Volt; Blue Mountain; held the first Tucson Twangfest in September 1998 with Red Meat, the Revenants, Al Perry, Creosote)

318 E. Congress
520-740-1986

ARKANSAS

Fayetteville

JR's Dickson St. Ballroom

Hosts a variety of Americana including the Bottlerockets, Son Volt, Charlie Robison, Lucinda Williams, Robert Earl Keen, and many more.

Little Rock

Vino's

Many alt. music styles (pp: Slobberbone; the Delta Angels)

7th & Chester
501-375-8466
//www.aristotle.net/seen/vinos/calendar.html

CALIFORNIA

NOTE: California has one of the most active Cajun dance scenes in the U.S. with many events not held at the regular nightclubs; for more information consult the Cajun Web Pages.

Los Angeles

*For detailed club/concert information see:

L.A. Weekly
//www.laweekly.com

and

Orange County Weekly
//www.ocweekly.com

The All-Star Lanes

Site for the monthly "Bowl-A-Rama," a rockabilly/psychobilly blow out with a consistently fine line-up of top acts from California and beyond; created and produced by Carlos Alvarado (pp: Horton Brothers, Hot Club of Cowtown, Dave Stuckey, Deke Dickerson, Smith's Ranch Boys, Groovy Rednecks, Cadillac Angels, Ronnie Dawson, Rosie Flores).

4459 Eagle Rock Blvd.
323-663-5589
//home.earthlink.net/~highoctane1/indexbowl.html
highoctane1@earthlink.net

Alligator Lounge

Alternative and Americana.

3321 Pico Blvd. (Santa Monica)
310-449-1843
//www.rockcitynews.com/clubs/alligator/

Bar Deluxe

"Hollywood's Rockabilly Roadhouse" featuring honky tonk, rockabilly, roots-rock

1710 N. Las Palmas (Hollywood)
213-469-1991
//www.black-kat.com/bardeluxe/
Bardeluxe@black-kat.com

Blue Cafe

Presents "Roadhouse Rockabilly Roots" every Sunday (pp: Bill Kirchen, the Hollisters, the Cousin Lovers...)

210 Promenade (Long Beach)
562-983-7111
//mediaraid.com/bluecafe/
Bbluecafe@aol.com

Blue Saloon

All manner of Americana including rockabilly.

4657 Lankershim Blvd. (N. Hollywood)
818-766-4644
//www.rockcitynews.com/clubs/bluesaloon

Dixiebell Restaurant

Hillbilly, honky tonk, rockabilly from California e.g. Red Meat, Jeff Bright.

9559 Imperial Hwy. (Downey)
562-803-4943

Foothill Club

Vintage dance hall offering many types of Americana.

1922 Cherry Ave. (Signal Hill)
310-494-5196

Highland Grounds

Home of the monthly "Western Beat Americana Showcase" in a coffeehouse setting.

742 North Highland (Hollywood)
213-466-1507
//www.highlandgrounds.com

Western Beat:
//www.electricearl.com/wbeat.html

Jack's Sugar Shack

Popular spot with lots of local and national alt. country; hosts the legendary Ronnie Mack's Barn Dance on Tuesday evenings

1707 N. Vine St. (Hollywood)
213-466-7005
//www.jackssugarshack.com

Linda's Doll Hut

"Live Music, Roadhouse Style": very alt. country friendly showcase especially for L.A. area artists such as Big Sandy, James Intveld, Dave & Deke, Rosie Flores, Ronnie Mack, et al. since 1990.

107 South Adams (Anaheim)
714-533-1286
//www.rockabilly.com/linda.html

or

//www.rockcitynews.com/clubs/dollhut/

McCabe's

Home of "McCabe's Variety Night" (acoustic, alt. rock) with connecting guitar shop.

3101 Pico Blvd. (Santa Monica)
310-828-4403
//www.infonorth.com/vnight/

The Rhino Room

Alternative club that has Wednesday nights designated for swing and/or rockabilly.

7979 Center Ave. (Huntington Beach)
714-892-3316

Sacramento

Old Ironsides

Alternative and Americana in a rustic setting.

1901 10th St.
916-443-9751
//www.rcip.com/ironsides/ironsides.htm.html

The Palms Playhouse

"A Cultural Oasis in Davis": very fine Americana and alt. country venue (pp: Dave Alvin, Pete Anderson, the Bad Livers, Austin Lounge Lizards, Jr. Brown, Del McCoury, et al.)

726 Drummond Ave. (Davis)
916-756-9901
//www.dcn.davis.ca.us/lacarrol/palms/palmhome.html

San Diego

The Belly Up Tavern

Famous Southern Cal nightclub booking blues, rock, rockabilly, Western swing, zydeco, etc.

143 S. Cedros Ave. (Solano Beach)
619-481-8140
//www.bellyup.com

Moonshines

Reopened January 17, 1999, with "The Salty Boogie Barndance" featuring the Smith's Ranch Boys.

4225 30th St. (North Park)

619-640-5310

Soul Kitchen

Rock on weekends but swing, bluegrass, etc. weekdays.

168 E. Main (El Cajon)
619-579-3735

Tio Leo's Lounge

"Coolest & Hottest Live Music in Town" e.g. rockabilly, jump swing, alternative rock (pp: the Lucky Stars, the Hollisters, Billy Bacon, Hot Club of Cowtown, the Hillbilly Boogiemen).

5302 Napa St.
619-542-1462
//www.tioleos.com/lounge.html
info@tioleos.com

San Francisco

Ace Cafe

Cozy Americana venue of **Pushing the Norton** compilation fame.

1539 Folsom. St.
415-621-4752

Bimbo's 365 Club

Historic nightclub offering alternative variety and host to Greaseball '98 Rockabilly Weekender with Kim Lenz, Jeff Bright, Dave Stuckey, Deke Dickerson, and more.

1025 Columbus Ave.
415-474-0365
//www.bimbos365club.com
bimbos@sirius.com

The Bottom of the Hill

Large club presenting the cream of local and national acts of many kinds.

1233 17th St.
415-626-4455
//www.sfstation.com/bars/bottomofthehill/

Cafe Du Nord

Good venue for alt. and Americana but especially locals like the Radio Ranch Straight Shooters, Red Meat, and the Sloe Gin Joes; has "Swingin' Sundays," both Eastern and Western.

2170 Market
415-861-5016
//www.cafedunord.com

Club Deluxe

Strong lineup of honky tonk, rockabilly, swing especially from the Bay area (pp: James Intveld, Jeff Bright, Red Meat).

1509-11 Haight St. @ Ashbury
415-552-6949
//www.clubdeluxe.com
info@clubdeluxe.com

DeMarco's 23 Club

Regular offerings of alt. country from California and beyond (pp: Wayne Hancock, the Hollisters)

23 Visitacion Ave. (Brisbane)
415-467-7717
//www.meer.net/~nuggett/DeM-pg1.html

DNA Lounge

Diverse schedule (previous host of the Grease Ball)

375 11th St.
415-626-1409
//www.dnalounge.com

Freight and Salvage Coffee House

West Coast's oldest acoustic/folk venue sponsored by the Berkeley Society for the Preservation of Traditional Muisc; presents all manner of traditional music.

1111 Addison St. (Berkeley)
510-548-1761
//www.bks.com/freight/

The Great American Music Hall

Sizable venue with a variety of music including alt., blues, bluegrass, country, Cajun, etc.

859 O'Farrell
415-885-0750
//www.musichallsf.com

Henflings Firehouse Tavern

Noted mostly for blues but also presenting a wider mix of Americana: Bad Livers, Deke Dickerson, Red Dirt Rangers.

9450 Hwy. 9 (Ben Lomond)
503-336-8811
//www2.cruzio.com/~henfling/
henfling@cruzio.com

The Ivy Room (Albany)

Good alt.country/Americana bar located outside San Francisco in Albany.

Corner of San Pablo and Solano

Paradise Lounge

Three, count 'em, three stages going at once with many musical styles including bluegrass, country, Cajun, etc.

308 11th St. at Folsom
415-621-1911

Slim's

Fair size club booking rock, country, Cajun, folk among others; one time host to the annual rockabilly "Grease Ball."

333 11th St.
415-255-0333
//sfstation.com/live/slims.htm

The Sweetwater

A potpourri of Americana

153 Throckmorton Ave. (Mill Valley)
415-388-2820
//www.globerecords.com/sweetwater/

San Jose

The Agenda Lounge

Mostly a jazz club, but Wednesday nights are set aside for rockabilly and swing.

399 South 1st St.
408-287-3991
//www.agendalounge.com

Fuel 44

Rockabilly, hillbilly bop, roots.

44 Almaden
408-295-7374
//www.fuel44.com

Santa Barbara

Cold Spring Tavern

The Cache Valley Drifters every Wednesday night.

COLORADO

Boulder

Penny Lane Coffee House

Primarily for a wide selection of acoustic acts.

1795 Pearl St.
303-443-9516

Breckenridge

Alligator Lounge

Roots music from bluegrass to rockabilly to Cajun.

320 South Main
http://www.rockski.net/alligator/

Denver

9th Ave. West

Home of "Tore Up!" on Wednesday night with the best in classic and contemporary rockabilly, Western swing, hillbilly boogie, and jump. (pp: Ray Condo, High Noon, the Ranch Girls, the Dalhart Imperials, Dave Stuckey).

9th & Acoma
303-572-8006
//www.bigk.com/bigk.html

Bluebird Theater

Once a porno house but now deals in Americana including alt. country (pp: the Bad Livers Jr. Brown, the Picketts, Wilco)

3317 E. Colfax Ave.
303-322-2308
//www.thebluebird.com/bluebird/

Herman's Hideaway

Blues, honky tonk, Cajun, roots-rock (pp: Big Sandy, Dale Watson, Dave Alvin)

1578 S. Broadway

303-778-9916
//www.hermanshideaway.com

Mercury Cafe

Eclectic Americana.

2199 California St.
303-294-9281

Swallow Hill Music Association

Acoustic and traditional for over 20 years including singer/songwriter (Richard Buckner, David Olney), Cajun, and more.

71 E. Yale
303-777-1003

FLORIDA

Gainesville

The Covered Dish

Recognized as one of the top venues in the region for its diverse musical tastes (pp: Will Oldham, the V-Roys); home of the "Raunch-o-Rama."

210 SW 2nd Ave.
352-377-3334
http://atlantic.net/~robg/dish/dish.html

Orlando

Sapphire Supper Club

Bills diversity of alternative music

54 N. Orange Ave.
407-246-1419
//www.sapphiesupperclub.com

Tampa Bay

Skipper's Smokehouse

Good roots venue including "Roots Wednesday" showcasing local and national talent.

910 Skipper Rd.
813-971-0666
//mbus.com/clubs/skippers.smokehouse/

GEORGIA

Athens

40 Watt

Alternative, country, folk
285 W. Washington St.
706-549-7871

Atlanta

*Check the weeklies for music calendars
Creative Loafing:
//wwwcreativeloafing.com
or
Flagpole:
//www.flagpole.com weeklies.

Austin Ave. Buffet

Birthplace of the Redneck Underground.

918 Austin Ave. NE
404-524-9274

The Star Community Bar

Meeting place for Atlanta's Redneck Underground, and one of the most famous alt. country venues; home of the annual Bubbapalooza Festival.

437 Moreland Ave.
404-681-9018
//www.creativeloafing.com/mall/starbar/
//users.aol.com/roboburger/starbar.htm

Smith's Olde Bar

Another fine alt. country watering hole (pp: Ex-Husbands, Seconds Flat, Shaver, Son Volt).

1578 Piedmont Ave.
404-875-1522

ILLINOIS

Champaign/Urbana

The Blind Pig Co.

General alt. with plenty of alt. country on the calendar (pp: the Honeydogs, the Cowslingers, the V-Roys, many more).

6 Taylor St.
217-351-7444
//www.shout.net/~blindpig/

Fat City

Americana.

505 S. Chestnut St.
217-356-7100

Chicago

*Check the calendars on the following web pages:

Centerstage
//centerstage.net/chicago/music/clubs/

and

Chicago Shows List
//www.tezcat.com/~andy/shows/byvenue.txt

Abbey Pub

Mainly a place for locals like Urban Twang, the Waco Brothers, the Riptones, Peatmoss, et al. but also touring acts such as the Mollys, Katy Moffatt, Tom Russell.

3420 W. Grace
773-478-4408
//centerstage.net/chicago/music/clubs/abbey-pub.html

Beat Kitchen

Eclectic with occasonal visits from local/regional performers e.g. The Riptones, Bucky Halker, Waco Brothers, et al.

2100 W. Belmont
773-281-4444

Chicago Folk Center

Formerly (until 1998) the venerable Old Town School of Folk Music, it offers a consistently fine schedule of Americana and roots variety (pp: Steve Earle, Alejandro Escovedo, Hot Rize, Dave Alvin, Steve Riley, the Jazzabels, and many more).

909 W. Armitage Ave.
773-525-7793

Double Door

Another of Chitown's many fine alt. country clubs (pp: Blue Mountain, Robbie Fulks, Farmer Not So John, Whiskeytown, and many, many others).

1572 N. Milwaukee
773-489-3160
//centerstage.net/chicago/music/clubs/double-door.html

Elbo Room

Mostly alt. rock but also alt. country (pp: Dave & Deke, Rosie Flores, Riptones)

2871 N. Lincoln
773-549-5549
//centerstage.net/chicago/music/clubs/elboroom.html

The Empty Bottle

Primarily alt. rock but often local and national alt. country acts as well (pp: Bodeco, Freakwater, Robbie Fulks, the Handsome Family, Jon Langford, the Scud Mountain Boys).

1035 N. Western
773-276-3600
//ww.emptybottle.com

Fitzgerald's

Home of the annual "American Music" and "Harvest Moon" festivals and the best in alt. country/Americana week in and week out.

6615 Roosevelt Rd. (Berwyn)
708-788-2118
//www.fitzgeraldsnightclub.com

The Hideout

Host to Honky Tonk Living Room, "Chicago's best country and country influenced music—country, alternative country, bluegrass, old-time, insurgent country, sturm and twang—in a cozy-as-your-living-room setting," the 1st and 3rd Thursdays each month; created (1998) and hosted by Kelly Kessler of Texas Rubies fame (pp: Edith Frost, Jimmy LaFave, Jon Langford, Volo Bogtrotters, Deanna Varagon, Jane Baxter Miller, Anna Fermin, Hillbillies From Space).

1354 W. Wabansia
773-227-4433
//www.bcity.com/honkytonk/
kykr@hotmail.com

Lounge Ax

Owned by Jeff Tweedy, it regularly presents alt. country acts (pp: the Bad Livers, Golden Smog, Moonshine Willy, the Old 97s, Wilco).

2438 N. Lincoln
773-525-6620
//www.loungeax.com

Schuba's Tavern

"Hard core honky tonk music nightly"; very supportive of alt. country artists (especially Chicago based), and the best from all over have played there.

3159 N. Southport
773-525-2508
//www.schubas.com

INDIANA

Bloomington

Second Story

Local/national acts from almost all genres.

201 S. College
812-336-2582

IOWA

Council Bluffs

Blue Ox Restaurant

Features "Country Roots" each Sunday which can range from bluegrass to Cajun to old-time.

3549 West Broadway
712-322-0097

Des Moines

Connie's Lounge

Good Midwestern venue on the alt. country circuit.

3839 Merle Hay Rd.
515-270-0412

Iowa City

Gabe's Oasis

Reputation as one of the area's top venues with a wide variety of music including such artists as the Bottle Rockets, Big Sandy, Dale Watson, Dave Alvin, et al.

330 E. Washington St.
319-354-4788

Gunnerz

Diverse venue especially favorable to local acts like Tom Jessen, High and Lonesome, and Bo Ramsey.

123 E. Washington St.
319-338-2010

KANSAS

Lawrence

The Bottleneck
Alternative club which frequently has the best in alt. country (pp: the Gourds, Robbie Fulks, Cheri Knight, the Damnations).

> 737 New Hampshire
> 913-842-5483

Liberty Hall
Historic building with Americana variety.

> 642 Massachusetts
> 785-749-1912
> //www.pilgrimpage.com/libertyhall/

Wichita

Artichoke Sandwich Bar
Acoustic music: bluegrass, folk, country (pp: Randy Erwin, Bell & Shore, Scroat Belly).

> 811 N. Broadway
> 316-263-9164
> //www.scoutserv.com/doodah/artichoke/music.html

KENTUCKY

Lexington

Lynagh's Music Club
One of the region's top clubs with a variety including lots of alt. country (pp: the V-Roys, Robert Earl Keen, Kelly Willis, the Old 97s, Joe Ely, et al.)

> 388 Woodland Ave.
> 606-255-6614
> //www.lexmusic.com/lynaghs/

Louisville

Butchertown Pub
Amidst the punk, you'll regularly find bluegrass and rockabilly (i.e. Cigar Store Indians).

> 1335 Story Ave.
> 502-583-2242

Newport

Southgate House
Varied offerings including alt. country (pp: Ass Ponys; Robbie Fulks).

> 24 East 3rd St.
> 606-431-2201
> //home.fuse.net/fabienne/
> ufofingertwin@hotmail.com

Whitesburg

Appalshop
One of the area's prime locales for bluegrass, folk, and blues. Home of the annual "Hillbilly Nation Celebration" and part of the Appalshop complex which includes Appal Records, film production, and WMMT radio.

> 306 Madison St.
> 606-633-0108
> //www.uky.edu/projects/appal/
> appalshop@igc.apc.org

LOUISIANA

*For detailed information on Cajun dance halls and other venues throughout Bayou Country consult:

> //www.cbu.edu/~smader/caz_ref2.html

Baton Rouge

Bayou Dance Pavillion
Zydeco Friday night, Cajun Saturday night.

> 35019 Alligator Bayou Rd.
> 888-3SWAMPS; 504-642-8297
> //www.alligatorbayou.com

Mulate's
Nightly Cajun dances.

> 8322 Bluebonnet Rd.
> 504-767-4794

Breaux Bridge

Harry's Club
Very popular Cajun hall with the natives on the weekends.

> 519 Parkway Dr.
> 318-332-5180

La Poussiere
Walter Mouton & the Scott Playboys home turf each Saturday evening.

> 1215 Grand Point Rd.
> 318-332-1721

Mulate's
Noted hot spot for great Cajun food and music.

> 325 Mills Ave.
> 318-332-4648
> //www.mulates.com

Eunice

Gilton's Club
The best bands, huge dance floor, lively dancers.

> Near the junction of Hwy. 95S and Hwy. 190
> 318-457-1241

Liberty Theater
Location for "Rendez-Vous des Cajins," a very popular two hour live radio broadcast (KEUN, KJJB, KRVS) each Saturday night hosted by Dr. Barry Ancelet and featuring 2-3 bands nightly playing while a live audience wildly dances and cheers in the background.

> 2nd St. and Park Ave.
> 318-457-6540

Savoy's Music Center
Music shop run by Marc and Ann Savoy which holds a weekly Saturday morning "Jam Session" (9:30-12) for Cajun musicians of all skill levels.

> Hwy. 190E
> 318-457-9563

VFW Post 8971
Homebase of Steve Riley & the Mamou Playboys.

> Hwy. 190E near Savoy's Music Center
> 318-457-1055

Henderson

Angelle's Whiskey River Landing
Cajun place built out over the water. Music/dancing Sundays starting at 4 p.m.

> About 15 mins. east of Breaux Bridge on Hwy. 347 south of I-10

Lafayette

Grant Street Dance Hall
A-1 club for Cajun, zydeco, and a variety of other music.

> 113 W. Grant St.
> 318-237-8513

Randol's
Cajun dining and dancing with bands like Al Berard & the Basin Brothers and File seven nights/week.

> 2320 Kaliste Rd.
> 800-YO-CAJUN; 318-981-7080

Lewisburg

Borque's
Rustic dance hall near Opelousas.

> 318-948-9904

Mamou

Brass Rail Lounge
The place to go for Saturday afternoon music/dancing after Fred's closes (see below).

> 6th. St.

Fred's Lounge
Renowned Cajun dance spot famous for Saturday morning live radio broadcasts and dances (9:30 a.m.-1 p.m.) courtesy of KVPI.

> 420 6th St.
> 318-468-5411
> (Mamou is about 10 miles north of Eunice)

New Orleans

Howlin' Wolf

Wide diversity of music on any given night.

828 S. Peters St.
504-529-2341

The Mermaid Lounge

Always noted for its eclecticism, it became a very good alt. country venue in the late 1990s with regular acts and special events like "Twang-O-Rama."

1100 Constance St.
504-524-4747
//www.geocities.com/bourbonstreet/6169/

Michaul's Restaurant

Cajun dancing every night but Sunday.

840 St. Charles Ave. (near the French Quarter)
504-522-5517

Mid-City Lanes Rock 'N' Bowl

A most unusual but fabulous venue with rockabilly on Tuesday and Cajun/zydeco Wednesday and Thursday nights plus blues, r&b, and rock on weekends. Dine, dance and bowl a few frames all in one evening!

4133 South Carrollton Ave.
504-482-3133
//www.neworleans.net/sndpages/clubmidcity.html

Mulate's

Cajun dancing nightly.

201 Julia St. (Near the French Quarter)
504-522-1492

Tipitina's

World renowned music club where Bruce Daigrepont hosts a *fais do-do* almost every Sunday at 5 p.m.

501 Napoleon Ave.
504-895-8477
//www.neworleans.net/sndpages/clubtipitinas.html

MAINE

Northeast Harbor

Neighborhood House

The local Austin-Acadia Connection group hosts 3-4 shows a year featuring mostly Texas singer/songwriters such as Christine Albert, Jimmie Dale Gilmore, Butch Hancock, and Jo Carol Pierce. Also had Fred Eaglesmith several times. Nice people, great music, *and* a pot luck dinner! They began publishing a newsletter in 1999.

Austin-Acadia Connection
c/o Lee Haynes & Dee Karnofsky
RFD 1, Box 1940
Bar Harbor, ME 04609

207-288-4365
olh@acadia.net
Neighborhood House: 207-288-4740

Ogunquit

Jonathan's

Acoustic; singer/songwriter

2 Bourne Ln.
207-646-4777
//www.jonathansrestaurant.com
Jonathans1@aol.com

MARYLAND

Annapolis

Ram's Head

Americana variety (pp: Austin Lounge Lizards, Derailers, John McEuen, Peter Rowan).

33 West St.
410-268-4545

Baltimore

8x10

Books a wide range of music.

10 E. Cross St.
410-625-2000

Roots Cafe at St. John's Church

Society for the Preservation of American Roots Music holds a concert/dance with various Americana artists on the 2nd and 4th Saturdays of each month at 8 p.m. (pp: The Grandsons, Ruthie & The Wranglers, Big Sandy, and many more).

27th & St. Paul Sts.
410-880-3883
//www.mindspring.com/~timhill/roots/

Bethesda

Twist & Shout

Mid sized venue that had one of the most consistently great selections of all kinds of alt. country and Americana until it closed its door for good on September 6, 1998.

MASSACHUSETTS

Boston

*A nice listing of "Twangin' Venues" is maintained by Stacey Taylor at the Hellcountry web site:

//www.hellcountry.com

The Attic

Alt. pop to roots-rock with acoustic duo the Coalboilers on Sunday night.

107-R Union St. (Newton)
617-964-6684
//www.unionst.com/attic.html

The Behan

Irish pub with rockabilly on Sunday night.

378 Center St. (Jamaica Plain)
617-522-5386

Bill's Bar

Hillbilly, country rock, roots, bluegrass.

5 Lansdowne St.
617-421-9678
//www.ultranet.com/pc/bills.html

Club Passim

Legendary club specializing in the best singer/songwriters.

47 Palmer St. (Cambridge)
617-492-7679
//www.clubpassim.com

Johnny D's Uptown

Good venue for alt. country including bluegrass, country, roots-rock, rockabilly (pp: Austin Lounge Lizards, Kate Campbell, the Hollisters, Kim Lenz).

17 Holland St. (Somerville)
617-776-9667
//www.johnnyds.com

Kendall Cafe

Home of the monthly "Hellcountry" showcasing alt. country from Bean Town and beyond and serving as "a collective force for twangin' change in the Boston music scene." Created and produced by Stacey Taylor.

233 Cardinal Medeiros Ave. (Cambridge)
617-661-0993
//www.hellcountry.com
stacey@hellcountry.com

Paradise Rock Club

Premier Boston club billing mostly touring groups (pp: Wilco, Son Volt, the Jayhawks)

967 Commonwealth Ave.
617-562-8804

TT the Bear's Place

Favorite with the locals for its diversity (pp: Freakwater, Martin Zellar, Charlie Chesterman, Wooden Leg).

10 Brookline St. (Cambridge)
617-492-0082
//www.tiac.net/users/ttbears/
Ttbears@tiac.net

The Upstairs Lounge

Atomic Lounge Thursday, Rockabilly Saturday, Swingin' Sunday.

65 Causeway St.
617-703-7364
//members.tripod.com/~kewlwerkz/

Northampton

Iron Horse Music Hall

Large venue for Americana/alt. country artists (pp: Salamander Crossing, Fred

Eaglesmith, Kim Richey, Cordelia's Dad, Junior Brown)

20 Center St.
//www.virtual-valley.com/ironhorse/

MICHIGAN

Ann Arbor/Detroit

The Ark

Long running club presenting all types of national alternative including acoustic country (pp: Dave Alvin, Jeb Roy Nichols, Steve Riley).

637 1/2 S. Main
313-761-1451
//www.a2ark.org

The Blind Pig

Popular spot for alternative & Americana.

208 S. First
313-996-8555

The Magic Bag (Ferndale)

Noted for its diversity of blues and country acts.

229 20 Woodward Ave. (Ferndale)
810-544-3030
//www.the magicbag.com

The Magic Stick

Leading local alternative venue which often includes the country kind; The Majestic Theater is connected and used mostly for bigger name acts.

4140 Woodward Ave.
313-833-0569

Lansing

Mac's Bar

Home of the weekly "Torch & Twang" nights sponsored by the Progressive Torch & Twang radio show on station WDBM and offering the best in alt. country; also hosts the annual "Torch & Twang Fest" (pp: Ex-Husbands, Robbie Fulks, Gringo, Lonesome Bob, Steve Owen, Ruthie & the Wranglers, the Steam Donkeys, the Riptones, Belle Starr, and more).

2700 E. Michigan Ave.

Progressive Torch & Twang Home Page:
//www.msu.edu/user/depolo/
Depolo@msue.msu.edu

The Ten Pound Fiddle

Presenting the best of traditional and acoustic music for almost 25 years.

855 Grove St. (East Lansing)
517-337-7744
//pilot.msu.edu/user/fiddle/

MINNESOTA

Minneapolis

*Details on Twin Cities venues and schedules at:

//twincities.sidewalk.com.

The 400 Bar

Mostly an alt. rock bar but also favorable to alt. country (pp: the Gourds, Sue Garner, the Sycamores).

400 Cedar Ave. S.
612-332-2903

First Avenue/7th St. Entry

Going strong for 25+ years with alternative acts including local and out-of-town alt. country like the Carpetbaggers, Golden Smog, the Honeydogs, Son Volt, SCOTS, Emmylou, Whiskeytown.

701 N. 1st Ave.
612-332-1775
//www.bitstream.net/bsu/tcguide/clubs/firstave/

Lee's Liquor Lounge

Small but great club for alt. country fans who especially like honky tonk and hillbilly bop (pp: Big Sandy, Wayne Hancock, the Derailers, Dale Watson)

101 Glenwood Ave. N.
612-338-9491

The Turf Club

Local and touring alternative including the country kind.

1601 University (St. Paul)
612-647-0486
//members.aol.com/turfclub/

MISSISSIPPI

Jackson

The Depot at Hal & Mal's

Americana including bluegrass, rockabilly, roots-rock (pp: Dash Rip Rock, Kudzu Kings).

200 S. Commerce St.
601-948-7000
//www.depotathalandmals.com

Oxford

Proud Larry's

Alternative variety including performers such as Mary Cutrufello and the Kudzu Kings.

211 South Lamar Blvd.
236-0050
//www.oxfordcenter.com/larrys/

MISSOURI

Kansas City

Davey's Uptown Ramblers Club

Rustic but very fine Americana club

3402 Main St.
816-753-1909
//www.idir.net/~daveys/cal.html

The Grand Emporium

Mostly a blues club but sometimes you'll find groups like Big Sandy, Dan Hicks, SCOTS et al.

3832 Main St.
816-531-7557

St. Louis

Cicero's

Premier indie/punk bar that was once a major stomping grounds for Uncle Tupelo, the Bottlerockets, and other area alt. country greats. Switched to a jazz/blues format in 1998.

6510 Delmar
314-862-04444
//www.vintagevinyl.com/ciceros

Hi-Pointe

Alternative variety.

1001 McCausland
314-781-4716

Mississippi Nights

Large capacity club mainly for big name national acts including alt. country.

914 N. 1st St.
314-421-3853

Off Broadway

Very alt. country friendly bar especially for local favorites like Belle Starr; home of "Twangfest," an annual showcase for alt. country/roots rock/Americana (pp: Belle Starr, the Waco Brothers, Edith Frost, the Ghost Rockets, One Riot, One Ranger, Meat Purveyors, and many more); inaugural held mid-June 1997 (see Festivals section for more details).

3509 Lemp
314-773-3363
Twangfest Home Page:
//www.twangfest.com
(also has information on Twangfest recordings).

NEBRASKA

Lincoln

The Zoo Bar

Mostly blues but also bluegrass, rockabilly, swing (pp: Dave Alvin, Billy Bacon, Kim Lenz).

136 North 14th St.
402-435-8754
//members.aol.com/frgtrs/zoo.htm

NEVADA

Las Vegas

Rockabilly's

What do you think!

3785 Boulder Hwy.
702-641-5800

NEW HAMPSHIRE

Portsmouth

The Elvis Room

Alternative with steady diet of alt. country (pp: Edith Frost, Wooden Leg, Wayne Hancock).

142 Congress St.
603-436-9189
//www.nh.ultranet.com/~dellis/elvis.html

NEW JERSEY

Hoboken

Maxwell's

Alternative variety.

1039 WashingtonSt.
201-798-0406
//www.nj.com/maxwells/

NEW YORK

Buffalo

Mohawk Place

The city's best venue for alt. country especially local (Scott Carpenter; Steam Donkeys) and touring acts.

47 E. Mohawk St.
716-855-3931
//www.wnywebshop.com/mohawk.htm

Ithaca

ABC Cafe

Wide variety of Americana.

308 Stewart Ave.
607-277-4770
//www.publiccom.com/abc/

New York City

9C

Small East Village bar where Greg Garing hosts his weekly alternative country showcase called the "Alphabet City Opry."

9th St. & Ave. C

The Bottom Line

An alternative mix including performers like the Mollys, Kelly Willis, and Kim Richey now and then.

15 West 4th St.
212-228-6300; 212-228-7880
//www.users.interport.net/~stoner3/blsched.html

The Fort at Sidewalk Cafe

"Honky Tonk Country" each Thursday night hosted by Rob Ryan with local acts such as Elena Skye & the Demolition String Band, Li'l Mo & The Monicats, Amy Allison & The Maudlins and a late night country jam.

94 Ave. A
212-473-7373
//members.aol.com/folkbro/fortweek.html

Louisiana Community Bar & Grill

All types of Americana throughout the week.

622 Broadway
212-460-9633
//www.interadcom.com/louis.html
LouComm@aol.com

Mercury Lounge

Offers a mix of alternative music.

217 E. Houston St.
212-260-4700
//webtunes.com/mercury/

Rodeo Bar

All kinds of music including frequent alt. country acts.

375 3rd Ave.
212-683-6500
//www.metrobeat.com/nyc/loc/rodeo-bar.html

Roger's Juke Joint

Live DJ, John Kopf of Trailer Trash hosts "Singin' a Beer & Drinkin' a Country Song," Saturday, 6-10 p.m. Also home to the yearly "TwangCore" showcase for local alt. country (pp: the Ghost Rockets, Lancaster County Prison, 5 Chinese Brothers, and the Disciples of Agriculture).

Coney Island High
15 St. Mark's Place (Manhattan)

The Wetlands

Holds weekly "Americana Night" and the "Ameripalooza Festival" and "Hank Williams Birthday Party" annually.

161 Hudson St.
212-966-4225
//www.wetlands-preserve.org

NORTH CAROLINA

*Schedules for alt. country venues in the Triangle area can be found at:

ChillWeb
//www.chapel-hill.nc.us/chillwebco.html

or consult

NEME's NC Music Calendar
//www.camelcity.com/ncmusic/

Carborro

Cat's Cradle

Alt. country variety (Jolene, Whiskeytown, Jr. Brown, Golden Smog).

300 E. Main St.
919-967-9053

Chapel Hill

The Cave

Especially supportive of local alt. country including Grasshopper Highway, Lou Ford, Mercury Dime, Two Dollar Pistols, et al.

452½ W. Franklin St.
919-968-9308
//www.caverntavern.com

Local 506

Major local alt. country venue and home of the annual "Honky-Tonk-A-Rama" and "Sleazefest" (see the Festivals section for details).

506 W. Franklin St.
919-942-5506
//www.sleazefest.com

The Skylight Exchange

Eclectic local roots, rock, old-time, etc.

405½ W. Rosemary St.
919-933-5550
//www.catscradle.com/sched/skylight.html

Charlotte

Double Door Inn

Home of the "Tuesday Night Americana Showcase" for local and touring acts (pp: Lilybandits, Rank Outsiders, Hollisters, Steve Owen).

greggm@charloote.infi.net

Durham

The Original Music Showcase

"The Best in Today's Acoustic and Traditional Country Music" in a concert hall setting (pp: Jerry Douglas, Tim O'Brien, Seldon Scene).

309 Morgan St.
919-560-3030

Pine Hill Farm

Rural ranch home where the unique "Topsoil House Concerts" are held. This is the brain-child of Steve Gardner (hosts the "Topsoil" program on local station WXDU) who wanted to create a special, totally acoustic setting for alt. country/Americana performers such as Robbie Fulks, Kevin Gordon, Kevin Johnson, Dan Levenson, and many more.

> For history, schedule, and directions see:
> //www.topsoil.net/houseconcerts.htm
> or e-mail
> Steve Gardner steve@topsoil.net

Raleigh

The Brewery

The alt. country/roots venue in North Carolina; home of the yearly "S.P.I.T.T.L.E. Fest" which stands for "Southern Plunge Into Trailer Trash Leisure and Culture" (pp: Redneck Greece, Mercury Dime, Six String Drag, V-Roys, Two Dollar Pistols, Drive By Truckers, Robbie Fulks, and the Backsliders).

> 3009 Hillsborough St.
> 919-834-7018
> SPITTLE Fest:
> //www.triw.com/brewery/index.html#spittle

The Hideaway

Friendly bar has no live music but instead a well-stocked jukebox full of great alt. country from near and far. Send CDs to Palmer Stacey, P. O. Box 17568, Raleigh, NC 27619.

> 2526 Hillsboro
> 919-821-4955

OHIO

*For Ohio venue information and schedules check out:

Cringe Magazine //www.cringe.com.

Cleveland

The Blind Pig

One of Northeast Ohio's premier venues and home to the the Thursday night alt. country showcase, "Made in America Live." Sponsored by the "Made in America" radio show on WERE, 1300 A.M., 9-10 p.m. Thursday.

> 1228 W. 6th St.
> 216-621-0001
> wwda@en.com

Wilbert's Bar & Grille

"Home of Cleveland's finest rock, roots, and blues" where everybody who's anybody in alt. country has played.

> 1360 W. 9th St.
> 216-771-BLUES

//www.wilberts.com

Columbus

Barley's Underground

All kinds of alternative.

> 467 N. High St.
> 614-228-2537

Stache's/Little Brother's

Ever' kinda alt. country you can think of.

> 1100 High St.
> 614-421-2025
> //www.littlebrothers.com

OKLAHOMA

Guthrie

Double Stop Music Hall

Owned and operated by master fiddler Byron Berline and presenting the Byron Berline Band and other bluegrass acts on Saturday nights plus a jam session on Sunday afternoons. Plays host to the annual Oklahoma International Bluegrass Festival and Fiddlefest. Adjoining is the Double Stop Fiddle Shop.

> 121 E. Oklahoma Ave.
> 405-282-6646
> //doublestop.com

Oklahoma City

The Blue Door

Singer/songwriter, bluegrass, Cajun, and more (pp: Dead Reckoners, Bad Livers, Gourds, Ray Wylie Hubbard, Kelly Willis, Guy Clark, Robert Earl Keen).

> 2805 N. McKinley
> 405-524-0738
> //www.okclive.com/bluedoor/

VZD's

Live music hub for 20+ years featuring local, regional, and national acts of all types (pp: Bottlerockets, Junior Brown, Cigar Store Indians, Red Dirt Rangers, Slobberbone).

> 4200 North Western
> //ww.okclive.com/vzd/

Tulsa

Cain's Ballroom

Renowned country/western dance hall most famous as the place where Bob Wills once set up shop; now it's an alternative club with a variety of musical styles.

> 423 N. Main St.
> 918-584-2306

OREGON

Ashland

Ashland Folk Music Club

All kindsof folk and acoustic music.

> Unitarian Fellowship
> 541-482-4154

Portland

Aladdin Theater

Located in old movie house (b. 1927) that was a porno theater for a while but then restored and now has eclectic selection of roots music: blues, country, folk, jazz, rock (pp: Junior Brown, Iris DeMent, Joe Ely, Jimmie Dale Gilmore, the Hellecasters).

> 3017 S. E. Milwaukee
> 503-233-1994
> //www.showman.com/aladdin.html

Belmont's

Acoustic, folk rock, roots rock.

> 3357 S.E. Belmont
> //www.teleport.com/~boydroid/dateven/belmonts/

PENNSYLVANIA

Bethlehem

Godfrey Daniels

Non-profit, member supported venue for old-time, bluegrass, s/s, Cajun, Celtic, and other roots.

> 7 East 4th St.
> 610-867-2390
> //www.godfreydaniels.org

Philadelphia

North Star Bar

Diversity of alt. country (pp: Robert Earl Keen, Bill Kirchen, Wayne Hancock, Junior Brown, Fred Eaglesmith, Mary Cutrufello).

> 2639 W. Poplar
> 215-235-STAR
> //www.northstarbar.com

Samuel Adams Brewhouse

Alternative venue including the country type on a fairly regular basis (pp: Cheri Knight, the Derailers, Charlie Chesterman, the Rolling Hayseeds).

> 1516 Sanson St.
> 215-563-2326
> //www.nightsscene.com/samueladams

Silk City

Variety with frequent alt. country (pp: Freakwater; rockabilly).

> 435 Spring Garden St.
> 215-351-9923

Tin Angel

Acoustic music venue (pp: the Bad Livers, the Gourds, John Hartford, Dale Watson, Frog Holler, Marah, and many more)

20 S. Second St.
215-928-0978
//www.tinangel.com

Pittsburgh

The Next Decade

Began to heat up as an alt. country venue in 1998 by presenting Mike Ireland, Ray Condo, Ruthie & the Wranglers and hosting the Rust Belt Rockabilly Weekender (October 2-3, 1998).

Atwood & Sennot
412-687-0990

Rosebud

A regular stop on the alt. country circuit especially on Wednesday nights which are set aside for "Twangburgh," a series of roots, Americana and twang music. On November 6-7, 1998, a festival of the same name was held with a stellar lineup including Robbie Fulks, Hazel Dickens, Greg Garing, Honky Tonk Confidential, Two Dollar Pistols, One Riot, One Ranger, Marah, Deliberate Strangers, Polish Hillbillies, and Sadies.

1650 Smallman St.
412-261-2221
//www.sportsrock.com/rosebud/

Twangburgh
//www.pitt.edu/~tikst/twangburgh/twang.html

RHODE ISLAND

Providence

The Century Lounge

Locale for the monthly "Boudin Barndance Roots Hoot" with Northeast talent such as the Sean Mencher Band, Jack Smith & Rockabilly Planet, and the Pulltabs. Created and hosted by Dan Ferguson who hosts the "Boudin Barndance" on local radio station WRIU.

150 Chestnut St.
401-751-CALL
Dan Ferguson Boudin Dan@aol.com

Lupo's Heartbreak Hotel

Roots-rock, rockabilly, swing in a big, big place.

130 Union St. near the Met Cafe
//www.lupos.com

SOUTH CAROLINA

Columbia

The Elbow Room Music Hall

Alternative including country from the Carolinas and beyond (pp: Jolene, Whiskeytown, Cigar Store Indians, Poor Little Fools, Robbie Fulks).

//www.elbowroom.com

Rockafella's

Alternative mix with groups like the Backsliders and Hypnotic Clambake occasionally on the schedule.

2112 Devine St.
//www.rockafellas.com

Greenville

The Handlebar Listening Room

Superb Americana variety (pp: Greg Brown, Peter Rowan, Jerry Douglas, Norman Blake, Jason & the Scorchers, Amazing Rhythm Aces, Guy Clark, Donna the Buffalo, and many more).

400 Mills Ave.
864-233-6173
//skydance.com/handlebar/
the handlebar@juno.com

TENNESSEE

Johnson City

The Down Home ("The Eclectic Music Room Since 1976")

Best alt. country venue in the area with regular shows by the likes of Robbie Fulks, Jerry Douglas, the V-Roys, Joy Lynn White, the Mystery Dates et al.; "Open Hoot" night on Wednesday.

300 W. Main St.
423-929-9822
//www.downhome.com

Knoxville

Mercury Theater

Popular alternative venue that often has roots-rock and other alt. country.

28 Market Sq.
423-637-8634

Memphis

The Poplar Lounge

Regular haunt for local alt. country groups such as the Pawtuckets and the River Bluff Clan.

2563 Poplar Ave.
901-324-1233

Nashville

*Venue details and schedules can be found in:

the weekly *Nashville Scene*
//www.nashscene.com

or at

City Search
//nashville.cityserach.com

12th & Porter

12th & Porter

Solid alt. country venue (pp: the Backsliders, Cigar Store Indians, Steve Earle, Townes, Van Zandt, John Prine).

114 12th Ave. N
615-254-7236

The Bluebird Cafe

Venue famous for singer/songwriters but also other types of alt. country.

4104 Hillsboro Rd.
615-383-1461
//www.bluebirdcafe.com

The Bluegrass Inn

Renowned "bluegrass and beer joint" featuring the "Hillbilly Spectacle," Joe Buck.

418 Broadway
615-726-2799
//nashville.cityserach.com

The Exit/In

"Legendary" with lots of alt. country/Americana highlighted by "Billy Block's Western Beat Roots Revival" on Tuesdays presenting a consistently fine lineup of alt. country talent.

2208 Elliston Pl.
615-321-4400
//www.exit-in.com

Western Beat Roots Revival
P. O. Box 128105
Nashville, TN 37212
615-383-5466
615-383-6331 (fax)
//www.westernbeat.com
westernbeat@home.net

Gibson's Caffe Milano

Diverse Americana (pp: Jimmie Dale Gilmore, Dale Watson, Webb Wilder, Raul Malo).

176 3rd Ave. N
615-255-0073
//www.nashville.citysearch.com

Robert's Western Wear

One of a kind alt. country venue for a taste of Nashville in the "good old days"; made famous as the homebase of BR5-49, their motto is "Boots and Beer" due to the fact that they are both bar and boot store in one.

416 Broadway
615-256-7937

Ryman Auditorium

Original home of the Grand Ol' Opry and still offering a variety of country music.

116 5th Ave. N
615-889-6611

The Station Inn

Very fine alt. country club, and the best one for local and national bluegrass acts (pp: Richard Greene; Cluster Pluckers); recently added a "No Depression" night

402 12th Ave. S
615-255-3307
//www.techpublishing.com/stationinn/
jt@stationinn.com

The Sutler

Top notch alt. country venue where you can see locals like Paul Burch as well as many touring acts such as Freakwater and Mount Pilot.

2608 Franklin Rd.
615-297-9195

Tootsie's Orchid Loune

"The World's Most Famous Little Honky Tonk!" Really, one of the most storied bars in country music history and still presenting live music everyday.

422 Broadway
615-726-0463
//nashville.citysearch.com
Lele302@aol.com

Ernest Tubb's Record Shop

Another "must see" on the Music City tour. Has held a "Midnite Jamboree" broadcast on WSM every Saturday night after the Grand Ol' Opry for many years. Until recently held at the old ETRS near the Ryman but now at the new store across from Opryland.

Music Valley Village
//www.etrs.net/mj.htm

TEXAS

Alpine

Railroad Blues

Out of the way Southwest Texas club that has become a regular stopping point for alt. country performers.

504 W. Holland
915-837-3103

Austin

*For venue information consult:

the *Austin Chronicle*
//www.auschron.com

or

Thursday's "XLent" section of the *Austin-American Statesman*
//www.austin360.com

The Backyard

Large, natural amphitheater in the Hill Country west of Austin that offers some big names in alt. country from Texas and beyond (pp: Don Walser, Chris Wall, Reckless Kelly, Lyle Lovett, Kelly Willis, Willie Nelson, Steve Earle).

13101 Hwy. 71 West
512-263-4146
//www.directevents.com/backyard.htm

Broken Spoke

"The last of the true Texas honky tonks and darn sure proud of it!" True Austin music landmark in operation for 30 years, they've had all the great country artists from Willie Nelson to Ernest Tubb to Bob Wills and regularly have the best of Austin's honky tonk artists including Gary P. Nunn, the Derailers, Don Walser, Dale Watson, Bruce Robison, Susanna Van Tassel, Ted Roddy, Clay Blaker. (My wife and I met and fell in love here.)

3201 S. Lamar
512-442-6189
//www.instar.com/bspoke/

Cactus Cafe

Intimate little spot on the University of Texas campus hosting a wide variety of Texas, national, and international acoustic music (pp: Lyle Lovett, Austin Lounge Lizards, Tim O'Brien, Ian Tyson, the Brother Boys, Topp Twins, and many more)

Texas Union Bldg.
24th & Guadalupe
University of Texas
512-475-6515
//www.utexas.edu/student/txunion/

Carousel Lounge

Vintage 1950s neighborhood lounge offering local swing, rockabilly, and honky tonk bands.

1110 E. 52nd
512-452-6790

Continental Club

Austin's premier alt. country venue for local, national, and international artists. Rockabilly, honky tonk, swing, and much more; Toni Price plays happy hour every Tuesday and the Hot Club of Cowtown each Wednesday; hosts annual salutes to Elvis, Hank, and Buck Owens. Small, dark, smoky and very cool! (pp: just about everyone).

1315 S. Congress
512-441-2444

Dessau Hall

Old, very roomy dance spot north of Austin that was hot for many years, fell on hard times in the early '90s then came back with a venegeance in 1997-1998 with a regular schedule of alternative music including mucho alt. country (pp: Derailers, Joe Ely, Reckless Kelly, Ray Wylie Hubbard).

13422 Dessau Rd.

512-252-1123

East 1st Garden Theatre

New place for alt. country (opened April 1998); first acts included Ray Condo, Shaver, Beausoleil.

4822-B E. Cesar Chavez (East 1st St.)
512-386-8686

Electric Lounge

Mostly an alternative rock club but regularly hosts local and national alt. country. In late 1998, they added a Thursday "Y'all Star" happy hour featuring local bands such as the Damnations TX preceded by John Dorn's famous country swing dance lessons.

302 Bowie
512-476-FUSE

Emo's

Noted alt. rock venue, but they have sometimes had artists like the the Bad Livers, Don Walser, Dale Watson, the Old 97s et al.

603 Red River
512-477-EMOS

The Filling Station

Restaurant/bar where Don McCalister, Cornell Hurd, and Ted Roddy often play.

801 Barton Springs Rd.
512-477-1022

Flipnotics

Cozy coffeehouse cafe presenting a wide variety of local alt. country (pp: the Gourds, Erik Hokannen, Shaun Young & His Texas Trio, Jean Caffeine, Michael Fracasso)

1601 Barton Springs
512-322-9750

Ginny's Little Longhorn Saloon

Tiny dive that is the subject of Dale Watson's "Honkiest Tonkiest Beer Joint."

5434 Burnet Rd.
512-458-1813

Gruene Hall

Located about 40 miles south of Austin (near New Braunfels) in historic German town. One time warehouse is now classic Texas dancehall with a full slate of Central Texas and touring alt. country acts (pp: Robert Earl Keen, Mavericks, BR5-49, High Noon, Monte Warden, Jack Ingram).

1281 Gruene
210-606-1281

Hole in the Wall

Tiny, very popular campus area dive serving mostly alt. rock but also alt. country (pp: Rick Broussard, Jon Langford, Jolene, Whiskeytown, the Walkabouts, the Meat Purveyors).

2528 Guadalupe
512-472-5599

Jovita's Cantina

Fine Mexican restaurant has early shows with local alt. country artists such as Don Walser, Wayne Hancock, Cornell Hurd, et al.

1619 S. 1st
512-447-7825

La Zona Rosa

Large venue hosting a variety of roots music.

4th & Rio Grande
512-472-2293

Liberty Lunch

The place in Austin for national touring independent acts; consistently voted best live venue (pp: SCOTS, Joe Ely, Son Volt, Wilco).

405 W. 2nd
512-477-0461
//www.texasmusicnet.com/libertylunch/

Rouse House Concerts

Texas singer/songwriter performances held periodically in a private home (pp: Butch Hancock, Darden Smith).

10219 Willifield
512-837-2333
//www.houseconcerts.com/txindex.htm
rouse_house@mail.utexas.edu

Saxon Pub

Long standing venue especially for singer/ songwriters.

1320 South Lamar
512-448-2552

Stubb's B-B-Q

Legendary restaurant/music venue reopened in 1996 and now books local and national alt. country talent in and outdoors (pp: the Derailers, Jack Ingram, the Old 97s, the Gourds, the V-Roys)

801 Red River
512-480-8341

Threadgill's Saloon

The original restaurant was made famous in the 1960s as a home of progressive country and the Threadgill's Troubadours weekly "Supper Sessions" in the 1990s. The latter was moved to a second, larger Threadgill's in 1997 which added a Saloon for a great weekly lineup of local honky tonk and swing with Don Walser, Dale Watson, Jeff Hughes, the Panhandlers, and Hot Club of Cowtown.

301 Riverside (at Barton Springs)
512-472-9304
//www.threadgills.com

Under the Sun

Vintage clothing/collectibles/record store sponsors regular in-store performances especially during SXSW (pp: High Noon, the Belmont Playboys, Billy Bacon, James Intveld, Chris Gaffney, Dale Watson).

1323A South Congress
512-442-1308

underthesun1@earthlink.net

Yard Dog

Actually an art space but derserves mention for legendary unofficial Bloodshot show- cases held there during SXSW.

1510 South Congress
512-912-1613

Bandera

The Cabaret

Dance hall and steak house in the "Cowboy Capital of the World" which books the best in Central Texas (pp: Bruce Robison, Don Walser).

801 Main
512-460-3095

Corpus Christi

Executive Surf Club

Variety including alt. country/Americana.

309 N. Water St.
884-7873

Dallas

*For venue info and calendars see:

The *Dallas Morning News*
//www.dallasnews.com

and

the weekly *Dallas Observer*
//www.dallasobserver.com

The Barley House

Cozy pub that has been favorite venue for Dallas alt. country acts such as the Old 97s, the Cartwrights, Homer Henderson, T. Texas Edwards and host to national acts as well; they sponsor the annual "Barley- palooza" and have issued several com- pilations of local alt. country music.

2916 N. Henderson
214-824-0306
//www.primeview.com/primeview/barleyho
use/

Club Clearview

Regular place for all types of "retro" including rockabilly.

2803 Main St.
214-939-0006

Gypsy Tea Room

In historic Deep Ellum, it had its grand opening March 26, 1998, with Steve Earle and since then has had the best in alt. country.

2548 Elm St.
214-74-GYPSY

Naomi's Lounge

Classic honky tonk joint specializing in local/Texas alt. country (pp: Cowboys & Indians, Mary Cutrufello, the Old 97s, the Cartwrights)

3001 Canton St.
214-741-0666

Poor David's Pub

Variety with frequent alt. country/Ameri- cana (pp: Kim Lenz, Dale Watson, Hillbilly Cafe).

2806 Elm (Deep Ellum)
214-939-0077

Sons of Hermann Hall

The best alt. country venue in Big D; located in an old two-story wooden building, the dancehall is on the second floor and the bar on the first; a regular stop on the circuit for just about everyone (pp: you name 'em).

3414 Elm St.
214-747-4422

Uncle Calvin's Coffeehouse

House concerts mostly by singer/song- writers from Texas and those who wish they were (pp: Erik Moll, Emily Kaitz, Ray Wylie Hubbard, Bill & Bonnie, Betty Elders).

1208 Grinnell Dr. (Richardson)
972-644-3734
//www.houseconcerts.com/txindex.htm
joejones@texasfolk.com

Denton

Rick's Place

Plenty of Texas based alt. country and more (pp: Slobberbone, Pat Green, Bruce Robison).

125 Avenue A
940-382-4141

El Paso

Wild Hare's Booze & Adventure

Alternative with frequent visits from touring alt. country acts.

4025 N. Mesa St.
915-532-3589

Ft. Worth

White Elephant Saloon

Historic dance hall in the Stockyards District with traditional country & western and Western swing nightly.

106 E. Exchange Ave.
817-624-1887

Houston

*The Space City Rock web site has a very thorough venues section.

//www.tenagra.com/~jhart/space_city.htm)

Fabulous Satellite Lounge

Americana variety.

3616 Washington Ave.
713-869-COOL
//www.fabsat.com

McGonigel's Mucky Duck

Strong showing for Texas and touring alt. country (pp: Hot Club of Cowtown, James McMurtry, Charlie Robison, Don Walser, the Mollys).

2425 Norfolk
713-528-5999
//www.mcgonigels.com

Old Quarter Acoustic Cafe

Legendary singer/songwriter venue where Townes Van Zandt recorded his landmark double album in 1977.

412 20th St. (Galveston)
409-762-9199
//www.phoenix.net/~icebreak/acoustic.html

Mineola

Piney Woods Pickn' Parlor

House concert series upstairs in the historic Beckham Hotel that presents s/s, bluegrass, and folk mostly from Texas every Saturday night at 8; located about 1 hour east of Dallas on Hwy. 80 (pp: Ray Wylie Hubbrad, Alan Munde, Joe Carr, Vince Bell, Emily Kaitz).

115 Commerce St.
903-569-2185
//topchoice.com/~beckham/pwpp.htm
randyb@southside.com

San Antonio

Cibolo Creek Country Club

Located way out in the boondocks in far north San Antonio, it's worth the drive for a variety of local and national Americana.

8640 E. Evans Rd.
210-651-6652

Flore's Country Store

Huge outdoor venue with picnic table seating and large concrete dance floor; regularly schedules the best of Texas alt. country.

In Helotes

Guadalupe Cultural Arts Center

Educational and promotional organization for Tejano/Conjunto music which hosts regular events and the annual Tejano Conjunto Festival.

1300 Guadalupe St.
210-271-3151
//www.guadalupeculturalarts.org

Urban Campfires

Monthly acoustic house concert presenting the best s/s from around the U.S. (pp: Christine Albert, Darden Smith, Ray Wylie Hubbard).

Lion's Field at Mulberry & Broadway
210-736-0987
//www.urbancampfires.com
info@urbancampfires.com

Stephenville

City Limits

The cream of Texas singer/songwriters e.g. Robert Earl Keen, Jack Ingram, Bruce Robison, et al.

1801 E. Washington
254-968-5222

UTAH

Provo

ABG's Funhouse

Private club for members only and their guests and regularly offering rockabilly, psychobilly, honky tonk, swing (pp: Jesse Dayton, Ditch Bank Okies, Slobberbone).

190 W. Center St.
//www.abgs.com
Abgs@abgsbar.com

Zephyr Club

Best in town with a variety of alternative (pp: Los Lobos, Mojo Nixon, Whiskeytown, Wayne Hancock, Lonesome Strangers, Atomic Deluxe).

301 South West Temple
801-355-9912

VERMONT

Burlington

Flynn Theater

Alternative venue that has been known to have groups like the Bad Livers among others.

165 Church St.
802-660-2088

VIRGINIA

*Plan 9 Music's monthly in-house publication has a concert calendar and is available at their stores throughout Virginia.

//www.plan9music.com

Alexandria

Birchmere

Leading folk club offering s/s, bluegrass, country, jazz (pp: Charlie Chesterman, Ian Tyson/Tom Russell, Junior Brown, Dieselhed).

3901 Mt. Vernon Ave.
703-549-5919
//www.birchmere.com

Cowboy Cafe (Alexandria)

Blues, folk, rock, rockabilly.

6151 Richmond Hwy.
703-660-2320

Annandale

Sunset Grille

Blues & rockabilly; Bill Kirchen is a regular.

7250 Columbia Pike
703-758-0928

Arlington

Cowboy Cafe North

Blues, folk, rock, rockabilly.

4792 Lee Hwy.
703-243-8010

Cowboy Cafe South

Blues, folk, rock, rockabilly. (pp: Honky Tonk Confidential; Grandsons).

2421 Columbia Pike
703-486-3467
//yp.washingtonpost.com/yp/cowboycafe/

Iota

Alternative venue often presenting Americana acts like the Gourds, Whiskeytown, Eugene Chadbourne, et al.

2832 Wilson Blvd.
703-522-8340

JV's Restaurant

50 year old establishment still presenting real, live hillbilly, honky tonk Wednesday-Saturday.

6666 Arlington Blvd. (Falls Church)
703-241-9504

Charlottesville

The Prism Coffeehouse

Top of the line bluegrass and other acoustic music (pp: Tony Rice, Norman Blake, Tim O' Brien).

214 Rugby Rd.
804-97-PRISM
//www.theprism.org
tunes@theprism.org

Richmond

Alley Katz

Hosts monthly "Capital City Barn Dance" showcase for local and national alt. country in the spirit of the 1950s "Old Dominion Barn Dance" (pp: Dirtball, Six String Drag, Michael Hurley, Used Carlotta, Drive By Truckers, Angry Johnny, Lancaster County Prison).

10 Walnut Valley
804-643-2816
Capital City Barn Dance
//www.geocities.com/SunsetStrip/7262/
barndance@geocities.com

Lucy's
Dirtball every Wednesday.
> 2811 W. Cary St.
> 804-355-LUCY

Moondance Saloon
Top alt.country venue in the area; home of the annual (but now defunct) "Route 1 South" festival.
> 9 N. 17th St.
> 804-788-6666
> //www.cvaweb.com/moondance/

WASHINGTON

Seattle
*Concert calendar available through:
//seattle.sidewalk.com

5th Street Theater
Folk/acoustic venue (pp: Iris DeMent, John Prine).
> 1308 5th Ave.
> 206-625-1418

Tractor Tavern
Very alt. country friendly venue; home of the annual "Rockabilly Ball," "Rockabilly Hell Night," and the "Hank Williams Revue."
> 5213 Ballard Ave. NW
> 206-789-3599

WEST VIRGINIA

Charleston

Empty Glass
Americana variety.
> 410 Elizabeth St.
> 304-345-9893

WISCONSIN

Neenah

Automatic Slim's
First rate alt. country fare (pp: Belmont Playboys, Derailers, Kim Lenz, Jack Ingram, Blazers, Hollisters, Damnations, Robbie Fulks, Deke Dickerson).
> 302 N. Commercial St.
> 920-720-7546

Combined Locks

Ryan's Bar & Concert Hall
Variety including roots-rock and rockabilly with "Rockabilly Thursdays" (pp: Ray Condo, Ronnie Dawson).
> 448 Prospect St.
> 414-788-9580
> //www.foxcitiesonline.com/pages/ryans/

CANADA

British Columbia

Vancouver

Rogue Folk Club
Non-profit organization presenting Celtic, folk, and roots concerts (pp: Stephen Fearing, the Mollys, Laurie Lewis).
> #31-1465 Lamey's Mill Rd.
> 604-736-3022
> //www.roguefolk.bc.ca/
> roguefolk@mindlink.bc.ca

Starfish Room
Alternative club with frequent alt. country (pp: Skydiggers, Ray Condo).
> 1055 Homer St.
> 604-682-4171
> //www.vanclubs.com/starfish2.htm

Ontario

Toronto

The Horseshoe Tavern
Best in the region for local and touring alt. country. The Skydiggers hosted a "Hogtown Hootenanny and Corn Roast" there in August, 1998 (pp: Neko Case, Sadies, Skydiggers, Bottlerockets, Richard Buckner).
> 370 Queen St. W
> 416-598-4753

Reverb
Alternative variety with the occasional singer/songwriter like Dave Alvin, Alejandro Escovedo or Peter Case.
> 651 Queen W

EUROPE

England

London
*Gig Guide for the UK is maintained by Bob Paterson and has an up-to-date Americana/roots music calendar for the London area.
//bobnetworks.co.uk/rumour/gig.nclk

12-Bar Club
DJ Bob Paterson (CMR) hosts a regular Americana showcase for UK and touring acts.
> 22-23 Denmark Place
> 0171 916 6989
> //bob.networks.co.uk/rumour/12-barlistings.htm

Bob Paterson
//www.ursasoft.com/bob/

bob@windbob.demon.co.uk

The Borderline
Tiny spot in the basement below a Tex-Mex restaurant, it has eclectic bookings that have included Johnny Dowd and the Glitterhouse Records alt. country revue with Neal Casal, Hazeldine, and the Good Sons.
> Orange Yard
> 5 Manette St.
> 0171 734 2095

Brady's Saloon
Home base for the Twisted Americana Music Club, a cabal of roots music enthusiasts, which sponsors regular performances by local bands and touring events such as a 1998 Bloodshot Records release party with Robbie Fulks, Jon Langford, and Rico Bell.
> 20 Atlantic Rd.
> Brixton
> Twisted AM Club
> //www.delta-music.co.uk/twisted2.html
> tim@tperry.demon.co.uk

Camden Town Hall
Home of the "Rockin' Ranch Party," a hot night of rockabilly music and dancing.
> Euston Road
> //www.rockabillyhall.com/chat-a-box.html

The Mean Fiddler
Irish, country, pop, rock with a main room for electric acts (the Jayhawks) and an acoustic space for singer/songwriters (Lyle Lovett) and such.
> 28A Hight St.
> 0181 963 094

The Spitz
In November 1998, Bob Paterson (CMR) began presenting a monthly alternative country/roots night.
> 109 Commercial Street
> 0171-392 9032
> //www.ursasoft.co.uk/bob/
> bob@windbob.demon.co.uk

The Tennessee Club
Popular Rock 'n' Roll Club specializing in 1950s style music including lots of rockabilly.
> White Hart Ln. & High Road
> The Kings Stables
> Woodgreen
> 0976 964086
> //www.rockabillyhall.com/TennClub.html

The Thunderbird
Rock 'n' roll; rockabilly.
> The Embankment
> Wellingborough
> //www.rockabillyhall.com/ThunderbirdClub.html

The Weavers

Best roots venue in London featuring English and U.S. s/s, Cajun, etc.

98 Newington Green Rd.
Outer Central
0171 226 6911

Whelans

"Traditional American Session" each week.

69 Copenhagen St.
Central
0171 833 3784

Finland

Helsinki

Semifinal Club

Home of "Goofin' Around Rock 'n' Roll," a weekly rockabilly showcase sponsored by Goofin' Records (pp: Hal Peters & His String Dusters, Mack Stevens).

Germany

Frankfurt

Texas Live Music Club

Americana venue with rockabilly, roots rock, etc. (pp: James Intveld)

Heidelberg

Schwimmbad Music-Club

Alternative variety including rockabilly, hillbilly bop, roots rock, etc.

Tiergartenstrasse 13
06221-470201
//www.smc.rheinneckar.de/

Munich

Blue Na Country Club

Home base of the Blue Na bluegrass band which also hosts the "Hillbilly Heaven Jamboree."

Gasthaus Steinberger
Hirschbachstrasse
Kirchdorf
//141.40.140.3/bluena/club.htm
bluena@lrz.tu-muenchen.de

Oklahoma Country Saloon

Country, bluegrass, old-time, Cajun/zydeco, hillbilly, rockabilly.

Schaftlarnstr. 156
0049/89/7234327
//www.rattlesnake-saloon.com
rattlesnake@rattlesnake-saloon.com

Rattlesnake Saloon

Country, bluegrass, old-time, Cajun/zydeco, hillbilly, rockabilly.

Schneeglockchenstr. 91
0049/89/1504035
//www.rattlesnake-saloon.com
rattlesnake@rattlesnake-saloon.com

Stemmen nr. Rintein

Gasthaus Brand

Americana/roots club (pp: Rose Maddox; Hillbilly Boogiemen).

Tuttlingen

S'urige

Americana/roots venue (pp: Jon Emery; James Intveld).

Ireland

Dublin

Whelans

"Highly eclectic mix of rock and roots in extremely congenial surroundings"; folk, Irish traditional, international rock, jazz, blues.

25 Wexford St.
478 0766

The Netherlands

Amsterdam

Cruise Inn

"Europe's No. 1 Rock 'n' Roll Club" offering the best in European and North American rockabilly, hillbilly bop e.g. Hillbilly Boogiemen, Ranch Girls, Barnstompers, Kim Lenz, Slap Sally Combo.

Zeeburgerdijk271-273
020-6927188
//www.ripe.net/home/john/cruise.html
djtex@bigfoot.com

Paradiso

Considered one of the best venues in the country, it regularly books alt. country artists like Steve Earle, Emmylou Harris, et al.

Weteringschans 6-8
//www.channels.nl/amsterdam/paradiso.html

Rotterdam

Rotown

Small, cafe setting but has good line-up of music including alt. country (pp: BR5-49, the Gourds, Wilco, Townes Van Zandt).

Utrecht

Tivoli

Large, very accessible venue on the regular alt. country circuit (pp: Steve Earle, Emmylou, the Gourds, Dale Watson)

NORWAY

Oslo

Cruise Cafe

Jazz, country, rock, Americana (pp: Junior Brown, Cactus Brothers, Tish Hinojosa, Asleep at the Wheel, Tom Pacheco, Darden Smith).

Stranden 3
Aker Brygge
2283-6430
//pluto.wit.no/pluto/uteliv/amplifile/Cruise Cafe.html

Gamla

Set up by Tom Russell in the 1980s as a honky tonk, it has become an important alt. country venue (pp: the Blazers, Greg Garing, 16 Horsepower, Tom Pacheco, Johnny Dowd, Hazeldine, Neal Casal)

Route 66

Country, roots.

Kirkegt. 30
2242-2910
//pluto.wit.no/pluto/uteliv/amplifile/Route66.html

Festival Guides

Americana Music Festivals

//www.gavin.com/issues/iss19960510/feature.html

Cajun/Zydeco Events

Covers Europe.

//dcpages.ari.net/dcmw/events/cz.html

Canadian Folk Festivals

//www.interlog.com/~ufojoe/

Cuzin' Isaac's Bluegrass Festival Guide

"The most informative bluegrass festival directory for the Northeast."

//www.geocities.com/SunsetStrip/3406/

Dirty Linen Festival Guide

Good resource in print or on-line.

//www.dirtynelson.com/linen/

Doggone Cat's Rockabilly Page

Comprehensive list of rockabilly weekenders world wide.

//members.aol.com/DoggoneCat/Hogwild.html

Festival Finder

Large list divided by category: alternative, bluegrass, Cajun, country, eclectic in North America.

//www.festivalfinder.com

Folk Festival Database

U.S. coverage.

//www.geocities.com/Nashville/7669/folkfest.html

Musi-Cal Festival Listing

Part of a big venue, concert database.

//www.calendar.com

Music Festivals From Bach to Blues: A Traveler's Guide, ed. Tom Clynes, Detroit: Visible Ink, 1996.

Excellent reference book for events all over North America.

Music Festivals (Mammoth Music Meta-List)

International in scope.

//www.vibe.com/vibe/mmm/music.html

Roots66: Rockin' Weekenders

Calendar for special rockabilly events worldwide.

//www.roots66.com/ste/events/weekend.htm

Rogue Folk Club World Resources

Links to festivals in Canada and Europe.

//www.roguefolk.bc.ca/

Wild Bop Marlon's Hillbilly, Rockabilly, Bluegrass, Western Swing, and Old-Time Country Music Events

Handy guide to festivals and weekenders in Europe and North America.

//www.geocities.com/Sunset Strip/Alley/5938/

Yahoo Festival List

Large and searchable by individual event or genres.

//www.yahoo.com/entertainment/music/events/concerts/festivals/

Festival/Event Directory

(*For special weekly and monthly alt. country events check the Venues section)

Accordion Kings (Summer)

Gathering hosted by Texas Folklife Resources to celebrate Texas ethnic accordion music: Tex-Mex, Cajun, German/Czech (pp: Flaco Jimenez, Santiago Jimenez, D. L. Menard, Valerio Longoria)

Old Settler's Park
Round Rock (north of Austin)
512-320-0022
//www.main.org/tfr/

Adams Avenue Roots Festival (April)

Going on 25 years with old-time, bluegrass, Cajun, hillbilly, and more (pp: Mary McCaslin, D.L. Menard, Smith's Ranch Boys)

Normal Heights
San Diego, California
//mall.turnpike.net/~walk/adamsave/busassn/rootsfestival/

American Music Festival (July)

Good music magnet at Fitzgerald's nightclub in Chicago (pp: Bottlerockets, Kelly Willis, Bill Kirchen, Cheri Knight, Hackberry Ramblers, the Old 97s, Dave Alvin, Skeletons, Robbie Fulks, Libbi Bosworth, Jimmy LaFave, Blue Mountain and more).

6615 Roosevelt Rd.
Berwyn (near Chicago)
//www.fitzgeraldsnightclub.com

Americana International (July)

"The greatest live music & American auto event"; vintage cars and sounds with the likes of the Tennessee Rhytm Riders, the Rim Shots, R. Cajun, and other honky tonk, old-time, etc.

County Showground
Newark, Nottinghamshire
England

Americanarama (August)

Roots music and barbeque in Buffalo, New York, hosted by the Steam Donkeys who in the first two years (1997-1998) welcomed the Cowslingers, Scott Carpenter, the Pine Dogs, and more.

Buffalo, New York
716-884-8142
//www.wnywebshop.com/donkey3.htm

Appalachian String Band Festival (End of July)

Major old-time gathering that some have called a life changing experience.

Clifftop, West Virginia
//www.wvlc.wvnet.edu/culture/string.html

Austin Acoustic Music Festival (Nov.)

Showcase for a wide variety of local performers including country, bluegrass, Cajun, Texas roots, and much more; hosted by different venue each year.

Austin, Texas
//monsterbit.com/aamf/

Barleypalooza (June)

Sponsored by the Barley House pub and featuring local and national alt. country (pp: the Old 97s, Slobberbone, the Gourds, the Grievous Angels).

2916 N. Henderson
Dallas, Texas
//www.barleyhouse.com/palooza/

Beeble Fest (October)

Put on by the Gourds who were joined for the inaugural in 1997 by the Old 97s, the Skeletons, the Damnations, and Jon Dee Graham.

Stubb's
Austin, Texas

Big, Big Country Festival

Glasgow's International Festival of Country Music (1997 line-up had Dale Watson, Alison Krauss, the Well Oiled Sisters, Tim O'Brien, Hank Wangford).

Glasgow, Scotland
//www.wonder.co.uk/bigbigcountry/

Big Muddy Festival (Late August)

Alt. country/Americana; 1st in 1997 with Jimmie Dale, Lucinda, Blue Mountain, the Delevantes, Robbie Fulks, Belle Starr, One Fell Swoop, and many more.

St. Louis

Bubbapalooza (late May)

Celebration of Atlanta's Redneck Underground that was the inspiration of Greg Dean Smalley back in 1992 and led to the infamous **Bubbapalooza, Vol. 1 & 2** compilations. It has been a platform mostly for area bands like Slim Chance, the Delta Angels, Redneck Greece, et al. but has over the years included outside groups e.g. Southern Culture on the Skids, the Steam Donkeys, Six String Drag, Whiskeytown, Ex-Husbands, Blacktop Rockets, Two Dollar Pistols, Lancaster County Prison, Dirtball and many other culprits.

Star Community Bar
Atlanta. Georgia
//users.aol.com/roboburger/starbar.htm
or
//www.sleazefest.com

Bumbershoot (late August)

Extravaganza with all kinds of alternative and Americana.

Seattle, Washington
//www.bumbershoot.org

Calgary Folk Festival (late July)

Major Canadian fete which always has a number of thematic alt. country "sidestages": in 1997, "De-ranged Country" hosted by Dave Alvin, "Bluebird Cafe" and "Country Cats" hosted by Fred Eaglesmith, "Under Western Skies" hosted by Giant Sand, "Country, Which Country?"; performers included Quartette, Buddy Miller, Vic Chesnutt, Kevin Welch, and many more.; in 1998, "Across the Sawdust Floor" hosted by the Corn Sisters with Billy Cowsill & Gillian Welch, "Variations on a Country Theme" with Richrad Buckner & Alejandro Escovedo, "The Grass is Always Bluer," "Giant Sandbox" hosted by Giant Sand, "Hardcore Troubadours" with Steve Earle & Gillian Welch.

//www.canuck.com/folkfest/

Canadian Music Week (March)

A Canadian version of SXSW.

Toronto
//www.cmw.net

Chicago Country Music Festival (June)

Includes representatives of bluegrass, old-time, rockabilly, Tex-Mex, honky tonk, and even HNC (pp: Ruthie & the Wranglers, Ex-Husbands, the Mollys, Reckless Kelly, the Waco Brothers, Anna Fermin's Trigger Gospel).

Grant Park
Chicago, Illinois

//www.ci.chi.il.us/tourism/festivals/country/

Chicago Folk & Roots Festival (July)

First held in July 1998 to commemorate the Old Town School of Folk Music's move and change of name to the Chucago Folk Center. Musical participants included Robbie Fulks and Del McCoury.

909 W. Armitage Ave.
773-525-7793

City Stages Music Festival (June)

Country, old-time, bluegrass, s/s, Cajun, roots (pp: Don Walser, Joe Ely, the Continental Drifters, the Hix, Balfa Toujours) since 1988.

Birmingham, Alabama
//citystages.org
Majordomo@citystages.org

CMJ Music Marathon

1,000 bands, 60 venues in the heart of the Big Apple; wide variety of alternative music and a good sampling of alt. country (pp: Blue Rags, Silos, Tommy Womack, Dolly Varden, Johnny Dowd, Skull Orchard, Damnations TX, Lambchop, Robbie Fulks...).

New York City
//www.cmjmusic.com/marathon/

Cosmic Americana Music Festival/GramFest (Fall)

To honor Gram Parsons, the "father of country rock"; held near the site of his untimely death, it presents musical tributes by a variety of alt. country performers from across the nation (pp: Sid Griffin, Polly Parsons & The Calamity Twins)

Joshua Tree, California
//www.primenet.com/~klugl/gramfest_main.html

Country Fried Fair (August)

A Northwest alt., progressive, authentic country event staged by Cravedog Records; participants have included Richmond Fontaine, Golden Delicious, Little Sue, the Flat Irons, and more).

Cloverdale, Oregon
//www.teleport.com/~swamp/cravedog.html

Country Jazz Fusion (November)

For almost 20 years, a one-night stand blending Western swing, jazz, and bluegrass; headliners have included Johnny Gimble, Buddy Emmons, and Byron Berlin backed by the Cameron University Jazz Ensemble.

Cameron Univeristy
Cameron, Oklahoma
580-581-5501
//www.cameron.edu

Cowboy Jubilee and Western Swing Festival (late October)

Celebration of local culture and music with the Texas Playboys, Asleep at the Wheel, Johnny Gimble and others

Old Settlers' Park
Round Rock, Texas (north of Austin)

Cringe Community Fest (late June)

Columbus, Ohio roots/rock with local alt. country acts (One Riot, One Ranger, the Lilybandits, the Haynes Boys et al.)

//members.aol.com/comfest/

Denver Rock N' Rhythm-Billy Weekend (mid-July)

One of the best and most popular hillbilly bop weekenders (pp: Big Sandy, Ray Condo, the Rollin' Rocks, the Lucky Stars, Mack Stevens, the Dalhart Imperials, the Ranch Girls, the Horton Brothers, Marti Brom, and many more.

3339 W. Moncrieff Pl.
Denver, Colorado 80211
//www.bigk.com
info@bigk.com

Dixie Rock-A-Billy Rumble (Jan./Feb.)

Organized by the Blacktop Rockets, held at the Star Bar, and featuring Sonny George and Kim Lenz among others.

Atlanta, Georgia

Down on the Farm (June)

Major European roots showcase where almost everybody who's anybody in U.S. and European alt. country/Americana has played.

Halden
Norway
//www.nordi.no/music/downfarm/

East Coast Blues & Roots Music Festival (Easter wknd.)

Down Under fete with a diversity of Australian and U.S. acts (pp: Steve Earle, Roger McGuinn, Southern Culture on the Skids, Buddy Miller).

Red Devil Park
Byron Bay
Australia
//www.byron-bay.com/blues/index.html

Edmonton Folk Music Festival

Another big Canadian gathering (pp: Steve Earle, Jimmie Dale, the Dead Reckoners, Tom Russell, Gillian Welch, Buddy Miller)

Edmonton, Alberta, Canada
//www.efmf.ab.ca/

Farm Aid

Willie Nelson's renowned fund raiser in behalf of America's beleaguered farmers has had many alt. country acts on the bill (pp: Steve Earle, Mary Cutrufello, Son Volt).

Fat Fry Music Festival (September)

Sponsored by KPIG radio and featuring Jerry Jeff Walker, John Hiatt, James Mc Murtry, Los Lobos, Blazers, Steve Riley, and so many more.

Aptos Village Park
Aptos, California (near Santa Cruz)
//gate.cruzio.com/~gpa/fatfry/

Festival Acadiens (September)

One of the top Cajun/Zydeco events in the world for over 20 years.

Lafayette, Louisiana
800-346-1958
//www.cajunhot.com
info@lafayettetravel.com

Finger Lakes Grassroots Festival of Music & Dance (Late July)

A really big Americana gathering with consistently fine variety; local groups like Donna the Buffalo and the Horseflies are frequent performers along with touring acts like Walter Mouton, Balfa Toujours, Kelly Willis, and the Hix.

Trumansburg, New York
//www.GrassRootsFest.org

Folk Alliance Conference (February)

Decade old event for contemporary folk music with showcases for alt. country acts (pp: Don Walser).

//www.folk.org

Folklore Society of Greater Washington (D.C.) MiniFestival (mid-September)

Features acoustic, bluegrass, old-time, roots, swing.

Silver Spring, Maryland

Gavin's In the Pines Americana Retreat

Conference for Americana radio and friends of the format with sessions on programming, production, etc. and performances by the likes of Robbie Fulks, Dale Watson, Fred Eaglesmith, Jimmie Dale Gilmore, the Hangdogs, Laurie Lewis, Wayne Hancock, Tim O'Brien and others.

http://www.gavin.com

Grain Belt Rock Review

Celebration of Midwestern alt. country held in January 1996 with groups including One Fell Swoop, the New Patrons of Husbandry, Stillwater, Sourpatch.

Off Broadway
St. Louis, Missouri

Greaseball (October)

"Two day celebration of rockabilly, Western swing, and rockin' country" from North America and beyond since 1995; held at different venue each year with 1998's at Bimbo's 365 Club (pp: Ray Condo, Dave & Deke, Ronnie Dawson, the Dalhart Imperials, Dale Watson, the Derailers).

San Francisco, California
//www.webcom.com/greasebl/
kaijupro@sirius.com (August Ragone)

Great Blue Heron Music Festival (July)

Another fine roots music gathering in Upstate New York held in a beautiful spot with lots of roots rock, Cajun, old-time, bluegrass, swing, and more (pp: Slobberbone, Tim O'Brien, Donna the Buffalo, Jazzabels, Y'all, the Hix).

P. O. Box 791
Sherman, NY 14701
gbhfest@servtech.com

Harvest Moon Music Festival (Octo- ber)

Another annual Americana event in the City of Big Shoulders (pp: Robbie Fulks, Hot Club of Cowtown, Shaver, V-Roys).

Fitzgerald's
Chicago, Illinois
//www.fitzgeraldsnightclub.com

Hemsby

"The greatest rock 'n' roll event in the world"; granddaddy of all rockabilly weekenders for 18 years and counting (pp: everybody in rockabilly and hillbilly bop).

Pontins Holiday Centre, Hemsby
Norfolk
England
//www.rockabillyhall.com

Hill Country Hoe-down (Mid-April)

Central Texas fest (1st in 1998) with the Damnations, 6 String Drag, Slobberbone, Alejandro Escovedo, the Gourds, the V-Roys, and more.

Dripping Springs, Texas

Hillbilly Nation Celebration (June)

Hosted by station WMMT and the Otis Campbell Society (pp: Kim Richey, Webb Wilder, the Possum Hollers).

Wise County Fairgrounds
Wise, Virginia
WMMT887@aol.com

Honky-Tonk-A-Rama

Tobacco Row alt. country gathering (pp: Mercury Dime, Trailer Bride, Ruthie & the Wranglers).

Local 506
Chapel Hill, North Carolina

Hootenanny Festival (July)

Rockabilly, hillbilly, Western swing, roots (pp: Steve Earle, Big Sandy, the Blasters, James Intveld, Deke Dickerson, the Supersuckers).

Oak Canyon Ranch at Irvine Lake
Orange County, California

International Country Music Conference (June)

Scholarly confab assembled each year in Music City to present papers on and discuss various aspects of "the history and contemporary status of Country Music" including precommercial, old-time, Nashville Sound, country rock, HNC, and alternative.

Belmont University
Nashville, Tennessee
//www.tntech.edu/www/ci/icmc.html
jakenson@tntech.edu (James Akenson)

Kerrville Folk Festival (Summer)

One of the best for over 25 years.

Quiet Valley Ranch
Hwy. 16
Kerrville ,Texas
//www.kerrville-music.com
info@kerrville-music.com

London International Cajun Music Festival (October)

c/o Erling Hagland
41 Gillam Way
Rainham, Essex
tratherf@sghms.ac.uk

Magnoliafest (October)

Formerly called "Big Cosmo's Sunshine Daydream Weekend" and still featuring "the finest in American roots-based acoustic and electric music" (pp; David Grisman, Peter Rowan, Old & In the Way reunion, Donna the Buffalo).

Spirit of the Suwannee Music Park
Live Oak, Florida (north of Gainesville)
//www.magmusic.com
comments@magmusic.com

Merlefest (April)

One of the major bluegrass/old-time events held in honor of Doc Watson's late, lamented son.

Wilkes Community College
Wilkesboro, North Carolina
//nomad.wilkes.cc.nc.us/links.htm

Midwest Regional Music Festival (October)

Americana fete like SXSW held at various St. Louis venues and offering (in 1997) several alt. country related showcases: "American Roots"; "If That Ain't Country..."; "Bloodshot Records Presents.." (pp: Kamikazee Cowboy, Guy Clark, the Riptones, Moonshine Willy, the Waco Brothers, and many more).

//www.mtix.com/mrmf/
mrmf@rftstl.com

My Way Jamboree (June)

Long-running international gathering of rockabiily, psychobilly, hillbilly bop (pp: Sonny George, Rosie Flores, Lester Peabody, Barnshakers, Rimshots).

Aitoo (near Tampere)
Finland
//www.algonquin.net/thebest/aitoo.html
(extensive review of MWJ '97)

Nashville River Stages (May)

Contemporary American music variety (pp: Steve Earle, Buddy & Julie Miller, Jason & the Scorchers, Jimmie Dale Gilmore, Jolene, Paul Burch).

Nashville, Tennessee
//www.nashvilleriverstages.com

National Cajun & Zydeco Festival (October)

The Met, Market Street
Bury, Lancashire
England

NeA Extravaganza

Perennial SXSW style music conference sponsored by the Nashville Entertainment Association with many alt. country showcases that have presented everyone from the Bad Livers to Whiskeytown.

P. O. Box 121948
Nashville, Tennessee
615-327-4308
//www.extravaganza.org
nea@isdn.net

Willie Nelson's 4th of July Picnic

Famous Central Texas party since 1973 where Outlaws and the new breed of alt. country share the stage.

Luckenbach, Texas
//www.luckenbachtexas.com/4thofjuly.html

North By Northeast (mid-June)

Canadian SXSW.

Toronto
//www.nxne.com
nxne@now.com

North By Northwest (mid-October)

The Pacific Northwest's answer to SXSW.

Portland, Oregon
512-467-7979
//www.sxsw.com

Old Settler's Music Festival (April)

For over ten years presenting top notch line-up of local and national Americana (pp: Jimmy LaFave, Don Walser, Bela Fleck, Tony Rice, Jerry Douglas, Peter Rowan, Del McCoury, Jimmie Dale Gilmore).

Old Settler's Park
Round Rock, Texas (north of Austin)
//www.bluegrassfestival.com

Orange Blossom Special I & II (June)

Glitterhouse Records festival in 1997 and 1998 to showcase some its impressive stable of alt. country artists such as Neal Casal, Hazeldine, the Good Sons, Go to Blazes, Hitchin' Post, Markus Rill.

Beverungen im Oberweserbergland
Germany
//staff-www.uni-marburg.de/~settler/orange.htm

Real Roots Festival

Sponsored by Munich Records and held in Holland on semi-annual basis (pp: Michael Fracasso, Jimmy LaFave, the Gourds, and many other roots/alt. acts).

Rhythm & Roots at Escoheag (September)

Superceded the long-time Big Easy Bash which died in 1997 and was held at the same location. Inaugural in 1998 had the same top lineup of Americana as its predecessor e.g. Dave Alvin, Doc Watson, Asleep at the Wheel, Steve Riley, Big Sandy, Fred Eagelsmith, Northern Lights, Balfa Toujours, Skip Gorman, Salamander Crossing to name just a few.

Stepping Stone Ranch
Escoheag, Rhode Island
888-855-6940
//www.rhythmand roots.com

Rockabilly Rebel Weekend (June)

Rockin' and jivin' in America's heartland produced by David Loehr of the James Dean Memorial Gallery (pp: Big Sandy, Kim Lenz, Ronnie Dawson, Derailers, Blacktop Rockets, Josie Kreuzer).

Fountain Square Theater
Indianapolis, Indiana
//our.tentativeness.net/rrw98/rrw6.htm
David Loehr dl@jamesdeangallery.com

RockyGrass: Rocky Mountain Bluegrass Festival (early August)

For over 25 years (pp: everybody in modern bluegrass).

Lyons, Colorado
//www.bluegrass.com/planet/
planet@bluegrass.com

Roots Music Gathering (September)

"A convocation of scholars, musicians, promoters, the media, culture bearers and music professionals who work within the area of music called Roots" sponsored by the Cutting Edge organization (1st in 1998). Activities include workshops, discussions, and showcases.

New Orleans, Louisiana
504-945-1800
//www.ikoiko.com/cuttingedge/roots.html
edge@bellsouht.net

Roots, Rock 'n' Rhythm (August)

Rockabilly, honky tonk, swing in The King's town. (pp: Sonny George, Ronnie Dawson, Rosie Flores, Dale Watson).

Memphis, Tennessee
//members.aol.com/bksnova/rabmemphis.html
BKSNOVA@aol.com

Route 1 South

Modest but very fine alt. country/Americana celebration that sadly came to an end after 1997.

Moondance Saloon
Richmond, Virginia

Rust Belt Rockabilly Weekender (October)

Iron City bopper blast (pp: Ronnie Dawson, Wayne Hancock, Ray Condo, Polish Hillbillies, Highway 13).

Next Decade
Pittsburgh, Pennsylvania
marciag@vms.cis.pitt.edu

Sacred Honk (October)

An L.A. alt. country event (b. 1994) for many of the city's leading performers including the Lonesome Strangers, Rick Shea, Patty Booker, Farmer Tan, the Radio Ranch Straight Shooters, Jann Browne, Patty Booker, and many more.

Sacred Grounds Coffee House
309 6th St. (San Pedro)
//www.eletricearl.com/sacred.html

Santa Barbara Rockabilly Roundup (January)

Put on for the past 10 years by local band, the Cadillac Angels (pp: Ronnie Dawson, Carl Perkins, James Intveld, Rosie Flores, the Paladins, Wanda Jackson)

Victoria Hall
Santa Barbara, California
//members.aol.com/jaydeebee1/roundup.html

Shake the Shack Rockabilly Ball (September)

Decade old Northwest 'bopper fete put on by KCMU radio and DJ Dr. Leon Berman, "The Proctologist of Rock 'n' Roll" (pp: Ronnie Dawson, Ray Condo, Deke Dickerson).

Tractor Tavern
5213 Ballard Ave. NW
Seattle, Washington
206-789-3599
//www.teleport.com/~oricet/shaketheshack/
Leon Berman stshack@nwlink.com or
800-824-1601

Singer Songwriter Festival

Swiss event that for the last 15 years has presented the best of s/s, roots-rock, country-rock, bluegrass, Western swing, and Tex-Mex from around the world; held at Frutigen until 1998 (pp: Tom Russell, John Prine, Iris DeMent, Christine Albert, the Old 97s, the Jayhawks, Doug Sahm, Santiago Jimenez, Don McCalister, Somebody's Darling, Joe Ely, Ian Tyson, the Good Ol' Persons and on and on).

Thun
Switzerland
//home.allgaeu.org/brosa/thune.html

Sleazefest (August)

Crazed celebration of "white trash culture" since 1994 (pp: SCOTS, the Old 97s, Whiskeytown, the Cowslingers, Hasil Adkins, Trailer Bride, Truckadelic, Cigar Store Indians).

Local 506
506 W. Franklin St.
Chapel Hill, North Carolina
//www.sleazefest.com
craigz@sleazefest.com

South By Southwest (mid-March)

Major music festival showcasing an increasing number of alt. country acts since 1987 and always accompanied by many excellent "unofficial" showcases.

Austin, Texas
//www.sxsw.com
sxsw@sxsw.com

Southern California Cajun & Zydeco Music Festival (June)

For over 10 years one of the major events of its type in California.

Rainbow Lagoon
Long Beach, California

S.P.I.T.T.L.E. Fest (early February)

Mostly Southern alt. country groups in celebration of redneck/white trash culture (1997: Mercury Dime, Redneck Greece, the V-Roys, 6 String Drag, the Backsliders, Robbie Fulks).

The Brewery
3009 Hillsborough St.
Raleigh, North Carolina
www.triw.com/brewery/index.html#spittle

Strawberry Music Festival (Memorial Day; Labor Day)

One of the top bluegrass, s/s, roots events since 1982 presented in two sessions (pp: Leftover Salmon, John Prine, Hot Rize, Emmylou Harris, Junior Brown, Big Sandy).

Camp Mather
Yosemite, California
//www.strawberrymusic.com

Summerfest (End of June-Beg. Of July)

"The Big Gig" with 13 stages and 100s of acts including alt. country/Americana (pp: the Jayhawks, Alejandro Escovedo, the Honeydogs).

Milwaukee, Wisconsin
800-273-FEST
//www.summerfest.com

Tejano Conjunto Festival (May)

Presented by the Guadalupe Cultural Arts Center to "celebrate the conjunto/button accordion tradition of Chicanos in South Texas" (pp: Tony De La Rosa, Seve Jordan, Valerio Longoria, Eva Ybarra, Santiago Jimenez, Mingo Saldivar).

Rosedale Park

San Antonio, Texas
//www.ondanet.com:1995/tejano/

Telluride Bluegrass Festival (late June)

Much more than just a bluegrass festival.

Town Park
Telluride, Colorado
//www.bluegrass.com/telluridepage.html

Torch & Twang Fest (October)

Alt. country event produced by local radio show "Progressive Torch & Twang" hosted by Doug Neal & Jamie DePolo on WDBM; inaugural (1997) featured Robbie Fulks, the Volebeats, Ruthie & the Wranglers, the Steam Donkeys, the Riptones, Holler, Belle Starr, One Fell Swoop while the next year included Steve Owen, the Weepers, the Sovines, the Ex-Husbands, Gringo and Lonesome Bob. P T&T also sponsors weekly alt. country showcases of the same name at the same venue.

Mac's Bar
2700 E. Michigan Ave.
Lansing
//www.msu.edu/user/depolo/nights.htm
nealdoug@egr.msu.edu
Depolo@msue.msu.edu

Troubadour Fest (September)

Singer/songwriter (pp: Iris DeMent, Fred Eaglesmith, Kimmie Rhodes, Slaid Cleaves).

Columbus, Ohio

Tucson Twangfest (September)

Honky tonk, country-rock in the desert Southwest; initial event in 1998 had Red Meat, Al Perry, the Revenants, and Creosote.

Rialto Theater
318 E. Congress
Tucson, Arizona

Twangburgh (November)

A "Steel City Hoedown" that grew out of a weekly roots music show of the same name and was inspired by Twangfest in St. Louis. The 1st in 1998 had Hazel Dickens, Robbie Fulks, Greg Garing, Honky Tonk Confidential, Two Dollar Pistols, Marah, Deliberate Strangers, One Riot, One Ranger, Polish Hillbillies, Sovines.

Rosebud
1650 Smallman St.
Pittsburgh, Pennsylvania
//www.pitt.edu/~tikst/twangburgh/twang.html
tikst@pitt.edu

TwangCore (December)

Showcase for Big Apple and other alt. country acts (pp: 5 Chinese Brothers, the Ghost Rockets, Lancaster County Prison, the Disciples of Agriculture, Drive By Truckers, Cheri Knight, Hangdogs, Dirtball, Tim Carroll). The first was in 1997.

Coney Island High, Roger Juke Joint
15 St. Mark's Place (Manhattan)

Twangfest (mid-June)

Pioneering alt. country/roots bash that grew out of discussions on the Postcard 2 online mailing list. The inaugural in 1997 had Belle Starr, the Ghost Rockets, One Riot, One Ranger, Edith Frost, the Meat Purveyors, and many of these returned for the 2nd along with Robbie Fulks, Kimmie Rhodes, and Mike Ireland. A CD compilation of acts associated with P2 and Twangfest was released as **Edges From the Postcard2**.

Off Broadway Club
St. Louis, Missouri
//www.twangfest.com

Viva Las Vegas Rockabilly Weekender (April)

One of the premier rockin' events (pp: Mack Stevens, Mac Curtis, Janis Martin, Marti Brom, the Rollin' Rocks).

Gold Coast Hotel & Casino
4000 W. Flamingo Rd.
Lost Wages, Nevada
//www.vivalasvegas.net
tom@vivalasvegas.net

Waiting for a Train: Jimmie Rodgers' America (September 20-21, 1997)

Conference, jamboree, and concert dedicated to the Singing Brakeman/Blue Yodeler with performances by Junior Brown, Guy Clark, the Delevantes, Iris DeMent, Steve Earle, Jimmie Dale Gilmore, Jason & the Scorchers, John Prine, Gillian Welch among others. Sponsored by the Rock and Roll and Country Music Halls of Fame and Case Western Reserve University.

Cleveland, Ohio

WestFest (October)

Michael Martin Murphey's celebration of the Old West with lots of country *and* western music; use to be held in Copper Mountain, Colorado but now in California (pp: Lyle Lovett, Steve Earle, Riders in the Sky, Asleep at the Wheel, Wylie & the Wild West, Ian Tyson, Don Edwards, Junior Brown).

Glen Helen Blockbuster Pavillion
San Bernadino, California

What The Folk Festival (June)

Americana event hosted by Todd Snider (pp: Steve Earle, the Bottle Rockets, Jack Ingram, Joe Ely).

Memphis, Tennessee

Wintergrass (Mid-February)

Bluegrass/newgrass concerts and workshops for five years running (pp: Sam Bush, Jerry Douglas, Peter Rowan, Del McCoury).

Tacoma, Washington
//www.halcyon.com/healey/wintergrass/

Winterhawk Bluegrass Festival (late July)

Old and newgrass at one of biggest in the Northeast (pp: the Freight Hoppers, Dry Branch, Pete Wernick).

Rothvoss Farm
Hillsdale, New York
888-WINTHWK
//www.inerport.net/~wntrhawk

Woody Guthrie Free Folk Festival (July)

In 1998, the year of a major Woody revival, came the 1st festival in his honor held in Guthrie's hometown. Over 7,000 attendees were treated to music by Arlo Guthrie, Kevin Welch, Jimmy LaFave, Ray Wylie Hubbard, Red Dirt Rangers, Bob Childers, Tom Skinner, and Billy Bragg who hosted a "Birthday Hootenanny" at the local Crystal Theater.

Okemah, Oklahoma
//www.galstar.com/~woody/
woody@galstar.com

RADIO & TELEVISION

PROMOTION

Americana

"Alternative country is the ONLY Alternative AND the ONLY Country...promoting **real** country music & country roots music to Gavin Americana reporters and anyone else with the courage, wisdom, foresight, & good taste to play it"

Moss Promotion
P. O. Box 941189
Atlanta, GA 31141
770-662-9463 or 496-0979
770-496-0216 (fax)
Amosspromo@aol.com

Broken Cherry Productions

Print & radio publicity for rockabilly, hillbilly, cowpunk.

//www.geocities.com/sunsetstrip/stadium/3429/
broken_cherry@hotmail.com

Counterpoint Music

Founded by Jon Grimson, a pioneer of the Americana radio format, this company promotes progressive, non-mainstream & roots country artists through radio, marketing, and consulting. Associated with the Americana music web site, and a leader in the first Gavin Americana "In the Pines" conference in September 1997.

//www.americana-music.com
jgrimson@americana-music.com

Jacknife

A3, Americana, College and Specialty Radio Promotions ("satisfied customers": Johnny Cash, SCOTS, Jolene, the Derailers, the Old 97s, Big Sandy, Don Walser, Whiskeytown, and many more).

8711 Burnet Rd., Ste. A-14
Austin, TX 78757

or

P. O. Box 33370
Austin, TX 78764
512-453-6122; 512-453-6502 (fax)
Jenni Sperandeo jdiva@io.com

Bill Wence Promotions

Americana, College, A3, Country radio promotion. Working with Red Meat, Kimmie Rhodes, Chris Wall, Amazing Rhythm Aces.

P. O. Box 39
Nolensville, TN 37135
615-776-2060; 615-776-2181 (fax)
//www.songs.com/wencepromo/
wencepromo@songs.com

RESOURCES

Bluegrass Radio Stations

Broken down by state with some links.

//www.bluegrass-music.com

BlueGrassRoots

Large list of radio stations with special focus on bluegrass and old-time shows.

//BGR.ee
BGR@BGR.ee

BRS Radio Directory

"The MOST comprehensive directory of radio stations on the Internet."

//www.radio-directory.com

Coalition for Eclectic Radio

Bay area organization devoted to keeping good radio alive; they publish *The Eclectic Ear* newsletter.

P. O. Box 883702
San Francisco 94188-3702
415-979-5390

Folk on the Radio

Massive database of acoustic, bluegrass, old-time, country, Cajun, etc. programs throughout the U.S. with history and description of each one.

//www.folkradio.org

Folk Radio Digests

Searchable archive of playlists for radio shows of DJs on the Folkdj-l mailing list.

//www.neverknow.com/folkdj-l/

Gavin Americana Charts

Clearinghouse for Gavin Americana (alt. country, blues, etc.) stations with articles, news, charts, links, etc.

//www.gavin.com

Gumbo Pages

Huge list of noncommercial radio stations in the U.S.

//www.gumbopages.com

International Bluegrass Music Association

A large catalog of stations is available by mail.

//www.ibma.org

KZSU List of Noncommercial Radio Stations

Stanford University station's large collection.

//kzsu.stanford.edu

M.I.T. List of Radio Stations on the Internet

Station WMBR's gigantic list categorized by country, state, call letters, and alphabetically.

//wmbr.mit.edu/stations/

OTR: Old-Time Music on the Radio

Project of the Old-Time Music Group which promotes and preserves radio broadcast of music drawing primarily from instrumental and vocal traditions of southern Appalachia; web site has both old-time music radio programming and compact disc databases.

//lupton.sas.upenn.edu/otr/otr.htm
jlupton@sas.upenn.edu

Rockabilly Radio

Directory of stations around the world with rockabilly programming.

//www.rockabillyhall.com/radio.html

Roots Radio Rockabilly

Selective online guide and links to rockabilly, hillbilly radio shows around the U.S., Australia, and Europe.

//www.geocities.com/sunsetstrip/backstage/
6273/radio.html

TML Music Pages Radio Roundup

Folk music resource directory for the Northeastern U.S. with listings for stations/programs featuring old-time, bluegrass, s/s, honky tonk, Western swing, roots, rockabilly et al. in New Jersey, New York, Connecticut, Rhode Island, Delaware and eastern Pennsylvania.

Traditional Music Line
P. O. Box 10598
New Brunswick, NJ 08906
732-699-0665

Viktoria Park Musik

Major web site for country music in Europe with big catalog of radio stations on the Continent and Great Britain.

//avus.de/viktoria/musik/country/index.htm

Yahoo List of Radio Stations

Major repository of radio stations divided into helpful categories.

//www.yahoo.com/entertainment/radio/stations

SYNDICATED PROGRAMS

Acoustic Cafe

Two hours of live interviews and performances from the best singer/songwriters: Peter Case, Alejandro Escovedo, Robbie Fulks, Jolene, Cheri Knight, Chris Knight, Roger McGuinn, Son Volt, Whiskeytown, Victoria Williams, and many more.

//www.mlive.com/cafe/

American Routes

PRI program hosted by Nick Spitzer from New Orleans and presenting Americana of all genres and eras.

University of New Orleans
1118 Royal St.
New Orleans, LA 70116
504-539-9637 (fax)
//amroutes.cc.emory.edu/
Amroutes@aol.com

The Country Eastern Radio Show

Hillbilly music intermixed with a variety ranging from punk to Tex-Mex. Hosted by Eddie Russell from KULM in Columbus, Texas and recorded for later broadcast in Ireland, Spain, and selected stations around the U.S.

Country Eastern West
108 Legion Cr.
Columbus, TX 78934

E-Town

NPR show from the Boulder Theater with Nick Forster (Hot Rize) and his wife Helen presiding over good music each week from the likes of Freakwater, Emmylou Harris, Sam Bush, Greg Brown, Cowboy Junkies, Steve Riley, and Steve Earle.

Boulder Theater
2030 14th St.
Boulder, Colorado
786-7030
//www.etown.org
etown@usa.net

The Fat Music Show

"Serving a high cholesterol smorgasbord of Americana music—from bluegrass and country western to comedy and rootsy rock and roll—to radio stations coast-to-coast since 1987."

P. O. Box 1869
Freedom, C 95019
//www.fatmusic.com/home.html
felton@fatmusic.com

The Folk Sampler

Bluegrass, old-time, blues and other acoustic from the foothills of the Ozarks with Mike Flynn since 1959.

P. O. Box 520
Siloam Springs, AR 72761
//www.folksampler.com
mikeflynn@folksampler.com

KingPup Radio Hour

Old-time and bluegrass "from high atop the Freckus Building in downtown Euphoria Falls, N.C." with Phil & Gaye Johnson.

//www.radioyur.com/kppg.html

The Midnight Special

Americana broadcast from WFMT Chicago with Rich Warren for over four decades.

P. O. Box 86
Urbana, Illinois 61801
//www.midnightspecial.org
folk@midnightspecial.org

Mountain Folk

"For people who enjoy bluegrass, folk and mountain music and such!" with your host East Side Dave.

P. O. Box 2266
Sinking Spring, PA 19608
//www.mountainfolk.com
MtnFolk@aol.com

Mountain Stage

Popular live radio performance that has had all the best of contemporary Americana and put out 19 CDs taken from shows over the years. Broadcast from West Virgina, hosted by Larry Groce.

600 Capitol St.
Charleston, WV 25301
800-RADIO-87, ext. 3
//www.wvpubrad.org/msindex.htm
wvapr@wvpubrad.org

New American Radio

Key place for artists in the Americana radio medium for over ten years; features cutting edge performers such as Terry Allen.

//www.somewhere.org/nar/nar_home.htm

A Prairie Home Companion

Perhaps the most famous of public radio's Americana variety programs hosted by Garrison Keillor with many guests from the world of alt. country (Riders in the Sky, Derailers).

Minnesota Public Radio
45 East Seventh St.
St. Paul, MN 55101
//phc.mpr.org
phc@mpr.org

Radio Bilingue

Only distributor of Spanish language programming for public radio including a number of music shows: "Musica Nortena" (traditional and contemporary accordion *conjunto*), "Onda Chicana" (contemporary Tex-Mex) and "Musica Internacional" (traditional variety from bluegrass to *charangos* to Celtic).

//www.radiobilingue.org

Rock-It Radio

1950's rock 'n' roll of all types (rockabilly, doo-wop, r&b) by vintage and contemporary artists.

P. O. Box 5617
Ventura, CA 93005
//members.wbs.net/homepages/r/o/c/rockitradio.html
rockitradio@earthlink.net

Truckin' Bozo Radio Network

All night program specializing in the good kind of country for the Knights of the Open Road.

888-860-TRUK
//www.thebozo.com
bozo@truck.net

Virtual Planet 3

RootsWorld editor Cliff Furnald takes to the air waves on WPKN in Bridgeprt, Connecticut to present 4 hours of international roots that often includes singer/songwriters such as Eddy Lawrence and James McMurtry plus Cajun and Tex-Mex.

244 University Ave.
Bridgeport, CT 06604
//www.wpkn.org/wpkn/cliff/

Woodsongs Old-Time Radio Hour

Folk & Americana variety show taped in front of a live audience at Planet III Record Studios in Lexington, Kentucky, and broadcast via satellite from World Radio.

P. O. Box 24187
Lexington, KY 40524
//www.poetusa.com/wsotro.html
radio@woodsongs.com

STATIONS/SHOWS*

*Information current as of

January 1, 1999.

UNITED STATES

Alabama

WEGL, 91.1 FM

"Psychobilly Freakout," Kristen Knotts, 8:30-10 p.m. Tues. (rockabilly music with roots in country & punk)

"The Backporch," 9-10 p.m. Wed. (bluegrass, folk)

"Twang," Doug Sherrard, 10-Mid. Wed. (alternative country) *DJ edits *Express Magazine* which reviews alt. country

Auburn University
116 Foy Union
Auburn 36849
844-WEGL
//www.wegl.org
wegl@mail.auburn.edu

Doug Sherrard:
twang@wegl.org
expressmagazine@mindspring.com

WUAL, 91.5 FM/WQPR, 88.7 FM

"All Things Acoustic," Jeremy Butler, 7:30-9:30 p.m. Fri.

"American Routes," 9:30-11 p.m. Fri.

"Bama Bluegrass," 7-9 p.m. Sat.

"Bayou Boogie," Herman Fuselier, 9-10 p.m. Sat. (Cajun/zydeco/swamp since 1992)

P. O. Box 870370, Suite 297
Phifer Hall
University of Alabama
Tuscaloosa 35487-0370
//www.wual.ua.edu/

All Things Acoustic:
//www.tcf.ua.edu/ata/
jbutler@tcf.ua.edu

Bayou Boogie:
//207.226.246.24/bayouboogie/

Alaska

KBBI Community Radio, 890 AM

Programming evenings and weekends runs the gamut of Americana.

3913 Kachemak Way
Homer 99603
907-235-7721
//www.alaska.net/~kbbi/
kbbi@alaska.net

KIYU, 910 AM

"Yukon River Ramble," 9-Mid. Mon.

"Banjo Signal," 7-8 p.m. Sat.

"Acoustic Accents," Bud Johnson, 9 p.m. Sun. (contemporary singer/songwriter)

P. O. Box 165
Galena 99741
//www.kiyu.com
kiyu@arctic.net

KMXT, 100.1 FM

"The Acoustic Music Hour," Jim Peterson, 3-4 p.m. Tues. and 1-2 p.m. Sat. (hosted by a mandolin/fiddle player in the local bluegrass band White Twang, this show features mostly old and newgrass but also s/s and other acoustic music)

718 Mill Bay Rd.
Kodiak 99615-7338
//www.ptialaska.net/~kmxt/
Kmxt@ptialaska.net

KNBA, 90.3 FM

"The Arctic Cactus Hour," Jim Stratton w/ Eric Smith, 7-8 p.m. Sat. (wide range of alt. country/Americana)

810 East 9th Ave.
Anchorage 99501
//www.alaska.net/~stratto/
stratto@dnr.state.ak.us
or
stratto@alaska.net

KTOO, 104.3 FM

"Crosscurrents," 8:30-10:30 a.m. M-F. (folk, rock, world, and more)

"Mule Train," 10 p.m.-1 a.m. Tues. (Country)

"Random Access Radio," David Youll, Sun. Eve. (Free form including s/s such as James McMurtry, Robert Earl Keen and Guy Clark.)

360 Egan Dr.
Juneau 99801
//www.juneau.com/KTOO/
ktoo@juneau.com

David Youll: DavidJuneau@aol.com

KUAC, 89.9 FM

"Folk Sampler," Mike Flynn, Noon-1 Sat. (old and new bluegrass, folk, blues, gospel, etc. centered on a weekly theme)

"Banjo Signal," Trudy Heffernan, 7-8 p.m. Sat.

"Funk Roots," Ray Funk, 7-8 p.m. Sun. (variety of roots styles including alt. country, rockabilly, swing)

University of Alaska at Fairbanks
Fairbanks 99707
//zorba.uafadm.alaska.edu/kuac/
fnssd@aurora.alaska.edu

Ray Funk
P. O. Box 72387
Fairbanks, AK 99707
rfunk@polarnet.com

Arizona

KXCI, 91.3 FM {Gavin Americana}

"Music Mix," Jamie Anderson, Suzanne Jameson, et al., 6 a.m.-6 p.m., M-F (blues, folk, rock, bluegrass, country)

"Ruby's Roadhouse," Carol Anderson, 7-9 p.m. Tues. (blues, rock, honky tonk)

"ZydeCajun Zone," Peter Bourque, 9-10 p.m. Tues.

"Al Perry's Clambake," 2 a.m.-5:30 a.m. Wed.

"Sunrise Serenade," Robert Bushkin, 6-8 a.m. Sat. (acoustic)

"Acoustic Alternatives," Don Gest, 8-10 a.m. Sat. (acoustic music not heard anywhere else)

"The Bluegrass Show," Victor Blue & Milo Solujic, 10-Noon Sat. a.m. (traditional/ progressive)

"Route 66," Michael Hyatt, Noon-2 Sat. (Carters, Patsy, Bob Wills and alt. country)

"Kid Squid's Mystery Jukebox," Kid Squid (David Squires), 2-5 p.m. Sat. (Bessie Smith to Hank to Ramones to Blasters; Tucson's #1 DJ for many years in a row)

"Bluegrass Gospel Show," A Mountain Boys, 10-Noon, Sun.

> 220 South 4th
> Tucson 85701
> //www.kxci.org
>
> Jamie Anderson: Tsunamiinc@aol.com
>
> Jim Foley (prog. dir.): foley@kxci.org
>
> Michael Hyatt: mnhyatt@azstarnet.com
>
> Suzanne Jameson: sqcomps@azstarnet.com

Arkansas

KABF, 88.3 FM

"Not Necessarily Bluegrass," 6:30-8 p.m. Mon. (contemporary bluegrass and progressive country)

"Ozark Mountain Hop," Janice Brewer, 6-9 p.m. Tues. (hot bluegrass)

"Country Collage," Uncle Jim and Red Ellis, 6-8 p.m. Wed. (traditional country)

"Pure Country," James Matthews, 6-8 p.m. Thurs. ("the best of country before it went Nashville")

"Best of Gospel Bluegrass," Vi Baker, 2-4 p.m. Sun.

> 1501 Arch St.
> Little Rock 72202
> //www.aristotle.net/kabf/
> kabf@aristotle.net

KUAF, 91.3 FM

"The Pickin' Post," 7-9 p.m. Sat. (bluegrass, country, folk)

> University of Arkansas
> 747 W. Dickson, Ste. 2
> Fayetteville 72701
> //www.npr.org/members/KUAF/

kuafinfo@comp.uark.edu

California

KALW 91.7 FM (since 1941, oldest non-commercial station west of the Mississippi)

"Folk Music & Beyond," JoAnn Mar & Bob Campbell, 5 p.m. Sat. (Americana/roots with different style showcased each week)

"Bluegrass Signal," Peter Thompson, 6-7 p.m. Sat. ("folk music in overdrive")

> 2576 Harrison St.
> San Francisco 94110
> //www.sfusd.kl2.ca.us/programs/kalw/kalw.htm
> KALWradio@aol.com
>
> Peter Thompson:
> bgsignal@worldnet.att.net

KALX, 90.7 FM {Gavin Americana}

"Vanessa or Nommi," 6-9 p.m. Wed. (eclectic mix including soul, country, r&b, bluegrass, folk, rock)

"Why Baby Why," Midnight-1 a.m. Wed. (showcase of roots, country, folk, bluegrass)

> University of California at Berkeley
> 26 Barrows Hall, #5650
> Berkeley 94720-5650
> 510-642-1111 (office)
> 510-642-KALX (DJs)
> //oms1.berkeley.edu/kalx/index.html

KAZU, 90.3 FM {Gavin Americana}

"Monday Morning Folk," J. T. Mason, 9-Noon (contemporary)

"Arden's Garden," Arden Eaton, 1-4 p.m. Mon. (rockin' country-bluesabilly; also on KPIG, Sat./Sun. 6-10 a.m.)

"Rosewood Gates," Robin Roberts, 9-Noon Tues. (folk; folk/rock)

"Out on the Dusty Trail," Mike McKinley & Aunt Bee, 9 a.m.-Noon Wed. (bluegrass to Hank Williams to western)

"The Sunny Side of Life," Uncle Jr. & Zeke., 9-Noon Thurs. (bluegrass/old-time, entertainment, comedy)

> P. O. Box KAZU
> Pacific Grove 93950
> 408-375-7275
> //www.kazu.org
> mail@kazu.org
>
> Arden Eaton: Muzicgirl@aol.com

KCBX, 90.1 FM

"Pickin' Up the Tempo," 8-10 p.m. Tues.

"Basically Bluegrass," 8-10 p.m. Thurs.

> 4100 Vachell Ln.
> San Luis Obispo 93401
> 800-549-8855
> //www.slonet.org/~ipkcbx/
> kcbx@slonet.org

KCPR, 91.3 FM

"Burnt Dog Rodeo," Gary Wells, 7-9 p.m. Mon. ("A whole bucket of twang": insurgent country, classic, rockabilly, folky; Carters, Freakwater, Townes Van Zandt, Uncle Tupelo, SCOTS)

> Cal Poly State University
> Journalism Department
> San Luis Obispo 93407
> 805-756-2955
> //www.kcpr.org
> kcpr@fix.net
>
> Burnt Dog Rodeo Page:
> //www.calpoly.edu/~sdalcerr/twang.html
>
> Gary Wells: gwells@polymail.calpoly.edu

KCRW. 89.9 FM

"The Open Road," Gary Calamar, 8-10 p.m. Sat. (Americana mix including alt. country of the "No Depression" variety)

> Santa Monica College
> 1900 Pico Blvd.
> Santa Monica 90405
> 310-450-5183
> //www.kcrw.org
>
> Open Road: openroad@kcrw.org

KCSB, 91.9 FM

"Festival Americana," Alex, 3-5 p.m. Wed.

"El Gigante," Ray Ramos, Sr., 6-8 p.m. Sun. (Tex-Mex; norteno; ranchera)

> University of California at Santa Barbara
> Attn: Music Director
> P. O. Box 13401
> Santa Barbara 93107
> 805-893-3757
> //www.as.ucsb.edu/kcsb

KCSN, 88.5 FM

"Bluegrass Express," Frank Javorsek, 7:30-10 a.m. Sat.

"Eclectic Americana Show," Skip Newhall, 2-5 p.m. Sat.; 3-5 p.m. Sun. (bluegrass, old-time, Western swing, Cajun, Blues, etc.)

"Classic Heartland" George Fair, 5-7 p.m. Sat. (country classics)

"Bluegrass Etc.," Frank Hoppe, 7:30-10 a..m. Sun. (bluegrass, old-time, gospel)

"City Billy," Rene Engel, 5-7 p.m. Sun. (classic & contemporary C&W)

"Down Home," Chuck Taggart, 7-9 p.m. Sun. (Roots and Traditional Music of the Americas: mix of all types of roots music with special emphasis on the musical styles of Southern Louisiana plus blues, bluegrass, country-rock, rael country, Tex-Mex; was on KCRW as "Gumbo" for many years until bounced in 1998; Chuck maintains the "Gumbo Pages" which have many links to Cajun sites and insurgent/alternative country such as the Passenger Side and Postcard 2 mailing lists plus "The Insurgent Country Roundup")

> University of California at Northridge
> 18111 Nordhoff St.
> Northridge 91330-8312
> 818-677-3090

//www.kcsn.org

Skip Marshall: skip@xxn.com

Frank Hoppe: fiddle@socal.com

George Fair: classicheartland@juno.com

Gumbo Pages: //www.gumbopages.com

Chuck Taggart: chuck@gumbo.org

KCSS, 91.9 FM {Gavin Americana}

"Fat Sunday," Texas Red aka Chip Meshew, 10 a.m.-1 p.m. (carrying on the tradition of renegade country station KFAT, 1975-1983 with real country and roots from honky tonk to Cajun; heavy Texas emphasis)

California State University, Stanislaus
801 West Monte Vista Ave.
Turlock 95383
209-667-3378
//kcss.csustan.edu/

Fat Sunday Forum:
//kcss.csustan.edu/fat/forum/

Texas Red: kcss@toto.csustan.edu

KDVS. 90.3 FM

"Old-Time/New Time," Genevieve, 4:30 p.m. Tues. (1 hr. old-time/bluegrass; 1 hr. experimental bluegrass/jazz)

"Tattoos & Pompadours," Bettie Sue, Noon-1:30 Thurs. (psychobilly, rockabilly, punk)

"Mr. Wagman's Neighborhood Where Morning Becomes Eclectic," Bill Wagman, 6-8:30 a.m. Wed. (folk, Celtic, roots rock, rockabilly, and "the occasional piece of cheese")

"Saturday Morning Folk Show," Peter Schiffman and Robyne Fawx, 9-Noon, Sat. (mostly folk but also alt. country)

1 Shields Ave.
UC Davis
Davis, CA 95616
916-752-9903
//www.kdvs.org

Bill Wagman: wjwagman@ucdavis.edu

Peter Schiffman:
schiffman@topaz.ucdavis.edu

KEGR, 97.7 FM

"American Roots," David Malbuff, 8-10:30 p.m. Thurs. (wide variety including many twangin' artists)

P. O. Box 103
Concord 94522

KFJC, 89.7 FM {Gavin Americana}

"Out Behind the Barn," Peggy O, 10-2 p.m., Tues. (bluegrass & beyond)

"Lubbock or Leave It," Joe Ed, 10 a.m.-2 p.m., Wed. (twangin', fishing & fun)

"The Big Guitar Show," Big Mike Destiny, 3-7 p.m., Sat. ("Twangin' tall boy can of whoop-ass rockabilly, twangin' footstompin' guitar bliss")

Foothills College
12345 El Monte Rd.
Los Altos Hills 94022
415-949-7260; FAX 415-948-1085
//www.kfjc.org

Out Behind the Barn:
//www.kfjc.org/peggyo/

Big Mike Destiny Web Page:
//www.kfjc.org/bigmike/

Big Mike Destiny:
Bigguitars@aol.com
or
myked@sbcinc.com

Joe Ed Web Page: //www.kfjc.org/joeed

Artists at the Edge of Obscurity Database:
//www.kfjc.org/
(record reviews by KFJC DJs)

KHSU, 90.5 FM

"Monday Night Folk Show," various DJs, 8-10 p.m. (traditional/contemporary)

"Tuesday Folk," Brooks Otis, Noon-1:30 p.m. (bluegrass, Western swing, old-time, Cajun, country, blues, old jazz)

"Wednesday Folk," Don, Noon-1:30 p.m. (diverse mix of folk and traditional country and "whatever else strikes his fancy")

"Bluegrass Express," Dave Sandlund, Noon-1:30 p.m. Thurs. (traditional/contemporary)

Humboldt State College
Arcata 95521
707-826-4807 (office)
//www.npr.org/members/khsu/

KKUP, 91.5 FM

"Monday Night Bluegrass," various hosts, 6-9 p.m.

"The Joint Is Jumpin'," Vida Lee, 10:30 p.m.-1 a.m. 1st Mon. (jump blues, r&b, Sun rockabilly)

"Don't Panic (It's Just Us Folks)," Lisa Atkinson, 10-1 a.m. Tues. (folk, bluegrass)

"New Wood," Peter Schwarz, 7-10 a.m. Thurs. (American, Celtic, bluegrass)

"Jumpin' & Jivin'," Vida Lee, 1-3 p.m. 3rd Thurs. (jazz, Eastern and Western swing, lounge)

"The Rhythm Range," Diana Dobro, 7-10 p.m. Thurs. (country folk, bluegrass)

"Friday Folk-Off," David Stafford & Mark Cook, 3-6 p.m. (eclectic folk)

"Captain Nashville," 6-9 a.m. 2nd Sat. (alternative folk, country, bluegrass)

"Swing Boogie,"Dave Barnett, Deadwood Dick, Sleepy John, 3-6 p.m. Sat. (bluegrass, country, Western swing)

"The Cupertino Barndance," Stompin' Steve Hathaway, 9-Mid. Sun. (classic & new bluegrass, honky-tonk, Western swing; Steve maintains the Western Swing Web Page)

P. O. Box 820
Cupertino 95015
408-260-2999
//www.kkup.com
webmistress@kkup.com

Peter Schwarz:
schwarz@almaden.ibm.com

Diana Dobro:
diana@newhomesmapguide.com

Dave Barnett: davencin@tdl.com

Western Swing Web Page:
//www.westernswing.com

Stompin' Steve Hathaway:
stevehat@best.com

Captain Nashville/David Borough:
//www.omix.com/music/denton/
borough@afm.net

KMUD, 91.1 FM

"The Bluegrass Show," Ron Stanley, 10-Noon Tues.

"Sharon's Country Closet," Sharon Byrd, 6-9 a.m. alt. Wed. ("today's most popular hillbilly rocksters plus legendary folk and country")

"Eclectic Roots," 11-2 a.m. Sun. (blues, country, jazz)

1144 Red way Dr.
Humboldt 95560
707-923-2513
//www.kmud.org
kmud@kmud.org

KNEW, 910 AM

"All Kinds of Country," Sully Roddy, 7-Midnight Sun. (classic country, bluegrass, old-time, Cajun, blues, etc.)

750 Battery St., Suite 200
San Francisco 94111-1524
415-291-0202

KPCC, 89.3 FM

"KPCC at Night: Alternative Music Until Midnight," 8-Mid., M-Th. (rock, folk, roots, Americana)

"Citybilly," 8-10 p.m. (classic and contemporary C&W and related styles)

"Friday Night Blues Review," Ellen Bloom & John "Juke" Logan, 8-10 (blues plus Cajun, country, roots)

Pasadena City College
1570 East Colorado Blvd.
Pasadena 91106-2003
818-585-7000
//www.kpcc.org
kpcc@pac.CD.cc.ca.us

KPFA, 94.1 FM; KPFB, 89.3 FM

"Sing Out!," Larry Kelp, 7-9 p.m. Mon. (folk and not-so-acoustic music)

"Free Form Music Mix," Michele Flannery, 9-11 p.m., M-Th. (eclectic mix including country punk)

"The Bonnie Simmons Show," 7-9 p.m. Thurs. (rock, country, folk)

"America's Back 40: The Hicks From Coast to Coast," Mary Tilson, 1-3 p.m. Sun. (all types of American roots music)

"Pig in a Pen"/"Panhandle Country," Ray Edlund or Tom Diamant, 3-5 p.m. Sun.

(bluegrass, old-timey, honky tonk, western swing, country jazz...)

> 1929 MLK Jr. Way
> Berkeley 94707
> 510-848-6767; 510-848-3812 (fax)
> http://www.kpfa.org
> kpfa@pacifica.org
>
> Tom Diamant c/o Arhoolie Records
> 10341 San Pablo Ave.
> El Cerrito, CA 94530
>
> Tom Diamant: tomd@flatrockrecords.com

KPFK, 90.7 FM {Gavin Americana}

"Folkscene," Roz & Howard Larman, 7-10 p.m. Sun. (all types of folk, roots music, Texas singer/songwriter since 1970; recorded, live music, and interviews)

> 3729 Cahuenga Blvd. West
> North Hollywood 91604
> //www.kpfk.org
>
> Folkscene //www.folkscene.com
>
> Howard Larman:
> howard13@ix.netcom.com

KPIG, 107.5 FM

Descendent of the famous KFAT, this station features Americana music all day plus "Cuzin Al's Bluegrass Show," 6-9 p.m. Sun.

> 1110 Main St., #16
> Watsonville 95076
> 724-PORK
>
> CyberSty: //www.kpig.com/
> (has "Pork Links" or connections to various Americana sites)
> sty@kpig.com

KRCB, 91.1 FM

"Eclectic Cafe," Cloud Moss, Tuesday p.m. (s/s, folk)

"Our Roots Are Showing," Chris Olson, Noon-5 p.m. Sat. (folk, s/s, bluegrass)

> 11375 Bodega Hwy.
> Sebastopol 95472
>
> Our Roots:
> //www.crl.com/~dreemer/roots.html
> dreemer@crl.com

KRSF (Noe Valley Community Radio), 97.7 FM

"Alt. Country/Twang," Sadie DeBauch, 8-10 p.m. Thurs.

> P. O. Box 77626
> San Francisco 94107
> //members.aol.com/~radiosf/sadie.htm
> RadioSF@aol.com

KSJV, 91.5 FM

"Musica Nortena," 5 a.m.-9 a.m. Sat. (Traditional & contemporary accordion *conjunto*)

"Onda Chicana," 9 a.m.-3 p.m. Sat. (contemporary Tex-Mex; *nortena* blended with jazz & country)

"Musica International," Carl Johnsen, 1-5 p.m. Sun. (international folk show that includes old-time string band, Cajun, bluegrass, and contemporary s/s)

> 5005 E. Belmont Ave.
> Fresno 93727
> //www.radiobilingue.org/ksjv/
>
> Carl Johnsen: ckj12@lennon.csufresno.edu

KSUN, 91.1 FM

"Butcher Pete's Rockin' Show," 1-3 p.m. Wed. (vintage rockabilly, neobilly, psychobilly for rockats; "a sleazy and greasy selection in the name of sex, fast cars, and teenage angst")

"Gallery 2," Jean, 10-Noon Fri. (rockabilly, punk, weird hillbilly, psychobilly, rock 'n' roll, Bulgarian folk and polka)

"I'm Just American," Seana Allen, Noon-3 p.m. Sat. ("country music at its best"—alternative/underground)

"I Heard That Being a DJ Would Get Me Laid...Boy Was I Wrong," Devin Robinson, 3-6 p.m. Sun. (indie rock including alt. country artists such as Son Volt with a little Hank Sr. thrown in)

> Sonoma State University
> 1801 E. Cotati Ave.
> Rohnert Park 94928
> 707-664-2621
> //www.sonoma.edu/ksun/
> ksun@sonoma.edu

KUCI, 88.9 FM

"La Onda Tejana," El Mafioso, 6-8 a.m. Wed. (Mexican music, Texas style)

"Trance Ranch Jiffy Loop," 3-6 p.m. Sat. ("Primitive interstellar Western...a honky tonk blend of Western styles flavored with ambianic valleys & cosmic beats")

> University of California at Irvine
> Irvine
> //www.kuci.uci.edu
> kuci@uci.edu

KUSP, 88.9 FM {Gavin Americana}

"Coast Ridge Ramble," Rachel Anne Goodman, 1-3 p.m. Sat. (all types of folk)

"Down on the Pataphysical Farm," Chris Jong or Leigh Hill, 1-3 p.m., Sun. (traditional/ modern bluegrass & old-time, Cajun since 1972)

"Lost Highway," Genial Johnny and Charlie Park, 3-5 p.m., Sun. (classic and alternative country plus Texas Country Roots)

> P. O. Box 423
> Santa Cruz 95061
> 408-476-2800
> //www.kusp.org
>
> Chris Jong: jong@kusp.org
>
> Genial Johnny Simmons: gjs@kusp.org

KVMR, 89.5 FM; 99.3 FM (Sacramento) {Gavin Americana}

"The Long and Dusty Road," Don Jacobson, 10 a.m.-Noon Mon. (10 years running featuring folk, bluegrass, blues, jazz, etc.)

"The Morning Show," Dan Bertsch, 7 a.m. Tues. (Y'alternative, neobilly, retrobilly technobilly)

"Harmony Ridge," Brian Terhorst, 7-10 a.m. Sat. (Bluegrass)

"County Line Bluegrass," Eric Rice, 10-Noon, Sat.

"Ragged But Right," Thomas Greener or "Hard Country," Rick Snelson, Noon-2 alt. Sats.(Cajun, country, folk, blues, zydeco)

"Rockin' & Stompin'," Wesley Robertson, 2-4 p.m. Sat. (Country-rock)

"Bayou Country: The Music of French Louisiana," Dale "LeBlanc" Johnson, 4-6 p.m. Sat.

"Loafer's Glory: Hobo Jungle of the Mind," U. Utah Phillipd, 11-Noon Sun.

> 401 Spring St.
> Nevada City 95959
> //www.kvmr.org
>
> Don Jacobson: dj@oro.net

KXLU, 88.9 FM

"Happy Trails," Robert Douglas, Mid-1 a.m. Fri. (recorded and live music show "specializing in C&W, roots and alternative forms of American roots music" from the L.A. area)

> Loyola Marymount University
> 7101 W. 80th St.
> Los Angeles 90045
> 310-338-2866
> //www.kxlu.org
> /www.thegrid.net/leondaniels/happytrails.html
>
> Robert Douglas 310-452-7339

KZFR, 90.1 FM, 107.1 FM (Redding)

"American Pastimes," Erik Mathisen, 3-5:30 p.m. Wed. (folk, bluegrass)

"Creole Stomp," Mary Riker, 10-Midnight Wed.

"Los Rancheras," Miguel Galvan, 3-6 a.m. Sun.

> P. O. Box 3173
> Chico 95927
> 916-895-0706
> //kzfr.org

KZSC, 88.1 FM

"The Fat Farm," Mary McCaslin, Noon-3 p.m. Wed. (off the wall country, folk, bluegrass and beyond with great contemporary s/s)

"Bushwacker's Club," Dangerous Dan and Juniper Jeff, 6-9 a.m. Fri. ("a sick & twisted romp across the American landscape")

> University of California at Santa Cruz
> Student Music East
> Santa Cruz 95061
> 408-459-2811

//www2.ucsc.edu/~kzsc/

Mary McCaslin:
//www.cruzio.com/~gpa/mary/

Mary McCaslin: marygreg@cruzio.com

Juniper Jeff Emery: jefmry@cruzio.com

KZSU 90.1 FM

"Hot Coffee & A Full Tank of Gas," Kara Whacked, 9-Noon Mon. (all acoustic folk, indie, country)

"Sunny Side Up," Bruce Ross, 9-Noon, Sun. (bluegrass, folk, alt. country, roots, Texas)

Stanford University
P. O. Box 6509
Stanford 94309
415-723-4389
//kzsu.stanford.edu/
(links to non-commercial radio stations)
info@kzsu.stanford.edu

Kara Whacked: karaw@kzsu.stanford.edu

KZYX, 90.7 FM {Gavin Americana}

"Humble Pie," Jimmy Humble, 6-7 p.m. Mon. & 9-11 a.m. Sat. (American roots, folk, acoustic)

"Lunch on the Back Porch," Diane Hering, 11-1 p.m. Sat. (bluegrass)

"Tubby Tunes," Long John Morehouse, 1-3 p.m. Sat. ("outlaw boogie, country deluxe...upbeat, irreverent tone of boogie & humor")

Philo 95466
//www.pacific.net/~kzyx/
kzyx@pacific.net

Jimmy Humble: jimmy@pacific.net

Long John Morehouse:
ttunes@envirolink.org

XHRM, 92.5 FM

"Music Without Boundaries," Kenny Weissberg, 9-Noon Sun. (Americana with a liberal dose of alt. country)

P. O. Box 80546
San Diego 92138

Kenny Weissberg: OtisSing@aol.com

Colorado

KAFM, 88.1 FM

Blues, folk, bluegrass, alternative, rockabilly and more.

Grand Valley Public Radio
Grand Junction, CO 81502

Mark Anderson: Slikkeeboy@aol.com

KGNU, 88.5 FM; 99.9 FM (Ft. Collins)

"Morning Sound Alternative," various hosts 9:30-Noon M-F (eclectic generally nonelectric mix of folk, acoustic, bluegrass, country, world, jazz)

"Afternoon Sound Alternative," 1-4 p.m. M-F

"Hwy. 322," Mike Bell, 7-8 p.m. Thurs. (folk revival, its roots and branches)

"Honky Tonk Heroes," John Baker, Michael C., et al., 6-9 a.m. Sat. (old & new country/ western music)

"Old Grass, Gnu Grass," various hosts, 9-Noon Sat. ("the oldest, the gnuest; you bet your grass!")

P. O. Box 885
University of Colorado
Boulder 80306
303-449-4885
//www.kgnu.org

John Baker: terraplane@h2net.net

KOTO, 91.7 FM {Gavin Americana}

Americana programming

P. O. Box 1069
Telluride 81435
//infozone.telluride.co.us/infozone/town/koto/koto.htm

Connecticut

WCNI, 91.1 FM

"Bon Temps Rouler," Bridget Ellis & Keith Harvey, 6-9 p.m. Sun. (Cajun, Conjunto, old-time, world)

"Not Exactly Nashville," Mike Trynosky, Noon-3 p.m. Sat. ("country music the way it oughta be!"; rockabilly, hillbilly, swing, the cream of Americana)

270 Mohegan Ave.
P. O. Box 4972
New London 06320
203-439-2853
//www.concoll.edu/noteworthy/

Mike Trynosky:
not_exactly_nashville@compuserve.com or twangbilly@cyberzone.net

WECS, 90.1 FM

"Simply Bluegrass," Amy Orlomski, 7:30-10 p.m. Sat

Willamantic 06226

WHUS, 91.7 FM

"Double A Diner," Bobby A., 8-10 a.m. Mon. (newgrass, alternative country, blues, jazz)

"Surfabilly Serenade," Dean Farrell, Mid-2 a.m. Sat. (best of rockabilly & surf from the 50s-90s)

"The Magic of Bluegrass," Suzie Colpitts, JT, and the Bluegrass Coyote, 1-4 p.m. Sun. (traditional/ contemporary bluegrass)

"Acoustically Sound," John Sloan, 4-7 p.m. Sun.

P. O. Box U-8R
2110 Hillside Rd.
University of Connecticut
Storrs 06269
203-486-4007
//www.whusfm.saup.uconn.edu
whusfm@uconnvm.uconn.edu

WPKN, 89.5 FM {Gavin Americana}

"Variety Show," Denise Manzari, 6-10 a.m. Mon.. (bluegrass, Celtic, Cajun/zydeco, folk, country, Tex-Mex)

"Virtual Planet 3," Cliff Furnald, 2-6 p.m. Mon. (syndicated show with roots of all types from all places hosted by the editor of *RootsWorld* magazine)

"Strangeland," Tom Frouge, 10-Mid. Mon. (Hillbilly, alt. country, outlaw, cowpunk, bluegrass, Western swing, rockabilly, Cajun and all that twang)

"Chris Teskey Show," 6:35-10 p.m. Wed. ("Teskey knows the old fellers from the hills and the young punks from out of Nashville"; country and bluegrass)

"On the Horizon," Mike Horyczun, 2-6 p.m. alt. Fris. (hot cutting edge folk, blues, acoustic; Mike's fetish—Austin/Nashville sound)

"Early Country Music," Dave Schwartz, 10-Midnight Sun. (Carters, Vernon Dalhart, Carson Robison...)

244 University Ave.
Bridgeport 06601
203-576-4895
//www.wpkn.org
wpkn@wpkn.org

VP3: //www.wpkn.org/wpkn/cliff/

WSHU, 91.1 FM

"Acoustic Connections," Walt Graham, 8-10 p.m. Sat. (bluegrass, folk, singer/songwriter)

5151 Park Ave.
Fairfield 06432
203-371-7989
//www.wshu.org
wienk@wshu.org

WWUH, 91.3 FM (West Hartford)/ WWEB, 89.9 FM (Wallingford)

"Folk Music on Toast," Ed McKeon, 6-9 a.m. M-F. (variety of acoustic from folk to bluegrass)

"UH Radio Bluegrass," Kevin Lynch, 9 a.m.-1 p.m. Sat. (old and new)

University of Hartford
200 Bloomfield Ave.
West Hartford 06117
203-768-4725
//uhavax.hartford.edu/~wwuh/
wwuh@uhavax.hartford.edu

Ed McKeon: EMcKeon@aol.com

Delaware

WVUD, 91.3 FM

"Roots," 9-Noon M-F ("folk music for all kinds of folks")

"Fire on the Mountain," Carl Goldstein, 10-Noon Sat. (bluegrass & old-time)

"Rural Free Delivery," John Lupton & George Mercer, 12-2 p.m. Sat. (in John's humble opinion "the best radio show in the history of the universe"; features a wide variety of country including honky tonk, old-time,

Western swing; classic and modern; John Lupton maintains the Brandywine Friends of Old-Time Music Page)

Perkins Student Center
University of Delaware
Newark 19716
302-831-2701
//www.udel.edu/wvud

Rural Free Delivery:
//www.sas.upenn.edu/~jlupton/rfd.html

John Lupton: jlupton@sas.upenn.edu

Brandywine Friends of old-time Music:
//www.sas.upenn.edu/~jlupton/bfotm.html

District of Columbia

WAMU, 88.5 FM

"Bluegrass Country," Jerry Gray & Ray Davis, 3-6 p.m., Mon-Fri. & 12-3 p.m., Sat.

"Old West Songs," Jerry Gray, 3-6 p.m., Sat.

"Bluegrass Overnight", Al Steiner, Bill Foster, Les McIntyre, Midnight-6 Sun.

"Stained Glass Bluegrass," Red Shipley, 6-10 a.m., Sun.

"The Eddie Stubbs Show," 2-5 p.m., Sun. (country & honky tonk)

American University
Brandywine Bldg.
4400 Massachusetts Ave. NW
Washington 20016-8082
202-885-1200
//soundprint.brandywine.american.edu/~wamu/

WAMU Bluegrass Bulletin Board:
//soundprint.brandywine.american.edu/~wamu/bulletin.html
wamu@capaccess.org

Al Steiner: asteiner@access.digex.net

Les McIntyre: les@american.edu

Eddie Stubbs
P. O. Box 148118
Nashville, TN 37214
//www.pond.com/~vanallen/stubbs.html

Florida

WLRN, 91.3 FM

"Folk & Acoustic Music," Michael Stock, 1-4 p.m. Sat. (s/s, bluegrass, old-time).

172 NE 15th St.
Miami 33132
305-995-2264
//www.wlrn.org/radio/

Michael Stock: mstock@dc.seflin.org

WMNF, 88.5 FM {Gavin Americana}

"Morning Show," var. hosts, 6-11 a.m. M-F (acoustic based mix with lots of alt. country of all types from the Austin Lounge Lizards to Lucinda Williams)

"Traffic Jam," Glen Hatchell, 4-6 p.m. M-F (eclectic show featuring roots rock, s/s, blues, and anything else that fits)

"This Is Bluegrass," Tom Henderson, 7-8 p.m. Mon.

"Bluegrass," Sid Flannery, 6-8 a.m. Sat.

"Sunday Folk Show," Jeannie Holton, Noon-2 p.m. Sat (lots of s/s e.g. Alvin, DeMent, Prine, Hinojosa, et al.)

1210 MLK, Jr. Blvd.
Tampa 33603
813-239-WMNF
//www.wmnf.org
wmnf@wmnf.org

Glen Hatchell: ghgator@ibm.net

WNSU, 92.9 FM

"Roots Music," Pete Agostinelli, 8-10 p.m. Sat. (blues, country, rockabilly, Western swing 1930-Present)

c/o Rosenthal Student Center
Nova Southeastern University
3301 College Ave.
Fort Lauderdale 33314
305-475-7419
//www.nova.edu/cwis/newsevents/wnsu.html

Pete Agostinelli:
600300a@bcfreenet.seflin.lib.fl.us

WUCF, 89.9 FM

"Acoustic/Folk Show," Paul Gerardi, 5-7 p.m. Sun.

"The Bluegrass Show," David Dees, 7-9 p.m. Sun. (on the air 10 years and hosted by an assistant dean and associate Prof. in sociology)

University of Central Florida
P. O. Box 162199
Orlando 32816-2199
407-823-3689
//Wucf.ucf.edu

Paul Gerardi: wordman@magicnet.net

David Dees: dees@ucflvm.cc.ucf.edu

WUFT, 89.1 FM

"Across the Prairie," Cathy DeWitt, 5 p.m. Sun. (traditional and modern s/s, bluegrass, old-time)

Weimar Hall
University of Florida
Gainesville

Cathy DeWitt: Cathydew@aol.com

Georgia

WMLB, 1170 AM {Gavin Americana}

Wide variety of Americana programming; Gavin Americana "Station of the Year 1996" and "Program Director (Chris Marino) of the Year 1997" plus *Atlanta* magazine's "Best Y'Alternative 1997." Marino was named Gavin Americana Editor to replace Rob Bleetstein in late 1997.

Cumming 30130
//www.wmlb.com
(includes Americana CD reviews)
twang@wmlb.com

WREK, 91.1 FM

"Back Alley Porch Roost," Andy Malkus, 9-10 p.m. Sun. (country, Western swing, rockabilly, bluegrass; "less Billy Ray and Reba, more Wanda and Hank")

Georgia Tech University
165 8th St. NW
Atlanta 30332
404-894-2468
//cyberbuzz.gatech.edu/wrek/

Andy Malkus: gt2238@prism.gatech.edu

WRFG, 89.3 FM

"Old Country & Bluegrass," Johnny Jones, 1-6 a.m. Mon.

"Amazing Grass," Cousin George, 7-9 p.m. Tues.

"Bluegrass Festival," 7-11 p.m. Wed.

"Harmony Grove," Jim Claxton, 7:30-9:30 a.m. Sun. (bluegrass)

"My Own House," alt. hosts, 9:30-11:30 a.m. Sun. (country & bluegrass)

"Zydeco," 11:30-1 p.m. Sun.

"Sagebrush Boogie," 5-6:30 p.m. Sun. (Western swing & country)

"Buck Dancer's Choice," Lewis Wills, 6:30-8 p.m. Sun. (traditional folk and lots of contemporary old-time too)

1083 Austin Ave. NE
Atlanta 30307

Lewis Wills: lw@atl.mindspring.com

WUOG, 90.5 FM

"Folk Scene," 2-4 p.m. Sun. (bluegrass, Cajun, Celtic, s/s)

"Dirt Roads & Honky Tonks," 4-6 p.m. Sun. (country from the classic to the "redneck underground")

University of Georgia
P. O. Box 2065, Memorial Hall
Athens 30602
706-542-8466
//www.uga.edu/~wuog/

Guam

KPRG, 89.3 FM

"Folkwaves," Jay MacDonald, 7-9 p.m. Tues. (mostly folk but also good sampling of alt. s/s especially from Texas)

303 University Dr.
UOG Station
Mangilao 96923
671-734-8930

Jay MacDonald: jjm@kuentos.guam.net

Illinois

WCBR, 92.7 FM

"Rural Electrification," Chris Schuba, 7-9 p.m. Tues. (classic and alternative country)

120 W. University
Arlington Heights 60004
847-255-5800

Chris Schuba: Schuba@aol.com

WDBX, 91.1 FM

"On The Backroad," Tom Hopkins, 10-Noon Wed. (wide variety of alt. country including s/s, bluegrass, etc.)

224 N. Washington St.
Carbondale 62901
618-457-3691

Tom Hopkins: tchopkins@midamer.net

WDCB, 90.9 FM

"Folk Festival," Bob Janis, 7-9 p.m. Tues. (folk, bluegrass)

"Strictly Bluegrass," Larry Robinson, 7-9 p.m. Wed. (hosted by a bluegrass musician in the group Running Fox)

"American Backroads," Greg Easterling, 10 p.m. Fri.

College of DuPage
22nd St. & Lambert Rd.
Glen Ellyn 60137
708-942-4200
//www.cod.edu/wdcb/

Scott Witt: scotwitt@delphi.com

Larry Robinson: Dobro28@aol.com

WEBX, 93.5 FM

Mostly alt. rock but playlists include Steve Earle, the Old 97s, BR5-49, et al.

University of Illinois
Champaign-Urbana 61820
//www.webxfm.com

WEFT, 90.1 FM

"From the Joshua Tree Inn," Kevin Elliott, 6-8 p.m. Tues. ("a place where folk, bluegrass, country, and rock music intersect, where folk isn't so self-conscious, country so commercial and rock so self-important. It's a place where musicians unite and the jamming continues far into the night filling the empty spaces over the vast lonesome desert...")

"Ridin' the Rails," Jan Warwick, 6-8 p.m. Wed. (Americana: folk, country bluegrass)

"Another Country," Radio Duff, 6-8 p.m. Thurs. (alt. country)

"Old McDonald's Country Breakfast," Donald Lemke, 4-8 a.m. Sat. (downhome blend of country, bluegrass, gospel)

"Old-Time Country Music Jamboree," Kent McConkey, 5-8 p.m. Sat. (old-time, bluegrass, country, gospel)

113 N. Market St.

Champaign 61820
217-359-9338
//www.prairienet.org/arts/weft/
Weft@prairienet.org

WFMT, 98.7 FM

"The Midnight Special," Rich Warren, 9-Mid. Sat. (Broadcasting an Americana mix; for over 45 years; syndicated)

5400 N. St. Louis
Chicago 60625

Midnight Special:
P. O. Box 86
Urbana 61801
//www.midnightspecial.org
folk@midnightspecial.org

WGLT, 89.1 FM

"Hillbilly Surf Hour," Steve Fast, Mid-1 Sat.

"Acousticity," Marc Boon, 8-Midnight Sun. ("flexible" folk, bluegrass, old-time, singer/songwriter, alternative country, Cajun, conjunto)

Illinois State University, WGLT
Campus Box 8910
Normal 61790-8910
//www.ilstu.edu/depts/wglt
wglt@ilstu.edu

WHPK, 88.5 FM

"Come All You Coal Miners," Pier, 4-5 p.m. Wed.

"Pinch of Joy, Dash of Misery," Jonathan Kriege, 5-6 p.m. Wed. (classic to insurgent country)

University of Chicago
Reynolds Club, Mitchell Tower
5706 S. University Ave.
Chicago 60637
312-702-8289
//student-www.uchicago.edu/orgs/whpk-radio/

Pinch of Joy:
//student-www.uchicago.edu/users/jdkriege/radio.htm

Jonathan Kriege:
jdkriege@midway.uchicago.edu

WIUM, 91.3 FM

"Folk Weekend," Jeff Holtz, 5-6 p.m. Sun.

"American Routes," Nick Spitzer, 7-9 p.m. (syndicated Americana variety)

Western Illinois University
429 Memorial Hall
1 University Circle
Macomb 61455
309-298-1873; Fax 309-298-2133
//www.wiu.edu/users/miwium/
WE-Radio@wiu.edu

WLUW, 88.7 FM

"Somebody Else's Troubles," Craig Kois, Tom Jackson, John Wright et al., 10 a.m.-Noon Sat. (wide variety with third Sat. hosted by Jackson and featuring American roots music)

"The New Orleans Music Hour," Tom Jackson, Noon-1 p.m. Sat. (Cajun, zydeco, blues, swamp pop, jazz)

Loyola of Chicago
820 N. Michigan Ave.
Chicago 60611
//www.luc.edu/depts/wluw/

Craig Kois: ckois@wpo.it.luc.edu

Tom ackson: Tjaxnoladj@aol.com

John Wright: jhwright@nwu.edu

WNUR, 89.3 FM

"The Folk Show," Amanda Johnson, 10 a.m.-1 p.m. Sun. (s/s, bluegrass, Celtic, etc.)

"Southbound Train," Jim Moran, Tony Becker & Keith Cook, 9-11 p.m. Sun. ("non-homogenized country" with lots of the alt./insurgent variety from Austin to Raleigh and all points in between; plus a dash of vintage country, bluegrass, rockabilly)

Northwestern University
1905 Sheridan Rd., #216
Evanston 60208-2660
708-491-7101
//www.wnur.org
wnur@nwu.edu

Amanda Johnson: ae-johnson@nwu.edu

Southbound Train:
//www.wnur.org/southbound/

Jim Moran: j-moran2@nwu.edu

WSIU, 91.9 FM

"Rural Route 3," Uncle Mark, 6-7 p.m. Sun. (bluegrass, old-time, country/western)

"Folk Sounds," 7-9 p.m. Sun.

SIUC Broadcasting Service
University of Southern Illinois
Carbondale 62901-6602
618-453-4343
//www.siu.edu/departments/cmcma/bs/fm/
tgodell@siu.edu

Uncle Mark: a971@siu.edu

WUIS, 91.9 FM

"Bluegrass Breakdown," Mark Mathewson, 6-8 p.m Sun.

University of Illinois at Springfield
Springfield 62794-9243
//www.uis.edu/~wuis/wuis2.html
wuis@uis.edu

Indiana

WAXT, 96.7 FM

"Singers & Songs," Rick Teverbaugh, Sun, eve. (Variety of singers and songwriters on any given show including Alison brown, Son Volt, Golden Smog, the Blacks and many more alt. Country artists; Rick also has a web site of the same name where he reviews CDs by the performers featured on his show.)

Rick Teverbaugh
P. O. Box 50

Anderson, IN 46015
765-641-0021

Singers & Songs: //indol.com
tever@indol.com

or

rickert@netdirect.net

WFHB, 91.3 FM {Gavin Americana}

"Rock! Everybody Rock!," Jodie, 6:30-9 p.m. (rockabilly, roots-rock, swing raw country)

"Breakfast Cafe," Sarah Flint, 6-9 a.m. Tues. (roots, rock-n-country)

"Those Friends of Mine," Mike Kelsey, 6-9 a.m. Wed. (bluegrass, old-time, s/s, Texas with lots of surprises)

"Crawfish Fiesta," Chet, 7:30-9 p.m. Fri. (Louisiana music from Cajun to R&B)

"Old-Time Train 45," Mechanic Mike, 10-Noon Sat. (bluegrass old and new)

"Rural Routes," var., 12-2 p.m. Sat. (bluegrass and other related acoustic music)

"Dark End of the Street," Gus Travers & Raymond Dubose, 2-4 Sat. (the best in country/western; R&B)

P. O. Box 1973
Bloomington 47402
812-323-1200
//www.wfhb.org
wfhb@wfhb.org

Mike Kelsey: kelsey@bluemarble.net

WMHD, 90.5 FM

"Rosie's Pickin' Parlor," Dave Voltmer and Jack Derry, 5-6 p.m. Sun. (playing bluegrass and old-time for 8 years but only during the school year, Sept.-May)

Rose-Hulman Institute of Technology
5500 Wabash Ave.
Terre Haute
812-877-8350
//www.rose-hulman.edu/users/groups/wmhd/html/index.html

Dave Voltmer: voltmer@rose-hulman.edu

WVPE, 88.1 FM

"The Back Porch," Al Kniola, 8-Mid. Sun. (traditional & contemporary bluegrass)

2424 California Rd.
Elkhart 46514
//www.wvpe.org
wvpe@skyenet.net

Al Kniola:
//www.hidwater.com/folkdj/wvpe881.html
acanola1@skyenet.net

Iowa

ICFR, 88.7 FM (Iowa City Free Radio)

"The Shady Grove," Norbert Sarsfield, Noon-2 p.m. Sun. (traditional and contemporary bluegrass, old-time, and folk)

308 E. Burlington
P. O. Box 219

Iowa City 52240

Norbert Sarsfield Sarsfield2@aol.com

KRUI, 89.7 FM

"Milk Cow Boogie," Dallas Clemmons, 3-5 p.m. Sun. (Americana with special focus on real/alt. country)

"American Rhythms," Eric Rothenbuhler, 5-7 p.m. Sun. (the roots of American music)

University of Iowa
811 Woodside Dr.
Iowa City 52246
//www.uiowa.edu/~krui/
krui@uiowa.edu

Dallas Clemmons: dallasc@pacbell.net

KUNI/KHKE, 90.9 FM

"Fresh Folk," Karen Impala, 1-3 p.m. Mon.

"Live Sets," 1-3 p.m. Tues.-Fri. (modern folk, bluegrass, s/s)

University of Northern Iowa
Cedar Falls 50613
//www.uni.edu/kuni/

Kansas

KANU, 91.5 FM

"Trail Mix/Flint Hills Special," Bob McWilliams, 1-7 p.m. Sun. (25 years running featuring two hours of bluegrass, then one hour of Celtic, one hour of old-time, followed by one hour of bluegrass, country, Cajun, folk rock etc.)

Broadcasting Hall
University of Kansas
Lawrence, KS 66045
//www.ukans.edu/~kanu-fm/

Bob McWilliams:
radiobob@falcon.cc.ukans.edu

KANZ, 91.1 FM (HPPR, High Plains Public Radio)

"Silver Rails," Lynn Boitano, 9 a.m. Sat. (sung, strummed, picked music)

"Western Swing & Other Things," Allen Bailey, 11 a.m.-Noon Sat. (Texas music: Western swing, cowboy, honky tonk)

"Folk Sampler," Mike Flynn, 10 p.m. Sat. (country, bluegrass, cowboy music etc.)

210 N. 7th
Garden City 67846
/www.westernkansas.net/publicradio/
hppr@westernkansas.net

KMUW, 89.1 FM

"Roots and Branches," Frank Dudgeon, 10-Mid. Fri. (traditional country, country blues, rock-abilly, folk, etc.)

3317 E. 17th
Wichita 67208
//www.knuw.org
kmuw@twsu.edu

Kentucky

WFPK, 91.9 FM

"Roots n' Boots," Michael Young (alt. country/Americana)

Michael Young
269 Coral Ave.
Louisville 40206
502-897-0435
Roots2@bellsouth.net

WKMS, 91.3 FM

"Music From the Front Porch," John McMillen, 9 a.m.-1 p.m. Sat. (old-time, bluegrass, s/s)

2018 University Station
Murray State University
Murray 42071

John McMillen:
bluegrass@mcc-uky.campus.mci.net

WKYU, 88.9 FM

"Barren River Breakdown," Erika Brady, Noon-2 p.m. Sat. (American roots music)

Western Kentucky University
Bowling Green 42101
502-745-5489
//www.wku.edu/wkyu-fm/

Erika Brady: erika.brady@wku.edu

WMMT, 88.7 FM ("Home of the Hillbilly Nation Celebration!") {Gavin Americana}

"Appalachian Mornings," Gentle Ben, 5-7 a.m. M-F (bluegrass, gospel, old-time)

"Kudzu Coffee Club," The Cuppa Family, 7-10 a.m. Mon. (old-time, bluegrass, folk)

"Songs From the Wood," Malta May, 11-2 p.m. Mon. (mix of Celtic, old-time)

"The Scuttle Gap Get-Together," Willard & Angie, 10:30-1:30 p.m. Tues.

"In the Mood," Jim B. 1:30-3:30 p.m. Tues. (variety of American music)

"Deep in Tradition," Buck Maggard, 3:30-6:30 p.m. Tues. (old-time, folk, bluegrass, humor)

"Kahula & Cappucino," 8-Mid., Tues. (Americana & folk)

"Biscuits Show," 7-10 a.m. Wed. (commentary mixed with country, rock, blues)

"Old-Time Music," Roy, 11-2 p.m. Wed.

"Ridin Around Listening to the Radio," Wylie Quixote, 4-7 p.m. Wed. (readings & great driving tunes)

"The Bluegrass Hillbilly," Noon-2:30 p.m. Thurs. & 8-10 a.m. Sat.

"Catfish John's Sunnyside Up Show," 3:30-6:30 p.m. Thurs. ("the finest bluegrass gospel this side of heaven")

"The Bluegrass Express," Verlin Sanders & Randy Wyatt, 7:30-10:30 p.m. Thurs. (classic local bluegrass sounds)

"The Normal Brothers Newgrass Show," 10:30 p.m.-1 a.m., Thurs.

"Acoustic Attitude," Susan Z., 12:30-3 p.m. Fri. (s/s)

"Country Bob's Virtual Radio," 4-6:30 p.m. Fri. (from "the Love Club" to the Cajun spotlight)

"From the Roots," 1-3 p.m. Sat. (traditional mountain music)

"Dirty Harry's Late Night Mix," 11 p.m-'til the dogs crawl back on the porch Sat. (classic country)

"Starvin' Marvin's Favorites," 3:30-6:30 p.m. Sun. (old-time, bluegrass, and local country)

> 306 Madison St.
> Whitesburg 41858
> //www.uky.edu/projects/appal/wmmt/wmmt. htm
> WMMT887@aol.com

WNKU, 89.7 FM {Gavin Americana}

"New Music," Laura Blackwood, 8 p.m. Wed. (alt. rock including alt. country, bluegrass, Cajun)

"Bluegrass," 6-9 a.m. & Noon-3 p.m. Sun.

"Folk City," Scott Levy, 9-Noon, Sun. (s/s, bluegrass etc.)

"Torch & Twang," Edward Cunningham, 3-5 p.m. Sun. (Americana)

> Northern Kentucky University
> P. O. Box 337
> Highland Heights 41076
> 606-572-7897
> //www.nku.edu/~wnku/
> wknu@nku.edu

WRFL, 88.1 FM

"Mary Gilmartin Show," Mary Gilmartin, 6:30-9 p.m. Thurs. (eclectic some alt. country)

"Jason Cebe Show," Jason Cebe, 9-Noon Fri. (alternative with good helping of "y'alternative" e.g. UT, Whiskeytown...)

"Blue Yodel #9," Terri Powell, 9-Noon Sat. (acoustic; bluegrass)

"Hard Travelin' Revue," Joe Gierlach, Noon-3 Sat. (old-time, bluegrass)

"The Hot Burrito Show," Bobby Ray, Noon-3 p.m. Sun. (classic and alt. country from GP to the Old 97s)

"Hoe Dad Hootenanny," Tom Moreland, 3-6 p.m. Sun. (rockabilly, surf, garage)

> University of Kentucky
> P. O. Box 777
> University Station
> Lexington 40504
> //www.uky.edu/~wrfl/
> wrfl@pop.uky.edu
>
> Jason Cebe: jrcebe0@pop.uky.edu
>
> Terri Powell: tpowel@pop.uky.edu

WSIP, 98.9 FM

"Bluegrass & the Bo Man," Bo McCarty, 8-Mid. Sun. (old and new grass with lots of links on McCarty's web page)

> Paintsville 41240
>
> Bo McCarty: //www.wwd.net/user/boman

boman@wwd.net

Louisiana

KAOK, 1400 AM

"Cajun and Zydeco," 6-8 a.m. M-F, 6 a.m.-8 p.m. Sat., 12:30-8 p.m. Sun.

> Lake Charles 70605
> 318-436-7541

KBON, 101.1 FM

Dedicated to the promotion and preservation of Louisiana music and culture and offering Cajun and other Louisiana music 24 hours a day!

> 109 S. 2nd St.
> Eunice 70535
> //www.whodat.net/~kbon/
> kbon-101fm@usa.net

KEUN, 1490 AM

"Cajun," 5-7 a.m. M-F, 7 a.m.-Mid. Sat.

"Rendesvous des Cajins," Dr. Barry Ancelot 5-8 p.m. Sat. (live from the Liberty Theater in Eunice)

"Live From Michot's Main St. Lounge in Basile," 8-10 p.m. Sat.

"Zydeco," 9 a.m.-6 p.m. Sun.

> Eunice 70535
> 318-457-3041
> //www.orion-cs.com/keun.kjjb/

KJCB, 770 AM

"Cajun and Zydeco," 7-9 p.m. M-Th., 9-11 a.m. Sat., Noon-2 p.m. Sun.

> Lafayette 70504
> 318-233-4262

KJEF, 1290 AM

Cajun music 24 hours a day, 7 days a week.

> Jennings

KLCL, 1470 AM

"Cajun and Zydeco," 9 a.m.-Noon Sat.

> Lake Charles 70605
> 318-433-1641

KROF, 105.1 FM; 960 AM

"Cajun and Zydeco," 6 a.m.-Sunset M-F (AM) and 6 a.m.-Noon Sat. & Sun. (FM)

> Abbeville 70510
> 318-893-2531

KRVS, 88.7 FM (Lafayette); 90.5 (Lake Charles)

"Bonjour Louisianne," Peter Bergeron, 5-7 a.m. M-F (traditional Cajun music in French)

"Zydeco est pas Sale," John Broussard and Melvin Caesar, 6-Noon Sat.

"Rendesvous des Cajin," Dr. Barry Ancelot, 5-7 p.m. Sat. (live from the Liberty Theatre in Eunice)

"Dirty Rice," Robert Broussard, Karl Fontenot, Todd Mouton, 8-10 p.m. Sat. (state's longest running Louisiana music show)

"Bayou Boogie," Herman Fuselier, 10-11 p.m. Sat. (zydeco and Cajun)

"Dimanche Matin/Bal de Dimanche," Donny Broussard, 6a.m.-3 p.m. Sun. (all French Cajun)

> University of Southwest Louisiana
> P. O. Box 42171
> Lafayette 70504
> //krvs.usl.edu
> djs1875@usl.edu

KVPI, 1050 AM (broadcasting French music since 1957)

"Cajun," 8-Noon, M-F

"Rendezvous des Cajin," Jim Soileau, 4-5 p.m. M-F

"Cajun Music Live From Fred's Lounge," Martel Ardoin 9:15-11 a.m., Sat. (perhaps the most famous of all Cajun radio shows; originates from dancehall in Mamou where locals cram its modest interior every week)

"T&J Show," Roland Manuel, 11 a.m.-Noon, Sat. (Cajun)

"Clento's Fais Do-Do," Clento Gotro, Noon-1, Sat. (Cajun)

"Zydeco," Noon-1 Sun.

> P. O. Box J
> Ville Platte 70586
> 318-363-2124

WRKF, 89.3 FM

"The General Store," Taylor Caffrey, Sat. a.m. (17 years of mostly folk but also alt. country from Steve Earle to Wayne Hancock)

> 3050 Valley Creek Dr.
> Baton Rouge 70808
> //www.wrkf.org
> The_General_Store@compuserve.com
>
> Taylor Caffery: tcaffery@iamerica.net

WWOZ, 90.7 FM

"Old-Time Country & Bluegrass," Hazel the Delta Rambler, 10-11:30 a.m. Sun.

"The Cajun Show," Charles LaBorde & Johnny Fasullo, 11:30 a.m.-2:30 p.m. Sun.

> P. O. Box 51840
> New Orleans 70151-1840
> 504-568-1234
> //www.wwoz.org
> wwoz@gnofn.org

WYNK, 101.5 FM

"Cajun Fais Do-Do," Tee-Mich Abed, 5-8 a.m. Sat. (15 years running)

> Baton Rouge
> teemich1@juno.com

Maine

WBOR, 91.1 FM

"Folk Routes & Detours," Suzanne Mitchell Shaver, 11-1 p.m. Mon. (heavy on American roots music including traditional and contemporary s/s, bluegrass, country, and more)

Bowdoin College
3725 College Station
Brunswick 04011
207-725-3210

Suzanne Mitchel Shaver: suzanne@ime.net

WERU, 89.9 FM

"Acoustic & Eclectic," 6-9 a.m. M-F

"Folk," 9-10 a.m. M-F; 6-10 a.m. Sat.

"Bronzewound," Manski, 8-10 p.m. Thurs. (bluegrass)

"Truckstop," 1-6 a.m. Sat. (Rock/country)

"Downeast Jamboree," Dan Avener & Rose the Record Lady, 7-8 p.m. Sat.

US Route 1, Box 170
East Orland 04431
//www.weru.org

WMPG, 90.9 FM

"Folkwaves: Hillbilly Hit Parade," Dave, 9-11 a.m. Mon. ("a real knee slapper")

"Folkwaves: In Your Ear," Deidre, 9-11 a.m. Tues. (politics, bluegrass, country, acoustic, local music and more)

"Folkwaves: Gas, Food, Lodging," Pat, 9-11 a.m. Wed. ("from the hollers of Appalachia to the Texas plains...fiddles, guitars, yodeling, longhorn cattle, lonesome widows, and lornfull lullabies")

"Evenin' Sun: American Roots Musics," Stephanie, 5-7 p.m. Wed. (part of a weekly series of roots shows; this one features blues, ragtime, Hawaiian, and 1920s-1930s hillbilly)

"Folkwaves: The Blue Country," Blizzard Bob, 9-11 a.m. Thurs. ("Hop a freight train and travel these highways and byways of this great land of ours in search of bluegrass and old-time country music")

"Folkwaves: Friday Quilting Bee," Michael Danahy, 9-11 a.m. ("not a folk show but a show about the folk process")

"Anondyne," Dan, Mid-2 Fri. ("A little bit of country, a little bit of r 'n' r, a whole lot of whiskey")

"The Rub Board Review," Brian, 7-9 a.m. Sat. (wake up dancing to Cajun/zydeco old and new plus New Orleans blues, soul, and r&b)

"Get Hot or Go Home," Matt, 2:30-5 p.m. Sat. ("Well, the old jukebox be throwin' out the beat, all the cats and gators will be shakin' their feet! The tunes I'll be playin' are right in the groove and I'll be tellin' you, man, you'll be startin' to move"; rockabilly)

University of Southern Maine
96 Falmouth St.
Portland 04103
207-780-4976
//www.usm.maine.edu/~wmpg/

wainberg@maine.edu

Maryland

WKHS, 90.5 FM

"Sleepy Hollow," Keith Brand, 6-10 a.m. Sat & Sun. (folk, old-time, bluegrass; originates from WXPN, Philadelphia)

"Nobody's Bizness," Clark Bjorke, 7-10 p.m. Sun. (as the title suggests the DJ plays whatever he wants based on the belief that "all music is folk music")

P. O. Box 905
Worton 21678

Nobody's Business:
//free.cyber-active.com/nobodys/
bjorke@dmv.com

WMUC, 88.1 FM

"Dave's Record Collection," Dave Sisson, 9-11 p.m. Sat. (eclectic blend of rock, folk, blues, comedy, spoken word; Hank to Hendrix)

University of Maryland
P. O. Box 99
College Park 20742
301-314-7868
//wmuc.umd.edu

WTMD, 89.7 FM (Towson)

"Detour: The Folk & Acoustic Music Show," Tony Sica & Paul Hartman, 5-7 p.m. Sun. (bluegrass, Cajun, old-time, s/s; Hartman is editor/publisher of *Dirty Linen* magazine)

Towson University
P. O. Box 150
Randallstown 21133
//www.towson.edu/wtmd/

Detour:
//www.charm.net/~dirtylin/detour.html

Tony Sica: tonysica@aol.com

Massachusetts

WADN, 1120 AM

"Tapestry," Ken Selcer, 7-10 p.m. Sun. (features s/s such as Tish Hinojosa, Gillian Welch)

10 Vineyard St.
Cambridge 02138
Ken Selcer //tiac.net/users/kselcer
kselcer@tiac.net

WBRS, 100.1 FM

"Southern Rail," Ofer Inbar, 1-3 p.m., Fri. & Sat. (contemporary and traditional bluegrass, country, folk)

Brandeis University
415 South St.
Waltham 02254-9110
617-736-5277
//www.wbrs.org

WCUW, 91.3 FM

"Crosstracks," Richard H. Fox, 6-9 a.m. M-F (variety of roots i.e. country, blues, jazz, alt. rock)

60 Bryn Mawr Ave.
Auburn 01501
//wcuw.org

Crosstracks: //foxy.net/newtrad.html
foxy@foxy.net

WERS, 88.9 FM

"Coffeehouse," 6-11 a.m. M-F (bluegrass, acoustic)

"Live at Club Passim," 3-5 p.m. Sun. (folk, acoustic)

Emerson College
126 Beacon St.
Boston 02116
617-578-8890
//www.emerson.edu/acadepts/mc/wers/

WGBH, 89.7 FM {Gavin Americana}

"The Folk Heritage," Dick Pleasants, 2-6 p.m. Sat. (all kinds of folk and what ever else Dick wants to play)

125 Western Ave.
Boston 02134
//www.wgbh.org

WHRB, 95.3 FM

"Hillbilly at Harvard," Cousin Lynn, 9 a.m.-1 p.m. Sat. (long running show playing a variety of traditional and contemporary country and bluegrass including independent and unsigned artists)

Harvard University
389 Harvard St.
Cambridge 02138-3900
617-495-4818
//www.whrb.org
whrb@hcs.harvard.edu

WICN, 90. 5 FM

"Against the Grain," David Richey, 8-Mid. Fri. & Sat. (alt. country of all types with a very generous sampling of Texas artists)

"Bluegrass Junction," Tom Banyai, 4-6 p.m. Sat.

6 Chatham St.
Worcester 01606
//www.wicn.org

Bluegrass Junction:
//www.hidwater.com/folkdj/wicndj.html

Tom Banyai: Tbanyai@aol.com

WMBR, 88.1 FM

"Debbie Does Dallas," Deb Rich, 6-8 a.m. Wed. (alt. & trad. country/western, Cajun, bluegrass)

"Troubadour," Bruce Sylvester, 2-4 p.m. Wed. (Hank Williams meets the Fugs—"an eclectic journey through traditional & contemporary acoustic"—American, British, Irish folk,, bluegrass, Cajun, rockabilly, r&b, country; "roots music w/o bounds or barriers")

"Backwoods," John Funke, 8-10 a.m. Sat. (vintage rock 'n' roll, country, r&b)

MIT
3 Ames St.
Cambridge 02142
617-253-4000
//wmbr.mit.edu

music@wmbr.mit.edu

backwoods@wmbr.mit.edu

rockingreg@wmbr.mit.edu

MIT List of Radio Stations on the Internet:
//wmbr.mit.edu/stations/list.html

WMFO, 91.5 FM

"The Roadhouse," 6-8 p.m. Mon. (roots, rock, country, Cajun, blues, more)

"Folk & Good Music Show," Morgan Huke, 2-5 p.m. Sat. (acoustic; eclectic)

"Living in America," Eric Bove, 3-5 p.m. Sun. ("tradition based folk and rock from America's melting pot")

Tufts University
P. O. Box 65
Medford 02153
617-625-0800
//www.tufts.edu/~wmfo/
wmfo@tufts.edu

WOMR, 92.1 FM

"Cajun Cafe au Lait & Grits," Joan LeBlanc, 6-9 a.m. Mon.

"Country Root Soup," Capt. Frank, 9:30-12:30 p.m. Tues.

"Bradford St. Bluegrass," Hillary Barnford, 5-8 p.m. Wed.

14 Center St., Box 975
Provincetown 02657
//www.capecodaccess.com/womr/index.html
womr@cca.com

WRSI, 95.3 FM

"Roadhouse," Moody Richard, 7-8 p.m. Sat. (blues, swing zydeco, rootsy rock etc.)

"The Back Porch," Jim Olsen, 8-Mid. Sun. (eclectic acoustic)

Greenfield
//www.wrsi.com
mail@wrsi.com

WSMU, 91.1 FM

"Hay Holler Wakeup," Scott MacKinnon, 6-8 a.m. M-F (bluegrass, Cajun, Celtic, folk, zydeco)

"Root 'n' Branch," Scott MacKinnon, 5-8 p.m. Sat. (bluegrass, Cajun, Celtic, folk, zydeco)

WSMU-University of Massachusetts at Dartmouth
285 Old Fall River Rd.
North Dartmouth 02747
508-999-8149, ext. 4

Root 'N Branch/WSMU:
//www.tiac.net/users/srprod/

Scott MacKinnon:
smackinnon@umassd.edu

WTCC, 90.7 FM

"Bluegrass," Dave Helman, 1-3 p.m. Sat.

P. O. Box 9000
Springfield 01101-9000

WUMB, 91.9 FM

"Acoustic Images," Dave Palmater, Jill Kaufman, Chuck Hall, 5-8 a.m. M-F (acoustic blues, bluegrass, s/s, traditional)

"Traditional Folk Music," Sandy Sheehan, 1-5 p.m. Sat. (blues, bluegrass, British Isles, Cajun, old-time)

University of Massachusetts at Boston
100 Morrissey Blvd.
Boston 02125-3393
wumb@umbsky.cc.umb.edu

WZBC, 90.3 FM

"Sunday Morning Country," George Hauenstein, 10 a.m.-2 p.m.

Boston College
107 McElroy
Chestnut Hill 02167
617-237-4433
/www.bc.edu/bc_org/svp/st_org/wzbc

Michigan

WCBN, 88.3 FM

"Free Roots," Funky Farmer (Chad Williams), 8-10 p.m. Wed. (the roots of American music: country, bluegrass, insurgents, blues)

"The Folk Show," Bob Wray & Freedom McLaughlin, 10 a.m.-1 p.m. Sat. ("not your daddy's folk music" but mostly acoustic based Americana including Richard Buckner, Steve Earle, Uncle Tupelo)

"Down Home Show," Funky Farmer, Tex, 2 O'Clock Cowboy, Jeff Stanzler, 1-4 p.m., Sat. ("for the twang deficient": honky tonk, bluegrass, old-time, Western swing, rockabilly, skronk)

"Go, Kat Go: The Rockabilly Show," Del Villarreal, 7-8 p.m. Wed. ("hot barn shakin' rockabilly from the 1950s-1990s plus western swing, hillbilly boogie")

530 Student Activities Bldg.
Ann Arbor 48109
313-763-3501
//www.wcbn.org

Free Roots: //www.wcbn.org/freeroot/
Folk Show:
//ai.eecs.umich.edu/people/wrayre/wcbn/folkshow.html
folkshow@wcbn.org

Down Home Show:
//www.wcbn.org/downhome/
(lots of alt. country links)
DownHomeShow@wcbn.org

Chad Williams: babooski@umich.edu

Funky Farmer: farmer@wcbn.org

Tex: jmanheim@umich.edu

2 O'Clock Cowboy: morayd@wcbn.org

Go, Kat Go: //www.wcbn.org/gokatgo/

Del Villarreal (David Thomas Rice):
gokatgo@wcbn.org

WDBM, 88.9 FM {Gavin Americana}

"Progressive Torch & Twang," Jamie DePolo and Doug Neal, 8-Midnight p.m. Tues. (alternative and hard core country since 1989 and including s/s, Cajun, bluegrass, rockabilly etc.; also sponsor a weekly "Torch & Twang" night and annual "Torch & Twang" festival)

G-4 Holden Hall
Michigan State University
E. Lansing 48824
517-353-4414
//www.wdbm.msu.edu

Progressive Torch & Twang:
//www.msu.edu/user/depolo/
(includes "Twang Links" to many key alt. country sites)

Jamie DePolo: depolo@msue.msu.edu

Doug Neal: nealdoug@egr.msu.edu

WDET, 101.9 FM

"Folks Like Us," Matt Watroba, Noon-3 Sat. (since 1986 and featuring all music with roots in tradition)

"Arkansas Traveler," Larry McDaniel, 3-5 p.m. Sat. (Bluegrass, acoustic)

6001 Cass Ave.
Detroit 48202
313-577-4146
//www.wdet.org

Matt Watroba: Mattw41@aol.com

WHND, 560 AM

"Rockin' Bones," Craig Maki, 6-8 p.m., Sat. (rockabilly)

22150 Greenfield
Monroe 48161

WKAR, 90.5 FM; 870 AM

"The Folk Tradition," Bob Blackman, 6-8 p.m. Sun. (hosted by veteran broadcasting folk music on this station for over 20 years; this program offers a wide variety of styles including bluegrass, blues, Cajun, Celtic, old-time, s/s, etc.)

Michigan State University
East Lansing 48824
//wkar.msu.edu
mail@wkar.msu.edu

Bob Blackman
P. O. Box 504
Haslett, MI 48840
Bob Blackman: blackman@wkar.msu.edu

Minnesota

KAXE, 91.7 FM

"Back Porch Harmony," 7-10 p.m. Fri.

"Folk City," Chad Haatvedt, 9-Noon Sun. (s/s including John Prine, Townes Van Zandt, et al.)

"Roots Americana," 1-4 p.m. Sun.

   1841 East Hwy. 169
   Grand Rapids 55744
   218-326-1234
   //www.kaxe.org
   comments@kaxe.org

   Chad Haatvedt: c3hotvet@uslink.net

KBSB, 89.7 FM

"The Twang Factor/Redneck Hour of Power," Todd Bodin & Chad Evans 9-Mid. Wed. (alt. country)

"Backporch Bluegrass," Arlan Wally, & Jerry, 6-9 p.m. Thurs.

   Bemidji State University
   Bemidji 56601
   218-755-2059
   //www.fm90.org
   fm90@fm90.org

KFAI, 90.3 FM; 106.7 FM

"Dakota Dave Hull Show," 9-11 a.m. Thurs. (country & western & swing hosted by one of the Upper Midwest's finest veteran musicians)

"Radio Rumpus Room," Jean Silverberg & Ron Thums, 9-10:30 p.m. Fri. (surf, hot rod, rockabilly, trad. & alt. country)

"Good 'n' Country," Ken Hippler, 3-5 p.m., Sat. ("real" country with Riders Radio Theater from 4-4:30 & local artists 4:30-5)

"Urban Folk," Bob Feldman, 11-1 p.m. Sun. (gritty edge contemporary folk, bluegrass, roots)

   1800 Riverside Ave.
   Minneapolis 55454
   //www.kfai.org
   kfai@kfai.org

   Ron Thums:
   //www2.bitstream.net/~rumpus2/
   rumpus2@bitstream.net

WELY, 92.1 FM; 1450 AM

"Ridge Runner Radio," Gregg Benson, Noon-6 p.m. Sat. (Bluegrass, vintage country, alt. country, Cajun, singer/songwriter)

   904 S. Central Ave.
   Ely 55731

   Gregg Benson:
   grim@sudand.sudan.umn.edu

Mississippi

WUMS, 92.1 FM

"It Came From the Garage," Paul Tucker, Noon-2 Sun. (all types of alternative including rockabilly and hard country from the 1940s-insurgent)

   University of Mississippi
   SMC, Farley Hall
   University 38677
   601-232-5395 (office)
   //www.olemiss.edu/orgs/wums

   It Came:
   //www2.dixie-net.com/kustom/
   kustom@dixie-net.com

Missouri

KCLC, 89.1 FM

"Bluegrass," Naomi Soule & Terry Moses, 6-9 p.m. Tues. (They also have a show on KDHX)

   Lindenwood College
   209 Kingshighway
   St. Charles 63301

   Naomi & Terry: nstm@anet-stl.com

KCOU, 88.1 FM

"Country Brunch," Jason Cafer, 11-1 p.m. Sun. (wide variety of country from traditional bluegrass, old-time, honky tonk, Western swing to Gram Parsons/FBB to Austin/Lubbock sound of Jimmie Dale Gilmore, Joe Ely, Butch Hancock, Terry Allen et al. to Uncle Tupelo, Bloodshot Records, Dave and Deke, etc.)

   101F Pershing Hall
   University of Missouri
   Columbia 65201
   314-882-7820
   //tiger.coe.missouri.edu/~kcou/
   kcou@cclabs.missouri.edu

   Jason Cafer:
   c638276@showme.missouri.edu

KDHX, 88.1 FM {Gavin Americana}

"Country Function & Bluegrass Junction," Gene Roberts and Larry Allen, 9-Noon Tues.

"Musique des Bayous," Al Boudreaux, 4-7 p.m. Tues. (Cajun, zydeco and all that's great from Southern Louisiana)

"Songwriters Showcase," Larry Weir, 9-Noon Wed. (variety of s/s mostly acoustic but occasionally more rocked up artists like Steve Earle)

"The Morning After," Sonny Boy Mason, 6-8 a.m. Sat. (Cajun, country, Tex-Mex, etc.)

"Blue Highways," Clint "The Voice" Harding, 8-10 a.m. Sat. (folk, bluegrass, s/s)

"The Bluegrass Show," Keith Dunning and Walter Wolz, 10 a.m.-Noon Sat. (old and new)

"Mid-Day Jamboree," Fred Gumaer, Noon-2 p.m. Sat. (classic c/w)

"The Acoustic Edge," Naomi Soule and Terry Mose, Noon-2 Sun. (bluegrass, s/s, folk rock, progressive country; favorite artists: Emmylou, Tom Russell, Steve Earle, Rankin Family)

"St. Louis Brain Sandwich," Jim Findlay, Jay Schober, and Mike Madonna, 2-4 p.m. Sun. (country and folk)

   3504 Magnolia
   St. Louis 63118
   314-664-3955
   //www.kdhxfm88.org/

   Gene Roberts: cfandbj@kdhxfm88.org

   Al Boudreaux:
   alboudx@kdhxfm88.org

   Larry Weir: songwriters@kdhxfm88.org

   Sonny Boy Mason:
   morningafter@kdhxfm88.org

   Clint Harding: bluehwys@mail.inlink.com

   Keith Dudding:
   bluegrassshow@kdhxfm88.org

   Fred Gumaer:
   mid-dayjamboree@kdhxfm88.org

   Naomi Soule/Terry Mose:
   nstm@anet-stl.com

   Jim Findlay: Mkmadonna@aol.com

KFAL, 900 AM {Gavin Americana}

"Country Sunrise," Chris Newbrough, 5-10 a.m. M-F (traditional country)

"Tennessee Hound Dog," Richard Burrell, 7-Mid. M-F & 6-Noon Sun. (bluegrass)

"Bluegrass Saturday Morning," Chris Newbrough, 5-11 a.m.

   1805 Westminster
   Fulton 65251
   //www.kfal.com
   kfal@sockets.net

KKFI, 90.1 FM

"Country Jesus & Hillbilly Blooze," Craig Rastorfer, 10-Mid. Thurs.

"Cuando Mexico Canto," Tony Aquilar, 6 p.m. Sat. (Mexican-American music)

"The Miguel Aguirre Show," 10 p.m. Sat. (Mexican-American music)

"Amanecer Ranchero," Raul Garcia, 8 a.m. Sun. (Mexican-American music)

"Coffeehouse," Bob Barnes & Jeanne Jaspers, 10 a.m. alt. Sun. (bluegrass and all kinds of acoustic)

   Kansas City
   //www.gazlay.com/kkfi/
   kkfi@gazlay.com

KOPN, 89.5 FM

"Roots & Branches," 10 p.m.-2 a.m. Sat.

"The Sunday Morning Coffeehouse," Steve Jerrett, 9-11 a.m. (bluegrass, folk, s/s, Celtic, traditional)

"Rootin' Tootin' Radio," Radio Ranger, 11-1 p.m. Sun.

"Alternative Americana," Jackson Buck, 1 p.m. Sun.

"String Benders," 7-9 p.m. Sun.

"High Lonesome Sound," 9 p.m. Sun. (bluegrass/newgrass)

   915 East Broadway
   Columbia 65201
   573-874-1139

//www.kopn.org
mail@kopn.org

Steve Jerrett:
sjerrett@mail.coin.missouri.edu

KTJJ, 98.5 FM

"Mid-America's best country and roots music for southeast Missouri and southwest Illinois" with classic and traditional country, bluegrass and Americana."

"Rooster Creek," Ron Lutz, 11:25 a.m Sat. (Live country)

"Bluegrass," Tennessee Hound Dog, 7-8 p.m. Sat.; 8-Noon Sun.

P. O. Box 461
Farmington 63640-0461
573-756-6476
//www.americana-music.com/americanahome/ktjj.html

KUMR, 88.5 FM

"Bluegrass for a Saturday Night," Wayne Bledsoe, 7-10 p.m. Sat. (hosted by the editor of *Bluegrass Now* magazine)

"The Mercantile Bluegrass Hour," Wayne Bledsoe, 8-9 p.m. Sun.

University of Missouri at Rolla
1870 Miner Cr.
G-6 Library
Rolla 65409-0130
//www.umr.edu/~kumr/
kumr@umr.edu

Bluegrass Now: //www.bluegrassnow.com

KWUR, 90.3 FM

"Sam Davis Show," 11 a.m.-2 p.m. Tues. (folk, bluegrass, rockabilly, swing)

Washington University
P. O. Box 1205
St. Louis
//kwur.wustl.edu/

Montana

KGLT, 91.9 FM {Gavin Americana}

"Cow Jazz," Deb Robiscoe, 9-Noon, Thurs.
"Bluegrass Traditions," Chris Mills, 9-Noon Sat.

P. O. Box 174240
Montana State University
Bozeman 59717
406-994-6483
//www.montana.edu/~wwwkglt
wwwkglt@montana.edu

Nebraska

KZUM, 89.3 FM

"Exposition Flyer," Eric Bachenberg, 7-8:30 p.m. Mon. (folk, bluegrass)

"Mystery Train," Dan Moser, 10-Mid. Non. (All kinds of American roots music, old and new)

"Tuesday Night Drive-In," Carl Anthony, 7-8:30 p.m. Tues. (folk, country, bluegrass)

"Home of Happy Feet," Kent Parfer, 7-8:30 p.m. Wed. (folk, bluegrass)

"Sugar Mountain," Ed Long, 7-8:30 p.m. Thurs. (folk, bluegrass)

"KZUM Hayride," John Schmitz, 7:30-9 p.m. Fri. (Western swing)

"La Onda Tejana," C. Casteneda, 1-2:30 p.m. Sat. (best in Tejano)

"Fiesta Mexicana," Roman Noriego, 3:30-5 p.m. Sun. (Tex-Mex)

Lincoln
402-474-5086
//www.kzum.org
info@kzum.org

Dan Moser: WheeSix@aol.com

Nevada

KUNR, 88.7 FM

"Back at the Bunkhouse," 2-3 p.m. Sun.

University of Nevada at Reno
Mail Stop 294
Reno 89557
//www.kunr.org
kunr@unr.edu

New Hampshire

WMVW, 93.5 FM

"Somewhat Acoustic," Annie Provenzano, 7-9 p.m. Mon. (s/s, bluegrass and more)

P. O. Box 88
Tamworth 03886

Annie Provenzano:
twocats@landmarknet.net

WNEC, 91.7 FM

"Music For the Mountain," Jon Colcord, 3-6 p.m. Sun. (bluegrass)

Simon Center
New England College
24 Bridge St.
Henniker 03242

Jon Colcord: jcolcord@ybp.com

WUNH, 91.3 FM {Gavin Americana}

Gavin Americana Station of the Year 1998.

University of New Hampshire
MUB
Durham 03824
603-862-2541
//www.wunh.unh.edu/
back.ogre@unh.edu

New Jersey

WBJB, 90.5 FM

"Bluegrass Jam," 8-11 a.m., Sun.

765 Newman Springs Rd.
Lincroft 07738
//www.monmouth.com/~wbjb/
wbjb@shell.monmouth.com

WBZC, 88.9 FM

"Burlington Co. Bluegrass," Nancy Longenecker & Joe Wills, 10 a.m.-1:30 p.m. Sat.

Burlington County College
Rt. 530
Pemberton 08068
//www.bcc.edu/radio

WDVR, 89.7 FM

"Western Melodies," Slim Edwards, 9-Noon Tues. (traditional cowboy/ western)

"Country, Bluegrass, Old-Time," Bill Moffett, 6-9 a.m. Wed.

"The Music of Love," Jenn Ellsworth, 9-Noon Wed. (bluegrass to blues)

"Country Roundup," Walt Allegar, Noon-3 p.m. Wed.

"Honky Tonk Roadhouse," Ted Lyons, 6-9 a.m.. Thurs. (country rock, folk rock, r&b)

"Currents and Traditions," Eileen Fisher, 10-Mid. Thurs. (folk music with a "twist")

"The Country Store," Frank Napp, 7-10 p.m. Fri. ("our premier traditional country program")

"Country Classics," Tom Wardle, 10-Mid. Fri.

"Country Tracks," Mike Mikels, 6-9 a.m. Sat.

"Radio Ranch," Len Brown, 9 a.m.-1 p.m., Sat. (real country and "Texas friendly music")

"Bluegrass Junction," R.W. Shamey, 1-4 p.m. Sat.

"Jukebox Saturday Night," Lavina Lozise & Tom Wardle, 8-11 p.m. Sat.

"Hep Cats and Neon Armadillos," Fred Boenig, 10-Mid., Sun. (an Americana music show featuring lots of alt. country)

"Americana on the Air" 8 p.m. last Fri. of each month (on air old-time music show)

P. O. Box 191
Sergeantsville 08557
609-397-1620
//www.frenchtown.com/wdvr/

Len Brown: LenB7291@aol.com

Fred Boenig: fboenig@ix.netcom.com

Eileen Fisher: e.fish-stoc@worldnet.att.net

Tom Wardle: djcowboy@erols.com

Mike Mikels: mmikels@cyberwar.com

WFDU/WFDQ, 89.1 FM {Gavin Americana}

"Traditions," Ron Olesko & Bill Hahn, 3-6 p.m. (bluegrass, blues, country, ethnic, and other traditional music)

1000 River Rd.
Teaneck 07666
201-692-2806
//alpha.fdu.edu/~emmert/wfdu.html

Traditions:
//www.hidwater.com/wfdu891.html

Ron Olesko: olesko@cnbc.nbc.ge.com

WFMU, 91.1 FM

"The Shrunken Planet," Jeffrey Davison, 6-9 a.m. Sat. (American & British roots music)

"Radio Thrift Shop," Laura Cantrell, Noon-3 p.m. Sat.

"Trash, Twang & Thunder," Meredith Ochs, 3-6 p.m. Sat. ("twang rock of now cowboys, gutbucket blues, front porch bluegrass, Americana soul of all sorts")

P. O. Box 1568
Montclair 07042
201-266-7901

Laura Cantrell: laura@wfmu.org

Meredith Ochs: meredith@wfmu.org

//wfmu.org
{for information about the "Catalog of Curiosities" which has a large selection of bizarre music, books, video, etc.}

wfmu@wfmu.org

WLFR, 91.7 FM

"Roadhouse Fever," Chip Lamey, 3-6 p.m. Mon. (alternative country & rockabilly; Chip publishes a magazine by the same name full of articles and reviews)

Pomona 08240
Roadhouse Fever
P. O. Box 54
Stone Harbor 08247

WNTI, 91.9 FM

"The Boneyard," Tim Carbone, 6:30-9:30 a.m. Tues. (Americana mix)

"JM's Country Corral," 10-Noon Tues. (classic & some alt. Country)

"Cookin' Country," Ron Febba, Noon-2 p.m. Wed. ("all the greats nobody plays anymore")

"The Nutt House," Bill Nutt, 3-6 p.m. Sat. (Celtic, Cajun, bluegrass, world)

"Death Valley Days," Ron Alden, 6-9 p.m. Sun. (country, bluegrass, jazz, folk, blues, gospel, world, film scores, contemporary compositions)

Centenary College
Hackettstown
Death Valley Days:
//www.goes.com/~deathvalley/

WRSU, 88.1 FM

"Sudzin Country," Herb Sudzin, 6-10 a.m. Sat./Sun. (bluegrass, classic and alt. country, Cajun)

"Homemade Music," Mark Corso, 10-Noon Sun. (bluegrass, acoustic)

Rutgers University
126 College Ave.
New Brunswick 08903
908-932-7800

Herb Sudzin: dsun@cybercomm.net

WTSR, 91.3 FM

"Legacy," Peter Kernast, 6-9 p.m. Mon.; 4-8 p.m. (various genres of roots music including folk, blues, Cajun, country, Celtic, bluegrass, world)

Trenton State College
Kendall Hall
Trenton 08650-4700
609-771-2420
//www.trenton.edu/~wtsr/
wtsr@tenj.edu

Peter Kernast: kernastp@pt.cyanamid.com

New Mexico

KGLP, 91.7 FM

"Morning Music Mix," Jamie Hoover aka Cow Patti, 9-11 a.m. M-F (blues, old-time, bluegrass, roots-rock, singer/songwriter, and more)

"Sounds From the Mother Road," Jamie Hoover, 10-Mid Mon. (Twangcentric program features real country/alternative country and all that twangs)

Gallup Public Radio
200 College Rd.
Gallup, NM 87301
505-863-7626; (fax) 505-863-7532

Jamie Hoover: jhoover@gallup.net

KRWG, 90.7 FM

"The Back Porch," David Brower.

New Mexico State University
Las Cruces
800-245-KRWG
//www.krwgfm.org
krwgfm@nmsu.edu

KSFR, 90.7 FM

"Terrell's Sound World," Stephen Terrell, 10-Mid. Sun. (from the guy who wrote "Picnic Time for Potatoheads," an eclectic show "where Merle Haggard, Pere Ubu, and James Brown can meet on equal footing"; every last Sunday or so, show mutates into "The Santa Fe Opry" with "country music as God intended "; hardcore, alternative, outlaw/insurgent, no depression; for more details see his section in this guide or his swell web site)

Santa Fe
505-438-1382

Stephen Terrell:
//members.aol.com/bluespud/
ROBOTCLAW@aol.com

KUNM, 89.9 FM

"Home of Happy Feet," Marilyn Altenbach, Karl Stalnaker, Barry Lauesen, 7-10 p.m. Tues. ("Folk music in the broadest sense of the word: bluegrass, blues, Cajun, zydeco, West-

ern swing, rockabilly, Tex-Mex, and more!"; very popular show for 12+ years)

"Folk Music USA," 9 a.m. Sat. (blues to bluegrass)

University of New Mexico
Albuquerque 87131
505-277-8018
//kunm.unm.edu
kunm@rt66.com

New York

WAMC, 90.3 FM

"Hudson River Sampler," Wanda Fischer, 8-10:30 p.m. Sat. (folk, blues, bluegrass)

P. O. Box 66600
Albany 12206
//www.wamc.org
webmaster@wamc.org

WBFO, 88.7 FM

"Bluegrass," Rob Campbell & Randy Keller, 9 p.m.-Mid. Sun. (old & new)

University of Buffalo
Buffalo 14260
//www.wbfo.buffalo.edu

WBNY, 91.3 FM

"Rooting About: The Folk & Roots Music Show," Al Riess, 9a.m.-1 p.m. Sat. (roots variety with good amount of alt. country material)

Buffalo State University
Buffalo 14222

Al Riess: riessaf@buffalostate.edu

WCDB, 90.9 FM

"The Rootsy Cosmopolitan Presents 'Alternative Country'," Evan Cooper, 8-11 p.m. Wed. (35-40% of show is one artist, genre, group, theme and the rest is recent alt. country releases)

University of Albany
Albany 12222
//www.albany.edu/~wcdb/
wcdb@albany.edu

Evan Cooper: ec7739@cnsibm.albany.edu

WFUV, 90.7 FM {Gavin Americana "Station of the Year, 1996"}

"City Folk," various hosts, 6 a.m.-8 p.m. M-F (huge variety of Americana all day long; Tuesday is "No Depression" day)

"City Folk: Sunday Breakfast," John Platt, 8-11 a.m.

Fordham University
Bronx 10461
718-365-8050
//www.wfuv.org

Americana A to Z (links to many artists):
//www.wfuv.org/americana.html

Top 50 Americana Classics:
//www.wfuv.org/classics.html

WICB, 91.7 FM

"Hobo's Lullaby," 10-Noon Tues.; 2-4 p.m. Sun. (acoustic, folk, bluegrass, world)

Ithaca
607-274-3217

WJFF, 90.5 FM

"Gumbo Shop," Maris Hearn, 7:30-9 p.m. Thurs. (eclectic folk)

"Ballads & Banjos," Sonja Hedlund, 6-8 a.m. Sat. (traditional/contemporary folk)

"Folk Plus," Angela Page, 11 a.m.-1 p.m. Sat. (Traditional/contemporary folk)

"Jambalaya," Jesse Ballew, 1-2:30 p.m. Sat. (bluegrass, country, folk, blues)

"Riverside Folk," Maureen Neville, 2:30-3:30 p.m. Sat. (bluegrass, old-time, country, Cajun)

P. O. Box 797
Jeffersonville 12748
914-482-4141
//www.zelacom.com/~wjff/
wjff@catskill.net

WKCR, 89.9 FM

"Honky Tonkin'", Doug Tuchman, 9:30-11 p.m. Tues. (honky tonk, country boogie, hillbilly, rockabilly 1940-1969)

"Moonshine," Josh Reid, 10-Noon, Sun. (bluegrass & old-time)

"Tennessee Border," Matt Matlack, Noon-2 p.m. Sun. (country and Western swing)

Columbia University
New York City 10025
212-854-5223
//www.columbia.edu/cu/wkcr/
wkcramerican@columbia.edu

WNEW, 102.7 FM

"Idiot's Delight," Vin Scelsa, 8 p.m.-2 a.m. (legendary eclectic folk/country/rock show with guest performances and lots of other good stuff)

New York City
//www.wnew.com

Idiot's Delight: //www.planet.net/id/

WNYU, 89.1 FM

"The Big Sky," Seth Madej, 8-? p.m., Thurs. (the whole enchilada of alternative country/ Americana styles past and present)

721 Broadway, 11th Floor
New York City 10003
212-998-1674
//www.rockonline.com/wnyu/

Seth Madej: Smadej@aol.com

WRHU, 88.7 FM

"Out Behind the Barn," Irv Simmer, 9-11 a.m. Sun. (traditional country & bluegrass)

Hofstra University
1000 Fulton Ave.
Hempstead 11550
516-463-5600

WRUR, 88.5 FM

"A Variety of Folk," Tom Bohan, 4-6 p.m. Fri. (s/s, oldtime, bluegrass)

CPU
Box 277356
Rochester 14627

Tom Bohan: tombohan@rpa.net

WSCP, 101.7 FM

Playlists include traditional classic and new country.

7890 N. Jefferson St.
Pulaski 13142
315-298-3185

WSLU, 89.5 FM (Upstate NY)

"String Fever," Barb Heller-Burns, 3-5 p.m. Thurs. (folk leaning to bluegrass)

Canton 13617
//www.ncpr.org

WSPN, 91.1 FM

"The Unkle Dave Show," David Larson, 3-6 p.m. Wed. (devoted to the origins of rock 'n' roll using various sources of blues and rhythm especially with reference to vocal harmony, doowop, and countrified aspects)

"Simpatico," Chris McGill, 9-Noon Sun. (acoustic, blues, bluegrass, folk)

Skidmore College
Saratoga Springs 12866
http://www.skidmore.edu/~wspn/

David Larson: dlarson@skidmore.edu

Chris McGill: cmcgill@skidmore.edu

WUSB, 90.1 FM

"The Ed Davis Show," 7-10 a.m. Mon. (bluegrass, country/western, Cajun, zydeco)

"The Geri Burgert Show," 8:30-10 p.m. alt. Mon. (bluegrass, folk, and related music)

"Always Acoustic," 6-7 p.m. alt. Tues. (country, blues, folk)

"Bluegrass Time," Buddy Merriam, 6:30-8 p.m. Wed.

"The Bayou," Chris LaPorta, 7-9 p.m. alt. Thurs.

"Morning Maniac Music," Gordon Healey, 7-9 a.m. alt. Sat. (jazz, bluegrass, acid rock plus discussions of race car driving)

"Sunday Street," Charlie Backfish, 9-11:30 a.m. Sun. (acoustic oriented show where you're likely to hear Cheri Knight, Salamander Crossing, Steve Earle, Katy Moffatt, and more)

"Down Home Country," Debbie De Waltoff, 11:30-12:30 p.m. Sun. (country/western, rock-abilly, Western swing from the 1920s-1990s)

SUNY at Stony Brook
Stony Brook 11794-3263
516-632-6500
//www.wusb.org
wusb@sunysb.edu

Charlie Backfish: CBackfish@aol.com

WVBR, 93.5 FM

"Salt Creek Show," Heather Dunbar, 6-10 a.m. Sun. (long running show with bluegrass and more)

"Bound for Glory," Phil Shapiro, 8-11 p.m. Sun. (30 years running makes it the oldest folk show in the U.S.; modern folk, bluegrass and more with in studio guests e.g. 5 Chinese Brothers, Eddy Lawrence, Y'All)

227 Linden Ave.
Ithaca 14850
//www.publiccom.com/web/wvbr/

Bound for Glory: bfg@wvbr.com

WVKR, 91.3 FM

"Hudson Valley Rag Shop," D. Brown, 6-8 p.m. Tues. (bluegrass, Celtic, comedy, folk)

"Pickin' Party," 9-10 a.m. Wed. (Bluegrass, old-time)

"Old-Time Country," 6-8 a.m. Sat.

Vassar College
P. O. Box 166
Poughkeepsie 12604
914-437-5476
//www.bestweb.net/~tish/wvkr/
wvkr@vassar.edu

D. Brown: brown@vassar.edu

WXYN, 91.3 FM

"Bluegrass Ramble," Bill Knowlton, 9-Mid. Sun. (long running show hosted by one of the great authorities on bluegrass music)

Syracuse

North Carolina

WCQS, 88.1 FM

"A Natural Bridge," Jim Magill, 10 a.m.-1 p.m. Sat. (contemporary folk and bluegrass with one hour devoted to a theme e.g. railroad songs, Texas s/s, etc., one hour to new releases, and one hour to live performances or taped interviews)

73 Broadway
Asheville 28801
Jim Magill, Warren Wilson College
P. O. Box 9000
Asheville 28815-9000

Jim Magill: gathering@warren-wilson.edu

WFDD, 88.5 FM

"Across the Blue Ridge," Paul Brown, 11-Noon & 8-9 p.m. Sun. (old-time, bluegrass, gospel, country)

P. O. Box 8850
Winston-Salem 27109
//www.wfu.edu/wfdd

Paul Brown: blueridge@wfu.edu

WFSS, 91.9 FM

"Countryside Jamboree," 7-9 p.m. Wed.

"Free Flight," Jim Graves, 7-10 p.m. Fri. (s/s including the likes of Steve Earle, Kevin Johnson, John Prine)

1200 Murchison Rd.
Fayetteville 28301
910-486-1381
//www.uncfsu.edu/w4/91.9

Jim Graves y00003@sbe1.uncfsu.edu

WNCW, 88.7 FM {Gavin Americana}

"Crossroads," 9-5 M-F; 10 p.m.-2 a.m. M,T,Th,F (Americana with lots of alt. Country)

"Goin' Across the Mountain," Russ Jordan 1-4 p.m. Sat. (bluegrass)

"Country Music Classics," Joe Bussard, 4-5 p.m. Sat.

"This Old Porch," John Fowler, 3-6 p.m. Sun. (old-time & traditional music)

P. O. Box 804
Spindale 28160
828-287-8000
//www.wncw.org
wncw@blueridge.net

WPAQ, 740 AM

Bluegrass & old-time Mon.-Fri. for over 25 years!

Mount Airy 27030

WVOT, 1420 AM

"Pickin' in the Pines," Skip Ogden, Sat. A.m. (bluegrass, old-time)

Wilson

Skip Ogden: cogden@ibest.net

WXDU, 88.7 FM

"Border Radio: Drive Time for Truckers," Rick Cornell, 5-7 a.m. Fri. (roots rock; alt. country; pure country)

"Topsoil," Steve Gardner, Noon-3 p.m. Sun. (formerly on KSCU in California until 1995; still featuring the best of old-time, bluegrass. Steve is also the creator and host of the excellent "Pine Hill Farm" house concerts; see the Topsoil web page for details)

P. O. Box 4706
Duke University
Durham 27706
919-684-2957
//www.duke.edu/~mea2/

Rick Cornell: cornellr@mindspring.com

Topsoil: //www.topsoil.net

Steve Gardner: steve@topsoil.net

WXYC, 89.3 FM

"Orange County Special," 10 a.m.-1 p.m. Sun. (traditional & neo-traditional bluegrass, blues, Latino, etc.)

"Southern Folklife Collection," 1-2 p.m. Sun. (sampling of UNC's huge archive of traditional music from the southeastern U.S.)

"Backyard BBQ," 7-8 p.m. Sun. (local music)

P. O. Box 51
Carolina Union
University of North Carolina
Chapel Hill 27599
919-962-8989
//www.wxyc.org
wxyc@unc.edu

Orange County Special: orancosp@unc.edu

North Dakota

KFJY, 90.7 FM {Gavin Americana}

"Into the Music," Bob Bertsch, 7-10 a.m. M-F & Noon-2 Sat.; Michael Olson, Noon-3 p.m. M-F & 9-Noon Sat./Sun.; Eric Deathrage, 3-6 p.m. M-F (s/s, alt. country, roots rock, and more since 1993)

University of North Dakota
P. O. Box 8117
Grand Forks 58202
//www.und.nodak.edu/org/nlpr/yfm.html
udkfjm@badlands.nodak.edu

Michael Olson:
miolson@badlands.nodak.edu

Ohio

WAIF, 88.3 FM

"Crawfish Fiesta," Neil Sharrow, 8-10 p.m. Tues. (one of the longest running shows of its kind covering Cajun, zydeco, r&b)

Mud Bug Productions
3260 Ashwood Dr.
Cincinnati 45213

Neil Sharrow: neil.sharrow@uc.edu

WBGU, 88.1 FM

"Country Craig Lummers," 7:30-Noon, M-W (eclectic range of country tunes)

Bowling Green State University
31 West Hall
Bowling Green 43402
419-372-2826
//ernie.bgsu.edu/

WCBE, 90.5 FM {Gavin Americana}

"Roots & Offshoots," Maggie Brennan, 9-11 p.m. Sun. (best mix of Americana; toe tappin' music of yesterday & today)

540 Jack Gibbs Blvd.
Columbus 43215
//www.wcbe.org

Maggie Brennan: mbrennan@iwaynet.net (Station and *Nash!* magazine co-hosted "A Night of Country Swingin', Boot Stompin' Twang" with One Riot, One Ranger, the Lilybandits, and the Handsome Family in 1997)

WCSB, 89.3 FM

"TTH's Folk Show," 7-9 p.m. Mon. ("finger pickin', foot stompin', beer drinkin', spirit liftin' music for folks of all sorts")

"La Preferida," Lilly Corona, 7-9 p.m. Thurs. (authentic Mexican show promoting Mexican culture and music including rancheras, nortenas, Tejano, cumbia, salsa and more)

"Lo-Fi," Keith, 9:30 a.m.-Noon, Fri. (surf-aholic rock-a-hillbilly)

"La Raza," Miriam, 3-5 p.m. Sat. (the best of Latin America including regional Mexican music: ranceras, nortenas, Tejano)

Cleveland State University
Route 956
Cleveland 44115
216-687-3523
//wcsb.org
wcsb@wcsb.org

Keith: choclat@choclat.com

WERE, 1300 AM

"Made in America," Cindy Barber, 9-10 p.m. Thurs. (alt. and real country hosted by local music journalist; sponsors the weekly "Made in America Live" showcase at The Blind Pig (Thursday nights).

6065 Timber Trail Dr.
Cleveland 44070
216-556-2395
(fax) 440-779-9901
wwda@en.com

WKSU, 89.7 FM

"Folk," 8-Mid. Sat./Sun. (old-time, bluegrass, s/s)

Kent State University
Kent
//www.wksu.org/folk/

WLFC, 88.3 FM

"The Natural Alternative," John Billerman, 6-9 p.m. Mon. (traditional & contemporary bluegrass)

2932 Gleneagle Dr.
Findlay 45840

John Billerman: john@mail.findlay.edu

WMUB, 88.5 FM

"The Oak Street Ramble," Janice McLaughlin, 11-1 p.m., Sat. (acoustic, bluegrass)

"Swinging on the Gate," Janice McLaughlin, 8-9 p.m. Sat. (singer/songwriter, contemporary folk, contemporary bluegrass, progressive old-time)

Amos Music Library
Miami University
Oxford 45056
//www.muohio.edu/wmub
jmclaugh@miamiu.acs.muohio.edu

WOBC, 91.5 FM

"Hickory Wind," Peter Galub, 11 a.m.-1 p.m. Mon.

"Doggoneit Billy Bob, Eat Yer Grits!," Cowtippin' Cathy & Loose Lucy, 11-Noon Wed. ("country music that will blow yer boots off...with commentary that's funny as all get out!")

"Hearts & Minds," John Pais, 8-10 p.m Thurs. (wide range of folk, bluegrass, and acoustic)

"North Coast Sunday," Sam Bergman, 10-12 Noon, Sun. (bluegrass, Cajun, Celtic, folk)

"Downhome Bluegrass," Freeman Morgan, 1-4 p.m. Sun.

Oberlin College
Wilder Hall, Rm. 319
Oberlin 44704
440-775-8107 (office)
440-775-8139 (studio)
//www.oberlin.edu/~wobc/
wobc@oberlin.edu

WOBO, 88.7 FM

"Prime Time Bluegrass," Jon Weisberger, 8-Mid. Thurs. ("the best in bluegrass, bluegrass, gospel, and new acoustic music")

P. O. Box 338
Owensville 45160
Jon Weisberger Home Page:
//home.fuse.net/jonweisberger/wobo.html

Jon Weisberger: jonweisberger@fuse.net

WOUB, 91.3 FM

"D28+5 Bluegrass," Ron Vigue, Deana Tribe, Pete Hart, 1-5 p.m. Sun. (On the air for over 20 years)

Ohio University
Athens
//www.tcom.ohiou.edu/pubradio/

WRUW, 91.1 FM

"All Things Acoustic," Luke Magee, 4 p.m. Mon. (eclectic mix of today's best singer/ songwriters)

"Alt. Country," Jeff, 7-9 a.m. Tues.

"When the Roses Bloom Again," Cousin Dave Wilson, 7:30-9:30 p.m. Thurs. (bluegrass, country, swing, Tex-Mex, Cajun, folk)

"Roll Away the Dew," Jimmie Wilson, 11-2 p.m. Sat. (long running folk show with traditional music, singer/songwriters, acoustic country old and new)

"Mucha Muchacha," Veronica Flores, 4 p.m. Sun. (Tejano, norteño, Latin)

11220 Bellflower Rd.
Case Western Reserve University
Cleveland 44106
216-368-2207
//www.cwru.edu/orgs/wruw/wruw.html
dk649@cleveland.freenet.edu

Alt. Country:
//www.drgw.net/~tex/show.html

WYSO, 91.3 FM

"Alchemy," Anne Williams, 9a.m.-Noon, M-F (folk; acoustic music)

"Potpourri," Ed Humphyrs, 4-6 p.m. Sat. (title says it all; expect to hear old-timey, bluegrass, Cajun, blues, world)

"Bluegrass Breakdown," 6-10 p.m. Sat.

"Midnight Ramble," 10-Mid. Sat. (C&W)

"Rise When the Rooster Crows," 6-8 a.m. Sun. (bluegrass; gospel)

Antioch College
Yellow Springs 45387
513-767-5420
//www.wyso.org
wyso@college.antioch.edu

Ed Humphrys:
ehumphrys@college.antioch.edu

Oklahoma

KKNG, 93.3 FM

"County Line Cavalcade," Richard Connor, 9-Mid. Sun. (a mix of classic and alternative country)

Oklahoma City

Richard Connor: ritocon@galstar.com

Oregon

KBOO, 90.7 FM

"The Hillbilly H?," The Mighty Hawk aka Wade Hockett, Noon-1 p.m., Mon. ("Folk music for people what ain't been to college")

"Tejano," Raul Cantu, 3:30-5 p.m. Tues.

"Root & Branch," Chris Nielsen, 11-12:30 p.m. Tues. (contemporary folk and roots from bluegrass to world with emphasis on new releases and European imports)

"Cooler Than Country," Paul Hodgen, 5:30-7:30 a.m. Wed. (bluegrass & parallel folk genres; 100% hand made music)

"American Hootenany," Richard Melling, 5:30-7 a.m. Fri. (folk, traditional, ethnic; rural and urban to 1950s)

"Movin' On," Linda Stein & Laurie Sonnenfeld, 11 a.m.-12:30 p.m. Fri. (bluegrass, blues, folk)

"Swing 'n' Country," alt. hosts, 6-9 a.m. Sat. ("country swing, old and new, liberally sprinkled with old country hits and non-hits")

"Music From the True Vine," Gareth Jenkins, Ian Joel, Gretchen Voll & Dee Ann Nelson, 9-Noon Sat. (bluegrass)

20 SE 8th Ave.
Portland 97214
503-231-8032
//www.kboo.org

KLCC, 89.7 FM/KLCO, 90.5 FM (Newport)

"Fresh Tracks," Liz Wise, Rooster, 9 a.m.-3:30 p.m. M-F (Americana variety)

"Heartwood Hotel," Cina Kraft, 7:30-10 p.m. Tues. (eclectic folk, s/s, new acoustic)

"The Saturday Cafe," Frank Gosar, 11 a.m.-1 p.m. (folk and s/s with a little bluegrass, ethnic, humorous, or old-timey)

"The Back Porch," Pete LaVelle, 9-11 p.m. Sat. (traditional, ethnic, folk ranging from Harry Belafonte to Flaco Jimenez to Cajun to western swing on any given show)

Lane Community College
4000 E. 30th Ave.

Eugene 97405
//www.klcc.org
klcc@efn.org

KMUN, 91.9 FM

"Hootin'," 6-8 p.m. Sat. (bluegrass)

"Country Swing," 2-4 p.m. Sun.

P. O. Box 269
Astoria 97103
503-325-0010
//www.kmun.org
kmun@seasurf.com

KORC, 820 AM

"Stringtime Serenade," Jim D'Ville, 10-Noon, Sat. (bluegrass, old-time)

235 SW Arrow #3
Waldport 97394

Jim D'Ville: dville@pioneer.net

KPSU, 1450 AM

"Walkin' the Line," 7-8 p.m. Tues. (old country, folk, blues)

"The Gumbo Ya Ya Hour," 5-7 p.m. Wed. (Cajun/zydeco)

"American Roots," 7-8 p.m. Fri. (honky tonk, blues, jazz, etc.)

"Unofficially American Roots," 8-10 p.m. Fri.

P. O. Box 751-SD
Portland 97207
//www.kpsu.org
kpsu@osa.pdx.edu

KRVM, 91.9 FM

"Miles of Bluegrass," Martin Anderson, 7-9 p.m. Mon

"Echoes From the Hills," Rich Evans, 7-9 p.m. Fri. (bluegrass)

"Jivin' John's Country Classics," John Etheredge, 9-10 a.m. Sat. (hot licks and hillbilly favorites from the 1920s-1960s)

"The FAT Music Show," Felton Pruitt, 10 a.m.-Noon, Sat. (music from the roots of KFAT)

"Acoustic Junction," Mike Meyer, 3-6 p.m. Sat. (modern acoustic with an emphasis on singer/songwriters with plenty of bluegrass, world, country, blues, Cajun, acoustic rock)

1574 Coburg Rd., Suite 237
Eugene 97401
503-687-3370
//www.krvm.com
krvm@krvm.com

Mike Meyer: mmeyer@proaxis.com

Martin Anderson: martin_a@efn.org

John Etheredge: etheredge@earthlink.net

KWVA, 88.1 FM

"Texas Chainsaw Acoustic Hour," Doug Tucker, 9-11 a.m. Sat. (Americana, alt. country, folk)

University of Oregon

Eugene
//gladstone.uoregon.edu/~kwva/

Doug Tucker: zora@pacinfo.com

Pennsylvania

WDIY, 88.1 FM

"Morning Mix," Carolyn Adams, 8:30-10:30 M-F (eclectic Americana format including blues, folk, country, etc.)

"Acoustic Eclectic," Otto Bost, 7-9 p.m. Mon. (s/s, bluegrass, humor)

"Echoes From the Hills," 7-9 p.m. Fri. (bluegrass)

301 Broadway
Bethlehem 18015
//www.wdiyfm.org

Carolyn Adams: carri@enter.net

Otto Bost:
//members.aol.com/folkdude/
FolkDude@aol.com

WEEU, 850 AM

60 hours of folk, bluegrass and mountain music per week. Home of the syndicated "Mountain Folk" show with "East Side" Dave.

Reading
///www.mountainfolk.com
MtnFolk@aol.com

WESS, 90.3 FM

"Roots & Wings," John McLaughlin, Noon-4 Mon. (since 1978 and featuring bluegrass, country, folk especially independent and d.i.y. artists)

English Department
East Stroudsburg State University
East Stroudsburg 18301-2999
717-424-3512
//www.esu.edu/wess/

John McLaughlin: johnmc@esu.edu

WITF, 89.5 FM

"The Chords Are Stacked," John Patterson, 8-10 p.m. Sat. (folk, blues, ethnic, bluegrass)

1982 Locust
Harrisburg
800-366-9483
//www.witf.org
witf@witf.org

WKVA, 920 AM

"Country The Way It Was," Ed Fisher, 10-Noon Sat. (traditional country, bluegrass, cowboy)

"Classic Country Music Hour," Noon- Sat.

Lewistown
717-242-1493

WPSU, 91.5 FM

"The Folk Show," various hosts, 6-7 a.m., 2-4 p.m. Sat; 11 a.m.-1 p.m. Sun. (eclectic including traditional folk, s/s, Celtic, bluegrass, old-timey, Cajun, acoustic blues)

123 S. Burrowes St., Suite 202
University Park 16801-3867
814-865-9191
//www.cde.psu.edu/edcomm/
tmhl@psuvm.psu.edu

WQSU, 88.9 FM

"Pure as Stone Country Music Jamboree" Dave Pearce, 9-Noon Sat.

"The Down Home Country Show," Larry Walters, Noon-2 Sat.

Selinsgrove
717-372-4100
//www.susqu.edu/orgs/wqsu-fm/wqsu.html
rbrown@susqu.edu

WRCT, 88.3 FM

"Fear & Whiskey," Carl Zimring, 7-10. p.m. Mon. (psychedelia, rock, soul, independent country)

Carnegie-Mellon University
5020 Forbes Ave.
Skibo Hall
Pittsburgh 15213
412-621-9728
//www.wrct.org
wrct@andrew.cmu.edu

Fear & Whiskey:
//www.andrew.cmu.edu/~cz28/fear.htm
cz28+@andrew.cmu.edu

WRDV, 89.3 FM; 91.9 FM (Trenton, NJ)

"Country Junction," Jack Boland

"Music in the Folk Tradition," Tor Jonassen, 10:30-11:30 p.m. Fri.

P. O. Box 2012
Warminster 18974
215-674-8002

WVIA, 89.9 FM

"Mixed Bag," George Graham with "George Graham's Weekly Album Reviews," 8 p.m. Fri. (he's done thousands of Americana reviews since 1973)

"Home Grown," George Graham, 9 p.m. Tues. (Regional music focus)

70 Old Boston Road
Pittston 18640
717-655-2808
//www.wvia.org

George Graham's Weekly Album Reviews:
//george.scranton.com/reviews.html
mixedbag@wvia.org

Home Grown:
//george.scranton.html/hgm_main.html

WXPN, 88.5 FM

"Morning Show," Michaela Majoun and Abby Goldstein, 6 a.m.-2 p.m. M-F (Texas music orientation)

"Sleepy Hollow," Keith Brand & Chuck Elliott, 6-10 a.m. Sat.; 6-10 a.m. Sun. (hosted by grad student/faculty member in communications at Temple and member of the Hix; he spins folk, old-time, bluegrass, etc.; this show can also be heard on WKHS in Baltimore)

3905 Spruce St.
Philadelphia 19104
//www2.xpn.org/xpn/

Keith Brand:
//www.iliad.com/xpn/sleepy/
kbphd@vm.temple.edu

WYEP, 91.3 FM

"American Sampler," Ken Batista, 7-Noon. Sun. (acoustic from blues to zydeco and in between)

"Bluegrass Jam Session and Traditional Ties," Bruce Mountjoy & John Trout, 8-Mid. p.m. Sun.

2313 E. Carson St.
Pittsburgh 15203
//www.wyep.org

Ken Batista: kbastita@pitt.edu

Rhode Island

WRIU, 90.3 FM {Gavin Americana}

"Traditions of Folk," Chuck Wentworth, 6-9 p.m. Mon. (a wide variety of roots music: blues, Cajun, country, folk, s/s, etc.)

"Boudin Barndance," Dan Ferguson, 6-9 p.m. Thurs. (a wide variety of roots music with lots of alt. country)

"Bluegrass," Mike Fishman, 6-9 p.m. Fri.

Rhode Island University
326 Memorial Union
Kingston 02881
401-789-4949

Dan Ferguson: BoudinDan@aol.com

South Carolina

NCC Radio, Channel 2 Scripps Howard Cablevision

"Folks on the Air," Page Turner, 8-10 p.m. Mon. (folk, old-time, bluegrass)

Newberry College
Wessels Library
2100 College St.
Newberry 29108

South Carolina Educational Radio Network

"The Bluegrass Sound," Larry Klein, 10 p.m. Sat. (active bluegrass, old-time and country musician who has done this show for over 6 years)

"Stay a Little Longer," Larry Hall, 7 p.m. Sun. (Western swing, cowboy)

1101 George Rogers Blvd.

Columbia 29201
//www.scern.org

Larry Klein: lklein@scsn.net

WSBF, 88.1 FM

"Startin' to Hate Country," Brian Townsend, 9-11 p.m. Thurs. (Alternative & classic country)

P. O. Box 2156
Clemson University
Clemson 29631-2156
//wsbf.clemson.edu
wsbf@clemson.edu

WSCI, 89.3 FM

"South to Louisiana," Gary Erwin aka Shrimp City Slim, 10-11 p.m. Fri. (zydeco, Cajun, swamp pop, etc.)

"La Noche Latina," Gary Erwin, 11 p.m. Fri. (All kinds of music from Latin America)

"Erwin Music" Gary Erwin, 4 p.m. Sun. ("a wild a wooly mix of world sounds and American roots")

Charleston

Gary Erwin/Shrimp City Slim:
//www.shrimpcityslim.com
emusic@shrimpcityslim.com

Tennessee

WANT, 98.9 FM

"Buried Treasure," Christi Ray (mix of classic, alt. and new country with in studio guests each week such as Tim O'Brien, BR5-49, the Hangdogs, Paul Burch, Hayseed, Kate Campbell)

"Fiddler's Grove Bluegrass Show," Mark Dyer, 7-10 p.m. Sun. (old and new)

P. O. Box 1025
510 Trousdale Ferry Pike
Lebanon 37087
615-449-3699

Mark Dyer: nero999@ix.netcom.com

WDVX, 89.9 FM

Broadcasts from a 16 foot camper and offers wide variety of alt. country including:

"Swing Set," Scott Carpenter, 10-11 p.m. Thurs. (Western swing, hillbilly boogie, country jazz)

"Tennessee Saturday Night," Shane Rhyne, 7 p.m.-10:30 p.m. Sat. (traditional old-time, bluegrass mixed in with lots of contemporary alt. country)

"Fringe," Shane Rhyne, 10:30-Mid. Sat. ("the frayed edges of mainstream music where rock, country, blues, and other roots music get tangled" or call it alternative country)

"Soppin' the Gravy" (bluegrass)

"Something Old, Something New" (classic then contemporary album)

"Cumberland Sunday Morning Show" (gospel bluegrass)

P. O. Box 27568
Knoxville 37927
423-494-2020
//www.wdvx.com
mail@wdvx.com

Swing Set
P. O. Box 191
Knoxville 37901
//www.w3street.com/swingset/
swingset@w3street.com

Shane Rhyne:
rhyne@east-tennessee-history.org

WETS, 89.5 FM

"Bluegrass Revue," 3-5 p.m. Tues.

Johnson City
//www.east-tenn-st.edu/wets.html

WEVL, 90.0 FM

"Southbound Line," 10-Noon Tues. (rockabilly)

"Hard Corn," Nancy Apple, 4-6 p.m. Tues. (mostly contemporary Americana but also lots of classic honky tonk)

"Barstool #1," Ed Dirmeyer, 8-10 a.m. Wed. (alt. country)

"Real Country," 10 a.m.-Noon, Wed.

"Hillbilly Jazz," 2-3 p.m. Wed.

"Old-Time Country Music Hour," 3-4 p.m. Wed.

"House Bayou," Tom Claypool, 4-6 p.m. Wed., Noon Fri. (Cajun, zydeco, swamp pop)

"Somethin' Else," Noon, Thurs. (Rockabilly)

"Bluegrass & Beyond," Brother Craig, 6 p.m. Thurs.

"Bluff City Barn Dance," The Ol' Ridge Runner, 6-10 a.m. Sat. (ten years of old-time, bluegrass, Western swing, etc.)

"Through the Cracks," Ed Dirmeyer, 1 p.m. Sat. (folk, rock, alt. country & everything in between)

P. O. Box 40952
Memphis 38174
901-528-0560
//wevl.org

Southbound Line:
//members.aol.com/bksnova/bksmemphis.html
Bksnova@aol.com

Nancy Apple: TheCowgirl@aol.com

Old-Time Country Music Hour:
Judydor@aol.com

Ed Dirmeyer: edirmeyer@worldnet.att.et

Brother Craig: brough@ix.netcom.com

Tom Claypool: HouseBayou@webtv.net

Bluff City Barn Dance:
//members.aol.com/Barndance1/index.htm
Barndance1@aol.com

WMTS, 88.3 FM

Country variety that includes some of the alternative kind.

"Gone Country," Brian Cassell, 10-Noon Fri.

P. O. Box 58
Middle Tennessee State University
Murfreesboro 37133
615-898-2636
//www.mtsu.edu/~wmts/
wmts@mtsu.edu

WQZQ/WZPC, 102.9 FM

"Western Beat Roots Revival," Billy Block, 7-Mid. Sun. (alt. country/Americana from the producer of the weekly Western Beat Showcase at the Exit/In)

Nashville
//www.westernbeat.com
westernbeat@home.net

WRVU, 91.1 FM

"George the Bluegrass Show," 2-4 p.m. Sun.

P. O. Box 9100
Station B
Nashville 37235
//www.vanderbilt.edu/wrvu
wrvu@ctrvax.vanderbilt.edu

WSM, 650 AM

Broadcasting the Grand Old Opry since 1925.

"The Eddie Stubbs Show," 7p.m.-Mid. M-F

"Orange Possum Special," H. Hensley, 6-8 p.m. Thurs. (Bluegrass)

"Friday Night Opry," Eddie Stubbs, 6-Mid.

"Classic Saturday, 6a.m.-10 a.m.

"Hipbilly Jamboree," Randy & Dole, 10-12 a.m. Sat.

"Saturday Grand Old Opry," 5p.m.-Mid.

"Ernest Tubb's Midnite Jamboree," Carol Lee Cooper, Mid-1 a.m. Sun.

Nashville
//www.country.com/music/wsm/

Texas

KAMU, 90.9 FM

"Brazos Valley Gold," Charlie Edwards, 7-9 p.m. Fri. ("country radio the way it used to be; the music is 'classical' country and the banter is 'hystorical' if not hysterical")

"The Bluegrass Hour," Rodney O'Connor, 7-8 p.m. Sat.

Moore Communications Ctr.
Texas A&M University
College Station 77843-4244
//www.rtis.com/reg/bcs/org/kamu
kamu-fm@tamu.edu

Rodney O'Connor: timakers@tamu.edu

KCTI, 1450 AM (Gonzales)

"Aaron Allan's Show," 1-4 p.m. M-F (vintage country, folk; Aaron is putting together the "Vintage Library Show" for syndication from the station's vast music archive)

c/o Aaron Allan
221 FM 86, #39

Luling 78648

KCWM, 1460 AM

"Vance's Country Western Jamboree," Ron Cole, 8:30 p.m.-12:30 a.m. Sat. (primarily Western swing and Texas artists)

1605 Ave. K
Hondo 78861-1838
210-741-KCWM
//www.crl.com/~rdcole/kcwm.html

Ron Cole: rdcole@crl.com

KEDA, 1540 AM (on air since 1966, it's the oldest Tejano station in the U.S.)

"Guero Polkas Show," 6-10 p.m. M-F

c/o Richard Davila, KEDA
510 S. Flores St.
San Antonio 78204

KEOS, 89.1 FM

"Gulf Coast Gumbo," 3-5 a.m. Mon. (from KPFT, Houston)

"Sounds of Texas & The World," 10 a.m.-3 p.m. M-F (from KPFT, Houston)

"Hickory Wind," Gary Varner, 7-9 p.m., Mon. (urban folk; country rock)

"High Lonesome," John Roths, 7-9 p.m. Tues. (bluegrass)

"Open Air," Judith Gennett, 10-Noon, Thurs.

"Eclectic Coffeehouse," Judith Gennett, 6-8 a.m. Fri. (roots, traditional, real folk, world)

"Cajun Bandstand," 6-9 a.m. Sat.

"Random Routes," Ruth Riegel, 9-Noon Sat. (alt. country/Americana)

"Pickin' & Swingin'," 3-5 p.m. Sun. (from KPFT, Houston)

P. O. Box 78
College Station 77841
409-779-5367
//www.rtis.com/keos/
L-parr@tamu.edu

Hickory Wind:
//snaefell.tamu.edu/~gary/hickorywind.html

Gary Varner: g-varner@tamu.edu

John Roths: jroths@vetmed.tamu.edu

Judith Gennett: judith@bihs.net

Ruth Riegel: ruth_riegel@odp.tamu.edu

KFAN, 107.9 FM

"Texas Rebel Radio": Americana format with at least 4 Texas artists/hour all day

"Humble Time," 6-7 p.m. Sat. (live show presenting unsigned Texas artists)

P. O. Box 311
Fredericksburg 78624
//www.texasrebelradio.com
txradio@texasrebelradio.com

KGRI, 99.9 FM

"The Texas Music Festival," Dave Rousseau, 5-8:30 a.m., Sun. (broadcasting traditional bluegrass, old-time and Western swing for over a decade)

P. O. Box 1400
Henderson 75653-1400
903-657-4528

KGSR, 107.1 FM

"Lone Star State of Mind," Kevin Connor, 10-Mid. Fri. (Texas variety)

505 Barton Springs Rd.
Austin 78704
512-472-1071
//www.kgsr.com

Kevin Connor: kevin@kgsr.com

KHYI, 95.3 FM {Gavin Americana}

First major market station with full-time alternative country/Americana playlist beginning in 1997; largest Americana station (25K watts) in the state and Gavin Americana "Station of the Year" in 1998.

"Bruce Kidder," 6a.m.-Noon M-F

"Brett Dillon Experience," 1-6 p.m. M-F

"Rusty Rhodes," 6-10 p.m. M-Thurs.

"Texas Music Revue," Little John & Boone, 6-10 p.m. Fri.

Plano (near Dallas) 75002
//www.khyi.com
khyi@swbell.net

KIKT, 93.5

Playlist is 30-40% Americana

Greenville 75401

KKZN, 93.3 FM

"Lone Star Radio," Abby Goldstein, 8-10 p.m. Sun. (Texas music with focus on Dallas/Ft. Worth area acts)

3500 Maple Ave., #1600
Dallas 75219
//www.933thezone.com

Lone Star Radio:
//www.broadcast.com/shows/lonestarradio/

Abby Goldstein: agoldste@dfwradio.com

KLLL, 96.3 FM

"West Texas Music Hour," Kenny Mines and/or Cary Banks, 9-10 p.m. Sun. (presenting West Texas artists from Bob Wills to Buddy Holly to the Lubbock Mafia)

Lubbock
806-763-1911
//www.klll.com
info@klll.com

KNBT, 92.1 FM {Gavin Americana}

"Crossroads Americana," Matson Rainer, 7-10 p.m. Sat. (Americana including folk, bluegrass, Texas artists)

1540 Loop 337 N
New Braunfels 78130
//www.nbradio.com
music@nbrradio.com

KNEL, 95.3 FM

"Hillbilly Hits," Tracy Pitcox, 6-Mid. Fri. (traditional country)

Hillbilly Hits Fan Club
1308 South Bridge, #7
Brady 76825
//www.hillbillyhits.com
webmaster@hillbillyhits.com

KNON, 89.3 FM {Gavin Americana}

"Texas Renegade Country," 4-6 p.m. M-F (Texas country & Americana with special focus on local singer/songwriters and live "in the studio" performances)

"Cajun & Zydeco," Leo Perron & T-Richard, 8-10 p.m. Mon.

"Tejano Block Party," Noon-4 p.m. M-F

"Rockabilly Revue," Cowhide Cole & Donna Rose, 8-10 p.m. Tues.

"Texas Music Revue," Little John, 6-10 p.m. Fri. (hardcore classic, s/s, hard edged Americana)

"Tejano," J.Y. Rodriguez, 1-5 p.m. Sat.

P. O. Box 710909
Dallas 75371
//www.knon.org

Texas Renegade Country:
//www.knon.org/renegade/

Rockabilly Revue:
//www.bbgun.com/rockabilly/
donna88@airmail.net

KOHM, 89.1 FM

"Roots Music," Lanny Fiel, 2-3 p.m. Sun.

"Roots Midnight Hour," Lanny Fiel, Midnight-1, Thurs. (recorded and live traditional music on both programs)

3716 27th St.
Lubbock 79410
//somewhere.org/nar/stations/kohm/main.html
info@somewhere.org

KOOP, 91.7 FM

"Ritmo Latino," 11-1 p.m. Mon. (Latin jazz to conjunto)

"Country Roots," John Hauser, 9-10 a.m. Tues. (thematic exploration of the traditions and sources of country music)

"Fais-Do-Do," Tom Mahnke, 10-11 a.m. Tues. (Cajun/zydeco from one of the area's foremost authorities and close personal friend of Stacy Keener)

"Country, Swing & Rock-a-Billy Jamboree," Rod Moag, 9-11 a.m. Thurs. (vintage music show hosted by the Pickin', Singin' Professer)

"New American Roots Music," Jim Caligiuri, 9-10 a.m. Fri. (new blues, country, Cajun, zydeco, bluegrass, folk, Tex-Mex)

"Strictly Bluegrass," 9-10:30 a.m. Sun.

P. O. Box 49340
Austin 78765

512-472-KOOP
//www.koop.org
koop@txinfinet.com

Jim Caligiuri:
jim_caligiuri@brahms2.tivoli.com

KPFT, 90.1 FM {Gavin Americana}

"Gulf Coast Gumbo," Gary Sapone, 3-5 a.m. Mon.

"KPFT Crossroads," Mary Ramirez, 10-Noon, M-F & 9-Mid., M-F (acoustic, folk, rock Texas)

"Afternoon Music," Leslie, 3-6 p.m. M-F

"Sounds of Texas and the World," Chris Knight, Noon-5:30 p.m. M-F (with various hosts)

"Zydeco Dawn," Wilfred Chavis, 4-6 a.m. Fri.

"Cajun Bandstand," Pe-Te Johnson, 6-9 a.m. Sat.

"The Lonestar Jukebox," Rick Heyquierdo, 9-Noon, Sat.

"Spare Change," Larry Winters, Noon-3 p.m. Sat. (Texas & acoustic music)

"Pickin' & Swingin'," Rick Gardner, 3-5 p.m. Sun.

"Night Sounds," Pat & Rose Leach, Mid-5 a.m. Sun. (folk, eclectic)

419 Lovett Blvd.
Houston 77006
713-526-4000
//www.kpft.org
ganter@kpft.org

KRJH, 92.5 FM

Americana format

Hallettsville-Yoakum

KSTX, 89.1 FM

"Sunday Night Session," David Furst, 7-8 p.m. (interviews, live & recorded music from Texas musicians e.g. Don Walser, Jimmie Dale, Jesse Dayton, Christine Albert, Libbi Bosworth et al.)

8401 Datapoint Dr., #800
San Antonio 78229-3295
//www.tpr.org/kstx/
kstx@tpr.org

KSYM, 90.1 FM {Gavin Americana}

"Third Coast Music Network," 8 DJs , 3-7 p.m. M-F; 2-6 p.m. Sat. & 6-10 p.m. Sun. (coordinated by Joe "X by God" Horn, each block offers twang, blues, rockabilly, jazz, Cajun, s/s; motto: "We're gonna do what we gotta do. Get out of our way or we'll kill you.")

"Bluegrass," Noon-2 Sun.

730 W. Summit
San Antonio 78212-2801
512-732-2104

Third Coast Music:
//www.accd.edu/tcmn/

Joe X. Horn: RMould5417@aol.com

KTRU, 91.7 FM

"Chicken Skin," David John, 7-10 p.m. Thurs. (running for almost 20 years playing bluegrass, country, folk)

Rice University
2nd Floor, Ley Student Ctr.
6100 S. Main St.
Houston 77005-1892
713-527-4098
//www.rice.edu/projects/ktru/

David John: chickskn@flash.net

KULM, 98.3 FM

"The Country Eastern Radio Show," Eddie Russell, 10-11 a.m. Sat. (hillbilly music intermixed with a variety from punk to Tex-Mex; also heard in Spain, Ireland, and Reading, Vermont)

Country Eastern West
108 Legion Cr.
Columbus 78934

KUT, 90.5 FM

"Blue Monday," Larry Monroe, 8-Mid. (blues & related)

"Phil Music," Larry Monroe, 8-Mid. Thurs. (Americana variety)

"Folkways," Sue Fawver, 9 a.m.-2 p.m. Sat. (long-running show of "real" Texas music, Western swing, bluegrass, old-timey, Cajun, Tex-Mex etc.)

"Live Set," 7 p.m., Sun.

"Texas Radio," Larry Monroe, 9 p.m.-Mid. Sun. (variety of Texas music old and new)

"Segway City," Larry Monroe Mid.-5 a.m. Sat./Sun. (another venerable Americana show)

CMB2 UT Austin
Austin 78713
//www.kut.org

Segway City: //www.ddc.net/segway/

Larry Monroe lm@ddc.net

Sue Fawver: suefawvr@onr.com

Live Set:
//wwwvms.utexas.edu/~wlmorgan/liveset/

KVRX, 91.7 FM

"Radiation Rock," Jaimey, 5 p.m. Sat. (Rockabilly; Western swing, hillbilly bop)

University of Texas Student Radio
Box D
Austin 78713-7209
512-471-5106
//www.utexas.edu/students/kvrx/index.html
Valerie@mail.utexas.edu

Radiation Rock:
blondebetty@mail.utexas.edu

Utah

KRCL, 90.9/91 FM; 89.7 FM (Moab); 96.5 FM (Park City) {Gavin Americana}

"Monday Breakfast Jam," various hosts, 6 a.m. (bluegrass, folk, country rock)

"Friday Breakfast Jam," Gary Timm, 6 a.m. (bluegrass and folk)

"Saturday Breakfast Jam," Jo Wilson, 8 a.m. (bluegrass and folk)

"Sagebrush Serenade," John, 10-1 p.m. Sat. & Phil Lanouette or Rick Stayner, 10 a.m.-2 p.m. Sun. (folk/country rock)

"Bluegrass Express," Tony Polychronis, 2-5 p.m. Sun.

"Fret 'N' Fiddle," Mark Cantor, 5:30-7 p.m. Sun. (folk/country music from mid-19th to mid-20th centuries)

230 South 800 West, Ste. 105
Salt Lake City 84101
801-363-1818
//www.krcl.org
mailman@krcl.org

Tony Polychronis: iama@xmission.com

Vermont

WGDR, 91.1 FM

"Acoustic Stage," Patti Garbeck, 7:30-9 p.m. Mon.

"Let the Bon Temps Roulet," George Thomas, 9-11 p.m. Mon. (Cajun/zydeco, old-time, blues)

"Kate Weeke's Show," 11 p.m. Wed. (Dylan-Petty-Hank-The Band)

"Radio Boogie," Jennifer Isaacs, 12:30-3 p.m. Sun. (new and old-time bluegrass)

Goddard College
Plainfield 05667
802-454-7762
//www.goddard.edu/wgdr/
wgdr@earth.goddard.edu

WJSC, 90.7 FM

"The Fancy Eatin' Table," Joe Farara, 5-7 p.m., Wed. (blues, Cajun/zydeco, conjunto, honky tonk, rockabilly)

Johnson State College
Johnson 05656
802-635-9572

WRUV, 90.1 FM

"Alien Folk," Mad Dog, 6-9 a.m. Tues. (since 1987 with a wide, wide variety from "truly folk"—Iris Dement, Ramblin' Jack, Tish Hinojosa et al. to "slightly weird"—Therapist John's Zip Code Revue to "truly alien"—Tracy and the Hindenburg Ground Crew; Mad Dog maintains a library of all folk music CDs on his playlist and a folk music search engine)

"The Old-Time," Kevin, 9 a.m.-Noon Wed,. (country, blues, bluegrass)

Billings Student Ctr.
University of Vermont
Burlington 05405
802-656-0796
//www.uvm.edu/~wruv/
wruv@moose.uvm.edu

WWPV, 90.1 FM

"Good Acoustics," Sam Ankerson, 10-Mid. Mon. (bluegrass, Celtic)

"Planet Jukebox," Tom Ayres, 8-10 p.m. Wed. (Americana/roots variety with all your alt. country favorites)

"The Folk Show," John Sheehey, 5-8 p.m. Thurs. (traditional and contemporary folk, bluegrass, Celtic, etc.)

Saint Michael's College
Winooski Park
Colchester 05439
802-654-2334
//personalweb.smcvt.edu/wwpv/
wwpv@smcvt.edu

Tom Ayres: toma@together.net

John Sheehey: jsheehey@smcvt.edu

Virginia

WAXM, 93.5 FM

"Wednesday Night Bluegrass/Sunday Night Bluegrass," 6 p.m.-5 a.m. Wed.-Thurs.; 6 p.m.-Midnight Sun. (straight ahead bluegrass on a large commercial station managed by a bluegrass fiddler)

Big Stone Gap 24219
//www.waxm.com

WBRF, 98.1 FM

"Folk & Beyond," Fred Boyce and Lisa K. Howard, Thurs. (bluegrass, folk and "beyond" from WTJU, Charlottesville)

Galax 24333

WCWM, 90.7 FM

"40 Acres & A Mule," 10-Mid. Thurs. ("granola rock")

"A Prairie Home Conflagration," Sean Atienza, Noon-2 p.m. Sat. (1 hour of bluegrass/old-time; 1 hour of punk)

College of William & Mary
Williamsburg
757-221-3287
//www.wm.edu/wcwm/

Prairie Home Conflagration:
//www.geocities.com/sunsetstrip/lounge/67 24/

WDCE, 90.1 FM (Richmond)

"The No-Garth Twang-A-Rama," Kactus Kimmy, Sun. night (the gamut of alt. country)

University of Richmond
P. O. Box 65
Richmond 23173
804-289-8698
//www.student.richmond.edu/~wdce/

WJMA, 96.7 FM

"Mike Hays' Twang Thang," 3-7 p.m. M-F

"Stained Glass Bluegrass," Red Shipley, 7-11 a.m. Sun.

"After Hours Bluegrass Jam," Lisa Howard, 6-Mid. Sun.

P. O. Box 271
Orange 22960
//www.gemlink.com/wjma/
Wjma@ns.gemlnik.com

The Twanger's (Mike Hays) Home Page:
//www.mikehays.realcountry.net/
(lots of links)

Mike@mikehays.realcountry.net
*In late 1998, Hays and Real.Country.net set up TwangCast.com, a 24 hour/day online broadcast of alt. country/Americana (//www.TwangCast.com).

WKEX, 1430 AM

All bluegrass, all the time!

Blacksburg

WNVA, 106.3 FM

"Original Downhome Bluegrass," Tom McConnell, 6 p.m.-4 a.m. M&W

P. O. Box 500
Norton, VA 24273
540-328-2244
//www.compunet.net/wnva/
wnva@compunet.net

WTJU, 91.1 FM

"Acoustic Windows," Aer Stephen & Tom Sears, Noon-2 Tues. (Celtoid, psychobilly, alt. country)

"Eclectic Country Rock," Pinetops Stephen & Lisa Spiro, Noon Thurs. (where Kitty Wells and Hank Williams hang out with Mojo Nixon and the Cowboy Junkies)

"Folk and Beyond," Phyllis White & Aer Stephen, 5-7 p.m. Thurs. (bluegrass, old-time, contemporary acoustic, and beyond)

"Sunset Road," Pete Marshall or Blue O'Connell, 5-7 p.m. Fri. (old-time, bluegrass, newgrass, folk, new acoustic, etc.)

"Leftover Biscuits," Bill Adams, 6:30-8 a.m. Sat. (traditional old-time and country)

"Atlantic Weekly I," John Hillstrom, 8:05-10:05 a.m. Sat. (bluegrass, old-time, swing, s/s)

"The Old Home Place," Jeff Vogelgesang, 6-8 p.m. alt. Sat. (bluegrass)

"Cajun Conspiracy," Aer Stephen, 8-9 p.m. Sat.

"The Prism Radio Coffeehouse," Fred Boyce, Noon Sun. (live performances by Vassar Clements, Gillian Welch, and many others since 1992)

University of Virginia
711 Newcomb Hall Station
Charlottesville 22904
804-924-0885
//www.virginia.edu/~wtju/
wtju@virginia.edu

Aer Stephen: stefek@juno.com

Lisa Spiro: lms4w@virginia.edu

Blue O'Connell:
rbo3x@uva.pcmail.virginia.edu

Bill Adams: BAJammin@aol.com

Pete Marshall: buster@cstone.net

Jeff Vogelgesang: uvogejp@michie.com

Prism Radio Coffeehouse:
//www.theprism.org

WVLS, 89.7 FM

"A Good Country Morning," 6-9 a.m. M-F

"Traffic Jam," 4-6 p.m. M-F (Americana)

"Steve's Show," 8-10 p.m. Mon. (Americana mix)

"Listen to the Radio," Mary Switzer, 6-8 p.m. Tues. (gospel, bluegrass, country)

"Country Plus," 10-Noon, Thurs.; 10-11 a.m. Fri. (country, Americana)

"Tom & Steve's Country," 6-8 p.m. Thurs. (country, bluegrass, gospel)

"TGIF Bluegrass," 2-3 p.m. Fri.

"Natural Blend," Noon-1 Sat. (bluegrass, Americana)

"Bluegrass, Folk, Americana," Tom Brody, 6-8 p.m. Sat.

"Pooh's Corner," Winnie Richardson, 8-10 p.m. Sat. (folk, acoustic, Americana)

"Bluegrass Reflections," Noon-4 Sun.

P. O. Box 185
Monterey 24465
//wvls.cfw.com
wvls@cfw.com

WXJM, 88.7 FM {Gavin Americana}

"Americana," 2-4 M-F (roots rock; blues)

"Bluegrass," 4-6 p.m. Sun.

James Madison University
Harrisonburg 22801
//www.jmu.edu/wxjm/
wxjm@jmu.edu

Radio Grass Twenty (Syndicated)

Weekly top 20 countdown of current bluegrass hits heard on 14 stations in 9 states

311 Fairway Ave,
Charlottesville 22902
800-232-6334
zone@cstone.net

Washington State

KAOS, 89.3 FM

"Cover the Earth," Juli Kelen, 10-Noon, Tues. (acoustic, Cajun, folk, world, jazz)

"American Anecdotes," Tom Foote, 6-8 p.m. Thurs.

"Retroactive," J. J. Syrja, 10:30-1 p.m. Sat. (r&b, roots rock, twang)

"The Acoustic Minstrel Show," Tom Wilson, 2-4 p.m Sun. (interviews & live performances by local & national musicians in bluegrass, folk, Celtic, acoustic)

Evergreen State College
TESC CAB 301
Olympia 98505
206-866-6000
//www.kaosradio.org
kaos@elwha.evergreen.edu

KBCS, 91.3 FM

"Roots & Branches," 3 p.m. M-F (old-time, Cajun, Tex-Mex, etc.)

"Risin' of the Sun," Jimi Boushey or Duane Adkins, 5 a.m. Sat. (traditional/contemporary music from the mountains, prairies, deltas of the South)

"Our Saturday Tradition," var., 8-Noon Sat. (bluegrass, Western swing, traditional country, and a bit of alt. country)

"Early Risers," Sonny Van Gelder, 5 a.m. Sun. (old-time, country, folk)

"Bluegrass Ramble," var., Noon-4 Sun..

Bellevue Community College
3000 Landerholm Cr.
Bellevue 98007
//prime.bcc.ctc.edu/kbcs/
kbcs@ctc.edu

Susan Madden: susnkbcs@halcyon.com

KCMU, 90.3 FM {Gavin Americana}

"The Variety Mix," various hosts, 6 a.m.-6 p.m.; 9 p.m.-6 a.m. M-F; 2 a.m.-6 a.m. Sat.; 9 p.m.-6 a.m. Sun. (includes the "Americana 40": roots, blues, jazz and *lots* of good old alternative country thanks to program director Don Yates who is also guardian of Postcard 2, the on-line alt. country mailing list)

"The Roadhouse," Jim Kelton, 6-9 p.m. Wed. (Americana 40 show with alt. country, rockabilly, classic country, roots)

"Swingin' Doors," Don Yates, 6-9 p.m. Thurs. (all types of alternative twang including honky tonk, Western swing etc.)

"Shake the Shack," Leon Berman, 6-9 p.m., Fri. (rockabilly and other uptempo Americana since 1987; Berman also hosts the long-running annual Shake the Shack Rockabilly Ball; see Festivals section for details)

University of Washington
P. O. Box 353755
Seattle 98195-3755
206-543-KCMU
//www.kcmu.org
{site for "Americana Top 40" and "Americana Archives" with hundreds of brief reviews of releases past and present plus playlists and links to labels}

kcmu@u.washington.edu

Leon Berman: stshack@nwlink.com

Don Yates: ctowndj@u.washington.edu

KKBY, 104.9 FM

"Honky Tonk Sundays," Icabod Caine, 10 a.m.- 10 p.m. (nationally syndicated show)

"Music With Madman Moskowitz," 5-10 p.m. Sun. (traditional country & novelty)

6310 16th St. East
Tacoma 98424
//www.thecowboy.com

Madman Moskowitz:
//idibbs.com/user/hightech/hrmosk.htm
mosk@halcyon.com

Icabod Caine: icky@cis.compuserve.com

KSER, 90.7 FM (Everett)

"Gator Gumbo," Rob Emery, 10-Mid. Wed.

14920 Hwy. 99, #150
Everett 98037-2300
206-742-4541
//www.dbailey.com/kser/
edkesr@aol.com

KVLR, 106.3 FM {Gavin Americana}

Nominated for 1995 Gavin Americana Roots Station of the Year for its eclectic programming including "Fat Music" with Felton Pruitt and Don Ashford.

Twisp 98856

KWCW, 90.5 FM

"Folkin' Excellent," Dana Leighton, 9-11 p.m. Wed. (folk, s/s, bluegrass)

Whitman College
Walla Walla 99362
//www.bmi.net/pfries/kwcw.html
leightdc@whitman.edu

Wisconsin

WERN, 88.7 FM

"Simply Folk," Judy Rose, 5-8 p.m. Sun. (all types of folk including bluegrass, Cajun, old-time, s/s)

821 University Ave.
Madison 53706-1412
//www.wpr.org

Judy Rose: rosej@vilas.uwex.edu

WORT, 89.9 FM

"Back To The Country," Bill Malone, 9-Noon, Wed. (1920s to the present with some alt./ insurgent country; host is author of many books on country including the seminal history *Country Music USA*)

"Mud Acres Bluegrass Special," Chris Powers, 9 a.m.-Noon Fri. (playing all types of bluegrass for the past 18 years)

118 S. Bedford St.
Madison 53703
608-256-2001
//netphoria.com/wort/

Bill Malone: wmalone@students.wisc.edu

WSUM, 91.7 FM

"Ho Down @ High Noon," Matt Spinner, Noon-2 Wed. (classic to insurgent country)

University of Wisconsin
Madison 53706
//msr.wisc.edu

Matt Spinner: mspinner@students.wisc.edu

WWSP, 90.0 FM

"Acoustic Revival," The Jester, 9-Noon, Sun. (country to bluegrass)

University of Wisconsin at Stevens Point
105 CAC Reserve St.
Stevens Point 54481
715-346-3755
//www.uwsp.edu/stuorg/wwsp/
wwsp@fsmailw.uwsp.edu

WYMS, 88.9 FM

"Sunday Night Folk Show," Mike Yuhas, 9-11 p.m. (bluegrass, Cajun, Celtic, folk and other acoustic music)

5225 W. Vliet
Milwaukee 53208
//www.wyms.org

Sunday Night Folk: //www.neverknow.com

Mike Yuhas: Folkdj@neverknow.com

Wyoming

KVOC, 1230 AM

"Bluegrass Plus," Steve Weih, 5-6 p.m. Sun. (hosted by musician and Shaker furniture maker who spins traditional bluegrass and old-time plus some country)

2323 E. 15th St.
Casper 82609
//coffey.com/business/shakerpine/shaker.html
sweih@coffey.com

CANADA

Alberta

CJSR, 88 FM

"Cheatin' & Hurtin' & Twangin'," Arthur & Mike, 9-11 a.m. Tues. (roots including folk, s/s, Celtic, bluegrass, country)

"Prairie Pickin'," Arthur Berman, 7-8 p.m. Thurs. (the only predominantly bluegrass show between Vancouver and Winnipeg)

Rm. 224, SUB
University of Alberta
Edmonton T6G 2J7

403-492-5244
//www.srv.ualberta.ca/~cjsrfm/
cjsrfm@gpu.srv.ualberta.ca

CJSW, 90.9 FM

"Vintage Voola," 3-4 p.m. Tues. (Rockabilly)

"Boot Heel Drag: The Country Show," 6:30-8 p.m. Tues.

"Folkcetera," Martin Kemp, 6-8 p.m. Thurs. (bluegrass)

"South Louisiana Gumbo," 7 p.m. Sun.

University of Calgary
Calgary T2N 1N4
403-220-3902
//www.cjsw.com
cjswfm@acs.ucalgary.ca

Martin Kemp: mkemp@acs.ucalgary.ca

CKUA, 94.9 FM

"Folk Routes," Tom Coxworth, 4-6 p.m., Sun. (bluegrass, Cajun, folk, hillbilly)

1007, 221 6 Ave. SE
Calgary T2G 4Z9
//www.ckua.org
ckua@freenet.edmonton.ab.ca

Tom Coxworth: folkrts@cadvision.com

CKUL, 99.7 FM

"The Tilted Kilt," Carol Watson, 10-Noon, Sun. (folk, eclectic folk, roots and traditional music from all over the world with a concentration on Canadian, British, and Scandinavian; also likely to hear Texas s/s such as James McMurtry, Robert Earl Keen, et al.)

University of Lethbridge
4401 University Drive West
Lethbridge T1K 3M4
403-329-2335
//www.uleth.ca/~ckul/

Carol Watson: watson@hg.uleth.ca

British Columbia

CFRO, 102.7 FM

"Blue Monday," Dinny, 2:30-4 p.m. (blues, jazz, folk, country)

"In the Pines," Paul Norton, 2:30-4 p.m. Sun. ("the most amazing showcase of swing, old-time, bluegrass music on the dial")

"What the Folk," Paul Norton, 4-5:30 p.m. Sun. (based on the philosophy, "It's all folk music, it just depends on who your folks are")

337 Carrall St.
Vancouver V6B 2J4
604-684-8494
//www.vcn.bc.ca/cfro/
cfrocoop@vcn.bc.ca

Paul Norton: norton@festival.bc.ca

CFUV, 101.9 FM

"Radio Folk," alt. hosts, 8-10 a.m. M-Sat. (folk/rock or "a pastoral ideal...music to graze by")

2nd Floor, UVIC SU
University of Victoria
P. O. Box 3035
Victoria V8W 3P3
//kafka.uvic.ca/~cfuv/
cfuv@uvic.ca

CIJR, 93.7 FM

"Pacific Bluegrass," 11 a.m.-Noon Sun.

Vancouver

CITR, 101.9 FM

"The Saturday Edge," Steve Edge, 8-Noon Sat. (folk/roots from all over the map)

CITR, Radio Room 233-235
6138 Student Union Bldg.
University of British Columbia
Vancouver V6T 1Z1
604-822-3017
//www.ams.ubc.ca/media/citr/citr.htm

Steve Edge:
//mindlink.net/roguefolk/
roguefolk@mindlink.bc.ca

New Brunswick

CHMA, 106.9 FM

"Bluegrass Jam," Wilson Moore

303 University Centre
Mount Allison University
Sackville E0A 3C0
//aci.mta.ca/theumbrella/chma/
cradio@mta.ca

CHSR, 97.9 FM

"According to Carmen," Carmen Kilburn, 4-6 p.m. Sun. (country, western, Cajun, Celtic)

P. O. Box 4400
SUB, University of New Brunswick
Fredericton E3B 5A3
506-453-4985
//www.unb.ca/web/chsr/
chsr@mi.net

CJSF, 93.9 FM

"Country/Blues," John "Hoog" Clark (alt. country & blues)

Simon Fraser University
Burnaby V5A 1S6
//www.schmooze.net/pwcasual/

Ontario

CFFF, Trent Radio, 96.3FM

"Smoking Grass," Dave Russell & Matt Elliot, 10-Mid. Mon. (the world of bluegrass from beginning to present with an emphasis on Canadian artists; also other roots acoustic)

"Grand Ole Country," George Moore, 9-Noon Tues. (old country emphasis)

"The Last Resort," Sahver Kuzucuoglu, 8-9 p.m. Fri. (ska, rockabilly, psychobilly, garage)

"The Good 'n' Country Show," Barb Bell and Barb Holtman, 8-Noon, Sat. (old, new, unusual)

Trent University
Peterborough K9H 3B4
//ivory.trentu.ca/www/tr/
Trent_radio@trentu.ca

Sahver Kuzucuoglu:
mkuzucuoglu@trentu.ca

Dave Russell: drussell@trentu.ca

Matt Elliot: melliot@trentu.ca

CFMU, 93.3 FM

"Bluegrass Show," Normand Paul, 8-9:30 p.m. Wed. (traditional)

"Texas Style Chili," Rob Schmidt, 6-9 a.m. Thurs. (pop, rawk, industrial)

"The Back Porch," Sean Maillet, 11-Noon Sat.. ("the door between hillbilly & pure country")

"Mole Matinee," Bruce Mowat, Noon-2 p.m. Sat. (garage, soul, modern jazz, C&W)

McMaster University
Hamilton Hall, Suite 319
Hamilton
416-525-9140
//www.freenet.hamilton.on.ca/
ip007@freenet.h.on.ca

CFRC, 101.9 FM

"Fill Yer Boots," Dickson Davidson, 1500-1700 Wed. ("kickin' bluegrass & a dustin' of good time country")

Carruther's Hall
Queen's University
Kingston K7L 3R6
//www.queensu.ca/cfrc/
cfrcfm@post.queeensu.ca

CHRW, 94.7 FM

"Hard Core Country," Fred Smith, 10-Mid. Wed. (emphasis on Canadian and alt. country from Roy Acuff to Martin Zellar; Acadian to Zydeco)

"Just Folk," John Gardi, 7-8 p.m. Fri. (Guthrie to the McGarrigles)

University of Western Ontario
London
//www.usc.uwo.ca/chrw/
chrw@usc.uwo.ca

CHRY, 105.5 FM

"The Live, Live Show," Ardene Shapiro, 1 p.m. Fri. ("Open roots" from Tom Waits to Townes Van Zandt)

York University
4700 Keele St., Rm. 258A
North York M3J 1P3
416-736-5293
//www.yorku.ca/org/chry/
chry@yorku.ca

CIUT, 89.5 FM

"The Great North Wind ," Steve Fruitman, 8-9 p.m., Mon. (mainly Canadian but also non-Canadian folk by a member of the Black Flies Cajun band and close associate of the Grievous Angels)

"Acoustic Workshop," Rick Fielding, 9-10 p.m Mon. (bluegrass, country, folk)

  91 St. George St.
  Toronto M5S 2E8
  //www.campuslife.utoronto.ca/groups/ciut/

  Great North Wind:
  //www.interlog.com/~gnwind/

  Steve Fruitman: gnwind@bigfoot.com

CJAM, 91.5 FM

"Daybreak in Dixie," 8-10 a.m. Sun. (bluegrass)

"Jump, Cat, Jump!," 8-10 p.m. Sun. (roots rock)

  University of Windsor
  401 Sunset Ave.
  Windsor N9B 3P4
  //www.uwindsor.ca/cjam/
  cjam@server.windsor.ca

CJET, 630 AM

"Rural Routes," Mike O'Reilly, 4-6 p.m. Sun.

  Smiths Falls

CKCU, 93.1 FM

"American Acoustic," Alan Weekes, 7:30-9 p.m. Wed. (the range of American folk from s/s to Tex-Mex)

  Carleton University
  1125 Colonel By Dr.
  Ottawa K1S 5B6
  613-788-2898
  //www.carleton.ca/~fyork/

  Alan Weekes: alanw@fultech.com

CKLN, 88.1 FM

"Acoustic Routes," Joel Wortzman, 7-8 p.m. Sun. (s/s with Canadian flavor)

"Radio Boogie," Steve Pritchard, 10-Mid. p.m. Wed. (old-tyme, bluegrass, Western swing, cowboy, Cajun 1920s-present)

  380 Victoria St.
  Toronto
  //www.sac.ryerson.ca/ckln/ckln.html
  ckln@sac.ryerson.ca

Prince Edward Island

CFCY, 630 AM

"Bluegrass Island," Charlie Hansen, 8 p.m. Wed. (the latest in bluegrass and roots with a Canadian focus)

  114 Kent St.
  Charlottetown C1A 7M7

Bluegrass Island:
//members.tripod.com/~bluegrassisland/bluegrassisland.html
chansen@auracom.com

Quebec

CKUT, 90.3 FM (Montreal)

"Pure Pop for Twisted People," 2-4 a.m. Thurs. ("Baroque post-industrial hillbilly lounge music")

"Folk Roots/Folk Branches," Mike Regenstreif, 9-11:15 a.m. Thurs. (s/s, acoustic blues, country, Western swing, Tex-Mex, bluegrass, etc.)

"Bluegrass Ramblings," Ross Harvey, 7-8 p.m. Sun.

  McGill University
  3480 MacTavish, Suite B-15
  Montreal PQ H3A
  514-398-6787
  //www.vub.mcgill.ca/media/ckut/
  dclear@po-box.mcgill.ca

  Mike Regenstreif:
  mregens@vax2.concordia.ca

Saskatchewan

CFCR, 90.5 FM

"Jumpin' the Blues," Dave Maenz, 9-10:30 p.m. Thurs. ("American music that counts": hot jazz, boogie woogie, Texas swing 1910s-1960s)

"Bad Booze Rodeo," 8-9 p.m. Sun. ("Nitro burnin' rockabilly with a dash of old country, truckin' and surf")

  Community Radio Society of Saskatoon
  P. O. Box 7544
  Saskatoon
  306-664-6678
  //www.lights.com/cfcr/
  aa076@sfn.saskatoon.sk.ca

  Brian Receveur: bcr418@mail.usask.ca

EUROPE

AUSTRIA

FM 106.1 (Austrian Cable TV & Radio) or Astra 1D (Satellite)

Shows broadcast from Country Music Radio UK.

"Rockin' Good Country," 19:00-21:00 Tues. (rockabilly and rockin' country)

"Rockabilly Show," Desperado Dell Richardson & Rockin' Roy Williams, 21:00-01:00 Fri. (Neorockabilly, psychobilly)

"Good Rockin' Tonight," Dell Richardson & Roy Williams, 10:00-01:00 Sun. (r 'n' r, rockabilly)

BELGIUM

ATL, 105.9 FM

"Roots Revival," Raymond Swennen, Wed. (alt. country/Americana from around the world)

  P. O. Box 42
  B-3960
  Bree
  (32) 89-472411

Radio Mol, 104.1 Mhz

"Nashville Rock," Geert Van Lommel, 21:00-22:00 Mon.

"Rawhide," Eric Van de Mert, 19:00-20:00, Thurs.

  Keirlandse Zillen 7/2
  B-2400 Mol

Radio USA, 106.8 Mhz

"On the Farm," Inge Boffgen, 9-10 Mon.-Fri.

"Country-Rock," Walter Wutys, 14:00-15:00, Mon.

"Rawhide Countdown," Eric Van de Mert, 21:00-23:00 Sun.

  Hundelgemsesteenweg 469
  B-9820 Merelbeke
  //ns.hookon.be/radio.usa/
  radiousa@hookon.be

CZECHOSLOVAKIA

ELDORADIO, 88.4 FM

American & Czech country & western, folksongs, bluegrass 24 hours/day.

  U Toi lvu 5
  Eeske Budijovice
  Eska Republika (Southern Bohemia)
  +420-38-801
  //www.eldoradio.cz
  live@eldoradio.cz

ESTONIA

Raadio Kuku, 100.7 FM (The Voice of the Cuckoo)

"Rohujuured/Grassroots," Jaanus Vainu, 9 p.m. Thurs. (country, bluegrass, roots since 1994)

"Kantri Alati Jaab/Country Forever," Jaanus Vainu, 10 p.m. Thurs. (began airing in 1992 when the first private radio stations in Estonia came into existence; show plays mostly traditional country; DJ maintains BlueGrass-Roots, an extensive Americana web site)

  Box 3657
  Tallinn, EE-0090
  //www.zzz.ee/kuku/
  kuku@kuku.kuku.ee

  BlueGrassRoots: //BGR.ee (gigantic web site for the radio program as well as links to

all types of American traditional/roots music)
BGR@BGR.ee

FINLAND

Radiomafia

"Kantrispaghetti" and "Rout 66," Teppo Nathila, Mon. eve. (modern roots/rock)

"Tutti Frutti Rock 'n' Roll," K.W. Blomqvist (rockabilly/hillbilly boogie)

//www.yle.fi/radiomafia/

FRANCE

RCF

"Country Unlimited and Lone Star Music," Jacques Spiry, Mid. Fri.; 1 p.m. Sun. (the only alternative country and new American roots music show on a national network)

Jacques Spiry
BP 1159
69203 Lyon Cedex 01
33 (0) 4 78 61 00 90
jacquesspiry@hotmail.com

RTL, Radio 22

"Country," Georges Lang, Sunday evening.

22 Rue Bayard
75008
Paris
//www.rtl.fr

Radio 666, 99.1 MhZ

"Sunglasses After Dark," David & Eddie, 8-9 p.m. Tues. (jump, jive, hillbilly, rockabilly)

"Highway 66," Eric Allart, 7-8 p.m. Wed. (country, bluegrass, Western swing, honky tonk)

Caen-Herouville

Radio Birotte

"Bluegrass Backup," Francois Galland.

Vierzon

Radio Canut, FR03, 102.2 Mhz

"Radio Canut Along the Navaro Trail," Bernard Boyat, 18:00-19:00 p.m. Sun. (country-rock, Cajun)

Lyon
//wwwperso.hol.fr/~lcombe/canut.htm
laurent.combe@hol.fr

Radio Enghien

"The Country Club," Raymond Cadou, Fri.

"Country & Souvenirs," Patrick Molis, Wed. (traditional/new country)

11, Avenue des Myosotis
95230 Soisy Sous Montmorency

TSF, 89.9

"Hayride," Jacques Dumery.

Bobigny

GERMANY

Radio Neckarburg, 101.2 FM

"Folk & Bluegrassladen," Hansjoerg Malonek, 8-9 p.m. Fri., twice per month (bluegrass, singer/songwriter, acoustic country)

Hansjakobstr. 8
78050 VS-Villingen

Radio Unerhort (RUM), 90.10 FM

"Insurgent Country/American Roots Music," Hans Settler, 10-Noon Sat. (Settler maintains Hans' Insurgent Country Page which is loaded with information on and links to alt./insurgent country)

Warburg
Hans' Insurgent Country Page:
//staff-www.uni-marburg.de/~settler/
settler@mailer.uni-marburg.de

Radio ZuSa, 95.5 & 88.0 FM

"Eine Kleine Weltmusik," Juergen Kramer, every 2nd Fri. (folk and traditional music from around the world with some alt. country artists)

Lueneburg (Northern Germany)

Juergen Kramer:
juergen.kramer@germany.com

IRELAND

Anna Livia, 103.8 FM

"Country Style," Liam Keane, 9-10 p.m. Wed.

"American Music Show," Sandy Harsch, 9:30-11 p.m. Fri. (the best in American country music)

"Route 103," Ray McGee, 10-Mid. Sat.

Dublin
//slarti.ucd.ie/annalivia/
ferlyn@indigo.ie

Riverside Radio, JRRI 6.230 khz 48 meter band (short wave)

"The Country and Eastern Show," Eddie Russell (re-broadcast of alt. country show originating from KULM in Columbus, Texas)

Waterford

ITALY

Radio Incontro Nuova Rete, 100.250 Mhz

"Jack and Coke," 10-Midnight Mon. (variety from blues to country, jazz to folk-rock to s/s)

c/o Claudio Cacchi
Via Domeniconi 15

47023 Cesena
//www.sirius.pisa.it/incontro/

NORWAY

P4 Radio Hele Norge

"Cool Country" and "Rune's Roots Restaurant," Rune Halland (two Americana shows with both new and alternative country)

Norge
//www.p4.no/
p4@p4.no
Cool.country@p4.no

PORTUGAL

Radio 2000, 96.7 FM

"BangBang," 8-10 p.m. Fri. (alternative and alternative country including the Schramms, Deliberate Strangers, Peter Stone Brown, and more)

AP 429
2001 905
Santarem
bangbangpopshow@mail.telepac.pt

SPAIN

RPEM, 107.8 FM

"The Country and Eastern Show," Eddie Russell (re-broadcast of alt. country show originating from KULM in Columbus, Texas)

Barcelona

SWITZERLAND

Schweizer Radio, DRS 3

"Country Special," Martin Schafer, Dienstag 21:00-23:00 (bluegrass, Western swing, country rock)

Postfach
CH-4024
Basel
//www.drs.ch/
guette@bidule.welcome.ch

UNITED KINGDOM

BBC Radio 1

"Roots Music," Andy Kershaw, 8:30-10:30 p.m. Mon. (West African kora to Johnny Cash)

//www.bbc.co.uk

BBC Radio 2, 88-90 Mhz

"Mike Harding Show," 20:00-21:00 Wed. (the best in folk/acoustic and roots music)

//www.bbc.co.uk
Mike Harding: mikeh@dent.demon.co.uk

BBC Radio Bristol, 95.5 FM

"My Style of Country," Kelvin Henderson, 18:00-20:00 Tues. (all kinds including alt.)

P. O. Box 194
Bristol
BS99 7QT
//www.bbc.co.uk

CMR (Country Music Radio) for Europe

Shows available all over Europe via satellite and cable.

"Whip Crack Away," Claiborne Mitchell, 18:00-20:00 Mon. (women in country)

"Folk Roots," Alan O'Leary, 20:00-22:00 Mon.

"Rockin' Good Country," Bryan Chalker & Dell Richardson, 18:00-21:00 Tues. (rockabilly, hillbilly)

"Hard Country," Bryan Chalker, 22:00-24:00 Wed.

"The Singer-Songwriter Show," Bob Paterson, 10-12 p.m. Thurs. (lots of alt. country/Americana including interviews and sessions; Bob is one of the most active promoters of Americana artists in the UK)

"Bluegrass on Friday," 18:00-20:00 Fri.; 19:00-21:00 Sun.

"Country Music," Bryan Chalker, 20:00-24:00 Fri.

"New Generation," Dell Richardson & Roy Williams, 20:00-24:00 last Fri each month (rockabilly)

"Saturday Night Party," Bryan Chalker, 20:00-24:00.

"The Americana Show," Tom Bridgewater, 17:00-19:00 Sun.

"Good Rockin' Tonight," Dell Richardson & Roy Williams, 21:00-24:00 Sun. (r 'n' r, rockabilly)

//www.countrymusic.org.uk/cmr/menu.htm

Bob Paterson:
//www.ursasoft.com/bob/
windmill@windbob.demon.co.uk

YUGOSLAVIA

Radio M

"Alternative Country/Americana,", Alexandr Lazarevic, Sat. (amazing program that features the best of alt. country from a dedicated and courageous DJ who is literally in the line of fire every week in his war-torn homeland).

P. Fah 80
11400 Mladenovac
Serbia
Yugoslavia
lavac@eunet.yu
+381 11 8220 554

ISRAEL

Radio West

"Radio West Show," Paul Graham, Sun. (s/s, contemporary bluegrass, and more)

P. O. Box 9029
Jerusalem 91090
Paul Graham: paul_g@netvision.net.il

SOUTH AFRICA

Radio UCT

"The Great Gig in the Sky," David Retief (alternative country)

retiefd@tredcor.co.za

AUSTRALIA

New South Wales

2MCE, 92.3 FM

"Cowboys & Outlaws," 2-4 p.m. Sat. & Sun.

"Bluegrass & More," 4-6 p.m. Sat. (bluegrass, folk, country)

Charles Sturt University
Panorama Ave.
Bathurst 2795
//www.csu.edu.au/communit/2mce/mcehome.htm
2mce@csu.edu.au

2NSB, 91.5 FM

"Smokey Dawson's Australian Country Music Showcase," 6-7 p.m. Fri.

Sydney
//www.dot.net.au/2nsb/
2nsb@dot.net.au

2RRR, 88.5 FM

"Weekend Country," Ken Date, 7-10 Sat. (all types of American & Australian country)

110 Chelmsford St.
Newtown 2042

Country Life, 103.1 FM

A free to air community broadcaster featuring classic and contemporary Australian country, bush music, Western swing, new country, country blues, cowboy, Cajun, old-time, bluegrass, folk/acoustic with a country flavor and more. On midnight to midday Monday-Friday.

Canberra
Barbara.Mason@atsic.gov.au

Queensland

Bay FM, 100.3

"Acoustic Harvest," Colin Nightingale, Fri. Eve. (most things acoustic including traditional Anglo/Celtic, s/s, Cajun, bluegrass, world, etc.)

"Doctor Hepocrates Rockin' Retro Radio Show"

P. O. Box 9035
Thornlands 4164
Colin Nightingale
5 Lavelle Ct.
Victoria Point 4165
//www.bit.net.au/~colin/
colin@bit.net.au

4ZZZ, 102.1 FM

"Rockabilly Show," Jason Myrdyez, 10-11 p.m. Wed. (mix of old and new with special emphasis on local bands)

P. O. Box 509
Fortitute Valley
Brisbane 4006
//www.4zzzfm.org.au/

South Australia

ABC Radio National

"Country Club," Richard Porteus, 5-7 a.m. Sat.; 10-Mid. Sun. (Bluegrass, old timey, acoustic country, folk)

P. O. Box 9994
Adelaide
porteus.richard@a2.abc.net.au

3DDD, 93.7 FM

"Hillbilly Hoot," 8-9 p.m. Mon. ("the best in country music performed live on the porch at 3DDD by local, interstate and international guests")

"Roots & Branches," 10-11 p.m. Thurs. (acoustic traditional, folk-rock, punk-folk, new country, s/s, world)

"Yodel Action," Allie Ayliffe, Terry Bradford, Tony Easton, 11 a.m.-1 p.m. Sat. (old-time country, alternative country including honky tonk, Cajun, Tex-Mex, rockabilly, Western swing)

"Cross Country," 1-3 p.m. Sat. (roots music dealing with bluegrass, c&w, r&b, folk blues, rockabilly, Western swing, Hawaiian, zydeco)

Adelaide:
//www.threed.suburbia.com.au/index.html

Yodel Action:
//www.skynet.apana.org.au/~brad/yodel/
brad@sa.apana.org.au

5UV, 531 AM

"Country Breakfast," Rob Tilmouth, 6-9 a.m. Sat./Sun. (Australian/U.S. alt. country)

"Bluegrass Unlimited," Bill Lawson, Noon-1 p.m. Sun.

228 North Terrace
University of Adelaide
Adelaide
//www.adelaide.edu/au/5uv/

Robert Tilmouth: rjt@wantree.com.au

Victoria

3BBB, 97.5 FM

"The Night Rider Show," Johnny From Dunnolly, Mid-6 Mon. & 11-Mid., Sun. (Aussie, U.S., independent label country)

"Red, Hot, & Blue," Mick, 7-9 p.m. Tues. (blues, country)

"The Country Club," Nick Pollock, 3-4 p.m. Wed. (latest & greatest in modern country)

"Wylde Country," Wendi, Noon-2 p.m. Sun. (modern & classic country from Australia & overseas)

Ballarat
//lin.cbl.com.au/3bbb/

Merv Romeo: merom@netconnect.com.au

3CR-AM, 855 Mhz

"Hot Damn Tamale," 2-4 p.m. Wed.

"Hillbilly Fever," Bruce Rowe & Tracey Beca, 11 p.m.-1 a.m. 2nd Sat. Each month (bluegrass)

Melbourne

3PBS, 106.7 FM

"Now Dig This," Hugo Armstrong, 3-5 p.m. Mon. (blues, rockabilly)

"No Depression," Sophie Best, 3-5 p.m. Thurs. (excellent alt. country show with in studio performances & interviews)

"Country Junction," Norm Burke & Paul McSherry, 9-10:30 a.m. Sun.

Box 210
St. Kilda
//home.vicnet.net.au/~pbsfm/
pbsfm@vicnet.net.au

Sophie Best: sophiebest@yahoo.com

3RIM, 97.9 FM

"Stephanie's Country Album," Stephanie Richards, Noon-2 p.m. Thurs. (left field country especially s/s, Texas country plus Australian country)

"Australian Country Bound," Doug Frampton, 2-4 p.m. Thurs. (old and new)

"Somethin' Country," 10:30-Noon Sun.

"Country Jamboree," Noon-2 Sun.

Mowbary College
Centenary Ave.
Box 979
Melton 3337

3RRR, 102.7FM

Had a very good alt. country show "High in the Saddle" originally hosted by Keith Glass and

then by Dave Dawson until March 1996. Current programs:

"Chicken Mary," Gary Young and Jimi Baeck, 2 p.m. Mon. (blues, rockabilly, r&b, soul)

"Rick E. Vengeances Old Folk Show," 2 p.m. Tues.

"Twang," Denise Hyland, 2 p.m. Sat. (music with rock, country, blues influences)

13 Victoria St.
Fitzroy
//www.rrr.apana.org.au/
3rrr@rrr.org.au

Western Australia

6RTR 92.1 FM

"Rock, Rattle 'n' Roll," Bob Hume, 7:30-9 p.m. Tues. (on-air since 1985 playing all types of roots, rockabilly & country)

"Folk West," Steve Barnes, Noon-2 p.m. Sun. (all folk/roots including country)

Box 7387
Nedlands6850
//rtrfm.iinet.net.au/
Rock, Rattle 'n' Roll:
//kali.murdoch.edu.au/~hopehume/rattle.html
(home of the Rockabilly Ring clearinghouse for rockabilly pages)

Robert Hume:
hope-hume@humpc61.edu.au

Folk West:
//www.iinet.net.au/~downesr/folkwest.html

Steve Barnes: barnes.s@per.dem.csiro.au

NEW ZEALAND

Christchurch

98 RDU, 98.3 FM

"Rural Delivery," Al or Dave, 9-11 p.m., Tues. ("songs from the cornfields of Iowa, bluegrass from the hills of Kentucky, stomps from the swamps of Louisiana, and the authentic Tex-Mex sound from the honky-tonks of Texas")

University of Canterbury
Private Bag 4300
UCSA Bldg.
90 Ilam Rd.
Ilam
//www.rdu.org.nz/rdu.html

Allan Murray:
a.murray@cantva.canterbury.ac.nz

Hastings

KCR, 1431 AM/88.5 FM

"Best of Bluegrass," Trevor JE Ruffell, 11-Noon M-F

"My Kinda Music," 6-7 p.m. Mon. (bluegrass)

"Way Out West," 10-11 a.m. Tues. (cowboy/western)

P. O. Box 919
//members.tripod.com/~ruffell/bayfolkhomepage.html
comus@xtra.co.nz

Trevor Ruffell: comus@xtra.co.nz

INTERNET BROADCASTS

*Below are Internet "listening stations" that broadcast music (including alt. country/Americana) 24 hours/day. Many individual radio stations and programs broadcast over the Internet; check their web pages:

Live Radio on the Internet:
//www.frodo.u-net.com/radio. htm

M.I.T. List of Bitcaster Radio Stations:
//wmbr.mit.edu/stations/bc.html
or
Peter Olmsted's list of Twangy online stations and shows:
//irc.leeds.ac.uk/~phy6pdo/music/radio/

Bluegrass Radio Network

Variety of weekly live and recorded programs including "Blue Highway" and "Into the Blue."

//www.bluegrassradio.com/

Freight Train Boogie

Online American roots music show (with special emphasis on alt. country) put together each week by Bill Frater.

//www.freighttrainboogie.com/ftradio.htm
frater@freighttrainboogie.com

Imagine Radio

Has link for KFAT, Americana radio.

//www.imagineradio.com

Live Concerts

Online broadcast of live events including acts like the Derailers, Richard Buckner, Peter Case, Wilco, Parlor James, Tarnation, etc.

//www.liveconcerts.com

LouisianaRadio.Com

Internet only showcase for Louisiana music past and present.

//www.louisianaradio.com

Net Radio Country MusicSites

Has alternative country programming under "Alt. Country"

//www.netradio.net/country/

NOMA Liquid Radio Network

Internet based music delivery system featuring acoustic, folk and independent artists.

//songs.com/liquidaudio/

The Spinner

Over 100 programs of uninterrupted music from a variety of genres including "Alt. Country," "Bluegrass," "Classic Country," "Country," "Folk."

//www.spinner.com

Tunes.Com

"World's Largest Listening Station" with categories including rockabilly, bluegrass, Cajun, country, folk & roots.

//www.tunes.com/tunes-cgi2/tunes/

TwangCast.com

24 hour a day broadcast of "real country" artists such as Mike Ireland, Dale Watson, Honky Tonk Confidential, et al. plus classic country and bluegrass. Part of the RealCountry network.

//www.TwangCast.com
mike@mikehays.realcountry.net

Western Beat's Roots Revival

Billy Block's fine weekly alt. country showcase from the Exit/In in Nashville.

//www.westernbeat.com

TELEVISION

Austin City Limits

Long running PBS Americana show that has showcased many of the top names in alt. country past and present
//www.klru.org/acl

Austin Music Network, Channel 15

Music videos and live tape of Texas artists including many alt. country acts.
//www.ci.austin.tx.us/music/

CMT's "Jammin' Country"

Weekly segment on Country Music Television with frequent alt. country videos.
//www.country.com/cmt/

Live From Cibolo Creek Country Club

Pilot for possible PBS series featuring musicians from central Texas performing at the CCCC north of San Antonio; 1st episode starred Terri Hendrix and Guy Forsyth.

Old-Time Country Music

Since 1989, local, regional, national artists recorded live at the Iowa Public TV station in Johnston (distributed to 55 stations in 15 states)

//www.iptv.org/iptv/otcmhome.html

Sessions at West 54th

PBS program presenting live performances by a variety of contemporary musicians including Emmylou Harris, Lucinda Williams, Gillian Welch, the Mavericks, Jimmie Dale Gilmore, Billy Bragg, and John Hiatt.

//www.sessionsatwest54th.com